Presidential Administration Profiles
for Students

Presidential Administration Profiles
for Students

Kelle S. Sisung, Senior Editor
Gerda-Ann Raffaelle, Editor

GALE GROUP

Detroit
San Francisco
London
Boston
Woodbridge, CT

Presidential Administration Profiles for Students

The Gale Group Staff

Editorial: Gerda-Ann Raffaelle, *Editor and Project Manager*; John F. McCoy, *Associate Project Editor*; R. David Riddle, *Assistant Project Editor*; Kelle S. Sisung, *Series Editor*; Kathy Droste, *Editor*; Bernard Grunow, *Associate Editor*

Graphic Services: Barbara J. Yarrow, *Graphic Services Manager*; Randy Bassett, *Image Database Supervisor*; Robert Duncan, Mike Logusz, *Imaging Specialists*; Pamela A. Reed, *Imaging Coordinator*; Christine O'Bryan, *Desktop Publisher*

Permissions: Maria Franklin, *Permissions Manager*; Margaret Chamberlain, *Permissions Specialist*; Mary K. Grimes, *Cataloger*

Product Design: Cynthia Baldwin, *Product Design Manager*; Pamela A. E. Galbreath, *Senior Art Director*

Production: Mary Beth Trimper, *Composition Manager*; Evi Seoud, *Assistant Production Manager*; Wendy Blurton, *Senior Buyer*

Data Entry: Ronald D. Montgomery, *Manager*; Gwendolyn Tucker, *Project Administrator*; Frances L. Monroe, *Data Entry Associate*

Graphics Creator: Eric E. Wisniewski

Copy Editor: Leslie Joseph

Indexer: Nancy Fulton

Copyright Notice

Copyright © 2000 by
Gale Group
27500 Drake Rd.
Farmington Hills, Michigan 48331-3535

Library of Congress Cataloging-in-Publication Data
Presidential administration profiles for students / Kelle S. Sisung, editor.
      p. cm. — (U.S. Government for students)
      Includes bibliographical references and index.
      ISBN 0-7876-2796-8 (hard)
      1. Presidents—United States—History. I. Sisung, Kelle S. II. Series.
      JK511.P78 1999
352.23 ' 0973—dc21
                                99-39017
                                   CIP

ISBN 0-7876-2796-8
Printed in the United States of America
10 9 8 7 6 5 4 3 2

Table of Contents

Table of Contents
by President Name

Advisors and Contributors

Advisory Board

A nine-member advisory board consisting of teachers, media specialists, and other experts on U.S. government was consulted to help determine the scope and content of *Presidential Administration Profiles for Students.*

Howard Ball: Professor of Political Science, University of Vermont

Marion J. Cannon: Library Media Specialist, Winter Park High School, Winter Park, Florida

Catherine Chauvette: Library Media Specialist, Fairfax County Public Library, Alexandria, Virginia

Fran Cohen: Library Media Specialist (retired), Conestoga High School, Berwyn, Pennsylvania

Michael D. Leahy, Ph.D.: Library Media Specialist (retired), Eastern High School, Bristol, Connecticut

Frank J. Orfei: History Department, Pelham Memorial High School, Pelham, New York

Harriet B. Sawyer: Social Studies Department Chair, Franklin High School, Livonia, Michigan

Jay A. Sigler, Ph.D.: Professor of Public Policy and Administration, Rutgers University

Lavonna Brown Williams: Educator, Minot Public School District, Minot, North Dakota; Bonneville Joint School District, Bonneville, Idaho

Contributors

Patrick Allitt, Ph.D.: Professor of History, Emory University. Dwight D. Eisenhower, Ronald Reagan, and Harry S. Truman profiles.

John Barnes: Woodrow Wilson profile.

Sheree Beaudry: Researcher. Gerald R. Ford profile (with Rita Koman, Ph.D.).

David Bernelle: James Monroe profile.

Robert Bolt, Ph.D.: Professor Emeritus of History, Calvin College. Grover Cleveland, Millard Fillmore, Theodore Roosevelt, William H. Taft, and Zachary Taylor profiles.

Daniel E. Brannen, Jr.: Attorney and writer. John Adams, John Quincy Adams, Thomas Jefferson (with Linda Miller, Ph.D.), and Franklin Pierce profiles.

Lloyd Carson: James Madison profile

Craig Collins: Researcher and writer. Andrew Jackson, John Tyler, and Martin Van Buren profiles.

Justus D. Doenecke, Ph.D.: Professor of History, New College of South Florida, Sarasota. Chester A. Arthur, James Garfield, and Herbert C. Hoover profiles.

Kenneth E. Hendrickson, Jr., Ph.D.: Hardin Distinguished Professor, Chair, Department of History, Midwestern State University, Wichita Falls, Texas. Lyndon B. Johnson, Richard M. Nixon, and Franklin D. Roosevelt profiles.

James W. Hilty, Ph.D.: Professor and former Chair of the History Department, Temple University, Philadelphia. John F. Kennedy profile.

Robert La Forte, Ph.D.: Professor of History, University of North Texas, Denton. Benjamin Harrison profile.

Thomas C. Mackey, Ph.D.: Associate Professor and Chair of the History Department, University of

Louisville. Abraham Lincoln, Andrew Johnson, Ulysses S. Grant, and Rutherford B. Hayes profiles.

Hannah Nordhaus: Writer and researcher, M.A. in history, University of Colorado. James Buchanan, George Bush, Jimmy Carter, Bill Clinton, and William McKinley profiles.

Jason Phillips, Ph.D.: Political science. William Henry Harrison and James K. Polk profiles.

Michael Robertson: Biography sidebars.

Thom Sherlock, Ph.D.: Associate Professor of Political Science, United States Military Academy at West Point. George Washington profile.

Walter E. Volkommer, Ph.D.: Professor, Department of Political Science, Hunter College of The City University of New York. Warren G. Harding and Calvin Coolidge profiles.

Preface

Presidential Administration Profiles for Students (*PAP*) is the third volume in the U.S. Government for Students series, preceded by *Federal Agency Profiles for Students* released in December 1998 and *Special Interest Group Profiles for Students* released in August 1999.
The purpose of the series is to provide an overall view of the workings of the United States government geared specifically to meet the curriculum needs of high school students, undergraduate college students, and their teachers. Each profile in a U.S. Government for Students volume will cover not only the basic facts found in such sources as the *United States Government Manual,* but will include the historical and political context, or the how and why. Furthermore, the series focuses on the relevancy and immediacy of government, explaining how an agency, a special interest group, or a presidential administration can impact the life of an average citizen and, in some cases, how a citizen can become actively involved in the federal government. While the series was designed to reflect curriculum standards, the general reader and researcher will also be able to find answers to their questions about the U.S. government.

PAP includes profiles of the 42 presidential administrations. Each profile includes a biographical sketch, which accounts for approximately ten percent of the entry, followed by a longer essay that focuses on the workings of the president's administration. Authors have attempted to glean how each administration has impacted the role of the Executive Branch in the U.S. government and its lasting impact on the country.

Advisory Board

Our advisory board, consisting of high school teachers, media specialists, and subject experts, assisted us in analyzing each presidential administration for its overall impact. Several PAP authors also graciously shared their expertise in an advisory capacity. We further relied on course curriculum supplied by our advisors that represented various school districts across the United States.

How Each Profile is Organized

Profiles are arranged in chronological order by administration. For additional access, readers should also refer to the second table of contents, which is organized alphabetically by president name, and the general index.

Biographical data includes full name, given name, popular name, birth date, birthplace, death date, death place, burial place, religion, education, spouse, children, political party, occupations, and age at inauguration.

The text of the biography attempts to provide the background for each president's decision to pursue a political career and tries to uncover what compelled them to seek the presidency. It is arranged in the following rubrics:

- **Early Life:** This rubric covers the president's life as a child and his family of origin. It presents early influences that may have directed the person toward a political career and the presidency.

- **Education:** Discusses the subject's educational achievements and any early interests that may have shown an inclination toward politics.

- **Family Life:** The focus of this rubric is the nuclear family of the president, including marriage, children, and life before, during, and when appropriate, following the "White House years." While a few presidents never had children, only James Buchanan remained a bachelor. A particular focus of this rubric is how the president's spouse fulfilled the role as first lady.

- **Career:** Covering each president's early career through the presidency, the career rubric examines the course that each president took to the White House in his professional life. It may include failed presidential campaigns.

- **Post-presidential Years:** These are the years following the presidency. Many former presidents remained very active and influential in public life, while others took up other pursuits. If an individual died in office, the circumstances of their death is discussed here.

The Administration portion of the entry focuses on the presidential years. The following rubrics are included:

- **Becoming President:** Covers from the first successful presidential campaign through all subsequent campaigns and describes the political backdrop, the campaign issues, the campaigns, and the outcomes of the elections. If an individual assumed the presidency from a previous president, those details are discussed. For instance, Lyndon Johnson's entry includes details of Johnson taking on the presidency after the assassination of John F. Kennedy.

- **Advisers:** Discusses the relationship of the president with his advisers. Will highlight those relationships that impacted the president's policy and actions.

- **Congress:** Examines the interaction of the president with members of Congress and Congress as a whole.

- **Judiciary:** Covers appointments to the Supreme Court by the president, landmark cases, and the influence the president had on the court through his appointments.

- **Changes in the U.S. Government:** Important changes that occurred during the administration, which may include the creation of cabinet posts or commissions, administrative changes, or a change that impacts the composition of the government, such as new states joining the Union, and amendments to the U.S. Constitution.

- **Domestic Issues:** An overview provides a broad brush look at the times, describing the economic and social conditions that existed at time of the administration. Areas for which the administration is known, such as civil rights or economics, are also introduced in the overview. Following the overview are the domestic events that were the highlights of the administration, including key legislation, firsts, use of emergency powers, and their impact.

- **Foreign Issues:** This rubric begins with an overview, which provides a look at the United States's place in the global community at the time of the administration. Coverage includes foreign trade, wars, treaties, and acquisition of land.

- **Legacy:** The legacy rubric explores what the president left to his successor and also the lasting impact of the administration. When there was sufficient information and space, authors provided the reactions to the administration by the public and by their contemporaries. For the most part this is intended to reinforce for the student the impact the administration had on government and life in the United States today.

- **Sources:** An alphabetical list of sources, including books and current periodicals quoted in the profile, with full bibliographic information.

- **Further Readings:** Lists other critical sources that may prove helpful for the student and researcher.

In addition, a *PAP* profile may contain one or more of the following supplementary sidebars:

- **Administration:** For quick reference, all entries contain an administration sidebar that furnishes the dates of the administration. It also includes the names of the vice president(s) and cabinet officers and their dates of service. Because cabinet officers are carried over from one administration to the next, with presidents oftentimes taking some time to make their own appointments, dates cited in sources consulted varied.

- **Fast Facts:** At-a-glance facts. Facts may reflect historical changes in the presidency being profiled or might illustrate the issues that have been discussed throughout the essay. Each fact is fully cited.

- **Biography:** An individual who was pivotal to a president's administration is profiled in a biography sidebar that includes birth and death dates, identifier, a brief sketch, and a thumbnail photo.

- **What they said:** Quotations by the president or about the administration.

Additional Features

In an attempt to create a comprehensive, one-stop reference tool for the study of the U.S. federal government, *PAP* also includes:

- Illustrations that depict historic events, notable individuals, and current issues along with maps.

- A chronology of over 750 key events in U.S. history that allows students to place each president in an historical context.

- A glossary containing over 400 political terms used throughout the profiles.

- A subject index for easy access to administrations, people, places, and events.

- Diagram appendices

We Welcome Your Suggestions

The editor of *Presidential Administration Profiles for Students* welcomes your comments and suggestions. Please direct all correspondence to:

Editor, *Presidential Administration Profiles for Students*
The Gale Group
72500 Drake Rd.
Farmington Hills, MI 48331-3535

Chronology

1492: Columbus discovers the Americas.

1565: St. Augustine, Florida, is founded by the Spanish.

1607: Over 140 men and boys form a settlement at Jamestown, Virginia; approximately one-half die before the end of the year. Jamestown becomes the second oldest town in North America, after St. Augustine, and the first permanent British settlement.

1614: Dutch found the colony of New Amsterdam.

1619: Martial law in Virginia is replaced by a general assembly of twenty-two burgesses, the first representative assembly in America.

1620: Off of present-day Cape Cod, Massachusetts, 41 male passengers on the *Mayflower* sign the Mayflower Compact, establishing a preliminary civil body politic and the authority to legislate laws as necessary. The people who debark are known as the Pilgrims.

1621: William Bradford becomes governor of Plymouth and serves at that post for 30 years.

1629: The Massachusetts Bay Company is formed by English Puritans allowing the company to have governmental autonomy once on the American mainland.

1630: English Puritans, sponsored by the Massachusetts Bay Company, found Boston and ten other settlements in Massachusetts.

1636: Plymouth colony inhabitants adopt the Great Fundamentals allowing for the establishment of a general court made up of the governor and two representatives from each town.

1640: The "Great Migration" to Massachusetts ends with the collapse of the reign of King Charles I and the beginning of the English Civil War; an estimated ten thousand Englishmen had come to New England by this time.

1643: Massachusetts, Connecticut, New Haven, and Plymouth form a confederation called the United Colonies of New England.

1644: Massachusetts Bay adopts a bicameral legislature.

1647: Rhode Island adopts its first constitution which declares separation of church and state and freedom of religious expression.

1660: Parliament passes the first of the Navigation Acts, which restricts the trade of New England merchants to England and the British West Indies by imposing taxes and duties on goods traded with other countries.

1675: King Philip's War begins and pits the New England Confederation against American Indian tribes led by Chief Philip of the Wampanoags. The two-year conflict results in great loss and destruction for both sides. Twelve New England towns are leveled, and for every 16 white men of fighting age, one loses his life.

1682: William Penn establishes his Frame of Government which allows for the creation of an assembly, council, and governor's office in Pennsylvania.

1685: The Dominion of New England is formed, and the following year Sir Edmund Andros is appointed governor.

1696: William III commissions the Board of Trade to oversee commercial (trade and fishing) and political (powers of appointment and legislative review) concerns in the American colonies.

1701: The Charter of Liberties, the constitution of Pennsylvania until the American Revolution (1775–83), establishes the only sustained unicameral (one-house) legislature in the colonies.

1702: As part of the War of the Spanish Succession (1702–1713), known as Queen Anne's War in America, James Moore, the English governor of South Carolina, attacks Saint Augustine, Florida, burning outposts and missions in Apalachee, or northern Florida.

1754–1763: The French and Indian War results in the British and Indian allies capturing Quebec and defeating the French.

August 17, 1754: The Albany Plan, formulated by Benjamin Franklin, is rejected. It would have joined the colonies in a defense against the French and would have established an intercolonial council to handle relations with the American Indians.

1763: The Treaty of Paris is signed, concluding the French and Indian War; Britain is given Canada and all French territory east of the Mississippi River and Florida.

1763: The Proclamation of 1763 prohibits colonists from settling west of the Appalachian mountains beyond the reach of British authorities. It is also issued to pacify the American Indians.

April 5, 1764: Parliament passes the Sugar Act, reducing the tariff on molasses imported into North America. However, it also sends custom agents and collectors to the colonies to strictly enforce the remaining laws in effect.

1765: Britain imposes the Stamp Act. This is the first internal tax levied on the colonies. Requiring the purchase of stamps to be affixed to a number of official documents, it affects mostly lawyers, clergymen, and printers.

October 7–25, 1765: Nine colonies represented at the Stamp Act Congress in New York protest Parliament's taxation of the colonies.

March 17, 1766: Parliament rescinds the stamp tax but insists it has the power to tax the colonies.

1767: The Townshend Acts, which impose a tax on goods imported into the American colonies, are passed by the British Parliament and contribute to a revolt against British rule.

May 16, 1769: After Virginia's House of Burgesses rejects Parliament's right to tax the colonies, the governor dissolves the assembly, which continues to meet privately, agreeing not to import British goods.

January 19–20, 1770: The Battle of Golden Hill, New York, results in one death as the Sons of Liberty skirmish with British soldiers trying to remove liberty poles from Golden Hill, Manhattan.

April 12, 1770: Parliament repeals all the Townshend duties except the one on tea.

November 2, 1772: The Boston town meeting creates a 21-member committee of correspondence to communicate with other towns in the colony and to defend the rights of colonists "as Men, as Christians, and as Subjects."

December 16, 1773: In the act that came to be known as the Boston Tea Party, a mob dumps a cargo of tea into Boston Harbor to protest Great Britain's tea tax.

May 20, 1774: The Massachusetts Government Act suspends the colony's charter.

May 27, 1774: A call for a Continental Congress goes out to consolidate action and support economic pressure to force Great Britain to rescind the Massachusetts Government Act.

September 5–October 16, 1774: The First Continental Congress meets in Philadelphia to work out constitutional issues; each state has one vote in this body.

October 18, 1774: The Continental Congress adopts the Continental Association, pledging to cease imports from Great Britain after December 1, 1774.

1775–1783: The American Revolution.

February 9, 1775: The king declares Massachusetts to be in rebellion.

May 5, 1775: The Second Continental Congress convenes for the purpose of uniting the colonies for military action.

June 14, 1775: The Department of the Army is founded as the Continental Army by the Second Continental Congress; George Washington is appointed its first commander in chief.

October 13, 1775: The Department of the Navy is founded; it is commissioned by the Continental Congress and plays a decisive role in the British decision to abandon the American colonies.

November 10, 1775: The U.S. Marine Corps is founded when two battalions of "marines" are authorized by the Continental Congress to serve in the Revolutionary War against Great Britain.

June 12, 1776: The Continental Congress appoints a committee led by John Dickinson to draw up a plan for a confederation.

July 2, 1776: The Continental Congress votes unanimously that "these thirteen colonies are, and of right, ought to be, free and independent states."

July 4, 1776: The Declaration of Independence is adopted.

November 15, 1777: The Continental Congress adopts the Articles of Confederation and Perpetual Union;

it requires the endorsement of all the state legislatures to take effect.

July 9, 1778: Delegates from 8 of the 10 states that have ratified the Articles of Confederation sign them.

September 13, 1779: John Jay, president of the Continental Congress, asks the states to collect taxes in order to pay requisitions to the federal treasury.

January 10, 1781: The Continental Congress creates a ministry for foreign affairs.

May 26, 1781: The Pennsylvania legislature charters the Bank of North America.

November 30, 1782: Benjamin Franklin, John Adams, Henry Laurens, and John Jay sign the preliminary peace agreement with British emissaries.

April 18, 1783: The Continental Congress proposes a revenue system as a way of paying the national debt.

September 3, 1783: The Treaty of Paris, which recognizes American independence, is signed by British and American negotiators.

December 23, 1783: George Washington resigns his commission as commander in chief of the Continental Army.

January 14, 1784: The Continental Congress ratifies the Treaty of Paris.

May 7, 1784: The Continental Congress appoints Thomas Jefferson to assist John Adams and Benjamin Franklin in negotiating commercial treaties with European nations.

January 11, 1785: The Continental Congress moves from Philadelphia to New York City.

May 20, 1785: The Continental Congress passes the Land Ordinance of 1785, revamping the system for settling western areas and setting aside land and revenue to support public education.

January 16, 1786: The Virginia legislature passes Thomas Jefferson's Bill for Establishing Religious Freedom, enacting the principles of religious toleration and separation of church and state.

August 29, 1786: Armed insurgents led by Revolutionary War veteran Daniel Shays begin closing courthouses in western Massachusetts after the legislature ignores their list of grievances.

January 25, 1787: Gen. William Shepherd and one thousand militiamen end Shays's Rebellion by thwarting an attack on the Springfield Arsenal.

May 25–September 17, 1787: The Constitutional Convention meets in Philadelphia to write what will become the Constitution of the United States of America. Delegates from all states except Rhode Island are present.

May 29, 1787: Edmund Randolph submits the Virginia Plan to the Constitutional Convention, proposing a bicameral legislature based on proportional representation, a national executive and judiciary, and a congressional veto of state laws.

May 31, 1787: The Constitutional Convention votes that the people should directly elect members to what will be the House of Representatives.

June 15, 1787: William Paterson presents the New Jersey Plan to the Convention, proposing to retain the unicameral national legislature (with each state having an equal vote) and to expand congressional control over trade and revenue.

July 11, 1787: The Constitutional Convention votes to count three-fifths of the slave population for taxation and representation purposes.

July 13, 1787: The Continental Congress passes the Northwest Ordinance, establishing the Northwest Territory (present-day Illinois, Indiana, Ohio, Michigan, Wisconsin, and parts of Minnesota). The Ordinance defines the steps for the creation and admission of new states and bars slavery in the area.

July 16, 1787: The Constitutional Convention approves the "Great Compromise," granting representation proportional to population in the House of Representatives and equal state representation in the Senate.

August 29, 1787: The Constitutional Convention decides to give Congress power to pass navigation acts, approves a fugitive slave clause, and forbids Congress from regulating the slave trade before 1808.

December 7, 1787: Delaware is the first of the original 13 states to ratify the Constitution.

December 12, 1787: Pennsylvania is the second of the original 13 states to ratify the Constitution.

December 18, 1787: New Jersey is the third of the original 13 states to ratify the Constitution.

January 2, 1788: Georgia is the fourth of the original 13 states to ratify the Constitution.

January 9, 1788: Connecticut is the fifth of the 13 original states to ratify the Constitution.

February 6, 1788: Massachusetts is the sixth of the original 13 states to ratify the Constitution.

April 28, 1788: Maryland is the seventh of the original 13 states to ratify the Constitution.

May 23, 1788: South Carolina is the eighth of the original 13 states to ratify the Constitution.

June 21, 1788: New Hampshire is the ninth of the original 13 states to ratify the Constitution.

June 25, 1788: Virginia is the tenth of the original 13 states to ratify the Constitution.

July 26, 1788: New York is the eleventh of the original 13 states to ratify the Constitution.

March 4, 1789: The first Congress to meet under the Constitution convenes in New York City.

April 30, 1789: George Washington, after unanimously being chosen by electors, is inaugurated as the first president of the United States. John Adams becomes vice president.

July 4, 1789: Congress, led by James Madison, passes the Tariff Act of 1789, creating a source of revenue for the federal government.

July 27, 1789: The Department of State is founded with the appointment of Thomas Jefferson as the first secretary of state; its highest concern is the protection of American interests at home and abroad.

July 31, 1789: The U.S. Customs Service is founded to collect the taxes on imported and exported goods, to document data relating to cargo and passenger ships, and to fine people or companies that defy the newly instituted laws.

September 1789: The Office of Attorney General is established.

September 2, 1789: The Department of the Treasury is founded to not only manage the nation's finances but also to provide leadership in setting its fiscal policy in order to plan the country's financial future.

September 11, 1789: Alexander Hamilton is appointed the first secretary of the Treasury.

September 24, 1789: Congress passes the Judiciary Act of 1789, creating a federal court system and giving the Supreme Court the right to review the constitutionality of state laws.

September 25, 1789: Congress, led by James Madison, submits the first ten constitutional amendments (later known as the Bill of Rights) to the states.

September 26, 1789: John Jay is appointed the first chief justice of the United States Supreme Court.

November 21, 1789: North Carolina is the twelfth of the original 13 states to ratify the Constitution.

November 26, 1789: President George Washington consults department heads on foreign and military affairs, establishing the practice of regular cabinet meetings.

February 2, 1790: The Supreme Court of the United States convenes for the first time with the responsibility of applying the Constitution and laws in deciding cases.

May 29, 1790: Rhode Island is the thirteenth of the original 13 states to ratify the Constitution.

July 1, 1790: Congress approves a site on the Potomac River (Washington, D.C.) as the future capital of the United States.

July 26, 1790: Congress passes Secretary of the Treasury Alexander Hamilton's program for assuming the states' debts; his program for funding the national debt by issuing interest-bearing securities is passed on August 4.

February 25, 1791: President George Washington signs a bill creating the First Bank of the United States after receiving conflicting opinions regarding the bank's constitutionality from Secretary of the Treasury Alexander Hamilton and Secretary of State Thomas Jefferson.

March 3, 1791: Congress passes an excise, or internal, tax on whiskey.

March 4, 1791: Vermont becomes the 14th state.

December 12, 1791: The First Bank of the United States opens in Philadelphia with branches in other cities.

December 15, 1791: The Bill of Rights becomes part of the Constitution. These ten amendments are intended to protect of freedom of religion, speech, and the press.

March 1, 1792: Congress passes the Presidential Succession Act. In case of the death or disability of the president and vice president, power will pass to the president pro tempore of the Senate followed by the Speaker of the House.

April 2, 1792: The U.S. Mint is founded by the Mint Act of 1792, which among other duties determines the materials, denominations, and inscriptions to be used in making U.S. coins.

June 1, 1792: Kentucky becomes the 15th state.

October 13, 1792: The cornerstone of the new executive mansion is laid in Washington, D.C.

November 1792: Federalist candidates George Washington and John Adams again compete for the presidential seat. Washington defeats Adams by an electoral vote of 132 to 77.

February 12, 1793: Congress passes the first Fugitive Slave Law, enforcing part of Article IV, Section 2, of the Constitution, which specifies that a person fleeing a state in which they are charged, must be returned to the state having jurisdiction of the crime.

February 13, 1793: In *Chisholm v. Georgia* the Supreme Court rules that states can be sued in federal court by citizens of other states.

March 4, 1793: President George Washington and Vice President John Adams are inaugurated for a second term.

April 22, 1793: Determined to keep the United States out of the war between France and Great Britain, President Washington issues the Proclamation of Neutrality.

September 18, 1793: President George Washington lays the cornerstone for the Capitol building in Washington, D.C.

June 5, 1794: Congress passes the Neutrality Act, forbidding Americans from joining foreign military forces or provisioning foreign vessels in American ports.

July–November 1794: Farmers in Pennsylvania resist officials trying to collect the whiskey tax. President George Washington and Secretary of the Treasury Alexander Hamilton lead a militia to enforce the law, but what became known as the Whiskey Rebellion is over by the time they arrive.

November 19, 1794: Jay's Treaty is signed in London, England. Terms include Great Britain's evacuation of posts in the Northwest Territory by 1796 and limited U.S. trade in the West Indies.

August 3, 1795: The United States and 12 Indian tribes in the Northwest sign the Treaty of Greenville, opening much of present-day Ohio to white settlement.

October 27, 1795: The United States and Spain sign the Pinckney Treaty, recognizing the 31st parallel as the southern boundary of the United States and granting Americans free navigation of the Mississippi River.

March 7, 1796: In *Ware v. Hylton* the U.S. Supreme Court declares a state law unconstitutional for the first time.

March 8, 1796: In *Hylton v. United States* the U.S. Supreme Court upholds the constitutionality of an act of Congress for the first time.

June 1, 1796: Tennessee becomes the 16th state.

December 7, 1796: In the nation's first contested presidential election, Federalist John Adams defeats Democratic-Republican Thomas Jefferson by a narrow electoral vote of 71–68; Jefferson becomes vice president.

March 4, 1797: President John Adams and Vice President Thomas Jefferson are inaugurated.

May 16, 1797: President John Adams recommends that Congress approve a three-man diplomatic mission to France, arm merchant vessels, create a navy, fortify harbors, and enlarge the army.

October 18, 1797: Three agents of French foreign minister Charles de Talleyrand (publicly identified as "X," "Y," and "Z") demand a bribe from the American envoys before negotiations can begin. Charles Cotesworth Pinckney responds: "No, no, not a sixpence!"

1798: The United States and France begin the "Quasi-War," an undeclared naval conflict in the Caribbean.

January 8, 1798: The Eleventh Amendment is ratified. It declares that states cannot be sued by citizens of another state or foreign country in federal court.

April 3, 1798: President John Adams releases diplomatic dispatches to Congress on the "XYZ Affair." Within a week the "XYZ Papers" are published in newspapers throughout the country, exciting outrage against France.

May–July 1798: Congress revokes all treaties with France and approves an enlarged army, a new Navy Department, harbor defenses, and the seizure of all French vessels interfering with U.S. shipping.

June 18, 1798: Congress passes the Naturalization Act, the first of four Alien and Sedition Acts, limiting freedom of speech and the press and the rights of foreigners. The act also increases the residency period required for citizenship to 14 years.

June 25, 1798: Congress passes the Act Concerning Aliens, allowing the president to deport any alien, during war or peace, judged "dangerous to the peace and safety of the United States"; President Adams never uses this authority.

July 9, 1798: Congress passes a direct tax on land, houses, and slaves to pay for the Quasi-War with France.

July 14, 1798: Congress passes the Act for the Punishment of Certain Crimes (the Sedition Act) by a vote of 44 to 41. The act imposes heavy fines and imprisonment on anyone convicted of writing, publishing, or speaking anything of "a false scandalous and malicious nature" against the government and its officers.

November 16, 1798: The Kentucky Resolutions, drafted by Thomas Jefferson and passed by the Kentucky state legislature, declare that states can judge the constitutionality of federal laws, and that the Alien and Sedition Acts are unconstitutional and thus "void and of no force."

February 1799: Farmers in Pennsylvania, led by John Fries, rebel against the direct tax of 1798. Federal troops put down Fries Rebellion, and the leader is convicted of treason but pardoned by President Adams.

November 22, 1799: The Kentucky state legislature passes resolutions reaffirming nullification as a proper constitutional solution.

1800: The Virginia state legislature passes a resolution proposing that freed slaves be resettled in Africa.

January 2, 1800: Free African Americans petition Congress in opposition to slavery and the slave trade. By a vote of 85 to 1, Congress refuses to accept the petition.

April 24, 1800: The Library of Congress is established by the "Act to Make Provision for the Removal and Accommodation of the Government of the U.S." While originally only members of Congress and other government officials are allowed to use the facilities, it later opens its doors to the public.

September 30, 1800: The United States and France sign an agreement ending the Quasi-War.

November 17, 1800: Congress convenes in Washington, D.C., for the first time, as the federal capital is moved from Philadelphia, Pennsylvania. The location had been selected by former president George

Washington during his administration. John Adams becomes the first president to live in the new Executive Mansion.

January 20, 1801: John Marshall is appointed chief justice of the United States, serving until his death in 1835.

February 17, 1801: John Adams receives 65 electoral votes and Thomas Jefferson and Aaron Burr each receive 73 votes, throwing the presidential election into the House of Representatives. On the thirty-sixth ballot Jefferson is elected, and Aaron Burr becomes vice president.

February 13, 1801: Congress passes the Judiciary Act of 1801, reducing the number of Supreme Court justices from six to five, establishing sixteen circuit courts, and increasing the number of judicial officers.

March 4, 1801: Thomas Jefferson is the first president to be inaugurated in Washington, D.C. His vice president is Aaron Burr.

April 6, 1802: Congress abolishes all internal taxes, including the unpopular whiskey tax.

April 29, 1802: After repealing the Judiciary Act of 1801, Congress passes a new Judiciary Act. It authorizes six Supreme Court justices, one session a year for the Supreme Court, and six circuit courts, each presided over by a Supreme Court justice.

August 1, 1802: The U.S. Military Academy is founded to serve as a training facility for military engineers.

August 25, 1802: The Patent and Trademark Office is founded with the mission of administering laws relating to patents and trademarks and advising the government on patent, trademark, and copyright protection.

February 24, 1803: In *Marbury v. Madison* the Supreme Court declares an act of Congress (the Judiciary Act of 1789) unconstitutional for the first time and expands its power of judicial review.

March 1, 1803: Ohio becomes the 17th state in the Union and the first to outlaw slavery from the beginning of statehood.

April 30, 1803: The United States purchases the Louisiana Territory from France for $15 million.

February 25, 1804: In the first congressional caucus Democratic-Republicans unanimously nominate President Thomas Jefferson for a second term and nominate George Clinton for vice president.

March 26, 1804: In the Louisiana Territory Act, the federal government declares for the first time that its intention is to move Indians living east of the Mississippi River to the West.

September 25, 1804: The Twelfth Amendment to the Constitution is ratified, providing separate ballots for president and vice president.

December 5, 1804: President Thomas Jefferson is reelected with 162 electoral votes over Charles Cotesworth Pinckney with 14 votes. George Clinton is elected vice president.

March 4, 1805: President Thomas Jefferson is inaugurated for a second term. His vice president is George Clinton.

March 29, 1806: Congress authorizes the construction of the National Road, connecting Cumberland, Maryland, with Wheeling, Virginia.

April 18, 1806: Congress passes a Non-Importation Act, prohibiting the importation of British goods in protest against the British seizure of American ships and sailors.

March 2, 1807: Congress decides to prohibit the African slave trade and importation of slaves into the United States as of January 1, 1808.

December 7, 1808: Democratic-Republican candidate James Madison is elected president with 122 electoral votes. The Federalist Charles Cotesworth Pinckney receives 47 votes, and George Clinton, the candidate of eastern Democratic-Republicans, receives 6 votes. Clinton is elected vice president.

March 4, 1809: President James Madison is inaugurated with George Clinton as vice president.

July 2, 1809: The Shawnee tribal leader Tecumseh begins forming a confederacy of Native American tribes.

September 30, 1809: William Henry Harrison, governor of Indiana Territory, signs a treaty at Fort Wayne by which American Indian tribes cede three tracts of land along the Wabash River.

October 27, 1810: President James Madison annexes West Florida between the Mississippi and Pearl Rivers after Americans in the region declare independence from Spain.

March 4, 1811: After the Senate votes against re-chartering the Bank of the United States, its charter expires.

November 7, 1811: American Indians under Tecumseh's brother, the Prophet, attack Governor William Henry Harrison's (president in 1841) army in the Battle of Tippecanoe; they are repulsed and Prophet's Town is burned. As a result Tecumseh and his followers cross into Canada, later joining British forces in the War of 1812.

November 20, 1811: Construction begins on the National Road, increasing the flow of settlers to the West.

December 24, 1811: Congress authorizes the completion of enlistments in the regular army, the enlistment of 25,000 additional regulars for five years' service and 50,000 volunteers for one year's service, and the call-up of one hundred thousand militia for six months' service at the president's request, and approves additional funds for the navy.

April 30, 1812: Louisiana becomes the 18th state in the Union.

June 18, 1812: After sending a war message to Congress, President James Madison signs the declaration of war against Great Britain, citing impressment, violations of American trade, and the incitement of American Indian warfare as the causes for hostilities with England.

December 2, 1812: President James Madison is reelected with 128 electoral votes. George Clinton, candidate of anti-Madison Democratic-Republicans and Federalists, receives 89 votes. Elbridge Gerry is elected vice president.

March 4, 1813: President Madison is inaugurated for a second term.

March 27, 1814: Tennessee militia led by Generals Andrew Jackson and John Coffee, defeat the Creek Indians at Horseshoe Bend in present-day Alabama.

August 29, 1814: British troops invade Washington and set fire to the White House. While the interior of the building is destroyed, the structure remains and is later restored.

September 13, 1814: As he watches the unsuccessful British attack on Fort McHenry at Baltimore, Maryland, Francis Scott Key composes the "Star Spangled Banner."

December 24, 1814: The United States and Great Britain sign a peace treaty at Ghent. Although it ends the war, the Treaty of Ghent does little to resolve the underlying issues which caused it. News of the treaty does not reach the United States until February, 1815.

January 5, 1815: The Hartford Convention, a forum for delegates to discuss ways and means of sectional defense and to take steps to revise the Constitution, ends with hints of secession. The delegates uphold a state's right to nullify federal law and propose constitutional amendments to limit the power of the federal government. After the signing of the Treaty of Ghent, these delegates come to be regarded as treasonous for opposing the war.

January 8, 1815: In the last major battle before news of peace reaches the United States, an American army led by Andrew Jackson successfully protects New Orleans from an attack by the numerically superior British. The Americans suffer only 21 casualties while inflicting more than 2,000. This victory makes Andrew Jackson a national hero, and convinces many Americans that the War of 1812 was won by the United States.

December 5, 1815: President James Madison urges Congress to approve a national bank, protective tariffs, and a program of national funding for transportation and education.

1816: The first postwar Congress charters the Second Bank of the United States and passes an internal improvements bill and the Tariff of 1816.

November 1816: James Monroe defeats Federalist Rufus King for the presidency, winning 183 electoral votes to King's 34.

December 11, 1816: Indiana is admitted to the Union as the 19th state.

March 4, 1817: James Monroe is inaugurated as president with Daniel D. Tompkins as vice president.

November 20, 1817: Settlers attack American Indians in Florida, igniting the First Seminole War. Spain is believed to support the Seminoles during the year-long conflict.

December 10, 1817: Mississippi is admitted as the 20th state of the Union.

1818: The Convention of 1818 between the United States and Great Britain sets the border between the United States and Canada at the forty-ninth parallel and establishes joint occupation of Oregon.

December 3, 1818: Illinois is the 21st state admitted to the Union.

1819: Under the Adams-Onis Treaty, Spain cedes Florida to the United States.

December 14, 1819: Alabama is admitted to the Union as the 22nd state.

March 2, 1820: As part of the Missouri Compromise, Congress prohibits slavery in the Louisiana Purchase north of 36°30' but, as part of the compromise, agrees to admit Missouri as a slave state.

March 15, 1820: Maine is admitted as the 23rd state of the Union.

November 1820: James Monroe wins reelection with 231 electoral votes out of 232 cast for the presidency.

March 4, 1821: James Monroe begins his second term as president.

August 10, 1821: Missouri becomes the 24th state of the Union.

December 2, 1823: President James Monroe delivers a message to Congress, warning European countries not to colonize or interfere with the Western Hemisphere. This policy comes to be known as the Monroe Doctrine.

March 30, 1824: Speaker of the U.S. House of Representatives Henry Clay defines his "American System" in a speech supporting a protective tariff that would generate revenue to fund internal improvements that would in turn expand the U.S. economy.

August 29, 1824: The Bureau of Indian Affairs is founded with the primary functions of acquiring American Indian lands and containing the American Indian people and their culture.

November 1824: John Quincy Adams, Andrew Jackson, Henry Clay, and William Crawford run for the presidency. Jackson wins the popular and electoral votes but fails to secure an electoral majority, requiring the House of Representatives to determine the winner.

1825: President James Monroe calls for the voluntary removal of Americans Indians from the East to lands west of the Mississippi River.

March 4, 1825: After the House selects John Quincy Adams as president, he is inaugurated with John Caldwell Calhoun as his vice president.

July 4, 1826: On the fiftieth anniversary of the Declaration of Independence, Thomas Jefferson and John Adams both die.

1828: The Democratic Party comes into power for the first time with the election of Andrew Jackson to the presidency, marking the return of the two-party system to national politics.

May 19, 1828: President John Quincy Adams signs the "Tariff of Abominations" into law that provides extremely high rates on imports of raw materials and manufactured goods. Southerners call it a "hateful law."

November 1828: John Quincy Adams fails to be reelected as president, winning only 83 votes to Andrew Jackson's 178 votes.

March 4, 1829: Andrew Jackson is inaugurated as president. His vice president is John Caldwell Calhoun.

April 13, 1830: At the annual Jefferson Day Dinner, in John C. Calhoun's presence, Andrew Jackson clearly warns against nullification of the 1828 Tariff of Abominations with his toast, "Our Federal Union, it must be preserved."

May 28, 1830: Jackson signs the Indian Removal Act to provide money to purchase land from the Creeks, Seminoles, Cherokees, Chickasaws, and Choctaws and to relocate them in present-day Oklahoma and Arkansas.

May 31, 1831: Congress adjourns before President Andrew Jackson acts on several improvement bills. Jackson thus institutes the concept of "pocket veto," or vetoing a bill by refusing to sign legislation before the end of the congressional session.

July 10, 1832: Jackson vetoes the charter for the Second Bank of the United States, claiming the bank is a "monster" because of its exclusive power.

November 1832: Andrew Jackson defeats Henry Clay for the presidency, winning 219 electoral votes to Clay's 49 votes.

November 1832: Believing that the states had the right to exempt themselves from federal laws with which they disagree, South Carolina nullifies the tariffs of 1828 and 1832 with the *Ordinance of Nullification.*

December 1832: At President Jackson's request Congress passes the Force Bill to compel South Carolina to abide by federal tariffs.

March 1, 1833: The Compromise Tariff of 1833 and Force Bill are signed into law.

March 4, 1833: Andrew Jackson is inaugurated for a second term. His vice president is Martin Van Buren.

March 28, 1834: The Senate votes 26 to 20 to censure Andrew Jackson for removing federal deposits from the Second Bank of the United States.

November 1835–1842: The Second Seminole War is fought in Florida when some Seminole Indians, led by Osceola, refuse to leave their land in defiance of an 1832 treaty.

June 15, 1836: Arkansas is admitted to the Union as the 25th state.

November 1836: Democrat Martin Van Buren becomes president after defeating three Whig opponents, Daniel Webster, Hugh Lawson White, and William Henry Harrison. Van Buren secures 170 electoral votes. Webster, his nearest competitor, wins 73 votes.

1837: The Panic of 1837 is the first real and lasting economic crisis the United States faces. Land speculation, a failed wheat crop, a 50 percent reduction in the price of cotton, and a crisis in several European banks combine to cause a widespread financial panic.

January 26, 1837: Michigan is admitted as the 26th state of the Union.

March 4, 1837: Martin Van Buren is inaugurated as president with Richard Johnson as vice president.

1838: The forced march of the entire Cherokee nation from Georgia along the Trail of Tears to Oklahoma, ordered by President Andrew Jackson, is carried out during the Van Buren administration.

November 1840: Whig William Henry Harrison defeats Martin Van Buren by an electoral vote of 234 to 60. Liberty Party candidate James G. Birney receives seven thousand popular votes.

March 4, 1841: William Henry Harrison is inaugurated as president with John Tyler as vice president.

April 4, 1841: President William Henry Harrison dies of pneumonia, and John Tyler becomes the first vice president to assume the presidency.

1842: The Webster-Ashburton Treaty settles the border between the United States and Canada in the Northeast.

November 1844: Democratic candidate James Polk defeats Whig Henry Clay and Liberty Party candidate James Birney with 170 electoral votes to Clay's 105.

March 3, 1845: Florida is admitted to the Union as the 27th state.

March 4, 1845: James Polk is inaugurated as president with George Mifflin Dallas as vice president.

October 10, 1845: The U.S. Naval Academy is founded to replace the U.S. Navy's former practice of relying on at-sea apprenticeships for midshipmen.

December 29, 1845: Texas is admitted as the 28th state of the Union.

May 13, 1846: The United States declares war on Mexico. The Senate votes 40 to 2 and the House votes 174 to 14 in favor of war.

June 15, 1846: The Senate ratifies a treaty with Britain fixing the Oregon Territory border at the forty-ninth parallel.

August 10, 1846: The Smithsonian Institution is established with funds bequeathed to the United States by English scientist and inventor James Smithson for "the increase and diffusion of knowledge."

December 12, 1846: The United States and New Granada (present-day Columbia and Panama) sign a treaty that gives the United States a right-of-way across the Isthmus of Panama.

December 28, 1846: Iowa is admitted as the 29th state of the Union.

February 2, 1848: American diplomat Nicholas Trist signs the Treaty of Guadalupe Hidalgo with Mexico. The United States receives California, New Mexico (including modern Arizona and Nevada), and Texas to the Rio Grande for $15 million.

March 10, 1848: The Senate ratifies the peace treaty with Mexico, 38 to14.

May 29, 1848: Wisconsin is admitted to the Union as the 30th state.

November 1848: Whig Zachary Taylor defeats Democrat Lewis Cass and Free-Soil candidate Martin Van Buren, with 163 electoral votes to 127 for Cass.

March 3, 1849: The Department of the Interior is founded to manage the sale and lease of federal lands; its focus later shifts to the conservation and protection of U.S. natural resources.

March 4, 1849: Zachary Taylor is inaugurated as president. His vice president is Millard Fillmore.

January 29, 1850: The Compromise of 1850 is introduced by Senator Henry Clay, admitting California as a free state, allowing the territorial legislatures of New Mexico and Utah to settle the slavery issue on their own, exacting a stronger fugitive slave law, outlawing the slave trade in the District of Columbia, and giving Texas $10 million to abandon its claims to territory in New Mexico.

July 9, 1850: President Zachary Taylor, an opponent of Henry Clay's compromise to end the conflict over slavery in the territory won from Mexico, dies. Vice President Millard Fillmore, who favors the compromise, becomes president.

September 9, 1850: California is the 31st state admitted to the union.

December 24, 1851: A fire at the Library of Congress in Washington, D.C., destroys two-thirds of its collection.

November 2, 1852: Democratic Party candidate Franklin Pierce defeats Whig candidate Winfield Scott and Free-Soil candidate John P. Hale to become president.

March 4, 1853: Franklin Pierce is inaugurated president. William Rufus De Vane King is vice president.

February 28, 1854: A coalition of Whigs, Democrats, and Free-Soilers meet in Ripon, Wisconsin, suggesting the name "Republican" for a new party pledged to bar slavery from the territories.

March 31, 1854: Commodore Matthew C. Perry signs the Treaty of Kanagawa, opening Japanese ports to American trade.

May 30, 1854: The Kansas-Nebraska bill is signed into law by President Franklin Pierce. Violent conflict between pro- and anti-slavery forces in the Kansas territory ensues.

January 15, 1856: A free state governor and legislature are elected in Kansas, which now has both a pro-slavery and anti-slavery government.

November 1856: James Buchanan wins the presidential election with 174 electoral votes over Republican candidate John C. Fremont.

March 4, 1857: James Buchanan is inaugurated as president with John C. Breckinridge as vice president.

October 19, 1857: A convention of pro-slavery Kansans meeting at Leocompton, Kansas, produces a constitution for the state with legalized slavery. It soon becomes apparent that a majority of Kansans oppose this Leocompton constitution.

February 2, 1858: President Buchanan recommends that Congress admit Kansas as a slave state under the Leocompton constitution. This issue splits the Democratic Party into northern and southern factions.

May 11, 1858: Minnesota is the 32nd state admitted to the union.

June 16, 1858: Abraham Lincoln, nominated for the Senate by Illinois Republicans, delivers his "House Divided" speech.

August 2, 1858: Given a chance to vote on whether or not to use the Leocompton constitution, Kansas voters overwhelmingly reject the document. They do so despite special incentives offered to the potential new state by Congress to vote in favor.

February 14, 1859: Oregon becomes the 33rd state.

November 6, 1860: Republican Abraham Lincoln defeats Northern Democratic presidential candidate Stephen A. Douglas with a vote of 180 to 12. Hannibal Hamlin becomes his vice president.

December 20, 1860: South Carolina secedes from the Union. Florida, Alabama, Georgia, Mississippi, Louisiana, and Texas soon follow.

1861–1865: American Civil War.

January 29, 1861: Kansas is admitted to the Union as the 34th state.

February 9, 1861: Jefferson Davis is elected president of the Confederate States of America.

March 4, 1861: Abraham Lincoln is inaugurated as president of the United States. Hannibal Hamlin is vice president.

April 12, 1861: In the first fighting of the Civil War, Confederate batteries fire on Fort Sumter rather than allow it to be resupplied.

April 17–May 20, 1861: Virginia, Arkansas, Tennessee, and North Carolina secede from the Union.

May 15, 1862: The Department of Agriculture is founded to enhance the quality of life for Americans by supporting the production of agriculture.

July 1, 1862: The Internal Revenue Service is founded; initially named the Bureau of Internal Revenue, it is created in response to the need for increased revenue to fund the War Department during the American Civil War.

August 29, 1862: The Bureau of Engraving and Printing is founded to produce paper currency as part of the U.S. Department of Treasury's plan to finance the American Civil War; it later becomes the sole manufacturer of the nation's currency and postage stamps.

January 1, 1863: The Emancipation Proclamation is declared in effect.

February 25, 1863: Congress creates a national banking system.

March 3, 1863: Congress passes the Conscription Act.

June 20, 1863: West Virginia is admitted as the 35th state.

November 19, 1863: Lincoln delivers the Gettysburg Address.

October 31, 1864: Nevada becomes the 36th state.

November 8, 1864: Abraham Lincoln is reelected as president of the United States; he defeats War Democrat George B. McClellan by a vote of 212 to 21.

1865: The Thirteenth Amendment abolishing slavery is ratified.

March 4, 1865: Abraham Lincoln is inaugurated for a second term with Andrew Johnson as vice president.

April 9, 1865: Robert E. Lee surrenders the Confederate Army at Appomattox Courthouse, Virginia.

April 15, 1865: Lincoln is assassinated at Ford's Theater by John Wilkes Booth; Andrew Johnson becomes president.

July 5, 1865: The U.S. Secret Service is founded with the mission of protecting U.S. leaders, visiting world leaders, and the integrity of U.S. financial systems.

April 9, 1866: A civil rights act is passed over President Johnson's veto.

June 13, 1866: Congress approves the Fourteenth Amendment to the Constitution which gives African Americans citizenship and guarantees all persons due process of law.

March 1, 1867: Nebraska becomes the 37th state.

February 24, 1868: The House of Representatives impeaches President Johnson.

May 16, 1868: The Senate acquits President Johnson of violating the Tenure of Office Act by one vote.

June 25, 1868: Alabama, Arkansas, Florida, Georgia, Louisiana, North Carolina, and South Carolina are readmitted to the Union by Congress.

November 3, 1868: Ulysses S. Grant defeats candidate Horatio Seymour in the presidential election by a vote of 214 to 80.

November 6, 1868: Red Cloud and other Lakota tribal leaders sign a treaty with U.S. government officials at Fort Laramie, Wyoming, establishing a reservation in nearly all of present South Dakota west of the Missouri River. This area includes the sacred Black Hills.

March 4, 1869: Ulysses S. Grant is inaugurated as the 18th president with Schuyler Colfax as vice president.

September 24, 1869: Black Friday on Wall Street occurs when financiers drive up the price of gold.

March 30, 1870: The Fifteenth Amendment, stating a right to vote regardless of race, color, or previous status of servitude, is declared to be in effect.

May 31, 1870: Congress passes the Enforcement Act to protect African American voters.

June 22, 1870: The Department of Justice is founded. Headed by the Attorney General, it is officially charged with the supervision of all federal law officers and attorneys, the control of immigration, and the investigation of federal crimes.

November 5, 1872: Ulysses S. Grant is reelected president over newspaperman Horace Greeley who was nominated by both the Liberal Republicans and the Democratic National Convention.

March 4, 1873: Ulysses S. Grant begins his second term as president. Henry Wilson is vice president.

September 18, 1873: Beginning of the financial panic of 1873.

January 14, 1875: The Specie Resumption Act limits greenbacks in circulation to $300 million, and provides for a return to specie payments by 1879.

March 1, 1875: Congress passes the Civil Rights Act; key provisions are held unconstitutional in the *Civil Rights* cases of 1883.

August 1, 1876: Colorado is admitted as the 38th state.

November 1876: The presidential election between Republican Rutherford B. Hayes and Democrat Samuel J. Tilden yields contested results. A special Electoral Commission is established by Congress to determine the winner.

March 2, 1877: The Republican dominated Electoral Commission declares that Rutherford B. Hayes won the disputed electoral votes of the 1876 election. This gives him the presidential election, with 185 electoral votes to Tilden's 184.

March 4, 1877: Rutherford B. Hayes is inaugurated as president with William A. Wheeler as vice president.

November 2, 1880: James Garfield defeats Hancock in a close presidential election, winning by an electoral vote of 2,114 to 155 and a popular vote of 4,446,158 (48.27 percent) to 4,444,260 (48.25 percent). The Greenback Labor Party candidate, James B. Weaver, gets 305,997 votes.

November 17, 1880: The United States and China sign a treaty that allows the United States to "regulate, limit, and suspend" Chinese immigration but not to ban it outright.

March 4, 1881: James Garfield is inaugurated as president. Chester A. Arthur is vice president.

July 2, 1881: President Garfield is shot by disappointed office seeker Charles J. Guiteau, who claims he was attempting to ensure that Vice President Arthur, a Stalwart who favors the spoils system, would become president.

May 6, 1882: Congress passes the Chinese Exclusion Act, suspending Chinese immigration to the United States for 10 years.

September 19, 1882: President James Garfield dies of complications from the wounds he sustained from his July shooting. Garfield is succeeded by Vice President Arthur the next day.

January 16, 1883: Congress passes the Pendleton Civil Service Reform Act, an attempt to depoliticize appointments of federal employees engaged in governmental operations and end the "spoils system." Signed into law by President Arthur, the act establishes a Civil Service Commission and specifies rules for a merit system based on competitive exams.

November 4, 1884: Democrat Grover Cleveland is elected president in an extremely close election, defeating Republican James G. Blaine. He is the first Democrat elected president since the Civil War. Protest movements represented by the Greenback Labor Party and the Prohibition Party win more than 300,000 votes (3.21 percent).

March 4, 1885: Grover Cleveland is inaugurated as president. Thomas A. Hendricks is vice president.

January 19, 1886: Congress passes a Presidential Succession Act; if both the president and vice president are unable to serve, they are succeeded by members of the cabinet in the order that their departments were created.

October 25, 1886: In *Wabash, St. Louis & Pacific Railway v. Illinois*, the Supreme Court rules that only the federal government, not the individual states, may regulate interstate railway rates.

November 1886: Samuel Gompers establishes the American Federation of Labor which emphasizes "bread and butter" unionism.

1887: American settlers in Hawaii force King Kalakaua to establish a constitutional government.

February 4, 1887: Congress passes the Interstate Commerce Act establishing the Interstate Commerce Commission, the first national regulatory commission, in an attempt to curb price fixing and other abuses by interstate railroads.

February 8, 1887: Congress passes the Dawes Act, which provides for the division of tribal lands among individual American Indians and the sale of "surplus" land to non-Indians.

November 6, 1888: Benjamin Harrison (Republican) narrowly defeats President Cleveland. Although Harrison wins the election in the Electoral College, Cleveland receives more popular votes. Minor-party candidates from the Union Labor and the Prohibition parties win nearly 400,000 votes, preventing either major party from gaining a clear majority.

March 4, 1889: Benjamin Harrison is inaugurated as president. Levi P. Morton is vice president.

November 2, 1889: North Dakota and South Dakota become states, followed by Montana on November 8 and Washington on November 11, becoming the 39th through 42nd states of the Union, respectively.

April 14, 1890: At a conference that began in Washington, D.C., on October 2, 1889, Western Hemisphere nations form the Pan-American Union.

July 2, 1890: Congress passes the Sherman Anti-Trust Act, which authorizes the federal government to initiate court proceedings to dissolve trusts or contracts in restraint of trade in an attempt to limit or prevent business monopolies.

July 3, 1890: Idaho becomes the 43rd state.

July 10, 1890: Wyoming becomes the 44th state.

1891: After succeeding her brother to the Hawaiian throne, Queen Liliuokalani issues an edict revoking the Constitution of 1887 and assuming autocratic powers, thus taking power away from the pro-American annexation faction.

March 3, 1891: The Immigration and Naturalization Service is created by the Immigration Act of 1891; originally called the Bureau of Immigration, it is the first federal agency in charge of enforcing immigration laws and standards.

November 8, 1892: Former president Grover Cleveland defeats incumbent Benjamin Harrison by more than 370,000 votes, becoming the only president to serve two non-connective terms.

January 17, 1893: Queen Liliuokalani of Hawaii abdicates the day after U.S. Marines land to back a rebellion led by pro-annexation American settlers.

February 1, 1893: Hawaii is proclaimed a U.S. protectorate with Sanford B. Dole as president of the provisional government.

March 4, 1893: Grover Cleveland is inaugurated to a second term as president. Adlai E. Stevenson is vice president.

May 5, 1893: Stock prices on Wall Street drop. More than 600 banks close their doors in June as the United States enters a financial depression that lasts four years.

October 3, 1893: Following a meeting of the National League for Good Roads, a lobbying group dedicated to the passage of national road legislation, the Federal Highway Administration is founded as the Office of Road Inquiry, an agency in the Department of Agriculture.

June 26–August 3, 1894: Supporting a strike against the Pullman railroad car manufacturers, the American Railway Union, led by Eugene V. Debs, strikes against most railroads. President Cleveland sends in federal troops to break up the strike, based on a court injunction prohibiting workers from interfering with the delivery of mail.

July 4, 1894: The Republic of Hawaii is proclaimed, and the government is recognized as a foreign power by President Cleveland on August 7.

August 27, 1894: Congress passes the Wilson-Gorman Tariff Act, which lowers the tariff rate; many see it as a victory for Democratic reductionism and a blow against Republican protectionism.

May 20, 1895: The Supreme Court in *Pollock v. Farmers' Loan and Trust Company* rules that the federal income tax provision of the Wilson-Gorman Tariff Act is unconstitutional.

January 4, 1896: Utah becomes the 45th state.

November 3, 1896: William McKinley is elected president, defeating Democratic candidate William J. Bryan with an electoral vote of 271 to 176.

March 4, 1897: William McKinley is inaugurated as president with Garret A. Hobart as vice president.

April 24, 1898: Spain declares war on the United States. Congress passes an official declaration of war on Spain the following day.

July 7, 1898: Recognizing the strategic military value of its base at Pearl Harbor, Congress approves the annexation of Hawaii by joint resolution.

December 10, 1898: A treaty ending the Spanish-American War is signed in Paris.

1899: The expansion of the federal government makes it one of the leading U.S. employers, reaching close to 250,000 by 1899.

1899: Secretary of State John Hay convinces Great Britain, France, Russia, Germany, Italy, and Japan to agree to an "Open Door" policy to assure all nations equal trading rights with China.

January 9, 1899: Congress ratifies the treaty with Spain, which is signed by President McKinley on February 10. The United States acquires Puerto Rico and Guam, and Spain grants independence to Cuba. The United States buys Spanish holdings in the Philippines, gaining control over the islands.

February 6, 1900: Theodore Roosevelt, hero of the Spanish-American War (1898) and governor of New York, declares that he neither could nor would accept the nomination for the vice presidency on the Republican ticket.

February 6, 1900: President McKinley appoints William Howard Taft, a U.S. circuit judge, head of the Philippine Commission to establish a civil government in the islands.

April 13, 1900: For the fourth time in eight years the House of Representatives adopts a resolution favoring a constitutional amendment for the election of U.S. senators by direct vote of the people instead of by state legislatures. The Senate finally concurs in 1911.

April 30, 1900: By act of Congress Hawaii is granted territorial standing in the United States, joining Alaska, Oklahoma, New Mexico, and Arizona as American territories. Sanford B. Dole is appointed governor of the new territory.

September 18, 1900: The first direct primary in the United States is held in Hennepin County, Minnesota.

November 6, 1900: Republican William McKinley wins the presidential election, running against Democrat and Populist Party nominee William Jennings Bryan, Prohibition Party nominee John G. Woolley, and Socialist Labor Party nominee Joseph P. Maloney.

March 3, 1901: The National Institute of Standards and Technology is founded to provide better measurements and more uniformity, precision, and control in laboratory and factory activities.

March 4, 1901: William McKinley is inaugurated for a second term as president; Theodore Roosevelt is sworn in as vice president.

June 10, 1901: President McKinley issues a statement declaring he has no interest in seeking a third term and would not accept the nomination.

September 14, 1901: After being shot by an anarchist seven days earlier, President McKinley dies. Theodore Roosevelt becomes president.

November 1901: Alabama adopts a new constitution that effectively disenfranchises African Americans (and some poor whites) by including literacy and property tests, as well as a measure known as the "grandfather" clause, which states that a person cannot vote if his grandfather was ineligible. It also denies suffrage to individuals convicted of certain "criminal" acts. Other southern states soon follow suit.

December 3, 1901: In his first State of the Union message to Congress, President Roosevelt calls for the regulation of business trusts "within reasonable limits" and becomes the first president to advocate the conservation of natural resources on public land.

March 6, 1902: The Bureau of the Census is founded, responsible for collecting information regarding the U.S. population and its economic and social institutions.

March 10, 1902: At President Roosevelt's instigation, Attorney General Philander C. Knox files to dissolve the Northern Securities Company under the Sherman Antitrust Act. This is the first major anti-trust action by the federal government.

July 8, 1902: The Bureau of Reclamation is founded to study, locate, and construct large-scale irrigation projects in the West.

February 14, 1903: The Department of Commerce is founded out of concern that the United States is not keeping up with its industrial competitors in promoting foreign trade.

April 27, 1903: The Supreme Court upholds the clauses in the Alabama constitution which effectively deny African Americans the right to vote.

November 18, 1903: The United States and Panama sign the Hay-Bunau-Varilla Treaty giving the United States permanent rights to a ten-mile-wide canal zone in return for $10 million and an annual payment of $250,000 after nine years.

March 14, 1904: The Supreme Court upholds the Sherman Anti-Trust Act in *Northern Securities Company v. United States*.

November 8, 1904: Theodore Roosevelt is elected for his first full term as president, defeating his Demo-

cratic opponent by more than 2.5 million votes. His opponents include Eugene V. Debs (Socialist Party), Silas C. Swallow (Prohibition Party), Thomas E. Watson (Populist Party), and Judge Alton B. Parker (Democratic Party).

January 20, 1905: President Roosevelt invokes the Roosevelt Corollary (asserting the right of the United States to intervene in Latin American internal affairs) for the first time, as the United States begins to supervise the payment of national and international debts owed by the Dominican Republic.

February 1, 1905: The Department of Forestry, created in 1881, is renamed the Forest Service; it is charged with studying forest conditions, disseminating forest information, and protecting and managing the national forests.

March 4, 1905: Theodore Roosevelt is inaugurated as president for a second term. He is the youngest elected president to date. His vice president is Charles Warren Fairbanks.

June 29, 1906: Congress passes the Hepburn Act, which puts teeth in the Interstate Commerce Act by permitting regulation of rates charged by railroads, pipelines, and terminals. President Roosevelt has strongly endorsed the act and helped guide it through Congress.

June 30, 1906: The Federal Food and Drug Act is passed.

September 29, 1906: The United States invokes the Platt Amendment (an amendment to Cuba's constitution allowing the United States to intervene to maintain order) and assumes military control of Cuba. The United States continues to govern Cuba until January 1909.

October 1, 1907: A downturn in the stock market touches off the Panic of 1907. At the request of the federal government J. Pierpont Morgan and fellow bankers bring $100 million in gold from Europe to restore confidence in the economy and end the currency panic that has caused runs on banks.

November 16, 1907: Oklahoma becomes the 46th state.

February 21, 1909: President Roosevelt sends the "Great White Fleet" of 16 battleships on a world cruise, partly to demonstrate that the United States is an important international power.

May 30, 1908: Congress passes the Aldrich-Vreeland Act, which frees banks to issue notes backed by commercial paper and bonds issued by state and local governments. At the same time, archconservative Nelson W. Aldrich is named as head of the National Monetary Commission, set up to review the entire financial structure of the United States.

June 8, 1908: At the urging of Gifford Pinchot, head of the U.S. Forest Service, President Roosevelt appoints a 57-member National Commission for the Conservation of Natural Resources, naming Pinchot as chairman. The commission's job is to compile the first list of all American natural resources.

July 26, 1908: The Federal Bureau of Investigation is created by Attorney General Charles J. Bonaparte as a corps of special agents to serve as the investigative arm of the Department of Justice.

November 3, 1908: Republican William Howard Taft wins the presidential election with 1,269,900 more votes than William Jennings Bryan. The Republicans maintain their majorities in both houses of Congress.

March 4, 1909: William Howard Taft is inaugurated as the twenty-seventh president of the United States. James S. Sherman is vice president.

July 12, 1909: Congress proposes the Sixteenth Amendment, which authorizes a federal income tax. It is ratified by the states in 1913.

March 17, 1910: Congressman George W. Norris (R-Neb.) introduces a resolution to limit the power of speaker of the house during Joseph G. Cannon's dictatorial speakership. The measure passes, indicating the growing strength of progressive Republicans.

June 18, 1910: Congress passes the Mann-Elkins Act, which extends jurisdiction of the Interstate Commerce Commission (ICC) to include telephone, telegraph, cable, and wireless companies. It also augments ICC regulation of railroads, and it establishes a Commerce Court (which is abolished in 1913).

June 25, 1910: Congress passes the Publicity Act, which requires members of Congress to report campaign contributions.

January 21, 1911: The National Progressive Republican League, founded by Sen. Robert M. La Follette of Wisconsin and other insurgent Republicans, issues its platform, which calls for direct election of U.S. senators, the initiative, the referendum, the recall, and other reforms.

July 24, 1911: The United States renews its commercial treaty with Japan. Among its provisions, the treaty reaffirms the "Gentlemen's Agreement" of 1907, in which President Theodore Roosevelt pledged to see that Japanese residents of the United States were well treated if Japan voluntarily prevented Japanese laborers from immigrating to the United States.

January 6, 1912: New Mexico becomes the 47th state.

February 14, 1912: Arizona is admitted as the 48th state.

June 22, 1912: Through his control of the Republican Party machine and the support of conservatives, Taft is nominated for a second term at the Republican National Convention in Chicago. Popular former president Theodore Roosevelt breaks with the

Republican Party to run for the presidency on the Progressive Party ticket.

August 2, 1912: Sen. Henry Cabot Lodge (R-Mass.) introduces a resolution—subsequently known as the Lodge Corollary—extending the Monroe Doctrine to pertain to foreign companies and non-European nations.

November 5, 1912: With the Republican vote split between Roosevelt and Taft, Democratic candidate Woodrow Wilson wins the presidential election, carrying forty of the forty-eight states. President Taft carries only Utah and Vermont. Eugene Debs, the Socialist Party candidate, is defeated for the fourth time.

March 4, 1913: Woodrow Wilson takes the oath of office and becomes the twenty-eighth president of the United States with Thomas R. Marshall as vice president.

March 4, 1913: The Department of Labor becomes a separate department from the Department of Commerce "to foster, promote, and develop the welfare of working people, to improve their working conditions, and to enhance their opportunities for profitable employment."

March 4, 1913: The Bureau of Labor Statistics is founded as part of the Department of Labor with the goal of protecting workers and improving their working conditions by providing accurate statistics.

May 31, 1913: The Seventeenth Amendment to the Constitution, providing for the direct election of U.S. senators, is officially adopted following ratification by thirty-six states. Previously senators were selected by state legislatures.

December 23, 1913: The Federal Reserve System is established by the Federal Reserve Act of 1913 to counter financial disruptions by coordinating the Federal Reserve banks and by controlling the "discount rate," or interest rate at which banks could lend each other money.

August 1914: World War I begins.

August 3, 1914: The Panama Canal opens.

September 1, 1914: The Federal Trade Commission is created and granted an unprecedented authority by the Federal Trade Commission Act of 1914 to investigate, publicize, and prohibit all unfair methods of business competition.

April 28, 1915: The U.S. Coast Guard is founded; over the years it becomes responsible for, among other things, patrolling U.S. shores for icebergs, performing lifesaving operations, and enforcing Prohibition laws and drug control policies.

May 7, 1915: The *Lusitania*, a British passenger liner, is sunk off the Irish coast by a German submarine. The dead include 128 Americans.

September 16, 1915: Haiti becomes a U.S. protectorate under the terms of a new ten-year treaty, which the Senate approves on 28 February 1916. U.S. Marines remain in Haiti until 1934.

June 3, 1916: Congress passes the National Defense Act, which provides for the expansion of the regular army to 220,000, authorizes a National Guard of 450,000 men, establishes the Reserve Officers Training Corps (ROTC) at colleges and universities, and makes provisions for industrial preparedness.

August 25, 1916: The National Park Service is founded to promote and regulate the use of national parks and monuments.

September 7, 1916: Congress passes the Shipping Act, which authorizes the creation of the U.S. Shipping Board to oversee the requisition of ships through the Emergency Fleet Corporation.

September 7, 1916: Congress passes the Workmen's Compensation Act, which offers coverage to half a million federal employees.

September 8, 1916: The U.S. International Trade Commission is founded as the United State Tariff Commission and is charged with the duty of providing Congress with trade information and statistics that would help members of Congress make rational decisions regarding tariff revisions.

November 7, 1916: Woodrow Wilson is reelected president, narrowly defeating Republican candidate Charles Evans Hughes who had resigned from the Supreme Court to run.

1917: Jeannette Rankin is elected to the House of Representatives. She is the first woman elected to Congress.

March 5, 1917: President Wilson is inaugurated for his second term in office.

April 4, 1917: The United States declares war on Germany.

July 24, 1917: Congress appropriates $640 million to develop an army air force. The goal is to build forty-five hundred planes by the spring of 1918.

November 6, 1917: An amendment to the New York State constitution gives women the right to vote in state elections.

January 8, 1918: In an address before Congress President Wilson puts forward his proposal for peace (the Fourteen Points).

March 19, 1918: To conserve energy during the war, Congress passes legislation that puts daylight saving time into effect.

September 14, 1918: Eugene V. Debs, who has been the Socialist Party presidential candidate in 1900, 1904, 1908, and 1912, is found guilty of making seditious statements that impede recruitment efforts and is sentenced to ten years in prison under the Espionage Act of 1917. His sentence is commuted by President Warren G. Harding in 1921.

1919: The Eighteenth Amendment, known as the Prohibition amendment, is ratified.

February 14, 1919: President Wilson delivers his proposal for a League of Nations to the Paris Peace Conference.

June 28, 1919: The Treaty of Versailles is signed, officially ending World War I.

September 25, 1919: After making his fortieth speech in support of the League of Nations, President Wilson collapses in Pueblo, Colorado, and is forced to return to the White House, where he suffers an incapacitating stroke from which he never fully recovers.

October 1919: The Volstead Act is passed to provide for the enforcement of the Eighteenth Amendment (the Prohibition Amendment).

1920: The Nineteenth Amendment, which grants women the right to vote, passes.

March 19, 1920: In a victory for opponents of the Treaty of Versailles, the Senate rejects U.S. membership in the League of Nations.

November 2, 1920: With his campaign slogan "back to normalcy," Warren G. Harding receives 404 electoral votes and 60 percent of the popular vote to win the presidency of the United States. He defeats the Democratic ticket of James M. Cox and Franklin D. Roosevelt.

March 4, 1921: Warren G. Harding is inaugurated as twenty-ninth president of the United States. Calvin Coolidge is vice president.

May 19, 1921: Harding signs the Emergency Immigration Act, restricting immigration to the United States from any European country to 3 percent of the individuals of that nationality in the United States at the time of the 1910 census. The act also creates an annual ceiling of 355,000 immigrants.

June 20, 1921: Alice Robertson of Oklahoma becomes the first woman to preside over the U.S. House of Representatives, remaining at the podium for thirty minutes.

August 25, 1921: Because the United States never ratified the Versailles Treaty, U.S. and German representatives sign a peace treaty in Berlin to officially recognize the end of World War I.

September 1, 1921: The General Accounting Office is founded and given the authority to interpret any laws concerning government payments, to investigate receipt and use of public funds, to recommend to Congress ways of making government expenditures more economical and efficient, and to standardize accounting systems, forms, and procedures among all government agencies.

October 3, 1922: Rebecca Felton of Georgia becomes the first female U.S. senator. Her term, to which the governor of Georgia appointed her following the death of Sen. Thomas Watson, lasts only one day.

April 9, 1923: The U.S. Supreme Court rules the minimum-wage law for women and children in Washington, D.C., to be unconstitutional in *Adkins v. Children's Hospital.*

August 2, 1923: President Harding dies in San Francisco on a goodwill tour of the country that took him all the way to Alaska.

August 3, 1923: Calvin Coolidge is sworn in as the thirtieth president of the United States.

May 17, 1924: Congress overrides President Coolidge's veto of the Veterans' Bonus Bill, which allocates $2 billion for veterans of World War I.

May 24, 1924: The United States decides that it must become more involved in international affairs after the tremendous loss of life in Word War I (1914–18); the Foreign Service is thus created by the Rogers Act of 1924 to better represent the country's political and economic interests abroad.

November 1924: President Calvin Coolidge is elected to his first full term as president. He defeats Democratic candidate John W. Davis by an electoral vote of 382 to 136.

March 4, 1925: Calvin Coolidge is inaugurated and begins his first elected term as president. Charles G. Dawes is vice president.

November 1928: Republican Herbert C. Hoover defeats Democratic presidential candidate Alfred E. Smith by an electoral vote of 444 to 87.

March 4, 1929: Herbert Hoover is inaugurated as the thirty-first president of the United States. Charles Curtis is his vice president.

June 18, 1929: President Hoover signs the reapportionment bill, which gives the president the authority to reapportion Congress after each decennial census if Congress fails to act. Hoover finds this legislation necessary because Congress has so far refused to reapportion congressional districts on the basis of the 1920 census.

October 29, 1929: Prices on the New York Stock Exchange collapse and the United State enters the Great Depression which will last into World War II (1939–45).

May 26, 1930: The National Institutes of Health is founded; it is originally a federal laboratory dedicated to the research of diseases, navigable stream pollution, and information dissemination.

July 21, 1930: President Hoover signs into law an act establishing the Veterans Administration.

July 26, 1930: The Food and Drug Administration is founded to enforce the regulations set out in the Food and Drug Act of 1906 and the Meat Inspection Act, establishing federal food standards and prohibiting the misbranding and adulteration of food and drugs.

September–October 1931: Hoarding of gold increases as the economic depression worsens; banks are failing in great numbers (522 close during October alone), and their depositors, uninsured by the government, lose most of their savings.

February 2, 1932: On the recommendation of President Hoover, Congress establishes the Reconstruction Finance Corporation, giving it wide-ranging power to extend credit to private banks and businesses.

February 27, 1932: Congress passes the Glass-Steagall Credit Expansion Act, making $750 million of the government gold reserve available for industrial and business needs.

November 1932: Democrat Franklin D. Roosevelt is elected to the presidency, defeating Republican president Herbert Hoover by a vote of 472 to 59.

February 6, 1933: The Twentieth Amendment to the U.S. Constitution, the "lame duck" amendment, is ratified. It moves the date of the presidential inauguration from March 4 to January 20 and sets the beginning of terms for senators and congressmen as January 3, which is also established as the first day of the new session.

March 4, 1933: Franklin D. Roosevelt is inaugurated president of the United States. John N. Garner is vice president.

March 5–13, 1933: Because bank runs and closings continue to sweep the country, President Roosevelt declares a "bank holiday," suspending regular bank business to provide a cooling-off period.

March 9–June 16, 1933: Congress convenes to deal with the banking crisis, beginning the "First Hundred Days" of the "First New Deal." Many emergency bills are passed, such as the National Industrial Recovery Act, the Emergency Banking Relief Act, the Agricultural Administration Act, and the Farm Credit Act.

May 18, 1933: The Tennessee Valley Authority is founded; originally established to provide flood control, navigation, and electric power to the people in the Tennessee Valley area, it grows to become the United States's largest electric power producing company.

June 12–July 27, 1933: At the London Economic Conference, European nations and the United States are unable to develop a plan for international cooperation in ending the wide fluctuation of exchange rates and reducing trade barriers.

July 26, 1933: The Farm Credit Administration is founded.

November 16, 1933: The United States formally recognizes the Soviet Union, sixteen years after the Bolshevik Revolution of 1917.

December 5, 1933: The Twenty-first Amendment repealing Prohibition is ratified.

1934: Congress passes the National Housing Act, which establishes the Federal Housing Administration (FHA).

January 1, 1934: The Federal Deposit Insurance Corporation (FDIC) is established to help restore the country's confidence in its banking system as a result of the bank failures of the Great Depression.

June 21, 1934: The National Mediation Board is founded to handle disputes between labor and management.

July 2, 1934: The Securities and Exchange Commission is founded to administer federal securities laws that curb fraudulent stock and investment practices.

July 26, 1934: The Federal Communications Commission (FCC) is founded to combine the functions of the Federal Radio Commission (regulating airwave use and radio licenses) with the telephone and telegraph policies previously regulated by the Interstate Commerce Commission and the Postmaster General.

January 4, 1935: The "Second New Deal" begins as President Roosevelt outlines a program for social reform that will benefit laborers and small farmers.

July 5, 1935: The National Labor Relations Board is founded by the Wagner Act, a response to an appeal by President Roosevelt for a greater degree of "industrial peace" so that economic recovery from the Great Depression could be achieved.

August 14, 1935: The Social Security Administration is founded to administer the new national old-age insurance program.

November 3, 1936: Franklin D. Roosevelt is elected to a second term as president in a landslide victory over Republican Alfred M. Landon of Kansas. There will be only 89 Republicans in the new House of Representatives and only 16 in the Senate.

January 20, 1937: President Roosevelt begins his second term, declaring, "I see one-third of a nation ill-housed, ill-clad, ill-nourished." John N. Garner is his vice president.

February 5, 1937: President Roosevelt requests that Congress pass legislation to increase the number of justices on the U.S. Supreme Court to as many as fifteen. His proposal is decried as "court packing" and fails.

July 22, 1937: Congress establishes the Farm Security Administration (FSA), which offers low-interest loans to sharecroppers and farm laborers.

September 2, 1937: President Roosevelt signs the National Housing Act, creating the U.S. Housing Authority.

December 12, 1937: Japanese planes bomb and sink the U.S. gunboat *Panay* on the Yangtze River in China; two American sailors are killed. Two days later Japan formally apologizes for the incident, but relations between Japan and the United States remain strained.

February 16, 1938: President Roosevelt signs the second Agricultural Administration Act, replacing the first AAA, which had been declared unconstitutional in 1936.

February 27, 1939: The U.S. Supreme Court rules wildcat strikes (strikes in violation of a contract) to be illegal.

April 14, 1939: President Roosevelt appeals to Adolf Hitler of Germany and Benito Mussolini of Italy to ensure European peace, and he calls for a world disarmament conference.

July 1, 1939: The Office of Management and Budget is founded with the responsibility of assisting the president in overseeing the preparation of the federal budget and supervising its administration in executive branch agencies.

September 3, 1939: Responding to the German invasion of Poland on September 1, Great Britain and France declare war on Germany. On the same day 30 Americans are killed when Germany sinks a British passenger ship; President Roosevelt restates U.S. neutrality.

September 8, 1939: The White House Office is founded; early staff positions involve mostly clerical duties. By the end of the twentieth century, the office grows to include more advisory and political positions.

September 8, 1939: Due to the conflict in Europe, President Roosevelt declares a limited state of emergency that gives him the ability to act quickly if needed.

October 11, 1939: The NAACP Legal Defense and Education Fund is organized and pledges an all-out fight against discrimination.

January 26, 1940: The 1911 U.S.-Japan Treaty of Commerce expires, and Secretary of State Cordell Hull informs the Japanese government that trade will continue only on a day-to-day basis.

May 25, 1940: President Roosevelt establishes the Office of Emergency Management.

June 30, 1940: The Bureau of the Public Debt is founded to borrow money needed to operate the government by issuing Treasury bills, notes, and bonds, guaranteeing repayment of the value plus interest to the owner.

September 27, 1940: The Tripartite Pact, a ten-year military and economic alliance among Germany, Italy, and Japan, is formalized. The three Axis powers pledge mutual assistance to one another in case of attack by any nation not already at war with another member. Observers see this pact as a clear warning to the United States.

October 29, 1940: Secretary of War Henry Stimson draws the first number in the Selective Service lottery, initiating the first peacetime draft in American history.

November 5, 1940: President Roosevelt is reelected in an electoral-college landslide against Republican Wendell L. Willkie but wins the popular vote by only 5 million ballots.

January 6, 1941: In his State of the Union Address, President Roosevelt asks Congress to support a "Lend-Lease program" that will allow Great Britain to borrow needed war supplies. He also outlines the "four essential freedoms" for which the Allies are fighting: freedom of speech, freedom of worship, freedom from want, and freedom from fear.

January 20, 1941: Franklin D. Roosevelt and Henry A. Wallace are inaugurated as president and vice-president. Roosevelt becomes the first three-term president.

February 3, 1941: The U.S. Supreme Court rules in *United States v. Darby Lumber Co.* that the Fair Labor Standards Act of 1938 is constitutional.

April 11, 1941: President Roosevelt establishes the Office of Price Administration (OPA) to control wages and prices for the duration of the war. Roosevelt informs Winston Churchill that the United States will extend its "security zone" to 26 degrees longitude—the middle of the Atlantic—and will commit American security patrols to these waters.

August 14, 1941: President Roosevelt and British prime minister Winston Churchill meet to discuss the Atlantic Charter, which becomes the blueprint for the United Nations.

November 17, 1941: In Washington, D.C., Japanese ambassador Nomura Kichisaburo and special envoy Kurusu Saburo suggest that war could result if the United States does not remove its economic embargo and refrain from interfering with Japanese activities in China and the Pacific.

December 7, 1941: Japan attacks Pearl Harbor, Hawaii, as well as U.S. bases in Thailand, Malaya, Singapore, the Philippines, Guam, Wake Island, and Hong Kong.

December 8, 1941: Calling the Japanese attack "a date which will live in infamy," President Roosevelt asks Congress for a declaration of war against Japan. Only one member fails to vote for the declaration: Representative Jeannette Rankin (R-Mont.), a committed pacifist who was against American involvement in World War I.

December 11, 1941: Germany declares war on the United States, with Italy following suit.

January 12, 1942: The National War Labor Board is established to settle labor disputes.

June 13, 1942: The Office of Strategic Services (OSS), the forerunner of the Central Intelligence Agency, is established with Maj. Gen. William "Wild Bill" Donovan as director.

November 8, 1942: Operation Torch begins with four hundred thousand Allied troops landing in Algeria and Morocco in northern Africa under the command of Gen. Eisenhower.

January 14, 1943: The Casablanca Conference begins. President Roosevelt and Prime Minister Winston Churchill decide to demand unconditional surrender from the Axis powers of Germany, Italy, and Japan.

May 1, 1943: In the name of "national security," President Roosevelt seizes all bituminous-coal mines in the eastern United States in response to wildcat strikes that threaten war production.

June 10, 1943: The Current Tax Payment Act takes effect, requiring the withholding of federal income taxes from individual paychecks on a regular basis. This act revolutionizes the collecting of taxes and gives government more power to spend than before.

December 17, 1943: Congress repeals all Chinese Exclusion Acts enacted throughout the century.

January 22, 1944: President Roosevelt creates the War Refugee Board to help resettle millions of refugees after the war.

March 29, 1944: Congress authorizes $1.35 billion to seed the United Nations Relief and Rehabilitation Fund, initiating a massive program to aid Europe's displaced millions.

April 3, 1944: In *Smith v. Allwright* the U.S. Supreme Court rules that African Americans cannot be denied the right to vote in the Texas Democratic primary.

June 6, 1944: The long-planned "Operation Overlord," the invasion of Nazi-occupied France, begins on D-Day on the beaches of Normandy in northern France. By day's end 150,000 troops successfully land. Within a week more than 350,000 troops are moving toward Germany.

June 20, 1944: The Battle of the Philippine Sea ends with the decisive defeat of Japanese forces.

July 22, 1944: The Bretton Woods Conference in New Hampshire, begun July 1, ends. Representatives of 44 nations, not including the Soviet Union, establish the International Monetary Fund (IMF) and the International Bank for Reconstruction and Development (the World Bank).

August–October 1944: The Dumbarton Oaks conference is convened by President Roosevelt, with delegates from Great Britain, China, and Russia in attendance, to work out proposals that will serve as a basis for the United Nations charter.

November 7, 1944: President Franklin D. Roosevelt wins reelection for a third time. Republican candidate Thomas E. Dewey is defeated by an electoral vote of 432 to 99.

January 20, 1945: Franklin D. Roosevelt is inaugurated for an unprecedented fourth term as president, with Harry S. Truman as vice president.

February 11, 1945: The Yalta Conference ends with President Roosevelt, Winston Churchill of Great Britain, and Joseph Stalin of Russia agreeing on the postwar division of Europe and Asia, on the treatment of war criminals, and on holding the first meeting of the United Nations to discuss further issues.

April 12, 1945: President Roosevelt dies of a cerebral hemorrhage. Truman is sworn in as president.

May 8, 1945: Germany surrenders, ending the European war. Victory in Europe (V-E) Day is declared in the United States as massive celebrations erupt.

August 6, 1945: The United States drops an atomic bomb on Hiroshima, Japan. The resulting devastation amazes even the scientists who created it. More than 50,000 people perish in seconds, and four square miles of the city are reduced to rubble.

August 9, 1945: An atomic bomb is dropped on Nagasaki in southern Japan, killing 40,000 Japanese civilians immediately. Japan announces its intention to surrender.

August 27, 1945: The Allies begin to divide Korea, with the Soviets occupying the territory north of the 38th parallel and the Americans the southern half of the peninsula.

September 2, 1945: Japan signs a formal surrender onboard the *U.S.S. Missouri* in Tokyo Bay.

September 6, 1945: President Truman announces his economic recovery plan to Congress. Later known as the "Fair Deal," the program promises full employment, a substantial raise in the minimum wage, the extension of Social Security, national health insurance, federal aid to education, and government-sponsored housing for the poor.

December 14, 1945: General Marshall is named special ambassador to China to make peace between the communist forces of Mao Tse-tung and the nationalist forces of Chiang Kai-shek.

December 31, 1945: President Truman dismantles the War Labor Board, replacing it with the Wage Stabilization Board in an effort to slow the pace of rapidly growing labor unrest.

January 10, 1946: The first General Assembly of the United Nations meets in London. Heading the American delegation are Secretary of State James F. Byrnes and former first lady Eleanor Roosevelt.

January 21, 1946: The United Steelworkers close down the nation's steel plants in a dispute over wage contracts.

February 20, 1946: The Employment Act of 1946 is passed by Congress, establishing the Council of Economic Advisers to help the nation's economy change from a high-production wartime economy to a civilian economy without a loss in stability or employment.

June 3, 1946: The U.S. Supreme Court rules in *Morgan v. Commonwealth of Virginia* that segregated seating on interstate buses is unconstitutional.

July 1, 1946: The Centers for Disease Control and Prevention is founded to eradicate communicable diseases; it later expands its activities beyond the bounds of infectious disease to include areas such as nutrition, chronic disease, and occupational and environmental health.

July 4, 1946: The United States grants political independence to the Philippines, but maintains the right to station ships and planes on Philippine territory at Subic Bay and Clark Air Base.

August 2, 1946: Congress passes the Legislative Reorganization Act, which requires registration of political lobbyists and the reporting of expenses.

November 9, 1946: Responding to pressures from business and conservatives, President Truman lifts price controls on most consumer goods even though recently enacted legislation is supposed to safeguard against this for six more months.

December 5, 1946: Despite conservative opposition, especially in the South, President Truman issues Executive Order 9809, creating the Committee on Civil Rights to investigate the treatment of African Americans in the United States—the first time in American history that a president focuses on civil liberties for racial minorities.

January 1, 1947: The Federal Mediation and Conciliation Service is founded to minimize interruptions of business that grow out of labor disputes and to settle labor and management disputes through conciliation and mediation.

March 12, 1947: Announcing his "containment policy," President Truman declares that the United States will provide $400 million to Greece and Turkey to fight communism. The Truman Doctrine will commit the United States to becoming a global anti-communist policeman.

June 23, 1947: Over President Truman's veto, Congress passes the Taft-Hartley Act (Labor Management Relations Act), which bans the closed shop by which only union members may be hired and which permits employers to sue unions for damages incurred in strikes. The act also allows the government to enforce an 80-day cooling-off period, forbids political contributions by unions, and requires union leaders to swear they are not communists.

July 18, 1947: The Presidential Succession Act is passed, making the speaker of the House of Representatives next in line for the presidency after the vice president. Following the speaker is the president pro tempore of the Senate and cabinet members according to rank.

July 26, 1947: The National Security Council is founded "to advise the president with respect to the integration of domestic, foreign, and military policies relating to the national security."

September 2, 1947: President Truman flies to Brazil to sign the Inter-American Treaty of Reciprocal Assistance (Rio Pact), in which nineteen American nations commit themselves to "collective defense against aggression."

September 8, 1947: The Joint Chiefs of Staff is founded as a collaboration of operations among the nation's military branches.

September 18, 1947: The Central Intelligence Agency is founded to gather and analyze intelligence information and to document the activities of foreign governments in order to better protect national security interests.

September 18, 1947: The Department of the Air Force is founded as its own agency, replacing the Army Air Force.

October 5, 1947: For the first time in the nation's history the president uses the new medium of television to speak to the American public.

October 18, 1947: The House Un-American Activities Committee (HUAC) launches an extensive investigation into Communist activities in the movie industry.

March 8, 1948: The U.S. Supreme Court rules in *McCollum v. Board of Education* that religious training in public schools is unconstitutional.

April 30, 1948: The International Conference of American States, with twenty-one members in attendance at Bogota, Colombia, establishes the Organization of American States (OAS).

May 14, 1948: Israel declares its independence from Britain as a sovereign state. The United States becomes the first nation to recognize the new country.

June 11, 1948: The Vandenberg Resolution passes in the Senate, allowing the United States to enter into collective security alliances outside the western hemisphere.

June 26, 1948: In response to the Soviet shutdown of all traffic from the West into Berlin on June 24, the United States initiates the Berlin airlift. For the next year nearly 275,000 flights will provide Berliners with 2.3 million tons of food and fuel.

August 3, 1948: Former communist Whittaker Chambers accuses Alger Hiss, a high-ranking State Department diplomat, of membership in the Communist Party, lending credence to right-wing charges that subversives have infiltrated the government.

November 2, 1948: Defying the polls and the political pundits, President Truman is reelected by a margin of 2.2 million popular and 114 electoral votes, defeating Republican Thomas Dewey, States Rights Party ("Dixiecrats") candidate Strom Thurmond, and Progressive Party candidate Henry A. Wallace.

January 20, 1949: President Truman is inaugurated for his second term with Alben W. Barkley as vice president. In his speech Truman emphasizes the importance of foreign aid.

March 2, 1949: To prove that the United States possesses intercontinental air-strike capabilities, the U.S. Air Force's B-50 bomber circumnavigates the globe.

July 21, 1949: The Senate ratifies the North Atlantic Treaty creating the North Atlantic Treaty Organization (NATO). The United States has never before concluded an alliance treaty with any European power during peacetime.

August 10, 1949: The Department of Defense is founded to create a command and interservice cooperation of land, sea, and air forces, both at home and in foreign countries where U.S. armed forces are stationed.

October 1, 1949: Mao Tse-tung announces the creation of the People's Republic of China. The United States does not recognize the new government.

October 26, 1949: The Fair Labor Standards Act is amended to raise the minimum wage from 40 cents to 75 cents an hour.

May 10, 1950: The National Science Foundation is founded, establishing the U.S. government's role in promoting and sponsoring scientific discoveries and projects.

June 1950–July 1953: The Korean War is fought.

1951: The Twenty-second Amendment, limiting the president's service to two terms, is ratified.

October 24, 1952: The National Security Agency is founded with the responsibility for the signals intelligence and communications security activities of the U.S. government.

November 4, 1952: Republican Dwight D. Eisenhower wins the presidential election by a popular vote of 32.9 million to 26.5 million and carries thirty-nine states to Democrat Adlai Stevenson's nine.

January 20, 1953: Dwight David Eisenhower is inaugurated president and Richard Nixon as vice president.

July 27, 1953: An armistice is concluded in Korea that leaves that country divided. The United States guarantees economic aid and military security for South Korea.

May 17, 1954: In *Brown v. Board of Education* the U.S. Supreme Court rules that racial segregation in public schools is unconstitutional.

1955: The United States opposes the entry of additional communist nations, especially "Red" China, into the United Nations.

1955: The eighty-fourth Congress has a record 18 women (16 in the House of Representatives, one in the Senate, and one nonvoting delegate from Hawaii).

November 6, 1956: President Eisenhower and Vice President Nixon are reelected in a landslide victory over Democrats Adlai Stevenson and Estes Kefauver (457 electoral votes to 74; 33.2 million popular votes to 24.1 million).

January 20, 1957: Dwight David Eisenhower is inaugurated for his second term as president with Richard Nixon as vice president.

May 18, 1957: The United States Commission on Civil Rights is founded with the mission of reporting to the president and Congress about all forms of discrimination throughout the United States.

September 24, 1957: President Eisenhower orders U.S. Army paratroopers to prevent interference with racial integration at Central High School in Little Rock, Arkansas.

April 1, 1958: The National Aeronautics and Space Administration is founded; it becomes the principal operating agency for manned space flight, space science, and launch-vehicle development, as well as a significant research-and-development source for space-flight technology and aeronautics.

August 2, 1958: The Federal Aviation Administration is founded with roots in the Air Commerce Act of 1926 which provides for the regulation of pilots and aircraft, for setting up a system of airways and navigational aids, and for fostering air commerce in general.

January 3, 1959: Alaska becomes the 49th state.

August 21, 1959: Hawaii becomes the 50th state.

November 16, 1959: The Department of Justice initiates a lawsuit in U.S. District Court to end "white primaries" in Tennessee, where blacks had been prohibited from voting.

May 5, 1960: The Soviet Union shoots down an American U-2 spy plane and captures the pilot, Francis Gary Powers. A conference between President Eisenhower and Soviet premier Nikita Khrushchev is consequently canceled.

November 1960: Republican vice president Richard Nixon is defeated in his bid for the presidency by Democrat John F. Kennedy, earning 219 electoral votes to Kennedy's 303.

1961: The Twenty-third Amendment grants voting rights in presidential elections to citizens who reside in Washington, D.C.

January 20, 1961: John F. Kennedy is inaugurated president with Lyndon B. Johnson as vice president.

March 1, 1961: President Kennedy establishes the Peace Corps by executive order.

April 17, 1961: Cuban exiles backed by the CIA invade Fidel Castro's Cuba at the Bay of Pigs. Cuba defeats the invaders by April 20, and the surviving members of the force are captured and imprisoned.

May 4, 1961: The Freedom Riders begin their bus travels to various southern cities, seeking to eliminate segregation in interstate transportation.

May 5, 1961: Slightly more than three weeks after Soviet cosmonaut Yuri Gagarin became the first human to fly in space, American astronaut Alan B. Shepard is launched in the *Freedom 7* spacecraft into space.

August 13, 1961: East Germany closes its borders with West Berlin and begins construction of the Berlin Wall.

November 3, 1961: Gen. Maxwell Taylor and State Department official Walt Rostow return from a fact-finding trip to South Vietnam and recommend quick military action.

February 19, 1962: John Glenn, a lieutenant colonel in the U.S. Marine Corps and pilot of the *Friendship 7* spacecraft who later becomes a senator from Ohio, is the first American to orbit Earth. He does so three times.

October 14, 1962: The United States discovers Soviet offensive missiles in Cuba and issues an ultimatum demanding their removal. Cuba is quarantined and placed under a U.S. naval blockade. After several days of tense confrontation, the Soviets agree to remove their missiles from Cuba on October 28.

August 28, 1963: Civil rights supporters march on Washington, D.C., and listen to Dr. Martin Luther King, Jr.'s now-famous "I have a dream" speech.

November 22, 1963: President Kennedy is assassinated while riding in a motorcade in Dallas, Texas. Lee Harvey Oswald is later charged with the murder. Subsequently, Lyndon B. Johnson is sworn in as president of the United States onboard Air Force One en route from Dallas to Washington, D.C.

1964: The Twenty-fourth Amendment passes. It bans the poll tax, which had been used to prevent many African Americans from voting.

June 10, 1964: The Senate invokes the cloture rule, ending a southern filibuster designed to prevent a vote on a civil rights bill—the first time cloture has successfully been invoked on civil rights legislation.

July 2, 1964: President Johnson signs the Civil Rights Act of 1964, the most extensive and far-reaching civil rights act since the Reconstruction.

August 3, 1964: U.S. ships are attacked in the Gulf of Tonkin by North Vietnamese patrol boats, prompting a retaliation by the United States and passage of the Tonkin Gulf Resolution, giving President Johnson congressional approval for all future actions he takes regarding the undeclared war in Vietnam.

August 20, 1964: President Johnson signs the War on Poverty Bill.

November 3, 1964: Johnson wins the presidential election. He defeats Arizona conservative Republican Goldwater in a landslide, carrying many Democrats into office.

1965: Johnson escalates the Vietnam War. By the end of the year there are more than 180,000 American troops there.

January 20, 1965: Lyndon B. Johnson is inaugurated for a second term. Hubert H. Humphrey is vice president.

March 2, 1965: U.S. aircraft begin bombing North Vietnam.

March 8, 1965: The first U.S. combat troops are sent to Vietnam; earlier forces had consisted primarily of military advisers and support personnel.

April 28, 1965: The United States invades the Dominican Republic, ostensibly to prevent a Communist takeover.

July 2, 1965: The Equal Employment Opportunity Commission is established under Title VII of the Civil Rights Act of 1964 to investigate and conciliate all claims of discrimination in the workplace on the basis of race, color, national origin, sex, and religion.

August 6, 1965: President Johnson signs the Voting Rights Act of 1965.

August 10, 1965: The Economic Development Administration is founded under the terms of the Public Works and Economic Development Act to target federal resources to economically distressed areas and to help develop local economies in the United States.

September 25, 1965: The National Endowment for the Humanities is founded after advocates of the humanities in the United States see the large investments being made for improvements in the sciences and argue that improving the disciplines of the humanities is equally important to the country's interests.

September 29, 1965: The National Endowment for the Arts is founded; since its creation, it has sponsored thousands of individual and organizational arts projects, supported the establishment of arts councils in every state, and worked to make the arts in America excellent and accessible.

November 9, 1965: The Department of Housing and Urban Development is founded to form an integrated approach to addressing housing and community development needs, taking into consideration the social, physical, and economic conditions that help communities thrive.

October 15, 1966: The Department of Transportation is founded as a cabinet-level agency responsible for creating and regulating policy for the entire transportation industry in the United States.

1967: The Twenty-fifth Amendment is ratified. It clarifies the circumstances under which the vice president becomes president, and allows for the possibility of the vice president serving as acting president if the president is temporarily incapacitated. It also establishes a method by which the vice president can be replaced.

March 31, 1968: President Johnson announces to a national television audience that he is halting the bombing of North Vietnam; he invites North Vietnam to begin peace negotiations. He also announces he will not run for reelection.

April 4, 1968: Civil rights leader Martin Luther King, Jr., is murdered in Memphis, Tennessee. Riots occur in many U.S. cities.

April 11, 1968: President Johnson signs the Civil Rights Act of 1968, directed at reducing racial discrimination practices in housing.

June 5, 1968: New York senator Robert F. Kennedy, brother of slain president John Kennedy, is shot and killed hours after winning the California Democratic presidential primary.

July 1, 1968: The Nuclear Non-Proliferation Treaty is signed by the United States, the Soviet Union, and many other nations.

November 5, 1968: Republican Richard Nixon wins the presidential election over Democratic contender Hubert Humphrey, from Minnesota.

January 20, 1969: Richard M. Nixon is inaugurated president with Spiro Agnew as vice president.

July 20, 1969: American astronauts Neil Armstrong and Edwin Aldrin are the first people to walk on the moon.

November 15, 1969: Over 250,000 march in Washington, D.C., to protest the Vietnam War. American opinion is deeply divided over the war effort; "hawks" call for increased military action while "doves" want to reduce military activity.

January 1, 1970: The Occupational Safety and Health Administration is founded with the goal of preventing injuries and deaths in the workplace and protecting the health of U.S. workers.

March 19, 1970: The National Highway Traffic Safety Administration is founded by the National Traffic and Motor Vehicles Act of 1966 that made auto design and manufacturing subject to federal regulation.

June 15, 1970: In *Welsh v. United States* the U.S. Supreme Court rules that the claim of conscientious-objector status can be argued on the basis of moral objection to war rather than long-standing religious belief alone.

September 22, 1970: President Nixon signs a bill authorizing a nonvoting congressional representative to the House of Representatives for the District of Columbia, the first since 1875.

December 2, 1970: The Environmental Protection Agency is founded as a coordinated and inclusive effort to control pollution in all its forms.

1971: The Twenty-sixth amendment lowers the voting age to 18.

February 11, 1971: The United States, the Soviet Union, and sixty-one other nations sign the Seabed Arms Control Treaty, banning nuclear weapons from the ocean floor.

April 7, 1971: The Supreme Court upholds court-ordered busing to achieve racial balance.

October 25, 1971: With the support of the United States, members of the United Nations vote to admit the People's Republic of China and expel Nationalist China (Taiwan).

January 22, 1972: In *Roe v. Wade* the Supreme Court decides that states cannot prevent a woman from obtaining an abortion during the first trimester of pregnancy.

February 1972: President Nixon travels to the (Communist) People's Republic of China, the most visible sign of an ongoing shift towards a more positive U.S. relationship with that nation.

February 14, 1972: President Nixon announces that he will take steps to limit the scope of court-ordered busing.

March 22, 1972: A proposed Twenty-seventh Amendment to the Constitution, prohibiting discrimination on the basis of gender, is passed by Congress and sent to the states for ratification. By the end of 1972, twenty-two of the necessary 38 states have ratified the amendment, also known as the Equal Rights Amendment.

April 7, 1972: The Federal Election Campaign Act goes into effect. The law sets limits and requires disclosures on personal contributions to political candidates.

May 22–30, 1972: President Nixon becomes the first American president to visit Moscow. While in the

Soviet Union he signs treaties on ballistic missiles and other strategic weapons.

September 12, 1972: The Senate approves President Nixon's $33.5-billion revenue-sharing plan that will disburse federal funds to state and local governments over a five-year period.

November 7, 1972: Richard Nixon defeats Sen. George McGovern for the presidency by 17,409,550 votes. McGovern wins electoral-college victories only in Massachusetts and the District of Columbia. The Democrats nevertheless retain their majorities in both houses of Congress.

November 27–30, 1972: Following a full collapse in the Paris peace talks, Nixon orders massive bombing raids against the North Vietnamese cities of Hanoi and Haiphong. The campaign continues for 11 days, pausing only for Christmas.

January 2, 1973: The Democratic Caucus of the House of Representatives votes 154 to 75 to cut off funds for the Vietnam War. Two days later the Senate Democratic Caucus votes 36 to 12 to cut off funds for the war.

January 20, 1973: Richard M. Nixon begins a second term as president.

January 30, 1973: Former Nixon campaign members James W. McCord and G. Gordon Liddy are convicted of breaking into and illegally wiretapping the Democratic party headquarters at the Watergate office complex.

February 27–May 8, 1973: Members of the American Indian Movement (AIM) exchange gunfire with federal agents in Wounded Knee, South Dakota. They seize a church and post office and hold them for 73 days to call attention to grievances they have against the federal government and tribal management.

April 30, 1973: The Watergate scandal continues to unfold. H. R. Haldeman, White House chief of staff; John Ehrlichman, domestic policy assistant; John Dean, presidential counsel; and Richard Kleindienst, attorney general, all resign their offices. In a televised address President Nixon denies any involvement in the Watergate break-in or cover-up.

May 14, 1973: The Consumer Product Safety Commission is created under the Consumer Product Safety Act and is charged with regulating consumer products, enforcing compliance with manufacturing safety standards, and developing a widespread consumer information system.

July 1, 1973: The Drug Enforcement Administration is founded to fight illegal drug use and trafficking.

July 31, 1973: Representative Robert F. Drinan (D-Mass.) introduces a resolution calling for President Nixon's impeachment on four grounds: the bombing of Cambodia; the unauthorized taping of conversations; the refusal to spend impounded funds;

and the establishment of a "supersecret security force within the White House."

October 10, 1973: Spiro Agnew resigns the vice presidency and pleads nolo contendere (no contest) to income-tax evasion in return for the dropping of other criminal charges. He receives a three-year suspended sentence and a $10,000 fine. Gerald Ford is sworn in as vice president on December 6.

October 20, 1973: President Nixon fires his Attorney General, Elliot Richardson, for refusing to obey Nixon's orders and fire Archibald Cox, the Special Prosecutor investigating Watergate. When Deputy Attorney General William Ruckleshaus also refuses to do so, Nixon fires him as well. Solicitor General Robert Bork then fires Cox, and disbands his 60 man investigative team. The public is outraged by these actions, which the media refers to as the "Saturday Night Massacre."

November 7, 1973: Over President Nixon's veto Congress passes the War Powers Act, requiring congressional approval for any commitment of U.S. armed forces abroad beyond 60 days.

December 6, 1973: Gerald Ford is sworn in as the new vice president. Appointed to the vice presidency under the guidelines of the 25th Amendment, he is the first vice president who was not elected to that office.

January 2, 1974: President Nixon signs into law a bill that requires states to lower speed limits to 55 miles per hour in order to receive federal highway funds. The bill is designed to help conserve energy.

May 31, 1974: The National Institute on Aging is founded after the federal government recognizes the need for a separate institute on aging at the 1971 White House Conference on Aging.

July 24, 1974: The Supreme Court rules, in *United States v. Richard M. Nixon,* that the White House has no claim to "executive privilege" in withholding the Watergate tapes from Special Prosecutor Jaworski. President Nixon turns over the tapes on July 30 and August 5.

August 8, 1974: In a televised address Richard Nixon announces his resignation from the presidency, effective at noon on August 9. He becomes the first president in American history to resign.

August 9, 1974: Gerald R. Ford is inaugurated as the thirty-eighth president of the United States. He is the first "unelected" president, having been appointed vice president the previous December.

August 20, 1974: President Ford nominates former New York governor Nelson A. Rockefeller for vice president. He is confirmed in December.

September 8, 1974: President Ford grants Nixon "a full, free, and absolute pardon" for any crimes he might have committed while in office. In opinion polls

Ford's popularity drops from 71 percent to 49 percent.

October 10, 1974: Congress passes legislation providing for public funding of presidential primaries and elections.

November 21, 1974: Over President Ford's veto Congress passes the Freedom of Information Act, increasing public access to government files.

February 24, 1975: The Congressional Budget Office is founded to give Congress more control over the nation's finances and to counter growing presidential power in budgeting.

April 14, 1975: The Federal Election Commission is founded, charged with enforcing the Federal Election Campaign Act of 1971, which had provisions requiring full reporting of campaign contributions and expenditures, limiting advertising in the media, and allowing corporations and labor unions to form Political Action Committees (PACs) through which they could solicit contributions.

May 2, 1975: The Labor Department announces an unemployment rate of 8.9 percent in April, the highest since 1941.

1976: *Viking I* and *Viking II* space probes land on Mars and send detailed information back to Earth about that planet's surface.

January 30, 1976: The Supreme Court upholds the provisions of the 1974 Campaign Financing Reform Act. It also requires that members of the Federal Election Commission be appointed by the president, not Congress.

May 11, 1976: The Office of Science and Technology Policy is founded to provide support and counsel to the president in matters of science and technology.

July 2, 1976: The Supreme Court upholds the death penalty laws of Georgia, Florida, and Texas. It strikes down death penalties in North Carolina and Louisiana.

November 2, 1976: Former Democratic Georgia governor James Earl "Jimmy" Carter defeats Republican Gerald Ford for the presidency. The Democrats retain majorities in both houses of Congress.

January 20, 1977: Jimmy Carter is inaugurated president of the United States. Walter Mondale takes the oath of office as vice president.

March 9, 1977: The Health Care Financing Administration is founded to more effectively coordinate Medicare and Medicaid and to address the issues created by escalating health care costs and the growing number of beneficiaries.

October 1, 1977: The Department of Energy is founded to oversee energy-related activities and programs and to incorporate nuclear technology as an alternative energy source within the United States.

October 1, 1977: The Federal Energy Regulatory Commission is created by the Department of Energy Organization Act of 1977 to establish and oversee U.S. energy policy.

April 18, 1978: The Senate ratifies a Panama Canal treaty that will turn control of the waterway over to Panama in 1999.

June 10, 1978: The National Council on Disability is founded as an advisory board within the Department of Education to address educational issues affecting the disabled.

June 28, 1978: The Supreme Court hands down the Bakke decision; it upholds a reverse discrimination ruling made after Allen Bakke was rejected twice for admission to California Medical School at Davis, because a special-admissions minority program reduced the number of positions available for whites.

October 6, 1978: The Senate votes to extend the deadline for ratification of the Equal Rights Amendment to June 30, 1982. Thirty-five states have approved the amendment, three short of the necessary thirty-eight.

January 1, 1979: The Federal Labor Relations Authority is created under Title VII of the Civil Service Reform Act, to oversee the certification of federal employees' bargaining units and to handle labor-management issues.

January 1, 1979: The United States recognizes the People's Republic of China and terminates its mutual defense treaty with Taiwan.

March 26, 1979: Egyptian president Anwar Sadat and Israeli prime minister Menachem Begin sign a formal peace treaty between their two nations in a ceremony held at the White House. The peace treaty, ending thirty-one years of warfare, was based upon negotiations mediated by U.S. president Jimmy Carter at Camp David in 1978.

March 31, 1979: The Federal Emergency Management Agency is founded with the primary mission to help the United States recover in the event of a nuclear attack; helping people recover from disasters is its secondary function. By the 1990s, however, the agency is transformed from a national defense-oriented agency to one that proactively assists people to recover from all types of disasters.

June 18, 1979: In Vienna the SALT II Accord, limiting production of nuclear weapons, is signed by President Carter and Soviet president Brezhnev.

June 27, 1979: The Supreme Court upholds the affirmative action program by ruling that an employer can establish voluntary programs to eliminate racial imbalance.

November 4, 1979: In Tehran several hundred Iranian militants storm the U.S. embassy and seize the diplomatic personnel. The militants announce they will release the hostages when the United States returns the shah, who is recovering from medical treatments

in a New York hospital, to Iran to stand trial. President Carter declares he will not extradite the shah.

January 4, 1980: President Jimmy Carter reacts to the Soviet invasion of Afghanistan on December 29, 1979, by withdrawing the SALT II arms-control treaty from consideration by the U.S. Senate. He also places an embargo on the sale of grain and some types of electronic equipment to the Soviet Union.

February 2, 1980: The news media report the results of a two-year sting operation (code name: Abscam) in which an FBI agent posing as a wealthy Arab offered bribes to elected officials. Among those arrested and eventually convicted on bribery or related charges are Sen. Harrison Williams Jr. (D-N.J.) and Representatives John W. Jenrette, Jr. (D-S.C.), Richard Kelly (R-Fla.), Raymond Lederer (D-Pa.), John M. Murphy (D-N.Y.), Michael Myers (D-Pa.), and Frank Thompson, Jr. (D-N.J.).

May 4, 1980: The Department of Education is founded; its predecessor was created by Congress in 1867 to collect information on schools and teaching that would help the states establish more effective school systems.

May 4, 1980: The Department of Health and Human Services is founded; its roots go back to the earliest days of the nation when the first marine hospital was established in 1798 to care for sailors.

August 20, 1980: The Defense Department announces the development of the Stealth aircraft, which can elude detection by radar.

November 4, 1980: Republican Ronald Reagan is elected president of the United States with 51.6 percent of the popular vote to 41.7 percent for incumbent Democratic president Jimmy Carter and 6.7 percent for third-party candidate John Anderson.

January 20, 1981: The Iran hostages are freed on the same day that Reagan is inaugurated as president and George Bush is inaugurated as vice president.

March 1981: President Reagan directs the CIA to assist "Contra" guerrilla forces opposed to the Marxist Sandinista government of Nicaragua.

April 11, 1981: President Reagan returns to the White House and a restricted work schedule after surgery and eleven days of hospitalization resulting from a March 30 assassination attempt.

September 29, 1981: President Reagan orders the U.S. Coast Guard to turn back boatloads of Haitian refugees fleeing their country without proper immigration papers.

1982: Because three-fourths of the states have failed to ratify the proposed Twenty-seventh (Equal Rights) Amendment, even after an extension, it dies.

October 1, 1982: The House of Representatives votes down a proposed constitutional amendment requiring a balanced federal budget.

December 8, 1982: Congressman Edward Boland (D-Mass.) successfully sponsors legislation making it illegal to use U.S. funds to overthrow the Sandinista government of Nicaragua. Congress renews the amendment in 1983, 1984, and 1985, extending it through the 1986 fiscal year.

March 23, 1983: President Reagan proposes the development of a defense shield—at least partly based in space—to intercept incoming missiles. Formally called the Strategic Defense Initiative (SDI), this proposal is popularly known as "Star Wars."

April 1983: The American public learns that the CIA assisted a Contra attack on Nicaraguan oil terminals.

October 25, 1983: U.S. troops invade Grenada after the assassination of Grenadan prime minister Maurice Bishop during a coup led by militant leftist Gen. Hudson Austin.

April 9, 1984: Nicaragua asks the International Court of Justice to rule that U.S. aid to the Contra rebels and its role in mining Nicaraguan harbors is illegal. On May 10 the court orders the United States to pay reparations to Nicaragua and to refrain from further involvement with the Contras. The United States contends that the court has no jurisdiction on the matter.

July 17, 1984: Congress passes a bill that will cut federal highway funding for states that fail to raise their minimum drinking age to twenty-one.

September 26, 1984: Congress passes a law requiring tougher health warnings on cigarette packages.

November 1984: Ronald Reagan is reelected as president of the United States, defeating Democrat Walter F. Mondale with 58.8 percent of the popular vote.

November 26, 1984: The United States and Iraq resume diplomatic ties, severed since 1967.

1985: Israeli intelligence tells the United States that Shiite Muslims will exchange western hostages for arms for Iran.

January 20, 1985: President Reagan takes the oath of office marking the beginning of his second term; George Bush is vice president. Because of the bitter cold, public ceremonies are postponed until January 21.

March 12, 1985: The United States and the Soviet Union reopen formal arms-control talks in Geneva.

1986: The national debt soars to over $2 trillion. The trade deficit worsens as does the budget deficit.

January 7, 1986: President Reagan declares a state of emergency between the United States and Libya, ordering U.S. oil companies out of Libya and ending trade and transportation between the two nations.

January 28, 1986: All seven astronauts aboard the U.S. space shuttle *Challenger* perish when their craft explodes. It is the worst accident in the history of the U.S. space program.

February 25, 1986: The United States recognizes the Philippine government of Corazon Aquino after the Reagan administration at first refused to acknowledge that outgoing president Ferdinand Marcos had attempted to prevent her election victory through vote fraud.

June 25, 1986: The U.S. House of Representatives approves $100 million in humanitarian and economic aid to the Contras in Nicaragua.

July 7, 1986: The Supreme Court declares unconstitutional a key provision of the Gramm-Rudman Act that would allow the comptroller general to decide precise spending cuts in each federal department.

September 27, 1986: Congress passes the most sweeping tax-reform bill since the 1940s.

October 2, 1986: Congress overrides President Reagan's veto of the Comprehensive Anti-Apartheid Act, which condemns racial separation in South Africa, institutes an embargo on most South African imports, and bans most American investment in that nation.

November 13, 1986: President Reagan says the United States has sent Iran a few defensive weapons and spare parts, but he denies any attempt to exchange weapons for hostages.

February 4, 1987: Congress overrides President Reagan's veto of a $20 billion Clean Water Act. It is identical to an act he vetoed successfully in 1986.

February 26, 1987: The Tower Commission report places chief blame for the Iran-Contra affair on National Security Council director Robert McFarlane, Lt. Col. Oliver North, Adm. John Poindexter, and former CIA director William Casey. It also criticizes the president for remaining too distant from the planning process.

April 2, 1987: Congress overrides President Reagan's veto of an $87.5 billion highway and transit bill that also allows states to raise speed limits to 65 MPH on interstate highways in sparsely populated areas.

October 19, 1987: Black Monday. The stock market plunges a record 508 points during one session.

November 18, 1987: In its final report on the Iran-Contra hearings Congress criticizes those involved in the operation for "secrecy, deception and disdain for the law."

December 8–10, 1987: During a summit meeting in Washington, D.C., President Reagan and Premier Gorbachev sign the Intermediate Nuclear Forces (INF) Treaty, agreeing to eliminate intermediate-range weapons from their nuclear arsenals.

March 22, 1988: Congress overrides President Reagan's veto of the Civil Rights Restoration Act, which extends federal anti-bias laws to an entire school or other organization if any of its programs receive federal funding.

September 13, 1988: President Reagan signs a bill extending the Fair Housing Act of 1968 to protect the disabled and families with children.

October 22, 1988: Congress passes a Taxpayer's Bill of Rights.

November 8, 1988: Republican vice president George Bush is elected president, defeating Democrat Michael Dukakis by a margin of 53.4 to 45.6 percent.

1989: The Communist party in Poland loses power in the national elections. New governments replace the Communist regimes in Romania, Bulgaria, and Czechoslavakia.

January 20, 1989: George Bush is inaugurated president with Dan Quayle as vice president.

January 23, 1989: The Supreme Court invalidates a Richmond, Virginia, affirmative action program calling it reverse discrimination.

March 15, 1989: The Department of Veterans Affairs is founded as the 14th department of the presidential cabinet.

October 1, 1989: The Office of Government Ethics is founded to ensure that employees of the executive branch of government perform their public duties in an ethical manner.

June 11, 1990: A proposed constitutional amendment to make the desecration of the American flag a crime fails in the House of Representatives.

July 26, 1990: The Americans with Disabilities Act is signed into law prohibiting discrimination on the basis of disability in employment, programs, or services provided by the government.

August 2, 1990: Iraqi forces, on the order of dictator Saddam Hussein, invade Kuwait; in response, President George Bush dispatches American military forces to the Persian Gulf.

October 22, 1990: President George Bush vetoes the Civil Rights Act of 1990 on the basis that the act would create "quotas" in the workplace.

November 15, 1990: The Clean Air Act is signed by President Bush, setting restrictions on automobile and utility emissions and the use of chlorofluorocarbons.

November 21, 1990: The Cold War is formally brought to an end with the signing of the Charter of Paris by the leaders of 34 North American and European nations.

1991: Forces from 34 nations, including the United States, overwhelm troops in Iraq and occupy Kuwait in Operation Desert Storm. On February 27, President Bush's popularity soars to 89 percent when he declares to Congress, "Kuwait is liberated."

July 31, 1991: The Strategic Arms Reduction Treaty is signed between the United States and the Soviet Union to reduce and limit strategic offensive weaponry.

October 23, 1991: After televised Senate Judiciary Committee hearings into charges of sexual harassment made against Clarence Thomas, a federal appeals court judge, by former colleague Anita F. Hill, Thomas is sworn as Court Justice of the Supreme Court of the United States.

December 21, 1991: Following continued economic and political deterioration, Soviet republics with the exception of Georgia sign a pact establishing the Commonwealth of Independent States. President Gorbachev resigns on December 25, heralding the official end of the Union of Soviet Socialist Republics (U.S.S.R.).

1992: Navy Secretary H. Lawrence Grant III is forced to resign after scandal erupts from the 1991 Tailhook Association convention in Las Vegas, Nevada, where women were assaulted by members of the navy. Three navy admirals are disciplined as a result of the incident.

May 7, 1992: The Twenty-seventh Amendment to the Constitution is ratified, barring pay raises for members of Congress between terms. It was originally proposed in September of 1789.

November 3, 1992: Arkansas Governor Bill Clinton defeats incumbent President George Bush to become the 42d president of the United States, winning 43 percent of the popular vote against Bush's 37 percent. A Democrat, Clinton's election breaks the 12-year Republican control of the White House. Also running as a presidential candidate is Ross Perot, who garners 19 percent of the popular vote.

December 9, 1992: Twenty-eight thousand U.S. troops are sent to Somalia in Operation Restore Hope, an effort to stem widespread famine and restore order among warring clans.

December 17, 1992: The North American Free Trade Agreement (NAFTA) is signed by the leaders of the United States, Canada, and Mexico to abolish most restrictions on trade between the countries.

January 20, 1993: Bill Clinton is inaugurated president with Al Gore as vice president.

January 25, 1993: The National Economic Council is founded by President Bill Clinton as an advisory council to help formulate and coordinate economic policy throughout the government in both domestic and international arenas.

February 5, 1993: The Family and Medical Leave Act is enacted, entitling eligible employees to take up to 12 weeks of unpaid, job-protected leave for specific family or medical reasons.

April 19, 1993: A 51-day standoff in Waco, Texas, occurring between members of the Branch Davidians, a religious group led by David Koresh, and federal law enforcement officers, ends with over 70 civilians and four federal agents dead.

March 3, 1993: The National Partnership for Reinventing Government is founded when President Bill Clinton appoints Vice President Al Gore head of the National Performance Review; Gore is given six months to study the problems associated with the federal government and then report recommendations for improvement.

November 30, 1993: President Clinton signs the Brady Bill, which requires a five-day waiting period for hand gun purchases. The bill is named after President Ronald Reagan's press secretary who was wounded while protecting the president in an assassination attempt.

May 6, 1994: An unprecedented sexual-harassment suit is filed against President Bill Clinton by a former Arkansas state employee, Paula Jones.

July 26–August 5, 1994: Congressional hearings take place concerning the Whitewater affair, questionable financial dealings that took place in the 1980s linked to President Bill Clinton and First Lady Hillary Rodham Clinton.

July 30, 1994: In *Madsen v. Women's Health Center, Inc.* the Supreme Court rules to inhibit pro-life activists from blocking public access of abortion clinics and from physically abusing persons entering or leaving the clinic.

August 28, 1994: U.S. forces occupy Haiti and force General C,dras to step down, restoring the elected president, Jean-Bertand Aristide, to power.

November 1995: Serbs, Muslims, and Croats of Bosnia sign a U.N.-brokered peace accord after the United States conducts limited air raids on the country, which led the warring parties to the negotiation table.

February 8, 1996: The Telecommunications Act is signed by President Bill Clinton; its objectives include allowing all Americans access to the Information Superhighway and developing technology that will allow parents to have more control over the type of television programming watched by their children.

April 9, 1996: President Bill Clinton signs a bill permitting line item veto, or the veto of specific spending or taxing provisions of legislation, modifying past stipulations that allowed a president to veto an entire bill only.

May 20, 1996: In *Romer v. Evans* the Supreme Court rules to overturn an amendment to the Colorado constitution that prohibits extending legal protection from discrimination to homosexuals, stating it violates the Fourteenth Amendment's equal protection clause.

June 13, 1996: The Supreme Court rules in *Shaw v. Hunt* that a redistricting plan in North Carolina assigning voters to a district based mainly on their race is unconstitutional, violating the Fourteenth Amendment.

June 26, 1996: The case of *United States v. Virginia* is decided by the Supreme Court, finding the male-only admission policy of the Virginia Military Institute (a public institute of higher learning) to be unconstitutional.

August 22, 1996: President Bill Clinton signs into law the Personal Responsibility and Work Opportunity Reconciliation Act, replacing previous welfare programs with one requiring work in exchange for monetary assistance.

November 1996: The Democratic National Committee has charges questioning its fund-raising practices. These charges arise from concern that the Committee has been illegally accepting contributions from foreign powers.

November 5, 1996: President Bill Clinton is reelected with 49.2 percent of the popular vote, defeating Republican candidate Bob Dole who receives 40.8 percent. Also running was Reform Party opponent Ross Perot, receiving 8.5 percent of the popular vote.

1997: Congress passes a bill reducing funds for Medicare by $115 billion over five years.

January 20, 1997: Bill Clinton begins a second term in office; Al Gore remains as vice president.

February 23, 1997: The first successful cloning of a mammal from the cell of an adult is reported. The effort was led by researchers at the Roslin Institute in Edinburgh, Scotland. The resulting clone, a sheep by the name of Dolly, had been born in July 1996.

May 27, 1997: Denying an attempt by President Bill Clinton to delay a sexual harassment lawsuit initiated by former employee Paula Jones, the Supreme Court decides in *Clinton v. Jones* that a serving president is not entitled to immunity for actions previous to or outside of office responsibilities.

June 26, 1997: In *Vacco v. Quill* and *Washington v. Glucksberg*, the Supreme Court rules that states may continue denying terminally-ill patients the right to a doctor's assistance in ending their lives.

June 26, 1997: The Supreme Court rules in *Reno v. American Civil Liberties Union* that a 1996 law prohibiting "indecent" material from being displayed on the Internet is unconstitutional, violating the First Amendment right of free speech.

June 27, 1997: In *Printz v. United States* the Supreme Court overturns a provision of gun control legislation (Brady Bill) requiring local law enforcement officers to perform background checks on potential handgun purchasers.

July 1, 1997: In an elaborate ceremony, Hong Kong is handed over to China from Britain after 99 years of being a British territory. Tung Chee-hwa is appointed as head of the Hong Kong Special Administration Region and a provincial legislature is sworn in. In response to protests about the takeover, Martin Lee, leader of China's Democratic Party, assures the public that the "flame of democracy will not be snuffed out."

July 4, 1997: *Pathfinder* makes the first successful landing of an American spacecraft on Martian soil in more than 20 years. Two days later, a small robotic vehicle called *Sojourner* is deployed to collect data about Mars's environment. Information received by NASA reveals similarities between the rock and soil content of Mars and Earth.

August 5, 1997: President Bill Clinton signs a federal budget bill promising to balance the budget by 2002.

January 16, 1998: Tobacco companies, sued by the state of Texas for Medicare funds lost treating individuals for smoking-related diseases, decide to settle for $15.3 billion over 25 years.

January 21, 1998: Reports of an alleged sexual relationship between President Bill Clinton and former White House intern Monica S. Lewinsky surface. President Clinton denies the allegations. If true, they would mean that Clinton had lied under oath during the investigation into the Paula Jones sexual harassment case.

February 1998: The 1999 U.S. budget proposed by President Bill Clinton is the first balanced budget since 1969; the $1.73 trillion budget has a surplus of $9.5 billion, which Clinton proposes spending on the ailing Social Security system.

March 4, 1998: The Supreme Court rules that sexual discrimination in the workplace extends to include same-sex sexual harassment in *Oncale v. Sundowner Offshore Services, Inc.*

May 22, 1998: The White House attempts to protect aides from testifying in accusations against the president by citing executive privilege; Federal judge Norma Holloway Johnson rules that the Secret Service must testify before the grand jury.

June 25, 1998: The Supreme Court rules in *Bragdon v. Abbott* that individuals with HIV, even if they are not suffering from symptoms of AIDS, are protected from discrimination under the Americans with Disabilities Act.

June 25, 1998: In *Clinton v. New York City* the Supreme Court strikes down the line-item veto law, stating that giving the president power to veto specific items in spending bills is unconstitutional and disrupts the balance of power.

August 7, 1998: Two bombs explode outside U.S. embassies in Kenya and Tanzania, killing 224 people (including 24 Americans). In retaliation, U.S.

missiles are fired at sites believed to be Islamic terrorist centers linked to the bombings.

August 17, 1998: In a televised statement, President Clinton admits to the nation that he did indeed have a relationship with former White House intern Monica Lewinsky that was "not appropriate."

September 9, 1998: Independent Counsel Kenneth Starr submits to Congress a 445-page report documenting evidence collected during an investigation of President Clinton, triggering the first impeachment review against a president since Watergate.

October 29, 1998: Seventy-seven-year-old John Glenn and six fellow astronauts take off aboard the space shuttle *Discovery*. Glenn was the first American to orbit the earth in 1962. The launch, the 123rd in the U.S. space program, makes Glenn the oldest person to go into space. NASA plans extensive medical studies on Glenn to determine how space travel affects older people.

November 1998: The House Judiciary Committee begins hearings on whether or not to recommend impeachment of President Clinton to the House of Representatives.

December 19, 1998: Accusing him of perjury and obstruction of justice, the U.S. House of Representatives vote along party lines to impeach President Clinton.

February 6, 1999: President Clinton is acquitted by the Senate, which cannot muster a majority to convict the president—much less the two-thirds vote needed to unseat Clinton.

March 24, 1999: After months of peace talks with Serbian leaders and attempts to establish peacekeeping forces in Kosovo, NATO launches massive air strikes against Yugoslavia.

April 20, 1999: Two high school students murder twelve students and one teacher in a shooting rampage at Columbine High School, Littleton, Colorado. A search after the incident uncovers more than 30 bombs planted around the school. Discussion follows on the merits of gun control legislation.

May 8, 1999: An accidental attack by U.S. warplanes on the Chinese embassy in Belgrade during the air strikes against Yugoslavia results in four deaths and 30 injuries. NATO Secretary-General Javier Solana offers the organization's "deep regret" for the incident, but relations between the United States and China suffer.

June 9, 1999: NATO and Yugoslav representatives sign a peace agreement for the withdrawal of Serb troops from Kosovo; the agreement had been approved by the Serbian senate on June 3. NATO ceases air strikes against Yugoslavia and makes preparations to send peacekeeping forces into Kosovo.

Washington Administrations

Biography

George Washington was the first and probably still the most revered of the U.S. presidents. A member of the economic and political elite of the English mainland colonies, he exhibited many of the moral qualities of this colonial elite: he was not personally ambitious and he had a strong sense of duty. He was, like a dozen other leading figures in U.S. history, the right person in the right place at the right time. Without Washington the American war for independence might not have succeeded. Without him the Constitution might never have gained enough support to be ratified. Finally, without Washington the country would never have had a living model for what was meant by "civic virtue" and service to the new nation. Washington's greatest contribution to the nation was simply the fact that a large portion of the U.S. population trusted him. In trusting him, they could begin to trust themselves and thus create the conditions of a viable representative democracy.

Full name: George Washington

Personal Information:

Born: February 22, 1732
Birthplace: Pope's Creek, Virginia
Died: December 14, 1799
Death place: Mount Vernon, Virginia
Burial place: Washington Family Vault, Mount Vernon, Virginia
Religion: Episcopalian
Spouse: Martha Dandridge Custis (m. 1759)
Occupation: Surveyor; planter; politician; general
Age at Inauguration: 57 years

Early Life

George Washington was born on February 22, 1732, in Westmoreland County, Virginia. His father was Augustine Washington, who was educated in England and was a prominent landholder and energetic businessman in Virginia at the time of George's birth. George Washington's mother was Mary Ball, whom Augustine, a widower, had married the previous year. Although little is known of the paternal line before Augustine, it has been suggested that King Henry VIII had given lands to George's English forebears. However, the Puritan Rev-

George Washington. (Painting by Stuart Gilbert. The Library of Congress.)

olution in England reversed family fortunes and John Washington, Augustine's grandfather, migrated to Virginia in 1657.

After his father's death in 1743, George Washington and his mother spent the next several years at the homes of family members and relatives. The most notable period was at Mount Vernon, one of the residences of Lawrence Washington, George Washington's elder half brother. Lawrence Washington, a retired naval officer, had named the 2,500-acre Virginia property after the British admiral under whom he had served. He was married to Anne Fairfax, the daughter of Col. William Fairfax, who was cousin and agent to Lord Fairfax, a prominent English aristocrat. The Fairfax connection exposed young Washington to the refined tastes of English high society. Contact with the Fairfax family also shaped George Washington's character and interests in more concrete ways. In 1748 the 16-year-old Washington assisted in plotting the lands of Lord Fairfax in the Shenandoah Valley of Virginia.

Despite considerable physical discomforts, Washington enjoyed his first encounter with the surveyor's profession. The following year, with the aid of Lord Fairfax, Washington was appointed official surveyor of Culpepper County. For the next two years Washington's body and mind were tempered by the demands and responsibilities of the job. His travels took him into the borderlands and the wilderness, stimulating a lifelong passion for western expansion and land speculation. Washington resented the English attempt in 1763 to dis-

courage settler migration beyond the headwaters of the Appalachian Mountains.

Following these formative experiences, the most significant event in Washington's young adulthood was his inheritance of Mount Vernon after the death of his half brother Lawrence in July 1752. At age 20 Washington became the master of one of the most important estates in Virginia. For the next 20 years Mount Vernon was at the center of Washington's life. He turned with equal enthusiasm to expanding and improving the house and its grounds, pursuing scientific, agricultural, and breeding techniques, and involving himself in local social and political affairs.

Education ♭

Little is known of Washington's early childhood and schooling, but it is evident that he did not receive the formal education afforded most children of the gentry. From ages seven to 15, he attended school periodically near Ferry Farm, the family residence on the Rappahannock River in Virginia. Washington had a natural talent for draftsmanship and practical mathematics, as well as an appreciation for reading and the fine arts. Most of Washington's early training emphasized practical skills, such as tobacco growing, animal husbandry, and elementary surveying, that would serve him well in later life. Unlike many of the Founding Fathers, Washington never learned French, the language of diplomacy, nor did he attend a university.

Family Life

On January 6, 1759, Washington married Martha Dandridge Custis, the wealthy widow of a prominent Virginia planter. Although the marriage was not a love match, it was based on affection, devotion, and respect. Martha Washington was by all accounts an efficient mistress of Mount Vernon. She also proved to be a social asset, serving as a gracious hostess to notables in the world of business and politics. This was no small matter given Washington's extensive involvement in Virginia's elite society. In the years prior to the American Revolution (1775–83), Martha Washington entertained as many as three hundred guests a year at Mount Vernon. Even more important to Washington were Martha Washington's children, John Parke ("Jacky") and Martha Parke ("Patsy") Custis, who were six-years-old and four-years-old, respectively, at the time of the marriage. Washington, who remained childless throughout life, treated Martha Washington's children as his own and was grief stricken when Patsy, an epileptic, died from a seizure in 1773. The unruly Jacky died during the American Revolution, and Washington adopted two of Jacky's four children, assuming the role of their father.

Washington's marriage endured these trials and weathered the Revolution and the presidency without significant strain. Martha Washington died on May 22, 1802, surviving her husband by less than three years.

Career

Washington was sufficiently wealthy to be able to spend extended periods of time away from the plantation, allowing him to concentrate his attention on politics and war. But in slack times he reveled in the routines of the gentleman farmer. His reputation for energy and attention to detail grew throughout Virginia. He tended corn and wheat, becoming one of the first farmers in the region to abandon tobacco as his main crop.

Early Military Service

Washington was awarded his first military appointment in 1752 as a major in the Virginia militia. Within two years he was participating in skirmishes that led to the French and Indian War (1754–63), a struggle between Britain and its American colonists on one side, and French forces and their American Indian allies on the other. Washington learned at least one valuable, if humiliating, experience as a soldier. In 1753 he was captured by French troops near Confluence, Pennsylvania. In return for his written admission that he was responsible for the "murder" of Cumon de Jumonville, a French officer, Washington and his men were allowed to return home.

In a subsequent engagement in 1754 at Fort Duquesne near present-day Pittsburgh, Pennsylvania, Washington's troops were ambushed and soundly defeated, with Washington's superior officer, the British general Braddock, dying of battlefield wounds. Although Washington had two horses shot from under him and his clothes pierced by four bullets, he emerged from this disastrous encounter unscathed. Moreover, his reputation as a soldier was enhanced. News spread that he had displayed considerable bravery and resourcefulness in the battle with the French, and that he had been largely responsible for the escape of the colonial and British forces. Washington resigned from military service in 1758 with the rank of brigadier general.

The French and Indian War was a formative experience for Washington. It helped mold his attitudes toward British colonial rule. During the war Washington became bitterly resentful of Britain's unwillingness to treat the colonial forces as competent equals, according British officers superior status and authority even if they held inferior rank to their colonial counterparts. When added to his other grievances against the British, these painful snubs set Washington against British rule.

Early Political Career

Shortly before retiring from military service in 1758 Washington won election to Virginia's colonial legislature, the House of Burgesses. This exposed him to a set of experiences shared by few people of his time: the practice of self-government. In contrast to other European monarchies, Great Britain allowed its colonies a significant degree of autonomy and self-government. This was partly to enlist the colonists' help in the day-to-day tasks of administering the colonies. The policy also reflected the new way that the English were beginning to think of themselves, as "free-born Englishmen" irrespective of differences in wealth or rank. This liberal creed also committed the English to listen to the colonies' petitions and complaints expressed through their elected assemblies, such as Virginia's House of Burgesses.

The cause of the increased tension between Great Britain and its mainland colonies was that, in light of the high costs of the recent war with France, the British Parliament decided that the colonies should pay more of the costs of maintaining the empire. Parliament levied a series of taxes on consumer goods shipped to the colonies (such as sugar, molasses, stamps, and tea). The colonial assemblies mobilized opposition to these new taxes. Using seventeenth-century British philosopher John Locke's language of mankind's "inalienable" rights to life, liberty, and property, the colonial assemblies argued that these new taxes deprived them of their "property" and that, in any case, the colonies were not truly represented in Parliament because they had not voted for the members of Parliament.

By the time Britain got around to suppressing the House of Burgesses in 1769, George Washington was moving from protest against British policies to opposition to British colonial rule. In 1774 Washington signed a resolution drawn up by Virginia legislators calling for a Continental Congress. The First Continental Congress met in September 1774 to sound out the level of anti-British unity between the colonies and to tighten the boycott of British goods. The rapid deterioration of relations with Parliament is evident from the fact that only a few months later in May 1775, the Second Continental Congress met in Philadelphia, Pennsylvania, to coordinate the military resistance against the British. Washington won election to both the First and the Second Continental Congresses.

Military Service During the Revolution

In June 1775 the delegates to the Second Continental Congress unanimously approved Washington's appointment as commander in chief of the infant Continental Army. This decision was based on a number of considerations, including the simple fact of Washington's commanding physical presence. (In a population whose average height was several inches shorter than today, he

Washington and his men encamped at Valley Forge, Pennsylvania, over the winter months of 1777 and 1778, anticipating the resumption of hostilities with the British in the spring. Many of Washington's men lost their lives during that bitter winter. (National Archives and Records Administration.)

stood over six feet tall). Also, the New England revolutionaries, who had thus far led the struggle against the British, saw the appointment of Virginia-born Washington as a way to bind the South to the revolutionary movement. The fact that Washington did not display aggressive political ambitions and did not seem likely to use his military powers for political purposes also weighed in his favor.

Washington now faced a difficult task. The colonials stood alone against the enormous power and prestige of Britain's armed forces, fielding a ragtag collection of national volunteers ("Continentals") and inexperienced state militia who served only for months at a time. There was no coherent system to produce and distribute munitions, supplies, and clothing, all of which were in short supply throughout the war. To make matters worse, there was no legitimate and effective national government to address these problems. Washington had to report to a weak Continental Congress and 13 quarrelsome state governments that jealously guarded their rights and prerogatives. Against all odds Washington overcame these problems. Skillfully maneuvering between domestic political and economic obstacles and periodic opposition from the Continental Congress, he forged an army that eventually stood toe-to-toe with British regulars, either winning the battles or retreating in good order.

The road to this outcome was long and hard. The heady first encounters with the Redcoats (British soldiers) at Breed's Hill in Boston on June 17, 1775, and the British evacuation of the city under American pressure eight months later, were followed by a string of defeats. Yet Washington was at his best when disaster seemed unavoidable. He turned the seemingly endless and demoralizing retreat from New York and through New Jersey into victory in late 1776 when he crossed the partly frozen Delaware River and defeated the numerically superior British and mercenary forces at Trenton (December 1776) and Princeton (January 1777). These bold and unexpected victories energized the American army and public, as did the victory of American forces under Horatio Gates over the British at Saratoga in October 1777. The French, sensing that the tide was turning against the British, began sending provisions and the diversionary presence of the French navy. The coup de grace came in October 1781 in a master stroke by Washington. Commanding the combined American and French forces, Washington brilliantly maneuvered to envelop Yorktown, Virginia, by land and by sea, trapping British general Lord Cornwallis and forcing him to surrender. The independence of the colonies was now assured. As the opponents met at Yorktown to discuss the terms of surrender, the shock and enormity of the American victory was poignantly underlined by the British band as it played "The World Turned Upside Down."

President

Washington had to hold the Continental Army together until the British finally vacated New York in April 1783. The following December he resigned his commission, having returned a month earlier to Mount Vernon, Virginia, to resume the quiet life of the plantation farmer. Because of the difficulties of governing under the Articles of Confederation, the forerunner to the U.S. Constitution, a constitutional convention restructured the government in 1787, giving more power to the central government and to its executive branch headed by a president. Washington was the obvious candidate to fill the role of president under this new Constitution. He was elected the first president of the United States and served two terms in that capacity, from 1789 to 1797. During his two terms in office the country grew more settled and prosperous, and the governing elite established a workable set of political precedents and institutions. Washington's wife, Martha Washington, also established an important precedent as a gracious hostess to the nation's preeminent polite society of diplomats and politicians.

Post-presidential Years

Washington's retirement from the presidency after two four-year terms did not end his public life. His most notable post-presidential service came in 1798 when John Adams, his successor, appointed him commander in chief as a war with France threatened to engulf the United States. It was an ill-considered appointment. Now old and no longer able to demonstrate the mental faculties of earlier years, Washington allowed himself to become involved in a factional power struggle. Although the war never materialized, the episode revealed that age had finally overtaken Washington, and that he would now finally depart the public stage. When his colleagues proposed soon thereafter that he come out of retirement and stand again for the presidency, Washington refused.

Washington's Death

On December 12, 1799, Washington spent several hours on horseback in harsh weather inspecting his estate at Mount Vernon. He contracted acute laryngitis and his health deteriorated rapidly. After instructing his secretary about his funeral arrangements, the old general died at 10:00 P.M. on December 14. Despite the divisive political confrontations that had marked his last years in office, news of his death plunged the nation into grief. Col. Henry Lee, the Virginia politician, captured the sentiments of most Americans when he wrote for Washington's eulogy:

> To the memory of the Man first in war, first in peace, and first in the hearts of his countrymen.

The George Washington Administrations

The first U.S. president, Washington commanded enormous prestige as the military leader of the American Revolution (1775–83) when he took office in 1789. Overcoming extraordinary political challenges, both foreign and domestic, he used his popularity and his considerable political and administrative skills to build a new federal government from scratch. Guided by the blueprint of the Constitution, Washington laid the foundation for an effective national government while remaining faithful to the republican and democratic principles enshrined in the document.

Washington Becomes President

The four years following the conclusion of the American Revolution (1775–83) revealed many weaknesses in the national government that had been established under the Articles of Confederation, and the forerunner to the U. S. Constitution. The political system established by the Articles favored the states over the national government, and lacked a strong executive or judiciary. Congress did not have the power to tax and was forced instead to request funds from the states, which the states were not compelled to pay. Nor could Congress regulate the commerce between states or with foreign governments. But perhaps most distressing, it did not have the power to maintain armed forces, a perilous defect for a young and infirm nation in a dangerous world. The 1786 to 1787 rebellion of Massachusetts small farmers, led by Daniel Shay, convinced the wealthy businesspeople and politicians of the young nation that they needed to redraft the Articles of Confederation.

Washington had long been vocal about the weaknesses of the Articles of Confederation. At first he believed that significant changes might reform the prevailing system, but he soon came to believe that an entirely new document was necessary—one that created a strong federal government. Washington was reluctant to reenter public service, even on so vital a question as the powers of the central government, but he agreed to attend the federal convention in Philadelphia, Pennsylvania, in May 1787, as one of Virginia's five delegates.

Once in Philadelphia, Washington was immediately and unanimously elected president of the convention. He argued forcefully and persuasively for a document that created a much stronger union and a viable federal authority. The result was a new document, the Constitution, which greatly enhanced the strength of the national government and also featured a powerful president. The U. S. Constitution was approved by the convention on September 17, 1787. Approval came in part because those who were concerned about the powerful national

Administration

Administration Dates
April 30, 1789–March 4, 1793
March 4, 1793–March 4, 1797

Vice President
John Adams (1789–97)

Cabinet

Secretary of State
Thomas Jefferson (1790–93)
Edmund J. Randolph (1794–95)
Timothy Pickering (1795–1800)

Secretary of the Treasury
Alexander Hamilton (1789–95)
Oliver Wolcott Jr. (1795–1800)

Secretary of War
Henry Knox (1789–94)
Timothy Pickering (1795)
James McHenry (1796–1800)

Attorney General
Edmund J. Randolph (1789–94)
William Bradford (1794–95)
Charles Lee (1795–1801)

Postmaster General
Samuel Osgood (1789–91)
Timothy Pickering (1791–95)
Joseph Habersham (1795–1801)

government believed that Washington would become the first president. Thomas Jefferson reflected this view, observing that he could overcome his concerns about the document "as long as we can avail ourselves of the services of our great leader, whose talents and whose weight of character I consider as peculiarly necessary to get the government so under way as that it may afterward be carried on by subordinate characters" (McDonald, p. 25).

Before the Constitution went into effect, the states had to approve it. The opponents of the Constitution, loosely called anti-federalists, constituted a broad coalition of forces who fielded a number of objections to the document. Many feared that the Constitution would institutionalize a system of political and economic oligarchy (or rule by a small elite), disregarding the rights of the

majority population. Southerners of all social and economic stripes were particularly concerned that the new government would usurp the powers of the states. Many of them also feared that the proposed system would benefit the northern merchants and manufacturers over the agrarians. Given the increasing unpopularity of slavery in the North, the southerners also feared that the North would eventually pass laws weakening or abolishing slavery.

The urban trading and manufacturing interests of the North generally favored a central government, with the power to erect protective tariffs against foreign competition and to improve the nation's infrastructure of roads, ports, and rivers. In addition to these economic interests, federalism had other supporters among those citizens, like Washington, who believed that the existence of the new nation depended on centralizing power. In the end the Federalists carried the day in the fight for ratification by the states. But they had to promise to adopt a supplementary Bill of Rights protecting the citizens and the states from a powerful and tyrannical federal government.

Like Jefferson, many U.S. citizens supported the new Constitution because they were reassured by the prospect of Washington as the first president. Given his vital role in securing the independence of the American colonies, Washington by now was widely viewed as a charismatic leader selflessly committed to the common good. Not surprisingly, the contest for president was a one-horse race. By present-day standards it was also a very unusual contest. Washington did not campaign for the office, and he made no public mention of whether he was even a candidate. Nevertheless, when the new Congress convened in 1789 and the votes of the electoral college were tallied, Washington emerged as the unanimous choice. He accepted the electors' decision and went to New York City, the temporary capital. John Adams, the runner-up in electoral votes, became vice president.

Washington's Second Term
Four years as president left Washington with deep reservations about serving a second term. He longed for private life, in part because the factional conflicts in his administration made public life disagreeable, and in part because he felt that he lacked the physical and intellectual strength to continue as president. Both Secretary of the Treasury Alexander Hamilton and Secretary of State Thomas Jefferson, whose political differences were becoming more marked, urged the aging Washington to stand for reelection. They feared that the young republic had yet to strike sufficiently deep roots to survive intact without Washington's leadership and charisma. Jefferson wrote to Washington that the "confidence of the whole union is centered on you . . . North and South will hang together if they have you to hang on . . ." (Emery, p. 320, 321). As in 1789 it was Washington's sense of duty, not political ambition, that determined his decision. Wash-

President Washington and the first U.S. cabinet (left to right): Washington; Secretary of War Henry Knox; Secretary of the Treasury Alexander Hamilton; Secretary of State Thomas Jefferson; Attorney General Edmund Randolph.

(Lithograph by Currier and Ives. Corbis. Reproduced by permission.)

ington allowed himself to be nominated and, in November 1792, he won unanimous reelection.

Washington's Advisers

An example of the improvised nature of government in the first days of the republic was the fact that Washington created the cabinet although it was not authorized by the Constitution. Establishing another significant precedent, Congress granted Washington unfettered power of appointment to cabinet posts. His cabinet (though it did not operate precisely as a modern cabinet does) included the heads of the major departments of the government: state, Treasury, war, and attorney general. Given his preference to govern by consensus, Washington consulted regularly with his cabinet, thus setting an important precedent for his successors. For the most part, Washington's chief advisers were also members of his cabinet.

Notwithstanding his own preference for consensus, Washington's two key advisers, Alexander Hamilton and Thomas Jefferson, had opposing viewpoints on the major political issues of the day. Born in the British West Indies in modest circumstances, Hamilton was secretary of the Treasury and the leader of the Federalists who supported a strong national government. An able administrator, Hamilton's ideas and programs were lightning rods for controversy. During the Constitutional Convention, for example, he had argued for a centralized political system

based on the British model. He felt that state governors should be appointed by the national government, ensuring that the states would be fully subordinate to federal authority. Although Hamilton had fiercely supported the Constitution in its final form, his opponents now quoted this earlier position in public debate.

Equally disturbing for his opponents was Hamilton's view of the social foundations of stable government. He had little confidence that the common man could exercise political power responsibly. Where others saw democracy Hamilton saw mob rule and anarchy. This fear seemed to be confirmed in France in 1793 when the French Republic descended into a bloody revolution. Never a strident monarchist as his critics claimed, Hamilton nevertheless believed that the federal government should rest less on popular consent than on the self-interested support of bankers and merchants. As secretary of the Treasury Hamilton crafted policies that nurtured these groups. He felt that without such a solid base of support, the federal government would never achieve stability.

Secretary of State Thomas Jefferson was Hamilton's political opposite. He was a brilliant thinker, an accomplished architect, a scholar, and a botanist (among many other pursuits). Like his friend and fellow Virginian James Madison, Jefferson read not only the great English writer John Locke, who summarized the experience of the turbulent seventeenth century in England, but also the French writer Montesquieu, who discussed the "sep-

Biography:

Alexander Hamilton

Secretary of the Treasury (1755–1804) Alexander Hamilton's rise to prominence began during the American Revolution (1775–83). As a trusted aide—and even adviser—to Gen. George Washington, Hamilton drafted many of Washington's important communications to high-ranking officers and was privy to Washington's wide-view perspective of the war itself. Despite his demanding schedule during this time, Hamilton also wrote articles and letters expressing his ideas on economic policy and his favor of a strong, central form of government that would unite the states under a common Union. In part because of his foreign birth, Hamilton's ideas were not biased or constrained by an attachment to the agenda of any one state or locality. Six months following Washington's inauguration as president of the new government, Hamilton was commissioned the nation's first secretary of the Treasury. This position was especially important given the pressing problem of paying off the national debt incurred as a result of the revolution. Hamilton's brilliant, yet controversial, program was contained in his three

major reports on the U.S. economy: "Report on Public Credit;" "Report on a National Bank;" and "Report on Manufacturers." When debate over his economic policies raged amongst members of Congress, Hamilton assumed leadership of the pro-administration party that supported his program, the Federalists. Washington hesitated to sign off on the measure and requested that his two top advisers submit their contrary opinions. His two advisers were

Thomas Jefferson and Hamilton. Arguing that Congress had exceeded its powers, Jefferson submitted a classic defense of a strict construction of the Constitution; affirming the bank's constitutionality, Hamilton submitted the best argument in U.S. political literature for a broad interpretation of the Constitution.

aration of powers" as part of the conditions of stable representative government. In contrast to Hamilton's modest background, Jefferson was a wealthy Virginia planter and a slaveholder who feared the rising economic power of the northeast and found Hamilton's vision of centralized government repugnant. He also was concerned that Hamilton's policies, resting as they did on elite self-interest, would erode the ideals of civic virtue and public service. Although a member of the gentry, Jefferson was an authentic populist, believing that the common man had both the intelligence and the good sense to govern himself. During Washington's presidency Jefferson emerged as the head of the "Democratic-Republicans," a loosely knit political block committed to the agrarian way of life and to states' rights—emphasizing the sovereignty of the states over the national government.

In the end, the issues were too divisive and the personalities too stubborn for compromise. Although he shared more in common with the agrarian Jefferson than with Hamilton, Washington came to side with Hamilton's pragmatism over Jefferson's idealism. Unable to maintain his political influence in Washington's second administration, an embittered Jefferson used his supporters to attack the president and Hamilton. In July 1793 he resigned from his cabinet post of secretary of state, profoundly unhappy about the course charted by Washington.

Washington's other cabinet appointments pale in comparison to Jefferson and Hamilton. Vice President John Adams and Attorney General Edmund Randolph, for instance, were good and competent administrators and men of principle, but they lacked the brilliance of the great antagonists, Hamilton and Jefferson. Washington also reached outside the cabinet for advice and counsel. One such adviser was Chief Justice John Jay, whom he called one of his "coadjutors" or assistants in government.

Washington and Congress

The unprecedented nature of government in Washington's administration meant that both the president and the Congress had to innovate in all areas where the Constitution was silent. This included questions of etiquette and the conventions of proper conduct within and between the different branches of government. In some ways there was continuity. Although the idea of a strong executive was a departure from the previous period, the Congress contained many of the same political leaders who had been prominent under the Articles of Confederation. Washington tried to establish sound principles for working with Congress based on a limited definition of the powers of his office. He took the doctrine of separation of powers very seriously, avoiding even the suggestion that he was treading on Congress's prerogatives and authority. He refused to speak for or against a candidate for Congress and maintained careful silence on issues being discussed in the legislature.

Washington's caution in shaping the role of the president also was evident in his belief that the veto should only be used when the constitutionality of a bill was in question (Flexner, *George Washington and the New Nation,* pp. 398, 399). In his two terms in office, Washington used the veto on only two occasions. Although Washington believed that the executive was the equal of the legislature, he also was cautious about exercising powers relative to Congress that were not explicitly sanctioned by the Constitution. He did not always adhere to these self limitations, but his careful and proper behavior toward Congress helped to avoid potential battles over political turf at a time when the new government could ill afford such conflicts.

Washington and the Judiciary

During Washington's two terms in office, the judiciary did not develop into an equal branch of government. Even more than the executive and legislative branches, the new Supreme Court found itself in uncharted territory. The Constitution of the United States created the basic framework for a government, however, the document contained many vague clauses and unanswered questions regarding the powers and responsibilities of the various branches of the federal government, including the judiciary. These so-called "Silences of the Constitution" left Congress with much discretionary power. The Constitution, in Article III, Sections 1 and 2, provided for an independent judiciary to consist of a Supreme Court and inferior courts. The general jurisdiction of the court system was defined in Section 2. Under Washington's guidance, the Judiciary Act of 1789 carried out this mandate by creating a Supreme Court, three circuit courts, thirteen district courts, and the office of Attorney General.

The newly created Court was not highly regarded, and many nominees refused to accept their appointments. Though the Court was given the authority, by the Judiciary Act, to review the rulings of state courts, there was very little business to decide at the outset, except staffing the Court and admitting attorneys to practice before it. Most of the government's earliest tasks turned out to be executive and legislative, rather than judicial. Washington's appointments included: John Jay, chief justice; John Rutledge; William Cushing; James Wilson; John Blair; James Iredell; Thomas Johnson; William Paterson; Samuel Chase; and Oliver Ellsworth, chief justice after John Jay.

Changes in the U.S. Government

Perhaps the most important change in government during the Washington years was the ratification of the first ten amendments to the U.S. Constitution, known as the Bill of Rights. The Federalists had promised a bill of rights during the great debate over the Constitution. The ratification of the amendments in 1791 helped cement support for the federal republic by guaranteeing important civil liberties, including freedom of religion, speech, the press, and assembly. The Tenth Amendment, not technically a part of the Bill of Rights, provided that powers not delegated to the U.S. government or denied to the states would remain the preserve of the states or of the people. Taken together, the first 10 amendments reassured the new nation that the federal government would be subject to constraints in its exercise of power.

The 13 original colonies all ratified the Constitution with Rhode Island being the last on May 29, 1790. Three newly formed states were admitted to the Union: Vermont (1791); Kentucky (1792); and Tennessee (1796). Finally, in what may have been a payback for Jefferson's and Virginia representative James Madison's agreement to drop their objection to Hamilton's plan for refunding the public debt, Congress decided in 1790 to build the permanent capital of the United States at a site near Virginia on the Potomac River (*See also,* Domestic Issues).

The Presidential Succession Act of 1792 was passed by the Second Congress, calling for a special election if both the presidency and vice presidency were vacated. Until the election, the president pro tempore of the Senate would serve as president.

Domestic Issues

For many citizens, Washington's presidency was a time of reconstructing lives and fortunes that had been disrupted by the American Revolution (1775–83). It was a time when frontier settlement breached the Allegheny Mountains, and pioneers came pouring through the Cumberland Gap into the Ohio River basin and the Northwest Territories, encroaching on the lands of American Indians as they went. Frontier farmers fleeing high land prices, banks, and mortgage foreclosures, engaged in subsistence farming and relied on barter or on cooperative labor for projects that required more than one family's labor. In a sense they were fleeing the government itself, with its military draft, its taxes, its courts, and its jails. This migration became the subject of many folktales and legends—like Daniel Boone and James Fenimore Cooper's rough-hewn literary hero, Leatherstocking.

This was also a time when the foundations of the national economy were being laid. The Constitution, for instance, stipulated that Congress had the power to collect taxes but that "all Duties, Imposts, and Excises shall be uniform throughout the United States." Thus, the

Biography:

John Jay

Jurist and Statesman (1745–1829) John Jay played an important part in the early years of America's history. A highly-respected moderate who supported the Patriot cause, Jay represented New York at the First and the Second Continental Congress. As such, Jay was instrumental in the drafting and passage of the U.S. Constitution. In addition, he collaborated with Alexander Hamilton and James Madison in writing the *Federalist*, a series of papers that explained the U.S. Constitution. Jay also played a major role in drafting New York's first constitution. Although considered an elitist, Jay believed that people are the source of government authority, and he was fearful of corruption and nepotism in the federal bureaucracy. In a move rare for the time, Jay attempted to insert a clause in the New York constitution forbidding slavery. The motion, however, did not pass. Serving as chief justice of New York until 1779, Jay inter-

preted the state constitution he had helped compose. In 1790 President George Washington offered Jay the position of chief justice of the U.S. Supreme Court. Jay established two precedents as chief justice: states were deemed subordinate to the national government, and national treaties were established as supreme over state laws. His term as chief justice ended in 1795. In the same year Jay was elected governor of New York. He served two terms but declined the bid for reelection in 1801. He also refused renomination as chief justice; after 28 years of public service Jay longed to retire.

---

states could not be tempted to erect tariff barriers between themselves. Victory over the British in the War of Independence promoted this spirit of national unification. But in some quarters, particularly in the South, national unification was perceived as a threat.

Continuing the debate between the Federalists and anti-federalists that had taken place during the debates over ratification of the Constitution (*See also,* Washington Becomes President), coalitions led by Thomas Jefferson and Alexander Hamilton formed to push for the creation of what each conceived to be an ideal government. Hamilton sought a strong national government, which protected and was supported by business, industry, and trade; he had little faith in the ability of the general population to rule itself. Jefferson argued that the farmer, and particularly the small farmers that constituted much of the U.S. population at that time, were the true basis of U.S. democracy. As such, they needed to be protected from plans such as Hamilton's, which would put the concerns of big business and the wealthy above those of the common man. Jefferson's coalition became known as the Democratic-Republicans, while the Federalists continued to support Hamilton under their existing name. Both groups were loose formations lacking internal cohesion and organizational strength. They were not yet political parties. Indeed, they were often reviled as factions, and feared as possibly a cause of anarchy, civil war, and dissolution of the republic.

This contest between Hamilton and Jefferson would dominate Washington's administration and was, at its

heart, a struggle between different sectional and class forces. Agriculture had dominated the economy of the American colonies, but its importance varied by region, causing the sectional differences to widen as time went on. Southern society had evolved into an agricultural aristocracy based on slavery. Jefferson considered agrarian life to be the wellspring of a nation's noble character and its political stability. New England was shaped by different economic forces. Lacking much fertile soil, the economy of New England developed an energetic mercantile culture that contrasted with the insular and stable life-style of the South. New England had given birth to influential merchant and business classes whose origins were often quite humble and whose wealth had little or no connection to the land. Although the middle colonies enjoyed a more mixed economy, they were inevitably and strongly influenced by the great trading and business centers of New York and Philadelphia, Pennsylvania. During Washington's first administration Hamilton brilliantly championed these sectional interests. On other issues, however, the lines were less clearly drawn. Western expansion, for example, found adherents in both camps.

Hamilton's Financial Program: The Funding and Assumption Plans

The most important initiatives of the Washington administration came from Secretary of Treasury Alexander Hamilton. Hamilton took his first major step toward creating a stronger government and a strong economy when, in his "First Report on Public Credit" (January 1790), he proposed that the federal government fund at par (at face value) all outstanding certificates of indebtedness issued during the American Revolution. These certificates were, in a sense, IOUs from the government of the United States to its creditors, whether foreign governments, private individuals (including farmers who had furnished provisions to the Continental Army as well as the soldiers themselves, who were owed back pay), or states. Hamilton argued that only by demonstrating its willingness to meet its financial obligations could the United States hope to attract the domestic and foreign capital needed for economic development.

But many legislators refused to support the bill. For one thing, the plan favored wealthy speculators. In the years since the War of Independence these speculators had bought at discount most of the privately-held certificates of indebtedness. Funding these debts at face value would result in profits for the speculators and nothing for those individuals who had been enticed into selling off their government securities at a fraction of their face value. Furthermore, since several of those states had already retired their debts, Hamilton's plan would require citizens of those states to pay a second time. After months of stalemate, in June 1790 the bill received sufficient southern support for passage in Congress. This was accomplished through a compromise stipulating that the permanent capital of the United States would be built on the Potomac River, offering southern politicians the prospect of greater national political influence.

The National Bank

In December 1790 Hamilton released his "Second Report on Public Credit," which proposed the creation of a national bank. The bank, modeled on the Bank of England, would serve a number of important functions. It would be the depository of government funds and facilitate the collection of taxes and the disbursement of funds. Equally important, the bank would provide a source of credit, and its notes would furnish a sound and relatively plentiful medium of exchange, the lifeblood of a strong economy.

Although the proposal commanded enough support to pass both houses of Congress, it heightened the fears of the federal government's growing power. In debate on the House floor, James Madison of Virginia attacked the proposal as unconstitutional since the Constitution did not explicitly give the federal government the power to create a national bank. His arguments caused President Washington to consider vetoing the bill after it had passed through Congress, even though he had submitted it as a formal legislative proposal. To avoid that possibility, in February 1791 Hamilton wrote the brilliant "Defense of the Constitutionality of the Bank," which predicted the decline of the national government unless the Constitu-

tion were understood to include "implied powers." In essence, Hamilton argued that the Constitution must not be interpreted as strictly defining everything that the government could and could not do, but rather as the guidelines and rules under which the specific activities of government were to be carried out. Washington, who had repeatedly suffered the consequences of weak government during the American Revolution, accepted Hamilton's view of implied powers and signed the bill. Although Washington balked at Hamilton's February 1791 "Report on Manufactures"—calling for tariffs to protect the country's infant manufacturing sector—the president was convinced that Hamilton's financial program as a whole was sound and essential.

Opposition to Hamilton's Program

Furious at Hamilton's growing power and influence on Washington, Madison and Jefferson counterattacked in February 1792, using a Republican newspaper, the *National Gazette,* which they helped to finance. The newspaper questioned Hamilton's policies, his character, and his motives. A journalistic war ensued with frequent attacks and counterattacks between the *National Gazette* and the staunchly pro-Hamilton newspaper, the *Gazette of the United States.* Although Madison and Jefferson were careful not to criticize Washington, the president was wounded by the attacks on Hamilton, rightly assuming that such attacks implied his complicity or gullibility, or careless attention to vital matters of state. Although Thomas Jefferson supported Washington's reelection in 1792, he resigned his post as secretary of state in mid-1793.

The Whiskey Rebellion

Criticism of Washington and his policies dogged the president into his second term. These critics included both the Democratic-Republicans in government led by Jefferson and various independent local organizations. They felt that the federal executive had grown too powerful, usurping the powers of Congress, and that special interests, born of Hamilton's and Washington's policies, threatened to destroy the values and virtues represented by the American Revolution. Washington's critics were further stimulated by the French Revolution, which had started in 1789. Remembering the support that the French had given the American Revolution, they watched with growing enthusiasm as the French people overthrew their king, proclaimed the slogan, "Liberty, Equality, Fraternity," and fought a long series of wars to defend their democracy against the monarchies of Europe.

In a direct tribute to this revolution, numerous local Democratic-Republican societies were founded in different parts of the country between 1793 and 1800. These groups fancied themselves the successors of the revolutionary era "Sons of Liberty," and they criticized President Washington for pulling back from U.S. treaty commitments to aid France should it ever come under attack.

Fast Fact

When Washington took office Congress voted him the salary of $25,000 per year. This was about 100 times what a skilled artisan in New York City might expect to earn in 1789. But Washington was also expected to pay for his official travel and entertainment out of this amount.

(Source: John Ferling. *The First of Men: A Life of George Washington,* 1988.)

Their members affected French revolutionary fashion, sporting pantaloons and three-cornered hats. They assembled in discussion clubs and trained in paramilitary tactics.

Meanwhile, unrest in western Pennsylvania was growing over Hamilton's policy of levying a high excise tax on whiskey, in order to help pay the cost of the debt assumption plan. This tax angered the region's farmers, who often used corn for currency and distilled the grain into whiskey for ease of transportation. When armed rioting broke out in the summer of 1794, Washington called on the rioters to disperse. When this failed, he used the power granted him in the Constitution to call up 12,000 militiamen. The rebel force evaporated before this imposing force could restore order. Two of the rioters were tried and condemned, but Washington pardoned them.

Washington publicly linked the Democratic-Republican societies to the Whiskey Rebellion. Although the societies as a whole did not instigate the Whiskey Rebellion, some of their members in western Pennsylvania did take an active part in the uprising. This was enough evidence for Washington, who was deeply concerned that these "self-created societies" must be discredited or else they might "destroy the government of this country" (Sharp, pp. 85-91, 100). Washington now associated more closely in his mind organized grassroots political activity with the potential for paralyzing government, or at worst, the emergence of popular anarchy, the very condition that the Federalists blamed for the bloodbath of the French Revolution. More generally, Washington, like most Americans of his class, viewed the Democratic-Republican societies as extra-constitutional entities that challenged their elite-centered conception of representative government. Much of the grassroots support for the popular societies dried up under the withering criticism of Washington and others. The popular societies also lost support when the French Revolution, with which they closely associated themselves, launched its frightful period of terror in 1793, in which 1,400 Parisians were executed. This drove off large numbers of previously sympathetic U.S. citizens.

Foreign Issues

The United States was in a difficult position when Washington took office in 1789. The American Revolution (1775–83) with Britain had ended only six years before, and tensions between the two nations remained high. Particularly troubling to the United States was Britain's refusal to abandon its forts in the northwestern part of the United States. Many Americans, however, still felt strong ties to the British, particularly in the North. Many northern merchants and businesspeople, the same who made up and were supported by Alexander Hamilton's Federalists, depended on trade with Britain for their livelihoods and did not want to see renewed conflict with that nation.

Yet at the same time, many Americans felt strongly about Britain's longtime enemy, France. France had provided crucial support for the colonies during the war, and most Americans were grateful to France for this help. Many of these Americans also felt that their revolution and new republican institutions would serve as a model for the rest of the world. These beliefs seemed to be confirmed by the start of the French Revolution shortly after Washington took office in 1789. Many people wanted the United States to aid France in its revolution and attempts to establish a representative government, including Thomas Jefferson and his Democratic-Republican supporters.

Thus the two major factions in Washington's government, the Federalists and the Democratic-Republicans, could add conflict over foreign affairs to their many disputes over domestic policy. While these domestic issues overshadowed foreign events for most of Washington's first term, the French declaration of war on Britain in 1793 put the United States into an increasingly difficult position. Meanwhile, the United States also faced problems along its western border. As increasing numbers of settlers moved over the Appalachian Mountains, many American Indian tribes reacted violently to incursions on their hunting grounds. Western settlers also demanded government action to secure their access to the Spanish port of New Orleans on the Mississippi River, through which most of their trade had to pass.

The Yazoo Land Grab

Although Washington wanted to suppress the American Indian forces that were attacking U. S. settlers, his attitude toward the American Indians differed from that of the settlers and other Americans who advocated violent conquest. He offered a glimpse of his moderate stance during the so-called Yazoo land grab. In 1787 the Georgia legislature, driven by voracious speculation, authorized the sale of sections of a vast tract of land between the Mississippi and the Yazoo Rivers (an area that stretches across the lower regions of present-day Alabama and Mississippi). The local tribes (Cherokees, Choctaws, and Chickasaws), allied with Spanish forces, and threatened to go to war to retain their hunting grounds.

Washington intervened, arguing that Georgia's sale of the Yazoo land violated federal treaties with the Chickasaw and the Choctaw tribes. Washington also confirmed earlier government policy by stating that the United States would not protect any of its citizens who settled in that area.

Washington also authorized other treaties that defused conflicts in the backwoods of Tennessee and Georgia between Indian tribes and encroaching white settlers. Amicable agreements were reached with the Creeks in the Treaty of New York in 1790 and with the Cherokees in the Treaty of Holston in 1791. In both cases American Indian lands taken by settlers were either returned or compensation was paid for them. New boundaries were settled for Indian lands with the hope that peace would be preserved, in Washington's words, "on the most humane principles" (Ferling, p. 411).

Western Expansion

Washington was opposed in principle to the forcible and wholesale dispossession of American Indians, being motivated in part by conscience and also by concern that American treatment of its native population not be compared to that of the brutal Spanish colonization of Mexico and Peru. Washington was supported in his opinion by much of the population of the eastern seaboard's population.

While Washington was able to uphold these principles when dealing with tribes in the east, the circumstances in the Northwest Territory were against a peaceful resolution. The tribes that occupied this region, located between the Great Lakes and the Ohio River, were tenacious and violent opponents of western expansion.

Whatever Washington's desires, a number of factors worked toward bloody resolution of the conflicting interests of American Indians of the Old Northwest. For one, the federal government, given the limits of its resources, would have been hard pressed to stop the seemingly inexorable flow of settlers into the region. For another, Washington saw great benefit to the influx of settlers, serving as they did as a counterweight to the continued British military presence south of the border with Canada. Ironically, matters were made worse for the Indians by their stunning defeats of government forces sent to pacify them in 1790 and 1791. These humiliating reversals and heavy loss of life enraged the government, motivating it to raise

and equip a four thousand-man army to fight against the tribes. Command of the force was given to Anthony Wayne, who had served with some distinction in the American Revolution.

After negotiations with the tribes that Washington had ordered failed to produce results, Wayne encountered and defeated in August 1794 a combined Indian force of some two thousand braves in the Battle of Fallen Timbers, near present-day Toledo, Ohio. This defeat, combined with the refusal of the British in Canada and in their forts south of the border to come to their aid, broke the will of the Northwest tribes to resist the settlers. The following year they signed the Treaty of Greenville, which opened much of the Northwest Territory and a small part of Indiana to white settlement. The influx of settlers stimulated by this agreement became still greater as the British honored the terms of Jay's Treaty (*See also*, Proclamation of Neutrality) and withdrew from their line of forts just inside U.S. territory in mid 1796. The movement of people into the region was such that Ohio was granted statehood only eight years later.

Proclamation of Neutrality

With the advent of war between Britain and France in 1793, the British Royal Navy began to seize U.S. cargoes and ships, especially in the French West Indies. The United States felt that these seizures were illegal and claimed the right to trade with all warring parties—in this case, both France and Britain—invoking one strand of international law that held "free ships make free goods." The British government embraced a competing, narrower definition that permitted greater latitude in the seizure of the cargoes of neutral ships.

American popular opinion, which still enthusiastically supported France's revolutionary experiment, was inflamed, and Congress prepared for war. Washington understood popular support for France, but as steward of U.S. interests he felt compelled to plot a sober and realistic course for the United States. Thus, while Europe plunged anew into warfare, Washington labored to keep the fragile republic out of harm's way. He was convinced that the nation would suffer great, perhaps irreparable, damage if it got caught up in the European war. To this end, Washington addressed the delicate problem of the United States's special relationship with France. Fifteen years earlier, when France sided with the Americans fighting the American Revolution, the United States signed the Franco-American Alliance of 1778, in which, among other things, the U.S. pledged to defend the French West Indies "forever against all powers." Other treaty provisions allowed French "privateers" to equip themselves and operate in U.S. ports. Privateers were armed private ships under government commission authorized to attack enemy vessels in time of war.

After the outbreak of war in Europe, Washington was unwilling to honor what he felt were unrealistic and dangerous obligations. For one thing, France appeared outnumbered on the European continent and likely to lose the war. More immediately, France was clearly weaker in naval power than Britain, and the United States had virtually no navy at all. Any official or unofficial aid to France ran the risk of bringing the weight of Britain and its ally, Spain, against the United States. Both Britain and Spain had colonial possessions that bordered the United States, as well as numerous American Indian allies. Defending the French West Indies, or allowing French privateers to operate out of U.S. ports, seemed destined to lead to defeat by the British. Other calculations were commercial in nature. Trade between Britain and the United States formed the bedrock of U.S. commerce, and eastern merchants lobbied against any action that supported France. Indeed, many of them favored siding with Britain.

After conferring with his advisers, Washington issued a Proclamation of Neutrality in April 1793. The proclamation declared that the United States would support neither France nor Britain in their war and maintained the right of the United States to trade with both nations. Through this proclamation, Washington hoped to protect U.S. shipping, without violating the treaties with France outright, or driving the United States into a war with Britain.

The Genet Affair

The French Revolution and the subsequent European war further inflamed and made more public the divide in Washington's cabinet between Hamilton and Jefferson. Here the pro-British sentiments of Hamilton and the pro-French stance of Jefferson overlaid the deeper ideological differences of the two giants in Washington's cabinet. Hamilton saw Jefferson's support for France as an infatuation with anarchic egalitarianism, while Jefferson viewed Hamilton's sympathy for Britain as confirmation of his opponent's misplaced admiration for the British political and economic system and of his disdain for individual and states' rights. Although neither Jefferson nor Hamilton advocated U.S. entry into the European war, the conflict induced the contending factions to hold to their positions even more firmly and appeal more vocally to public opinion for support.

Jefferson and the Democratic-Republicans recognized that they held the high ground in their battle with the Hamiltonians for public support. Pro-French sentiment, buttressed by Britain's violations of U.S. neutrality, was so strong in the United States that the advent of the Great Terror, in which 1,400 Parisians were executed, and the execution of the King of France in 1793 at first had little negative impact.

Despite Jefferson's expectations that he could exploit pro-French sentiment, the so-called Genet Affair set in motion forces that he did not anticipate or control. In April 1793 Edmond Genet, the new French minister to the United States, arrived in Charleston, South Carolina. The stakes were high for Genet, whose mission

was to secure U.S. support for France. Despite the recent Proclamation of Neutrality, Genet was determined to draw the United States into the war in support of France. Although Genet was snubbed by Washington, the enthusiastic pro-French crowds that greeted him during his travels in the United States helped sustain the envoy's reckless schemes. Indeed, the U.S. neutrality proclamation and the arrival of the French envoy were catalysts for a wave of strident criticism of Washington, who so recently had been above public attack. Newspapers and broadsheets charged that the president's neutrality proclamation and treatment of Genet had broken faith with a sacred ally; usurped the role of Congress, which, it was said, alone had the right to review the treaties with France; and revealed Washington's distaste for republicanism. The most unflattering criticism of Washington was leveled by the popular associations of Democratic-Republicans who celebrated the French Revolution as the embodiment of republican idealism (*See also*, Whiskey Rebellion).

Emboldened by the popular support he was receiving, in the spring of 1793 Genet began licensing U.S. ships to act as privateers against British merchantmen and recruited U.S. citizens to man them. Much more dangerous was Genet's attempts to organize private U.S. expeditions against Canada, Spanish Florida, and Louisiana. If any of these plans had been implemented, Britain and its allies obviously would have viewed them to be acts of war by the United States, and would have prompted a military response.

Jefferson, who had initially construed Genet's mission as benevolent and therefore politically useful, now strongly warned him against further violations of U.S. neutrality. Apart from his concerns for U.S. neutrality, Jefferson feared that the brash Genet and his outspoken public criticism of Washington would alienate Americans from France, and in so doing, weaken the Democratic-Republicans who were closely associated with the French cause. Although Virginia legislators James Madison and James Monroe, Jefferson's allies, were reluctant to cut their ties to Genet, the secretary of state supported the decision of Washington's cabinet to demand that the French recall Genet.

As Jefferson predicted Genet's provocative behavior eventually backfired: Genet's escalating public attacks on Washington inflamed U.S. patriotism, prompting renewed support for the president. Mass assemblies across the United States adopted Federalist resolutions condemning Genet and supporting the president. Genet was replaced by the French in early 1794.

Jay's Treaty

Although both Britain and France had long attacked U.S. shipping bound for each other's ports, Britain escalated and broadened its assault in 1793, creating a firestorm of protest in the United States. The United States had no navy to speak of, but it did have a strong merchant marine, and Britain's rough treatment of U.S. trading vessels strained U.S.-British relations to the breaking point. To make matters worse, the British forces in the disputed Northwest Territory (along the disputed Canadian border) began to add a new fort to their existing chain of fortifications. They also foiled Washington's efforts to conclude a durable peace with the region's American Indian tribes, who were reportedly told by the British governor general of Canada to prepare for war with the United States.

Reacting to London's provocative behavior, Democratic-Republicans and Federalists again attacked each other, strongly disagreeing over what to do. Democratic-Republican leaders in Congress demanded harsh retaliatory measures against British commerce, ranging from the imposition of high tariffs on British imports, which would have drastically increased the price of those products in U.S. markets, to the implementation of a total embargo against British goods. For their part, Washington and the Federalists were determined to prevent an escalation of the conflict. Federalists in Congress successfully turned back these calls for prohibitive sanctions against Britain and instead enacted relatively mild sanctions against both Britain and France for their violations of U.S. shipping rights.

These actions enabled the Federalists to project an image of their readiness to retaliate but also their even-handedness and moderation. Britain itself helped to cool tempers somewhat by relaxing its cargo-seizure policy in March 1794, enabling the United States to resume trade with the French West Indies. New French attacks on U.S. shipping also blunted attacks against Britain. Nevertheless, a Democratic-Republican measure that would have cut off all trade with Britain introduced in the Senate in April 1794 resulted in a tie vote. It failed with the tie-breaking ballot of the vice president, John Adams.

Having forestalled direct retaliation against Britain, which Washington was certain would lead to war, the president then turned to positive efforts at defusing the conflict. He dispatched Chief Justice John Jay to Britain to negotiate a settlement. The appointment itself sent a powerful signal to Britain of U.S. conciliation: Jay was a vigorous supporter of Hamilton, who was avowedly pro-British.

When the text of the treaty arrived in the United States in March 1795, it reignited political warfare between the Democratic-Republicans and the Federalists. The treaty failed to resolve the most divisive issue: Britain refused to recognize the United States's expansive interpretation of the rights of neutrals. The treaty also prevented the United States from imposing discriminatory tariffs on British goods, and provided for the payment of pre-Revolutionary War debts still owed to British businesspeople. Nevertheless, Britain also made considerable concessions. It agreed to evacuate its forts in the disputed territories by early 1796 and to compensate the owners of U.S. ships seized in the West Indies. The com-

Fast Fact

When Washington received the flamboyant and reckless envoy of the revolutionary French government Citizen Genet, he made a point to address him under the portrait of the late French monarch, Louis XVI, who had been guillotined in 1793.

(Source: John Ferling. *The First of Men: A Life of George Washington*, 1988.)

pensation package was particularly significant because approximately 250 U.S. vessels had been seized by mid-1794, making the West Indies the scene of the most serious violations by far of U.S. neutrality.

Widely viewed as a humiliating and one-sided document, Jay's Treaty was roundly condemned in U.S. popular opinion, and Washington suffered the indignity of scattered calls for his impeachment. Many Americans were incensed that the treaty stripped the United States of the weapon of trade sanctions, which were viewed as the only lever that could budge Britain on the neutrality issue. The Democratic-Republicans also charged that the treaty was yet another effort by the Washington administration to bring the United States closer to Britain and away from any sympathetic treatment of France.

Washington, however, supported the treaty, once again fearing war with Britain without it. Amid renewed criticism of his judgment and character, Washington brought his still considerable prestige and power to bear on the issue of ratification. With the aid of committed Federalists, the treaty was assured passage. But a high price was paid for the treaty in terms of moving the nation still further from Washington's long-standing hope that the republic, through the goodwill of its leaders, could achieve elite and popular consensus on common goals. Instead, the treaty further polarized elite and popular opinion. It also widened and hardened the breach in Congress between New Englanders and much of the Middle Atlantic states, on the one hand, and the South, on the other. In the vote in the House of Representatives over whether or not to support the treaty, 79 percent of those supporting Jay's Treaty were from New England or Middle Atlantic states, while over 73 of those rejecting it were from southern states (Bell, pp. 24, 25).

As for Washington's public reputation, the treaty dealt the president a grievous blow. Stripped of the iconic status he had enjoyed in the presidential elections of 1789 and 1792, Washington now wanted to announce his retirement for fear that the mounting criticism would leave the impression that he was being forced out of office. Indeed, the Democratic-Republicans now were in open revolt, defining their political identity further by declaring their opposition to Washington. Washington's own ambassador to Paris, the Democratic-Republican James Monroe, openly attacked the Jay's Treaty and Washington himself to Monroe's French hosts.

Despite its significant shortcomings and divisive political repercussions, Jay's Treaty must be judged an important achievement. By working to normalize relations with Britain, the treaty helped protect U.S. security and promoted economic development during the vital formative years of the republic. Though the Democratic-Republicans argued that the treaty was unfair, Jay's Treaty was apparently the only alternative to war with Britain.

Pinckney's Treaty

During Washington's second term the United States also faced a growing crisis in its relations with Spain. Spain controlled much of the territory to the south and the west of the United States. Of particular importance was Florida, the northern border of which was in dispute, and New Orleans, in the Louisiana territory. All trade on the Mississippi River had to pass through New Orleans, which meant that almost all contact and trade between the western settlers and the Eastern United States traveled through that city. The Spanish denied Americans the right to travel freely through New Orleans. They also charged Americans a duty for offloading their goods in New Orleans so they could be transferred to ocean-going vessels. The financial hardships imposed by these practices greatly angered western settlers.

Spain was relatively weak militarily in New Orleans and Florida, however. They had only thinly populated the Louisiana Territory, and as the U.S. settlers protested the restrictions placed in them more vehemently, Spain felt vulnerable to attack or subversion by these settlers. Spanish anxiety intensified with the news of Jay's Treaty, which Spain thought might lead to closer Anglo-American relations and open the way to a British or U.S. attack on its possessions. Facing these potential threats, Spain decided to negotiate with the United States. The result was Pinckney's Treaty of 1795, a resounding success for U.S. diplomacy. Spain accepted the United States's version of its boundary between the United States and Spanish Florida, as well as the U.S. interpretation of neutrality. Most importantly, the United States was given free navigation of the Mississippi River and the right of free deposit in New Orleans for three years. This meant that goods brought down the Mississippi River could be unloaded at New Orleans to be reloaded aboard ocean-going vessels for shipment to the East Coast or to foreign ports. The fact that Pinckney's Treaty secured the right of deposit was immediately applauded by western-

ers who had been near rebellion over the failure of the government to safeguard their economic interests.

The Washington Administration Legacy

When Washington left office in March 1797, his most immediate legacy was that of an uneasy peace. Through Jay's Treaty and Pinckney's Treaty, Washington had addressed the greatest foreign policy concerns of his administration, without drawing the United States into war. However, relations with Britain would remain uneasy, as violations of U.S. neutrality continued. Within 15 years the United States would be drawn into war with Britain, over many of the same issues that faced Washington.

Domestically, Washington's immediate legacy was his defense of the Constitution and of a strong federal government. While he preferred to seek consensus on most issues, Washington took a stand against popular associations, opposed the Yazoo land grab, and supported the formation of a national bank. Through actions such as these, Washington boosted the power and the authority of the federal government. He did this carefully, however, working hard to keep his actions within the bounds of the Constitution, and avoiding the appearance of tyranny as much as possible. When John Adams took office on March 4, 1797, he inherited from Washington a government that was far more powerful, and a nation that was much more unified, than what had existed eight years earlier.

One legacy of the Washington administration of which the first president would not be proud was the often bitter division between the Federalists and the Democratic-Republicans. This division led to angry debates and criticism of Washington's policies, especially in his second term. The strains of his last year in office were evident in Washington's *Farewell Address to the Nation,* which was published in September 1796.

Clearly stung by the mounting attacks against him, Washington pointed to his selfless devotion to duty, reminding the reader that he had not sought a second term in office. The address then passed quickly to an assessment of the internal and external threats to the integrity of the United States. Fearful of associations based on factional interests, Washington stressed the need for a political philosophy grounded in mutual gain and selfless dedication to the community. He directly confronted the problem of "the spirit of party," referring to the belief of some democrats that factions might place useful checks on government, protecting democratic practice and liberty. For Washington, however, any gains would be greatly outweighed by the costs. Party spirit, if left to develop, would eventually spark a "fire not to be quenched." Faction and party would place the union, the basis of political stability and economic prosperity, in peril. At the very least, parties would be unable to generate "consistent and wholesome plans" benefiting the whole nation if they came to power. At the worst, Washington feared a descent into the violence and repression of the later stages of the French Revolution. Despite this warning, however, the Democratic-Republicans and the Federalists had already taken on many of the characteristics of political parties.

Lasting Impact

Washington left an indelible mark on the United States, providing the nation with a model of selfless public service and a foundation of sound domestic and foreign policies. Perhaps most important, Washington provided a sense of national identity and purpose for the U.S. political community.

Washington held the United States together at a time when it could easily have fallen apart. Although his prestige as commander of the revolutionary army aided him in this task, it would have been insufficient by itself. Rather, Washington achieved still greater authority by placing himself above sectional and group interests. Although his harshest critics thought otherwise, Washington's behavior was judged to be nonpartisan by a sufficient number of his contemporaries to enable him to lay the foundation for legitimate and effective government. Through careful observation of the limits placed on his power by the Constitution, Washington lessened fears that a strong executive would lead to despotism or a leader with unlimited power. Yet at the same time, he exerted the power of the federal government when, as in stopping the Whiskey Rebellion, he felt it was necessary to strengthen and safeguard the Union. Although the foundation laid by Washington would eventually crack under the weight of recurring sectional disputes over states' rights and slavery, by then the federal government was strong enough to survive the crises of secession and civil war.

Washington also established many important precedents for the presidents who followed him. Washington refused a third term primarily out of the desire to ensure that the next president of the United States be chosen in free elections, rather than have the vice president ascend to the presidency when, as Washington expected, he died in office. An unintended consequence of this action was the development of a tradition of serving no more than two terms as president. Another action that Washington took on his own that became an important part of the political system was his formation of a cabinet of frequently consulted advisers.

Even looking beyond Washington's role in the formation of a strong United States, Washington's contributions to U.S. politics and policy are substantial. His *Farewell Address to the Nation* may be the best summary of the successes and failures of his administration. In his address Washington denounced the rise of "factions" and

the "spirit of the party" in U.S. politics. Despite the fact that most of Washington's contemporaries agreed with him on the danger of factionalism, Washington's warnings were unable to stop the rapid development of party politics in the United States. In truth, the transformation of the Federalist and Democratic-Republican factions into full-fledged political parties was already well underway. Accustomed to defining the public good at the state level, where most people shared the same interests and values, Washington's contemporaries were frustrated in their attempts to do the same at the national level, where heterogeneity and divergent interests replaced the familiar political and social landscape of the home state. Partisanship was the natural, if regrettable, product of this shift of power from state to national government.

Not surprisingly, the *Farewell Address to the Nation* also discussed the question of foreign relations. With Jay's Treaty and the Proclamation of Neutrality in mind, Washington justified his behavior with a simple yet powerful argument. Pointing to the dangers of entangling alliances, he stated that the "great rule of conduct" for the United States should be to promote commercial relations while having "as little political connection as possible" with foreign powers. Why, Washington asked, should we "entangle our peace and prosperity" in the continual upheavals and conflicts of Europe? For the next century and more after his farewell address, the United States followed Washington's advice to avoid political alliances with European powers. After Washington's retirement, national tempers gradually cooled over the issue of whether France or Britain should receive U.S. support, and even Democratic-Republican leader Thomas Jefferson came to value a policy of neutrality toward the European powers. Until World War I (1914–1918) the United States for the most part maintained a studied distance from European politics, developing strength as a nation as well as extending its global commercial reach. When the United States finally cast off its isolationism and strode onto the world political stage, it was no longer the fragile republic whose fate, as Washington had feared, could be sealed by involvement in European conflict. Now it was the involvement of the United States, in World War I and then World War II (1939–45), that helped determine the political and economic future of Europe.

Sources

Bell, Rudolph. *Party and Faction in American Politics.* Westport, Conn.: Greenwood Press, 1973.

Brookhiser, Richard. *Founding Father: Rediscovering George Washington.* New York: Free Press, 1996.

Carman, Harry J., Harold C. Syrett, and Bernard W. Wishy. *A History of the American People.* Vol. 1. New York: Knopf, 1964.

Combs, Jerald. *The Jay Treaty: Political Battleground of the Founding Fathers.* Berkeley, Calif.: University of California Press, 1970.

DISCovering U.S. History. Detroit: Gale Research, 1996.

Draper, Theodore. *A Struggle for Power: The American Revolution.* New York: Vintage Books, 1997.

Emery, Noemie. *Washington: A Biography.* New York: G. P. Putnam, 1976.

Encyclopedia of World Biography. Detroit: Gale Research, 1997.

Ferling, John. *The First of Men: A Life of George Washington.* Knoxville, Tenn.: University of Tennessee Press, 1988.

Flexner, James Thomas. *George Washington and the New Nation.* Little, Brown, 1970.

————. *George Washington: Anguish and Farewell, 1793–1799.* Boston: Little, Brown, 1972.

————. *Washington: The Indispensable Man.* Boston: Little, Brown, 1969.

Freeman, Douglas Southall. *George Washington, a Biography.* 7 vols. New York: Scribner's Sons, 1948–57.

McDonald, Forrest. *The Presidency of George Washington.* Lawrence, Kans.: University Press of Kansas, 1974.

Morison, Samuel Eliot. *The Oxford History of the American People.* New York: Oxford, 1965.

Phelps, Glenn A. *George Washington and American Constitutionalism.* Lawrence, Kans.: University Press of Kansas, 1994.

Reuter, Frank T. *Trials and Triumphs: George Washington's Foreign Policy.* Fort Worth, Tex.: Texas Christian University Press, 1983.

Schwartz, Barry. *George Washington: The Making of an American Symbol.* New York: Free Press, 1987.

Sharp, James Roger. *American Politics in the Early Republic: The New Nation in Crisis.* New Haven, Conn.: Yale University Press, 1993.

Smith, Richard Norton. *Patriarch: George Washington and the New American Nation.* New York: Houghton Mifflin, 1993.

Further Readings

DeConde, Alexander. *Entangling Alliance: Politics and Diplomacy under George Washington.* Durham, N.C.: Duke University Press, 1958.

Hirschfeld, Fritz. *George Washington and Slavery.* Columbia, Mo.: University of Missouri Press, 1997.

Tebbel, John William. *George Washington's America.* New York: Dutton, 1954.

Washington, George. *The Diaries of George Washington.* 6 vols. Edited by Donald Jackson. Charlottesville, Va.: University Press of Virginia, 1976–80.

————. *The George Washington Papers: Basic Selections from the Public and Private Writings of George Washington.* Edited by Saul K. Padover. New York: Harper, 1955.

John Adams Administration

Biography

Described by third U.S. president Thomas Jefferson as the central "pillar" of support for the Declaration of Independence, John Adams played an important political and ideological role during the United States's early efforts to grow from a fledgling union into a respected nation. A prolific writer and accomplished politician and diplomat, Adams's words and actions trumpeted the importance of commitment to a government composed of strong, independent branches.

Early Life

John Adams was born in Braintree (now Quincy), Massachusetts, on October 30, 1735. His father, John Adams, was a farmer and cordwainer (a maker of leather goods) who served as a church deacon, town selectman, and lieutenant in the local militia. His mother, Susanna Boylston, had three sons: John, Peter, and Elihu. Elihu died in 1775 in the American Revolution (1775–83).

As a boy, Adams loved the outdoors and found farm life in rural Braintree agreeable. On one occasion, responding to his father's exasperation at his son's lack of devotion to schoolwork, young Adams declared that he would be a farmer. His angry father reacted by taking Adams to gather thatch in a marsh under the hot sun. When asked at the end of the day if he still liked farming, Adams responded yes. Even later in life as he achieved distinction in the world of politics, Adams always was grateful to return to his farm in Quincy.

Full name: John Adams

Personal Information:
Born: October 30, 1735
Birthplace: Braintree (now Quincy), Massachusetts
Died: July 4, 1826
Death place: Quincy, Massachusetts
Burial place: First Unitarian Church, Quincy, Massachusetts
Religion: Unitarian
Spouse: Abigail Smith (m. 1764)
Children: Abigail Amelia; John Quincy; Susanna; Charles; Thomas Boylston
Education: Harvard College, BA, 1755
Occupation: Farmer; teacher; attorney; politician
Political Party: Federalist Party
Age at Inauguration: 61 years

John Adams. *(Painting by C. W. Peale. National Archives and Records Administration.)*

Education

Adams spent his school days at a public Latin school and was taught by two private tutors. Despite Adams's simple rural background, his parents believed strongly in the importance of formal education and decided that their son should go to Harvard College in Cambridge, Massachusetts, to become a clergyman.

Founded by Puritans in 1636, Harvard was mainly an institution for the training of clergymen and schoolmasters when Adams attended. Life at Harvard had a monastic quality in those days. After morning prayers at six and a breakfast of bread and milk, classes were held from eight until noon. The midday meal of meat and vegetables was followed by outdoor activities and prayers at five. The evening was set aside for study and a late supper, both accomplished by candlelight.

Based on his family's social standing, Adams was seated 14th among the 28 incoming students, but he soon ranked academically in the top three of his class. The Harvard curriculum was based on the classics, consisting largely of logic, rhetoric, Latin, and Greek. Mathematics, climatology, and physics also were required. Adams joined a play-reading group and began to apply himself diligently to his studies.

After graduating from Harvard in 1755, the 19-year-old Adams moved to Worcester, Massachusetts, a town 30 miles west of Boston. There he started to teach grammar school, having decided against going into the ministry. An independent streak and refusal to accept unquestioningly the doctrine of the Church may have contributed to his decision. While teaching, Adams began to study law. Upon completing his legal training around 1758, Adams returned to his parents' home, was admitted to the Boston, Massachusetts, bar, and began to practice law.

Family Life

On October 25, 1764, John Adams married Abigail Smith, the daughter of a well-known Congregational minister in Weymouth, Massachusetts. Abigail Adams was intelligent, vivacious, warm, and enormously loyal to her husband. Their marriage was marked by mutual devotion and intellectual respect. It also brought Adams wide social connections that contributed to his eventual political success. The primary strains in their marriage occurred during times of separation, such as when Abigail Adams remained at home in Quincy, Massachusetts, while John Adams was in Europe as a diplomat or in the capital as president.

Abigail Adams herself was a prolific writer of correspondence, from which we know her thoughts concerning the important issues and people of the day. When American independence was near, Abigail Adams suggested to her husband that Congress "Remember the Ladies" and protect them from the "unlimited power" of men, whom she described as "Naturally Tyrannical" (Ferling, p. 172). Abigail Adams and John Adams both were opposed to slavery as immoral and contrary to Christianity.

Within the first decade of their marriage, they had five children: Abby, John Quincy, Susanna, Charles, and Thomas Boylston. Their children were a source of both great sorrow and joy. Susanna died when she was only one year old. Charles, a hopeless alcoholic with whom Adams had strained relations, died from his disease in 1800. Abby, who was very dear to both of her parents, suffered during her marriage to Colonel William Smith, who went heavily into debt and was often away from home chasing after speculative business ventures. Abby's parents ultimately watched her die in their home from breast cancer in 1813. Thomas Boylston, who also battled alcoholism, enjoyed moderate success as a lawyer. John Quincy, also a lawyer, had a successful political career, including appointment by his father as minister to Prussia in 1797. In 1824, less than two years before his death, John Adams had the paternal honor of seeing his son elected as the sixth president of the United States. John Quincy was the first son of a president to attain that position.

Sadly, Abigail Adams did not live to see her son's presidency. After long battles with illnesses caused by rheumatism, she predeceased her husband by almost eight years on October 28, 1818. In the days following her death, Adams wrote to Thomas Jefferson in December: "We shall meet and know each other in a future State. . . . I cannot conceive that [God] could make such a Species as the human merely to live and die on this Earth" (Peabody, p. 405).

Career

In the 1760s Adams continued to study law and slowly built his law practice. He also began to involve himself in the maelstrom of revolutionary politics. When the French and Indian Wars ended in 1763, victorious Britain had accumulated a large debt. To remedy this, the British parliament enacted a series of tax and custom duty laws that became known as the Intolerable Acts. American colonists protested, believing it was unfair to be taxed by a legislature in which they had no representation.

After Britain's enactment of the Revenue Act, or Sugar Act, of 1764 and the Stamp Act of 1765, John Adams's cousin Sam Adams organized groups of protesters in Boston, Massachusetts. After listening to his cousin and attending some of the meetings, John Adams emerged as an effective spokesman against British imperial policy. In August of 1765 Adams published the first of four essays in the *Boston Gazette* that later were published in Britain under the title *Dissertation on the Canon and Feudal Law*. Adams described how the American colonists' love of liberty led them to emigrate to America to establish civil governments "in direct opposition to the cannon and feudal systems" that prevailed in Britain (Ferling, p. 47). Adams warned that his generation might have to make great sacrifices to retain their liberty.

In addition to his political activism, Adams continued to advance in the legal profession. He generally worked on cases involving divorce, wills, rape, and trespassing. Adams defended John Hancock, signer of the Declaration of Independence, against smuggling charges brought by British customs officials. His most important case in this period, however, came in 1770 when he defended Captain Thomas Preston, the officer in charge of British troops at the Boston Massacre. The massacre occurred when British soldiers fired upon a crowd of colonists, who may have goaded them into violence. When five colonists were killed, the incident became a rallying point for revolution. Believing that all men—even those who were despised—had the right to a fair trial, Adams agreed to defend Preston. While greatly criticized for it, Adams won the case.

American Revolution Politics and Diplomacy

Revolutionary passions intensified in the 1770s. In 1774 Adams was chosen to attend the First Continental

Fast Fact

When Adams arrived in the new capital in November 1800, Washington, D.C., was a muddy collection of public and private buildings still under construction amidst fields and forests. On the evening of November 1, 1800, Adams was the first president to sleep in the White House. The next day he closed a letter to his wife Abigail Adams with the following: "I pray Heaven to bestow the best of Blessings on this House and all that shall hereafter inhabit it. May none but honest and wise Men ever rule under this roof." Three weeks later in his last annual address to Congress, Adams paid homage to George Washington, who had died the previous December, and to the new federal city that bore Washington's name: "May this territory be the residence of virtue and happiness! In this city may that piety and virtue, that wisdom and magnanimity, that constancy and self-government, which adorned the great character whose name it bears be forever held in veneration! Here and throughout our country may simple manners, pure morals, and true religion flourish forever!"

(Source: Ralph Adams Brown. *The Presidency of John Adams,*1975.)

Congress in Philadelphia, Pennsylvania, which sought to discuss and solve the problems of imperial relations. For a number of reasons, including his distaste for war and fear of the consequences of openly advocating revolution, Adams recommended a system of coequal parliaments in America and Britain joined by common allegiance to the crown. In April of 1775, however, with knowledge that the Congress had disclaimed parliament's authority to use trade with America to raise revenue for Great Britain, British troops set out to crush the rebellion by attacking the colonists' arsenals in Concord, Massachusetts. Adams wrote in his *Autobiography* that the battles "changed the instruments of warfare from the Penn to the Sword."

In May of 1775 Adams attended the Second Continental Congress in Philadelphia, where he supported George Washington as the man to lead the Continental Army. Once fighting broke out and as it intensified, Adams came to believe that resolution with Britain was impossible and independence was necessary. Adams developed plans for the colonies to adopt new governments modeled on their colonial regimes. He presented this proposal to Congress in February of 1776 in a pam-

Biography:

Abigail Adams

Farmer; First Lady (1744–1818) Abigail Adams was the first lady to the second president of the United States, John Adams, and mother of the sixth president of the United States, John Quincy Adams. She lived during a pivotal time in U.S. history and her role as first lady was behind-the-scenes, but definitely not passive. Her husband's service to the nation and the need for her to care for their family and working farm, were circumstances that necessitated long periods of separation from one another. It is through the voluminous amount of correspondence between them during these times that we know the notable influence she had on her husband and his responses to the trying issues of the times. Her letters were also the intellectual and emotional bond that supported him. While it was very unusual for women of that period to conduct business affairs, Adams traded stock, hired help, coped with tenants, bought land, oversaw construction, and supervised planting and harvest-

ing. At a time when women were not allowed to vote and married women were not allowed to own property, Adams implored her husband to ". . . remember the ladies and be more generous and favorable to them than your ancestors." While their separations—once an overseas separation lasted five years—meant a life of loneliness

and hard work for Adams, her husband would consult her before accepting any appointment. In letters to friends Adams wrote that seeing him off she'd be "very sensible and heroic," but her heart would feel "like a heart of lead."

---

phlet entitled "Thoughts on Government." In July Adams seconded a motion in Congress for a formal declaration of independence. Thomas Jefferson, who wrote the historic document, called Adams "the pillar of its support on the floor of the Congress, its ablest advocate and defender against the multifarious assaults it encountered" (Brown, p. 10). Congress issued the Declaration of Independence on July 4, 1776.

In late 1777, Congress elected Adams commissioner to France. Upon his arrival in Paris, Adams learned that France already had granted diplomatic recognition to, and contracted treaties of commerce and amity with, the United States. Adams thus spent the next year and a half trying to secure badly needed loans for Congress, transmitting lengthy letters on European affairs, and learning with mixed fascination and repugnance about the ways of French court and national life. Upon learning that one of his fellow commissioners, Benjamin Franklin, had been appointed sole U.S. diplomatic agent in France, Adams returned to Boston in 1779. That fall he was elected from Braintree, Massachusetts, to the state constitutional convention. For the next few months he devoted his time to drafting what became the new Massachusetts constitution.

In 1779 Congress selected Adams as commissioner to negotiate peace with Britain. Adams embarked in mid-November and arrived in Paris on February 9, 1780. He and the other two U.S. commissioners, diplomats Benjamin Franklin and John Jay, eventually ignored their

instructions to make no agreement without first consulting the French foreign minister—they feared (correctly) that France wished to pressure the United States into peace arrangements inconsistent with the United States's national interests (for example, leaving certain coastal areas in British hands). The U.S. commissioners concluded provisional articles of peace and sent the results home to Congress. These were signed as the Treaty of Paris on September 3, 1783.

Before returning permanently to the United States, Adams spent three frustrating years as U.S. envoy to the Court of Saint James in London, England, attempting without success to negotiate a commercial treaty and other diplomatic issues remaining after the revolution. Rebuffed by British officials and unsupported by a weak Congress, Adams finally asked to resign. Formal letters of recall were sent in February of 1788. During the last year and a half of his stay, he composed the three-volume *Defense of the Constitutions of Government of the United States of America,* an extended effort to defend the U.S. concept of balanced government against contemporary European criticism.

Vice President

From 1789 to 1797 Adams served as vice president for two terms under George Washington. Washington and Adams were Federalists, a political party led by Treasury secretary Alexander Hamilton that favored strong powers for the federal government. Secretary of

State Thomas Jefferson was leader of the Republican Party, which equated a strong federal government with the English monarchy, and instead favored government by the individual states. These parties grew out of differences between Federalists and anti-federalists in 1787 concerning the power of the federal government and the composition of the legislative branch by the U.S. Constitution. The factions ratified the Constitution only after a compromise that created a Senate with equal representation for each state (preferred by the Federalists) and a House of Representatives with representation weighted by state population (preferred by the anti-federalists).

While Adams was vice president, his family resided on a modest income in Philadelphia, Pennsylvania (then the nation's capital). Abigail Adams was ill much of the time but did her best to provide a cheerful and warm environment for herself and her husband, despite their dislike for Philadelphia and longing for their farm in Massachusetts. Adams faithfully discharged his vice presidential responsibilities, which he admitted were insignificant.

The presidential campaign of 1796 between John Adams and Thomas Jefferson displayed the ongoing differences between Federalists and Republicans. Federalists wanted a strong military for defense and a national bank for financing commercial development. Republicans feared that a national military could be used against the states, and that a national bank would lead to financial ruin for borrowers paying high interest rates. The campaign also foreshadowed a split in the Federalist Party. Extreme Federalists, led by Hamilton, favored alliance with Britain and opposition to France in the European wars that began after the French Revolution in 1793. Moderate Federalists, led by Adams, preferred maintaining peace with, and independence from, all foreign nations.

President

John Adams won the election and took office in March 1797, with Thomas Jefferson as his vice president. (The U.S. Constitution at that time gave the vice presidency to the man who received the second most electoral votes.) Adams's cabinet, inherited from Washington and dominated by Hamilton's followers, would prove difficult to control.

International problems dominated Adams's presidency. Britain and France, themselves engaged in war in Europe, were the chief sources of conflict. The United States faced challenges to its independence, neutrality, and freedom on the seas as Britain and France both captured U.S. merchant ships, seized their cargoes, and impressed U.S. sailors into foreign naval service. The United States responded by creating the Department of the Navy in 1798 and strengthening its naval and military forces. The ensuing maritime conflicts were all but an official declaration of war until the United States and

What They Said . . .

Letter to Mrs. Adams, July 3, 1776

"Yesterday the greatest question was decided which ever was debated in America; and a greater perhaps never was, nor will be, decided among men. A resolution was passed without one dissenting colony, that those United Colonies are, and of right ought to be, free and independent States."

"The second day of July, 1776, will be the most memorable epocha in the history of America. I am apt to believe that it will be celebrated by succeeding generations as the great anniversary festival. It ought to be commemorated as the day of deliverance, by solemn acts of devotion to God Almighty. It ought to be solemnized with pomp and parade, with shows, games, sports, guns, bells, bonfires, and illuminations, from one end of this continent to the other, from this time forward for evermore."

(Source: John Bartlett. *Familiar Quotations: A collection of passages, phrases, and proverbs traced to their source in ancient and modern literature,* 1992.

France signed the Treaty of Môrtefontaine in 1800 (*See also,* Foreign Issues).

In 1798 Congress passed the Alien and Sedition Acts (*See also,* Domestic Issues). A response to Federalist insecurities brought about by international and political tensions, the acts severely restricted freedom of speech and impeded the naturalization of foreigners. Although Adams did not openly support the acts, neither did he discourage or veto them. Along with federal taxes needed to finance the navy and the military, the Alien and Sedition Acts contributed to growing civil unrest in the United States. They were strongly criticized by Thomas Jefferson and became issues in the presidential election of 1800, which Jefferson won.

Post-presidential Years

At the age of 65, John Adams left Washington, D.C. (the nation's capital since 1800), to return to his beloved farm in Quincy, Massachusetts, where he would pass the remaining 25 years of his life. He worked on the farm as much as his physical condition and energy would allow, continued to write essays and articles, and corresponded with family and friends. Adams wrote his *Autobiography,* which he never finished, in spurts from 1802 through 1806. Abigail Adams, his wife of 54 years, died in 1818. Her death was a profound loss to Adams.

Adams resumed friendship with Thomas Jefferson, his vice president and third president of the United States, around 1811, when they began an active correspondence that would last until their deaths. The two discussed politics, philosophy, theology, and personal matters. On July 4, 1826, 50 years after signing the Declaration of Independence, Adams died in his home in Quincy. His last words reportedly were "Thomas Jefferson survives" (Ferling, p. 444). Adams did not know, nor could he have, that Jefferson had died earlier that same day.

The John Adams Administration

Partisan politics in the United States intensified during John Adams's presidency. Federalists, who supported a strong national government, lined up against Republicans, who favored power residing in the states. While war raged in Europe, controversy raged at home over how to handle foreign relations with France and Great Britain. Adams, himself a moderate Federalist, struggled with both Federalists and Republicans over the primary domestic issues of taxes and the development of a strong military. The competing political philosophies ultimately led to fracture of the Federalist Party and victory for the Republicans in the election of 1800.

Adams Becomes President

The Campaign of 1796

The election of 1796 was the first presidential competition between political parties—the Federalists and the Republicans. These parties had developed from factions that struggled over construction of the U.S. Constitution in 1787. Federalists had supported a strong federal government with a legislative branch composed of representatives chosen equally from the states. Anti-federalists (forerunners to the Republican Party) preferred a federal government with limited powers, and a legislative branch with representation weighted by state population. The compromise, a Senate with equal representation for each state and a House of Representatives with representation weighted by state population, allowed both parties to ratify the Constitution. In the ensuing years, however, Federalists continued to prefer strong powers for the federal government, while Republicans preferred power in the states with minimal inter-ference from the federal government. Republicans resided primarily in the South, where their desire to protect the institution of slavery shaped their preference for state governmental power.

During George Washington's eight years in office, the United States had savored the success of the American Revolution (1775–83) and the establishment of a new government under the U.S. Constitution. Toward the end of Washington's administration, however, philosophical differences between Federalists and Republicans grew, largely concerning relations with Great Britain and France, who were at war. Federalists generally favored Great Britain, which stood for a strong national government by officials from the upper class of society. Republicans generally favored France, whose people had overthrown the French monarchy in 1793 in the wake of the United States's successful revolution.

The United States, however, had problems with both countries. Great Britain and the United States had signed Jay's Treaty in 1795 to resolve differences that developed after the Treaty of Paris ended the American Revolution in 1783. France viewed Jay's Treaty as a breach of treaties of commerce and alliance it had signed with the United States during the revolution. France had assumed that after the American Revolution the United States would ally with France. The United States found itself in the middle of the European wars as both Great Britain and France captured U.S. merchant ships and impressed U.S. sailors into foreign naval service (*See also,* Foreign Issues).

In the midst of this turmoil, in September 1796, George Washington announced that he would not seek a third presidential term. The Federalists turned to John Adams, who had been Washington's vice president for eight years, as their presidential candidate. Thomas Pinckney of South Carolina was Adams's vice presidential running mate. The Republicans believed that Thomas Jefferson, who wrote the Declaration of Independence and served with Adams in the Washington administration, was the only man with enough stature to challenge Adams. They selected Aaron Burr of New York as his running mate.

As was the practice in those times, Adams did not campaign on his own behalf. Nevertheless, supporters conducted a fierce campaign in the press. Led by Alexander Hamilton, who had been secretary of the Treasury under Washington, Federalists charged Jefferson with being a French supporter and an atheist (someone who denies the existence of God). Federalists often reminded the electors of Jefferson's flight from his home in Charlottesville, Virginia, when the British army invaded in 1781. Republicans accused Adams of being a monarchist, made fun of his portliness, and attacked Jay's Treaty and Alexander Hamilton's economic policies.

The campaign foreshadowed an emerging split in the Federalist Party. Alexander Hamilton, acknowledged leader of the Federalists, disagreed with Adams on issues such as relations with Europe and the necessary and proper economic strength of the national government, including the role of national banks and paper currency. Hamilton also knew that he would be unable to exercise much influence over Adams, who was fiercely independent. Hamilton, however, feared a Jeffersonian presidency even more. Some historians thus accuse Hamilton of scheming to have Adams's vice presidential candidate, Thomas Pinckney, win the election. Despite Hamilton's influence, most Federalists supported John Adams.

Under the U.S. Constitution at the time, electors chosen by the states cast their ballots, and the presidency and the vice presidency went to the candidates with the first and second most votes. Adams, in his position as vice president and thus president of the Senate, opened and read the results before Congress in February 1797: John Adams, 71 votes; Thomas Jefferson, 68; Thomas Pinckney, 59. John Adams thus was elected president of the United States, and his opponent, Thomas Jefferson, became vice president.

John Adams's inauguration occurred in Philadelphia, Pennsylvania, then the nation's capital, on March 4, 1797. George Washington attended dressed in a sleek black suit and powdered hair. Adams was nervous the night before but soon relaxed as he launched into his inaugural address. In a balanced speech that was well received by all but the most extreme Federalists, Adams pledged his commitment to the U.S. Constitution, dedication to a strong national government and commerce, respect for the constitutions of the individual states, and determination for the United States to maintain peace and neutrality with the nations of Europe. Oliver Ellsworth, chief justice of the U.S. Supreme Court, then administered the oath of office—the first time the oath was administered as such—and John Adams began his service as the United States's second president.

The Campaign of 1800

The political party of the presidency changed for the first time in history with the election of 1800. It was the first time in the history of the world that a major country peacefully changed the political orientation of its leadership. Adams was the Federalist candidate, this time with running mate Charles C. Pinckney of South Carolina, a Revolutionary War soldier and hero during the XYZ Affair (*See also,* Foreign Issues). The Republicans again nominated Thomas Jefferson and Aaron Burr.

The dominant issues were taxes and the military, peace negotiations with France, and the Alien and Sedition Acts of 1798. Adams found support mainly in the New England states, which had vested interests in the commerce cultivated by strong federal programs. Jefferson found support in a growing national desire to return to the principles of democracy that had ignited the American Revolution.

Administration

Administration Dates
March 4, 1797–March 4, 1801

Vice President
Thomas Jefferson (1797–1801)

Cabinet
Secretary of State
Timothy Pickering (1795–1800)
John Marshall (1800–01)

Secretary of the Treasury
Oliver Wolcott Jr. (1795–1800)
Samuel Dexter (1801)

Secretary of War
James McHenry (1796–1800)
Samuel Dexter (1800)

Attorney General
Charles Lee (1795–1801)

Secretary of the Navy
Benjamin Stoddert (1798–1801)

Postmaster General
Joseph Habersham (1795–1801)

The campaign and election reflected fracture within the Federalist Party. Hamilton and the extreme Federalists attacked Adams's insistence on peace with France, his resistance to building an army, and his failure to enforce the Alien Acts (*See also,* Domestic Issues). Hamilton supported Pinckney, and even expressed a desire for Jefferson over Adams, claiming that he would rather the government sink at the hands of the opposition party. Hamilton wrote a searing attack of the president entitled *Letter Concerning the Public Conduct and Character of John Adams.* Adams resisted the urge to respond, and instead stood on the strength of his record. While Adams declined to campaign openly, he made numerous appearances and speeches in the months before the election, often referring to his political service during the American Revolution.

On December 5, 1800, the electors met in their respective state capitals to cast their ballots. As the votes trickled in, it became apparent that New York and South Carolina would be the pivotal states. As it turned out, the Republicans swept both states, and Jefferson and Burr ended up in a tie for the presidency with 73 votes each. While Adams ran a close second with 65 votes, the elections for the House of Representatives more strongly reflected a nationwide preference for Republicans and a return to the principles of democracy.

After the House of Representatives resolved the tie vote, Jefferson was inaugurated on March 4, 1801. In a move that has received much historical criticism, Adams did not attend. Instead he left for Quincy, Massachusetts, that same morning. Some say that there was no evidence that Adams was invited to the inauguration. Whatever the reason, Adams's absence put an exclamation point on the exit of the Federalists and the beginning reign of the Republicans.

Adams's Advisers

In 1797 there was no precedent for a changing presidential administration, and thus no custom for the cabinet members to offer their resignations to the incoming president. In the midst of this, Adams made what he later called one of the biggest blunders of his presidency. He decided to retain Washington's cabinet instead of making his own personal selections. Adams believed that successful government depended on experienced men. He also saw how difficult it was for Washington to fill the low-paying cabinet positions with competent men after Treasury Secretary Alexander Hamilton and Secretary of State Thomas Jefferson resigned late in Washington's presidency. Also, politically, Adams feared that dismissing a Federalist cabinet would cause a rift in the party. What he did not know was that such a rift was destined during his presidency.

Hamilton was the root of the troubles in Adams's cabinet. An extreme Federalist, Hamilton favored peaceful relations with Great Britain and war with France. Unfortunately for Adams, Hamilton exercised great influence over two members of the cabinet: Secretary of State Timothy Pickering and Secretary of War James McHenry. A third, Secretary of the Treasury Oliver Wolcott Jr., shared Hamilton's preference for Great Britain.

Relations were tense from the outset. Early in March of 1797, Adams proposed sending James Madison of Virginia, a Republican, to head a bipartisan diplomatic mission to France. Wolcott objected to the selection of Madison and offered the resignation of the entire cabinet if Adams pursued the idea, which he did not. It was one of the few times that Adams would capitulate so easily. While Adams frequently consulted his entire cabinet, usually in writing, he believed that final decisions were his to make alone. Four years of rejecting the suggestions of his Hamiltonian cabinet made Adams's presidency uncomfortable.

Pickering and McHenry proved to be particularly treacherous. Both men withheld information from Adams and supplied secret information to Hamilton and Adams's other critics. Their actions and opposition to peace with France precipitated a cabinet crisis in 1800. It began on May 5 when a dinner meeting between Adams and McHenry erupted into an argument. Adams accused McHenry of manipulating George Washington, who still acted as an adviser to Adams, to have McHenry's true boss, Hamilton, elevated to the head of the national army (*See also,* Domestic Issues). McHenry submitted his resignation the next day. Four days later Adams requested Pickering's resignation. When Pickering refused because he needed the salary, Adams dismissed him on May 12.

Adams replaced Pickering with John Marshall of Virginia, who had served on the president's first diplomatic mission to France in 1797. Adams named Samuel Dexter, a Boston, Massachusetts, lawyer who had served in both houses of Congress, to be the new secretary of the Treasury. Along with Benjamin Stoddert as secretary of the navy, a position created in 1798, Adams finally had a cabinet he could work with during the last nine months of his presidency.

Adams did not have any official advisers beyond his cabinet. His administration was before the days of White House advisers and press secretaries, a time when the total federal government employed only two thousand people, and the executive records fit into seven packing cases. (In the summer of 1798, Adams personally hired his wife's nephew to be his secretary, but only to handle clerical functions such as copying and filing.) Adams, however, received unofficial advice in active correspondence with family members, including his wife when she resided at the farm in Quincy, Massachusetts, and his son John Quincy, who was stationed in Europe at various diplomatic posts. While Abigail Adams certainly did not participate actively as first ladies have in later administrations, she was an intelligent woman whose opinion Adams respected.

Adams and Congress

Adams was in office during the Fifth and Sixth Congresses, in which the Federalists had a slight majority. Adams believed strongly in the separation of powers and did not try to interfere with the work of Congress. Although he occasionally disagreed with legislation, Adams was the first of seven presidents who never exercised the veto power.

At a time when British and French attacks on U.S. ships threatened both her independence and commerce, Adams was committed to strengthening the U.S. Navy. He once told the Boston Marine Society that "Floating Batteries and Wooden Walls have been my favorite System of Warfare and Defense. . . for three and twenty years" (Brown, p. 72). In both his inaugural address and early congressional addresses, Adams asked Congress to join his commitment to naval expansion. Congress refrained at first, waiting for the result of Adams's first diplomatic mission to France, but eventually passed legislation to create the Navy Department in April 1798 and the U.S. Marine Corps in July 1798. Congress also passed legislation to increase the size of the navy and its power on the seas.

The bitterness that marked Federalist and Republican relations during the Adams administration is colorfully illustrated by the Lyon-Griswold Affair. It began in January 1798 when Representative Roger Griswold, a Federalist from Connecticut, insulted Representative Matthew Lyon, a Republican from Vermont, who thereupon spat tobacco juice in Griswold's face. When the House of Representatives declined to expel Lyon after its first ever censure motion, or official reprimand, Griswold attacked Lyon on the floor of Congress with a hickory cane, and Lyon defended with fire tongs. The incident led to riots in the U.S. capital in May. In an unrelated incident, Lyon later was convicted under the Sedition Act and served four months in prison for an article he published in the *Vermont Journal* (*See also*, Domestic Issues).

The Adams administration saw the first impeachment trial of a U.S. senator. William Blount of Tennessee, who owned a great deal of land in the southwest, plotted with the British minister to the United States to drive Spain out of Florida and the Louisiana Territory to encourage settlement and land sales. When a letter by Senator Blount containing his plans came into Adams's hands, Adams gave it to the Senate for investigation. The Senate expelled Blount in July 1797, and the House impeached him. The Senate eventually dropped the charges on the grounds that no further action could be taken beyond his dismissal.

Adams and the Judiciary

In terms of impact on the future of U.S. government, the appointment in 1800 of Secretary of State John Marshall to chief justice of the U.S. Supreme Court was one of Adams's most significant presidential actions. Marshall served as chief justice for 34 years and authored one of the Supreme Court's most important decisions, *Marbury v. Madison,* in 1803 (*See also*, Thomas Jefferson Administration). In it Marshall staked out a strong role for the federal judiciary: "It is emphatically the province and duty of the judicial department to say what the law is." To help Americans discern what the law is, Marshall ended the practice whereby each justice wrote his own opinion in every case, and instead encouraged one majority opinion.

Adams also appointed two associate justices to the Supreme Court; Bushrod Washington of Virginia in 1798

The U.S.S. Constitution, *nicknamed "Old Ironsides," symbolized President Adams's conviction that the United States needed to expand its naval forces in order to become a strong nation and military power.* (Painting by Marshall Johnson. National Archives and Records Administration.)

and Alfred Moore of North Carolina in 1799. Most controversial, however, was his appointment of federal judges in the waning days of his administration. In 1799 Adams had recommended legislation to reorganize and increase the number of federal courts and judges. The legislation failed to pass. However, after the election of 1800, when Republicans won the presidency and a majority in both houses of Congress, defeat prompted the lame duck Federalists to pass the Judiciary Act Adams wanted. Under the act, Adams made mostly Federalist judicial appointments until the last days of his administration, creating a tradition of packing the courts with so-called midnight judges. Although incoming president Thomas Jefferson and others criticized him for his conduct, Adams thought a Federalist judiciary was necessary if the government's system of checks and balances was to operate properly with a Republican president and Congress.

Changes in the U.S. Government

Although the United States was preoccupied with foreign crises during most of Adams's presidency, the

U.S. government experienced some important changes at home. In 1798 Congress created the Navy Department (which formerly was under the domain of the War Department) and the U.S. Marine Corps. Other notable changes included adoption of the Constitution's Eleventh Amendment. The Eleventh Amendment was written to limit the power of federal courts to hear cases brought by individual citizens of one state against the state government of another. The amendment has been interpreted in many different ways by the Supreme Court over the years, but at the time of its writing, the effect was such that the individual states were protected against suit in federal court by individuals of other states.

In 1798 the U.S. Public Health Service was established, and Adams reacted to the yellow fever epidemic of the prior summer by urging Congress to consider health legislation. While no states were added to the Union during Adams's presidency, the Mississippi and Indiana Territories were created in 1798 and 1800, respectively. The Library of Congress, today the world's largest repository of recorded information, was established on April 24, 1800.

A matter of great symbolic importance was the relocation of the federal capital from Philadelphia, Pennsylvania, to Washington, D.C., in 1800. President George Washington had selected the location during his administration.

Domestic Issues

The United States was just 20 years old, and the Constitution eight, when Adams began his presidency. Foreign issues would command the young nation's attention during the next four years. Europe was embroiled in war and revolution. Despite peace treaties with both Great Britain and France, both countries were attacking U.S. ships on the high seas and impressing U.S. sailors into foreign naval service (*See also,* Foreign Issues). Adams immediately faced questions concerning development of the U.S. Navy and the military.

The country debated how to maintain its independence. Federalists, largely comprising Americans in growing urban areas, favored a strong national government to support the development of commerce. Republicans, which included farmers and frontiersmen, equated a strong national government with a monarchy and lack of support for their local, agrarian needs. As a farmer who grew up within earshot of the Atlantic Ocean, Adams understood the importance of both agricultural and commercial strength. Adams was a Federalist, however, and he placed less faith in democracy than Thomas Jefferson and the Republicans. At a time when communication and transportation were slow, rural and frontier Americans were isolated from and distrustful of the urban centers of commerce, politics, and power, residing mainly on the East Coast. Tensions between the political parties reflected tensions between Americans.

Amidst the strife, former Treasury secretary and undisputed Federalist leader Alexander Hamilton sought expansion and fortification of the national army. Republicans feared Hamilton's domestic intentions for use of the army. Virginia, Jefferson's home and a bedrock of republicanism, responded by raising taxes 25 percent to finance expansion of the state militia and the manufacture of arms. Writing of those times ten years later, Adams said: "To despatch all in a few words, a civil war was expected" (Brown, p. 120).

In light of the need for national unity, a curious aspect of Adams's presidency was the amount of time he spent away from the capital. While George Washington was absent only 181 days in eight years in office, Adams was absent 385 days in four years, seeking his beloved farm and family in Quincy, Massachusetts. His opponents criticized him for this, while his supporters beseeched him to spend more time in Philadelphia then the U.S. capital. Such a practice would eventually become impossible with the growth of the nation and the president's responsibilities. The public and the press, however, continue the tradition of paying attention to the president's whereabouts in times of crisis.

Adams counterbalanced his absence from the capital by responding personally to correspondence received from fellow Americans. Whether in the capital or at home in Quincy, Massachusetts, Adams made a habit of spending between six o'clock in the morning and noon each day reading and responding to these many addresses.

Military Buildup

Naval Expansion

When John Adams took office, the United States's military was paltry. Compared to Great Britain's dominant navy, and France, with the world's largest army, the United States had an army of only 1,600 men and a navy without a warship. Adams immediately sought naval expansion. He believed that a strong navy was necessary to defend the United States from the threat of war with France and to protect the United States's developing commerce and fishing. French and English attacks on U.S. merchant ships, especially in the West Indies, were particularly problematic. Skyrocketing maritime insurance rates reflected the gravity of the situation.

Adams also felt that a strong navy was essential to independence from Great Britain. While extreme Federalists supported naval expansion, they believed that outright alliance with Great Britain was the better solution. Republicans opposed a large navy, partially because they felt no threat from France, and partially because they felt that naval expenditures for the sake of commerce were at the sacrifice of agrarian interests.

In the first session of the Fifth Congress in 1797, before tensions with France had escalated to undeniable proportions (*See also,* Foreign Issues), Congress blocked Adams's efforts to arm all merchant ships and defeated a bill to add 15,000 men to the army. However, Congress did authorize arming merchant ships in the East Indies and the Mediterranean, even though the ensuing naval conflicts were primarily in the West Indies. Congress passed the bill to add 12 frigates to the navy, with a close Senate vote of 16 to 13. A year later in May 1798, Congress created the Navy Department. Under Secretary Benjamin Stoddert, a Revolutionary War veteran, the navy drafted articles of governance (a system of management or government) and built and redesigned ships. By the winter of 1799, the United States's navy was strong enough to serve Adams's goals of defense, commerce, and independence.

Washington and Hamilton Gain Command of the Army

Development of the U.S. army under Adams did not receive much attention until spring 1798, when foreign relations with France deteriorated after a diplomatic insult (*See also,* Foreign Issues). Federalists, led by Alexander Hamilton, wanted a strong national army. Republicans feared that a domestic army would be used by a tyrannical government against its own people. Republicans instead favored development of the state militias. Adams believed that the expense of a national army was wasteful compared to the benefits that would be derived from naval expansion. In 1798, however, he signed a congressional bill to increase the army by 10,000 troops. Because the army leadership was beset with problems, the army never saw action.

In May and June 1798, Hamilton wrote to George Washington expressing his desire to serve as second-in-command in a Washington-led army. Secretary of State Timothy Pickering also wrote to Washington to cast doubt on Adams's military ability and to support Hamilton's desire for a Washington-Hamilton led army. Unaware of this correspondence, Adams wrote to Washington seeking his military advice and suggesting that Washington should return to lead the army. Before receiving a response, Adams submitted Washington's name to the Senate for nomination as the new lieutenant general and commander in chief. The Senate quickly and unanimously confirmed the nomination. The Federalists too wanted a strong army led by Washington and hoped that Hamilton would be his second-in-command.

After receiving confirmation of his appointment, Washington wrote to Hamilton that it was essential that he have confidence in his subordinates, whom he preferred to be Hamilton and Charles C. Pinckney of South Carolina. Washington suggested, however, and correctly so, that it was up to Adams to decide who would be second-in-command.

Adams suggested that Washington's subordinates be ranked as they were in the American Revolution: former secretary of war Henry Knox, Pinckney, and Hamilton.

Adams's cabinet, especially the extreme Federalist James McHenry, secretary of war, wrote many letters urging him to make Hamilton second-in-command. In a bold move, Washington wrote directly to the president suggesting that he would resign if he could not choose his officers. In his response, Adams asserted his presidential authority on the matter and Washington agreed with him. In the end, however, acceded to Washington's wishes making Hamilton Washington's second-in-command of the United States's standing army. Nevertheless tensions between Adams and the extreme Federalists increased and the Republicans continued to fear the antidemocratic implications of a large standing army.

Alien and Sedition Acts

Partisan politics during Adams's presidency resulted in a limitation on civil liberties. In the summer of 1798, at the height of tensions with France, Congress passed and Adams signed four statutes called the Alien and Sedition Acts. The Naturalization Act increased the length of residence required for U.S. citizenship from five to 14 years. The Alien Friends Act allowed the president to deport, without explanation, any alien he deemed to be dangerous to peace. The Alien Enemies Act allowed the president to deport the citizens of any country with which the United States was at war. The Sedition Act penalized conspiracies against federal law and "false, scandalous, and malicious" accusations against the federal government.

Historians claim that international tensions were merely an excuse for the Alien and Sedition Acts, which really were a Federalist effort to silence their Republican critics. When enforcing the Sedition Act, the Adams administration targeted Republican newspaper editors. Biased Federalist judges made impassioned speeches when instructing juries about the law of sedition, which one newspaper defined as follows: "It is Patriotism to write in favor of our government—it is sedition to write against it" (Dauer, p. 165.) The Sedition Act curiously had an expiration date of March 3, 1801, when the Republicans were destined to attain the presidency and control of Congress. The Federalist-dominated Congress passed the Naturalization Act because most immigrants were joining the Republican Party.

Adams eventually embarked on a mission of peace with France and never sought to enforce the Alien Acts. Soon after their enactment, however, many French aliens voluntarily left the country to avoid prosecution. While Secretary of State Timothy Pickering frequently asked Adams to sign orders for the deportation of French aliens who remained in the United States, Adams declined to do so. This added to the growing rift between Adams and the extreme Federalists.

In later years Adams would blame Hamiltonian influence for enactment of the Alien and Sedition Acts. Hamilton, however, appeared to be opposed at least to the Sedition Act. He feared that it could lead to civil war

Fast Fact

U.S. citizens saved more than eight million dollars in insurance rates after the navy was enlarged (in 1798), a sum more than twice the total naval expenditures between 1794 and 1798.

(Source: Ralph Adams Brown. *The Presidency of John Adams*, 1975.)

and wrote to Treasury Secretary Oliver Wolcott saying the United States should not establish a tyranny. Historians blame Adams for whipping up national fervor against France in addresses in the wake of the XYZ Affair (*See also,* Foreign Affairs). Adams also signed the acts into law without exercising his option to veto them—he later claimed that Congress had the votes to override a veto.

The public debate caused by the Alien and Sedition Acts increased civil unrest. The Republican legislatures of Virginia and Kentucky passed laws declaring the acts to be unconstitutional in their states, and there was talk of seceding from the Union. Republicans sought to have the laws repealed in 1800, and the laws were an issue in the presidential election campaign later that year.

Taxes and the Fries Rebellion

Financing the federal government, especially its standing army, became increasingly expensive during the Adams administration. The annual federal budget nearly doubled from 1796 through 1800. In July 1798 the Federalist-controlled Congress passed the so-called Window Tax, a direct tax based on land, houses, and slaves at 50 cents per head. The tax placed the greatest burden on Republican farmers and plantation owners in the South.

Americans who lived through the American Revolution (1775–83) remembered the revolts against the British monarchy over taxation, and many sought to defy the U.S. tax collectors. When three citizens in eastern Pennsylvania were jailed in early 1799 for their refusal to pay the land tax, a rebellion ensued. Led by John Fries, a county auctioneer, nearly 150 men marched to Bethlehem, Pennsylvania, and forced the federal marshal to release the prisoners.

The federal government acted swiftly. Adams issued a statement ordering the cessation of insurgent activity. Federal troops made 29 arrests, and the rebellion quickly subsided. Fries stood trial with his supporters and was

sentenced to death for treason with two others. Although they gained a retrial on a technicality, they petitioned Adams for presidential pardons.

Adams's consideration of the matter lasted well into 1800. He studied the common law of treason and the details of the rebellion. Adams also wrote to his cabinet members to solicit their advice. Attorney General Charles Lee, Treasury Secretary Oliver Wolcott, and Secretary of the Navy Benjamin Stoddert ultimately recommended no pardon. In a letter to Wolcott on May 21, 1800, Adams rejected their advice. He had decided that the Fries rebellion was riotous, but was not an effort to overthrow the federal government. Adams's decision probably reflected a belief that the death penalty would decrease confidence in the federal government and inflame civil unrest. Adams's decision contributed to his unpopularity among the extreme Federalists.

Impact of Domestic Policy

Adams was caught in the middle of the Federalists and the Republicans at a time when partisan politics ascended in the United States. He initially was liked by Americans, thanks in part to his association with the Washington administration. As Adams charted a course of executive independence, however, he made enemies in both parties. His personal attention to the voluminous addresses he received kept him in touch with the wishes of the nation. His inability to satisfy everyone attests more to the practical limitations of the position than to personal failure to discharge his duties.

Historians are both critical and laudatory of Adams's domestic accomplishments. They have denounced his failure to oppose the Alien and Sedition Acts, and otherwise have applauded his refusal to serve blindly the interests of even his own political party. More than anything else, however, historians agree that Adams's greatest achievements lie in the realm of foreign affairs, which shaped and often overshadowed the domestic issues of the young country.

Foreign Issues

Foreign conflict dominated John Adams's presidency. The conflict derived from the United States's continuing need to fortify its independence by developing commercial strength. This required access to New England fisheries, profitable trade in the Caribbean, and access to major waterways and ports both on the U.S. continent (i.e., the Mississippi River and New Orleans, Louisiana) and in Europe. Cultivating these avenues of commerce inevitably led to conflict with Great Britain, France, and Spain.

When the United States declared its independence from Great Britain in 1776, France quickly extended recognition of the United States and eventually contributed soldiers to the United States's war effort. In 1778 the United States and France signed a Treaty of Commerce, which provided that French warships with the spoils of war would be permitted entrance into U.S. ports. They also signed a Treaty of Alliance, promising that neither country would separately make peace with Great Britain until Great Britain recognized the United States's independence. This began an international tug-of-war between France and Great Britain, with the United States in the middle, that would last through Adams's presidency.

The Treaty of Paris between Great Britain and the United States in 1783 marked the conclusion of the American Revolution (1775–83). John Adams had negotiated the treaty for the United States along with U.S. diplomat, and later first Supreme Court chief justice, John Jay, and U.S. diplomat Benjamin Franklin. The treaty resolved boundary disputes, clarified the United States's fishing rights in New England, and provided for the United States to repay prewar debts. France immediately viewed the treaty as a violation of the Franco-American Treaty of Alliance.

France and Great Britain Go to War

In the wake of the French Revolution of 1789, by which France overthrew its monarchy, France declared war on Great Britain in 1793. Under the Treaties of Alliance and Commerce, France immediately sought assistance from the United States, including access to U.S. ports for France's warships. President George Washington, however, declared the United States's neutrality and declined to provide assistance. This further soured relations with France, despite the fact that many Americans favored France in the conflict.

Meanwhile, relations with Great Britain under the Treaty of Paris also had deteriorated. Americans refused to repay pre-Revolutionary War debts. Great Britain refused to abandon military forts along the United States's northern border and refused to give U.S. ships access to British ports. With the eruption of war with France in 1793 and a shortage of British soldiers, Great Britain began the practice of capturing U.S. ships and impressing U.S. sailors into service in the British navy. Great Britain also announced a policy of condemning neutral trade with France in the West Indies, and thereupon began capturing U.S. merchant vessels in the Caribbean.

Although he did not condone Great Britain's behavior, President Washington, like Adams, believed that neutrality with the nations of Europe was the United States's best strategy for long-term success. Washington sent John Jay to London, England, to engage in diplomatic negotiations. Jay's Treaty of 1795, however, secured few concessions from Great Britain beyond the agreement to remove Great Britain's military from U.S. soil by June

1796. The treaty said nothing about the impressment of U.S. sailors and failed to open Great Britain's ports to U.S. ships, except for ships under 70 tons in the West Indies. Although the Senate ratified the treaty at Washington's urging, Americans and Frenchmen alike were outraged by the alliance. France reacted in 1796 with a decree resolving to treat U.S. ships as Great Britain did. France thus began capturing U.S. merchant ships and their cargoes, especially in the West Indies, and impressing U.S. sailors.

This was the climate when Adams entered the presidency in March 1797. For the next four years Adams struggled between avoiding war with France while standing up to its attacks on the high seas. Most historians refer to the ensuing naval conflicts as a quasi-war. Adams's policy drew fire from extreme Federalists who criticized his failure to ask Congress to declare war, and Republicans, who were angry that Adams did not treat France the same way he did Great Britain by ignoring them. The political tensions reflected animosity between Americans, who became bitter at the United States's treatment by both Great Britain and France.

John Adams's greatest accomplishment was avoiding a full-scale war with France while maintaining neutrality with Great Britain. Adams knew such a result was essential for the United States to maintain independence and garner respect from Europe, while developing the commerce it would need to continue its constitutional experiment. The cost of his success was political failure in the presidential election of 1800.

U.S.-French Relations

Shortly before Adams's administration began, President Washington sent Federalist Charles C. Pinckney of South Carolina to Paris, France, to replace James Monroe, a Republican sympathizer, as minister to France. The executive branch of France's government was a commission of five men collectively called the Directory. Within the first 10 days of his presidency, Adams learned that the Directory had both refused to accept Pinckney as Monroe's replacement and ordered him to leave the country. Weeks later Adams learned that on March 2, 1797, largely in response to news of Adams's election, the Directory issued a decree abrogating the treaties of 1778 and committing to seize neutral ships carrying British goods.

Adams had contemplated sending an envoy, either Vice President Thomas Jefferson or James Monroe, both Republicans, to negotiate peace with France. Jefferson and Monroe both had declined. Adams now called a meeting of his cabinet and a special session of Congress to discuss how to react to France's treatment of Pinckney and the Directory's decree. The cabinet immediately contacted Federalist leader and former Treasury secretary Alexander Hamilton for advice. At the time, Hamilton felt war with France was contrary to public sentiment, and he supported a Republican envoy so that his political enemies would have to take the blame for the envoy's inevitable failure.

Adams was pleased when his cabinet recommended diplomacy instead of war. He nonetheless addressed the special session of Congress in May 1797 with harsh words for France. He insisted that their treatment of Pinckney and aggressions on the seas could not be accepted by an independent United States, and he asked for increased naval and military spending. Federalists applauded the speech, while Republicans thought it would incite war. Debate over the proposed military spending led one western congressman to advise New England to secede from the nation and build its own navy rather than spend the money of the nation's farmers. Domestic tensions rose.

In the following weeks Adams outlined his proposal to send a bipartisan commission consisting of Charles Pinckney; John Marshall, a Federalist judge; and Elbridge Gerry, a Republican friend. Adams considered himself and Gerry to be the only two men in the United States not shackled by partisanship. Federalists saw the appointment of the Republican as both a softening toward France and an unwarranted political favor. The commissioners nonetheless set out for Paris in July 1797.

XYZ Affair

Adams charged Pinckney, Marshall, and Gerry with negotiating a treaty similar to Jay's Treaty of 1795 with Great Britain. Under no circumstances were they to offer assistance to France in its war with Great Britain. While the commissioners were to seek absolute freedom on the seas and compensation for French capture of U.S. merchant ships, such terms were secondary to the primary goal of arriving at a neutral commercial treaty.

The French Directory selected Minister of Foreign Relations Charles Maurice de Talleyrand-Perigord to negotiate with the U.S. commissioners. While France truly desired peace with the United States, it viewed Jay's Treaty as a threat. France intended to use the negotiations to reverse the United States's supposed alliance with Great Britain while obtaining support for its war effort.

When the U.S. commissioners were assembled in Paris in October 1797, Talleyrand sent unofficial secret agents to speak with them. The secret agents communicated the Directory's displeasure with Adams's address to the special session of Congress the previous May. They stated that before the U.S. commissioners could expect an official reception from France, the United States would have to apologize for Adams's words, pay a bribe of $250,000, and advance a loan to assist France with its war efforts.

While the suggestion of a bribe was consistent with European diplomacy at the time, the U.S. commissioners were shocked by the amount. In keeping with their orders, they were unalterably opposed to making a loan. As informal talks dragged into 1798 with no progress,

the secret agents threatened the U.S. commissioners' personal and national safety. A rift then developed between Gerry and his fellow commissioners. Gerry supported moderate concessions to avoid full-scale war. The Directory ultimately ordered Marshall and Pinckney to leave the country and allowed Gerry to remain in Paris to continue talks. He remained for many months without resolving the dispute.

The wheels of diplomacy turned slowly as transportation from Europe often took between one and two months. It was not until March 4, 1798, that the Adams administration received dispatches from the commissioners. Secretary of State Timothy Pickering read the message first and then raced to the president's house broiling with anger. Adams also was angered as he read the message, which revealed France's refusal to receive the commissioners and the secret agents' insulting threats and demands.

Adams immediately reported the failure of the mission to Congress without disclosing the details. Congress asked to see the diplomatic dispatches, but Adams refused citing executive privilege. This led the Republicans to believe that Adams had made up the whole thing. When Adams finally agreed, he sought to protect the U.S. commissioners by deleting the names of the secret agents and instead inserting the letters X, Y, and Z. Americans reacted to the news with hostility. Republicans were forced to justify their support for France while Federalists, including Attorney General Charles Lee and Pickering, called for war. Adams included such a request in initial drafts of a presentation to Congress, but he eliminated it as too dangerous for the United States.

While there never was an official declaration of war, which the Constitution reserves for Congress, Adams revoked Washington's order that forbade the arming of U.S. merchant ships. Congress passed laws abrogating all treaties with France and authorizing seizure of all French ships that endangered U.S. commerce. Adams and the Federalist Congress then seized on the opportunity to expand the navy and the military. This also is when Congress enacted the Alien and Sedition Acts (*See also,* Domestic Issues). In the summer following the XYZ Affair, Adams often appeared in public in full military uniform with a sword at his side, and he enjoyed the height of his popularity with the Federalists.

After military expansion was complete and the United States had time to calm down, Adams addressed the third, and last, session of the Fifth Congress in December 1798. The president saw how civil unrest threatened to undo the United States, such as the Fries Rebellion of 1799. (*See also,* Domestic Issues). He sought to relieve these tensions by reaching out for peace with France while maintaining the United States's dignity. In his address, Adams announced that the United States did not want war with France but would continue military development and would not disgrace the United States by sending an uninvited envoy to France. According to Adams, however, intelligence reports suggested that France's Directory might be ready to receive a U.S. ambassador. Adams insisted that such a step was possible only on invitation from France. Adams thus continued to hold out for peace.

Peace with France

Adams appointed his final diplomatic mission to France in February 1799. Letters between Talleyrand and Gerry suggested that France was interested in peace. John Quincy Adams, John Adams's son, later sixth U.S. president, who was in Europe as minister to Prussia, agreed with this assessment. Talleyrand also wrote a letter expressing France's intention to receive a new U.S. envoy "with the respect due to the representative of a free, independent, and powerful country" (Ferling, p. 375). Although it was not an official communication directly from France, Adams accepted it as an invitation to achieve peace with France while maintaining the United States's dignity.

Without consulting his cabinet or Congress, Adams nominated U.S. Ambassador to the Netherlands William Murray in February, 1799, to be an envoy to France. The nomination reached Congress as the House of Representatives was debating a bill for expansion of the army. In the words of Secretary of State Timothy Pickering, the Federalists were "thunderstruck." Pickering and the Federalist press immediately voiced strong opposition to the mission—their political platform and success depended in large part on war with France. Adams persisted, driving the final stake into his relations with the extreme Federalists. To avoid defeat of his nomination of Murray, however, Adams agreed to add two more envoys to the mission: Oliver Ellsworth, the chief justice of the U.S. Supreme Court, and William Davie, Federalist governor of North Carolina. Adams stipulated that the commissioners would not embark for Paris until he had assurances that France would receive them as the United States's representatives for peace. Talleyrand sent a letter with such assurances directly to Adams.

Adams returned to his home in Quincy, Massachusetts, in March 1799, and would receive much criticism for remaining there for over half a year. In October he finally returned to the capital—now temporarily in Trenton, New Jersey, due to yellow fever in Philadelphia, Pennsylvania—at the urging of Secretary of the Navy Benjamin Stoddert. In Trenton Adams listened to the advice of his cabinet. Secretary of War James McHenry, Treasury Secretary Oliver Wolcott, and Pickering urged him to cancel the mission to France, while Attorney General Charles Lee argued that further delay would close a window of opportunity for peace. Hamilton left his command of the army to visit the president for a few days. While he opened with military matters, Hamilton ultimately launched into a lecture concerning affairs in Europe and his counsel against the mission to France. Still, Ellsworth and Davie embarked from Rhode Island on November 3, 1799, to meet Murray in Europe.

Fast Fact

Commissioners Negotiate with Napoleon's Government: When the commissioners arrived the French Directory had been replaced by a new government controlled by Napoleon Bonaparte, who was engaging in successful military campaigns throughout Europe. Bonaparte's goal was to strengthen France by establishing peace with the United States and opening up commercial relations. Bonaparte also did not want to curtail his successful war efforts by sending the United States into Britain's arms. Bonaparte appointed Talleyrand as minister of foreign relations under the new government, and Talleyrand received the U.S. commissioners in Paris.

While the meetings between the negotiators were cordial, conflict soon developed. The Americans' instructions, drafted by Pickering and finalized by Adams, were to secure recognition of abrogation of the treaties of 1778, establish freedom of navigation for neutral vessels with neutral cargo, and get reparations for damage caused by French attacks on U.S. merchant ships. Adams insisted that the commissioners never concede the latter demand, and that they finish their negotiations by April 1, 1800. Adams hoped that success would boost his campaign for reelection.

Bonaparte hoped to take the opportunity to turn the United States against Great Britain. He instructed France's negotiators to secure recognition of the existence of the treaties of 1778, under which the United States had granted France access to U.S. ports during wartime. The United States felt it could not do so under Jay's Treaty of 1795. France ultimately insisted that the United States either recognize the treaties of 1778, or drop its demand for reparations. The negotiations deadlocked for months on these issues.

In September 1800 the U.S. commissioners sought to break the stalemate by setting aside the issues of the old treaties and reparations. They instead proposed that the United States and France negotiate a provisional treaty to restore normal, peacetime political and commercial relations. France accepted this proposal. The two countries signed the Treaty of Môrtefontaine on October 3, 1800, at Bonaparte's brother's country estate, Chateau Môrtefontaine, from which the treaty got its name.

While France published the treaty that month, the official copy did not reach Adams until December 11, 1800, after the electors had cast their ballots in the presidential election. The treaty received mixed reactions in the United States. Republicans and moderate Federalists accepted it, though not enthusiastically. Extreme Federalists denounced it as worthless. The Senate ratified the treaty in February 1801 only after deleting article two, which called for further negotiations concerning both reparations and the treaties of 1778. Adams felt that acceptance of the entire treaty was the better course, but he preferred the Senate's ratification to no treaty at all. The second and final session of the Sixth Congress then returned the navy to a peacetime status.

Twelve years after leaving the White House, Adams reflected on his presidency and said he would defend his "missions to France, as long as I have an eye to direct my hand, or a finger to hold my pen. They were the most disinterested and meritorious actions in my life. I reflect upon them with so much satisfaction that I desire no other inscription over my gravestone than: 'Here lies John Adams, who took upon himself the responsibility of the peace with France in the year 1800'" (Brown, p. 174).

Hamilton Seeks to Wrest Louisiana and the Floridas from Spain

When Adams took office, Spain controlled the territories of Louisiana and the Floridas. Louisiana stretched from what is now Canada to Santa Fe, New Mexico, and from the Mississippi River to the Rocky Mountains. Florida included a strip of coast land from present-day Florida to New Orleans, Louisiana. In 1795 Spain and the United States had signed the Treaty of San Lorenzo (also known as Pinckney's Treaty), by which they agreed to negotiate their border disputes in the southwest United States. Spain further agreed to surrender a piece of land called the Yazoo Strip that stretched from the Mississippi River to Georgia. Spain also promised to remove forts along the Mississippi River, to allow Americans unlimited navigation of the river, and to grant Americans the right to store goods untaxed in the port city of New Orleans.

Spain soon dishonored the treaty, and some Americans in the southwest voiced support for a war. This comment appeared in the *Porcupine Gazette:*

> A war with Spain is absolutely necessary to the salvation of this country, if a war with France takes place, or if the Spaniards have ceded Louisiana to France. They must both be driven into the Gulf of Mexico, or we shall never sleep in peace. Besides, a war with Spain would be so convenient! There is nothing but dry blows to be gotten from

the penniless sans-culottes; but the wealth of Spanish America would be a salve for every sore. It would be the cream of the war with Spain (Brown, p. 140).

Meanwhile, France wanted to regain Louisiana from Spain, and there were rumors that Great Britain intended to invade Louisiana from Canada. In the midst of this convergence of interests, a Venezuelan adventurer named Francisco de Miranda devised a plan to use the U.S. Army and the British navy to liberate South America from Spanish rule. The United States's prize for participation was control of Louisiana and Florida. The British were interested.

Miranda approached Alexander Hamilton with his scheme. By August 1798, after becoming second-in-command of the U.S. Army, Hamilton was looking for a role for the army (*See also,* Domestic Issues). Over the next year Hamilton corresponded with Rufus King (U.S. ambassador to Great Britain), Miranda, Secretary of State Timothy Pickering, and Secretary of War James McHenry to develop plans for the invasion of Spanish territory in the southwest. At the same time he sought to expand and arm the United States's ground forces. Hamilton had his eyes set not only on Florida and Louisiana, but on Central and South America as well.

Miranda outlined his proposal in a letter to Adams in March 1798, but Adams declined to respond. The president was aware of Hamilton's and the cabinet's efforts to plan for war, however, he felt that Americans in the southwest preferred peaceful commercial development. Adams also disliked the idea of a naval alliance with Great Britain during the latter's war with France, while the United States sought to establish naval independence. The president did not want to alienate Great Britain, so he remained silent in response to his cabinet's inquiries concerning Miranda's proposal. Adams opted for peace yet again, and Hamilton never got the opportunity to attack Spain in the southwest. By a secret treaty in 1800, Spain eventually ceded Louisiana to France.

Great Britain Interferes with U.S. Shipping

Although Great Britain and the United States had a mutual enemy in France during Adams's presidency, relations between the two countries also deteriorated. Jay's Treaty of 1795 had created two commissions to address the questions of Great Britain's payment for U.S. property destroyed during the American Revolution and the United States's payment of prewar debts. These commissions disbanded without success during Adams's presidency, and Great Britain maintained its military presence along the United States's northern border.

The conflict reached the high seas as well. British destruction of French merchant ships sailing from the West Indies led to the latter's increased reliance on U.S. merchant ships. Even after June 1798, when Congress passed a law outlawing commerce with France, U.S. merchants still profited from the carriage of French goods from the West Indies. These ships became targets for the British navy. On February 1, 1799, a Jeffersonian journal called the *Aurora* printed statistics showing that British warships inflicted 10 percent more damage on U.S. merchant ships than did French privateers in the previous six-month period.

The naval warfare took its toll in casualties on the British navy as well. British naval shortages in its war with France led to the capture and impressment of U.S. merchant sailors into the British navy. The impressment policy infuriated American patriots. That period saw the height of British indiscretion. In mid-November 1799, the British H.M.S. *Carnatic* stopped the U.S. warship *Baltimore,* which was escorting merchant ships to Havana, Cuba. The *Carnatic* prevented the ships from entering the harbor, ordered the *Baltimore* to prepare to be boarded, and removed 55 of its crew members, most of whom were returned. The Adams administration was outraged. The captain of the *Carnatic* was transferred upon complaints from Secretary of State Pickering. Adams himself wrote to Great Britain to protest the practice of impressment. Adams also dismissed the captain of the *Baltimore* without trial and ordered the U.S. Navy to resist future impressment.

In the end, however, the Federalists never reacted as strongly against British naval indiscretion as they did against France. Republicans saw the hypocrisy in this unequal treatment, but were powerless to handle the situation otherwise without control of the presidency and Congress.

Impact of Foreign Policy

Adams's foreign policy received both praise and criticism from both parties. When he talked tough against France, Federalists cheered; when he extended an olive branch for peace, they jeered. Republicans, especially Vice President Thomas Jefferson, generally felt the best foreign policy was to take care of business at home and leave Europe to itself. Conversely, while Federalists supported Adams's tough talk in 1798, his ultimate decision to pursue peace finished Adams with the Hamilton and the extreme Federalists. The cost of peace for Adams was the presidential election in 1800.

Politics aside, Americans judged Adams from the perspective of their own economic positions. Commercial interests in urban areas desired free commerce on the high seas. Rural farmers sought peace to avoid the burden of an expensive national military. Interestingly, then, Americans truly desired economic prosperity through peaceful relations. In spite of this, political passions and the lure of the wealth through other nations attracted everyone like a magnet to the brink of war.

While historians disagree over the wisdom of Adams's decisions, motives, and intellectual passions, they agree that avoidance of full-scale war was the pinnacle of his presidency. Adams feared, probably correctly, that war spelled doom for a young nation with an untested army and a fledgling navy.

The Adams Administration Legacy

Adams left the White House after delivering peace to the United States. To be sure, the Thomas Jefferson administration had to handle unfinished business. Changes in the settlement with France had to be resolved—the countries eventually agreed to abrogate the old treaties of 1778 and to forgive France's obligations for property seized during the quasi-war. As for Great Britain, the Jay's Treaty commissions had disbanded during Adams's presidency without resolving post-Revolutionary War issues. Adams, however, had charted a course for peace that proved to be invaluable as the United States sought territorial expansion, namely purchase of the Louisiana Territory from Napoleon Bonaparte, under the Jefferson administration.

Popularity and Public Opinion

Adams, perhaps unintentionally, also accomplished something else that Jefferson wanted. By his friendship with and political support of people such as John Marshall and Elbridge Gerry, Adams brought moderate Federalists and Republicans together on middle ground. Adams's failure to win reelection was less a reflection of public sentiment against him and more an indication of the departure of support by the extreme Federalists. Indeed, excluding New York, Adams received more electoral votes in 1800 than he had in 1796. Jefferson was able to use this middle ground to enjoy a popular presidency.

The Press and Media

If the people liked Adams even as he returned to his farm in Quincy, Massachusetts, the press did not reflect their sentiment. Adams, in fact, blamed both the Federalist and the Republican newspapers for his downfall. While the press only began attacking Washington toward the end of his administration, Adams was roasted from the time of his address to Congress in May 1797 until he left the capital in March 1801. This baptism marked the beginning of a tradition of inhospitable presidential-press relations. Adams once wrote to a friend: "Regret nothing that you see in the papers concerning me. It is impossible that newspapers can say the truth. They would be out of their element" (Brown, p. 144).

During Adams's presidency Federalist newspapers carried essays written by Adams's critics, including Federalist leader Alexander Hamilton, that accused Adams of conspiring with Republicans for peace with France. Republican papers, most notably the *Aurora* in Philadelphia, Pennsylvania, denounced Adams as a monarchist who sought a dynasty with Great Britain. In 1801 the

Republican press did not hide its pleasure when Adams and the Federalists lost control of the federal government. As Adams sat down in 1802 to write his *Autobiography* (which he never finished), he sought to set the record straight: "My Excuse is, that having been the Object of much Misrepresentation, some of my Posterity may probably wish to see in my own hand Writing a proof of the falsehood of that Mass of odious Abuse of My Character, with which the News Papers, private letters and Public Pamphlets and Histories have been disgraced for thirty Years" (Brown, p. 143).

Lasting Impact

When Adams was president, the federal government still was working out the practicalities of operating under the lofty ideals of the U.S. Constitution. Adams set an example in favor of a strong, independent executive branch of government. He made his own decisions concerning the matters entrusted to his discretion. He regularly rejected the ill advice of his department heads, whom he viewed as advisers with no constitutional power. While his failure ever to veto legislation is mostly due to the fact that the Federalists controlled both houses of Congress, his refusal to interfere with Congress was consistent with his philosophy of government.

President Adams also sought to govern based on the pulse of the nation. One historian has compared Adams's and seventh president of the United States Andrew Jackson's view of the presidency "as the one agent of government chosen by *all* the people and thus able to act in the best interests of the entire nation rather than of a faction, section, or special interest" (Brown, p. 212). By charting a course of independence from political dogmatism and then losing his bid for reelection, Adams probably influenced future administrations in favor of party loyalty, for better or for worse.

Most importantly, Adams set an example for the peaceful resolution of foreign conflict. Adams's philosophical and religious studies, not to mention his experience in national and international politics and diplomacy, taught him that the nature of humanity made it hunger for power. Adams sought to check that weakness. Perhaps his example has not been followed by future generations of presidents. Perhaps Adams knew it was futile: "All Parties have been violent Friends of Order, Law, Government, and Religion, when in Power; and all Parties libelous, Seditious, and Rebellious, when out of power. Such is our destiny" (Brown, p. 145).

Sources

Bartlett, John. *Familiar Quotations: a collection of passages, phrases, and proverbs traced to their sources in ancient and modern literature.* 16th ed., Boston: Little, Brown, and Company, 1992.

Brown, Ralph Adams. *The Presidency of John Adams.* Lawrence, Kans.: The University Press of Kansas, 1975.

Brown, Walt. *John Adams and the American Press: Politics and Journalism at the Birth of the Republic.* Jefferson, N.C.: McFarland and Company, 1995.

Dauer, Manning J. *The Adams Federalists.* Baltimore: The Johns Hopkins Press, 1968.

DeConde, Alexander. *The Quasi-War: The Politics and Diplomacy of the Undeclared War With France, 1797–1801.* New York: Charles Scribner's Sons, 1966.

Ferling, John. *John Adams: A Life.* Knoxville, Tenn.: The University of Tennessee Press, 1992.

Kane, Joseph Nathan. *Facts About the Presidents: A Compilation of Biographical and Historical Information.* 6th ed. New York: The H. W. Wilson Co., 1993.

Kurtz, Stephen G. *The Presidency of John Adams: The Collapse of Federalism, 1795–1800.* Philadelphia: University of Pennsylvania Press, 1957.

Nelson, Michael, ed. *CQ's Encyclopedia of American Government: The Presidency A to Z,* Washington, D.C.: Congressional Quarterly, Inc., 1994.

Peabody, James Bishop, ed. *John Adams: A Biography in His Own Words.* New York: Newsweek, 1973.

U.S. Congress. Senate. Secretary of the Senate. *Presidential Vetoes, 1789-1988.* 103d Cong., 2d sess., S. Pub. 102-12.

Further Readings

Adams, John. *Diary and Autobiography.* Edited by L. H. Butterfield. Vol. 3. New York: Atheneum, 1964.

Chinard, Gilbert. *Honest John Adams.* Boston: Little Brown, 1933.

Gibbs, George, ed. *Memoirs of the Administrations of Washington and John Adams.* 2 vols. New York: The Subscribers, 1846.

Handler, Edward. *America and Europe in the Political Thought of John Adams.* Cambridge, Mass.: Harvard University Press, 1964.

Howe, John R., Jr. *The Changing Political Thought of John Adams.* Princeton, N.J.: Princeton University Press, 1966.

Miller, John Chester. *Crisis in Freedom: The Alien and Sedition Acts.* Boston: Little Brown, 1951.

Onuf, Peter S. *Federalists and Republicans.* Vol. 8 of *The New American Nation, 1775–1820.* New York: Garland Publishing, Inc., 1991.

Smith, Page. *John Adams.* 2 vols. Garden City, N.J.: Doubleday, 1962.

Walsh, Correa Moylan. *The Political Science of John Adams: A Study in the Theory of Mixed Government and the Bicameral System.* New York: G. P. Putnam's Sons, 1915.

Jefferson Administrations

Biography

Thomas Jefferson, the son of a Virginia planter family, was one of the principal builders of the American Republic. He is best remembered as the author of the Declaration of Independence, which he based on the principle that humanity is entitled to government that does not interfere with life, liberty, and the pursuit of happiness. Jefferson's distinguished service in early U.S. government included five years as secretary of state under George Washington, four years as vice president under John Adams, and eight years as president, during which he usually remained loyal to the republican principles he promoted in his writings. Jefferson was the leader of his party even after retiring from the presidency to his home in Virginia.

Early Life

Thomas Jefferson was born into a well-established family in Goochland (now Albemarle) County, Virginia. Jefferson's father, Peter Jefferson (1708–57), was a self-educated man who became a planter, surveyor, justice of the peace, and eventually a legislator in the Virginia House of Burgesses, the legislative body of Virginia's colonial government under Great Britain. Jefferson's mother, Jane Randolph (1720–76), was the daughter of a wealthy and socially prominent Virginia family that owned slaves and plantations. Thomas Jefferson was born on April 13, 1743. He was the third of ten children.

Jefferson's father instilled in his son a spirit of discipline and hard work. He taught him to read, write, and keep accounts, as well as to ride, shoot, and hunt. When

Full name: Thomas Jefferson
Popular name: Sage of Monticello

Personal Information:
Born: April 13, 1743
Birthplace: Shadwell, Virginia
Died: July 4, 1826
Death place: Charlottesville, Virginia
Burial place: Monticello, Charlottesville, Virginia
Religion: Deism
Spouse: Martha Wayles Skelton (m. 1772)
Children: Martha Washington; Jane Randolph; an unnamed son who died in infancy; Mary; Lucy Elizabeth who died in infancy
Education: Attended College of William and Mary
Occupation: Farmer; lawyer
Political Party: Democratic-Republican Party
Age at Inauguration: 57 years

Thomas Jefferson. (The National Portrait Gallery/Smithsonian Institution.)

his father died in 1757, 14-year-old Jefferson assumed the responsibility of being the oldest male in a home with six girls and two boys. He was a tall, shy, red-haired boy with a keen interest in books, who loved to ride horseback, play the violin, and take long walks in the woods with his sister Jane, whom he adored.

Education

Lacking formal education himself, Peter Jefferson made sure that his son attended private Anglican schools and had the best tutors, under whom young Jefferson studied English, Latin, Greek, and French. In 1760 Jefferson enrolled at the College of William and Mary, a popular school in Williamsburg, Virginia, for young men of his social standing. There he became friends with several influential people. Dr. William Small, a professor of mathematics and philosophy, inspired Jefferson's interest in science. George Wythe, the foremost jurist in Virginia, taught Jefferson about the virtues of republican government operated by and at the will of the people.

Jefferson, who often referred to his college town as "Devilsburg," favored books and studies over his peers' preference for drinking, gambling, and cockfighting. He diligently mastered various subjects including calculus, Greek and Spanish grammar, and classical literature. While Jefferson closed his mind to subjects incapable of

experiment, such as metaphysics and theology, he also developed a morality that was the foundation for religion in his life. After two years and one month at William and Mary, Jefferson left to study law under George Wythe in Williamsburg. William and Mary granted him an honorary degree in 1782.

Family Life

On January 1, 1772, Jefferson married Martha Wayles Skelton, a widow who had a four-year-old son who died shortly after the wedding. Martha Jefferson was the educated daughter of a wealthy Williamsburg, Virginia, lawyer. With the land and slaves they inherited from their fathers, the Jeffersons were one of the wealthiest families in Virginia, guaranteeing Jefferson a role in Virginia politics.

The newlyweds moved into Monticello, a mansion Jefferson designed as an amateur architect, in Charlottesville, Virginia. Together they had six children, three of whom died in infancy. Jefferson's happiest years were spent at Monticello between 1772 and 1782 with his wife and his daughters, Martha and Mary. The happiness ended tragically with his wife's death on September 6, 1782, shortly after the birth of their daughter Lucy Elizabeth. Tragedy struck again when Lucy died of the whooping cough at the age of two on October 13, 1784, while Jefferson was in France as a diplomatic agent.

Jefferson's only remaining daughters, Martha and Mary, gave him 12 grandchildren in all. The grandchildren were a source of great pleasure for Jefferson, who willingly assumed the financial burden for their food, clothing, and education.

Career

When Jefferson left William and Mary in April 1762 to study law under George Wythe in Williamsburg, Virginia, Jefferson was not really interested in being a lawyer. He even scoffed at the legal profession's wordy and unethical methods, but he wished to extend his years of scholarship. Thus Jefferson studied for five years under Wythe and was not admitted to the bar until 1767, after which he developed a successful and lucrative law practice. Jefferson's practice gave him frequent contact with the leading men of the Virginia bar, including Patrick Henry, an advocate of revolution against Great Britain. All the while Jefferson continued to supervise his tobacco plantation.

The American Revolution (1775–83)

In 1769 Jefferson was elected to the Virginia House of Burgesses, where he served until 1774. In 1774 Jefferson and a small group of legislators prepared a resolution to support the Boston Tea Party, a colonial protest against the British tax on tea. The British-appointed governor of Virginia reacted by dissolving the House, prompting its members to hold a meeting in Williamsburg to adopt a plan of action. Although illness prevented his attendance, Jefferson submitted a paper that was published as *A Summary View of the Rights of British America.* The paper contained some of the arguments that later appeared in the Declaration of Independence. It helped establish Jefferson's reputation as a writer.

After the American Revolution began in April 1775, Jefferson attended the Second Continental Congress, which assembled in Philadelphia, Pennsylvania, in May. Five days after he arrived, Jefferson and John Dickinson, a Philadelphia lawyer, were selected to draft a declaration supporting war with Great Britain. In it Jefferson compared Great Britain's treatment of its colonial subjects to slavery. Jefferson justified such rhetoric with his ownership of slaves on his tobacco plantation.

On June 7, 1776, Jefferson, Massachusetts legislator John Adams, American statesman Benjamin Franklin, and two others were selected by the Second Continental Congress to draft a second document, the Declaration of Independence. The committee deferred to Jefferson, who labored at the document for 17 days. By listing the pursuit of happiness, rather than property, as one of the inalienable rights of men, Jefferson broke with the traditional concept of the purpose of government and established a unique foundation for America's own. After Franklin and Adams made a few changes, the committee sent the document to Congress on June 28. The lawyers in Congress rewrote it considerably (to Jefferson's dismay), and Congress approved it on July 2, signing it on July 4.

In September 1776 Jefferson resigned from Congress to return home to be with his children and his ailing wife. By October he was in Williamsburg for the autumn session of the Virginia House of Delegates, Virginia's legislative body under its newly declared independence. There Jefferson struck up a lifetime friendship with James Madison, who would be Jefferson's secretary of state and then president himself. While in the House of Delegates, Jefferson worked on a committee to revise Virginia's entire legal code, a step Jefferson saw as necessary for eliminating the trappings of monarchy, or undivided rule by a single person such as a king. The code that the committee submitted to the House in June 1779 was itself a revolution. It required that all citizens receive free public education, because Jefferson thought the spread of knowledge was essential to the preservation of freedom and independence. The code also proposed freedom of religious worship and separation of religion from government. Jefferson believed that partnership between religion and government inevitably led to oppression. Within six years virtually the entire code was enacted into law in Virginia.

Jefferson was a talented amateur architect. He designed Monticello at Charlottesville, Virginia, between the years of 1772 and 1782. Monticello served as Jefferson's home both before and after his presidency as well as the family's burial ground. (Corbis. Reproduced by permission.)

From 1779 to 1781 Jefferson served as Virginia's governor. Jefferson's conduct, including his retreat from British forces near the capital in Richmond to Monticello with his family, was investigated by the Virginia legislature shortly before the end of his second term. Although the legislature cleared him of wrongdoing the investigation insulted Jefferson, who resigned as governor. The episode was used by his political enemies during future presidential campaigns (*See also,* John Adams Administration). After resigning as governor Jefferson wrote his only published book, *Notes on Virginia.* Originally a response to requests for information from the United States's French allies, the book ended up being a philosophical treatise on a wide range of subjects, including politics, religion, and law.

After the victory over Great Britain, Jefferson served as a member of the Continental Congress from 1783 to 1784. The Congress was the new country's governing body under the Articles of Confederation, the forerunner to the U.S. Constitution, adopted by the Second Continental Congress in 1777. Jefferson drafted many documents, including a plan to use a decimal system of dollars and coinage for U.S. currency. From 1784 to 1789 he served as minister to France, initially working with John Adams and Benjamin Franklin in an unsuccessful attempt to negotiate commercial treaties. Jefferson's time in Europe increased his disdain for monarchy and commerce, and strengthened his commitment to an agrarian way of life and republican government in the United States.

Secretary of State

Jefferson sailed home from France in October 1789 and arrived at Monticello before Christmas. As the United States launched a new government under the newly adopted U.S. Constitution, President George Washington called upon Jefferson to be the first secretary of state. Jefferson had mixed reactions about the Constitution. He liked the idea of dividing governmental power into three branches, but he was concerned about the federal government's overall power and the Constitution's lack of protection for individual rights.

Jefferson sparred almost immediately with secretary of the Treasury Alexander Hamilton. Hamilton envisioned the United States as a commercial nation with a complex pattern of industry, production, and international trade. Jefferson saw it as a collection of self-sufficient farms virtually independent from contact with other nations. Hamilton favored channeling power through the federal government, while Jefferson preferred to restrict power to the individual states. Out of their differences grew the first political parties—the Federalists led by Hamilton and the Democratic-Republicans (or Republicans) led by Jefferson.

One of the principal disputes between Jefferson and Hamilton concerned the institution of a national bank. Hamilton saw it not only as constitutional but essential to developing U.S. commerce. Jefferson feared that corruption inevitably would develop if the federal government got into the business of borrowing and lending money, benefiting the financial speculators, the merchants, and the wealthy to the detriment of the nation's farmers. Hamilton won the argument when Washington signed the bank bill on February 25, 1791. Jefferson left the office of secretary of state at the end of 1793 because he sensed that Washington favored Hamilton's policies.

Vice President

George Washington decided not to run for a third term, and in 1796 Thomas Jefferson received the Republican nomination for president. The Federalists nominated Jefferson's old friend but now political adversary, John Adams. Under the Constitution at the time, the state appointed electors who voted for the president and the vice president but did not distinguish between the two offices. This allowed for Federalist Adams to become president with 71 electoral votes and Republican Jefferson to become vice president with 68. As vice president, Jefferson saw little action during the next four years.

The United States, however, saw a lot of action in a naval, "quasi-war" with France from 1798 to 1800, as a result of the United States's friendly relationship with Great Britain, France's foe, during the Washington administration. In the heat of the crisis in the summer 1798, Congress passed the Sedition Act to curb Republican criticism of the Adams administration, and the Alien Acts to limit the naturalization of immigrants, most of whom were joining the Republicans (*See also,* John Adams Administration). Although he was vice president under Adams, Jefferson drafted the Kentucky Resolutions of 1798, which declared the Alien and Sedition Acts to be unconstitutional and unenforceable in that state. While the resolutions reflected Jefferson's concerns for freedom of speech, they more importantly reflected his opinion of the supremacy of states' rights over the power of the federal government.

President

Adams, who was a moderate Federalist, lost the support of extreme Federalists by failing to declare war officially against France and by ultimately negotiating a peaceful resolution to the conflict. Because of this split in the Federalist Party, as well as growing support for individual and states' rights, Jefferson won the presidential election of 1800.

As president, Jefferson demonstrated political leadership by developing the Republican Party and, through it, his influence in Congress. During the first of his two terms, Jefferson governed by his Republican ideals of limited power in the federal government. He cut the number of federal officials and reduced the size of the army and the navy. Jefferson convinced Congress to abolish most direct taxes, which had worked to the disadvantage of American farmers. He abandoned regal customs such as bowing, replacing it with handshaking. While he did not undo the national bank, he worked to reduce the size of the national debt.

However, Jefferson also understood that the federal government sometimes had to exercise its authority even if the constitutional basis for action was vague. With the 1803 Louisiana Purchase Jefferson doubled the size of the country and secured the important port of New Orleans for agrarian interests along the Mississippi River.

He did this even though the Constitution contained no language explicitly giving the federal government the right to annex land. In this instance, Jefferson's reluctance to expand the limits of federal power was overridden by his commitment to provide land in the west for the individual "yeoman" farmer.

Jefferson's second presidential term was less successful. At the outset Jefferson announced to friends that he intended to retire at the end of the term, causing Republicans in Congress to split into factions over nominating his successor. British interference with U.S. merchant shipping heightened tensions with the former mother country, while Napoleon Bonaparte's France treated the United States little better. Unable to negotiate peace with either country, Jefferson persuaded Congress to pass a general embargo, forbidding international trade by U.S. merchants. Frustrated and contradicting his own philosophy, Jefferson called on the federal military to seize suspected violators and to crush protests and outright disobedience. Jefferson left office embattled and embittered in March 1809.

Post-presidential Years

Upon Jefferson's return to private life he became known as the "Sage of Monticello." In early December 1811, Jefferson resumed a friendship with Adams that had been interrupted by their political feud. They struck up a lively correspondence that would continue to the end of their lives. An avid architect, Jefferson in retirement busied himself in drawing up blueprints for many buildings that still stand today, including the capitol in Richmond and the University of Virginia. His primary activity, farming, was his sole means of support.

Never a good steward of his inherited wealth, Jefferson's later years were troubled by a growing mass of unpaid debts. This preoccupation with paying off his creditors led Jefferson in 1814 to sell his personal library to the Library of Congress, which had been created at the start of the century. The Jefferson collection consisted of 15,000 books and replenished the original collection, which was mostly destroyed during the War of 1812. Today the Library of Congress contains one of the world's largest collections of recorded material.

During his final years Jefferson developed a plan for a public education system in Virginia consisting of three parts: elementary, high school, and university. Early in 1818 the Virginia legislature approved money for the University of Virginia. Jefferson spent the next six years building the university, which opened in 1825, when Jefferson was 82.

Jefferson suffered from disease and the frailties of old age in his final year of life. On July 4, 1826, the 50th anniversary of the signing of the Declaration of Independence, both Jefferson and John Adams were dying.

At one point Adams muttered "Thomas Jefferson survives," not knowing Jefferson had preceded him to death a few hours earlier. Jefferson was buried next to his beloved wife Martha and daughter Mary on a hill at Monticello, his home in Charlottesville, Virginia, under a simple stone obelisk containing an inscription he wrote himself: "Here was buried Thomas Jefferson, Author of the Declaration of American Independence, of the Statute of Virginia for religious freedom, and Father of the University of Virginia."

The Thomas Jefferson Administrations

With the presidential election of 1800, the United States replaced its Federalist John Adams with Republican Thomas Jefferson. The fact that this transfer of power was accomplished without bloodshed prompted Jefferson to proclaim it a "revolution." After his inauguration Jefferson set out to implement his republican ideals by limiting the power of the federal government—cutting direct taxes, eliminating federal positions, and reducing military size and spending. With the Louisiana Purchase of 1803, which doubled the size of the United States, Jefferson hoped to encourage agricultural growth. The contradiction between Jefferson's politics of restraining federal power while actually having to make important executive decisions occasionally led Jefferson to trample on some of his ideals even as he pursued others.

Jefferson Becomes President

The Campaign of 1800

The international crises that plagued the John Adams administration, plus a growing fear of exaggerated federal power, paved the way for Thomas Jefferson's victory in 1800. Adams angered extreme Federalists when during his administration he failed to declare war against France for its seizing of U.S. merchant vessels bound for Great Britain during France's ongoing war with Great Britain. On the other hand, the Republicans denounced Adams's so-called "quasi-war" with French privateers in the West Indies from 1798 to 1799. They pointed out that Adams had failed to take up arms against similar British attacks on U.S. shipping. They also protested the direct taxes necessary to fund the expanded military.

In the election campaign the Democratic-Republicans (or Republicans) in Congress nominated Jefferson for president with Aaron Burr of New York for vice president. The Federalists renominated John Adams for the presidency, with Charles Pinckney of South Carolina as their vice presidential candidate. In addition to the foreign affairs crises presented by the ongoing war

Administration

Administration Dates
March 4, 1801–March 4, 1805
March 4, 1805–March 4, 1809

Vice President
Aaron Burr (1801–05)
George Clinton (1805–09)

Cabinet
Secretary of State
James Madison (1801–09)

Secretary of the Treasury
Samuel Dexter (1801)
Albert Gallatin (1801–14)

Secretary of War
Henry Dearborn (1801–09)

Attorney General
Levi Lincoln (1801–05)
John Breckinridge (1805–06)
Caesar A. Rodney (1807–11)

Secretary of the Navy
Benjamin Stoddert (1798–1801)
Robert Smith (1801–09)

Postmaster General
Joseph Habersham (1795–1801)
Gideon Granger (1801–14)

---

between Great Britain and France, the size of the military, and the issue of taxes, the campaign also focused on the Alien and Sedition Acts of 1798. These laws were designed to curb Republican criticism of the Adams administration and to reduce the naturalization of foreigners, most of whom joined the Republican Party. The Republicans denounced these laws as infringements on the right to free speech. In the fall of 1798 Jefferson and Madison secretly authored the "Virginia and Kentucky Resolutions," which argued that the right to judge the constitutionality of federal laws ultimately rested in the states and that the Alien and Sedition Acts, were null and void. The rhetoric of the campaign reflected the Federalists' preference for a strong federal government and national commerce, and the Republicans' preference for "states rights" (keeping the preponderance of governmental power in the states) and an agriculture-based national economy.

Jefferson actively campaigned by authoring anonymous pamphlets and newspaper editorials, but, as was the tradition at the time, he did not make public speeches. The campaign, however, tarnished the reputations of both presidential candidates. The Republicans accused Adams of scheming to marry one of his sons to a daughter of the king of England to form an Anglo-American monarchy. For their part, the Federalists accused Jefferson, who supported freedom of religious expression, of being an atheist (someone who denies the existence of God).

The Constitution at the time did not distinguish between presidential and vice presidential candidates. It provided only that each elector vote for two persons, with the presidency and the vice presidency going to the men with the most and second most votes, respectively. Under this system, Jefferson and Burr tied with 73 electoral votes each in the December election. Adams received only 65 votes. The Constitution provided for the tie to be broken by the House of Representatives, which was dominated by the Federalists. On the 36th ballot, the Federalists, led by former secretary of the Treasury Alexander Hamilton who had become disenchanted with Adams's moderate views, decided the election in Jefferson's favor. Republican victories in congressional elections gave their party control over the legislative and the executive branches of the federal government.

On March 4, 1801, Jefferson was administered the oath of office by his cousin and political foe, Chief Justice John Marshall. President Adams failed to attend, leaving Washington, D.C., the morning of the inauguration and putting an exclamation point on the decline of Federalist power. Jefferson's inaugural address appealed to the Federalists by promising to sustain the federal government in all its vigor and to continue the policy of paying off the national debt. He warned that government by the will of the majority could not trample on the rights of the minority. Jefferson emphasized, however, that the federal government should be concerned with foreign affairs and should allow the states to administer local matters. As for foreign affairs, Jefferson advised against "entangling alliances" with foreign governments, a theme borrowed from first president George Washington's "Farewell Address." Jefferson made a bid for national unity by exclaiming "we are all Republicans, we are all Federalists." Then he set out to undo a lot of what the Federalists had done in the prior 12 years under Washington and Adams.

The Campaign of 1804

By the election of 1804, the Federalists were so hopelessly disorganized and defeated that tensions were running high. That summer, Vice President Aaron Burr, dissatisfied with his position in the federal government, ran as the Federalist candidate for governor of New York, and Federalist Alexander Hamilton supported the Republican nominee. When Burr lost, he challenged Hamilton to a duel for insults made during the campaign and inflicted fatal gunshot wounds. Hamilton's death weighed heavily on the Federalist Party during the presidential campaign later that year. They nominated Charles Cotesworth Pinckney of South Carolina for president and Rufus King of New York for vice president. Both men had served under John Adams, Pinckney as a delegate to France and King as minister to Great Britain.

Jefferson was at the top of his political career during the campaign, though personally suffering from the death of his daughter Mary. The Republican caucus, a gathering of Republican congressmen, nominated Jefferson with George Clinton of New York replacing Burr as his running mate. Jefferson even got significant support in Federalist New England, where Massachusetts elector and former president John Adams voted for him. The Republican campaign proudly proclaimed the achievements of Jefferson's first administration, including the elimination of taxes, reduction of land and naval forces, reduction of the public debt, and preservation of domestic tranquility with the peaceful acquisition of the Louisiana Territory. Jefferson won the electoral votes in every state except Connecticut and Delaware, and his popularity helped Republicans increase their majority in both houses of Congress.

Jefferson delivered his Second Inaugural Address in a voice so low that few could hear him. He talked about the United States's friendship with other nations, and he appealed for greater national unity. He praised the accomplishments of his first term by observing "It may be the pleasure and pride of an American to ask what farmer, what mechanic, what laborer, ever sees a tax gatherer of the United States?" (Cunningham Jr., p. 276). Although his second term began with peace and prosperity, it would end with foreign and domestic strife. Shortly after his reelection, Jefferson privately announced that he would follow Washington's precedent and not seek another term. As Republicans no longer had a formidable opponent in the Federalists, they deteriorated to infighting among themselves over selection of Jefferson's successor.

Jefferson's Advisers

Thomas Jefferson had a much more successful presidency than his predecessor John Adams, in part due to the men he selected for his cabinet. Adams felt obliged to keep George Washington's cabinet as his own, a decision that led to political frustration. Jefferson selected his own trusted and competent men using two criteria: proven competence and loyalty to the Jeffersonian ideals of republicanism. While he tried to avoid undeserved political appointments, Jefferson chose half of his cabi-

net from New England to unite the North with the South. Initially, then, Jefferson was able to coordinate the executive branch without internal Republican squabbles.

Jefferson's most influential advisers were secretary of the Treasury Albert Gallatin and secretary of state James Madison. Gallatin was a Swiss-born American immigrant who had settled in Pennsylvania and rose quickly through the Republican ranks. Gallatin occasionally argued in private with the president, but he carried out policy loyally once Jefferson made a final decision. Gallatin was on friendly terms with most Republican congressmen since he had served as the floor leader in the House of Representatives. Gallatin's and Jefferson's primary goal was the reduction and eventual elimination of the public debt. Gallatin worked toward this goal with a skill for figures and finances that rivaled former Treasury secretary Alexander Hamilton, a master of financial wizardry. By the end of Jefferson's second term, Gallatin had reduced the federal debt from approximately $80 million to $57 million.

James Madison, the only southerner in Jefferson's cabinet, was Jefferson's foreign affairs counterpart to Gallatin. Jefferson's lifetime protégé since their days in the Virginia House of Delegates during the American Revolution (1775–83), Madison was one of the ablest and most interesting cabinet members. From Washington, D.C., he supervised diplomatic negotiations in Europe, including those that resulted in the Louisiana Purchase of 1803. Madison's wife Dolley Madison often served as hostess at the President's House (later called the White House), where Jefferson was the first presidential widower.

Jefferson assembled a cabinet of qualified men, exercised a loose rein, and was open to their ideas. All business went through the department heads, who gave Jefferson daily summaries concerning their area of responsibility. Jefferson typically responded in writing to all but the most important matters, cutting down on the number of meetings to minimize argumentative debates. Jefferson solicited ideas from his cabinet when he prepared his annual address to Congress. Except for the most important matters, Jefferson injected democracy into the executive branch by exercising one vote along with each cabinet member, with the majority vote prevailing. Few cabinets since have functioned as effectively as Jefferson's.

Jefferson and Congress

Jefferson served during the Seventh, Eighth, Ninth, and Tenth Congresses, each having a Republican majority in both houses. During his first term, Jefferson used the Republican majority to establish a productive rapport with Congress. While he respected the separation of powers, Jefferson took seriously the presidential privilege of making recommendations to Congress. During

Biography:

Albert Gallatin

Secretary of the Treasury, politician, diplomat, banker (1761–1849) Albert Gallatin immigrated to the United States as a teenager in 1780 from Switzerland seeking adventure in the "freest country in the universe." After becoming a landowner in Pennsylvania, he quickly became a political leader. Both as a businessman and politician, Gallatin demonstrated early on his keen sense of finance and was the man who proposed the creation of the House Ways and Means Committee, an agency established to receive input from the Treasury and to superintend all government finances. He was a strong opponent of government debt and led the way in proposing measures to curb a growing deficit. After being elected president of the United States in 1800, Thomas Jefferson named Gallatin head of the Treasury Department. Gallatin went to work right away and made pledges and proposals to eliminate the excise tax and to pay off the national debt by 1817. He argued for the promotion of manufacturing and for the construction of a nation-

wide network of roads and canals with federal aid. For most of President Jefferson's two terms in office, Gallatin's plans were successful. It was the Embargo Act of 1807 and other efforts by the United States to avoid involvement in the Napoleonic Wars that derailed his agenda. In 1811 Gallatin urged rechartering the Bank of the United States, but Congress refused and the nation entered the war of 1812 with its monetary system in disarray. Gallatin's tenure stretched almost 15 years and is still one of the longest on record. During James Madison's presidency, Gallatin moved into diplomatic service and distinguished himself in this capacity for the balance of his political career.

his first term, Jefferson only had to suggest legislation and it was almost always enacted, making aggressive governmental reform not only possible but easy.

Jefferson courted politicians with three dinner parties each week at the presidential mansion that brought together carefully selected members of Congress, the executive branch, and foreign diplomats. Political discussions were forbidden. Outside of these social occasions, Jefferson minimized official contact with Congress. A stronger writer than orator, Jefferson delivered his usually brief annual address to Congress in writing. Like John Adams before him, Jefferson never exercised the veto power.

During Jefferson's first term, Congress acted aggressively to implement his agenda for reversing Federalist policies. Congress repealed the Alien Acts (1798) limiting the naturalization of immigrants, while Jefferson pardoned the Republicans who had been convicted under the Sedition Act (1798), which prohibited Americans from speaking against the government during the Adams administration. Congress then abolished direct taxes, which the Federalists had used to fund the military, leaving the United States dependent on import duties for revenue. Reduction in military size and spending followed, resulting in an increased reliance on the state militias. Gallatin's plan for reducing the national debt also involved reducing the number of federal employees, a measure Congress also implemented.

At the outset of his second term Jefferson indicated he would not seek a third, and Republicans in Congress split into factions over nominating his successor. This depleted Jefferson's strength in Congress. With a reduced military and increased reliance on import duty revenues, the United States now was even more vulnerable to the whims of Great Britain's foreign policy, independence from which was, ironically, one of Jefferson's main goals. As war between Great Britain and France escalated yet again, Congress busied itself mainly with enacting Jefferson's embargo policy, designed to keep the United States out of the conflict by cutting Europe off from U.S. trade (*See also,* Foreign Issues). The policy was a disaster, and Congress repealed the embargoes at the end of Jefferson's second term.

Jefferson and the Judiciary

Jefferson entered office hoping to reduce the Federalist dominance in the judiciary. To this end, he sought to repeal the recently enacted Judiciary Act of 1801, and eliminate many Federalist judge's jobs. The plan, however, presented a constitutional problem. Federal judges have lifetime tenure under the Constitution, purposefully to insulate them from the vacillating whims of the masses. Dismissing those who simply had not received their signed commissions arguably violated that tenure. Jefferson was undaunted by this technicality. "On great occasions," he wrote, "every good officer must be ready to risk himself in going beyond the strict line of the law, when the public preservation requires it; his motives will be a justification" (McDonald, p. 49).

Republicans introduced a repeal bill into the Senate in January of 1802. Debate proceeded along party lines, but the vote was a tie. Vice President Aaron Burr, as president of the Senate, cast a deciding vote for the Senate to reconsider the legislation, thus alienating himself from Jefferson and the Republican Party. The bill eventually passed after further debate and amendments, and the House signed it in March. A few days later Congress passed another act postponing the next meeting of the Federalist dominated Supreme Court for a year. Weeks later it passed the Judiciary Act of 1802 to reenact the elements of the Judiciary Act of 1801 that were favorable to the Republican Party. Jefferson signed the bills into law, and thus won the first round of his attack on the judiciary.

Marbury v. Madison (1803)

Jefferson's dispute with the Federalist influence in the federal judiciary continued in the Supreme Court ruling in *Marbury v. Madison* (1803). Just before he left office, Adams rewarded a number of loyal Federalists with "midnight appointments" to federal jobs. One such appointment was that of William Marbury to a patronage job as justice of the peace in the District of Columbia. When Secretary of State James Madison took office under Jefferson, however, he refused to process Marbury's appointment because he wanted to give the job to a Republican. Marbury then petitioned the Supreme Court for a writ of mandamus—an order forcing Madison to deliver the commission.

The chief justice of the Supreme Court was the brilliant Federalist John Marshall, who had earlier served as Adams's secretary of state. In 1803 Marshall ruled that although Marbury was entitled to the position, the Supreme Court could not force Madison to complete the process of appointment. This contradicted the Judiciary Act of 1789, which stated that the Supreme Court did have the power to issue such writs. Marshall, however, ruled that this part of the Judiciary Act of 1789 was itself unconstitutional. The reason was that nowhere did the Constitution explicitly impute this power to the Supreme Court. Thus, by giving up the relatively unimportant power of issuing writs of mandamus, Chief Justice John Marshall established for the Supreme Court and the federal judiciary a much more powerful competency: the right to rule on the constitutionality of acts of Congress. Although Jefferson did not intend this result, the *Marbury* case gave the judicial branch power equal to the legislative and the executive branches of government and rounded out the system of checks and balances that structured the Constitution.

Impeaching Federal Judges

Jefferson also used impeachment to attack Federalist judges. This raised an important constitutional question—what constitutes "high Crimes and Misdemeanors, the constitutional criteria for impeachment," making a federal servant removable from office? Jefferson's first target was John Pickering, a New Hampshire federal district court judge who was a violent alcoholic. Pickering was impeached by the House, judged guilty by the Senate, and removed from office in 1803.

While Pickering's drunkenness really was not constitutional grounds for removal, the Republicans' next target was even more controversial. Supreme Court Associate Justice Samuel Chase had aroused Republican hatred with his insults of Republican lawyers and the unrestrained vigor with which he had tried violations of the Sedition Act of 1798, which prohibited antigovernment rhetoric. Chase once ordered the federal marshal to strike from the jury panel "any of those creatures or persons called democrats" (Padover, p. 326). The last straw was a speech Chase made to a grand jury in May 1803 in which he lamented Maryland's recent adoption of universal manhood suffrage, the right of all men to vote regardless of property holdings: "The modern doctrines by our late reformers, that all men in a state of society are entitled to enjoy equal liberty and equal rights, have brought this mighty mischief upon us; and I fear that it will rapidly progress until peace and order, freedom and property, shall be destroyed" (McDonald, p. 81). Chase thus was a political enemy who had committed no crimes. Jefferson, who had opposed the Sedition Act in 1798, pursued him nonetheless in a letter to Congressman Joseph Nicholson of Maryland: "Ought this seditious and official attack on the principles of our Constitution, and on the proceedings of a State, to go unpunished?" (McDonald, p. 81).

The impeachment proceedings lasted throughout January and February 1805. In a trial that set the stage for later presidential impeachments of Andrew Johnson and Bill Clinton, Chase supported a strict constructionist interpretation of "high Crimes and Misdemeanors," arguing that his noncriminal behavior did not qualify as such. Congressman John Randolph of Virginia, who led the House managers' prosecution in the Senate, argued for a democratic interpretation, giving the will of the people free reign to decide when a public servant is unfit or too dangerous to remain in office.

The impeachment ultimately failed as the Senate adopted the legalistic view that Justice Chase had not committed any high crimes or misdemeanors. It was the first in a succession of political defeats in the second term for Jefferson, who thereafter gave up on impeachment as a political weapon. Jefferson was, however, able to inject some republicanism into the Supreme Court with his appointments of William Johnson of South Carolina in 1806, Brockholst Livingston from New York in 1806, and Thomas Todd from Kentucky in 1807.

Biography:

John Marshall

Politician; Chief Justice of the Supreme Court (1755–1835) Given his upbringing, it's no wonder that John Marshall grew up to be one of the most influential leaders of his time. His decisions helped to define the balance between our three branches of government—the executive, judicial, and legislative. Throughout his childhood and into adulthood, Marshall benefited from the influence and encouragement of his father's friend, George Washington. He served under Gen. Washington during the American Revolution (1775–83) and his admiration for Washington grew, along with his resolve to help shape the new nation. After the war, Marshall distinguished himself both in his law practice and in his place on Virginia's House of Delegates. In 1801 President John Adams appointed Marshall chief justice of the Supreme Court. Marshall's readings of the Constitution gave rise to constitutional law and the concept of judicial precedent. In his *Marbury v. Madison* ruling of 1803, Marshall declared the power of the Supreme Court to invalidate any act of Congress that the Court deemed

unconstitutional. Two additional Court rulings proscribed—under Marshall's guidance—the same Court purview over any state legislative acts or state court rulings. Throughout his 34-year Court tenure, Marshall emerged as a man well regarded for his fairness, acute intellect, and his belief in a strong central government. This latter trait, coupled with his strict reading of the Constitution, brought him into conflict with many of the

day's leading Democratic-Republicans—chief amongst them, President Thomas Jefferson. Although Marshall and Jefferson were cousins, they were fierce opponents and almost continually fought throughout President Jefferson's term in office.

Changes in the U.S. Government

The Constitution originally did not distinguish between presidential and vice presidential candidates during elections. Each elector could vote for two candidates, with the person receiving the most votes becoming president, and the runner-up, vice president. This system resulted in a tie vote for the presidency between Jefferson and Aaron Burr in the 1800 election (*See also,* Jefferson Becomes President). Although they had promoted Burr as their vice presidential candidate to secure additional support for the party, the Republicans had always intended for Jefferson to be president. The fact that the Federalist-controlled Congress could have voted to make Burr, and not Jefferson, president was very disturbing. To address this problem, the Republicans devised the Twelfth Amendment to the U.S. Constitution, which provided for the electors to vote separately for the president and vice president. At first the amendment failed to pass Congress. Small states feared it would eliminate their ability to get a man into the executive office in the seat of vice president. Northern states felt that efforts at constitutional amendment should be directed at eliminating the provision that counted slaves as three-fifths of a person for determining the number of seats each state had in the House of Representatives. Congress eventually passed the amendment, and it was ratified by the requisite number of states in time for the election of 1804.

On March 1, 1803, Ohio was admitted as the 17th state of the nation. Treasury secretary Albert Gallatin convinced Congress to remind Ohio that the federal government retained lands it claimed as national in the Ohio Territory. In exchange the United States would set aside 136th of the land in each township for public schools, and further would contribute five percent of the net proceeds from sales of federal lands in Ohio to build roads to the Ohio River from the navigable waterways that led to the Atlantic Ocean. These provisions dated back to the Northwest Territories Acts of the 1780s that Jefferson had helped to draft. Ohio accepted the proposal, and the electors there contributed to Jefferson's landslide reelection in 1804. Also during Jefferson's presidency, the United States doubled its size with the Louisiana Purchase (*See also,* Foreign Issues), and territories were created in Michigan and Illinois.

Jefferson elaborated the doctrine of executive privilege, by which presidents ever since have resisted investigation of their presidential papers. In 1807 former vice president Aaron Burr was on trial for treason for an alleged scheme to take New Orleans, West Florida, and Mexico by force (*See also,* Domestic Issues). Chief Justice Marshall, who presided over the trial, subpoenaed papers in President Jefferson's possession concerning the incident and ordered him to appear in court to testify. Jefferson gave the district attorney only those documents he deemed to be essential to the administration of justice and refused to travel to Richmond, Virginia, to appear as a witness. Battles over executive privilege would play major roles in future governmental investigations, such as during investigations of and impeachment proceedings against presidents Richard Nixon and Bill Clinton.

Jefferson introduced many customs and eliminated others to inject democracy into the conduct of U.S. government. He replaced the custom of bowing with handshaking when receiving visitors at the President's House (later called the White House). And he often greeted domestic and foreign officials dressed in slippers and trousers rather than official state dress. This behavior alienated Jefferson with British minister Anthony Merry, who was offended at a dinner party when Jefferson escorted secretary of state James Madison's wife rather than Merry's wife to sit next to him at the round dinner table. Jefferson responded by explaining that the United States was a republic where everyone is treated equally.

Domestic Issues

In 1800 agriculture was still the principal livelihood of Americans, as the industrial revolution lay decades into the future. Jefferson fantasized that the United States should develop as a country dotted with small, self-sufficient, family-run farms. Each region would have its own specialty—rice, cotton, and tobacco plantations in the South, grain and livestock farms in the mid-Atlantic states, lumberyards and fisheries in the North. People would govern locally, largely without interference from the national government, which instead would concern itself primarily with the foreign policy of minimizing intercourse with foreign nations.

The Federalists under George Washington and John Adams, however, had set up national institutions that propelled the United States forever away from Jefferson's agrarian ideal. Washington's secretary of the Treasury, Alexander Hamilton, saw the United States's strength in the commerce that was developing in metropolitan areas, where master craftsmen, shopkeepers, lawyers, importers, and exporters pursued the U.S. dream of capitalistic wealth. Hamilton sought to support this growth by establishing a national bank to lend money to aspiring capitalists. National banking naturally led to public debt, accumulated to enable the bank to act as a money-lender. The interest that came with borrowing and lending money profited bankers at the expense of the people, and the national government itself had to raise taxes to finance its interest burden. On top of this, the Federalist plan for international commerce meant financing a large military for defense when relations with Europe went sour, requiring further increase in taxes.

Domestic reform aimed at reversing these Federalist policies dominated Jefferson's first term in office. His primary goal was to reduce both taxes and the national debt. In Jefferson's opinion, taxes prevented the work-ing classes from improving their lot in life, so he supported the elimination of all direct taxes except on items consumed by the wealthy, such as wine. Jefferson saw a similar evil in debt, profiting money changers at the expense of farmers. Under Jefferson, Treasury secretary Albert Gallatin masterminded a program that cut the federal debt from approximately $80 million to $57 million in eight years. Reducing debt and taxes also meant reducing spending, so Jefferson cut federal jobs and the size of the military. At the same time, Congress created the military academy at West Point, New York, to train a capable yet small army. By the end of his first term, Jefferson had "reversed the flow of history" by voluntarily limiting the power and the resources of the federal government (McDonald, p. 52).

During Jefferson's second term, foreign affairs dominated his attention, and division among Republicans in Congress over nominating Jefferson's successor prevented him from accomplishing much domestic reform. The most significant exception was the abolition of the slave trade as of January 1, 1808.

Yazoo Land Fiascoes

During Jefferson's presidency, sectionalism, greed, and politics converged in Georgia, where speculation in frontier lands led to ownership disputes and conflicting lawsuits in both state and federal courts. American Indians who claimed much of this land sought protection of their rights under treaties signed during the Washington administration. The state of Georgia largely ignored these treaties and sold the lands to speculators, including the Yazoo Land Companies formed in 1789. Georgia, in fact, sold some lands many times over, canceling previous transactions as fraudulent. A group of speculators from Connecticut and Massachusetts called the New England Mississippi Land Company bought 11 million acres of such land from Yazoo, only to find Georgia declared their title to be worthless. Finally, with the Judiciary Act of 1801, Federalists had committed jurisdiction over land disputes exclusively to federal courts, where Federalist judges were sure to protect the interests of Federalist land speculators.

Jefferson sought to clean up this mess in favor of Republican interests. He began with an act of appeasement by appointing one of the leading New England speculators, Gideon Granger of Connecticut, as postmaster general. Jefferson then appointed secretary of state James Madison, Treasury secretary Albert Gallatin, and attorney general Levi Lincoln to negotiate a resolution of disputed ownership with Georgia. In 1802 the United States agreed to pay Georgia $1.25 million for the purchase of Georgia's western lands, which later would become the states of Alabama and Mississippi. In addition the United States agreed to liquidate Indian land claims in Georgia and to set aside one-tenth of its acquired lands to compensate Yazoo claimants. By the time this agreement was approved and fulfilled by Congress in Jefferson's second term, the United States would spend as much for the Georgia lands as it did for the entire Louisiana Purchase (*See also,* Foreign Issues). When Republicans split over nominating Jefferson's successor, Republicans, led by Virginia congressman John Randolph, criticized the resolution as fraudulent. Years later the deal would be the basis for President Andrew Jackson's Trail of Tears, a policy of removing American Indians from their Georgia homelands and pushing them into unsettled western territory.

Lewis and Clark Expedition

As a scientist, Jefferson was interested in exploring the U.S. continent west of the Mississippi River to the Pacific Ocean. He knew that flora and fauna waited to be discovered and added to the body of U.S. knowledge. The only problem was that the Louisiana Territory, as far as Jefferson knew, was the property of the king of Spain. However, Spain had given the territory to France in a secret treaty in 1800. Then, in a historical coincidence, France sold the Louisiana Territory to the United States shortly after Jefferson announced and sought funding for an expedition in early 1803 (*See also,* Foreign Issues). Jefferson now could launch the expedition without encroaching on foreign territory.

In the spring of 1804 a 35-member expedition led by U.S. Army officers Meriwether Lewis and William Clark left from their fort near St. Louis, Missouri. Their goal was to create maps, gather specimens of plants and animals, collect data on soil and weather, and observe every detail of the new territory. The expedition explored the Missouri River; crossed the Continental Divide with the help of Sacajawea, a Shoshone Indian woman; boated down the Columbia River; and made it to the Pacific Ocean in November 1805. They stayed there until March 1806 before heading back for St. Louis. Although Lewis and Clark failed to discover a Northwest Passage (a river flowing to the Pacific Ocean from within Missouri), they returned with survey information that sparked further exploration and eventual western settlement.

The Burr Conspiracy

After the election of 1804, Aaron Burr was a defeated man looking for revenge (*See also,* Jefferson Becomes President). He had lost the election for New York governor, been ousted as vice president, and was indicted in both New York and New Jersey for the duel that resulted in former Treasury secretary Alexander Hamilton's death. Seeking refuge, Burr traveled to Tennessee to see his daughter and then visited with locals west of the Appalachian Mountains, where he devised a plan. History is unclear what Burr's plan was. It may have been a patriotic (but illegal) plot to attack Spanish territory in the west and the Floridas to claim them for the United States. There also is evidence that it was a treasonable plot to engineer the secession of New England and the western regions from the United States. Whatever it was, Burr recruited men for his scheme during his

travels. One recruit was future president Andrew Jackson, head of the Tennessee militia and a foe of Spain who pledged to support Burr in a march against the Spanish southwest. Another was James Wilkinson, governor of upper Louisiana and commander of U.S. forces defending the United States against the Spanish southwest.

Foreign affairs added to the confusion surrounding Burr's plans. Spain was claiming that the sale of Louisiana to the United States was illegal under the agreement by which Spain had ceded that territory to France (*See also,* Foreign Issues). Spain was also refusing to recognize that the Floridas were included in that sale. In his annual address to Congress in December 1805, Jefferson adopted a hostile stance toward Spain. In this situation, Burr traveled to Washington in late 1805 and early 1806 to solicit financial and military support for his plan. There he met with British minister Anthony Merry, who pledged naval backing when he heard that Burr and western Americans planned to attack the Spanish southwest. Burr also met with Spanish minister Don Carlos Casa Yrujo and suggested that with Spanish support, the westerners would secede from the United States and join the Spanish crown. Finally, Burr had many dinners with President Jefferson, although neither man kept a record of what they discussed.

Burr ultimately set up headquarters on Blennerhassett Island in the Ohio River in present-day West Virginia to gather forces and supplies. When Spain began to march against New Orleans, Louisiana, to stand up to Jefferson's threats, Wilkinson led the U.S. Army against them, and Burr marched southward from his headquarters. Larger forces intervened as French emperor Napoleon Bonaparte conquered Prussia and issued his Berlin Decree, in which he insisted on peace between Spain and the United States (*See also,* Foreign Issues). Further, Wilkinson had sent a letter to Jefferson betraying Burr and his plans. Desiring an alliance with France to offset escalating problems with Great Britain, Jefferson canceled military action in New Orleans and, in December 1806, issued an order that "sundry persons," meaning Burr and his companions, cease at once from conspiring to attack Spanish possessions.

Burr fled for Florida but was apprehended and sent to Washington. Jefferson had Burr indicted for treason, but the trial became a Republican embarrassment presided over by Chief Justice John Marshall. Marshall instructed the jury that Burr technically could not have committed treason if he was not present, as he had not been, at the gathering of men on Blennerhassett Island in the Ohio River on December 10, 1806, the basis for the indictment for treason. Based on this the jury found Burr not guilty, and Jefferson fumed over continuing problems with the federal judiciary.

Slave Trade

While Jefferson opposed both slavery and the slave trade, he remained a slaveholder himself until his death.

After Jefferson purchased Louisiana from the French he put together an expedition to explore the new territory, which was headed by U.S. Army officers, Meriwether Lewis and William Clark. The expedition explored the Missouri River, crossed the Continental Divide with the help of Sacajewea, a Shoshone Indian woman, and boated down the Columbia River before arriving at the Pacific Ocean. (Corbis. Reproduced by permission.)

As a public figure, however, he regularly spoke out against the slave trade as "piratical warfare" (Channing, p. 105). As president, Jefferson backed up those words with action. To secure adoption of the U.S. Constitution, the framers had to include a provision prohibiting the federal government from regulating the slave trade for 20 years. That moratorium would expire in 1807. Jefferson used his annual message in December 1806 to ask Congress to prohibit "those violations of human rights which have been so long continued on the unoffending inhabitants of Africa, and which the morality, the reputation, and the best interests of our country have long been eager to proscribe" (Channing, p. 106).

Sectionalism in Jefferson's time often pitted the commercial interests on the eastern seaboard against interior agricultural interests. Passing legislation to abolish the slave trade from Africa aroused sectional debates that foreshadowed later divisions between the North and the South. The Senate began with a bill that proposed the total prohibition of slave trade from Africa effective January 1, 1808. The House bill was more controversial in its details. It proposed that illegally imported slaves be forfeited to the federal government and that coastal domestic trade in slaves be prohibited in vessels under 40 tons (a measure meant to prevent the smuggling of slaves). Northerners objected to the former provision, offended by the notion that the federal government would become a slaveholder. Southerners balked at the latter, speculating that any regulation of the domestic aspect of slavery was the first step towards abolition. Debate also raged over the penalty for importing slaves. Some wanted imprisonment, others death.

In the end New England and Pennsylvania lined up on Jefferson's side against Virginia and the southern states. The bill that passed outlawed trade from Africa effective January 1, 1808, and penalized a violation with imprisonment, a fine, and forfeiture of cargo. Forfeited slaves were to be turned over to the authorities of the state where the vessel was seized, and state authorities also would be responsible for handling violations of the prohibition on coastal trade by vessels under 40 tons. In the end, the act reduced the slave trade but did not eliminate it. Southern states had no intention of punishing coastal domestic trade, and importation from Africa even continued. In the midst of debate over passage of the bill, Congressman John Randolph of Virginia foretold that if there ever were division in the Union, the split would be between the free and the slave states.

Impact of Domestic Issues

As president, Jefferson usually set an example that commitment to government by and for the people did not have to be empty rhetoric. He backed up his republican philosophies by limiting the power of the federal government and eliminating the trappings of monarchy from its customs. He proved that a United States that relied on international trade for revenue and taxed only the products consumed by the wealthy did not have to bury the working class under oppressive taxes. He supported freedom of speech by allowing the Sedition Act, passed in 1798 to curb antigovernment speech, to expire without reenactment. Finally, whether intentionally or otherwise, Jefferson urged the first step toward the abolition of slavery by supporting elimination of the slave trade.

As happens so often, however, Jefferson's ideals were his undoing. Jefferson's aggressive reform came during a time when the world powers of Great Britain and France were temporarily at peace and the United States had no need for a strong military. When tempers flared in Europe during Jefferson's second term, the United States was unprepared to defend itself and its international trade. Conflict in Europe led to conflict at home.

Foreign Issues

Jefferson's foreign policy objective was to protect U.S. independence by maintaining peace, but avoiding alliances with foreign nations. To this end Jefferson initially set out to recall all U.S. diplomats from their foreign posts. He also hoped to acquire the port city of New Orleans at the mouth of the Mississippi River in Louisiana, ensuring farmers west of the Appalachian Mountains a place to launch their goods into international trade. These objectives were part of Jefferson's overall plan to see the United States develop into a self-sufficient nation of farmers.

During the George Washington and John Adams administrations, the United States had been caught in the middle of a power struggle between Great Britain, France, and Spain for world domination. U.S. commercial interests at the time depended heavily on carrying goods to and from the West Indies, Great Britain, and continental Europe. When Great Britain and France were at war, they viewed U.S. vessels carrying their enemy's goods as appropriate targets. English and French vessels both attacked U.S. merchants on the high seas, captured their cargoes, and forced U.S. sailors into foreign naval service. Federalist policy had been to ignore such treatment by Great Britain while protesting to France, resulting in a naval, quasi-war between the United States and France from 1798 to 1800 (*See also,* Career).

Three developments shaped the course of foreign affairs for Jefferson during his first term. The United States and France made peace at the Convention of Mortefontaine in October 1800. In October 1801 Great Britain and France signed a peace agreement that five months later would become the Treaty of Amiens. These developments allowed Jefferson to embark on a domes-tic policy that involved slashing military size and spending. Finally there was a secret agreement by which Spain ceded the Louisiana Territory to France, retaining West and East Florida for itself. While this development made the Louisiana Purchase possible, Jefferson was unaware of the transaction until after he took office in March 1801, and so he initially thought Spain posed an immediate threat to U.S. independence at home.

While at peace with France, Jefferson's initial foreign policy concerned Great Britain, Spain, and the American Indians. Most importantly, the United States needed to maintain the rights of navigation on the Mississippi River and storage of goods in the port city of New Orleans, rights the United States had negotiated with Spain during the Adams administration. As for the American Indians, Jefferson sought to pacify them in the northwest and the southwest so as not to interfere with frontier development. Meanwhile, the United States had to keep an eye on Great Britain, who retained holdings in Canada and South America and was allied with Spain. In this environment, the United States made the greatest real estate transaction in history, acquiring the entire Louisiana Territory from France for $15 million.

In 1802 war erupted again between Great Britain and France. From 1804 through 1807 both countries issued a series of orders designed to strangle the enemy by controlling ocean trade. Great Britain prohibited ships carrying French goods from sailing in the English channel, between Great Britain and France, while France prohibited ships carrying English goods from harboring on the European coastline. U.S. vessels were subject to confiscation by either belligerent if they obeyed the rules of the other. In addition, British ships patrolled the U.S. coast to intercept and inspect U.S. ships for enemy goods and to search for British deserters.

As Jefferson and Congress cut the size of the United States's army and navy to cut expenses and reduce the national debt, the United States was in no position to go to war. Jefferson thus decided to cut off all European powers by enacting an embargo, legislation prohibiting U.S. merchants from engaging in international trade. Enforcing the embargo against U.S. shippers in New England led to civil rights violations. Jefferson left office in 1809 at the low point of his popularity as the United States was on course for war with Great Britain in 1812.

Napoleon Bonaparte Targets Santo Domingo

Santo Domingo, present-day Dominican Republic, was a lucrative source of trade for the young United States, whose ships carried U.S. foodstuffs and European arms to the half-Spanish, half-French Caribbean island. The island was a sugar colony where plantations were operated by slaves. After Spain ceded its half to France, slaves led by General Pierre Dominique Toussaint L'Ouverture revolted against their masters in 1795 and established their own government. Under President John Adams the United States established diplomatic relations with Toussaint to maintain the valuable commercial trade. Republicans opposed this policy of trading with rebellious slaves.

When Jefferson took office, French emperor Napoleon Bonaparte had a two-part plan to establish French dominance in the United States that involved occupying New Orleans, Louisiana, and reestablishing control in Santo Domingo. Bonaparte sent diplomat Louis Pichon to discuss the latter plan with the Jefferson administration around July 1801. Bonaparte's plans for Santo Domingo were favorable to Republicans, who were frightened by stories that slaves had successfully revolted against their masters, slaughtering many in the process. Jefferson promised Pichon that as long as France made peace with Great Britain (which it did in October), the United States would supply military and naval support as well as cut off trade with Toussaint to allow France to recapture the island.

Bonaparte's brother-in-law, General Victor E. Leclerc, sailed from France for Santo Domingo in late 1801. Despite the United States's promise of assistance, Leclerc had orders from Bonaparte to cut off U.S. shipping after restoring the island to French control. The orders were part of Bonaparte's plans to weaken the United States so that France could dominate North America. When Leclerc arrived in Santo Domingo, he went beyond Bonaparte's orders by seizing the 20 U.S. ships in port and imprisoning some of their masters. The United States protested through its minister in France, Robert Livingston, but Jefferson did not press the issue. He wanted to establish trade with the island after France reestablished control. Leclerc scored many early victories, including tricking Toussaint into sailing to Paris, France, to be decorated when he actually was to be imprisoned. Yellow fever eventually struck the French troops, however, and the slaves rallied under new leadership, killing 20,000 French soldiers, including Leclerc, in a matter of weeks. The defeat was one of the factors that led Bonaparte to sell Louisiana to the United States.

Louisiana Purchase

In one sense the Louisiana Purchase from France in 1803, which in one stroke doubled the size of the United States, was the chance result of a constantly changing set of geopolitical developments. The renewed hostilities—now called the Napoleonic Wars—between Great Britain and France; Napoleon's reluctance to fight the United States on a distant second front; and the inability of French troops, after almost 10 years of war, to defeat an intractable slave rebellion in Santo Domingo convinced Napoleon Bonaparte to sell the Louisiana Territory to the United States. In another sense, the Louisiana Purchase was hardly an accidental development. The Mississippi River and the port of New Orleans were of immense strategic importance to the United States's western trade

and transportation. Likewise, the fabled richness of western lands impressed Jefferson as a source of homesteading opportunities for coming generations of "yeoman" farmers. These observations convinced Americans that this vast frontier land must either be assimilated into the United States or else it would become a dangerous power vacuum inviting foreign invaders.

The Louisiana Territory stretched northward from New Orleans to Canada and westward to the Rocky Mountains and comprised land in the current states of Arkansas, Colorado, Iowa, Kansas, Louisiana, Minnesota, Missouri, Montana, Nebraska, North Dakota, Oklahoma, South Dakota, and Wyoming. Under the Treaty of San Lorenzo, or Pinckney's Treaty, with Spain in 1795, the United States had secured shipping rights on the Mississippi River and the right of deposit in New Orleans—the right to store goods awaiting shipment. In a secret treaty in 1800, however, Spain, which was not powerful enough to defend Louisiana from the United States, ceded the territory to France. Rumors of Spain's cession reached Jefferson early in his administration. Jefferson wrote to James Monroe, then governor of Virginia, that cession of Louisiana to France was "very ominous" to the United States, who would have difficulty defending itself against France's superior army.

In the winter of 1801, as the French general Leclerc was landing in Santo Domingo to retake the island for France, Jefferson got confirmation of Spain's cession of Louisiana to France. The news went public in March 1802. Jefferson approached Napoleon indirectly by sending a famous letter to the U.S. minister in France, Robert Livingston. Jefferson suggested that occupation of New Orleans by France would force the United States to forge an alliance with Great Britain to dominate the seas, take Louisiana by force, and acquire the Spanish territories in the New World. Jefferson also made an offhand suggestion that perhaps France would cede to the United States not only New Orleans but also West Florida, which Jefferson thought France also had received from Spain.

In the summer of 1802, Bonaparte instructed French general Claude Victor to gather forces and supplies in Holland to sail for New Orleans that winter. Then in November, Spain, which had not yet turned possession over to France, unexpectedly closed the port of New Orleans to all foreign shipping and withdrew the United States's right of deposit. The source of the order was unclear, but the United States assumed it was France. Federalists immediately called for war. Then Jefferson got information that Pierre S. Du Pont de Nemours, Jefferson's French friend who had read and then delivered Jefferson's letter to Livingston, believed that France would be willing to sell New Orleans and West Florida for $6 million. As France still owed the United States $4 million for U.S. claims stemming from the quasi-war during the Adams administration, Jefferson dreamed he might seal the deal for a mere $2 million. Jefferson convinced Congress to appropriate that much money for the

Fast Fact

When Jefferson was president, 19 out of 20 Americans lived on farms or in villages with fewer than 2,500 people.

(Source: Forrest McDonald. *The Presidency of Thomas Jefferson,* 1976.)

cause, and then appointed James Monroe as minister to France in early 1803.

Du Pont's belief was misinformed, and Bonaparte originally had no intention of selling New Orleans. But circumstances changed drastically between the time of Monroe's appointment and his arrival in Paris, France. General Claude's fleet was frozen in port in Holland and unable to sail for New Orleans. General Leclerc was killed along with 20,000 French soldiers in their failed attempt to recapture Santo Domingo. Finally, France was on the eve of returning to war with Great Britain after temporary peace under the Treaty of Amiens, and Bonaparte needed money to finance the effort. Under the circumstances, Bonaparte offered to sell the entire Louisiana Territory to the United States at a price of $15 million. Although it was well beyond what they were authorized to spend, Monroe and Livingston accepted the offer as too good to refuse and signed a purchase treaty in May 1803.

Jefferson was thrilled with the prospect of acquiring Louisiana but embarrassed by the fact that he could not find authority in the Constitution to make the deal. Usually Jefferson was a "strict constructionist," interpreting the Constitution as strictly as possible to give the federal government the minimal authority necessary for its operation. Jefferson initially drafted a constitutional amendment to accompany the Louisiana Purchase Treaty, but he later dropped the amendment and accepted secretary of the Treasury Albert Gallatin's opinion that the purchase was constitutional under the president's authority to make treaties.

While the Senate ratified the treaty, Federalists, who wanted to acquire Louisiana for free by force, used the purchase as an opportunity to criticize Jefferson's contradictory domestic policy—the cost of the purchase increased the public debt by 20 percent. More problematically, the United States learned that when Spain had ceded Louisiana to France, Bonaparte agreed not to resell it to another country. In theory, then, Jefferson had bought territory he had no authority to buy from a country that had no authority to sell. Federalists scoffed at the transaction and its high price tag as nothing more than U.S. tribute to France. In the end, however, Federalists lacked the power to derail the purchase, Spain lacked the power to dispute the United States's ownership, and the territory gave the United States dominance in the New World.

Tripolitan War

When Jefferson took office, the Barbary States on the coast of North Africa, including Tripoli, Tunis, Algiers, and Morocco, regulated trade in the Mediterranean Sea by demanding tributary payments from foreign powers who wished to sail there. Prior to its independence, the United States was protected by the tribute paid by Great Britain. After the United States declared independence from Great Britain, the Barbary States demanded a separate tribute from the United States. Presidents Washington and Adams paid out more than $2 million during their administrations.

Jefferson reluctantly continued the practice until May 1801, when Tripoli suddenly cut down the flag at the U.S. consulate, issued a declaration of war, and demanded more money from the United States. (Tripoli believed that the other Barbary States were receiving a disproportionate share.) Jefferson decided to challenge the entire tributary practice. Without declaring war Jefferson dispatched four vessels to engage in a spirited defense of U.S. shipping in the Mediterranean. The naval war, also known as the Barbary War, lasted four years and frustrated secretary of the Treasury Albert Gallatin's desire to finance interest payments for the Louisiana Purchase by cutting naval expenditures.

Tripoli secured its greatest victory in 1804, when the 38-gun U.S. frigate *Philadelphia* struck a reef while pursuing a vessel near Tripoli's harbor. The *Philadelphia* was seized and used against the rest of the American fleet. The tide turned in the United States's favor later that year when Lt. Stephen Decatur and his crew entered the harbor disguised in a captured Mediterranean vessel, set fire to the *Philadelphia,* and then escaped killing thousands of Tripolitans without losing a man. The United States eventually paid $60,000 in ransom to Tripoli for release of the crew of the *Philadelphia,* but its naval victories ended Tripoli's demands for tribute, and the parties signed a peace treaty in June 1805.

Although Jefferson refused to admit it, once again he had stretched the constitutional justification for his actions as president. The Constitution gives Congress—not the president—the power to declare war. This recalls other points in his administration—like the Louisiana Purchase—when Jefferson let his pragmatism override his Republican reverence for a strict construction of presidential power under the Constitution.

Jefferson Targets West Florida

After Jefferson purchased the Louisiana Territory from France, Spain claimed that the territory of West

Florida, which stretched from New Orleans to Pensacola, Florida, was not included in its cession to France, and thus was not part of the United States's purchase. Jefferson nonetheless was determined to take West Florida to increase control over the Gulf of Mexico. Shortly after Congress approved the Louisiana Purchase, it passed the Mobile Act on February 24, 1804, to establish statutory claim to West Florida.

In the summer of 1804, despite diplomatic efforts to get him to pronounce otherwise, Napoleon Bonaparte declared that West Florida had not been included in the sale to the United States. Jefferson sent James Monroe to Europe to resolve the dispute. Monroe went first to Paris, France, in October 1804, to seek France's assistance. He was unsuccessful. While Monroe was en route from Paris to Madrid, Spain, in December, Spain declared war against Great Britain, thereby allying itself with France and making Monroe's mission hopeless. Receiving reports of these failures back home, Jefferson proposed war with Spain to his cabinet, which advised that war would be too expensive. Meanwhile the Republican press began to carry stories of the dangers posed by the United States's Spanish neighbors to the south.

A year later, with the matter unresolved, Jefferson had intelligence reports suggesting that Bonaparte might compel Spain to sell West and East Florida for up to $10 million if the United States would align itself with France. In his annual message to Congress on December 3, 1805, Jefferson recounted U.S. grievances against Spain and the failure of negotiations to secure the claim to West Florida. Jefferson recommended fortification of U.S. harbors, construction of gunboats to defend coastal cities, and organization of an army or militia to defend against aggression on the Spanish frontier. In a secret message at the same time, however, Jefferson asked Congress to appropriate money for purchase of the Floridas.

The suggestion offended Republican congressman John Randolph of Virginia, who clung dearly to the ideals that had swept the party into power in 1800. Randolph felt the secretive plan, following on the heels of the questionable Louisiana Purchase, was a dangerous expansion of presidential authority. Randolph called for a return to conservative Republican principles, including a limited national government and a strict separation of powers between the president and Congress. Randolph's efforts marked a growing rift in the Republican Party, which was headed for a power struggle over nominating Jefferson's successor for the election of 1808.

Despite Randolph's efforts, the appropriations bill passed and was signed into law on February 13, 1806, but to no avail. As Bonaparte increased his European strength with a succession of successful military campaigns that reduced his need for cash, France abandoned the idea of supporting sale of the Floridas and instead demanded that Spain and the United States make peace between themselves. As maritime relations with Great Britain were beginning to worsen, Jefferson went along

with Bonaparte's suggestion and temporarily abandoned his efforts to acquire West Florida (Spain ceded Florida to the United States in 1819 as part of the Adams-Onis Treaty [*See also*, James Monroe Administration]).

Commercial Warfare

When war resumed between Great Britain and France in 1803, Great Britain's navy dominated the seas while France's army dominated the European continent. Both countries dared not leave their area of strength, and instead pursued a strategy of trying to starve the other country into submission by blocking enemy trade with neutral countries, including the United States. By a series of orders between 1804 and 1806, Great Britain cut off the United States's lucrative carriage of goods to Europe from the West Indies and imposed a blockade of coastal traffic along the European coastline. Bonaparte responded in November 1806 with the Berlin Decree, establishing a largely unenforceable blockade and prohibition of trade with Great Britain, and declaring that ships entering European ports with English cargoes would be seized.

Further aggravating matters, Great Britain continued the practice of stopping U.S. merchant ships in U.S. and British waters as well as on the high seas to recapture deserters from the Royal British Navy, a practice that often accompanied the capture and impressment of Americans into British naval service. Two incidents in particular led to U.S. cries for war. In April 1806 off the coastline of New York, the British man-of-war H.M.S. *Leander* announced its intention of searching a U.S. merchant ship by firing a shot across her bow. The shot hit a small U.S. sloop and killed a crewman. Then in June 1807, the British H.M.S. *Leopard* hailed the U.S. naval frigate *Chesapeake* off the coast of Norfolk, Virginia, and demanded the return of suspected deserters. When Commodore James Barron refused to be boarded, the *Leopard* fired, killing three men and wounding 18.

Although Jefferson ordered Great Britain's ships out of U.S. waters after the *Chesapeake* incident, he was opposed to war. Instead, Secretary of State James Madison convinced Jefferson to pursue a policy of commercial warfare by cutting off the importation of English goods. The problem with this plan, which Treasury secretary Albert Gallatin opposed, was that taxes on imports were the United States's primary source of revenue after over five years of tax cuts under Jefferson. Jefferson ultimately rejected Gallatin's protests, for in his heart he believed the United States would fare better by limiting its reliance on international commerce and developing self-sufficiency grounded in a strong agriculture.

The Embargo Acts

The first session of the Ninth Congress passed the first in a series of embargo acts during the winter of 1805. It was a limited embargo, prohibiting only the importation of British goods that could be acquired elsewhere or produced in the United States, and allowing the continued importation of such valuable revenue generators as Jamaican rum and Birmingham hardware. Enforcement of the act was suspended until November 1806 (it actually did not go into effect until December 1807), and Jefferson sent James Monroe and Maryland senator William Pinckney to Great Britain to negotiate terms for commercial peace. Monroe and Pinckney signed a treaty in December 1806, but Jefferson refused to sign it or send it to the Senate for ratification—it failed to eliminate the British practice of impressment (forcing captured U.S. sailors into British service), and an addendum tacked on at the last minute required the United States to refuse to comply with Bonaparte's Berlin Decree. Jefferson still wanted Bonaparte's assistance with obtaining the Floridas, and would need France as an ally if conditions with Great Britain led to war. Further Bonaparte had effectively exempted the United States from operation of the Berlin Decree in European ports.

In January 1807 Great Britain issued orders to strengthen its blockade of the European coast. Later in the year, Bonaparte decided to enforce the Berlin Decree against the United States. In Bonaparte's opinion the United States's failure to go to war with Britain in light of British seizure and impressment was a sign that the United States was allied with his enemy. Toward the end of 1807 the United States learned of two further orders from Great Britain: that it would continue the practice of impressment and extend it to warships as well, and that all ships trading with France must first enter a British port to pay taxes and obtain a license. U.S. international commerce was faced with strangulation.

The Jefferson administration responded by proposing a series of embargo acts that prevented U.S. ships from sailing to foreign ports unless specifically authorized by the administration. Congress passed the acts in December 1807 and January 1808. Madison, a staunch supporter of the policy, saw the acts as prohibiting trade even with foreign vessels in U.S. ports. This policy became law in an act passed in March 1808 preventing the export of any goods.

The Enforcement Act: Through enforcement of the embargo acts, which were designed to avoid war with Europe, Jefferson waged war in the United States. Citizens who depended on shipping for their livelihood, particularly those in the New England states, regularly violated the embargoes. In April 1808 Jefferson convinced Congress to pass the Enforcement Act, which contained two key provisions. It empowered collectors to seize and inspect ships on the mere suspicion that they might be violating the embargo. This flew in the face of the Fourth Amendment, which prohibits the federal government from making an arrest without probable cause, stronger than mere suspicion that there has been a violation. The act also empowered Jefferson to use the army and the navy to enforce the embargo acts.

Civil disobedience and military enforcement entangled and escalated during the remainder of the year. Americans were wounded and some died. The Republican who was swept into power on a platform of limited government exited trampling civil rights with the exercise of unlimited executive authority. Although Madison won the presidential election in 1808, northern Republicans and Federalists joined together in Congress to repeal the embargo acts effective March 4, 1809. While Congress replaced the embargo with an act prohibiting trade only with Great Britain and France, nobody truly expected them to be enforced by the Madison administration, and indeed they were not.

The embargo thus died with Jefferson's presidency. In a letter to his friend du Pont on the next to last day of his administration, Jefferson wrote, "Within a few days I retire to my family, my books and farms. . . . Never did a prisoner, released from his chains, feel such relief as I shall on shaking off the shackles of power" (Cunningham, p. 319).

The Jefferson Administration Legacy

Jefferson left his successors a stronger and larger nation, but one that would have to face serious challenges, especially in the field of foreign policy. While Jefferson technically avoided "entangling alliances," his foreign policy drew the United States further into the maelstrom of European politics. With the Louisiana Purchase, the United States increased its resources and therefore its strength, inevitably leading to antagonism with Great Britain, France, and Spain. While Jefferson desired to minimize the United States's dependence on the European powerhouses, he increased it by eliminating direct taxes, leaving the United States to rely on import duties for revenues. When the United States was caught in the middle of European war without adequate defenses during his second term, Jefferson's embargo policy was a commendable strategy for keeping the United States out of harm's way. When the embargo failed, Jefferson learned the hard way that the pursuit of happiness by some Americans would make it impossible for the United States to avoid trade with the other powerful nations in the world.

Still, Jefferson cannot be held responsible for all of the difficulties posed for an infant republic trying to formulate a foreign policy by Europe in flames. All in all, Jefferson had a very successful administration and, until the last years of his second term, a popular one. If history had a gauge, the president who slashed taxes while doubling the size of the United States's frontier surely would measure as one of the most popular. His landslide reelection in 1804 reflected the widespread appeal of his republican ideals. Sadly his success fell apart toward the end of his second term as the Republican Congress succumbed to infighting over Jefferson's successor. Congressman John Randolph of Virginia and the conservative Republicans saw the administration wavering from the ideals that brought it to power. The foreign and domestic strife at the end of Jefferson's second term spelled trouble for the first term of Jefferson's successor, James Madison.

Jefferson's enemies were staunch Federalists who feared the nationwide trend away from government by and for the moneyed classes. If the Federalists were a minority, however, their press spoke against Jefferson loudly and clearly, attacking his financial policies, military reduction, and foreign relations. Their most scathing attacks, however, were personal. A reporter in 1802 printed a story accusing Jefferson of fathering illegitimate children by Sally Hemmings, one of his slaves. Jefferson never denied the charge, but its validity still is subject to dispute.

Jefferson's support of religious freedom and separation of church and state led Federalists to accuse him of atheism. This charge is false. Jefferson was a Deist. He believed in a distant and benign organizing principle to the universe rather than in the stern and wrathful God of the Puritans and other Protestant groups. In this belief, however, he reflected the religious sensibilities of a good many Americans.

Still the Federalists equated Jeffersonian republicanism with the destruction of the society they coveted in the United States. Jefferson never responded publicly to these attacks on his religious belief or his morals.

Lasting Impact

Historians generally give Jefferson high marks for injecting democracy into the federal government. A balanced analysis must also point out the occasions when Jefferson neglected certain of his ideals in order to pursue pragmatic goals, such as his support of the Chase impeachment, the enforcement of the embargo acts, and support of Napoleon Bonaparte's efforts to reestablish control over the slaves on Santo Domingo. A balanced appraisal of Jefferson's lasting impact on U.S. politics must also note that his Republican commitment to limiting the power of the federal government and championing states' rights did not prevent him from occasionally concentrating power in the federal government and adopting, for all his criticism of Federalist leader Alexander Hamilton, an elastic construction of the Constitution rather than a strict construction. The Louisiana Purchase and the Barbary War clearly show this.

Jefferson's election in 1800 marked the success of the greatest constitutional experiment of all time—a government constructed to allow peaceable change in power at the whim of the people. John Adams's deathbed statement that "Thomas Jefferson survives" remains true today. Modern Republicans (who, despite their name, are not directly related to Jefferson's Democratic-Republicans)

Fast Fact

The terms of the Louisiana Purchase called for the United States to pay France $11,250,000 with 6 percent bonds that were irredeemable for 15 years, plus $3,750,000 in gold or U.S. Treasury notes, which France would use to pay debts stemming from the naval, quasi-war of 1798–1800. The total purchase price of $15 million amounted to four cents per acre.

(Source: Forrest McDonald. *The Presidency of Thomas Jefferson,* 1976.)

fight for a minimal role for the federal government in the day-to-day affairs of corporate America. Democrats fight to keep religion out of government. Both parties debate their differences in a press and media that usually enjoys unrestrained freedom of speech. All of these are ideals for which Jefferson fought.

For the general public, Jefferson served to humanize the presidency, to make the president another American rather than another monarch. In the minds of Americans Jefferson stands with other great U.S. presidents, such as George Washington and Abraham Lincoln, as a symbol of the United States's most cherished ideals, individual freedom and equality for all in a lifetime pursuit of happiness.

Sources

Brodie, Fawn M. *Thomas Jefferson: An Intimate History.* New York: W. W. Norton, 1974.

Channing, Edward. *The Jeffersonian System: 1801–1811.* Vol. 12 of *The American Nation: A History.* New York: Harper and Brothers, 1906.

Cunningham, Noble E., Jr. *In Pursuit of Reason: The Life of Thomas Jefferson.* Baton Rouge, La.: Louisiana State University Press, 1987.

DeConde, Alexander. *The Quasi-War: The Politics and Diplomacy of the Undeclared War with France 1797–1801.* New York: Charles Scribner's Sons, 1966.

Graff, Henry F. *The Presidents.* 2d ed. New York: Charles Scribner's Sons, 1997.

Kane, Joseph Nathan. *Facts About the Presidents: A Compilation of Biographical and Historical Information.* 6th ed. New York: H. W. Wilson, 1993.

McDonald, Forrest. *The Presidency of Thomas Jefferson.* Lawrence, Kans.: The University Press of Kansas, 1976.

Padover, Saul K. *Jefferson.* New York: Harcourt, Brace, 1942.

Peterson, Merrill D., ed. *The Portable Thomas Jefferson.* New York: Viking Press, 1975.

Smith, Page. *Jefferson: A Revealing Biography.* New York: American Heritage, 1976.

Further Readings

Boorstin, Daniel. *The Lost World of Thomas Jefferson.* Chicago: University of Chicago Press, 1948.

Burtstein, Andrew. *The Inner Jefferson: Portrait of a Grieving Optimist.* Charlottesville, Va.: University of Virginia Press, 1995.

Ellis, Joseph. *American Sphinx: The Character of Thomas Jefferson.* New York: Knopf, 1997.

Fliegelman, Jay. *Declaring Independence: Jefferson, Natural Language, and the Culture of Performance.* Stanford, Calif.: Stanford University Press, 1953.

Maier, Pauline. *American Scripture: Making the Declaration of Independence.* New York: Alfred Knopf, 1997.

Malone, Dumas. *Jefferson and His Time.* 6 vols. Boston: Little and Brown, 1948–81.

Onuf, Peter, ed. *Jeffersonian Legacies.* Charlottesville, Va.: University Press of Virginia, 1993.

Onuf, Peter, and Nicholas Onuf. *Federal Union, Modern World: The Law of Nations in an Age of Revolutions, 1776–1814.* Madison, Wisc.: Madison House, 1993.

Peterson, Merrill D. *Thomas Jefferson and the New Nation, A Biography.* New York: Oxford University Press, 1970.

Samuelson, Richard. *Thomas Jefferson and John Adams: Poles Together.* Charlottesville, Va.: Seminar Press University of Virginia Continuing Education, 1997.

Sheldon, Garret Ward. *The Political Philosophy of Thomas Jefferson.* Baltimore: Johns Hopkins University Press, 1991.

Madison Administrations

Biography

James Madison of Virginia was considered the father of the U.S. Constitution. An early supporter of American independence and an advocate of religious tolerance and individual rights, he was one of the main authors of the Constitution. A flexible and powerful political thinker, Madison was willing to change his positions when necessary to achieve his overall vision of a United States balanced between the power of the individual, the states, and the federal government. Along with statesmen John Jay and Alexander Hamilton, he wrote *The Federalist Papers,* urging the ratification of the Constitution and the establishment of a strong national government. Yet he also helped to draft the Bill of Rights, to protect individual citizens from government coercion. As president, Madison led the nation through the controversial War of 1812 with Great Britain.

Full name: James Madison

Personal Information:

Born: March 16, 1751

Birthplace: Port Conway, Virginia

Died: June 28, 1836

Death place: Montpelier, Virginia

Burial place: Family cemetery, Montpelier, Virginia

Religion: Episcopalian

Spouse: Dolley Dandridge Payne Todd (m. 1794)

Children: John Payne Todd (stepson)

Education: College of New Jersey (now Princeton University), BA Princeton, N.J., 1771

Occupation: Politician; landowner; congressman; secretary of state

Political Party: Democratic-Republican Party

Age at Inauguration: 57 years

Early Life

James Madison Jr., the fourth president of the United States, was born on March 16, 1751. He was raised on his paternal grandparents' plantation at the foot of the Blue Ridge Mountains in Virginia. This would be his official home for the rest of his life and would come to be known as Montpelier. The Montpelier plantation produced tobacco and grains. It consisted of about four thousand to five thousand acres and about one hundred slaves.

Madison was the eldest of seven surviving children born to James Madison Sr. (1723–1801) and Eleanor (Nelly) Rose Conway Madison (1731–1829). James himself was a small and somewhat sickly child. He was sub-

James Madison. (Portrait by Stuart Gilbert. National Archives and Records Administration.)

Education

Madison's formal education began at age 11 when he was tutored in logic, philosophy, and the classics. He excelled in Latin, as well as Greek, French, algebra, geometry, geography, and literature. In 1769, at age 18, Madison entered the College of New Jersey at Princeton (later Princeton University). His course work included study of important thinkers of the Scottish Enlightenment such as Francis Hutcheson and Adam Ferguson, who upheld individual rights over the power of the state. As distinguished from traditional Calvinist Presbyterians, these thinkers had a more hopeful view of humanity; they showed great confidence in humankind's inherently moral nature and respect for humankind's power of reason. Madison also debated with his friends about the writings of John Locke, a leading advocate of religious liberty and of representative government. While at Princeton Madison was an active and popular student. He engaged in normal undergraduate mischief while remaining a serious scholar.

After graduating in 1771 after two years rather than the typical three, Madison remained at Princeton for an additional six months of study. He began reading the law on his own, but never found it sufficiently interesting to entice him to become a practicing lawyer. When he left New Jersey in April 1772, he was still unsure of his career.

ject to seizures through much of his life. By adulthood, he had grown to only about 5 feet 4 inches tall and weighed about 100 pounds. His father was the largest landowner in the county and a man of influence in local affairs, serving variously as county lieutenant, sheriff, justice of the peace, and church vestryman. James's relationship with his mother was very warm and affectionate, and they remained close until her death at 98 years of age.

One important event in Madison's childhood was the French and Indian War (1754–63). Bloody war stories raised apprehensions of savage American Indian attacks in colonial America. Though no attacks ever occurred east of the Blue Ridge Mountains, these lurid tales and bloody accounts prejudiced Madison's view of American Indians for the rest of his life. They also excited his interest in the area beyond the mountains—the West. It was also on the plantation that Madison became aware of the evils of slavery. He would spend his entire life trying to reconcile his contradictory feelings about slavery. On the one hand he observed that slavery debased both the slave and the slaveholder. On the other, the plantation owner's economic interest in keeping slaves snared Madison as it did his colleague, third U.S. president Thomas Jefferson. Like Jefferson, Madison never freed his slaves, and he kept a slave as his body-servant (for personal dressing and grooming) until his death. Yet his strong feelings for individual liberty led him to openly disapprove of slavery throughout his life.

Family Life

James Madison did not marry until he was 43 years old. Described as shy in public but eloquent in private, Madison mustered the courage to ask a mutual friend, Aaron Burr, to arrange an introduction to the beautiful and sociable Dolley Payne Todd. Dolley Todd was a widow with one son, John Payne Todd (a spendthrift who would one day bring financial ruin on his parents). Dolley Todd and James Madison married on September 15, 1794. The marriage cost Dolley Madison her religion, as she was expelled from the Society of Friends for marrying outside of the Quaker religion.

Dolley Madison was a striking beauty, a stylish dresser (after she left the Quaker religion), and an accomplished conversationalist. She served frequently as hostess for presidential dinners during the administration of President Thomas Jefferson, Madison's friend, whose wife had died before he assumed the presidency. While serving as hostess, Dolley Madison invited interesting people to the White House, not just diplomats. And although the matter struck some observers (including her husband) as frivolous, by insisting on the society of talent and wit rather than office and wealth, Dolley Madison blazed new trails in the field of nation-building. At one such party in which a Washington haberdasher was invited, the wife of the British minister sniffed that the affair seemed more like a "a harvest-home supper" than a formal dinner. Dolley Madison smiled and observed that in her view "abundance was preferable to elegance; that circumstances formed customs, and customs formed taste." This being the case, she said that she did not hesitate "to sacrifice the delicacy of European taste for the less elegant, but more liberal fashion of Virginia" (Boller, p. 41). When she became first lady, she did make her wishes known regarding the need to upgrade the presidential official residence. Upon Madison's election as president in 1808, she invited a number of senators and congressmen to tour the White House and prevailed upon them to appropriate sufficient funds to renovate. Dolley Madison became one of the most popular people in Washington, D.C.

Career

Madison's presidential years were not the high point of his career. More an intellectual force than a political leader, Madison made his mark on U.S. history as the main author of the Constitution prior to his years as president. Madison's main contributions were as a philosopher of representative democracy.

Virginia Politics

During the American Revolution (1775–83), Madison accepted a military commission as a colonel; but because of poor health he never fought in battle. Instead, he involved himself in revolutionary politics on the state level in Virginia. As delegate to the Virginia Convention in 1776, Madison served on a committee to draw up a declaration of rights and a state constitution. After the Virginia Convention adopted the proposed constitution, the delegates declared independence from Britain. During his short stay in the Virginia legislature (he was elected in 1776 but lost a reelection bid in 1777), Madison met Thomas Jefferson and formed a lifelong friendship, during the course of which they worked together to gain passage of a bill guaranteeing religious liberty for Virginia's citizens.

From 1778 to 1779 Madison served on the Virginia Council of State under Governors Patrick Henry and Thomas Jefferson. Along with other new states, Virginia reacted to the excessive power that the king's British governors had wielded over the colonies by limiting the powers of the executive branch of state government. Thus, Virginia required that all actions of the governor had to be approved by the council. Madison soon found this type of government made the executive branch cumbersome and inefficient. The experience impressed upon Madison of the need for a stronger executive branch of government, a lesson that shaped his approach to drafting the U.S. Constitution. Madison served in the Continental Congress, the national legislative body that preceded the U.S. Congress, from 1780 to 1783. As he began to lean toward a stronger national government, Madison also advocated adequate financial support for the Continental army.

Madison returned to the Virginia state legislature in 1784. At that time there was a movement underway to make the Episcopal Church the state church in Virginia. Governor Patrick Henry had proposed a tax to support the Episcopal Church. After that attempt failed, Henry's group proposed expanding the proposed tax benefits to all Christian churches. Finally, they tried to broaden support by calling for a tax to support all teachers of the Christian religion. Madison fought the measure at every stage. His tract of 1785, *A Memorial and Remonstrance against Religious Assessments,* outlined his conviction that such taxes threatened the individual's right of free conscience and undermined the equality of citizens. He urged his fellow Virginians to maintain "an asylum to the persecuted and oppressed of every nation and religion." He was a firm believer in the separation of church and state—a concept that he later drafted into the Bill of Rights, the first 10 amendments to the U.S. Constitution. Madison also pressed for legislation to decriminalize heresy and to eliminate a religious test for a person to hold public office.

Madison and the Constitutional Convention

In 1786 Madison attended the Annapolis Convention in Maryland—a meeting of the young nation's political leadership to consider what to do about the depression that gripped the economy shortly after the conclusion of the American Revolution. The war had created a demand for domestically manufactured goods because of the British blockade of American ports. The end of the war brought a deluge of manufactured goods from Europe. This threatened the infant manufacturing sector in the United States. Another cause of the economic downturn was that the Articles of Confederation left the regulation of commerce up to the individual states. Attempting to protect their own markets for farm or manufactured products from domestic as well as foreign competition, or just to raise revenues, the states were levying taxes on goods shipped across state lines. Interstate trade was being crippled by these tariffs. Representatives at the Annapolis Convention failed to solve the trade problems, but they did petition the Continental Congress to convene a conference to address the weaknesses in the Articles of Confederation. As it was, Congress could not enact laws because nine out of 13 states had to vote for a new law and rarely were there 10 states present. Furthermore, without a chief executive, law enforcement was up to the individual states, and no central courts existed to handle disputes between states. Amendments to the articles required a unanimous vote, and the Continental Congress did not have the authority to levy taxes, make commercial treaties, regulate interstate commerce, or raise an army. And although the Continental Congress could issue currency, so could the states.

From 1780 to 1783, Madison served in the Continental Congress, the national legislative body that preceded the U.S. Congress. (Corbis. Reproduced by permission.)

Architect of the U.S. Constitution

George Washington presided over the Constitutional Convention when it convened in Philadelphia, Pennsylvania, in 1787, and all the states sent delegates except Rhode Island. The convention was handed the task of coming up with a document that addressed all the problems of the Articles of Confederation. The main debate revolved around the question of representation—large states versus smaller states. Madison drafted the large state plan (the Virginia Plan). It provided for a lower house elected by the people and an upper house elected by the lower house. The small states put forward the Patterson Plan (presented by William Patterson of New Jersey) recommending equal representation of all the states in Congress. The conflict was resolved in the Connecticut Compromise (July 1787), which provided for a two-house legislature—the upper (Senate) with an equal representation of all states, and the lower (House of Representatives) with representation apportioned according to the population of the state. After the Connecticut Compromise in July, Madison involved himself in what is known as the Great Debate (August 6 to September 10), which hammered out the specifics of the new constitution. Madison took a leading role in drafting the document, which prescribed a stronger role for central government while preserving political stability through a system of checks and balances between the different levels and branches of government. Madison borrowed from the French political philosophers the idea of a system of

countervailing power where state governments, a bicameral federal legislature, an independent judiciary, and an elected president exercise sovereign power on behalf of the people.

The Federalist Papers

When the Constitutional Convention finished its work in 1787, it faced the task of winning ratification. Special conventions of delegates elected by qualified voters had to approve the new constitution in at least nine states. Success was by no means assured. Many ordinary citizens, including veterans of the American Revolution, felt that the Constitution gave too much power to the federal government and threatened the liberties of individual citizens. People of this political persuasion came to be known as "anti-federalists." They cautioned against trading the tyranny of British king George III for a regime of homegrown authoritarians. In response to anti-federalist criticisms published in New York, a group of the Constitution's supporters published *The Federalist Papers,* a series of 85 essays. They appeared in the *New York Independent Journal* under the name of Publius. The real authors were Alexander Hamilton (delegate to the Constitutional Congress, later secretary of the Treasury under George Washington), John Jay (later chief justice of the Supreme Court), and James Madison. The anti-federalist argument drew on two centuries of experience with Great Britain. They held that tyranny thrived in the concentration of power. By definition, the way to secure liberty was to disperse power and settle outstanding public issues through the democratic vote. The Federalists, including Madison, held that although sovereignty rested with the people, the public good could better be secured through the deliberations of informed and dispassionate representative legislators than through the direct action of the people. Under the system of representative democracy, legislators would be less likely to be driven to unwise action by a temporary passion or by narrow interests. Madison also argued against the popular belief that liberty was best protected by local government through state legislatures. He felt that a federal government, because of its size and diversity, would better advance the public good and protect liberty. It would not be as easily dominated by local interests or factions as the state legislatures. In the end, Madison and his coauthors convinced the nation of their case. The Constitution was ratified in the summer of 1788.

The Bill of Rights

Madison's nationalist perspective and his association with Federalists and northerners like Hamilton and Jay gained him enemies in his home state of Virginia. Patrick Henry and other Virginia politicians blocked Madison's bid for the U.S. Senate, but Madison was able to win election to the House of Representatives where he served from 1789 to 1797. While serving in the House of Representatives, Madison helped to author the Bill of Rights. Madison's version included 19 different items. In 1791 the states approved 10 of them. These became the first 10 amendments to the Constitution. These amendments protected individual liberties against encroachment by government and assured that basic freedoms, such as the right to speak freely, were protected—even against the democratic majority.

Madison and Jefferson and the Formation of Political Parties

One of the things that makes James Madison interesting is that he changed his political positions to take into account the changing political situation. During the period when the relatively weak Articles of Confederation were in force (from 1783 to 1788), Madison argued for a stronger central government. But once the Constitution was in force, Madison turned his attention to the defense of individual and states' rights. Not only did he advocate the establishment of a bill of rights, he also helped to found a political party—the Democratic-Republicans—that was dedicated to making sure that the central government did not infringe on the liberties of its citizens. Led by Representative Madison and the nation's first secretary of state, Thomas Jefferson, the Democratic-Republicans stood in opposition to the Federalist policies that came to dominate the presidential administrations of George Washington and John Adams.

Madison as Secretary of State

In the election of 1800 the Democratic-Republican Thomas Jefferson won the presidency. In 1801 he appointed Madison secretary of state. Madison assumed the office as conflicts with Britain and France were intensifying as a result of the Napoleonic Wars (1793–1815). Until 1803 U.S. ships traded with all parties with little interference, but during Jefferson's second term both Great Britain and France tried to stop the United States from trading with their opponent by establishing blockades, seizing ships, and in the case of the British, even "impressing," kidnapping, U.S. sailors to serve on their warships. Neither Madison nor Jefferson were able to do much to stop these affronts by the powerful European nations. Instead, their attempts to force Great Britain and France to cooperate with the United States by restricting their access to U.S. trade with an embargo hurt the economy of the northeastern United States, and gave new strength to the deteriorating Federalist party. Nevertheless, the Democratic-Republicans kept control of Congress in the 1808 elections, and their candidate for the presidency, James Madison, was victorious.

Madison as President

James Madison, the fourth president of the United States, served for two terms. Madison's administration was dominated by the continuing conflict with Great Britain. Pressured by the "war hawks" in Congress, and unable to resolve the situation through diplomacy, Madison asked for and received a declaration of war against Great Britain in 1812. Leading the federal government in its first war in defense of the national interest, Madison did so with a limited means of communicating with the citizenry to gather support, a government with few financial or bureaucratic resources, and a small and ineffective military. While several attempts to conquer Canada were failures, and Washington D.C., was attacked and burned, Britain was unwilling to devote itself to a long war with the United States on the heels of its battles with France, and peace was made in 1814. Although little was gained by the War of 1812, the very fact that the United States had stood up to the powerful military of Great Britain and held onto its own gave Americans a new sense of unity and confidence.

During the final years of his presidency, in the wake of the war, Madison was able to turn his attention to domestic issues. He recommended the building of canals and roads and the establishment of a national university and new national bank. His endorsement of the bank was striking in that it revealed an evolution in his thought. Undogmatic in his philosophy, he was flexible when he felt it would serve the interests of the nation. As the first president to guide the Constitution through a war, Madison had learned that a more advanced financial system would improve military preparedness as well as foster the growth of the economy as a whole. Committed to securing U.S. economic independence and prosperity, his administration concluded a limited trade agreement with the erstwhile enemy, the British, in 1816. By the time his second term ended the next year, the United States was stronger than ever before, and Madison's term ushered in what came to be known as the "Era of Good Feelings" for his successor, James Monroe.

Post-presidential Years

After the end of his second term in 1817, Madison followed the two-term tradition set by President Washington and retired to Montpelier, Virginia. He avoided public activities, but he spent a good deal of time corresponding on public issues. He advised President James Monroe on foreign affairs, arranged his own papers for posthumous publication and, like his predecessor, Jefferson, involved himself in scientific agriculture. He supported Jefferson's new University of Virginia, and even became the rector (leading officer) upon Jefferson's death. He continued his outspoken opposition to slavery and headed the American Colonization Society, which supported efforts to relocate slaves to Africa, for a short time. (The United States supported the creation of Liberia for freed slaves in 1823 during the James Monroe presidency.) Though Madison was a critic of slavery, he felt the United States would never reconcile itself to a free black population. Madison died in 1836 without freeing his slaves. Dolley Madison moved back to Washington, D.C., after his death and resumed a major role in the capital's social scene. She died on July 12, 1849, at the age of 81 almost destitute. The expense of her spendthrift son's debts had forced her to sell Madison's papers to a sentimental Congress. She had even sold Montpelier. In 1858 her remains were moved to the Madison family plot at Montpelier.

The James Madison Administrations

The War of 1812, which came to be known as Madison's war, dominated the Madison administration. As president, Madison had to deal with the initial resistance to the war, the inept prosecution of the war, and the problems of ineffectual military command. Support or nonsupport for the war was partisan and regional. In the end, the Treaty of Ghent, which ended the war, reaffirmed the boundaries that existed before the war. Despite this, when the War of 1812 came to an end it was remembered as a U.S. victory that inaugurated a period of patriotic consensus known as the "Era of Good Feelings" under Madison's successor, James Monroe.

Madison Becomes President

Campaign of 1808

During the Washington administration the two-party system had emerged particularly in the cabinet where the factions struggled over the new country's finances. The Federalists prevailed through the Federalist presidency of John Adams until the formidable Democratic-Republican Thomas Jefferson won the election of 1800.

On domestic issues, the Democratic-Republicans spoke for the southern planters and the small "yeoman" farmers. The Federalists supported the expansion of trade and manufacture, higher protective tariffs, and strong monetary policies—all under the political tutelage of the wealthy urban classes. In foreign relations, the Democratic-Republicans favored the French Revolution and remained hostile to monarchist Britain, while the Federalists championed Great Britain. Compared to former Treasury secretary and undisputed Federalist leader Alexander Hamilton's extreme nationalism, the Democratic-Republicans (including Madison) favored limited federal power and supported the election of Jefferson in 1800. The Democratic-Republican Party retained control of the presidency through the administrations of Jefferson, Madison, and James Monroe. When Andrew Jackson won the presidential election in 1828 the victorious party became known simply as the Democrats.

It was not until Andrew Jackson's tenure (1828–36) that anything resembling a modern U.S. presidential election took place. In Madison's time, the party leaders (the caucus of party members in Congress) picked the candidate, and the candidate did little public campaigning. In the election of 1808, Madison was supported by Jefferson's wing of the Democratic-Republican Party. His chief rival for the party nomination was fellow Virginian James Monroe, a prominent diplomat and politician. Governor George Clinton of New York attracted the support of northeasterners who wanted to break the hold of the Virginians over the presidency (John Adams was the only U.S. president up to that time who was not from Virginia).

The Federalists supported Charles Cotesworth Pinckney of South Carolina. Although Madison lost four of the five New England states and part of New York, he won the election with 122 electoral votes to Pinckney's 47. (George Clinton also received six electoral votes.)

Campaign of 1812

In May 1812 the Democratic-Republican Party leadership nominated Madison for his second term as president. Partly to achieve regional balance, Madison chose Elbridge Gerry of Massachusetts as his running mate. George Clinton had died in office in April 1812. DeWitt Clinton, the maverick Democratic-Republican lieutenant governor of New York and nephew of George Clinton,

Administration

Administration Dates

March 4, 1809–March 4, 1813
March 4, 1813–March 4, 1817

Vice President

George Clinton (1809–12)
Elbridge Gerry (1813–14)

Cabinet

Secretary of State

Robert Smith (1809–11)
James Monroe (1811–17)

Secretary of the Treasury

Albert Gallatin (1801–14)
George W. Campbell (1814)
Alexander J. Dallas (1814–16)
William H. Crawford (1816–25)

Secretary of War

William Eustis (1809–13)
John Armstrong (1813–14)
James Monroe (1814–15)
William H. Crawford (1815–16)

Attorney General

Caesar A. Rodney (1807–11)
William Pinkney (1811–14)
Richard Rush (1814–17)

Secretary of the Navy

Robert Smith (1801–09)
Paul Hamilton (1809–12)
William Jones (1813–14)
Benjamin W. Crowninshield (1815–18)

Postmaster General

Gideon Granger (1801–14)
R. Jonathan Meigs Jr. (1814–23)

---

ran against Madison, attacking the War of 1812 as without cause and Madison as an incompetent leader of the war effort. Clinton, who received widespread Federalist support throughout the northeast, sought to appeal to both supporters and opponents of the war by demanding a stronger war effort while at the same time asking for a quick return to peace. His confusing positions failed him, and Madison carried 128 electoral votes and 11 states, against Clinton, who received 89 electoral votes and carried seven states.

Madison's Advisers

Madison had problems with his cabinet from the very beginning. He made his appointments with an eye towards creating geographical balance and making alliances with powerful forces inside the party. Cabinet positions were not much sought after since they did not pay well and conveyed little prestige. Most departments of government had small budgets and consisted of just a few clerks. The most reliable member of Thomas Jefferson's cabinet had been the Swiss-born secretary of the Treasury, Albert Gallatin. Though not well liked by his fellow Democratic-Republicans, Gallatin had proved his worth by reducing the federal deficit. Madison wanted to make Gallatin secretary of state in his own cabinet, but

he gave in to Senate opposition and reappointed him head of the Treasury Department. Gallatin also distinguished himself as an able negotiator when Madison dispatched him to Ghent, in Belgium where he negotiated the peace treaty ending the War of 1812 (*See also,* Foreign Issues). Along with retired president Thomas Jefferson, Gallatin was Madison's most valuable adviser.

Madison's other cabinet selections nearly crippled his presidency. Given the strained relations with Great Britain, and the fact that Jefferson's Embargo Act was in place (which imposed a ban on goods leaving U.S. ports) when Madison assumed the presidency. The positions of secretary of war and secretary of the navy were critical. But Madison appointed men with little military experience. Secretary of War William Eustis had been a congressman and a surgeon during the American Revolution (1775–83). He was forced to resign after the campaign against Canada failed during the War of 1812. Paul Hamilton served as secretary of the navy from 1809 to 1812. Hamilton called for building up the U.S. fleet and waging a war of harassment, while avoiding pitched battles with the much stronger British navy. (The British had 80 ships compared to a dozen ships in the U.S. fleet.) Unfortunately, Paul Hamilton was an alcoholic, and Madison had to replace him after an episode of public drunkenness. Madison's secretary of state, Robert Smith, was allied with a group of disgruntled senators (*See also,* Madison and Congress) and Madison fired him in 1811, replacing him with future president James Monroe. Although Madison's cabinet choices, especially Eustis and Hamilton, brought him justified criticism, the disorganized state of the cabinet was in large part a result of an immature, understaffed, and unprofessional government attempting to conduct one of the most difficult executive functions—war.

Madison and Congress

Madison was president during the Eleventh, Twelfth, Thirteenth, and Fourteenth Congresses. The Democratic-Republicans held a strong majority in both houses throughout his presidency. More and more the West was figuring into national politics, and political leaders were coming from that part of the country.

The "War Hawks"

In 1810 a new, younger, and more belligerent group of national leaders from the West were elected to the twelfth Congress. Upon taking office, they elected 34-year-old Kentucky representative Henry Clay as Speaker of the House and proceeded to call for war against Great Britain. These "war hawks," including Thomas Hart Benton of Missouri and John C. Calhoun of South Carolina, were concerned over Great Britain's repeated violations of the nation's neutrality, the impressment of U.S. seamen, and British incursions into U.S. waters. They also attributed American Indian uprisings in Ohio, Michigan, and Indiana to the British. Two Shawnees, Chief Tecumseh and his brother Tenskwatawa (known as the Prophet) had been attempting since about 1805 to build an Indian confederation to halt white encroachment. In 1810 American Indian attacks targeted frontier settlers. Democratic-Republicans attributed the uprising to the agitation of British agents. Additionally they were pushing for war in the hopes of bringing about the annexation of Canada, Florida, and Texas.

Opponents of War

Northern Federalists, many of whom were merchants engaged in trade relationships with the British, opposed war. However, in June 1812 Madison gave in to the saber rattling war hawks and asked for a declaration of war. It was passed later that month by both the House and the Senate, although only by a slim margin. At the time there were not sufficient revenues to support a war, and Madison's failure to provide strong leadership produced little enthusiasm in Congress for war preparations. Congress passed no war tax and made no provision to increase the navy. The governors of the New England states failed to supply state militias to fight the war. Troops sometimes refused to cross outside the boundaries of their particular state.

Furthermore, there was fierce opposition to the war by a group of Democratic-Republicans senators known as the Invincibles. Led by Senator Samuel Smith of Maryland, who had the support of his brother, Secretary of State Robert Smith (*See also,* Madison's Advisers), the Invincibles had opposed Thomas Jefferson's programs and now carried their opposition over to Madison. These senators favored the British and preferred the occasional seizure of ships over the suspension of trade.

Another example of Madison's ineffectual relations with Congress was his failure to renew the charter of the Bank of the United States (BUS). Anti-federalist feelings among the Democratic-Republicans, and personal dislike of Treasury Secretary Gallatin underlay opposition to the bank. Gallatin argued that the bank was necessary to finance the war effort. Madison's political enemies were so obstructionist that Gallatin offered to resign. However, Madison intervened and asked for Secretary of State Robert Smith's resignation. Smith refused and demanded to be fired in order to smear the administration in the press. He charged Madison with being in collusion with the French. In order to repair this political disaster, Madison fired Smith and asked fellow Virginian James Monroe to become secretary of state.

Congress and the First Amendment

Madison, like his predecessor Jefferson, tried to avoid vetoing bills. However, on several occasions he was forced to because of the antagonism directed his way from Congress. His first vetoes resulted from controversies over religious freedom. Congress had passed a bill that gave a small parcel of land in the Mississippi Territory to the Salem Meeting House Baptists. Another bill proposed the incorporation of an Episcopal church in Alexandria, Virginia (then part of the District of Columbia), thereby giving government endorsement to the Episcopal Church. Madison, who years before had written the separation of church and state into both the Virginia state constitution and the Bill of Rights, refused to sign either bill. In the Mississippi case he cited the First Amendment, which prohibits the government establishment of religion. In the Alexandria case, he noted that the bill violated not only the prohibition against the establishment of religion but gave the Church a state-sanctioned role in education and in caring for the poor. Madison argued that these functions were a "public and civic duty" that the state could not confer upon a church.

Madison and the Judiciary

The relationship of the Democratic-Republican Party to the Supreme Court had been strained ever since the John Adams administration (*See also,* John Adams Administration). The relationship between Madison and the judicial branch of government was shaped in large part by the decisive actions of the Federalist head of the Supreme Court, John Marshall. Coincidentally, Madison's name is attached to the 1803 decision *Marbury v. Madison* in which Marshall succeeded in expanding judicial authority (*See also,* John Adams Administration).

During his own administration Madison continued to uphold the power of the judicial system and sought to strengthen the system of checks and balances. One example of this was the case of *Olmstead v. Rittenhouse.* Olmstead, a U.S. prisoner on a British ship, managed to overtake his captors and claimed the ship as a sea prize (a ship or cargo captured during wartime). He then encountered a U.S. ship, and this ship confiscated the sea prize for the state of Pennsylvania. Olmstead took the state of Pennsylvania (Rittenhouse was the state treasurer) to court to get the prize returned. In 1803 the federal courts ruled in favor of the plaintiff (Olmstead), but a decade later Justice John Marshall was still trying to get Pennsylvania to pay Olmstead. Eventually, Marshall ordered a federal marshal to arrest the defendants, but Simon Snyder, the Democratic-Republican governor of Pennsylvania, called out the state militia to protect them. The governor asked President Madison to intervene on the side of the state, but Madison responded that the executive of the United States is not only unauthorized to prevent the execution of the decree sanctioned by the Supreme Court, but is required to carry it out. Madison came down against his own party and on the side of a balance between the separate branches of government.

Madison very much wanted to reduce the influence of the Federalists and John Marshall in the Court while maintaining regional balance. His opportunity came with the death of one of the justices, William Cushing. After considering Levi Lincoln, the first attorney general in the Jefferson administration as a replacement for Cushing, Madison fixed upon Alexander Wolcott of Connecticut. When his confirmation was defeated in the Senate (nine for and 24 against), Madison decided to wait. Then, while the Congress was not in session, Justice Samuel Chase of Maryland died, creating a second vacancy. Madison settled on his comptroller of the Treasury, Gabriel Duvall of Maryland. For the second position, Madison, against Jefferson's opinion, chose Congressman Joseph Story of Massachusetts. He had offered the position to John Quincy Adams, then U.S. minister to Russia, but Adams did not want it. Both Duvall and Story were confirmed when Congress reconvened in 1811 with such little difficulty that the vote was not even recorded.

Changes in the U.S. Government

The War of 1812 has been credited as the event that finally gave the United States a sense of nationhood. Prior to the war personal allegiances were usually focused on the state or the locality. The war pulled the country together and focused its attention on the greatness of the nation. To U.S. citizens at that time, the nation had stood up to Great Britain, the preeminent military power in the world. This was a genuine source of pride for an underdeveloped, agricultural country with no real professional military and little industry. The fact that the nation survived despite its disorganized leadership made both possible and necessary the task of innovating a system of government.

Another important aspect of the government during Madison's presidency was that the Constitution proved to be both effective and durable. Despite all of the problems with the states over militias and finances, the Constitution suffered no important change during those years. It established the framework of relations between the different branches and levels of government.

During the Madison administration, Louisiana was admitted as the 18th state to the Union on April 30, 1812; and Indiana was admitted as the 19th state on December 11, 1816.

Domestic Issues

When Madison was sworn in for his first administration, the United States consisted of 17 states and a large new territory extending from the Ohio River to the Rocky Mountains (the Louisiana Purchase). Nearly 85 percent of the population lived on farms or plantations. Voting was limited to white males, and in many areas—especially in the South—even white males faced disenfranchisement, or deprivation of the right to vote, due to property requirements. The U.S. population was between seven and eight million, and there were about four million slaves. American Indians east of the Mississippi River were gradually losing control of their homelands to American settlers, a trend that would be hastened by their unsuccessful alliance with the British during the War of 1812.

Communication in the interior was poor. There were no railroads, and roads, canals, and bridges were primitive at best. The United States played the same trading role in relation to Europe that it had in colonial days. It exchanged agricultural goods—such as cotton, corn, fish, furs, wheat, and bacon—for comparatively exotic goods like silks, spices, sugar, wine, calicoes, and lace. Farm communities depended on long-term credit, and farmers had little cash. They traded shares of their crops for rented land or for the necessities that they got from merchants.

Rechartering the Bank of the United States

When Alexander Hamilton, secretary of the Treasury under President George Washington, urged the charter of the first Bank of the United States (BUS) in 1791,

Thomas Jefferson, Washington's secretary of state, felt that the Constitution did not give the government power to create a bank. Nevertheless, Hamilton prevailed and the first BUS was incorporated for 20 years in 1791. It was located in Philadelphia, Pennsylvania, and had a 25-member board of directors and eight branch offices. It served as a fiscal agent of the U.S. government, which was its principal stockholder and customer. Though it was profitable, many Democratic-Republicans, who favored a weak central government, bitterly opposed it, claiming it was unconstitutional, that it favored northern money interests, and that it violated states' rights and responsibilities. Because of this opposition, the charter was not renewed in 1811. After the charter expired, there was disorder. State banks did not have the specie (gold and silver) reserves to back the paper currency they issued. Furthermore, the federal government no longer had a safe depository for its funds. At the conclusion of the War of 1812, there was a spirit of nationalism, and the Democratic-Republicans were more objective and receptive to the bank. Congress granted a second 20-year charter in 1816.

The Bonus Bill

Although sounding a bit like a Federalist in his support for the second national bank, Madison remained a strict constructionist, favoring states' rights and urging a strict interpretation of the Constitution. One of his final acts in office was to veto a Bonus Bill that was supported by powerful senators, John C. Calhoun of South Carolina and Henry Clay of Kentucky. This legislation proposed that $1.5 million left over from the charter of the BUS in 1816 be used to build roads and canals. Madison himself had repeatedly cajoled the Congress to pass legislation for much needed internal improvements. However, he also felt the Constitution required an amendment to allow Congress to increase its powers to carry out such public works. Madison felt the general welfare clause of the Constitution was not broad enough to cover such spending. To Clay's and Calhoun's surprise, Madison's veto was sustained after he left office. Madison was asserting the responsibility of the president to protect the Constitution, and the principle that precedence was a proper guide to determining constitutionality. The original signers of the Constitution had not considered canals and roads within their jurisdiction, and Congress should not open a new area of authority without a clear amendment to do so. So, although he supported the activity, he rejected the legislation.

Foreign Issues

The United States engaged in active commercial relations with Europe in the early years of the nineteenth century. Foreign trade was profitable, but troublesome. By flying a neutral flag and trading with both of the main belligerents in the Napoleonic Wars (1803–15)—France and Great Britain—the U.S. merchant marine was making money. But in June 1807 a British frigate, the *Leopard,* fired on a U.S. warship, the *Chesapeake,* inside U.S. territorial waters. The British boarded the U.S. ship, removed four deserters from the British navy, and hung one of them. Madison's predecessor, Thomas Jefferson, responded to the challenge in an unexpected way—one that was guaranteed to hurt the U.S. economy much more than the British. He simply imposed a total embargo on goods leaving U.S. ports.

This self-imposed blockade was a remarkable policy decision. For one thing, it certainly demonstrated how anxious Americans were to avoid the humiliation of being boarded and searched for deserters from the British navy. But it also stirred the pot of factionalism in the United States, because the Federalists, mostly wealthy merchants and bankers, were heavily engaged in shipping on the northeast coast and most hurt by the embargo. They might be angry at the British for boarding ships and impressing sailors, but they were much more worried about their profits from trade. With the exception of smuggling, the embargo stopped trade. U.S. exports dropped from $108 million in 1807 to $22 million a year later. For example, exports in sea island cotton fell from almost nine million pounds in 1807, to only one million in 1808. Wheat brought 40 percent less in 1809 than in 1804. By 1809 U.S. farm prices were depressed and merchants were suffering. New England merchants and bankers, who tended to be Federalists, were particularly upset at the reductions in trade; but Democratic-Republican plantation owners from the South and farmers from the mid-Atlantic states also were suffering.

The War of 1812 (1812–14)

Fervor mounted as the war hawks, led by Henry Clay and John C. Calhoun (*See also,* Madison and Congress), persuaded Madison and members of Congress that the British were aiding the American Indians, impressment was on the increase, and the economy was stagnating with Britain controlling the seas. When the War of 1812 began, the United States had a navy with 17 ships and an army with fewer than five thousand troops. The U.S. War Department consisted of only the secretary and 11 clerks, and none of these had over a year of experience. The officer corps consisted of a few men left over from the American Revolution (1775–83) and some untried youth. However, the war hawks in Congress were clamoring for war, because they wanted to claim more territory for the young republic. The United States was not only unprepared for war, it had no idea how unprepared it was. With the U.S. population of almost eight million and Canada, then still a British colony, with a population of only 500,000, many of whom were American Indians, Democratic-Republicans thought taking Canada would involve simply marching in.

On August 24, 1814, British troops entered Washington, D.C. Retaliating for the U.S. raid on Canada's capitol city of York, the British set the Capitol, the White House, and other public buildings on fire. (National Archives and Records Administration.)

The U.S. strategy was to invade Canada and take control of the St. Lawrence River. The generals planned a three-pronged attack. One army, commanded by Henry Dearborn, was to advance along Lake Champlain, between New York and Quebec, and take Montreal. Meanwhile, Gen. Stephen Van Rensselaer was supposed to attack across the Niagara River into western New York. Gen. William Hull was to attack across the Detroit River and take Fort Malden near Windsor, Ontario. Yet even with the British military officers still fighting French emperor Napoleon in Europe, all three attacks failed. The campaigns in one way or another all were stymied by overextended lines of supply, inexperienced generals and troops, and widespread refusal of the militia to cross outside U.S. territory. Many in the state militia refused even to cross outside their own state. For them, sovereignty stopped at the state line. While they were willing to defend their state, they would not risk their lives for their country. The writing of the Constitution had allowed the political luminaries like Madison to think through the questions of sovereignty and the balance of authority between states and the nation. But now these same issues were being raised in a very different arena, perhaps with less eloquence but certainly with more urgency. Each soldier had to decide what to do when his commander ordered him to march across the border into Canada. Capt. Zachary Taylor's (later president of the United States) sole U.S.

victory in the northern campaign during his defense of Fort Harrison against an assault by American Indians, was fought well south of the border with Canada in Indiana territory.

Tide Turns for the United States

At sea, the British were able to drive off most of the U.S. navy, but the Americans were able to win a few small battles. The most notable of these was the sinking of the HMS *Guerriere* by the USS *Constitution*.

In the following year, 1813, there was a somewhat more successful invasion of Canada. On September 10, 1813, a victory by Oliver Hazard Perry near Detroit, Michigan, destroyed the British fleet on Lake Erie. This defeat forced a British retreat to the east. In pursuit, the Americans burned the Canadian capital at York, and a victory was gained over a combined British and American Indian force at the Battle of the Thames (Moraviantown) under the armies of William Henry Harrison, who would later become the ninth president of the United States. In that battle, the Shawnee Indian leader Tecumseh was killed while fighting alongside the British. However, a second attempt at Montreal, with one force invading up from Lake Champlain and another advancing down the St. Lawrence from Lake Ontario, failed. In the end, U.S. forces were never able to establish control over Canada.

Biography:

Tecumseh

Chief; warrior (1768–1813) Of all the attempts by American Indians to resist white encroachment, few efforts equal those put forth by Tecumseh. The young Shawnee grew up to be a distinguished warrior, angry at white settlers who drove his people further and further west after purchasing land from individual tribes. An eloquent speaker, Tecumseh argued that no land could be sold by any single tribe because all lands belonged to all tribes. He centered his argument around the 1795 Treaty of Greenville, which was made between the U.S. government and all American Indian tribes. The treaty guaranteed title of all unceded land to the tribes in common. Tecumseh further argued that if American Indians acted as a group, they would embody the strength of a collective whole. Aided by his bother, Tenskwatawa (Prophet), Tecumseh attempted to unite all tribes, from the Great Lakes to the Gulf of Mexico, in organized opposition to white encroachment. Tecumseh and his brother urged

their people to forego the sale of Indian land, to reject European ways, and to renew Indian traditions. They were further aided by the British who, seeking allies against American troops, supplied Tecumseh with weapons, munitions, and clothing. During the Battle of Tippecanoe the number of Indian casualties

was great, and cost Tecumseh many followers who became disillusioned to his cause. During the War of 1812, a much-diminished band of warriors fought with Tecumseh alongside British troops. Tecumseh held the rank of brigadier general when he was killed by forces of William Henry Harrison at the Battle of the Thames.

In early 1814 after defeating Napoleon in Europe, the British turned their attention to the U.S. war. Both the British and many Americans believed that the United States would be defeated. While the British blockade around the U.S. coast was effective in cutting off U.S. trade, the British strategy of a three-pronged attack against the United States proved largely unsuccessful. The British navy did enter Chesapeake Bay, an inlet of the Atlantic in Virginia and Maryland; and, in retaliation for burning York, burned Washington. However, even after an all-night bombardment of Fort McHenry in Baltimore, Maryland, Britain could not take the city. (This was the battle that inspired Francis Scott Key to write the "Star Spangled Banner"). A British drive across New York with an army of 10,000 troops was beaten back at Plattsburgh, New York, and Capt. Thomas MacDough won the naval battle of Lake Champlain. The British troops retreated back to Canada, fearful of running out of supplies. When news of the U.S. victory at Plattsburgh reached peace negotiators at Ghent, Belgium, the British eased their territorial demands.

A third British force suffered a defeat at the hands of Gen. Andrew Jackson at the Battle of New Orleans in Louisiana. It is now clear that this battle actually took place after the signing of the peace treaty; but since news of the U.S. victory and the signing of the treaty in Europe arrived almost simultaneously, Americans felt this battle also had helped win the war. This victory changed public perception of Madison. It was no longer Madison's

war but a U.S. victory. He became almost immediately a very popular president.

Treaty of Ghent

The United States was represented by the negotiating team of John Quincy Adams, Albert Gallatin, Henry Clay, James Bayard, and Jonathan Russell. The British had agreed to a meeting at Ghent, Belgium, as an alternative to mediation by Czar Alexander I, of Russia. Mediation under the czar between Britain and the United States had been going on since before the war, starting in 1809. The British went into the negotiations for ending the war with strong demands. They saw themselves as victors, or likely victors, once they turned their full force against the United States. Their demands were for no U.S. fishing off the Grand Banks (possibly the richest fishing area in the world off the shores of Newfoundland); a U.S.-Canada-Indian boundary favoring British traders and trappers; expanded Canadian territory in the Northwest; the removal of U.S. naval forces from the Great Lakes; and complete British navigational access to the Mississippi River basin.

But after the U.S. victory in Baltimore and the British retreat at Plattsburgh, British public opinion became so angered at the United States, that newspapers and members of the British Parliament demanded the national hero and conqueror of Napoleon at Waterloo in Belgium, the Duke of Wellington, be sent to command

British troops. Wellington, however, declined the offer indicating that he had no expectation of success in the United States and, furthermore, he indicated he really was not in full support of the war. This was the turning point.

Britain was war weary. It was tired of war taxes. Its alliance with Russia against France was shaky, and discussions at the Congress of Vienna, an international conference that was called to create a balance of power and to preserve peace in Europe after the fall of Napoleon, were not going well. Another concern was that the victory over France was not secure, and some thought that Napoleon might rally. This led the British to compromise with the Americans. Both parties agreed to return the boundaries as they were before the war; the treaty provided for restoration of all conquered territory and for the appointment of a commission to determine the disputed U.S.-Canada border. The remaining issues were set aside for later consideration. An agreement was signed December 24, 1814.

End of the War and the Hartford Convention

One of the major impacts of the British blockade was to increase New England's hostility toward what was called Madison's war. By 1814 opposition to the war was so great that the leading Federalists of New England met in Hartford, Connecticut. They proposed several constitutional amendments that they felt would prevent such a war from happening again. Although a move to secede from the Union was headed off, the Hartford Convention passed a number of resolutions for a restructured relationship between the northeastern states and the rest of the nation, including a single term presidency and a two-thirds congressional vote to admit new states or declare war. But the Hartford Convention coincided with the announcement of the end of the War of 1812. This coincidence threw the loyalty of the Federalists at Hartford into doubt. The timing of the end of the war cast the Hartford conventioneers in such a negative light that it signaled the end of the Federalist Party.

Westward Expansion

Another outcome of the War of 1812 was the continuation of westward expansion. The western migration that in the end would turn the United States away from Europe and towards its own interior got an important boost from the Louisiana Purchase and the Lewis and Clark expedition of 1804 to 1806 (*See also,* Thomas Jefferson Administration). Many New Englanders had lost their jobs in the shipping industry during the course of the war and decided to migrate west to begin a new life. The War of 1812 gave Americans the security to continue westward expansion because several hostile American Indian forces were put down on the western frontier during the course of the war. The fact that U.S. attention was focused on the West meant that it held a relatively isolationist posture in relation to Europe. It would be more than a century before the United States would become involved in another European war. In the

Fast Fact

When it became known that the British were moving to attack Washington, D.C., during the War of 1812, Dolley Madison remained at the White House to supervise the removal of documents and other items, including the famous portrait of George Washington by Gilbert Stuart. The British later burned the White House, so these actions saved many priceless historical artifacts.

(Source: Michael Nelson, ed. *The Presidency A to Z,* 1994.)

1840s the ideology of westward expansion would become known as the United States's "manifest destiny."

The Madison Administration Legacy

Madison, although very popular by the end of his second administration, retired in the two-term tradition of his predecessors. His handpicked successor, James Monroe, was fortunate that the British enthusiasm for war had finally played out. Madison left the presidency a very popular figure.

Madison's greatest contributions came before the presidency as architect of the Constitution and his ability to foresee the kinds of political institutions the nation would need. As a president, Madison was not particularly effective. He failed to lead the people of the United States in what was a serious struggle for survival. Madison hobbled his own effectiveness and reputation with unwise cabinet appointments and with a seeming inability to communicate a sense of strong leadership to the Congress and the people.

Despite Madison's inability to lead and mobilize, the war was perceived in the end to have been won. This inspired a new sense of unity and national strength in a public that was still used to thinking of itself as citizens of a particular state first, and the United States second. The war solidified the hold of the United States in the Mississippi River basin, and helped to foster the idea of a coast-to-coast empire.

Even though the war nearly split the Union, it had been fought to establish the United States's neutrality rights and that had largely been accomplished. The Constitution held up despite the criticism it received in the Hartford Convention. Madison's final two years in office were dedicated to improving the infrastructure of the country. He proposed the rechartering of a national bank and the founding of a national university, suitable memorials to one of the architects of a new nation and a believer in democracy.

Sources

Boller Paul F., Jr. *Presidential Wives: An Anecdotal History.* New York: Oxford University Press, 1988.

Hickey, Donald R. *The War of 1812: A Forgotten Conflict.* Champaign-Urbana, Ill.: University of Illinois Press, 1990.

McCoy, Drew R. *The Last of the Fathers: James Madison and the Republican Legacy.* New York: Cambridge University Press, 1989.

Nelson, Michael, ed. *The Presidency A to Z.* Washington, D.C.: Congressional Quarterly, Inc., 1994.

Peterson, Merrill D., ed. *The Founding Fathers: James Madison.* New York: Harper and Row, 1974.

Rutland, Robert Allen. *The Presidency of James Madison.* Lawrence, Kans.: University Press of Kansas, 1990.

Staggs, J. C. A. *Mr. Madison's War.* Princeton, N.J.: Princeton University Press, 1983.

Taylor, George Rogers, ed. *The War of 1812: Past Justifications and Present Interpretations.* Westport, Conn.: Greenwood Press, 1974.

West's Encyclopedia of American Law. Minneapolis/St. Paul, Minn.: West Publishing, 1998.

Further Readings

Coles, Harry L. *The War of 1812.* Chicago: University of Chicago Press, 1965.

Doyle, William. *The Oxford History of the French Revolution.* New York: Oxford University Press, 1989.

Drake, Benjamin. *Life of Tecumseh.* Cincinnati, Ohio: Anderson, Gates and Wright, 1858. Reprint, North Stratford, N.H.: Ayer Company Publishers, 1988.

Edmunds, R. David. *Tecumseh and the Quest for Indian Leadership.* Boston: Little Brown, 1984.

Hamilton, Alexander, John Jay, and James Madison. *The Federalist.* New York: Random House, 1937.

Madison, James. *The Papers of James Madison.* 3 vols. Washington, D.C.: Langtree & O'Sullivan, 1840.

Matthews, Richard K. *If Men Were Angels: James Madison and the Heartless Empire of Reason.* Lawrence, Kans.: University Press of Kansas, 1996.

Rutland, Robert. *James Madison and the American Nation, 1751–1836: An Encyclopedia.* New York: Simon and Shuster, 1996.

Whitaker, Arthur P. *The Mississippi Question, 1795–1803: A Study in Trade, Politics, and Diplomacy.* New York: Appleton-Century, 1934.

Monroe Administrations

Biography

Monroe was the last of the Revolutionary War (1775–83) heroes to serve as U.S. president. A Virginia landowner and a member of the political and social elite, Monroe enjoyed great opportunities but also assumed considerable responsibilities. He studied law under Thomas Jefferson as a youth and then embarked upon a life in politics, becoming the country's first career politician.

Early Life

James Monroe was born in Westmoreland County, Virginia, on April 28, 1758. Like Presidents George Washington and James Madison before him, both of whom were also born in Westmoreland County, Monroe left the area as a youth and was not associated with it in his adult life. His father was Spence Monroe and his mother, Elizabeth Jones Monroe. In his autobiography, written after he left the presidency, Monroe gave little detail about his early life. Spence's grandfather, Andrew Monroe, had emigrated from Scotland in 1650 after receiving a land grant, but by the time of James's birth, Spence, a descendant of one of Andrew's younger sons, owned only five hundred acres. This amounted to enough of an estate to make the Monroes part of the gentry, but at the lower end of the scale. Like many young men of his time who were raised on a plantation, young Monroe was given a great degree of freedom, and he developed a lasting interest in riding and hunting. He also developed an interest in farming, and continued throughout his life of public service to regard himself as a farmer by profession.

Full name: James Monroe

Personal Information:
Born: April 28, 1758
Birthplace: Virginia
Died: July 4, 1831
Death place: New York, New York
Burial place: Gouverneur Vault, Second Street Cemetery, New York, N.Y.; moved in 1858 to Hollywood Cemetery, Richmond, Va.
Religion: Episcopalian
Spouse: Elizabeth Kortright (m. 1786)
Children: Eliza; Maria
Education: Attended College of William and Mary
Occupation: Farmer; lawyer; diplomat; legislator; governor
Political Party: Democratic-Republican Party
Age at Inauguration: 58 years

James Monroe. (The Library of Congress.)

Of all of Monroe's relatives, only one was politically active, Elizabeth Monroe's brother Joseph Jones. Jones was a patriot who served in the Virginia House of Burgesses prior to the revolution, and then in the Congress from 1777 to 1783. Later, he was appointed to the Virginia Supreme Court, where he served for 16 years until his death in 1805. Monroe and his uncle became especially close after Spence Monroe died in early 1774, leaving James, the eldest son, the estate as well as the responsibility of completing the education of his brothers and sister and seeing them established in life. With his uncle's help, James Monroe managed the family's affairs, but he acquired more than advice. His uncle gave him an introduction into the world of politics.

Education

Monroe's formal education began at the age of 11, when he was enrolled at Campbelltown Academy. It was considered to be the best school in the entire colony of Virginia and had a total enrollment of only 25 students. At Campbelltown Monroe became friends with his classmate John Marshall, the future chief justice of the United States. The two remained close until political differences in the 1790s placed them in opposite camps.

Monroe studied at Campbelltown for more than four years, until his father died, and his uncle Joseph, execu-

tor of the estate, removed him from the school. Encouraged by his uncle to pursue a career in politics, Monroe entered William and Mary College in June 1774.

At William and Mary, which was in the colonial capital of Williamsburg, Monroe began his course of study, but the political activity of the day quickly turned the focus more toward politics and away from math, Latin, and letters. The long conflict between the king of England and the American colonists was reaching a climax, and the center of action was the city of Williamsburg, where the students began to take an active part in the rebellion against the crown. At the age of 17, Monroe took part in a raid against the governor's palace, where he and 23 others removed two hundred muskets and three hundred swords and gave them to the Williamsburg militia. In the spring of 1776 Monroe left the college and enlisted in the Third Virginia Infantry.

After spending two and one-half years fighting for independence in the American Revolution (1775–83), Monroe returned to Virginia, unsure of what he would do next. It was at this time that Monroe was introduced by his uncle Joseph to the governor of Virginia, the internationally renowned Thomas Jefferson. Jefferson had a decisive influence on Monroe's life, advising him to prepare for a career in politics by studying law. So Monroe reentered William and Mary in 1780 and began reading law under Jefferson's direction. Monroe and Jefferson quickly developed a strong and lasting friendship. When later that year the capital of Virginia was moved to Richmond, Monroe left the college and followed his mentor Jefferson.

Family Life

Monroe married Elizabeth Kortright on February 16, 1786, when he was 27 years old and she was 20. Elizabeth Monroe has been described as a person who, in public, seemed cold and reserved, but in private, "she was a devoted wife and a doting mother, possessing to the full the domestic virtues then so highly prized—a complete absorption in the affairs of her family and household and a total detachment from the world of politics and business" (Ammon, p. 62). The two were married in New York, where they met while Monroe was serving as a member of the Continental Congress, the precursor to the U.S. Congress. The two stayed there only a short time. In October of 1786, when Monroe's term in Congress was over, the two moved to Virginia. In December of that same year they had their first child, Eliza. Their other two children, a son who died as an infant, and their second daughter, Maria, were born more than a decade later. The family eventually settled on an estate in Virginia that Monroe named Oak Hill, while maintaining a second home in Albemarle, Virginia, not far from the homes of his friends Thomas Jefferson and James Madison.

Eliza Monroe married George Hay when she was in her early twenties. Twenty years her senior, Hay was a well-known lawyer and was active in Virginia politics. After he and Eliza were married, he became Monroe's close friend and intimate adviser. In fact, for much of Monroe's presidency George and Eliza lived in the White House. While Eliza remained close to her father's political life and was actively involved in it (to the extent that women could be at the time), Maria Monroe was much more removed. She lived in the White House for only about a year, and after her marriage to her cousin Samuel Gouverneur at the White House, she moved to New York and rarely visited Washington or Virginia.

Career

Monroe in the Military

Monroe always considered himself a farmer by profession, but in reality he was the country's first career politician. From the time he entered William and Mary in 1774, he had been interested in a career in politics. He first served his country not as a politician, however, but as a soldier. Soon after he and John Mercer had enlisted in the Third Virginia Infantry in 1776, he was made an officer. Such a quick rise in that era was not uncommon for educated men of reputable families.

Within months the Third Virginia joined George Washington's army at Long Island, New York, where the bulk of the fighting against Great Britain was taking place. During his two and one-half years of military service, Monroe participated in some of the American Revolution's (1775–83) most historic occurrences. He was with Washington when he crossed the Delaware, and he spent the bitterly cold winter at Valley Forge. Monroe spent most of his service as an aide to Gen. Lord Stirling, one of George Washington's brigade commanders.

After two years as an aide, Monroe longed for his own command, but the surplus of officers made such advancement impossible. So he left his position with Stirling and sought to raise his own regiment in Virginia (this was both a common and a necessary measure at the time). At the recommendation of Gen. Washington, the Virginia legislature appointed Monroe a lieutenant-colonel. Still, he was unable to recruit enough soldiers to fill the ranks of a regiment. Though his preference at the time was continued military service, Monroe was sitting on the sidelines, frustrated and disappointed.

Monroe Enters Politics

In the spring of 1780 Monroe decided to return to a career in law and politics. He studied law with Thomas Jefferson, then governor of Virginia, for two years, then turned to politics, winning election in 1782 to the Virginia legislature. After one year, at the age of 25, he was named as a delegate to the Continental Congress, the forerunner to today's U.S. Congress, where he served until 1786. Jefferson was also a delegate at the time, and he introduced Monroe to another prominent Virginian, James Madison. The three would maintain a lifelong association, which would be upset only briefly by a rift between Madison and Monroe.

In Congress one of Monroe's primary concerns was the need for a stronger central government. He led a committee that drafted an amendment to the Articles of Confederation (the first written constitution of the United States) that would allow the government to regulate commerce. However, no action was taken on the measure. When action was finally taken to revise the Articles, at the Constitutional Convention in 1787, Monroe, though serving again in the Virginia legislature, was not selected as a delegate. (This was done out of a concern for Monroe's finances, which throughout much of his life remained troublesome. However, Monroe was very upset at not being included.) Notwithstanding his views in Congress, Monroe adopted an anti-federalist position, opposing the ratification of the Constitution because he believed it created a central government that was too strong. This reflected the high degree of centralization of power represented by the Constitution, compared to the Articles of Confederation.

By 1790 Monroe had spent four years in private life. He did serve in the Virginia legislature for much of that period, but outside the debates over ratification of the Constitution, that position was not full time. Though he enjoyed his private life and was pleased to be getting his finances in order, Monroe agreed, at the urging of his friends and colleagues, to represent Virginia in the Senate from 1790 to 1794. During that same period, Jefferson and Madison served as secretary of state and as a representative from Virginia. In the Senate Monroe was a leader and a founder of the newly developing Republican Party (later called the Democratic-Republican Party), which generally opposed the programs of Treasury Secretary Alexander Hamilton. Hamilton and the Federalists favored what the Republicans considered to be an overly powerful executive branch.

In 1794 Monroe left the Senate to accept an appointment from President George Washington as ambassador to France, the same post his friend and mentor Jefferson had once held. In the position for almost three years, Monroe was sent to improve tense relations with France, which was undergoing its own revolution. However, as Washington's administration became increasingly sympathetic to the Federalists, Monroe was recalled from the post in December 1796 for being too conspicuously pro-French. He returned home to private life in a political setting that was highly partisan.

Though not in any elected office, Monroe remained actively involved in politics, and was elected in 1799 as governor of Virginia for three one-year terms. After that Monroe served in several diplomatic posts for President

Thomas Jefferson, who was elected in 1800. In 1803 Monroe negotiated the treaty with French emperor Napoleon which gave the Louisiana Territory to the United States (*See also,* Thomas Jefferson Administration). Upon completing that mission, he was appointed ambassador to England, a post he held from July 1803 until his return back to private life in the United States in December 1807. Jefferson also dispatched Monroe to Spain on a special mission for six months in 1805.

It was the mission to England that caused the rift between Monroe and Madison, then serving as secretary of state. A commercial treaty Monroe had negotiated with the British in 1806, following renewed fighting between Britain and France, was rejected by Jefferson and Madison and not presented to the Senate for ratification. Monroe felt slighted and misled by his two old friends. He had worked tirelessly to negotiate the treaty, believing he was fully representing the president's wishes. Jefferson did not sign it because it failed to address the issue of U.S. sailors being captured by and forced into the British navy. Its rejection served to chill the relationship he enjoyed with Jefferson and Madison. While Jefferson quickly repaired relations with Monroe, those with Madison continued to be strained. Monroe even allowed himself to be nominated for president in 1808, which put him directly against Madison, who went on to win the election. The break did not last long. Two years into his administration, Madison sought the experience and advice of his colleague, and offered Monroe the post of secretary of state, which was quickly accepted. Monroe served at this post until his election as president in 1816, though he did, for a time during the War of 1812 against the British, also serve as secretary of war.

As the Madison administration came to a close, Monroe turned his sights on the presidency. Though he faced some opposition in his own party, once he had overcome that there were no serious challengers for the office.

Monroe as President

When Monroe, now 58 years old, took office in what became known as "The Era of Good Feelings," the country was still recovering from the recent war with Great Britain and was refocusing its energies on domestic matters. Monroe and the Congress spent much of their time on issues involving the admittance of new states, territorial expansion across the continent, and the subsequent federal role in building an infrastructure in these new areas. The admittance of Missouri to the Union proved to be a particularly difficult problem, as the role of slavery in new states sparked a crisis between the northern and southern states. "The Missouri Compromise" was reached after two years of bitter debate in the country, but only after the Union had been threatened with dissolution.

Monroe faced other crises as well, such as the country's first economic depression and war with Spain, yet he emerged from them without any great damage to his presidency or his reputation.

Monroe came to be most remembered throughout history because of his foreign policy regarding Latin America. His principles for action became known as the Monroe Doctrine, and they called on the European powers to abandon their plans for further colonization in the Western Hemisphere, leaving what remained in the Americas as land for the Americans who lived there. (American Indians, however, were not considered at the time as "Americans" whose territory should be left alone, leaving room for expansion by the United States and Latin American countries.)

When Monroe finished his two terms as president he was given high marks for his performance. He never enjoyed great influence with Congress, and political rivalries within his own administration often made it difficult to work with the legislative branch. Yet he was usually quite successful in achieving his desired results.

Post-presidential Years

Monroe did not immediately leave the White House after his term of office ended. His wife Elizabeth Monroe was too sick to travel, and so the Monroes stayed for a few weeks until she was well. After the strain and turbulence of eight years in the White House, Monroe was eager to return to his home in Oak Hill, Virginia.

Monroe continued to see and communicate with his friends, former presidents Thomas Jefferson and James Madison, who lived nearby. He also served, along with his two friends, as a board member for the University of Virginia, which was founded by Jefferson, and Monroe continued in that capacity after Jefferson died.

After leaving the presidency, Monroe avoided partisan political involvement. He used his influence to get George Hay, his son-in-law, an appointment as a federal judge, and his other son-in-law, Samuel Governeur, appointed postmaster for New York, but otherwise he stayed out of politics. He refused both a diplomatic assignment to the Panama Congress in 1826, and an offer to run as vice president on the John Quincy Adams ticket in 1828. He did, however, serve in 1829 as president of the Virginia Constitutional Convention, his last act of public service.

One of Monroe's greatest worries in his retirement concerned his finances. When he left office, he was more than $75,000 in debt. While he was able to sell some land to retire part of the debt, he also asked Congress to settle his claims for payment, which dated back to his first mission to France. As part of several diplomatic delegations before becoming secretary of state in 1811, Monroe had taken on significant financial burdens, for which he had not been properly compensated by the U.S. government. Congress took up the request for more than

$53,000 in 1825, but only awarded Monroe $29,000 in the following year. Considering the decision a challenge to his integrity and honesty, and in great need of money, Monroe resubmitted his claim. However, because of congressional factionalism, the issue was delayed for several years, and payment of an additional $30,000 was made in February 1831, only months before his death.

In 1830 Monroe suffered two tragedies. Within two days of each other, his wife Elizabeth, and George Hay, his friend and counsel died. After his wife's death, Monroe's health began to quickly deteriorate, and he died the following summer, on the Fourth of July, the anniversary of Thomas Jefferson's and second U.S. president John Adams's deaths and the signing of the Declaration of Independence.

The James Monroe Administrations

A veteran of the American Revolution (1775–83), and the last of the "Virginia Dynasty" who rose to the office after serving as secretary of state, Monroe presided during "The Era of Good Feelings," a period of peace, national expansion, and the absence of party rivalry. Monroe is best known for the Monroe Doctrine, a foreign policy statement which declared that the Americas were to be considered off limits to further colonization by European powers.

Monroe Becomes President

The Campaign of 1816

The campaign for president in 1816 was not conducted like modern campaigns. Prior to 1840 candidates remained above the fray. There was no formal campaign of making speeches, shaking hands, and getting out to meet the people by touring the country. State legislatures, electors, and Congress played the greatest roles in presidential elections, and it was through exercising influence among these groups that candidates met with success or failure. Monroe and his opponents all enjoyed solid reputations, of which influential people were familiar, and campaigning for votes would have been considered undignified.

Of all the presidential candidates in 1816, Monroe could claim the greatest experience in politics and government. Daniel D. Tompkins was governor of New York, Rufus King was a senator from the same state, and William Crawford of Georgia had served as secretary of war for President James Madison. (All were Republicans except for King, who was a Federalist.) Democratic-Republicans at that time were referred to as Republicans. Yet it was Monroe who brought to the campaign a long record of service in domestic politics combined with extensive diplomatic experience abroad. And as Madison's secretary of state, he had served in the position that had come to be seen as a necessary stepping stone to the presidency. Monroe also benefited from his close association with U.S. presidents Thomas Jefferson and Madison. Monroe was considered by many of his contemporaries as the most prominent public character of his time, the logical choice to assume the presidency.

Monroe's strongest opponent was William Crawford, who received support from the important electoral state of New York and could claim many backers in Congress.

Though Monroe's supporters were concerned for a time that Crawford might win, in the end the congressional Republican caucus, responsible for nominating a candidate, favored Monroe over Crawford by a vote of 65 to 54. Crawford did nothing to challenge Monroe after that, for he did not wish to jeopardize his chances of being part of the Monroe administration, in which he became secretary of the Treasury.

While the caucus vote was not binding, it was an indication that most of the Congress, as well as the state legislatures, who provided recommendations to their respective delegations, supported Monroe, and would deliver that support when the electoral college voted in December. Rufus King, Monroe's only opponent in the election, later wrote that the election was never in doubt once Monroe received the nomination. His assessment was entirely correct. Monroe won all but three states and captured 183 electoral votes to King's 34, while Daniel Tompkins was elected vice president.

The Campaign of 1820

If there was little drama surrounding the election in 1816, there was even less in 1820 when Monroe ran unopposed. It was the least contested presidential election since George Washington had been elected unanimously in 1789, and nothing like it has occurred since. Monroe was a popular and respected president, and so no one sought to challenge him from within his own party. Nor was there a challenger from any other party. The Federalists had disappeared as a national entity by then, and no new party had yet arisen. All the prominent politicians of the day were Republicans.

The nominating process existed that year only as a formality. In April the Republican Party convened a congressional caucus to make its nomination. While there was a failed effort to replace Daniel Tompkins as vice president, no one was offered as a challenge to Monroe, so the caucus adjourned after passing a motion that it was not expedient to nominate anyone.

When the electoral ballots were cast in December, Monroe won all but one of the 232 total. William Plumer,

Administration

Administration Dates

March 4, 1817–March 4, 1821
March 4, 1821–March 4, 1825

Vice President

Daniel D. Tompkins (1817–25)

Cabinet

Secretary of State
John Q. Adams (1817–25)

Secretary of the Treasury
William H. Crawford (1816–25)

Secretary of War
John C. Calhoun (1817–25)

Attorney General
Richard Rush (1814–17)
William Wirt (1817–29)

Secretary of the Navy
Benjamin W. Crowninshield (1815–18)
Smith Thompson (1819–23)
Samuel L. Southard (1823–29)

Postmaster General
R. Jonathan Meigs Jr. (1814–23)
John McLean (1823–29)

a former Federalist senator from New Hampshire, voted for John Quincy Adams. While it has been said that Plumer voted for Adams so that George Washington would be the only unanimously elected president, Plumer said that he disapproved of Monroe's economic policies and that the president did not have the weight of character that the office required.

Monroe's Advisers

Monroe as president carefully guarded his executive power and was often intimately involved with the details of his administration's policies. Though he often solicited advice, it was always clear that final authority rested with Monroe. When he sought advice he generally relied on his cabinet, but he also looked to the judgment of his son-in-law, George Hay. Hay was the president's friend, confidant, and perhaps his most trusted adviser, living in the White House for much of Monroe's presidency. He managed Monroe's run for office, helped during the crisis over Missouri, and, when apart from Monroe, continually exchanged letters with him.

Monroe often convened his cabinet for consultation and discussion, especially when issues of national importance were at stake. He also routinely consulted the cabinet on the subject and wording of his annual messages to Congress. An excellent record of all these discussions was kept by Secretary of State John Quincy Adams, who kept an extensive diary. Monroe was most interested in foreign and defense matters, and thus he took a greater part in formulating policy in these areas than he did in others. Adams's diary reveals that he and Monroe worked very closely together, seeing each other almost every day. The two had an excellent relationship, as they shared a common view of the interests and objectives of the United States.

In defense matters, Monroe's primary interest was in strengthening the country's defenses. Having learned the value of military fortifications during the War of 1812, Monroe made their improvement one of his highest priorities. To this end he maintained a close working relationship with his secretary of war, John Calhoun. In other areas, there is a less extensive record about Monroe's interactions with his remaining cabinet members. However, this is due not only to the lack of a committed and thorough diarist like Adams, it is also because Monroe had less interest in other departments and so gave most of his other cabinet secretaries a freer hand.

Monroe had particular trouble maintaining harmony within his cabinet as the presidential election of 1824 approached. As most of the candidates for president were cabinet members—Adams, Calhoun, and Treasury Secretary William Crawford all ran, (as well as Speaker of the House Henry Clay and Andrew Jackson, later seventh president of the United States)—divisions often ran deep. Crawford in particular enjoyed considerable support in Congress, and it was often his supporters who were responsible for defeating legislation the president and other cabinet members supported. In one instance in 1822, two of Monroe's military appointments were rejected by the Senate. As those who had voted against the two were Crawford supporters, the secretary's relationship with Monroe was severely strained. As a result, Crawford offered to resign. Monroe rejected the resignation, but stressed that it was necessary to have the cabinet's full cooperation once a decision was made. Though the president was able to reassert his authority, he was never able to contain the competition among his advisers to be his successor.

Monroe and Congress

Monroe made himself very accessible to members of Congress, who were welcomed to call on him at the White House. Monroe also exercised influence over Congress through several department offices. As Congress had little staff or services, it was often dependent on the executive branch for information, data, and sometimes even legislative language, practices that continue to this day.

At the same time, there were several influences that diminished the president's effectiveness with Congress. First of all there was the popular and powerful Speaker of the House, Henry Clay of Kentucky. One of the country's great legislators (who ran unsuccessfully for president), he wielded great power in the House of Representatives due to his office as well as his personal stature. Clay might not have been able to force Monroe's hand, but neither could the president succeed in Congress without Clay.

A second factor that limited Monroe's influence with Congress was, ironically, the absence of party rivalry. Monroe's tenure in office coincided with a temporary end of partisan politics. The Federalists were finished as a party, but nothing had replaced it yet. This was a circumstance Monroe had welcomed, believing that strict partisanship was detrimental to U.S. political life. However, presidents are usually able to count on party cohesion and discipline in Congress to win votes, and to the extent that this did not exist, blocs in Congress formed around different personalities. As factions revolved around individuals, and alignments on different issues varied, Monroe often found it exceedingly difficult to be effective with Congress, for he could not appeal to members of Congress in the name of party unity.

Monroe and the Judiciary

During Monroe's presidency, little of his attention was devoted to judicial matters outside of appointments to the federal courts. He made one appointment to the Supreme Court, Smith Thompson of New York, who served from 1823 to 1843. Notable as Monroe was for his constitutional literalism and strict construction, he stayed well out of judicial business, as it was not a presidential concern. Paradoxically, it was during Monroe's presidency that the Supreme Court handed down two decisions that permitted the government to greatly expand the scope of its power and control. One was *Cohens v. Virginia* (1821), in which the Court ruled that it had the authority to take appeals from state courts. This ruling was based on the grounds that the Constitution, laws, and treaties of the United States could only be uniformly applied and remain supreme if the Supreme Court could review the actions of state courts.

The other case, and the most notable case during Monroe's presidency, was *McCulloch v. Maryland* (1819), in which the State of Maryland sought to challenge the constitutionality of the Second Bank of the United States (known as the BUS). The state of Maryland had imposed a tax on branches of the bank operating in the state. When this action was challenged by James McCulloch, the bank's cashier, the State of Maryland took the bank to court. When the case went before the Supreme Court, the state argued not only that it had the power to tax a bank within its jurisdiction, but also that Congress did not have the power to charter a corporation such as the BUS.

Three days after hearing the case, Chief Justice John Marshall handed down the Court's unanimous opinion. The decision was in favor of the bank, but Marshall did much more than permit the bank to operate and avoid paying state taxes. In his ruling, Marshall wrote that though the Constitution may not expressly allow Congress to charter a national bank, it was not meant to foresee every contingency. Rather, the Constitution marked only "great outlines," with the result that the federal government could exercise not only its enumerated powers, but "implied powers" as well. Implied powers were those considered "necessary and proper" for carrying out the specified functions of government. Since Congress did have the power to collect taxes, regulate commerce, raise armies, and declare war, it also should have the means to exercise such power. The bank was one such method. Furthermore, Marshall wrote, Maryland could not tax the bank because it was an instrument of the United States, like courts, the mails, and customs.

The idea of implied powers was a significant break with past practice, and the ruling caused an outcry among those who saw the power of Congress as strictly limited in scope. Former presidents James Madison and Thomas Jefferson in particular both opposed the ruling and believed that it would allow the government to claim vast powers it was never intended to have.

The ruling kept the bank in business for another 13 years, but it was not until the twentieth century when Marshall's opinion had its greatest impact. By allowing for a broad interpretation of the Constitution, it became the virtually undisputed cornerstone for the federal government's involvement in the economy and various social, scientific, and educational programs.

Changes in the U.S. Government

Few changes in the U.S. government occurred during James Monroe's presidency. He served in an era when chief executives understood the power of their office to be rather limited, and before the institutions and functions of the U.S. government had much opportunity to grow. For the most part, the government that Monroe inherited was very much the same when he left office, sustaining only modest growth in most departments. One exception was the office of the attorney general, occupied throughout most of Monroe's presidency by William Wirt. Until Monroe, the job was considered to be part time, whereby the president could receive advice on legal matters and include another voice in his cabinet. Monroe asked the Congress to appropriate funds to provide an office and a clerk for the attorney general.

What did change during the Monroe years was the size of the United States itself. Five new states were added during his tenure—Missouri, Maine, Alabama, Mississippi, and Illinois—while the territory of Florida was acquired from the Spanish. Reflecting this growth, the General Land Office and the Post Office doubled in size. Moreover, the United States established that its western boundary extended, in the Oregon Territory, as far as the Pacific Ocean.

Domestic Issues

Monroe served as president during an unusual time in U.S. history notable for the absence of party rivalry. Coined by a Boston newspaper, "The Era of Good Feelings," it was a period of time in which Monroe's Republican Party was the only national party after the bitter division sparked by the War of 1812 had subsided. The Federalists had all but disappeared, leaving the Republicans the rewards of victory, but also the perils of factionalism within their own party. In such a setting, the country redirected its energies toward domestic issues.

The Era of Good Feelings

"The Era of Good Feelings" has been used to describe the period of Monroe's presidency. However, it was not only a moniker applied to the period by historians. It was coined during Monroe's first year in office and accurately describes Monroe's goals for the country. Coming to office after the bitter divisions caused by the War of 1812 with the British had subsided, and after the Federalist Party had become a marginal force in national politics, Monroe found that the primary threats to national unity had greatly diminished. He sought to capitalize on this by promoting a sense of common purpose, devoid of partisan rivalries and political factionalism. One of his primary goals, in fact, was the elimination of all parties. So after taking the oath of office on March 4, 1817, he turned less to governance and instead decided to emulate his predecessor, George Washington, by traveling throughout the country to foster a spirit of unity. The timing was ideal. The White House was not yet ready for occupancy, as it was still undergoing repairs after its destruction in the War of 1812. Congress was not in session and would not reconvene until December, and Monroe did not have all of his cabinet seats filled.

Traveling as a private citizen and paying for the trip out of his own pocket, Monroe spent 16 weeks visiting a host of cities, and in each he was met with open arms

and given a hearty welcome. His trip to Boston, a stronghold of the Federalists, was meant as a demonstration of the words of his inaugural speech that the American people constituted a single family with a common set of interests. It worked. Federalists and Republicans wholeheartedly received the president. The entire affair prompted one Boston newspaper to refer to the times as "the era of good feelings," thus giving the period a name to last through the ages.

Nevertheless, Monroe's goodwill did not extend so far as to give any leading Federalist an appointment in the government. He feared causing any resentment in his own party, and he did not wish to embolden the Federalists. Still, by 1819, every New England state except Massachusetts was controlled by the Republicans, and in Congress there was only a handful of Federalists, who usually supported the administration with more enthusiasm than many Republicans.

The Panic of 1819

The first major U.S. economic depression came during Monroe's first term. Known as the panic of 1819, it was precipitated by many factors—a drop in exports, rising imports, overexpansion of credit, and the financial mismanagement of the Second Bank of the United States. After the War of 1812, the bank adopted a very generous policy in making loans, providing easy money to private borrowers. Moreover, the bank's operations were not closely supervised, and soon the bank had overextended itself, threatening its very existence. At this point the bank reversed course, and began to rapidly limit borrowing. This reduction in credit exacerbated problems that had already begun to develop, so much so that by the middle of 1819, the price of land was falling rapidly, unemployment was rising, and loans were virtually impossible to obtain. The result was financial ruin for many people, something that had been relatively unknown in the United States on such a vast scale.

Since so many people were unable to borrow, buy land, or even work, they blamed the bank and its mismanagement for their problems. Congress began an examination of the bank, and its investigation found a series of improprieties on the part of the directors. In contrast to the bank's directors, President Monroe received very little criticism for the state of the economy. Unlike presidents in the late twentieth century, those in Monroe's era received neither credit nor blame for economic performance. Thus, changes were made in the bank's operations, but no government action was taken to try and alleviate the depression's worst effects. In an age in which none of the primary functions of government involved managing and stabilizing the economy, there was little thought that either the president or Congress should or could do anything to end the downturn. One observer wrote that "the people . . . are now eating the bitter fruit of excessive Banking" (Cunningham, p. 84). The solution, therefore, did not involve government, it

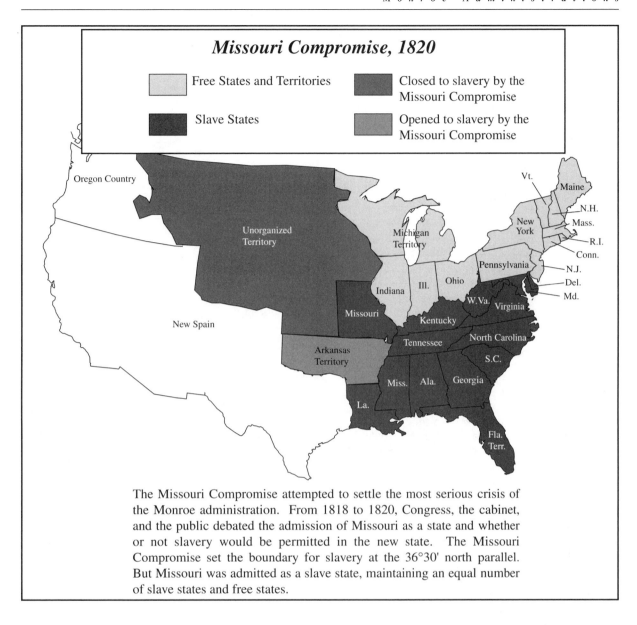

Missouri Compromise, 1820

- Free States and Territories
- Slave States
- Closed to slavery by the Missouri Compromise
- Opened to slavery by the Missouri Compromise

The Missouri Compromise attempted to settle the most serious crisis of the Monroe administration. From 1818 to 1820, Congress, the cabinet, and the public debated the admission of Missouri as a state and whether or not slavery would be permitted in the new state. The Missouri Compromise set the boundary for slavery at the 36°30' north parallel. But Missouri was admitted as a slave state, maintaining an equal number of slave states and free states.

lay in industry and economy—working harder and spending less.

The Missouri Compromise

The controversy that resulted in what became known as the Missouri Compromise was the most serious crisis of the Monroe administration.

In 1819 the territory known as Missouri petitioned the U.S. Congress for admission as a state. The petition was met with fierce opposition by northern congressmen. There were many slave-owners living in Missouri, and the northern congressmen did not want to admit a new slave state. In fact, they had recently proposed a constitutional amendment banning slavery in any new state. Congress recessed without voting on either issue.

In December, when Congress reconvened, Speaker of the House Henry Clay again introduced the petition from the Missouri Territory. This time, no constitutional amendment was proposed, only an amendment to the Missouri statehood bill, specifying that no new slavery be allowed in the state, and that all slaves already there be set free over a period of time. This proposal, offered by Representative James Tallmadge of New York, had the effect of taking the routine business of admitting a new state into the Union and turning it into a bitter dispute. It produced the most important debate about slavery since the ratification of the Constitution in 1789, and its merits were discussed far beyond Washington.

The argument, which was about much more than Missouri, consisted of two distinct positions. On one side it was advanced that Congress had no authority to force any state to admit or prohibit slavery. The Constitution says that each state government must be republican in form, but it says nothing about slavery in any single state. Therefore, it was argued, each state maintained the right to decide its own position with regard to slavery.

On the other side of the debate the argument consisted of two parts. The first was that Congress did have the power to prescribe conditions for admission into the Union. Thus, it was legitimate for legislation about slavery to be one of those conditions. The second part, and what lay at the core of the argument, was a strong opposition to slavery altogether. It was considered by its opponents to be both morally wrong and incompatible with freedom and republican institutions. This debate, which lay at the heart of the country's first great sectional crisis, pitted North against South, with northerners willing to see slavery as a national problem in which all shared some measure of guilt, and southerners refusing to debate the morality of slavery, while embracing its constitutionality.

As the debate continued through yet another congressional session, passions ran high throughout the country. What was especially ominous is that people began to talk openly of dissolving the Union. The stalemate was reflected in Congress, where the House approved the Tallmadge Amendment and the Senate rejected it. Seeking a solution, Henry Clay helped to forge a compromise, the first of many for which he would be remembered in his long career in Congress. Rather than threaten disunion, Clay and others in early 1820 reached an agreement whereby Missouri and Maine would be admitted to the Union at the same time. Missouri would be a slave state while Maine would be a free state. This would preserve the sectional balance in Congress, where the number of slave states and free states would be equal. It was further agreed that slavery would be excluded forever in all territories north of the latitude 36°30', excluding the state of Missouri. With this formulation, both sides received enough to be satisfied, and the controversy that almost split the Union was put to rest. However, the compromise did not end the larger sectional conflict, it only resolved the immediate crisis. The issue would only be fully resolved by the American Civil War (1861–65), 40 years later.

Foreign Issues

As a young, dynamic, and increasingly powerful nation, the United States was not only expanding west into the vast Louisiana Territory it had recently purchased from France, its leaders also were interested in additional acquisitions, such as Florida, and in forging a relationship with the countries of Latin America.

The Monroe Doctrine

The Monroe Doctrine was James Monroe's most notable contribution to the formulation and conduct of U.S. foreign policy, living on, in many different interpretations, more than a century and a half after his presidency. Contained in a series of statements in his annual address to Congress in December 1823, and only dubbed "The Monroe Doctrine" years after it was pronounced, the declaration of principles and interests Monroe made to Congress gave voice to American attitudes and actions toward Latin America.

Monroe made this announcement as a response to the revolutions in South America, which had succeeded in the early 1800s in freeing the region from Spanish control. By 1821 all the countries of South America had declared and achieved their independence. President Monroe, from the time he took office, had been reluctant to grant formal recognition to the new republics for fear of harming U.S. relations with Spain. Though the United States was not an ally of Spain, Monroe did not want to risk war over Latin American independence, nor did he want to jeopardize negotiations over Florida, which the United States was seeking to purchase from Spain at the time. Thus his administration's policy, despite the objections of Speaker of the House Henry Clay and much of Congress, was to maintain a course of impartial neutrality and consider the conflict between Spain and its colonies as a civil war. However, by early 1822 Florida was entirely in U.S. hands. Moreover, Latin America had proven its ability to maintain its independence. Therefore, Monroe chose this time to officially recognize the new governments and establish diplomatic relations, an action highly welcomed by the new republics (to this day, in fact, there is a statue of James Monroe in the capital of Bolivia).

By the following summer, civil war in Spain itself ended in victory for the monarchy, prompting concerns that Spain, with the help of France and other continental monarchies, might try to retake its former colonies in the Americas. This was considered unacceptable not only in Latin America, but also in Great Britain and the United States. In a spirit of cooperation (but also calculated self-interest), the British made a proposal to the United States that the two countries make a joint declaration: both would oppose any effort by the Spanish to revive its empire in the Americas, as well as any new colonization. The proposed statement also included a declaration that opposed any country taking certain lands in North America and the Caribbean, Cuba and Texas in particular. Monroe and his cabinet were divided as to how to respond to the offer. While Secretary of War John Calhoun approved of the idea, Secretary of State John Quincy Adams opposed it. Recognizing that American and British interests were similar, and that the power of the British navy would be able to prevent Spanish intervention in Latin America, Adams saw no reason to bind the United States to a set of promises that would also place restrictions upon U.S. expansion into Cuba and Texas. Monroe also consulted former presidents Thomas Jefferson and James Madison, both of whom suggested he accept the offer. However, in the end Monroe took

The Monroe Doctrine, in declaring the Americas off-limits to further European colonization, represented a bold step in U.S. foreign policy. European leaders were surprised at this aggressive move on the part of the United States.

(Corbis. Reproduced by permission.)

Adams's advice. In so doing Monroe could respond not only to Spain, but also to Russia and Great Britain, which were both interested in annexing part of the Oregon Territory on the Pacific.

In his annual message to Congress in 1823, Monroe declared that, "the American continents, by the free and independent condition which they have assumed and maintain, are henceforth not to be considered as subjects for future colonization by any European power . . . we should consider any attempt on [Europe's] part to extend their system to any portion of this hemisphere as dangerous to our peace and safety." He further asserted that, "any interposition for the purpose of oppressing them" could only be viewed as "the manifestation of an unfriendly disposition toward the United States" (Richardson, pp. 776, 789).

With these words, Monroe sought not only to declare the Western Hemisphere off limits to Europeans, but to outline a particular relationship within the region, one in which the United States stood above other countries in the region, acting as both the arbiter and guarantor of Latin American and Caribbean independence. Whether intended by Monroe or not, his doctrine has provided the context and often the rationale for the use of American power and influence in the region ever since it was pronounced, often with little or no consultation with the countries in question.

Florida

Closer to home, and an even greater issue of contention with Spain, was the problem of Florida. Not only was it an area coveted by Monroe and his predecessors, it was an area from which the Seminole Indians staged raids into U.S. territory. The Seminoles used the Spanish colony as a sanctuary and would not be controlled by the Spanish. This activity, seen not only as a threat to the physical security of white settlers in the area, but also as a threat to national honor, provoked outrage in the United States and demands that the raids be stopped.

Thus near the end of 1817, Monroe sent orders to Gen. Edmund Gaines, and Gen. Andrew Jackson, who shortly took command from Gaines, to attack the Seminoles and pursue them into Florida if necessary. However, the order explicitly stated that no Spanish outposts should be attacked.

Jackson proceeded to carry out his orders, but he went further than directed. Accusing the Spanish of giving aid and refuge to the Seminoles, Jackson seized the Spanish fort at St. Marks. After that he turned to Pensacola, Florida, seizing not only the Spanish fort there but the entire city. The general's actions prompted protests by the Spanish, French, and British, and also in Congress, where the general and the administration were accused of overstepping constitutional authority. Only

In what was eventually called the First Seminole War, President Monroe ordered Gen. Andrew Jackson to attack the Seminole Indians of Florida. Jackson later became the seventh president of the United States. (The Library of Congress.)

Congress had the power to make war, and this, it was argued, was exactly what Jackson had done. In both Congress and the cabinet a debate ensued about how President Monroe should react, and whether Pensacola and the Spanish forts should be returned to Spain. In the cabinet, John Quincy Adams argued that Pensacola should be held, but Monroe and the rest argued that the taking of Pensacola was an act of war, and that it must be restored to Spain. Monroe's decision was well received around the country. Though Americans tended to share the goal of acquiring Florida, the manner in which Jackson had seized Florida prompted a great deal of criticism.

While the seizure of Pensacola and the Spanish forts were quickly reversed (wounding the pride and honor of Andrew Jackson), Spanish hold on the territory proved to be only temporary. Jackson's conquests, which became known later as the First Seminole War, gave added impetus to negotiations with Spain, which had already been underway regarding Florida. Within months Secretary of State Adams and the Spanish ambassador to the United States negotiated an agreement, signed on February 19, 1819. It provided for the United States to assume control of Florida and pay five million dollars in claims on Spain's behalf. It also settled border disputes with Spain in Louisiana and on the West Coast.

The Monroe Administration Legacy

When James Monroe left office in March of 1825, he turned over the office to his secretary of state, John Quincy Adams. Monroe left his successor without immediate problems or great crises to confront—the country was at peace, new states and the Florida Territory were acquired, economic prosperity had returned, and the sectional conflict over the expansion of slavery had been solved for the time being. In addition, Monroe had strengthened the power of the presidency in the conduct of foreign affairs, while leaving to his successor a country that had gained a degree of stature in the world.

At the same time, Monroe's ideal of national unity and the absence of parties never materialized. "The Era of Good Feelings," however, did not meet its defeat at the hands of a single cause. It was merely left behind. James Monroe's presidency marked the approaching end of an era. Monroe was the last Revolutionary War (1775–83) veteran to occupy the office, and the last of the Virginia Dynasty. Of the country's first five presidents, all but John Adams were Virginians. By 1824 other parts of the country, including the quickly-expanding West, were gaining power and had grown resentful of Virginia's stronghold on national politics. Finally, after John Quincy Adams was elected in 1824, the country decisively moved away from a system, informal though it was, of electing notable, prominent individuals from the country's unofficial aristocracy. Rather, the extension of the franchise (the right to vote), the growth of Andrew Jackson's wing of the party, the emergence of new factions, and the rise of a large-scale popular democracy changed the face of politics in the country forever.

Lasting Impact

In spite of these great changes that left the political landscape greatly altered in the years after Monroe, his presidency did leave a lasting legacy in two areas. The first, the case of *McCulloch v. Maryland* (1819), was something that Monroe really had little involvement in. Yet the Supreme Court decision from that period has turned out to be one of the most significant that has ever come from the Court. In arguing that the Congress could pass any law "necessary and proper" to carry out its constitutional responsibilities, Chief Justice Marshall and the Court determined that the Constitution need not be interpreted with only a strict construction. The decision made it possible for the document to be "a living thing, capable of growth, capable of keeping pace with the advancement of the American people and ministering to their changing necessities" (Levy, p. 1235).

The second of Monroe's legacies is directly attributable to him: the Monroe Doctrine. Monroe's statement about U.S. interests in the Western Hemisphere has served as a foundation for U.S. foreign policy in Latin America and the Caribbean ever since Monroe developed it. It represents to this day a sense in the United States that the country has legitimate interests in the Western Hemisphere, and that the United States may act on those concerns with a greater degree of autonomy than it may anywhere else in the world. In the early twentieth century Theodore Roosevelt expanded the doctrine, to suit his purposes in intervening in the affairs of Latin America, and later during the Cold War the Monroe Doctrine served to (usually implicitly) justify and guide U.S. policy in the hemisphere. Preventing the spread of a foreign ideology, Communism, and its European sponsor, the Soviet Union, was by extension similar to preventing the direct influence of outside powers in the region. Such reasoning and the policies they produced were sometimes controversial, but they rarely violated the long accepted principle that the United States maintained legitimate reasons to intervene in Latin America and the Caribbean.

Sources

Ammon, Harry. *James Monroe: The Quest for National Identity.* New York: McGraw-Hill, 1971.

Congressional Record. 58th Cong., 3d Sess., 6 December 1904.

Cunningham, Noble. *The Presidency of James Monroe.* Lawrence, Kans.: University Press of Kansas, 1996.

Degregorio, William. *The Complete Book of U.S. Presidents.* 5th ed. New York: Wings Books, 1996.

Kane, Joseph Nathan. *Facts About the Presidents.* 6th ed. New York: H.W. Wilson, 1993.

Levy, Leonard, ed. *Encyclopedia of the American Constitution.* Vol. 3. New York: Macmillan, 1986.

Monroe, James. *The Autobiography of James Monroe.* Syracuse N.Y.: Syracuse University Press, 1959.

Richardson, James. *A Compilation of the Messages and Papers of the Presidents.* Washington, D.C.: Government Printing Office, 1896–99.

Further Readings

Adams, John Quincy. *The Diary of John Quincy Adams.* Edited by David Allen. Cambridge, Mass: Harvard University Press, 1981.

Dangerfield, George. *The Era of Good Feelings.* New York: Harcourt, Brace, 1952.

John Quincy Adams and American Continental Empire: Letter, Papers, Speeches. Chicago: Quadrangle Books, 1965.

LaFeber, Walter. *The American Age: U.S. Foreign Policy at Home and Abroad, 1750 to the Present.* 2d ed. New York: W. W. Norton, 1994.

May, Ernest. *The Making of the Monroe Doctrine.* Cambridge, Mass.: Belknap Press of Harvard University Press, 1975.

Molineu, Harold. *U.S. Policy toward Latin America.* Boulder, Colo.: Westview Press, 1986.

Moore, Glover. *The Missouri Controversy, 1819–1821.* Lexington, Ky.: University of Kentucky Press, 1953.

Rogin, Michael Paul. *Fathers and Children: Andrew Jackson and the Subjugation of the American Indian.* New York: Vintage Books, 1976.

Tindall, George Brown. *America: A Narrative History.* 2d ed. Vol. 1. New York: W. W. Norton, 1988.

John Q. Adams Administration

Full name: John Quincy Adams
Popular name: Old Man Eloquent

Personal Information:

Born: July 11, 1767
Birthplace: Braintree (now Quincy), Massachusetts
Died: February 23, 1848
Death place: Washington, D.C.
Burial place: First Unitarian Church, Quincy, Massachusetts
Religion: Unitarian
Spouse: Louisa Catherine Johnson (m. 1797)
Children: George Washington; John; Charles Francis; Louisa Catherine
Education: Harvard College, 1787
Occupation: Lawyer; politician; U.S. senator; diplomat
Political Party: Democratic-Republican Party
Age at Inauguration: 57 years

Biography

Eldest son of John Adams, the second president of the United States, John Quincy Adams was a child of the American Revolution (1775–83). As a diplomat under presidents George Washington, John Adams, and James Madison, John Quincy Adams developed a foreign policy founded on the principle of independence from foreign nations. As secretary of state under James Monroe, Adams formulated this policy into the Monroe Doctrine, declaring that the United States would not tolerate European interference in the affairs of the American continents. After an unsuccessful presidency, Adams ended his illustrious career with 18 years in the House of Representatives, where he successfully opposed "gag" rules that prevented antislavery petitions from being read on the floor of the House.

Early Life

John Quincy Adams, the eldest son and second child of John and Abigail Adams, was born in Braintree (now Quincy), Massachusetts, on July 11, 1767. As the son of the second president of the United States, Adams was raised in the governing class of the new nation. His background was an apprenticeship to high office. He accompanied his father on diplomatic missions to Europe, and he was steeped in the culture of New England's Puritan society that held piety, independence of spirit and mind, ambition, and learning in high regard. In this environment Adams developed a hard-nosed tendency to favor morality over popularity.

Education

John Quincy Adams was, arguably, the most intelligent and, for his time, the best prepared president that the country ever had. His education began at home, where he learned reading, writing, and arithmetic from his parents. He also read history and literature, and became proficient in Latin, Greek, and French. In Europe with his father between 1778 and 1780, Adams studied at private schools in Paris, France, Amsterdam, and at the University of Leiden in the Netherlands. Returning to the United States, he enrolled as a junior at Harvard College in 1785 and graduated with a baccalaureate degree in 1787. Following in his father's footsteps, Adams studied law in Newburyport, Massachusetts, and was admitted to the bar in 1790.

Family Life

In 1797 in London, England, Adams married Louisa Catherine Johnson, daughter of the U.S. consul to London. The couple had three sons who grew to maturity, George Washington, John, and Charles Francis, and one daughter, Louisa Catherine, who died as an infant. Adams's sons would struggle under the high expectations inherited from their father and grandfather's service as presidents of the United States.

As first lady Louisa Catherine Adams was a social hostess when not bedridden by poor health. She was frustrated by her husband's refusal to advance his presidency by being more social and rewarding friends and supporters with political appointments. As congressional opposition made the presidency the low point of Adams's political career, his consequent depression made it the low point in his marriage.

Career

John Quincy Adams's diplomatic career began when he was still legally a minor, serving as secretary to the U.S. minister to Russia in 1781 and then secretary to his father in Paris, France, during negotiations in 1783 to end the American Revolution (1775–83). Although he practiced law for a short time in Boston, Massachusetts, beginning in 1790, Adams's greater interest in politics led him to political journalism and then to appointment by President George Washington as minister to the Netherlands in 1794. After his father's election to the presidency in 1796, Adams served as minister to Prussia, in present-day Germany, where he negotiated an important treaty of commerce.

In 1801 Adams renewed his law practice in Boston. Politics soon won out over his interest in the law, however, and he stood successfully for election in 1802 to

John Q. Adams. (The Library of Congress.)

the Massachusetts State Senate. In 1803 the state legislature elected him to the U.S. Senate. (At that time U.S. senators were chosen by the state legislatures.) As the son of one of the founders of Federalism—a political tendency that championed ratification of the Constitution and supported strong central government—he was expected to carry on his father's Federalist policies.

Adams's independence of mind and his dedication to a national, rather than a regional, perspective, plus the popular backlash against the Alien and Sedition Acts of 1798, which toughened requirements for citizenship and punished public criticism of the government, and other undemocratic excesses of Federalism during his father's presidency, led him to break with Federalism. Instead, he supported important aspects of the agrarian, states' rights, Republican politics of Thomas Jefferson, third president of the United States. He voted frequently in favor of Jefferson's agenda, including for the Louisiana Purchase in 1803, which nearly doubled the size of the United States, and for the Embargo Acts in 1807, which hampered New England shipping commerce by prohibiting trade with foreign nations. He paid the political price for his nationalist politics when the Massachusetts legislature elected his replacement before the end of his term in 1808, prompting him to resign. He soon joined the Democratic-Republican Party. The Jeffersonian Republican Party, of which Adams was a part, was distinct from the current Republican Party that originated in the antislavery politics of the 1850s.

Secretary of State

In 1809 Republican president James Madison appointed Adams minister to Russia and later to a U.S. delegation to negotiate the end of the War of 1812 with Great Britain. During the ensuing "Era of Good Feelings," Adams served as secretary of state under President James Monroe from 1817 to 1825 (*See also,* James Monroe Administration). Adams was considered a brilliant secretary of state. He pursued the United States's traditional policies of independence from Europe and expansion of the United States's continental holdings.

Adams negotiated or helped to negotiate three important treaties that gained new territory or stabilized existing agreements. In the aftermath of the War of 1812 he hammered out an arms reduction agreement with Great Britain. The treaty, negotiated in 1817, was called the Rush-Bagot Treaty. It restricted the number of warships that Great Britain and the United States could deploy on the Great Lakes. He also negotiated the Convention of 1818, which established the boundary between British Canada and the United States at the 49th parallel from the Lake of the Woods (in present-day Minnesota) to the Rocky Mountains in the West. In 1819 Adams brokered the Adams-Onis Treaty with Spain. The treaty was a result of Gen. Andrew Jackson's brazen occupation of much of Spanish Florida, supposedly as part of his war with the Seminole Indians. In a piece of diplomatic footwork that exhibited Adams's talents, he was able to convince his diplomatic counterpart, Onis, that Spain was militarily unable to prevent such incursions. Onis therefore agreed to cede Florida to the United States for free. The rest of the treaty defined the southern boundary of Spain's Louisiana Territories from the west side of what would become Texas all the way to the Pacific Ocean north of present-day California and New Mexico. In return the United States agreed to assume $5 million in claims of U.S. citizens against Spain.

In 1823 the British suggested to the Americans that the two nations issue a joint declaration of noninterference of other European powers in the Western Hemisphere. Although he favored good relations with Great Britain, Adams opposed a joint declaration and recommended instead that the United States issue such a declaration on its own. President Monroe released his famous message, the Monroe Doctrine, announcing that the United States would not tolerate European interference in, or colonization of, the independent countries in the Western Hemisphere. As Monroe's secretary of state, Adams was a principal author of the Monroe Doctrine (*See also,* James Monroe Administration).

President

The skills that made John Quincy Adams a brilliant diplomat—his capacity for cold calculation and his steady determination to hold to a course once adopted—contributed to the failure of his presidency. His intellectual arrogance meant that he never learned the art of com-

promise. On top of this, the manner of his elevation to the presidency created hostility and rancor that precluded compromise, even if Adams had wanted to compromise. He was elected by the House of Representatives with the help of candidate Henry Clay's supporters after none of the top four candidates (Tennessee war hero Andrew Jackson, Treasury secretary William Crawford, Speaker of the House Henry Clay, and Adams) received a majority of the electoral votes in 1824. When President Adams appointed Clay secretary of state, then a stepping-stone to the presidency, Jackson's supporters charged Adams and Clay with making a "corrupt bargain." Jacksonian opposition in Congress frustrated virtually all of Adams's presidential initiatives, including his national improvement plan for bankruptcy laws, an astronomical observatory, a national university, and support of manufacturers. Due in large part to Adams's determination to give coveted political appointments to the most competent men, including enemies instead of friends and supporters, Adams lost the election of 1828 to Andrew Jackson.

Post-presidential Years

Adams left the White House in 1829 with the intention of retiring to his ancestral home in Quincy, Massachusetts, to pursue literary interests. In 1830, however, the citizens of Quincy convinced Adams to run for the U.S. House of Representatives, where he served with distinction from 1831 until his death in 1848. Adams received the nickname "Old Man Eloquent" for his speeches before the House. His crowning achievement was in orchestrating opposition to the "gag rules" that prevented antislavery petitions from being read on the floor of the House. Adams believed the rules violated the First Amendment of the U.S. Constitution, which protects freedom of speech and the right to petition the government. After eight years, the House discarded the "gag rules" in 1844.

In 1848 Adams suffered a stroke and collapsed on the House floor. He was carried to the Speaker's room to lay for two days until he died on February 23.

The John Quincy Adams Administration

John Quincy Adams's presidency was the low point of his political career. Opposition from Adams's chief opponent in the 1824 presidential election, Andrew Jackson, and his supporters in Congress made it impossible for Adams to accomplish most of his plans for national improvement. From a political standpoint, Adams was particularly inept, failing to reward his own supporters with appointments in the executive office. After four years of struggling, Adams lost the election of 1828 to Jackson by a wide popular and electoral margin.

Adams Becomes President

The Campaign of 1824

Following the War of 1812, the United States enjoyed what was called an "Era of Good Feelings," continued from the James Monroe administration. Republicans governed without strong opposition from the ailing Federalist Party. The national consensus appeared to be so strong that political parties no longer seemed to be necessary. Until a delayed postwar depression in 1819, U.S. manufacturers that had started up during the war to replace British imports thrived. The panic of 1819, however, played havoc with the manufacturing sector, disrupted the credit structure, and caused extensive hardship, not only to merchants and manufacturers, but also to farmers, many of whom lost their land.

The Republican Party, which dominated the presidency since Thomas Jefferson's election in 1801, produced the only viable candidates in 1824. Mounting divisions among the Republicans, however, would soon spoil this brief period of consensus. In the election of 1824 a minority of Republicans in Congress nominated William H. Crawford of Georgia, Monroe's secretary of the Treasury, for the presidency. The Tennessee state legislature nominated Andrew Jackson, hero of the Battle of New Orleans during the War of 1812 and famed American Indian fighter in the South, who until the election was on friendly terms with Adams. The Kentucky state legislature nominated Henry Clay, Speaker of the House of Representatives. The Massachusetts legislature nominated John Quincy Adams.

Like his father, Adams did not campaign on his own behalf. Borrowing from Shakespeare, he called it the Macbeth Policy: "If chance will have me king, why, chance may crown me, Without my stir." When pressed to be more active, Adams explained, "He who asks or accepts the offer of aid to promote his own views necessarily binds himself to promote the views of him from whom he receives it" (Bemis, p. 20). Adams's campaign depended almost entirely on unorganized groups of Republican supporters in the New England states, New York, and Pennsylvania.

The most important issues of the day were whether the United States should impose tariffs on imports to protect domestic manufacturers, and whether the government had the authority to fund internal improvements, such as roads and canals, to stimulate growth. Underlying these issues was the more fundamental question of the power of the national government versus the power of the states. However, as the Republican candidates were afraid of alienating voters with the issues, the campaign became a clash of personalities. Jackson's supporters por-

Administration

Administration Dates
March 4, 1825–March 4, 1829

Vice President
John Caldwell Calhoun (1825–29)

Cabinet
Secretary of State
Henry Clay (1825–29)

Secretary of the Treasury
Richard Rush (1825–29)

Secretary of War
James Barbour (1825–28)
Peter B. Porter (1828–29)

Attorney General
William Wirt (1817–29)

Secretary of the Navy
Samuel L. Southard (1823–29)

Postmaster General
John McLean (1823–29)

trayed him as a national hero, the man of the people, and branded Adams as a descendant of the Federalist Party, which had been friendly to the English monarchy. Adams's supporters touted his accomplishments as a diplomat and secretary of state, and painted Jackson as a brutal tyrant who hung deserters from his army during the War of 1812. When the electors cast their ballots, Jackson received the most votes with 99, but none of the candidates received the majority necessary to win the election. (John C. Calhoun, Monroe's secretary of war who had entered the campaign but dropped out early to run for vice president, won that post easily.)

In accordance with the Twelfth Amendment of the U.S. Constitution, the House of Representatives decided the election by casting their votes for the top three candidates. It soon was apparent that Clay's supporters could dictate the outcome by transferring votes to either Jackson or Adams. Clay and his supporters met with both candidates, and when the House met to vote on February 9, 1825, Adams won by a bare majority of 13 states to Jackson's seven and Crawford's four. (Adams would subsequently name Clay secretary of state, leading Jackson and his supporters to call it a corrupt bargain and to promise congressional opposition to Adams.)

The day after the election, Adams humbly presented a written acceptance to a formal delegation from the House, saying that he would commit the election to another popular vote if the Constitution allowed. At his inauguration on March 4, 1825, Adams described the United States as a union no longer divided by partisan politics, indicating his Federalist conception of the United States as a union over the Republican concept of the United States as a republic of sovereign states. Adams paid tribute to the scientific and exploratory accomplishments of the Monroe administration, which foreshadowed his aggressive program for national improvement. Finally Adams acknowledged that he was a minority candidate who would have to work hard to earn the support of Congress, the states, and the people.

The Campaign of 1828

In October of 1825 the Tennessee legislature nominated Jackson for the presidential election of 1828. Adams would run again, but after three years of opposition from the Jacksonians in Congress, he had nothing substantial to show for his presidency. The campaign of 1828 was bitter. Adams's supporters accused Jackson and his wife of adultery without explaining that before they wed neither knew that her divorce from her first husband was not final. Jackson's supporters circulated a false story that Adams had given Czar Alexander I the sexual services of his wife's maid while Adams was minister to Russia. In the end Jackson won by a large margin in both the electoral and the popular votes. Adams's failure as president, his refusal to develop a supportive political machine, and the South's and the West's opposition to the growing power of the federal government all contributed to Adams's defeat. Like his father, Adams was not invited to, and did not attend, his successor's inauguration.

Adams's Advisers

When Adams became president in 1825, he offered to retain his predecessor's entire cabinet, including William H. Crawford as secretary of the Treasury who had run against Adams in the presidential election. This meant Adams only had to appoint secretaries of state and war. Adams offered the former position to Speaker of the House Henry Clay, whom he thought was best qualified, and the latter to Andrew Jackson. Clay and Jackson were Adams's other opponents for president in 1824. Adams even reached out to the Federalists by nominating one of the leading Federalists, Rufus King of New York, as minister to Great Britain, a post King held during John Adams's administration. John Quincy Adams's goal was

to unite not only the Republican Party but the whole country, geographically and politically, in the aftermath of the election.

Adams's cabinet plan failed. Crawford refused to remain in the cabinet and Jackson declined to accept the war post. Southern slave-holding Republicans were enraged by the nomination of King, who had opposed the extension of slavery into Missouri in 1819. Most damaging, however, was Adams's nomination of Clay as secretary of state. Since the tradition of the time was that the secretary of state generally succeeded the current president, it looked as if Clay had thrown his support to Adams in return for the lucrative appointment to secretary of state (*See also,* Adams Becomes President). An enraged Jackson and his supporters in both the House and the Senate called it a "corrupt bargain" and vowed to oppose Adams's administration for the next four years. As Speaker of the House in the waning days of the Eighteenth Congress, Clay immediately called for an impartial investigation, which found no basis for the allegation. The Senate confirmation vote, however, of only 27 to 10 in favor of Clay, foreshadowed trouble for Adams from the Senate.

Adams had an ally in Secretary of State Clay, who hoped to succeed him as president. While Clay counseled Adams to soften some of his aggressive proposals for national improvement, he outwardly supported the president's final decisions. When Adams prepared his annual address to Congress, he consulted each member with a draft either individually or as a group. Adams, however, frequently overburdened himself by tending to minuscule details, such as the appointment of minor officers, rather than delegating such tasks to his advisers.

Adams tried to govern without political patronage. It did not work. Postmaster General John McLean of Ohio was the biggest political enemy in the cabinet. He professed loyalty to Adams while working covertly for Jackson. Late in his presidency when Adams learned of McLean's disloyalty, including his recommendation of a Jacksonian to the postmaster position in Philadelphia, Pennsylvania, during the campaign of 1828, Adams still declined to replace McLean. Adams vowed to discharge federal officers, even political enemies, only for misconduct in their official business, a principle contributing to his defeat in 1828.

Adams and Congress

Adams served during the Nineteenth and the Twentieth sessions of Congress. A majority in the House of the Nineteenth Congress, including Speaker John W. Taylor from New York, was friendly to Adams's administration. The Senate, however, comprised a majority of Jackson supporters who vowed to oppose Adams when he appointed Clay secretary of state.

The Erie Canal opened for traffic during the administration of John Quincy Adams, who championed the improvement of roads and canals during his administration. (Archive Photos. Reproduced by permission.)

Without support from the Senate, most of Adams's proposals either failed to receive consideration or were defeated as bills. The main exception was funding for surveys and construction of roads and canals. The National Road, the United States's first highway, which stretched from Maryland to Virginia, was extended to Zanesville, Ohio, during Adams's presidency. The Erie Canal opened for traffic on October 26, 1825, and Adams turned over the first shovel of dirt for construction of the Chesapeake and Ohio Canal on July 4, 1828.

After the interim election of 1826, Adams became the first president to face a hostile majority in both houses of Congress. On the advice of his cabinet, he softened requests for national improvement in his remaining congressional addresses. The damage, however, already was done. Congress had no intention of adopting any of Adams's proposals. Adams left office after four years without successfully proposing a single significant legislative program.

Yet the Jacksonians in Congress, who concentrated on taking over the House in 1826 and the presidency in 1828, failed to enact significant legislation of their own design. Indeed, Adams once quipped that if a foreigner observed U.S. politicians, he would think their sole business was electioneering. Whether because Congress failed to pass any significant legislation or because he faced significant opposition, Adams became the third president who never exercised the veto power.

Adams and the Judiciary

Adams's administration was a quiet time for the federal judiciary. The Supreme Court announced no significant decisions. A bill to enlarge the membership of the Supreme Court to allow Adams to appoint two new justices failed to pass Congress. Although Adams occasionally ran into Chief Justice John Marshall during their daily, early morning walks around the capital, Adams's distaste for socialization kept him from having much contact with members of the federal judiciary. During his presidency Adams appointed one associate justice, Robert Trimble of Kentucky, to the Supreme Court.

Changes in the U.S. Government

The greatest change during the quiet Adams administration was the birth of the Democratic Party, which came to power with Andrew Jackson's election in 1828. Prior to Jackson's election, Democratic-Republicans had stood virtually unopposed for the presidency since Thomas Jefferson's campaign for a second term in 1804. In Jefferson's time, Republicans supported reduction of federal power, leaving the task of government to the individual states. Adams's plans for national improvement sounded more like his father's Federalist policies, which advocated a strong national government. These policies were repugnant to some Democratic-Republicans, especially in the South, who coveted states' rights as essential to the protection of slavery. Their split from the Republicans to form the Democratic Party marked the return of the two-party system to national politics.

Domestic Issues

The economic panic of 1819 continued to reverberate throughout the political landscape of the 1820s. New England shipping interests had suffered from Great Britain's blockade during the War of 1812. The end of the war in 1815 spelled relief for them, but new problems soon followed. The domestic manufacturers that had sprung up to produce the goods traditionally imported from Great Britain during the British blockade in the 1812 conflict suffered when the British "dumped" finished goods on the U.S. market after the war ended in 1815. These episodes of instability sapped the credit system and brought on waves of financial contractions as bankers foreclosed on loans and farmers lost their land.

During Adams's presidency, however, the economy was recovering and was entering a phase of economic expansion. This appeared to be an omen for political stability. The country offered other indications that crises could be managed and that successful government was possible. For one thing, political reform seemed to be taking place without undue turmoil. Both in the North and in the South, the states were beginning to enact the democratic franchise reforms. (Often associated with Andrew Jackson's reign, the states during Adams's administration were already competing with one another for a growing labor force by granting the right to vote to all white men irrespective of property ownership.) Even the great and dangerous question of slavery appeared to be manageable. The Missouri Compromise of 1819 had prohibited slavery in U.S. territories north of Missouri's boundary at 36° 30' north latitude. Many, including Adams, believed that they could manage democracy and do so without undue factional conflict. They were soon to be proven wrong.

The "American System"

Adams responded to the challenge of international economic competition by supporting a major effort championed by Secretary of State Henry Clay to create the conditions in which the economy could round itself out and the manufacturing sector of the economy could expand. Clay called this program the "American System." As secretary of state himself, Adams had written that self-reliance and self-improvement were a nation's primary right and obligation. His first presidential address to Congress in December of 1825 thus proposed an ambitious program of national improvement. It envisioned an improved economic infrastructure of improved roads and canals, and it called for the creation of a naval academy, a national university of Washington, D.C., a national astronomical observatory, plus the passage of bankruptcy laws and federal debt reduction. This proposal commanded the support of congressional leaders like Henry Clay and John C. Calhoun of South Carolina who at the time were both committed nationalists.

For Adams, the program of national improvement was necessary not only to revitalize the economy, but also to sustain the country's long-term growth. The plan was really a reversion to Federalism, which relied on the federal government to assist in national economic development. Supporters of Andrew Jackson criticized Adams's proposals as unconstitutional, reflecting the ongoing debate over the respective powers of the state and the federal governments. Underlying this debate was the South's fear that federal power would lead to interference with slavery, a pillar of the South's economic strength.

Treasury Secretary Richard Rush, for one, attempted to implement the American System. With the Board of Internal Improvements under his jurisdiction, Rush supervised Adams's plan to survey the country to develop roads and canals. Congress, however, approved only moderate funding for actual construction and repairs. Rush also worked to reduce the federal debt. Hardheaded opposition from Jackson's supporters in Congress, however, defeated most of the plan. Southern opposition to nationalization of the bankruptcy laws, Adams's land policies, and protective tariffs prevented the substantial national development and improvement that Adams sought.

Indian Land Policy

Economic expansion depended largely on the removal of American Indians from their valuable, fertile homelands into undeveloped western territory. During Thomas Jefferson's presidency, land speculators and American Indians held conflicting titles to land in western Georgia. To resolve the dispute, the federal government purchased lands west of Georgia's boundary in exchange for $1.25 million and a promise to satisfy the Indian claims to territory within Georgia's boundary. Subsequent efforts to satisfy these claims and to remove the Indians westward went slowly.

Soon after Adams became president, the Senate ratified a treaty by which the Creek Indian tribe agreed to exchange its land in Georgia for land west of the Mississippi River. However, the Creek negotiator, William McIntosh, son of a Scottish trader and Creek woman, only represented a minority of the Creek tribe and was killed in a fire set by protesting Creek Indians. When Adams learned of these developments, he received a delegation of Creek Indians who, with Secretary of War James Barbour, negotiated a new treaty. The new arrangement ceded Creek territory in Georgia east of the Chattahoochee River, about two-thirds of what McIntosh had ceded.

The incident sparked a conflict that reflected the ongoing struggle between state and federal power. Governor George M. Troup of Georgia vowed to remove the Indians and survey land for development under the original treaty with McIntosh. When the Creeks attacked the surveyors, Governor Troup ordered the state militia to the scene. Adams responded by threatening to send in the federal military. In the end, the entire dispute was resolved with a third treaty, executed in November 1827, by which the Creeks again ceded all of their land in Georgia. Out of the incident Andrew Jackson found a friend in the State of Georgia, where as president he would support forcible removal of Indians in a program known today as the Trail of Tears (*See also,* Andrew Jackson Administration).

Tariff of Abominations

After the War of 1812 New England manufacturers faced stiff competition from Great Britain. British manufacturers produced cheaper products that British shippers sold in the United States at a loss, because they recouped the money in the lucrative trade in the West Indies. To protect the United States from this competition, the federal government passed legislation in 1816 and again in 1824 imposing duties on selected imports. The South opposed these tariffs because it preferred Great Britain's cheaper products, and because it needed the lucrative British market for its own cotton crops. Like other important issues, the debate over tariffs reflected the struggle between state and federal power.

During the summer of 1827, manufacturers and farmers from the New England and mid-Atlantic states sought higher tariffs from the federal government. Led by Martin Van Buren, U.S. senator from New York, Jackson's supporters responded with a scheme to use the issue to destroy support for Adams in both the North and the South in the upcoming election of 1828. They drafted legislation with a tariff schedule so abominable, later referred to as the Tariff of Abominations, that if it passed Congress, Adams would lose support whether he signed it or vetoed it. The schedule lowered the tariff on woolens and increased the tariff on molasses and articles for shipbuilding, both contrary to New England's desires. Then in the name of protection, action the South thought was unconstitutional, it raised the tariffs on items for which nobody sought protection. Although not an Adams supporter, Senator John Randolph of Virginia quipped during congressional debates that the bill concerned no manufactures except that of the next president. Despite its flaws Congress passed the bill and Adams signed it, thus, according to biographer Samuel Flagg Bemis, "if anything more was necessary to finish John Quincy Adams in the South and even in the Northwest the Tariff of Abominations did it" (Bemis, p. 90).

Fast Fact

When Great Britain completely closed the British West Indies to U.S. trade effective December 1, 1826, the United States's lucrative exports to those islands dropped from $2,079,000 in 1826 to $1,000 in 1829.

(Source: Mary W. M. Hargreaves. *The Presidency of John Quincy Adams,* 1985.)

Foreign Issues

The United States was at peace during Adams's presidency. This gave Adams the chance to pursue foreign policies that dated back to Presidents George Washington and Thomas Jefferson—maintaining U.S. independence by avoiding alliances with foreign nations, while securing recognition of the United States's freedom to use the seas unmolested by foreign privateers and navies. Indeed, these policies were at the heart of the doctrine of noninterference that Adams, as secretary of state under James Monroe, had molded into the Monroe Doctrine. Negotiation of commercial treaties was an important component of these policies, and the Adams administration signed nine in four years, more than in any other four-year period prior to the American Civil War (1861–65).

Trade with the West Indies

The United States, however, continued to struggle with trade relations with the major powers of Great Britain and France. Claims for repayment of debts stemming from France's capture of U.S. merchant vessels during the Napoleonic Wars (1803–15) remained unresolved. Great Britain's policy of excluding U.S. trade vessels from the lucrative British West Indies, a remnant of the War of 1812, continued to be a topic of negotiation. When Great Britain completely closed the British West Indies to U.S. trade effective December 1, 1826, U.S. exports dropped to almost nothing. The matter remained unresolved when Adams left office. One of the administration's rare successes with Great Britain was negotiation of a treaty for payment of $1,204,960 as compensation for U.S. slaves carried off during the War of 1812.

Biography:

Henry Clay

Statesman; Politician (1777–1852)   American states-man Henry Clay had a real genius in the art of compro-mise and diplomacy. He was so adept at striking a bal-ance between opposing factions that he became widely known as the Great Compromiser. Clay was born to a middle-class Virginia family and blessed with a quick mind, a flair for oratory, and an ability to charm both men and women with his easy, attractive manner. Dur-ing his exhaustive career in public service, Clay was a U.S. representative, a senator, secretary of state, and a presidential candidate in three unsuccessful campaigns. Clay had a tireless ambition and loved to drink and gam-ble—no drawback in an age that celebrated both vices. Though Clay was a leading "War Hawk" whose clamor for hostilities helped bring about the War of 1812, he was also one of the commissioners who negotiated the 1814 Treaty of Ghent, ending that war. In 1820 it was Clay above all who engineered the Missouri Compromise,

striking a balance between free and slave states. Although Clay was a slave owner, his view on the subject was mod-erate. He effectively played his views to one side and his ownership status to the other, commanding the trust of each. When Clay backed out of the 1824 presidential election, he threw his support to John Quincy Adams who then won handily and named Clay his secretary of state. Many believe that Clay's greatest coup was the Com-promise of 1850 whereby he alone, some argue, should be credited with averting (at least for a while) the Amer-ican Civil War.

Boundary Disputes

Boundary disputes also occupied the Adams admin-istration. The United States and Great Britain claimed conflicting boundaries in both Maine and the current state of Oregon. Secretary of State Henry Clay supervised var-ious negotiations, some conducted by U.S. minister to Great Britain Albert Gallatin, who had served as secre-tary of the Treasury under Thomas Jefferson. Clay also supervised negotiations with Mexico over the Texas boundary. These matters all went unresolved during Adams's presidency.

The Congress of Panama

By 1826 six Latin American countries (Mexico; Central America; Colombia; Peru; Chile; and the Provinces of Rio de la Plata, near present-day Uruguay and Argentina) had obtained independence from Spain. With plans to liberate Cuba and Puerto Rico, the region engaged in ongoing war with the former mother country. Haiti, a French colony populated by African slave descendants, had secured independence in name only. In this environment, the countries of Latin America decided to convene in Panama in September of 1825 to discuss the ongoing wars with Spain and to negotiate treaties of alliance.

The Congress of Panama invited the United States to attend with the hope that the United States would offi-cially extend the Monroe Doctrine to the newly inde-pendent Latin American states. Adams wanted to send a U.S. delegation not only to coordinate enforcement of the Monroe Doctrine, but also to work on freedom of the seas for U.S. merchant vessels, which were being seized in connection with the wars with Spain. After seeking to postpone the meeting, Adams used his first address to Congress on December 5, 1825, to recommend a dele-gation. Then he nominated U.S. minister to Colombia Richard C. Anderson of Kentucky and Congressperson John Sergeant of Pennsylvania for the mission in a spe-cial address to the Senate in late December. Determined to oppose Adams, Jacksonians called it a deviation from the United States's policy of avoiding alliances with for-eign nations. Underneath the opposition, however, was the South's repugnance at the thought of attending a con-gress that would include black delegates from Haiti, who had fought for independence by revolting against their slaveholders.

Senate hearings on the issue dragged into 1826. In March, as Senator John Randolph of Virginia spoke in opposition to the mission, he referred to Adams's earlier nomination of Henry Clay for the State Department as the "combination of the Puritan with the black-leg," meaning swindler (Bemis, p. 553) (*See also,* Adams Becomes Pres-ident). Clay challenged Randolph to a duel, and in April they met and fired their pistols without harm. While the Senate ultimately approved the mission and the House appropriated the necessary funds, the victory was in vain. Anderson died on his way to Panama, and Sergeant arrived after the congress had adjourned. The United

States would not again reach out for collaboration with Latin America until early in the twentieth century.

The Adams Administration Legacy

Despite Adams's defeat in 1828, there was a solid minority who supported his administration's goals. The most prominent pro-Adams newspaper, the *Daily National Journal,* regularly carried editorials, many written by Adams and his secretary of state, Henry Clay, that supported their proposals for national improvement. In contrast, the *United States Telegraph* spent four years denouncing the "corrupt bargain" between Adams and Clay, and criticizing their "unconstitutional" efforts to increase the power of the federal government over the states. In the end, however, even Adams had to sum up his presidency as a fiasco:

> When I came to the Presidency the principle of internal improvement, was swelling the tide of public prosperity, till the Sable Genius of the South saw the signs of his own inevitable downfall in the unparalleled progress of the general welfare of the North, and fell to cursing the tariff and internal improvement and raised the standard of Free Trade, Nullification and State Rights. I fell, and with me fell, I fear never to rise again, certainly never to rise again in my day the system of internal improvement by National means and National Energies. The great object of my Life therefore as applied to the Administration of the Government of the United States, has failed. (Bemis, p. 150–1)

Lasting Impact

As secretary of state and diplomat, Adams is credited by historians with developing a foundation for U.S. foreign relations based on independence, freedom of the seas, and commercial reciprocity. As a representative in the House from 1831 to 1848, Adams helped to lay a foundation for the abolition of slavery. As a president with many principles and few accomplishments, however, Adams's impact on U.S. government is an unfortunate lesson. In his biography of Adams, historian John T. Morse observed of Adams's time as president that "there was opening an issue as great as has ever been presented to the American people—an issue between government conducted with a sole view to efficiency and honesty, and government conducted very largely, if not exclusively, with a view to individual and party ascendancy" (Morse, p. 200–201). No president before or since John Quincy Adams has been as unbiased in his politi-

cal appointments, and as unwilling to compromise his morals for the sake of success. But time has proven that politics rarely rewards such principles.

Sources

Bemis, Samuel Flagg. *John Quincy Adams and the Foundations of American Foreign Policy.* New York: Alfred A. Knopf, 1969.

———. *John Quincy Adams and the Union.* New York: Alfred A. Knopf, 1970.

Encyclopedia of World Biography. Vol. 1. Detroit: Gale Research, 1998.

Graff, Henry F., ed. *The Presidents: A Reference History.* 2d ed. New York: Charles Scribner's Sons, 1997.

Hargreaves, Mary W. M. *The Presidency of John Quincy Adams.* Lawrence, Kans.: University Press of Kansas, 1985.

Hecht, Marie B. *John Quincy Adams: A Personal History of an Independent Man.* New York: Macmillan, 1972.

Historic World Leaders. Vol. 4. Detroit: Gale Research, Inc., 1994.

Kane, Joseph Nathan. *Facts About the Presidents: A Compilation of Biographical and Historical Information.* 6th ed. New York: H.W. Wilson, 1993.

Morse, John T., Jr. *John Quincy Adams.* Boston: Houghton, Mifflin and Company, 1882.

Nagel, Paul C. *John Quincy Adams: A Public Life, A Private Life.* New York: Alfred A. Knopf, 1997.

Further Readings

Adams, Charles Francis, ed. *Memoirs of John Quincy Adams, Comprising Portions of His Diary from 1795 to 1848.* 12 vols. Philadelphia: J. B. Lippincott, 1874–77.

Ford, Worthington C., ed. *Writings of John Quincy Adams.* 7 vols. New York: Macmillan, 1913–17.

Ketcham, Ralph. *Presidents Above Party: The First American Presidency, 1789–1829.* Chapel Hill, N.C.: University of North Carolina Press, 1984.

Lipsky, George A. *John Quincy Adams: His Theory and Ideas.* New York: Thomas Y. Crowell, 1950.

Nagel, Paul C. *Descent from Glory: Four Generations of the John Adams Family.* New York: Oxford University Press, 1983.

Jackson Administrations

Full name: Andrew Jackson
Popular name: Old Hickory; The Hero of New Orleans

Personal Information:

Born: March 15, 1767
Birthplace: Waxhaw, South Carolina
Died: June 8, 1845
Death place: Nashville, Tennessee
Burial place: The Hermitage Estate, near Nashville, Tennessee
Religion: Presbyterian
Spouse: Rachel Donelson Robards (m. 1791 and 1794)
Children: Andrew, Jr.
Occupation: Attorney; judge; soldier; legislator
Political Party: Democratic (Democratic-Republican) Party
Age at Inauguration: 61 years

Biography

The first of the United States's "log cabin" presidents, Andrew Jackson rose from humble backcountry origins to become a U.S. congressman and senator, a renowned military hero, and the seventh president of the United States. Among many Americans, especially those of the western frontier, he was acclaimed as a symbol of the new American: self-made, strong through closeness to nature, and endowed with a powerful moral courage.

Early Life

Andrew Jackson was the only member of his immediate family to be born in the United States. In 1765 his father, also named Andrew, and mother, Elizabeth Hutchinson Jackson, had come to America from the northeastern coast of Ireland with two sons, Hugh and Robert. The family immigrated to the Waxhaw settlement in South Carolina, where Elizabeth's sisters lived. The elder Andrew tried with difficulty to cultivate the red clay soil of South Carolina, but he had little success and died suddenly in 1767. A few days after his burial, on March 15, Elizabeth Jackson gave birth to her third son, whom she named Andrew after his dead father.

For the first 10 or 12 years of his life, Andrew was raised in the home of his aunt and uncle. His mother, a devout Presbyterian, always hoped Andrew would some day become a minister, but from the start Andrew gave few indications that he was destined for the clergy. As a boy he was wild and reckless and was reported to be generally foul-mouthed. He loved to play practical jokes, and at times he exhibited a streak of cruelty that led some to consider him a bully. He also had a quick temper. Because he was sensitive to criticism, he frequently got into fights with other boys.

The most significant event of Jackson's youth was almost certainly the American Revolution (1775–83). Jackson's oldest brother, Hugh, died from exhaustion after the battle of Stono Ferry, and Robert died of small-pox contracted while he and Andrew were being held in a British prison camp. Upon his release from the camp, Andrew was nursed back to health by his mother, before she died after tending to other prisoners of war in Charleston, South Carolina. At the age of 14 Jackson found himself orphaned by the war and possessed of a lifelong hatred for the British. A year later he traveled to Charleston to claim an inheritance left to him by his grandfather. The inheritance amounted to more than three hundred pounds and would have been enough to give Jackson a good stake in life—but he squandered it in an alarmingly short period of time, mostly on drinking and gambling. He left Charleston humbled by the experience and determined to improve his behavior and make a fortune for himself.

Education

As the youngest in the family, Andrew Jackson was better educated than his brothers, but he was certainly less learned than any of the U.S. presidents before him. (He was the first president since George Washington not to attend college.) As a boy Jackson attended several schools in the Waxhaw district, where he learned to read, write, and perform bookkeeping tasks. He also studied Greek and Latin but seemed to remember little of what he had learned. In general he was a poor student who showed little regard for the rules of the English language, and he was a famously bad speller all his life. Still, as president he could be forceful and eloquent in both writing and speech.

As a teenager Jackson decided that the way for him to make his fortune was to enter the legal profession. In 1784 he traveled to Salisbury, North Carolina, where he entered the law office of Spruce McCay to learn his new occupation. While Jackson worked hard during the day, he spent very little time with his law books in the evenings, preferring to drink and carouse at the local tavern or to attend the local dancing school. He did manage to learn some law during that time, and in 1787 he left Salisbury to work at the office of Colonel John Stokes, a brilliant North Carolina lawyer. Jackson completed his legal training under Stokes, and in September of 1787, at the age of 20, he was admitted to the North Carolina bar.

Family Life

Andrew Jackson and his wife, Rachel Donelson Jackson, never had children of their own, but throughout most

Andrew Jackson. (The Library of Congress.)

of their marriage the Jackson estate was populated by many children. Jackson served as guardian for several children whose fathers had died, and in 1810 Rachel and Andrew were allowed to legally adopt her orphaned nephew, whom they christened Andrew Jackson, Jr. While Jackson could be rough and impatient with adults, he was said to be surprisingly tender and indulgent with children. The circumstances of Jackson's marriage to Rachel Jackson proved to be politically damaging when he became a candidate for president. He first met her in 1788 while a boarder in her mother's house in Nashville, Tennessee. At the time, Rachel Robards was separated from her husband, a Kentuckian named John Robards. Robards quickly grew resentful of Jackson's presence in the Donelson home, and with good reason—Jackson and Rachel Robards soon fell in love. Rachel Robards did attempt a reconciliation with her husband in 1790, but it failed. It was Andrew—and not one of Rachel's brothers, who would have been a more appropriate escort—who went to Kentucky to bring the young woman home. While traveling the two heard that Robards had been granted a divorce in Virginia, and they married without hesitation.

But Robards did not actually have a divorce; he had merely been granted permission to file for divorce in a court of law. The divorce was not actually granted until 1793. Andrew and Rachel Jackson were shocked by the news; both sincerely believed they had been married, but in the eyes of the law their marriage was illegal. In January 1794 the two exchanged vows a second time. In the

Fast Fact

With his fiery temper, Jackson was one of the few serious pistol duelists in U.S. history. His opponents included a Nashville lawyer named Charles Dickinson (whom Jackson killed in 1806); John Sevier, governor of the Tennessee Territory; and Thomas Hart Benton, the Missouri legislator. Jackson's gunfights left him with at least one bullet lodged permanently in his body, and he suffered from lead poisoning late in his life.

(Source: Robert Remini. *Andrew Jackson,* 1966.)

---

presidential campaign of 1828, famous for its mudslinging and name-calling, Jackson's opponents made much of this "adulterous" relationship. Not long after Jackson's victory—about two months before he took office—Rachel Jackson died. She had a history of heart trouble, and the strain of dealing with attacks on her character, accompanied by her fear of assuming the role of first lady, apparently contributed to a fatal attack. Jackson was grief-stricken, and forever blamed his political opponents for her death.

Career

Shortly after passing the North Carolina bar, Andrew Jackson headed west with several of his friends for the Tennessee territory. In the frontier town of Nashville, Jackson quickly established himself as an able prosecutor, trying cases that dealt mostly with land titles, debts, and sales. His record as a lawyer quickly earned him an appointment as attorney general for a district in the Southwest Territory, and financial success allowed him to begin constructing his family plantation near Nashville, which he called the Hermitage.

In 1795 Jackson became involved in a land deal of his own that went sour: he sold a large parcel of land to a Philadelphia merchant named David Allison, who offered a down payment and promissory notes to cover the rest of the purchase. After the deal Jackson wrote some promissory notes of his own, based on the income expected from the deal. But in 1797 Allison went bankrupt, defaulted on the sale, and left Jackson deeply in debt. It took Jackson years to recover, and the ordeal forever convinced him that paper money and debts were the tools of swindlers and cheats. This opinion proved to be

a highly influential factor in the "Bank War" that occurred in Jackson's second term as president (*See also,* Domestic Issues).

In 1796 Jackson was elected as the new state's first congressional representative, an office he held from 1796 to 1797. After a brief five-month stint as a U.S. senator, Jackson grew bored with the legislative life and ran for a seat on the Tennessee Superior Court, an election that he won easily. As a judge in the state's highest court, Jackson became known as a capable and impartial dispenser of justice. He served for a period of six years.

Military

Andrew Jackson's military career began in 1802 when he won election to the major-generalship of the Tennessee state militia (military leaders in those days gained offices through election rather than promotion). In the early part of the War of 1812 (1812–14), during a harsh winter's march, Jackson earned the respect of his troops as a physically tough general who sacrificed his own comfort to see to the needs of his men. The men affectionately referred to him as "Old Hickory," a name used throughout his life by friends and enemies alike. In the famous Battle of New Orleans in 1815, General Jackson commanded the troops that held the city against a British invasion. The battle took the lives of only 13 Americans, compared to over two thousand for the British. Jackson's victory was due to a number of factors—luck, serious British mistakes, and the surprising accuracy of U.S. sharpshooters—but General Jackson received full credit as the mastermind of this overwhelming defeat. At the war's end he became a national hero, considered by many to be destined for the White House.

Jackson's exploits as an American Indian fighter during his military service were renowned for different reasons and actually caused serious political problems in his later presidential campaigns. Jackson and his Tennessee volunteers were the primary fighting force in the Creek War of 1813, fought to repel an uprising by the Creek Indians who were allied with the British. They defeated the Creeks decisively in the Battle of Horseshoe Bend in Alabama.

The First Seminole War of 1817–18 was fought to deter raids on Georgia settlements. Jackson's troops tended to kill American Indians indiscriminately—men, women, and children alike—and they burned and looted every Indian village they found. During the Creek War Jackson had several soldiers executed for desertion. At times during the campaigns Jackson appeared to be acting on his own, regardless of orders. In 1818 he invaded Florida (then a Spanish territory) in response to reports that the Seminoles were staging their raids from there. He crushed the Seminole Indian invaders and executed two British citizens who were believed to have been helping the Seminoles. Afterwards, having heard rumors of a British invasion into the United States from the town

Biography:

John Caldwell Calhoun

Politician (1782–1850) John C. Calhoun was raised in South Carolina, the son of a wealthy judge, legislator, and slave owner. This southern upbringing probably played a large part in directing the course of his life including his successes along with his tragic legacy: his insistence that the Constitution should be based upon the "truth" of the inequality of man and on the principle that people are not equally entitled to liberty. Calhoun's political career began in the South Carolina legislature and took him all of the way to the vice presidency, first under President John Quincy Adams and then under President Andrew Jackson. Disagreements erupted between President Jackson and Vice President Calhoun over states' rights. Calhoun argued for the right of a state to "nullify" a federal enactment injurious to its' interests if the state believed the law to be unconstitutional. This was what Calhoun's home state of South Carolina did in response to the 1828 Tariff of Abominations, which protected northern manufacturing interests but dealt a severe eco-

nomic blow to the South's economy. After a few years had passed, Jackson threatened military force to collect unpaid duties from South Carolina. In an unprecedented action and huge upset to the administration, Calhoun resigned the vice presidency and fled to South Carolina where he immediately took a seat on the state legislature to defend his state's cause. Only through diplomatic

intervention by Henry Clay was the crisis ended. Though he served other stints as both a U.S. senator and a secretary of state, Calhoun spent the rest of his years entrenched in southern, sectional politics arguing to preserve slavery.

---

of Pensacola, Florida, the general undertook an even more extraordinary action, the seizure of an entire Spanish town. He informed the Spanish governor that he would be taking control until the Spaniards could assure the United States they would not allow British invaders into their ports. The evidence is not conclusive about whether Jackson had an order to invade Florida. One order from General Edmund Gaines authorized him to pursue the Seminoles across the border but not to attack if they were sheltered in a Spanish port. Yet the will of the James Monroe administration to possess Florida was well-known. Jackson's orders from Monroe were intentionally vague—with carefully worded suggestions, but not orders, that he should take care of the Spanish. Afterwards, Monroe and John C. Calhoun (then secretary of war) denied authorizing the invasion but Jackson escaped punishment because he had enough high-level support. A high-profile campaign for his censure, however, was led by none other than Henry Clay, an influential senator from Kentucky and a critic of the Monroe administration. The incident created an international uproar that was quietly settled in 1819, when the Spanish sold Florida to the United States, which was the goal of the James Monroe administration all along.

Jackson's conduct during the Indian campaigns earned him a reputation among journalists and many Washington legislators as a coward, tyrant, and murderer. Among the general population, however, Jackson's popularity as a no-nonsense military leader grew. He was

bold and sometimes cruel in dealing with his enemies, but in the eyes of the public—especially settlers in the U.S. South and West—he was the man to keep them safe from foreign invasions. Jackson's popularity won him another election to the U.S. Senate representing his home state of Tennessee, where he served from 1823 to 1825.

The Jackson Presidency

Jackson was first elected president in 1828. He was 61 years old. His first term was marked by a deepening alienation between him and his vice president, John C. Calhoun. Calhoun played a part in the "Eaton Affair," in which vicious accusations were cast against the morality of the wife of John Eaton, Jackson's friend and secretary of war. Jackson and Calhoun also clashed on the issue of nullification, whereby if a state objects to a law, it has the right to block its enforcement. Calhoun's home state of South Carolina attempted to nullify the tariffs of 1828 and 1829. When Jackson called for a bill authorizing military suppression of South Carolina's defiance, it took a compromise tariff, engineered by Henry Clay, to avoid confrontation. With the relationship between Jackson and Calhoun all but destroyed, Jackson's secretary of state, Martin Van Buren, became Jackson's running match for the campaign of 1832. One of the most tragic events of the nineteenth century, the forced march of thousands of Cherokees along the "Trail of Tears" into Indian Territory (what is today Oklahoma), was allowed by Jackson's 1830 Indian Removal Act.

Jackson's second term was dominated by his campaign to abolish the Second Bank of the United States (BUS). He forced the removal of federal deposits from its vaults and distributed them among a group of "pet banks"—a move that led to powerful protests from Senate members, many of whom declared the president's actions unconstitutional. His last months in office were tainted by the financial crisis caused by these drastic measures. During his second term, however, his administration achieved several important advances in foreign policy: the reopening of British West Indian ports to U.S. commerce, the settling of outstanding claims against France, and the establishment of diplomatic relations in several key Asian ports. One of Jackson's last official acts was the recognition of the independence of Texas, though he resisted the issue of annexation.

Post-presidential Years

After the 1837 inauguration of his successor, Martin Van Buren, Jackson retired to his estate in Tennessee, the Hermitage. He remained a powerful force in the Democratic Party despite his distance from national politics, his age—now 70—and his poor health. As the nation suffered through a financial panic and deepening depression, Jackson publicly supported much of Van Buren's economic agenda, including the Divorce Bill, which ultimately established a U.S. Treasury that was independent of private banking interests.

Jackson was disappointed to learn that his friend Van Buren was opposed to Texas annexation. Because Jackson considered Texas to be an indispensable component of U.S. security, he switched his allegiance to James K. Polk, the Democratic Party's candidate, for the 1844 presidential campaign. He lived just long enough to see Texas join the Union as a state. In June of 1845 Jackson, then 78 years old and suffering from tuberculosis and dropsy, died quietly in his bed at the Hermitage, surrounded by friends, children, and grandchildren.

The Andrew Jackson Administrations

Andrew Jackson presided over one of the most remarkable periods of political change in U.S. history, in which circumstances seemed destined to provide wealth and political opportunity to the many, instead of an aristocratic few. Jackson's rise to power contributed to the birth of the Democratic Party, and through his insistence that the president alone represented the will of the whole nation, he signaled a shift in U.S. government toward a strong executive.

Jackson Becomes President

The Campaign of 1828

In the early nineteenth century the nation found its way of life being reshaped by a number of factors: the surge of settlers into the western United States, the impact of the Industrial Revolution, the advent of great U.S. cities, and dramatic advances in transportation. Andrew Jackson's rise to power in this era was no coincidence. In a time when many Americans were growing tired of being governed by a "Virginia Dynasty" that they viewed as being elitist, corrupt, and detached, Jackson, was considered the champion of the popular majority. The Virginia Dynasty referred to the early hold of Virginians on the presidency—only one of the first five presidents, John Adams, was not from Virginia. George Washington was from Virginia, and presidents Thomas Jefferson, James Madison, and James Monroe were all Virginians as well and had been nominated through a caucus system over which Virginian politicians had a powerful hold.

The presidential election of 1824 lent credibility to the idea of a selfish and underhanded system at work in government. Jackson, running against Kentucky senator Henry Clay, secretary of state John Quincy Adams, and former secretary of the treasury William Crawford, captured most of the popular and electoral votes but failed to gain an overall majority in the electoral college. The selection of a president then fell to the House of Representatives, of which Henry Clay was Speaker. Though Clay had finished last in the balloting and was therefore eliminated from consideration, he still believed Jackson to be his most powerful political rival and used his influence to gain John Quincy Adams the presidency. When Clay was later named to Adams's cabinet, Jackson's followers denounced the "corrupt bargain" that had gotten Adams into the White House.

U.S. voters were reminded of this corrupt bargain by Jackson's supporters in the election of 1828—considered by many historians to be one of the dirtiest presidential campaigns in history. The election turned out to be a strictly Jackson-Adams contest. Jackson and his followers officially split with Adams's party, the National Republicans, and called themselves the Democrats. Almost no issues of substance were addressed by the campaign. Instead, Jackson's followers depicted Adams as an elitist with European tastes who had spent extravagant sums of money on elegant White House furniture. In particular, they made a great fuss over Adams's purchase of a billiard table, which they portrayed as the toy of a gambler and aristocrat. One of the most outrageous claims against Adams was that he had procured the services of a prostitute for the Russian minister when he was U.S. minister to Russia—a charge that was never substantiated.

Although Adams did not stoop to mudslinging, his supporters launched attacks that were as disgraceful as the Democrats'. Charges that Jackson and his wife were

Administration

Administration Dates
March 4, 1829–March 4, 1833
March 4, 1833–March 4, 1837

Vice President
John Caldwell Calhoun (1829–32)
Martin Van Buren (1833–37)

Cabinet

Secretary of State
Martin Van Buren (1829–31)
Edward Livingston (1831–33)
Louis McLane (1833–34)
John Forsyth (1834–41)

Secretary of the Treasury
Samuel D. Ingham (1829–31)
Louis McLane (1831–33)
William J. Duane (1833)

Rogert B. Taney (1833–34)
Levi Woodbury (1834–41)

Secretary of War
John H. Eaton (1829–31)
Lewis Cass (1831–36)

Attorney General
John M. Berrien (1829–31)
Roger B. Taney (1831–33)
Benjamin F. Butler (1833–38)

Secretary of the Navy
John Branch (1829–31)
Levi Woodbury (1831–34)
Mahlon Dickerson (1834–37)

Postmaster General
John McLean (1823–29)
William T. Barry (1829–35)
Amos Kendall (1835–40)

---

adulterers (*See also,* Family Life) and that his pious mother had been a common prostitute stung Jackson acutely. Black-bordered handbills with the shapes of coffins printed on them were distributed as campaign material. They cited Jackson's numerous pistol duels and his hanging of mutinous militiamen during the Creek War as evidence of his barbarism.

The Election
In the end all this sleazy campaigning had little effect on voters. The party organization assembled by Jackson, vice-presidential candidate John C. Calhoun, and the New York politician Martin Van Buren—along with Jackson's widespread popularity—decided the election of 1828. Jackson won 56 percent of the popular vote, and a 178 to 83 victory in the electoral college. In March of 1829 he took the oath of office and delivered an inaugural address in which he vowed to undertake "the task of reform, which will require particularly the correction of those abuses that have brought the patronage of the Federal Government into conflict with the freedom of elections, and the counteraction of those causes which have disturbed the rightful course of appointment and have placed or continued power in unfaithful or incompetent hands."

Jackson's election was interpreted by the general population as the end of government control by the com-

mercial aristocracy of Virginia. Though Jackson was a bit of a Tennessee aristocrat himself, and by no definition a common man, his coming to power was expected to establish a link between the central government and the masses of people from all over the country. This heralded the advent of what came to be known as Jacksonian Democracy. His view was generally that government's task was to break down barriers, such as social and economic obstacles, so people could develop their abilities and enjoy the rewards of their work. Also he held that the president, being the only nationally elected official, reflected the will of the people and therefore should vigorously exercise his powers. While he held that government should generally leave people alone, as president he believed wholly in the indivisibility of the federal Union, on which the American society was founded. He fought hard to maintain a single, indissoluble Union.

The Campaign of 1832
The campaign of 1832 was memorable for several reasons. It was the first in which presidential candidates were selected by nominating conventions, which took over from the state legislatures the responsibility for naming candidates. The first national party platform was published, and for the first time there was a third-party ticket in the field, though the party—the Anti-Masonic Party—was a short-lived movement. It was formed in

reaction to a particular social phenomenon of the day: a growing suspicion of the secrecy of the Society of Freemasons. The Freemasons, originally a loose fraternity of free-thinking men, had in the United States become more of a social club for wealthy, upper-class farmers, merchants, and bankers whose ranks included both Andrew Jackson and Henry Clay. However, when a New York bricklayer named Morgan, who had written an exposé of the practices (mostly symbolic rituals) of the Freemasons, was mysteriously murdered, the Anti-Masonic Party was formed with the express purpose of wresting control of the government from the Freemasons, and combating secrecy in a supposedly free and open society.

The platform of the Anti-Masons was based on a charge of nationwide conspiracy for which there was not much evidence (Morgan's murder was likely the work of a few men), and the party did not play a significant role in the campaign. It was to be a contest between the two fragments of the Republican Party. For the Democratic-Republicans, Jackson's nomination was a given; the function of the Democratic convention was simply to select a vice-presidential candidate. Martin Van Buren was overwhelmingly nominated over the out-of-favor John C. Calhoun. The National Republicans nominated their leader, Kentucky congressperson Henry Clay, and the fight was on.

The presidential campaign of 1832, unlike Jackson's first, had a real issue. Clay had made sure the issue would be the future of the Second Bank of the United States (BUS), an institution to which Clay knew Jackson was opposed. The bank's charter was not up for review until 1836, and Jackson was willing to wait until then to set about dismantling it. Clay, however, saw the issue as a means by which he could gain the White House. He convinced bank president Nicholas Biddle to reapply for the bank's charter four years early, in the campaign year of 1832. Clay thought Jackson could either veto the charter, thereby opposing a congressional majority and angering the Eastern aristocrats, or he could give in and allow the charter to be renewed, alienating the westerners who had elected him.

But in staking his presidency on the issue of the BUS, Clay had made a serious political miscalculation. He appeared to believe that the U.S. presidency was still decided by the moneyed classes—a belief that Jackson had already proven wrong in 1828. Confident that this would continue to be a major factor of U.S. politics, Jackson promptly vetoed Congress's approval of the bank's charter. Congress was unable to override the veto, and the Bank issue was set before the American people to decide in the coming presidential election.

The National Republicans, helped along by a seemingly endless stream of money and propaganda by Nicholas Biddle, pointed to Jackson's veto as just the latest proof that he was a tyrant who had trampled the Bill of Rights. The Democrats, however, decided to address the issue as little as possible: a nationwide campaign of parades, songs, and barbecues was accompanied by the old arguments about rich versus poor and the privileged versus the working class, and about Andrew Jackson as the only "man of the people" in the contest. The election results showed that the national sentiment had not changed since 1828. Jackson claimed a 219 to 49 majority in the electoral college.

Jackson's Advisers

Prior to Jackson's election the executive cabinet was known as the organization where U.S. presidents were cultivated. Jackson's appointments, however, were notoriously mediocre; among them, only his secretary of state Martin Van Buren was a first-rate officer with the intelligence and shrewdness to have much influence over policy formation. This was not because Jackson chose his officers poorly. He chose a weak cabinet purposely, because he meant to dominate it. He believed firmly in the doctrine of "executive supremacy"—it was the president, and not the legislature or the courts, who alone represented and symbolized the will of the American people. As one historian put it, "While [he] intended to listen to their ideas, his vision of President-Cabinet relations involved secretaries who functioned as lieutenants, carrying out policies they had little voice in deciding" (Belohlavek, p. 25).

The Kitchen Cabinet

There was a group of greater consequence who advised Jackson: a clique of men known by jealous adversaries as the Kitchen Cabinet, so-called because it included several men without official titles with whom Jackson met in informal sessions. The group consisted of Jackson's closest friends and most trusted political allies, including his good friend John H. Eaton, the secretary of war. The other principal members of the Kitchen Cabinet were William B. Lewis, a friend from Tennessee; Amos Kendall, editor of a pro-Jackson newspaper in Kentucky and a fellow enemy of Kentucky senator Henry Clay; Duff Green, editor of the *United States Telegraph,* the leading Jackson political organ; and Isaac Hill, editor of the *New Hampshire Patriot* and later, with the help of Jackson, a New Hampshire senator. Van Buren and Eaton were also trusted advisers who met informally with Jackson.

Because Jackson saw his cabinet secretaries as clerks rather than advisers, he discontinued the practice of holding regular cabinet meetings. So the Kitchen Cabinet was certainly more powerful than the actual cabinet. Though generally more influential than Jackson's formal cabinet, the Kitchen Cabinet's role in forming policy has been historically overrated. Jackson himself was the policy maker. Composed largely of journalists, the Kitchen Cabinet helped Jackson to perceive, and in turn shape, popular thought. In this way they did help to direct his policy. Ultimately, it was Jackson (critics sometimes called him King Andrew I) who decided the administration's course of action.

Martin Van Buren and John Calhoun

Toward the end of Jackson's first term, Martin Van Buren was emerging as the clear choice as Jackson's right-hand man and successor, helped along by both his own political shrewdness and by a succession of political blunders on the part of Vice President John Calhoun. When Calhoun perceived Van Buren's threat to his future presidency, he launched an effort to strike down his political opponents in the cabinet. Unwisely, the secretary he pursued most vigorously was Eaton, Jackson's close friend—and even more unwisely, his attacks centered on the character and reputation of Eaton's wife, Peggy. After Rachel Jackson's death, caused in the president's opinion by the slander of malicious propagandists, the president was especially offended and upset by these attacks. Calhoun and President Jackson also differed substantially on the issue of states rights. When Jackson later learned that in 1818, Calhoun the legislator had voted to censure the general after his Florida campaign, Calhoun's days were numbered. By 1831 Jackson had forced Calhoun's resignation and purged the cabinet of his followers. Van Buren became the next vice president at the beginning of Jackson's second term.

Jackson was known as "King Andrew" reflecting the dominance he held during his term, especially over Congress. Because the president was directly elected, he felt the presidency reflected best the will of the people and should prevail.

Jackson and Congress

Jackson presided over the Twenty-first, Twenty-second, Twenty-third, and Twenty-fourth sessions of Congress, each of which was composed of a majority of Democratic members in both the House of Representatives and the Senate. The opposition party, the National Republicans (later the Whigs), was led by figures such as Kentucky senator Henry Clay and Massachusetts senator Daniel Webster. While Jackson's executive decisions did spark much legislative debate, some of it quite heated, he generally prevailed due to the strength of his majority.

When Jackson's majority did not prevail in Congress, his belief in "executive supremacy" was made clear—"King Andrew" defied and dominated Congress as few presidents in history have done. The six presidents before him had exercised the veto a total of 10 times, but Jackson alone wielded it 12 times during his two terms, including seven uses of the "pocket veto." A pocket veto allows a bill to fail through inaction. If Congress adjourns before the president can return the vetoed bill within the specified 10 days, the bill is considered "pocketed" and does not become a law. The pocket veto, used first by James Madison, was employed by Jackson as a relatively quiet, noncontroversial way to sink congressional legislation with which he did not agree.

Jackson and the Judiciary

In the years since the Jackson administration, it has been accepted in U.S. government that in the interpretation of the Constitution, the Supreme Court holds ultimate supremacy. To Jackson, this was questionable. He saw no reason why the Supreme Court should act as the final arbiter of constitutional issues. His views on this subject were complicated, however, by the fact that Chief Justice John Marshall was a political enemy who had supported John Quincy Adams and Henry Clay during the election of 1828. It was often difficult to tell whether Jackson's reactions to the Court's opinions were due to political convictions, or to his personal feelings on the matter at hand.

The best example of Jackson's sometimes contradictory approach to the judiciary is the Court's decision during the Georgia controversy of his first term, involving the Cherokee Indians. (*See also,* Domestic Issues).

Biography:

Daniel Webster

Lawyer; Politician (1782–1852) In the course of his life, Daniel Webster succeeded in making a name for himself on both the political and judicial fronts. Webster was a devout Federalist, which meant that he supported the idea that the states should exist under the control of a strong, unifying federal government. Though shared by many others, his position was still radical at a time when most people regarded the union of states as a loose and non-permanent partnership that could be dissolved. Serving in both the House and Senate, Webster could always be found leading the resistance to any legislation or attempt by any state, to usurp power from the federal government. In 1832, as a senator representing Massachusetts during Andrew Jackson's presidency, Webster was engaged in a Senate debate with Congressman Robert Y. Hayne of South Carolina. In the course of the debate, Webster made a now-famous, stirring, and emotional declaration of his passionate attachment to the idea of a strong, inseparable Union. His com-

mitment was echoed in his support for President Jackson's enforcement of state challenges to federal government edicts. Webster was a frequent guest in the White House until relations began to crumble following President Jackson's veto of the proposed recharter of the Bank of the United States. Webster had interests in the bank and vigorously condemned the president. In 1934

Webster voted with the Senate majority to censure President Jackson for removing government deposits from the bank. Webster eventually made his own failed run at the presidency before losing his fortune to speculation in middle western real estate.

When Georgia began to enact laws extending their authority over Cherokee lands—an action in strict contradiction to U.S. treaties with the Cherokees—the Supreme Court struck down these laws as unconstitutional. President Jackson, however, refused to enforce the decision mandated by the Supreme Court, on the constitutional grounds that Congress did not have the power to regulate commerce with Indian tribes. The president made the assertion that he was not empowered to enforce the law against a state. This is an extraordinary position, given that a year later Jackson came down hard on the "nullies" in South Carolina who made similar arguments for states's rights. The president's constitutional arguments seem to have fallen short in this instance, and appear to have been a rationalization of his lack of sympathy for the American Indians and his animosity toward Marshall.

Following Marshall's death in 1835, Jackson appointed Roger Brooke Taney as chief justice of the Supreme Court on March 15, 1836. Jackson's associate justice appointments were as follows: John McLean (1829); Henry Baldwin (1830); James Moore Wayne (1835); and Philip Pendleton Barbour (1836). As chief justice, Taney is best remembered for his controversial opinion in the 1857 *Dred Scott v. Sandford* case. In speaking for the majority, Taney ruled that Congress had no authority to outlaw slavery in the U.S. territories. This decision voided the Missouri Compromise, a plan meant

to keep the balance between slave states and free states, and helped speed the onset of the American Civil War (1861–65). Taney wrote that blacks, whether slaves or free, were not citizens as defined in the Constitution; they were "beings of an inferior order, (with) no rights which the white man was bound to respect."

Changes in the U.S. Government

Jacksonian Democracy

By the 1820s and 1830s the swelling population of the U.S. frontier helped transform U.S. government into something that more closely resembled true democracy. One by one, states began to eliminate property requirements for suffrage, extending the right to vote to all adult white males. While this still eliminated a good portion of the population, namely women and African Americans, it nevertheless transformed the federal government into one that more closely resembled the will of the masses. Candidates were more directly chosen by the will of the people, rather than by a caucus of political bosses.

Because Jackson saw himself as reflecting the will of the people, he also assumed a dictatorial role and saw the presidency as superior to the Supreme Court and the Congress. So he became the main beneficiary of this new populism, so much that this new type of democracy was called Jacksonian Democracy. While he did not create the new democracy, he was the only politician in possession of the shrewdness and backwoods credentials that would allow him to ride this new political sentiment to the presidency. Jackson was a symbol of the shift of U.S. political influence from the conservative eastern seaboard to the new states on the other side of the Appalachians.

The "Spoils System"

In his first inaugural address Jackson had promised to clean house in Washington. No party had been overturned in government since 1800, and many government offices suffered from complacency—or worse, incompetence and corruption. A few officeholders in 1828 had actually had their commissions signed by President Washington and had lingered on into their eighties, performing virtually no work for their salaries. To Jackson, the quickest way to reform was to sweep out this old, worthless corps and bring in his own followers—rewarding them as he punished the supporters of his predecessors.

Jackson is thus recognized by historians as having initiated one of the most troublesome and demoralizing practices in U.S. democracy. Though the "spoils system," from New York senator William Marcy's classic 1832 remark: "To the victor belong the spoils of the enemy" (Remini, p.110), was hardly new to U.S. government, and though Jackson actually only replaced fewer than 2,000 out of 11,000 officers, he did employ the system to a greater degree than any of his predecessors. Some of Jackson's officers, it was later revealed, had openly bought their posts with campaign contributions. Fairly or not, Jackson bears much historical blame for promoting the practice of patronage and undermining public service by subordinating professional merit to political considerations.

During Jackson's administration two states were admitted to the Union. Arkansas became the 25th state on June 15, 1836, and Michigan the 26th on January 26, 1837.

Domestic Issues

The remarkable changes in the U.S. domestic environment before and during Jackson's presidency presented the government with a host of new problems. While the nation continued to expand into its western frontier, resulting in the growth of an independent pioneer population who profited from skyrocketing land values, the Industrial Revolution had produced powerful urban centers in the North and the East. The nation's expansion into the American frontier created new tensions among settlers and American Indians. Rural Americans clamored for more land, some of which was legally occupied by the American Indians under previous treaties with the federal government. At the same time, the rise to prominence of Northern cities left many Americans in the South, who still relied on a primarily agricultural economy, feeling overlooked and even victimized by a government that appeared to be growing more sympathetic to urban interests. Both of these circumstances sparked fresh debate about the issue of states rights. Citizens in certain states, unhappy with the restrictions imposed on their way of life by officials in faraway Washington, began to assert that it was the states, and not the central government, which held ultimate sovereignty in the United States. In a country that had existed for only about a half century, this question had not yet been settled to anyone's satisfaction. Increasingly the United States was becoming divided into two sectional interests: the wealthy and rapidly growing urban North, and the traditional agricultural society of the South.

Indian Removal: The Trail of Tears

Prior to Jackson's arrival in the White House, Presidents James Monroe and John Quincy Adams had each tried to handle the problems resulting from the rapid settlement of the lands west of the Appalachians, where white settlers were coming into frequent contact with large American Indian tribes. Various treaties had been negotiated with the tribes, but continued frontier expansion forced renegotiation after renegotiation. While many of the tribes, faced with a combination of lures and threats, agreed to removal further west, some rebelled and many of them were crushed by General Jackson, the infamous Indian fighter.

The Cherokees of Georgia were a tribe who had seemed to win the fight to stay in their ancestral homeland. Like the Creeks, Choctaws, and Chickasaws, they were a practical people who had adopted many white ways and worked them to an advantage. The Cherokees raised cash crops and kept African American slaves. Both their houses and their language had become a mixture of Cherokee and white influences; in 1821 a half-Cherokee named Sequoya developed an alphabet for a new written tribal language, in which newspapers and books were printed. The tribe was widely considered to have run one of the best school systems in the South.

Under treaty with the United States the Cherokees were entitled to remain in their ancestral Georgia homeland and to be recognized as a semisovereign nation within the United States. Holding fast to their treaty, they resisted every federal inducement and threat to remove them. Nevertheless, the state of Georgia was resolute in its drive to get rid of the Cherokees. While the Cherokees had friends in Congress, there were no sympathizers to be found in the Georgia legislature. The people of Georgia wanted the Cherokee lands and were willing to ignore the federal government to get them. The state legislature tested its authority by trying and convicting a

Jackson's signing of the 1830 Indian Removal Act allowed the forced 1,200-mile march from Georgia to what is now Oklahoma. On the course of the "Trail of Tears" over four thousand Cherokees died and the ones that made it to Oklahoma were demoralized and were never able to recover from the horrific event. (The Granger Collection, New York. Reproduced by permission.)

white missionary for a crime committed in Cherokee territory. The conviction was appealed to the Supreme Court, then led by Chief Justice John Marshall, Jackson's adversary. While Marshall did not believe any more than Jackson that whites and Indians could live peacefully side by side, he was adamant that the United States honor its contracts. He ruled that the state of Georgia had no authority in Cherokee territory, threw out the conviction, and clearly proclaimed that the State of Georgia could not force the Cherokees to yield their homeland.

Defiance

To Georgians the matter was not settled. The state had gone largely for Jackson in the election of 1828, and the people knew that as a lifelong Indian fighter the president was not likely to stand up for the Cherokees. In an act of sheer defiance, the state held onto its prisoner, manipulated a few unscrupulous Cherokees into signing fraudulent agreements that gave away the land, and undertook the forced removal of the entire tribe from Georgia. President Jackson, learning of the Georgia controversy, was quoted as saying: "John Marshall has made his decision. Let him enforce it" (McDonald, p. 177).

The president proved not only willing to overlook Georgia's defiance of the federal government; he soon sanctioned it by signing the 1830 Indian Removal Act

into law. Under this legislation the lands formerly held under treaty by American Indians within the states were exchanged for new lands west of the Mississippi River. Georgia engineered the tragic march thereafter known as the "Trail of Tears," the forcible 1,200-mile migration of the Cherokees and other southeastern tribes to what is now Oklahoma. Over four thousand Indians died on the march—two thousand of them in camps, waiting for the march to begin. Eventually, about 15,000 Cherokees made it to Oklahoma, a bitter and demoralized people who would never fully recover from the horrors of their forced march.

Jackson's role in the Trail of Tears has been roundly denounced by many historians, who claim that the president let his own personal history, emotions, and antagonism for John Marshall get in the way of the Constitution. At every turn Jackson allowed the State of Georgia to undermine existing authorities of the U.S. government, and he set a hateful precedent for federal treatment of American Indians. On the other hand, some think the president's conduct in the Georgia controversy was entirely detached, practical, and unemotional—he would never knowingly have allowed a state to nullify the authority of the U.S. government, but he also knew that an attempt to force the people of the South and the West to abide by the U.S.-Indian treaties was a doomed effort. The laws were, essentially, unenforceable, and the president was merely responding to the will of the people.

The Tariff of 1828 and Nullification

Just before Jackson took office in 1828, Congress passed an extremely high protective tariff. No legislators completely favored the tariff, but it was accepted by the majority and signed into law by John Quincy Adams. Specifically, the tariff imposed duties on imported goods to protect the prices of goods manufactured in the industrial North. The South, which was the least prosperous U.S. region because of declining land productivity and an increasingly costly system of slave labor, had no such protections for its agricultural products. Southern farmers and plantation owners were squeezed at both ends, forced to buy manufactured goods from the North on a closed market, and forced to compete on an open international market with their cotton or tobacco exports. Foreign markets reacted by imposing their own tariffs.

Ironically, the Tariff of 1828—denounced in the South as the "Tariff of Abominations"—had been masterminded by Jackson's supporters in Congress. It was designed specifically to alienate Southern voters, driving them away from the Adams administration into the waiting arms of Jackson. The tariff did just that, but a year later President Jackson was left holding the bag. Most southerners hated the tariff, but the cotton planters of South Carolina were especially angry. Trade reprisals from Europe had denied the South its market, and South Carolina's land was becoming depleted because of the adverse effects of cotton on the soil. It also was facing increased competition from the rich cotton land in the Southwest. However, a constitutional majority had decided that this was the way trade would be administrated in the United States.

Calhoun Proposes Nullification

It was the Constitution, however, to which South Carolina's most prominent politician, Vice President John C. Calhoun, turned to solve the problems presented by the tariff. In 1829 he secretly wrote and distributed copies of *The South Carolina Exposition and Protest,* a pamphlet with a novel and ingenious interpretation of the Constitution. Calhoun argued that the Union had not been formed directly by the people of the United States; it had rather been formed by the people through the individual states, of which they were citizens. It was the states, and not a single federal government, who were sovereign. The states themselves were the indivisible units of government that had formed an agreement, the Union, for their mutual benefit.

Obviously, Calhoun argued, South Carolina was not benefiting from the Tariff of 1828. When a state objected to a law passed by a majority in the Union, as South Carolina objected to the tariff, it had the right to nullify the law (block its enforcement) within its borders until three-quarters of the other states overruled its decision. At this time the state could choose to yield to the will of the other states, or to secede entirely from the Union. Though a highly provocative document, the *Exposition* did not have much immediate effect in the South; for the time being, South Carolina remained largely alone in its outrage. But the dangerous theories of nullification and secession had been presented to the American people and were destined to work their destruction. Despite his conduct in the Georgia controversy, Jackson was an ardent supporter of the Union, and the *Exposition* had identified a new political enemy for him: his own vice president.

The South had supported Jackson in 1828, and after his election southerners fully expected him to pull the tariff rates down, especially after his passive "defense" of Georgia's rights in the Cherokee affair. But they were mistaken. Jackson did sympathize with southerners, but he also wanted to preside over a debt-free nation, and tariff revenues were an element in his plan. When Congress passed a new tariff in 1832, its rates were more modest than those of the Tariff of Abominations. But they were still considered outrageous and protective, especially in South Carolina. The state was now ready for drastic action. In the state elections of 1832 the "nullies" won a two-thirds majority, and the new state legislature promptly announced that the existing federal tariff was null and void within the borders of South Carolina. It further threatened to withdraw from the Union if the Washington government attempted to collect the duties by force.

Jackson Responds

President Jackson declared that if South Carolinians refused to collect the tariff and send the proceeds to Washington, he would personally lead an army into the state. For a brief moment violence seemed imminent. But again, no states joined South Carolina in their dramatic protest, and Kentucky senator Henry Clay proposed an 1833 compromise tariff that would reduce the tariff's existing rate. Despite bitter debate, the tariff was eventually squeezed through Congress.

Neither Jackson nor the "nullies" won a clear victory in this contest, though South Carolina did come away with a lower tariff, which was what it had wanted from the start. After the conflict had subsided, Jackson expressed fears that the next logical step in the assertion of states rights was secession. His fears proved prophetic in 1860, when South Carolina became the first state to secede from the Union at the outset of the American Civil War (1861–65). While it is true that Jackson may have done more to squash the sentiment of nullification and secession at its roots, it is also probable that the only way he could have accomplished this was through military force. In hindsight it seems that only the tragedy of the American Civil War could permanently resolve the question of secession. In its far-reaching and disastrous consequences for the United States, the concept of nullification became perhaps the most significant issue of Andrew Jackson's presidency.

Internal Improvements and the Reach of the Federal Government

Jackson was both a westerner and a strict Constitutional constructionist: as one, he understood the need for roads and canals on the American frontier; as another, he questioned the constitutionality of the federal government paying for them. In 1830 he vetoed an appropriations bill for the construction of a road between Maysville and Lexington, Kentucky. He told Congress that he was not personally against the road, but that since it was to be built entirely within the boundaries of one state, rather than linking two or more states, it was unconstitutional for the federal government to pay for it. If the Constitution were amended to authorize such projects, he said, he would approve them.

In his veto of the Maysville Road, Jackson's true intent appears to have once again been obscured by politics and his personal feelings. Construction of the Maysville Road would have been undertaken entirely within the home state of Kentucky senator Henry Clay, Jackson's political rival, and would have added greatly to Clay's popularity there. Later, Jackson approved similar bills for internal improvements when the expenditures promised to boost his own popularity.

Because of politics and his own emotional involvement with certain issues, Jackson's stance on states's rights is difficult to pin down with certainty. While he began his political career clearly in line with the conservative ideas of Thomas Jefferson, including an inclination toward states's rights and laissez-faire economics (or the doctrine that government should not interfere in economics), he appeared to take a more active view later in his administration. He went on to support a strong central government (of which he was the "supreme executive") that was more involved in the affairs of the states—but often, the ultimate influence in his policies was political expediency. He continued throughout his presidency to worry over the constitutional difficulties involved in public works. Generally, he seemed to rely on a simple formula—if a public works project would work for him and the Democrats, he was for it; if it promised to benefit his opponents, he was against it.

The Bank War

Jackson had voiced his opposition to the Second Bank of the United States (BUS) shortly after his 1829 inauguration, but given all the pressing issues of his first term, the bank did not become a high priority. In 1832, however, it would become, along with the nullification controversy, one of the two defining issues of his presidency.

Through 29 strategically located branches, the BUS controlled about a third of all U.S. bank deposits and han-

dled about $70 million in transactions each year. Jackson, as a land speculator who had been burned in the 1795 Allison ordeal (*See also, Career*), was wary of an institution that held such immense power over the nation's money supply.

The Nature of the Second Bank of the United States

During Jackson's term the bank was led by Nicholas Biddle, a conservative Philadelphian under whom the bank flourished. The BUS acted as the government's financial agent, paying government bills out of its accounts, providing vaults for its gold and silver, investing deposits, and selling bonds. Biddle took pride in the public service provided by his bank, as well as its annual profits, but the fact remained that the bank was not a government institution. It was successful primarily because it controlled such a huge portion of the U.S. money supply, but its policies were made not by elected officials but by a board of directors responsible to shareholders. The bank was opposed by three main groups: the western bankers, who thought it was unfairly restraining their land speculations; the growing financial community of New York, who wanted looser control of the nation's money supply; and "hard-money" folks such as Andrew Jackson, who were simply opposed to any person or institution that issued paper money in quantities greater than it could redeem in gold and silver.

Opponents' charges of corruption and concentrated power at the BUS were justified. The bank had fallen into the hands of a wealthy clique, and the range of its beneficiaries was becoming narrower. However, the BUS did serve some positive functions. It kept the western banks under some restraint, issued sound bank notes, and reduced overall bank failures. It helped the West expand by making credit reasonably available, and it was also a safe depository for the government's funds. It did have a monopoly of surplus federal funds, but that monopoly had been authorized by Congress. The bank was a highly important and useful institution.

Biddle was aware of Jackson's opposition to the bank, and he was also aware that the president intended to run for another term in office. This meant that the Jackson administration might extend into 1836, the year the bank's charter would come up for reauthorization. Biddle lobbied hard to gain the president's favor: he made loans to several key Jackson supporters and designed a plan to retire the national debt, which was a particular goal of Jackson's. But Jackson was unmoved, and Biddle turned to Congress for support. It was here—and not in the White House as many had expected—that the first shot in the Bank War was fired.

Clay and Biddle Challenge Jackson

Henry Clay, Jackson's nemesis and a presidential hopeful, convinced Biddle in January 1832 to reapply for the bank's charter, four years before its 1836 expiration.

Clay knew full well that a majority of Congress would support the charter and put Jackson on the spot. If Jackson vetoed the charter, he would oppose a congressional majority and anger the moneyed classes of the East. In Clay's eyes this created the opportunity for Clay to win the presidential election by promising to save the bank. If Jackson gave in and signed the bill, he would alienate the westerners who had voted him into office. Either way, Clay reasoned, it would be a victory for him.

Clay's political gamble on the bank failed (*See also,* Jackson Becomes President), as soon as Jackson won his second term he arranged for the demise of the BUS. Soon after his inauguration he began to deposit government funds not with the BUS, but into several dozen state institutions, his so-called "pet banks." The new depositories were selected because of their pro-Jackson sympathies, and they were reputed by Jackson's enemies to be weak and unstable institutions. While this is only partly true (they were certainly not as stable as the BUS), this was the first in a series of events that would nearly bring the financial structure of the country crashing down. In a fit of spite, Biddle began to call in loans with unnecessary severity, apparently to force reconsideration of the bank's charter. The result was a wave of bank failures that wiped out the savings of thousands of citizens, which was precisely the kind of outcome Jackson had feared from the immense power of the BUS.

The Specie Circular

The nation's teetering financial structure soon swung dramatically in the other direction, however; under pressure from the business community, Biddle reversed his policy, increasing the nation's money supply and making loans to other banks. A boom in land speculation occurred, in which Jackson's "pet banks" proved to be among the most irresponsible investors. By 1836, when the BUS breathed its last breath, land values had soared, the number of state banks had more than doubled, and more credit was issued than could possibly be redeemed in any short period of time. Government land sales totaled $25 million in 1836. Since there was no Second Bank of the United States to slow things down, Jackson put an end to all land sales by issuing the Specie Circular in July, which required that government lands be paid for in gold and silver coin. Paper money was no longer acceptable.

While he stopped the runaway speculation, Jackson also created a full-blown financial panic. Many western speculators were unable to pay their debts to the government and went bankrupt. The Specie Circular drained gold and silver supplies from the East, creating a depression there. Jackson's financial policy, based largely on ignorance and stubbornness, was perhaps the biggest disaster of his administration. While few today would argue that the Second Bank of the United States should have remained a chartered institution, Jackson's method of bringing it down was reckless. The damage done to the U.S. economy ruined the career of Martin Van Buren,

Fast Fact

The traditional symbol for the Democratic Party, the donkey, was first used as an attack on Jackson by the Whigs, his political opponents. They intended the "jackass" to be a satire on Jackson's supposed ignorance.

(Source: Morison, Commager, and Leuchtenburg. *A Concise History of the American Republic,* 1983.)

his successor, and lasted well into the 1840s. In 1841 alone, 28,000 Americans declared bankruptcy.

In hindsight, an institution such as the Second Bank of United States probably never should have been chartered without the kind of regulatory oversight that is provided today by the Board of Governors of the Federal Reserve System. The BUS granted loans to secure political influence, and retaliated against opposition by disrupting business and threatening government. The fall of the BUS may have been the most important economic development of the nineteenth century, and the federal banking system of today is designed intricately and carefully to avoid the kind of financial panic that was created in 1836. What the nation needed in 1836, however, was a government program that would provide an effective means of regulating a banking system, that would benefit all classes of people. It is doubtful, given Jackson's personality and the prevailing 1830s philosophy of limited government, that the Jackson administration could have pulled this off. Instead, President Jackson did what he could—he destroyed the bank, roots and all.

Foreign Issues

The United States, one of the world's youngest nations in the early nineteenth century, had yet to spread its wings in terms of foreign affairs. As a nation created through revolution, it had remained relatively isolated and opposed to meddling in the affairs of other countries as well as to the intrusion of foreigners into its own territory. But the fact remained that as a young nation situated on the opposite side of the globe from Europe, Africa, and Asia, the United States had much work to do in establishing relations with the rest of the world. As the

European colonial powers continued to battle for influence in North and South America, the United States took the position that it was proper for them to keep these nations from encroaching into their sphere of influence.

As a former general and frontiersman, President Jackson could not claim much of a background in foreign diplomacy. This was in contrast to his predecessor, John Quincy Adams, who had undergone diplomatic training in both the Hague, Netherlands, and St. Petersburg, Russia. But Jackson, despite his reputation for a hair-trigger temper, in the end enjoyed greater diplomatic success than his more diplomatically seasoned rival. He did not let his lack of experience discourage him from pursuing a vigorous foreign policy that actively promoted and defended the nation's interests abroad. Jackson borrowed ideas from two former presidents, George Washington and James Monroe. In his 1796 Farewell Address, Washington envisioned a United States that would dominate the continent of North America while its commerce reached out to the world. However, Washington had fervently proposed neutrality and nonentanglement in foreign affairs that did not concern the United States. The celebrated Monroe Doctrine of 1823, an expression of post-1812 United States nationalism whereby Europe was prohibited from any further colonization in the Western Hemisphere and restrained from interfering in affairs there, seemed a follow-up to this philosophy. It sounded a warning to the colonial powers of Europe and Russia to keep their imperial hands off the territories of the Western Hemisphere.

To these traditional elements of U.S. foreign policy, Jackson added his own personal brand of conservatism and applied them all to the two prominent foreign concerns of the day: the expansion of foreign trade and the settlement of claims against various European nations who had seized or damaged American property during the Napoleonic Wars of 1803–15. Jackson's foreign policy, like other policies of his administration, bore the stamp of the president alone, and not the cabinet or even his secretary of state. He believed in the necessity of growth for the nation's cotton, tobacco, and grain markets overseas. Accordingly, he was concerned with advancing U.S. commercial interests around the world, but strongly opposed to involving the United States in alliances, revolutions, or wars unless they posed a threat to U.S. security. While Jackson was aggressive and sometimes forceful in his pursuit of U.S. interests abroad, his record does not fully deserve the label of "brass knuckles diplomacy" that is often used to describe it. At times he could be very tactful; he was harsh and assertive only when he felt it would produce the results he was seeking. He was an ardent nationalist who intended to fight for U.S. interests around the globe. Although Jackson sometimes argued and threatened approaching the brink of war, the United States never really came close to involving itself in any foreign wars during his administration.

The British West Indies

Perhaps one of the most successful examples of Jackson's surprising skill at conciliation occurred in dealing with Great Britain. The United States desperately wanted a resumption of trade with the Caribbean islands of the British West Indies, which had been broken off by Great Britain when the John Quincy Adams administration had refused to comply with trade restrictions imposed in 1825 by the British government. Adams had demanded trade in the islands as an absolute right and retaliated by forbidding the export of U.S. goods in British ships to the islands. He pushed for preferential treatment of U.S. ships entering West Indian ports, while at the same time refusing to remove U.S. duties on British ships engaged in the same trade. When Great Britain attempted a compromise, Adams rejected it outright. Thus Adams managed to close off a very profitable market that southern agricultural and northern industrial interests had formerly enjoyed.

Jackson, a man who had fought against British dominance for most of his life, knew immediately upon being elected to his first term that the issue of the British West Indies would have to be among the most important of his immediate priorities; given their pasts, the two nations could not afford to be on bad terms. He quickly informed the British that in electing him president, the American people had rejected the foreign policy of the previous administration. He assured them that the new government could be expected to address the problem fairly and with a sense of compromise. A lowering of the tariff rates imposed on the British in 1828 were in order. Where Adams had claimed trade with the West Indies as a right, Jackson requested it as a privilege. The British reacted favorably to Jackson's accommodating gesture, and frank discussion of the problem commenced almost immediately.

Jackson's lack of experience in foreign affairs was soon apparent, however. Privately, he nearly lost patience with the slow pace of negotiations that ensued, and he suggested to his secretary of state, Martin Van Buren, that perhaps more vigorous measures would be required. He held his tongue, however, and in the end Louis McLane, minister to Britain, hinted that an act of Congress authorizing President Jackson to grant privileges to Britain might be met with a reciprocal gesture. President Jackson arranged for the legislation to be passed in 1830, and Great Britain removed its trade restrictions. Jackson completed the accord in October by issuing a proclamation which stated that the ports of the United States and the British West Indies were open without duties against ships of either nation or their cargoes.

The Maine/Canada Boundary

Jackson further nurtured good relations with the British by adopting a deferential posture on the question of the boundary between the state of Maine and Canada—then a British territory. The boundary had been unresolved since the end of the American Revolution (1775–83). When Maine had become a state in 1820, additional pressure to define the border was placed on Washington. It was another unresolved issue that Jackson inherited from Adams, and it was a thorny one, involving land grants that went back as much as two hundred years. Despite loud protests from the residents of Maine, Jackson accepted Britain's compromise line, which yielded 8,000 of the 12,000 disputed square miles to the United States. Jackson quietly engineered compensation to Maine landholders for their sacrifice, and instead of becoming an incendiary domestic issue, the matter was settled in relative peace.

Texas, Sectionalism, and the Question of Annexation

Since becoming president, Jackson had wanted to buy the territory of Texas from Mexico. He found, after five years of negotiations, that Mexico would not budge and that Texas was not for sale. Mexican officials appeared to invite trouble in the territory in 1823 when they granted huge tracts of land to a United States citizen, Stephen Austin, and about three hundred of his followers. By 1835 these settlers numbered 30,000, and they were tired of being told what to do by Mexico's government on issues such as slavery, immigration, and states rights. These tensions were touched off when General Antonio Lòpez Santa Anna, the Mexican dictator, revoked rights granted to the settlers by the 1824 constitution of Mexico. The Texas Revolution was under way.

The fighting began in 1835, with Sam Houston, an old Indian-fighting sidekick of Jackson, in command of the Texas army. Jackson lent support to the rebels by ordering General E. P. Gaines to cross the Texas border, ford the Sabine River, and penetrate 50 miles into the territory—for the expressed purpose of protecting the United States from possible Indian attacks. Meanwhile, Houston defeated General Santa Anna at the Battle of San Jacinto, forced the Mexican president to grant Texan independence, and immediately appealed to the United States to recognize its independence—or even better, to annex it as a territory.

With his goal of sovereignty over the Texas territory close at hand, Jackson wavered. He was an ardent nationalist, but he was also pragmatic. The idea of either recognition or annexation made him uneasy for two reasons. First, it was likely to start a war with Mexico; and second, recognizing Texas as an independent republic—a move that could only be interpreted as a prelude to Texas statehood—would touch off the volatile issue of slavery at a time when the president was trying to engineer the election of his successor Martin Van Buren. If Texas statehood was made imminent, slavery and anti-slavery forces, in both Congress and Jackson's own Democratic Party, would fight for control of the state. Jackson did not want his party split by such an issue dur-

ing Van Buren's campaign, so he did nothing until the election was over. On March 3, 1837, the day before he left office, Jackson officially recognized Texas independence.

Jackson's predictions for Texas ultimately came true. The United States did fight a war with Mexico over the territory (1846–48), and Texas did contribute to the firestorm of national debate on the question of slavery (*See also,* Polk Administration). When Jackson left office, the issue was only a couple of decades from tearing the nation apart.

Jackson's careful handling of the Texas question marks one of the first times that the issue of slavery showed its influence in U.S. politics. Jackson, a plantation owner himself who at one time owned about 150 slaves, probably did not think it to be such a significant issue. He did recognize, however, that in the political environment of the 1830s, there were many people in the United States who did find the issue to be significant. Along with the nullification controversy (*See also,* Domestic Issues), the question of Texas annexation was a sign that a sectional storm was brewing in the United States.

The French Claims Crisis

The event in foreign affairs that earned Jackson his reputation for "brass knuckles diplomacy" was the crisis surrounding the so-called French Spoilation claims. The long-standing controversy was created by claims from U.S. citizens against France for the destruction of their property during the Napoleonic Wars (1803–15). Most of these claims involved U.S. ships and goods that had been illegally seized by France during the wars. In 1831, after stalling for nearly two years, the Paris government belatedly agreed to pay the United States several million dollars as compensation.

Implementation of this treaty depended entirely on its approval by the French Chamber of Deputies and the subsequent appropriation of the money. Months and then years passed without the French government making a single move, and by 1833 Jackson was beside himself. He replaced the U.S. minister to France with Edward Livingston, who immediately put pressure on the government for payment. The French government did more than ignore U.S. demands this time; in the spring of 1834, the French Assembly actually defeated a bill to appropriate the money.

Jackson's patience had run out. In his annual 1834 message he recommended that if provision were not made for repayment of the debt, a law be passed authorizing the seizure of French property in the United States so that the debt could be paid off with the proceeds. Though the French seemed to have been inviting such an insult for some time, they claimed to be appalled by Jackson's statement. The Paris government broke off diplomatic relations, recalling their representatives. The U.S. delegation in Paris was likewise shut down, and as talk

Fast Fact

When Jackson paid off the national debt in 1835, he became the first, last, and only president of a debt-free United States.

(Source: "Andrew Jackson," in the Internet Public Library <http://www.ipl.org/ref/POTUS/ajackson.html/#cabinet>, 1999.)

of war spread, Jackson was urged by many advisers to apologize. But he saw no reason to ask pardon for demanding repayment of a legitimate debt.

The possibility of war was overstated, but the affair did catch the attention of the British, who stepped in to make sure its French ally did not spend its strength in a dispute with the United States. Meanwhile, the House of Representatives backed up the president's statement, passing a three-million dollar fortifications bill to be implemented as the need arose. The Senate wisely killed this bill, however, and Henry Clay, chairman of the Senate Foreign Affairs Committee, introduced a resolution in the upper house declaring it imprudent for the president to threaten such reprisals, no matter how just the U.S. claim.

The people, however, supported Jackson and admired his strong-arm tactics. Nobody, clearly, would bully the United States while Old Hickory was in the White House. Jackson's popular support, British mediation, and the increasing embarrassment of the French government finally resulted in the French Chamber of Deputies voting for the funds to pay the debt in the spring of 1835. The government added the stipulation that the money would not be turned over until Jackson apologized for the threat contained in his 1834 address to Congress—a condition that Jackson angrily refused, sensing another French dodge. Still, he desired the whole ordeal to be over with, and in his annual message to Congress he denied any intention to "menace or insult" (Remini, p. 176) the French government. He insisted, however, that the honor of the United States prohibited his offering of anything resembling an apology for stating the clear truth.

The French, anxious for an escape from this ugly situation, carefully interpreted Jackson's statement as an apology, though he protested loudly that none had been offered. Repayment was begun, and by the spring of 1836, just in time for the new presidential campaign, the president announced to the nation that four of the six install-

ments of the debt had been paid off, and that friendly relations with France had been restored. In their 1836 campaign the Whigs had hoped to hurt the Democratic candidate, Martin Van Buren, with references to the administration's crude and ill-mannered diplomacy. But once again Jackson's appeal to the general public engendered a large measure of national pride, due in no small part to the work of the president and his Democrats.

Asia: Quallah Battoo and the Roberts Treaties

In Asia, a part of the world dominated by European trade prior to Jackson's presidency, the United States was anxious to expand trade. Since the days of Marco Polo, the thirteenth century Italian explorer, the riches of the Orient, including spices, tea, and silks, had enriched European trade, and the United States wanted to benefit as well. Some inroads had already been made. In 1790, a seafaring merchant from Salem, Massachusetts, had earned a 700 percent profit on the first large cargo of pepper to be imported from Sumatra (a mountainous island in what is now western Indonesia), while another Salem merchant opened the coffee trade with the Red Sea port of Mocha in 1798. The United States, however, often found itself at a disadvantage in Asia. Many of the Europeans, who had been the first westerners to arrive in these Asian ports, had either colonized these lands or negotiated treaties that would make it difficult for competitors.

Except for the pepper trade, Americans had paid little attention to the East Indies before Jackson's presidency, focusing instead on the resumption of trade in the neighboring British West Indies. But by 1831 U.S. merchants had taken control of Sumatran commerce; the world pepper price was set in the market in Salem. Unfortunately, the region became politically unstable for two reasons: the bottom dropped out of the pepper market in 1830, leaving merchants and natives alike desperate for profits; and control of the island was still being disputed by the British and the Dutch, leaving it governed by a loosely organized confederation of native tribes. It was into this tense environment that the U.S. merchant ship, the *Friendship* sailed on a routine voyage in 1831. The ensuing events would seize the attention of the entire United States and spark a new direction in Jacksonian foreign policy.

Quallah Battoo

During an early morning loading at the west Sumatran port of Quallah Battoo, while the *Friendship* was being loaded with pepper cargo, it was suddenly attacked by a band of native Malays who killed two seamen and seriously wounded three others before seizing the ship. By the time the *Friendship's* captain, Charles Endicott, had enlisted the help of other merchants to recapture the ship, the vessel had been stripped of everything but its cargo: over $12,000 in gold and silver, $8,000 worth of opium, and everything else of value had been stolen.

When news of the assault reached the United States, politicians from the states on the seaboard demanded government intervention. The president had no policy that applied to Southeast Asia, and it is questionable whether, prior to the *Friendship* affair, Jackson or his advisers could have located Sumatra on a map. But such a brazen attack on a U.S. merchant ship was considered by Jackson to be a blow to the national honor. He quickly decided to take a firm stand in that part of the world. After investigating the incident, Jackson dispatched the naval captain John Downes to demand restitution and immediate punishment of the murderers from Quallah Battoo's tribal leader, the rajah. If the natives did not comply within a reasonable period of time, Downes was to take the murderers prisoner, retake the stolen property, and destroy the ships and fortifications of the Malay pirates.

Downes arrived in Quallah Battoo almost exactly a year after the assault, and, sensing hostility from the natives, reinterpreted his orders. Instead of attempting discussion with the rajah, Downes and his men stormed Quallah Battoo and engaged in several hours of bloody fighting, killing over a hundred natives. When no stolen cargo was found in the village, Downes and his men looted the town and set fire to the village. Over the next few weeks, frightened rajahs from surrounding regions visited Downes and professed their undying friendship for the United States.

When word of Downes's actions reached Washington, the capital was already in chaos: Congress was debating the tariff, and Jackson was preparing his veto of the Second Bank of the United States (*See also,* Domestic Issues). Political opponents in both Congress and the press roundly denounced the barbarity of the diplomatic mission, in which dozens of noncombatants were killed without any prior attempt at negotiation. Not surprisingly critics also framed the assault as an abuse of executive power—Jackson was making war without waiting for a declaration from the legislative branch. Though the fault was Downes's, not the president's, Quallah Battoo was a serious blemish on Jackson's foreign affairs record—though it was seen by many Americans as an unpleasant but necessary lesson, invited by savage pirates who dared violate the rights of U.S. traders.

Roberts Treaties

After the Quallah Battoo affair was finally sorted out, it was clear that the president meant to expand and protect U.S. trade in the Pacific. He was aided in this endeavor by the former naval officer and explorer, Edmund Roberts, who had already urged the Jackson administration to explore the untapped trade potential of the East African and Persian Gulf lands controlled by the Islamic leader of Muscat. In 1831, awakened by the Quallah Battoo assault, Jackson dispatched Roberts to visit Muscat (Oman), Siam (now Thailand), Japan, and Cochin China (Vietnam)—an empire that had been visited by only two or three U.S. ships—for the purpose of estab-

lishing trade. The Roberts missions produced treaties with both Muscat and Siam in 1833, opening these countries to U.S. trade on a most-favored-nation basis, whereby the participants receive the same tax benefits. The Cochin China mission failed, and unfortunately the emissary grew sick and died before attempting to establish diplomatic ties with Japan.

The Roberts's missions are among the most underrated accomplishments of the Jackson presidency. In exploring the diplomatic possibilities in Southeast Asia and Japan, the Jackson administration opened the door for a wholesale expansion of trade and healthy diplomatic relations with a previously neglected part of the world. The treaties with Siam and Muscat, the first treaties between the United States and Far Eastern countries, established a strong commercial foothold for the nation in an area where it had been handicapped by its own ignorance and disinterest. The Roberts missions also sparked interest in the rising Pacific nation of Japan, which would be visited 20 years later and opened to trade by Commodore Matthew Perry and diplomat Townsend Harris during the Franklin Pierce administration.

The Jackson Administration Legacy

Seventy years old and in poor health, Jackson did not stand for a third term. Instead, he engineered the nomination of his protégé, Martin Van Buren, as the Democratic candidate for the 1836 campaign. The party that Jackson had helped to create did not question the choice of the outgoing president, and in fact Van Buren was an able politician, though his leadership remained to be tested.

So total was Jackson's domination of the federal government during his administration that by 1836 a new party had formed among the National Republicans, led by Henry Clay and Democrats who had defected from Jackson. They had defected for several reasons: Jackson's indiscriminate use of the veto; his treatment of the Indians; his war against the bank; and his perceived bullying of South Carolina. This new party called themselves the Whigs, after the party opposed to the English monarchy. It was the hope of the Whigs to end the reign of King Andrew I and his successors. But this opposition to Jackson proved to be all that united the Whigs, and they ran a weak and confused campaign against Van Buren who won a comfortable victory.

Van Buren found himself the unfortunate inheritor of two sizable problems. On the domestic front, he was forced to take charge of an economy that was in ruins. The panic of 1837 and the ensuing depression, one of the worst in U.S. history, were in part a result of Jackson's destruction of the Second Bank of the United States and his Specie Circular. It would be many years before the economy would recover, and Van Buren's reputation as a president would forever be tarnished by his inability to pull the country out of the depression. In recognizing the independence of Texas the day before he left office, Jackson also left Van Buren to resolve a nasty foreign affairs crisis with an infuriated Mexican government.

Jackson's hold on the Democrats remained closely linked to the issue of Texas annexation. In the presidential campaign of 1844, when Van Buren failed to come out strongly in favor of annexation, Jackson switched his support to James K. Polk. Polk agreed with Jackson that Texas should become part of the Union. Polk's nomination and victory in 1844 and the ensuing complications in domestic and foreign affairs can, in part, be traced to the residual popularity of Andrew Jackson.

Lasting Impact

Debate over the importance of the Jackson presidency has not ceased since the end of his second term. There is no doubt that through his forceful application of executive power and privilege, he expanded the significance of the presidency. In his eight years in office he vetoed more bills than had been vetoed in the previous 40 years. His presidency is often cited as the starting point in the trend toward federal centralization of the government, a principle that Jackson often claimed to oppose, but which he enjoyed while in office.

Jackson also enhanced the prestige of the presidency as the leader of a national political party with mass appeal. For the first time a presidential candidate was chosen not behind closed doors by caucus or committee, but by an open appeal to the people of the party. As a presidential candidate, Jackson was not a figurehead, manipulated to prominence by behind-the-scenes party operatives, but a true leader, a war hero, and a champion of the masses. He benefited from, and presided over, an age of entrepreneurship in which most Americans believed government should not grant privileges to one group that it would withhold from another—a very rudimentary form of the arguments of the Civil Rights movement, hatched in a time when the ownership of slaves was just beginning to be questioned on a fairly large scale.

Jackson's popularity with the masses allowed his emphasis on reform to trickle down to the state level during his administration. Reforms in prisons, schools, and mental hospitals were widely undertaken. The idea that all Americans, and not just the aristocratic, propertied classes, should participate in the nation's political affairs, was gaining increased acceptance. Of course, the nation still had far to go— "all Americans" at the time meant "all white males." Women and former African slaves would have to fight their own battles for suffrage later in U.S. history.

In foreign affairs Jackson was among the most influential presidents of his era; his Asian treaties were of immeasurable value to the nation. More important, he formulated and implemented the most expansive and assertive foreign policy since Thomas Jefferson. In doing so, he further extended the power of the chief executive beyond the traditional realm of domestic affairs, and he helped set a precedent for the more dynamic diplomatic actions of modern presidencies.

Sources

Bailey, Thomas A. *The American Pageant: A History of the Republic.* 3d ed. Lexington, Mass.: D.C. Heath and Company, 1966.

Belohlavek, John M. *Let the Eagle Soar! The Foreign Policy of Andrew Jackson.* Lincoln, Neb.: The University of Nebraska Press, 1985.

Conlin, Joseph R. *The American Past: A Survey of American History.* San Diego, Calif.: Harcourt Brace, 1990.

Davis, Burke. *Old Hickory: A Life of Andrew Jackson.* New York: Dial Press, 1977.

Gatell, Frank Otto, ed. *Essays on Jacksonian America.* New York: Holt, Rinehart, and Winston: 1970

Kane, Joseph Nathan. *Facts About the Presidents.* New York: H.W. Wilson, 1993.

McDonald, William. *Jacksonian Democracy 1829–1837.* New York: Harper and Brothers, 1906.

Morrison, Samuel E., Henry Steele Commager, and William E. Leuchtenberg. *A Concise History of the American Republic.* New York: Oxford University Press, 1983.

Ogg, Frederic Austin. *The Reign of Andrew Jackson: A Chronicle of the Frontier in Politics.* New Haven, Conn.: Yale University Press, 1919.

Remini, Robert V. *Andrew Jackson.* New York: Twayne Publishers, 1966.

———. *Andrew Jackson and the Bank War: A Study in the Growth of Presidential Power.* New York: Norton, 1967.

———. *The Legacy of Andrew Jackson: Essays on Democracy, Indian Removal, and Slavery.* Baton Rouge, La: Louisiana State University Press, 1988.

Schlesinger, Arthur Meier. *The Age of Jackson.* New York: Little, Brown; 1946.

Sellers, Charles Grier. *Andrew Jackson: Nullification and the State-Rights Tradition.* Chicago: Rand McNally, 1963.

Wallace, Anthony F. C. *The Long Bitter Trail: Andrew Jackson and the Indians.* New York: Hill and Wang, 1993.

Further Readings

Historic World Leaders. Vol. 4. Detroit: Gale Research, 1994.

Latner, Richard B. *The Presidency of Andrew Jackson: White House Politics, 1829–1837.* Athens, Ga.: University of Georgia Press, 1979.

Ratner, Lorman. *Andrew Jackson and his Tennessee Lieutenants: a Study in Political Culture.* Westport, Conn.: Greenwood Press, 1997.

Remini, Robert Vincent. *Andrew Jackson and the Course of American Empire.* New York: Harper and Row, 1977.

Rogin, Michael Paul. *Fathers and Children: Andrew Jackson and the Subjugation of the American Indian.* New York: Knopf, 1975.

Syrett, Harold C. *Andrew Jackson: His Contribution to the American Tradition.* Westport, Conn.: Greenwood Press, 1953.

Van Buren Administration

Full name: Martin Van Buren
Popular name: The Little Magician; The Red Fox of
Kinderhook

Personal Information:
Born: December 5, 1782
Birthplace: Kinderhook, New York
Died: July 24, 1862
Death place: Kinderhook, New York
Burial place: Kinderhook Cemetery, Kinderhook, New York
Religion: Dutch Reformed
Spouse: Hannah Hoes (m. 1807)
Children: Abraham; John; Martin; Smith Thompson
Education: No formal education
Occupation: Politician; diplomat; vice president of the
United States
Political Party: Democratic-Republican Party
Age at Inauguration: 54 years

Biography

One of the first "professional politicians" to rise to
the presidency, Martin Van Buren made the most of a
modest upbringing and a poor education in the small
upstate village of Kinderhook, New York. Serving as a
U.S. senator, secretary of state, and vice president before
assuming the presidency, he carried on the strong tradition of democracy that had been established by his political patron, Andrew Jackson.

Early Life

In 1782, at the time of Martin Van Buren's birth,
the town of Kinderhook, in upstate New York, was home
to seven families of Van Burens. While predominantly
Dutch in descent, the inhabitants of Kinderhook were
generally well-established and thoroughly American.
Martin's father, Abraham Van Buren, was a tavernkeeper
who had inherited a number of interests from his various
relatives, including a farm and six slaves, and he and his
family were kept busy maintaining their various
resources.

When he was 39, Abraham married a widow named
Maria Hoes Van Alen, who at the time was raising three
children of her own. Martin was the third of five children born to Abraham and Maria.

Education

Like his immediate predecessor in the White House,
Andrew Jackson, Van Buren had little formal education.

As a child his studies in the crude village schoolhouse in Kinderhook, New York—which were not regularly held anyway—were often interrupted as Martin was called away to work on the family's farm or in the tavern. He attended enough school to learn a little Latin and some grammar and rhetoric, and he left the school at the age of 14 to work as an apprentice to one of the town's best lawyers, Francis Sylvester. It was while working for Sylvester that his real education would begin in the study of law.

Van Buren's lack of a formal education was rarely an issue in his political life, but it was true that late in life he regretted not having had more educational opportunities. He never seemed at ease among some of the elite statesmen in the nation's capital. Though he authored volumes of pamphlets, letters, reports, and public statements throughout his life, he is said not to have released them until after his friends had thoroughly checked the documents for spelling, punctuation, and grammar.

Family Life

In 1807 Van Buren married a young woman, Hannah Hoes, who was a distant relative and had been an acquaintance since childhood. Their first son, Abraham, was born while the newlyweds were still living in Kinderhook, New York. The following year the new family moved to nearby Hudson, a growing town, for two reasons: to accommodate Martin's rapidly advancing legal career and to live near schools better than the small village schoolhouse Martin had attended.

Three more sons followed during the family's years in Hudson, but the last died in infancy. In 1816 the Van Buren family moved to the state capital, Albany, where their fourth and last surviving son was born. After suffering through two years of failing health, Hannah Van Buren died at the age of 35 in 1819, probably of tuberculosis. Martin, obviously grief-stricken, did not return to work for several days. He never remarried; it was his daughter-in-law, Angelica Van Buren, wife of eldest son Abraham, who later acted as first lady.

Career

After six years of studying law, Van Buren passed the New York bar in 1803. He returned to Kinderhook, New York, to establish his private practice. As a Jeffersonian Republican, Van Buren's practice often consisted of defending—very often, successfully—the interests of local farmers and merchants in land and contract disputes against the landed gentry, who were typically Federalists. By 1807 his reputation as a lawyer had grown beyond Kinderhook, and he was admitted as a counselor to the New York Supreme Court.

Martin Van Buren. (The Library of Congress.)

A year later, in 1808, Van Buren was appointed to his first political office, surrogate of Columbia County, New York (a surrogate is an officer with jurisdiction over the settling of wills and estates). He held that position until 1812, when he was elected to the state senate. At this time a power struggle was being conducted between two factions of his political party, the Democratic-Republicans. Van Buren became the leader of his faction, popularly known as the Bucktails, and their support helped him win the post of state attorney general in 1815. In this position he helped build what is considered by many historians to be the first modern political machine, the Albany Regency, a network of high-ranking politicians who operated on the spoils system (making appointments based on patronage rather than merit) and used their collective power to defeat the efforts of political rivals.

Van Buren was elected to the U.S. Senate in 1821 and, serving until 1827, helped put together the coalition that won the 1828 presidential campaign for the Democratic-Republican candidate, Andrew Jackson. Van Buren, riding the wave of pro-Jackson sentiment in New York, ran for the governorship in 1827 and won. He ran primarily to promote the Jackson candidacy, and it was no surprise when, a few months after the election, he resigned as governor to accept Jackson's offer to become secretary of state.

Once inside Jackson's cabinet, Van Buren's political skills flourished. He became one of Jackson's most trusted and influential political advisers, the *de facto* leader of Jackson's intimate circle of counselors, known as the Kitchen Cabinet. During the end of Jackson's first term, Van Buren, capitalizing on the political blunders of Vice President John C. Calhoun, conducted a masterful behind-the-scenes campaign to become Jackson's vice-presidential running mate for the campaign of 1832. It was this political slickness that earned Van Buren the nicknames the Little Magician and the Red Fox of Kinderhook, which were not names that were ever used by his friends or allies.

As vice president, Van Buren voiced some concern over Jackson's war with the Second Bank of the United States (known as the BUS)—but his concern was merely political, a fear that Jackson's removal of government deposits from the bank would create a schism in the party. After crushing the bank, Jackson retired with his popularity intact—but the effects of his Bank War would hit his successor hard.

Van Buren's Presidency

Van Buren was elected president in 1836. He was 54 years old. Van Buren's presidential term seemed doomed from the outset. Saddled with the financial panic of 1837 and a subsequent depression, in addition to his reputation as Andrew Jackson's groomed pet, Van Buren struggled to restore economic and financial stability to the nation while remaining loyal to the spirit of Jackson's policies. Without Jackson's domineering personality, however, Van Buren was unable to build widespread support for his policies even within his own party.

Post-presidential Years

After being voted out of office in 1840, Van Buren at first traveled about the country trying to revive his political career and plot a run in the 1844 presidential campaign. When Democrats (as the Democratic-Republicans were now called) learned of his opposition to the annexation of Texas and the expansion of slavery, however, his candidacy was essentially sunk. At the nominating convention of 1844, James K. Polk of Tennessee emerged as the Democratic candidate and won the election easily.

After becoming alienated from his own New York Democrats, who were more and more leaning toward the support of Polk, Van Buren invested his political hopes in the abolitionist Free Soil Party for the election of 1848. His defection split the Democratic vote in New York, and the Whig candidate, Zachary Taylor, won the presidency. Afterward, Van Buren had very little to do with political life, though he did serve the Democrats as an adviser. He traveled around Europe for several years, writing his autobiography, and then retired in 1855 to Lindenwald, his estate in Kinderhook. He died on July 24, 1862.

The Martin Van Buren Administration

Martin Van Buren was president during the nation's first terrible economic depression, and to this day his administration is defined by the Panic of 1837. Lacking the dynamic personality that had made Andrew Jackson so popular, Van Buren nevertheless guided the nation peacefully through a period marked by tense relations with Britain and a worsening sectional crisis in the United States.

Van Buren Becomes President

The Campaign of 1836

There was growing conflict within the Democratic Party by 1835, with the line being drawn between conservative members, who were friendly to banks, and the "Locofocos" who sided with the working class and advocated a hard-money currency (silver and gold coin). In the hope of heading off these deepening divisions, Jackson arranged for the party's nominating convention to be held soon, more than a year before the election. Van Buren, Jackson's handpicked successor, was easily nominated, but his disappointed rivals made the party's overall support for their candidate lukewarm at best.

Fortunately for the Democrats, their opponents the Whigs were even less unified, unable to agree on a single candidate to run against Van Buren. They adopted an unusual strategy: they would run three Whig candidates, each of them popular within a specific region. With no single candidate gaining an overall majority of the vote, the Whigs reasoned, the election would then be referred to the House of Representatives, where Speaker and Whig leader Henry Clay of Kentucky could engineer a victory for the party. Because the only thing the Whigs appeared to agree upon was their intense dislike of Jackson, their strategy was to attack Van Buren as a lapdog, a career politician who was without convictions or principles of his own. At the same time, ironically, they accused him of being a northern candidate who was opposed to slavery, in order to alarm southern Democrats enough to withdraw their support.

Van Buren adopted a low profile for the election, rarely appearing in public. Instead, he wrote letters to close associates defining his own positions and soliciting their support. His carefully delineated proposals, all moderate in nature, seemed in some ways to vindicate his reputation as a slick politician and fence sitter. To Democrats, he professed approval for the economic policies of the Jackson administration and pledged to veto any bill for a national bank. But he did accept the idea of depositing federal funds in the state banks. To the Whigs, Van Buren explained that previous antislavery measures he had supported in New York had nothing to do with his real feelings about slavery—he was simply trying to prevent his political opponent, DeWitt Clinton (governor of New York from 1817 to 1823), from exploiting the issue for political gain. On slavery, Van Buren adopted stances that were designed to appease both sides. He resisted the pressure of southern Democrats to speak out in favor of annexing or even recognizing the independent republic of Texas, which would surely tilt the sectional balance in favor of the slave states. On the other hand, he declared publicly his opposition to any effort by Congress to abolish slavery in the District of Columbia.

The Democrats and Van Buren prevailed over the divide-and-conquer strategy of the Whigs. Van Buren won 170 electoral votes, with the remaining 124 scattered among his Whig opponents, but the popular vote was much closer—approximately 762,000 to 735,000. To many, the election was less an endorsement of Van Buren than an embrace of Andrew Jackson's residual glory, which was helped along by a fractured Whig party.

Campaign of 1840

Van Buren's bid for a second term in 1840, in which he ran as the incumbent against the Whig's sole candidate, William Henry Harrison, was unsuccessful. Like Andrew Jackson, Harrison was an aged war hero, having defeated the confederated American Indian army in 1811 in present-day Indiana.

In nominating Harrison, the Whigs succeeded in turning party images on their heads. Branded by the Whigs as the pampered elitist who had presided over the financial panic of 1837, Van Buren simply could not overcome Harrison's folksy war-hero image. He was not even a unanimous choice among his own party, but the Democrats decided that nominating another candidate would amount to admitting a mistake in 1836. The election was surprisingly close, with Harrison winning the popular vote by the narrow margin of 1.2 million to Van Buren's 1.1 million votes, but the electoral college overwhelmingly went for Harrison, 234 to 60.

Van Buren's Advisers

Van Buren's presidency was noteworthy for its hands-off approach to the activity of the executive departments. He generally allowed his secretaries to pursue their own courses, and some of his most trusted advisers were cabinet members who had served with him under President Jackson. Amos Kendall, who remained postmaster general under Van Buren, became a close adviser. For advice on foreign affairs, Van Buren generally relied on the judgment of his secretary of state, John Forsyth, who had held the post since 1834 and was strongly loyal to Van Buren and the Democratic Party.

It may have been that he was never quite comfortable with the scope of national politics, because for his

Administration

Administration Dates
March 4, 1837–March 4, 1841

Vice President
Richard Mentor Johnson (1837–41)

Cabinet
Secretary of State
John Forsyth (1834–41)

Secretary of the Treasury
Levi Woodbury (1834–41)

Secretary of War
Joel R. Poinsett (1837–41)

Attorney General
Benjamin F. Butler (1833–38)
Felix Grundy (1838–39)
Henry D. Gilpin (1840–41)

Secretary of the Navy
Mahlon Dickerson (1834–38)
James K. Paulding (1838–41)

Postmaster General
Amos Kendall (1835–40)
John M. Niles (1840–41)

closest and most trusted advisers, Van Buren tended to stick with his associates from New York. In particular, his old friend and Albany Regency (*See also,* Career) man, Silas Wright, who during Van Buren's administration served in the U.S. Senate, was a key adviser on legislative affairs and an important architect of Van Buren's domestic programs. Likewise, the chairman of the House Ways and Means Committee, Churchill C. Cambreleng, was a former Regency member who helped shape Van Buren's domestic policies and articulate them to House members.

Van Buren and Congress

Van Buren presided over the Twenty-fifth and Twenty-sixth sessions of Congress, both of which held a

MARTIN VAN BUREN 1837–1841

The route Martin Van Buren took to reach the White House began in his hometown of Kinderhook, New York. Popularly known as "Old Kinderhook," the Democrats used the abbreviation "OK" for Van Buren's campaign slogan, thus the origin of OK, meaning correct. (Corbis. Reproduced by permission.)

slight Democratic majority (30 of 52 senators in the Twenty-fifth Congress were Democrats, while the House was composed of 108 Democrats, 107 Whigs, and 24 others). With the intraparty factionalism that was characteristic of the time, however, the terms Whig and Democrat did not mean much; in 1837 Whigs and conservative Democrats could outvote those Democrats loyal to Van Buren. The president's efforts to influence legislative outcomes, then, were generally unsuccessful, due to his inability to discipline the conservative wing of his own party. For example, while Congress did pass most of Van Buren's programs designed to deal with the panic of 1837, the keystone of the plan, a bill establishing an independent treasury, was blocked by the House until 1840—just months before Van Buren's term expired (*See also,* Domestic Issues).

In general, even Democrats loyal to Van Buren were displeased with his leadership, especially his low-profile method of building support. In the case of his independent treasury proposal, they charged that after presenting it to Congress he seemed to leave it entirely up to chance. They also criticized the indirect manner in which Van Buren dealt with members of Congress; rather than communicate with them directly, he often sent advisers to convey messages back and forth between himself and lawmakers.

Van Buren and the Judiciary

Shortly after Van Buren had taken office, Postmaster General Amos Kendall rejected a $120,000 claim filed by a powerful contractor, Stockton and Stokes, on the grounds that the sum was not a legitimate claim but the product of sloppy bookkeeping and overbidding. The solicitor of the Treasury, who had close personal ties to Stockton and Stokes, ruled that Kendall should not only credit the contractors with the $120,000 in question, but also pay an additional $40,000. The Senate concurred with this decision. Kendall immediately complied with the first order, but he refused to pay the additional award, for which he could find no justification.

Kendall argued that as a member of the executive branch, he was under no obligation to comply with the "recommendation" of the Senate or a later writ of mandamus (used only when all other judicial remedies fail), issued by the circuit court in the District of Columbia, ordering him to comply. Van Buren supported Kendall's refusal, but their interpretation of the power of the executive branch was later shot down by the Supreme Court in *Kendall v. U.S. Ex. Rel. Stokes* (1838). In this case the Court made the distinction that the determination to pay the claim was not an exercise of the executive's "discretionary power" but merely a "ministerial" act—in other words, simply part of the postmaster general's job description.

As a result of this decision, Van Buren attempted to further executive independence in his 1838 message to Congress, in which he asked the legislature to pass a bill that would explicitly take away the mandamus power from the Washington, D.C. Circuit Court. Though the Senate passed a bill conforming to the president's wishes, the House took no action, and the circuit court retained the right to compel certain actions from members of the executive branch.

Van Buren made three appointments to the U.S. Supreme Court: John Catron, John McKinley, and Peter V. Daniel.

Changes in the U.S. Government

Under Navy Secretary James K. Paulding, the U.S. Navy undertook an exploratory expedition that left Norfolk, Virginia, in 1838. The expedition eventually circumnavigated the globe, covering 87,780 miles, by way of Hawaii; San Francisco, California; and Singapore, before sailing into New York Harbor in 1841. Unlike foreign expeditions ordered by Jackson, Van Buren's predecessor, and Tyler, his successor, these voyages were not concerned with commercial interests but were mostly scientific in nature. As a result of this expedition, samples of plants and animals from throughout the world were gathered for study and improved maps were created. Once home, the vast collections were installed with the National Institution, an organization heavily influenced by Paulding and War Secretary Joel Poinsett. The National Institution was the direct predecessor of the Smithsonian Institution.

However, the main change in government associated with the Van Buren administration was the introduction of an independent treasury, whereby government funds would be deposited in a network of subtreasuries in various cities (*See also,* Domestic Issues), thus removing funds from the private sector.

Domestic Issues

In many ways Martin Van Buren could not have picked a worse time to become president of the United States. The surging economy of the mid-1820s to 1830s, based largely on land speculation and entrepreneurial extension, came crashing down around him as soon as he had taken office, and much of his work was devoted to fighting off the depression. A rising sectional consciousness also continued to divide the nation, with abolitionists and other northerners strongly condemning the prospective annexation of Texas. Expansionists, on the other hand, increasingly called for annexation and the

Fast Fact

The abbreviation "O.K." used to stand for "Old Kinderhook," Van Buren's home in New York. O.K. became the designation for Democratic clubs in New York during the campaign of 1840, and the Whigs, who could not figure out what the term meant, invented a conversation between Andrew Jackson (a famously bad speller) and Postmaster General Amos Kendall to explain it: "These papers, Amos, are all correct. I have marked them O.K. (oll korrect)." In this way the word "okay" entered the English language.

(Source: Samuel Eliot Morison, Henry Steele Commager, and William E. Leuchtenburg. *A Concise History of the American Republic,* 1983.)

removal of American Indians to territory west of the Mississippi River. Van Buren, with shaky support in Congress, was unwilling to alienate either wing of his own party; he often found himself pursuing policies designed to please both sides—but pleasing neither.

The Panic of 1837

Before leaving office Andrew Jackson had succeeded in bringing down the Second Bank of the United States, known as the BUS. The BUS was a nationally-chartered bank which, in Jackson's view, was a corrupt institution that favored wealthy Americans. After engineering the abolition of the bank, Jackson distributed federal deposits among banks (thereafter known as his "pet banks") in several states. A surge in land speculation by western investors, fueled in part by the questionable lending practices of these very pet banks, endangered the stability of the banking system. Jackson himself was uncomfortable with the amount of land that was being purchased on credit, and in 1836 he issued his famous Specie Circular, his proclamation that all government lands (by now, at least $25 million worth) could be paid for only in "hard money"—silver or gold coin.

The Specie Circular stopped further speculation dead in its tracks, but other factors (including a failed 1836 wheat crop, a 50 percent reduction in the price of cotton, and a crisis in several European banks that caused them to call in loans from U.S. investors) combined to cause a widespread financial panic. Westerners, unable to pay their debts, went bankrupt. Easterners, with their banks drained of gold and silver, went into a deep depression, the first real and lasting economic crisis for the United States. Grain prices were sent so high that three weeks before Van Buren took office, mobs in New York City attacked warehouses and broke open flour barrels. Unemployment reached unprecedented levels as factories closed their doors.

The problem was left for Van Buren's to handle. He took the view that the less governmental interference there was in the economy, the better, but he did take some practical measures to increase the nation's money supply. These included suspension of the Specie Circular, postponement of the collection of import duty bonds, extension of the time for old deposit banks to repay borrowed Treasury funds, a temporary issue of treasury notes, and postponement of the delivery of transfer payments to the states. He also developed his Divorce Bill, known today as the Independent Treasury Bill, to remove all government funds from private banks and deposit them in government vaults, in order to completely divorce them from the political process. They would also not be invested in any form of private enterprise.

The Divorce Bill was probably the only constructive measure undertaken by the Van Buren administration, and it was debated so hotly that it did not pass until 1840. Congressional Whigs, who had been most responsible for delaying the bill's passage and who still favored the establishment of a national bank, were able to suggest that Van Buren's policies, while they may not have caused the depression, had done nothing to make it go away. They branded him Martin Van Ruin, a name that stuck to Van Buren into his unsuccessful campaign for reelection.

Indian Policy and the Seminole Wars

In order to accommodate the rising tide of expansionism, Van Buren began his presidency by announcing his clear intention to continue Andrew Jackson's policy of moving American Indian tribes to lands west of the Mississippi River. One of most tragic events in U.S. history, the forced march of the entire Cherokee nation from Georgia along the Trail of Tears, was ordered by President Jackson, in direct opposition to previous federal treaties and a recent Supreme Court ruling (*See also,* Andrew Jackson). But the Trail of Tears march was carried out in 1838, under Van Buren's watch. Driven relentlessly by General Winfield Scott's troops, several thousand Cherokees died on the way to Oklahoma. Van Buren defended the march, saying the government was simply trying to keep the Cherokees out of harm's way.

While Van Buren deemed the Trail of Tears march successful, he could not make a similar claim for the increasing problem with the Seminole Indians in Florida Territory. The problem went as far back as 1817 and 1818, when General Andrew Jackson had been sent to fight Seminoles who had attacked settlements in Georgia and Alabama. Jackson had made removal treaties with Seminole chiefs in 1832 and 1833, but by 1835 most Seminoles and their chief, Osceola, were directly defying these treaties.

Shortly after Van Buren took office, Osceola was lured into a trap by an army flag of truce and thrown into prison. Van Buren then ordered General Thomas S. Jesup to take command in Florida and step up the army's efforts. In the battle of Lake Okeechobee, begun on Christmas Day 1838, Colonel Zachary Taylor (later president of the United States) led more than one thousand men deep into the Florida swamps to face the Seminole renegades. This was the single biggest conflict of the war that would become a war of attrition and last until 1842. By 1840 the war had cost the administration more than $30 million and placed Van Buren in poor standing among northerners opposed to the war. Southern expansionists, however, were pleased with his efforts. Between 2,500 and 3,000 Seminoles were killed or captured during the course of the war, along with several hundred African Americans who lived among them. All of them were simply turned over to southern planters as slaves. The war ended on August 18, 1842, by a proclamation of President John Tyler. About three hundred surviving Seminoles were allowed to remain on a reservation in Southwest Florida.

Foreign Issues

If the domestic situation was not alarming enough for Van Buren, he also faced a foreign policy crisis immediately upon taking office. Just before leaving office, his precursor Andrew Jackson, who had long wanted to annex the nearby territory of Texas, had precipitated a crisis with Mexico. Within months Van Buren also faced the prospect of war with Great Britain, over northern boundaries and interference in a Canadian rebellion.

In his inaugural address, Van Buren stated clearly that the United States was to be a nation that would always seek peace before war, unless its rights were directly invaded. He also declared his intention to stay out of the foreign affairs of other countries, and to "observe strict neutrality in their controversies" (Inaugural Address, March 4, 1837). Throughout his administration, Van Buren managed to adhere to this principle, though he was urged on several occasions by his advisers to get the United States involved in a war.

Mexico and Texas

President Jackson had long had an eye on the Mexican territory of Texas, and in 1835 he had even sent U.S. troops to interfere in Texas's war for independence from Mexico. However, he feared a war with Mexico and the political firestorm that would be generated over the inevitable follow-up issue: whether Texas might become

Biography:

Osceola

Seminole Chief (1804–38) In his brief life, Osceola distinguished himself with his brave struggle against a nation intent on advancing its borders onto the lands of a native people. Though a full-blooded member of the Creek nation, Osceola's mother took him to Florida as a young boy, to live amongst the Seminoles. At the age of twelve, Osceola took up arms and joined the Seminoles in their battle against U.S. troops during the War of 1812. During the next 20 years, Osceola rose to prominence amongst the Seminole tribe for his role as intermediary between the U.S. Indian agent stationed in the area and restless tribesmen. In 1832 pressure from the United States to move the Seminoles to an area west of the Mississippi River led to a push for the Seminole chiefs to sign removal treaties. When approached to sign on behalf of his tribe, Osceola signified his refusal by plunging a knife through the document. He was arrested for his defiance. After convincing his captors that he would push for

approval of the treaty, he was released. Immediately upon his release, Ocseola gathered warriors together and brutally murdered U.S. agents, effectively beginning the Second Seminole War which raged on through President Martin Van Buren's administration. Fighting for two years and leading Seminole warriors alongside fugitive slaves, Osceola won many fierce battles. Osceola's warriors were so successful that the U.S. Army suffered public ridicule. It was during a flagged truce that Gen. Thomas S. Jesup ordered Osceola's arrest. The captured 37-year-old Seminole chief died in prison three months later of unknown causes.

---

a free or a slave territory of the United States. Jackson postponed recognizing Texas as an independent republic, let alone proposing its annexation to the United States—until three days before leaving office. Then he influenced the Senate to recognize Texas's independence, thereby infuriating the Mexican government.

Van Buren was the president who was forced to deal with the crisis. He was much more sensitive to the sectional divisiveness of the Texas issue, and his concerns were justified; immediately after Jackson recognized Texas, northerners claimed it was a conspiracy among the slaveholding states of the South to grab power. In 1837, eager to join the United States, the newly independent republic of Texas sent their minister to Washington, D.C., to formally request their admission into the Union. Because Van Buren had made his intentions clear to the cabinet and lawmakers—many of whom desired annexation but could not argue with the wisdom of the refusal—the proposal was politely rejected, without much discussion.

The Amistad *and Slavery*

The fine line Van Buren constantly walked between northern and southern sectional interests is perhaps best illustrated by the *Amistad* incident, which took place in the summer of 1839. Two slave dealers named Jose Ruiz and Pedro Montez had bribed officials in Havana, Cuba, to issue papers certifying that 52 men, recently captured in Africa, were in fact *ladinos,* or Spanish-speaking

slaves from Cuba, who were merely being transported to plantations eastward along the U.S. coast (Cuba was a Spanish possession in 1839). At the time the United States had outlawed the African slave trade but permitted the trade and transport of American-born slaves. Four days after the slave dealers' ship, the *Amistad,* had left Havana, the Africans freed themselves from their chains, killed the captain of the ship, and demanded to be taken back to Africa. Instead, Ruiz and Montez steered toward the U.S. coast, where the ship was captured near Long Island Sound. The captives were accused of piracy and held in prison to await trial in federal district court.

The immediate reaction of Van Buren and his cabinet revealed a willingness to appease the nation's proslavery interests—whenever those interests did not involve a change in the nation's sectional balance. Spanish authorities in the United States demanded that the slaves be returned to their Spanish owners, and Attorney General Felix Grundy and Secretary of State John Forsyth agreed, assuring the Spanish ambassador that the administration would return the slaves as soon as the court had ruled. Van Buren, expecting a favorable outcome, signed an executive order for the slaves to be escorted back to Cuba by the navy schooner *Grampus.*

Abolitionists had other ideas, and they organized a committee to defend the captives and publicize the case. When the district court and the court of appeals ruled against Van Buren's administration, Grundy brought the case to the Supreme Court of the United States, where

---

Fast Fact

When forming his cabinet, Van Buren invited fellow New Yorker and celebrated author Washington Irving (author of "Rip Van Winkle" and "The Legend of Sleepy Hollow") to become secretary of the navy. Irving, fearing the political reaction to such an appointment, declined.

(Source: Major L. Wilson. *The Presidency of Martin Van Buren*, 1984.)

former President John Quincy Adams defended the slaves. Adams, then 73 years old, had not appeared before the Supreme Court since 1809. His impassioned defense of the captives was based primarily on the fraudulent certification papers, but also on the principles of freedom and equality. The Supreme Court decided in favor of the defense and set the captives free.

The *Amistad* case dragged on in appeals throughout 1840 and 1841, and Van Buren's clearly proslavery handling of the case was much debated in the press during the campaign year. Predictably, he won credit in the South and infamy in the North.

Great Britain-U.S. Relations

The Caroline

The greatest threats to peace during Van Buren's administration involved two separate crises with Great Britain. The first was sparked in 1837, when rebellion broke out in Canada, then a British colony, against British rule. At the time, many Americans in the North were understandably not fond of the British and would not have minded seeing them disappear entirely from the North American continent. Some forward-looking expansionists, in fact, looking to counterbalance what they saw as the inevitable annexation of Texas as a slave territory, openly advocated the Canadian rebellion and the later annexation of all of Canada.

Despite an 1818 treaty of neutrality, many northern Americans were determined to aid the Canadians in their cause. The situation reached a breaking point in December 1837, when an American steamer, the *Caroline* based in Buffalo, New York, was observed by the British to have crossed into Canada on three occasions, unloading supplies to the Canadian rebels. The *Caroline* was seized by Canadian loyalists and boarded by

force. The crew were expelled and the ship was set afire and sunk.

Against the advice of several advisers, Van Buren was determined to avoid war. Before he had even taken up the issue of the *Caroline* with the British minister in Washington, he issued a proclamation of U.S. neutrality in the conflict. He also sent General Winfield Scott into the region to persuade the Americans to stop aiding the Canadian rebellion. Later in the year, after more skirmishes, Van Buren issued a second, more strongly worded declaration, emphasizing his peaceful intentions toward the British government. As more Americans were tried and convicted in U.S. courts of violating the 1818 treaty of neutrality, the appetite for rebellion and talk of Canadian annexation fizzled out. Van Buren had managed to maintain the peace—but never managed to receive an official apology or reparations for the loss of the *Caroline*.

The Aroostook War

The nation was brought even closer to war with Britain over the disputed boundary between the state of Maine and the Canadian territory of New Brunswick. The boundary defined at the end of the American Revolution (1775–83) was not completely clear, and a compromise engineered by President Andrew Jackson had not sufficiently laid the matter to rest. Shortly after taking office, Van Buren engaged Great Britain in discussions about the border, but tensions in the area were mounting. In 1838 Canadian lumberjacks began cutting timber in the Aroostook Valley, an area claimed by the United States. This led to a series of skirmishes—popularly referred to as the "Aroostook War"—between the Maine and the New Brunswick militias, and much posturing on the part of the opposing governors.

The situation worsened for several months until Van Buren intervened, working out an agreement that typically mixed demands with concessions to the British. He stressed to the constituents of Maine (who later burned him in effigy for the reminder) that the boundary was an issue to be worked out between the two national governments. By the summer of 1839 the United States and Britain were talking over an arrangement to submit the boundary to arbitration, but Van Buren's term would expire before the boundary was finally settled. The final Main/Canada border was established by the Webster-Ashburton Treaty, during the subsequent Tyler administration.

The Van Buren Administration Legacy

After being voted out of office in 1840, Van Buren distinguished himself with his graciousness. He paid a personal visit to his Whig successor, William Henry Harrison, at Harrison's Washington hotel, and invited him to be the guest of honor at one of Van Buren's renowned dinner parties. Van Buren also offered to vacate the presidential mansion early, in order to allow Harrison and his family to move in before inauguration day.

Because of Van Buren's insistence on maintaining peace, Harrison and the Whigs were handed the leadership of a nation that was not involved in a foreign war. But Harrison and the Whigs also inherited an institution they loathed: Van Buren's Independent Treasury. They promptly dismantled it in 1841, but by this time the economy was on the mend and the Whigs could not convincingly claim credit for overcoming the crisis. It was also up to Harrison's administration—which was destined to end only a month after his inauguration, upon his death—to finally decide upon the question of annexing Texas.

While Van Buren's American Indian policies are typically denounced by historians and critics, some point out that he was quick to curb other expansionist tendencies in the South. It may have been that Van Buren was simply trying to satisfy the expansionist urges of southerners without tipping the sectional balance of the Union. Whatever his reasons, his approach to the growing conflict with American Indians helped continue a tragic tradition in the U.S. government's handling of Indian affairs.

The political skill that had ultimately won Van Buren the White House was not enough to make him into a strong statesman who could lead his party, and he was considered by the Whigs and the conservative Democrats to be a slick career politician who had ridden Jackson's coattails to power.

Lasting Impact

While the Whigs did succeed in destroying the sole activist accomplishment of Van Buren's presidency, the Independent Treasury, this was only temporary. The Democrats, victorious again in 1846, revived the institution, which remained a part of the federal government until it was merged with the new Federal Reserve System in 1921.

Van Buren's reputation suffers today, as it did then, from an unfavorable comparison with his predecessor, Andrew Jackson, and his unfortunate association with many events that were well beyond his control. While the condemnation of Van Buren as a purely political animal, devoid of principle, has some basis in history (his continuation of Jackson's brutal American Indian policies are an example), it is also true that the issues on which Van Buren equivocated most, slavery and the annexation of Texas, were based on a principle in which Van Buren passionately believed—the preservation of the Union.

Maintaining peace in the face of war was probably his most significant, and today his most undervalued,

achievement. Van Buren's refusal to annex Texas, viewed by many contemporaries as a typical evasion of a difficult issue, has been interpreted by some historians as a merciful granting of "repose" to a nation troubled by sectional conflict. By 1862, the year Van Buren died, the American Civil War (1861–65) had already begun to destroy the Union he had worked to preserve.

Sources

Alexander, Holmes. *The American Talleyrand: The Career and Contemporaries of Martin Van Buren, Eighth President.* Harper and Brothers, 1935.

Bailey, Thomas A. *The American Pageant: A History of the Republic.* Boston: Little, Brown, 1966.

Bancroft, George. *Martin Van Buren to the End of His Public Career.* New York: Harper and Brothers, 1889.

Conlin, Joseph R. *The American Past, Part One: A Survey of American History to 1877.* San Diego, Calif.: Harcourt Brace, 1990.

Lynch, Denis Tilden. *An Epoch and a Man: Martin Van Buren and His Times.* New York: H. Liveright, 1929.

Morison, Samuel Eliot, Henry Steele Commager, and William E. Leuchtenburg. *A Concise History of the American Republic.* New York: Oxford University Press, 1983.

Nash, Gary B., et al. *The American People: Creating A Nation and a Society.* Vol. 1. New York: Harper and Row, 1990.

Niven, John. *Martin Van Buren: The Romantic Age of American Politics.* New York: Oxford University Press, 1983.

Remini, Robert Vincent. *Martin Van Buren and the Making of the Democratic Party.* New York: Columbia University Press, 1959.

Shepard, Edward Morse. *Martin Van Buren.* Boston: Houghton Mifflin, 1894.

Sloan, Irving, ed. *Martin Van Buren: 1782–1862.* Dobbs Ferry, N.Y.: Oceana Publications, 1969.

Wilson, Major L. *The Presidency of Martin Van Buren.* Lawrence, Kans.: University Press of Kansas, 1984.

Further Readings

Cole, Donald B. *Martin Van Buren and the American Political System.* Princeton, N.J.: Princeton University Press, 1984.

Curtis, James C. *The Fox at Bay: Martin Van Buren and the Presidency, 1837–1841.* Lexington, Ky.: University Press of Kentucky, 1970.

Mushkat, Jerome, and Joseph G. Rayback. *Martin Van Buren: Law, Politics, and the Shaping of Republican Ideology.* DeKalb, Ill.: Northern Illinois University Press, 1997.

Van Buren, Martin. *The Autobiography of Martin Van Buren.* Washington, D.C.: U.S. Government Printing Office, 1920.

W. H. Harrison Administration

Full name: William Henry Harrison
Popular name: Old Tippecanoe; Old Tip

Personal Information:

Born: February 9, 1773
Birthplace: Charles City County, Virginia, Berkeley Plantation
Died: April 4, 1841
Death place: Washington, D.C.
Burial place: William Henry Harrison Memorial State Park, North Bend, Ohio
Religion: Episcopalian
Spouse: Anna Tuthill Symmes (m. 1795)
Children: Elizabeth Bassett; John Cleves Symmes; Lucy Singleton; William Henry, Jr.; John Scott; Benjamin; Mary Symmes; Carter Bassett; Anna Tuthill; James Findlay
Education: Hampden-Sydney College, Virginia; University of Pennsylvania Medical School
Occupation: Soldier; politician; diplomat
Political Party: Whig Party
Age at Inauguration: 68 years

Biography

Born into one of Virginia's most aristocratic families, William Henry Harrison entered the military at an early age, attained national recognition for his victory over the American Indian leader Tecumseh at the Battle of Tippecanoe, and was promoted to general during the War of 1812. He went on to enjoy a long career in frontier and national politics that culminated in his victory of the presidential election of 1840. He died, however, after only one month in office, and his administration is known as the shortest in U.S. history.

Early Life

William Henry Harrison was born into one of the oldest, wealthiest, and most highly respected families in the English colony of Virginia. Of English ancestry, Harrison was a direct descendant of King Henry III (1207–72) through his paternal grandmother. He was born in 1773 on the Harrison family plantation, Berkeley, in Charles City County, Virginia. He was the youngest of seven children born to Benjamin Harrison V and Elizabeth Bassett. Very little is known about his early childhood except that it was spent at Berkeley in activities such as swimming, fishing, and horseback riding. William Henry grew up during the tumult of the American Revolution (1775–83) and experienced its effects firsthand. At the age of seven he and his family were evacuated to another Harrison estate, Lower Brandon, on the James River (also in Virginia), as German mercenary soldiers and American loyalist troops under the command of Brigadier Gen. Benedict Arnold raided and ransacked Berkeley.

Although William Henry Harrison did not display any particular interest in politics during his youth, his father was one of the most important figures in revolutionary and newly independent Virginia politics. An outspoken opponent of British colonial policy, Benjamin Harrison V sat in the Virginia House of Burgesses (1748–75); was one of seven Virginians to sign the Declaration of Independence; was a member of the Continental Congress, a forerunner to the U.S. Congress, (1774–77); was elected, over Thomas Jefferson, to the position of Speaker of the Virginia House of Delegates (1778–81); and served as governor of Virginia (1781–84). He continued his political career in the Virginia state legislature until his death in 1791, whereupon he was replaced by none other than John Tyler, the father of the vice president of the same name who would replace William Henry Harrison after his untimely death in office 50 years later.

Education

Harrison's schooling began as a young child on the Berkeley plantation where he and his siblings attended classes taught by private tutors. Unlike his older brothers who entered into business or studied law, Harrison was interested in natural history and decided to pursue a medical degree. In 1787, at the age of 14, he enrolled in Hampden-Sydney College in Hampden-Sydney, Virginia. Although the school was little more than a log cabin at the time, its headmaster was a well-respected physician. While at Hampden-Sydney Harrison founded a literary society, but it was military history that fascinated him. Harrison later left Hampden-Sydney for the University of Pennsylvania Medical School in Philadelphia, but the death of his father left him with too little money to continue his education.

Family Life

Anna Tuthill Symmes was born July 25, 1775, in Flathook, New Jersey. She was well-educated and had attended the Clinton Academy in Easthampton, New York, and a private school in New York City. In 1795 her father, Colonel John Cleves Symmes, a chief justice in the New Jersey Supreme Court who served in the Continental Congress, acquired over 500,000 acres in what is now southwestern Ohio. Appointed to a judgeship in the Northwest Territory, he relocated the family to an area near modern-day Cincinnati. On a visit to relatives in nearby Lexington, Kentucky, in the spring of 1795 she met William Henry Harrison who happened to be in town on military business. The two fell in love and eloped on November 25, 1795, in North Bend in what is today Ohio. It was not until Harrison achieved fame as a soldier in the years ahead that he was accepted by Judge Symmes.

William Henry Harrison. (National Portrait Gallery. Reproduced by permission.)

By all accounts the Harrisons had a happy marriage. Their family life was marred by tragedy, however, as six of their 10 children suffered untimely deaths prior to their parents. Anna Harrison was also quite ill at times. Just a month before her husband was inaugurated as president she fell sick and was unable to accompany him to Washington, D.C. Harrison's daughter-in-law Jane Irwin Harrison, the widow of Colonel William Henry Harrison Jr., acted as the temporary mistress of the White House while Anna Harrison recuperated. Sadly the president died before Anna Harrison was well enough to join him in Washington. She survived her husband by almost 23 years and was the first presidential widow to be awarded a pension.

Career

In August 1791, shortly after dropping out of the University of Pennsylvania, Harrison had a fortuitous meeting with Virginia governor Richard Henry Lee, a family friend who was visiting Philadelphia. He suggested that Harrison join the army. By September Harrison had been appointed an ensign in the First U.S. Infantry Regiment of Virginia and set off for Fort Pitt on the Ohio River. From there he continued on to Fort Washington (what is now Cincinnati) in the Northwest Territory as part of a contingent charged with protecting settlers from attacks by the local American Indian inhabitants of the region. Harrison was promoted and commended several times. By 1797 he had reached the rank of captain, but he resigned from the army to pursue his growing political and commercial ambitions.

Harrison Enters Politics

Harrison's first significant foray into the world of politics came in 1798 when he was appointed by President John Adams as secretary of the Northwest Territory. The Northwest Territory, created by Congress in 1787, was the region that is currently the states of Ohio, Michigan, Illinois, Indiana, and Wisconsin, as well as a small part of Minnesota. In 1799 the political status of the Northwest Territory was upgraded—its population having risen to the point that it was allowed to govern itself and elect its own representatives in Washington—and Harrison was elected the area's first delegate to the House of Representatives.

Governor of the Indiana Territory

In 1801 President John Adams appointed Harrison governor of the Indiana Territory, the western half of the newly divided Northwest Territory. Harrison served in this post for the next 12 years. During his tenure as governor he was known for his attempts to establish law and order in the territory. He was also admired for his success in negotiating treaties with the local American Indians (such as the Sac and Fox Treaty of 1804 and the Treaty of Fort Wayne of 1809), which ceded control over millions of acres in what are now the states of Indiana, Illinois, Wisconsin, and Missouri to the United States. Not all of the tribes in the area acknowledged the legitimacy of these treaties, however. Foremost among Harrison's and the U.S. government's opponents were the Shawnees, led by two half-brothers Tecumseh and the Prophet.

Under orders from Washington, Harrison led a force of army regulars and militiamen to attack the Shawnees and their allies. Ambushed while they slept near Tippecanoe Creek, in west central Indiana, Harrison was able to rally his troops and defeat Tecumseh after suffering heavy losses. This greatly demoralized the American Indian resistance in the territory and made Harrison into a hero throughout Indiana and Ohio. It was here that he aquired the nickname "Old Tippecanoe" as a result of his exploits.

Harrison Returns to the Military

Harrison resigned his position as governor of the Indiana Territory to take part in the War of 1812 (1812–14) with Great Britain. Originally he was commissioned a major general in command of the Kentucky militia, which was detailed to protect the Northwest Territory from combined Anglo-Indian attack. On the strength of his reputation from Tippecanoe, and with the support of powerful Kentucky representative Henry Clay, he quickly rose to the rank of brigadier general. Given the mission of recapturing Detroit, Harrison defeated the British and Indian forces at the Battle of the Thames near Chatham, Ontario, and secured the United States's northwest flank. His victory made him into a national hero.

Harrison Reenters Politics

Shortly after the War of 1812 Harrison resigned from the army over differences with Secretary of War John Armstrong. He retired to his farm in North Bend, Ohio, to spend time with his family and pursue a variety of commercial ventures. However, by 1816 he was having serious financial difficulty and looked toward a return to political life as a means to provide for his large family. Harrison was elected to the Cincinnati seat in the U.S. House of Representatives in 1816, where he became an ally of Henry Clay. When his House term expired in 1819 Harrison returned home whereupon he defeated William Gazely of Cincinnati for a seat in the Ohio State Senate where he served until 1821. His political good fortune was short-lived though, as he was defeated in a bid for the U.S. Senate in 1821 and the U.S. House of Representatives in 1822. He was finally returned to political office in 1825 as a U.S. senator, a position that he occupied until 1828. Although Harrison had little knowledge of diplomacy, Henry Clay made overtures to President John Quincy Adams that resulted in Harrison's appointment as U.S. minister to Colombia. Soon after his arrival in the Colombian capital of Bogota in February 1829, he clashed with Colombia's ruler Simon Bolivar, who accused him of complicity in a local uprising. Upon Andrew Jackson's assumption of the presidency in 1830, Harrison was recalled from his overseas post to the United States.

Harrison's Political Fortunes Turn

The next several years were hard on the Harrisons. Returning to his home in North Bend, Ohio, in 1830, Harrison's business ventures and farming activities proved unsuccessful. In 1834, his family in a state of financial depression, Harrison accepted the mundane position of clerk of the Ohio Court of Common Pleas. A dramatic turnaround in his political fortunes began in 1836, however, when he was nominated as one of the newly created Whig Party's candidates for president. Although he was defeated by Democrat Martin Van Buren of New York, Harrison proved himself the most popular of the three Whigs who stood in the presidential election of 1836. This made him one of the most viable candidates for the Whig presidential nomination in 1840. Thanks to the adroit campaign strategy of the Whig leadership, "Old Tippecanoe" was able to narrowly defeat incumbent Van Buren in 1840 to become the ninth president of the United States.

Harrison as President

While the Whig Party had chosen Harrison as their presidential candidate, this was primarily due to their feeling that he was more likely to win an election than the party's true leaders, senators Henry Clay and Daniel Webster. These and other powerful Whigs were expected to be the ones who controlled the presidency, not Harrison. It will never be known if Harrison was truly willing to serve such a reduced role as president. He caught pneumonia during his inauguration and died after only one month in office, on April 4, 1841.

Post-presidential Years

Of William Henry Harrison's 10 children only one followed in his father's footsteps by pursuing a career in politics. His fifth child, John Scott Harrison (1804–78), was elected as a Whig representative from Ohio to the U.S. House of Representatives. He served from 1853 to 1857 during the Thirty-fourth and Thirty-fifth Congresses. John Scott Harrison was also the only man to be both the son of one president and the father of another. His son, Benjamin Harrison (1833–1901), was elected the 23d president of the United States in 1888.

The William Henry Harrison Administration

William Henry Harrison was the first Whig to become U.S. president. Given the Whigs's commitment to weakening the power of the executive branch after years of its expansion under the control of the Democrats, Harrison's administration was plagued from the outset by rumors that the newly elected president was destined to be little more than a figurehead for more powerful party members. Although Harrison demonstrated a willingness to take independent action, he died after only one month in office, bequeathing the struggle for control over the Whig Party and the national agenda to his successor, Vice President John Tyler.

Harrison Becomes President

The Campaign of 1840

The presidential election of 1840 occupies an important place in the annals of U.S. politics. Utilizing an array of "modern" public relations techniques and a militant pattern of campaigning that brought voters out by the tens of thousands, the Whig Party was able to transform William Henry Harrison into a folk hero of immense popular appeal. Elaborating and improving upon the campaign strategies that had proven so successful for Andrew Jackson into the presidency in 1828, the Whigs were able

to wrest control of the White House for the first time since their emergence as a national political party in the early 1830s.

Founded in 1834 as an alternative political force to President Andrew Jackson and his Democratic Party, the Whigs were a catchall party that did not really coalesce into a unified national opposition movement until the latter part of the decade. Little of substance actually united the disparate elements that made up the Whigs but for a shared grievance against the "imperial" tactics of Democratic president Jackson, who was known derisively as "King Andrew" for his aggressive use of executive power.

The Whig's First National Convention

Because of the recession of 1837, incumbent president Martin Van Buren appeared vulnerable in the 1840 campaign. Eschewing their 1836 campaign strategy altogether, in which they ran three candidates in the hopes that between them they would deny Democratic candidate Van Buren a majority, the Whig leadership opted to unite behind a single candidate in 1840. On December 4, 1839, the Whigs met in Harrisburg, Pennsylvania, in their first national convention. Of the possible candidates for the presidential nomination, Senator Henry Clay of Kentucky was clearly the front-runner. One of the founders of the Whig Party and a figure at the center of U.S. politics for the past two decades, Clay was one of the most widely known politicians of his day. Yet, Whig strategists were not sure if Clay was their party's best chance at the presidency. While Clay was a brilliant politician and a skilled orator, he was tarnished by his previous losses in the presidential elections of 1824 and 1832.

What the Whig strategists wanted was a new name and a fresh face around whom the entire nation could be mobilized. Just as the Democrats had done with Andrew Jackson so successfully in the past, the new generation of Whigs wanted a nominee who could be turned into a national folk hero. As far as the Whig strategists were concerned, the two most viable candidates for their party's nomination were William Henry Harrison and Gen. Winfield Scott. Both were soldier heroes with national reputations who had achieved notoriety for their service in the War of 1812. Harrison's and Scott's lack of political experience in Washington compared with Clay's was deemed far less important than their perceived potential to garner votes. Once either got into the White House more skilled and able Whig leaders could effectively manage the presidency behind the scenes.

The Whig convention was notable in a number of regards. It was the first to adopt the unit rule by which all the votes of a state delegation are cast for the candidate who receives a majority of the state's votes. This was especially detrimental to Clay as he had strong minority support in both Pennsylvania and New York. It was also the first convention to invite the newspaper press

Administration

Administration Dates

March 4, 1841–April 4, 1841

Vice President

John Tyler (1841)

Cabinet

Secretary of State

Daniel Webster (1841–43)

Secretary of the Treasury

Thomas Ewing (1841)

Secretary of War

John Bell (1841)

Attorney General

John J. Crittenden (1841)

Secretary of the Navy

George E. Badger (1841)

Postmaster General

Francis Granger (1841)

to the proceedings. After the first ballot was cast Clay led the field with 103 votes to Harrison's 97 and Scott's 57, but he did not command a majority. In the second ballot the New York delegation shifted its support from Scott to Harrison, giving the latter more than enough votes to secure the nomination. Pushed aside by the party he helped to found, Clay was frustrated, disappointed, and angered. While publicly he threw his support behind the convention's outcome, privately he stewed. After four days of meetings John Tyler, a former senator from Virginia, was selected by the Whig nominating committee to be Harrison's running mate. No platform was adopted at the convention in order to avoid commitment to issues that might unveil and exacerbate divisions within the party.

The Democratic Convention

Although his popularity suffered badly as a result of the 1837 economic depression that occurred during his presidency, incumbent president Martin Van Buren of New York was the unquestioned front-runner in the Democratic Party. At the party's national convention in Baltimore, Maryland, on May 4, 1840, Van Buren was nominated without dissent on the first ballot. Unlike the Whigs, the Democrats did compose a party platform. It called for strict construction of the Constitution, meaning that the government would have no power beyond what was explicitly laid out in the Constitution, and opposed federal funding for infrastructure improvements internal to a single state, federal assumption of state debts, unequal protective tariffs, a national bank, and congressional interference in the slavery issue.

The Presidential Campaign

The election of 1840 was the first truly modern presidential campaign, relying on mass mobilization of voters, patriotic songs, banners and trinkets, extensive use of the media, and a full-scale public relations war that focused almost entirely on the personal images of the candidates rather than the issues. Through deft planning and tight organization throughout the ranks of the party the Whigs were able to create a momentum behind Harrison that the Democrats were unable to counter. The Whig strategy was simple: avoid any discussion of potentially divisive public policy questions and concentrate entirely on simple slogans and symbols to get as many people into the election spirit as possible. Tremendous effort was put into developing a public image of Harrison as an honest, kindly, rustic man of the people, while Van Buren was denigrated as a dandified aristocrat who was out of touch with the common man. Harrison's exploits at the Battle of Tippecanoe Creek were rehashed as the public was encouraged to identify with "Old Tip," defender of the settler. Cheers of "Tippecanoe and Tyler too!" were heard across the nation.

The Democrats attempted to counter the swelling popular momentum for Harrison with its own public relations machine and a call to refocus the campaign on substantive policy issues. Harrison was attacked as a sham hero, a "Granny" (he was 67 in 1840), while the Whig party was linked with the old Federalist Party and abolitionism (i.e., advocacy of the abolition of slavery).

The Whig machine proved unstoppable, however, and those running the campaign were more adept at the public relations game than their Democratic counterparts. Over 80 percent of the electorate voted in 1840. Only two other presidential elections, those of 1860 and 1876, brought more citizens to the polls. When the final election results were tallied in November 1840, Harrison and Tyler had 52.9 percent of the popular vote to Van Buren's and Johnson's 46.8 percent. At the congressional level the Whig triumph was just as pronounced. In both the House and the Senate previous Democratic majorities had been reversed and Whigs now controlled both chambers. Relegated to the role of opposition for the better part of the last two decades, the Whigs found themselves in control of the commanding heights of the national political system.

The "slogan ball" of the 1840 Harrison campaign popularized the expression "keep the ball rolling." Huge Harrison balls, over 10 feet in diameter and covered with slogans, were rolled from town to town. (Archive Photos. Reproduced by permission.)

Harrison's Advisers

The biggest issue surrounding the Harrison administration was the extent to which the new president would be merely a figurehead for more powerful personalities in the Whig Party. Opposed to the imperial style of executive leadership exercised by President Andrew Jackson and continued by Van Buren, the Whigs were committed to a redefinition of the relationship between the president, Congress, and the cabinet so that the executive abuses of the past would be reigned in. In accordance

with this goal the Whig philosophy of presidential-cabinet relations asserted that the cabinet should guide and direct the president. While the president presided over his official advisers in name, decisions were to be reached by majority with the president accorded one vote equal in stature to those of the cabinet members.

Even before Harrison had taken the oath of office rumors circulated that he was destined to become little more than the puppet of Kentucky senator Henry Clay, an outcome that followed closely with Clay's own intentions after being cast aside in the previous election. Clay

Fast Fact

The word "booze" entered the English language as an outgrowth of the Whig presidential campaign of 1840 when a distiller from Philadelphia, E. G. Booz, began putting his whiskey into log-cabin shaped bottles to promote Harrison's candidacy.

(Source: William Nesbit Chambers. *History of American Presidential Elections, 1789–1968,* 1971.)

turned down Harrison's offer of the prestigious office of secretary of state, preferring to remain in the Senate in preparation for another run at the presidency. It was clear, however, that Clay still expected to have a great deal of control over Harrison. Harrison, while he subscribed to the Whig's philosophy of a weakend presidency, was not actually willing to give up so much power that he became simply one among equals. While at times he allowed his cabinet to overrule him, he was prepared to, and on occasion did, act independently of their wishes.

Harrison and Congress

Harrison died before the first special session of the Twenty-seventh Congress convened in May 1841.

Harrison and the Judiciary

The only major event that took place in the judiciary under Harrison was the Supreme Court's decision in the case of *United States vs. The Amistad,* handed down on March 9, 1841, five days after Harrison took office. In this case a group of Africans, who had been kidnapped and sold into the Spanish slave trade, were charged with murder and piracy after seizing control of the slaver's ship, the *Amistad,* and running aground on Long Island, New York.

The attorney for the United States argued that existing treaty law demanded that the ship and its cargo be returned to its Spanish owners. Arguing for the defense was former president John Quincy Adams, who eloquently presented the case that the Africans could in no way be considered slaves. The Supreme Court ruled for the Africans, thereby affirming the lower court's deci-

sion, accepting Adams's argument that they were never citizens of Spain and were illegally taken from their homes where they were free men. While acknowledging that the United States did have certain obligations to Spain under existing treaties, Justice Joseph Story declared that these responsibilities were not intended to take away the equal rights of [the Africans]. Shortly after the Court's ruling the Africans sailed back to their homeland in West Africa.

Changes in the U.S. Government

William Henry Harrison was the first president to die in office. Although the Constitution was clear in its stipulation that the incumbent vice president was the first in line to the presidency in such an instance, there were no precedents to guide the nation in the process of installing Vice President John Tyler as Harrison's successor. The Constitution was silent, for instance, on whether the successor simply occupied the office of the president, serving in the capacity and under a title of "acting president," or whether he actually became the president, with all the attendant rights, privileges, and responsibilities. It was only as a result of Tyler's persistent demanding that he be treated as the president, rather than simply a temporary occupant of the vacated office, that such a precedent now governs the succession issue.

Domestic Issues

While Harrison died before he had a chance to enact any policies, something of his goals are known from his inaugural address. He sought to reform the presidency, limiting presidents to one term and ending the practice of presidents initiating legislation and otherwise intruding on Congress. He also sought to reform the civil service, making competence not political affiliation, the deciding factor in getting jobs with the government.

The Death of a President

William Henry Harrison arrived in Washington, D.C. as president-elect on his birthday, February 9, 1841. Age 68 when he took the oath of office the following month, he was the oldest man prior to Ronald Reagan to be inaugurated president. Although it was cold and stormy, Harrison delivered his inaugural address outside without a hat, gloves, or coat. Almost six thousand words in length, Harrison's inaugural speech took over one hour and forty minutes to deliver, the longest on record. He caught a cold at the ceremonies that by late March had been diagnosed as pleurisy (pneumonia). He managed to improve slightly at the beginning of April, but shortly after midnight on April 4, 1841, he died.

Foreign Issues

The United States's emergence as a world power was many years away when Harrison took office in 1841. Relations with Europe monopolized U.S. politicians interest in the international arena. Disputes with Great Britain over Canada's territorial boundaries and the support of U.S. citizens for a Canadian rebellion against British colonial rule in 1837 threatened to bring the two countries to hostilities. Little was accomplished during Harrison's brief tenure, however, and the Anglo-American disputes were bequeathed to the Tyler administration.

The William Henry Harrison Administration Legacy

Because Harrison died so shortly after becoming president his administration did not leave a lasting imprint on the U.S. political system or the nation. The campaign of 1840 that brought him to power, though, established many important precedents. The use of the unit rule to nominate a candidate at conventions, the exploitation of the mass media to build a candidate's public image, and the direct communication of the candidate to the voters through public speeches on the campaign trail are all features of modern elections that are as commonplace today as they were groundbreaking over 150 years ago when the Whigs utilized them to unseat the Democrats. Harrison's death also led to the establishment of the precedent that the person who succeeds to the presidency actually becomes the president, and not just a temporary occupant of the vacated office.

Sources

Chambers, William Nesbit. "The Election of 1840." In *History of American Presidential Elections, 1789–1968*, Vol. 1. Edited by Arthur Schlesinger, Jr. New York: Chelsea House Publishers, 1971.

Cleaves, Freeman. *Old Tippecanoe: William Henry Harrison and His Time*. New York: Charles Scribner's Sons, 1939.

Cornell Legal Information Institute. "The Amistad Revolt." 12 February 1998. <http://www.law.cornell.edu/amistad/revolt.htm> (4 July 1999).

———. "The First Amistad Case." 12 February 1998. <http://www.law.cornell.edu/amistad/summary.htm> (4 July 1999).

DeGregorio, William A. *The Complete Book of U.S. Presidents*. New York: Dembner Books, 1989.

Encyclopedia of World Biography. Vol. 7. Detroit: Gale Research Inc., 1998.

Goebel, Dorothy Burne, and Julius Goebel Jr. *Generals in the White House*. Garden City, N.Y.: Doubleday, Doran, 1945.

Peterson, Norma L. *The Presidencies of William Henry Harrison and John Tyler*. Lawrence, Kans.: University Press of Kansas, 1989.

Further Readings

Edmunds, R. David. *Tecumseh and the Quest for Indian Leadership*. Boston: Little, Brown, 1984.

Goebel, Dorothy B. *William Henry Harrison: A Political Biography*. Indianapolis, Ind.: Indiana Library and Historical Department, 1926.

Green, James A. *William Henry Harrison: His Life and Times*. Richmond, Va.: Garrett and Massie, Inc., 1941.

Gunderson, Robert G. *The Log-Cabin Campaign*. Lexington, Ken.: University of Kentucky Press, 1957.

Sugden, John. *Tecumseh: A Life*. New York: Henry Holt and Co., 1998.

Tyler Administration

Full name: John Tyler
Popular name: The Accidental President; His Accidency

Personal Information:

Born: March 29, 1790
Birthplace: Greenway Plantation, Virginia
Died: January 18, 1862
Death place: Richmond, Virginia
Burial place: Hollywood Cemetery, Richmond, Virginia
Religion: Episcopalian
Spouse: Letitia Christian (m. 1813); Julia Gardiner (m. 1844)
Children: Mary; Robert; John; Letitia; Elizabeth; Anne
    Contesse; Alice; Tazewell; David Gardiner; John
    Alexander; Julia Gardiner; Lachlan; Lyon Gardiner;
    Robert Fitzwalter; Pearl
Education: College of William and Mary, 1807
Occupation: Lawyer; legislator; governor; vice president
Political Party: Democratic Party; Whig Party
Age at Inauguration: 51 years

Biography

John Tyler was born into one of the most prominent families in Virginia and was raised by his father to believe in the principles of Jeffersonian Republicanism—limited federal government and the rights of states to govern themselves. His political career began at the early age of 21, when he joined the Virginia state legislature.

Early Life

John Tyler was born on March 29, 1790, at Greenway Plantation in Charles City County, Virginia. He came from a family steeped in American tradition: his father, John Tyler, a governor of Virginia and a judge of the U.S. district court, had been a friend and associate of American revolutionaries Patrick Henry, Thomas Jefferson, and Benjamin Harrison (father and great grandfather to William Henry Harrison, ninth president of the United States, and Benjamin Harrison, 23d president of the United States).

Little is known of Tyler's boyhood. His mother, Mary Armistead Tyler, died when he was just seven years old, and the elder John Tyler took on the job of raising his son with great enthusiasm. As a boy, President Tyler was said to be gentler than his stern father, universally well behaved, and a good student. The Virginia Tylers were wealthy tobacco planters who owned plantations and slaves, and in the tradition of the South, Tyler was raised by his father to be a strict "constructionist"—one who believes the powers of the federal government should be limited to those explicitly expressed in the Constitution.

Education

After attending a rural school near Greenway, in Virginia, Tyler left in 1802—at the young age of 12—to attend the preparatory school of the College of William and Mary, in Williamsburg, Virginia. In 1804 he enrolled in the college itself. The curriculum was dominated by classical languages and English literature, but Tyler was also introduced to history and political economy. His academic career was very successful, and he graduated in 1807 at the age of 17.

After returning to Charles City County, Virginia, Tyler, already bent on pursuing a political career, began the study of law under his father. When his father became governor of Virginia in 1809, Tyler studied in the Richmond, Virginia, office of Edmund Randolph, a brilliant lawyer who had been U.S. attorney general under President George Washington. Tyler was admitted to the bar in 1809.

Family Life

Tyler married Letitia Christian in 1813, on his 23d birthday. Like Tyler, his wife was a product of the Virginia plantation aristocracy. The couple had eight children, seven of whom lived to maturity, including the eldest son Robert, who went on to mount a political career of his own. Later stricken by illness, Letitia Tyler became an invalid after 1839 and was confined to a wheelchair. It was Robert's wife, Priscilla Cooper Tyler, who assumed the duties of White House hostess. Letitia Tyler died in 1842.

Two years later, in 1844, President Tyler married the young New York socialite Julia Gardiner. After overcoming some initial criticism (she was 30 years younger than the president), Julia Gardiner Tyler acted as first lady for the final eight months of Tyler's term. She then retired with him to his Virginia plantation. Together, she and Tyler had an additional seven children.

Career

Tyler's rapid rise to prominence, made much easier by his father's good name, began when he was licensed to practice law at the age of 19. Two years later he was elected to the Virginia House of Delegates, where he served from 1811 through 1816. He later served in the U.S. House of Representatives from 1817 to 1821, as governor of Virginia from 1825 to 1827, and in the U.S. Senate from 1827 to 1836. Throughout his early career Tyler never wavered from his staunch support of states's rights. As a strict constructionist he opposed the Bank of the United States (referred to as the BUS), on the grounds that the Constitution did not provide Congress with the

John Tyler. (Daguerrotype by Matthew Brady. The Library of Congress.)

power to charter it. He also was against internal improvements at federal expense.

In fact, one of Tyler's first politically important acts was to introduce a censure of Virginia's U.S. senators in 1811 (Tyler was a state legislator at the time, and U.S. senators were chosen by state legislators). The senators had supported the charter of a national bank, against the explicit instructions of the state legislature. During his early career Tyler was a Democrat who supported the programs of President Andrew Jackson, but Tyler soon became disillusioned with what he perceived to be Jackson's lack of respect for states's rights. He was persuaded in 1839 to run on the Whig ticket as a vice presidential candidate. After the Whigs's presidential candidate, William Henry Harrison, won the election, Tyler served as vice president until Harrison died about one month later.

President

After Harrison's death, Tyler's strong demand for the full title and resulting powers of the presidency helped set a precedent for a procedure which had been vaguely defined by the Constitution. Once in office, however, it was clear that Tyler had not been placed on the Whig ticket because of his own beliefs. He opposed many key elements of the Whig platform, including the establishment of a national bank, and didn't hesitate to use the presidential veto to reject bills with which he did not agree. From the start, his relations with Con-

Fast Fact

Tyler's second wife, Julia, devoted herself to volunteer work for the Confederacy during the American Civil War (1860–65), and found herself in dire poverty after the South's loss. Until 1958, there was no federal law providing automatic pensions for presidential widows, but Congress, in 1880, voted to grant Julia Gardiner Tyler $1,200 a year.

(Source: *The First Ladies,* The White House [http://www.whitehouse.gov/WH/glimpse/firstladies])

gress were soured. As a result, Tyler's domestic achievements were almost entirely negative, consisting largely of rejected Whig programs. Tyler capitalized on a growing spirit of expansionism in the United States when he fostered the 1845 annexation of Texas, an event which highlighted the troublesome issues of slavery and sectionalism for Americans, and which eventually led to war with Mexico.

Post-presidential Years

Cast out by the Whigs and rejected as a candidate by the Democrats, who chose the "dark horse," or long shot, James Polk, Tyler did not mount an 1845 campaign for the presidency. He retired to his Virginia plantation, Sherwood Forest, shortly after leaving office. He remained active in politics, however, and in 1861 he led a peace mission to Washington from the southern states in an effort to avert the impending American Civil War (1861–65). Tyler met with President Buchanan, but mostly served as a figurehead and seldom participated in the debates. The Convention produced ten compromise measures, designed mainly to preserve some measure of slavery in the South. The U.S. Senate, however, defeated these proposals resoundingly. After the mission failed, Tyler supported the South's secession from the Union. He was elected to the Confederate House of Representatives, the legislative body for the 11 southern states that seceded from the Union, but he died in 1862, at the age of 71, before he could assume his seat. One morning, Tyler had a fainting spell at the breakfast table, took to his bed, and died several days later from bronchitis.

The John Tyler Administration

In his strenuous demand to be considered more than merely an "acting president," John Tyler set the precedent that all subsequent vice presidents have followed in assuming the presidency. In an administration known mostly for political paralysis, Tyler nonetheless guided the nation through a successful period in foreign relations, and—for better or for worse—settled the question of Texas annexation just prior to leaving office.

Tyler Becomes President

Campaign of 1840

In 1840 the Whigs ran against incumbent president Martin Van Buren with the aging war hero, William Henry Harrison, who had defeated the Shawnee Chief Tecumseh at the Battle of Tippecanoe in 1811. In many ways the campaign was not seriously undertaken by the Whigs, who declined to issue a platform and added Tyler—a southerner who had split with Jacksonian Democrats—to pull in southern votes. Tyler was not, however, a true Whig. As a strict constructionist, he did not support the establishment of a national bank or the funding of internal improvements, which were not provided for in the Constitution. As a loyal southerner, he rejected tariffs that would protect northern financiers and lower the income of southern farmers and plantation owners. These beliefs would later lead Tyler into vicious battles with the Whigs in Congress.

Harrison died after only a month in office. While the Constitution provided for the vice president's assumption of the president's "powers and duties" on such an occasion, it left the exact nature of this assumption unclear. After some debate over Tyler's status as president, Tyler took the oath of office on April 6, 1841. Two days after Harrison was buried, Tyler issued a brief address—referred to by some as an "inaugural address," though he did not designate it as such. In this speech he outlined the principles for governing that he would follow in his administration. He generally avoided specific issues that would bring him into conflict with the Whigs, and for the time being there was little objection to his status being equal to that of an elected president. Tyler never appointed a vice president.

Also contributing to the awkwardness of Tyler's succession was the increasing importance of expansionism and slavery in the political system of the 1840s. John Tyler grew up in the world of the original southern Democratic Party shaped by Andrew Jackson's opposition to strong central government and his dedication to preserving the slave system. This program proved a powerful draw for the Democratic Party in the South. When reforms were enacted in the 1830s and 1840s giving poor white males the right to vote, the Democrats' strong appeal among small farmers in the South gained even more clout at the polls. Although he approved of the states's rights agenda, as an aristocratic southerner, Tyler was repelled by Jackson's machine politics and by his franchise reforms. So he joined the anti-Jackson coalition called the Whig Party. But, even though he did not like what the Democrats had become, he also did not agree with the Whigs who, in the North, were moving in the direction of repudiating states's right. Thus Tyler found himself the vice presidential nominee of a political party with which he shared few core beliefs. This was aggravated by the fact that the vice presidency had already become a symbolic office useful mainly for "balancing the ticket" during election campaigns. This worked fine until a sitting president died. Then everything was up for grabs, as the presidency devolved on a man whose politics had never been considered.

Tyler's Advisers

Tyler began his administration in the unusual position of having no close friends or advisers in the cabinet he inherited from President Harrison. Instead, he began to rely for support on a group of strong states's-rights supporters, dominated by men from his home state of Virginia: congresspeople Nathan Beverly Tucker, Thomas Gilmer, Henry Wise, and Francis Mallory; Abel P. Upshur, a judge of the General Court and later a Tyler cabinet member; and Senator William C. Rives, Tyler's staunchest supporter in the Senate. The closeness of this group led enemies such as Senator Henry Clay of Kentucky to cry out against the "Virginia Cabal" that was, he accused, effectively governing the nation under Tyler. Several biographers of Tyler have pointed out, however, that while this clique was in the habit of offering much advice to Tyler, he was as likely to reject it as to accept it. He was generally suspicious of their motives and stubborn in his own convictions.

There was only one friend and adviser whom Tyler seemed to trust unconditionally—Littleton Waller Tazewell of Virginia, with whom Tyler had served in the Senate. Tazewell was considered to be one of the South's great intellectuals of the time, and because he had not supported the Harrison-Tyler ticket in 1840, Tyler trusted him as someone who would make no demands on him as president.

Because Tyler did not stick to the Whig party line, each member of Tyler's first cabinet withdrew their support and resigned. Even during this hostile period, however, Tyler held regular cabinet meetings and occasional special sessions. This adherence to routine was not out of any real desire for advice, however; many of Tyler's own appointments were strictly political moves, and while he professed an interest in hearing the views of his department heads, he believed he alone was responsible for all official actions. (*See also,* Domestic Issues).

Administration

Administration Dates
April 6, 1841–March 4, 1845

Vice President
None

Cabinet
Secretary of State
Daniel Webster (1841–43)
Abel P. Upshur (1843–44)
John C. Calhoun (1844–45)

Secretary of the Treasury
Thomas Ewing (1841)
Walter Forward (1841–43)
John C. Spencer (1843–44)
George M. Bibb (1844–45)

Secretary of War
John Bell (1841)
John C. Spencer (1841–43)
James M. Porter (1843–44)
William Wilkins (1844–45)

Attorney General
John J. Crittenden (1841)
Hugh S. Legaré (1841–43)
John Nelson (1843–45)

Secretary of the Navy
George E. Badger (1841)
Abel P. Upshur (1841–43)
David Henshaw (1843–44)
Thomas Walker Gilmer (1844)
John Y. Mason (1844–45)

Postmaster General
Francis Granger (1841)
Charles A. Wickliffe (1841–45)

Tyler and Congress

Tyler presided over the Twenty-seventh and Twenty-eighth sessions of Congress. The Whigs held a slight majority in each Senate session, while the midterm elections of 1842 saw a radical turnaround in party com-

Fast Fact

Tyler's relations with Congress were so strained that the legislature withheld any funds for the operation and maintenance of the White House. Tyler was forced to pay for heating and lighting out of his own pocket.

(Source: Norma Lois Peterson. *The Presidencies of William Henry Harrison and John Tyler,* 1989.)

---

position in the House—it went from a 133 to 102 Whig majority to a 142 to 79 Democratic majority. Tyler interpreted these election returns as a confirmation of popular support for his administration, but they more likely demonstrated support for the annexation of Texas—supported by Democrats and opposed by Whigs. It was this newly elected Congress that for the first time in history overrode a presidential veto for a 1845 tariff bill.

Tyler's presidency is known for its bad relations with Congress. The ill will began immediately after President Harrison's death, with congressional Whigs, led by Senator Henry Clay of Kentucky, urging Tyler to continue with the Whig agenda—an agenda with which Tyler had never really agreed. Then followed a series of vetoes that enraged Whig members of Congress: successive drafts of bills establishing a national bank; protective tariff bills; and bills for funding internal improvements were all vetoed by Tyler. This led to overt efforts, especially in the House, to limit the powers of the executive branch.

While these conflicts were rooted in political discord, they were also the manifestation of an issue that had not yet been determined in U.S. government—whether the legislature or the executive was the seat of power.

Tyler and the Judiciary

Because of his poor relations with the Whig Senate, Tyler earned the unfortunate distinction of having more Supreme Court appointees—six—rejected than any other president, past or present. When Justice Smith Thomspon died in 1843, the Senate rejected several nominees before accepting Samuel Nelson, the chief justice of the New York Supreme Court, more than a year later. Before that vacancy could be filled, another seat had opened upon the death of Justice Henry Baldwin. The Senate, prefer-

ring to have the justice appointed by the following administration (which it assumed would be Whig leader Henry Clay of Kentucky), managed to take Tyler to the end of his term without approving an appointee.

The Supreme Court under Chief Justice Roger Taney (1836–64) established over time a reputation for leaning toward the power of the states, but several cases during the Tyler administration contradict this characterization. Probably the most controversial, *Prigg v. Pennsylvania* (1842), led to the Court's conclusion that the Constitution, along with the Federal Slave Act of 1793, gave the federal government the exclusive power to deal with fugitive slaves, and that individual states had no authority to pass their own fugitive slave laws.

Changes in the U.S. Government

The most significant precedent established by the Tyler administration had to do with the accession of the vice president to the presidency. From the beginning Tyler's assumption of the office and its full powers and duties was questioned, especially by members of Congress, who pointed out the Constitution's vagueness on the subject. Kentucky senator Henry Clay and many other congresspeople addressed Tyler as an "acting" president, but Tyler, for the moment backed by the late president Harrison's cabinet, insisted that he, as well as every other vice president after him who assumed the presidency, would be regarded as the real and full president, regardless of the form of accession. Subsequently, all vice presidents who have assumed the office have followed the example established by Tyler, and this procedure was further codified in the Twenty-fifth Amendment to the Constitution, ratified in 1967.

Just prior to leaving office, Tyler signed a congressional act granting statehood to Iowa and Florida. Under the principle of balanced representation, Florida was signed in as a slave state; Iowa as a free state. Also in the last days of his administration, Tyler engineered the passage of a joint resolution for the annexation of Texas, which would become a state under the presidency of James Polk and lead the U.S. into a war with Mexico (*See also,* Domestic Issues).

Domestic Issues

When John Tyler assumed the office of president in 1841, the population of the United States had nearly doubled over the past 20 years—from 9.6 million to more than 17 million. As the population grew it began to move westward, and as these migrations increased, the precarious matter of slavery continued to create intense animosity between North and South. The Democratic predecessor, Martin Van Buren, had avoided any expansion that might agitate the sectional divide, but as the newly free republic of Texas voiced its desire to join the Union, southern expansionists began to clamor for annexation.

Within the government itself there was little agreement over what kind of nation the United States should be, or how it should be governed. The old Federalist/Anti-Federalist Party division (*See also,* Thomas Jefferson Administration) had given way to a new two-party system which, on the surface, appeared not to have a firmly established identity. On one side were the Democrats, who had been all but invented by President Andrew Jackson during his administration (1829 to 1837). On the other side were the Whigs, who defined themselves simply by their opposition to one or another aspect of Jackson's leadership. Many Democrats—such as the young John Tyler—disagreed with at least some of Jackson's principles. And many Whigs—such as the old John Tyler—could agree on little else other than their dislike of Jackson. It appeared that the new party system was in for a shake-up, and Tyler's presidency proved to be the catalyst.

The election of William Henry Harrison to the White House was, for the Whigs, a landmark in their party's short history. (Harrison was the first Whig to win the presidency.) With a president in office who seemed to agree with Senator Henry Clay of Kentucky and his Whig congressional majority, the party began immediately to implement the goals of their first administration. This proved to be a formidable task, since the divisive issues of slavery and territorial expansion soon caused fissures even among the Whigs. Although most Whigs looked askance at the Mexican War (1846–48) and the expansion of slavery into any land that might be acquired as a result of the conflict, the sentiment on these issues varied greatly within the Whig Party. There were southern Whigs, like Alexander Stephens, who took fairly moderate positions early in the debate over slavery, but whose attitudes hardened as the controversy over slavery and states's rights became increasingly embittered in the 1840s and 1850s. (Stephens ended his political career as vice president of the Confederacy.)

The Bank Bills and a "President Without a Party"

When Tyler became president the leading Whigs were wary. They knew that Tyler was not a Whig and that he sympathized with southern planters who were opposed to nearly everything the Whig majority hoped to accomplish. Still, Senator Clay, hopeful that Tyler would conform to the wishes of the party that had brought him into office, immediately began drafting bills that would abolish the Independent Treasury System (an institution put into place by the previous Democratic president, Martin Van Buren) and establish a third Bank of the United States (referred to as the BUS).

Tyler readily agreed to repeal the Independent Treasury—but, opposed all his life to a central national bank, he had already warned Clay not to try to establish one. Though Clay and the Whigs knew he would not approve, they presented bills that referred to the bank by another name, in the hope that the president could be brought around. Not only was Tyler not fooled by the attempts but he was insulted. After a bill to establish a "Fiscal Bank" was flatly vetoed, the Whigs presented Tyler with a bill to install a "Fiscal Corporation," which he also vetoed.

Tyler had vetoed many Whig bills in his administration, but his refusal to approve a national bank—a cornerstone of the Whigs's "American System" proposed and drafted by Clay, was the final straw. A Whig caucus met and formally expelled Tyler from the party, and his entire cabinet (except for Secretary of State Daniel Webster, who was involved in diplomatic negotiations with the British) resigned. In addition, a serious effort at impeachment was undertaken in the House. Tyler's enemies began to refer to him as "His Accidency," a reference to the manner in which he had gained his office.

Texas Annexation

When the republic of Texas, populated primarily by American settlers, had fought and won the war for its independence from the Mexican nation in 1837, expansionists in the United States immediately began to argue for its annexation. These expansionists were primarily southern Democrats who understood that the new state of Texas would become a slave state, swinging the balance of government power in their direction. By now, the issue of slavery was so controversial among the states that it became the first issue around which questions of territorial acquisitions were discussed. Tyler's Democratic predecessor, Martin Van Buren, was concerned about annexing Texas for two reasons: he did not want to provoke a war with Mexico, which still considered Texas to be a Mexican possession; and he did not want to upset the sectional balance that existed in the federal government. When the newly independent republic of Texas sent their minister to Washington to formally request their acceptance into the Union, Van Buren ignored the issue.

After his breakup with the Whigs, Tyler, a career politician, knew where he stood. The Whigs primarily represented the northern urban (mostly abolitionist) voting centers. In order to build political support for a run at the presidency in 1845, he would need to look to southerners like himself. And the only issue that could rally southerners around him would be the annexation of Texas.

The British unwittingly played into Tyler's hands. As the other New World power, they were anxious to check the spread of the United States into areas that might threaten their possessions. As a nation that had already abolished slavery and the slave trade, Britain also hoped to obstruct the advance of that institution. After Texas won the war for independence against Mexico, Britain was the first to formally recognize it as an independent state and sent a number of abolitionists into the territory to establish trade and diplomatic ties. The southern press promptly published scare stories about the British agitators infiltrating Texas. Tyler came under increasing pressure to act on the annexation question.

After Secretary of State Webster resigned to join the other Whigs in their condemnation of Tyler, the president sent his new secretary, John C. Calhoun of South Carolina, to deal with the British and to negotiate a treaty of annexation with Texas. The outspoken Calhoun unwisely released a letter to the press that he had written to a British minister. The letter explained that among other reasons, Americans wanted to annex Texas in order to protect slavery, an institution that was essential to the prosperity of the Union. Northerners seized on this letter as proof that the push for annexation was simply a proslavery grab for power, and the treaty was overwhelmingly defeated in 1844.

True to Tyler's intent, annexation became the premier issue of the forthcoming election, and both his prospective opponents, Clay and the Democratic frontrunner, former president Martin Van Buren, were opposed to it. Unfortunately, Tyler had so successfully whipped southerners into a proannexation frenzy that during their Democratic convention they denied Van Buren the nomination and instead selected former speaker of the house James Polk, who favored annexation. Without his party's support, Tyler was for all purposes bumped out of the race.

He was still, however, intent on achieving annexation for his administration, and his political shrewdness sprang forth just weeks before his term ended. He knew that the stumbling block to annexation was the Senate, where a two-thirds majority was required for approval of a treaty. So Tyler suggested that annexation be achieved by a joint resolution, which only required a simple majority in both houses. The motion easily passed, over the outrage of northern opponents, and on March 1, 1845—with only three days remaining in his presidency—Tyler signed the resolution.

Foreign Issues

Tyler's tenure in office coincided with a rising tide of expansionist sentiment among many Americans, who became emboldened by the independence of Texas. As annexation grew imminent, many Americans began to make noises about acquiring California, a Mexican possession, and the Oregon Territory—an area jointly occupied by the British and the Americans. For the president the challenge would be to balance the desire for territorial expansion with the desire to maintain peace.

The paralysis of domestic legislation under Tyler has tended to overshadow some real achievements of the administration in foreign affairs—many of them engineered by Secretary of State Daniel Webster, who would later resign to join the Whig condemnation of Tyler.

Looking to the Pacific—The Sandwich Islands and Trade with China

Secretary of State Webster believed that one way to moderate the belligerence of many western expansionists was to gradually increase the influence of the United States in the Pacific. Prior administrations had paid little attention to outposts in the Pacific, such as the Hawaiian Islands (known then as the Sandwich Islands), but U.S. merchants and missionaries were already deeply involved there, particularly in whaling and sugar planting.

The islands were then led by the Hawaiian monarchy, and though Webster was opposed to claiming them as a protectorate, he advised Tyler to make U.S. interests clear to the rest of the world—especially to France and Britain, who also had commercial interests in the islands. In an 1842 message to Congress, Tyler announced a policy that became known as the Tyler Doctrine: while acknowledging that the location of the Sandwich Islands made them a frequent stopping point for ships of all nations, Tyler stated that U.S. whaling ships were most dependent on the ports. In addition, Americans owned far more island property than citizens of any other nation. Though the United States did not wish to assert control over the islands, it would consider an attempt by any other nation to do so as a serious offense. In effect, Tyler extended the principles of the Monroe Doctrine (President James Monroe's warning to European colonial powers to stay out of the Americas) far west, to the Sandwich Islands.

Tyler's message also asked Congress to authorize funding for a mission to China, for the negotiation of a commercial treaty. The English/Chinese Opium Wars, fought over Britain's illegal import of opium, had just ended there, and Britain had won some concessions that were alarming to Webster. Britain now had access to more Chinese ports than any other world power, and in addition they had taken permanent possession of Hong Kong, on the southeast coast of China. To Webster and Tyler, the exclusion of the United States from these lucrative ports of trade would be a disaster.

After some squabbling over the cost of the mission—about $40,000—Congress finally agreed to fund it, and Massachusetts congressperson Caleb Cushing was chosen commissioner. Cushing was to be respectful to the representatives of the Chinese government, but he was to avoid any suggestion of U.S. inferiority to Britain. Cushing's mission was a success, and in 1844 the Treaty of Wanghia—the first bilateral agreement between China and the United States—was signed.

Trade between the United States and China later flourished. Webster and Tyler had clearly defined U.S. interests in the Pacific, and their efforts served as a strong precedent to the "Open Door" policy that would define U.S. foreign relations during the late nineteenth and early twentieth centuries.

The Webster-Ashburton Treaty

The greatest foreign policy controversy of Tyler's administration was the continued dispute over the nation's northeastern boundary, between the state of Maine and the British Canadian territory of New Brunswick. The boundary defined at the end of the American Revolution (1775–83) was not completely clear, and during the Martin Van Buren administration (1837–41) armed skirmishes had broken out among Americans and Canadians in the disputed area of the Aroostook River valley. Van Buren negotiated an end to the Aroostook War (1839) but was unable to settle upon a final boundary before he left office.

In 1842 the British government took a step to make sure that this persistent dispute be put to rest. Lord Ashburton, a nonprofessional diplomat who had married an American woman, was sent to Washington to negotiate a settlement.

What Britain wanted out of the settlement, Ashburton pointed out, was an unimpeded overland route from the coastal port of Halifax, Nova Scotia, to the city of Quebec, and the disputed territory would clearly obstruct such a route if it belonged to the United States. Webster was willing to grant this and ceded about five-twelfths of the land in dispute. Ashburton, in a generous mood, sweetened the deal by ceding territory in northern New York and Vermont—to which the United States had no claim—and also about 6,500 square miles of land near Lake Superior.

The Webster-Ashburton Treaty was promptly denounced by critics in both countries, who saw the treaty as mere capitulation. But after Webster's treaty had been negotiated, every outstanding issue between Britain and the United States—except for the status of the Oregon Territory—had finally been settled. Upon completing the treaty, Webster, alienated by the president's exploitation of the Texas annexation issue, joined the other Whigs in resigning his cabinet post. The foreign policy accomplishments of the Tyler administration—which, thanks to Webster, were considerable—had effectively come to an end.

The Tyler Administration Legacy

On March 2, 1845, the eve of Tyler's exit from office, the Tylers hosted a gala cabinet dinner—at which president-elect James Polk and his wife, Sarah, were honored guests—to celebrate the passage of the joint reso-

Fast Fact

The tradition of playing the song "Hail to the Chief" whenever a president appears at state functions was started by Tyler's second wife, Julia Gardner Tyler.

(Source: *John Tyler,* The Internet Public Library [http://www.ipl.org/POTUS/jtyler.html])

lution approving the annexation of Texas. Thus, much of the work that Polk had pledged to do had already been accomplished by Tyler. However, the real difficulties of Texas annexation—the war with Mexico and the escalating animosity between the North and the South—were Polk's to handle. Likewise, it would be up to Polk to finally settle the controversy of the Oregon Territory.

In annexing Texas, Tyler was arguably hastening the inevitable. It was the will of a proannexation majority, after all, that had voted Polk into office. The shooting war that followed with Mexico and the deepening sectional crisis that resulted would almost certainly have ensued without Tyler's resolution. But Tyler's critics were upset with the way in which annexation had been accomplished. A joint resolution was not the means by which the Constitution had determined such treaties were to be approved, and it again raised the accusation first put forth when Tyler demanded to be treated as an elected president, that he was only a strict "constructionist" when this principle served his political purposes. According to John Quincy Adams, an outspoken Tyler critic, the resolution was "the heaviest calamity that ever befell myself and my country. . . I regard it as the apoplexy of the Constitution." (*The Memoirs of John Quincy Adams,* quoted in *The Presidencies of William Henry Harrison and John Tyler,* by Norma Lois Peterson).

Lasting Impact

History has generally been unkind to the Tyler administration. Most accounts of his presidency focus on his battles with Congress, and he is often blamed for the stubbornness with which he resisted the efforts of congressional Whigs to enact their programs. But Tyler's resistance to the Whigs and Henry Clay's high-handed tactics strengthened the office of the presidency, and in particular gave greater credibility to all later vice presidents who happened to succeed to the office. Though the Whigs expelled Tyler from the party, they did not succeed in making the presidency a tool of the legislature.

The foreign policy accomplishments of the Tyler administration also are overlooked. With the help of Secretary of State Daniel Webster, Tyler smoothed a relationship with Britain that had been growing hostile. These good relations may have helped to establish the relatively peaceful settlement of the Oregon border under President Polk. Webster and Tyler also managed to firmly establish the United States as an important international presence in the Pacific region, in both the Sandwich Islands (Hawaii) and China.

Despite these successes, there is plenty of evidence to support the suggestion that Tyler remained throughout his presidency a servant of the culture from which he had come—the slaveholding southern plantation aristocracy. His insistence on states's rights, according to critics, at times showed him to be a protector of his own provincial interests, rather than a statesman with a national vision. His presidency illustrated the difference between northern and southern Whigs, which led eventually to the establishment of the Whigs as a primarily northern, urban party. The way in which Texas annexation was engineered by his administration, along with Tyler's persistent advocacy of the southern cause, appeared to deepen the sectional division that ultimately led the nation into the American Civil War (1860–65).

Sources

Bailey, Thomas A. *The American Pageant: A History of the Republic.* 3d ed. Lexington, Mass.: D. C. Heath, 1966.

Bowers, Claude G. *John Tyler (Address at the unveiling of the bust of President Tyler in the State Capital, Richmond, Virginia, June 16, 1931)* Salt Lake City, Utah: Richmond Press, 1932.

Chitwood, Oliver Perry. *John Tyler: Champion of the Old South.* New York: Russell and Russell, 1964.

Conlin, Joseph R. *The American Past, Part One: A Survey of American History to 1877.* New York: Harcourt Brace, 1990.

Merk, Frederick. *Fruits of Propaganda in the Tyler Administration.* Cambridge, Mass.: Harvard University Press, 1971.

Morgan, Robert J. *A Whig Embattled: The Presidency under John Tyler.* Lincoln, Nebr.: University of Nebraska Press, 1954.

Peterson, Norma Lois. *The Presidencies of William Henry Harrison and John Tyler.* Lawrence, Kans.: University Press of Kansas, 1989.

Seager, Robert. *And Tyler Too: A Biography of John and Julia Gardiner Tyler.* New York: McGraw-Hill, 1963.

Further Readings

Ellett, K. T. *Young John Tyler.* Richmond, Va.: Dietz Press, 1976.

Tyler, Lyon G. *The Letters and Times of the Tylers.* 3 vol. New York: Da Capo Press, 1970.

Wise, John Sergeant. *Recollections of Thirteen Presidents.* New York: Doubleday, Page, 1906.

Polk Administration

Biography

Raised in the fertile frontier territory of Middle Tennessee, James K. Polk enjoyed a long and illustrious career in politics that took him from the Tennessee state legislature to the U.S. Congress and, after a brief stint as governor of Tennessee, the U.S. presidency. A protégé of seventh U.S. president Andrew Jackson, Polk spent his entire political life attempting to bring his mentor's Democratic visions into being.

Early Life

Of Scotch-Irish ancestry, the first Polks arrived in the United States late in the seventeenth century and became farmers on Maryland's Eastern Shore. Here they organized the earliest Presbyterian congregation in the New World. Over the years the Polk clan migrated westward, settling in significant numbers by the end of the eighteenth century in Mecklenburg County, North Carolina. It was in this rural community that James Knox Polk, named after his maternal grandfather, was born on November 2, 1795.

The eldest of 10 children born to Jane Knox and Samuel Polk, James Polk's early life was shaped by the religious convictions of his mother, the rigors of a frontier upbringing, and his poor health. Jane Knox was a devout Presbyterian who instilled in her son the values of duty, self-reliance, and personal achievement, characteristics that contributed to Polk's later reputation as one of the hardest working men ever to occupy the Oval Office. Ironically, despite the central role that Presbyterianism played in Polk's upbringing, a quarrel between

Full name: James Knox Polk
Popular name: Young Hickory; Napolean of the Stump

Personal Information:

Born: November 2, 1795
Birthplace: Mecklenburg County, North Carolina
Died: June 15, 1849
Death place: Nashville, Tennessee
Burial place: State Capitol Grounds, Nashville, Tennessee
Religion: Presbyterian; Methodist
Spouse: Sarah Childress (m. 1824)
Education: University of North Carolina, BA, 1818
Occupation: Lawyer; legislator; governor
Political Party: Democratic Party
Age at Inauguration: 49 years

James Knox Polk. *(The Library of Congress.)*

Samuel Polk and the local minister, James Wallis, over the former's refusal to profess his commitment to the faith, prevented James from being baptized. It was not until he was on his deathbed that he completed the ceremony, as a Methodist.

In 1806 Samuel Polk followed his father and others who had left the increasingly populous North Carolina countryside to settle in the newly opened Duck River valley of Middle Tennessee. James, aged 11 at the time of the arduous 500-mile journey across the Blue Ridge Mountains, spent the next several years helping his father, a successful farmer, surveyor, and land speculator, carve out a new life in this frontier setting. Unfortunately James was plagued with poor health as a child and could not participate in many of the rugged activities that such a life demanded. In fact, at the age of 17 he was forced to undergo an emergency surgery to remove a gallstone. James miraculously survived the operation, conducted without the benefit of antiseptics or anesthesia. His successful recovery from such a close brush with death assuaged some of his former feelings of inadequacy and instilled in him a strong sense of determination and confidence in his abilities. His father arranged an apprenticeship for him with a local merchant after his recuperation, but James despised the work and persuaded his father to allow him to further his education instead.

Although it would be several years before Polk's official career in politics began, his upbringing in Mid-

dle Tennessee undoubtedly influenced his political beliefs. Tennessee was the political birthplace of former president Andrew Jackson, and the Polks were some of the strongest supporters of his populist philosophy which asserted that presidential authority is derived from the will of the people. Samuel Polk and Jackson were well acquainted. James grew up admiring Jackson immensely and a strong personal friendship later developed between the two. James Polk became one of Jackson's strongest supporters during his time in the House of Representatives and fought fiercely to advance the Jacksonian agenda once he became president.

Education

Polk received only rudimentary schooling during his childhood in the North Carolina and Tennessee frontiers and still had difficulty with basic spelling at the age of 18. His first encounter with formal classical education came in 1813 when he was allowed to enroll in a small Presbyterian academy near Columbia, Tennessee, run by Rev. Robert Henderson. Polk spent one year there studying Greek and Latin, and despite his background, proved himself one of the school's finest students. His success greatly impressed his father, and in 1814 Polk transferred to the larger Murfreesboro Academy, 50 miles south of Columbia. Under the tutelage of the Presbyterian schoolmaster Samuel Black, Polk rose to the top of his 1815 graduating class.

Polk continued his successful academic progress at the University of North Carolina at Chapel Hill, another Presbyterian institution, where he was admitted as a sophomore in January 1816. An extremely diligent student, he earned a reputation for hard work, which, in the absence of innate genius, led to his graduation in 1818 with honors in both mathematics and classics. It was during his tenure at Chapel Hill, as a member of the Dialectic Society, that he developed and perfected the oratorical skills that would prove so valuable to his subsequent political successes.

Polk returned to Tennessee in early 1819 to study law. He was able to secure employment in the prestigious office of Judge Felix Grundy and moved to Nashville to undertake his legal education. In late 1820 Polk was admitted to the Tennessee bar.

Family Life

Sarah Childress, daughter of a wealthy and prominent merchant, tavern owner, planter, and land speculator, was introduced to James Polk through her brother, his classmate at the University of North Carolina. She received the best schooling possible for a woman in her position at the time, having attended the Moravian

Female Academy in Salem, North Carolina. After several years of courtship she and James Polk were married New Year's Day, 1824; she was 20 years old and he was 28. The wedding was held at the Childress plantation outside Murfreesboro and was considered one of the most important social events in Middle Tennessee.

As first lady Sarah Polk's principal responsibility was to administer to the social aspects of her husband's administration. In the course of entertaining the numerous guests who passed through the White House she developed a reputation for warmth, charm, and friendliness. This led many of those with whom she came into contact during her husband's presidency to call on her at Polk Place in Tennessee long after her husband had died. She also served as an informal information officer for the president. Each day the first lady read the major newspapers, marked those articles that she thought were most important for her husband to examine, and stacked them at the foot of his desk. The Polks never had any children.

Career

In 1819 Polk successfully ran for the position of clerk to the Tennessee Senate in Murfreesboro, the state capital. He served in this capacity while he completed his legal education and was reelected to the same position in 1821.

After passing the Tennessee bar in 1820, Polk worked in Columbia, Tennessee, to build up a private legal practice. He achieved some degree of success, especially after he and state senator Aaron V. Brown formed a partnership in 1822. With his father, Polk was also involved in some land speculation involving previously unsettled tracts in the westernmost quarter of Tennessee.

In 1823 Polk decided to run for the Tennessee House of Representatives, where he served for two years.

Polk Enters National Politics

Having attained success in Tennessee politics, Polk harbored national political ambitions, which were to make him a major figure in Washington over the next 14 years. Drawing on the strong base of local support (and family connections) that he had developed in Middle Tennessee, Polk was elected to the U.S. House of Representatives in 1825 from Tennessee's Sixth Congressional District. He served seven consecutive terms in the House (1825–39), with three presidential administrations (John Quincy Adams, Andrew Jackson, and Martin Van Buren).

During John Quincy Adams's administration Polk regularly opposed the Whig agenda of raising tariffs (taxes on goods imported into a country) and spending federal money on internal improvements (such as roads and harbors). His political star really began to shine,

however, when Andrew Jackson became president in 1829. A close personal friendship developed between the two, and it was not long before the president considered Polk his most important and powerful ally in the House. Polk's rise to congressional power began with his appointment to the House Ways and Means Committee where he was thrust into the center of controversy over the future of the Bank of the United States, the tariff, and internal improvements. These issues were at the very heart of Jackson's Democratic agenda (*See also,* Domestic Issues). As chairman of the Ways and Means Committee, Polk used his considerable power and influence to support Jackson's decision to remove federal deposits from the National Bank. It was his commitment to Jackson during this so-called "bank war" that solidified Polk's reputation as the administration's chief spokesman in the House. Polk's ascent continued when he was elected Speaker of the House in 1835. He was reelected Speaker in 1837, and continued his support for the Democratic Van Buren administration.

Polk Campaigns for the Vice Presidency

Although the economic crisis of 1837—brought on by rampant land speculation and overextension of credit by banks— cast a pall over the prospects of the Democratic Party and President Van Buren in the upcoming 1840 presidential election, Polk believed that the time was right for him to make a push for a more prominent national position. With hopes of receiving the Democratic vice presidential nomination, Polk retired from the U.S. Congress in 1839 and returned to Tennessee in time to campaign for the gubernatorial election. Polk won the election, but despite considerable backing from Jackson, he did not get the vice-presidential nomination. Even had he received the vote, his goal of an executive position would have remained unfulfilled, as Whig candidate William Henry Harrison defeated Van Buren in the election.

Polk sought reelection as governor in 1841, but lost to Whig candidate James C. Jones. Out of political office for the first time in 16 years, Polk returned to his law practice in Columbia while he waited for a chance to avenge himself in the next election. With thoughts of a vice-presidential nomination in the 1844 national election on his mind, he sought to unseat Jones in the gubernatorial race of 1843. Defeated once again, Polk's political future was far from assured. It therefore came as a tremendous surprise to Polk, not to mention his Whig opponents, when the Democratic Party nominated him as their candidate for president in 1844.

Polk Becomes President

James K. Polk defeated Whig candidate Henry Clay in the 1844 presidential election to become the 11th president of the United States. He was 49 years old at his inauguration. He served one term in office, from March

Fast Fact

Polk was the first Speaker of the House of Representatives to become president.

(Source: Joseph N. Kane. *Facts About the Presidents*, 1993.)

4, 1845, to March 3, 1849. Polk's administration is best remembered for its success in expanding the United States to the Pacific coast through a combination of war and diplomacy and his aggressive use of the executive power of the presidency to achieve his domestic and foreign policy goals.

Post-presidential Years

Worn down physically from his years of hard work in the White House, Polk looked forward to a retreat from public life. A year before he left office he had purchased the former home of Judge Felix Grundy in Nashville, Tennessee, as a retirement retreat, renaming it Polk Place. After the inauguration of his successor, Zachary Taylor, Polk embarked on a one-month tour of the southern United States before returning to Tennessee. He arrived at Polk Place in a greatly weakened condition, having possibly contracted cholera during his visit to New Orleans, Louisiana. James Polk died on June 15, 1849, at the age of 53, just three months after leaving office. His wife, Sarah Childress Polk, lived for another 42 years.

After James Polk died Sarah Polk turned the inside of Polk Place into a memorial to her late husband. She served as a hostess to the Polk estate for visitors and acted as a curator to what amounted to a James Polk museum. She saved all letters, papers, and manuscripts connected with her husband's political career, and they are now deposited in the Library of Congress.

The James K. Polk Administration

Best remembered for his expansionist foreign policies that brought the United States into war with Mexico (1846–48), Polk also presided over one of the most far-reaching and successful domestic legislative agendas in the nineteenth century. The first dark horse candidate (a politician who unexpectedly receives a nomination) of a major party to become president, Polk dominated his cabinet and the Congress with a brand of executive leadership not seen since his mentor and friend Andrew Jackson occupied the White House.

Polk Becomes President

The Campaign of 1844

The election of James K. Polk as president in 1844 was one of the most surprising events in the annals of U.S. election history. While he had been considered as a possible vice-presidential candidate, a stalemate between former president Martin Van Buren, whose reputation and popularity suffered during the recession of his administration, and Michigan senator Lewis Cass led the Democratic Party to select Polk as a compromise candidate during its national convention in Baltimore, Maryland, May 1844. After nine rounds of balloting, Polk, a man who had never expressed any public presidential ambitions, became the first dark horse candidate (a politician who unexpectedly receives a nomination).

The balloting in Baltimore glaringly illustrated that the Democratic Party had emerged from its defeat in the presidential election of 1840 leaderless, mutinous, and fractured. Initial hopes that Polk's nomination could act as a unifying force were short-lived, even though he was able to regain the executive branch for his party. Once in office Polk's policies and management style exacerbated intraparty cleavages, which ultimately split the party in 1848 and assured victory for Whig candidate Zachary Taylor in the next national election.

Upon accepting his party's nomination, Polk declared that he would not seek reelection. By committing himself to a single term Polk sought to assure himself the backing of the two most powerful Democrats, Van Buren and John Calhoun of South Carolina, both of whom intended to run for the presidency again in 1848. George M. Dallas of Pennsylvania accepted the vice-presidential nomination on the second ballot, rounding out the Democratic ticket.

The Democratic platform of 1844 reiterated the party's positions from previous years on most counts. It called for strict construction of the Constitution and opposition to a national bank, an excessive tariff, federally funded internal improvements, federal assumption of state debts, and federal interference in the domestic institutions of the states (i.e., slavery). Yet it also called for the annexation of Texas and the "reoccupation" of all of the Oregon territory from Great Britain.

Polk's opponent in the 1844 presidential race was the undisputed leader of the Whigs, Henry Clay of Kentucky.

Clay was a key figure in national politics having served in Congress since 1806, except for time spent as secretary of state and in two failed bids for the presidency. Theodore Frelinghuysen of New Jersey was nominated for vice president. The Whig platform, the first to be formally adopted by the party, called for a well-regulated currency, high tariffs, restrictions on the presidential veto, distribution of the proceeds from the sale of public lands, and a one-term presidency.

The campaign between Polk and Clay was waged mostly in the press and largely revolved around issues of personal character. Democrats portrayed Clay as an aristocrat out of touch with the common voter. For its part, the Whig press harped on the controversy surrounding the Democratic convention and sought to cast Polk as a mediocre and obscure figure unqualified to hold the nation's highest office. The refrain "Who is James K. Polk?" emanated from the Whig camp throughout the election. Polk was also denounced as little more than a puppet of Andrew Jackson and derided as a tool of southern, slaveholding sectional interests. The Democratic press recast Polk's commitment to Jackson as a badge of honor nicknaming him "Young Hickory" (Jackson being "Old Hickory").

Election Issues

Historians have generally agreed that Polk's victory over Clay can be attributed to the candidates' handling of three issues: Texas annexation, the tariff, and the immigrant vote. The incorporation of Texas into the Union became a contentious issue in the election of 1844 as a result of then Secretary of State John Calhoun's linking of annexation to the defense and expansion of slavery. By casting the issue in such sectionally volatile divisive terms, annexation became a measure of a candidate's stance on slavery. While Polk came out squarely for annexation, Clay initially equivocated, fearing that it would provoke a war with Mexico and alienate the anti-slavery faction of the Whigs. This hurt him severely in the South. Clay began to vacillate, trying to regain support in the South, but only succeeded in alienating anti-slavery abolitionists in the North.

On the tariff issue it was Polk's pragmatism that made the difference. Although he had been a stalwart supporter of low tariffs throughout his political career, Polk recognized that he needed support from the protectionist forces in the North, especially Pennsylvania, in order to win the election. He was able to assuage the protectionists' fears that he was not, as the Whig press labeled him, an untrammeled "free-trader," and he carried Pennsylvania.

In an election whose outcome was decided by less than 39,000 votes, each vote mattered a great deal. By uniting with anti-immigrant forces Clay pushed many foreign-born U.S. voters into the hands of the Democrats. In New York the Liberty Party garnered 16,000 votes that otherwise would have gone to the Whigs had Clay been

Administration

Administration Dates
March 4, 1845–March 4, 1849

Vice President
George Mifflin Dallas (1845–49)

Cabinet

Secretary of State
John C. Calhoun (1844–45)
James Buchanan (1845–49)

Secretary of the Treasury
George M. Bibb (1844–45)
Robert J. Walker (1845–49)

Secretary of War
William Wilkins (1844–45)
William L. Marcy (1845–49)

Attorney General
John Nelson (1843–45)
John Y. Mason (1845–46)
Nathan Clifford (1846–48)
Isaac Toucey (1848–49)

Secretary of the Navy
John Y. Mason (1844–45; 1846–49)
George Bancroft (1845–46)

Postmaster General
Charles A. Wickliffe (1841–45)
Cave Johnson (1845–49)

able to assure voters of his antislavery credentials. As it turned out Polk won New York by only five thousand votes and turned the tide in a race that was neck and neck up to that point. He went on to win the election, defeating Clay by 1.4 percent of the popular vote.

Polk's victory was a bitter tonic for the Whigs and the last chance at the presidency for Clay. While many Democrats rejoiced in their recapture of the White House, Whigs had a less sanguine interpretation of events. Upon seeing a Democratic victory banner flying in Washington on the morning after the election results were known, a Vermont Whig exclaimed, "That flag means Texas, and Texas means civil war, before we have done with it" (Sellers, p. 797).

Polk's Advisers

In an effort to promote party unity and assure the smooth functioning of the cabinet Polk attempted to structure his appointment decisions around three criteria: that he have no holdovers from the previous administration; that the cabinet would have representatives from all geographic regions; and that his advisers pledge to devote themselves to his administration.

There were several potential obstacles to Polk's plan. Several friends of Polk, and of Vice President Dallas, were in the outgoing administration's cabinet. The thorniest of these issues was what to do about the powerful southern leader and secretary of state, John Calhoun, whom Polk could not afford to estrange. The problem resolved itself, however, when Calhoun voluntarily stepped down from his position and pledged his support to the new administration. Polk managed to convince all but his friend John Mason, who became attorney general, to move on.

Of the six available cabinet positions Polk sought to fill them with one Democrat each from New York, Pennsylvania, New England, Virginia, the Deep South, and Tennessee. Remarkably, Polk was able to get his cabinet to conform to these regional desires, but, rather than promoting party unity, his appointments exacerbated infighting. James Buchanan, for instance, who accepted the most prestigious secretary of state position, was from Pennsylvania, but he happened to be Vice President Dallas's chief political rival in that state. It was Polk's selection to fill his New York quota, however, which proved disastrous to the party as a whole. For secretary of war he chose William Learned Marcy, a rival of powerful New Yorker and former president Martin Van Buren.

Historians of the Polk administration have made routine reference to the president's authoritative management style and explicitly expressed intention to oversee even the most minute detail of policy formation. But Polk's relationship with his advisers was characterized more by consensus and cohesion than dominance. The president constantly sought out the advice, aid, and support of his advisers, especially his close personal friends John Mason, first serving as attorney general and later as secretary of the navy, and Cave Johnson, the postmaster general. By one count the president convened the cabinet a total of 364 times over his four years in office (Bergeron, p. 36).

Polk and Congress

Polk presided over the Twenty-ninth and Thirtieth sessions of Congress with the forcefulness and savvy that allowed him to enact one of the most wide-ranging legislative agendas of a president in the nineteenth century. Yet while he was very successful in getting Congress to support his administration's goals on matters of domestic economic policy, Polk was less able to influence the legislative branch in foreign affairs. Democrats enjoyed a majority over the opposition Whigs in both the House and the Senate during the Twenty-ninth session, but this superiority in numbers did not assure easy acceptance of Polk's legislative agenda. Democratic control, for instance, was undermined by superior Whig leadership. This was especially the case in the Senate, where powerful Whig fixtures such as Daniel Webster of Massachusetts, William S. Archer of Virginia, and John M. Clayton of Delaware returned to their seats in Congress while the Democratic ranks were weakened by losses to the cabinet or to other branches of government. Divisions within the Democratic Party were also almost as wide as those between Democrats and Whigs on some issues, such as the Pennsylvania Democrats' opposition to the Walker Tariff of 1846 (*See also,* Domestic Issues). Intraparty rivalry was also rampant, with the struggle for Senate supremacy between John Calhoun of South Carolina and Thomas Hart Benton of Missouri being only one example. In the Thirtieth Congress Whigs were able to secure a narrow majority in the House, which they used to harass and otherwise obstruct Polk's legislative agenda and to oppose the administration's support of the Mexican War (1846–48). There were also issues raised during the Thirtieth session, such as the expansion of slavery into the newly acquired territories of Oregon, California, and New Mexico, which divided Congress along sectional rather than party lines, and brought large sections of both chambers into conflict with the president's policies.

Set against this backdrop Polk's congressional victories are all the more remarkable, and his failures more easily understood. Following the footsteps of his mentor, Andrew Jackson, Polk firmly believed that the office of the president, and not Congress, embodied the nation's general will and represented the American people. He intended to lead the legislative branch, and he did so firmly. Polk utilized his veto power three times, twice to sink internal improvement bills and once to thwart an attempt to get the U.S. government to compensate U.S. property holders for French depredations on U.S. shipping in the 1790s (French Spoilations Bill).

Polk and the Judiciary

While there were no landmark cases decided by the Supreme Court during Polk's four years in office, he did face the challenge of filling two vacancies on the Court. In keeping with his views on political patronage, Polk maintained a tight grip on the appointment process and viewed the opportunity of filling the vacancies as a chance to smooth relations between the disparate wings of the Democratic Party. Polk was able to assure that the justices were "original Democrats" who believed in strict construction of the Constitution, states's rights, union-ism, and limited government.

In filling Supreme Court positions, Polk once again made the regional identity of his appointees a primary concern. Under the Judiciary Act of 1789 it was the duty of Supreme Court justices to preside over the regional circuit courts. Polk was determined to appoint people who were natives of the regions over which they would preside. For New England his choice was Senator Levi Woodbury of New Hampshire. Popular with both former president Martin Van Buren and South Carolina senator John Calhoun, he was confirmed easily and took his seat on September 20, 1845. A vacant seat in Pennsylvania proved thorny, however. Secretary of State Buchanan and Vice President Dallas, both from Pennsylvania, fought to put one of their men on the Court. It took over a year for a compromise to be reached with the appointment of Robert Cooper Grier.

Changes in the U.S. Government

The Polk years were not a time of substantial administrative innovation, but several developments are worth noting. Polk demanded that all of his cabinet sec-retaries personally review their departmental reports and submit them to him before they were passed on to Congress, therein establishing the first comprehensive executive branch budget. It was also during Polk's years in office that postage stamps were first introduced by Postmaster Gen. Cave Johnson. The presidential elec-tion of 1844 was also the last time that there was no uniform date for national elections. On January 23, 1845, an act was passed designating the first Tuesday after the first Monday in November of every even-numbered year as election day. This formula is still in use today. The Department of the Interior was created on the last day of the Thirtieth Congress, March 3, 1849, and transferred a number of offices from other departments to its control. It was and is the nation's principal conservation agency, responsible for more than 549 million acres of public lands. No amendments to the Constitution were passed or ratified during Polk's term and no states were admit-ted to the Union.

Domestic Issues

The domestic setting in which James K. Polk emerged and governed was a challenging one for the nation. The country was on the move again, successfully emerging from the traumatic economic depression that had begun in 1837 and had lasted for several years. Opti-mism about the United States's future, bolstered by expansion of the country's railways, western settlement, technological innovations like the telegraph, and large population increases, fostered a renewed sense of nation-alism. The social and political reforms begun in the 1820s and 1830s gained momentum in the 1840s as well. In the North in particular the temperance (or anti-alcohol) and antislavery movements began to take on crusade-like fea-tures, the latter exacerbating sectionalism and fomenting cleavages within the Democratic Party.

As a Jackson protégé, President Polk launched a full-scale attack on the very principles of the "American Sys-tem" of government associated with U.S. statesman Alexander Hamilton and Henry Clay. Their program called for active governmental supervision and interven-tion in the economy. Its prime components were a high protective tariff to develop manufacturing industries, a national bank, and federally funded internal improve-ments. Through his successful reform of the Whig Tariff of 1842, his institution of an independent treasury system operated on hard-money principles, and his opposition to the use of federal funds for internal improvements, Polk presided over one of the most transformative domestic legislative agendas in the nineteenth century.

Yet Polk's triumphs not only reflected the culmina-tion of Jacksonian Democracy, but also sowed the seeds for its eventual demise. A son of the South, Polk was a slaveholder and cultivated cotton in Tennessee. An oth-erwise astute observer of the political climate, Polk failed to recognize throughout his four years in office how pow-erful a force the abolitionist movement was becoming, and how his expansionist foreign policies in Texas, Ore-gon, California, and New Mexico had domestic reper-cussions through their elevation of the slavery issue to the center of political debate. Polk's presidency was thus a passage from the waning of the Jacksonian era in U.S. politics to the prospect of civil war.

Walker's Tariff

True to his Jacksonian pedigree, Polk had been a firm and consistent opponent of protective tariffs throughout his political career. In addition to believing that the fos-tering of special industries was not a legitimate function of the government, Polk opposed high tariffs on the grounds that they unjustly favored manufacturers in the North to the detriment of southern agrarian interests. He also felt that tariffs produced an unnecessary accumula-tion of funds in the national treasury, which led to demands for internal improvements at federal expense. In 1842 the John Tyler administration enacted a protective tariff. Polk made it his most important domestic goal to strike down this tariff. The reform that the administration was able to force through Congress in the summer of 1846 represented a severe blow to the domestic economic agenda of Clay and the Whigs.

Instead, Polk based a new tariff on the results of a survey distributed in 1845 to importers and customs offi-cials in an effort to better understand the effects of tar-iff rates on national revenues. With the survey Treasury Secretary Walker attempted to determine the level at which duties became so high as to reduce the volume of imports, thereby decreasing revenue. While Polk, Walker, and many other Democrats were opposed to high tariffs, they were not advocates of pure "free trade" (as Whigs often charged them). They supported tariffs, but only for the purpose of generating revenue for the federal government in balance with its level of expenditures. Walker's survey was thus aimed at establishing a "revenue tariff" based on hard statistical data. While it entailed substantial reduction in existing levels of protection, it in no way did away with duties altogether. On July 3, 1846, by a margin of only 19 votes, the House passed the Walker Tariff.

The Constitutional Treasury

The second pillar of Polk's Jacksonian domestic economic agenda was the reestablishment of an independent treasury system in which federal monies were deposited directly in the Treasury instead of privately controlled banks. Polk's predecessor, John Tyler, thwarted Whig attempts to resurrect the controversial Bank of the United States (BUS), a private bank that had served as a federal repository until dismantled by Andrew Jackson. The country returned to the system of state, or "pet," banks previously dismantled by Van Buren, which were in control of federal funds when Polk assumed office.

Polk opposed the idea of depositing federal monies in banks on pragmatic, constitutional, and philosophical grounds. Following the thinking of Democratic predecessors Jackson and Van Buren, Polk believed that national and state banks had proven themselves unworthy custodians of public funds in the wake of their role in the devastating economic collapse of 1837. A strict constructionist (one who adheres strictly to the Constitution), he also did not see any provision in the Constitution that allowed private corporations (i.e., banks) to use government funds for profit or speculation.

In his inaugural address, Polk called for the founding of what he termed a "constitutional treasury" identical to Van Buren's independent treasury system. A year later, in March 1846, the House considered the administration's bill on this matter. The constitutional treasury bill did not really create anything at all; it simply required for and authorized the executive branch to collect government revenues in gold and in silver and to deposit them in the Treasury Department's vaults until they were disbursed in the course of ordinary governmental business transactions. The bill also stipulated that fireproof vaults be constructed to hold these deposits and that they be formally declared the "Treasury of the United States."

When the bill came up for a vote in the House in April 1846, it passed by an overwhelming majority, 122 to 66. Not a single Whig voted for it and not a single Democrat voted against it. The bill's fate in the Senate in August was identical. The most remarkable aspect of the bill's passage was the lack of controversy. The issue that had been at the heart of the Jacksonian domestic

vision and the subject of fierce debates had lost its old fervor, as new issues such as slavery and territorial expansion became the central political issues.

Internal Improvements

Whereas both the call for tariff reform and institution of an independent treasury emanated from the executive branch, the third major domestic issue reform during Polk's tenure, internal improvements, was a congressionally initiated measure. On two occasions Congress presented to Polk bills authorizing the use of federal funds for improvement of the nation's transportation infrastructure, and in both cases Polk vetoed the legislation.

In accordance with his strong Jacksonian beliefs, Polk had opposed federally funded internal improvements throughout his political career. A strict constructionist, Polk viewed such demands as unconstitutional, and as a proponent of limited government he rejected such federal activism. He also viewed such expenditures as unnecessary drains on the national treasury, a position that he came to hold all the more dearly once war with Mexico placed increased demands on federal funds.

Economic expansion and western settlement, however, created keen congressional interest in improving the nation's infrastructure. Thanks to strong support from western Democrats in both the House and the Senate, a rivers and harbors bill calling for the appropriation of almost $1.5 million in federal monies for improvements throughout the country was presented to the president in July 1846. In addition to haranguing its inexpediency and unconstitutionality Polk vetoed the measure in August on the grounds that its proposed projects benefited local rather than national interests, and that acceptance would initiate a scramble for public money that would eventually bankrupt the Treasury. An attempt to overturn the veto failed in the House shortly thereafter.

The supporters of improvements were not dissuaded, however, and yet another rivers and harbors bill was passed in March 1847. Because the bill was presented only one day before Congress adjourned, Polk was able to squash it with a pocket veto by simply failing to sign it (pocketing it) until Congress adjourned and the bill died. But he was eager to present a full message on the matter once the legislature reconvened. In December Polk delivered to the House an eloquent and elaborate justification for his position in which he presented himself as a guardian of the Constitution and the Treasury and urged states to raise their own revenue rather than persist in their efforts to get the U.S. government to bankroll their pet projects.

Slavery

Slavery had been a major factor in U.S. politics for decades but, mindful of the issue's divisiveness, politicians consciously worked to keep it off the national political agenda. The slavery issue was allowed to reach the center of the political stage as a direct issue only once prior to the Polk administration in the struggle that led to the Missouri Compromise of 1820. The Missouri Compromise prohibited slavery north of Missouri's southern border— with the exception of Missouri itself, which was allowed to enter the Union as a slave state. A slaveholder himself, Polk's expansionist policies forced the nation to debate the terms on which territory acquired through war and diplomacy would be governed and eventually admitted into the Union. Although the president did not anticipate such a development, his administration's expansionistic policies exacerbated sectionalism, paving the way toward national dissolution.

Slavery emerged at the center of political debate in the second half of the 1840s as a result of two mutually reinforcing trends. There was a rising tide of antislavery opinion in the North to which politicians were becoming more and more sensitive, and northern Democratic congresspeople were growing increasingly resentful of their southern compatriots and of an administration that appeared to pander to their interests.

Yet the slavery question was not directly raised in Congress until the summer of 1846 when, in the very last days of the Twenty-ninth session, it came up in consideration of a military appropriations bill for the war with Mexico (*See also,* Foreign Issues). As the bill was being considered on the floor of the House on August 8, David Wilmot, a Democrat from Pennsylvania, offered an amendment prohibiting slavery within any new territory acquired through the war. The amended bill passed but was not acted upon in the Senate before Congress adjourned.

Slavery in the Territories Debated

In his attempts to negotiate peace with Mexico and establish a territorial government for Oregon (which had been acquired from Great Britain in 1846), the president tried to take slavery out of the issue. But the issue of slavery would not go away. Secretary of State Buchanan, backed by the rest of the cabinet, recommended that the Missouri Compromise line might be extended all the way to the Pacific as a means of silencing once and for all the mounting slavery agitation. Polk, however, refused to commit himself. He still hoped that Congress could reach a compromise on its own.

As congressional debate progressed on the subject two distinct camps emerged. On one side stood the Wilmot Proviso advocates, comprised of northern Democrats and Whigs who did not want slavery in the new territories, and on the other side stood Calhoun Democrats from the South (*See also,* Foreign Issues). It was not until August 1848 that the Senate finally passed a House-sponsored bill establishing a government for Oregon but prohibiting slavery there. With the people of Oregon clamoring for protection from Indians, and when his own recent attempts at brokering a compromise became a failure, Polk reluctantly

signed the bill. He also warned, however, that he would veto any bills prohibiting slavery in territories south of the Missouri Compromise line.

Polk Fails to Find a Compromise

The election of Gen. Zachary Taylor, a Whig, as president in November 1848 made Polk fearful that unless he was successful in bringing California and New Mexico into the Union before his term expired the territories might be allowed (even encouraged) to develop into independent republics. Unable to get support for his idea of extending the Pacific Ocean-Missouri Compromise line, Polk prepared to veto any bills that would prohibit slavery in the new territories. However, no bills establishing governments in the new territories made it out of Congress before it adjourned. Thus, despite all of the efforts to resolve the issue, Polk's presidency ended without determining the status of slavery in the territories acquired from Mexico.

Foreign Issues

Polk entered the presidency with no experience in foreign affairs, for although he was a well-known politician, his reputation and experience lay in the realm of domestic party politics. His administration is remembered first and foremost, however, for its foreign policies. As president, Polk was an ardent expansionist who sought to increase the power and prestige of the United States through territorial acquisitions. Under his leadership Texas was brought into the Union, sole control of the Oregon territory south of the 49th parallel was assumed from Great Britain, and the provinces of California and New Mexico were detached from Mexico in the course of a protracted war. Polk was an ardent supporter of the Monroe Doctrine, President James Monroe's 1823 statement that the United States would not stand for European interference in the Western Hemisphere, and strove to limit European influence in the Americas. Like his mentor Andrew Jackson, he approached cross-Atlantic relations from a standpoint of distrust and suspicion. Lacking any diplomatic skills, Polk conducted foreign affairs in a bellicose and self-righteous style in the belief that brinkmanship (pushing a dangerous situation) was the only way to interact with the United States's international adversaries and competitors. Polk's foreign policy, in the words of historian David Pletcher, "epitomized the self-centered, aggressive nationalism prevalent in the Mississippi River valley during much of the nineteenth century" (Pletcher, p. 605).

Texas Becomes a State

Prompt annexation of Texas was a key component of the Democratic Party platform of 1844, and Polk's avowed commitment to this goal had figured prominently in his electoral victory over Whig candidate Henry Clay.

Fast Fact

The U.S. casualty rate during the 17 months of the Mexican War exceeded 25 percent, and may have totaled 35–40 percent if later injury and disease-related deaths are considered. In this respect the war was the most disastrous in U.S. military history.

(Source: Seymour V. Connor. "Mexican War," *Grolier Multimedia Encyclopedia*, 1995.)

Indeed, Polk's election was taken in many quarters as an implicit endorsement of annexation. It was also one of the most volatile and divisive issues to face the fledgling administration as it touched on the slavery question and threatened to ignite a war between the United States and Mexico. While Polk was successful in bringing the territory into the Union, his handling of the Texas question opened him up to charges of saber rattling and duplicity, and historians still debate the extent to which Polk purposefully used annexation to provoke a war with Mexico in order to acquire even more territory.

In the early 1820s, in an effort to increase its tax revenues and strengthen its economy, the Mexican government encouraged U.S. immigration into its northern province of Texas. Lured by its rich soil and the offer of cheap land, thousands of U.S. settlers made their way to the territory. By 1835 over 30,000 Americans, mostly southerners and their slaves, had settled in Texas. Friction arose between them and the Mexican government over their desire to legalize slavery, which Mexico had made illegal in the province in 1830, and their efforts to develop closer economic and cultural ties with the United States. Sporadic fighting between the Mexican authorities and the Texas settlers began in 1835 and, in 1836 the Texans proclaimed their independence. Initially the U.S. settlers had trouble defending themselves against the Mexican forces led by Gen. Antonio Lopez Santa Anna, suffering terrible defeats at the Alamo mission in San Antonio and at Goliad. Their fortunes improved, however, under the able leadership of Gen. Sam Houston. At the battle of San Jacinto, Santa Anna was captured and forced to sign a treaty granting independence to Texas. While many in the new republic envisioned the eventual creation of a great nation in the southwest stretching to the Pacific that might rival the United States, others, like Texas's first president Sam Houston, sought amalgamation with the United States. Fears that annexation of Texas would exacerbate sectionalism in the

Union and provoke a war with Mexico, however, kept presidents Jackson, Van Buren, and Harrison from taking the steps necessary to incorporate the territory.

In the months between Polk's election and his assumption of office, Texas had become the most important and contentious issue in the John Tyler administration. Urged on by his secretary of state John Calhoun, Tyler sought to fast track annexation before he left office. As a lame duck (or outgoing) president whose administration was mired in controversy, annexation of Texas was a way for Tyler to restore prestige to his tarnished image. On March 1, 1845, just three days before Polk took over, Tyler signed a joint congressional resolution providing for annexation under a plan cobbled together by both the House and the Senate.

As president-elect during the annexation debate, Polk played an important, and subsequently controversial, role in fostering congressional support for Tyler's and Calhoun's goals. For a variety of reasons, foremost among them Texas's support of slavery and Mexico's unwillingness to give up its claims to the territory, opposition to annexation was rife within Congress. The House, in a close vote divided along sectional lines, adopted Tyler's annexation resolution on January 25, 1845, but the Senate was filled with antiannexationists who had solidly rejected the administration's desires once before. In order to avert another rejection Senator Robert Walker of Missouri, at Polk's behest, introduced a compromise amendment that added a provision permitting the renegotiation of the treaty terms between Texas and the United States once the new president came to power. As many as five previously resistant Democratic senators voted for the amended resolution, thereby allowing the bill to pass on February 27, 1845. Once he became president, however, Polk refused to abide by the terms of the amendment and allowed the resolution, in its current terms, to be presented as a fait accompli to Texas. Scholars disagree on the extent to which president-elect Polk purposefully deceived members of the Senate to attain the votes necessary for annexation, but his actions left those involved feeling duped and manipulated.

Washington's decision to annex Texas was viewed in the Mexican capital of Mexico City as tantamount to a declaration of war and caused an immediate rupture of diplomatic relations between the countries. Thus when Polk took office U.S. relations with its southern neighbor were poor, and war between the two countries was being openly discussed. Fearing that Mexico might invade Texas to try to thwart annexation the republic requested military protection from the United States. In response Polk ordered Gen. Zachary Taylor to move his three thousand U.S. troops stationed at Fort Jessup, Louisiana, into Texas territory and a naval squadron under the command of Commodore John Stockton into the Gulf of Mexico off the coast of Galveston. On June 28, 1845, Taylor's forces took up defensive positions in Corpus Christi, the westernmost point of Texan occupation.

Under the military protection of Taylor and Stockton Texas completed the formalities of joining the Union. On July 4, 1845, the Texan Congress accepted the U.S. government's terms for annexation, rejected continued independence and a peace treaty with Mexico, and began drawing up a state constitution. It was formally adopted in October. On December 29, 1845, Texas was admitted as the 28th state. Because the annexation resolution left the disposition of Texas's domestic affairs solely up to the Texans themselves, Texas entered the Union as a slave state. In addition to aggravating sectional tension Texas's slaveholding status left abolitionists and other Polk opponents, particularly many northern Democrats, convinced that the president was a tool of southern, proslave interests.

The Anglo-U.S. Crisis Over the Oregon Territory

Just as the dispute between the United States and Mexico over the boundary of Texas led these two countries to war in 1846, so too disagreement over control of what was then known as the Oregon Territory brought the United States to the brink of war with Great Britain. Unable to resolve their competing claims to Oregon, Great Britain and the United States signed a joint occupation agreement in 1818 for this half-million square mile area in the Pacific Northwest. The Oregon Territory included the present states of Oregon, Washington, and Idaho, parts of Montana and Wyoming, and half of British Columbia. The treaty, renewed in 1827, allowed citizens of both countries equal access to the territory. Both countries could terminate the agreement at any time by giving the other country 12 months' notice of its intention to abrogate, at which point both countries were obligated to divide the area along a mutually acceptable boundary.

The major controversy between the United States and Great Britain pertaining to Oregon was how far north legitimate U.S. claims to the territory extended. The region's commerce was dominated by U.S. merchants and traders, but the British also had a trading presence and forts in the region operated by the Hudson's Bay Company. U.S. settlement was very sparse though, numbering only 1,200 U.S. citizens at the time Polk became president. None of them lived north of the Columbia River, far from the northernmost limits of the U.S. claim at the 54 degrees 40 minutes parallel. Under the previous administration, talks had commenced between Great Britain and the United States over termination of the joint occupancy agreement and a plan, sponsored by the U.S. ambassador in London, Edward Everett, to extend the boundary between the United States and Canada at the 49th parallel from the Rocky Mountains to the Pacific coast, bending it in such a way that Britain would retain control of Vancouver Island. Little was accomplished to resolve the matter by the end of Tyler's term, leaving the issue to the new administration.

It was therefore with great anticipation that those supporters of pressing maximal U.S. claims, subsequently known as the "All-Oregon" men, greeted President Polk when he assumed office. Great Britain's expressed unwillingness to relinquish all of Oregon, however, led to the development of a countercoalition whose members, including Secretary of State Buchanan, Senator Calhoun, and most Whigs, favored compromise at the 49th parallel lest the issue escalate into war.

In his inaugural address Polk reiterated that U.S. claims were clear and unquestionable, but he omitted any reference to pressing them to their fullest extent. Historians are now in general agreement that Polk was privately disposed towards compromise and in no way desired a war with Great Britain, but he felt compelled to take a more aggressive public stance to appease the All-Oregon movement and force the British to abandon their claims south of the 49th parallel. Polk's saber-rattling inaugural pronouncements prompted shock and dismay in the London press. Prime Minister Sir Robert Peel and Foreign Secretary Aberdeen, however, were less inclined to believe that Polk would risk war with Britain over the issue given the close trade relationship that existed between the two countries. Thus they viewed Polk's statements as directed more to a domestic audience than to London.

Bowing to the sentiments of his cabinet, Polk authorized Buchanan in May 1845 to offer the British negotiator Richard Pakenham a compromise agreement at the 49th parallel, allowing the British free use of ports south of that line. For reasons that are still not fully understood, Pakenham rejected Buchanan's offer without submitting it to London for consideration and issued a scathing retort. This caused a serious diplomatic row that derailed the negotiations. Buchanan cautioned against any hasty response, and the threat of war in Mexico diverted the president's attention for a while. At the end of August, however, Polk withdrew the U.S. settlement proposal and renewed claim to all of Oregon.

From September through November 1845, the British and Buchanan continued to strive for a diplomatic solution, and Polk remained steadfast in his outward opposition to any compromise. In his first annual message to Congress in December 1845, Polk laid out in great detail his position on Oregon and invoked the Monroe Doctrine declaring that North America was off limits to any European power as a basis for his stance. Western expansionists such as Senator Lewis Cass of Michigan rallied behind the president and exclaimed their willingness to go to war for all of Oregon with the nationalistic slogan "Fifty-Four Forty or Fight!" Though he still did not want a war with Great Britain, Polk was willing to confront Great Britain in order to defend the United States's prestige.

Despite Polk's bravado, the British continued to appraise the situation from a pragmatic standpoint. Rather than match Polk's incendiary remarks tit-for-tat they restrained themselves secure in the knowledge of growing domestic opposition to Polk's tough public stance on Oregon. When the new Congress convened, a new coalition of moderates desirous of compromise had developed.

In early February the new U.S. ambassador in London, Louis McLane, informed Polk that the British were poised for a compromise at the 49th parallel. The dispatch also noted in passing that British warships had set sail for Canada. Though McLane in no way suggested that this was an aggressive action taken in direct response to the Oregon controversy, it created a great stir in Polk's cabinet. As the prospect of war with Mexico grew more probable, Polk was eager to diffuse the situation with Great Britain. Accordingly, on February 24, 1846, he instructed McLane to inform Aberdeen that Polk was ready to submit to the Senate a notice resolution calling for compromise at the 49th parallel and free British navigation rights on the Columbia River. Calhoun and his moderates in the Senate supported the president, and on April 23 a resolution publicly declaring the terms of compromise was approved by both chambers of Congress.

Providing for an extension of the 49th parallel to the Pacific coast with Vancouver Island granted in its entirety to the British, the Buchanan-Pakenham Treaty of 1846 was essentially the same as the proposal initially considered, and rejected, in 1843. It is still in force today as the boundary between the United States and Canada.

All of the political divisiveness over Oregon would become even more salient as the government grappled with the next major challenge emanating from the acquisition of Oregon, how the issue of slavery should be handled as territorial governments sprung up on new U.S. land.

War With Mexico: April 1846-February 1848

Upon entering office President Polk confided to his secretary of the navy George Bancroft that he had two foreign policy goals for his administration: acquire Oregon from the British and gain control of the Mexican province of California. Possessing valuable ports like San Francisco and Monterey from which it was envisioned that the United States could enter into lucrative trade relations across the Pacific Ocean, California was also an attractive area for U.S. settlement.

The annexation of Texas and the subsequent stationing of U.S. troops west of the Nueces River, which Mexico claimed as its border, ruptured U.S.-Mexican relations and put the two countries on a collision course. Relations at the time were further complicated by Mexico's failure to pay U.S. debts totaling more than $3 million by the mid-1840s. When war broke out between the two countries in April 1846 along the Rio Grande Polk declared that the only thing he desired was a swift peace. But observers of the war effort began to suspect that the administration desired more than peace and settlement of the Texas boundary and U.S. claims disputes. As U.S.

military operations escalated "Mr. Polk's War," as the conflict was sardonically referred to by its critics, was exposed as the expansionist war of conquest that it was always intended to be.

Early Negotiations

While prepared to go to war with Mexico to acquire California if need be, Polk preferred diplomacy. In November 1845, months before hostilities broke out, Polk sent John Slidell, a former congressperson from Louisiana, to Mexico in secret to negotiate a settlement. But Slidell's mission failed because neither the incumbent Mexican regime or the insurgents would meet with the Slidell delegation. The Slidell mission left Mexico in protest on March 15, 1846.

Diplomacy having failed to accomplish his administration's expansionist goals in the Southwest, Polk was inclined to consider more aggressive measures. When Mexican troops opened fire on a U.S. reconnaissance patrol near the Rio Grande on April 25, Polk had the incentive he needed. On May 12, 1846, he signed a congressional declaration: The United States and Mexico were now officially at war.

The War Begins

The first crucial decision facing Polk as commander in chief of the U.S. armed forces was selection of a leader for the U.S. war effort. This was a very thorny issue for the president because the two most qualified and obvious choices for the position, Gen. Zachary Taylor and Gen. Winfield Scott, were both ardent Whigs. Polk initially selected Scott to assume overall command of U.S. troops but replaced him with Taylor only two weeks later. In order to win the war Polk needed to trust both men with vital military campaigns, yet their very success rebounded favorably on the Whigs and made both generals into potential contenders for the upcoming presidential election in 1848.

The Mexican forces were roughly four to six times the size of the U.S. army. The troops were also well-armed, disciplined, and battle-hardened, having just emerged triumphant from revolution, compared to U.S. forces that were largely volunteers. Furthermore the Rio Grande theater was hundreds of miles from main U.S. population centers and Washington, D.C., making supply, reinforcement, and communication difficult. The Mexican leader Mariano Paredes y Arrillaga, therefore believed that the United States would not be able to defeat him on the battlefield. He also believed that domestic opposition to the war could be counted on to sap Polk's desire to fight. Thus, when the Mexican army was twice defeated by Gen. Taylor, at Palo Alto and Resaca de la Palma, Paredes was stunned. He was now the one facing domestic opposition and even open revolt, and he fled the country. The war continued under interim President Valentin Gomez Farias until former president Santa Anna returned from exile in Cuba.

Holding to the idea of Manifest Destiny, President Polk sought to annex the land north of Mexico in present-day Texas. The result was a war with Mexico. Although it was dubbed "Mr. Polk's War" by its critics, the successful capture of substantial Mexican territory made the war popular with most Americans. (Archive Photos. Reproduced by permission.)

The Wilmot Proviso, Hopes for Peace

President Polk welcomed Santa Anna's return because he had indications that Santa Anna was inclined towards a peace settlement on U.S. terms. In anticipation of a settlement, Polk came before Congress with a special message requesting $2 million to negotiate a treaty with Mexico and to pay for any concessions that may be made. This was the first official, public avowal of the administration's territorial aims in the war and it was met with an uproar. David Wilmot, a Van Buren supporter piqued by Polk's refusal to appoint several of his constituents to office, took the floor on August 8, 1846, and introduced an amendment barring slavery from any and all territory acquired from Mexico with the use of the congressionally appropriated funds. The measure, thereafter known as the Wilmot Proviso, was adopted by a vote of 83 to 64. The amended request for funds was passed by the House but reached the Senate so late, and the Wilmot Proviso was so strongly opposed, that it failed to reach a vote before Congress adjourned in December.

Contrary to his intimations, Santa Anna had no desire to acquiesce to the United States, and upon his return he took control of the Mexican army and prolonged the war for more than another year. Polk ordered Gen. Taylor to press across the Rio Grande into Mexican territory. Unable to halt Taylor's advance, in February 1847 Santa Anna's forces retreated to Central Mexico to take up defensive positions around Mexico City.

The previous summer Californians near Sacramento had rebelled against Mexican rule and proclaimed independence as the Bear Flag republic, stating that they wished to join the United States. Meanwhile, U.S. Brigadier Gen. Stephen Kearny invaded New Mexico. By early 1847 U.S. military governments were in control of both territories.

Santa Anna's refusal to capitulate to U.S. terms in the fall of 1846 brought a change in U.S. war strategy. In addition to ordering Taylor's forces on the offensive in northern Mexico, Polk and Secretary of War William Marcy decided to open a second front to the south, at Vera Cruz, from which a march on Mexico City could be initiated. After all his attempts to find alternates failed, Polk reluctantly appointed Gen. Scott to lead the Vera Cruz mission. In February 1847, Scott's army of 12,000 landed at Vera Cruz and succeeded in capturing the city by the end of the month. He then began his arduous march inland toward the capital, which surrendered on September 13. With the fall of Mexico City Santa Anna resigned and fled the country, leaving his successor, Pedro Maria Anaya, to conduct peace negotiations with the victorious Americans.

Biography:

Winfield Scott

Military Leader (1786–1866) A brigadier general before the age of 30, Winfield Scott made his life out of a long, successful military career during which he became only the second man after President George Washington to attain the rank of lieutenant general. Scott was a studied military tactician who was twice awarded the congressional gold medal, first for his service in the War of 1812 and later following the Mexican-American War (1846–48). His rank and stature, coupled with his own political aspirations, placed him in direct contact with every presidential administration he served under. During some administrations, this contact was favorable and during others it was beset with more conflict than contact. Following the War of 1812, Scott was offered the position of secretary of war by President James Madison, but declined. Conversely, President James Polk perceived Scott to be a strong political rival and campaigned unsuccessfully to have Scott court-martialed following the

Mexican-American War. Five years later, Scott did accept the Whig Party's nomination for president, but lost the election. This military tactician was a keen negotiator as well, and several presidents relied on Scott to negotiate favorable resolutions to internal conflicts as well as conflicts at both borders. At the start of the American Civil War (1861–65), President Abraham Lincoln listened to Scott, general in chief of the army since 1841, and used his "divide and contain" strategy as a means for defeating the Confederacy during the Civil War. When Scott passed away a few years later at 79, President Lincoln eulogized him saying, "We are. . . his debtors."

The Treaty of Guadalupe Hidalgo

Nicholas P. Trist, the chief clerk of the State Department, was dispatched to negotiate a treaty that would establish a border along the Rio Grande and cede to the United States the territories of California and New Mexico. He was authorized to pay up to $30 million. Despite several setbacks, the final version of the treaty arrived in Washington on February 19, 1848, and included everything that Polk had originally desired. By a vote of 36 to 14 the Senate approved the treaty in early March. On May 25, 1848, the Mexican Congress ratified the Treaty of Guadalupe Hidalgo, officially bringing the war to an end. In return for a payment of $15 million and the assumption of all U.S. claims against Mexico, Mexico ceded all of California and New Mexico to the United States and agreed to recognize the Rio Grande as the border of Texas.

In light of victory, support for "Mr. Polk's War" was enthusiastic. Military success seemed to confirm the popular notion of Manifest Destiny that the nation was destined to expand to the Pacific Ocean. In fact by the time Trist's treaty arrived in Washington, a movement calling for the conquest and annexation of all of Mexico had been gaining momentum and could count among its members Secretary of State Buchanan and Treasury Secretary Walker. Despite these sentiments, the war effort was far from universally endorsed. Public dissent was particularly pronounced in the Northeast. Abolitionists, pacifists, and clergy denounced the war as a duplicitous

attempt to extend slavery into Mexican territory and a violation of the very democratic and republican principles upon which the country was founded. Congressional opposition existed from the outset as well, led by the Whigs, who were later joined by the Calhoun Democrats and, after the introduction of the Wilmot Proviso in the fall of 1846, the antislavery Van Burenites as well. For all their protests, however, both Whigs and renegade Democrats voted for the men, material, and funding that Polk requested out of fear of being labeled unpatriotic had they taken steps to impede the administration's prosecution of the war.

The Polk Administration Legacy

Polk tried to solve the slavery question in a way that would preserve national and party harmony, but to no avail. By the end of the 1840s slavery had become the most burning issue in U.S. politics, a status that it retained for the next 25 years. In July 1848, in anticipation of the upcoming presidential election, the Democratic Party officially splintered. Dissident Democrats joined with Conscience Whigs and the Liberty Party to form the Free Soil Party. They nominated Martin Van Buren as their candidate and ran on a platform dedicated to the exclusion of slavery from the West.

The first historians to reflect on Polk's presidency were Whigs whose interpretation of events were, unsurprisingly, critical. He was maligned as an agent of proslavery southern annexationists who schemed to strengthen the Democratic Party and duped the country into supporting a war of conquest to expand slavery (Horn, pp. 454–55). The publication of Polk's personal diary in 1910, however, allowed scholars to gain new insight into the man and his policies, thereby allowing for a more balanced view of his administration. He is now lauded for his integrity and hard work while in office and is recognized for his success in accomplishing his stated policy goals.

Lasting Impact

Polk's vision of the president as the embodiment of the nation's will led to his own brand of leadership that strengthened the executive branch's power vis-á-vis the other branches of government. Following the precepts of his mentor, Andrew Jackson, Polk dominated the legislature and his cabinet, leading one historian to conclude that he was perhaps the strongest chief executive before the Civil War (1861–65). The first president to preside over a full-scale war since James Madison, Polk set the precedent of effective civilian leadership of U.S. forces in his capacity as commander in chief during the Mexican conflict.

Under Polk's leadership the territory controlled by the United States expanded by one-third. His aggressive diplomacy on Oregon and victory in war with Mexico added over 1.2 million square miles to the United States and set the stage for the United States's emergence as a Pacific power. It also led to the eclipse of British influence in the Western Hemisphere and European recognition of U.S. dominance along the northern Pacific coast and in the Gulf of Mexico. February 2, 1998, represented the 150th anniversary of the signing of the Treaty of Guadalupe Hidalgo, but the events still have political significance. A Republican-sponsored bill, the Guadalupe-Hidalgo Treaty Land Claims Act of 1997, seeks to create a presidential commission to review claims by thousands of Hispanic families in New Mexico who say their lands were stolen by corrupt lawyers and local officials in violation of the 1848 treaty.

Territorial expansion, however, came at a price. It fueled the feelings of U.S. chauvinism and militarism stirred up by notions of Manifest Destiny, thereby paving the way for future U.S. aggressiveness in Central and Latin America. It also worsened sectional quarrels and ruptured the Democratic Party by thrusting discussion of slavery to the top of the nation's political agenda. It is for these reasons that scholars looking back on the Polk presidency identify it as a crucial point in U.S. history when the nation began its slide toward disunion.

Sources

Bergeron, Paul H. *The Presidency of James K. Polk.* Lawrence, Kans.: University Press of Kansas, 1987.

Brinkley, Alan. *American History: A Survey.* Vol. 1. New York: McGraw-Hill, 1995.

Brooke, James. "Hot Issue in Northern New Mexico: Fine Print of an 1848 Treaty." *New York Times,* 19 February 1998, A10.

Bumgarner, John Reed. *Sarah Childress Polk: A Biography of a Remarkable First Lady.* Jefferson, N.C.: McFarland, 1997.

Connor, Seymour V. "Mexican War." *Grolier Multimedia Encyclopedia,* 1995.

DeGregorio, William A. *The Complete Book of U.S. Presidents.* New York: Wings Books, 1997.

Encyclopedia of World Biography. Vol. 7. Detroit: Gale Research, 1998.

Ferrell, Robert H. "Oregon Question." *Grolier Multimedia Encyclopedia,* 1995.

Foner, Eric. "The Wilmot Proviso Revisited." *Journal of American History* 56, no. 2 (September 1969): 262–79.

Graebner, Norman A. "James Polk." In *America's Ten Greatest Presidents,* edited by Morton Borden, 113–38. Chicago: Rand McNally and Co., 1961.

Horn, James J. "Trends in Historical Interpretation: James K. Polk." *North Carolina Historical Review* 42, no. 4 (Autumn 1965): 454–64.

Kane, Joseph N. *Facts About the Presidents.* New York: The H. W. Wilson Co., 1993.

McCormac, Eugene I. *James K. Polk: A Political Biography.* New York: Russell and Russell, 1965.

Nelson, Michael, ed. *Congressional Quarterly's Guide to the Presidency.* Washington D.C.: Congressional Quarterly, 1989.

Polk, James K. *Polk: The Diary of a President, 1845–1849.* Edited by Allan Nevins. New York: Capricorn Books, 1968.

Pletcher, David M. *The Diplomacy of Annexation: Texas, Oregon and the Mexican War.* Columbia, Mo.: University of Missouri Press, 1973.

Schroeder, John H. *Mr. Polk's War: American Opposition and Dissent, 1846–1848.* Madison, Wis.: The University of Wisconsin Press, 1973.

Sellers, Charles G. *James K. Polk, Jacksonian: 1795–1843.* Princeton, N.J.: Princeton University Press, 1957.

———. *James K. Polk, Continentalist: 1843–1846.* Princeton, N.J.: Princeton University Press, 1966.

———. "Election of 1844." In *History of American Presidential Elections, 1789–1968.* Vol. 1, edited by Arthur M. Schlesinger Jr., 747–861. New York: Chelsea House Publishers, 1971.

Further Readings

Johannsen, Robert W. *To the Halls of the Montezumas: The Mexican War in the American Imagination.* New York: Oxford University Press, 1985.

Mahin, Dean B. *Olive Branch and Sword: The United States and Mexico, 1845–1848.* Jefferson, N.C.: McFarland and Co., 1997.

Taylor Administration

Full name: Zachary Taylor
Popular name: Old Rough and Ready; Old Zach

Personal Information:

Born: November 24, 1784
Birthplace: Montebello, Virginia
Died: July 9, 1850
Death place: Washington, D.C.
Burial place: Congressional Cemetery, Washington, D.C.; moved to Zachary Taylor National Cemetery, Louisville, Kentucky
Religion: Episcopalian
Spouse: Margaret "Peggy" Mackall Smith (m. 1810)
Children: Ann Mackall; Sarah Knox; Octavia Pannel; Margaret Smith; Mary Elizabeth; Richard Taylor
Education: Little formal education
Occupation: Farmer; soldier
Political Party: Whig Party
Age at Inauguration: 64 years

Biography

Dubbed Old Rough and Ready by the soldiers he commanded, the name was a tribute to Zachary Taylor's willingness to share in physical hardship and combat with the men he commanded. Taylor was never pretentious and did not care for pomp and circumstance or external appearances. Yet, he became a Mexican War (1846–48) hero and eventually president of the United States.

Early Life

When Zachary Taylor was born on November 24, 1784, his father, Richard Taylor, had already secured a land grant of one thousand acres in Kentucky. When he was less than a year old, Taylor moved with his parents from their home in Virginia to a log house five miles east of the village of Louisville, Kentucky. Louisville was a frontier town still in danger of American Indian attacks. Although his parents were not poor, life on the frontier was not easy. The future president had little formal education. On the frontier practical knowledge was imperative—for example, he quickly learned how to load and fire a muzzleloader.

Besides the fact that Taylor's father had fought in the American Revolution (1775–83), two of his boyhood chums may have influenced his decision to become a soldier. One, George Croghan, was a nephew of the famous Revolutionary War hero George Rogers Clark. The second, Robert Anderson, graduated from the U. S. Military Academy at West Point, New York, in 1824 and later was the Union commander at Fort Sumter at the start of the American Civil War (1861–65).

Education

On the frontier Zachary Taylor had little formal education. At an early age Elisha Ayer tutored the future president. Ayer testified that his protégé was "quick in learning and still patient in study" (Hamilton, p. 28). Later Kean O'Hara accepted Taylor as one of his pupils. Taylor biographer Holman Hamilton stated that Taylor's correspondence "bears eloquent evidence that the instruction of Ayer and O'Hara did not fall on barren soil" for Taylor's hand was "bold and firm, the mode of expression clear and forceful, if lacking in grace."

Family Life

Margaret Mackall Smith married Zachary Taylor on June 21, 1810, at the age of 21. Although raised as a lady by well-to-do parents, she, like her husband, was considered unpretentious. Peggy Taylor, as her husband affectionately called her, proved to be a highly competent partner for her soldier husband. She was devoted to her children, and sought a good education for them. She was more deeply religious than her husband who, though attending the Episcopalian Church, never formally joined. Illness limited her activities as first lady so that her daughter Mary Elizabeth "Betty" Bliss performed many of the functions that otherwise would have been hers. The Taylors were a devoted couple, which made for a very successful marriage. Margaret Taylor died on August 18, 1852.

Career

Zachary Taylor was a career soldier until he became president. Taylor's military career began in 1808 when President Thomas Jefferson commissioned him as a first lieutenant in the U.S. Army. In 1812 he distinguished himself with his defense of Indiana's Fort Harrison after the fort had been attacked by Shawnee Indians led by Indian chief Tecumseh. Later, as a colonel, he fought American Indians in the Black Hawk War in 1832 and the Seminole Indians in Florida during the late 1830s. While Taylor served in the military, he also purchased land and slaves in Louisiana, and lived at his plantation there when not on duty.

After the United States annexed Texas in 1845, President James Polk got a declaration of war against Mexico from Congress to defend the border. Taylor was in command of the U.S. troops when Mexican soldiers crossed the Rio Grande, the river dividing the United States and Mexico, on April 25, 1846, at Matamoros, Mexico. The attack on Taylor's forces marked the unofficial beginning of the Mexican War (1846–48). Taylor's troops withstood the attack and went on to score a number of victories that climaxed in the February 1847 Battle of Buena Vista.

Zachary Taylor. (The Library of Congress.)

The Mexican War ended officially on July 4, 1848, when President Polk proclaimed the Treaty of Guadalupe Hidalgo in effect. Military action had ended in late 1847. The U.S. Senate ratified the treaty on March 10, 1848, and the Mexican Congress did the same on May 25, 1848. As a result of the war, the territorial boundaries of the United States were greatly expanded. The present states of Arizona, Nevada, California, and Utah, and also parts of New Mexico, Colorado, and Wyoming all were ceded to the United States by Mexico. The Mexican Cession, as it was referred, was a mixed blessing, because it did much to revive the slavery issue. The nation now had to decide whether slavery would be extended into this recently acquired land.

As for Zachary Taylor, the Mexican War made him a national war hero. Without the war, few Americans would ever have heard of him. This alone propelled him into the White House. Taylor was nominated for the presidency by the Whigs in 1847 and won the election in 1848. During his presidency slavery and its extension westward was the all-encompassing issue. Taylor died in office on July 9, 1850, with the issue far from being resolved.

Post-presidential Years

During a hot Fourth of July celebration in Washington, President Taylor spent two hours in the broiling sun listening to Independence Day oratory. Upon his return to the White House, he drank freely of iced water and chilled milk while eating cherries and other raw fruits and vegetables. He did this in spite of warnings concerning the Asiatic cholera epidemic. The president soon fell ill and eventually died about 10:30 P.M. on July 9, 1850. At noon on July 10, Taylor's vice president, Millard Fillmore, officially became president when he took the oath of office in the chamber of the House of Representatives.

The Zachary Taylor Administration

Ironically, Zachary Taylor, who had achieved his fame in war, as president sought to find a peaceful resolution to the sectional controversy over slavery that raged during his presidency. He died in the second year of his presidency, leaving the quest to his vice president and successor Millard Fillmore.

Taylor Becomes President

The Campaign of 1848

After the successful military campaigns Zachary Taylor had waged during his military career (*See also,* Career), he was a prime candidate for the Whig Party's presidential nomination in 1848. Although the prominent Kentucky congressperson Henry Clay was a chief contender, Taylor, backed by President James Polk, received the nomination on the fourth ballot. As it turned out, another Mexican War hero, Winfield Scott, came in second, with Henry Clay finishing third and Daniel Webster of Massachusetts fourth. Millard Fillmore of New York gained the vice presidential nomination on the second ballot.

In 1848 the Democrats nominated Lewis Cass of Michigan for president and William O. Butler of Kentucky for vice president. Martin Van Buren (eighth president of the United States), once a Democrat, felt the Democratic Party had increasingly fallen under the dominance of southern politicians. He, too, ran for president, on the third party ticket of the Free Soil Party.

In the campaign Lewis Cass came out against the Wilmot Proviso, which would have prohibited the extension of slavery into any territory acquired from Mexico. Instead, he favored squatter sovereignty, which would have permitted residents in new territories to decide whether slavery should be allowed. Taylor, a slave owner himself, sidestepped the issue. The Free Soil Party adamantly opposed the extension of slavery.

Taylor was a military hero who, like Dwight Eisenhower in 1952, came across as a national and not a partisan candidate. Arthur Schlesinger in his *History of American Presidential Elections 1789–1968* quotes Taylor, "I am not expected to force Congress, by the coercion of the veto, to pass laws to suit me or pass none. This is what I mean by not being a party candidate. And I understand this is good Whig doctrine—I would not be a partisan President and hence should not be a party candidate, in the sense that would make one."

In the fall election Van Buren failed to capture a single electoral vote, but he did attract enough popular votes from antislavery Democrats to assure Taylor's election. Taylor received 163 electoral votes to 127 for Cass. Taylor drew 47 percent of the popular vote, to 43 percent for Cass, and 10 percent for Van Buren. Because March 4, 1849, was a Sunday, Taylor was inaugurated on March 5.

Taylor's Advisers

Knowing few politicians personally and having little or no experience in the political arena, Taylor was handicapped when he assumed the presidency. He abhorred the spoils system (honoring those faithful to the party with plum jobs in the administration) and so made his cabinet selections based on merit rather than patronage. This alienated many party regulars; however, Taylor was not bothered by this circumstance when he first took office. He believed that domestic issues were primarily the responsibility of the legislature. Later it would prove problematic as he tried to resolve sectional differences between the North and the South.

Taylor picked a leading Whig senator, John M. Clayton of Delaware, for secretary of state; Clayton advised Taylor on further cabinet nominees. Clayton's major contribution to the Taylor administration was the successful negotiation of the Clayton-Bulwer Treaty with Great Britain (*See also,* Foreign Issues).

Senator William H. Seward of New York, who had promoted Taylor's presidential candidacy and later became Abraham Lincoln's secretary of state, strongly opposed the extension of slavery. Taylor, although a slaveholder himself, was influenced by Seward. Taylor eventually supported allowing states to choose for themselves whether or not slavery would be allowed within their borders, and he endorsed the quick entrance of California to the Union as a free state. He did not back the idea of a compromise whereby concessions would be made to the South in order to maintain peace (*See also,* Domestic Issues).

Taylor and Congress

Perhaps because he had so little political experience, Taylor failed to recognize the need of winning over influential members of Congress to his side. Kentucky senator Henry Clay, a leading Whig who had also vied for the 1848 nomination, complained, "I have never before seen such an Administration. There is very little cooperation or concord between the two ends of the Avenue. There is not, I believe, a prominent Whig in either House that has any confidential intercourse with the Executive" (Bauer, p. 265). Other Whig leaders like Daniel Webster and Robert C. Winthrop, both of Massachusetts, and John Bell of Tennessee also were slighted. Thus, several Whigs were not enthusiastic with Taylor's proposals for dealing with the problems that arose from the acquisition of the Mexican Cession (land acquired through the Mexican War (1846–48)), such as letting the new states make their own decisions on whether or not to allow slavery.

At the beginning of the Thirty-first Congress, which sat from March 4, 1849 to March 3, 1851, the Democrats had control of the Congress by a count of 35 Democrats to 25 Whigs, with two Free Soilers added to the mix. In the House there were 113 Democrats, 108 Whigs, nine Free Soilers, and one from the American Party. There also was one independent and one vacancy.

Zachary Taylor was one of the few presidents who never exercised the veto.

Taylor and the Judiciary

During his brief presidency Taylor made no appointments to the Supreme Court. The chief justice of the Supreme Court during the time Taylor was president was Roger B. Taney, who was staunchly anti-Whig.

Changes in the U.S. Government

Congress established the Department of the Interior, originally called the Home Department, on March 3, 1849, two days before Zachary Taylor became president. This new department brought under one head the Office of the Census, the Office of Indian Affairs, and the General Land Office. Taylor named the first secretary of the interior—Thomas Ewing of Ohio.

Domestic Issues

When Zachary Taylor assumed the presidency on March 5, 1849, the American Civil War (1861–65) was still 12 years away. However, at the time Taylor took office slavery was already the consuming issue. In the early 1820s the Missouri Compromise was established, whereby in the Northwest Territory (west of the Mississippi River) slavery was to be allowed south of the 36 degrees 30 minutes line while north of that line (except

Administration

Administration Dates
March 4, 1849–July 9, 1850

Vice President
Millard Fillmore (1849–50)

Cabinet
Secretary of State
James Buchanan (1845–49)
John M. Clayton (1849–50)

Secretary of the Treasury
Robert J. Walker (1845–49)
William Morris Meredith (1849–50)

Secretary of War
George W. Crawford (1849–50)

Attorney General
Reverdy Johnson (1849–50)

Secretary of the Navy
John Y. Mason (1846–49)
William Ballard Preston (1849–50)

Postmaster General
Cave Johnson (1845–49)
Jacob Collamer (1849–50)

Secretary of the Interior
Thomas Ewing (1849–50)

---

for Missouri) slavery was prohibited. Thus, as part of the compromise Maine was admitted to the Union as a free state and Missouri as a slave state, maintaining the balance between slave states and free states.

Following the Mexican War (1846–48), decisions had to be made concerning the status of slavery in the Mexican Cession, land that was added to the United States in the aftermath of the war. It was an area that today includes the states of California, Arizona, Utah, Nevada, and parts of New Mexico, Colorado, and Wyoming. In 1846 the House of Representatives passed the Wilmot Proviso, which banned slavery in any territory acquired from Mexico. The Senate, however, refused to approve it. The status of slavery in the Mexican Ces-

Fast Fact

Because March 4, 1849, fell on a Sunday, Zachary Taylor was not inaugurated until March 5, the day after President Polk's term ended. Because of this, Missouri senator David R. Atchison, president pro tempore of the Senate, later claimed that he had been president of the United States for one day. At that time, the law called for the president pro tempore of the Senate to assume the presidency if there was no president or vice president.

(Source: Elbert B. Smith. *The Presidencies of Zachary Taylor and Millard Fillmore,* 1998.)

sion would consume much of Taylor's time and energy during his brief presidency.

Zachary Taylor and the Compromise of 1850

In 1848 gold was discovered in California. Soon thousands of adventurers from around the world poured into the area. Convinced that statehood was essential to maintain an orderly society, responsible Californians, encouraged by President Taylor, drafted a constitution excluding slavery and forthwith applied to Congress for admission into the Union. In his annual message to Congress on December 4, 1849, Taylor recommended immediate admission of California as a free state.

Southerners vehemently opposed Taylor's proposal because at the time of California's request there were 15 free states and 15 slave states. The admission of California would upset that balance.

Senator Henry Clay of Kentucky realized that the South would not tolerate the admission of California without concessions. Therefore on January 29, 1850, he introduced a series of resolutions designed to pacify both the North and the South, originally referred to as the Omnibus Bill.

Clay proposed that California be admitted as a free state, but that the territorial governments in New Mexico and Utah be organized without mention of slavery. To further placate the South a stricter fugitive slave law was proposed. Furthermore, slavery would continue to be legal in Washington, D.C., the nation's capital, although slave trade would be prohibited. Clay also included a provision that set the boundary between New Mexico and Texas (a slave state), and one that called on

the national government to assume debts that Texas had incurred prior to the time when it joined the Union.

Although President Taylor wanted California admitted immediately without mollifying the South, and therefore opposed compromise, both northern and southern senators realized that could not realistically be accomplished. They ignored the president's recommendation and launched into one of the greatest debates ever witnessed on the floor of the U.S. Senate.

Clay, of course, strongly favored the compromise proposals, as did Senator Daniel Webster of Massachusetts, who on March 7, 1850, gave such a passionate, articulate speech that forever after it has been remembered as Webster's Seventh of March Speech.

Another giant in the Senate, John C. Calhoun of South Carolina, stood in opposition to the compromise. Too weak to speak himself, Calhoun sat silently on March 4, 1850, as one of his younger colleagues, Senator James Mason of Virginia, delivered Calhoun's speech on ways the Union could be saved. Calhoun had less than a month to live before he died on March 31. Senator William H. Seward of New York was also opposed to the compromise, but for other reasons. He was against slavery altogether, and in his opposition to any concessions to slaveholders he appealed to a "higher law," apparently the law of God.

Some historians believe that when President Taylor died on July 9, 1850, in the midst of the debate, and Vice President Millard Fillmore became president, the chances of enacting what came to be called the Compromise of 1850 were enhanced. Whereas Taylor opposed the compromise, Fillmore favored it.

Following Taylor's death the Compromise of 1850 was effected by the passage of five laws between September 9 and September 20, 1850. This legislation followed the outline that Senator Henry Clay had drawn at the start of the debate.

Foreign Issues

In the middle of the nineteenth century when Zachary Taylor became the United States's 12th president, the continental United States was about the size that it is today. During the 1840s Americans insisted that Manifest Destiny dictated that the United States should extend from the Atlantic Ocean to the Pacific Ocean. In 1846 the United States and Great Britain agreed to divide the Oregon Territory along the 49th parallel, giving the United States sole possession of the area south of that line.

When two years later Mexico ceded the Mexican Cession to the United States (*See also,* Domestic Issues), Manifest Destiny seemed to have been fulfilled. Many Americans felt that God had blessed the United States in a special way and that in a certain sense the United States was superior to other nations. The United States faced the second half of the nineteenth century with an air of confidence, which at times bordered on arrogance.

The Clayton-Bulwer Treaty

When the United States expanded to the Pacific Ocean, the need for an inter-oceanic waterway through the Central American isthmus seemed imperative. At the time it appeared that a Nicaraguan site would be the most feasible. Great Britain, with an empire spanning the globe and with Caribbean holdings such as Jamaica and the British Honduras, also had interest in an isthmian canal.

A conflict with Britain seemed possible when during James Polk's administration (1845–49) a Polk envoy, Elijah Hise, signed a treaty with Nicaragua pledging U.S. protection for Nicaragua against the British in exchange for the right of way for an inter-oceanic canal. This treaty awaited ratification when Taylor assumed office.

At the eastern Caribbean end of the proposed canal stood a small town called San Juan. It was inhabited by Mosquito Indians, who claimed to be independent of Nicaragua. Great Britain recognized these Indians as a separate, independent nation and changed San Juan's name to Greytown. Later British sailors seized, for a time, Tigre Island, which was at the western end of the proposed waterway.

In 1850 neither Britain nor the United States wanted war over this issue. Therefore, when Sir Henry Bulwer, the new British minister to the United States, arrived in early 1850, he immediately began conferring with Secretary of State John M. Clayton. By February 3, 1850, the two had hammered out a tentative agreement. After receiving reactions from their respective governments, the two signed what came to be called the Clayton-Bulwer Treaty. Under the terms of the treaty both nations agreed never to seek exclusive control of an isthmian canal. The proposed waterway would be left neutral and unfortified with the citizens from both nations accorded equal treatment. The treaty was ratified on April 19, 1850.

The Taylor Administration Legacy

Taylor died after suddenly becoming ill. Public reaction was one of sorrow mixed with surprise, because his illness had been so brief. On July 13, 1850, an estimated 100,000 thronged Washington, D.C., especially along the funeral route.

While Taylor resolved potential conflicts with Britain and France during his administration, he left the issue of slavery to his vice president and successor Millard Fillmore. Senator Henry Clay of Kentucky had offered a series of compromise measures between the North and the South in the form of what was called the Omnibus Bill, a precursor to his Compromise of 1850

A miner digs for gold in California during the gold rush in the mid-1850s. The issue of California statehood caused furious debate between the North and the South over whether California would be admitted as a free state or a slave state. (Archive Photos. Reproduced by permission.)

(*See also,* Domestic Issues). Several observers believe that Taylor's death on July 9, 1850, was fortuitous for the nation because Fillmore had supported the Omnibus Bill, which, although defeated, led to the passage of a series of separate bills called the Compromise of 1850. The Compromise of 1850, in turn, delayed the onset of the American Civil War (1861–65) for another decade.

The signing of the 1850 Clayton-Bulwer Treaty demonstrated that the United States wished to improve relations with Great Britain. (*See also,* Foreign Issues). Although Taylor had been a soldier engaged in combat much of his life, he sought peaceful resolutions to conflicts. However, it was also demonstrated that the United States would not back down when Taylor believed the U.S. cause to be just.

Lasting Impact

While Taylor was not a seasoned politician, he refused to be merely a Whig figurehead. Taylor was a southerner who, in the course of his short presidency, put preservation of the Union above all else. Although an outsider to the world of politics, he did not relinquish his power—rather he pursued his goals despite the setbacks his lack of experience caused. However, his lack of leadership skills resulted in few lasting changes.

Sources

Bailey, Thomas A. *A Diplomatic History of the American People.* New York: Appleton-Century-Crofts, 1969.

Bauer, K. Jack. *Zachary Taylor: Soldier, Planter, Statesman of the Old Southwest.* Baton Rouge, La.: Louisiana State University Press, 1985.

DeGregorio, William A. *The Complete Book of the U.S. Presidents.* New York: Dembner Books, 1984.

Encyclopedia of World Biography. Vol. 15. Detroit: Gale Research, 1998.

Hamilton, Holman. *Zachary Taylor: Soldier of the Republic.* New York: Bobbs-Merrill, 1941.

———. *Zachary Taylor: Soldier in the White House.* New York: Bobbs-Merrill, 1951.

Nevins, Allan. *Ordeal of the Unions.* 2 vols. New York: Charles Scribner's Sons, 1947.

Schlesinger, Arthur, Jr., ed. *History of American Presidential Elections 1789-1968.* New York: Chelsea House, 1971.

Smith, Elbert B. *The Presidencies of Zachary Taylor and Millard Fillmore.* Lawrence, Kans.: University Press of Kansas, 1988.

Further Readings

Bauer, K. Jack. *The Mexican War, 1846–1848.* New York: Macmillan, 1974.

Craven, Avery O. *Civil War in the Making: 1815–1860.* Baton Rouge, La.: Louisiana State University Press, 1959.

Dyer, Brainerd. *Zachary Taylor.* Baton Rouge, La.: Louisiana State University Press, 1946.

Hamilton, Holman. *Prologue to Conflict: The Crisis and Compromise of 1850.* Lexington, Ky.: University of Kentucky Press, 1964.

Morison, Samuel E. *The Oxford History of the American People.* New York: Oxford University Press, 1965.

Rayback, Joseph G. *Free Soil: The Election of 1848.* Lexington, Ky.: University of Kentucky Press, 1970.

Fillmore Administration

Biography

Born into humble circumstances on the frontier, Millard Fillmore overcame the shortcomings of his early education to become a successful lawyer. Hard-working and handsome, Fillmore enjoyed a successful political career in the early days of the Whig party in New York, leading to his nomination for the vice presidency in 1848. Fillmore succeeded to the presidency after the death of Zachary Taylor in 1850, and while in that office made it his priority to help resolve the nation's struggle over slavery.

Early Life

The story of Millard Fillmore demonstrates vividly that in the United States a person of very humble birth can rise to be president. On January 7, 1800, Millard Fillmore was born in a log cabin on the frontier in western New York State. Millard's father was a poor and rather unsuccessful farmer. As a boy, Fillmore learned to hoe corn, mow hay, harvest wheat, and cut logs for the fireplace. Not until he was 19 years old did he attend school. There was never much time for fun and relaxation, but Fillmore did occasionally hunt and fish in Lake Skaneateles near his home in New York. When Fillmore reached the age of 14, his father apprenticed his son to a clothmaker. The future president disliked his mentor so much that within four months he was back at home. His father found another clothmaker, and Fillmore moved to New Hope, New York, to learn the trade.

Full name: Millard Fillmore
Popular name: The American Louis Philippe

Personal Information:
Born: January 7, 1800
Birthplace: Locke Township, New York
Died: March 8, 1874
Death place: Buffalo, New York
Burial place: Forest Lawn Cemetery, Buffalo, New York
Religion: Unitarian
Spouse: Abigail Powers (m. 1826); Caroline Carmichael McIntosh (m. 1858)
Children: Millard Powers; Mary Abigail
Education: Attended an academy at New Hope, New York
Occupation: Lawyer; legislator; vice president of the United States
Political Party: Whig Party
Age at Inauguration: 50 years

Millard Fillmore. *(The Library of Congress.)*

books that sparked a similar interest in him. The two fell in love and after a long courtship were married on February 5, 1826. In time Fillmore and his wife built a large personal library.

Abigail Fillmore advanced her husband's career by continuing to teach to provide family income while Fillmore studied to become a lawyer and establish a legal practice. When she became first lady, Abigail Fillmore discovered the White House had no library. Her husband, with congressional approval, obtained funds to create a library of some nine hundred volumes. Even though she was a devoted wife who provided intellectual companionship and financial support when needed, Abigail Fillmore was always quite frail.

President Fillmore took great pride in his two children. His daughter, Mary Abigail Fillmore, was well educated, a talented musician, and fluent in both French and Spanish. Because of his wife's frail health, Fillmore relied heavily on his daughter to arrange and participate in the White House's social functions. In effect, his daughter became Fillmore's White House hostess. Both Fillmore's wife and daughter died soon after he left office. Abigail Fillmore died on March 30, 1853, after 27 years of marriage, and Mary Abigail Fillmore died on July 26, 1854.

On February 10, 1858, Fillmore married for the second time. Caroline McIntosh was the widow of a prominent Albany, New York, businessman named Ezekiel C. McIntosh. At the time of her second marriage she was 52. The two were prominent in Buffalo, New York, society. They purchased a mansion on Niagara Square in Buffalo where Caroline Fillmore continued to live until her death on August 11, 1881. Fillmore had died in 1874.

Education

Because his parents were poor and lived on the frontier, Fillmore had little formal schooling. Young Fillmore had to help the family survive in a harsh environment. As a boy, Fillmore did learn to read, but there was not much to read except the Bible and a few spelling and reading books. When at the age of 17 his neighbors organized a circulation library, Fillmore eagerly participated. At 19 he enrolled in the Academy of Good Hope in New Hope, New York. It was a small institution that did not compare to the more prestigious schools on the U.S. East Coast.

Soon Millard Fillmore was on his way to becoming a lawyer. He never attended a law school, but he learned by studying and working in the office of County Judge Walter Wood in Montville, New York, and later in the office of lawyers Asa Rice and Joseph Clary in Buffalo, New York. In 1823 Fillmore formally became a lawyer when he was admitted to the bar.

Family Life

While Fillmore was attending the Academy of Good Hope in New Hope, New York, he met Abigail Powers, who was a 21-year-old teacher at the academy. Powers significantly influenced Fillmore with her interest in

Career

In 1823 Millard Fillmore began practicing law in East Aurora, New York, after being admitted to the bar earlier that year. He was a successful lawyer and eventually formed a partnership with N. K. Hall and S. G. Haven in Buffalo, New York.

When he entered politics he supported the National Republicans, later called the Whigs, favoring the national bank, tariffs to protect U.S. industry, and internal improvements sponsored by the federal government. In 1828 he was elected to the New York State Assembly where he served three one-year terms. As a state legislator he successfully promoted a bill abolishing imprisonment for debt and one establishing a state bankruptcy law.

In 1832 Fillmore won a seat in the U.S. House of Representatives. After two years he headed back to Buffalo to practice law, but returned to the House after his election in 1836. He then served three consecutive terms in the House of Representatives. In his last term as chair of the powerful House Ways and Means Committee, he drafted and successfully backed the Whig-sponsored Tariff Act of 1842, which raised enough revenue to reduce the national debt.

By this time the Whig Party was the second major political party in the United States. Thus, as a congressman who seemed to be a rising star, he was nominated for governor in 1844 by the Whigs. His opponent was Democrat Silas Wright who, according to historian Benson Grayson, "had represented New York state in the United States Senate where he had been regarded as one of the ablest members of that body." He was handicapped by lukewarm support from powerful New York Whigs William Seward and Thurlow Weed. Associated with the liberal wing of the Whig party, they opposed slavery and worked to attract new immigrants to the Whig party. Fillmore, while opposed to slavery, regarded it as untouchable in the states where it existed and also sympathized with those who were hostile to immigrants. Fillmore lost the election by only ten thousand votes.

After his unsuccessful bid for governor of New York in 1844, Fillmore won election as New York comptroller in 1847 by the largest plurality that a Whig had ever garnered over a Democrat in New York State. After only holding that office for a short time the Whigs nominated him for U.S. vice president. He was chosen because of his strong showing in New York and the fact that they needed someone to balance the ticket—the presidential nominee was Zachary Taylor, a southerner. He became president on July 10, 1850, following the death of Zachary Taylor on the previous day.

When Fillmore became president, the U.S. Congress was in the midst of a debate that eventually produced the Compromise of 1850 (*See also,* Zachary Taylor Administration). Unlike his predecessor, Fillmore backed the proposals leading to the compromise, which was intended to avert civil war and, at least for the time being, put the slavery issue to rest. These proposals were adopted by the Congress in September 1850.

Yet even after the Compromise of 1850 was passed, the slavery question continued to haunt Fillmore and his country all during his presidency. The publication of *Uncle Tom's Cabin* in 1852—the most effective and controversial anti-slavery book ever published—and the Fugitive Slave Act of 1850—which required the federal government to enforce the return of fugitive slaves to their masters—kept the coals smoldering until the day Fillmore left the White House.

In foreign affairs, President Fillmore is best remembered as the president who opened Japan to the United States by sending Commodore Matthew C. Perry's expedition to that faraway Asian country. Although Perry did not reach Japan until Fillmore left office, the plans were drawn while Fillmore was at the helm.

Fast Fact

When Millard Fillmore visited Great Britain in 1855, Oxford University offered him an honorary degree. Fillmore refused to accept it saying, "I had not the advantage of a classical education and no man should, in my judgment, accept a degree he cannot read."

(Source: Robert J. Rayback. *Millard Fillmore: Biography of a President,*1959.)

Post-presidential Years

After Fillmore failed to win renomination in 1852, he retired. His support of the Fugitive Slave Bill significantly hurt his chances of renomination. After traveling extensively both in the United States and in Europe, Fillmore accepted the presidential nomination of the American Party, better known as the Know-Nothing Party, for the 1856 election. According to Elbert B. Smith who wrote *The Presidencies of Zachary Taylor and Millard Fillmore,* Fillmore supported the American Party because he was convinced that the Republican Party, which had evolved from the Whig Party, was a sectional party, which would divide the country. In the 1856 election Fillmore garnered 21 percent of the popular vote but only carried Maryland in electoral votes.

After losing the election, Fillmore returned to Buffalo, New York; he married Caroline McIntosh in 1858. In his retirement Fillmore was active in Buffalo's civic affairs where he was the first president of the Buffalo Historical Society, first chancellor of the University of Buffalo, and a trustee of the local library.

On February 13, 1874, he suffered a stroke and then a second stroke on February 26. He died on March 8. He was 74 years old.

The Millard Fillmore Administration

Brought to the White House by the death of his predecessor, Zachary Taylor, Millard Fillmore suddenly had to face the slavery issue as president. He conscientiously sought to avert civil war by strongly supporting the Compromise of 1850. Believing that the United States should become more involved in Asia, he authorized Commodore Matthew C. Perry's famous voyage to Japan.

Administration

Administration Dates
July 10, 1850–March 4, 1853

Vice President
None

Cabinet
Secretary of State
John M. Clayton (1849–50)
Daniel Webster (1850–52)
Edward Everett (1852–53)

Secretary of the Treasury
William M. Meredith (1849–50)
Thomas Corwin (1850–53)

Secretary of War
George W. Crawford (1849–50)
Charles M. Conrad (1850–53)

Attorney General
Reverdy Johnson (1849–50)
John J. Crittenden (1850–53)

Secretary of the Navy
William B. Preston (1849–50)
William A. Graham (1850–52)
John P. Kennedy (1852–53)

Postmaster General
Jacob Collamer (1849–50)
Nathan K. Hall (1850–52)
Samuel D. Hubbard (1852–53)

Secretary of the Interior
Thomas Ewing (1849–50)
Thomas M. T. McKennan (1850)
Alexander H. H. Stuart (1850–53)

Fillmore Becomes President

Campaign of 1848

In 1848 the Whigs nominated Zachary Taylor for president. The Taylor camp's choice for vice president was Abbott Lawrence, a Massachusetts textile manufacturer. However, on the second ballot Millard Fillmore, backed by several delegates who had supported Kentucky senator Henry Clay's bid for the top spot on the ticket, won the vice presidential nomination. In the weeks that followed Fillmore reached out to assure Taylor of his wholehearted support. Apparently Fillmore was successful for shortly before the election on October 2, 1848, Taylor (as quoted in Grayson) wrote:

> Attempts no doubt will continue to be made to sow distrust and discord between us but . . . all efforts to place either of us in a false attitude towards the other, or to lessen the mutual confidence and support which strongly unite us, will have no countenance ever at my hands.

As a New Yorker, Fillmore was somewhat suspect concerning his stand on slavery. Fillmore assured southerners that while he did not favor slavery, he strongly felt that the Constitution protected slavery in the states where that institution existed. In November the Taylor-Fillmore ticket won the 1848 election. The Taylor administration was marked by his strong support for states's rights, whereby the issue of slavery would be left for the individual states to decide. He was opposed to the compromise that was proposed that would satisfy both the North and the South. Taylor died on July 9, 1850, in the midst of a major congressional debate over slavery (*See also,* Domestic Issues). It was left to Millard Fillmore, who was sworn in as president on July 10, 1850, to lead the nation through this crisis.

The Campaign of 1852

In 1852 President Fillmore was a reluctant candidate. In 1851 he indicated privately that he had no desire to serve another term. He preferred to return to his Buffalo, New York, home. The Whig Party was divided with the southern Whigs favoring the nomination of President Fillmore or Senator Daniel Webster from Massachusetts. Both Webster and Fillmore had backed the Compromise of 1850. However, as president, Fillmore sought to enforce the Fugitive Slave Act, which had evolved from the Compromise of 1850 (*See also,* Domestic Issues).

Fillmore's support for the Fugitive Slave Act, which required the federal government to enforce the return of fugitive slaves to their masters, antagonized individuals like Senator William H. Seward of New York, who adamantly opposed slavery. Seward strongly objected to the renomination of Fillmore. Other northern Whigs followed Seward who not only opposed the Fugitive Slave Act but had also opposed the Compromise of 1850. These Whigs supported Winfield Scott, a Mexican War hero just as Zachary Taylor had been. If those favoring Webster or Fillmore had united it seems likely that the reluctant Fillmore would have been nominated.

At the Whig convention held in June, Fillmore led on the first ballot with 133 votes. Scott had 131 votes and Webster had 29 votes. It was not until the 53rd ballot that Scott was nominated. At one point Fillmore supporters offered to throw their support to Webster if Webster could muster at least 40 votes. Webster never gained that minimum. As the balloting continued, support for Fillmore began to erode, and when finally the Webster delegates switched to Scott, Scott gained the nomination.

Fillmore's Advisers

When Fillmore became president, he knew that Taylor's cabinet was fundamentally opposed to what became known as the Compromise of 1850 being worked on by Massachusetts senator Daniel Webster. Upon taking office he accepted the resignations of all seven members of the Taylor cabinet and appointed his own members, who would not interfere with the compromise efforts.

Fillmore's key advisers were members of his cabinet, with Secretary of State Daniel Webster being closest to the president. Another well-known cabinet member was Attorney General John J. Crittenden who had served in the U.S. Senate and as attorney general in the William Henry Harrison and John Tyler administrations. Crittenden promoted compromise between the North and the South on slavery.

Fillmore and Congress

Millard Fillmore presided over the Thirty-first Congress, which was sitting when he took office, and the Thirty-second Congress, which was elected in 1850. In both of these sessions the Democratic Party had the majority. President Fillmore had some political experience, so even though he was a Whig, he was able to work with the opposition party. The best example of this was the enactment of the Compromise of 1850. Another evidence of bipartisanship is the fact that he is one of the few presidents who never exercised the veto. Some of the congressional leaders with whom Fillmore had to work included Henry Clay of Kentucky, Jefferson Davis of Mississippi, Stephen A. Douglas of Illinois, and Thaddeus Stevens of Pennsylvania.

Fillmore and the Judiciary

President Fillmore appointed one person to the Supreme Court, Benjamin R. Curtis of Massachusetts. When the famous *Dred Scott* case was decided in 1857, rendering the Missouri Compromise unconstitutional, Curtis wrote one of the two dissenting opinions (*See also,* James Buchanan Administration). Curtis also later served as President Andrew Johnson's chief defense counsel when Johnson was impeached.

The most significant Supreme Court decision handed down during Fillmore's presidency was *Cooley v. Board of Wardens of Port of Philadelphia* (1851). In this case Justice Curtis ruled that where commerce was strictly national or interstate the federal government had exclusive jurisdiction (the authority to apply the law), but that in local commerce a state legislates in the absence of any federal regulations.

At a time when states's rights was becoming a significant issue, the Cooley case reaffirmed the right of the national government "to regulate commerce with foreign nations and among the several states," as stated in the Constitution. At the same time it recognized the right of a state to regulate commerce within its own boundaries if not prohibited by the Constitution.

This case also became significant when later it came time to introduce legislation regulating the railroads. The federal government assumed the right to enact such legislation. In 1887 the Congress passed and President Grover Cleveland signed the Interstate Commerce Act, establishing the Interstate Commerce Commission.

Changes in the U.S. Government

The Compromise of 1850 (*See also,* Domestic Issues) brought a number of changes to the United States. Most significantly, California was admitted to the union as the 31st state on September 9, 1850. The Compromise also led to the enactment of a Fugitive Slave Law that for the first time made the federal government responsible for the recovery of runaway slaves. On March 2, 1853, the Washington Territory was created out of the northern part of what was then Oregon.

Domestic Issues

The decade of the 1850s saw the South prospering as cotton prices went higher. The North also enjoyed good times economically. For example, the production of Pennsylvania anthracite coal increased from 4.1 million tons in 1850 to 10.9 million tons in 1860. Pig iron foundries turned out 563,000 tons in 1850; the production rose to 821,000 tons in 1860. Canals were giving way to railroads, which opened the prairies to profitable settlement. Wages were rising along with production. Inventions such as Cyrus McCormick's reaper for harvesting wheat and Eli Whitney's cotton gin helped increase agricultural production. The telegraph as well as the railroads were linking the United States.

The slavery issue was at the forefront of political debate when Fillmore became president. The rapid westward expansion of the United States presented many questions over whether slavery should be extended. Many northerners wanted the west to be closed to slavery, and there were many who vocally called for the abolition of slavery throughout the United States. Proponents of slavery in the South, who feared the growing anti-slavery sentiment in the North, wanted to increase the political and

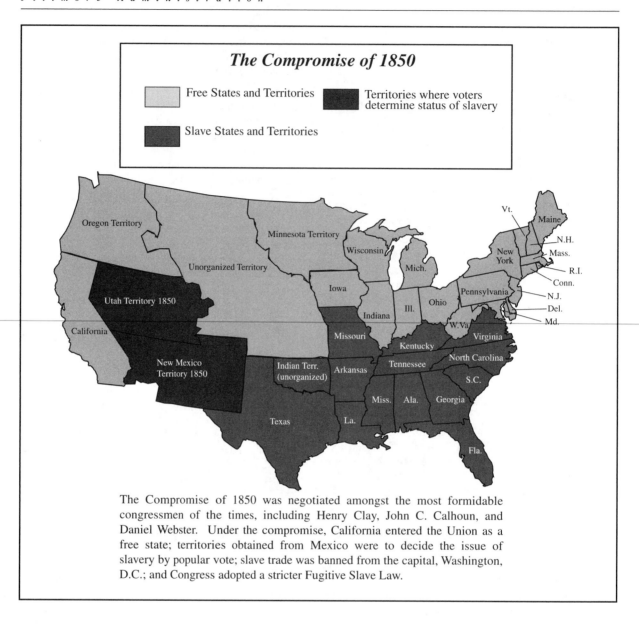

The Compromise of 1850

Free States and Territories

Slave States and Territories

Territories where voters determine status of slavery

Oregon Territory

Minnesota Territory

Wisconsin

Mich.

Vt.

Maine

N.H.

Mass.

New York

R.I.

Conn.

N.J.

Del.

Md.

Unorganized Territory

Iowa

Ill.

Ohio

Pennsylvania

Utah Territory 1850

Indiana

W.Va

California

Missouri

Kentucky

Virginia

New Mexico Territory 1850

Indian Terr. (unorganized)

Arkansas

Tennessee

North Carolina

S.C.

Miss.

Ala.

Georgia

Texas

La.

Fla.

The Compromise of 1850 was negotiated amongst the most formidable congressmen of the times, including Henry Clay, John C. Calhoun, and Daniel Webster. Under the compromise, California entered the Union as a free state; territories obtained from Mexico were to decide the issue of slavery by popular vote; slave trade was banned from the capital, Washington, D.C.; and Congress adopted a stricter Fugitive Slave Law.

economic clout of the slave-holding sections of the United States, to better protect their "property" and their way of life.

The Compromise of 1850

When Millard Fillmore assumed office on July 10, 1850, the United States had only recently won the Mexican War (1846–48) and taken over a large tract of land called the Mexican Cession. The all-consuming issue when Fillmore became president concerned the status of slavery in this new acquisition, which included the present states of Arizona, Nevada, California and Utah and parts of New Mexico, Colorado, and Wyoming.

With the United States growing so rapidly, the South wanted as much territory opened to slavery as possible, while anti-slavery advocates in the North wanted as little as possible. Early in 1850 Kentucky senator Henry Clay had advanced a number of proposals that were designed to resolve the question of slavery in this new territory. Under one umbrella called the Omnibus Bill, resolutions concerned with the organization of the Mexican Cession were presented to the Senate by a select committee on May 8, 1850. A second bill called for prohibition of slavery in the District of Columbia. The Omnibus Bill encountered stormy weather when leaders like Senator William H. Seward from New York, Senator Jefferson Davis from Mississippi, and President

Zachary Taylor opposed the measure. Northerners such as Seward felt the bill gave too much to the slave states, while southerners such as Davis wanted greater protections for slavery than the bill offered, and for months Congress struggled to reach an agreement.

Although his predecessor, Zachary Taylor, had opposed Clay's bill, when Millard Fillmore became president after Taylor's death he made it known that he favored Clay's resolutions. With the weight of the executive branch now on his side, Clay and his supporters began to see light at the end of the tunnel. From September 9 through September 20, 1850, five laws were enacted that came to be called the Compromise of 1850. Under this legislation California was admitted into the Union as a free state, a concession to the North. Utah and New Mexico were organized as territories with the understanding that the residents in these territories would decide the status of slavery when each territory applied for statehood. This idea, known as popular sovereignty, gave both sections hope that they could gain control of the territories. Texas agreed to relinquish its claims on territory in New Mexico, in exchange for $10 million. In a concession to the South, a federal Fugitive Slave Act was passed, which made it easier for slaveowners to recover slaves who had fled to freedom in the North. There was also a compromise on slavery in the nation's capital—slavery remained legal there, but the trading of slaves within Washington, D.C. became illegal.

The Compromise of 1850 provided both sides with some of what they wanted, enough so that the bills passed, but neither the North nor the South was truly satisfied. The South felt vulnerable to political action by the North, with its higher population, where many still called for the abolition of slavery. While the Compromise of 1850 ended congressional debate on the slavery issue, the public debate was far from over.

Foreign Issues

With the acquisition of the Mexican Cession, land acquired after the Mexican War (1846–48), the boundaries of the continental United States expanded to about what they are today. The borders of the United States extended across the continent from the Atlantic Ocean to the Pacific Ocean. The successful war had demonstrated the strength of the United States, and encouraged Americans to seek greater opportunities and national influence abroad. Increased trade with the Far East was of particular interest. At the same time, however, the United States had long followed a policy of keeping out of the often violent international politics of the European powers.

Thus, the Fillmore administration tried to encourage foreign commerce while the United States remained at a distance from the political affairs of other nations. Fillmore in his first annual message to Congress stated that it was "an imperative duty" of the United States "not to interfere in the government of internal policy of other nations."

President Fillmore Sends Commodore Matthew C. Perry to Japan

For almost two and a half centuries Japan had been closed to foreigners except for very restricted trade with the Dutch. With Americans desiring increased foreign trade, President Fillmore in 1852 authorized an expedition to Japan under the command of Matthew C. Perry. The goals of this expedition included the opening of Japan to U.S. commerce, an arrangement whereby protection would be afforded U.S. seamen and property involved in shipwrecks along the Japanese shoreline, and an agreement whereby Americans engaged in foreign trade could obtain provisions, water, and fuel in Japan.

Although Perry did not arrive in Tokyo, Japan, until after Fillmore left office, he did carry a letter from President Fillmore with proposals he wanted the Japanese to consider. In 1854 the Japanese signed a treaty opening Japan to U.S. trade. The Japanese also agreed to provide care for shipwrecked U.S. sailors and to furnish supplies to Americans as they were needed.

Portugal

The Fillmore administration can be credited with settling amicably a lingering conflict with Portugal. An agreement was reached with Portugal settling U.S. claims stemming from the War of 1812 when the British had been able to capture a U.S. ship called the *General Armstrong,* because the Portuguese had allowed the British to seize the ship in Portuguese waters. In 1828 the United States and Portugal had another encounter when the Portuguese took money from the U.S. ship *Shepherd,* charging that the captain had taken money illegally from Portuguese soil. Portuguese courts found the captain innocent, but the money was never returned. When Zachary Taylor became president he was determined to collect the money and settle the matter of the *General Armstrong.* The Portuguese foreign minister rejected the *General Armstrong* claims, but promised to look into the *Shepherd* incident. Even though Portugal decided to pay everything but the *Armstrong* claim, Taylor still recalled James Clay, the U.S. representative in Portugal.

When Fillmore became president, Secretary of State Daniel Webster and the Portuguese minister in Washington signed an agreement on February 26, 1851, whereby Portugal promised to pay all the claims except those involving the *Armstrong.* It was agreed that France's Louis Napoleon would arbitrate the *Armstrong* claims. On November 30, 1852, Louis Napoleon rejected the U.S. claim thus ending the controversy.

The Fillmore Administration Legacy

Although President Fillmore fervently hoped that the Compromise of 1850 would permanently settle the conflict over slavery, by the time he left office it was apparent that it had not. The publication of Harriet Beecher Stowe's anti-slavery novel *Uncle Tom's Cabin* in 1852 and flagrant violations of the Fugitive Slave Act in the North did much to stir passions in both the North and the South. Eventually the issue was to be settled by a tragic war between the two sections.

Lasting Impact

Some would argue that Millard Fillmore was an unsuccessful president because the Compromise of 1850 failed to provide a lasting solution to the slavery issue. However, the compromise did delay the eventual conflict and thus allowed the North to strengthen itself so that when the war came, the North was better prepared.

Fillmore revered the U.S. Constitution. He believed that it was his obligation to enforce the laws of the land even though he might not agree with a particular law. This he did when he enforced the Fugitive Slave Act, even though this was often unpopular. He demonstrated that if the United States is to be a nation of laws and not one of chaos, all laws had to be enforced equally.

In foreign affairs he demonstrated some vision when he authorized the Perry expedition to Japan. He seemed to sense that the day was coming when the United States would significantly benefit from increased commerce with the world and particularly with Asia.

Sources

Encyclopedia of World Biography. Vol. 5. Detroit: Gale Research, 1998.

Grayson, Benson L. *The Unknown President: The Administration of President Millard Fillmore.* Washington, D.C.: University Press of America, 1981.

Griffis, William E. *Millard Fillmore: Constructive Statesman, Defender of the Constitution, President of the United States.* Ithaca, N.Y.: Andrus and Church, 1915.

Potter, David M. *The Impending Crisis, 1848–1861.* New York: Harper and Row, 1976.

Rayback, Robert J. *Millard Fillmore: Biography of a President.* Buffalo, N.Y.: Buffalo Historical Society, 1959.

Smith, Elbert B. *The Presidencies of Zachary Taylor and Millard Fillmore.* Lawrence, Kans.: University Press of Kansas, 1988.

Further Readings

Boller, Paul F. *Presidential Anecdotes.* New York: Oxford University Press, 1981.

Hamilton, Holman. *Prologue to Conflict: The Crisis and Compromise of 1850.* Lexington, Ky.: University of Kentucky Press, 1964.

Morison, Samuel E. *"Old Bruin": Commodore Matthew C. Perry, 1794–1858.* Boston: Little, Brown, 1967

Nevins, Allan. *Ordeal of the Union.* 2 vols. New York: Charles Scribner's Sons, 1947.

Van Deusen, Glyndon. *William Henry Seward.* New York: Oxford University Press, 1967.

Pierce Administration

Biography

Franklin Pierce, whose father served in the American Revolution (1775–83), inherited a devotion to Jeffersonian principles of the sovereign power of the individual states. In his early career as both an attorney and a politician, Pierce remained loyal to these foundations of the Democratic Party, as popularized by President Andrew Jackson. His loyalty included a commitment to the constitutionality of slavery, and his support for that institution during his presidency led to a deterioration of the relationship between the North and South.

Early Life

Franklin Pierce was born in a log home on November 23, 1804, among the hills of Hillsborough County, New Hampshire. Franklin's father, General Benjamin Pierce, was a veteran of the American Revolution (1775–83) who was active in local politics. Anna Kendrick Pierce, Franklin's mother and Benjamin's second wife, was known as a lively and tender soul. The seventh of his father's nine children, Franklin enjoyed a rural boyhood fishing and swimming in the ponds and creeks of backwoods New Hampshire.

Education

As a boy Pierce studied at Hancock Academy and Francestown Academy, both in New Hampshire. At the

Full name: Franklin Pierce
Popular name: Young Hickory of the Granite Hills

Personal Information:
Born: November 23, 1804
Birthplace: Hillsborough County, New Hampshire
Died: October 8, 1869
Death place: Concord, New Hampshire
Burial place: Old North Cemetery, Concord, New Hampshire
Religion: Episcopalian
Spouse: Jane Means Appleton (m. 1834)
Children: Franklin; Frank Robert; Benjamin
Education: Bowdoin College, Brunswick, Maine, 1824
Occupation: Attorney; politician; soldier
Political Party: Democratic Party
Age at Inauguration: 48 years

Franklin Pierce. *(The Library of Congress.)*

Career

After graduating from Bowdoin College, Pierce studied law under Levi Woodbury, who was secretary of the Treasury under presidents Andrew Jackson and Martin Van Buren, and practiced law for a few years. Pierce then joined the Democratic Party and served in the New Hampshire legislature from 1829 to 1833, the U.S. House of Representatives from 1833 to 1837, and the U.S. Senate from 1837 to 1842. Pierce, who was an alcoholic, resigned as senator in 1842 for the sake of his wife Jane, who hated politics, and also to avoid the social pressures to drink.

In 1842 the Pierces returned to New Hampshire, where Franklin opened a law practice in Concord and became involved in local politics. After declining President James Polk's invitation to serve as U.S. attorney general, Pierce served from 1846 to 1848 as brigadier general in the Mexican War (1846–48).

Presidency

In recognition of his loyalty to the Democratic Party and in the absence of a strong candidate with widespread appeal, Pierce won the Democratic nomination for president and the election in 1852. Racked with self-doubt from the recent death of his son Benjamin, Pierce delegated most tasks to his cabinet and was an ineffective leader. President Pierce supported slavery as a property right protected by the U.S. Constitution. His administration is remembered for civil unrest in the territory of Kansas, where pro- and antislavery forces clashed over whether to extend the so-called "peculiar institution" of slavery in the United States.

age of 16 he entered Bowdoin College in Brunswick, Maine. When after two years Pierce learned he was ranked at the bottom of his class, he resolved to study each day between midnight and four A.M., thereby graduating fifth in a class of 13 students.

Family Life

In 1834 Franklin Pierce married Jane Means Appleton, the daughter of a Congregational minister and former Bowdoin College president. Although Jane Pierce gave her husband strong social connections, her Calvinist, Federalist upbringing made her disdain Pierce's Democratic politics. Her poor health added to the family's difficulties, but Jane and Franklin loved each other deeply and got along very well.

Tragedy haunted the Pierces as they lost each of their three children. Their first born, Franklin, died at just three days old and Frank Robert at age four. Benjamin, their last child whom Jane Pierce doted upon, was crushed to death before his parents' eyes at age 11 in a train wreck, only a few months before Pierce's inauguration in 1853. Jane and Franklin were physically unharmed, but the loss of their only remaining son destroyed what was left of Jane's mental and physical health and may have crippled Franklin's confidence.

Post-presidential Years

The first elected president to fail to be renominated by his party, Pierce retired to Concord, New Hampshire, in 1857 to care for his ailing wife. He continued to follow politics, denounced the abolitionists (those who lobbied for the abolition of slavery), and became depressed at the election of President Abraham Lincoln and the start of the American Civil War (1861–65). Jane Pierce died in December 1863, and Franklin Pierce passed away, largely to be forgotten by history, on October 8, 1869.

The Franklin Pierce Administration

Franklin Pierce's presidency began three years after the Whig and Democratic Parties reached a legislative compromise in 1850 to set aside the divisive debate over slavery. Economic interests and a minority of enlightened moral objectors, however, were destined to reopen the question. The Pierce administration helped reignite the debate by enforcing the compromise's Fugitive Slave Act, which required the return of escaped slaves to their owners in the South and by supporting the Kansas-Nebraska Act of 1854, which repealed the Missouri Compromise of 1820 (*See also*, James Monroe Administration). Thus, Pierce's administration contributed to the further deterioration of relations between North and South.

Pierce Becomes President

The Campaign of 1852

In the mid-1800s, the Whigs and the Democrats were the two major political parties in the United States. Whigs generally wanted a federal government that actively supported internal improvement through the use of a national bank and paper money. Democrats generally opposed federally funded improvements and supported states's rights. As both parties had pro- and anti-slavery constituents, the federal government sought to patch up the most troublesome aspects of the slavery question with legislation called the Compromise of 1850. Supported by Senator Stephen Douglas, a Democrat from Illinois, and signed into law by Whig President Millard Fillmore, the most controversial part of the compromise was the Fugitive Slave Act, which set up a mechanism for returning runaway slaves to their owners. This was becoming an important issue since abolitionist mobs (those advocating an end to slavery) would sometimes break into jails to liberate the runaway slaves awaiting extradition.

In the temporary spirit of national unity that followed the Compromise of 1850, winning the election of 1852 required nominating a candidate who was not known for strong positions and would support the Compromise. On its 49th ballot the Democratic National Convention nominated Franklin Pierce, a handsome, charming man who had been loyal to Democratic politics and who believed that slavery was a property right protected by the U.S. Constitution. In an undeserved comparison to Andrew Jackson, who had been called Old Hickory, Pierce received the nickname Young Hickory of the Granite Hills.

Despite a fairly close popular vote between Pierce and Whig candidate Winfield Scott, Pierce received 254 of 296 electoral votes and was inaugurated on March 4, 1853. Pierce was the first and only president to affirm rather than swear the oath of office, a choice he made on religious grounds based on Matthew 5:34-7, which enjoins the reader to use moderate language and not to swear.

Administration

Administration Dates
March 4, 1853–March 4, 1857

Vice President
William Rufus De Vane King (1853)

Cabinet
Secretary of State
William L. Marcy (1853–57)

Secretary of the Treasury
Thomas Corwin (1850–53)
James Guthrie (1853–57)

Secretary of War
Charles M. Conrad (1850–53)
Jefferson F. Davis (1853–57)

Attorney General
Caleb Cushing (1853–57)

Secretary of the Navy
John P. Kennedy (1852–53)
James C. Dobbin (1853–57)

Postmaster General
Samuel D. Hubbard (1852–53)
James Campbell (1853–57)

Secretary of the Interior
Alexander H. H. Stuart (1850–53)
Robert McClelland (1853–57)

Democrats Nominate James Buchanan in 1856

Franklin Pierce was the only president elected to office who sought but did not receive renomination by his party. After watching four years of Pierce's ineffective leadership, civil disaster in Kansas, and the U.S. growing interest in the new Republican Party, which rallied around opposition to slavery, the Democrats nominated James Buchanan, a party loyalist who served under Pierce as U.S. minister to the Court of St. James in England. Buchanan won the national election on a platform that stressed the importance of maintaining national

Biography:

Stephen Arnold Douglas

Congressman; Politician (1813–61) Whatever Stephen A. Douglas lacked in stature, he made up for in aggressiveness, audacity, and in a consuming political ambition. Douglas taught himself with borrowed books and, at age 27, was the youngest judge ever to sit on the Illinois Supreme Court. Beginning in his early thirties, Douglas occupied a seat first in the U.S. House of Representatives and later in the Senate. It was as a senator, during President Franklin Pierce's administration, that Douglas drafted the legislation that would both mark and upset his career. Modern historian Allan Nevins called Douglas's Kansas-Nebraska Act, rescinding the Missouri Compromise of 1820, "the worst Pandora's box in our history." When President Pierce, with his signature, put the act into law, he sparked a small, but bloody, civil war in the territory of Kansas. Overnight, Americans were referring to the new territory as Bleeding Kansas. Douglas returned home to campaign for his job, this time against a rising star. The campaign debates between the opposed Abraham Lincoln and Stephen Douglas are famous today. Douglas was ardently opposed to the rights of African Americans to citizenship and attacked as "monstrous heresy" Lincoln's insistence that, "the Negro and the white man are made equal by the Declaration of Independence and by Divine Providence." Douglas won reelection to the Senate, but soon found himself running against Lincoln again, this time for the presidency. Despite their differences, Douglas said to Republicans who had nominated Lincoln for the 1860 presidential ticket, "Gentlemen, you have nominated a very able and

a very honest man." This time, it was Lincoln who was victorious. Although Douglas first sought to effect a compromise between the Southern and Northern states, after the Confederacy attacked the Union's Fort Sumter in 1861, Douglas publicly supported Lincoln's efforts to restore the United States through force.

unity in the face of Republican agitation over the slavery question.

Pierce's Advisers

Franklin Pierce was the first president who appointed a new cabinet after his election, and then retained each member during his entire administration. This was in light of the fact that Pierce's goal was to award all factions of the Democratic Party, who were often at odds with each other, with important positions. Once in place, the cabinet ran the executive branch with little interference from Pierce, who lapsed into a sort of paralysis in part due to the trauma of witnessing his child die in a train wreck shortly before his inauguration. For whatever reason, Pierce proved to be incapable of executive decision.

William L. Marcy, Pierce's secretary of state, was a Democrat who remained loyal to the party when the antislavery Democratic "Barnburners" of 1848 left to join the Free Soilers, a small rural party opposed to slavery. Marcy oversaw the efforts of U.S. diplomats to expand U.S. territory and international trade during Pierce's administration. One of Marcy's most memorable actions was the "dress circular" of June 1, 1853, by which he encouraged all U.S. diplomats to wear "the simple dress of an American citizen" rather than the host country's formal garb.

Attorney General Caleb Cushing was a former Whig who supported the foreign expansionist goals of the Young America sect of the Democratic Party. (The "Young Americans" rebelled against the leadership of older party members. They demanded that the Democratic Party adopt policies that would help spread U.S. democracy throughout the globe.) Cushing wrote daily editorials for the *Washington Union* and supported the property rights of slave owners. He also backed the right of southern postmasters to exclude abolitionist (or antislavery) materials from the mails.

Jefferson Davis, who would head the Confederate states when they split from the Union during the American Civil War (1861–65), presided over the War Department in Pierce's cabinet at a time when the United States's sole military conflict was with the American Indians. Davis also oversaw efforts to determine the location of a railroad to the U.S. West Coast (linking this obviously internal improvement to military affairs), which he hoped would be in the South to the benefit of southern economic interests.

Postmaster General James Campbell, a Catholic with only local political experience, focused on eliminating fraud and the two million dollar annual deficit in his department. He won congressional support for a system for registering mail and using postage stamps. Secretary James Guthrie sought to inject public integrity into the Department of the Treasury as he worked to reduce the national debt. In an era of frontier expansion and growing industrial development, Secretary of the Interior Robert McClelland was overwhelmed with managing land, American Indian, pension, and patent issues. Secretary of the Navy James C. Dobbin took a small navy with low morale and convinced Congress to approve spending for six new steam frigates and five smaller sloops-of-war.

Pierce and Congress

Pierce served as president during the Thirty-third and the Thirty-fourth Congresses, in which the Democrats had a slight majority—a fact that renders curious Pierce's almost total lack of accomplishment. In fact, it was Congress that sold Pierce on the only major legislation passed during his presidency—the Kansas-Nebraska Act of 1854 (*See also,* Domestic Issues).

During his relatively inactive presidency Pierce exercised the veto power nine times, mostly to block federal spending for internal improvements, including a bill sponsored by prominent social reformer Dorothea Dix to use 12 million acres of public land to fund institutions for the indigent mentally ill. As Pierce lost popularity in the second half of his presidency, the Thirty-fourth Congress overrode his veto five times.

Pierce and the Judiciary

The Supreme Court played no important role in the federal government during the Pierce administration. Although federal commissioners tried some cases under the Fugitive Slave Act of 1850, which required the return of escaped slaves to their owners in the South, the Supreme Court did not announce its *Dred Scot* decision to uphold the constitutionality of slavery until days after Pierce left office. During this time Pierce made only one appointment to the Supreme Court, Associate Justice John Archibald Campbell of Alabama on March 22, 1853.

Changes in the U.S. Government

Pierce delivered on his promise to govern with integrity and economy. Only military spending grew considerably during Pierce's presidency. In addition to the departmental reforms made by his cabinet (*See also,* Pierce's Advisers), Pierce supported an 1853 act of Congress that limited the total number of clerks in federal civilian service and standardized their pay. Another law introduced the civil service examination. Civil servants were often selected as a political payback. This law helped to ensure that clerks were qualified for the positions to which they were nominated.

Domestic Issues

During Pierce's presidency the United States still was more a collection of states, regions, and territories than a nation. Local rather than national issues dominated the peoples' attention. Although farming was a way of life for many Americans, the Jeffersonian ideal of a country dotted with small, self-sufficient, family-run farms was being swallowed up by the commercialization of agriculture. The gathering steam of the Industrial Revolution was responsible for this trend, as well as for the cities' higher material standards of living, unsafe working conditions, and pollution.

Waves of immigrants came from Ireland and Germany, giving rise to a strong anti-Catholic sentiment among the largely Protestant American people. Americans and immigrants alike continued to settle in unsettled territories in the West. They traveled as far as the rapidly growing city of Chicago, Illinois, by train, but the country still had not succeeded in linking the coasts by rail.

Slavery was the most important national issue of the day, in spite of the politicians' effort to sweep it under the rug with the Compromise of 1850. The compromise had been a series of measures meant to resolve the slavery issue and forestall civil war (*See also,* Zachary Taylor Administration). Except for the abolitionists, who opposed slavery on moral grounds, division over the question was economic, pitting wealthy southerners against northerners who feared that the nation's wage labor system was in jeopardy as slavery spread into new territories and even threatened to overrun the North. Thus, many of the northerners who opposed slavery did so not out of sympathy for slaves but out of fear of the cheapening of wage labor. The anxiety that accompanied the debate over slavery produced new political phenomena, such as the appearance during the 1854 midterm elections of a new political party—the American, or Know-Nothing party—which ran on an antislavery, anti-Catholic, and antiforeigner platform.

The Kansas-Nebraska Act of 1854

The Missouri Compromise of 1820 had provided that the westward extension of the southern boundary of Missouri would divide freedom and slavery in territories being established in the west. By 1852 settlement of lands in the Nebraska Territory, which stretched westward from Missouri to the Rocky Mountains and northward to

Biography:

Dorothea Lynde Dix

Nurse; Teacher; Reformer (1802–1887) At just 12 years of age, young Dorothea Lynde Dix escaped a bleak, poverty-stricken home filled with loneliness and despair, and made her way to Boston Massachusetts. Before she was 20, Dix opened an academy for daughters of the well-to-do and filled her time conducting a free school for poor children. Her pure love of teaching made her schools a success. Illness forced Dix to briefly abandon full-time teaching. When she recovered, she volunteered to teach Sunday school at a Massachusetts jail where she was horrified to learn that the cells of the insane prisoners had no heating, even in the coldest weather. This encounter sparked a lifelong crusade beginning with a two-year tour throughout Massachusetts, during which time she took notes on the deplorable conditions she found in jails, workhouses, almshouses, and hospitals. In her controversial, but successful reform-winning address to the Massachusetts legislature, Dix wrote, "I proceed, gentlemen, briefly to

call your attention to the present state of insane persons confined within the Commonwealth in cages, closets, cellars, pens; chained, naked, beaten with rods, and lashed into obedience." In 1848 Dix took her fight nationwide, successfully passing an appropriations bill for asylums through both houses of Congress. Her delight was short-lived as the bill was quickly vetoed by President Franklin Pierce. Discouraged, Dix continued her campaign overseas where she effected reforms in almost a dozen countries. Except for her dedicated service as a hospital nurse during the Civil War (1861–65), Dix continued her reform efforts in the United States until her death.

Canada, created both the need and the opportunity for territorial legislation. Stephen A. Douglas, Democratic senator from Illinois with land interests in the West, sponsored legislation that would create two territories and ultimately states Nebraska and Kansas. To allow slavery in Kansas, which was north of the boundary set by the Missouri Compromise, the bill called for repeal of the compromise. When the bill passed in May 1854, northerners saw it as proof that the relative minority of wealthy slave owners in the South controlled the government in Washington, D.C.

Bleeding Kansas

After Pierce signed the Kansas-Nebraska Act into law in 1854, many pro-slave Missourians, called "border ruffians" because of their unruly behavior, crossed over into Kansas and illegally voted to elect a pro-slavery territorial government in Kansas headed by governor Andrew H. Reeder. Antislavery interests from New England and other northern states responded by founding the New England Emigrant Aid Company and recruiting free-soil, or antislavery, farmers to establish an antislavery government. Their supporters in the northeast outfitted them for the trek west and also furnished them with rifles, which they called "Beecher's Bibles" after the New York abolitionist Henry Ward Beecher. The pro-slave "border ruffians" were a violent bunch, but so were the anti-slave forces. John Brown was a fanatical abolitionist who in 1855 used a broad sword to massacre five pro-slavery settlers at Pottawatomie Creek, Kansas. On Jan-

uary 24, 1856, President Pierce sent a special message to Congress in which he recognized the pro-slavery government in Kansas. The violence that erupted between the two factions led Americans to refer to the territory as Bleeding Kansas.

In the summer of 1856 Free-Soil senator Charles Sumner of Massachusetts, who had fought against slavery since entering the Senate in 1851, delivered a scathing speech to the Senate. He accused the Pierce administration of trying to force slavery on the territory of Kansas and personally attacked many southern senators, including Andrew Pickens Butler of South Carolina. Two days later as Sumner sat at his desk in the Senate, a relative of Senator Butler, Congressman Preston S. Brooks of South Carolina, attacked Sumner with a walking stick. Sumner fell to the ground bleeding from scalp wounds and was unable to return to active service until 1859. The incident marked the hostility between pro- and antislavery Americans.

The Garner Incident

Under the Fugitive Slave Act of 1850 all Americans were obliged to help return escaped slaves to captivity. A slave owner only had to make a written or oral claim of ownership to institute proceedings against an escaped slave. A federal commissioner then decided the facts and received a fee of $10 if he decided for the slave owner and $5 if he decided for the slave. The slave had no right to testify. Northerners resented this system, especially because of their forced participation in efforts to return slaves to captivity.

In early 1856 eight escaped slaves, including Margaret Garner and her three children, hid in Cincinnati, Ohio, from their Kentucky owners. One of their masters got an arrest warrant under the Fugitive Slave Act and found them in hiding. As federal officers approached, Margaret Garner cut her daughter's throat to prevent her return to slavery but was stopped before she could kill her two sons. Commissioner John L. Pendery returned the slaves to Kentucky, where their owner hid Garner from Kentucky authorities who wanted to return her to Cincinnati to face murder charges. While slave owners won this battle, the incident brought national attention to the slaves' desire to be free from captivity, contrary to the propaganda that slaves were content.

Foreign Issues

Except for continuing conflict with American Indians, the United States was not engaged in war during the Pierce administration. The country did, however, still face the usual international tensions resulting from competing commercial interests. In 1845 John L. O'Sullivan, editor of *United States Magazine and Domestic Review* had called for the "fulfillment of our manifest destiny to o'erspread the continent." This "manifest destiny" became a powerful idea for many Americans, and a rallying cry for the expansion of the United States. Pierce was swayed by this expression of imperialist ideology just as he was influenced by the "Young America" movement and tempted by several expansionist foreign policy goals (*See also,* Pierce's Advisers). A dizzying array of foreign policy objectives faced Pierce during his four years as president. He improvised some successes but was unable to win very many foreign policy victories. One sign of Pierce's ineffectiveness as a leader was that he was unable to impose order or strategic priority on the nation's expansionist appetites.

With Canada, which had begun to seize U.S. fishing boats in the early 1850s, the United States negotiated a treaty giving them expanded fishing rights off Canada's shores, and giving both countries duty free admission of certain raw materials. Negotiations Pierce began with Denmark resulted after Pierce left office in a treaty in which Denmark eliminated the tolls that it charged merchant ships in the Danish Sound.

Pierce's expansionist policy was less successful than his trade negotiations. The only major acquisition came under the Gadsden Purchase Treaty, by which the United States purchased 39 million acres of land from Mexico for $15 million, giving the continental United States the borders it has today. The only other acquisition was the 1856 possession of the Guano Islands south of Hawaii, which contained rich deposits of bird droppings that were valuable as fertilizer to U.S. farmers. Pierce's attempt to convince Congress to support the annexation of Hawaii itself was less successful, as southern senators refused to vote for the entry of another non-slave state. On the other hand, Commodore Matthew C. Perry's naval expedition to Japan forced its isolationist government to open two ports to U.S. ships (*See also,* Millard Fillmore Administration).

Cuba

In the most significant foreign policy activity of Pierce's foreign policy, the United States failed utterly in its attempt to annex Cuba, then a possession of Spain. As a strategic defensive position and one of the remaining vestiges of monarchy in the New World, Cuba had attracted the attention of presidential administrations dating back to Thomas Jefferson. U.S. efforts under Pierce to obtain Cuba included diplomacy by U.S. minister to Spain Pierre Soulé to purchase Cuba from Spain; the Ostend Manifesto, by which diplomats including James Buchanan, at that point minister to Great Britain, recommended war if Spain declined to sell Cuba; and private plans to assemble men and material to invade Cuba and take it by force, a tactic called "filibustering" that Pierce's administration tacitly condoned.

In this environment Spain and the United States reached the brink of war when Cuban officials seized a U.S. vessel, the *Black Warrior,* for a violation of harbor regulations. Pierce's cabinet called for war while Secretary of State William L. Marcy sent Minister Soulé to request compensation from Spain. Both efforts failed as Spain negotiated a private resolution with the owners of the *Black Warrior.* Ultimately relations with Spain cooled down, as did the United States's efforts to annex Cuba.

The Pierce Administration Legacy

Despite the disappointments of Pierce's foreign policy efforts, he was more successful in international affairs than in his domestic policies. At a time when the powerful nations in Europe still viewed the United States as an upstart country, Pierce's efforts to expand international trade and acquire new territory allowed the country to continue growing into a powerful presence in international affairs.

Further, perhaps Pierce's failures in domestic affairs were not entirely his fault. Although he received an overwhelming majority of electoral votes in 1852, he was a compromise candidate who was nominated on the Democratic convention's 49th ballot after its failure to agree on a strong leader. This was a built-in limitation to his chances of success. Pierce's failure to attain renomination in 1856, however, reflects the voters' impatience and embarrassment with the bloodshed in Kansas and the president's utter failure to take the lead on a single important piece of legislation.

Lasting Impact

Pierce's attempts to govern by cajoling and charming his critics clearly failed. Despite his capitulation to the South's agenda on the questions of the Kansas-Nebraska Act and the Fugitive Slave Act, extreme southern newspapers branded him a Free Soil Democrat, while Whig newspapers denounced his catering to the interests of southern slaveholders. Historians today generally agree that Pierce was an ineffective president, although it probably was impossible for any president to prevent the country from hurtling toward civil war.

Franklin Pierce's political fate illustrates the danger of failing to be in touch with popular opinion in the United States. Slave owners only comprised a minority of wealthy southerners. Pierce's insistence on protecting slavery under the Constitution while denying the government's ability to spend federal money for internal improvements mirrors ongoing debates over both civil rights for minorities and the desirable amount of federal involvement in the day-to-day affairs of Americans.

Pierce's failure to see the slavery debate smoldering beneath the Compromise of 1850 and his catering to the interests of southern slave owners contributed in 1854 to the birth of the Republican Party, which would elect Abraham Lincoln in 1860. The bloodshed in Kansas that Pierce allowed to take place can be seen as the first battle of the American Civil War (1861–65).

Sources

Anbinder, Tyler. *Nativism and Slavery: The Northern Know Nothings and the Politics of the 1850s.* New York: Oxford University Press, 1992.

Encyclopedia of World Biography. New York: McGraw-Hill, 1973.

Gara, Larry. *The Presidency of Franklin Pierce.* Lawrence, Kans.: University Press of Kansas, 1991.

Gienapp, William E. *The Origins of the Republican Party: 1852–1856.* New York: Oxford University Press, 1987.

Godwin, Parke, ed. *Political Essays.* New York: Dix, Edwards and Co., 1856.

Hawthorne, Nathaniel. *Life of Franklin Pierce.* Boston: Ticknor, Reed, and Fields, 1852.

Kane, Joseph Nathan. *Facts About the Presidents: A Compilation of Biographical and Historical Information.* 6th ed. New York: H. W. Wilson, 1993.

Miller, Barry O. "Political Influences on Foreign Relations: Pierce, Marcy, Buchanan, 1852–1856." Master's thesis, Pennsylvania State University, 1963.

Nichols, Roy Franklin. *Franklin Pierce: Young Hickory of the Granite Hills.* Rev. ed. Newtown: American Political Biography Press, 1993.

Ray, P. Orman. *The Repeal of the Missouri Compromise: Its Origins and Authorship.* Cleveland, Ohio: The Arthur H. Clark Company, 1909.

Further Readings

Carroll, Ann Ellis. *Review of Pierce's Administration Showing Its Only Popular Measure to Have Originated with the Executive of Millard Fillmore.* Boston: J. French and Co., 1856.

Craven, Avery. *The Coming of the Civil War.* Rev. ed. Chicago: University of Chicago Press, 1957.

———. *The Growth of Southern Nationalism, 1848–1861.* Baton Rouge, La.: Louisiana State University Press, 1953.

Nevins, Allan. *Ordeal of the Union.* 2 vols. New York: Charles Scribner's Sons, 1947.

Potter, David M. *The Impending Crisis, 1848–1861.* New York: Harper and Row, 1976.

Webster, Sydney. *Franklin Pierce and His Administration.* New York: D. Appleton, 1892.

Buchanan Administration

Biography

James Buchanan was an affable, conciliatory man who was a fixture in the Democratic Party of the mid-nineteenth century. As a legislator, Buchanan helped build the Democratic Party, and sided with southern politicians as tensions over slavery began to rise in the Congress. As a diplomat and secretary of state, Buchanan defended U.S. interests abroad, and played a major role in the establishment of the current boundaries of the United States. Buchanan was chosen for president because of his good relations with both northern and southern politicians and his ability to avoid controversy. He proved unable to defuse the ever-increasing tensions over slavery, however. His term in office is best remembered for the secession of the South from the Union, which led to the American Civil War (1861–65) only weeks after he left office.

Full name: James Buchanan
Popular name: The Old Public Functionary

Personal Information:
Born: April 23, 1791
Birthplace: Mercersburg, Pennsylvania
Died: June 1, 1868
Death place: Lancaster, Pennsylvania
Burial place: Woodward Cemetery, Lancaster, Pennsylvania
Religion: Presbyterian
Spouse: None
Education: Dickinson College, Carlisle, Pennsylvania
Occupation: Lawyer; politician; diplomat
Political Party: Democratic Party
Age at Inauguration: 65 years

Early Life

Buchanan was born on a farm near Mercersburg, Pennsylvania. His father, James Buchanan, Sr., a merchant and farmer, emigrated from County Donegal, Ireland, to the United States in 1783. In 1788 Buchanan, Sr., married Elizabeth Speer, a native of Lancaster County, Pennsylvania. The couple had eight children. When James Buchanan, Jr. was five years old, the family moved the five miles from their log cabin at Cove Gap, Pennsylvania, to Mercersburg, where Buchanan spent the remainder of his childhood.

James Buchanan. (The Library of Congress.)

Education

Buchanan studied at Old Stone Academy in Mercersburg, Pennsylvania, until 1807, when he was admitted to Dickinson College in Carlisle, Pennsylvania. He was a good student who excelled in problems of logic and metaphysics, but he was prone to getting into disciplinary trouble. He was suspended in his first year for "disorderly conduct." Buchanan pledged to change his ways, and he graduated in 1809. In December of that year he moved to Lancaster, Pennsylvania, to study law under James Hopkins. A talented student of legal concepts, he was admitted to the bar in 1812.

Family Life

In 1819, at the age of 28, he became engaged to Anne C. Coleman, the 23-year-old daughter of a wealthy Lancaster, Pennsylvania, family. In December of that year, however, the couple quarreled, and Coleman broke off the engagement. She then went to visit relatives in Philadelphia, where she died suddenly on December 9, 1819. There has been speculation that her death was a suicide. The source of the quarrel is unknown—according to some rumors, Coleman came to suspect that Buchanan was marrying her for her fortune. When Buchanan died, the executors of his estate, on Buchanan's request, destroyed unexamined materials

explaining the reasons for the quarrel. Buchanan was apparently devastated by his fiancée's death. Although Buchanan was reported to have had romantic attachments in his later years, he never married. Instead, he threw himself into politics.

Career

Buchanan practiced law in Lancaster, Pennsylvania, after his admission to the bar in 1812. In 1814 he was elected to the Pennsylvania assembly as a member of the Federalist Party. He won election to the U.S. House of Representatives in 1820, and as a leading member of the new Democratic Party in Pennsylvania, he was an early supporter of Democrat Andrew Jackson's presidential aspirations. When Jackson became president in 1828, Buchanan was sent to St. Petersburg as the U.S. minister to Russia, where he spent two years negotiating commercial and maritime treaties. When Buchanan returned to Pennsylvania, he was elected to the U.S. Senate in 1834, serving there until 1845. As a senator in a chamber increasingly divided by the North-South tensions over the issue of slavery, Buchanan frequently sided with southern interests, supporting, for example, southern demands that the Senate dismiss petitions calling for the abolition of slavery without consideration, the so-called gag rule.

Secretary of State

At the 1844 Democratic convention, Buchanan was one of the leading contenders for the presidential nomination, but he lost to James K. Polk of Tennessee. After Polk won the election, he named Buchanan his secretary of state. Although Buchanan was initially a moderating influence on Polk's vision of the United States's "manifest destiny" to expand its boundaries, Buchanan soon came to lead the charge for more territory. Buchanan successfully negotiated a treaty with England over the Oregon Territory, establishing the United States's northwestern boundaries with Canada at the 49th parallel (*See also,* Polk Administration). His dealings with Mexico did not resolve themselves as peacefully, however. When Mexico refused to meet U.S. demands concerning the annexation of Texas, the Mexican War (1846–48) broke out. When Mexico surrendered in 1848, Buchanan unsuccessfully called for the rejection of the Treaty of Guadalupe Hidalgo, which established the current southern border of the United States. He favored instead the annexation of even greater areas of Mexico, including the Baja Peninsula. He also tried, but failed, to secure the purchase of Cuba from Spain for $120 million.

Minister to Britain

After Polk's presidency ended, Buchanan retired to Wheatland, the estate near Lancaster, Pennsylvania, that he had recently purchased. He was a contender for the Democratic presidential nomination in 1848 and 1852 but was passed over for more charismatic candidates. In 1853 Democratic president Franklin Pierce appointed Buchanan minister to Great Britain. Buchanan served in England from 1853 to 1856, keeping a conveniently low profile on the U.S. political stage as the sectional tensions over slavery between the North and the South continued to build. He did help to draft the controversial Ostend Manifesto in 1854, however. That document, later repudiated by the Pierce administration, called for the U.S. acquisition of Cuba, by force if necessary. The annexation of Cuba was a popular cause in the South, because pro-slavery forces saw the Caribbean island as a potential new slave state that could bolster the sagging political strength of the slaveholding population.

President

In 1856 Buchanan returned to the United States. Having been abroad during much bitter debate over slavery, Buchanan was able to win the Democratic nomination and the presidency by appearing to be above the sectional fray. He took power in March 1857, as the furor over slavery in the territories built to a fever pitch. Buchanan had always been sympathetic to southern concerns, and in an attempt to satisfy discontented southerners he sided with them in many of the political confrontations of his presidency. Buchanan was unable to reconcile the differences between the North and the South, however. His continuing support of slavery alienated northern voters, and they threw their support to the Republican Party in the four-way presidential election of 1860.

When Abraham Lincoln won the presidency in 1860, the states of the lower South, believing Lincoln to be hostile to slavery, seceded from the Union. Buchanan refused to take direct action against these rebellious states, believing it to be outside his authority, and tensions rose unchecked for the next several months. By the time Buchanan left office in March 1861, the nation faced the gravest political crisis in its short history. Only a few weeks later, the first shots would be fired at Fort Sumter, South Carolina, and the North and the South would begin the bloodiest war in U.S. history.

Post-presidential Years

Buchanan retired to his estate in Wheatland, in Lancaster County, Pennsylvania, after Lincoln's inauguration. His retirement was not a peaceful one: many Americans held Buchanan responsible for the American Civil War (1861–65), and he found himself so unpopular that, for a time, he was unable to leave his house. Buchanan fell violently ill as the attacks mounted. When he recovered, he embarked upon a crusade to restore his reputation. He cut off his relationships with Confederate lead-

ers (those in charge of the southern states that had seceded) and used every possible opportunity to offer his public support for Lincoln and the Union war effort. He also wrote a memoir, *Mr. Buchanan's Administration on the Eve of the Rebellion,* defending his decisions as president and refuting attacks on his administration. Although he would never be a popular president, he did, in the end, manage to salvage his good name and reputation to some extent. He died on June 1, 1868, at the age of 77.

The James Buchanan Administration

Slavery was the only issue in United States politics during the 1850s—the most important quality in a president during those years was that he be acceptable to both North and South. James Buchanan had avoided taking positions on the issue of slavery in the new territories, and he ascended to the presidency on the power of his centrist reputation. His conciliatory posture on the slavery issue, however, only exacerbated the North-South tensions that flared into hostilities only weeks after he left the White House.

Buchanan Becomes President

The Campaign of 1856

The campaign of 1856 took place at a time when the nation was undergoing a major political realignment that was driven, like almost all of the politics of the 1850s, by the sectional tensions over slavery. The bloody battles in Kansas polarized North and South and widened sectional divisions within the political parties.

The 1856 election marked the debut of two new national parties—the "Know Nothings" and the Republicans. The "Know Nothings"—officially, the American Party—were a coalition of former Whigs and some northern Democrats. Their slogan, "Americans must rule America," reflected growing fears among native-born Protestants that Irish Catholic immigrants streaming into the nation's ports were stealing jobs and precious resources. The party had begun as a secret organization in July of 1854—their name derived from members' habit, when asked about the new party, of responding with a cryptic "I know nothing." The party was short-lived, however: their official opposition to federal interference on the slavery issue would ultimately split the party along North-South lines, just as it divided every other national party in the 1850s. The Know Nothings ran former president Millard Fillmore as their presidential candidate, with Andrew J. Donelson, nephew of former president Andrew Jackson, running for vice president.

Administration

Administration Dates
March 4, 1857–March 4, 1861

Vice President
John Cabell Breckinridge (1857–61)

Cabinet
Secretary of State

William L. Marcy (1853–57)
Lewis Cass (1857–60)
Jeremiah S. Black (1860–61)

Secretary of the Treasury

James Guthrie (1853–57)
Howell Cobb (1857–60)
Philip F. Thomas (1860–61)
John A. Dix (1861)

Secretary of War

John B. Floyd (1857–60)
Joseph Holt (1861)

Attorney General

Jeremiah S. Black (1857–60)
Edwin M. Stanton (1860–61)

Secretary of the Navy

John C. Dobbin (1853–57)
Isaac Toucey (1857–61)

Postmaster General

James Campbell (1853–57)
Aaron V. Brown (1857–59)
Joseph Holt (1859–60)
Horatio King (1861)

Secretary of the Interior

Robert McClelland (1853–57)

The Republican Party also formed in 1854, from a coalition of antislavery Whigs and Democrats disgusted with the battles over slavery in Kansas. Like the Know Nothings, the Republicans were white, northern Protestants. But, unlike their new rival, the Republicans considered slavery, not immigration, to be the nation's greatest evil. The Republicans argued that a strong federal government was necessary to deal with the issue of slavery; to encourage economic development; to pay for railroad, harbor, and river improvements; and to protect native industry (mostly located in the North) by levying high tariffs on imports. In addition, the Republicans favored limiting the size of farms in the west, which would make it economically unfeasible for slavery to be used in that region. In their first national election in 1856, the Republicans nominated military hero John C. Fremont. Famed for his explorations around the U.S. West, Fremont had settled in California, where he made a fortune in the gold rush and served as one of California's first two U.S. senators. As a presidential candidate, Fremont was vocal in his opposition to slavery but silent on most other issues.

While the Whigs had collapsed into northern and southern factions, as well as becoming part of the Know Nothing and Republican parties, the Democrats tried desperately to hold their party together. Buchanan seemed the best candidate to do so. All three candidates—incumbent President Franklin Pierce, Senator Stephen Douglas of Illinois, and Buchanan—respected southern sovereignty and upheld the constitutionality of slavery. But Buchanan, who had spent the previous three years in London, England, as U.S. minister to Great Britain, had avoided involving himself in the violent controversy over slavery in the territories. Buchanan came from a northern state that was crucial to Democratic victory. Having spent much of his 30 years in politics ingratiating himself to Southerners, however, he was also agreeable to the South. After 16 ballots, Senator Douglas—who would later become one of Buchanan's strongest critics—withdrew from the race to allow Buchanan to win the nomination. Buchanan named John Cabell Breckinridge of Kentucky—a southerner who supported slavery but opposed the extension of slavery into the territories—as his running mate.

The Democrats attempted to hold the middle ground on the slavery issue, endorsing the Compromise of 1850, which had been temporary measure to forestall civil war, and the Kansas-Nebraska Act (*See also,* Domestic Issues). In addition, they supported the construction of a transcontinental railroad. Their main draw in 1856, however, was that the southerners had threatened secession if Fremont and the Republicans won the presidency. This threat encouraged those who still hoped for a peaceful resolution to the slavery controversy to vote for Buchanan. Buchanan won the election, but the results were by no means decisive. He took the race with 45 percent of the vote; Fremont won 33 percent, Fillmore 22 percent. Buchanan carried every southern state and the lower North—Pennsylvania, New Jersey, Illinois, Indiana, and California. Fillmore also had a strong showing in this region and carried Maryland. In a remarkable showing for a two-year-old party, Fremont and the Republicans carried 11 free states and lost the others by only a scant margin.

Buchanan's Advisers

Buchanan hoped that he could balance his cabinet with representatives of all of the major political positions of the time. Buchanan's closest friends during the important process of selecting a cabinet, however, were anything but balanced. His most trusted advisers—Secretary of the Treasury Howell Cobb, a slave owner and Unionist; John Slidell, a Louisiana politician; Indiana senator Jesse Bright, who also owned slaves in Kentucky; and Virginia governor Henry Wise—were all southerners or pro-southern northerners.

Buchanan's cabinet, too, was comprised of mostly old-fashioned, southern-leaning politicians who tended to represent views very close to his own. Buchanan's cabinet consisted of four slaveholding southerners and three northerners, only one of whom—Secretary of State Lewis Cass, who was widely regarded as too old and impaired to be of any worth—agreed with the North on the issue of slavery. Buchanan surrounded himself with rural politicians and lawyers who shared with Buchanan what historian Elbert Smith called "a partial and highly antiquated view of the realities in 1857." By neglecting the growing political strength of the industrial North, and by underestimating the northern antipathy to the spread of slavery, Buchanan assured himself a difficult presidency. In December 1860, when the Republicans won the presidential election and his southern friends in his cabinet and in Congress departed for the Confederacy, Buchanan found himself facing the secession crisis alone.

Buchanan and Congress

Buchanan presided over a fragmented and hostile Congress, and he sought to resolve the growing conflicts between North and South through compromise and constitutional argument. Every political choice he made, however, seemed to anger the North without appeasing the South. Even before his inauguration, he clashed with antislavery advocates over the *Dred Scott* decision, which voided the right of Congress to ban slavery from the territories (*See also,* Buchanan and the Judiciary). Shortly after he became president, Buchanan squandered much of his remaining goodwill with northerners in Congress when he supported Kansas's pro-slavery Lecompton constitution, even though the majority of Kansas voters opposed it (*See also,* Domestic Issues).

The Kansas issue was essentially a question of who would control Congress in the future: if Kansas was admitted as a free state, the southerners would lose the balance of power in Congress. Buchanan put great pressure on Congress to accept the Lecompton document and admit Kansas as a slave state, in order to appease the South, but he ran into immediate opposition from his own political party. Stephen Douglas of Illinois, the Democrats' most powerful and popular senator, believed strongly in the principle of popular sovereignty (allowing the people to decide what they want) and opposed Buchanan's meddling on the matter. With Buchanan's own party divided against him, Buchanan's relations with Congress grew increasingly fractious.

While Democrats controlled Congress when Buchanan took office in 1857, the Republicans won control of the House of Representatives for the first time in 1859. This made Buchanan's ability to lead even more tenuous, and made southerners less willing to work within the bounds of the Union to solve the slavery problem.

Congress passed little legislation during the Buchanan years, spending most of its energy on the constitutional questions of slavery and territorial expansion, which was being settled in the states and the courts, not in Congress. In addition, Buchanan initiated little significant legislation of his own.

Buchanan and the Judiciary

Buchanan appointed one Supreme Court justice, Nathan Clifford of Maine. Clifford had previously served as attorney general under James Polk. Like all of Buchanan's battles with Congress, the confirmation of Clifford, considered more a loyal Democrat than a notable scholar, was also heated. The Senate narrowly confirmed Clifford after a fervent debate.

The Dred Scott *Case*

Buchanan's relations with the judicial branch is best remembered for his controversial role in the *Dred Scott* case, decided by the Supreme Court two days before his inauguration in March 1857. Dred Scott, a slave, had traveled with his master from Missouri, a slave state, to live in Illinois, and in federal territory, neither of which allowed slavery. Scott's owner died, and in 1846 Scott sued his master's widow for freedom, on the grounds that living in the free territory had made him free. When the case reached the Supreme Court, Chief Justice Roger Taney of Maryland dismissed Scott's suit. Taney, joined by five pro-slavery justices on the nine-member court, wrote in his opinion that African American slaves were not citizens of the United States, and that the framers of the Constitution had never intended for African Americans to be citizens. Therefore, Scott had no standing to sue. This claim alone was enough to cause anger throughout the North, but Taney went further. Taney declared the federal ban on slavery in the territories unconstitutional because it deprived citizens of their property (slaves) without due process of law. This decision not only implied that slavery could not be banned in federal territories, but that the states of the North might be forced to accept slavery on the grounds that their state bans were unconstitutional. This decision stunned northerners, and they vowed to seek a reversal.

Buchanan involved himself personally in the Court's deliberations, a contact between the executive and judicial branches that is considered highly inappropriate, if not illegal. Shortly before the Court reached a decision, Buchanan wrote a letter to a northern justice, urging him to side with the Southerners on the court. Buchanan, apparently, hoped that the Court would issue a sweeping ruling on slavery in the territories that would settle the troubling question for good. The *Dred Scott* decision, however, did anything but quiet down the agitation over slavery. Instead, it reinforced northern fears of a conspiracy of "Slave Power" Southerners to circumvent the will of the majority of Americans, in order to perpetuate slavery.

Changes in the U.S. Government

Minnesota, Oregon, and Kansas all joined the Union during the Buchanan years. Admitted as free states, the growth of the nation in many ways precipitated the dissolution of the Union, by tipping the electoral power towards non-slaveholding states.

Certainly the most significant event during the Buchanan years—indeed, during any president's term—was the departure of the southern states from the Union. Buchanan came to the presidency determined to do whatever he could to hold the Union together—and this, in his opinion, meant following a conservative course of defending the South and the constitutional right to slavery. Every effort to keep the South happy, however, made northern voters intensely unhappy. And northerners' discontent with the political situation, along with the continuing growth of the northern population while the South held steady, fueled the Republican victory in 1860, which in turn drove southerners out of the Union.

Domestic Issues

By the 1850s the issue of slavery had divided the United States into two ideologically separate societies. Americans in the North had grown increasingly opposed to any further expansion of the nation's "peculiar institution." Northerners objected to slavery on both moral and economic grounds: some believed that slavery was wrong; others felt that the presence of slave labor provided an unfair advantage against free men competing in the labor market. Southerners, even those who did not own slaves, had grown to feel more and more strongly that slavery was an integral element of their regional identity. To take away slavery was to take away the South's independence.

Both sections saw the fate of the new western territories, and in particular Kansas, as the key to the future of slavery. Northerners wanted slavery to be banned in the federal territories; southerners wanted to expand slavery into the West. If the antislavery forces won out, the slaveholding states would become a rapidly shrinking minority in the United States, vastly outnumbered in Congress. If slavery were to expand, however, then the number of slave states would remain relatively equal to the free states, and they would be able to protect their way of life from hostile legislation in the Senate.

Behind the ideological divide that separated North and South lay major social and economic differences. The rate of urban and industrial growth in the North in the mid-nineteenth century was greater than in any other area in the world. U.S. population growth, which occurred mainly in the North and the West, and the expansion of the railroads, which linked the West to the Northeast, meant that the South was losing both economic and political clout. Meanwhile, the South remained a rural, agricultural society. Investments in land and slaves tied southerners to their farmland, preventing the development of major industrial cities and manufacturing centers. As the North grew in population and wealth, the South became increasingly desperate to protect its way of life. Buchanan, although a northerner, in many ways belonged more to the world of the South. He was firmly rooted in the idea of a pre-industrial, rural United States.

Kansas

The issue of whether Kansas would be a slave state or a free state had been a problem for the two previous presidential administrations, and Buchanan had been elected in part because he had been abroad during the violent and controversial battles between pro- and antislavery forces in Kansas. Buchanan was not an advocate of slavery—he had always felt that it was morally wrong—but he also believed that the federal government had the obligation to protect slavery in the states where it already legally existed. His position on the issue of slavery in the territories, however, was not initially clear.

Under the Kansas-Nebraska Act of 1854, Kansas had been allowed to organize as a slave or a free territory, depending on the choice of its settlers. Hoping to influence the vote on the issue, supporters of both slavery and abolition (to abolish slavery) came pouring into Kansas. Soon after Buchanan became president Kansas began preparing to write a constitution that would settle the slavery question in Kansas once and for all. Buchanan appointed his friend, fellow Pennsylvanian Robert Walker, as Kansas's territorial governor. Walker, a slaveholder, was known as a man of integrity, and Buchanan charged him with overseeing what was sure to be a hotly contested election in June of 1857 to name delegates to Kansas's constitutional convention.

The violence of the previous years had subsided in Kansas, but the political tensions had only become more pronounced. The anti slavery "free-staters" announced that they would boycott the election to name delegates

Biography:

Roger Brooke Taney

Politician; Supreme Court Chief Justice (1777–1864)
Roger Brooke Taney was born to a proud, land-owning, slaveholding, Maryland family at the time the United States was formed. He was instructed from a young age by a private tutor and then went on to college at age 15, graduating with honors a few years later. He then studied law and emerged as one of his state's most promising young lawyers. From there Taney worked many years in state politics before being appointed chief justice of the Supreme Court in his late fifties by President Andrew Jackson. Taney's career in the High Court would span almost 30 years. His opinions and decisions showed that he was a firm supporter of private property, was a moderate states' rightist, sided against the doctrine of implied contract in a court challenge, and promoted the expansion of interstate commerce. Unfortunately, Taney's aristocratic upbringing characterized his opinions on slavery, and he wrote the majority opinion in the *Dred Scott v. Sanford* case which came before the Court during the

Buchanan administration. In his vehemently criticized opinion, Taney held that African Americans could not become citizens of the United States because they were deemed as inherently inferior by the Constitution. He went on to opine that Congress could not prohibit slavery because slaves were property and property rights were protected under the Fifth Amendment to the Con-

stitution. It was only years after the passions of the Civil War had subsided—and years after his death—that Taney's great contribution to the development of our constitutional government—contributions that preceded and were outside of the *Dred Scott* case—were recognized and acknowledged.

---

to the constitutional convention. The free-staters feared that election fraud would give control of the convention to pro-slavery delegates, and they chose not participating at all to avoid giving an appearance of legitimacy to a process they were sure would be corrupt. With many free-staters not participating, the remaining voters elected a fiercely pro-slavery delegation to the constitutional convention in Lecompton, Kansas.

Shortly after the convention was seated in Lecompton, elections were also held for a new territorial legislature. Walker, who had become convinced that the majority of voters in Kansas did not want it to be a slave state, persuaded the free-staters to participate in these elections. While the election returns initially showed that the pro-slavery forces had won a narrow victory, Walker soon discovered that thousands of fraudulent votes had been cast for slavery advocates, including 1,601 names copied directly from the Cincinnati, Ohio, city directory. After throwing out the fraudulent votes, the free-staters were found to have won control of the territorial legislature for the first time.

The pro-slavery delegates attending the constitutional convention in Lecompton, meanwhile, drafted a constitution that would make slavery legal in Kansas. Buchanan, who had promised Southerners that Kansas would be a slave state, was determined to accept the constitution, even though it was now evident that the majority of settlers in Kansas opposed slavery. He dismissed

Walker, who believed the constitutional convention to be fraudulently elected, and ignored the advice of Walker's replacement, who also argued that the constitution was illegitimate. Although it clearly sidestepped the requirement that state constitutions be approved by popular sovereignty, Buchanan submitted the Lecompton constitution to the U.S. Senate for approval.

Northerners were outraged by Buchanan's actions—not only had the president ignored the evidence of voter fraud, but he refused to hold a referendum in Kansas to allow the inhabitants to vote on whether or not they wanted the Lecompton constitution. Northern Democrats, led by Illinois senator Stephen Douglas, a passionate advocate of popular sovereignty, refused to support Buchanan on the grounds that the people of Kansas had been denied a chance to vote for their own government. The Lecompton document passed the Senate but died in the House of Representatives. When the constitution was referred back to Kansas voters for approval in 1858, they overwhelmingly rejected it. At Buchanan's urging, they held another referendum, and again, the Lecompton document failed. Kansas was admitted as a free state in 1861.

The Panic of 1857

In August 1857 the Ohio Life Insurance Company of Cincinnati, Ohio, shut its doors, spurring a wave of bank runs across the country that plunged the nation into economic depression. A number of factors contributed to the crash: the price of gold dropped precipitously in the wake of the California gold rush, and the end of the Crimean War in Europe meant a significant decline in U.S. food exports. In the northern United States, which was embarking on an unprecedented stint of economic growth, unsecured debt had piled up that could not be repaid, and the railroads and a number of banks found themselves without funds. Holding to the economic theories of the time, Buchanan refused to tamper with the economy, even as unemployment rose and people begged for food and shelter in the streets of northern cities. The prolonged recession lasted until the eve of the American Civil War (1861–65).

Northern Republicans saw the recession as another failure of Democratic policies: the nation would have been insulated from recession, they believed, had Democrats permitted the passage of Republican legislation to raise tariffs, give western land to homesteaders, and fund transportation projects. The Democrats' insensitivity to northern workers, they said, reflected that party's capitulation to southern slaveholding interests.

The South, meanwhile, had weathered the downturn well. The European demand for cotton remained high, and few southern banks failed. The financial crisis in the North actually bolstered southern arguments about slavery—it convinced southerners of the superiority of their slave-supported economic system and reinforced their belief that northerners were greedy materialists who did not take care of their own. Southerners resisted the Republicans' proposed interventions, believing they were aimed at enriching the North at the expense of the South. Every crisis, it seemed, exacerbated the tensions between North and South.

The Mormons

Although most of Buchanan's attentions were occupied in matters dividing North and South, he did manage to solve a long-standing problem on the western frontier. The Mormons—followers of a religion founded in 1830 by a man named Joseph Smith—had fled from the East in the 1840s in the face of growing hostility. Their leader, Brigham Young, had brought his Mormon followers to Salt Lake City, Utah, where he established a church-run government. Even removed from the general population, however, the Mormons continued to arouse hostility among Americans dismayed by reports of church-dominated political and economic practices, and the open acknowledgment of polygamy, the practice of marrying multiple wives. Federal troops attempting to force Brigham Young to accept a governor appointed in Washington had periodically engaged in battle with the Mormons in the years since their arrival in Utah, and the situation had deteriorated into bloodshed in the mid-1850s.

When Buchanan became president he sent 2,500 federal troops to bring Utah under federal control. After the Mormons fled Salt Lake City and threatened to destroy

their city rather than surrender, Buchanan agreed to compromise. He sent his friend Thomas L. Kane, who had lived with the Mormons and had written a favorable book about them, to negotiate an agreement with Young in Utah. After some haggling, Young and Kane reached an agreement: Washington would rule the Utah Territory in temporal, or secular, affairs, while the Mormons would remain autonomous in religious matters. In April 1858 Buchanan announced pardons for all Mormons who would submit to the federal government.

John Brown's Raid on Harper's Ferry

John Brown was a militant abolitionist (someone seeking to abolish slavery) originally from New England. Brown moved to the Kansas territory to support anti-slavery activities there, and became famous for his brutal murder of five pro-slavery settlers there. His actions made Brown something of a celebrity among the abolitionists of New England, who supported him while he was in hiding from the law. Brown, an intensely religious man, had come to believe that he was God's personal instrument in the battle for human freedom, and when the violence subsided in Kansas, he developed a more ambitious scheme. His plan was to seize the federal arsenal at Harper's Ferry, Virginia, then arm and incite the local slaves to rebellion that, he believed, would spread throughout Virginia and the South. He convinced some of his New England admirers to fund the training of a small "army."

On October 16, 1859, John Brown and 22 followers captured the Harper's Ferry arsenal by force. The nearby slaves—who had not been informed of their role in the insurrection—did not respond to Brown's ill-conceived plan, but the Virginia militia and a detachment of the United States Marines did. President Buchanan sent Colonel Robert E. Lee to command the troops, who put a quick end to the raid, wounding Brown and killing or capturing most of his force.

While most northerners decried Brown as insane and condemned his actions, a vocal group of abolitionists hailed Brown as a hero. Southerners, meanwhile, saw the raid as evidence of a broad-based northern conspiracy to destroy the institution of slavery altogether. The State of Virginia tried Brown on a charge of treason, sentencing him to hang. After Brown hanged a few days later, southerners, upset at the outpouring of northern grief at Brown's death, began to support the idea of southern secession. While northerners came to regard Brown as a martyr to the cause of human freedom, southerners saw him as evidence that the North sought not only to contain slavery, but to do away with it.

The Secession Crisis

Every political event in the first three years of Buchanan's presidency seemed to exacerbate the increasing divide between North and South. Economic downturns, territorial expansion, court rulings all seemed to drive northerners towards the Republican Party and southerners closer to the logic of secession.

The election of 1860—a four-way contest between two northern candidates and two southerners—split the nation for good. Buchanan, who had planned to hold the presidency for only one term, declined to run, and the Democratic Party split into two factions. Northern Democrats nominated Illinois senator Stephen Douglas, an ardent critic of Buchanan, while Buchanan's remaining adherents nominated Vice President John C. Breckinridge of Kentucky. A number of former Whigs from the upper South, meanwhile, formed the Constitutional Union Party and nominated John Bell of Tennessee. And the Republicans nominated Abraham Lincoln (*See also, Abraham Lincoln Administration*). In essence, the presidential campaign of 1860 divided into two separate, sectional races—Breckinridge versus Bell in the South; Lincoln versus Douglas in the more populous North. Lincoln, benefiting from the split in the Democratic Party, won the presidency with 39 percent of the vote.

The Lower South Secedes

Many Southerners feared that the election of a Republican to the presidency would be the beginning of the end for slavery. Much as they had done to Republican presidential nominee John C. Fremont in 1856, many Southerners threatened to secede from the United States if Lincoln won. Four days after Lincoln's victory, the South Carolina legislature called a convention to consider secession, and in December 1860 the delegates voted unanimously to leave the Union. By February 1861, six other states—Mississippi, Florida, Alabama, Georgia, and Texas—had joined South Carolina to form the Confederate States of America, with Jefferson Davis as its president.

Buchanan was forced to deal with the secession crisis until Lincoln took office in March of 1861. Buchanan took the position that secession was illegal, but he also held that the federal government could not constitutionally use force against the states, even to keep them in the United States. Afraid to limit the options of the incoming administration, and even more fearful of driving the other southern states to secede, Buchanan refused to act forcefully. He instead proposed a plan for amending the Constitution to protect slavery. It was acceptable to no one. Others made more energetic attempts at conciliation. Kentucky senator John J. Crittenden proposed a package of amendments that would extend the Missouri Compromise line—the invisible line that had, until 1854, divided slave states from free states—all the way across the country. Former president John Tyler proposed a similar compromise, which also would guarantee that some of the new territories admitted to the Union would remain slave states. But with the battle lines drawn, neither side would accept a middle course.

Fast Fact

In response to President Buchanan ordering a $250 reward for his capture or death, John Brown offered a bounty of $2.50 for Buchanan.

(Source: Kenneth Davis. *Don't Know Much About History,* 1990.)

Buchanan believed that military action against the Confederate States was permissible only to protect federal property, such as the Union forts in the South, but when Fort Sumter, in the Charleston, South Carolina, harbor, came under threat, he refused to act, determined not to be the aggressor. In January 1861 Buchanan sent a warship, the *Star of the West,* to reinforce Union soldiers surrounded by Confederate forces at Fort Sumter. Confederate shore batteries fired upon the ship, and it abandoned its mission. A few months later, this same scenario, with Abraham Lincoln now in the White House, would provoke the first shots of the American Civil War.

Foreign Issues

In the years before James Buchanan took office, the United States had grown from a small agricultural nation to an empire that stretched across the North American continent. Buchanan, an ardent expansionist, was instrumental in the nation's growth—as secretary of state under James Polk he had helped orchestrate the nation's expansion. He believed passionately in the ideology of "manifest destiny," the nation's mission to extend to the edges of the continent.

As president, Buchanan is remembered as somewhat more forceful in the foreign policy realm than he was in the domestic arena. Buchanan ran his own State Department. His elderly, ailing secretary of state, Lewis Cass, was apparently unfit for either administration or policy-making, chosen mainly to be a figurehead who could represent northerners in Buchanan's cabinet without threatening southerners. Buchanan often was bold and decisive in foreign policy. He signed treaties that facilitated U.S. trade with three continents, and persuaded the British—who had unsuccessfully tried to establish a colonial foothold in Central America—to give up all claims to the Central American isthmus.

Latin America

With the crumbling of the Spanish Empire in Central and South America in the early nineteenth century, many Americans saw an opportunity for the United States to extend its borders to the west and the south. Many politicians, Buchanan included, believed that the expansion of the United States into Mexico, Cuba, and other former Spanish colonies would provide an economic boost to the nation. The nation's victory in the Mexican War (1846–48), led only to the heated debates over slavery in newly acquired territory that would ultimately sink Buchanan's presidency.

By the time Buchanan became president, the former Mexican territories had been incorporated into the United States, but the U.S. position in relation to the rest of Central and South America had not yet been resolved. Buchanan spoke strongly of his desire to eliminate all European influence in Central America and to establish U.S. control there by purchase, annexation, or intervention. But Republicans and many northern Democrats in Congress opposed any further acquisition of former Spanish colonies, believing that the admission of new states to the Union would only make the debate over slavery in new U.S. territories worse.

Many historians argue that Buchanan's foreign policy revealed the same weakness as his domestic policy: his capitulation to pro-slavery southerners. An attempt to annex slaveholding Cuba, for example, and the escapades of Tennessee adventurer, William Walker, who spent the latter half of the 1850s attempting to conquer Nicaragua and reestablish slavery there, were seen by many in the North as attempts to expand the pro-slavery population in the United States. While Buchanan never endorsed these private military expeditions into Central America, some historians believe they had his tacit permission—again, as a balm to southerners looking to expand the nation's slave territory and increase slaveholders' electoral clout.

The Buchanan Administration Legacy

When Buchanan left office in 1861, he was leaving behind him as serious a crisis as had ever presented itself in U.S. history. The United States was no longer united; seven states had announced their secession from the Union, with the other slave states clearly considering joining them.

Buchanan had done nothing of significance to prevent the secession or to remedy it after it occurred. Historians disagree on the consequences of this inaction. Some believe that Buchanan showed admirable restraint: had he acted more forcefully, they say, he may have hastened the secession of the upper South, and put the federal government in the position of having fired the first

shots of the American Civil War (1861–65). Other historians, however, believe that Buchanan's insistence that the federal government lacked the authority to put down secession only encouraged the South. Either way, it was left to Buchanan's successor, Abraham Lincoln, to solve the problems of secession.

Lasting Impact

Buchanan will always be remembered, whether fairly or not, as the president who brought the nation to the verge of civil war. The slavery issue dominated Buchanan's administration, and his attempts to deal with the problems it presented were singularly unsuccessful. The secession of the lower South occurred under his watch, and he did nothing useful to either prevent it or to mend the situation. His successor, Abraham Lincoln, did act forcefully to bring the South back into the Union, and he is, by contrast, one of the most esteemed presidents in U.S. history.

There is a sense among historians that Buchanan was lacking in the qualities necessary for the demanding years preceding the American Civil War. Buchanan was a centrist who sought to take refuge from the controversies of the day by cloaking himself in "constitutionalism." His essentially conservative philosophy of life and politics, his respect for law and property, led him to search for safe, but ultimately untenable, compromises in a time that demanded more forceful action. "He exemplified the new generation of professional politicians," writes historian Michael Birkner, "who believed an ounce of compromise was worth a pound of principle" (Birkner, p. 23).

A few historians do argue that Buchanan was unfairly stigmatized by the political crises of the 1850s, that "little went right and much went wrong" during his presidency, and that no person could have changed the course of events (Birkner, p. 29). While Buchanan certainly did not bring on the American Civil War, he did not appear to have the fortitude to stop it. At very best, he postponed it for four years.

Sources

Binder, Frederick Moore. *James Buchanan and the American Empire.* London: Associated University Presses, 1994.

Birkner, Michael J., ed. *James Buchanan and the Political Crisis of the 1850s.* London: Associated University Presses, 1996.

Davis, Kenneth C. *Don't Know Much About History.* New York: Avon Books, 1990.

Goldfield, David, et al. *The American Journey: A History of the United States.* Vol. 1. Upper Saddle River, N.J.: Prentice Hall, 1998.

Smith, Elbert B. *The Presidency of James Buchanan.* Lawrence, Kans.: The University Press of Kansas, 1975.

Further Readings

Buchanan, James. *The works of James Buchanan, comprising his speeches, state papers, and private correspondence.* Edited by John Bassett Moore. Philadelphia, London: J.B. Lippincott Company, 1908–11.

Curtis, George Ticknor. *Life of James Buchanan, Fifteenth President of the United States.* New York: Harper and Brothers, 1883

Updike, John. *Buchanan Dying.* New York: Summit Books/Simon and Schuster, 1978.

Lincoln Administrations

Full name: Abraham Lincoln
Popular name: Old Abe; the Rail-Splitter; Father Abraham;
the Great Emancipator

Personal Information:

Born: February 12, 1809
Birthplace: Hodgenville, Kentucky
Died: April 15, 1865
Death place: Washington, D.C.
Burial place: Oak Ridge Cemetery, Springfield, Illinois
Spouse: Mary Todd (m. 1842)
Children: Robert Todd; Edward Baker; William Wallace;
Thomas (Tad)
Education: Self-educated
Occupation: Farmer; lawyer; congressman
Political Party: Republican Party
Age at Inauguration: 52 years

Biography

Gangly, self-conscious, and taller than average, Abraham Lincoln stood out in any crowd. Friends knew him to be brimming with both funny stories and bouts of self-doubt; his adversaries in law and politics knew him as a crafty lawyer and a formidable political opponent. To his children and his wife, Lincoln was indulgent and tolerant. Lincoln's unique combination of political skills and personal strengths had a tremendous impact on U.S. history as he led the United States through the turmoil of the Civil War (1861–65).

Early Life

From his birth on February 12, 1809, until his inauguration as president on March 4, 1861, the early life of few presidents has been as exhaustively studied as Abraham Lincoln's. Since the traits and influences on the boy mold the man, scholars have searched extensively for information on the young Lincoln. Yet much of his early life remains mystery and speculation, since little evidence has survived. It is known that Lincoln was born in a log cabin situated along Nolin Creek just south of the city of Hodgenville, Kentucky. He was the second child of Thomas Lincoln and Nancy Hanks Lincoln, and was named Abraham after his paternal grandfather.

As a young child, two trends shaped the young Lincoln: first, the death of close relatives and friends and, second, his family's frequent moves. In 1812 his mother gave birth to another son, Thomas Lincoln, who died in infancy the next year. In 1818 close family friends (Thomas and Elizabeth Hanks Sparrow, Lincoln's great-aunt and her husband) died of "milk sickness," a not uncommon disease on the midwestern frontier brought on by drinking the milk of cows that had eaten poisonous plants. Even more tragically for Lincoln his mother died in 1818 of the same disease; he was nine years old. The person whom he felt closest to in early life, his sister Nancy (called Sarah) Aaron Grigsby, would die during childbirth in January 1828.

In addition to these emotional dislocations were his family's physical dislocations. His father moved the family both to escape the confusing land title problems encountered in Kentucky and to search for better farm land. In 1816 the family moved from Kentucky across the Ohio River to southwest Indiana and settled on Little Pigeon Creek in Perry (later Spencer) County. The family constructed and lived in a three-sided shelter for several weeks until a log cabin could be built. His family lived in Indiana until 1830, when Thomas Lincoln moved them again, this time into Illinois settling in Macon County near Decatur.

In addition to the death of family and friends and their physical relocations, a new family member influenced the young Lincoln, his stepmother. About 14 months after the death of his birth mother and after the family's move to Indiana, Lincoln's father returned to Kentucky and remarried. He wed a widow from Elizabethtown, Kentucky, Sarah Bush Johnston, who already had three of her own children from a previous marriage; the Lincolns knew her from their time in Kentucky. Over time, Abraham Lincoln came to be very close to his stepmother and she, in turn, came to feel strongly about Lincoln. What few records that have survived from Lincoln's childhood were kept and preserved by his stepmother.

Education

While his father could write his name, for the most part the Lincoln family was illiterate and possessed little formal education. Lincoln attended school infrequently during his childhood, never for more than a few months, but he did learn the rudiments of spelling, grammar, and math.

Lincoln also developed a passion for reading and self-improvement and through his reading he became self-educated. Besides the family Bible (which he absorbed thoroughly and deeply), Lincoln read books such as Mason Locke Weem's *The Life and Memorable Actions of George Washington,* Daniel Defoe's *Robinson Crusoe,* William Grimshaw's *History of the United States,* and Thomas Dilworth's *A New Guide to the English Tongue.* By the early 1830s Lincoln was reading the works of William Shakespeare and Robert Burns, and through his work in stores as both clerk and proprietor, he improved his math skills.

Abraham Lincoln. *(The Library of Congress.)*

Beginning in 1834 Lincoln borrowed law books, read them, and taught himself the rules of law. He read the standard treatises and handbooks of the day such as Sir William Blackstone's *Commentaries* and Joseph Chitty's *Precedents in Pleading.* On September 9, 1836, Lincoln passed an oral bar examination and received a license to practice law. Self-education in Lincoln's era was not uncommon, but the depth, breadth, and sophistication Lincoln gained from his efforts was exceptional.

Family Life

Taller than average, muscular, and self-conscious, Lincoln was reportedly uncomfortable around women his own age. In 1831 Lincoln met the daughter of tavern keeper James Rutledge in New Salem, Illinois; her name was Ann Rutledge. Lincoln continued an on-again and off-again relationship with her until her death on August 25, 1835, probably from typhoid fever. In late 1836 Lincoln started a courtship with 28-year-old Mary Owens who was visiting her sister at New Salem, Illinois, at the time. Lincoln proposed to her in 1837, but she rejected his offer in August of that year and the courtship ended.

In 1839 Lincoln met Mary Todd, the daughter of a prominent Kentucky Whig banker and the cousin of his law partner John T. Stuart. They began a long and occasionally stormy relationship. The next year Lincoln was reelected to the Illinois legislature, and he and Mary Todd became engaged. But on January 1, 1841, Lincoln broke off his engagement during a bout of self-doubt and depression. In the summer of 1842 Lincoln reignited his courtship of Mary Todd, and on November 4, Lincoln and Mary Todd married in the parlor of her sister's home in Springfield, Illinois. The couple first moved into Mary's rooms at the Globe Tavern. The next year, after the birth of their first son, Robert Todd Lincoln, the new family moved into a rented cottage. In May 1844 Lincoln bought a house in Springfield at Eighth and Jackson Streets for $1,500; they lived there until 1861 when the Lincolns took up residence in the Executive Mansion in Washington, D.C.

Career

In addition to family tragedies, relocations, and remarriages, the hard physical work of living, farming, and surviving on the midwestern frontier influenced and molded the young Lincoln. Attending school only occasionally and with his father's assumption that the boy would become a farmer and therefore did not need much schooling, the young Lincoln spent a great deal of time out-of-doors at work in the fields, mills, and forests.

Lincoln was impatient under the discipline and oversight of his father, and while proficient enough at agricultural work, he apparently disliked the prospect of making farming a living. As he grew older, Lincoln sought opportunities to try new tasks and visit new areas. While he continued to live with his parents and help on the farm, in the late 1820s and early 1830s Lincoln also traveled down the Mississippi River to New Orleans, Louisiana, on two occasions to sell farm products. These experiences gave him firsthand exposure to slavery for the first time. Lincoln's parents belonged to a Baptist congregation that had split from the larger Baptist Church as a protest against slavery. While Lincoln never joined an organized church, it is likely that his parents' dislike for the institution of slavery, and what he saw of it during these youthful trips to the South, contributed to his distaste for slavery. In 1831 Lincoln moved out of his father's house and moved to New Salem, Illinois. There he worked at a mill and as a clerk in a general store.

Early Politics

Through his travels and his exposure to business and commerce, Lincoln became convinced that the middle west needed "internal improvements," a cause that he supported throughout his career. By internal improvements, Lincoln meant government-subsidized flood control dams, canals, turnpikes, and roads. In particular, Lincoln believed that improvements on the Sangamon River west of Decatur, Illinois, were needed to foster trade and commerce and to make the area grow economically. He

advocated such improvements in his first known political speech in 1830, and he followed up that interest in 1832 by deciding to run for political office.

During his campaign for the Illinois legislature, fighting broke out with American Indian tribes in the region, in what became known as the Black Hawk Indian War. Lincoln enlisted in the local militia. Following the practices of the day, militiamen elected their officers, and Lincoln was chosen to be their captain. In the end, Lincoln's unit did not see combat during the war. Lincoln's absence from his county in northern Illinois before the elections, however, greatly hurt his chances of election, and he finished eighth out of the 13 candidates.

Having lost the election to the Illinois legislature and without a formal profession to fall back on, Lincoln pondered whether to become a blacksmith and move to a new town or to continue in the business and political world in the New Salem area. He chose to stay. Along with a friend, Lincoln opened a new general store, which quickly went into debt and closed in 1833. Lincoln accepted the minor political office of postmaster, and he became a deputy county surveyor. He also continued working as an occasional hired hand and boarded with a variety of families, moving every few months.

Lincoln ran for the Illinois State House in 1834 and was elected as a member of the Whig Party from Sangamon County. He took his seat in December 1834, at the capital at Vandalia, Illinois, and roomed with John T. Stuart. Stuart lent Lincoln his law books and encouraged Lincoln to study the law. It was during this first session of the legislature that Lincoln first met an up-and-coming Democratic lawyer and politician from Chicago, Illinois, Stephen A. Douglas. As a legislator Lincoln consistently promoted government involvement in the economy to aid business, such as funding river improvements and underwriting canal and railroad bonds.

In 1836 Lincoln's borrowing of Stuart's law books paid off when he passed the requirements of the bar (minimal as they were at the time) and embarked on a career as a lawyer. In time Lincoln built his law practice into one of the most important in the state, and he practiced in both the state and the federal courts. For example, in 1849 Lincoln appeared before the U.S. Supreme Court to argue an appeal from Illinois concerning Illinois's statute of limitations on nonresident aliens—he lost the case.

During this time Lincoln also stayed active in Illinois politics. He was part of the nine-member delegation from Sangamon County in 1837 that successfully lobbied for the moving of the Illinois capital away from Vandalia, in southern Illinois, to Springfield, closer to the growing population areas of central and northern Illinois. Lincoln then moved to Springfield. He continued to serve in the Illinois legislature until 1842 and made two unsuccessful bids for Speaker of the House.

Biography:

Jefferson Davis

President; Military Leader (1808–89) While every man on the street knows that Abraham Lincoln was president of the United States during the American Civil War (1860–65), some forget that people in the southern states pledged allegiance to a leader by the name of Jefferson Davis, president of the Confederate States of America. Davis was a U.S. senator from Mississippi and major southern spokesman who announced his state's secession in an eloquent address on the Senate floor. Knowing the challenges that would now face the South, Davis only reluctantly accepted the Confederate presidency when it was offered to him. The South had a much smaller population base from which to draw an army from than the North, few weapons and no factories or means to replenish them, no warships, and less than half the mileage of usable railroad track. It should have been a clear northern victory, but Davis's supreme military acumen, coupled with his success in elevating his cause

from a quest for continued slavery to a crusade for independence, was effective to the point of prompting serious doubts on the part of President Lincoln about whether the North could win. When the long, bloody war finally ended in southern defeat, Davis found himself the object of intense hatred in both the North and

the South. While southerners blamed him for their defeat, northerners accused him of complicity in Lincoln's assassination. Tired and bankrupt in spirit, health, and the wallet alike, Davis returned from two years' postwar imprisonment to write *Rise and Fall of the Confederate Government.*

Lincoln Enters National Politics

In 1842, when Lincoln decided not to run for the Illinois house and with his marriage to Mary Todd, his life took a new turn. He set his sights on national politics, his new family, his support of the Whig Party in Illinois, and his demanding legal career.

Four years later, after expanding his law practice and personal reputation, Lincoln decided to run for the U.S. House of Representatives as a Whig. He won the election and took his seat in Congress in December 1847, during the debates over the Mexican War (1846–48). Lincoln distinguished himself as a loyal party member by opposing the Mexican War, despite its popularity in Illinois. When Lincoln did not run for reelection (he believed that political offices should rotate), the new president, Whig Zachary Taylor, offered Lincoln the governorship of the territory of Oregon in 1849. Lincoln declined in the hopes of a position at the General Land Office, which was not offered to him. Lincoln then returned to his law practice in Springfield, and tried to rebuild his political reputation, which had suffered from opposition to the Mexican War.

In 1854, in response to the Kansas-Nebraska Act, Lincoln decided to reenter politics. Proposed by Stephen A. Douglas, now a U.S. senator from Illinois, the Kansas-Nebraska Act would have allowed slavery's expansion into areas of the Midwest where slavery had been prohibited by the Missouri Compromise of 1820. Lincoln ran for election to the Illinois legislature, won the seat,

but declined the office in order to be available for the U.S. Senate race. Although he led on the first ballot by the Illinois legislature (at that point state legislatures elected U.S. senators), his support slipped away on later ballots. Lincoln then gave his support to Democrat Lyman Trumbull, who also opposed the Kansas-Nebraska Act; Trumbull was elected to the Senate on the 10th ballot.

In the years that followed, Lincoln was instrumental in organizing the Illinois opposition to the Kansas-Nebraska Act, which became the foundation of the emerging Republican Party. Lincoln attended the first Republican National Convention in Philadelphia, Pennsylvania, in June 1856, and was considered for the party's vice presidential candidate. He went on to campaign in Illinois for Republican Party presidential candidate, John C. Frémont, who lost the election to Pennsylvania Democrat James Buchanan.

The Lincoln-Douglas Debates

In 1857 Lincoln spoke out against the recent Supreme Court decision in *Dred Scott v. Sanford*. This ruling denied all rights to African Americans and cleared the way for the movement of slavery into the west. It also undercut the fundamental principle of the fledgling Republican Party: the nonextension of slavery into the federal territories. The next year Lincoln was involved in what would become one of the most memorable political events of U.S. history: the Lincoln-Douglas debates.

Illinois's Republican Party nominated Lincoln as their choice for the Senate seat held by Democrat Stephen Douglas.

In accepting his nomination, Lincoln delivered one of his best-known speeches, the "House Divided" speech. In this speech Lincoln spoke to the crisis before the country, beginning by quoting from scripture:

> A house divided against itself cannot stand. I believe this government cannot endure, permanently half *slave* and half *free*. I do not expect the Union to be *dissolved*—I do not expect the house to *fall*—but I *do* expect it will cease to be divided. It will become *all* one thing, or *all* the other. Either the *opponents* of slavery, will arrest the further spread of it, and place it where the public mind shall rest in the belief that it is in the course of ultimate extinction; or its *advocates* will push it forward, till it shall become alike lawful in *all* the States, *old* as well as *new*—*North* as well as *South.* . . .

On July 9, 1858, Lincoln attended a speech by Senator Douglas in Chicago, Illinois, responding in print to Douglas's speech the next day. Lincoln followed Douglas around the state delivering his own speech and responding to Douglas's. Douglas refused Lincoln's offer to share the stage for their political speeches, but Douglas agreed to debate Lincoln seven times in August, September, and October 1858; Douglas defending the Kansas-Nebraska Act and its extension of slavery into the federal territories and Lincoln attacking Kansas-Nebraska and arguing against the extension of slavery into the federal territories. In the November elections, the Republicans won a plurality of the vote, but the Democrats maintained their hold on the Illinois Senate. Douglas was then reelected by the state senate. Lincoln gathered together the newspaper clippings of the debates and saw that they were published in 1860.

The Lincoln Presidency

Although he lost the Illinois Senate race of 1858, Lincoln's name had become known among Republicans nationally, and he received his party's nomination for president in 1860. On November 6, 1860, Lincoln won a four-way contest for the presidency, winning a plurality of the popular vote and receiving 180 of the 303 electoral votes. Republicans also won majorities in both the new House and the Senate.

The campaign, which had been centered almost entirely on the future of slavery, split the Democratic Party along northern and southern lines and demonstrated the deep divisions between the North and the South. Seven southern states, fearing that the new Republican government would try to abolish slavery and force its will on the states, claimed to secede from the Union between Lincoln's election and his inauguration on March 4, 1861. A month after Lincoln took office, South Carolina fired on the Union's Fort Sumter in the harbor of Charleston, South Carolina, and the nation launched itself into four years of bloody civil war to preserve the Union.

From the beginning, the North's goal as proclaimed by Lincoln was the restoration of the Union, but with the Emancipation Proclamation of January 1863, Lincoln added to the war's goals the end of slavery. The initial fighting saw many victories for the South, but gradually the North's advantages in men and material began to show. Military successes in July 1863 at Gettysburg, Pennsylvania, and Vicksburg, Mississippi, turned the war decisively in favor of the North.

These military victories, as well as favorable state elections in Ohio and Pennsylvania, had Lincoln looking forward to reelection in November of 1864. He was unanimously renominated by the "National Union" Party (the Republican Party was renamed for the 1864 election in an attempt to reach out to so-called war Democrats—those against emancipation but for a military end to the war). Buoyed by the siege of the Confederate capital and the capture of Atlanta, Georgia, by Union troops, Lincoln won 55 percent of the popular vote and 212 of the 233 electoral votes cast in defeating the Democratic Party's candidate, Gen. George Brinton McClellan. On March 4, 1865, Lincoln delivered his famous second inaugural address, urging a gentle hand toward southerners in the postwar world. The southern Confederacy soon collapsed, and on April 9, 1865, Confederate Gen. Robert E. Lee surrendered near Appomattox Courthouse in Virginia, effectively ending the war. Lincoln made his last public speech on April 11 regarding reconstruction of the nation.

Post-presidential Years

On April 14, 1865, Lincoln was shot while at Ford's Theatre in Washington, D.C. Lincoln lost consciousness after being shot and was carried to a house across the street. He died early on April 15, 1865. Chief Justice Salmon P. Chase administered the presidential oath of office to Vice President Andrew Johnson of Tennessee at approximately 10:30 A.M. that morning.

Secretary of War Edwin Stanton took charge of the investigation of Lincoln's death. Lincoln's assassin, a sympathizer with the Confederate cause named John Wilkes Booth, initially escaped, but he died during an attempt to capture him at Port Royal, Virginia, on April 26. Eventually, eight people were tried by a military tribunal for the conspiracy to kill President Lincoln, Vice President Andrew Johnson, and Secretary of State William Seward. Four were executed, the others sentenced to life imprisonment.

Lincoln's oldest son, Robert Todd Lincoln (born August 1, 1843), also distinguished himself as a businessman and public servant. After graduating from Harvard College in 1864, Robert Todd Lincoln studied law at the Harvard Law School. During the American Civil War (1860–65) he left school to serve on the staff of Union Gen. Ulysses S. Grant. He then completed his degree and became a corporate lawyer in Chicago, Illinois. Robert Todd Lincoln would later serve as secretary of war to Presidents Garfield and Arthur in the 1880s, and was the U.S. minister in Great Britain from 1889 to 1893. He then left public service and reentered the business world. In 1911 he became chairman of the board of the Pullman Company. Robert Todd Lincoln died on July 26, 1926, at his family's retreat at Manchester, Vermont.

The Abraham Lincoln Administrations

Abraham Lincoln consistently ranks as one of the most important presidents in U.S. history. Not only did he direct and manage the country through the political and constitutional crises of secession and civil war, Lincoln also led and educated the public about the war's goals, oversaw the military, managed internal domestic politics, and discouraged foreign intervention. And throughout this maelstrom of war, politics, and personal tragedy, Lincoln maintained his great dignity, humility, and humanity. Few men have had as great an impact on the United States as Lincoln.

Lincoln Becomes President

The Campaign of 1860

Although he lost the Illinois Senate race of 1858, Lincoln's name became nationally known among Republicans and he was considered a serious presidential candidate. Known for his support of business, his support of free labor (meaning white property-owning workers), his opposition to the spread of slavery into the Great Plains, and his moderate position on tariffs, Lincoln carved an attractive political niche for himself. Lincoln visited the eastern states early in 1860 on a speaking tour and developed an extensive following.

In the tradition of the day, Lincoln did not travel to the Republican National Convention in Chicago, Illinois, held from May 16 to May 18, 1860, but his supporters were there in force. While prominent Lincoln backers such as Judge David Davis of Illinois (whom Lincoln would later appoint to the Supreme Court) worked to convince delegates to support Lincoln, less prominent supporters filled the balcony and cheered wildly every time Lincoln's name was mentioned. Lincoln faced many strong challengers for the nomination, including Edward Bates of Missouri, Senator Salmon P. Chase of Ohio, Senator Simon Cameron of Pennsylvania, and Senator William H. Seward of New York, many of whom had more experience in national politics than Lincoln.

On the third ballot Lincoln prevailed over his opponents, receiving 364 votes and the presidential nomination. The convention selected Hannibal Hamlin of Maine as the party's vice presidential nominee. The party platform opposed the expansion of slavery into the federal western territories; pledged not to interfere with slavery within states; endorsed a protective tariff to aid U.S. business; and supported a homestead act, federal support for a transcontinental railroad, and other internal improvements including banking reform.

Lincoln's Opponents

The Democratic Party held its convention during late April and early May at the Hall of the South Carolina Institute in Charleston, South Carolina. Led by William Lowndes Yancy of Alabama, southern Democrats demanded a party platform calling for a federal slave code to protect slavery in the West. This demand was too extreme for the northern Democrats. Led by Senator Stephen A. Douglas of Illinois, Northern Democrats favored a policy of accommodating slavery in the West through "popular sovereignty," which would allow the people in the western areas to decide for themselves whether or not to protect slavery. With the two sides still deadlocked on a candidate or platform after 57 votes, the convention adjourned, with an agreement to meet again in Baltimore, Maryland, in June.

A month later, however, divisions had only grown deeper. Southern Democrats boycotted the convention at the Front Street Theater in Baltimore, Maryland, from June 18 to June 23, splitting the party. Without the southerners present, the northern Democratic Party convention went smoothly nominating Douglas for the presidency on the second ballot, and Herschel Vespasian Johnson of Georgia for the vice presidency. Their platform supported Douglas's solution of popular sovereignty over slavery in the West without a federal slave code, federal monies for a transcontinental railroad, and other internal improvement projects.

Southern Democrats also met in Baltimore five days after the northern Democratic Party convention closed. Meeting at the Maryland Institute Hall in June 1860, they nominated current vice president John Cabell Breckinridge of Kentucky for president and Joseph Lane of Oregon for the vice presidency. For their platform the southern Democrats called for a federal slave code to protect slavery in the federal territories and an explicit guarantee to slave owners that they could take their property into the federal territories.

A fourth political party formed during the politically stormy summer of 1860. Essentially the last remnants of the old Whig Party, they called themselves the Constitutional Union Party and essentially hoped to defuse the political situation by ignoring it. Meeting in Baltimore on May 9 to May 10, 1860, the party adopted a simplistic platform of platitudes supporting "the Constitution of the Country, the Union of the States, and the enforce-

Administration

Administration Dates

March 4, 1861–March 4, 1865
March 4, 1865–April 15, 1865

Vice President

Hannibal Hamlin (1861–65)
Andrew Johnson (1865)

Cabinet

Secretary of State

Jeremiah S. Black (1860–61)
William H. Seward (1861–69)

Secretary of the Treasury

John A. Dix (1861)
Salmon P. Chase (1861–64)
William P. Fessenden (1864–65)
Hugh McCulloch (1865–69)

Secretary of War

Joseph Holt (1861)
Simon Cameron (1861–62)
Edwin M. Stanton (1862–68)

Attorney General

Edward Bates (1861–64)
James Speed (1864–66)

Secretary of the Navy

Isaac Toucey (1857–61)
Gideon Welles (1861–69)

Postmaster General

Horatio King (1861)
Montgomery Blair (1861–64)
William Dennison Jr. (1864–66)

Secretary of the Interior

Caleb B. Smith (1861–62)
John P. Usher (1863–65)

---

ment of the laws" and saying nothing about the key issue of the expansion of slavery into the federal territories. For president the Constitutional Union Party chose John Bell of Tennessee, and for vice president Edward Everett of Massachusetts.

The Election

The election of 1860 had four major candidates but, in reality, there were two separate, two-way contests, with Douglas and Lincoln contesting for the northern free labor states and Breckinridge and Bell contesting for the slave labor states. On the surface, the key issue of the election of 1860 was the question of the extension of slavery into the federal territories, but as the campaign built, it became clear that the Republican Party itself was the issue. Southerners feared that Lincoln and the "black Republicans" favored immediate emancipation of African Americans, the confiscation of their property in persons, and the trampling of their right to hold slaves under state law. As time passed southern leaders more and more feared the political results if the Republicans won the election of November 1860, to the point that they claimed a national administration led by Republicans would be unacceptable and secession would be southerners' only option. Republicans stressed again and again that their party platform stated their opposition to

the expansion of slavery into the West but their respect of slavery within states. But in the midst of the passions and fears of the time, few southerners were listening.

On election day, November 6, 1860, the results showed a solid win for Lincoln and the Republicans. The Republicans polled the majority of the popular votes, 1.8 million, with Douglas next with 1.3 million, followed by Breckinridge with 850,000, and Bell with 600,000. Lincoln's win signaled a change in policy at the national level and confirmed many southerners' worst fears about federal limitations on their slave property, an overly powerful central government, and their future within the Union.

The Campaign of 1864

Occasionally lost in the history of the American Civil War (1860–65) era is the presidential election of 1864. Lincoln was not certain that he would either receive the Republican Party nomination, or win reelection in November 1864, because so much depended on the successes of the military that he could not predict or control. There were many prominent opponents within his own party, including some of Lincoln's cabinet. Lincoln also faced the facts that no president had been elected to a second term since Andrew Jackson in 1832, nor had any sitting president been renominated by his party since 1840.

Lincoln's strongest challenger within the Republican Party was Secretary of the Treasury Salmon P. Chase. Chase believed himself not just equal to Lincoln in talent but more willing to press ahead quickly on emancipation, or freeing the slaves in the South. Working within the traditions of the time, Chase did not openly campaign to unseat Lincoln for the Republican nomination but instead allowed his friends to promote his candidacy. And his friends proved his undoing. In February 1864 a pro-Chase pamphlet circulated by prominent Republican congressmen appeared in the Midwest. Several days later Chase's political manager, Senator Samuel C. Pomeroy of Kansas, circulated a letter touting Chase's strengths and denigrating Lincoln's abilities. The "Pomeroy Circular" ended up hurting Chase's chances, however, because it caused a pro-Lincoln reaction within the Republican Party.

Within the next few months, 14 Republican-controlled legislatures or state conventions passed resolutions supporting Lincoln's renomination. By the time the Republicans gathered at the Front Street Theater in Baltimore, Maryland, on June 7 to June 8, 1864, Lincoln's renomination was no longer in doubt. In order to reach out to Democratic supporters of the war, the Republicans called themselves the "National Union" Party. To back up their claims of representing the entire Union, the Republicans selected Andrew Johnson of Tennessee, the only southern Democratic senator not to follow his state out of the Union, as their vice presidential candidate.

Northern war weariness, relative lack of successes on the battlefield, and the internal dispute among the Republicans over Reconstruction (*See also*, Domestic Issues), led Lincoln to believe that he would not be reelected in 1864. Lincoln wrote a memo on August 23, 1864, saying that he did not believe that he would be reelected and therefore it was his duty to assist in the transfer of power to the new administration. Lincoln took the memo to the cabinet and had them endorse it, without telling them what it said.

The Democrats

Lincoln had good reason to be concerned about his prospects for reelection, as the Democrats remained a powerful political force. After being removed from command of the Union armies, Gen. George B. McClellan had returned to New Jersey and supported Democratic candidates for political offices. McClellan also let it be known that he was available for the Democratic Party nomination of 1864.

McClellan was a so-called war Democrat—he opposed emancipation but sought a military end to the rebellion. This position put him at odds with the peace Democrats—who also opposed emancipation but favored a negotiated end to the war. When the Democrats met in Chicago, Illinois, from August 29 to August 31, 1864, the two competing wings of the party agreed to nominate the war Democrat McClellan as their presidential nominee (and George Hunt Pendleton of Ohio as their vice presidential nominee) and let the peace Democrats write the party platform. The Democratic Party platform therefore put peace with the Confederates, or southerners who had seceded from the Union, first, and restoration of the Union second. McClellan now faced a situation where he was expected to run on a platform that he opposed. In the end, McClellan ignored the party's platform and emphasized his own feeling that preservation of the Union was the nation's first priority, and peace was second.

The Election

On November 8, 1864, the voters of the northern and midwestern states went to the polls and gave Lincoln a solid victory. In raw numbers Lincoln and Johnson received 2.2 million votes, or 55 percent of the popular vote, and McClellan received 1.8 million votes, or 45 percent of the popular vote. McClellan carried only three politically minor states: Kentucky, New Jersey, and Delaware. Crucial in some states and remarkable for their numbers was the soldier vote. Some states had legislation that allowed troops to be polled while in the field. Troops from states that did not poll the field troops were often given furloughs to return home to vote. Among those in the service and literally risking their lives against the rebellion, Union soldiers gave Lincoln 78 percent of their votes.

Lincoln's reelection demonstrated not only his popularity and the popularity of his administration, it demonstrated the North's determination to see the war concluded without compromise to southerners and slavery. It was a message not lost on either northern public opinion, the Confederates, or the Lincoln administration.

Lincoln's Advisers

As president Lincoln actively sought advice from a large number of people, both civilian and military. For the most part, he relied upon his cabinet officers to run their departments. However, Lincoln maintained overall control, and when he felt major decisions or changes were necessary, he acted. In an effort to strengthen and unify the Republican Party, Lincoln appointed many of his most powerful opponents within the party to his cabinet. While several of these men proved very capable, they were also ambitious and hoped to use their positions to enhance their power.

Lincoln's relationship with his secretary of state is an example. William H. Seward ran against Lincoln for the Republican presidential nomination in 1860 and was still bothered by his defeat. Seward accepted Lincoln's offer to become secretary of state thinking that he would play the role of an older, wiser, "premier" to Lincoln, who had little experience in national politics. During the height of the secession crisis of March and April 1861, Seward led the cabinet in urging Lincoln to reach a compromise with the South. As such, he opposed the idea of resupplying Fort Sumter (*See also,* Domestic Issues). By March 20, however, public opinion had shifted to the point that Seward was the only cabinet officer who still opposed resupply.

Unhappy with his inability to influence policy, and unwilling to embarrass himself by backing down from his earlier position, Seward presented a position paper to Lincoln on April 1, 1861. In this paper Seward proposed abandoning Fort Sumter, but more extreme were his foreign policy proposals. In essence, Seward suggested entering into war with France and Spain in order to unite the country behind the national government through a foreign war. Seward's letter went on to say that strong leadership would be needed to challenge these European powers, and he suggested that he could provide that leadership.

Lincoln responded to Seward's note that same day. As to who should lead the cabinet and the administration, Lincoln politely but firmly rejected Seward's offer. Lincoln told Seward that he welcomed his suggestions, but he also made it clear that he, as president, would lead the administration. Lincoln also rejected Seward's suggestion not to resupply Fort Sumter and dismissed his idea of foreign intervention. After this response, Seward backed down, realizing that he could not control Lincoln.

For domestic and foreign policy Lincoln relied on a talented group of cabinet officers, some of whom were also his political rivals. Secretary of State William H. Seward oversaw the nation's foreign policy. After resolving his initial difficulties with Lincoln, he proved highly effective, particularly in his role in preventing Great Britain or France from coming to the aid of the Confederacy, as the southern states that seceded were referred. Seward was greatly aided by the steady hand, the appreciation of European politics, and the great prestige of the U.S. ambassador in London, England, Charles Francis Adams—the son and grandson of former presidents John and John Quincy Adams.

Secretary of the Treasury Salmon P. Chase was another one of Lincoln's rivals in the Republican Party. He successfully oversaw the taxing and spending policies of the Lincoln administration and managed the controversial expansion of the money supply through the use of paper money, known as greenbacks.

Simon Cameron, Lincoln's first secretary of war, was an important Pennsylvania politician and another candidate for the Republican presidential nomination in 1860. Lincoln needed to reward Pennsylvania with a cabinet post as well as appease Cameron. Unfortunately the monumental task of organizing, enlisting, training, equipping, and directing the ever-expanding U.S. Army and Navy overwhelmed Cameron. He awarded military contracts to his friends, which embarrassed the Lincoln

administration and undermined public confidence in the war effort. As a result, on January 15, 1862, Lincoln replaced Cameron with fellow Pennsylvanian Edwin M. Stanton. A Democrat, Stanton had served as attorney general in the James Buchanan administration. By appointing Stanton, Lincoln reached out to the "war" Democrats, the loyal opposition of the North. Lincoln and Stanton worked well together, and Stanton brought honesty, efficiency, and respectability back to the War Department.

Gideon Welles, the secretary of the navy, was another important adviser to Lincoln. Welles guided the building up of the ocean and river navy and offered his opinion to Lincoln on many military and domestic issues. Welles also is known for his diary, an important source of information on Lincoln, his administration, and the American Civil War.

Military Advisers

Lincoln was less successful in finding effective generals for the Union war effort than he was in building and controlling his cabinet. Over the course of the war, Lincoln turned to what became a blur of generals in his search for effective military leadership. Not until March 1864 did Lincoln find a general and a command structure to press forward the war effort.

During the secession crisis and the early stages of the war, Lincoln turned to Gen. Winfield Scott for advice. A highly respected hero of the Mexican War (1846–48) and the highest-ranking officer in the military, Scott was 71 years old at the outset of the war and no longer capable of leading troops in the field. He did, however, develop a war plan for the Union to follow. His plan, which called for the blockading of Confederate ocean ports and the use of the navy in the Mississippi River to split the Confederacy in half, would prove an important part of the Union strategy.

Recognizing that Scott was too weak from old age to manage the war, Lincoln eased him out in the fall of 1861. His replacement was Gen. George Brinton McClellan. McClellan caught the attention of Lincoln and the general public with his successful actions in western Virginia. Appointed to lead the Army of the Potomac (the Union's main military force in the east) in July 1861, he also was appointed the overall commander of the army in November. A skilled administrator, McClellan performed well in building up the strength of the Union army. In the field, however, McClellan proved extremely cautious with his troops and was unable to make significant headway against the Confederate army and its leader, Gen. Robert E. Lee.

When McClellan took his army south to attack Richmond, Virginia, in the summer of 1863, Lincoln appointed a new general in chief to manage the army as a whole. For this position Lincoln chose Gen. Henry W. Halleck, who had been in overall command of the

Union's western armies. Halleck succeeded in the role of the army's chief administrator, but he was unable to lead McClellan into the aggressive action that Lincoln considered necessary. When McClellan's attack on Richmond failed, Lincoln chose to remove McClellan from command in November 1863.

With the removal of McClellan, Lincoln also needed a new field commander. It took him until March of 1864 to find one who suited his needs. Gen. Ulysses S. Grant, who had won a series of important victories in the West, was given command of the entire Union army, and came east to take personal command of the Army of the Potomac. Halleck served as chief of staff under Grant, continuing to manage the army as Grant took to the field. Over the course of late 1864 and early 1865, Grant led the Union to victory.

Lincoln and Congress

Three Congresses met during the Lincoln administration: the Thirty-seventh, Thirty-eighth, and Thirty-ninth Congresses. Because southerners removed themselves from the halls of Congress leaving the Republicans and a small number of northern Democrats in control of the Senate and the House of Representatives, Lincoln and Congress experienced good personal and political relations. However, differences did emerge within the respective parties.

The Democrats

Among the Democrats, two general groups appeared: the peace Democrats and the war Democrats. Peace Democrats supported the continuation of the Union but wanted a negotiated end to the conflict. They also opposed the blockade of the Confederacy, Lincoln's expansion of the army, and the issuance of paper money (greenbacks) to fund the war effort. War Democrats wanted the Union restored militarily, not through negotiations with the secessionists and, as with all Democrats, they opposed emancipation of the slaves.

The Republicans

The Republicans in Congress were roughly divided into three groups—the conservatives, the moderates, and the Radicals. The conservative Republicans supported Lincoln, but counseled a go-slow policy on issues such as confiscation of slaves and southern property and the war effort. Many opposed the emancipation of African Americans and, once emancipation occurred, opposed the recruitment and use of African American troops as well as voting by African Americans.

The Radical Republicans were at the opposite end of the spectrum from conservatives. Their name is misleading for they adopted the term "radical" themselves, by which they meant that they went to the root (the radical) of the issues. The Radicals strongly favored emancipation, even immediate emancipation, based on their revulsion of slavery, and they felt that Lincoln moved too slowly toward making emancipation a war goal. Radicals aggressively supported the war's efforts and sought to punish the South for its treason, which for them included depriving wealthy southerners of their personal property—their slaves.

The rest of the Republicans were the moderates. As their name implied, the moderates fell somewhere between the conservatives and the Radicals in their opinions. Lincoln himself was a moderate, and while their exact positions could vary greatly, most moderates supported Lincoln's conduct of the war and handling of emancipation.

The Radicals were the most vocal of the branches of the Republican Party, and as such they received a great deal of attention both then and today. The moderates were the largest group in Congress, however, and research shows that when congressional bills were voted on, the moderates and the conservatives, together with the war Democrats, controlled policy making in Congress.

Legislation

With Republicans in control and southerners out of Congress a lot of important nonmilitary legislation that southerners had blocked in the past became a reality. In particular, bills supported by the Lincoln administration and passed by Congress in 1862 and 1863 included the Homestead Act, the Land-Grant College Act (the Morrill Act), the Pacific Railroad Act, as well as the Legal Tender Act, the Internal Revenue Act, and the Confiscation Act. Such legislation provided cheap land for western development, educational institutions in the Midwest and the West, and an intercontinental railroad linking the vast country together, and proved momentous for postwar economic development. These acts formed what historian Leonard P. Curry has described as a "blue print for modern America."

Reconstruction

The Lincoln administration was so well in tune with both public opinion and the Republican majorities in the Senate and the House that Lincoln exercised the presidential veto power only once. At issue was what would become known as Reconstruction—who should direct the reconstruction and readmission of states back into the Union, the Congress or the president, and what standards must the reconstructed states meet to be readmitted?

On December 8, 1863, the Lincoln administration proposed a "Proclamation of Amnesty and Reconstruction." Under this relatively easy and fast reconstruction plan to bring rebellious states back into the nation, Lincoln offered a pardon and a restoration of property, except slaves, to persons who would swear an oath of

Biography:

Frederick Douglass

Activist; Editor; Author (1817–95) After escaping north to freedom from the bonds of slavery in his early twenties, Frederick Douglass began his life as one of the most ardent and effective abolitionists. Douglass used both the pen and podium as his weapons against pro-slavery sentiment. His success on both fronts was meteoric. In 1845, his autobiography, *Narrative of the Life of Frederick Douglass, an American Slave,* was published and immediately became a best-seller. Douglass's moving and eloquent lectures were popular in Europe as well as in the United States. For the 1860 presidential election, Douglass backed Abraham Lincoln, even though Lincoln did not support Douglass's two strongest viewpoints: that African Americans should be allowed to fight in the Union Army and that a decree should be issued declaring the freedom of all southern slaves. President Lincoln eventually came to agree with Douglass's point of view. In 1862 Lincoln delivered the *Emancipation Proclamation,* and a year later an all-African American regiment

was formed. In 1863 Douglass met with President Lincoln to share his concerns over the inferior treatment of African American soldiers fighting in the Union Army. The following year, President Lincoln called a second meeting with Douglass. Lincoln shared his doubts about his ability to win the war and asked Douglass to draw up plans for leading slaves out of the South should the Union face imminent defeat. For Douglass, the North's victory in the American Civil War was shallow, doing little more than guaranteeing the freedom of the slaves. Douglass spent the remaining 30 years of his life in a tireless campaign to promote the civil rights and liberties of African Americans across the nation.

---

future allegiance to the Union (high Confederate officials and officers were excluded). Once 10 percent of the population who had voted in 1860 had taken the oath, they could establish a loyal government by electing state officers and apply for presidential recognition. Under this plan, loyal citizens in several states started the process of reconstruction, particularly in Louisiana and Arkansas. But Congress controls its own membership, and it would be up to Congress to decide whether to readmit the representatives of an executively recognized state back into the nation and seat their representatives.

To the Radicals and many moderates in Congress, Lincoln's 10 percent plan did not sufficiently punish the rebels. And as the casualty figures climbed in early to middle 1864 and northern public opinion solidified for punishing the South, Congress proposed its own plan for Reconstruction. Called the Wade-Davis Bill (after its sponsors, Senator Benjamin F. Wade of Ohio and Congressman Henry Winter Davis of Maryland), it passed Congress in July 1864 after five months of contentious debate. The Wade-Davis Bill differed from Lincoln's 10 percent plan in a number of important ways. It set the minimum percentage taking the oath to participate in Reconstruction at 50 percent, not 10 percent. Furthermore, instead of swearing an oath of future allegiance, the Wade-Davis Bill demanded that persons swear the "iron clad oath," an oath that they had never supported the rebellion. This 50 percent would not elect state officers but establish a state constitutional convention to

rewrite their state constitution providing protections for the newly freed African Americans. Congressional Republicans wanted to reward southern Unionists for their support throughout the conflict and, at least some Radicals hoped, use the iron clad oath to allow African Americans into the political process, since they had never voluntarily supported the rebellion.

Although the Wade-Davis Bill passed Congress almost unanimously, Lincoln was opposed to it. Congress went out of session soon after passing the bill, and Lincoln chose to simply not sign the bill, voiding the bill in a process known as a pocket veto. Lincoln explained his veto by saying that he did not want to be committed to any single plan for Reconstruction. Further Lincoln wanted to encourage and nurture those states that had begun Reconstruction under Lincoln's terms—specifically Arkansas and Louisiana. This veto greatly angered the bill's supporters, but Lincoln's 10 percent plan remained the only Reconstruction plan in place at the time of Lincoln's death in 1865.

Lincoln and the Judiciary

Lincoln left an important impression on the judiciary through his appointment of Republicans, both to the Supreme Court and to the lower federal judiciary. No appointment demonstrated the change in direction of the country with the Republicans more than the appointment of Salmon P. Chase as chief justice of the Supreme Court on December 6, 1864. Chase, who had built his reputation as an opponent of slavery, replaced Chief Justice Roger B. Taney, author of the infamous *Dred Scott* decision of 1857 (*See also,* Buchanan Administration). In the 1869 case *Texas v. White,* Chase would write the Lincoln administration's view of the nation into constitutional law when he described the nation as "an indestructible Union of indestructible States."

Chase was the last and most famous of Lincoln's five appointments to the Supreme Court. The others were Noah Hayes Swayne of Ohio on January 24, 1862; Samuel Freeman Miller of Iowa on July 16, 1862; David Davis of Illinois on October 17, 1862; and Stephen Johnson Field of California on March 10, 1863. In time, Miller became an important member of the Court, and Justice Field would become one of the most respected justices in the late nineteenth century.

One important case regarding Lincoln's war powers reached the U.S. Supreme Court during his administration. In 1863 the Supreme Court considered a case that challenged the legality of Lincoln's April 19, 1861, declaration of a naval blockade of the South. At issue was whether or not Lincoln possessed the constitutional authority to declare a blockade without permission from Congress. Congress was not in session when Lincoln declared the blockade, and only in July of 1861 did it pass a resolution authorizing Lincoln's actions.

The owners of some ships seized between the time of the president's proclamation and Congress's authorization went to federal court and challenged the legality and constitutionality of the presidential blockade. When the lower federal courts rejected their challenges, the owners appealed and the Supreme Court combined their actions into one case, the *Prize Cases* (1863). In a five-to-four decision (with all three of Lincoln's appointees voting in the majority), the Court upheld Lincoln's actions as a valid use of the emergency powers inherent in the president's war powers. Southern sympathizer Chief Justice Roger B. Taney strenuously dissented, arguing that the Constitution did not explicitly provide for such emergency powers, and that the Constitution's grant to the president to wage war did not extend to suppressing an internal rebellion.

Changes in the U.S. Government

One new cabinet position was created during the Lincoln administration, the Department of Agriculture on May 15, 1862. Two new states gained admission to the Union during Lincoln's administration: West Virginia on June 19, 1863 (its territory having been captured from Virginia), and, on October 31, 1864, Nevada became part of the Union. The Thirteenth Amendment to the Constitution, which outlawed slavery, was passed by Congress

on January 31, 1865. Lincoln would not live to see its ratification in December.

On another level, a major change had occurred in the country with Lincoln's election and the withdrawal of southerners from Congress. Popular ideas that had languished in Congress because of southern opposition became law, such as the Homestead Act of 1862 (*See also,* Lincoln and Congress). The Lincoln administration provided adequate and active government to maintain the Constitution, build the nation, defeat the rebellion, and remove the blot of slavery. This aggressive use of federal government power was a dramatic change from the administrations of the decades before the American Civil War (1860–65), which tended to defer to Congress and the states. While some presidents, such as George Washington and Andrew Jackson, had employed strong federal leadership in crisis situations, Lincoln and the Republicans changed the nature of the country by firmly asserting the supreme power of the federal government, and by directly involving the federal government in people's lives. Lincoln and his supporters considered the United States a nation, not merely a loose union of states, and they stressed the strength of the federal government to preserve the country and the Constitution even in the face of a domestic insurrection. And the Lincoln administration did so by finding adequate powers within the existing federal Constitution (especially the president's oath and war powers) to craft a more perfect Union.

Domestic Issues

Two domestic issues dominated the Lincoln administration: the American Civil War (1860–65) and the related issue of slavery. All other issues including the currency questions, race relations, preventing European intervention in the Civil War, nonmilitary legislation, and eventually questions of reconstruction after the war hinged on the execution of the war effort and decisions regarding slavery.

The Birth of the Confederacy

On December 20, 1860, South Carolina voted to secede from the Union. The South Carolinians feared that when Lincoln became president and the Republicans took control of Congress in March of 1861, they would act to end slavery across the United States. Mississippi, Florida, Alabama, Georgia, Louisiana, and Texas, the so-called Deep South, soon followed South Carolina. These states banded together and began to form the government that would become the Confederate States of America. In an attempt to maintain public calm, Lincoln spent the secession winter balancing a cabinet, working on his first inaugural speech, but saying nothing publicly about the secession.

This cartoon depicts Union attitudes toward the South at the beginning of the Civil War. As the Confederate States of America formed under the leadership of Jefferson Davis, the North believed traitors like Davis should hang for their crimes. (Currier and Ives lithograph. National Portrait Gallery. Reproduced by permission.)

Privately Lincoln and the rest of the Republicans tried to reassure southerners that the forthcoming administration would not endanger them nor their property within current states. Republicans had no plan to abolish slavery in the South, or in the District of Columbia (which they would control once in office), nor did they envision any interference with the interstate slave trade. But the Republicans would not compromise on the nonexpansion of slavery into the federal territories.

Southerners met in Montgomery, Alabama, beginning on February 4, 1861, and wrote a constitution for the so-called Confederacy, which strengthened protection for slavery and the right of a state to protect slavery. They nominated Mississippian Jefferson Davis as provisional president and Alexander Stephens as provisional vice president. They scheduled elections and inaugurations for 1862 and established a Confederate Congress. In one of its first acts, the Montgomery meeting authorized an army of 100,000 men. With these actions southerners launched the Confederacy.

Attempts at Compromise

While the secession crisis was clearly serious, there were still many people who hoped that a compromise

could be reached that would keep the South in the Union. Certainly recent history suggested that compromise was possible. Politicians had compromised the issue of slavery a number of times, most recently with the Compromise of 1850, just 10 years earlier.

A peace conference convened by the Virginia legislature in February 1861 proved a failure when representatives of the seceded states refused to attend. Meanwhile, both the U.S. House and the U.S. Senate established committees to discuss the slavery issue. Senator John J. Crittenden of Kentucky proposed that the Missouri Compromise line of 36 degrees 30 minutes be extended all the way across the country to the Pacific Ocean. Republicans, however, were unwilling to accept such an expansion of slavery into the West. Congress did agree to a new amendment to the Constitution. This proposed Thirteenth Amendment would have protected slavery where it existed against federal interference. It had significant Republican support, as it did not extend slavery, but this proposal came too late. Only two states had ratified the amendment before the beginning of the American Civil War made it meaningless.

The Inauguration of President Lincoln

Southern sympathizer and Maryland chief justice Roger B. Taney administered the oath of office of the president of the United States to Abraham Lincoln on March 4, 1861. Lincoln well understood the political and legal tensions in the country, the potential threat of the Confederacy, and the importance of his inaugural speech in setting the tone for his administration. While restating his party's commitment not to interfere with slavery within states, Lincoln also forcefully argued that the Union was perpetual and secession was wrong. Because southern states had taken over most of the federal installations in the South (with the notable exceptions of Fort Pickens in Pensacola Bay, Florida, and Fort Sumter in the harbor of Charleston, South Carolina), Lincoln pledged his administration to "hold, occupy, and possess" its property and collect all federal taxes and fees. He implied that force might be needed, but only so much force as was necessary to achieve these goals.

In the final two paragraphs of his speech, Lincoln explained that it was up to southerners to solve the constitutional and political crisis of secession. He reached out to southerners and their shared history and heritage in urging them to change their course. Lincoln read:

> In *your* hands, my dissatisfied fellow countrymen, and not *mine,* is the momentous issue of civil war. The government will not assail *you.* You can have no conflict, without being yourselves the aggressors. *You* have no oath registered to Heaven to destroy the government, while *I* shall have the most solemn one to 'preserve, protect, and defend' it.

> I am loath to close. We are not enemies, but friends. We must not be enemies. Though passion may have strained, it must not break our bonds of affection. The mystic chords of memory, stretching from every battle-field, and patriot

grave, to every living heart and hearthstone, all over this broad land, will yet swell the chorus of the Union, when again touched, as surely they will be, by the better angels of our nature.

By crafting his speech in reassuring and vague language on whether the Lincoln administration would use force against the South, Lincoln hoped to give himself as much political room to maneuver as possible. He did not want to alienate and perhaps lose to the Confederacy the upper South states such as Maryland, Virginia, North Carolina, Kentucky, Tennessee, Arkansas, and Missouri. Reactions to Lincoln's first inaugural speech divided along sectional lines with northern Republicans hailing its moderate, prudent, nonconfrontational tone and message, and southerners dismissing the speech.

The American Civil War

Fort Sumter

After Lincoln's inauguration, national interest focused on Forts Pickens and Sumter. Fort Pickens sat just outside Pensacola Bay, Florida, and was relatively easy to resupply. Lincoln ordered the fort reinforced on April 6, 1861. Located within the harbor of Charleston, South Carolina, Fort Sumter was in a different situation altogether. The fort was vulnerable to attack by land, and the Confederacy could prevent supplies from reaching it.

As one of the last areas of Union control in the South, Fort Sumter had become particularly symbolic for both sides. For the North, the fort and its commander, Maj. Robert Anderson, had come to symbolize resistance to the belligerent southerners. To southerners, Fort Sumter represented an affront to their attempt to establish the southern Confederacy. As a result Sumter became more important politically and symbolically than for its military value.

Lincoln's administration faced a dilemma: without resupply and reinforcement Major Anderson could only hold out until April 15, 1861. If the federal government used force to get supplies and new troops into the fort, then the Lincoln administration faced the prospect of starting a war with the seceded states. Such an action might alienate the remaining southern states and drive them into the Confederacy. On March 20 Lincoln accepted a plan not to militarily reinforce Sumter but to send in unarmed supply ships on a "mission of humanity" to support the men of the fort. In this way, if southerners fired on the resupply ships, they, not the Lincoln administration, might be blamed for starting a war. On April 6 Lincoln sent word to the Confederate commander in Charleston, Gen. Pierre G. T. Beauregard, that the resupply ships were on their way and not to interfere with them. The next move was up to the Confederates.

On April 9, after discussing the issue, Jefferson Davis and the Confederate cabinet decided that Fort Sumter had to be taken. After his surrender demand was rejected by Maj. Anderson, Gen. Beauregard prepared to

The Gettysburg Address

Abraham Lincoln seldom made speeches rallying support for the Union war effort as president. The leading spokesman for the North was instead Edward Everett of Massachusetts. Thus it was Everett who was invited to deliver the main address at the dedication of a cemetery on the site of the Gettysburg battlefield on November 19, 1863. After Everett's oration, however, President Lincoln offered some brief dedicatory remarks:

"Four score and seven years ago our fathers brought forth on this continent, a new nation, conceived in Liberty, and dedicated to the proposition that all men are created equal.

"Now we are engaged in a great civil war, testing whether that nation, or any nation so conceived and so dedicated, can long endure. We are met on a great battle-field of that war. We have come to dedicate a portion of that field, as a final resting place for those who here gave their lives that this nation might live. It is altogether fitting and proper that we should do this.

"But in a larger sense, we can not dedicate—we can not consecrate—we can not hallow—this ground. The brave men, living and dead, who struggled here, have consecrated it, far above our poor power to add or detract. The world will little note, nor long remember what we say here, but it can never forget what they did here. It is for us the living, rather, to be dedicated here to the unfinished work which they who fought here have thus far so nobly advanced. It is rather for us to be here dedicated to the great task remaining before us—that from these honored dead we take increased devotion to that cause for which they gave their last full measure of devotion—that we here highly resolve that these dead shall not have died in vain—that this nation, under God, shall have a new birth of freedom—that government of the people, by the people, for the people, shall not perish from the earth."

take the fort by force. On April 12, 1861, at 4:30 A.M., Confederate shore batteries fired on Fort Sumter and the U.S. flag that flew over the fort in the harbor. For 36 hours the cannonade continued, destroying a large part of the fort. Hopelessly outmatched and almost out of supplies, the federal garrison surrendered on April 14.

As a result of the battle over Fort Sumter, Virginia, North Carolina, Tennessee, and Arkansas declared their

What They Said . . .

In the early years of the Civil War, Lincoln consistently refused to make freedom for the slaves a priority of his administration and the war effort, despite pressure from abolitionists and Radical Republicans. On August 22, 1862, Lincoln responded to an attack on his policies by influential newspaper editor Horace Greeley with a letter that read in part:

"My paramount object in this struggle *is* to save the Union, and is *not* either to save or to destroy slavery. If I could save the Union without freeing *any* slave I would do it; and if I could save it by freeing *all* the slaves I would do it; and if I could save it by freeing some and leaving others alone I would also do that. What I do about slavery, and the colored race, I do because I believe it helps to save the Union; and what I forbear, I forbear because I do *not* believe it would help to save the Union . . . . I have here stated my purpose according to my views of *official* duty; and I intend no modification of my oft-expressed *personal* wish that all men every where could be free."

(Source: Abraham Lincoln. "Letter to Horace Greeley," as cited in *The Internet Public Library: Presidents of the United States,* 1999.)

secession and joined with the Confederacy. Maryland, Missouri, and Kentucky wavered between limited involvement and limited neutrality. The United States's Civil War had begun.

Presidential Action

On April 15, on the basis of his oath as president to "preserve, protect, and defend the Constitution of the United States" and employing his war powers as commander in chief, Lincoln called 75,000 state militiamen into federal service for 90 days. On April 19 Lincoln announced a naval blockade of the Confederacy. On May 3 he again enlarged the military on his own authority, issuing a call for men to enlist for three-year terms of service. In order to ensure order and suppress the supporters of rebellion in the border states, Lincoln suspended the legal writ of *habeas corpus* in border areas. With this writ suspended, the military could arrest and hold civilians waging war on the Union without having to turn them over to civilian courts for trial. All of these actions were unprecedented for a president acting without direct authorization from Congress, which was out

of session until July 1, 1861. When Congress convened, however, it retroactively approved all of Lincoln's orders (*See also,* Lincoln and the Judiciary).

The Battlefield

There were three major theaters of operation during the American Civil War. With the capitals of the Confederacy, Richmond, Virginia, and the Union, Washington, D.C., only one hundred miles apart, the eastern theater had the most attention. It was in this region, between Richmond and Washington, D.C., that many of the war's most famous and bloody battles would be fought. The Shenandoah valley of Virginia, on the western side of the Blue Ridge Mountains from Washington and Richmond, also saw a great deal of fighting.

The other major area of ground warfare was in the west. The western theater of operations was initially focused on the Mississippi River and included movements through Missouri, Kentucky, and Tennessee. On the river itself, the navy's gunboats played an important role.

The shorelines and ocean surrounding the Confederacy were also an important battleground. One of Lincoln's first wartime actions was to order a blockade of the South, cutting off the Confederacy from outside supplies. Many of the major ports of the Confederacy were also subject to attack from the sea. With its far superior shipbuilding capabilities, this is one area in which the Union dominated from the beginning.

Many in the North hoped for and expected a quick victory over the Confederacy, but the War Department and the U.S. officer corps were poorly prepared for civil war. The army was small and poorly trained. Many of the nation's best officers, with combat experience from the Mexican War (1846–48), were now serving the Confederacy. Winfield Scott, the commander of the U.S. army when the war began, worked out a plan to defeat the Confederacy over time. Labeled the Anaconda Plan by the media, Scott's plan was fairly simple: establish a naval blockade around the Confederacy, check any aggressive military movements from the Confederacy, and take control of the Mississippi River, dividing the western and eastern states of the Confederacy from each other.

Scott's plan reflected the clear advantages in men and material that the Union had at the beginning of the war. The population of the North was much larger than that of the South, and it had most of the nation's industry. Scott believed that if the Confederacy could be prevented from gaining supplies from the outside, it would eventually collapse. Neither the northern public nor the Lincoln administration wanted to sit and wait, however. Lincoln recognized that the southern will to fight was much stronger than that of the North, and throughout the war he feared the possibility of the northern public growing tired of the fighting and demanding negotiated peace with the Confederacy. From the outset of the war, Lincoln believed that a decisive Union victory would be necessary to restore the Union.

Thus, with the northern newspapers and the public crying "On to Richmond!" Lincoln ordered Scott to send an army to attack the Confederate capital. Union and Confederate forces met at a creek named Bull Run, 25 miles southwest of Washington. There, the Union army was soundly defeated and forced to flee back to Washington.

McClellan Takes Command: With the defeat at Bull Run, Lincoln reassessed the situation and concluded that Scott was correct and that the Union needed to prepare for a longer war. Lincoln chose Gen. George B. McClellan, who had gained some notoriety for his victories in western Virginia, to be the commander of the Army of the Potomac (the main eastern army of the Union). When the aged Gen. Scott stepped down from overall command in November 1861, Lincoln appointed McClellan to this position as well. McClellan's task was to train, organize, and equip a large army and to use that army to defeat the Confederacy in the east. In the first task, he excelled. As a field commander, however, McClellan proved very cautious. He consistently refused to mount a major attack on the Confederacy until well into 1862.

The Union Offensive: While McClellan continued to hold his troops out of battle in the east in early 1862, the Union saw a number of successes in the western theater. In February Gen. Ulysses S. Grant led a combined force of infantry and river gunboats to capture Forts Henry and Donelson in Tennessee. This gave the Union control of the Tennessee and Cumberland Rivers, and paved the way for the capture of Nashville, capital of Tennessee, in February 1862. In April Grant's army suffered a surprise attack near Shiloh Church in West Tennessee. Although Grant held his ground, casualties were high and his offensive was temporarily halted. While Grant rebuilt his strength, an attack from the ocean succeeded in capturing the key Confederate port of New Orleans, Louisiana.

In the east McClellan proposed to transport the Army of the Potomac by sea to a point on the James Peninsula about 25 miles south of Richmond. From there McClellan believed he would be able to press forward to capture the Confederate capital. Put into action in May 1862, McClellan's plan might have worked if he had pursued it aggressively, but as was characteristic of McClellan, he moved too slowly. Despite his superior numbers, McClellan felt the Confederates outnumbered him. Lincoln refused to send any of the defensive troops around Washington to reinforce McClellan, and while they argued, the Confederates launched a counterattack

The Confederacy Counterattacks: Under the command of Gen. Robert E. Lee, the Confederates used superior tactics to drive the larger Union army away from Richmond. With Richmond safe, Lee divided his forces and sent Gen. Thomas Stonewall Jackson back into

northern Virginia to threaten Washington. McClellan had no choice but to abandon the peninsula campaign and rush back up the Chesapeake to help defend the capital, only again to go too slowly and arrive after the Union defeat at the Second Battle of Bull Run from August 29 to August 30, 1862.

After the Second Battle of Bull Run, Lee and Jackson moved their army into Maryland, in an attempt to cut off Washington from the rest of the Union. McClellan followed, and on September 17, 1862, the armies clashed at Antietam, Maryland. The resulting battle was the single bloodiest day of the American Civil War. In less than seven hours of fighting, both sides suffered more than six thousand dead and 17,000 wounded. While McClellan forced Lee back into Virginia, he refused to aggressively pursue Lee. Thus the Confederate army escaped damaged but intact. Lincoln, tired of McClellan's refusal to pursue and engage the Confederates, removed him from command in November 1862. Lincoln also decided to use the occasion of the Union "victory" at Antietam to announce his preliminary emancipation proclamation (*See also,* Domestic Issues: Emancipation). With this announcement, Lincoln added the emancipation of the slaves to the original goal of the war, the restoration of the Union.

Meanwhile in the west the Confederates took advantage of the fact that the Union did not really have sufficient forces to control all of the territory they had conquered. Confederate raiders and guerrilla fighters harassed Union garrisons, blew up bridges and railroad tracks, and generally tied down Union soldiers there, preventing any Union advances in the West.

The Tide Turns: In late 1862 and early 1863, McClellan's replacements fought a series of losing battles with Lee, and were themselves replaced as Lincoln sought a general who could lead the Union to victory. In the west the Union had recovered from the raids of the previous year, and Grant led an army to lay siege to the Confederate fortress guarding the Mississippi River at Vicksburg, Mississippi.

Hoping to weaken the already damaged northern resolve and revive the possibility of European involvement in the war on the side of the Confederacy (*See also,* Foreign Issues), Lee moved his army north into Pennsylvania in June of 1863. The latest commander of the Army of the Potomac, Gen. George Meade, moved to block Lee, and the two armies clashed on July 1 at the town of Gettysburg, Pennsylvania. In three days of fighting at Gettysburg, the Army of the Potomac dealt Lee a major defeat. Having lost nearly a third of his men, Lee was forced to retreat on July 4.

At the same time that Lee was losing at Gettysburg, Grant was successfully concluding the siege of Vicksburg. The city surrendered to Union forces on July 3, 1863. Four days later the last Confederate fort on the Mississippi River, Port Hudson, was captured. With these victories, the Mississippi River came under Union con-

The September 17, 1862, Battle of Antietam resulted in one of the bloodiest fights between Confederate and Union soldiers. While there was no clear victor, President Lincoln considered the Maryland battle a Confederate defeat and used the occasion to introduce a preliminary emancipation proclamation. (National Archives and Records Administration.)

trol, and the states of Alabama, Texas, and Louisiana were cut off from the rest of the Confederacy.

The victories at Gettysburg and Vicksburg marked a decisive change in the war in favor of the Union. The Confederacy had now lost too many men and supplies to realistically threaten another invasion of the North. However, Lee continued to hold his ground in Virginia, and the offensive in the west was moving forward slowly. The northern public was becoming increasingly weary of the war. With no end in sight Lincoln feared they would not reelect him in 1864, and instead select a candidate who would negotiate for peace (*See also,* Lincoln Becomes President).

The Conclusion of the War

Still frustrated with the refusals of his eastern generals to take the offensive, Lincoln appointed Ulysses S. Grant the general in chief of the Union armies and brought him east to command the Army of the Potomac in March 1864. In the west, Gen. William Tecumseh Sherman replaced Grant.

Grant promptly took his army into the field, coordinating an attack on Lee in Virginia with an attack on Atlanta, Georgia, by the western army. In a series of battles in May and June, Grant gradually pushed Lee toward Richmond. Unlike his predecessors, Grant kept his forces engaged with Lee despite heavy casualties, refusing to allow the Confederate general to withdraw. These high casualties brought much criticism from the northern press, but Lincoln supported Grant. Grant had hoped to cut off Richmond and force its surrender by capturing the vital rail junctions at Petersburg, Virginia, to its south, but Lee dug in at Petersburg and refused to budge. The two armies settled into a siege.

In the west Sherman was initially stopped outside of Atlanta by Confederate troops. By September 1864, however, Sherman had cut off Atlanta's supplies and forced the Confederates to retreat. This victory helped secure Lincoln's reelection, as it truly began to appear that an end to the war was near. Sherman, determined to break the South's will to fight, began his famous "march to the sea" after capturing Atlanta. Moving largely unopposed while half his army held the Confederates in check to the north, Sherman's troops destroyed everything in their path as they marched to capture the port of Savannah, Georgia, on December 20.

The siege at Petersburg continued into the spring of 1865. On April 1, however, Union cavalry captured the last rail link into Petersburg, cutting off that city and Richmond from the rest of the Confederacy. Lee attempted to retreat into North Carolina but was blocked by Grant. On April 9, 1865, Lee surrendered to Grant near Appomattox Courthouse, Virginia. With the surrender of the remaining Confederate troops in North Carolina nine days later, the war was over.

Funding the Civil War

One of the areas where the United States was least prepared for a massive war was in its finances. Because of a deep cultural suspicion of banks and the power they wielded, no central bank or banking system existed. Instead, the federal government handled its finances through a vast series of state banks whose bank notes were only as good as a bank's reputation and its limited reserves. While in peacetime this system sufficed, it was woefully inadequate to meet national needs in wartime. But tinkering with the money supply and the nature of money was emotional and politically dangerous. Much of the public trusted only specie or "hard" money, namely gold and silver, although they also would use bank notes backed by specie. As a result, the federal government's policies toward war funding changed, but slowly.

At first, in 1861, Secretary of the Treasury Salmon P. Chase continued to fund the war the way the federal government had funded peace—by borrowing from the banks. In the fall of 1861, Chase negotiated a loan with the state banks for $150 million. Chase also attempted to raise funds through the sale of government bonds, but this proved unsuccessful because the bonds had to be purchased with specie, which most people did not possess in large quantities, and because Union losses on the battlefield led to low confidence in the federal government. In August 1861 Congress attempted to address the funding problem by passing the first ever income tax in the United States, 3 percent on all incomes over $800. This was only a halfway measure, however, as the congressmen, fearful of the political fallout from the new tax, postponed its implementation until January 1863.

The Legal Tender Act

Spurred on by Chase and the nation's bankers, in early 1862 Congress again worked to address the need for war funds. With only a limited supply of specie circulating in the economy, and demand for capital increasing due to the war effort, the supply of money was becoming tight and the government was running short of funds. Congress acted on February 25, 1862, by passing the Legal Tender Act. This law provided for the first official paper currency of the United States. Called "greenbacks" for their color, this paper currency was not directly backed by specie, thus they were "soft" money.

To the surprise of many, the greenbacks worked. With greenbacks the federal government met its obligations to creditors and soldiers, expanded the money supply, encouraged the wartime economy, and overcame the money crisis of 1862. Further, whereas the Confederate government had always employed paper currency and had begun to experience high inflation because of it, the federal Treasury notes did not inflate for several reasons. First, just as nonmonetary events weakened the 1861

bond offering, the timing of the 1862 greenbacks was fortuitous. Military successes boosted public and investor confidence in the federal government just as the greenbacks gained circulation, thereby strengthening the new paper money. The federal government further demonstrated its financial strength by issuing another $500 million in bonds.

Also, and unlike the Confederate government, at Chase's urging Congress passed a series of new taxes to support the government and the greenbacks. On July 1, 1862, Lincoln signed a tax measure that raised existing taxes and placed new taxes on practically everything. Under this authority income taxes were set at 3 percent on incomes for $600 to $10,000, and 5 percent on incomes above $10,000. In 1864 these figures would be raised again to 5 percent on incomes over $600 dollars and 10 percent on incomes over $10,000. In addition, the tariffs on most imported goods were raised, and new taxes were instituted on business, inheritances, and domestic consumer goods such as tobacco and liquor.

A National Banking System is Established

Also at Chase's and Lincoln's urging, Congress established a national banking system that remained in place until Congress established the Federal Reserve system in 1913. In February 1863 Congress passed the National Bank Act (amended and expanded in 1864), which allowed state banks to receive a federal charter and to issue national bank notes. Congress's goal with this act was to drive the unstable state banks out of business and establish a national uniform currency. The conditions for a national charter also were devised so as to encourage state banks to buy Treasury bonds, helping to fund the war effort.

Through its efforts, the Lincoln administration was able to both secure funding for the northern war effort and reform the fiscal system of the United States. The combination of new taxes, the sale of Treasury bonds to the banks and to an increasingly confident public, and the expansion of the currency through the use of greenbacks, proved sufficient to fund the war.

Emancipation

Perhaps no issue is more identified with Lincoln, his administration, and the American Civil War era than the end of slavery. While some Radical members of the Republican Party were abolitionists, and sought an end to slavery throughout the United States, the goals of Lincoln and most other Republicans were initially more modest. Before the American Civil War, Lincoln and the Republicans feared that slaveholders would come to dominate the federal territories in the West, effectively closing those areas to free white labor. The Republicans of 1860 also feared that southerners would find a way to build on Justice Roger B. Taney's language in the 1857 Supreme Court decision of *Dred Scott,* which had found that the federal government could not restrict slavery in the territories.

During the election and in his famous first inaugural address, Lincoln stated time and again that he and the Republicans did not want to abolish slavery, but only to prevent its spread. The fact that much of the South seceded after Lincoln's election demonstrates that Lincoln's promises were not believed. Nevertheless, when the American Civil War began, the federal government's only goal was to restore the southern states to the Union, not to abolish slavery. The difficulty with this position was that to restore the Union without ending slavery would leave intact the same problems that led to the rebellion in the first place. Despite his moral opposition to slavery, Lincoln supported the party's stance of not interfering with slavery within states. As he considered himself the president of all the states, including those that had been illegally taken over by secessionists, Lincoln felt that he must respect the legally established institutions of the South, including slavery.

Confiscation and Contraband

The war's dynamics and, ironically, the Confederacy's use of slave labor, changed Lincoln's and his administration's position. As much of its working-age white male population joined the military, the Confederacy became increasingly reliant on slave labor to support its rebellion economically. Slaves worked in munitions and iron factories; they worked the fields that grew the food to feed the Confederate armies and population; they built military forts and defense systems; and they worked in the Confederate army as cooks, servants, teamsters, and musicians. Abolitionists and Radicals in the Republican Party used these facts to their advantage in the push to end slavery. Weaken the rebellion by weakening its labor force became their argument. In August 1861 Congress passed the First Confiscation Act, which allowed the army to seize all property, including slaves, used to support the rebellion.

Slaves themselves forced the Lincoln administration and the Republicans to rethink the issue of slavery by escaping into Union army lines. Under the law, these slaves were still the property of their owners and ought to have been returned. Some owners appeared in federal camps and went to state and federal courts after the war had started to regain their property. Many Union officers refused to return fugitive slaves, however. One such officer, Gen. Benjamin Butler in command of Fortress Monroe on the tip of the James Peninsula, Virginia, in refusing to return fugitive slaves who had been working on nearby Confederate fortifications, referred to the slaves as "contrabands of war." The name "contraband" stuck and came to refer to any slaves who had escaped into union army positions.

Both Congress and the Lincoln administration debated and struggled with the contraband and slavery question. As Union troops advanced in 1862, "contrabands" swamped Union commanders. Led by the Radicals, Congress nibbled at slavery's fringes. In April 1862 Congress abolished slavery in Washington, D.C., a longstanding dream of the abolitionists. On July 17, 1862, Congress passed the Second Confiscation Act, which allowed the seizure of all persons in rebellion against the United States and explicitly stated that all slaves who came into federal army lines "shall be deemed captives of war and shall be forever free." Here started emancipation as war policy and American Civil War goal, but Lincoln did not actively pursue the confiscation route to emancipation.

The Emancipation Proclamation

Lincoln hoped for a gradual emancipation and in fact feared the effect that moving too quickly might have in the loyal slave states still in the Union. He also felt that there was not strong support for emancipation among the general public. So Lincoln bided his time on the slavery issue, waiting for the right moment to take decisive action. In mid-1861 and again in early 1862, Lincoln revoked proclamations by Union generals that freed slaves in the area under their control.

On March 6, 1862, Lincoln sent to Congress a proposal for a gradual, 30-year emancipation in the loyal slave states, with compensation paid to slave owners by the federal government. Republicans overwhelmingly supported the bill, but the opposition of Democrats and representatives from the border states led to its failure in July. The failure of the bill convinced Lincoln that he would have to take action himself.

On July 22, 1862, Lincoln presented to his cabinet his decision to make a preliminary emancipation proclamation. While the cabinet was in favor of the proclamation, Secretary of State Seward suggested, and Lincoln agreed, to wait until after a Union victory before making the announcement. The Battle of Antietam, on September 17, 1862, provided Lincoln with the opportunity he sought. On September 22, 1862, Lincoln issued the preliminary Emancipation Proclamation. Based on his temporary presidential war powers, the preliminary Emancipation Proclamation declared that on January 1, 1863, all slaves in the states or portions of states that were in rebellion against the United States at that time would be forever free. Further, in this preliminary proclamation Lincoln ordered the military to protect and enforce the act, and Lincoln promised that loyal citizens whose property was freed by the proclamation would be compensated for their losses.

To no one's surprise none of the rebellious states gave up the war before the end of the year. On January 1, 1863, President Lincoln signed the Emancipation Proclamation. In the proclamation, Lincoln stated: ". . . I do order and declare that all persons held as slaves within said designated States, and parts of States, are, and henceforward shall be free; and that the Executive government of the United States, including the military and naval authorities thereof, will recognize and maintain the freedom of said persons."

This proclamation is much misunderstood, for on the day it was signed the proclamation actually freed no one from slavery. The "designated states" were only those states that were a part of the Confederacy. In order to ensure the continued loyalty of the slave states in the Union, the proclamation left slavery intact there. Similarly, the proclamation did not include areas of the Confederacy that were under Union control, such as New Orleans, Louisiana, or West Virginia. While it was widely expected that slavery in these areas would eventually be abolished, the only areas immediately affected by the Emancipation Proclamation were those in active rebellion against the United States.

Ironically, then, Lincoln freed the slaves only in areas where he had no control at the time of the proclamation. Lincoln chose this course because, while he wanted to free the slaves for a variety of reasons, he was not willing to allow emancipation to interfere with the war effort by turning loyal southerners against the Union. Furthermore, many in the North disliked African Americans, and while they might want to see an end to slavery, this did not mean they wanted to accept former slaves as equals. They also feared what the former slaves might do now that they were free. In the Emancipation Proclamation, Lincoln addressed these fears when he called upon the freed slaves to refrain from violence, and he encouraged them to "labor faithfully for reasonable wages." However, the proclamation also declared that African Americans would be recruited into the Union army and navy "to garrison forts, positions, stations, and other places, and to man vessels of all sorts." In time African Americans also would serve on the fighting lines, and by the end of the war one in eight Union soldiers was African American.

The Thirteenth Amendment

The Emancipation Proclamation was only a temporary measure, based on the president's war powers. After it was announced, Congress went to work to make emancipation a permanent part of the U.S. legal and constitutional order. In June 1864 the Congress almost passed a Thirteenth Amendment to the Constitution outlawing slavery, but the Democrats possessed just enough votes in the House to prevent its passage. Union victories and the reelection of Lincoln in 1864 convinced the opponents of emancipation in Congress that an amendment would soon be passed, with or without them. Thus, on January 31, 1865, Congress passed the Thirteenth Amendment to the Constitution. The amendment went to the states for ratification and, while Lincoln did not live to see its ratification, the states ratified the Thirteenth Amendment on December 6, 1865, officially ending slavery in the United States and making emancipation permanent.

Foreign Issues

The American Civil War (1860–65) dominated foreign affairs during Lincoln's presidency as much as it did domestic issues. At the beginning of the war, the Confederacy expected, even counted on, British and French support and perhaps open intervention in the war. The South was the world's largest supplier of cotton, and southerners were convinced that the huge demand for cotton in Great Britain and France would mean that those countries would have to support the South in order to protect their own economies. Both the Union and the Confederacy sought European aid throughout the war.

However, both the United Kingdom and France developed alternative sources of cotton, specifically in Egypt and India, as southern cotton sat on docks and in the warehouses of the South rotting for lack of a market. King cotton turned out not to be so royal after all.

Union Naval Blockade

On April 19, 1861, in response to the firing on the Union's Fort Sumter in Charleston, South Carolina, Lincoln declared a naval blockade around the Confederacy. This blockade immediately became a point of contention between the United States and Great Britain. On May 14, in response to the blockade and pursuant to international law, the British issued a proclamation of neutrality. The French soon followed with their own proclamation. With these actions, Great Britain and France acknowledged the Confederacy as an official belligerent in a war. This stopped short of recognizing the Confederacy as a new nation, but it did give the Confederacy a certain amount of official recognition, allowing it to negotiate for loans with European banks and trade for much needed weapons. As neutrals, Britain and France hoped to continue their trade relations with southern states without entering the war. The British action was cheered in the South since many believed the move was preliminary to British recognition of the Confederacy. In the North the action caused outrage, and the diplomatic situation was tense in the early months of the Lincoln administration.

The Trent Affair

Tensions between the United States and Great Britain nearly boiled over in November 1861. It had become standard practice for U.S. warships to stop and search British ships headed for neutral ports and search for contraband goods destined for the Confederacy. On November 8, 1861, between Cuba and St. Thomas in the Virgin Islands, the U.S.S. *San Jacinto,* captained by Charles Wilkes, stopped a British trade ship, the *Trent,* and removed two Confederate commissioners headed for London, England, and Paris, France, James Mason of Virginia and John Slidell of Louisiana. Wilkes took them first to Fort Monroe, Virginia, and then on to prison in Boston, Massachusetts.

While hailed in the North as a brave act in preventing the rebels to reach their destinations, the British government was outraged at having their ship stopped and passengers removed. Searching for contraband and cargo was one thing, but removing persons was something else entirely. International law was unclear whether commissioners were "contraband" and therefore could be removed. The British prepared and sent a harsh diplomatic note to the Lincoln administration (but not an ultimatum), demanding an apology and the release of Mason and Slidell.

For a time it looked like Great Britain and the United States might be headed for war. Neither Lincoln nor the British government wanted war over this relatively minor issue, however. When the British suggested that perhaps Wilkes had acted without orders, Secretary Seward used that technicality to admonish Wilkes for his actions. Mason and Slidell were released, and although no apology was issued, the two Confederate representatives were allowed to travel to Europe.

The Laird Rams

Near the beginning of the war Georgian James D. Bulloch arrived in Liverpool, England, and set about the task of building warships for the Confederacy. A British statute explicitly prohibited the "equipping, furnishing, fitting out, or arming" of any warships to be used against a country at peace with Great Britain, so the construction of warships for the Confederacy seemed to be illegal. Bulloch argued that "building and constructing" ships did not fall under the scope of the law, and despite protests from U.S. diplomats, Great Britain was willing to go along with the Confederacy at this early stage of the war.

Two ships, the *Florida* and the *Alabama*, were built at Liverpool for the Confederacy. Fast ships designed to attack the Union's ocean-going commerce rather than its navy, the two commerce raiders caused substantial damage to Union shipping, especially the *Alabama*. Great Britain's willingness to construct and sell these ships to the Confederacy placed a strain on U.S.-British relations that would not be resolved until years after the end of the war.

In addition to commerce raiders, Bulloch also contracted with the Laird shipbuilding company to build two ironclad rams for the Confederacy. These heavily armored ships, designed with underwater rams on their bows to tear into wooden Union ships, were expected to be the most powerful ships afloat at the time. Bulloch did everything he could to disguise the ships' true destinations, and U.S. minister to Britain, Charles Francis Adams, lobbied the British Foreign Office not to let the ships leave their construction site. On September 5, 1863, Adams reached the end of his patience and sent a note to the head of the Foreign Office, explaining that if the rams left their berths, then the consequences would be dramatic. As Adams explained, "It would be superfluous in me to point out to your Lordship that this is war."

The next day the British detained the ships. It is now known that the British government had decided to detain the ships before Adams's note arrived, but at the time it appeared that Britain had backed down in the face of the resolute policy of Adams in London and Secretary of State William H. Seward in Washington, D.C. Britain eventually bought the rams for its own Royal Navy.

The Confederacy and Europe

Public opinion in Britain, especially in the first half of 1862, appeared to favor the Confederacy. With Gen. George B. McClellan's failure on the James Peninsula (*See also,* Domestic Issues), and the apparent success of the Confederacy to maintain itself, and before other sources of cotton began to flow in large amounts to the cloth producing areas of Britain, many in Britain pushed for support for the Confederacy.

During this period the leadership of Britain discussed a joint British and French mediation of the conflict, and if that failed then recognizing the Confederacy on its own. Meanwhile, however, British cloth manufacturers were finding new supplies of cotton in Egypt and India. Then, before action was taken to aid the Confederacy, events in North America once again changed European public opinion. Confederate Gen. Robert E. Lee's defeat at Antietam and retreat into Virginia raised questions about the possibility of a Confederate defeat. More importantly, Lincoln's issuance of the preliminary Emancipation Proclamation on September 22, 1862, was very well received by the public in Britain, which had long been antislavery. With the Union solidly on the side of personal freedom and the South clearly on the side of slavery, the European powers could not endorse the Confederacy without angering much of their population. Although Confederate success at Chancellorsville, Virginia, in mid-1863 briefly revived talk of French and British recognition, the subsequent Confederate defeats at Gettysburg and Vicksburg ended any realistic hope of European recognition or mediation.

Overall, the Lincoln administration managed to avoid embroiling the country in a foreign war while fighting a civil war. Furthermore, as it turned out, the domestic decision of embracing emancipation combined with Union victories prevented both European intervention and European diplomatic recognition of the Confederacy. Thus, the European countries effectively accepted the Lincoln administration's belief that the states of the South were not out of the Union but had been taken over by illegal and unconstitutional bands of secessionists and traitors.

The Lincoln Administration Legacy

One of the great ironies of the American Civil War (1860–65) is that the United States emerged stronger than when it entered the war. The war effort boosted the industrial economy of the North, and the problems with the U.S. economy that the war exposed were successfully resolved by legislative reforms of the banking and currency system. The domestic agenda of the Republicans, which included such landmark legislation as the Homestead Act and the Morrill Land-Grant College Act, also boosted the economy and helped speed the development of the western United States during and after the war.

Still, as the war drew to a close, the Lincoln administration faced many problems. The most significant: what to do with former slaves and former rebels. Lincoln began to address the issue of reincorporating the South into the Union in 1863 with his proclamation of amnesty and reconstruction. In this area, Lincoln favored reconciliation and forgiveness, and defended his policy both with the veto of the Wade-Davis Bill and with his words. In the famous last paragraph of his Second Inaugural Address can be glimpsed Lincoln's hope for a swift end to the war and a quick healing of the wounds. On March 4, 1865, as the conclusion of the war drew near, Lincoln said:

> With malice toward none; with charity for all; with firmness in the right, as God gives us to see the right, let us strive to finish the work we are in; to bind up the nation's wounds; to care for him who shall have borne the battle, and for his widow, and his orphan—to do all which may achieve and cherish a just, and a lasting peace, among ourselves, and with all nations.

Ten days later the American Civil War claimed another casualty when John Wilkes Booth shot Abraham Lincoln at Ford's Theatre in Washington, D.C. Lincoln died early the next morning, but his administration had successfully piloted the nation through the storm-tossed seas of the Civil War and of emancipation. It was left to his successors to solve the problems of bringing the southern states back into the Union, referred to as the Reconstruction.

Lasting Impact

It is no surprise that Lincoln is routinely ranked as the United States's best and most important president, and that the same can be said for the administration he headed. Guiding the country through a civil war, modernizing the monetary system, navigating the problems of domestic and party politics, avoiding foreign policy problems, and moving four million people from slavery to freedom would test the fortitude and character of any president and administration, but Lincoln's administration passed the test.

Lincoln succeeded in keeping the United States together, and in doing so he fundamentally and forever changed the nature of government in the United States. The American Civil War and the constitutional amendments that arose out of it settled the question of state versus federal power in favor of the latter. Lincoln also did much to establish the idea of strong presidential leadership. Although he was not the first strong president, he became a model for all those who followed him. Perhaps the most remarkable aspect of this pivotal era in U.S. history, however, was that Lincoln and his administration preserved both the nation and its constitutional structure. For all their innovations, Lincoln and his administration did not challenge the fundamental structures of the United States. The Constitution proved more than adequate to protect itself when led by talented, creative, committed, and dedicated people.

Besides the Lincoln administration's example of aggressive and determined leadership in the face of adversity in resisting secession and defeating rebellion, emancipation formed the other lasting legacy of the administration. Lincoln and his administration sought a middle ground on the emotional and explosive issue of emancipation between the urging of the abolitionists and the Republican Radicals for immediate and uncompensated emancipation, and the Democrats who urged the continuation of the institution of slavery. When Lincoln moved against slavery, he did so as a necessary war measure, as a complementary and supplementary measure to the first war goal—preservation of the nation.

By permanently removing slavery from the country through the success of the federal army and the ratification of the Thirteenth Amendment, the Lincoln administration ended the institution of persons as property and began the search for legal equality before the law for all Americans regardless of race. Race relations and racism continues to test and challenge U.S. culture, but through emancipation the Lincoln administration freed the slaves and began to establish African Americans on a more equal status with whites.

Sources

Curry, Leonard P. *Blueprint for Modern America: Nonmilitary Legislation of the First Civil War Congress.* Nashville, Tenn.: Vanderbilt University Press, 1968.

————. *Equal Justice Under Law: Constitutional Development, 1830–1880.* New York: Harper and Row, 1982.

Fehrenbacher, Don E., ed. *Abraham Lincoln: Speeches and Writings, 1832–1858.* New York: The Library of America, 1989.

————. *Abraham Lincoln: Speeches and Writings, 1859–1865.* New York: The Library of America, 1989.

Historic World Leaders. Detroit: Gale Research, 1994.

Hyman, Harold M. *A More Perfect Union: The Impact of the Civil War and Reconstruction on the Constitution.* New York: Alfred A. Knopf, 1973.

Lincoln, Abraham. "Letter to Horace Greeley." *The Internet Public Library: Presidents of the United States.* 1999. <http://www.potus.com/alincoln.htm> (8 July 1999).

McPherson, James M. *Battle Cry of Freedom: The Civil War Era.* New York: Oxford University Press, 1988.

———. *Ordeal By Fire: The Civil War and Reconstruction.* New York: Alfred A. Knopf, 1982.

Paludan, Phillip Shaw. *The Presidency of Abraham Lincoln.* Lawrence, Kans.: University Press of Kansas, 1994.

Further Readings

Basler, Roy, et al., eds. *The Collected Works of Abraham Lincoln.* 9 vols. New Brunswick, N.J.: Rutgers University Press, 1953–55.

Foner, Eric. *Free Soil, Free Labor, Free Men: The Ideology of the Republican Party before the Civil War.* New York: Oxford University Press, 1970.

Franklin, John Hope. *The Emancipation Proclamation.* Garden City, N.Y.: Doubleday, 1963.

Gienapp, William E. *The Origins of the Republican Party.* New York: Oxford University Press, 1987.

Hyman, Harold M. *American Singularity: The 1787 Northwest Ordinance, the 1862 Homestead and Morrill Acts, and the 1944 G.I. Bill.* Athens, Ga.: The University of Georgia Press, 1986.

———. *Era of the Oath: Northern Loyalty Tests During the Civil War and Reconstruction.* Philadelphia, Penn.: University of Pennsylvania, 1954.

Neely, Mark E., Jr. *The Fate of Liberty: Abraham Lincoln and Civil Liberties.* New York: Oxford University Press, 1991.

———. *The Last Best Hope of Earth: Abraham Lincoln and the Promise of America.* Cambridge, Mass.: Harvard University Press, 1993.

Paludan, Phillip Shaw. *A People's Contest: The Union & Civil War, 1861–1865.* Lawrence, Kans.: University Press of Kansas, 1996.

Potter, David M. *The Impending Crisis, 1848–1861.* New York: Harper and Row, 1976.

Silbey, Joel H. *A Respectable Minority: The Democratic Party in the Civil War Era, 1860–1868.* New York: W. W. Norton, 1977.

Thomas, Benjamin P., and Harold M. Hyman. *Stanton: The Life and Times of Lincoln's Secretary of War.* New York: Alfred A. Knopf, 1962.

Andrew Johnson Administration

Biography

A tailor by trade, Andrew Johnson entered politics on behalf of the laboring people of eastern Tennessee. Throughout his political career Johnson identified with and advocated for the interests of the working class. His passion for political debate aided his rise from obscurity to the U.S. Senate. Because of his loyalty to the Union during the American Civil War (1861–65) Abraham Lincoln tapped Johnson to become his vice president in March 1865, and upon Lincoln's death on April 15, 1865, Johnson assumed the presidency. The battles between Johnson and Congress over the fate of the former Confederacy led to an unprecedented attempt to remove President Johnson from office.

Full name: Andrew Johnson

Personal Information:
Born: December 29, 1808
Birthplace: Raleigh, North Carolina
Died: July 31, 1875
Death place: Carter's Station, Tennessee
Burial place: Andrew Johnson National Cemetery, Greeneville, Tennessee
Spouse: Eliza McCardle (m. 1827)
Children: Martha; Charles; Mary; Robert; Andrew Jr.
Education: No formal education
Occupation: Tailor; legislator
Political Party: Democratic Party
Age at Inauguration: 56 years

Early Life

Born in a log cottage at Casso's Inn, Raleigh, North Carolina, on December 29, 1808, Andrew Johnson started from the humblest of beginnings. His father, Jacob Johnson, held a series of jobs including porter, tavern servant, constable, and bank janitor. Although illiterate like his wife, Jacob Johnson was a respectable member of his community serving as a militia captain and as a sexton (a minor church official) of the Presbyterian Church. Andrew Johnson's mother, Mary "Polly" McDonough, married Jacob Johnson in 1801. They had two sons, William and Andrew.

In December 1811 Jacob Johnson dove into a pond to save two men from drowning. He never fully recovered from the exhaustion of the event. While tolling the church bell the next month as part of his duties as sex-

Andrew Johnson. *(The Library of Congress.)*

ton, Jacob collapsed and died. Andrew Johnson was only three years old. Mary Johnson supported her family by sewing, weaving, and washing. A few years later, she remarried. Her new husband, Turner Dougherty, was a poor provider.

In 1822 in order to provide her boys with a skill to support themselves, their mother apprenticed them to a local tailor. Young Andrew learned the trade well and throughout his life took pride in his skill as a tailor. It was during his apprenticeship that a local minister taught Andrew Johnson the barest of rudiments of reading and writing. He and his brother worked as apprentices for two years before they fled in 1824 because they feared punishment for an incident of rowdiness that they became involved in. The boys ended up in Tennessee. In 1826 Johnson returned to Raleigh, North Carolina, and convinced his mother and stepfather to move with him to Tennessee. Only 17 years old, Johnson chose Greeneville in eastern Tennessee as his new home and opened a tailor shop there.

Education

Andrew Johnson received no formal schooling. While Johnson was an apprentice, however, the shop foreman, James Litchford, and a local minister, Dr. Hill, read aloud to the apprentices as they worked; a typical workshop practice in the early nineteenth century. From

these two men Johnson learned the fundamentals of reading. This experience of listening to the words of the important orators of Great Britain, such as William Pitt the younger and Charles James Fox, stirred and influenced Johnson. Johnson continued to educate himself during his years of wandering, but his wife would be his best teacher. Better educated than Johnson, Eliza McCardle Johnson encouraged her husband to read and write, tutored him, and taught him some math skills.

Family Life

Andrew Johnson met Eliza McCardle soon after arriving in Greeneville, Tennessee. They quickly grew to love each other and married on May 17, 1827. They would have a long marriage that produced five children: Martha, Charles, Mary, Robert, and Andrew Jr. Throughout their marriage, Andrew and Eliza Johnson remained devoted to each other and to their home in Greeneville, Tennessee. They left it only during the American Civil War (1861–65) and during Johnson's presidency. By middle age, Eliza Johnson developed what was called "slow consumption." She became a semi-invalid and reclusive. Eliza Johnson joined her husband in Washington, D.C., after he assumed the presidency, but her health prevented her from overseeing White House social life or playing a public role in Johnson's administration. Johnson's daughter, Martha Patterson, took on the role of White House hostess as a result.

Career

Andrew Johnson always considered himself a plain workingman. He achieved success as a tailor, and his business grew. In time he became a full-time politician representing the working people of Tennessee against what he perceived as the monopoly of power wielded by the landed aristocrats of the state. Johnson grew up in a political culture defined during the era of President Andrew Jackson, when the common man gained political standing, and he held strongly to those beliefs throughout his life.

With his gregarious and combative personality and his passion for arguments and making speeches (aided by his much admired and powerful speaking voice), Johnson was elected in 1828 to be alderman of the village. Two years later he became mayor of Greeneville and served in this capacity until 1833, all the while running his growing tailor business.

Johnson Serves in the Tennessee State Legislature

In 1835 Andrew Johnson was elected to the state House of Representatives. Favoring limited government spending, Johnson voted against a bill for internal improvements (roads) for Tennessee as being too costly. Unfortunately for Johnson, the people of Greeneville and eastern Tennessee wanted more and better roads, and they did not reelect him to the Tennessee lower house in 1837.

After reconsidering his position on internal improvements, Andrew Johnson was again elected to the Tennessee House of Representatives in 1839. He continued his support for the free, nonslaveowning white laborers of eastern Tennessee against the slaveowning areas of middle and western Tennessee. In 1840 Andrew Johnson became affiliated with the Democratic Party and in 1841 ran for a seat as a Tennessee state senator, which he won. As a state senator, Johnson developed a reputation as a tough politician, a tough talker, and, at times, a bully unwilling and perhaps unable to compromise on key issues. He proposed to repeal the state law that gave slaveholders greater representation than nonslaveholders, which passed the state senate only to fail in the state house. Johnson also proposed creating a new nonslave-holding state out of the eastern mountain areas of Tennessee, Virginia, North Carolina, and Georgia. This idea also failed.

U.S. Representative

Between 1843 and 1853 Andrew Johnson served as a U.S. congressman. Like his hero, seventh U.S. president Andrew Jackson, Johnson was a Democrat who supported the federal Union and the U.S. Constitution. This position put him at odds with the Democratic slaveowning elite in Tennessee (and the South generally), who had begun their drift away from the Union. In general, however, Johnson voted along the Democratic Party line.

Johnson's most notable success as a congressman was his 1846 proposal for the nation's first homestead legislation, which he negotiated through the House before the bill failed in the Senate. Inexpensive homesteads in the West assisted free white small farmers and exactly fitted Johnson's idea of whom the country's future should be built upon. But because the bill might close the West to slavery's expansion, most southern congressmen and senators opposed Johnson's idea. The bill finally passed in 1862, 16 years after Johnson's original proposal.

Governor

Through clever political maneuvering in 1853, Johnson received the Democratic Party nomination for the Tennessee governorship. Nevertheless, his chances looked bleak since his Whig opponent was none other than the "Eagle Orator" of Tennessee, Gustavus A. Henry, a direct descendant of American statesman Patrick Henry. Johnson's hard work, pluck, and skill as a speaker served him well, and he defeated Henry in 1853. Two years later Johnson was reelected governor. During his governorship Johnson signed into law the

state's first public school system, a state library, and a system of agricultural and mechanical fairs to improve the state's agricultural economy.

U.S. Senator

In 1857 Johnson was elected to the U.S. Senate. There he renewed his efforts for a federal homestead act, receiving the most opposition from southern Democrats and the most support from northern Republicans (who hoped the West would be populated by free white laborers). A weak homestead bill actually passed both houses of Congress in June 1860, only to have President James Buchanan veto it because he feared it offended the Democrats of the Deep South. Southern votes preserved Buchanan's veto and Johnson fumed at the arrogance of the aristocratic elites who denied cheap federal land in the West to small farmers.

While Johnson supported the southern wing of the Democratic Party in the elections of 1860, he was above all committed to the United States and the Constitution. Not even the victory of Abraham Lincoln and the Republicans that year shook him from this commitment. This strong nationalism won him acclaim in the North but condemnation in the South.

After Lincoln's election in 1860, tensions between the North and the South reached the breaking point. Over the following several months many southern states seceded from the Union. They formed their own government, called the Confederacy. Other slave states remained in the Union, but with mixed feelings.

Tennessee stayed away at first from secession, supporting Johnson's position on the Union and the Constitution. But after April 14, 1861, with the South's firing on Fort Sumter in South Carolina marking the beginnings of the American Civil War (1861–65), Tennesseans wavered in their support. Governor Isham B. Harris opened negotiations with the Confederacy regarding a "military league," and the legislature ordered a popular referendum on whether to leave the Union. Senator Andrew Johnson returned from Washington, D.C., to campaign against leaving the Union. Despite his efforts and eastern Tennessee's vote against secession, Tennesseans overall voted to join the Confederacy. Johnson left the state. After Confederate authorities forced his wife and children to leave their Greeneville home, they made their way to Union-held Nashville, Tennessee, where Johnson joined them when not in Washington. Once the war began, Johnson supported Lincoln's emergency powers as Lincoln sought to restore the Union. Johnson was the only southern senator not to resign his seat and follow his state into treason.

Military Governor

In March 1862, to reward his Union loyalty, Lincoln offered Johnson the military rank of brigadier general and the position of military governor of Tennessee,

Fast Fact

Andrew Johnson married Eliza McCardle on May 17, 1827, at the age of 18 years and 139 days; he remains the president who married at the youngest age.

(Source: Joseph Nathan Kane. *Facts About the Presidents,* 1993.)

once the western Union army pushed Confederate forces out of western and central Tennessee. Wielding extraordinary powers to discharge executive, legislative, and judicial functions, Johnson's job was to restore order in Tennessee and to build a new pro-Union government for the state. During his three years as military governor, Johnson levied taxes, dismissed civil officials unwilling to take the federal oath of allegiance, shut down opposition newspapers, arrested pro-Confederate ministers who used their pulpits to support disunion, and arrested and punished captured guerrillas. Because Johnson believed the war's goal was the restoration of the Union, not the emancipation of the slaves, he persuaded Lincoln to exempt the entire state of Tennessee from the January 1, 1863, Emancipation Proclamation, which freed slaves in Confederate states still at war.

Vice President

In the summer of 1864 Lincoln and the Republican Party reached out to northern Democrats and southern Unionists and changed the name of their party to the National Union Party. Lincoln, who liked Andrew Johnson, prevailed on the 1864 Republican Party convention to drop his first vice president, Hannibal Hamlin of Maine, and to replace him with the southern Unionist Democrat, Andrew Johnson. Republicans granted Lincoln's wish and nominated Johnson for the vice presidency. Lincoln and Johnson soundly defeated the Democratic candidate George B. McClellan of New Jersey in the November 1864 general election. In February 1865 Johnson left Nashville and traveled to Washington for the March 4, 1865 inauguration as vice president of the United States.

On inauguration day, Johnson, still suffering from an earlier fever, felt faint when he reached the Capitol, so he asked outgoing vice president Hannibal Hamlin if he had some whiskey. Hamlin did and Johnson swallowed two large doses of the "medicine." Unfortunately, the alcohol combined with the heat in the Senate Cham-

ber, and his infirmness from fever, impaired Johnson's speech and judgment. He delivered an embarrassing, rambling speech. Several Republican senators reportedly hid their faces in their hands at Johnson's behavior. There is no evidence to suggest he had a drinking problem but there is no doubt that this unfortunate incident greatly damaged his public image.

Embarrassed by his own behavior, Johnson met with Lincoln only once while serving as vice president, on the afternoon of Friday, April 14, 1865. No record exists of what Lincoln and Johnson discussed, but clearly Johnson stood on the margins of policy decisions, like many vice presidents. That night John Wilkes Booth shot Lincoln at Ford's Theatre in Washington, D.C. Lincoln slipped into unconsciousness immediately. He died the following morning.

President

At a little past 10 o'clock in the morning on April 15, 1865, Chief Justice Salmon P. Chase administered the presidential oath of office to Andrew Johnson. A Tennessee plebeian, a tailor, had become president at a key moment in the nation's history—Reconstruction. Inheriting a cabinet from Lincoln and believing he, not Congress, was best able to direct and guide the rebuilding of the defeated South and its re-admittance into government, Johnson set about the task of reestablishing the nation after a long and bloody civil war.

Johnson's combative personality, his inability to compromise easily, and his southern social heritage, values, and conservatism set him at odds with the congressional Republicans who, ironically, had raised him to the nation's highest executive office. His term was marked by constant losing battles with Congress. These battles reached their peak when Johnson was impeached and nearly removed from office in 1868.

Post-presidential Years

In 1868, even though the Democrats had a sitting president in the person of Andrew Johnson, they chose not to nominate him for the presidency. Because of Johnson's record as president, the Democrats knew that they needed someone other than Johnson to face the Republican's nominee, popular war hero Ulysses S. Grant. Grant won in November 1868, and neither Grant nor Johnson wished each other's company at the inauguration. As a result, Johnson spent the morning of March 4, 1869, tying up loose ends at the White House and, just past noon, he entered a carriage and drove off.

Johnson returned to a hero's welcome in Greeneville, Tennessee. He threw himself into local and state Democratic political affairs, just as he had before the presidency, and he ran for political office again. In 1869 he lost an election to the U.S. Senate. Three years later he unsuccessfully ran for a seat to the U.S. House of Representatives. In 1874 and into 1875 Johnson tried to sway enough state senators for a second try for the U.S. Senate. His electioneering paid off when the Tennessee legislature elected him senator by one vote. Taking his Senate seat on March 4, 1875, he joined the institution that had impeached and almost convicted him. Johnson became the first and so far the only ex-president to sit in the United States Senate.

At the end of Congress's session, Johnson returned to Tennessee. On July 28, 1875, while visiting his daughter Mary Johnson Brown Stover, he suffered a stroke that paralyzed him on one side. Johnson regained consciousness and instructed his family not to call either a doctor or a minister. He suffered another stoke the next day and died on July 31, 1875. Johnson left detailed instructions for his funeral. His body was wrapped in an American flag, and his head rested on a copy of the United States Constitution. Johnson was buried at a spot he had selected and marked by a willow tree grown from a sprig found at Napoleon's tomb on St. Helena Island in the South Atlantic. The ailing Eliza Johnson died in early 1876, surviving her husband by only six months.

The Andrew Johnson Administration

Reconstruction, the process of rebuilding and establishing an acceptable political system in the South following the American Civil War (1861–65), consumed—even overwhelmed—the Johnson administration. Although nominally a member of the wartime National Union party, Andrew Johnson was a Democrat by background, and usually found himself opposed by a Republican-controlled Congress. A combative man by nature, Johnson's unwillingness to accept the will of Congress and the new political realities of the post-Civil War world led to impeachment. Johnson escaped removal from office by one vote, but the trial made it clear that Congress, and not the president, would determine Reconstruction policy.

Johnson Becomes President

On the night of Friday, April 14, 1865, when President Abraham Lincoln was shot by John Wilkes Booth in Ford's Theater, in Washington, D.C., Andrew Johnson had been vice president for little more than a month. Nevertheless, Johnson also had been targeted by the Lincoln conspirators: George Atzerodt was supposed to assassinate Johnson, but Atzerodt had lost his nerve, gotten drunk, and missed his chance to assassinate the vice

president. Secretary of State William H. Seward, third in line for the presidency, was also attacked and wounded.

Knowing that Lincoln was unconscious, Johnson waited at the Kirkwood House, where he lived, for news. At about 7:30 A.M. Saturday, April 15, 1865, word reached Johnson that Lincoln had died. At a little past 10 o'clock in the morning, with some of Lincoln's cabinet members and some congressmen present, Chief Justice Salmon P. Chase administered the presidential oath of office to Andrew Johnson in the Kirkwood House.

When Andrew Johnson became president, Reconstruction confronted not only the new president, but all of the nation's political leaders as well. Southern states needed political and economic rebuilding after the American Civil War (1861–65), and a political process needed to be developed to bring southern states back into the nation and to repair race relations (*See also,* Domestic Issues). In its various manifestations, Reconstruction policy defined Johnson's administration in popular culture and in history.

Election of 1868

Having escaped removal from office by impeachment in May 1868 (*See also,* Domestic Issues), Johnson began his campaign to secure the 1868 Democratic Party presidential nomination. Johnson needed to show the South that he was not beaten by impeachment and that he could still stand up to the Republicans. He vetoed the Arkansas readmission bill, which not only provided for black suffrage but also required all voters to declare their belief in racial equality, a clause designed to eliminate most white voters. Johnson also vetoed an omnibus readmission bill that would have readmitted the Republican-controlled states of North Carolina, South Carolina, Florida, Georgia, Alabama, and Louisiana. To no one's surprise Congress easily overrode both of Johnson's vetoes, and the readmission bills took effect.

Johnson also sought to improve his chances for his party's nomination when on July 4, 1868, the day the Democratic Party's convention opened, he issued a presidential amnesty to everyone who had participated in the American Civil War. Those currently under indictment such as Jefferson Davis, the ex-president of the Confederacy, were not included. Although his proclamation had no legal affect, its purpose was not really to establish an amnesty but to sway Democrats to support him for the presidency.

Johnson Fails to Win the Nomination

But the delegates to the Democratic National Convention were not swayed. Even though they had a sitting president, they chose not to nominate him because he possessed so much negative political baggage. Because of Johnson's record as president, and because of his impeachment, the Democrats knew that they needed

Administration

Administration Dates
April 15, 1865–March 4, 1869

Vice President
None

Cabinet

Secretary of State
William H. Seward (1861–69)

Secretary of the Treasury
Hugh McCulloch (1865–69)

Secretary of War
Edwin M. Stanton (1862–68)
John M. Schofield (1868–69)

Attorney General
James Speed (1864–66)
Henry Stanberry (1866–68)
William M. Evarts (1868–69)

Secretary of the Navy
Gideon Welles (1861–69)

Postmaster General
William Dennison Jr. (1864–66)
Alexander W. Randall (1866–69)

Secretary of the Interior
John P. Usher (1863–65)
James Harlan (1865–66)
Orville H. Browning (1866–69)

someone other than Johnson to face the most popular person in the United States at the time, Union general Ulysses S. Grant. On July 7, 1868, the Democratic Convention started to vote on possible nominees, and on the first ballot George H. Pendleton of Ohio polled 105 votes and Johnson 65. But as the ballots continued, Johnson's support eroded away until only the Tennessee delegation supported him. On the 21st ballot a dark horse, or unexpected, former candidate, the governor of New York Horatio Seymour, received enough votes to achieve the party's nomination.

Johnson's Advisers

President Johnson kept his own counsel and, like many presidents, reserved decision making on the largest issues to himself. He discussed strategy and policy with a handful of close friends and cabinet members and then ran the idea or decision past the whole cabinet. There were several people whom Johnson relied on more than others for policy decisions and in defending himself against impeachment.

Once Secretary of State William Henry Seward recovered from wounds suffered the same night as Lincoln's assassination, he exercised great influence over Andrew Johnson. He became one of Johnson's primary advisers on foreign affairs. Henry Stanbery of Ohio, a Republican identified with the conservative wing of his party, supported Johnson throughout his administration as attorney general and served as one of Johnson's defense attorneys during impeachment. Orville H. Browning, another conservative Republican and an ex-senator from Illinois, served as Johnson's secretary of the interior and trusted adviser. Another holdover from the Lincoln administration, Gideon Welles of Connecticut, stayed at his post as secretary of the navy throughout the Johnson years, helping Johnson navigate national politics.

Preston King of New York, a conservative Republican, former Democrat, and ex-senator from New York, and Wisconsin senator James Doolitle, another conservative Republican, were two of Andrew Johnson's closest friends during his administration. Pennsylvania Democrat Jeremiah S. Black, attorney general and secretary of state during the Buchanan administration, assisted Johnson in preparing veto messages as well as serving on Johnson's defense team against impeachment.

Johnson and Congress

Johnson's term included the Thirty-ninth (1865–67) and the Fortieth Congresses. Both of these Congresses were completely dominated by the Republican Party (or, as it was called in the Thirty-ninth Congress, the Unionist Party). The Republicans were not an entirely unified voice, having conservative, moderate, and radical wings. The conservatives were most likely to agree with Democrats and with President Johnson. The Radicals were the most extreme, calling for extensive reform. But the moderate Republicans, which had counted Lincoln among their members, were the largest group and, through cooperation with one of the other wings, could control policy.

Lincoln had advocated a lenient Reconstruction policy based on the fact that the southern states had never really seceded because no state could legally leave the Union; blame for the rebellion rested on a few individual southerners. He primarily sought to regain the South's loyalty. Some Republicans in Congress, however, particularly the Radicals, wanted greater control over the

Reconstruction process. These congressmen tended to feel that white southerners as a whole should be punished for the rebellion, and that Reconstruction should include strong federal measures to ensure that African Americans' rights were protected.

In the first few days and weeks of the Johnson administration, Republicans believed that the new president supported their goals and timing for Reconstruction. Powerful Radical Republicans such as senators Charles Sumner of Massachusetts, Zachariah Chandler of Michigan, congressmen Thaddeus Stevens of Pennsylvania, and George Julian of Indiana lobbied the new president to support their policies. They convinced themselves that Johnson believed as they did, particularly on the issue of African American suffrage. However, Johnson's whole life and political career had been waged to aid the southern small white farmers against the landed aristocracy of the South. He had never joined the Republican Party and he continued to refer to himself as a "Jacksonian Democrat." As such, Johnson had little interest in African Americans and their legal status in the states and localities. Johnson opposed undue federal government spending throughout his political career, opposed excessive federal powers generally, believed that the state and local governments were safer for persons and property than the federal government, and supported emancipation only because it helped the little people of the South while hurting the aristocrats. As a result, when Johnson announced presidential Reconstruction policy, he dismayed and infuriated the Radical Republicans (and, at times, the moderate Republicans).

When Johnson repeatedly vetoed key legislation and when he openly defied Congress, Republicans believed that they had to seek Johnson's removal from office through impeachment. While Johnson was impeached for violating the Tenure of Office Act, which was passed over his veto only months before, the real issue was who would control the Reconstruction process (*See also,* Domestic Issues). Johnson's acquittal, by one vote, avoided his removal from office, but the trial weakened his position to the point that Congress's plan for Reconstruction became the path the nation followed.

Andrew Johnson exercised his veto power 29 times and saw his veto overridden by Congress 15 times. Among the key bills Congress passed, Johnson vetoed, and Congress enacted into law over the president's veto were the nation's first civil rights act, the 1866 Civil Rights Act; the Freedman's Bureau Act of 1866; the Tenure of Office Act; and all four of Congress's Reconstruction Acts (*See also,* Domestic Issues). Johnson's resistance to Congress encouraged white southerners to resist congressional Reconstruction as well, including the granting of greater legal, constitutional, and political rights to African Americans. Johnson's resistance earned him allies among southerners, but made enemies of the legislators and people of the North.

Johnson and the Judiciary

During Andrew Johnson's administration there were no appointments made to the U.S. Supreme Court, but the Court did hand down a series of key decisions. Chief Justice Salmon P. Chase also carried out his constitutional duty during Johnson's impeachment by presiding over the Senate and acting as chief judge as it heard the House of Representatives's case against the president.

In *Texas v. White* (1869), a case about whether creditors could recover monies loaned to the Confederate government of Texas, the Supreme Court took the opportunity to write into U.S. constitutional law the status of the states during the American Civil War (1861–65) and describe the nature of nation. In the case, Chief Justice Chase took the Lincoln administration's position regarding secession and the American Civil War: the states had never been out of the Union, and the state governments had been taken over by illegal groups of conspirators. Therefore, monies lent to an illegal Confederate government were not recoverable.

In the case of *Ex Parte Milligan* (1866), decided after the war ended, the Supreme Court struck down as unconstitutional the trial of civilians by a military commission if normal civilian courts are open. The Court held that such military commissions failed to provide adequate procedural due process to the accused, and that Congress lacked the power to establish such commissions in areas where the normal business of the federal and state courts was uninterrupted by the war. This case is often cited as an example of the individual's right to protection from arbitrary government prosecution.

In the cases of *Ex Parte Garland* (1867) and *Cummings v. Missouri* (1867), the Court struck down a federal and state test oath requirement. Oaths had been used widely prior to and during the American Civil War to ensure loyalty and fidelity to the nation. In 1865 Congress passed the Federal Test Act requiring persons to swear not just to future loyalty to the nation, but to past loyalty as well, called at the time the "iron clad" oath. Persons wishing to become federal attorneys had to make such pledges. Missouri, as it proceeded through its Reconstruction process, adopted a similar state statute for ministers, attorneys, and persons seeking public office. Test oaths not only guaranteed loyal people for federal and state offices but also served a partisan purpose since only persons loyal to the Republican Party (including African Americans) could truthfully swear such an oath. In a close five-to-four decision the Supreme Court struck down such test oath statutes as unconstitutional restrictions on office holding. More politically, the Supreme Court's decision appeared to undermine Congress's Reconstruction plans, which included both reconstructing southern states and building a strong Republican Party in the South based on African American votes. In the short term, however, the effects of these decisions were limited. Congress was unwilling, and President Johnson unable, to enforce them.

Changes in the U.S. Government

Congress established temporary military districts to reestablish loyal state governments in an effort to streamline the process of Reconstruction (*See also,* Domestic Issues). These temporary military districts did not last as most of the states of the former Confederacy received readmission to Congress in 1868. White resistance to Reconstruction in Texas and Mississippi delayed their return until 1869 and 1870, respectively.

The Thirteenth and The Fourteenth Amendments

While President Lincoln had declared the slaves of the Confederate states to be free with his Emancipation Proclamation, there was still a need to formally alter the laws of the United States to make slavery illegal. To this end, Congress developed what would become the Thirteenth Amendment to the Constitution. Passed by Congress on January 31, 1865, this Amendment stated that:

> Neither slavery nor involuntary servitude, except as a punishment for crime, whereof the party shall have been duly convicted, shall exist within the United States, or any place subject to their jurisdiction.

When this amendment was ratified by the states in December 1865, it abolished slavery within the United States.

In January 1866 the Joint Committee on Reconstruction suggested to the rest of Congress an amendment reducing the representation in Congress of any state that did not recognize African American citizenship and African American voting privileges. While this idea passed the House, the Senate rejected it, and the joint committee worked to craft an amendment with African American citizenship as the baseline for Reconstruction. They ultimately crafted the Fourteenth Amendment, the first section of which reads:

> All persons born or naturalized in the United States, and subject to the jurisdiction thereof, are citizens of the United States and the State wherein they reside. No State shall make or enforce any law which shall abridge the privileges or immunities of citizens of the United States; nor shall any State deprive any person of life, liberty, or property, without due process of law; nor deny to any person within its jurisdiction the equal protection of the laws.

Passed by Congress on June 13, 1866, the amendment was ratified by the states on July 9, 1868. The Fourteenth Amendment established a new definition of citizenship in the United States. All persons, including African Americans, born in the United States are citizens of the United States. Futhermore, the amendment made it clear that national citizenship was primary and state citizenship secondary. The later half of the first section contains what are known as the Due Process Clause and the Equal Protection Clause, because they prohibited the states from treating citizens in an unfair or arbitrary manner, or from discriminating against certain people or groups of people. A later section of the Fourteenth Amendment overrode the provision of the Constitution which declared that slaves would be counted as three-fifths of a person for the purposes of determining a state's representation in Congress. The Fourteenth Amendment also declared the debts of the Confederacy to be void, and prohibited the leaders of the Confederacy from holding public office.

Domestic Issues

As the American Civil War (1861–65) drew to a close, there remained hard regional feelings. The economy slowed down when the war ended and the South was concerned about whether its agrarian economy could survive without slavery. The western regions of the country sought funding to build a transcontinental railroad linking the mountains and the far West to the markets of the Midwest and the eastern seaboard. However, Reconstruction was the central issue with which the young country was preoccupied during the Johnson administration.

Reconstruction

The most important issue by far that faced Johnson during his administration was what to do with the defeated states of the former Confederacy, the collective name for the southern states that had seceded from the Union. The key issues were who would govern the southern states, how the reintegration of the southern states would work, and who would ensure the freedom and protection of former slaves. Abraham Lincoln began to address this problem in December 1863, when he issued a "Proclamation of Amnesty and Reconstruction." With the exception of high-level officers and officials of the Confederacy, all southerners would be pardoned for their role in the rebellion. Once 10 percent of the eligible voters of a state in 1860 swore an oath of future loyalty to the nation, they would be allowed to elect a new state government. This government would then have to accept the Emancipation Proclamation (*See also,* Lincoln Administration) and free the slaves before the state would be allowed to resume its normal place in national affairs.

Some in Congress did not approve of Lincoln's plan, considering it too lenient. In July 1864 congressional Republicans proposed their own plan, the Wade-Davis Bill, named for its sponsors, Benjamin Wade of Ohio and Henry Winter Davis of Maryland. This plan increased the percentage of loyal voters required to form a government to 50 percent, and those voters would have had to take an oath of not just future loyalty but of past loyalty as well— the "iron clad oath" (*See also,* Johnson and the Judiciary).

In order to protect those states that had begun Reconstructing under his 10 percent plan and to maintain a presidential presence in Reconstruction, Lincoln pocket-vetoed (held the bill until Congress adjourned) the Wade-Davis Bill, infuriating the radical wing of his own political party. The Reconstruction issue thus remained unresolved when Johnson took office in 1865.

Johnson's Reconstruction Plan

On May 29, 1865, seeking to continue Lincoln's moderate Reconstruction plan, Johnson issued an "Amnesty Proclamation" and a plan for North Carolina's Reconstruction, which would be a model for other southern states. It provided for a general pardon to all persons who had been in rebellion, except for high-ranking military officers and wealthy civilians. Their property would be returned to them (except for slaves), and they would be required to take an oath of future loyalty to the nation. Those persons at the upper end of the Confederate military and civil life would have to apply to President Johnson in person for a pardon to restore their right to hold office and vote. Johnson appointed a provisional governor for the state, W. W. Holden, and instructed Holden to call a state constitutional convention elected from loyal voters of 1861 who had accepted the president's amnesty proposal. Most of the southern states acted quickly to put Johnson's plan into action. New governments were elected, and constitutional conventions held. Most conventions repudiated their Confederate debts and provided for state elections to the governorship, the legislature, and the judiciary. Representatives and senators were also elected and were ready to join Congress when it reconvened in December 1865.

Black Codes

Throughout mid-1865, as the South reconstructed along Johnson's lines, Congress was in recess. Many southern states, while they had formally abolished slavery, had gone on to establish Black Codes. Reflecting white fears of African American violence and white southern unwillingness to accept the ramifications of emancipation, Black Codes prohibited African Americans from owning guns, knives, and property, prohibited their testimony in court against whites, mandated that African Americans labor for ex-masters, prohibited them from voting, and other similar restrictions. Often, southern state legislators simply took their previous slave code and reenacted it after substituting the word "black" for "slave," thus recreating slavery in all but name.

Johnson was willing to accept these kinds of laws. In many ways Johnson still believed in the traditional system of U.S. government from before the American Civil War, when states were largely in control of their own affairs. If African Americans could not vote for state constitutional delegates, or if the new state legislatures restricted African American liberties, well, traditionally American states had made those decisions and Johnson was comfortable letting states continue to do so.

Congress Rejects Johnson's Plan

When Congress convened in December 1865 most Republican congressmen were very concerned by the course Reconstruction was taking. They were distressed by the Black Codes and by the speed and lack of congressional involvement in Reconstruction. Many southern states had already completed Reconstruction under the terms laid out by Johnson and Lincoln, and to the Republican's dismay their representatives and senators were ready to rejoin the Congress.

Republican leadership in both houses of Congress met and agreed not to seat any of Johnson's Reconstructed representatives. According to the Constitution, Congress controls its own membership, and the Republican leadership instructed the clerks of the House and the Senate to ignore the southern states when calling the roll, effectively shutting out Johnson's reconstructed governments. It did not help the cause of the southern states that some of the new southern representatives and senators were the same people who seceded four years earlier, and some of those men wore their Confederate uniforms to the Congress to retake their seats. Without southern states present, Congress established the Joint Committee on Reconstruction to study Reconstruction options and to report its findings.

The Freedman's Bureau Acts

One of the first issues the new Congress took on was the future of the Freedman's Bureau. To clarify the role of the federal government in assisting former slaves, Congress passed and Lincoln signed into law the first Freedman's Bureau Act in March 1865. Lasting for the duration of the war and one year afterwards, the Freedman's Bureau was housed in the War Department with the goal of coordinating food and supplies to the freed slaves and white war refugees. The bureau was also directed to assist those persons in settling on abandoned lands. Many lawyers and northern reformers joined the bureau, and they used special Freedman's Bureau courts to protect African Americans against assaults and the newly passed state Black Codes.

Johnson was opposed to the use of the federal government's power to protect African Americans in the South, but Congress supported it. In February 1866, with large majorities, Congress passed a second Freedman's Bureau Bill. This second bill expanded the Freedman's Bureau's term and power and explicitly charged it with protecting African Americans from oppressive state laws. Despite the strong support for the bill by Congress, Johnson vetoed it. Democrats hailed Johnson's veto as a defense of the South and their property rights, and attempts to pass the bill over his veto could not attract the required two-thirds majority and failed. Johnson felt vindicated, but his victory was short lived. A few months later, as anti-Johnson sentiment grew in Congress, it passed a slightly different Freedman's

Biography:

William Henry Seward

Lawyer; Politician; Secretary of State (1801–1872)
William Henry Seward has been called one of the nation's greatest secretaries of state. Seward's career began as a trial lawyer, a New York governor, and then a U.S. senator. As a trial lawyer in 1846, Seward defended two mentally ill African Americans who were brought to trial on the charge of murder. His defense was eloquent and his *Argument in Defense of William Freeman* was published and hailed as "the finest forensic effort in the English language." Appointed secretary of state by President Abraham Lincoln upon his election in 1860, Seward handled the office with the dignity and firmness necessary to usher the nation through the politically charged and delicate Civil War era. His tactful pressure and veiled threats are credited with keeping nations that officially recognized or sided with the Confederacy, from directly intervening on behalf of the Confederacy. Seward was a longtime, staunch opponent of slavery and his views on this and most other issues closely paralleled those of President Lincoln. In fact, he was regarded as one of President Lincoln's most loyal defenders and personally urged him to run for the presidency again in 1864. Following President Lincoln's assassination, Seward remained secretary of state and backed fully the Reconstruction proposals of President Andrew Johnson. Under this administration, Seward also

helped crowd France out of Mexico, settled the Alabama Claims, and coordinated the purchase of Alaska from Russia. His loyalty remained unbridled throughout the impeachment proceedings brought against President Johnson. Seward spent his last days travelling around the world before dying at home at age 71.

Bureau Bill. Johnson vetoed it, but Congress overwhelmingly overrode this veto.

The Civil Rights Act of 1866

Also making its way out of the Senate Judiciary Committee was the nation's first civil rights act. Aimed to provide federal guarantees of rights for African Americans in their localities and in their state courts, the Civil Rights Bill of 1866 struck back at the Black Codes. In fact, once passed, the Civil Rights Act of 1866 nullified the southern Black Codes. The bill, designed to enforce the Thirteenth Amendment, which specifically ended slavery and involuntary servitude, declared African Americans citizens and provided a long list of rights persons were entitled to because they were citizens. These rights included the right to make and enforce contracts, the right to sue and be sued, the right to give testimony, and the right to own and sell land.

The bill passed the Senate in February 1866 by a vote of 33 to 12, and it passed the House of Representatives the next month, by a vote of 111 to 33. Stung by Johnson's earlier veto of the Freedman's Bureau Bill, and believing that Johnson would accept the civil rights legislation since he had made no objection to the proposal, it came as a shock to many Republicans a few weeks later when Johnson sent a message to Congress vetoing the bill. Johnson argued that the bill was unconstitutional because it intruded on states's powers, and in his mind

was another step in a dangerous trend toward centralization of power in the federal government. Also in his veto message, Johnson argued that African Americans were not ready for full citizenship and that it would "operate in favor of the colored and against the white race" (Richardson, p. 6:405).

Historian Albert Castel calls Johnson's veto of the Civil Rights Act "one of the greatest blunders of his presidency—perhaps the greatest. He turned friends into enemies, united Moderates and Radicals, and made the issue between him and Congress not the African American's political rights, on which he probably could have won, but their civil rights, on which he was doomed to lose." Johnson's veto was eventually overridden.

Military Reconstruction Acts

After impressive wins in the congressional elections in the fall of 1866, Republicans were ready to take control of Reconstruction away from Johnson. Congress had sent the Fourteenth Amendment to the states for ratification in June (*See also,* Changes in the U.S. Government). Although it was clear that they would not be readmitted unless they accepted the amendment, only Tennessee had done so. Ten states remained out of the Union. Attacks on African Americans, ranging from single assaults to urban race riots, were a common occurrence throughout the South. Northern public opinion demanded that these issues be addressed.

In January 1867 the Joint Committee on Reconstruction proposed a bill for the military government of the South. Based on the argument that the southern states remained politically disorganized, this bill allowed Congress (not the president) to use military courts for civil purposes. After debate in the appropriate committees, the bill passed. In March 1867 President Johnson vetoed the bill arguing that it was unconstitutional. He believed it denied citizens the right to due process, which it did since it imposed military law on civilian populations. Congress overrode Johnson's veto the same day it received Johnson's veto message. The Military Reconstruction Act became the law of the land.

Under the First Military Reconstruction Act (three more would eventually be passed), Congress divided the 10 unrestored states into five military districts under the command of army generals. These generals received orders to maintain law and order in their districts and to use troops to protect all persons (including African Americans) and their property. For all practical purposes Johnson's reconstructed southern state governments ceased to exist. Specifically, Congress directed the commanders of the five military districts to register eligible African American and white voters who would then vote for delegates to a new state constitutional convention. Because any person who had voluntarily participated in the rebellion was excluded from political participation, a majority of the white voters of the southern states were eliminated from the political process. These new southern state constitutions would be submitted to the voters of the states for approval and had to include a guarantee of African American suffrage. Once each state had adopted its new constitution, the registered voters would elect a new state legislature and governor. These congressionally reconstructed governments, backed by the military, would then have to ratify the Fourteenth Amendment to be readmitted to the Union.

Not surprisingly, Johnson's southern state governments and white southerners in general resisted the Military Reconstruction Act. Three more Military Reconstruction Acts were eventually passed to deal with this problem. All were passed by Congress, vetoed by Johnson, then written into law over Johnson's veto by Congress.

Although approximately 100,000 people were excluded from voting in elections, southern states began to write up new constitutions. These new congressional state Reconstruction governments provided for universal male suffrage and an equality before the law regardless of race (broader suffrage than existed in many northern states at the time). Many of these state constitutions brought about other reforms such as reorganizing urban governments, updating the penal laws, reapportioning taxes and election district lines, and establishing free public education for children. As the southern states accepted their new constitutions and ratified the Fourteenth Amendment, Congress readmitted them into the nation and allowed their representatives to rejoin the House and Senate. In June 1868 Congress readmitted Alabama, Arkansas, North Carolina, South Carolina, Georgia, Florida, and Louisiana. Delays meant that Texas and Virginia were not readmitted until 1869 and Mississippi not until 1870; by that time those states also had to ratify what would become the Fifteenth Amendment, designed to grant African Americans the right to vote. Still, the readmission of the southern states into the nation and into Congress did not mean the end of Reconstruction. Federal troops remained posted in the major southern cities and state capitals to support the Reconstruction governments, controlled by northern Republicans.

The Tenure of Office Act

On the very day that Johnson vetoed the First Military Reconstruction Act, in March 1867, he confronted two other important pieces of Republican legislation both aimed at limiting his power as president. One was a bill that limited Johnson's ability to interfere with military Reconstruction operations, by requiring that his orders go through the general in command of the army, who he would also be prevented from removing without congressional approval. The current commanding general, Ulysses S. Grant, was a supporter of congressional Reconstruction, so Johnson did not want to sign the bill. However, these changes were part of a larger bill, one that would provide the army with its funding. Since Johnson did not want to be responsible for delaying the payment of the military, he signed the bill.

The other piece of legislation Johnson was faced with was the Tenure of Office Bill. This legislation prohibited the president from removing from office any person whom the Senate had approved. Johnson well understood that it was designed to prevent him from removing any military or civilian officer engaged in congressional Reconstruction. Particularly controversial was the status of cabinet officers, all of whom are approved by the Senate. Several of Johnson's cabinet members were men who he had kept from Lincoln's administration, and some of them favored Congress's plans over the president's. Even the Republican sponsors of the bill were unsure about the idea of restricting Johnson's control of his own cabinet. Some argued that any president, even one they disliked, ought to be able to place people he trusted in his cabinet. Thus, to cover cabinet officers the Tenure of Office Bill stated vaguely that they should hold their office "during the term of the President by whom they may have been appointed, and for one month thereafter, subject to removal by and with the advice and consent of the Senate." The bill did allow the president to make ad interim, or temporary, changes when Congress was not in session, but these would have to be approved later. As expected, Johnson vetoed the bill, Congress overrode his veto, and the Tenure of Office Bill became law.

The Impeachment and Trial of President Andrew Johnson

In early 1867, knowing of President Johnson's hostility to their Reconstruction plans, House Republicans established an investigative committee to examine how to impeach and remove the president for obstructing Congress's will. Impeachment is an eighteenth century administrative procedure to remove holders of high office. Seldom used because of its cumbersome nature (and the American preference for removing officeholders at the polls), when impeachment had been used in the United States, it was employed to remove incompetent or disabled federal judges from their bench. Under the Constitution an officer could be impeached for "high crimes and misdemeanors," but the Constitution did not define what constituted high crimes and misdemeanors. Simply because Republicans disliked Johnson's meddling with their Reconstruction plans, could they impeach and remove him? No one knew for sure, but Johnson's aggressive defense of his vetoes and his continued resistance to congressional Reconstruction made impeachment only a distant possibility unless he broke the law. In July 1867 the committee could find no grounds for impeachment. Nevertheless, Radicals continued their pressure for impeachment. It was no surprise, then, that when Johnson violated the Tenure of Office Act some months later, his opponents in Congress sought to remove him from office.

Johnson Violates the Tenure of Office Act

Johnson's secretary of war, Edwin Stanton, was a holdover from the Lincoln administration who supported the Radicals in Congress and opposed Johnson's Reconstruction plan. He refused to resign, considering it important that the Radicals have a voice on Johnson's cabinet. Johnson finally decided to remove Stanton from his office. First, he attempted to replace him legally. In August 1867, with Congress not in session, Johnson removed Stanton from his position and replaced him with Ulysses S. Grant on an ad interim basis. When Congress reconvened in December 1867, however, the Senate rejected Johnson's removal of Stanton from office and Stanton resumed his post. Johnson still wanted to get rid of Stanton, and in February 1868, with the Senate in session, he removed Stanton from office and replaced him with General Lorenzo Thomas, in direct violation of the Tenure of Office Act.

Johnson is Impeached by the House of Representatives

Johnson's violation of the Tenure of Office Act was the presidential action the Radicals and some Moderates had been waiting for, an impeachable action by Johnson. On February 24, 1868, the U.S. House of Representatives adopted the following resolution by a vote of 126 to 47: "That Andrew Johnson, President of the United States, be impeached of high crimes and misdemeanors."

House members applauded the action and Andrew Johnson became the first impeached United States president. On March 2 and 3, 1868, the full House accepted the 11 articles of impeachment drawn up by the House Judiciary Committee. Most of the articles dealt with Johnson's alleged violation of the Tenure of office Act.

Hoping to be rid of Johnson quickly, the Radicals expected impeachment to be swift; Johnson's guilt was self-evident and impeachment a necessary evil to remove an obstructionist president. On March 13, 1868, with Chief Justice Salmon P. Chase presiding over the Senate, President Andrew Johnson's attorneys appeared in the Senate and asked for a delay of 40 days to prepare their defense. After a heated debate—the Radicals wanted to start that very day—the Senate agreed to a 10-day delay and, on March 23, the Senate granted Johnson's lawyers another delay of six days. As a result, Johnson's impeachment trial took up the months of April and May 1868. Instead of a fast impeachment, delay worked to Johnson's advantage and raised concerns about the process and about the charges in the minds of some moderate Republican Senators.

Johnson is Tried in the Senate

When the trial finally started, Johnson's defense team out-argued the House's prosecution team. Johnson's lawyers had prepared a multipart defense for the president. His attorneys argued, first, that the Tenure of Office act was unconstitutional. They cited examples from English and U.S. history demonstrating that the removal power (completely within the president's power, they argued) was separate from the appointing power (a concurrent power with the Senate). Second, even if the act was constitutional, reasoned his attorneys, Stanton had been appointed by Lincoln, not Johnson, and Johnson had merely acquiesced to his staying in the office and thus could remove him at any time. Because Stanton was not his appointee, Johnson could remove him without violating the Tenure of Office Act. Third, since Stanton remained on the job (he had refused to physically relinquish his office), Stanton was still in office and therefore Johnson had not violated the act. Fourth, by attempting to remove Stanton from office, Johnson hoped to test the constitutionality of the Tenure of Office Act, not commit a high crime or misdemeanor and hardly a criminal act. Lastly and most significantly, Johnson's lawyers stressed that impeachment was a judicial proceeding, not a political one; therefore, the normal judicial procedures and standards for criminal behavior ought to guide the Senators in their decision making.

Since Johnson had committed no crime by his attempt to remove Stanton, he could not, and should not, be convicted of committing "high crimes and misdemeanors." This last point spoke to the heart of the impeachment issue—was impeachment a "trial" or more of a political event? The real reason that Republicans wanted to remove Johnson was political—he was impeding their Reconstruction plans. The Senate was reluctant,

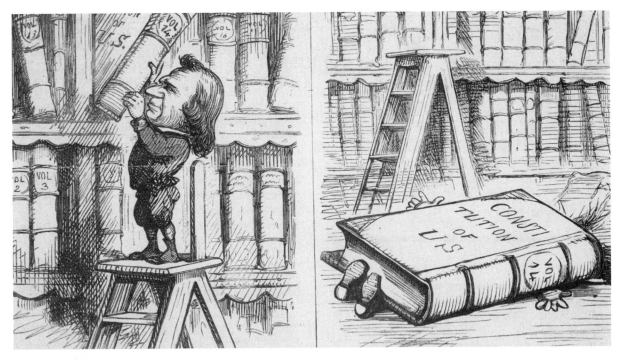

This political cartoon depicts Andrew Johnson being crushed by the same Constitution he was trying to uphold. His opposition to Congress's Reconstruction plans brought about his impeachment. (Archive Photos. Reproduced by permission.)

however, to turn what was supposedly a trial for violating the Tenure of Office Act into a purely political matter. Thus the Senate voted early on in the proceedings to allow the chief justice to decide all questions of law, evidence, and procedure unless the Senate overruled him. In effect, this decision made the proceedings a trial with the chief justice as the presiding officer and the senators acting like associate judges.

Led by Radical Benjamin Butler of Massachusetts, the House prosecution team met each of Johnson's defenses, but only ineptly. Believing that the Republican-dominated Senate was sure to convict Johnson, the prosecution team did not work as hard as it should have to win its case. They argued that the Tenure of Office Act was constitutional, and Johnson (together with Thomas) had knowingly violated the law and ought to be punished. Prosecutors conceded the obvious—that impeachment was inherently political—but they defended impeachment by arguing that without it as a tool to restrain unfit presidents, how could the nation be protected?

On May 16, 1868, the Senate began its balloting on Johnson's impeachment. Republicans believed that they had the greatest chance of conviction on the broadest of the articles of impeachment, so they decided to vote on Article Eleven, which summed up all the previous articles. After the call of the roll, 35 senators voted "guilty" and 19 voted "not guilty"—one vote short of the requisite two-thirds needed for conviction. Johnson was

acquitted on the votes of northern Democratic senators, and seven Republicans who voted not guilty. With these seven Republicans under enormous political and public pressure, the Senate took up the second article of impeachment and the vote was again 35 to 19. Having defeated that article, the Senate took up the third article and again the vote was 35 to 19. As the seven Republican senators stood firm, it became clear that impeachment would fail. At that point in the proceedings the Senate voted to adjourn and not take up the issue again. The trial was over.

Many explanations have been offered as to why the seven Republican senators refused to convict Johnson. They have been hailed as statesmen, rising above politics and making a decision based on principle, but that explanation is probably too simple. The man who would replace Andrew Johnson, the president pro tempore of the Senate, Benjamin Wade, was undoubtedly a factor: Johnson had no vice president, as at the time no method existed to fill that office if the vice president succeeded the president as he did. Wade was known to favor the continued circulation of paper money, the wartime "greenbacks"; thus he was a soft money man while those who voted to acquit Johnson were overwhelmingly for hard money (gold and silver).

Johnson also helped his own case by softening his positions. He withdrew Thomas's name to head the War Department and submitted that of General John M. Schofield instead. Schofield served with distinction dur-

Fast Fact

Andrew Johnson, who was a tailor before entering politics, was the first president whose background was not in the law or the military.

(Source: Joseph Nathan Kane. *Facts About the Presidents*, 1993.)

son used his message to take some further shots at Republican money policy hoping to tie the Republicans to hard money, banks, and the business community at the expense of the small people of the country. Johnson also proposed four constitutional amendments: the direct election of the president and vice president, and limiting presidents to one four-year term (the Twenty-second Amendment of 1951 limits presidents to two consecutive four-year terms, while the direct election of presidents has not been adopted); clarification of the succession to the presidency (the Twenty-fifth Amendment of 1967 specifies the succession); the direct election of senators (adopted in 1913 with the Seventeenth Amendment); and limiting the number of years federal judges can serve (not adopted but often considered).

ing the American Civil War and had enforced the Reconstruction acts in Virginia, making him relatively attractive to Congress. Also, instead of holding up the Reconstruction constitutions of Arkansas and South Carolina as he had a tendency to do, Johnson sent them directly to Congress, a step that pleased its members. By these actions, Johnson signaled that he was backing off just enough from his obstructionist position to allow the Senate Democrats and the conservative and a few moderate Republicans to vote not guilty.

Other Domestic Issues

After failing to gain the 1868 Democratic presidential nomination, Johnson harassed Republican initiatives with his veto power and aided Democratic causes as best he could. Johnson did not tour the country on behalf of Democratic presidential candidate Horatio Seymour of New York, but he could and did encourage southern white Democratic voters to support Seymour and to resist Republican reconstructed governments. In July 1868 Johnson vetoed a bill excluding from the upcoming meeting of the electoral college the three unreconstructed states of Texas, Mississippi, and Virginia—which would vote for Seymour if allowed in the college. Yet again Congress quickly overrode Johnson's veto, but this veto was meant only to draw attention to the extremes the Republicans were willing to go to remain in power. Johnson also pocket-vetoed a bill refunding the national debt. Foreshadowing the political disputes over hard and soft money in the decades to come, the bill reassured both the pro- and anti-greenback elements in the country (and highlighted an issue that the Democrats hoped to exploit in the fall). Johnson's veto meant that, although they did not need it, the Republicans could not use the money question effectively during the upcoming elections.

Although Republican candidate Ulysses S. Grant won the November 1868 election, President Johnson still had one major role to play—to deliver his State of the Union message to Congress on December 9, 1868. John-

Foreign Issues

Reconstruction, and the political power struggle between the president and Congress left the Johnson administration little time for foreign issues. Much like President Abraham Lincoln, Johnson left U.S. foreign policy in the capable hands of Secretary of State William H. Seward of New York, while he battled Congress over Reconstruction. With the American Civil War (1861–65) over the United States was rapidly expanding, especially in the West. Most of the foreign policy initiatives of this period were to continue or support this expansion. Seward attempted to negotiate the purchase of a number of territories, including Cuba, Puerto Rico, Hawaii, and the Virgin Islands. Most of his proposals failed, due in large part to the poor relationship between Congress and the Johnson administration. There were some successes, however, most notably with Alaska and China.

The Alaska Purchase

In March 1867 the Russian government decided that the defense of its Alaska claims would be too costly if, as expected, U.S. settlers moved into the area. Further, Russia's imperial treasury needed monies, and the selling of the Alaska territory would stabilize its finances. As a result, Russia's representative to the United States, Baron Edouard de Stoeckl, received instructions to sell Alaska.

President Johnson needed some positive news as Congress took the Reconstruction initiative away from him, so de Stoeckl's timing fitted the needs of the administration. At first Secretary Seward and de Stoeckl met to discuss only U.S. fishing and shipping rights, but it became clear in the meeting that the Russians sought to dispose of the whole territory. After a few days of negotiations, de Stoeckl and Seward reached an agreement for the United States to purchase the Alaska territory for $7 million in gold. Later negotiations added a further $200,000 to the deal. Seward and de Stoeckl completed and signed the treaty early on March 30, 1867. The Sen-

Biography:

Thaddeus Stevens

Politician (1792–1868) Thaddeus Stevens was a mid-nineteenth-century Pennsylvania congressman who was known for his long-standing, staunch opposition to slavery and African American oppression. A congressman during House debates over the Compromise of 1850, Stevens was noted for his fierce, outspoken attacks against southern slaveholders. The start of the American Civil War found Stevens as chairman of the powerful House Ways and Means Committee where he helped to secure passage of legislation needed to finance the Union Army's fight. Along with other Radical Republicans, Stevens campaigned hard urging President Abraham Lincoln to adopt uncompromising war policies against the South. He advocated controversial steps like the use of African American soldiers in the Union Army and confiscation of Confederate property. In the postwar period, Stevens served on the Joint Committee on Reconstruction guiding legislation like the passage of the Fourteenth Amendment to the Constitution, which affirmed equal rights for all citizens. Many of his proposals for restruc-turing the southern states challenged the existing social fabric and were too radical for most northerners to accept. In bitter legislative conflict, Stevens rallied the support of other radical congressmen to successfully override President Andrew Johnson's own, more-conservative course of Reconstruction to substitute his own. A few years later, Stevens sat on the committee that drafted the articles of impeachment against President Johnson and

then managed the case before the Senate. Months after Johnson's acquittal, Stevens passed away. His unconventional request to be buried in a "black cemetery" was to "illustrate in my death the principles which I advocated through a long life—Equality of Man before his Creator."

---

ate ended its session later that day, before it had time to consider the treaty. Johnson called a special session of Congress for April 1. After a good deal of lobbying, Seward had enough votes to ratify the treaty. On April 9, 1867, by a vote of 37 to 2, the United States accepted the treaty.

Newspapers of the day dubbed the treaty Seward's Folly, since most people at the time considered Alaska a practically useless frozen wasteland. In retrospect, however, Alaska's price was cheap, and its acquisition a genuine positive achievement for the Johnson administration. By adding Alaska to U.S. holdings, President Johnson and Secretary Seward added an area to the country twice the size of Texas, an area known to hold gold (they could not have anticipated later oil strikes), and they eliminated Russia's claim to territory in North America.

The Burlingame Treaty of 1868

Another diplomatic success came in late May 1868 when the U.S. envoy to China arrived in Washington with a delegation sent by the Emperor. Anson Burlingame, a former U.S. envoy to China, sought trade advantages from the Chinese so Americans could reach the huge Chinese market. On Secretary Seward's part, he wanted cheap Chinese labor to immigrate to the western states of the United States to help develop the area. The Burlingame Treaty of July 1868 defined the rights and status of Americans in China and of Chinese in America, allowed a U.S. consulate to open in China, and allowed unrestricted Chinese immigration to the United States. To irritate Johnson, the Senate postponed ratification of the treaty until President Grant's administration, even though the real work on the treaty had been accomplished during Johnson's administration.

The Johnson Administration Legacy

When Andrew Johnson left the presidency in March 1869, the politics of Reconstruction still divided the country. Federal troops occupied the southern state capitals, and the occasional race riot erupted as African Americans (and their white supporters) tested the limits of freedom. In rural areas of the South unreported and unpunished assaults on blacks continued as white southerners demonstrated their intransigence to accepting blacks as political or legal equals. In the North, Midwest, and Far West the economy had rebounded from its immediate post-war dip, and industrialization increased its pace after being slowed by the demands of the war.

Southerners and northerners with southern sympathies supported the Democrats and some liked Johnson's resistance to the Republicans, but Johnson's own tough personality and his tainted image from his impeachment acquittal removed Johnson as a serious Democratic leader in 1869. Republican majorities entered Congress in 1869 stronger than ever, supported by a Republican president and confident in their abilities to set national policy due to their broad public support throughout the North, Midwest, and Far West. As expected, the Republicans in the next few years built on their political, legal, and constitutional achievements stretching back to the Abraham Lincoln administration.

Modern historians who deplore the nation's inability in the late 1860s to transform southern race relations into more modern sensibilities routinely rate Andrew Johnson as one the nation's worst presidents. Johnson did have a low opinion of African Americans but that opinion simply made him a man of his times, little different from the majority of white southerners (which he ultimately always was), and white northerners. Abraham Lincoln was never a race equalitarian and certainly neither were other better presidents such as Johnson's political hero, Andrew Jackson. Without glossing over Johnson's failure to recognize that the outcome of the American Civil War and black emancipation changed the country, it is still true that Johnson was not alone in his unwillingness to alter the form of U.S. constitutional government he defended by resisting secession in Tennessee. His vetoes of needed legislation such as the Civil Rights Act of 1866 and the Freedman's Bureau Act ironically prompted Congress to draft a constitutional amendment, the Fourteenth, which cemented even deeper changes in the old prewar Constitution Johnson defended.

A politician of his times and so thoroughly embedded in his social and political culture that he could not envision a future much different than his present, Johnson was simply a normal individual. A competent representative and a capable person, Johnson may have made an average to slightly above average president in an era when Reconstruction did not occupy every tongue and pen. But the times of his presidency were against him. One of the great "what if" questions is whether even Lincoln could have ridden the storm of Reconstruction. It is not surprising that Johnson could not. Because of his pugnacious personality and his sincere belief that it was Congress who had cast off the limitations of the Constitution and was out of control, Johnson badly damaged his own reputation and his administration's reputation.

Lasting Impact

Johnson was an American success story, one of the few truly rags-to-riches stories of a man who heard the call to public service. His administration was not without successes such as the key purchase of Alaska and the Burlingame Treaty with China, which did provide access to the Chinese market for U.S. businesses. His devotion to the nation and the Constitution led him to the highest administrative office in the land. Yet given the historical context of Reconstruction, Johnson proved to be exactly the wrong sort of leader the country needed in the 1860s. Although political tempers cooled and Johnson regained his seat in the U.S. Senate in 1874, his missteps and failures constitute much of the history of his administration.

Also remembered from his presidency, of course, is his impeachment. Because of the lessons learned from the nation's first impeachment of a president, congressmen, senators, and scholars began to consider impeachment as a judicial and an administrative process, not a political technique. To convict in an impeachment process, the prosecution bore the burden of proving that the impeached official committed a crime in order to remove that official from office. Presidential impeachment would not come up again until the late 1990s and President Bill Clinton's administration.

Perhaps too often lost in the institutional analysis of the Johnson administration are Johnson's personal qualities as president. Instead of buckling under to the Republican Party, Johnson stood his ground. Perhaps he stood his ground in the wrong way and on the wrong issues, but Johnson stood by what he believed. Johnson defended the institution of the presidency against congressional government. A man of his times who misunderstood the changing race relations issue since the American Civil War, Johnson maintained his allegiance to the Constitution and its divisions of powers and duties between president and Congress as well as between the states and the federal center. Because his political enemies won all the key political battles during his administration, Johnson's administration has been judged a failure. But that judgment has to be tempered by Johnson's personal integrity and the knowledge that congressional Reconstruction did not solve all of the nation's problems, especially the race relations issue.

Sources

Benedict, Michael Les. *The Impeachment and Trial of Andrew Johnson.* New York: W. W. Norton, 1973.

Castel, Albert. *The Presidency of Andrew Johnson.* Lawrence, Kans.: The University Press of Kansas, 1979.

Kane, Joseph Nathan. *Facts About the Presidents.* 6th ed. New York: H. W. Wilson, 1993.

Kelly, Alfred H., Winfred A. Harbison, and Herman Belz. *The American Constitution: Its Origins and Development.* 7th ed. New York: W. W. Norton, 1983.

McKitrick, Eric L. *Andrew Johnson and Reconstruction.* Chicago: The University of Chicago Press, 1960.

Richardson, James D. ed. *A Compilation of the Messages and Papers of the Presidents, 1789–1897.* Washington, D.C.: Government Printing Office, 1896–99.

Trefousse, Hans L. *Impeachment of a President: Andrew Johnson, the Blacks, and Reconstruction.* Knoxville, Tenn.: The University of Tennessee Press, 1975.

Further Readings

Benedict, Michael Les. *A Compromise of Principle: Congressional Republicans and Reconstruction, 1863–1869.* New York: W. W. Norton, 1974.

Cox, LaWanda, and John H. Cox. *Politics, Principle, and Prejudice: Dilemma of Reconstruction America, 1865–1866.* New York: Macmillan, 1963.

Hyman, Harold M. *The Reconstruction of Justice Salmon P. Chase: In re Turner and Texas v. White.* Lawrence, Kans.: The University Press of Kansas, 1997.

Mantell, Martin E. *Johnson, Grant, and the Politics of Reconstruction.* New York: Columbia University Press, 1973.

Nelson, William E. *The Fourteenth Amendment: From Political Principle to Judicial Doctrine.* Cambridge, Mass.: Harvard University Press, 1988.

Stampp, Kenneth M. *The Era of Reconstruction, 1865–1877.* New York: Alfred A. Knopf, 1965.

Thomas, Lately. *The First President Johnson: The Three Lives of the Seventeenth President of the United States of America.* New York: William Morrow, 1968.

Grant Administrations

Full name: Ulysses S. Grant
Given name: Hiram Ulysses Grant
Popular name: Unconditional Surrender Grant

Personal Information:

Born: April 27, 1822
Birthplace: Point Pleasant, Ohio
Died: July 23, 1885
Death place: Mount McGregor, New York
Burial place: Grant's Tomb, New York, New York
Religion: Methodist
Spouse: Julia Boggs Dent (m. 1848)
Children: Frederick Dent; Ulysses S. Jr.; Ellen (Nellie) Wrenshall; Jesse Root
Education: United States Military Academy, West Point, 1843
Occupation: Soldier
Political Party: Republican Party
Age at Inauguration: 46 years

Biography

The son of an Ohio tanner who was working as a clerk at his father's store when the American Civil War (1861–65) began, Ulysses S. Grant rose from humble beginnings to become a general and a president. His successes during the American Civil War made him one of the most popular men in the United States by the war's end, popularity that carried over to his two terms as president. Moody but not glum in personality, modest but confident, loyal to those loyal to him even to a fault, and determined to finish every job he started, Grant personified nineteenth-century values of strong character and hard work.

Early Life

Hiram Ulysses Grant was born on April 27, 1822, to Hannah Simpson Grant and Jesse Grant, a tanner. When Grant was just an infant his father moved the family to Georgetown, Ohio, in order to be closer to the raw materials needed for his tanning business. It was in and around Georgetown that Hiram Grant grew up. As a child Grant showed no interest in his father's tanning business. While his father saw horses as a source for his leather products, Grant was drawn to them as sources of wonder. Throughout his life Grant knew how to handle and appraise horses.

Due to his father's success in the business world, Grant's childhood was not a stressful one. He helped with the chores around the house such as hauling wood and, as Grant said in his famous *Memoirs* "all the work done with horses." Put off by the sights, smells, and noises of the tannery business, the young Grant was at best ambivalent about pursuing a business career. By his middle teens Grant's next step was unclear to him and to his parents.

Education

The Grant family could afford better than average education for their children. Ulysses Grant's schooling began in Georgetown, Ohio, in a school run for profit by John D. White, where Grant learned the fundamentals. He attended the Maysville Academy in Maysville, Kentucky, from 1836 to 1837, and the following year attended the Presbyterian Academy in Ripley, Ohio. While Grant was a good student, particularly in mathematics, he was certainly not an outstanding one. His father's ambitions led him to ask Representative Thomas L. Hamer for an appointment to the United States Military Academy for his son, and in 1839 Grant left for West Point, New York.

By this time Grant had already been tinkering with his name. His given name, Hiram Ulysses Grant, resulted in the initials "HUG," which he understandably disliked. As a result, Grant began inverting his middle and first names so the initials became "UHG," and he began to refer to himself as Ulysses Grant and not Hiram Grant. But, unknown to him, his name was about to change again. Congressperson Hamer forgot or did not know that Grant's first name was Hiram, so when he filled out Grant's appointment papers he listed "Ulysses" as his first name. Hamer then listed Grant's mother's maiden name, "Simpson," as his middle name; this name resulted in Ulysses Simpson Grant. Ulysses adopted the name as his own from that day forward.

At West Point during his cadet years, Grant surprised himself with his academic abilities. While not outstanding, he held his own far better than he had expected. His skills with horses and his horsemanship did stand out and he finished first in his class in the subject. While at the academy Grant became friends with his roommate, Frederick Tracy Dent, the brother of Grant's future wife. Grant graduated from West Point in 1843 finishing 21st in his class of 39 cadets. Because of his horsemanship, Grant requested assignment in the dragoons (cavalry), but due to his average grades and the elite nature of the dragoons, the army denied his request and assigned him to the infantry.

Family Life

Ulysses S. Grant met his wife, Julia Boggs Dent, when he and his friend Frederick Dent were assigned to a barracks in St. Louis, Missouri, near Dent's home. Julia Dent grew up in a world of moderate comfort with a few family slaves to help around the house. She received a

Ulysses S. Grant. (Colonial Press.)

normal education for girls at the time and developed some abilities in art and music. She was noted for her strong personality. Grant visited the Dents and became enamored with Julia and she with him. In 1844 the couple became engaged. They saw each other only once between 1844 and 1848, while Grant served in the Mexican War (1846–48). On August 22, 1848, they were married at Julia's home.

Typical of service families, from their marriage until Ulysses Grant's death on July 23, 1885, the couple occasionally spent months apart. From all indications, theirs was a relation of mutual dependence with Julia Grant being very much the "boss" (their family term). The couple had four children: Frederick, Ulysses Jr., Ellen, and Jesse.

Julia Grant stayed as close to her husband during the American Civil War (1861–65) as circumstances allowed. She divided her time between wherever Grant established his headquarters and her family's residence in St. Louis, Missouri. In March 1864 when President Lincoln promoted Grant to the rank of lieutenant-general and put him in overall charge of Union forces, Julia Grant followed and moved the family to Washington, D.C.

Julia Grant greatly enjoyed being first lady and attending the many parties, receptions, and events. Although sometimes criticized for her less than refined looks and speech, she was regarded as a warm and capable hostess who made the White House the social center of official Washington. Julia Grant did insist, however, that the White House's grounds be closed to provide security for her family. Previously the mansion's grounds had been open to the general public.

Career

Before the American Civil War (1861–65), Ulysses S. Grant's career can be described as halting. He served well, even with distinction during the Mexican War (1846–48), and was promoted to first lieutenant. A series of assignments to peacetime military posts did not appeal to him. Although promoted to captain while serving on the West Coast, Grant hated being apart from his family and fed his depression with alcohol. Grant recovered, resigned his commission, and returned to Missouri to support his family. Unfortunately, his military training left him poorly prepared to pursue farming. Before the outbreak of the Civil War, Grant had to swallow his pride, return to his father's store in Galena, Illinois, and work as a clerk.

The American Civil War

What made Grant famous and eventually led him to the presidency was the American Civil War. Never a friend of slavery, yet tolerant of those who owned slaves, Grant's patriotism accounts for his staying with federal forces during the secession crisis from 1860 to 1861. On April 18, 1861, two nights after Confederate forces fired on Fort Sumter, South Carolina, a mass meeting was held in Galena to discuss military recruitment. As the only West Point-trained person in town, Grant chaired the meeting. He set about raising volunteers for service and even went with them to Springfield, Missouri, as they began their training.

In June 1861 the Illinois governor appointed Grant as a colonel, commanding the Twenty-first Volunteer Infantry Regiment. In August 1861, as the Lincoln administration expanded the army to meet the crisis of war, Grant received promotion to brigadier general, commander of the southeast Missouri district, and was assigned to Cairo, Illinois. From Cairo, Grant began his noted military campaigns.

Grant proved himself an able leader in several incidents during 1861 and 1862, including the battle of Shiloh in Tennessee, the bloodiest battle of the war to that point. These early victories, coming at a time when other Union generals were performing poorly, first brought him to national attention. Grant spent late 1862 and early 1863 attempting to capture the Confederate fortress at Vicksburg, Mississippi. After several failed attempts, Grant laid siege to Vicksburg in June 1863. When the city surrendered on July 4, 1863, Grant had achieved control of the entire Mississippi River for the

Union. This victory, combined with the Union victory at the battle of Gettysburg, Pennsylvania, electrified northern public opinion and proved the key turning point of the American Civil War.

President Lincoln placed Grant in charge of the Mississippi Department as a major general, and Grant pushed steadily deeper into the Confederacy. In March 1864 Lincoln appointed Grant the overall commander of Union forces. Grant took personal command of the eastern Union troops and led them on an offensive to capture the Confederate capital of Richmond, Virginia. Beginning with the Battle of the Wilderness and spreading southwest, Union and Confederate forces battled until Richmond and Petersburg, Virginia, were besieged by the late fall of 1864. This situation continued until April 1865, when Grant outflanked the Confederates and moved on Richmond proper. On April 2, 1865, the Confederates abandoned Richmond. A week later, on April 9, 1865, Grant accepted Confederate General Robert E. Lee's unconditional surrender, effectively ending the war.

Grant's victories throughout the war made him the most popular man in the United States. Congress recognized his immense standing by commissioning him general of the army on July 25, 1866; a position held previously only by General George Washington.

Politics

While the war was won, Grant's political battles had just begun. Grant felt torn between his duty to serve the army and President Andrew Johnson, his commander in chief, and his personal support for the Republican policies put forth in Congress, which Johnson opposed. Grant believed that Johnson's plans for Reconstruction (the rebuilding of the South after the war and its reintegration into the Union) were too easy on white southerners. He preferred instead the plans of the Republicans for a longer, more demanding Reconstruction. Grant and Johnson clashed in the summer of 1867 over the use of the army in the president's plans for Reconstruction, and over Johnson's wish to remove pro-Republican generals and replace them with more pro-Johnson generals.

President

Grant took office on March 4, 1869. In his two terms in office, he struggled with the issues of currency reform and Reconstruction. Among his achievements, he forcibly protected the rights of African Americans to vote in the South, and he developed a new and less violent approach to interacting with American Indians. He also managed to settle an outstanding dispute with Great Britain, without breaking the international peace that the United States enjoyed throughout his presidency. However, Grant's achievements have long been

Appointed by Lincoln as overall commander of the Union forces in 1864, Ulysses S. Grant pushed steadily deeper into the Confederacy, bringing about Gen. Robert E. Lee's surrender at the Appomattox Courthouse on April 9, 1865. The surrender effectively put an end to the Civil War. (Photograph by Timothy O'Sullivan. The Library of Congress.)

overshadowed by his failures. His initially bold action in defense of Reconstruction faded over the years, as the northern public grew weary of the ongoing and often bloody struggle. By the end of his administration Reconstruction would have effectively ended. Numerous scandals also hurt the Grant administration, including several that implicated close advisers to Grant in bribe-taking and influence-peddling. Grant himself was never involved in unethical activities, and he remained an extremely popular war hero throughout his eight years in office.

Post-presidential Years

While many in his party wanted Grant to run for a third term, he did not want to spend another four years in the White House. He was succeeded in 1877 by fellow Republican, Rutherford B. Hayes. Grant spent the next two years traveling the world with his family, followed by a year visiting the American South, Cuba, and Mexico. In 1880 Republicans again pushed Grant to run for president. Grant made it known that he did not wish

Fast Fact

Three of Grant's groomsmen at his 1848 wedding to Julia Boggs Dent—James Longstreet, Cadmus Marcelus Wilcox, and Bernard Pratte III—were among the Confederate troops who would surrender to Grant at Appomattox Courthouse in 1865, ending the Civil War.

(Source: Geoffrey Perret. *Ulysses S. Grant: Soldier & President,* 1997.)

to be nominated, but a draft Grant movement emerged anyway at the party's convention. Grant led the initial voting, but after the party deadlocked James A. Garfield was chosen as a compromise candidate.

Money problems occupied most of the rest of Grant's life. Grant had never saved much money for retirement and what money he had he and Julia Grant spent. The Grants's many friends and admirers would often come to their aid. Through the help of his son Ulysses Grant Jr., Grant became president of the Mexican Southern Railroad and moved into a house in New York City purchased for him by friends. Grant also invested his life savings in his son's investment firm. When financial scandals drove the firm out of business, Grant went deeply into debt and relied on friends to make ends meet.

In order to pay the bills, Grant consented to writing a few articles on his American Civil War (1861–65) experiences for the *Century* magazine. His friend, Samuel "Mark Twain" Clemens, urged him to write his memoirs. Grant, a lifetime cigar smoker, knew he was developing throat cancer and agreed to write his memoirs in order to ensure his wife an income after he was gone.

In late 1884 and 1885 Grant wrote out longhand his memoirs, *Personal Memoirs of U. S. Grant.* The work was a financial success and remains one of the best memoirs produced by a U.S. president and an important account of the American Civil War. Grant did not live to witness this success, however. On July 23, 1885, only a few days after finishing his memoirs, he died from throat cancer.

On August 8, 1885, an estimated one million people lined the streets of New York City to witness the passing of Grant's funeral procession. Grant rested in a temporary cemetery until a tomb could be built for him on the far upper west side of New York City. He was

reinterred in the magnificent Victorian tomb that bears his name in 1897.

The Ulysses S. Grant Administrations

While Grant himself was extremely popular during his lifetime, historically his administration has been heavily criticized. Grant's poor choices in appointments led to corruption and numerous scandals and, although Grant was not involved in any of them directly, they have forever damaged his legacy. Grant is also criticized for having taken a weak stand on Reconstruction (the rebuilding of the South after the American Civil War [1861–65] and its readmittance to the Union), and on the protection of former slaves in the South. Yet Grant used troops to enforce Reconstruction when white resistance reached new levels, and his administrations maintained the country at peace in world affairs.

Grant Becomes President

The Campaign of 1868

In 1868 Grant was the most popular man in the United States because of his long and successful career as a soldier in the American Civil War (1861–65). This, along with his known support for congressional Republican's Reconstruction policy, was enough to assure him of the Republican nomination. On May 21, 1868, at the Republican National Convention in Chicago, Illinois, Grant won the nomination unanimously. The convention then selected Speaker of the House of Representatives Schuyler Colfax of Indiana as his vice presidential running mate.

Democrats met in New York City, in the city's Democratic Party's headquarters, Tammany Hall, from July 4 to July 9, 1868. The Democrats had a sitting president in Andrew Johnson, but his near removal from office by Congress earlier that year made him an unattractive candidate. After several days of balloting, the Democrats chose Horatio Seymour as their candidate. Seymour was a true dark horse, or unexpected, candidate. The governor of New York had not sought the nomination and won it only as a compromise between the supporters of other, more prominent politicians. For his running mate, the convention selected Francis Preston Blair Jr., of Maryland, a close friend of President Johnson.

Grant avoided taking strong positions during his campaign and in general relied on his immense popularity. Seymour campaigned on a policy of an immediate end to Reconstruction's restrictions on the political

Administration

Administration Dates
March 4, 1869–March 4, 1873
March 4, 1873–March 4, 1877

Vice President
Schuyler Colfax (1869–73)
Henry Wilson (1873–75)

Cabinet

Secretary of State
William H. Seward (1861–69)
Elihu B. Washburne (1869)
Hamilton Fish (1869–77)

Secretary of the Treasury
George S. Boutwell (1869–73)
William A. Richardson (1873–74)
Benjamin H. Bristow (1874–76)
Lot M. Morrill (1876–77)

Secretary of War
John M. Schofield (1868–69)
John A. Rawlins (1869)
William T. Sherman (1869)

William W. Belknap (1869–76)
Alphonso Taft (1876)
James D. Cameron (1876–77)

Attorney General
Ebenezer R. Hoar (1869–70)
Amos T. Akerman (1870–72)
George H. Williams (1872–75)
Edwards Pierrepont (1875–76)
Alphonso Taft (1876–77)

Secretary of the Navy
Adolph E. Borie (1869)
George M. Robeson (1869–77)

Postmaster General
John A. J. Creswell (1869–74)
James W. Marshall (1874)
Marshall Jewell (1874–76)
James N. Tyner (1876–77)

Secretary of the Interior
Jacob D. Cox (1869–70)
Columbus Delano (1870–75)
Zachariah Chandler (1875–77)

---

process in the South, and support for the use of paper money. While Seymour closed the gap between himself and Grant, Grant won the election handily. Grant drew over three million votes and Seymour received 2.7 million votes. More impressive was Grant's success in the electoral college where he carried 26 states versus eight states for Seymour. He received 214 electoral votes, 72.79 percent, to Seymour's 80, or 27.21 percent. As Grant and the Republicans analyzed the election results, they discovered that the key voters in his election were the newly enfranchised African Americans of the reconstructed states of the South, who had voted almost entirely Republican. The need to protect these Republican votes was a major source of motivation for the drafting of what would later become the Fifteenth Amendment.

On March 4, 1869, incoming president Grant did not take the traditional carriage ride to the Capitol with the outgoing president, Andrew Johnson. Relations had soured between the two men and neither wanted to see the other. At approximately 12:30 P.M., Chief Justice Salmon P. Chase swore Ulysses S. Grant into office; he

became the nation's 18th president and, to that time, the nation's youngest president at age 46 years, 311 days old. His inaugural speech centered on the need to reduce the national debt.

The Campaign of 1872

Dissatisfaction with Grant grew among the radical wing of the Republican Party during Grant's first administration. The corruption of some of the federally backed reconstructed governments horrified the radicals and led to suspicions of corruption within the Grant administration. As a result of their unhappiness, a branch of the Republican Party, calling themselves the Liberal Republicans, broke away in 1872. They held their convention in Cincinnati, Ohio, on May 1, 1872, and nominated New York newspaper editor Horace Greeley for president. For his running mate the Liberal Republicans selected Benjamin Gratz Brown of Missouri. Their platform stated that they recognized the equality of all men, called for an amnesty for former Confederates, and reform of the civil service.

Greeley's candidacy as part of a small, splinter party probably would have been inconsequential, except that the Democrats nominated Greeley as well. Hoping to drive a wedge in the Republican Party and defeat Grant by supporting a Liberal Republican, the Democrats met in Ford's Opera House in Baltimore, Maryland, July 9 to July 10, 1872. They nominated the Greeley/Brown ticket to oppose Grant in the November 1872 elections.

Republicans met in Philadelphia, Pennsylvania, from June 5 to June 6, 1872, and unanimously renominated Grant for the presidency. Because of the failing health of Vice President Schuyler Colfax, the Republicans chose Senator Henry Wilson of Massachusetts as Grant's second term running mate. Their party platform pledged to continue Reconstruction, to lower the national debt, maintain tariffs, and an eventual return to hard money.

The campaign of 1872 is notable for the formation of another party, the People's Party, also called the Equal Rights Party. While they won few votes, the party's candidates of Victoria Claflin Woodhull and Frederick Douglass were the first female presidential nominee and the first African American vice presidential nominee.

On November 5, 1872, Grant won a second term as president with a larger popular and electoral vote than in 1868. While members of his party might have become disenchanted with Grant, the voters were not and swept Grant into office over Greeley and the Liberal Republicans and Democrats. Grant received 3.6 million and Greeley 2.8 million of the popular votes; he polled 286 of the electoral votes to Greeley's 66 electoral votes. Greeley's defeat at the polls combined with the illness and death of his wife took its toll. He died on November 29, 1872, just three weeks after his election defeat. On March 4, 1873, Grant took the presidential oath of office for a second time and pledged to continue to heal the wounds of the American Civil War and Reconstruction and reduce the national debt.

The Campaign of 1880

Although Grant declined to be nominated for a third consecutive term in 1876, he still had many supporters at the Republican National Convention of 1880. When the incumbent president, Rutherford B. Hayes, declared he would not seek a second term, Grant's supporters put him forward as a candidate. It is unclear if Grant actually wanted another term. He did not make any public statements for or against his candidacy. Grant initially held a commanding lead in the balloting, but when he could not secure the nomination, a compromise was found in James A. Garfield.

Grant's Advisers

Grant reserved major decisions for himself and relied on only a small group of trusted advisers for advice.

In keeping with his military background, Grant used a staff to present him with options and then decided the issue himself. This style did not always sit well with his fellow Republicans in the House and the Senate, who considered it their duty, even right, to advise and consult with the president and have the president act on their advice. In accordance with this governing style, Grant chose cabinet officers who he felt would competently carry out his policies, rather than attempting to appease various Republican leaders by appointing them or their favorites to high office. Grant also tended to rely on people that he personally knew and trusted. On more than one occasion, his personal loyalty would be tested by accusations of corruption and scandal surrounding some of his appointees (*See also,* Domestic Issues).

Until his untimely death due to tuberculosis, few people were as close to Grant and trusted by him as his first secretary of war, John A. Rawlins. A member of Grant's wartime staff, Rawlins was one of the few men who could challenge Grant's opinions. When Rawlins died in early 1869, Grant lost a valued friend and adviser. Hamilton Fish was another important adviser. As secretary of state for Grant's entire term, he exerted substantial influence over U.S. foreign policy, and his able diplomacy won reparations from Great Britain.

After Rawlins's death Grant established a staff of three ex-colonels to advise him and run the executive mansion–Horace Porter, Orville Babcock, and Frederick T. Dent, his old West Point roommate. Their presence gave Grant's presidency an air of a military camp. Robert Douglas, the son of the late senator from Illinois, Stephen A. Douglas, also joined Grant's staff for a time.

While not a formal political adviser to the president, Julia Grant also was influential as she and Grant spoke about the issues of the day, and they trusted each other completely. Her influence over Grant's decisions is still in scholarly debate.

Grant and Congress

Grant presided over the Forty-first through the Forty-fourth sessions of Congress during his two terms. Throughout this period Republicans controlled both the House and the Senate, the one exception being the Democrat-controlled House of 1875–76. Despite this Republican dominance, Grant often had difficulty working with Congress. Many Republican leaders in Congress were angered by Grant's failure to consult them on major appointments and policy. Further, while the many corruption scandals of Grant's term also touched Congress, they tainted the administration far more. That appearance of weakness encouraged Congress to resist presidential initiatives.

Another issue that colored Grant's relationship with Congress was Grant's own perception of the presidency.

The first African Americans to serve in the U.S. Congress (seated, left to right): Hiram R. Revels, Benjamin S. Turner, Josiah T. Walls, Joseph H. Rainey, R. Brown Elliot, (standing, left to right) Robert C. De Large, and Jefferson F. Long. All Republicans, they were elected during the period following the Civil War known as Reconstruction, when the federal government actively protected the voting rights of the recently freed slaves. (National Portrait Gallery. Reproduced by permission.)

Having been raised in the Jacksonian era of President Andrew Jackson (1829–37), with its minimal government with most decisions being made by Congress and the states, Grant failed to understand the changed world of the post-Civil War United States. Further, Grant also failed to appreciate the president as party leader, as evidenced by his selecting a cabinet without seeking the advice and support of other Republicans.

As a result of Grant's own perception as the administrator of policy established by Congress, his administration initiated few acts. In 1871 Grant asked for and Congress established the nation's first Civil Service Commission. Civil service was new to the United States; it meant that government jobs ought to go to those persons who possessed the skills to do the jobs, not politically connected persons. Civil service struck at the existing patronage system, which allowed politicians to assign government jobs as they saw fit, and thereby reward their supporters with profitable jobs. Grant only tentatively supported the idea, and when Congress did not renew the commission in 1872, Grant did not protest.

Reconstruction could still force the administration to act, as it did in 1870 and 1871. As southern whites increased their resistance to Reconstruction, they turned to intimidation and terror against the carpetbaggers

(white northerners who came South after the war), the scalawags (white southerners who supported Reconstruction), and African Americans. Their violence became so widespread in the western counties of North Carolina and South Carolina that Grant asked for and Congress provided him with measures to deal with the violence. These included the Force Bill of 1870, which authorized the president to send troops into those areas declared in rebellion, and the Ku Klux Klan Act of 1871, which further expanded Grant's ability to use federal power to put an end to the power of vigilante groups such as the Klan (*See also,* Domestic Issues).

Grant and the Judiciary

Grant appointed five men to the Supreme Court during his two terms, but on several occasions they were not his first choice. In 1869 Grant appointed Edwin M. Stanton of Pennsylvania as an associate justice, and the Senate quickly confirmed his appointment. But Stanton died on December 24, 1869, before taking his seat. At the same time as Stanton's appointment, Grant sent the nomination of his attorney general, Ebenezer Rockwood Hoar, to the Senate for confirmation to fill another associate justice's seat. Because of opposition by Senator

Biography:

Horace Greeley

Publisher; Politician (1811–72) It was one week before the 1872 presidential election that Horace Greeley's wife passed away. Her death, coupled with Greeley's personal humiliation over his election defeat by Ulysses S. Grant, unbalanced Greeley's mind, and he died in a private mental hospital later that year. But Greeley's death did not come before the sum of this man and his life's work was revealed in his nationwide presidential campaign. Greeley was in his early twenties when he started a literary and news magazine that survives today, the *New Yorker*. He proved a capable editor and the success of the magazine gave rise to another publication, intended for a general readership and called the *New York Tribune*. Greeley's editorial policy for both publications reflected his strong belief that progress demanded a serious effort to better society. He promoted the politically radical writings of renowned Socialists while at the same time publishing editorials that reflected less progressive ideas like his opposition to women's suffrage and divorce reform.

He was his paper's most important and prolific commentator and both he and his paper soon gained national importance. During and after the American Civil War (1861–65), Greeley's editorial focus centered on the abolishment of slavery and his high profile led President Abraham Lincoln to call upon him to probe peace possibilities in a meeting arranged with Confederate agents.

After the war, Greeley met with corruption-weary Radical Republicans to form a new party, the Republican Liberal party. It was the new party's choice of Greeley as their first presidential nominee that started him on his fateful candidacy.

Charles Sumner of Massachusetts, Hoar's nomination failed to receive Senate approval. In place of Stanton and Hoar, Grant nominated men more attuned to the Senate's wishes. Joseph P. Bradley of New Jersey and William Strong of Pennsylvania were both confirmed by the Senate in 1870. In 1872 Ward Hunt became Grant's final associate justice appointment.

Grant also ran into trouble over the nomination of a chief justice after the death of Salmon P. Chase. While several persons expressed their interest in the position, including associate justice Noah H. Swayne, New York senator Roscoe Conkling, secretary of Treasury Benjamin H. Bristow, and the U.S. minister to Spain, Caleb Cushing; Grant selected his then attorney general George H. Williams of Oregon. Unfortunately, several senators disliked and distrusted Williams, and when Williams's wife pressed too hard for his appointment she embarrassed the administration and Grant was forced to withdraw Williams's name. Several other names were put forward before Grant, and the Senate agreed on Morrison R. Waite of Ohio in January 1874.

The Slaughterhouse Cases

One of the U.S. Supreme Court's most important decisions during the Grant administration was the *Slaughterhouse Cases* of 1873. This case was the first time that the Supreme Court was called upon to interpret the Fourteenth Amendment (*See also,* Andrew Johnson Administration), and its decision had a powerful and long-lasting impact.

The case began in New Orleans, Louisiana, when a number of butchers went to court to stop the closing of their butcher shops. Louisiana had decided to concentrate all butcher shops in New Orleans into one business, a state-mandated monopoly, in order to protect the public's health. But the businesspeople not favored by the monopoly sued Louisiana to stop the monopoly, arguing that their rights to earn a living under the new Fourteenth Amendment's "due process" and "privileges and immunities" clauses were being violated. The local and state courts ruled against the business owners. When they appealed to the Supreme Court, the Court combined several cases into one case for decision, the *Slaughterhouse Cases*.

In a split five-to-four decision, the majority of the Supreme Court upheld the monopoly legislation. Writing for the majority, Justice Samuel F. Miller dismissed the butchers' claim that the regulation violated any Fourteenth Amendment rights. This decision was based on a traditional understanding of the rights of U.S. citizens— an understanding that predated the American Civil War (1861–65)—that most rights were conferred and protected by the states in which people lived rather than the national government.

Under this interpretation, the Fourteenth Amendment applied only to those rights that had long been the responsibility of the federal government, such as the right to receive protection abroad, to engage in interstate commerce, and to petition the national government. Any other rights were purely a matter for the states to control; the Fourteenth Amendment, it was decided, did not transfer responsibility for citizens' rights from the states to the federal government. Therefore, the butchers lost their appeal because the monopoly was legal under Louisiana state law.

The greatest impact was not on butchers, however, but on African Americans. Ironically, while the Fourteenth Amendment was ratified to provide African Americans with citizenship and rights, the Miller opinion in *Slaughterhouse* held that any rights African Americans might have would have to be determined in state courts and were primarily state rights—not federal rights that the national government was obligated to protect. Without such national protection, African Americans were left at the mercy of hostile, white majorities, particularly in the South. This limited interpretation of the Fourteenth Amendment would last well into the twentieth century.

Changes in the U.S. Government

Under pressure from the Liberal Republicans in 1871, the Grant administration agreed to establish the Civil Service Commission to oversee the awarding of government jobs. While in theory a sound idea, the political reality was different. Patronage ruled the era and politicians wanted to control government jobs in order to award them to their loyal supporters. Civil service threatened that patronage system, and the commission, without strong support by Grant, died in 1872.

Unlike civil service reform, which did not become a permanent part of the federal government bureaucracy until later, a new constitutional amendment was proposed, passed by Congress, and ratified by the states during Ulysses S. Grant's administration: the Fifteenth Amendment. Analysis of the 1868 election results had revealed to Republican leaders that the newly enfranchised African American population of the South had provided Grant with his victory in the presidential election. In order to maintain this advantage, the Republicans sought some federal guarantee of the right to vote for African Americans. However, the Republicans wanted to avoid taking control of the voting process, which had traditionally been administered by the states.

What emerged from Congress and was ratified by a sufficient number of states on February 3, 1870, was a negative amendment. It read: "The right of citizens of the United States to vote shall not be denied or abridged by the United States or by any State on account of race, color, or previous condition of servitude." Contrary to popular impression, this amendment did not provide anyone with the right to vote. Rather, it prohibited states from denying someone the vote on account of their race. Significantly, it did not prohibit other restrictions on voting, such as poll taxes, grandfather clauses, and literacy tests. All of these were in wide use throughout the United States when the Fifteenth Amendment was enacted, and in many places such restrictions were used to effectively deny African Americans the right to vote. Not until the mid-twentieth century would such barriers become illegal.

Domestic Issues

The United States was in the midst of a complicated process of growth, integration, and shifting values when Grant came into office. The Republican Party of the North controlled the national government and was in command of efforts to reintegrate the southern states into the Union. The methods and goals of this process, called Reconstruction, were a subject of much debate, however. Another contentious issue was money. The federal government had begun using paper money that was not redeemable for gold during the American Civil War (1861–65), and debate raged over whether the procedure should continue. These issues were set against a backdrop of general economic prosperity, particularly in the industrialized North. The completion of the transcontinental railroad early in Grant's first term symbolized the expansion of the United States from ocean to ocean. This increasing development in the West led to new political pressures and may have prompted Grant's reform of federal policies on American Indians.

Reconstruction

During the administration of Andrew Johnson, Congress had seized control of Reconstruction policy and set about rebuilding the South on its own terms. While President Johnson had opposed these congressional plans, Grant was in agreement with them and expected to leave the matter primarily in their hands. Under congressional Reconstruction, southerners who had supported the rebellion, which included almost all whites, were prohibited from voting. The state governments thus came under the control of recently freed African Americans and whites who had moved south after the war. These governments, Republican dominated in an area where whites were strongly Democratic, set about establishing a new political system, one in which African Americans would be equal to whites. The Reconstruction governments were very unpopular, and federal troops were in place throughout the South to protect them.

Black voting particularly irritated whites in the South, and by the late 1860s and early 1870s a few whites turned to threats and terror to keep blacks away from the polls. These private actions took the form of vigilante groups such as the Knights of the White Camilla and, the most notorious of all, the Ku Klux Klan. In order to protect black voting rights, Congress, with Grant's full support, passed what came to be known as the Force Acts, which were designed to give the federal government the authority to enforce the Fourteenth and Fifteenth Amendments.

In May 1870 the First Enforcement Act prohibited state officials from discriminating against voters on the basis of race, made bribery and intimidation of voters a federal crime, and outlawed conspiracies to prevent citizens from exercising their federal rights. This was followed in February 1871 with the Second Enforcement Act. Designed to control anti-black riots on election day in cities, it placed elections in cities over 20,000 in population under direct federal supervision.

Best known of the Force Acts was the Third Enforcement Act, also known as the Ku Klux Klan Act. This act made it a federal crime to deny the equal protection of the laws and privileges and immunities of citizens. Most significantly, President Grant received the power to effectively declare martial law in places where violations of the act were taking place. He could suspend legal due process and use military forces to suppress conspiracies to deprive citizens of their civil rights. Grant ordered the army into the western counties of North Carolina and South Carolina where the worst of the violence was taking place. Once in place, the army crushed the illegal bands of intimidators and assisted the federal prosecutors in indicting persons accused of denying the civil rights of African Americans. By 1872 Grant's actions backed by the Enforcement Acts had destroyed the Ku Klux Klan and other such vigilante groups. (Another Ku Klux Klan would be founded in 1915.)

Redemption

Both Grant and the Congress, however, had become concerned about how long southern states would be under federal oversight and, reflecting northern public opinion, they became tired of the continuing problems of Reconstruction. Gradually southern states that had drafted acceptable state constitutions and had ratified the Thirteenth, Fourteenth, and Fifteenth Amendments to the Constitution had the restrictions on their voting rights removed. As federal troops left the southern states and the predominately Democratic white southerners regained control of the state governments, a so-called redemption of that state occurred.

By 1871 the states of Virginia, North Carolina, and Georgia had been redeemed. In 1872 Congress regularized the redemption process by passing the Amnesty Act. This legislation affected approximately 150,000 ex-Confederates, restoring to them their political rights, including voting. Only about five hundred white southerners still had their political rights suspended after the Amnesty Act's passage. With their right to vote restored, white voting majorities overwhelmed the Reconstruction Republican dominated southern governments and redeemed southern states. In 1873 Texas was redeemed, followed by Alabama and Arkansas in 1874, then Mississippi in 1876. South Carolina, Louisiana, and Florida

would not be redeemed until after the 1876 presidential elections during the administration of Rutherford B. Hayes.

The Money Question

In the nineteenth century, different varieties of money possessed emotional qualities for people. Soft money, meaning paper money like the greenbacks that came into use during the American Civil War, struck many people as unsafe since it was not directly supported with gold reserves. Large businesses in particular favored specie or hard money, such as gold. Yet soft money had its supporters. More paper money in circulation meant inflation, and inflation helped farmers, laborers, and small businesses pay their debts.

Upon entering office Grant instructed his secretary of the Treasury, George S. Boutwell, to withdraw the greenbacks from circulation, but to do so slowly. This go-slow approach was politically attractive since the greenbacks would remain in circulation (which the Democrats wanted), but would be decreasing in the overall money supply (which the Republicans wanted). This policy was reflected by the Public Credit Act of March 1869, which declared that the government would redeem its bonds with specie, rather than greenbacks.

Although this policy encountered a few bumps, for most of Grant's first term it worked well. But at the beginning of Grant's second administration, the economy went into a steep decline. The panic of 1873 started when a series of banks failed due to their overspeculation in the gold market. When the banks failed, businesses failed, and unemployment followed. Bank failures also meant a decrease in the money supply and deflation. Congress responded to this economic downturn by passing the Inflation Bill of 1874. The Inflation Bill authorized the president and the Treasury Department to raise the amount of greenbacks in circulation from $356 million to $400 million. This action would increase the money, lead to inflation, and, it was hoped, help to slow if not reverse the economic slump.

On April 21, 1874, Grant vetoed the Inflation Bill. Grant feared that the bill would be the first of many such inflation bills, and if it was not successful it would set a dangerous precedent; Congress would simply print more unsupported money. Highly unpopular at the time, Grant's veto reflected the conventional economic beliefs of his time, that any government interference in the economy, even to aid those in need, would cause more problems that it solved. The recession continued, causing hardship for many small businesspersons, farmers, and workers.

In 1875 Congress passed and Grant signed the Specie Resumption Act, which pledged to put the nation back on the gold standard by January 1, 1879. Grant and the hard money Republicans were determined to maintain stability of the nation's currency, and that goal meant a currency of specie and gold reserves, not greenbacks. This policy aided bankers, investors, and large businesses at the expense of some smaller economic actors, but it also maintained the respectability and viability of the dollar at home and abroad.

Indian Policy

Indian policy formed an unexpected area of change and development during Grant's administration. Apparently Grant did not hold the prejudices against American Indians that most of his culture did in the nineteenth century. During the American Civil War, a Seneca Indian named Ely S. Parker served on his staff. An able aide, Grant eventually raised Parker to the brevet rank of brigadier general. When Grant assumed the presidency, he appointed Parker to be his commissioner of Indian Affairs.

After the Civil War, ongoing conflict in the West had continued between the Plains Indians, white settlers, and the army. On the reservations corrupt government agents sold government supplies intended for the American Indians, pocketing the profits themselves. Agents sold alcohol and weapons to the American Indians, knowing that this would lead to violence and that the army would have to be called in to quell the disturbance. Grant took several steps to remedy this situation. He appointed Parker to head the federal government's Bureau of Indian Affairs and developed an independent committee to provide him advice and suggestions on how to deal with the American Indians. This commission, the Board of Indian Commissioners, was supposed to last for only one year, but it proved so successful that it was retained until 1934. Grant, Parker, and the board all agreed that if the American Indians were to survive in the modern United States four conditions had to be met.

First, the treaty system would have to be abandoned. As the board noted treaties were confusing, contradictory, and useless. Grant agreed. From 1871 onward the federal government looked upon the American Indians as wards of the country, not independent domestic nations. Second, American Indians would have to be treated as individuals, not as tribes. Third, tribes would have to be contained on reservations. And fourth, American Indians would have to be educated to learn farming and adopt Christianity in order to fit into American society. This four-part plan formed Grant's "Peace Policy" for the American Indians.

In spite of these changes, relations between whites and American Indians remained poor. The army was still the primary means of controlling American Indians who were not on reservations. It is estimated that the army and the American Indians fought two hundred battles during Grant's administration. This includes the famous June 1876 Battle of the Little Big Horn near Billings, Montana, where General George Armstrong Custer led his divided forces against a strong encampment of American Indians. He and much of his Seventh Cavalry command paid with their lives. In retaliation the army redoubled its efforts to capture and place the last remaining roving American Indians on western reservations. Custer's death cast a pall on the nation's centennial celebrations of July 4, 1876, but in the long run Grant's Peace Policy lasted. While it severely hurt the tribal nature of the American Indians, it also moved the federal government into a more active and honest role in managing Indian affairs than had existed previously.

Political Scandals

While Grant's administrations made important contributions to Reconstruction policy, financial policy, and Indian policy, his administration is best known for its scandals. In the unregulated economy and market of the late 1860s and 1870s, there was much opportunity for quick wealth through speculation and government fraud, and many examples were uncovered during Grant's administration. These scandals never involved Grant himself, but they weakened his ability to work with Congress and greatly damaged his reputation in the long run.

Black Friday

One of the earliest scandals of the Grant administration involved the gold market. Two of the most notorious Wall Street speculators, James Fisk and Jay Gould, developed a scheme to corner the market, or buy up all of the available gold. By buying up so much gold, they would drive up its price. Before this false rise in gold prices could collapse, Fisk and Gould calculated that they could sell their gold to other speculators and make a tidy profit.

What Fisk and Gould needed to make their plan work was access to information about whether or not the federal government would sell additional gold to prevent the price from rising. At this point Grant's sister, Virginia Grant, married a New York financier, Abel R. Corbin, and Corbin provided the link to the Executive Mansion. While visiting his newly married sister in Boston, Massachusetts, in June 1869, Grant met Corbin who, in turn, introduced Grant to Gould. Grant returned to New York on a steamer owned by Fisk, where Fisk and Gould spoke to Grant about the gold supply without revealing their intentions. At the time they concluded that Grant would take action to stop a rise in gold prices. However, later that summer the unsuspecting Grant mentioned to Corbin that he was now planning on decreasing government sales of gold. This was the news that Corbin, Fisk, and Gould had been waiting for. They began buying up as much gold as they could.

The conspirators made a mistake when they had Corbin write Grant a letter asking him not to permit gold sales in the fall. For the first time it occurred to Grant that his brother-in-law might be speculating in the gold market. Grant had his wife add a note to Corbin in a letter to stop speculating. When her letter reached Corbin on Thursday, September 23, 1869, Corbin, Fisk, and

Gould realized that their scam was about to come undone. The next day Grant instructed the secretary of the Treasury, Boutwell, to sell $5 million of gold, increasing the amount in circulation by one-third and ruining Gould's and Fisk's attempt to corner the market. Over the summer Corbin, Fisk, and Gould had driven the price of gold up from $140 to $162 an ounce, but with the federal government's sale gold fell to $135 an ounce. This rapid fall in gold's value wiped out speculators and caused many banks and businesses to fail. For this reason Friday, September 24, 1869, is still referred to as "Black Friday."

Congress investigated the scandal and the whole plan was revealed. Fisk and Gould admitted to instigating all events and the report submitted by the chairman of the joint congressional committee, James A. Garfield of Ohio (later to become the 20th U.S. president), found no improprieties committed by Grant other than having a few meals with Fisk, Gould, and Corbin.

Crédit Mobilier

In the heat of the 1872 presidential election, the *New York Sun* revealed that beginning in 1868 a large amount of Union Pacific Railroad stock had been given away or sold below value to important federal politicians. As an investigation discovered, the Crédit Mobilier Co., the branch of Union Pacific that was responsible for building the recently completed transcontinental railroad, had used fraud and, when necessary, bribes in the form of Union Pacific stock to secure millions of dollars of unnecessary funding for the project. These government funds, as well as much of Union Pacific's own money, was kept by the leaders of the scam. Among the officials implicated in the scandal were both Grant's first and soon-to-be second vice presidents, Schuyler Colfax and Henry Wilson.

The Whiskey Ring

Ever since the late eighteenth century the federal government had taxed whiskey. During the American Civil War Congress increased the tax on whiskey even more to help pay the costs of the war. This tax increased the monies raised from whiskey, and it also raised opportunities for corruption and graft. Tax collectors simply filed fraudulent tax returns and kept the extra monies for themselves. This system of fraud became routinized in places like Chicago, Illinois; Milwaukee, Wisconsin; and St. Louis, Missouri.

In 1874 Grant replaced outgoing secretary of the Treasury William A. Richardson with Benjamin H. Bristow. Bristow hoped to make a name for himself by cracking down on the widespread fraud involving whiskey. On May 10, 1875, the Treasury seized numerous distilleries for failing to pay adequate taxes, arrested dozens of the Treasury's own agents, and seized a great deal of documentation. An old friend of Grant's, General John McDonald, was charged with defrauding the government of millions of dollars through his position as the super-

visor of the Internal Revenue Service in St. Louis, Missouri, a position Grant had appointed him to. Grant's personal secretary, Orville Babcock, was also implicated. Grant refused to believe that someone he trusted as much as Babcock could be corrupt. Grant toyed with the idea of traveling to St. Louis to testify on Babcock's behalf, but the cabinet urged him not to be so directly involved. Instead, Grant swore a deposition and forwarded it to be read at Babcock's trial. In spite of overwhelming evidence that Babcock knew of the frauds, and possibly even directly profited from the tax evasions, the jury acquitted Babcock of bribery and conspiracy; Grant's deposition saved his aide from conviction. Babcock did not return to the White House staff; but Grant did appoint him the chief inspector of lighthouses.

The Impeachment of William Belknap

Corruption reached Grant's cabinet room as well. William W. Belknap became Grant's secretary of war after the death of John Rawlins in 1869. Belknap's second wife, Amanda Tomlinson Bower Belknap (who was the sister of his first wife), had an "arrangement" with Caleb P. Marsh, the sutler at Fort Sill, Oklahoma. Sutlers were merchants who had a monopoly on the sale of food, clothing, and other necessities and luxuries to the soldiers and dependents at a base. At a large base like Fort Sill, a sutler could make a substantial income. Belknap's first wife had helped secure the position for Marsh, and in return he paid her a percentage of his earnings. Amanda Belknap continued to collect from Marsh once she married William Belknap. A congressional investigation committee was about to make this "arrangement" public in March 1876. When Grant first learned of Belknap's problems, he demanded and received his immediate resignation. This did not stop the House of Representatives from impeaching Belknap after a lengthy investigation, making Belknap the first cabinet official ever impeached in the United States. However, the Senate did not convict Belknap in their impeachment proceedings, largely because he had already left office.

Foreign Issues

Foreign affairs played a secondary role during the administrations of Grant. With relative peace abroad but the problems of Reconstruction and a major recession at home, the public had little interest in foreign affairs. The only pressing issue that Grant faced coming into office were outstanding claims against Great Britain for its assembly and protection of Confederate warships during the American Civil War (1861–65). Grant did have foreign policy interests of his own and made some effort to put them into practice during his administration. In particular Grant sought to expand U.S. influence in the Caribbean basin. He sent several surveys to Panama to explore the feasibility of a canal, but it would be many years before real action was taken on this issue. Conflict with Congress over foreign policy, and particularly with Senator Charles Sumner of Massachusetts and the Senate Foreign Affairs Committee, cut short Grant's other plans for the region.

Santo Domingo

The island nation of Santo Domingo, in the Caribbean Sea, possessed a fine harbor at Samaná Bay that Grant hoped to purchase. President Andrew Johnson's secretary of state, William Seward, had tried to purchase Samaná Bay from the Dominicans, but nothing had come from his efforts. Grant and his secretary of state Hamilton Fish renewed negotiations with the island's president, Buenaventura Báez. Báez came up with a plan to sell the harbor to the United States and keep half of the monies for himself. Grant sent one of his secretaries, Orville Babcock, to Santo Domingo to investigate Báez's offer and assess the island's and the harbor's worth. Much to Grant's and Fish's surprise, when Babcock returned in August 1869 he brought with him a signed treaty of annexation. Fish disavowed this treaty and made Babcock return to the island the following November with authority from the State Department to try to lease the harbor at Samaná Bay for the United States. Babcock also took with him $100,000 and weapons; the money was used to encourage Báez to agree to the deal and the weapons were offered to assist Báez with any opposition. This time Babcock brought back a treaty of annexation, and, in case this treaty was unacceptable, a long-term lease agreement for the harbor.

Yet Grant still had a problem—Senator Charles Sumner, the head of the Senate Foreign Relations Committee, was key if Grant hoped to have his treaty approved by the Senate. Sumner and Grant did not like each other, and Sumner was displeased by Grant's unwillingness to include him in his foreign policy decisions. Nevertheless, Grant met with Sumner on January 2, 1870, and Sumner reportedly told him that he would support Grant's plan.

With what Grant thought was Sumner's blessing, he pressed the Senate to ratify the treaty for Samaná Bay. Unfortunately, once the bribe for Báez and the weapons to assist him became known, key senators announced their opposition to the treaty. Even more importantly, Senator Sumner refused to support the treaty after all. Instead, he led his Foreign Affairs Committee to a three-to-two vote against ratification of the treaty and refused to even discuss the proposed lease. When the full Senate voted on the treaty in March 1870, it fell short of the required two-thirds majority. A revised version of the treaty also failed ratification in 1871. Grant took these losses hard and never forgave Sumner for his opposition.

Alabama *Claims*

During the American Civil War Great Britain allowed the Confederacy, made up of the southern states that had seceded from the Union, to buy and build commerce raiders, fast ships designed to capture or destroy enemy commercial shipping while avoiding enemy warships, in its ports. One of these ships, the *Alabama*, became particularly notorious in the North for its successful attacks on Union shipping. After the war's conclusion northerners and the ship owners who had been injured by the *Alabama* wanted the British to pay for the damages and apologize for allowing the ships to operate out of supposedly neutral British ports. Americans demanded more than $20 million in compensation. At the end of President Johnson's administration, a tentative deal was struck with the British in which they agreed to pay a smaller fee, which represented the actual losses to U.S. shipping. Britain did not agree to apologize.

Grant disliked the deal and said so before he took office. He believed that the British ought to be held more accountable for their actions and ought to pay more of the *Alabama* claims. Congressional leaders, including Charles Sumner, agreed with Grant. Sumner convinced Grant to appoint one of his friends, John Lothrop Motley, as the new ambassador to London, England, with orders to squeeze greater concessions out of Britain. Sumner took the floor of the Senate in 1869 and denounced the Johnson treaty. He went on to claim that the commerce raiders had so lengthened the war and done such a huge amount of damage to Union shipping that the British ought to be made to pay at least $110 million in compensation, and perhaps be made to pay for the entire cost of the Civil War. Many in the press and public were enthusiastic about Sumner's speech, and there was talk of an annexation of Canada, or even war with Great Britain, over the *Alabama* claims. In spite of the uproar caused by Sumner's speech, negotiations continued without any effect for over a year.

In time the British suggested independent arbitration of the dispute, and Grant appointed a new ambassador, Robert C. Schenck, with instructions to negotiate a treaty for the arbitration of the claims. This treaty was then presented to the Senate for ratification. Sumner's nationalistic outburst had cost him much respect among his Senate colleagues, and they voted to ratify the Treaty of Washington on June 17, 1871. In the end, the arbiters awarded the United States $15.5 million in damages. While the apology and repayment for the indirect cost of the *Alabama* and other commerce raiders that Grant had hoped for were left out, he still had reason to be proud. The award exceeded what Johnson's administration had achieved, and it was reached without resorting to violence.

The Grant Administration Legacy

Grant succeeded in addressing many of the pressing concerns of his day; when Rutherford B. Hayes succeeded Grant in 1876, he inherited few long-standing problems. Reconstruction was effectively over, with only a few states still under the control of Reconstruction governments. While some controversy still surrounded the greenbacks, particularly in light of the depression that the nation had been in since 1873, Grant's fiscal policies had maintained the fundamental soundness of the U.S. currency and economy. In addition, Grant had settled the *Alabama* claims, the only pressing matter in foreign affairs to arise during his administration. Political corruption also was a part of Grant's legacy, however. While Grant himself was still seen as honest, and was extremely popular for the rest of his life, scandals such as the Whiskey Ring and the improprieties of his secretary of war, William Belknap, left his successor with the need to repair the damaged reputation of the presidency and the government.

Lasting Impact

Grant's reputation as president has not benefited from time. He left office as one of the most popular presidents ever, but over time his achievements have faded and his failings grown. Grant came to the presidency as one of the least prepared men ever to hold the office. Long service as an army officer, a hardscrabble existence before the American Civil War (1861–65), and the rapid rise to greatness because of his generalship during the war, did not give Grant the experience and skills necessary to manage the rough and tumble world of party and national politics in the late 1860s and 1870s. Grant felt strongly that he needed to find people who would be loyal to him and put them in key offices to carry out his policies. In a few cases, notably Secretary of State Hamilton Fish, this principle served Grant well; but Grant failed to grasp that loyalty to him did not always equate with personal honesty. In far too many cases, Grant's loyal friends failed him by taking bribes and engaging in other scandalous abuses of the power and the trust he had given them.

Grant also is associated with the failure of Reconstruction to truly reform the politics and society of the South and give African Americans a place in the United States as equals. By the time Grant left office, Reconstruction was effectively over. It is unfair, however, to say that Grant himself ended Reconstruction. Proposal and ratification of the Fifteenth Amendment occurred under Grant, in an attempt to assist African Americans (and Republican vote totals) in the South. Grant's use of federal troops to put down vigilantes under the Enforcement Acts further demonstrates his willingness to take strong action to defend the voting rights of African Americans. But northern public opinion grew weary of the constant problems of the South, and over the eight years of Grant's administration northern commitment to protecting African American rights faded. Grant's administration reflected this trend but did not create it.

Yet Grant did have several positive achievements in other areas. Grant's Peace Policy for dealing with American Indians, although criticized since for separating individuals from their tribes and educating American Indians away from their own culture, was a genuine reform for its time. Instead of the hit-or-miss approach of the treaty system, widely abused by both sides, all American Indians were treated as wards of the state, more in need of assistance than military suppression. It is not surprising that Grant's Peace Policy failed in its goal of assimilating the majority of American Indians; it is surprising that Grant's administration tried at all given the deep prejudices of the day. Grant also deserves credit for his foreign policy. He succeeded in settling the most difficult issue of his time, the *Alabama* claims, and maintained peaceful international relations throughout his eight-year term.

Historians have long rated Grant as one of the United States's greatest generals, while also rating his presidency as one of the United States's least successful. However, Grant's accomplishments as president tend to be overlooked, and he receives more than his due share of blame for the corruption of his time and the unwillingness of Americans to continue the forceful protection of African American rights.

Sources

Hesseltine, William B. *Ulysses S. Grant: Politician.* New York: F. Ungar, 1935.

Historic World Leaders. Vol. 4. Detroit: Gale Research, 1994.

McFeely, William S. *Grant: A Biography.* New York: W. W. Norton, 1981.

Perret, Geoffrey. *Ulysses S. Grant: Soldier & President.* New York: Random House, 1997.

Simpson, Brooks D. *Let Us Have Peace: Ulysses S. Grant and the Politics of War and Reconstruction, 1861–1868.* Chapel Hill, N. C.: University of North Carolina Press, 1991.

Further Readings

Anderson, Nancy Scott. *The Generals—Ulysses S. Grant and Robert E. Lee.* New York: Knopf, 1988.

Arnold, James R. *The Armies of U. S. Grant.* London: Arms and Armour, 1995.

Carpenter, John A. *Ulysses S. Grant.* New York: Twayne Publishers, 1970.

Grant, Ulysses S. *Personal Memoirs of U. S. Grant.* Hartford, Conn.: C. L. Webster, 1885.

Nevins, Allan. *Hamilton Fish; The Inner History of the Grant Administration.* New York: F. Ungar Publishing Co., 1957.

Simon, John Y., ed. *The Personal Memoirs of Julia Dent Grant.* New York: Putnam, 1975.

Hayes Administration

Biography

A well-liked and capable lawyer, Rutherford B. Hayes came to the public eye through his military service during the American Civil War (1861–65) which propelled him first to Congress and then to the Ohio governor's office. The sincerity of his desire to heal the wounds of the Civil War and Reconstruction were never questioned, even if historians have criticized his policies as president.

Early Life

On October 4, 1822, Sophia Birchard Hayes gave birth to a son whom she named after her recently deceased husband, Rutherford Hayes Jr. Her husband had been a successful store owner but contracted typhus and died the July before Hayes was born. As a baby, Hayes was so weak that his mother did not expect him to survive. To support the family including two other young children, she rented their farm for one-third of the crop and one-half of the fruit it produced, and her younger brother, Sardis Birchard, helped the family financially.

On January 20, 1825, Hayes's older brother, Lorenzo, fell through the ice while skating and drowned. This tragedy combined with the early death of Rutherford Jr. affected Hayes's mother in two ways: first, she consoled herself through religion and, second, she became extremely protective of her two remaining children, two-year-old Rutherford B. Hayes and his four-year-old sister, Fanny Arabella.

Full name: Rutherford Birchard Hayes
Popular name: Old 8 to 7

Personal Information:

Born: October 4, 1822
Birthplace: Delaware, Ohio
Died: January 17, 1893
Death place: Fremont, Ohio
Burial place: Spiegel Grove State Park, Fremont, Ohio
Religion: Methodist
Spouse: Lucy Ware Webb (m. 1852)
Children: Birchard Austin; James Webb Cook; Rutherford Platt; Joseph Thompson; George Crook; Fanny Hayes; Scott Russell; Manning Force
Education: Kenyon College, B.A., 1842; Harvard University Law School, L.L.B., 1845
Occupation: Lawyer; general; legislator; governor
Political Party: Republican Party
Age at Inauguration: 54 years

Rutherford Birchard Hayes. (The Library of Congress.)

In part because of the stable environment in which he grew up, reinforced by the positive example of his uncle Sardis Birchard, early in his boyhood and young manhood Hayes displayed a noted quality—self-assurance. Not rigid or intolerant (Hayes was also known as a warm person and conversationalist), he had a quiet confidence in himself and his abilities throughout his career.

Education

Hayes's mother first taught him the fundamentals of reading and writing. He also received some early education at a private elementary school and some private tutoring by a local lawyer. He attended preparatory school beginning at age 15; his uncle Sardis Birchard paid for his schooling. Hayes started college at Kenyon College in Gambier, Ohio, when he was 16. In 1842 he graduated first in his class. After graduation he spent a year reading law in a law office, but his uncle wanted Hayes to attend the Harvard Law School in Cambridge, Massachusetts, because of the strength of its law faculty and especially because Justice Joseph Story of the U.S. Supreme Court and Simon Greenleaf, one of the nation's leading treatise writers, taught there. In August 1843 Hayes entered the Harvard Law School where he studied with both distinguished law professors. He graduated in January 1845 with a bachelor of laws.

Family Life

Hayes returned to Ohio to begin his law practice. He became interested in a young woman, Lucy Webb, who attended the Wesleyan Female College and was an ardent Methodist, abolitionist, and prohibitionist. Hayes was skeptical of religion and social reform throughout his life, but despite of these differences they married on December 30, 1852. Devoted to each other, their marriage proved to be fulfilling, fruitful, and long-lasting. The couple had eight children, five of whom, four sons and a daughter, lived to maturity.

Lucy Ware Webb Hayes was almost nine years younger than her husband. Because she was adamant in her opposition to alcohol and firmly committed to prohibition, she refused to serve alcohol at the formal receptions in the executive mansion. For this reason the press nicknamed her "Lemonade Lucy." She died of a stroke on June 25, 1889.

Career

Upon graduation from the Harvard Law School in 1845, Rutherford B. Hayes had returned to his uncle's town of Lower Sandusky (now Fremont), Ohio, and began his law practice, which never attracted much business. Hayes moved to Cincinnati, Ohio, where he opened another law practice that was eventually more successful.

Always interested in politics, Hayes attended lectures and occasionally gave speeches on the issues of the day. In September 1853 Hayes defended his first runaway slave case, and because of his concern about the spread of slavery into the western territories, Hayes joined the newly formed Republican Party.

In December 1858 the city solicitor (attorney) of Cincinnati was killed in a railroad accident. The city council chose Hayes to replace him because of his competence as a lawyer and because of his moderate positions on the issues before the city. This post would be the first of several for Hayes due to his skills and his moderate positions. He held the position of city solicitor until April 1861.

Becoming an ardent Republican, Hayes was glad when the American Civil War (1861–65) broke out as it was proof to him that the federal government was finally defending itself. Hayes was commissioned a major in the Twenty-third Ohio Volunteer Infantry.

During the course of the war, he participated in over 50 engagements and was wounded four times in battle. His military career culminated in his promotion to major general in March 1865. He resigned from the army in June 1865 because he had been elected to Congress.

Congress

Because of his excellent war record, Hayes's political supporters in Cincinnati decided to run him for an unfinished term in Congress in 1865 while Hayes was still in the military. With his war record and skills as a lawyer Hayes won an easy victory. As a Republican congressperson, Hayes generally voted and sympathized with the Radical Republicans, those Republicans most committed to ensuring African American citizenship. Because of those sympathies, Hayes came to oppose President Andrew Johnson for his handling of Reconstruction (*See also,* Andrew Johnson Administration). He voted in favor of impeaching President Johnson (though Johnson did end up keeping his job). Hayes decided not to run for reelection to Congress in 1868; instead, he decided to return to Ohio and run for governor.

Governor

As governor of Ohio from 1868 to 1873, Hayes supported universal manhood suffrage (the right to vote), hard-money policies (gold and silver as opposed to "soft" money such as paper money), and the ratification of the Fifteenth Amendment guaranteeing the African American vote. He advanced a series of other causes while Ohio's governor such as state civil service reform, budget cutting, promotion of education in the state including the establishment of the Ohio State University, and better treatment for the mentally ill. He refused to break the tradition in Ohio of not running for a third term and turned down his party's nomination in 1872.

Hayes ran for Congress in 1872 but lost because he spent most of his time campaigning on behalf of Ulysses Grant's reelection as president. Hayes thought that Grant might appoint him to the cabinet, but Grant merely offered him the position of assistant U.S. treasurer in Cincinnati, which he declined. Hayes returned to practicing law in Fremont, Ohio. His uncle, Sardis Birchard, died in January 1874 and left his estate to Hayes.

In 1875 the Republicans asked Hayes to once again accept the nomination for governor. His supporters argued that if he won the Ohio governorship early in 1876, that win would place him in a strong position for the presidential nomination later that year. Hayes relented and accepted the nomination. He went on to win the election by over 5,000 votes.

President

Hayes became president at the age of 54. His victory in the governor's race brought him national attention, and he was considered for the Republican Party presidential nomination in 1876. Hayes succeeded in his bid for president, despite a tough party convention, a disputed election, and a special commission called to count the votes from tainted state elections. His moderate positions and policies, and his luck, carried him into the executive mansion on March 4, 1877. As president Hayes is

Fast Fact

Lucy Hayes was the first first lady to graduate from college, the Wesleyan Female College in Cincinnati, Ohio, in 1850.

(Source: Ari Hoogenboom. *The Presidency of Rutherford B. Hayes,* 1988.)

best remembered for ending Reconstruction and the federal protection of African American voting rights in the South. While this was an honest attempt to meet the desires of a public weary from the social strife that followed the end of the American Civil War (1861–65), Hayes's presidency is poorly regarded by historians.

Post-presidential Years

After completing his administration and attending the inauguration of his successor and fellow Ohioan, James A. Garfield, Hayes returned to Fremont, Ohio. He promoted education by serving as the director of the George Peabody Educational Fund and the John F. Slater Fund, groups that worked to provide education to African Americans and whites without access to schools. He also served on the board of several Ohio universities. Hayes continued his work in favor of prohibition and also became involved with prison reform.

On June 21, 1889, Lucy Hayes suffered a stroke and on June 25, 1889, she died.

On a trip to Cleveland, Ohio, on January 14, 1893, to take care of business as trustee of Western Reserve, Hayes suffered a heart attack. On the evening of January 17, 1893, he died at home in Spiegel Grove, Ohio. Democratic president Grover Cleveland attended Hayes's funeral on January 20, 1893, as did Ohio governor (and future president) William McKinley.

The Rutherford B. Hayes Administration

Hayes's presidency signaled the end of a key and controversial era in American history—Reconstruction.

Administration

Administration Dates
March 3, 1877–March 4, 1881

Vice President
William Almon Wheeler (1877–81)

Cabinet
Secretary of State
Hamilton Fish (1869–77)
William M. Evarts (1877–81)

Secretary of the Treasury
Lot Myrick Morrill (1876–77)
John Sherman (1877–81)

Secretary of War
George W. McCrary (1877–79)
Alexander Ramsey (1879–81)

Attorney General
Alphonso Taft (1876–77)
Charles Devens (1877–81)

Secretary of the Navy
George M. Robeson (1869–77)
Richard W. Thompson (1877–80)
Nathan Goff Jr. (1881)

Postmaster General
James N. Tyner (1876–77)
David M. Key (1877–80)
Horace Maynard (1880–81)

Secretary of the Interior
Zachariah Chandler (1875–77)
Carl Schurz (1877–81)

Because he entered under a cloud due to the disputed election of 1876 and because of his pledge not to run for a second term if elected, many considered Hayes's administration an interim presidency only. Yet during his four years in office, Hayes addressed the issues of his time such as the end of Reconstruction, civil service reform, currency reform, and foreign policy questions such as Chinese immigration restrictions.

Hayes Becomes President

The Campaign of 1876
Rutherford B. Hayes won the Ohio governorship for the Republican Party in a year when the Republicans nationally fared poorly at the polls. Although they had overseen policy since the 1860 national election, had guided the nation through the maelstrom of civil war and the Reconstruction policy and politics, northern political opinion had grown weary of both the "southern problem" and Reconstruction—when the southern states were gradually reintegrated into the Union (*See also,* Andrew Johnson and Grant Administrations). Northern voters also had grown weary of the scandals and political embarrassments during the eight years of the Ulysses S. Grant administration. As a result, in 1875 and 1876, Democrats showed surprising strength at the polls in northern states, especially in the urban centers. Republicans needed a winner in 1876. Hayes was a popular figure in the key state of Ohio, a veteran of the Union Army in the American Civil War (1861–65) who had been wounded in combat, and a known moderate on issues such as civil service reform and currency reform. When he won the governorship of Ohio for the third time in 1876, his advisers told him he was well positioned with the party and the country for a shot at the Republican nomination for president that summer.

Hayes favored business development, which continued the hard money policies of the Grant administration, minimal government spending (except in times of war), and a commitment to the three Civil War amendments guaranteeing African American citizenship and equality before the law. Significantly, Hayes had not been touched by the corruptions of the Grant administration. Hayes represented a clean slate for the Republicans.

The Party Conventions
Republicans met in Cincinnati, Ohio, in June 1876. Hayes's supporters packed the galleries and the street outside. Nevertheless, Hayes remained a dark horse candidate—not expected to win the nomination.

Representative James G. Blaine of Maine was favored to win the nomination. He had the support of many of the East Coast Republicans and had been campaigning informally for the nomination for months. However, there were allegations of corruption and at least the suspicion that Blaine had been involved with some of the scandals of the Grant administration. On the seventh ballot Hayes won the Republican Party presidential nomination by five votes. William Almon Wheeler of New York was chosen by the convention to be Hayes's vice presidential running mate.

In late June 1876, the Democrats met in their own convention in St. Louis, Missouri. The front-runner in the Democratic field was the reform governor of New York, Samuel J. Tilden. Trained as a lawyer, Tilden had entered public service and made a reputation as an opponent of the corrupt William M. Tweed Ring in New York City. He then took on the corruptions involved with the Erie Canal. Tilden held a strong hand for the fall elections: he contrasted well against Grant and the Republicans, the hard times since the panic of 1873 worked to the Democrats' favor, Tilden carried the reform banner, and the Democrats took a moderate position on the hard versus soft money debate.

The Election

Three small parties ran candidates in 1876 and received votes. Most important of the third parties was the Greenback Party, which nominated Peter Cooper of New York and Samuel Fenton Cary of Ohio. Greenbackers favored taking the country off the gold standard and shifting the currency of the country to paper money. This inflationary currency would aid small farmers and laborers to pay their debts. The Greenbackers received over 81,000 votes in the fall election. Also running were two other third parties: the National Prohibition Reform Party, which sought to institute national prohibition of alcohol, and the American National Party, a minor splinter group. Neither party polled more than 9,500 votes.

When voting began on November 7, 1876, prospects for victory looked dim for Hayes and the Republicans. However, the returns from the three southern states still under Republican-controlled Reconstruction governments could not be reconciled. The Republicans in these states sent one set of election returns to Congress with Hayes as the victor, and the Democrats sent another with Tilden as the victor. It also came out that one of the Oregon presidential electors held a federal office, which violated the Constitution. Altogether, 20 electoral votes were disputed, 19 from South Carolina, Florida, and Louisiana, and one from Oregon. Tilden tallied 184 electoral votes and needed only one of those disputed votes to be elected president; while Hayes, with only 165 electoral votes, needed them all.

Unclear Results

All the Constitution provides for in regards to electoral college votes is that they be "directed to the President of the Senate" who "shall, in the Presence of the Senate and House of Representatives, open all the Certificates and the Votes shall then be counted." (The Constitution of the United States of America, Section II). There was no provision for determining which set of ballots should have been counted as valid.

In January 1877 congressional leaders formed a special joint committee, an Electoral Commission, which would decide which electoral ballots were valid. The Electoral Commission was composed of 15 members appointed by Congress: five from the House of Representatives, five from the Senate, and five associate justices of the U.S. Supreme Court. While both parties and both candidates approved this ad hoc extra-constitutional solution, the key issue was not which branch of government the commissioners represented, but rather their political party affiliation. The Republican-dominated Congress managed to control the selection process for the Electoral Commission, which ended up having eight Republicans and seven Democrats. After deliberating the disputed election returns, the electoral commission voted eight to seven to accept the results from the Republican-controlled state governments. During this process, Oregon Republicans managed to replace the disqualified elector with a Republican elector who cast his vote for Hayes. This meant that all the disputed votes went to Hayes.

Hayes and his political allies worked to coax the Democrats and reluctant Republicans into supporting the results of the Electoral Commission. Hayes promised that his administration would look favorably upon internal improvements for the South, especially railroad expansion, and would not challenge the Democrats' choice for the Speaker of the House. Also, Hayes's supporters courted moderate Republicans and Democrats by pledging to remove the last federal troops from the southern states and to end Republican-controlled Reconstruction governments in the South. (This would allow white majorities to return to office.)

Victory for Hayes

On March 2, 1877, at 4:10 in the morning, two days before the end of President Grant's term, the Senate president announced that the electoral vote was 185 for Hayes and 184 for Tilden. Hayes won the presidency and earned the nickname "old 8 to 7." Hayes won even though he had polled fewer votes in the general election, having received only four million votes to Tilden's 4.3 million votes.

Because March 4 fell on a Sunday that year, and Hayes refused to violate the Sabbath even to be inaugurated president of the United States, on Saturday evening March 3, Hayes attended a dinner in the executive mansion with President Grant and Chief Justice Morrison R. Waite. After dinner, Waite swore Hayes into office in order to avoid a gap in administrations. On Monday, March 5, 1877, Hayes reaffirmed the presidential oath of office in a public ceremony on the steps of the nation's capitol.

Hayes's Advisers

Typical of the presidents of his era who worked with almost no staff help, President Rutherford B. Hayes relied on his cabinet officers for advice. In particular, the reformer Carl Schurz at the Department of the Interior provided Hayes with important advice. However, when a large and important decision had to be made,

Hayes consulted with his cabinet but reserved the final decision for himself. Hayes understood that he was responsible for the decisions of his administration, and while cabinet officers made recommendations, the ultimate responsibility for the decision rested with the president.

Hayes and Congress

Hayes was president during the Forty-fifth and Forty-sixth Congresses. Throughout his single term of office, Democrats controlled the House of Representatives. Republicans controlled the Senate until 1879, but their majority was not large or solid. With his pledge not to run for a second term, Hayes had hoped to appear to be "above" politics and patronage, which had tarnished previous Republican administrations. Unfortunately for Hayes, his pledge proved to be politically unwise because politicians in both parties treated him as a lame duck, or interim president.

Hayes initiated little new or dramatic legislation fearing what the Democratic House might do with it. Where Hayes and Congress clashed was not on administration initiated legislation, but on legislation proposed by the Democratic House. In particular, Hayes consistently vetoed soft money measures passed by the Congress. Although soft money was intended to ease the money supply and thereby aid debtors over creditors, Hayes and most Republicans supported a tighter money supply to maintain stability in the currency. Only one major soft money measure became law, over President Hayes's veto, and it was the 1878 Bland-Allison Act (*See also,* Domestic Issues). Hayes then used executive orders to limit the effects of the act.

Hayes and the Judiciary

President Hayes made two appointments to the U.S. Supreme Court. By far his most important appointment was his first, Kentuckian John Marshall Harlan. Harlan believed as Hayes did in expanding the role of the federal government, in defending the civil rights of individuals including African Americans within states, and in restraining monopoly power in the economy. Harlan dissented from the opinions of his fellow justices so often that he earned the nickname, "the Great Dissenter." His most famous dissent came in *Plessy v. Ferguson* (1896), which sanctioned the growing movement to allow segregation of citizens on public accommodations like railroads, as long as equal but separate facilities were provided. This policy of Jim Crow, legally supported segregation of the races, lasted in law until the key twentieth-century case of *Brown v. Board of Education* (1954), where the Court relied on Harlan's dissent to overturn school segregation (*See also,* Eisenhower Administration).

Hayes's other appointment was federal circuit judge William Burnham Woods. His area of expertise was patent law and equity issues. But Woods disappointed Hayes in not being as committed to individual and African American rights as Harlan.

Two major decisions were made by the Court during the Hayes administration. One dealt with the power of the states to regulate private property, *Munn v. Illinois* (1877), and the other dealt with private segregation, *Hall v. DeCuir* (1878). *Munn* grew out of farmers' discontent with grain warehouse monopolies. In an eight-to-one decision, Chief Justice Morrison R. Waite argued that Illinois' regulations of grain warehouses were valid uses of state power since the legal rule had always been that private property "affected with a public interest" (as stated in his opinion) could be regulated. Since privately owned grain elevators affected so many people, Illinois could regulate them.

Continuing the retreat from federal oversight of African American rights, the Court handed down the case of *Hall v. DeCuir* (1878). In *Hall* the Court held that the Fourteenth Amendment, which granted African Americans U.S. citizenship, did not affect or prohibit private discriminations on common carriers such as railroads, streetcars, or riverboats. Under this decision states could not force privately owned businesses to integrate their passengers. Other decisions such as the better known case of *Plessy v. Ferguson* (1896) built on this precedent.

Changes in the U.S. Government

Hayes relied on presidential executive orders and on his power as commander in chief to affect policies. On issues such as civil service reform—making federal employment based on a merit system instead of on patronage connections—Hayes could and did issue executive orders instructing the establishment of civil service examinations. He often infuriated members of his own party by making such orders, but Hayes genuinely believed in civil service reform and he sought to limit political patronage.

Acting as commander in chief, Hayes simply issued orders to the troops occupying the South during Reconstruction and the army moved out of its southern barracks; politically, removal of the troops was more difficult, but the actual movement of the troops was accomplished through executive orders (*See also,* Domestic Issues).

Domestic Issues

On March 5, 1877, in the course of his inaugural address, President Rutherford B. Hayes touched upon the

Biography:

John Marshall Harlan

Supreme Court Justice; Attorney (1833–1911) At the time he was appointed justice of the U.S. Supreme Court in 1877, and for decades thereafter, Judge John Marshall Harlan practically stood alone as a voice in high federal office championing equal rights for African Americans. His controversial stance would have cost him his job were it not for the lifetime appointment to the Court. He received his appointment from President Rutherford B. Hayes after he single-handedly ensured Hayes the Republican Party's presidential nomination in 1876. Upon taking the bench, Judge Harlan began a long record of dissents in civil rights cases in which his dissenting vote on behalf of the rights of African Americans was always a minority vote and usually the single dissent. His most famous dissent was in the *Plessy v. Ferguson* (1896) case. Judge Harlan argued that a Louisiana law segregating blacks into separate railroad cars was a violation of the Fourteenth Amendment to the Constitution which states that, "No state shall make or enforce any law which

shall abridge the privileges or immunities of citizens of the United States." Judge Harlan's literal interpretation of the Constitution in this case was typical and exemplified his belief that the document should never be subject to any form of subjective interpretation. Harlan's belief in equality for all men was consistent and unbiased to an extraordinary degree. Once as a candidate in the race

for the Kentucky governorship, Harlan represented an alleged member of the Ku Klux Klan who was accused of participating in a lynching. Responding to outrage at his actions, Harlan contended that every man, whatever his politics, deserved as good a lawyer as he could pay for.

---

issues his administration would address: the South and its future, civil service questions, currency problems, and foreign affairs. Reconstruction, the rebuilding of loyal southern state governments and of southern race relations on a basis other than master and slave, had dominated national politics since at least the close of the American Civil War in 1865 (*See also,* Andrew Johnson Administration and Grant Administration). Reconstruction's end during the Hayes administration reflected more the nation's weariness of the "southern question" than the reconciliation of the issues of the Civil War era. As Reconstruction waned, Americans focused attention on the growing domestic economy.

The federal government between 1862 and 1872, had contributed a lot to the growth of industry and the railroads (*See also,* Grant Administration). Millions of dollars in aid and over a million acres were granted to the railroads for construction. Speculation accompanied prosperity only to come to ruin with the panic of 1873 when European investors removed their capital after widespread business failures in Europe. The New York Stock Exchange closed for 10 days to cool off the crisis, but the depression would linger through the 1870s. The depression created unprecedented levels of misery. Over one million workers lost their jobs and millions more had their wages cut. These conditions became the catalyst for the confrontations that were to come between labor and owners. In particular, the workers' role and power in U.S. industry became an issue, which was dramatically

demonstrated in the summer of 1877 with the Great Railroad Strike.

The South

Towards the reconstructed South, Hayes repeated his known position that the region should have "wise, honest, and peaceful local self-government." Hayes believed his presidency did not represent an end to Reconstruction; instead, as historian Brooks D. Simpson has explained, Hayes believed his presidency was "an opportunity to implement a new southern policy." The Republican governments that emerged in the South during Reconstruction had several bases of support—the enfranchised African American freedmen, settlers from the North who were derided as "carpetbaggers" (because they supposedly brought only a small suitcase made of carpet and sought to make their fortune by exploiting the South), and native white southerners who were mostly from the hills and had historically fought domination by the plantation owners. Opposition Democrats referred to them as scalawags. Hayes sought to reconcile with white southerners, and he hoped they would join the Republican Party and make the South into a two-party region like the North and the Midwest.

Troop Removal

Hayes removed the last of the federal troops from the South too slowly for Democrats and too quickly for

---

Republicans. Hayes was committed to putting aside hard feelings, but he was also concerned about simply deserting southern Republican governments. During the disputed election and in the first few months of his administration, Hayes heard reports of the corruption of the Republican-led carpetbag southern governments. He also heard responsible white southerners pledge to protect Republicans and African Americans within their states. In response to these pledges, Hayes decided to remove the troops from South Carolina. He issued the orders on April 3, 1877, and on April 10 the troops left the capital of Columbia; the next day a redeemed white Democratic government took possession of the statehouse.

Next, Hayes ordered the removal of the troops from the Louisiana capital of Baton Rouge on April 24, 1877. Crowds cheered and the church bells rang as the federal troops left and the Democrats reclaimed the statehouse from the Republicans. These troops were the last federal forces in a state capitol (troops having been withdrawn from Florida late in President Grant's administration), and their removal signaled the federal government's withdrawal from overseeing southern governments and race relations. In spite of white assurances to Hayes about the treatment of African Americans, African American legal and political disenfranchisement continued. Nevertheless Hayes continued to be optimistic that southern states would honor their pledges to uphold African American rights.

Sectional Reaction in Congress

In the summer and fall of 1877 Hayes toured the South where he was warmly welcomed. To him, it appeared that his new southern policy was working and the war wounds were healing. But when Congress reconvened in special session in October 1877 in order to pass an appropriation for the army, old animosities reemerged. Southern congressmen attached riders to the army appropriation, which cut off money for federal poll watchers (official observers during elections) in southern states. Southerners hated this federal oversight of their elections while Republicans claimed (probably correctly) that, without federal poll watchers, no African Americans could vote in the South. Five times in various forms an appropriation bill passed Congress with a rider attached denying monies for federal poll watchers, and five times President Hayes vetoed the measure as contrary to his new southern policies. Clearly Hayes's conciliatory policies only emboldened southerners to resist federal oversight even more aggressively. Ending Reconstruction did not result in harmony between the sections. Ending Reconstruction meant ending most federal influence over southern affairs.

The Great Strike of 1877

The economy was poor when Hayes became president. Railroads and industry had overexpanded (originally supported by the Civil War), agricultural prices were low causing insufficient farm purchasing power,

and there were many outstanding unsound loans. Railroads began to cut wages further in the summer of 1877. Employees of the Baltimore and Ohio line in Martinsburg, West Virginia, were the first to go on strike in protest of the wage cuts. State militia were poorly equipped and many refused to take action against the strikers, having friends and family amongst them. The governor and railroad owners appealed to President Hayes to send in federal troops. Hayes hoped that the workers and the companies would solve their own problems, but he reluctantly sent troops in after federal court orders were issued that stated that strikers were in contempt of court. Strikes spread across the country. Collectively the strikes came to be called the Great Strike. In the summer of that year, the eastern half of the nation's rail system was brought to a stop by strikes; there was violence and widespread rioting. By the time the strikes were over more than a hundred people had died and more than a thousand strikers were jailed. In response to the strike a few of the railroads restored wages and pledged to negotiate with the workers on workplace issues. But for the most part the companies, backed by the state militias and federal troops, ended the Great Strike. In time passions cooled and order returned to the railroads, but worker discontent about unannounced wage cuts and longer hours continued—the seeds of organized labor had been sown.

The Bland-Allison Act Passes

Tied to workers' concern about their wages was the nation's hard money, anti-inflation policies. Hard money, meaning specie such as gold and silver, possessed more than monetary value for people in the late nineteenth century. Hard money represented stability, honesty, and careful management of the currency, while soft money, meaning paper money, the greenbacks, meant an inflationary, risky, and an unstable currency. During the American Civil War, Secretary of the Treasury Salmon P. Chase had funded the federal war effort by allowing the printing and circulation of greenbacks, and the removal of the greenbacks from the currency was part of the Republican platform beginning with the Grant administration. In January 1875 Congress passed and President Grant signed the Resumption Act pledging to gradually remove the greenbacks from circulation, redeeming greenbacks for gold beginning January 1, 1879. This deflationary policy hurt debtors such as workers and small farmers since they had to repay their loans in hard money, which they had taken out in soft money. It helped creditors such as the major corporations and banks, which received their soft money loans back in hard money.

Silver mining interests in the West feared that the market for their ore would disappear if the nation adopted an all gold standard as many hard money supporters hoped. In the fall of 1877, silver interests managed to get a silver coinage bill through Congress, the Bland-Allison Bill, named for the bill's sponsors, Representative Richard P. Bland of Missouri and William B. Allison of Iowa. It required the government to purchase and coin

In the summer of 1877 conditions between railroad laborers and owners came to a boiling point with the Great Railroad Strike. Prior to the strike over 100 million railroad workers had been laid off due to the economic depression in the early 1870s and severe wage cuts were put into effect. (Archive Photos. Reproduced by permission.)

silver in limited quantities. The reasoning was that by coining silver there would be more money in circulation. This inflationary bill passed not only with strong Democratic support but also strong Republican support. Hayes opposed the Bland-Allison Bill. He supported stability in the currency, and he supported a hard money policy because he believed such a policy was a safer course. Hayes vetoed the bill on February 28, 1878. Congress passed the Bland-Allison Act over Hayes's veto and it became law. Hayes limited the act's effectiveness by issuing executive orders that limited the amount of silver minted into coins and the number of coins in circulation. Although a reduced amount of greenbacks remained in circulation, the nation remained on a gold standard, and hard money continued to underlie the nation's growing economy.

Civil Service Reform

Hayes had pledged at his inauguration a reform of the civil service, federal and state employees. Ever since the presidency of Andrew Jackson, winning political office meant distributing political appointments to one's friends and supporters—the spoils system. By Hayes's era, those in Congress believed they had a "right" to decide appointments within their districts or states, and to do so without oversight or interference by the president or anyone else. Carl Schurz, reformer and secretary

of the interior, favored the development of a professional civil service in which examinations would be administered to determine an applicant's skills. However, a merit system such as this one threatened politicians and their ability to reward their supporters with jobs. Not surprisingly most officeholders opposed civil service reform.

In April 1877, as he took his final steps to remove the last federal troops from the South, Hayes also pressed forward on civil service reform. His most important target was the New York customhouse. New York's customhouse was a lucrative position because it was controlled by New York's senators, especially Roscoe Conkling, and because of the opportunity it provided for graft. By undervaluing imported goods and overvaluing expenses and damages, customhouse officials could skim enormous amounts of money into their own pockets, some of which they kicked back to the politicians who appointed them to their offices. At the time, the collector of the customs was a Conkling protégé (and future president of the United States), Chester A. Arthur. A commission investigating the New York customhouse recommended cutting staff and continuing the minor exams already required (in actuality these were easily avoided or fraudulently passed). The commission did not suggest that Arthur be removed from office, but Hayes sought Arthur's removal to reform the customhouse and to strike a blow at Senator Conkling. In response, Conk-

Fast Fact

On February 15, 1879, President Hayes signed "an act to relieve certain legal disabilities of women." This act opened eligibility to practice before the U.S. Supreme Court to any woman lawyer of good moral character who had practiced for three years before any state Supreme Court. On March 3, 1879, Belva Ann Lockwood of Illinois became the first woman admitted to practice before the Court.

(Source: Joseph Nathan Kane. *Facts About the Presidents,* 1993.)

ling attacked Hayes and his civil service reform proposals on the floor of the Senate as an attack on senatorial courtesy, whereby a president is expected to support appointments made by members of his own party in their home states. When the Senate voted on whether to accept Hayes's appointments or side with Conkling and the spoils system, Hayes lost; the Senate rejected Hayes's candidates for offices in the New York customhouse and accepted Senator Conkling's candidates. Even Republican senators for the most part voted against Hayes in order to protect their patronage power within their respective states.

Despite losing the customhouse controversy, Hayes continued to support civil service reforms established by executive (*See also,* Changes in the U.S. Government) order such as in the Department of Interior where Secretary Schurz had established a merit system. While widespread and true movement toward a professionalized civil service did not occur during his administration, Hayes adopted the unpopular position of civil service reform as a necessary governmental reform.

Foreign Issues

With a small army and navy, Hayes's administration did not participate in the European imperialist frenzy of seizing overseas colonies. While some U.S. politicians called for purchasing Mexican land for American and railroad expansion, Hayes resisted such imperialist dreams. The United States concentrated its efforts on its own domestic development and played only a limited role in world affairs in the late 1870s. Three areas of conflict did attract the administration's attention: bandits on the border of the United States and Mexico, the treatment of

Chinese immigrants in California, and the question of a canal through Panama. As with domestic policy, no grand foreign policy breakthrough emerged during Hayes's single term of office, but he dealt adequately with foreign policy issues when they arose.

Mexican Bandits

Bandits had been striking settlers along the U.S.-Mexican border and then retreating into Mexico safe from pursuit. In order to prevent further border raids by Mexican bandits, Hayes ordered the army to the border. Further, he said that the army could cross into Mexico if it was chasing bandits and raiders. This decision infuriated Porfirio Díaz who had come to power after a coup that overthrew Sebastian Lerco de Tejada in November 1877. In response Díaz sent troops to Mexico's northern border. While Díaz's show of force played well with the Mexicans, the government only nominally controlled the border areas, which is the reason the bandits operated so freely in that region. While open fighting between the United States and Mexico did not break out, neither did the raids by bandits stop, which kept U.S. armed forces on the border and tensions simmering. When the Díaz regime had consolidated its power in early 1880 and was able to effectively limit banditry along the border, Hayes revoked the army's authority to chase bandits into Mexico.

Chinese Immigration

Chinese immigration to California became a political issue in that state and for the nation during Hayes's administration. Although only about 8 percent of the California population was from China in 1880, there were large concentrations of Chinese in certain areas of the state. For instance, the percentage of Chinese in San Francisco reached 30 percent in 1880. Because whites feared that cheap Chinese labor would take jobs away from them, an anti-Chinese backlash occurred in California. A California constitutional convention was called to update and revise the state's constitution. Under the California Constitution of 1878, the Chinese, as well as the mentally challenged, mentally ill, and criminals were not allowed to vote. It also prohibited Chinese from working on any public works in the state.

These provisions would not stand scrutiny by the federal courts, but such actions sent a message of a strong anti-Chinese sentiment in California. In response, the House of Representatives passed a bill limiting any ship from bringing more than 15 Chinese to any U.S. port. Further, the Senate added a rider to the immigration bill abrogating two sections of the Burlingame Treaty (1868)—the section allowing voluntary immigration between China and the United States and the section protecting each other's nationals while they lived in the other country. This exclusion bill found wide support in California and other western states, while reformers and old abolitionists recoiled at the harshness of the measure.

When the bill reached President Hayes on March 1, 1878, he vetoed it. While no friend of the Chinese and while he personally identified with the fears of the white workers in California, Hayes opposed the bill.

Hayes turned to William H. Seward, who had served as consul and minister to China, for a solution. Seward suggested that Hayes open negotiations with the Chinese and rethink the Burlingame Treaty's open immigration policy and U.S.-Chinese trade relations. American negotiators wanted to maintain open trade relations with China because European powers were beginning to establish their own "spheres of influence" in and around Chinese ports. Not until the 1890s would the United States's Open Door policy be articulated during the William McKinley administration, but Hayes's negotiators certainly sought to push relations in that direction. In time, a new treaty was negotiated with the Chinese, which was signed on November 17, 1880. Under this treaty the United States could regulate, limit, and suspend Chinese immigration, but not prohibit it altogether. In return, the Chinese received a pledge that the United States would not be a part of the opium trade into China; the treaty also prohibited the Chinese from importing opium into the United States. While not ratified until 1881, after Hayes left office, this corollary to the Burlingame Treaty soothed feelings both in the United States and in China. In 1882, bowing to continued pressure from western state representatives and senators, Congress did suspend Chinese immigration to the United States for 10 years.

Panama

Nineteenth-century Americans and Europeans dreamed of two canals: one connecting the Red Sea with the Mediterranean Sea, and one connecting the Atlantic and Pacific Oceans. Ferdinand de Lesseps of France engineered what became the Suez Canal, connecting the Red Sea with the Mediterranean Sea; it opened for traffic on November 17, 1869. In 1879 de Lesseps turned his attention to the dream of a Central American canal. At an international conference de Lesseps suggested a way to build a sea-level canal linking the two oceans, and to do so by 1882. Almost immediately de Lesseps encountered opposition. U.S. engineers who had surveyed the isthmus of Panama understood that a sea-level canal was not practical; only a canal with locks would be feasible for the terrain. Also, de Lesseps was French and his involvement worried both the Americans and the Mexicans about possible French expansion into the Western Hemisphere. Hayes's administration cited the Monroe Doctrine, which banned expansion of European influence in Latin America as reason to oppose the French plans. Mexico also feared a return of the French after Napoleon III's attempt to make Maximilian the Mexican emperor in the late 1860s.

Hayes outlined the United States's position in a special message delivered on March 8, 1880. In this presidential message, he expressed his own and the nation's policy towards a Panama canal: "The policy of this country is a canal under American control." He criticized foreign schemes for building such a canal and warned foreign investors not to look to their governments to protect their investments if a non-American canal was built. A canal between the oceans would be so important to the United States that the country could not allow Europeans to build or control such an engineering feat. De Lesseps's plan eventually foundered due to a lack of U.S. investors, but also due to Hayes's nationalistic stance. A canal through Panama would have to wait until the Theodore Roosevelt administration, and when a canal was built it was with U.S. money and under U.S. control.

The Hayes Administration Legacy

When James A. Garfield assumed the presidency in March 1881, he found that Hayes had left the country and the economy in good order. While the wounds of the American Civil War (1861–65) could still be felt, Reconstruction and its problems finally lay in the nation's immediate past. Because Hayes continued the hard money policies of the Grant administration, the economy had remained under control and was growing at a prudent pace, even though those policies had begun to be controversial among farmers and industrial workers. And Hayes kept his pledge to serve only one term.

Although popular culture then and since has caricatured Hayes as inept or worse, his record in office suggests differently. Entering the executive mansion under the cloud of the disputed election of 1876–77 and attacked as "Rutherfraud" Hayes, Hayes upheld his public promises to end Reconstruction and return home rule to those southern states still under carpetbag governments. Hayes's commitment to end the separations in the country over the Civil War led him to support the withdrawal of the troops, and his optimistic nature caused him to misread southerners and how they would treat African American citizens. Hayes, a Republican, confronted a Democratic House of Representatives and, after the midterm election of 1878, a Senate also controlled by Democrats. This political reality sharply limited any new initiatives Hayes might have undertaken. As a result of this politically divided government, Hayes resorted to using his executive powers and his veto to achieve ends he sought or to stymie policies initiated by Democrats. Hayes's political luck and acumen allowed him to rise in the Republican Party and to achieve the presidency; his integrity and abilities allowed him to be effective in the limited channels available to him.

Lasting Impact

What lasts from the administration of Rutherford B. Hayes is the knowledge that a dramatic and key era in U.S. history closed during his term in office—the era of the American Civil War and Reconstruction. The United

States was well on its way to becoming modern through large-scale industrial development, urban growth, massive foreign immigration, and all the growing pains associated with those developments. Just as Hayes's administration was the closing of one era, it was the opening of another, one of national industrial development to world power. For the next 50 years (with notable bumps along the way), the country prospered as the Gilded Age, Progressive Era, and the 1920s rushed by. Not until the Great Depression in the 1930s and the new mechanisms for dealing with the depression would a truly new era in U.S. history emerge.

Sources

Davison, Kenneth E. *The Presidency of Rutherford B. Hayes.* Westport, Conn.: Greenwood Press, 1972.

Encyclopedia of World Biography. Vol. 7. Detroit: Gale Research, 1998.

Hoogenboom, Ari. *The Presidency of Rutherford B. Hayes.* Lawrence, Kans.: University Press of Kansas, 1988.

Kane, Joseph Nathan. *Facts About the Presidents.* 6th ed. New York: H.W. Wilson, 1993.

———. *Rutherford B. Hayes: Warrior and President.* Lawrence, Kans.: University Press of Kansas, 1995.

Simpson, Brooks D. *The Reconstruction Presidents.* Lawrence, Kans.: University Press of Kansas, 1998.

Further Readings

Barnard, Harry. *Rutherford B. Hayes and His America.* Indianapolis, Ind.: Bobbs-Merrill, 1954.

Robinson, Lloyd. *The Stolen Election: Hayes versus Tilden—1876.* Garden City, N.J.: Doubleday, 1968.

Rutherford B. Hayes Presidential Center. <http://www.rbhayes.org> 1999. (25 June 1999).

Williams, Charles Richard, ed. *Diary and Letters of Rutherford Birchard Hayes: Nineteenth President of the United States.* 5 vols. Columbus, Ohio: Columbus Ohio State Archeological and Historical Society, 1922–26.

Williams, T. Harry, ed. *Hayes: The Diary of a President, 1875–1881.* New York: David McKay, 1964.

Woodward, C. Vann. *Reunion and Reaction: The Compromise of 1877 and the End of Reconstruction.* Boston: Little, Brown, 1951.

Garfield Administration

Biography

James Garfield was an intelligent and good-natured man who was affectionate with friends and family. A gifted orator and extremely ambitious, Garfield became a successful politician after the American Civil War (1861–65). Yet he never set out to be president and was genuinely stunned when he won the Republican nomination as a dark horse candidate and went on to win the presidency. Seen as a sober and honorable man who lacked the vision and imagination of a great leader, Garfield's true capabilities as president were never tested, as he was assassinated only months after his inauguration.

Early Life

James Abram Garfield was born into a working class family in Orange Township, Ohio, on November 19, 1831. Garfield was named for his father and for a brother who had died in infancy. His parents, Abram and Eliza Garfield had met in their native Worcester, New York, and married in 1820. They moved to Orange Township, Ohio, near Cleveland, and raised two sons and two daughters. Abram Garfield worked on the railroad and as a farmer. When Garfield was only 18 months old his father caught a cold and died soon after. The loss of his father affected Garfield for the rest of his life. After his father's death young James grew very close to his mother, whom he helped support and to whom he credited his successes. The young Garfield worked for a short time as a barge driver on one of Ohio's canals. Later, Horatio Alger wrote a campaign biography for Garfield titled *From Canal Boy to President.*

Full name: James Abram Garfield

Personal Information:
Born: November 19, 1831
Died: September 19, 1881
Burial place: Lake View Cemetery, Cleveland, Ohio
Religion: Disciples of Christ
Spouse: Lucretia Rudolph (m. 1858)
Children: Eliza Arabella; Harry Augustus; James Rudolph; Mary; Irvin McDowell; Abram; Edward Abram
Education: Williams College, Williamstown, Massachusetts, B.A., 1856
Occupation: Teacher; soldier; politician
Political Party: Republican Party
Age at Inauguration: 49 years

James Abram Garfield. (The Library of Congress.)

Education

Garfield was an early achiever who learned to read at home by age three. He attended the district school near Orange Township, Ohio, and then Geauga Academy at Chester, Ohio. In 1851 Garfield enrolled at the Eclectic Institute in Hiram, Ohio, and transferred to Williams College in Williamstown, Massachusetts, as a junior. He was active in the college's debate, literary, and theological societies and graduated in 1856.

Family Life

On November 11, 1858, James Garfield married Lucretia "Crete" Rudolph in Hiram, Ohio. Garfield met Crete Rudolph at the Geauga Academy and was attracted to her quick intelligence and desire for learning. The couple set up housekeeping in Hiram and eventually had five children who lived to maturity, Harry, James, Mary, Irwin, and Abram. Crete Garfield played a very small role in the White House due to her own illness and the death of her husband six months after he became president. After her husband's death, Crete Garfield eventually settled with her children at Lawnfield, the estate Garfield had purchased in Mentor, Ohio, where she lived a quiet and private life until her death in 1918.

Two of Garfield's sons went into careers of public service. Harry Garfield was chairman of the price com-

mittee of the U.S. Food Administration, then fuel administrator under Woodrow Wilson He earned the Distinguished Service Medal in 1921. James Garfield served in the Ohio State Senate from 1896 to 1900, on the U.S. Civil Service Commission from 1902 to 1903, and as commissioner of corporations in the Department of Commerce and Labor from 1903 to 1907. In 1907 President Theodore Roosevelt appointed James Garfield secretary of the interior, a position he held to the end of Roosevelt's administration in 1909.

Career

Garfield worked his way through college as a teacher, carpenter, and janitor. After graduation Garfield became an instructor and eventually the president of the Eclectic Institute in Hiram, Ohio. Bored with campus life, Garfield began to study law on his own and became involved with Republican politics. Garfield was elected to the Ohio State Senate in 1859 as a strong opponent of slavery. When the American Civil War (1861–65) broke out, Garfield supported President Abraham Lincoln and the military efforts to maintain the Union. Garfield joined the Union Army in 1861.

Military Service

Garfield served in the Union military from August 1861 to December 1863, rising from the rank of lieutenant colonel to major general. Garfield successfully led his troops in many battles, including the battle of Shiloh in April 1862. After contracting camp fever at Shiloh, he recuperated in Hiram for two months. At the battle of Chickamauga in September 1863, Garfield relayed information from flank to flank, which earned him the promotion to major general. Having been elected to Congress in 1862, Garfield resigned his commission in December 1863.

U.S. Representative

Garfield easily defeated his opponent in his first run for Congress, and was reelected eight times, serving from 1863 to 1880. During the American Civil War, Garfield was a member of the Radical caucus within the Republican Party (who wanted the South severely punished for the war). He supported confiscation of rebel property and the execution or exile of Confederate, or southern, leaders. After the war ended, Garfield's views became more moderate, and he tried to reconcile the Radicals to President Andrew Johnson's more lenient Reconstruction policies. (Reconstruction had attempted to restructure southern society and create a place for ex-slaves in that society.) During Johnson's impeachment trial, however, Garfield voted with the Radicals against Johnson. (*See also,* Andrew Johnson Administration). Garfield eventually became known as a knowledgeable spokesman on financial and economic matters. During the Rutherford B. Hayes administration (1877–81), Garfield was the leader of the Republican minority in the House of Representatives. In 1880 he was elected to the U.S. Senate, but he declined his seat after being elected president.

President

James Garfield took the oath of office as president on March 4, 1881, but was shot by a frustrated political office seeker, Charles J. Guiteau, on July 2, 1881. About two months later, on September 19, 1881, Garfield died from complications caused by his wounds. His tenure as president was very short and much of his six-month term was spent as an invalid. Garfield was still adjusting to his new role as president when he was shot, but he managed to appoint his cabinet. Unfortunately, no one would ever know what Garfield could have accomplished as president.

Post-Presidential Years

Garfield died while he was still president. He was shot by Charles Guiteau, an unsuccessful applicant for a political patronage job, as Garfield strolled with Secretary of State Blaine across the waiting room of a train station in Washington, D.C. Garfield was on his way to visit his wife, who was ill, in Elberon, New Jersey. After being taken to the White House, the president was operated on to remove bone fragments from his wounds in his arm and his midsection. Repeated probing of the wounds by unsterilized instruments and doctors' hands led to blood poisoning. On September 6, the president requested to be taken to Elberon. There, in addition to blood poisoning, he contracted bronchopneumonia and died on September 19, 1881. Garfield lay in state in the Capital rotunda where over one hundred thousand mourners paid their respects before his burial at Lake View Cemetery in Cleveland, Ohio.

The James A. Garfield Administration

Garfield was assassinated only a few months after taking office, not giving him the time to prove himself as president. A relative unknown in national politics at the time of his election, Garfield was faced with the entrenched power and interests of his better known party members when he entered office. Some historians infer that he might have attempted to challenge these interests had he lived. Though Garfield seemed to be at least obliquely confronting the power of the national parties and the spoils system of patronage, whether or not he could have overcome them will never be known.

Garfield Becomes President

The Campaign of 1880

When James Garfield went to the Republican National Convention in Chicago, Illinois, in 1880, he had no intention of running for president. In fact, Garfield went to the convention to try to help John Sherman of Ohio win the nomination. Former president Ulysses Grant was favored to win the nomination and had the backing of conservative members of the party, known as the Stalwarts. Moderate Republicans, known as "Half-Breeds", divided their support between Sherman and James G. Blaine of Maine.

As the convention repeatedly voted, none of the three top contenders received the majority of votes needed to win the nomination. As the voting dragged on, delegates began to consider Garfield the ideal compromise candidate and urged him to break with Sherman and declare his own candidacy. Garfield refused to do so, but delegates began casting votes for him anyway. The number of votes for Garfield increased with each ballot, and on the 36th ballot the Blaine and Sherman delegates gave the majority of votes to Garfield. Chester A. Arthur of New York, a Stalwart, was chosen to balance the ticket. Garfield was genuinely stunned at the turn of events, but he accepted the nomination as the will of his party.

Garfield's campaign against Democrat Winfield S. Hancock of Pennsylvania, a military administrator, was unique primarily because of Garfield's lack of participation. Garfield had done nothing to gain the nomination, and he did little active campaigning. Garfield stayed at home in Mentor, Ohio, and received supporters. He left the politicking to other party officials in what came to be known as the "front porch campaign."

The campaign and the candidates were both rather lackluster as there were few significant differences between the parties' positions on issues. Only the tariff, or duties changed on foreign goods brought to the United States, divided the parties. The Republicans supported a high tariff and the Democrats favored a limited tariff. Garfield narrowly won the presidential election with 48.3 percent of the vote to Hancock's 48.2 percent.

Garfield's Advisers

Garfield chose his cabinet with the intent of having all factions of the Republican Party represented. He also chose independents from the Midwest and the South. Garfield hoped to create a cabinet of advisers that would help him make decisions that would be acceptable to a cross section of U.S. political interests. Garfield also felt a cabinet with varied perspectives could help create compromise solutions to divisive issues that might arise. Garfield grew friendly with Secretary of State James G. Blaine but did not have enough time to build strong rela-

Administration

believed that the president should make suggestions to Congress but never interfere with the legislative process. Garfield saw the presidency as an administrative position and separate from the responsibilities of legislators.

Administration Dates

March 4, 1881–September 19, 1881

Vice President

Chester A. Arthur (1881)

Cabinet

Secretary of State

William M. Evarts (1877–81)
James G. Blaine (1881)

Secretary of the Treasury

William Windom (1881)

Secretary of War

Alexander Ramsey (1879–81)
Robert T. Lincoln (1881)

Attorney General

Charles Devens (1877–81)
Wayne MacVeagh (1881)

Secretary of the Navy

Nathan Goff Jr. (1881)
William H. Hunt (1881–82)

Postmaster General

Horace Maynard (1880–81)
Thomas L. James (1881–82)

Secretary of the Interior

Carl Schurz (1877–81)
Samuel J. Kirkwood (1881–82)

Garfield and the Judiciary

Stanley Matthews of Ohio became a Supreme Court associate justice during Garfield's administration, although he was not originally nominated by Garfield. Rutherford B. Hayes had appointed Matthews shortly after Garfield had been elected, but the Senate refused to confirm him as a snub to Hayes. When Garfield took office, he reappointed Matthews as a courtesy to Hayes and requested the Senate to respond quickly. Ultimately, the full Senate confirmed Matthews by only one vote. Later in his career, Matthews spoke for the Court in *Yick Wo v. Hopkins* (1886), ruling that discriminatory administration of just laws violates the Fourteenth Amendment's clause on equal protection under the law.

Changes in the U.S. Government

Though Garfield's administration created no direct changes in the U.S. government, it did influence future changes. When Garfield was shot by a man who had been denied a political patronage job, the problem of the political spoils system drew national attention. The tragedy prodded his vice president and successor, Chester Arthur, to advocate for civil service reform, even though he had been at the center of patronage politics in New York. Desire to avoid other violent incidents was the impetus for Congress to legislate such reform in the Pendleton Act of 1883 which created the modern civil service system.

Uncertainty over who would become president if there was no vice president or something happened to the vice president, was another issue Arthur raised after Garfield's death. However, the issue of presidential succession was not finally resolved until the passage of the Twenty-fifth Amendment in 1967.

tionships with his cabinet or test their ability to work as a cohesive team.

Garfield and Congress

Garfield's short term as president coincided with the Forty-seventh Congress. There was an equal number of Republicans and Democrats in the Senate and a slight Republican majority in the House of Representatives, with 147 Republicans and 135 Democrats. Garfield

Domestic Issues

When Garfield was elected president, the U.S. public was ready to move past the horrors of the American Civil War (1861–65), and its aftermath into a brighter future. The economy was strong, thanks to expanding productivity brought about by new technology, but workers, many of whom had undergone the transformation from farm life to factory work, often felt disconnected from their rural upbringing and, for many of them, their foreign roots. Political activity was a way for people to come together and (especially for foreign workers) to feel a part of American society.

Yet participation in U.S. political life frequently meant involvement in the political spoils system, where voters gave money, votes, or campaign labor to a party or candidate in return for jobs, contracts, and other favors. This system had become an embarrassment as politicians and citizens alike realized that government had ceased to work in the interest of all the people, and instead acted in the interest of those in political favor. Party functionaries routinely raised campaign money by assessing contributions from holders of political jobs. This guaranteed mass involvement in campaigns, because the only way to make back the money that they had contributed was to make sure that their candidate won the election. This unhealthy system resulted in political scandals that plagued the Ulysses S. Grant administration (1869–77) and spilled over into the Rutherford B. Hayes administration (1877–81). By the time Garfield took office, the president of the United States was expected to spend much of his work day meeting with "office seekers," who expected to be rewarded for their political loyalty. The spoils system not only created problems for Garfield during his short administration, it would ultimately lead to his death.

Battle with Conkling

Under the patronage system, one of the most important tasks of the new president was to hand out jobs. After his election, Garfield appointed a man to the powerful position of collector of customs of the Port of New York who was not the choice of the state Republican political boss, Senator Roscoe Conkling. Conkling had thrown his weight behind Garfield, convincing Republican conservatives (Stalwarts) to support his candidacy. In return, Conkling expected to be consulted on government appointments. Garfield ignored Conkling's demands. The outraged Conkling resigned his Senate seat in protest and intended to get reelected to show the president just how much power he commanded among New York voters. This elaborate ritual was acted out in the full glare of the media. Conkling never got the revenge he sought because Garfield died at the height of the conflict.

Post Office Scandal

Another scandal broke shortly after Garfield's election. In isolated western states the Post Office had contracted with private stagecoach agencies to deliver the mail. Certain contractors would submit low bids for their services, win the contracts, then petition Congress for increased funds to improve services. Congressmen who voted in favor of the increases received kickbacks from the contractors. Congressional inquiries into the situation had stalled. Only five days after his inauguration, Garfield asked Postmaster General Thomas L. James to proceed with an investigation and to institute reforms. A month later several officials in the Post Office Department had resigned or been fired. At the time of Garfield's death, lawyers were preparing a case for prosecution. President Arthur would eventually proceed with the Post Office investigation.

Garfield's Assassination

On July 2, 1881, as President Garfield was on his way to Elberon, New Jersey, to visit his wife who was ill, he was shot in the Baltimore and Potomac train station. Garfield was hit twice; a superficial wound in the arm, and a more serious wound to his midsection where the bullet lodged in his spinal column. Garfield was taken to the White House and operated on to remove bone fragments. Despite early optimism regarding his chances for recovery, Garfield grew steadily weaker. As doctors probed his wounds with their unsterilized hands and instruments, Garfield developed infections that further weakened his condition.

Early in September, at his request, Garfield was moved to Elberon. There he contracted bronchopneumonia. He died on September 19, 1881. His body laid in state in the Capitol rotunda where over one hundred thousand mourners paid their respects before his burial at Lake View Cemetery in Cleveland, Ohio. James Garfield was 49 when he died.

The nation was shocked at Garfield's assassination and looked to newly sworn-in President Chester A. Arthur for leadership. Arthur assured the country that he would act swiftly to reform the political spoils system that had led to Garfield's death. Garfield's assassin, Charles J. Guiteau, had supported Garfield in the 1880 election and had come to Washington, D.C. to request a diplomatic position as his reward. When Guiteau was refused, he began stalking the president and shot him three weeks later. Guiteau had a history of mental instability and pleaded not guilty to Garfield's murder by reason of insanity. The jury in his trial deliberated only one hour before finding him guilty. Guiteau was executed by hanging on June 30, 1882.

Foreign Issues

Foreign affairs was of little interest to most Americans in the age when Garfield became president. The aftermath of the bloody American Civil War (1861–65) and the "amoral fatigue" that many voters felt at the failure of Reconstruction in the South (which had attempted to restructure southern society and create a place for ex-slaves in that society) led them to turn away from national and international affairs, and concentrate instead on their own communities. As president, Garfield did appear to have a foreign policy agenda at least slightly more forward-looking than the voters. His earlier speeches in Congress seemed to indicate that he believed in commercial expansion overseas and in reciprocal trade, where mutual agreements on tariff reduction were made with other countries to allow goods to flow back and forth. He was also wary of Great Britain's attempts to secure trade agreements that excluded the United States, and he felt diplomatic efforts to protect the nation's economic interests overseas should be increased. Further, Garfield saw the building of a canal in Central America as important to U.S. trade. Such a canal would allow goods and materials to be transported more quickly, and thus more cheaply, between the eastern and the western United States, and to other countries. It would be another 20 years before such a canal, the Panama Canal, became a reality.

The Garfield Administration Legacy

Garfield left to his successor, Chester A. Arthur, little in the way of an ongoing agenda. His term in office was too short to verify first impressions of the path he intended to take the nation. He did show some independence in his dispute with New York Republican Party boss, Roscoe Conkling.

Lasting Impact

The circumstances of Garfield's death suggested that politics by patronage needed to be reformed. The message of reform that he seemed to be delivering was reinforced by the assassination itself. It was an unintended demonstration of the debilitating effect of patronage and graft on U.S. politics. Though the patronage system had been a matter of concern for many years—at least since the Ulysses Grant administration—Garfield's assassination made the public and politicians alike realize how serious the problem had become. Garfield's successor, Chester A. Arthur, a product of the spoils system himself, made civil services reform a high priority in his

administration. In addition, although historians generally do not rank Garfield in presidential ratings, it is important to note that his short-lived administration sought to reconcile many different political views by appointing officials who would work for compromises.

Sources

Clancy, Herbert J.*The Presidential Campaign of 1880.* Chicago: Loyola University Press, 1958.

Dinnerstein, Leonard. "Election of 1880," *Running for President: The Candidates and Their Images,* edited by Arthur M. Schlesinger Jr. Vol. 1. New York: Simon and Schuster, 1994.

Doenecke, Justus D. *The Presidencies of James A. Garfield & Chester A. Arthur.* Lawrence, Kans.: University Press of Kansas, 1981.

Jordan, David M. *Roscoe Conkling of New York: Voice in the Senate.* Ithaca, N.Y.: Cornell University Press, 1971.

Morgan, H. Wayne. *From Hayes to McKinley: National Party Politics, 1877–1896.* Syracuse, N.Y.: Syracuse University Press, 1969.

Muzzey, Davod Saville.*James G. Blaine: A Political Idol of Other Days.* New York: Dodd, Mead, 1934.

Further Readings

Peskin, Allan. *Garfield: A Biography.* Kent, Ohio: Kent State University Press, 1978.

Pletcher, David M. *The Awkward Years: American Foreign Relations under Garfield and Arthur.* Columbia, Mo.: University of Missouri Press, 1962.

Reeves, Thomas C. *Gentleman Boss: The Life of Chester Alan Arthur.* New York: Knopf, 1975.

Smith, Theodore Clark. *The Life and Letters of James Abram Garfield.* 2 vols. New Haven, Conn.: Yale University Press, 1925.

Arthur Administration

Biography

Chester A. Arthur was an easygoing man who successfully hid his deepest feelings under layers of charm and wit. He was well mannered and enjoyed the finest clothes and the ceremonial trappings of the presidency. Arthur was not overly ambitious in his own career, but he gave much of his time and energy to promoting the careers of other members of his party. Arthur was an honest man who always aspired to do a good job and successfully met his responsibilities. His private life was kept very private, and his professional life was conducted without scandal.

Early Life

Chester Arthur was born on October 5, 1829, in North Fairfield, Vermont, to William Arthur and the former Malvina Stone. Arthur's father was a Baptist minister whose work made it necessary for the family to move several times during Arthur's youth. Arthur was the fifth of nine children. The large family and frequent moves helped Arthur to develop his outgoing and friendly personality.

Education

Arthur's education began at home where he was tutored by his scholarly father. He then attended an academy in Union Village, New York, for a short time before

Full name: Chester Alan Arthur

Personal Information:
Born: October 5, 1829
Birthplace: North Fairfield, Vermont
Died: November 18, 1886
Burial place: Rural Cemetery, Albany, New York
Religion: Episcopalian
Spouse: Ellen Lewis Herndon (m. 1859)
Children: William Lewis Herndon; Chester Alan II; Ellen Herndon
Education: Union College, 1848
Occupation: Teacher; attorney; politician
Political Party: Republican Party
Age at Inauguration: 51 years

Chester Alan Arthur. *(The Library of Congress.)*

enrolling at the Lyceum in Schenectady, New York. There he became editor of the school newspaper and got his first taste of politics when he joined other students at rallies to support Senator Henry Clay of Kentucky, the renowned legislator and statesman, for president. He entered Union College in Schenectady in 1845 and graduated in the top third of his class in 1848. He taught school while studying law and was admitted to the bar in 1854.

Family Life

On October 25, 1859, Chester Arthur married Ellen "Nell" Lewis Herndon in New York City. Ellen Herndon's father was a naval officer. Her mother came from Virginia. The Arthurs had three children; William Lewis who died at age four, Chester Alan, and Ellen Herndon. The Arthurs were known to have a strong marriage, but one that was strained by Arthur's absences due to his American Civil War (1861–65) service and later his political activities. Despite their problems, Arthur was inconsolable when his wife contracted pneumonia and died in 1880. Arthur always regretted that his wife did not live to see him become president. Arthur's sister, Mrs. Mary McElroy, served as his official hostess in the White House during his administration.

Career

Chester Arthur began his career as a teacher and school principal to support himself while he studied law. Once he passed the bar in 1854, he joined the law firm he had clerked for, and two years later he formed his own law partnership with a friend. Two of Arthur's first and most well-known cases involved discrimination against African Americans. Arthur, a strong abolitionist (someone who supported abolishing slavery), felt these cases gave him an opportunity to contribute to the antislavery movement. During this time Arthur also became a supporter of the newly formed Republican Party and its candidates for governor and president.

Military Service

Arthur joined the New York state militia in 1858. He rose through the ranks, and after the American Civil War (1861–65) began he was ultimately promoted to the position of quartermaster general of New York. In this position he was responsible for raising regiments to fight on the battlefields and maintaining the troops. Arthur also participated in direct combat on occasion and despite encouragement to join and lead combat troops by the troops themselves, Arthur remained in the quartermaster position at the request of the governor. Arthur resigned from the militia in 1862, when a Democrat was elected governor of New York.

Collector of the Port of New York

Arthur returned to the practice of law and continued to work to elect Republican candidates, including Roscoe Conkling, a powerful New York politician, to the U.S. Senate. His party rewarded Arthur's loyalty and hard work by electing him chairman of the executive committee of the New York Republican Party. In 1871 Republican president Ulysses S. Grant appointed Arthur collector of the Port of New York, the most important political position (and potentially the most lucrative) outside of Washington, D.C. In this position, Arthur was responsible for collecting 75 percent of the taxes from ships that landed in ports within his jurisdiction, which included the coast of New York State, the Hudson River, and parts of New Jersey. Though Arthur did a good job, new Republican president, Rutherford B. Hayes, dismissed him under the cloud of scandal that hung over the Grant administration. Grant's administration had rewarded political supporters with government jobs instead of filling positions with the most qualified applicants. This is referred to as the "spoils system." The removal of Arthur was not based on his competence, but on the fact that he was a powerful politician. After his dismissal, Arthur returned to practicing law.

Vice President

Arthur's hard work paid off in 1880, when he was nominated as the vice presidential candidate for the

Republican Party. The presidential candidate was James Garfield of Ohio. Both men were surprised at their nomination, as they had come to the convention to support other men. When the delegates could not agree on the leading candidates, Garfield and Arthur became the unexpected compromise candidates. The two politicians' long careers of public service helped them get elected by a narrow margin. Arthur had just begun to adjust to his position as vice president, when Garfield was shot on July 2, 1881, and died of his wounds 80 days later. Chester A. Arthur became president on September 20, 1881.

President

When Arthur became president he worked hard to convince the American people that he was an able administrator, not just a beneficiary of the spoils system that the public had come to hate. He supported civil service reform and encouraged bipartisan cooperation in Congress. Arthur urged that the United States build a canal in Nicaragua, in Central America, to be owned and operated by the United States. He advocated a number of other measures, most of which were passed after his administration. Despite his desire to become president on his own, Arthur had offended too many old friends with his reforms, and not made enough new friends, to be nominated for president in 1884.

Post-presidential Years

After leaving the White House in 1885, Arthur resumed practicing law but was able to do very little because of poor health. As president Arthur knew that he was suffering from Bright's disease (a kidney ailment which, at that time, was fatal). Arthur's health steadily deteriorated, and his last public appearance was at a retirement dinner for a friend in December 1885. On November 17, 1886, Arthur suffered a paralyzing stroke and, without regaining consciousness, died the next day on November 18, 1886.

The Chester A. Arthur Administration

A career politician with a background in machine politics, Chester A. Arthur succeeded to the presidency after the assassination of President James Garfield. As president Arthur sought to govern in accordance with the best interests of the American people, even when they were against the interests of the powerful politicians and political systems that he had long been associated with. In doing so, Arthur turned out to be a much better president than anyone expected.

Arthur Becomes President

President James Garfield was shot on July 2, 1881. His vice president, Chester Arthur, went to Washington, D.C., to await developments. As the president's condition improved, Arthur returned to his Manhattan, New York, home where he was spending the summer months. When Garfield's health took a turn for the worse, Arthur refused to return to Washington for fear it would appear he was eager for the president's death. Late on September 19, 1881, a messenger arrived at Arthur's home to tell him the president had died. Arthur was sworn in as president early the next day by New York Supreme Court Justice John R. Brady at Arthur's home in New York. On September 22, 1881, Arthur took a second oath at the United States Capitol.

Arthur's Advisers

Chester Arthur inherited the cabinet of James Garfield when he took office and maintained it through December 1881. Many cabinet members eventually resigned, despite Arthur's requests that they continue to serve. Several of those who resigned refused to work with Arthur, who they felt was part of a party machine of which they disapproved. Only Robert Lincoln (son of Abraham Lincoln) remained in the cabinet in his position of secretary of war during the entire Arthur administration.

As Arthur began to distance himself from his former party associates and to support reform measures, he attempted to create new associations with like-minded officials. Unfortunately Arthur was viewed with suspicion by reform politicians due to his past links with the party spoils system, appointing people to positions as political favors rather than based on merit, and he was unable to form new political bonds. Thus Arthur had no close public advisers, and he kept his private life, including any confidants, very private. Arthur was also a strong administrator and expected department heads to administer their departments while he attended to executive duties, with little consultation between them.

Arthur and Congress

Chester Arthur was president during the Forty-seventh and Forty-eighth Congresses. In the Forty-seventh Congress, the Senate had equal numbers of Republican and Democratic members and the Republicans held a majority of seats in the House of Representatives. In the Forty-eighth Congress, the Republicans held a majority of seats in both chambers. Arthur enjoyed an amiable relationship with Congress.

One of the reasons for this smooth relationship was that Arthur left Congress alone and did not challenge con-

Administration

Administration Dates
September 20, 1881–March 4, 1885

Vice President
None

Cabinet

Secretary of State
James G. Blaine (1881)
Frederick T. Frelinghuysen (1881–85)

Secretary of the Treasury
William Windom (1881)
Charles J. Folger (1881–84)
Walter Q. Gresham (1884)
Hugh McCulloch (1884–85)

Secretary of War
Robert Todd Lincoln (1881–85)

Attorney General
Wayne MacVeagh (1881)
Benjamin H. Brewster (1882–85)

Secretary of the Navy
William H. Hunt (1881–82)
William E. Chandler (1882–85)

Postmaster General
Thomas L. James (1881–82)
Timothy O. Howe (1882–83)
Walter Q. Gresham (1883–84)
Frank Hatton (1884–85)

Secretary of the Interior
Samuel J. Kirkwood (1881–82)
Henry M. Teller (1882–85)

---

gressional initiatives. On the other hand, Arthur made many suggestions in his annual messages to Congress. Members of Congress were willing to hear the president's suggestions, but they did not feel compelled to act on them because their political bases were more secure than the president's. Arthur believed that Congress was responsible for the legislative affairs of the country (a field in which Arthur had little experience), while the president's role was to oversee administrative affairs.

Thus, Arthur's major interaction with Congress was through the use of the presidential veto. In 1882 Arthur vetoed an internal improvements bill claiming that it was an extravagant expenditure of public money. Probably Arthur's most important veto was a bill to exclude Chinese laborers from the United States (*See also,* Domestic Issues).

Arthur and the Judiciary

During his administration, Arthur made two appointments to the Supreme Court. His first appointee was Horace Gray of Massachusetts, a former state supreme court chief justice and renowned legal scholar, who brought a great knowledge of precedent decisions to the Court. Gray distinguished himself when he wrote the majority opinion in *Julliard v. Greenman* (1884), which gave the government the right to issue paper money in times of peace as well as war.

Samuel Blatchford of New York was Arthur's second appointee, after Arthur's old friend, political boss Senator Roscoe Conkling, declined to serve. Blatchford was a former circuit court judge who was known for his expertise in patent law. Blatchford wrote the pro-business majority opinion in *Chicago, Milwaukee, and St. Paul v. Minnesota* (1890), when he ruled that corporations whose rates were subject to state regulation could sue states in court.

Also under Arthur's presidency, in 1883 the Supreme Court delivered several stinging setbacks to the rights of African Americans. The Court ruled unconstitutional the Supplementary Civil Rights Act of 1875, a law which provided that all persons, regardless of race, were entitled to "the full and equal enjoyment of the accommodations, advantages, facilities and privileges of inns, public conveyances on land or water, theaters, and other places of public amusement." In his third annual message, the president declared that he would unhesitatingly support any civil rights legislation that Congress might pass. Congress, however, refused to act.

African Americans had already been rebuffed the previous year in *United States v. Harris* (1882), in which the Court ruled, in effect, that Reconstruction (the process of bringing southern states that had seceded during the American Civil War [1861–65] back into the Union) was over, and that the protection of the federal government did not apply to the murder of a black person in Tennessee. Only in *Ex parte Yarbrough* (1884) could African Americans take some comfort. The Court ruled that Congress could punish efforts to prevent citizens from voting in federal elections. The Court's position with regard to minority populations was accurately reflected in *Elk v. Wilkins* (1884), ruling that American Indians were no more subject to the protections of the Fourteenth Amendment (which defined U.S. citizenship) than were the "children of subjects to any foreign governments."

Changes in the U.S. Government

The most significant change in government during the Arthur administration was the passage of the Pendleton Act in 1883, which established the precedent for the modern civil service system (*See also,* Domestic Issues).

Arthur's administration also upgraded the military arm of government by making improvements to the military. The Naval War College was established in Newport, Rhode Island, and a new naval advisory board was created to direct the growth of the naval system. And in 1883 Arthur signed a bill authorizing the building of the nation's first three steel-plated ships, which would replace wooden vessels.

Finally, on May 17, 1884, Congress passed a law establishing a territorial government in Alaska.

Domestic Issues

The political climate of the United States in the 1880s was somewhat sluggish. One historian remarked that "the great questions of the Civil War had been settled, but the problems of postwar expansion were not yet in sharp outline" (Graff, pp. 273–74). Many of the achievements in the field of domestic issues during the Arthur administration were modest and custodial: they include measures like adopting standard time, building a repository for the Library of Congress, and establishing a constitutional amendment dealing with presidential succession. Possibly the most important for the future of the country was civil service reform.

Civil Service Reform

In the years prior to the Arthur administration, more and more Americans called for an end to the political spoils system. It is ironic that Arthur, a lifelong participant in party patronage, helped to dismantle the system by signing the Pendleton Act into law in 1883. Although only 10 percent of federal employees were initially covered by the act, it created the modern civil service system in which applicants for government jobs were to be tested, classified by their test results, and then placed in appropriate positions. The new law also banned obligatory political contributions or service from civil servants (government workers). A bipartisan, three-man Civil Service Commission was established to oversee the system. Arthur angered many of his old political friends when he signed the bill. In fact, soon after the bill's passage, the Postal Service (run by Arthur's former political allies) was soon investigated for violating provisions of the Pendleton Act.

Chinese Exclusion Act

Beginning in the late 1840s, large masses of Chinese laborers immigrated to the western United States.

Fast Fact

Arthur refused to live in the White House until it had been cleaned out and renovated. Twenty-four wagon loads of furniture, clothing, and other items were removed and auctioned to the public, thereby losing forever many historical treasures.

(Source: Barbara Seuling. *The Last Cow on the White House Lawn and Other Little-Known Facts About the Presidency,* 1992.)

Initially their inexpensive labor was seen as a godsend by the mining, railroad, and construction industries. But as the laborers became owners of their own successful businesses, white Americans grew increasingly hostile towards them because they feared the business competition. Further, after the completion of the transcontinental railroads and in the midst of a general economic depression that settled in during the last third of the nineteenth century, white workers feared that cheap "coolie labor" would soak up the available jobs. Violence against Chinese people became common on the West Coast, and a third-party movement called the Workingman's Party championed the issue of Chinese exclusion. The Democratic Party in California took up the issue of exclusion, as did the national American Federation of Labor (AFL). During the 1870s western politicians convinced Congress to pass an exclusionary bill that explicitly targeted Chinese immigration. The president at that time, Rutherford B. Hayes, vetoed the bill.

In 1882 Senator John Miller of California attempted to address the issue again by introducing a new bill. The new bill would have ended Chinese immigration for 20 years, as well as deny citizenship to Chinese residents. Southern senators supported the bill on racial grounds and felt it strengthened "the white man's government." The bill passed in Congress by large majorities.

Almost immediately Arthur vetoed the bill. Although Arthur understood the fears of the westerners, he felt that 20 years was an unreasonable period to exclude Chinese immigration. Arthur was also hesitant to offend Asian trade partners, and he demanded that Congress revise the bill. Arthur signed the revised bill, known as the Chinese Exclusion Act of 1882. The new measures reduced the exclusion period to 10 years, but it still denied U.S. citizenship to all Chinese. In addition to its immediate effect of blocking further Chinese immigration, the bill also set a post-Civil War precedent for future, and greater, exclusion policies.

Mongrel Tariff

In 1882 Arthur created a tariff commission to review the taxes or duties that were paid on foreign goods imported into the United States. The commission's recommendation that duties be greatly reduced created arguments in Congress. Free traders wanted the tariff schedule reduced or even eliminated. Protectionists wanted the tariff schedule maintained or increased. The final bill, referred to as the Mongrel Tariff of 1883, was signed by Arthur and reduced duties, but by less than 1.5 percent. Ultimately, the bill satisfied no one, and it began a decades-long battle over tariff issues.

Foreign Issues

A few short years after Chester Arthur's presidency, U.S. opinion makers had once again embraced the goal of a larger role for the United States in the world. The concept of the United States's "manifest destiny" to "o'er-spread the continent"—a notion that dated back to the western migration of the 1840s just before the war with Mexico—was, by the end of the century, being applied to a larger mandate to carry the U.S. flag and the Christian religion to the benighted regions of the Pacific Ocean. The confidence of these end-of-century Americans stemmed in part from the fact that most of the emerging leaders of that generation, such as Teddy Roosevelt, 26th U.S. president, had never fought a war. They yearned to "earn their spurs" in war. The leaders of James Garfield and Arthur's generation, however, had seen all too much of war. The American Civil War (1861–65) had chastened them. They were ready to profit, if they could, from foreign trade and commercial contact with the people beyond the United States's borders, but they, and the American people that they served, did not look forward to foreign adventures. Perhaps in part because of this reluctance, Arthur's record of foreign policy efforts is a mixed one.

Setbacks

The Arthur administration faced many setbacks in foreign policy. It was unable to mediate a war between Peru and Chile, a conflict that had begun in April 1879. Early in December 1881, Secretary of State James G. Blaine, a temporary holdover from the Garfield administration, convinced Arthur to send a special mission, composed of U.S. diplomat William Henry Trescot and Blaine's son Walker, to the parties involved. When Blaine's replacement, Frederick T. Frelinghuysen, took office, he terminated the mission because it had been unsuccessful. Frelinghuysen also canceled a Pan-American Conference that Blaine had hoped would bring peace to the Peru-Chile war, as well as to a dispute between Mexico and Guatemala.

Another Frelinghuysen initiative was to do away with the Clayton-Bulwer Treaty, an agreement made in 1850 with Great Britain that recognized British rights over any canal built through any part of Central America. In May 1882 the secretary wrote the U.S. minister in London, England, denying that the treaty ever applied to Panama, and claiming that joint rights would create endless problems. The United States, he said, should establish the only protectorate over any canal built across the Central American isthmus. Britain's foreign secretary, Lord Granville, simply replied that the terms of the 1850 treaty remained in force.

The Arthur administration did negotiate a treaty with Nicaragua giving the United States co-ownership over a canal strip there. However, when the Senate voted on the agreement in January 1885, the bill fell nine votes short of the two-thirds needed for ratification. It met with a variety of objections: the cost would far outweigh any advantage; it would produce confrontation with Great Britain; holding land in any foreign country was unconstitutional; and any effort to turn Nicaragua into a United States "colony" was unwise. The administration also negotiated reciprocal trade agreements with Mexico, Cuba, Puerto Rico, and the Dominican Republic, but Congress refused to act. Congresspersons who felt the agreements would create unfair competition for domestic industries made sure the treaties were not ratified.

The Arthur Administration Legacy

When Arthur left office in 1885, he left his successor, Grover Cleveland, a government that was running smoothly. Whatever his limitations, Arthur was a gifted administrator who brought organization and efficiency to the executive office. The public's concerns over Arthur's past in party politics had proven largely unfounded given his support of civil service reform. However, they still viewed Arthur with some suspicion, and his insistence on privacy made it difficult for the public to warm up to him. His reluctance to meet with the press left the media irritated and inclined to paint a less than flattering picture of Arthur as president. He was criticized for enjoying the trappings of the presidency, more than the office itself. It was reported that he arrived at the office late, left early, and spent much of his time entertaining guests. Yet Arthur was given credit for his conduct after Garfield's death and his calm strength as he assumed the presidency.

Lasting Impact

Historians tend to agree that Arthur was a much better president than anyone expected him to be, but he still is ranked as an average president. Arthur's disassociation from the party politics and spoils system he had spent his adult life in, revealed him to be a man who could be transformed by the power and the aura of the presidency. Clearly, his administration's most significant and long-lasting legacy is the civil service reform that accompanied his personal reform. Though Arthur did not create the legislation establishing equitable processes for government hiring, he did not oppose the bill and enforced it after signing it. The civil system remains an effective alternative to political favoritism.

Sources

Bryce, James. *The American Commonwealth,* 3 vols. London: Macmillan, 1888.

Clancy, Herbert J. *The Presidential Election of 1880.* Chicago: Loyola University Press, 1958.

Doenecke, Justus D. *The Presidencies of James A. Garfield & Chester A. Arthur.* Lawrence, Kans.: University Press of Kansas, 1981.

Hoogenboom, Ari. *Outlawing the Spoils: A History of the Civil Service Reform Movement, 1865–1883.* Urbana, Ill.: University of Illinois Press, 1961.

Howe, George Frederick. *Chester A. Arthur: A Quarter-Century of Machine Politics.* New York: Dodd, Mead, 1935.

Seuling, Barbara. *The Last Cow on the White House Lawn & Other Little-Known Facts About the Presidency.* New York: Ivy Books, 1992.

Weisberger, Bernard A. "James A. Garfield and Chester A. Arthur." *The Presidents: A Reference History.* Edited by Henry F. Graff. New York: Simon and Schuster Macmillan, 1997.

Further Readings

Jensen, Richard J. *The Winning of the Midwest: Social and Political Conflict, 1888–1896.* Chicago: University of Chicago Press, 1971.

Jordan, David M. *Roscoe Conkling of New York: Voice in the Senate.* Ithaca, N.Y.: Cornell University Press, 1971.

Morgan, H. Wayne. *From Hayes to McKinley: National Party Politics, 1877–1896.* Syracuse, N.Y.: Syracuse University Press, 1969.

Peskin, Allan. *Garfield: A Biography.* Kent, Ohio: Kent State University Press, 1978.

Pletcher, David M. *The Awkward Years: American Foreign Relations Under Garfield and Arthur.* Columbia, Mo.: University of Missouri Press, 1962.

Reeves, Thomas C. *Gentleman Boss: The Life of Chester Alan Arthur.* New York: Knopf, 1975.

Cleveland Administrations

Full name: Grover Cleveland
Given name: Stephen Grover Cleveland

Personal Information:

Born: March 18, 1837
Birthplace: Caldwell, New Jersey
Died: June 24, 1908
Death place: Princeton, New Jersey
Burial place: Princeton Cemetery, Princeton, New Jersey
Religion: Presbyterian
Spouse: Frances Folsom (m. 1886)
Children: Ruth; Esther; Marion; Richard Folsom; Francis Grover
Education: High School
Occupation: Lawyer; governor
Political Party: Democratic Party
Age at Inauguration: 47 years

Biography

Grover Cleveland was a conservative and an honest man. Many of his contemporaries shared his conservative reaction to the immense changes that the United States was going through in the last years of the nineteenth century, though few shared his honesty. He was the only president to serve two nonconsecutive terms. Throughout his life he demonstrated courage and integrity, not flinching to do what he thought was right even if what he said or did cost him popularity.

Early Life

Grover Cleveland grew up with few privileges. The son of a Presbyterian pastor who moved from church to church, Cleveland was born in 1837 in Caldwell, New Jersey. His parents named him after a family friend, Rev. Stephen Grover, who had faithfully served the Caldwell church for nearly 50 years before Grover's father succeeded him.

Born in the manse (the pastor's house) in Caldwell, Grover Cleveland was the fifth child in a family that eventually grew to nine children. His parents moved to Fayetteville, New York, in 1841. In 1851 the Clevelands moved to Clinton, New York, where Cleveland's father became director of the American Home Missionary Society. In 1853, shortly after Rev. Richard Cleveland was appointed pastor of a church in Holland Patent, New York, he died. This death ended any hopes that Cleveland had for more formal education.

Still, Cleveland believed that his upbringing as the son of a Christian minister had a significant strengthening influence on him throughout his entire life. Although he did not aspire to become a clergyman, Cleveland exhibited some of the same traits as his father. President Cleveland's honesty, integrity, work ethic, forthrightness, tenacity, and willingness to take responsibility were also characteristic of his father.

Education

When he was 11 years old, Cleveland was enrolled in the Fayetteville Academy in Fayetteville, New York. Soon his family moved to Clinton, New York, and from 1850 to 1851 Cleveland studied Latin and mathematics at the Clinton Liberal Institute. He dreamed of attending college, but when his father died in 1853 Cleveland began working to help support his large family. Somewhat later while living in Buffalo, New York, he studied law while he was associated with Rogers, Bowen, and Rogers, one of the leading law firms in Buffalo. In 1859 he officially became a lawyer when he was admitted to the bar.

Grover Cleveland. (The Library of Congress.)

Family Life

When 21-year-old Frances Folsom married 49-year-old Grover Cleveland on June 2, 1886, she became the youngest first lady in the history of the United States. Cleveland, who also set a record by becoming the only president ever to be married in the White House, had known his wife since she was an infant and had been good friends with her father, Oscar Folsom. Cleveland served as her guardian when her father died without having prepared a will. Cleveland held traditional views on women and the family. At one point not long before his marriage he observed, "A good wife is a woman who loves her husband and her country with no desire to run either" (Boller, p. 167).

Young though she was, Frances Cleveland proved to be a gracious and mature first lady. She arranged numerous formal dinners and receptions cheerfully. Biographer Rexford Tugwell said she "carried herself gallantly" always in good humor. "She met the inevitable small crises without becoming flustered and won the affection of everyone around her" (Tugwell, p. 198).

The Clevelands had three daughters and two sons. The first child, Ruth, died at age 12 from diphtheria, still a scourge around the turn of the century. Esther, born in 1893, became the only child of a president to be born in the White House. The Clevelands' third child, Marion, worked from 1943 to 1960 as community relations adviser for the Girl Scouts of America at its New York headquarters. Richard Folsom Cleveland, the first son of Grover Cleveland, became a conservative Democrat like

his father. In 1932 at the Democratic National Convention he seconded the nomination of Albert C. Ritchie, Maryland's governor. Later he became active in the ultra-conservative American Liberty League and opposed the reelection of Franklin D. Roosevelt. Cleveland's youngest child, Francis Grover Cleveland, was born in 1904. He later graduated from Harvard with a degree in drama.

Career

After Cleveland was admitted to the bar in 1859, he successfully practiced law in Buffalo, New York, where he became active in the Democratic Party. In 1862 he was selected as a delegate to the Democratic city convention. The same year he served in an elective office for the first time when he was elected supervisor of his ward (city electoral district). Shortly thereafter, he was appointed Erie County's assistant district attorney.

With the advent of the American Civil War (1861–65), two of Cleveland's brothers enlisted on the Union side. Grover Cleveland stayed home to provide for his mother and younger sisters. When drafted for military service, he hired a substitute to serve in his place. This practice, which was legal during the American Civil War, came back to haunt him politically after the war. Military service during the civil war defined a whole generation of politicians. With the exception of

Cleveland, all the presidents from Grant through McKinley had served in the Union army. Being a veteran gave a candidate what amounted to a character reference with the voters. This may have accounted for Cleveland's defeat in 1865 when he ran for district attorney of Erie County and probably impacted his other candidacies as well.

Sheriff

After losing the race for district attorney in Erie County, Cleveland practiced law with Isaac K. Vanderpoel, and later with Albert P. Laning and Oscar Folsom (father of his future bride). In 1870 he ran—successfully this time—for election as sheriff of New York's Erie County. Sheriff Cleveland earned a reputation of honesty, and that would go with him throughout his entire public life. For a long time, favored contractors and vendors had been routinely shortchanging the community. They overcharged for goods and services or billed for goods and services that were unnecessary. To cover their tracks they bribed officials. Cleveland insisted on genuine competitive bidding on goods and services purchased by the city. He required that the city auditor confirm the legitimacy of accounts presented to him. During Cleveland's tenure as sheriff, contractors doing business with Erie County were expected to completely fulfill their obligations or risk being run out of business. Cleveland stood out as a fearless and incorruptible politician.

When Cleveland completed his term as sheriff at the end of 1873, he resumed his law practice in a new firm headed by Lyman K. Bass and Wilson S. Bissell. For a time Cleveland was less active in public life. This changed in 1881 when the Democrats nominated him for mayor of Buffalo, New York. Cleveland won the election by appealing to the Buffalo citizens who were concerned about corruption in high places.

Mayor

As mayor of Buffalo Cleveland demonstrated the same fortitude and integrity. In June 1882, the city council passed a resolution awarding a street-cleaning contract to George Talbot, who had put in a bid that significantly exceeded the bids of five other contractors. It seemed obvious that the aldermen had awarded this contract to Talbot knowing that Talbot would reward them for their votes. Mayor Cleveland would have none of this. In ringing tones he vetoed the resolution declaring that it was a "time for plain speech." He said, "I withhold my assent from the same, because I regard it as the culmination of a most bare-faced, impudent, and shameless scheme to betray the interests of the people, and to worse than squander the public money" (Nevins, p. 85). So often did Cleveland refuse to assent to similar actions taken by the council that he affectionately became known as the "Veto Mayor."

Governor and Tammany Hall

Cleveland was able to leverage his reputation for good government into nomination for higher office. In 1882 the New York Democrats were looking for a candidate for governor who would appear to be independent of Tammany Hall, the political machine of the Democratic Party in New York City. Tammany Hall was the most famous of all the big city political machines. It emerged from the welter of immigrant poverty in New York City during the 1860s and early 1870s under "Boss Tweed" (William M. Tweed). A kind of unofficial social welfare system, Tammany Hall facilitated the distribution of jobs, the mediation of conflicts between the community and the police or court system (often just by bailing a father out of jail for drunkenness so that he could go back to work to feed his family), and even the subsidy of funeral expenses for the final laying to rest of the most destitute of its constituency. The key figure in this system was the ward leader, who did most of the legwork in servicing the population and in getting them to the polls on election day with clear instructions on which candidates to vote for.

This system harvested massive amounts of votes, and it used these votes to enrich itself. The Tweed machine redirected large sums of money from the city coffers into its own pockets. The total money siphoned off into the Boss Tweed Tammany regime has been estimated at anywhere between $30 million to $200 million. Eventually, the "good government" forces in both parties became sensitized to the corruption question, and political cartoonists like Thomas Nast lampooned Boss Tweed so that opposition to the Tammany machine became a popular position. Progressive reform forces in both parties, like Jane Addams, the founder of Hull-House in Chicago, Illinois, and of the "settlement house" movement (which ministered to the moral and physical needs of the downtrodden immigrant populations of the big cities), opposed the political machines and lobbied for reform.

Cleveland accepted the Democratic nomination for New York governor in 1882 and won election in November. As governor Cleveland forthrightly opposed the campaign of Tammany Hall politician Thomas F. Grady for the post of state senate. Grady had consistently opposed the "good government" forces. In the end, Grady withdrew from the contest. These reform efforts brought Cleveland a sterling reputation among other municipal reformers. As governor, Cleveland also demonstrated that he could cooperate with Republicans by signing a state civil service bill introduced in the legislature by another future president, Theodore Roosevelt. As an alternative to the back-room network of appointment to office that the political machines offered, Cleveland supported the state civil service bill. He appointed distinguished reformers to the new civil service commission. He also instituted closer scrutiny of state banking practices and sought to preserve some one-and-a-half million acres around Niagara Falls, near Buffalo, for the public to enjoy.

Biography:

Jane Addams

Activist; Feminist (1860–1935) Like a small minority of privileged women of her time, Jane Addams was expected to assume the traditional, domestic role. On the other hand she was given the opportunity to pursue a higher education at schools of similar caliber to men's institutions. The conflicting combination of traditional expectations and an nontraditional education was especially difficult for Addams, a woman with strong ambitions instilled by her father. Addams was characterized by other traits as well: compassion and moral purpose. In 1889 Addams found her moral purpose and, with a friend, opened Hull-House in the Chicago slums just days after her twenty-ninth birthday. The purpose of Hull-House was to help the underprivileged by providing "a center for higher civic and social life, to institute and maintain educational and philanthropic enterprises, and to investigate and improve the conditions in the industrial districts of Chicago." Their efforts to provide hot lunches, child care services, English instruction, lectures,

and parties began locally during the Cleveland administration, spread to the national level, and ultimately involved Addams in national political reform. She led campaigns for protective labor laws for women, for elimination of child labor, and for women's suffrage. Her centers also provided women of the times a place to develop meaningful careers outside of the home. Addams argued

that women possessed special talents apart from men and that they had the special responsibility to emphasize the "humane impulse in world affairs." Her pleas for peace during World War I (1914–18) garnered her much criticism, but in 1931 she was co-winner of the Nobel Peace Prize for those efforts.

Cleveland Nominated for President

In 1884 the national Democratic Party nominated Cleveland for president. During the Democratic convention Edward S. Bragg from Wisconsin remarked on the fact that the voters seemed to "love Cleveland for his character, but they love him also for the enemies he has made." By this time in Cleveland's political life he was firmly identified with the "character question." The most memorable aspect of his political profile is his character. He was a man of courage and integrity. His political positions, on the other hand, were traditional. He was a conservative Democrat who stood for sound currency and a gold standard to back up the currency, and he continued the traditional Democratic hostility to the protective tariff as a tax against consumers. As a general principle he stood for limited government, and in foreign policy he adopted an "anti-imperialist" position and criticized the rising agitation for a U.S. territorial empire.

Cleveland defeated Republican James G. Blaine of Maine in 1884 and became the first Democratic president since James Buchanan was succeeded by Republican Abraham Lincoln in 1861. During Cleveland's first term as president the Congress passed and he signed the Interstate Commerce Act, the Hatch Act, the Presidential Succession Act, and the Dawes Act (*See also,* Domestic Issues). This was a reasonably productive collaboration for a president who was trying to reassert the dignity

and power of the executive branch that had slipped notably in the post-Civil War period. In 1888 the Democrats renominated Cleveland, who lost to Republican Benjamin Harrison in the November election. Cleveland returned to the practice of law until 1892, when for the third time the Democrats nominated him for president. Cleveland rebounded to win the presidential election for a second time.

Soon after Cleveland returned to the White House the "panic of 1893" beset the nation. The depression resulted in wage cuts and labor unrest. Cleveland again showed his conservative orientation by aiding the railroad interests and sending federal troops to Illinois to break the 1894 Pullman strike. This hurt his popularity among the working-class voters, but a larger problem for his diminishing popularity was his conservative refusal, even during the worst depression to that point in U.S. history, to use the power of the government to intervene in the economy. On this matter he summed up his position with the remarkable statement that, "though the people support the Government, the Government should not support the people." In the midst of this turbulent period, Cleveland suffered a personal crisis when doctors diagnosed a cancerous tumor in the roof of his mouth. Once again demonstrating strength of character, he kept his surgery and recovery silent, rather than risk further public uncertainty and financial panic.

Post-presidential Years

After completing his second term and retiring from politics in 1897, Cleveland settled in Princeton, New Jersey. In 1899 Princeton University appointed him Henry Stafford Little Lecturer in Public Affairs. Later he served on Princeton's board of trustees when future U.S. president Woodrow Wilson was president of Princeton. Between 1900 and 1906 he wrote several articles for the *Saturday Evening Post*. In 1906 he became involved as a consultant in the reorganization of the Equitable Life Assurance Society. Fittingly, Cleveland's last words were, "I have tried so hard to do right." On June 24, 1908, at 8:40 P.M. he died of heart failure at his Princeton home.

The Grover Cleveland Administrations

Grover Cleveland was the only president to serve two nonconsecutive terms. A conservative Democrat, he stuck doggedly to his ideals; however, he did little to mollify discontented farmers and could not unite his own party. After being defeated by Benjamin Harrison in the election of 1888, he came back to regain the presidency in 1892 but found the country sliding into the worst economic depression of the nineteenth century. Despite his integrity and commitment, his policies lacked the imagination to unite the country on a course to economic recovery.

Cleveland Becomes President

The Campaign of 1884

The 1884 presidential campaign proved to be one of the nastiest that the nation had ever witnessed. Issues such as the tariff, the restrictions on trusts, and civil service reform took a backseat to a dialogue concerning the morality of each candidate. The Republicans nominated James G. Blaine of Maine. Blaine had been Speaker of the House of Representatives, and it appeared that he had personally profited when he used his influence on behalf of the Little Rock and Fort Smith Railroad in 1869 to preserve a land grant that the railroad had been in danger of losing. Afterwards he acted as an agent for the railroad's bonds, pocketing a generous commission for himself. Democrats scoffed at his denials and chanted, "Blaine! Blaine! James G. Blaine! Continental Liar from the State of Maine!" The *New York Times* denounced Blaine as "a prostitutor of public trusts, a scheming jobber, and a reckless falsifier."

Because of all the controversy surrounding Blaine's nomination a segment of Republicans called the Mug-

wumps indicated that they would support a reform-minded Democrat, enhancing Cleveland's chances for the Democratic nomination. Cleveland had demonstrated as New York State governor his unwillingness to maintain the "spoils system," whereby government jobs are awarded based on political patronage rather than merit and advocated reform at every level of government. He was particularly instrumental in standing up to the New York City political machine, Tammany Hall, and the powerful politicians who controlled it. On July 11, 1884, the Democrats nominated Cleveland on the second ballot.

During the campaign the Republicans sought to taint the image of "Grover the Good," as one Republican sarcastically called Cleveland, by trumpeting Cleveland's affair with Maria Halpin. In 1874 Cleveland had allegedly fathered an illegitimate child with a Buffalo, New York, widow named Maria Halpin. It was true that Cleveland among others had sexual liaisons with Halpin. Although there was no proof that he was the father, he had assumed responsibility for the child's upbringing. When the situation became known to the public, Cleveland told his staff not to hide the truth.

As the campaign continued, the Republicans taunted Cleveland and the Democrats with, "Ma, ma, where's my pa?" Democrats retaliated with "Gone to the White House, ha, ha, ha!" A thoughtless rhetorical misstep by a Republican clergyman late in the campaign turned the tide when he referred to the Democratic Party as the party of "Rum, Romanism, and Rebellion." It was a thinly veiled slight on Irish Democrats. "Romanism" referred to their Catholicism; "Rebellion" to the fact that the southern block of the Democratic Party had seceded from the Union to defend slavery in 1861, while the northern section of the party had obstructed the Civil War policies of the now-revered Abraham Lincoln; "Rum," of course, connoted the ethnic slur of alcoholism among the Irish.

The incident alienated Catholic voters in general and Irish Americans in particular, whose faith and patriotism had been ridiculed. With a 77.5 percent voter participation rate, the election was close enough (48.5 percent for Cleveland to 48.2 percent for Blaine) for this to make a difference. The remark, which was not repudiated by Blaine, may well have scuttled Republican hopes. There were a lot of Catholic immigrants in New York City, and Cleveland won the huge block of electoral votes from New York State by only 1,149 votes out of 1,125,000 votes cast.

Defeat in 1888

In the election of 1888, although Cleveland received 100,000 more votes than his opponent, he lost to Republican candidate Benjamin Harrison. This campaign was lower key than the first one, and the election revolved somewhat more around the issues. The Republicans advocated a high protective tariff (a tax on imported

Administration

Administration Dates
March 4, 1885–March 4, 1889
March 4, 1893–March 4, 1897

Vice President
Thomas Andrews Hendricks (1885)
Adlai Ewing Stevenson (1893–97)

Cabinet

Secretary of State
Frederick T. Frelinghuysen (1881–85)
Thomas F. Bayard Sr. (1885–89)
Walter Q. Gresham (1893–95)
Richard Olney (1895–97)

Secretary of the Treasury
Hugh McCulloch (1884–85)
Daniel Manning (1885–87)
Charles S. Fairchild (1887–89)
Charles Foster (1891–93)
John G. Carlisle (1893–97)

Secretary of War
Robert T. Lincoln (1881–85)
William C. Endicott (1885–89)
Stephen B. Elkins (1891–93)
Daniel S. Lamont (1893–97)

Attorney General
Benjamin H. Brewster (1882–85)

Augustus H. Garland (1885–89)
William H. H. Miller (1889–93)
Richard Olney (1893–95)
Judson Harmon (1895–97)

Secretary of the Navy
William E. Chandler (1882–85)
William C. Whitney (1885–89)
Benjamin F. Tracy (1889–93)
Hilary A. Herbert (1893–97)

Postmaster General
Frank Hatton (1884–85)
William F. Vilas (1885–88)
Donald M. Dickinson (1888–89)
John Wanamaker (1889–93)
Wilson S. Bissel (1893–95)
William L. Wilson (1895–97)

Secretary of the Interior
Lucius Q. C. Lamar (1885–88)
William F. Vilas (1888–89)
John W. Noble (1889–93)
Hoke Smith (1893–96)
David R. Francis (1896–97)

Secretary of Agriculture
Norman J. Colman (1889)
Jeremiah M. Rusk (1889–93)
Julius Sterling Morton (1893–97)

---

goods to protect manufacturing interests and jobs), while Cleveland promised to lower tariffs for the sake of consumers. The Republicans also promised generous pensions to Union veterans of the American Civil War (1861–65). Cleveland made no promises on this issue. Republicans raised a lot of money in the business community, which feared Cleveland's anti-tariff policies. With Tammany Hall undermining his campaign, Cleveland even failed to carry his home state of New York. Harrison carried the large states and won the election by an electoral college vote of 233 to 168.

The Campaign of 1892

Cleveland sought the presidential nomination again in 1892. Throughout the Benjamin Harrison presidency, Cleveland had maintained his relationships with the conservative Democratic leadership of the eastern seaboard.

He felt that his stance on tariff reduction and his reform mindedness would help him regain the presidency. This election did revolve around campaign issues which had begun to reflect the serious economic problems that would characterize the 1890s.

Harrison presided over what came to be known as the Billion Dollar Congress. He was able to carry out the Republican Party platform (Republicans controlled both houses of Congress) and lower tariffs. He also authorized veterans' pensions and many "pork barrel" projects, which are government projects awarded to a political supporter's home state. The surplus of federal funds was wiped out, and the Republicans lost control of the House of Representatives in the 1890 congressional elections. Consumers held the Republicans responsible for the sharp increase in the cost of living, and farmers blamed the Republicans for failing to raise agricultural prices.

Cleveland promised that his conservative agenda would bring back prosperity.

Neither party addressed well the concerns of farmers who were already in the midst of a depression. Farmers formed an alliance in the form of a third political party, the Populist (or People's) Party. The Populist Party grew out of the Farmers' Alliance movements of the 1880s and 1890s. These grassroots movements were composed of farmers in the West and the South who were suffering a sustained drop in farm commodity prices. The farmers advocated for the coinage of silver, which would put more money in circulation to buy farm products. This would be inflationary (causing a rise in prices) and would allow farmers to repay their debts with cheaper money.

In 1892 the Populist Party nominated James B. Weaver of Iowa for president. Weaver got over a million votes and won 22 electoral votes (all from western states). So the Populist Party made its presence known with 8 percent of the popular votes. But the Democrats' Grover Cleveland won with approximately 43 percent (277 electoral votes), followed by Harrison with approximately 46 percent (145 electoral votes).

Cleveland's Advisers

Grover Cleveland had no kitchen cabinet or informal circle of advisers. He depended on his formally constituted cabinet for counsel. He listened carefully to each cabinet officer before making a decision on administration policy.

First Term Cabinet

Secretary of State Thomas Bayard was Cleveland's chief foreign policy adviser. He placed great emphasis on peaceful negotiations as the means to avoid confrontations with other nations. Under Bayard the State Department tried to settle disputes over fishing rights in the North Atlantic by Canadian and American fishermen. He negotiated the Bayard-Chamberlain Treaty of February 15, 1888, which allowed U.S. fishers more rights in Canadian waters if Congress removed tariffs on Canadian fish products. Republicans killed the bill in the Senate. However, Bayard was able to work out temporary agreements that actually lasted for a long time. Secretary Bayard also initiated civil service reform in his State Department, whereby merit and not party allegiance would determine one's qualifications for government jobs.

In Daniel Manning, the secretary of the Treasury, Cleveland found a man who opposed silver coinage and the purchase of silver by the U.S. government, deeming it inflationary (See also, Domestic Issues). Perhaps Secretary of War William Endicott's most controversial action was his approval of the proposal to return Confederate flags captured during the American Civil War

(1861–65) to southern states that claimed them. Secretary of the Navy William C. Whitney inaugurated the Naval War College at Newport, Rhode Island. Secretary of the Interior Lucius Lamar stood with President Cleveland in his attempt to save some public land for settlers who wanted to move to the West.

Second Term Cabinet

Cleveland also retained able and dedicated individuals for his cabinet during his second term. The most influential members of this team were Secretary of State Walter Q. Gresham, Secretary of the Treasury John G. Carlisle, Secretary of War Daniel S. Lamont, and Richard Olney who served as attorney general and then secretary of state. These men shared Cleveland's understanding of the world and of the United States's place in it.

Cleveland and his cabinet worked well together, providing mutual support on initiatives and policies. Cleveland supported his first secretary of state Walter Gresham's position on the annexation of Hawaii (See also, Domestic Issues) and his succeeding secretary of state Richard Olney's Olney Corollary to the Monroe Doctrine. Olney expanded on the concept of the Monroe Doctrine, which barred European powers from extending their control into the Western Hemisphere, by justifying the United States's political and economic domination of the Caribbean (See also, Foreign Issues). Secretary of the Treasury Carlisle supported Cleveland's positions on lowered tariffs and silver and helped develop policy in those areas.

Cleveland and Congress

First Term Congresses

In his first administration, Cleveland presided over the Forty-ninth and Fiftieth sessions of Congress. In the Forty-ninth session the Republicans controlled the Senate 42 to 34, while the Democrats had a majority in the House of Representatives of 182 to 141 (with two representatives from third parties). In the Fiftieth session the majorities were more slender. There were 39 Republicans and 37 Democrats in the Senate, and in the House 167 Democrats sat with 152 Republicans along with six third-party representatives.

One of Cleveland's main goals in his relations with Congress was to restore the balance between the executive and the legislative branches. Powerful congressional leaders had tended to dominate policy in years past. Since Andrew Johnson's impeachment trial in 1868 for a Reconstruction policy (policy to reincorporate rebellious southern states after the end of the American Civil War [1861–65]) that differed from that supported by Congress, there was a tendency for Congress to lead and the president to follow. With this in mind Cleveland asked for the repeal of the 1867 Tenure of Office Act. A relic of the Reconstruction Congress's battle with President Andrew Johnson, this law prohibited the president from dismissing federal officeholders without the consent of the Senate. Cleveland gained repeal of this legislation in March 1887. He also successfully fought Republican efforts in the Senate to limit executive appointive powers.

However, he initiated little new policy. He governed in a manner designed to prevent corruption rather than provide leadership for a constructive agenda. He exercised the veto power much more frequently than did any of his predecessors. Whereas Chester A. Arthur, the man Cleveland succeeded, had used the veto 12 times, Cleveland vetoed 414 bills sent to him by the Congress. Congress overrode Cleveland's vetoes only two times. He vetoed many special pension bills for veterans, claiming that the bills were based on farfetched claims (*See also,* Domestic Issues).

Although the Senate was under Republican control and the House under Democratic control, there were some significant pieces of legislation that were enacted. The Interstate Commerce Act of 1887 began federal regulation of railroads (*See also,* Changes in the U.S. Government). Other legislation included the Indian Emancipation, or Dawes Act, which offered land and citizenship to American Indians; the Hatch Act, which established agricultural experiment stations; and the Presidential Succession Act, which determined who would succeed to the presidency in the event neither the president nor the vice president could lead the country. Cleveland signed this bill on January 19, 1886.

Second Term Congresses

In his second administration Cleveland presided over the Fifty-third and Fifty-fourth sessions of Congress. In the Fifty-third session the Democrats controlled both houses, whereas in the Fifty-fourth session the Republicans had control of both houses.

Relations between the president and Congress were not harmonious. Cleveland's call for repeal of the Sherman Silver Purchase Act, which provided for the production of silver coinage, split his own party (*See also,* Domestic Issues). When the Democrats gained control of the Senate in 1894, they passed a watered down version of a tariff reduction bill backed by Cleveland—the Wilson-Gorman Act of 1894. Cleveland assailed the measure, charging that it contained "inconsistencies and crudities which ought not to appear in tariff laws or laws of any kind," but he allowed it to become law (Nevins, p. 587).

In his second administration, President Cleveland used the veto 170 times. His predecessor, Benjamin Harrison, had vetoed acts 44 times, and his successor, William McKinley, 42 times. Congress overrode five Cleveland vetoes.

Cleveland and the Judiciary

First Term Court

Grover Cleveland appointed two justices to the Supreme Court during his first administration. Lucius Q. C. Lamar of Mississippi had been secretary of the interior before becoming a Supreme Court justice in 1888. President Cleveland also named Melville Fuller of Illinois chief justice in 1888.

During Cleveland's administration the Supreme Court proved to be quite conservative. In *Santa Clara County v. Southern Pacific Railroad* (1886) the Court ruled that a corporation was a legal person and was thus protected by the Fourteenth Amendment's Due Process clause, which states that no state may "deprive any person of life, liberty, or property without due process of law." The railroad lawyers thus argued that the regulatory legislation being passed by Populist-influenced state legislatures violated their clients' right not to be deprived of their property without due process.

In *Wabash, St. Louis and Pacific Railroad Company v. Illinois* (1886), the Supreme Court declared that a state may not regulate the portion of interstate commerce that occurs within the boundaries of the state. This decision, considered a victory for the railroads, hampered a state's effort to regulate powerful railroads that sometimes demonstrated little concern for the public's interest (despite the fact that they had benefited significantly from government support), particularly by rate gouging. This caused an uproar among farmers who were dependent on the railroads to transport farm products.

Second Term Court

During his second administration, Cleveland again had the opportunity to make two more Supreme Court appointments, Edward D. White of Louisiana and Rufus W. Peckham of New York. Three significant decisions reflected the Supreme Court's continued conservatism. In *United States v. E.C. Knight* (1895) the Court ruled that the Sherman Antitrust Act applied only to monopolies in interstate commerce, not to monopolies in manufacturing. In 1895 the Court decided that levying of a federal income tax was unconstitutional in *Pollock v. Farmers Loan & Trust Company*. In 1896, in what came to be called the "separate but equal doctrine," the Court in *Plessy v. Ferguson* declared that if facilities are equal, segregation did not constitute discrimination.

Changes in the U.S. Government

Although it had no immediate impact, perhaps the most important change in government during Cleveland's first term was the signing of the Interstate Commerce Act on February 4, 1887. The Interstate Commerce Act created the Interstate Commerce Commission (ICC), the United States's first regulatory commission, which came into existence over the issue of railroads. The commission, consisting of five members appointed by the president and approved by the Senate, was charged with overseeing railroad management to insure "reasonable and just" railroad rates, to guarantee fair competition, and to eliminate discrimination in rates and service. Enforcement depended on the diligence of the commission and the courts. The ICC eventually became a large and active body regulating not only railroads, but also trucking, air transportation, and telecommunications.

The ICC was also important at the time of its passage because it entailed a new vision of what the government was supposed to do. It is interesting that this new regulatory function of government, destined to become such an important aspect of the government's relationship with the economy and with business during the Progressive period, the New Deal years, and the post World War II (1939–45) presidencies of Harry Truman through Lyndon Johnson, was enacted during the first term of the laissez-faire conservative, Grover Cleveland. Eventually the ICC was incorporated into the Department of Transportation, a cabinet-level agency created during the Lyndon B. Johnson presidential administration.

Cleveland also supported the civil service bill, the Pendleton Act of 1883, which was passed during the Chester Arthur administration. He appointed distinguished reformers to the new civil service commission and insisted that merit be the criterion for appointment to government posts.

Recognizing that the nation's farmers were beset with financial problems, Cleveland signed into law an act elevating the Department of Agriculture to cabinet rank in January 1889. The department had reached 488 employees in 1889 and was branching out into many different fields, including inspecting and grading food, the quarantining of foreign animals, and the investigation of adulterated food. Cleveland named Norman J. Colman the first secretary of agriculture.

The Presidential Succession Act, passed in 1886, extended the line of succession to the presidency, after the vice president, to the cabinet heads in the order in which their departments were created. This would endure until the Harry Truman administration when it was changed to pass after the vice president to the Speaker of the House.

On January 4, 1896, Utah was admitted to the union as the 45th state.

Domestic Issues

In 1885 Grover Cleveland became the first Democratic president since James Buchanan left office in 1861, just before the American Civil War (1861–65).

Buchanan's successor, Abraham Lincoln, was a strong leader, but the succeeding presidents were not. Andrew Johnson, Lincoln's successor, was impeached when he failed to endorse Congress's Reconstruction policy (the policy for reincorporating rebellious southern states back into the Union after the end of the American Civil War). The trend toward a strong Congress and a weak executive continued.

Cleveland was elected president based on the reputation he had earned as the reform governor of the state of New York by standing up to the powerful political machines that controlled New York City, Tammany Hall. Supported by the Mugwumps (Republicans who had switched camps due to the corruption that tainted the candidacy of the popular James G. Blaine of Maine), Cleveland entered office with a mandate to clean up the federal government and restore the former prestige to the presidency (*See also,* Cleveland Becomes President).

However, the economy was beset with problems during both of Cleveland's terms causing poverty and discontent amongst farmers and laborers. Seven years before Cleveland's first election, the Great Railroad Strike of 1877 portended a future of labor unrest. Against this backdrop, industrial empires continued to expand and thrive. It was the "Gilded Age" and the "captains of industry" and finance paraded their wealth in castles they had built for themselves in Newport Beach, Rhode Island, and other exclusive neighborhoods. But underlying this scene the "labor question" and poverty amongst farmers loomed.

Perhaps as much as any president in U.S. history, Cleveland believed that the role of government was passive and custodial: it had to maintain the integrity of the currency backed by the gold standard, avoid protectionist tariffs that favored one sector of the economy against another, and in general stay out of the way of economic life.

Cleveland and the Grand Army of the Republic

The Grand Army of the Republic (GAR) was the veterans' organization formed after the American Civil War, which lobbied for veterans' pensions among other activities. Although President Cleveland believed that civil war veterans should be respected, he did not think that pensions should be allocated to every veteran. Thus, he vetoed the Dependent Pension Bill of January 1887, which would have granted a $12 per month pension to any Union veteran who claimed that he was incapable of earning a living by physical labor, even though the incapacity did not result from war service. This bill even extended the pension to the parents or widow of a dead veteran if they claimed they were unable to support themselves by daily labor. Cleveland's veto was angrily denounced by the GAR.

To pacify veterans, Congress passed hundreds of individual pension bills that granted pensions to some soldiers whose claims had been rejected by the Pension Bureau. The Pension Bureau considered each application for a pension and found that in some cases the veteran had suffered no ill effects from Civil War service. Many veterans whose applications for a pension were turned down, requested a pension be given to them directly by Congress. Although Cleveland signed most of these individual pension bills, he vetoed 228 of them, further incurring the wrath of the GAR.

The Cleveland administration continued to be a thorn in the side of the GAR when in June 1887 Secretary of War William Endicott approved a proposal to return captured Confederate battle flags to the South.

Cleveland and the Indian Emancipation or Dawes Act

When Cleveland assumed the presidency about 207,000 American Indians inhabited the United States. In an attempt to assimilate these American Indians, most of whom lived on tribal reservations, President Cleveland supported a bill sponsored by Senator Henry Dawes of Massachusetts. Congress passed the Dawes Act in 1887, which upon tribal agreement gave the president the power to allocate from 40 to 160 acres to an individual living on a reservation. Tribal lands not taken by individuals would be purchased by the federal government with the understanding that the funds would be used to assist and educate Indians. Furthermore, the rights of U.S. citizenship eventually would be extended to Indian landowners. Indian landowners were barred from practicing tribal customs and practices. Essentially the act provided for the dissolution of Indian tribes as legal entities. Reformists and philanthropists felt that this redistribution of land was necessary because private property was the basis for responsible citizenship.

Unfortunately the American Indians were not accustomed to farm life. They were unfamiliar with farming and assigned poor land. Most Indians rejected the offer in favor of retaining their culture. In 1924 Congress granted citizenship to all American Indians, and the 1934 Wheeler Howard Act, passed during the Franklin Roosevelt administration, restored the tribe as the center of Indian life.

Cleveland and Tariff Reform

The Republican Party had gained control of the presidency during the American Civil War. Backed mainly by business leaders and urban laborers who depended on manufacturing for their livelihood, the Republican majority in Congress passed the Morrill Tariff Act of 1861. Since that time tariffs remained very high. Import tariffs generated revenue for the government, but they were mainly a means of creating a protective umbrella to preserve a portion of U.S. business from foreign competition. Lowering the tariff would force U.S. business to compete with foreign companies. Democrats, who tradi-

Fast Fact

On June 28, 1894, President Cleveland signed a bill making the first Monday in September a legal holiday. It was called Labor Day.

(Source: John F. Marszalek. *Grover Cleveland: A Bibliography,* 1988.)

---

tionally represented the farming sector of the economy and the consumer interests of the working classes, generally supported tariff reduction, because the consumer would usually benefit from lower prices.

As the U.S. manufacturing economy was maturing near the end of the nineteenth century, some observers were beginning to worry about the problem of overproduction. It appeared that the domestic market was inadequate to absorb the increased productivity of U.S. manufacturers. The obvious solution to this was foreign trade. But the protective tariffs in place stifled foreign trade. Potential trading partners had erected their own trade barriers.

Cleveland Appeals for Lower Tariffs

Although Cleveland had advocated tariff reductions prior to 1887, in that year he decided to lead the fight for tariff reform by devoting his entire 1887 annual message to that issue. This he did in spite of advice that his reelection in 1888 would be jeopardized by his refusal to delay the battle for tariff reform. Replied Cleveland, "What is the use of being elected or reelected unless you stand for something?"

In his address to the Congress, the president argued that high tariffs were a form of taxation that was the most onerous for low-paid workers and struggling farmers. He bluntly described U.S. tariff laws as "vicious, inequitable, and an illogical source of unnecessary taxation." The House of Representatives responded by passing a bill introduced by Congressman Roger Mills of Texas reducing tariffs an average of 7 percent. However, the Republican-dominated Senate pigeonholed the Mills Bill and stalled the reductions that Cleveland sought.

After Cleveland lost his 1888 bid for reelection, he reflected on his 1887 message to the Congress calling for tariff reform. Said Cleveland, "My friends all advised me not to send it in. They told me that it would hurt the party; that without it, I was sure to be reelected, but that if I sent it that message to Congress, it would in all probability defeat me; that I could wait until after the election and then raise the question." Cleveland, however, demurred because he felt the people should know where he stood before the election. It would not be fair to the country to do otherwise. Concluded Cleveland, "Perhaps I made a mistake from the party standpoint; but damn it, it was right" (McElroy, p. 300).

The Wilson-Gorman Tariff Act

When Benjamin Harrison took office in 1889, he renewed the Republican commitment to high protective tariffs to benefit the northeast manufacturing. What became known as the McKinley Tariff passed through a political maneuver called logrolling; to get enough votes to pass the tariff measure the eastern Republicans agreed to support a more generous silver coinage law. The 1890 tariff placed the highest tax ever on imports. This happened despite underlying economic uncertainty.

When Cleveland returned to office in 1893 he again pursued a tariff reduction plan in order to stimulate foreign trade. The Wilson-Gorman Act, a tariff reduction bill, was passed more or less intact by the House of Representatives, but the Senate weakened the language and inserted so many exceptions that Cleveland denounced the resulting legislation. But, since he did not think that the support existed in Congress to improve on it, he let it stand and did not veto it. It would not be until the Woodrow Wilson administration that significant legislation to lower tariffs would be passed.

Panic of 1893

Cleveland's popularity would decline during his second term. As a result of the overexpansion of the economy in the previous period, the depression of 1893 was the most severe economic crisis to that point in the nation's history. Millions of U.S. farmers, workers, and small businessmen were thrown out of work. Sixteen thousand businesses failed during the first year of the depression, including 491 banks and 156 railroads. This depression left about 2.5 million unemployed, which meant one out of every six men was idle.

When the railroad workers went on strike against the Pullman Car Company in 1894, President Cleveland called out the federal troops to break the strike, arguing that the government had an obligation to make sure that the mail was delivered. A conservative on economic matters, Cleveland also resisted the temptation to use government policies to revive the economy. Some observers urged "cheaper money" backed by government holdings of silver as well as gold—a position that many farmers, small businessmen, and fellow Democrats believed would stimulate investment and recovery. But Cleveland stood by the gold standard and called for the repeal of the Sherman Silver Purchase Act of 1890.

Coxey's Army

Cleveland's refusal to aid the victims of the economic collapse provoked the largest national protest demonstration to that date in Washington, D.C. Jacob Coxey, a Ohio businessman, was a Populist leader who was very concerned about the plight of the U.S. farmer and currency reform. In January 1894 he announced a plan to petition Congress to raise $500 million to build roads. According to Coxey, the fund could be put to work building roads and repairing public edifices. The government could pay the laborers in "greenback" paper dollars, money not backed by gold, which would put money back in circulation and end the depression. The petition became known as the "petition in boots," because Coxey called for a march to Washington.

The word traveled across the country and poor and homeless began the trek to Washington. In the West, as many as 50 trains were commandeered by Coxey's Army, who rode in the boxcars until the authorities caught up with the trains. Thousands of people were part of Coxey's march, though only a few hundred were present when Coxey tried to speak at the Capitol building on May 1, 1894. The police dispersed the demonstrators. However, after this other small armies were formed in an effort to take their pleas for economic relief to Washington.

Repeal of the Sherman Silver Purchase Act

The U.S. monetary system from the time of the Bland-Allison Act in 1878 had been coining silver at a ratio of 16:1, with gold having 16 times the value of silver. With the deepening depression in the 1890s, silver interests were clamoring for more silver coinage. This was a part of the Populist agenda (*See also*, Cleveland Becomes President). Farmers reasoned that the coinage of silver would increase the amount of money in circulation and cheapen the money, allowing more farm products to be purchased. They further reasoned, as did other debtors, that loans and mortgages could be paid off with cheaper currency. President Benjamin Harrison backed the silver interests and endorsed the passage of the Sherman Silver Purchase Act of 1890, whereby the Treasury would purchase 4.5 million ounces of silver monthly to be coined into money.

President Cleveland believed that the Sherman Silver Purchase Act was a contributing factor to the panic of 1893. He argued that the silver act had helped drain the federal Treasury of gold, by requiring the Treasury to purchase such a large amount of silver each month. He called Congress into special session requesting repeal of that measure.

Congress convened on August 7 to consider the president's request. After spirited debate, the House of Representatives repealed the Sherman Silver Purchase Act on August 28 by a vote of 239 to 108. By a count of 48 to 37 the Senate voted to do the same thing on October 30. Although Cleveland considered this a victory, it was costly in that it left the Democratic Party divided. Many rank and file Democrats believed that freeing up the currency market would stimulate the economy and make it easier for debtors to avoid bankruptcy, a common enough occurrence during the depression of 1893.

Pullman Strike of 1894

The Pullman Palace Car Company, which manufactured railroad sleeping cars, was owned by George Pullman who also owned the town in which the workers lived. Workers paid rent for their homes to the company. During the panic of 1893, the Pullman Palace Car Company, while continuing to pay 8 percent dividends to shareholders, reduced the wages of its employees by an average of 25 percent without lowering the rents of the workers in the company-owned housing. On May 11, 1894, almost 2,500 employees began a strike forcing the closure of the shops. This local strike expanded into a much more disruptive transportation strike when members of the American Railway Union led by Socialist Eugene V. Debs refused to handle Pullman cars. Soon railroads throughout the country were tied up.

When a federal court injunction prohibiting the strike as a hindrance to interstate commerce was ignored and violence ensued, Attorney General Richard Olney urged President Cleveland to dispatch federal troops to ensure the movement of the U.S. mail. President Cleveland ordered troops to be sent in despite protests by Illinois governor, John Peter Altgeld, who felt that the state could meet the challenge. Cleveland's actions effectively broke the strike.

Foreign Issues

Beginning with the Monroe Doctrine (advanced by President James Monroe in 1823), the U.S. foreign policy posture had generally been one of not becoming involved in the political affairs of nations outside the Western Hemisphere. The Monroe Doctrine clearly warned Europe that the United States would protect the smaller republics of Central and South America from interference by the European powers. Over time the United States itself occasionally intervened in the affairs of these smaller republics. With regard to the rest of the world, however, until the last decade of the nineteenth century U.S. foreign policy did not contemplate getting involved in building an empire as Great Britain had done. Beginning in the 1890s, there was an increasingly vocal tendency within the foreign policy establishment, as well as from diverse sectors of U.S. society, to advocate that the United States set about acquiring its own empire. To many of these supporters, an U.S. empire might offer a solution to the problems of overproduction. In acquiring an empire, the United States would be gaining employment for its unemployed, a market for its unsold goods, and a new "frontier" for the western frontier that the U.S.

Census Bureau in 1890 announced no longer existed. There were many who opposed this drive for empire, however, and they called themselves "anti-imperialists." Grover Cleveland was among that number.

Cleveland Withdraws the Hawaiian Annexation Treaty

During the administration of President Benjamin Harrison, U.S. sugar interests in Hawaii fomented a revolution against the national government headed by Queen Liliuokalani. John L. Stevens, the U.S. minister in Hawaii, encouraged the rebellion and at the appropriate time arranged for the landing of 150 soldiers from the USS *Boston*.

When the Hawaiian queen saw the troops, and Stevens almost immediately acknowledged the insurrectionist government as legitimate, she surrendered her authority under protest. Strongly favoring annexation by the United States, Stevens stated, "The Hawaiian pear is now fully ripe, and this is the golden hour for the United States to pluck it" (Bailey, p. 430). Less than a month before Cleveland was to assume office, a treaty of annexation was presented to the Senate.

Five days after he assumed the presidency, Cleveland withdrew the treaty. After careful investigation, Cleveland believed that Queen Liliuokalani had been wronged and that she should be restored. Cleveland did not want the United States to act immorally. Because of opposition at home and in Hawaii by the white insurrectionists, however, he was unable to undo the revolution. The best he could do was delay annexation. Eventually, President William McKinley signed a treaty of annexation in July 1898, which made Hawaii part of the United States.

The Venezuelan Crisis

For many years Great Britain and Venezuela had disputed the boundary line between Venezuela and British Guiana. During Grover Cleveland's second administration the controversy became more heated when Britain refused to allow the United States to arbitrate the disputed border and then occupied the Nicaraguan port of Corinto.

As a result of what was perceived a violation of the Monroe Doctrine, Secretary of State Richard Olney issued what came to be called the Olney Corollary to the Monroe Doctrine. The Monroe Doctrine had warned European powers not to attempt to extend their powers into the Western Hemisphere. The Olney Corollary took this a step further, allowing the United States to intervene in South American affairs if there is a perceived threat to the United States. By insisting that the United States be allowed to arbitrate Olney declared, "Today the United States is practically sovereign on this continent, and its fiat is law upon the subjects to which it confines

Workers of the Pullman Palace Car Company went on strike in 1894. President Cleveland supported the owners and dispatched federal troops to intercede. Railway officials are shown removing spikes placed in the tracks by the strikers. (Archive Photos. Reproduced by permission.)

its interposition." When British Foreign Secretary Lord Salisbury finally responded, he said that this matter had nothing to do with the Monroe Doctrine.

Somewhat uncharacteristically, Cleveland belligerently urged Congress to establish a committee to investigate the dispute. Cleveland implied that after an investigation, the United States would determine the boundary line with or without British consent and would fight to maintain it. Britain, also facing challenges in Europe, wanted peace with the United States. In time Britain cooperated by providing the Americans with relevant data. In February 1897 Britain and Venezuela signed an agreement establishing an arbitration board, which in October 1899 handed down its decision. By that time Anglo-American relations had improved considerably as they would continue to do as the new century dawned.

The Cleveland Administration Legacy

The United States remained in the grips of depression when Cleveland's second term came to a close. In fact, his own party, the Democratic Party, nominated William Jennings Bryan of Nebraska for president in

1896. Bryan, also the candidate of the Populist Party that year, advocated free and unlimited coinage of silver, which to a gold Democrat like Cleveland was anathema. Although Bryan campaigned vigorously, the U.S. people elected Republican Party candidate William McKinley as their president. Grover Cleveland returned to private life where he continued to take interest in U.S. politics although never running for public office again.

Partially because of the panic of 1893 Cleveland's presidency was one of frustration. Cleveland was rejected because of his determination to do what he thought was right even though it may have been unpopular. During both administrations he insisted that tariffs be lowered, but once again, the influence of industrial manufacturing on the government prevented this outcome. His stubborn attachment to the issue was an illustration of his moral consistency. It also showed how out of touch he was. The country was on the brink of the Progressive era in which the government would become much more involved in the economy. Cleveland belonged to an earlier era of government noninterference in the economy.

When the panic of 1893 beset the country, Cleveland became convinced that the Sherman Silver Purchase Act had weakened the monetary standards of the country. He called for the repeal of the act, even though he realized that this would divide his own party. In fact, he misdiagnosed the problem, which had to do instead with a crisis in overproduction associated with an industrializing economy. A later Democrat, Franklin D. Roosevelt, was to fight an even more serious depression with actions that Cleveland would not have accepted. Work programs, legislation to aid different segments of U.S. society, and deficit spending may have worked better than repeal of the silver act, but Cleveland's conscience would not allow that. In retrospect one must applaud Cleveland's integrity while at the same time question whether other policies might have been more effective in combating the panic of 1893.

Lasting Impact

Biographer Allan Nevins wrote that the Cleveland administration did not represent a change in politics so much as a change in spirit. Americans expected Cleveland to demonstrate "a greater honesty and earnestness than his predecessors." Grover Cleveland was able to deliver on that promise because he possessed in abundance the moral qualities of honesty and steadfastness. In that sense he brought to an end the "age of excess" that characterized post-Reconstruction era politics. Although his solutions to the problems that he encountered were traditional, conservative, and not very effective, he did succeed in restoring the prestige and the power of the presidency.

One poll of historians ranked him among the "near great" presidents, just below Lincoln, Washington, Wilson, Jefferson, Jackson, and the two Roosevelts. In more recent polls, however, his standing has steadily declined (Murray and Blessing, p. 15). Cleveland's personal strengths were those that resonated with the celebrated values of the nineteenth-century Protestant middle class from which he sprang—discipline, square dealing, personal autonomy, attention to duty, and diligent hard work. These traits shaped his leadership and limited it. He was not very agile, enterprising, or elastic on the job. The transforming twentieth-century expansion in the powers of the presidency and in the responsibility of the federal government to provide public remedies for social distress, make Cleveland's performance seem in retrospect to have been too often negative and narrow. In his own day, and on his own terms, he functioned consistently as a national sheriff of public law and order.

Sources

Bailey, Thomas A. *A Diplomatic History of the American People*. New York: Appleton-Century-Crofts, 1969.

Boller, Paul F., Jr. *Presidential Wives: An Anecdotal History*. New York: Oxford, 1988.

Bolt, Robert. *Donald Dickinson*. Grand Rapids. Mich.: Wm. B. Eerdmans Publishing Co., 1970.

Encyclopedia of World Biography. Vol. 4. Detroit: Gale Research, 1998.

Marszalek, John F. *Grover Cleveland: A Bibliography*. Westport, Conn.: Meckler Corporation, 1988.

McElroy, Robert. *Grover Cleveland: The Man and the Statesman*. New York: Harper and Brothers, 1923.

Merrill, Horace S. *Bourbon Leader: Grover Cleveland and the Democratic Party*. Boston: Little, Brown, 1957.

Morison, Samuel E. *The Oxford History of the American People*. New York: Dodd, Mead, 1965.

Murray, Robert K., and Tim H. Blessing. *Greatness in the White House*. 2d ed. University Park, Penn.: Pennsylvania State University Press, 1994.

Nevins, Allan. *Grover Cleveland: A Study in Courage*. New York: Dodd Mead, 1932.

Tugwell, Rexford G. *Grover Cleveland*. New York: Macmillan, 1968.

Welch, Richard E., Jr. *The Presidencies of Grover Cleveland*. Lawrence, Kans.: University Press of Kansas, 1988.

Further Readings

Blodgett, Geoffrey. *Gentle Reformers: Massachusetts Democrats in the Cleveland Era*. Cambridge, Mass.: Harvard University Press, 1966.

Garraty, John A. *The New Commonwealth, 1877–1900*. New York: Harper and Row, 1968.

Lindsay, Almont. *The Pullman Strike*. Chicago: University of Chicago Press, 1942.

Nevins, Allan, ed. *Letters of Grover Cleveland*. Boston: Houghton Mifflin, 1933.

Wiebe, Robert H. *The Search for Order, 1877–1920*. New York: Hill and Wang, 1967.

Benjamin Harrison Administration

Full name: Benjamin Harrison
Popular name: Little Ben

Personal Information:

Born: August 20, 1833
Birthplace: North Bend, Ohio
Died: March 13, 1901
Death place: Indianapolis, Indiana
Burial place: Crown Hill Cemetery, Indianapolis, Indiana
Religion: Presbyterian
Spouse: Caroline Lavinia Scott (m. 1853); Mary Scott Lord
  Dimmick (m. 1896)
Children: Russell Benjamin; Mary Scott; Elizabeth
Education: Miami University, Ohio, B.A., 1852
Occupation: Lawyer; politician
Political Party: Republican Party
Age at Inauguration: 55 years

Biography

Heir to a family political legacy that included a signer of the Declaration of Independence and a former president, Benjamin Harrison was a career politician. Although pleasant in social circumstances, in politics Harrison was often cold, aloof, and at times uncommunicative. He made decisions on his own and had very few close friends. While at times this made for a difficult relationship with his colleagues, Harrison appealed to the electorate because of his powerful oratory, pious attitude, and his calls to remember the cause and sacrifices of the Civil War (1861–65) in which he and many other Americans had served. Elected president in 1888, Harrison had a difficult and unproductive relationship with Congress, which led him to concentrate on a foreign policy that was unusually aggressive for his era.

Early Life

Benjamin Harrison was the grandson of William Henry Harrison, ninth president of the United States; the great-grandson and namesake of Benjamin Harrison, who signed the Declaration of Independence; and the son of U.S. Congressman John Scott Harrison and his second wife, Elizabeth Ramsey Irwin Harrison. It was this distinguished parentage that would ultimately draw him into politics. He was the fifth of his father's children; second of 10 children of his father's second marriage. Born and raised on his grandfather's farm in North Bend, Ohio, he spent his youth in a rustic setting, attended a log cabin school, and was tutored at home with some of his brothers and sisters.

Education

At 14 Harrison entered Carey's Academy in Cincinnati, Ohio, and three years later enrolled as a junior at Miami University in Oxford, Ohio. He became intrigued by the challenges of a career in the legal profession, and following graduation in June 1852 he read law at a firm in Cincinnati. He was admitted to the Ohio bar in 1854. Harrison and his wife, Caroline Harrison, moved to Indianapolis, Indiana, in 1855 where he formed a law partnership with William Wallace, son of former Indiana governor David Wallace and brother of novelist-soldier-politician Lew Wallace.

Family Life

Harrison had met his future wife while a student at Miami University, where her father, the Reverend John W. Scott, was a faculty member. After a two-year courtship during which Harrison agonized over whether he was ready for matrimony, Harrison wed Caroline Lavinia Scott in 1853. Their first child, Russell Benjamin Harrison (1854–1936), was born the next year and a daughter, Mary Scott ("Mamie") Harrison (1858–1930), was born four years later. The family's daily activities were governed by three things: religion, politics, and the law. Harrison was a deacon and elder in the Presbyterian Church that the family attended in Indianapolis. Before studying law he had briefly considered a ministerial calling. He believed that the church was responsible for the moral character of its members and he organized his life accordingly.

Because Caroline Harrison suffered from tuberculosis, her widowed niece, Mary Scott Lord Dimmick, joined the family in Washington, D.C., to help with the duties of White House hostess. Caroline Harrison died during her husband's last year in office, and to the consternation of his children he married the niece in 1896. The next year his third child, Elizabeth Harrison (1897–1955), was born.

Career

Harrison served as Indianapolis city attorney from 1856 to 1861 and became active in Republican Party affairs, ultimately as secretary of the Indiana Republican State Committee. Capitalizing on his family name and his good record as a public servant, he was elected Supreme Court reporter for Indiana in 1860.

Harrison had been excited by Abraham Lincoln's visit to Indianapolis in 1861 and shared Lincoln's anti-slavery views. He joined the army in July 1862, and helped raise the 70th Regiment of Indiana Volunteers to fight. Appointed its colonel, he spent the majority of his

Benjamin Harrison. (The Library of Congress.)

time commanding troops guarding the Louisville and Nashville Railroad. Later, his unit served in the offensive in Georgia under William Tecumseh Sherman. Harrison was cited for gallantry following the battles of Resaca (May 14) and Peach Tree Creek (July 20) in 1864. He was made brigadier general on February 23, 1865, shortly before the end of the war. As was often the case with men interested in public office, Harrison was furloughed home after the fall of Atlanta in September 1864 to run for political office.

After being discharged on June 8 of that year Harrison joined the firm of Porter, Harrison, and Fishback in Indianapolis and immersed himself in politics and law. He left office as Indiana's Supreme Court reporter in 1869 and won local renown as both a public prosecutor and defense attorney. His attempt to become the state's governor failed in 1876, but he reemerged as a Republican Party leader. President Rutherford B. Hayes appointed Harrison as one of three civilian members on the Mississippi River Commission in 1879, where he made regional political contacts and gained national visibility. Led by the Corps of Engineers, the commission recommended means to improve navigation and promote flood control along the waterway.

After helping James A. Garfield win the presidential nomination in 1880, Harrison was considered for a cabinet position but chose to run for the U.S. Senate instead. He was elected by the Indiana legislature in 1881. (Popular election of U.S. senators did not come about until 1913 when the Seventeenth Amendment was passed.) As a senator he championed issues he would later advocate as a candidate for the presidency, including the protective tariff, the merit system of civil service, natural resource conservation, national funding of education, and civil rights laws. His reelection bid failed in 1887.

President

With the support of Republican leader and former presidential candidate James G. Blaine, Harrison received the 1888 presidential nomination of the Republican Party. Levi P. Morton, the Wall Street tycoon, was chosen as his running mate. Harrison ran a "front porch" campaign, remaining at home in Indianapolis while delegations from across the nation came to hear him speak. Harrison concentrated on the benefits of a protective tariff, and the shortcomings of the incumbent, Grover Cleveland. Although the Harrison-Morton ticket lost the popular vote to Cleveland and Allen G. Thurman (5,540,050 to 5,444,337), they won the more populous northern states and therefore defeated Cleveland in the Electoral College, 233 to 168.

Harrison was 55 years old when he became president. His four years in office were a time of dissatisfaction. While he could inspire crowds with his speeches, his relationships with individuals were poor. Additionally, his idealism regarding patronage—he favored appointing qualified candidates not necessarily the most important party workers—did not square with the needs of those who helped elect him. These factors led to a poor relationship with Congress. While Harrison did see some legislation he supported pass Congress, including higher tariffs and pensions for Civil War veterans, others suffered from his lack of congressional support. Harrison did preside over a notably active period in U.S. foreign affairs, as he strengthened the navy and aggressively pursued U.S. interests abroad. Harrison ran for reelection in 1892 against Democrat and former president Grover Cleveland. Attacked for his high tariff policies and the high expenditures of the federal government, Harrison failed to win reelection, and left office in 1893.

Post-presidential Years

Following defeat Harrison returned to Indianapolis to resume legal practice. Over the next several years he worked on many prominent cases, including a dispute between British Guiyana and Venezuela. During this time Harrison also published *This Country of Ours* (Scribners, 1898). In 1901 Harrison caught a cold that turned into pneumonia. He succumbed to complications on March 13, at the age of 68. After his death his wife published lectures he had given at Stanford University in 1894 as *Views of an Ex-President.*

The Benjamin Harrison Administration

The presidency of Benjamin Harrison was a time of shifting priorities in U.S. politics. Harrison's aggressive pursuit of U.S. interests abroad helped to establish the United States as a major power in world politics, after a century of self-imposed non-involvement. On the domestic front, the Harrison administration saw changes in how the government dealt with public lands, and the beginnings of a new policy towards business. Harrison had a poor relationship with Congress, however, due to his unwillingness to reward powerful Republicans with government jobs, and his sometimes difficult personality. This contributed to the defeat in Congress of some of his most ambitious programs, such as federal protection of African American voting rights in the South.

Harrison Becomes President

The Campaign of 1888

Harrison was a dark horse candidate for president (i.e., he was not expected to be the party nominee prior to the convention). According to a quotation in one of his biographies, "The Presidency overtook and surprised Harrison while he was going away from it rather than toward it" (Socolofsky and Spetter, p. 7). Although somewhat exaggerated the quote does reflect his minimal preparations for winning the nomination at the Republican Convention in Chicago in June 1888. Of course he was not without supporters, primarily Louis T. Michener, his closest political associate, and Philadelphia banker Wharton Barker. The Republicans found themselves without an established candidate, however, after James G. Blaine, who had run for president in 1884, declined to seek the presidential nomination. Harrison was selected on the eighth ballot on the basis of his support for a protective tariff, and his successful service during the Civil War (1861–65). New York City banker Levi P. Morton was selected as Harrison's running mate.

Harrison was running against President Grover Cleveland, who the Democrats easily nominated for a second term. Cleveland and the Democrats had already supplied Harrison with his major campaign issue. In 1887 Cleveland and his party endorsed a reduction of the protective tariff (a tax on imported goods intended to protect local manufacturing interests) with the enactment of the Mills Bill of 1888. Republicans in Congress successfully blocked the Mills Bill, but used this attempt by Cleveland to reduce the tariff to gain votes with laborers and business in the industrialized northeast, which supported protective tariffs. Harrison also wanted to emphasize protection of African American voting rights in the campaign. These rights were routinely denied African Americans throughout the South, despite the Fourteenth and Fifteenth Amendments. At the urging of his campaign managers, however, Harrison concentrated his efforts on the tariff issue.

Most historians believe that the tariff issue and the effectiveness of the "front porch" campaign determined the election's outcome. Republicans, endorsed by industrial capital, outspent Democrats, who were favored by investor and banking capital. Republicans used their funds to bring people to Harrison's home to meet with him, to flood the nation with pamphlets and circulars supporting the party ticket, to finance speakers and rallies across the country, and provide walking-around-money for their local agents. Harrison also "waved the bloody shirt," by invoking the memories and patriotism of Civil War veterans to encourage them to vote for him.

Despite the success of Harrison's tactics, Cleveland won a slight plurality of about 100,000 popular votes in the November elections. Harrison, however, won the strategic states of New York and Indiana (51 electoral votes), making them the only two states that changed their vote from the 1884 election in which Cleveland became president. With population growth elsewhere giving the Republicans a few more votes in the electoral college, Harrison won the presidency with 233 electoral college votes to Cleveland's 168.

The Campaign of 1892

Harrison had become unpopular with party leaders during his term due to his cold personality and his unwillingness to take their advice. Furthermore he did not reward his colleagues and supporters with government jobs. However, there were no other strong candidates in the Republican Party. Harrison was nominated for a second term on the first ballot of the June 1892 convention. A new candidate for vice president was chosen, Whitelaw Reid of New York. At their convention, the Democrats once again nominated Grover Cleveland as their candidate, making this the first election in history where both major candidates had experience as president. Adlai E. Stevenson was the Democratic vice presidential candidate.

Harrison's wife was seriously ill throughout the campaign and died two weeks before the election. Thus, Harrison did little to promote himself to the people and, out of respect for the Harrisons, Cleveland also refrained from personally campaigning. The Democratic Party, nevertheless, was unrestrained in its criticism of the McKinley Tariff of 1890 (*See Also,* Domestic Issues). The new Republican-sponsored tariffs had led to major increases in the price of consumer goods, angering many in the lower and middle classes. The strike at the Carnegie Steel Company in Homestead, Pennsylvania, was also damaging to Harrison. Despite the fact that the company's profits were increasing because of tariff protections, Carnegie Steel ordered a pay cut. When unionized workers protested, they were locked out of their jobs. Violence ensued, and the

Administration

Administration Dates
March 4, 1889–March 4, 1893

Vice President
Levi Parsons Morton (1889–93)

Cabinet
Secretary of State
Thomas F. Bayard Sr. (1885–89)
James G. Blaine (1889–92)
John W. Foster (1892–93)

Secretary of the Treasury
Charles S. Fairchild (1887–89)
William Windom (1889–91)
Charles Foster (1891–93)

Secretary of War
William C. Endicott (1885–89)
Redfield Proctor (1889–91)
Stephen B. Elkins (1891–93)

Attorney General
Augustus H. Garland (1885–89)
William H. H. Miller (1889–93)

Secretary of the Navy
William C. Whitney (1885–89)
Benjamin F. Tracy (1889–93)

Postmaster General
Donald M. Dickinson (1888–89)
John Wanamaker (1889–93)

Secretary of the Interior
William Freeman Vilas (1888–89)
John W. Noble (1889–93)

Secretary of Agriculture
Norman J. Colman (1889)
Jeremiah M. Rusk (1889–93)

national guard was eventually called in to guard the steel mills and restore order. Democrats cited the events in Homestead as further proof that the Republicans, who continued to support protective tariffs, were on the side of big business.

In the November elections, Grover Cleveland and the Democrats scored an impressive victory. Cleveland was elected president with 46 percent of the popular vote and 277 electoral college votes, to Harrison's 43 percent of the popular vote and 145 electoral votes. The Populist Party, running James Weaver as their first ever presidential candidate, had a surprisingly strong showing. Their platform of government and fiscal reform, centering on free silver, gathered an impressive 8.5 percent of the popular vote, and won the states of Colorado, Idaho, Kansas, Nebraska, and two other electoral college votes for a total of 22.

Harrison's Advisers

As president, Harrison did what he had done for most of his life, he depended primarily on his own counsel when making decisions. He consulted cabinet heads on actions affecting their departments, but he never relied heavily on their advice nor did he rely on recommendations from informal advisers. In deferring to party politics, Harrison named the powerful Blaine as secretary of state, but chose persons much like himself for other cabinet positions, even though powerful Republicans opposed them. Harrison's unwillingness to appoint men to office that other powerful Republicans favored made him many enemies in his own party.

Harrison appointed his best friend, William Henry Harrison Miller attorney general, but even though Harrison was at ease with Miller, his old companion did not exert any special influence on the president. The same could be said of a trusted college classmate in Congress, Representative John Anderson of Kansas, who dined with the Harrisons weekly. In most respects Harrison remained what he was essentially throughout his life, a loner.

Harrison and Congress

Harrison's endorsement of the GOP (Grand Old Party) platform of 1888 and his cooperation on most issues with the Republican controlled Fifty-first Congress (1889–91) produced the major legislation of his administration. Losses in the election of 1890 gave Democrats a majority in the House of Representatives and halted the Republican's legislative agenda during the Fifty-second Congress (1891–93).

Although Harrison believed that a president should not initiate a domestic program, he pushed for the passage of legislation he supported. He used receptions and dinner parties to influence members of Congress and at times threatened to veto legislation to get changes made. Sometimes he had cabinet members serve as emissaries to Congress to get bills amended. For their part, Demo-crats used delaying tactics, such as the silent or disappearing quorum, to block action before they gained control of the House in 1891. For a silent quorum the Democrats would ask for a quorum call and then not answer to their names. Speaker of the House Thomas B. Reed, going against tradition, checked them by having members in attendance, who refused to answer the roll call, marked present and counted to make a quorum. For his effort he earned the nickname "Czar Reed."

Because of the president's view that Congress should legislate the party program, many of the important bills considered by the Fifty-first Congress bore the names of powerful senators and congress people who initiated them. While not all bills passed, they included: the McKinley Tariff, the Sherman Antitrust Act, the Sherman Silver Purchase Act, the Morrill Pension Act, and the Lodge Force Bill.

Harrison and the Judiciary

Harrison appointed four people to the Supreme Court during his presidency. They were justices David J. Brewer, Henry Billings Brown, Howell E. Jackson, and George Shiras Jr. Jackson, who was confirmed on the last day of Harrison's presidency, March 3, 1893, was a Democrat from Tennessee. He was selected because of that party's victory in 1892 and because he was a personal friend of Harrison and the incoming president, Grover Cleveland. The others, of course, were loyal Republicans. Although the foursome did not always agree on matters, they normally adhered to the Court's states' rights, laissez-faire, or free enterprise, philosophy. These views dominated several landmark cases they later helped decide.

One other judicial event of note that took place during Harrison's administration resulted from Harrison's desire to help the Supreme Court reduce its backlog of cases. The Judiciary Act of 1789 had established circuit courts which performed both trial and appellate functions. Over the years their appellate activity fell into disuse and despite an effort to update the system in 1869 by creating circuit judgeships, the Supreme Court still handled the bulk of this duty. Congress passed the Evarts Act (Judiciary Act of 1891) to remedy the matter by handing all appellate work to the newly created United States Circuit Courts of Appeals. Henceforth these courts would determine which cases went on appeal from lower federal courts to the Supreme Court.

Changes in the U.S. Government

Under Harrison six states were admitted into the Union in 1889 and 1890. Harrison favored statehood for all six states, although he was active on behalf of only

Biography:

Queen Liliuokalani

Queen; Musician; Composer (1838–1917) Queen Liliuokalani was the last of the traditional Hawaiian rulers before the islands were annexed by the United States. Her efforts to reverse the tide of U.S. intrusion and restore native Hawaiian self-determination were dignified but futile. Liliuokalani was born Lydia Kamakaeha to two native Hawaiian high chiefs at a time when Western influences were becoming a strong presence. In addition to religion, Christian missionaries brought Western-style education, government, laws, and economic growth with the establishment of sugar cane plantations. Because of this, there were drastic social and political changes happening during the years that Liliuokalani was growing up. Schooled by the missionaries, she was one of the first generations to learn formal spoken and written English. She excelled in school and was a talented poet and musician. Liliuokalani composed two of her country's best known songs: "He Mele Lahui Hawaii," the island's national anthem, and "Aloha Oe" ("Farewell to Thee"), the first

Hawaiian song to enjoy widespread popularity outside of the islands. Otherwise strong and determined, Queen Liliuokalani's downfall was her misplaced faith in President Grover Cleveland and his power to restore her to power. On the basis of President Cleveland's non-committal responses to her pleas, Liliuokalani waited several years, all of the while urging patience and calm amongst her people and encouraging faith in the United States. As time passed, the islands became strategically important, and independence was no longer an option. A beloved heroine of her people, Liliuokalani spent the last years of her life out of the public eye composing songs and preserving examples of native Hawaiian music.

North Dakota, South Dakota, Washington, and Montana. Wyoming and Idaho secured their entry into the Union through constitutional conventions. Harrison also issued the proclamation that opened the land rush (or "Harrison's Horse Race") into the unassigned lands of modern-day western Oklahoma in 1889, although that state's entry into the Union would not occur for nearly another 20 years.

Domestic Issues

By the time Harrison became president during the so-called "Gilded Age" of U.S. history, the United States had assumed world leadership in industrial production. The term, which historians took from Mark Twain and Charles Dudley Warner's 1874 novel, *The Gilded Age,* implies that although the times seemed attractive the appearance was deceptive, merely a gild. Despite the criticism implicit in the term "Gilded Age," a great deal of the infrastructure of modern, corporate industrialism was laid during these years. Not only was the United States now the world's leading producer of goods creating the wealthiest society in history, many cultural and social improvements were being made and the intellectual groundwork for twentieth-century progress in the country was being laid. This was the era in which national labor unions arose, when groups agitating for women's

rights and suffrage coalesced, when numerous professional associations were created, and when the nation's major cities were built.

The McKinley Tariff

The McKinley Tariff was passed in 1890 to fulfill the Republican Party's main commitment in the campaign of 1888: a strong protective tariff. Reacting to the growing political power of industry within the U.S. economy, Republicans wished to sustain industrial expansion and economic development. The law was designed to protect U.S. markets from the influx of foreign goods, benefiting both industry and labor. Laborers' wages would not be depressed by the importation of commodities produced by cheaper foreign labor. The act was also designed to protect and foster what were once regarded as "infant industries," but which by this time were no longer small. These included industrial giants such as Carnegie Steel, Standard Oil, and the American Sugar Refining Company. Overall the McKinley Tariff created the highest tax on imports ever levied in U.S. history.

As had been the case historically, the tariff divided late nineteenth century political parties. In general Democrats opposed it, while Republicans supported the measure. Still, a compromise had been necessary to secure its passage. Western Republicans, reflecting agricultural interests, were generally in favor of lower tariffs or trade reciprocity. To secure their votes for the McKin-

Fast Fact

In the nineteenth century many politicians sought votes by appealing to strong anti-British feelings among Irish immigrants. During the presidential campaign of 1888, an enterprising Republican named Charles Osgoodby sent a letter to the British minister in Washington. In this letter, Osgoodby posed as an American of British descent named Murchison, who was seeking advice on whether voting for Cleveland or Harrison would most benefit England. Just as Osgoodby had hoped, the British minister responded that President Cleveland would be the best choice. When the "Murchison Letter" was made public, it created national headlines. President Grover Cleveland denied that he was pro-British, and dismissed the British minister, but the letter still helped Harrison win the anti-British vote.

(Source: Paul F. Boller, Jr. *Presidential Campaigns,* 1996.)

ley bill, eastern Republicans had to accept in part a more generous silver coinage law.

The Silver Purchase Act

Of all the issues raised in the late nineteenth century, money was the most persistent and cataclysmic. It ultimately spawned a major third party movement in the South and the West, the People's Party of America, or Populism. The struggle was between those who wanted an increased money supply and those who favored a steady supply of currency. Each side believed their ideas were best for the economy and the nation. Farmers, industrialists, and debtors were normally inflationists (wanting prices to rise), while commercial and banking interests, urban labor, and creditors favored stability. Farmers believed more money in the system would mean higher agricultural prices and more income. Likewise, industrialists thought it would increase the amount of money available for loans and lower interest rates. Debtors, including both farmers and industrialists, felt more money cheapened what money was available and made loans easier to repay. On the other hand, urban labor believed that wages would not keep pace with prices and opposed an increase. Bankers and traders also felt that as the value of money fluctuated business activity would be stifled by uncertainty. Creditors, which included bankers

and to some extent merchants, believed the value of their loans would shrink as a debased currency was used to repay them.

Early arguments over the money supply were about greenback dollars, or paper money, in circulation. Greenbacks were a legal tender currency that was not convertible to gold and were originally issued to help fund the American Civil War (1861–65). This paper money was supported by confidence in the government but did not have metallic, i.e., gold or silver, backing. To combat the depressionary effects of the economic panic of 1873, inflationists wanted even more issued. Even though their efforts spawned the National Greenback Party, they were largely a failure by the late 1870s.

After that silver money became the issue, beginning with the passage of the Bland-Allison Act of 1878, whereby the government during the Hayes administration resumed the coinage of silver at a rate of 16 to one— that is 16 ounces of silver was worth one ounce of gold. Under Harrison the Sherman Silver Purchase Act of 1890 was passed, replacing the Bland-Allison Act. The act required that the Treasury purchase 4.5 million ounces of silver monthly to be coined into money, the law nearly doubled what Bland-Allison had done. Now out of office, former president Grover Cleveland, a sound money man (preferring to maintain high gold supplies) or "gold bug" to detractors, denounced the Sherman Act as a "dangerous and reckless experiment."

The Sherman Antitrust Act

As U.S. business grew in scope, agitation for a national law limiting the size of individual production entities developed. At a time when large businesses and monopolies called trusts were coming to dominate U.S. business, many Americans longed for the presumed pristine days of competition among small producers. Business leaders such as oil magnate John D. Rockefeller argued in favor of big business, which they felt could use mass production, research and development, and optimal market sizing to lower costs and prices while improving products. Of course, big business also made the men who controlled it, like Rockefeller, extremely rich.

In practice, the arguments of big business generally prevailed, and consolidation into trusts continued. Republicans in particular supported and were supported by business interests. Nevertheless, Harrison and Congress responded to public concerns by enacting the Sherman Antitrust Act in 1890. The law provided that "every contract, combination, or conspiracy, in restraint of trade or commerce among the several states, or with foreign nations, is hereby declared illegal." Despite this seemingly strong language, the law was largely symbolic. Neither Harrison nor his immediate successors enforced the act with any strength. In time, however, the Sherman Antitrust Act became an important check on business unification beginning with Theodore Roosevelt's administration.

The Morrill Pension Act

Influenced by the Grand Army of the Republic (GAR) veterans' group and by their own backgrounds, Republicans supported generous pension legislation in the post-Civil War era. Their cause was abetted by the presence of what many considered a surplus in the U.S. Treasury. Harrison's first commissioner of pensions, James R. ("Corporal") Tanner, commander of New York's GAR, had championed pensions for all Union veterans for years. The Morrill Dependent Pension and Disability Act of June 27, 1890, fulfilled not only Corporal Tanner's dreams but also Kansas representative Edmund N. Morrill's when it granted pensions to veterans of the Union Army who had served for at least 90 days and were then or thereafter physically or mentally disabled and unable to earn a living. It also provided pensions for minor children, dependent parents, and widows who had married veterans before 1890.

Lodge Force Bill

Protection of African Americans' voting rights in the South was of special interest to President Harrison and Republicans. They had made it part of the party platform in 1888 and subsequently a major issue when Massachusetts congressman Henry Cabot Lodge's special committee filed the Federal Elections Bill, which was debated and passed by the House of Representatives in July of 1890. The Force Bill, as the measure came to be known, required that U.S. district judges appoint bipartisan election supervisors to inspect voter registration books and attend to elections in all congressional districts to make certain African Americans were not unjustly kept from voting.

With overwhelming support from Republicans, the bill passed the House by six votes during the first session of the Fifty-first Congress. The measure was stalled in the Senate, however, where southern leaders and their northern Democratic allies made a deal with western silver interests to block it. Nevertheless, in January 1891 the bill was taken up in the Senate, forcing southern Democrats to filibuster (long speeches intended to delay or obstruct legislation). Unable to break the filibuster, the Senate moved on to other considerations. The Lodge Force Bill was dead and with it a chance to change the course of U.S. history. If the bill had passed and if it had worked as planned, African American voting would have had a monumental effect on civil rights much earlier than it did.

The Land Revision Act

In the nineteenth century many laws had been passed to encourage and aid the settlement of the western United States. By the time Harrison became president, however, many people were concerned that the land was being exploited. Many scientists and progressive reformers believed that the federal government should encourage rational planned management of public lands. To address some of these concerns, the Land Revision Act of 1891 was passed. The Land Revision Act of 1891 also created a national forest program, authorizing presidents to set aside portions of the public domain as forest reserves. For this reason the Act is sometimes referred to as the Forest Reserve Act. Harrison subsequently created the first fifteen forest reserves in the United States, encompassing more than 22 million acres. Harrison's actions were early moves in the conservationist crusade that followed, and Gifford Pinchot, who became chief forester under President Theodore Roosevelt, considered it the most significant act in the history of forestry in the United States.

Foreign Issues

A variety of factors contributed to the Harrison administration's development of a foreign policy that emphasized expansion. One reason was the presumed need for foreign markets to ensure prosperity by providing purchasers for surplus agricultural and industrial production's. A less tangible cause, but probably more important determinant, was a growing sense of national greatness fostered by preservation of the Union through the American Civil War (1861–65) and the rapid economic growth that followed. A religious people, many in the United States believed God had marked them to carry their civilization beyond North America to the world's less fortunate. Many who were less charitable or religious in their opinions believed that the white "Anglo-Saxon race" was the most advanced people of the earth, and therefore had the right to control other peoples. Whichever motivated individuals to act, Harrison became president at a time when many Americans supported an expanded role for the United States in world affairs.

Expansion of the Navy

Harrison's secretary of the navy, Benjamin F. Tracy, was a strong supporter of the ideas put forward by U.S. Navy Captain Alfred T. Mahan. Mahan argued that if the United States needed to expand and modernize the navy in order to protect its merchants and exert U.S. power in crucial overseas markets. A modern, steam-powered, navy would also require anchorages and coaling stations far from U.S. shores, in order to supply the fleets with fuel.

With Harrison's approval, Tracy set about developing a modern battleship fleet and strategic naval doctrine. He reorganized the Navy Department and saved the recently established Naval War College from opponents who wanted to eliminate it. Tracy also helped shepherd the Naval Act of 1890 through Congress. This act authorized the construction of a two-ocean navy, centered on state-of-the-art battleships. The three *Oregon* class battleships built under the act during Harrison's term were among the most powerful warships afloat.

Latin America

Pan Americanism

In the summer of 1888, the Cleveland administration had issued a call for a Pan-American Conference, at which the United States and the other nations of the Western Hemisphere could gather to promote peace, understanding, and commerce. Seventeen nations responded, and a conference was scheduled for October 2, 1889. When the conference convened, the United States was represented by Secretary of State Blaine, who while serving as Secretary of State to President Arthur eight years earlier, had attempted to sponsor a similar conference. Blaine hoped to establish a customs union in the Americas, as well as a system for arbitrating political disputes among the nations. While Blaine did not get his ambitious program through, the International Bureau of American Republics was created—two decades later it would become the Pan-American Union. Another achievement indirectly related to the conference, which lasted until April 1890, was the decision to give President Harrison, as part of the McKinley Tariff Act of 1890, the power to write reciprocal trade agreements with Latin American states. This led to eight such reciprocal agreements. In a broader perspective, the idea of reciprocity introduced a third element into the argument between protectionists and those who favored only a revenue tariff.

The Baltimore Affair

Despite the recent conference, relations between the United States and its southern neighbors suffered a setback in 1891. In that year, revolutionaries in Chile ousted the country's U.S.-backed president, Jose Balmaceda. During the fighting U.S. officials had the navy seize a Chilean merchant vessel, the *Itata,* to keep it from carrying supplies to the rebels, and they placed a small flotilla off of Chile's coast. Captain W. W. Schley, commander of the squadron, made the mistake of giving shore leave in Valparaiso, Chile, to crew members of one of these ships, the *U.S.S. Baltimore.* An angry mob of Chileans attacked the Americans at the True Blue Saloon, killing two sailors and injuring 17. Upon hearing of the deaths, President Harrison, in a special message to Congress, made the attack an affair of honor and demanded that Chile either apologize and pay reparations or face the consequences.

Rather than confront the military wrath of the United States, the Chilean government quickly complied with the ultimatum. While the incident hurt U.S. relations with Latin America, it did have some beneficial effects. Harrison's vigorous and firm actions supported the new, more active role for the United States in foreign affairs and helped gain support in Congress for the ongoing expansion of the navy.

Samoa

The United States's contact with the South Pacific islands of Samoa began early in the nineteenth century when whalers used it as a port of call. In the 1870s, the U.S. Navy established a refueling base at Pago Pago. By 1889 several decades of competition among English, German, and U.S. interests nearly led to fighting when German and U.S. warships challenged each other in Apia Harbor in Samoa. A typhoon scattered the vessels and eased tensions. Hoping to avoid war, Harrison and Secretary of State Blaine dispatched emissaries in April 1889 to the "New Samoan Conference" in Berlin, where the three powers established a tripartite supervision of the islands. The United States has controlled the eastern portion of the Samoan Islands since this time.

Hawaii

Initial U.S. interest in Hawaii began with missionaries, the Pilgrims of the Pacific, in the 1820s. By the 1880s the islands' sugar crop, which American and European residents controlled, and the desire for a naval station at Pearl Harbor, dominated the United States's interest. In 1890 the McKinley Tariff, which ended tariffs on sugar imported to the United States, caused a rapid decline in sugar prices in the United States and seriously damaged the Hawaiian economy, which was tied to the U.S. market. The powerful American sugar planters in Hawaii began to consider it advantageous to have the islands become part of the United States because they would then be supported by government sugar subsidies. However the new Hawaiian queen, Liliuokalani, wanted to assert greater authority over the constitutional monarchy that had been established in 1887.

Queen Liliuokalani's efforts to strengthen the monarchy occasioned an uprising led primarily by U.S. planters, who successfully disbanded the monarchy and established the Republic of Hawaii. The U.S. minister to the islands, John L. Stevens, was deeply involved in the revolution, authorizing the use of U.S. troops from the cruiser *Boston.* He later proclaimed an American protectorate over the islands. While not encouraged by Harrison to do these things, when Stevens and Hawaiian leaders adopted a plan of annexation, the president embraced it. Harrison's interests in Hawaii differed from those of Stevens. He was concerned about Japan's growing presence there and the navy's desire to occupy Pearl Harbor as U.S. territory. In the closing days of his administration, he sent a treaty of annexation to the Senate for ratification. President Cleveland, who believed it unfair, recalled it a week after assuming office. While Harrison's attempt to annex Hawaii failed, five years later, in the midst of the Spanish-American War, the next Republican administration acquired Hawaii by joint resolution of Congress.

Canadian Sealing

The Pribilof Islands in the Bearing Sea, which the United States owned, were home to vast seal herds and off limits to foreign hunters. Thus, sealers of other nations began pelagic sealing, or gathering catches on the high seas, beyond the three-mile limit. Canadians were the most active in this practice, which was decimating the herds. To protect the seals and U.S. interests, Congress empowered the president to assume dominion over the waters of the Bering Sea. The British, acting on the behalf of its Canadian commonwealth, protested the United States's assertion, causing Secretary of State Blaine to accuse the British of acts near to piracy. However, before the affair could mushroom into a major controversy, both countries agreed to arbitrate the matter. In 1893 an international tribunal established a 60-mile zone around the Pribilofs in which sealing was forbidden for a number of years.

The Harrison Administration Legacy

Few of Harrison's domestic initiatives had any long-lasting effect. The McKinley Tariff ultimately proved to stifle business growth and anger workers, just the opposite of what the president and the Republicans wanted to do in 1890. The Silver Purchase Act, which was in effect for only two years, likewise was of secondary importance. Harrison failed outright in his attempt to implement federal protection of African American voting rights, at least in part because he was unable to marshal support within his own party. The only major domestic success for Harrison proved to be his generous pension legislation. Even this act, while satisfying public demands, proved a serious drain on government funds in the years after following its passage.

While Harrison's impact on the domestic front was ultimately minor, in foreign affairs he had many significant achievements. The expansion and modernization of the navy and the securing of the U.S. position in Samoa greatly improved the ability of the United States to influence events away from its borders. Harrison's attempt to annex Hawaii, while blocked by the Cleveland administration, further demonstrated that the United States was willing and able to act on the international stage.

Lasting Impact

Historians tend to downplay the transitional role Harrison's four years in office played in U.S. government. While not the first to view government as a positive force in U.S. affairs, Harrison did more than his contemporaries in creating what he believed were beneficial programs. The idea that government could and should correct economic and subsequent social ills paved the way for the ideological stance taken a decade later by progressive reformers.

Moreover, by creating coherent naval and foreign policies, Harrison made the switch from a passive to an interventionist nation easier, and interventionist is what the U.S. became in the last decade of the nineteenth century and throughout the twentieth century. His administration was the first presidency to link a forceful foreign policy stance to the need for a powerful military. Others had achieved as much in reaction to developments, as in the case of James Polk and Mexico (*See also,* Polk Administration), but Harrison prepared for unforeseen eventualities. Harrison also began the process of acquiring an overseas empire for the United States, by gaining control over part of Samoa and targeting Hawaii for annexation. Only five years after Harrison left office the United States annexed Hawaii and easily won the Spanish-American War (1898), resulting in the acquisition of the Philippines and Puerto Rico.

Sources

Boller, Paul F., Jr. *Presidential Campaigns.* New York: Oxford University Press, 1996.

Herrick, Walter R., Jr. *The American Naval Revolution.* Baton Rouge, La.: Louisiana University Press, 1966.

LaFeber, Walter. *The New Empire: An Interpretation of American Expansion, 1860–1898.* Ithaca, NY: Cornell University Press, 1963.

Marcus, Robert D. *Grand Old Party: Political Structure in the Gilded Age, 1880–1896.* New York: Oxford University Press, 1971.

Morgan, H. Wayne. *From Hayes to McKinley: National Party Politics, 1877–1896.* Syracuse, NY: Syracuse University Press, 1969.

Sievers, Harry J. *Benjamin Harrison.* 3 vols. Chicago, Ill.: H. Regnery Co., 1952–68.

Socolofsky, Homer E., and Allan B. Spetter. *The Presidency of Benjamin Harrison.* Lawrence, Kans.: University Press of Kansas, 1987.

White, Leonard D. *The Republican Era, A Study in Administrative History, 1869–1901.* New York: Macmillan Co., 1958.

Further Readings

Muzzey, David Saville. *James G. Blaine: A Political Idol of Other Days.* Port Washington, NY: Kennikat Press, 1963.

White, Leonard D. *The Republican Era, 1869-1901: A Study in Administrative History.* New York: Macmillan, 1958.

Williams, R. Hal. *Years of Decision: American Politics in the 1890s.* New York: Wiley, 1978.

McKinley Administrations

Full name: William McKinley
Given name: William McKinley, Jr.

Personal Information:

Born: January 29, 1843
Birthplace: Niles, Ohio
Died: September 14, 1901
Death place: Buffalo, New York
Burial place: Adjoining Westlawn Cemetery, Canton, Ohio
Religion: Methodist
Spouse: Ida Saxton (m. 1871)
Children: Katherine; Ida
Education: attended Allegheny College, Meadville, Pennsylvania
Occupation: Teacher; lawyer; congressman; governor
Political Party: Republican Party
Age at Inauguration: 54 years

Biography

At the turn of the twentieth century William McKinley—an amiable man with a talent for political administration—became a fixture on the U.S. political scene. As a congressman, governor, and president, McKinley supported and protected U.S. business. In a period of social and economic upheaval when tensions between industry and labor were high, McKinley's talkative and easygoing personality made him a reassuring figure to business and the general public.

Early Life

William McKinley Jr. was born in Niles, Ohio, the seventh of nine children, to William and Nancy Allison McKinley. Young William was in many ways a child of U.S. industry: his father was a pig iron manufacturer. At the age of nine, McKinley's family moved to Poland, Ohio, near Youngstown, so that the children could receive a better education.

Education

McKinley attended Poland Academy, a Methodist seminary, for eight years. Soon after entering to academy, he publicly committed himself to the Methodist faith at a revival meeting. He remained an involved Methodist throughout his life. At Poland Academy McKinley participated in debating clubs and eventually became president of the local debating society.

After completing his studies at Poland Academy, McKinley attended Allegheny College in Meadville, Pennsylvania, for a year. He was forced to drop out of college, however, due to poor health and financial difficulties. After serving in the American Civil War (1861–65) McKinley returned to Ohio and studied law at the office of county judge Charles E. Glidden (*See also,* Career). In 1866 McKinley briefly attended law school in Albany, New York. After winning admission to the Ohio bar, he began practicing law in March 1867.

Family Life

McKinley married Ida Saxton, the daughter of a wealthy Canton, Ohio, businessman, on January 25, 1871. Less than a year later, their first child, Katherine, was born. Ida McKinley was pregnant with a second child two years later when she learned that her mother had died. Ida McKinley went into premature labor, delivering a sickly baby who died within the year. A few months later, the couple also buried their only surviving child, Katherine, who had contracted typhoid fever. Ida McKinley herself developed epilepsy and soon became dependent on her husband. McKinley was very devoted to his fragile wife— even as president he carefully tended to her needs.

William McKinley. (The Library of Congress.)

Career

Military Service

In 1860 when health and finances forced McKinley to discontinue his studies at Allegheny College, the future president took a job as a clerk for the Poland, Ohio, post office. In 1861, however, when the American Civil War began, McKinley enlisted in the 23d Ohio Volunteer Regiment in western Virginia. The regiment was under the command of future president Maj. Rutherford B. Hayes. In 1862, at the Battle of Antietam, in Maryland, McKinley, a commissary sergeant, drove a mule team through heavy enemy fire to supply troops at the front. He was quickly promoted to second lieutenant and became brigade quartermaster for Hayes. Other promotions followed, and McKinley left the army in July 1865 as a brevet major.

Legislator

After passing the Ohio bar in 1867, McKinley immediately became involved in politics. He campaigned for his former commander, Rutherford B. Hayes, in the Ohio gubernatorial campaign of 1867. Living in Canton, Ohio, McKinley was elected to his first political office, prosecuting attorney for Stark County, in 1869. From there McKinley became increasingly active in the Republican Party, and in 1876 he was elected to the U.S. House of Representatives.

McKinley served in Congress from 1877 to 1891, with the exception of one term (the boundaries of his district were changed in 1882, but McKinley recaptured the seat in 1884). McKinley's greatest interest in Congress was economic and monetary policy. Serving on the House Ways and Means Committee, McKinley supported the establishment of high taxes on imported goods, or tariffs. McKinley felt that high tariffs were necessary in order to protect U.S. industry from foreign competition, and that such protection would lead to an expansion of the U.S. economy and higher wages. As the chairman of the Ways and Means Committee in 1890, McKinley convinced his colleagues in Congress to enact his program. The 1890 McKinley Tariff imposed the highest tariffs that the United States had ever placed on imports. The public blamed the McKinley Tariff for rising consumer prices, however, and voted McKinley out of office in 1891.

Governor of Ohio

McKinley was not long deterred by his defeat in Congress. In 1891 he won the Ohio governor's seat. In a time of intense labor and agrarian unrest, Governor McKinley attempted to please both labor and industry, and in many respects he succeeded. McKinley contributed to relief funds for strikers and supported laws favorable to labor, but he also was well known for his general support of industry. McKinley, a popular governor, easily won reelection in 1893, in the midst of the worst depression to hit the nation up to that point in history. The depression of

1893, coming as it did with a Democratic president, Grover Cleveland, in office, bolstered the hopes of Republicans that they could win back the presidency.

Already a prominent Republican, McKinley had served as the chairman of the Republican National Convention in 1892, establishing himself as a presidential prospect for the 1896 election. In 1896 McKinley won the Republican nomination and ran in the general election against youthful Democrat William Jennings Bryan, who had inspired working-class and western Americans with his fiery oratory in support of "free silver," or the unlimited coinage of silver, and against big business. McKinley and his campaign staff portrayed Bryan as a hotheaded incompetent who would shut down businesses and turn the U.S. economy upside down. McKinley won the election by 600,000 popular votes.

President

Soon after McKinley became president the depression began to ease and the nation returned to prosperity. With U.S. workers receiving better wages and farmers selling their goods for higher prices, the labor and agrarian protests of the early 1890s subsided. McKinley pursued a conservative course, emphasizing social stability and economic growth. In foreign policy, however, he was more of an activist, committing the nation to a course of territorial and economic expansion that would alter the United States's relationship with the rest of the world. Under McKinley the United States annexed Hawaii, fought the Spanish-American War (1898), acquired territorial control over Puerto Rico and the Philippines, and asserted itself as a player in the international marketplace. McKinley won reelection easily in 1900, but he died in office, the victim of an assassination.

Post-presidential Years

On September 6, 1901, while visiting the Pan American Exposition in Buffalo, New York, Leon F. Czolgosz, a deranged millworker and anarchist shot President McKinley twice at point-blank range. His wounds were not properly dressed, and as a result McKinley died of gangrene eight days later. After McKinley's death, Vice President Theodore Roosevelt became president of a shocked and mourning nation, finishing out the last three years of McKinley's term.

The William McKinley Administrations

As president, William McKinley believed that the strength of the nation and the success of U.S. businesses were firmly linked. The McKinley administration solid-

ified the connections between government and industry both at home and abroad. In a time of domestic prosperity, McKinley sought to extend U.S. economic influence into the international arena, committing U.S. forces to the Spanish-American War (1898) and steering the nation towards a new imperialism.

McKinley Becomes President

The Election of 1896

McKinley—who had been a leader of the Republican Party for over 20 years—was the logical choice for the Republican nomination in 1896. In his bid for the nomination, McKinley relied on the generous funds and the skillful political organizing of Cleveland, Ohio, industrialist Mark Hanna, who had helped McKinley win the Ohio gubernatorial race in 1891. Hanna encouraged McKinley to travel the country and speak on the importance of raising tariffs to protect U.S. businesses. McKinley gave nearly four hundred speeches in eight weeks, logging 10,000 miles through 17 states. The strategy paid off at the St. Louis, Missouri, convention; McKinley easily won the nomination, beating House Speaker Thomas B. Reed of Maine in the first ballot.

The Republican Party platform was unabashedly pro-business, supporting policies designed to help U.S. businesses compete in the world economy. These included continued support for the gold standard (gold based currency), the acquisition of Hawaii, the construction of a canal across Central America, and a significant expansion of the U.S. navy. In addition, the platform called for the exclusion of illiterate immigrants and the creation of a national arbitration board to settle labor disputes.

William Jennings Bryan

The Republican Party was relatively united around McKinley's candidacy, but the Democratic battle for the nomination proved to be more tumultuous. The depression of 1893 heightened long-standing demands that the U.S. economy be reformed to eliminate what some saw as undue favoritism to big business, at the expense of laborers and farmers. At the Democratic convention in July 1896, southern and western delegates argued for a platform that curbed the excesses of big business, lowered tariffs, and placed stricter control on trusts and railroads. "Free silver" (or using silver as well as gold for currency) was also a major issue (*See also,* Domestic Issues). Many of these ideas were borrowed from the Populists, a new party that had been winning elections in the South and the West by calling for reforms and regulation of big business.

At the Democratic convention, William Jennings Bryan, a handsome 36-year-old congressman from Nebraska, sought the party's nomination for president. Speaking on the issue of free silver, Bryan delivered what

Administration

Administration Dates
March 4, 1897–March 4, 1901
March 4, 1901–September 14, 1901

Vice President
Garret Augustus Hobart (1897–99)
Theodore Roosevelt (1901)

Cabinet
Secretary of State
Richard Olney (1895–97)
John Sherman (1897–98)
William R. Day (1898)
John M. Hay (1898–1905)

Secretary of the Treasury
John G. Carlisle (1893–97)
Lyman J. Gage (1897–1902)

Secretary of War
Daniel S. Lamont (1893–97)
Russell A. Alger (1897–99)
Elihu Root (1899–1904)

Attorney General
Judson Harmon (1895–97)
Joseph McKenna (1897–98)
John W. Griggs (1898–1901)
Philander C. Knox (1901–04)

Secretary of the Navy
Hilary A. Herbert (1893–97)
John D. Long (1897–1902)

Postmaster General
William L. Wilson (1895–97)
James A. Gary (1897–98)
Charles E. Smith (1898–1902)

Secretary of the Interior
David R. Francis (1896–97)
Cornelius N. Bliss (1897–99)
Ethan A. Hitchcock (1899–1907)

Secretary of Agriculture
Julius S. Morton (1893–97)
James Wilson (1897–1913)

---

would become one of the most famous political speeches in U.S. history. "You shall not press down upon the brow of labor this crown of thorns," Bryan said, "you shall not crucify mankind upon a cross of gold" (Isaak, p. 476). Bryan's impassioned speech against the enormous concentration of wealth by businessmen and bankers in the new industrial economy swayed the convention to the free silver camp, and won him the nomination on the fifth ballot.

The Campaign
The election of 1896 took place in the midst of the most debilitating depression the nation had ever experienced. In 1893 two of the nation's largest corporations collapsed under the weight of overexpansion and crushing debt, triggering a stock market crash and a wave of bank failures. Within six months more than eight thousand businesses, 156 railroads, and four hundred banks had failed; farm prices had tumbled; and up to one million workers—20 percent of the labor force—had lost their jobs. The presidential candidates were judged by the public in terms of how they would help the nation recover.

During the general election campaign, Bryan took his revival-style oratory to the people of the United States, traveling 18 thousand miles to deliver his "Cross of Gold" speech six hundred times to an estimated five million people. McKinley, meanwhile, remained in Canton, Ohio, where he met with delegations of the press and the party faithful in a "front porch" campaign.

With the business and financial community petrified at the prospect of Bryan and his populist rabble-rousers winning the White House, cash flowed into Republican coffers. The McKinley campaign spent as much as seven million dollars on the race, while Bryan raised only $300,000. McKinley won with 51.1 percent of the popular vote, besting Bryan by 600,000 ballots, becoming the first successful candidate to win a majority of the popular vote since Ulysses S. Grant. While Bryan had won the votes of farmers with his support of free silver, industrial workers and businessmen in the populous northeast voted predominately for McKinley and his call for protective tariffs.

The Election of 1900
Soon after McKinley took office, the economy recovered from the long depression of the mid-1890s, and his administration was one of general prosperity.

McKinley, a popular president who campaigned on the slogan of "Four More Years of the Full Dinner Pail," was ensured the Republican nomination. The biggest debate at the 1900 Republican National Convention in Philadelphia, Pennsylvania, was over the selection of a new running mate for McKinley, since Vice President Garret A. Hobart had recently died in office. Although McKinley's adviser Mark Hanna strongly disliked New York governor and Spanish-American War hero Theodore Roosevelt, the convention delegates gave Roosevelt the nod.

McKinley again ran against William Jennings Bryan, and once again McKinley avoided the campaign trail. In his place, McKinley sent Hanna to stump against Bryan. With the end of the depression and the passage of legislation during McKinley's first term (*See also,* Domestic Issues), the currency debate was no longer a major issue. The Democratic Party focused its campaign on criticism of McKinley's imperialistic military and economic forays into the former Spanish territories. The Democrats condemned U.S. annexation of Cuba and the Philippines, but most Americans supported the Spanish-American War (1898) and the nation's foreign acquisitions. McKinley won reelection by almost one million votes.

McKinley's Advisers

Ohio industrialist Mark Hanna was McKinley's closest adviser throughout his political career. Hanna had groomed McKinley for national office, backing his friend's run for Ohio governor in 1891, raising money for his campaigns, and crafting the strategies that twice won McKinley the presidency. After McKinley was elected, he offered to reward Hanna with the secretary of the Treasury post, but Hanna asked instead to fill the Senate seat vacated by Ohio senator John Sherman, who had left the Senate to become secretary of state. During McKinley's years in office, Hanna was also, without question, the president's most influential adviser on all matters of domestic policy—with Hanna's guidance McKinley charted a cautious political and economic course that won him the praise of U.S. business interests.

Although McKinley had initially been reluctant to acquire new territories, he soon acceded to the wishes of his cabinet and allowed them to set the course for U.S. policy abroad. Under this system, John Hay, secretary of state from 1898 to 1905 under both McKinley and Theodore Roosevelt, became one of the most influential and widely respected secretaries of state in U.S. history. Hay played a major role in all foreign policy decisions of the McKinley administration, and he helped engineer the expansion of the United States into Cuba, Puerto Rico, and the Philippines.

McKinley's second secretary of war, Elihu Root, also was an influential force in the administration. Root, a lawyer, was charged with administering the nation's new territorial acquisitions. A sincere believer in the doctrine of imperialism, Root argued that U.S. "progress" would be a civilizing force in the new territories, regardless of whether these territories desired the often-oppressive assistance of the United States. "Government does not depend upon consent," Root explained. "The immutable laws of justice and humanity require that people shall have government, that the weak shall be protected, that cruelty and lust shall be restrained, whether there be consent or not" (Bacon and Scott, p. 42).

McKinley and Congress

McKinley, like many of his predecessors, conceived of his role as president as an essentially conservative one, carrying out the decisions of Congress but rarely initiating his own policies. Because of the large Republican majorities in Congress, McKinley did not need to worry that the voice of Congress would be vastly different from his own.

McKinley's 15 years as a congressman served him well as president. He knew from experience how to exert the kind of gentle pressure to which Congress would respond. He often invited members of Congress to visit him at the White House. His secretary of war, Elihu Root, reported that McKinley "had vast influence with Congress. He led them by the power of affectionate esteem, not by fear. He never bullied Congress" (Morgan, p. 275). McKinley also was meticulous about helping those who helped him, rewarding his supporters with powerful and lucrative appointments. All of this meant that when he did need something done, McKinley knew who to call and how to shepherd legislation through Congress quickly and quietly. After the explosion of the U.S.S. *Maine* precipitated the hostilities that would lead to the Spanish-American War for instance (*See also,* Foreign Issues), McKinley called powerful Republican congressman Joseph Cannon of Illinois to the White House. A $50 million appropriation for the war effort followed quickly.

McKinley and the Judiciary

McKinley appointed only one justice to the Supreme Court. In 1898 he nominated Joseph McKenna of California, who had previously served as McKinley's attorney general, to the High Court.

The two most important decisions the Supreme Court made during McKinley's term had to do with the tariff status of the former Spanish colonies that the United States had won in its war with Spain. They dealt with the question of whether or not Cuba, Puerto Rico, and the Philippines were subject to the same high tariffs as other countries importing goods to the United States.

At the end of 1900 a series of cases came before the Supreme Court that attempted to answer this question, and

Biography:

William Jennings Bryan

Lawyer; Politician; Secretary of State For most of his career William Jennings Bryan carried the moniker the "Great Commoner," because his politics favored the values and protests of the common man who felt pressured and disadvantaged by the urban, industrial forces shaping the nation in the post-American Civil War era. Bryan was a great orator and his rhetoric addressed complex social and economic issues in a simple and straightforward manner that was accessible to the common man. Bryan began his career practicing law but soon after entered politics. At the 1896 Democratic Convention, Bryan won the presidential nomination and ran a strong race against Ohio governor William McKinley. Bryan lost that election and two subsequent attempts but stayed in the public eye by writing articles, launching a weekly newspaper, and making extensive speaking tours. In 1912 Bryan helped Woodrow Wilson to capture the party's nomination and was rewarded by President Wilson with an appointment as secretary of state. On the domestic front, Bryan helped secure passage of the Federal Reserve Act. On the international front, Bryan worked to negotiate arbitration treaties with 30 countries in hopes of preventing war. When World War I (1914–18) erupted in Europe, Bryan led the call for a neutrality. When the passenger ship, the *Lusitania* was sunk and President Wilson entered the United States in war, Bryan resigned his post. It was Bryan's last public appearance before his death in 1925 that most people today know him for. In 1924 Bryan appeared as prosecutor for the state of Tennessee in the Scopes "Monkey" trial where he opposed the teaching of theories of evolution in public schools.

---

the Court issued a confusing and often contradictory set of answers. In *De Lima v. Bidwell* (1901) the majority ruled that because Puerto Rico was not a foreign country, it was illegal to impose duties and tariffs on goods imported from there. The majority opinion in *Downs v. Bidwell* (1901), however, declared that the passages of the Constitution that dealt with trade and revenue did not apply to Puerto Rico. It was within the constitutional power of Congress, the Court ruled, to collect duties from the new U.S. territories. The Supreme Court generally concluded that the rights of citizenship enunciated in the Constitution did not apply to the new territories. The Spanish colonies, with their very different populations, would not be integrated into the Union as states—rather, they would be held as the colonial possessions of a budding empire.

Changes in the U.S. Government

McKinley, a conservative in domestic matters, did little to change the form of the federal government. In foreign matters, however, McKinley was an activist. During his time in office the nation acquired far-flung foreign territories ranging from the Caribbean islands of Cuba and Puerto Rico, to the South Pacific islands of Hawaii and the Philippines. The question of how to govern the new U.S. possessions would reverberate for years (*See also, Foreign Issues*).

Domestic Issues

Soon after McKinley took office the deep depression of the mid-1890s began to ease. The passing of the economic crisis also helped diminish the political crises of the previous years, as labor and agrarian protests began to subside. Still, the end of the depression by no means heralded a return to the nation's agricultural roots. By the late 1890s, the United States had become an urban, industrial country whose economy was dominated by large, wealthy corporations. Wealth and power had become concentrated in the hands of a very small number of people. At the same time many less fortunate Americans were living in dire poverty. McKinley, however, did not believe it was his role to address these matters. McKinley had supported business and industry throughout his career, and he resisted the recurring calls by Americans to regulate or reform the enormous power of the "trusts" that had formed monopolies over the nation's railroad, oil, and steel industries.

The Dingley Tariff

McKinley had been a passionate proponent of higher tariffs in Congress, and the first order of business when he became president was to raise the tariff rate yet again. On March 15, 1897, less than two weeks after his first inauguration, McKinley called a special session of Congress to introduce a measure to increase taxes on

Fast Fact

McKinley was the first president to harness the telephone for campaigning. During his 1896 front porch campaign, McKinley telephoned 38 of his campaign managers to discuss the race for president.

(Source: Joseph Kane. *Facts About the Presidents*, pp. 155–6.)

imported goods. The legislation, drafted by chairman of the House Ways and Means Committee Nelson Dingley, a close friend of the president's, raised duties to the highest point in U.S. history.

McKinley sought higher tariffs primarily as a means to protect U.S. manufacturers from low priced European goods. Other nations tended to respond to high U.S. tariffs by setting their own tariffs on U.S. products to be very high, which made it difficult to sell U.S. manufactured goods and crops abroad. Shortly before he died, McKinley came to believe that the high tariffs he had long advocated for were hurting U.S. business interests abroad more than they were helping them at home. With the United States's new productive capacities now creating goods to sell to the vast markets opening up in Asia, McKinley began to call for reciprocal agreements with trading partners abroad. In a speech the day before he was assassinated, McKinley called for tariff reform, to promote the "universal brotherhood of man" through increased international commerce (Kane, p. 156).

The Currency Question

One of the driving issues of the election of 1896 had been the question of the basis of the U.S. currency. In the nineteenth century all paper money was backed by precious metal (called specie) held in the U.S. Treasury's coffers. This meant that paper money could be traded for gold or silver if presented to a bank or to the Treasury. Up until the 1870s the United States had recognized both gold and silver as a basis for the dollar. The official ratio of the value of silver to the value of gold was 16 to 1—16 ounces of silver equaled one once of gold. But when the value of gold dropped in the wake of the California gold rush, silver's value on the open market was higher than this ratio. Owners of silver held onto their silver or sold it to industry, and the U.S. mint, in turn, stopped coining silver. In 1873 Congress had officially discontinued silver coinage.

By the end of the 1870s, however, the market value of silver had dropped, making it more economical to trade silver for paper money. As credit and currency contracted during the depression of 1893, it became clear that Congress had foreclosed a method of expanding the currency, and tempers began to rise over what came to be called the "Crime of 1873." Many Americans soon concluded that a cabal of big bankers had conspired to "demonetize" silver in favor of the gold standard (or a gold-based economy).

The most eager proponents for a return to what they came to call "free silver"—the free and unlimited coinage of silver—were westerners. Silver miners in the West wanted the government to buy their surplus silver above the market value, and struggling farmers in the West and the South believed that an increase in the amount of currency available would raise the prices for farm products and ease the burden of their mounting debts. Silverites came to consider the gold standard an instrument of tyranny to ensure that money remained in the hands of the rich. They further claimed that if the money supply was not expanded, demand for currency would surpass the available supply of gold, with serious negative effects on the economy. Advocates of the gold standard, meanwhile, believed that a limited gold supply assured the stability and long-term value of a gold-based currency. Easterners, particularly bankers and business interests, supported the gold standard, and they aligned with Republicans. The issue proved to be an explosive one.

In the 1896 election McKinley had said he would support a policy of bimetallism—allowing both silver and gold to be traded for paper money—but only if the United States's largest trading partners abroad also would agree to back their currency with silver. McKinley—who devised his policy to assuage both silver and gold advocates—was well aware that an international agreement of this sort was highly unlikely. When he became president, McKinley sent a commission to Europe to explore the possibility of a silver agreement with Great Britain and France, but, as he had anticipated, the effort was futile.

By 1898 it seemed that advocates for the gold standard had been right: the depression had lifted, U.S. businesses had set out on another round of expansion, and U.S. farm prices had rebounded. This was due in large part to luck. Without an enormous increase in the nation's gold stockpiles in the late 1890s—prompted by the discovery of new gold supplies in Alaska, South Africa, and Australia and of new technology for extracting ore—the silverites' predictions of insufficient currency for the economy to function may have come to pass. With the increase in the amount of available gold, however, the government was able to continue issuing currency without purchasing silver. The Gold Standard Act, reaffirming the nation's commitment to the gold standard, was passed by large Republican majorities in 1900.

Foreign Issues

While the United States had always been prone to fits of expansion, it had previously annexed land directly adjoining its existing boundaries. The trans-Appalachian West, the Louisiana Territory, the former Mexican territories, and Oregon had all been acquired to provide land for the nation's expanding population and to fulfill the perceived "manifest destiny" of the United States to expand across the continent.

When McKinley took office in 1896, settlers had spread across the nation, but the nation was still quite isolated from the affairs of the larger world. Unless there was a direct threat to the United States, Americans preferred to stay out of world affairs. Under McKinley, however, the nation's expansionist urges would take on a new character. Rather than acquiring new land for settlement, McKinley's foreign policy was aimed at creating new markets abroad for U.S. business. Under the guidance of McKinley and his secretary of state John Hay, the United States would join the European powers—England, Spain, France, and others—in the imperial push to colonize the nonindustrial world.

The Annexation of Hawaii

Since the early nineteenth century, the islands of Hawaii had been an important stop for ships sailing the trade routes to China, and in 1887 the United States negotiated a treaty with Hawaii permitting a naval base at Pearl Harbor on the island of Oahu. A growing number of Americans had settled among the large population of Polynesian natives on the Hawaiian islands, where many came to work for U.S.-owned sugar plantations. These U.S. sugar planters had been exempted from the usual tariffs on foreign sugar in 1875, but in 1890 this exemption was ended. Facing serious reductions in their profit, many U.S. planters decided that the best way to regain their exemption from tariffs was for Hawaii to become part of the United States.

In 1893 the U.S. planters staged a successful revolution to overthrow Hawaii's nationalist queen Liliuokalani and called for U.S. protection. While Republican president Benjamin Harrison agreed to annex Hawaii shortly before leaving office, his successor, Democratic president Grover Cleveland, refused to accept the annexation. In 1898, soon after taking office, McKinley approved the Hawaii annexation treaty, agreeing with the supporters of annexation that it was the United States's destiny to save and civilize Hawaii (and to make it profitable for U.S. sugar planters). The treaty languished in the Senate for a year, until the war with Spain and the expansionist frenzy it created tipped the balance in favor of annexation.

The Spanish-American War

By 1898 Cuba and Puerto Rico were the only two remaining vestiges of Spain's empire in the Americas.

Since 1868 Cubans had been fighting a long and fruitless battle for independence from Spain. In 1894 Cuba rebelled again, and the Spanish forces responded with a savagery that shocked many Americans. Despite calls for intervention, President Grover Cleveland refrained from involving U.S. troops in the hostilities, proclaiming U.S. neutrality. Pressure to send troops to Cuba continued to mount, however, driven in part by the florid, often distorted, reports on Cuba published by "yellow" newspapermen William Randolph Hearst and Joseph Pulitzer, who were engaged in a ferocious circulation war in New York City.

When McKinley became president, he took a stronger stand, formally protesting Spain's "uncivilized and inhuman" conduct in Cuba. Spain, in response, granted the island limited autonomy and curtailed the brutal persecution of the Cubans. In February 1898, however, two events occurred which ensured that the United States would lend military assistance to the Cuban fight for independence. First, the *New York Journal* printed the contents of a letter sent from the Spanish minister in Washington, Enrique Dupuy de Lome, to a friend in Havana, Cuba. In it the minister described McKinley as a weak man, a tool of public opinion, a "bidder for the admiration of the crowd" (Morgan, p. 356). Despite similar criticism of McKinley from some U.S. politicians (Theodore Roosevelt had once described his president as having "no more backbone than a chocolate éclair"), the attack, coming from a foreigner, raised a tremendous national furor (Brinkley, p. 566).

A week later with antipathy towards Spain running high, the U.S. battleship *Maine* exploded and sank in Havana harbor, killing 266 people. The ship had been sent to Cuba a month before to protect U.S. interests in Cuba against Spanish loyalists, and many Americans assumed that the Spanish had sunk the ship (Later evidence, however, would point to an accidental explosion inside one of the engine rooms). The country began preparing for war. Congress unanimously appropriated $50 million for military maneuvers, and Americans began chanting "Remember the *Maine!*" in a national call for revenge. On April 25, 1898, McKinley requested and received a declaration of war against Spain.

"A Splendid Little War"

The struggle in Cuba proved to be short and relatively easy, with Spanish forces already weakened by the Cuban rebels. Only 460 Americans were killed in battle, while some 5,200 died of malaria, dysentery, typhoid, and other tropical diseases. Still, the army proved to be ill prepared for large-scale combat—it took U.S. forces five days to get ashore in Santiago harbor, even with the enemy offering no opposition. Despite the U.S. military's incompetence, however, it quickly overpowered the Spanish army. By July 16, less than three months after the declaration of war, U.S. forces had surrounded Spanish forces in Santiago, Cuba, and forced them to surrender. At the same time, U.S. troops landed in Puerto Rico, meeting virtually no opposition.

The U.S.S. Maine *sunk in Havana Harbor in 1898 after a mysterious explosion of undetermined origin. Its sinking was the spark that ignited the Spanish-American War.* (U. S. Army Military History Institute.)

Soon after the declaration of war, Commodore George Dewey received orders from then-Assistant Secretary of the Navy Theodore Roosevelt to attack Spanish naval forces in the Philippines. On May 1, 1898, six days after the declaration of war, Dewey's forces sailed into Manila Bay in the Philippines and destroyed the outdated and ineffective Spanish fleet. Only one U.S. soldier died in the battle, of heatstroke. Spanish forces surrendered the city of Manila several months later.

On August 12 Spain signed an armistice agreement recognizing Cuban independence, ceding Puerto Rico to the United States, and accepting U.S. occupation of the Philippines until the two nations reached a final agreement. What had begun as an expedition to help the Cuban rebels fight off their oppressive Spanish rulers had ended with the United States seizing Spain's remaining colonies.

The Philippines

The U.S. victory over the Spanish provoked a storm of debate in Congress and the nation at large concerning the U.S. presence in the Philippines. While it made some defensive sense to control Cuba, a nearby Caribbean island, the idea of controlling a densely populated archipelago (a group of islands) thousands of miles away seemed less than logical. Still, McKinley and many of his Republican colleagues in Congress felt that there was no alternative. Returning the territories to Spain would

be cowardly and dishonorable, according to McKinley. As Massachusetts senator Henry Cabot Lodge explained:

> The President cannot be sent back across the Atlantic in the person of his commissioners, hat in hand, to say to Spain with bated breath, I am here . . . to tell you that we have been too victorious and that you have yielded us too much and that I am very sorry that I took the Philippines from you (Spielman, p. 146).

Nor could McKinley envision turning the islands over to another imperial power, such as Britain or France. The final option—granting independence to the islands—was irresponsible, McKinley said, because the Filipinos were "unfit for self-government." Instead, it was the American responsibility "to take them all and to educate [them], and uplift and Christianize them, and by God's grace do the very best we could by them" (Brinkley, p. 572).

Others, however, questioned the United States's new role in the world. After the Spanish agreed to an offer of $20 million for the islands, the treaty encountered stiff resistance in the Senate from a powerful group of anti-imperialists who argued against the annexation. The fate of the treaty stood in peril for weeks until it received the unlikely support of Democratic presidential contender William Jennings Bryan. Bryan secretly helped McKinley gain some support for the treaty among anti-imperialist Democrats, in the hopes of making the occupation of the Philippines a campaign issue in 1900.

On February 6, 1899, Congress ratified the treaty. That same day the United States received news of a

Filipino insurrection against U.S. occupation. The Filipinos, who had been rebelling against Spanish rule well before 1898, now commenced a struggle against U.S. authority. For the next four years the Americans attempted to force the Filipinos to submit. The war in the Philippines was one of the United States's longest and most vicious engagements, with 200,000 U.S. troops involved in the war and 4,300 U.S. deaths. It is likely that at least 50,000 Filipinos were killed in the struggle. The Filipinos, who attacked their occupiers using guerrilla tactics, were soon subject to the same brutal subjugation that Americans had found so horrifying when perpetrated by the Spanish in Cuba. By the summer of 1901, the fighting began to wane as the rebellion exhausted itself. The military soon transferred authority over the islands to a civilian governor, William Howard Taft. The United States, a country founded on outrage against the injustices of colonial rule, had become an imperial power in its own right.

China

The Open Door Notes

The United States's interest in Hawaii and the Philippines was fueled in part by the need for way stations on the trade route to China. By 1900 England, France, Germany, Russia, and Japan were all vying for dominance over the huge but politically weak Asian nation. U.S. businesses, also eager for their own piece of the China trade, soon grew to fear that they would be cut out of trade in the region altogether. McKinley, who wanted to protect U.S. interests in China without committing to another foreign war, issued a statement in September 1898 demanding the right to access to China. "Asking only the open door for ourselves, we are ready to accord the open door to others." The "Open Door Notes," as the principle came to be called, became the basis for U.S. policy in the region: the United States should be able to trade freely with the Chinese without interference from other foreign powers. The policy, however, met with scorn from nations trying to establish their own monopoly over trade in China (Brinkley, p. 579).

The Boxer Rebellion

In August 1900 McKinley saw an opportunity to assert U.S. rights in the region. After the Boxers, a secret Chinese martial arts society, laid siege to the entire foreign diplomatic corps in the British embassy in Beijing, China, the United States participated in an international expeditionary force that put the rebellion down and rescued the diplomats. McKinley and his secretary of state, John Hay, agreed to lend troops to the international coalition in order to exercise some influence over China's future. In return for his help in putting down the rebellion, McKinley won support for his Open Door policy. China maintained its territorial integrity, and the United States retained access to its lucrative trade.

The McKinley Administration Legacy

Under William McKinley the United States entered the international arena. When McKinley took office, the nation was in the midst of the most debilitating economic depression thus far in its history and was largely isolated from world affairs. By the time McKinley died in his second term as president, the nation had entered into a period of prosperity and growth, and moved into a new era of international involvement. With the beginning of the twentieth century, the United States was poised to spread its gospel of economic growth to the larger world.

Lasting Impact

McKinley, from early in his political career, believed that the health of U.S. business was inseparable from the health of the nation, and that the highest political good was to create an environment where U.S. industries could flourish. Soon after McKinley became president, the nation entered an era of explosive growth. Under McKinley's watch, the nation increased not only in terms of population and productivity, but also in international stature. For the first time in its history, the United States acquired territory far from its North American center and actively sought involvement in world affairs. McKinley broke with the traditional U.S. policy of acting only to defend its interests in Western Hemisphere and established a new precedent of actively supporting U.S. commercial interests abroad. McKinley's forays into the international arena were aimed largely at creating new markets abroad for U.S. business, and his Open Door policy for China would become a major component of U.S. foreign policy. By the time McKinley died, the United States had redefined its relationship with the greater world, acquired a far-flung overseas empire, and had entered the twentieth century poised to become a great power.

Sources

Bacon, Robert, and James Scott, eds. *The Military and Colonial Policy of the United States: Addresses and Reports by Elihu Root.* Cambridge, Mass.: Harvard University Press, 1916.

Brinkley, Alan. *The Unfinished Nation: A Concise History of the American People.* Vol. 2, *From 1865.* 2d ed. New York: McGraw Hill, 1997.

Coletta, Paolo, ed. *Threshold to American Internationalism: Essays on the Foreign Policies of William McKinley.* New York: Exposition Press, 1970.

Isaak, Robert. *American Political Thinking.* New York: Harcourt Brace, 1994.

Kane, Joseph Nathan. *Facts About the Presidents: A Compilation of Biographical and Historical Information.* New York: H. W. Wilson, 1993.

Morgan, Howard. *William McKinley and His America.* Syracuse, N.Y.: Syracuse University Press, 1963.

Spielman, William. *William McKinley: Stalwart Republican.* New York: Exposition Press, 1954.

Further Readings

Filler, Louis, ed. *The President Speaks: From William McKinley to Lyndon B. Johnson.* New York: G. P. Putnam's Sons, 1964.

Glad, Paul. *McKinley, Bryan and the People.* New York: Lippincott, 1964.

Gould, Lewis. *The Presidency of William McKinley.* Lawrence, Kans.: Regents Press of Kansas, 1980.

Hoyt, Edwin Palmer. *William McKinley.* Chicago: Reilly and Co., 1967.

Leech, Margaret. *In the Days of McKinley.* New York: Harper, 1959.

Mayer, George. *The Republican Party, 1854–1966.* New York: Oxford University Press, 1967.

Theodore Roosevelt Administrations

Biography

At the outset of the twentieth century, Theodore Roosevelt became the United States's first modern president by asserting that the president, and not Congress, was the ultimate representative of the people. He popularized the Progressive movement at home and insisted that the United States had to play a greater role in world affairs. Roosevelt was the bride at every wedding, the baby at every christening, and the corpse at every funeral—always on center stage. His lust for life and living, his dynamic personality, and his everlasting curiosity made him a natural-born leader, and he was admired by many.

Early Life

Although destined to become the leader of a reform movement that revitalized U.S. democracy, Theodore Roosevelt was born into an affluent family high on the social ladder. His forebears had been among those early Dutch settlers who colonized New Amsterdam, later called New York. Roosevelt's father, also named Theodore, operated a successful glass-importing business before becoming a New York City banker. Roosevelt's mother, Martha Bulloch, was a Georgian. Known for her sense of humor, she was ever the southern lady—never quite willing to reconcile herself to the South's defeat in the American Civil War (1861–65). Roosevelt's father, on the other hand, was a staunch Lincoln Republican.

Roosevelt's father was a significant influence in his life. The younger Roosevelt said in his autobiography that his father was "the best man I ever knew," while at

Full name: Theodore Roosevelt
Popular name: Teddy; TR

Personal Information:
Born: October 27, 1858
Birthplace: New York City, New York
Died: January 6, 1919
Death place: Oyster Bay, New York
Burial place: Young's Memorial Cemetery, Oyster Bay, New York
Religion: Dutch Reformed
Spouse: Alice Hathaway Lee (m. 1880); Edith Kermit Carow (m. 1886)
Children: Alice Lee; Kermit; Theodore Jr.; Ethel Carow; Archibald Bulloch; Quentin
Education: Harvard College, B.A., 1880
Occupation: Politician; rancher; civil service commissioner; police commissioner; assistant secretary of the navy; soldier; governor; writer
Political Party: Republican Party
Age at Inauguration: 42 years

Theodore Roosevelt. *(Theodore Roosevelt Collection, Harvard College Library.)*

the same time "the only man of whom I was ever really afraid" (Roosevelt, pp. 8–10). The older Roosevelt made it clear that he would not tolerate cruelty, idleness, cowardice, or untruthfulness. Roosevelt senior was also very involved in charity and founded the Children's Aid Society. Throughout his life, TR, as he came to be called, reflected his father's zest for life and sense of duty. Roosevelt later wrote that his father's example spurred him to teach a mission class three years before going to Harvard and then all four years while he was in college. By word and by deed, Roosevelt's father shaped his son who some day would lead the United States into the twentieth century.

As a boy Roosevelt was, by his own words, "a sickly boy afflicted by asthma as well as poor eyesight" (Roosevelt, p. 32). Then, something happened that would change his life. One summer Roosevelt was riding by himself to Maine's Moosehead Lake. On the stagecoach he was taunted by two boys. Infuriated, Roosevelt lashed out at them with his hands. He soon discovered that he was incapable of inflicting much harm. Roosevelt's father explained to his son that his fine mind was not matched by his body and "without the help of the body the mind cannot go as far as it should. You must make your body" (Pringle, 12). This incident and these words spurred Roosevelt to do exactly that. He began by learning to box, and quickly branched out into other athletic pursuits, most of which he continued doing while he was in the White House. As a result he was not only fit but, as he himself said, he trained his

"soul and spirit" to become a man who lived "the strenuous life" (Roosevelt, p. 58).

Education

Roosevelt never enrolled in a public school. He was mostly instructed by private tutors until he entered Harvard College in 1876. As a collegian Roosevelt took no interest in writing themes or forensics. Because he did not think he would enter public life, he never studied elocution or practical debating. His main interests were scientific. He thoroughly enjoyed the study of natural history, and for a time he dreamed of becoming a scientist. He abandoned this goal because, Roosevelt said, at Harvard "they treated biology as purely a science of the laboratory and microscope" failing to understand "the great variety of kinds of work that could be done by naturalists. I had no more desire or ability to be a microscopist and section-cutter than to be a mathematician" (Roosevelt, pp. 29–30). Although Roosevelt decided not to become a scientist, his interest in conservation and the great outdoors never diminished. His first published work, *The Summer Buds of the Adirondacks,* gave evidence of his love of nature, which led to his promotion of conservation throughout his life and behind which he would eventually throw the weight of his presidency.

Roosevelt was elected to the national honorary society Phi Beta Kappa and graduated from Harvard on June 30, 1880, with a bachelor of arts degree. He was 21st in a class of 158. Roosevelt's formal education ended after he enrolled for a short time at the Columbia Law School following his days at Harvard. During those formative years he read voraciously and traveled extensively in Europe.

Family Life

On his 22nd birthday, October 27, 1880, Roosevelt married Alice Hathaway Lee who was 19. On February 12, 1884, Lincoln's birthday, Alice Roosevelt gave birth to a daughter also named Alice. Two days later, on St. Valentine's Day, tragedy struck the Roosevelt's home when both Roosevelt's mother and wife died on the same day.

Roosevelt married for the second time on December 2, 1886, in London, England. With his second wife, Edith Kermit Carow, Roosevelt had five children: Theodore Jr., Kermit, Ethel, Archibald, and Quentin. If Roosevelt can be called the United States's first modern president, then his wife was the country's first modern first lady. One of her many innovations was making Isabelle "Belle" Hagner the first social secretary ever for a president. She also scheduled regular evening musicals where concert artists like the cellist Pablo Casals performed. Further, Edith Roosevelt directed the successful remodeling of the White House.

On July 14, 1918, Roosevelt's youngest son Quentin died in action during World War I (1914–18). The Germans had shot down his plane. Ever imbued with a sense of duty to country, Roosevelt wrote, it was "very dreadful" to hear of Quentin's death but "it would have been worse if he had not gone" (Pringle, p. 483). During World War II (1939–45) Roosevelt's son, Brig. Gen. Theodore Roosevelt, died of a heart attack in France, shortly after the D-day invasion on June 6, 1944.

Career

After graduating from Harvard in 1880, Roosevelt studied law. However, he soon gave that up. Although he realized "that the lawyer can do great work for justice and against legalism," he felt that "some of the teaching of the law books and of the classroom seemed to me to be against justice" (Roosevelt, p. 61). Roosevelt took a much greater interest in politics. In 1880 he joined the Republican Party, which he would later say was the only choice for "a young man of my bringing up and convictions" (Roosevelt, p. 62).

State Representative

On November 9, 1881, at the age of 23, Roosevelt was elected to the New York state assembly representing New York City's 21st district. He took office on January 2, 1882. Roosevelt began to make a name for himself when in March 1882 he called for an investigation of former attorney general Hamilton Ward and state Supreme Court Justice T. R. Westbrook, both accused of using their positions to assist a group of stock speculators in taking over the Manhattan Elevated Railway Company. Although leaders from both parties had little stomach for such action, the resolution was approved and hearings ensued. The *New York Evening Post* declared that "Mr. Roosevelt accomplished more good than any man of his age and experience has accomplished in years" (Pringle, p. 52). Although careful not to alienate influential members of his own party, Assemblyman Roosevelt in the time that he served established himself as a leader who favored social and political reforms.

Rancher

Although Roosevelt thoroughly enjoyed politics, he wrote in his autobiography that he did not believe "any man should ever attempt to make politics his only career." Roosevelt lived up to that credo. As an author he wrote and published numerous books and articles throughout his life. He also tried his hand as a rancher. In the spring of 1884, following the deaths of his wife and mother, Roosevelt refused nomination for a fourth term in the state assembly and traveled to the Dakota Ter-

ritory. In time he became the owner of two ranches. "I do not believe there ever was a life more attractive to a vigorous young fellow than life on a cattle ranch in those days" (Roosevelt, p. 106).

Roosevelt biographer Henry Pringle wrote that the Harvard-trained cowboy "wearing eyeglasses and christened Four-Eyes" was able to win the respect of his fellows "is no small tribute to his character." Pringle related that the first time Roosevelt engaged in a roundup "one or two hardened cowboys nearly fell from their saddles as he called in his high voice to one of the men: 'Hasten forward quickly there!'" (Pringle, p. 68). The phrase was not soon forgotten as often thereafter thirsty cowboys urged bartenders to "hasten quickly" after ordering a drink.

Return to Politics

Roosevelt returned to the East and politics in the fall of 1886 when the Republicans nominated him to be mayor of New York City. The lure of reentering public life and his second marriage, this time to Edith Carow, were the encouragement he needed to head back home. He campaigned energetically but came in third behind Abram S. Hewitt, the winning Democratic candidate, and Henry George, the United Labor Party's nominee.

In 1888 the Republicans recaptured the White House when Benjamin Harrison defeated the incumbent Grover Cleveland. By this time Roosevelt was eager to return to public service. Thus, he accepted an appointment by the new president to the United States Civil Service Commission, even though he knew that Harrison was not a reformer and that the position paid a mere $3,500 annually. As a civil service commissioner Roosevelt promoted civil service reform by vigorously promoting the merit system, which calls for civil servants to be appointed on the basis of competency and not political affiliation. He helped revise civil service exams by insisting that prospective candidates possess practical skills as well as theoretical knowledge.

In 1895 Roosevelt undertook a new challenge when he became president of the New York Police Board. As a police commissioner he quickly developed a reputation as a reformer who refused to appoint people based on connections or money, despite the wishes of his party bosses. As one *New York World* writer put it, "We have a real Police Commissioner. His teeth are big and white, his eyes are small and piercing, his voice is rasping. He makes our policemen feel as the little froggies did when the stork came to rule them. His heart is full of reform. . . ." When William McKinley won the 1896 presidential election, Roosevelt returned to Washington as assistant secretary of the navy. When the United States declared war on Spain in April 1898, Roosevelt resigned from this desk job saying he strongly felt that Cuba should be free from Spanish rule.

The Spanish-American War

Roosevelt helped form what popularly came to be called the Rough Riders. The Rough Riders were a regiment of volunteers that Roosevelt helped recruit just as the Spanish-American War began in April 1898. As a formal part of the U.S. military, their official name was the First United States Volunteer Cavalry. Leonard Wood commanded the Rough Riders, and Roosevelt was second in command and held the rank of lieutenant colonel. Roosevelt explained that the Rough Riders got their nickname "doubtless because the bulk of the men were from the Southwestern ranch country and were skilled in the wild horsemanship of the great plains" (Roosevelt, p. 238). It was in Cuba during the Spanish-American War that Roosevelt became a war hero by leading his Rough Riders in a successful charge up San Juan Hill. Roosevelt's exploits on the battlefield helped him become a prime contender for high political office.

Governor of New York

In 1898 New York Republicans led by Senator Thomas C. Platt needed a gubernatorial candidate to counter negative publicity resulting from a scandal over state land contracts. Although wary of Roosevelt and his reform tendencies, the newly acclaimed war hero filled the bill. Thus the Republicans nominated Roosevelt who went on to score a narrow victory in the general election.

As governor of New York Roosevelt demonstrated his political skills by promoting certain reforms without completely breaking with the conservative Platt. Perhaps the bill most vigorously opposed by many members of his own party was one calling for a tax on corporation franchises. Although legislators sought to tone down the measure, Roosevelt finally pushed through an effective piece of legislation.

Vice President

By 1900 Platt and his followers had seen enough of Governor Roosevelt. Thus they began touting their governor for the 1900 vice presidential nomination. John "Cactus Jack" Garner, one of Franklin D. Roosevelt's vice presidents, reportedly once said that his office was not worth a bucket of warm spit because the vice president had so little power. Thus, with some reluctance, Roosevelt agreed in 1900 to run with incumbent president William McKinley, who was somewhat hesitant to be teamed with a man who might rock the boat.

Once gaining the nomination, Roosevelt campaigned vigorously, insisting that under Republican leadership the United States would prosper at home and be more respected abroad. In eight weeks he logged some 21,000 miles while speaking in 24 states. On November 6, 1900, the McKinley-Roosevelt ticket soundly defeated the Democrats led by William Jennings Bryan. On Inauguration Day, March 4, 1901, Roosevelt took the oath of office as vice president of the United States. Roosevelt was not to hold this office long. On September 6, 1901, anarchist Leon Czolgosz, with his bandaged hand concealing a pistol, fatally wounded McKinley in Buffalo, New York. When McKinley died on September 14, Roosevelt, at the age of 42, became the 26th president of the United States.

President

Initially Roosevelt moved cautiously, but as leader of the United States, the Progressive movement, and the Republican Party, he did step into action. In giving life to the Progressive reform movement, he worked with congressional leaders, particularly Republicans, and convinced many Americans that the people's interests were prime. He seemed to take the people's side when he challenged large corporations, settled a coal strike, promoted conservation, and supported legislation designed to protect consumers. Abroad, he upheld the interest of his nation by building the Panama Canal and promoting peace in Europe and Asia. He had vision to ascertain that the United States's interests in the twentieth century were linked to events far from his nation's shores.

Post-presidential Years

After Roosevelt was elected in 1904, he immediately stated that he would not seek reelection. He firmly believed that the no third term tradition was a wise custom that he would not violate. Roosevelt served as chief executive until William H. Taft succeeded him on March 4, 1909. Although Taft was his chosen successor, Roosevelt in time became unhappy with him, as Taft was not aggressive in his pursuit of reform as Roosevelt had been. In order to carry on the Progressive movement that he felt Taft had failed, Roosevelt sought the Republican presidential nomination in 1912. In his autobiography he states that he had not violated the no third term tradition as he felt it only applied to consecutive terms. Roosevelt was unable to defeat Taft and gain the nomination, despite an emotional speech given at the 1912 Republican convention in which he proclaimed that "we stand at Armageddon, and we battle for the Lord" (Harbaugh, p. 407). He bolted his party and became the leader of the Progressive, or Bull Moose, Party. Running as a third-party presidential nominee, he finished second to the Democrats' Woodrow Wilson. Taft finished a distant third.

After the United States entered World War I on April 6, 1917, Roosevelt sought permission to raise a volunteer division and to assume command of one of its brigades. Wilson's refusal to grant permission estranged the old warrior from the president. On January 6, 1919, Roosevelt died peacefully in his sleep at his Sagamore Hill home in Oyster Bay, New York.

In 1898 at the beginning of the Spanish-American War, Teddy Roosevelt founded a group of volunteer fighters known as the Rough Riders. Roosevelt (center) was second in command and gained fame for successfully taking control of San Juan Hill, Cuba. (The Library of Congress.)

The Theodore Roosevelt Administrations

At the outset of the twentieth century, Theodore Roosevelt, one of the United States's most popular and dynamic leaders, became the first modern U.S. president. In leading the Progressive movement, he advanced the stewardship theory, which meant that the president should always represent the interests of the people, and he developed a program to achieve this known as the Square Deal.

Abroad, he believed the interests of the United States mandated greater involvement in world affairs.

Roosevelt Becomes President

Vice President Theodore Roosevelt became president on September 14, 1901, following the death of President William McKinley. He had run with McKinley as a Republican in 1900. The Democrats had nominated

Administration

Administration Dates

September 14, 1901–March 4, 1905
March 4, 1905–March 4, 1909

Vice President

Charles W. Fairbanks (1905–09)

Cabinet

Secretary of State

John M. Hay (1898–1905)
Elihu Root (1905–09)
Robert Bacon (1909)

Secretary of the Treasury

Lyman J. Gage (1897–1902)
Leslie M. Shaw (1902–07)
George B. Cortelyou (1907–09)

Secretary of War

Elihu Root (1899–1904)
William H. Taft (1904–08)
Luke E. Wright (1908–09)

Attorney General

Philander C. Knox (1901–04)
William H. Moody (1904–06)
Charles J. Bonaparte (1906–09)

Secretary of the Navy

John D. Long (1897–1902)
William H. Moody (1902–04)
Paul Morton (1904–05)
Charles J. Bonaparte (1905–06)
Victor H. Metcalf (1906–08)
Truman H. Newberry (1908–09)

Postmaster General

Charles E. Smith (1898–1902)
Henry C. Payne (1902–04)
Robert J. Wynne (1904–05)
George B. Cortelyou (1905–07)
George V. Meyer (1907–09)

Secretary of the Interior

Ethan A. Hitchcock (1899–1907)
James R. Garfield (1907–09)

Secretary of Agriculture

James Wilson (1897–1913)

Secretary of Commerce and Labor

George B. Cortelyou (1903–04)
Victor H. Metcalf (1904–06)
Oscar S. Straus (1906–09)

William Jennings Bryan for president and Adlai E. Stevenson for vice president that year. The Republican campaign slogan had been "Four Years More of the Full Dinner Pail," meant to symbolize full employment and a high standard of living, continuing the gains made during McKinley's first administration (1897–1901).

While McKinley remained rather aloof, his running mate traveled and spoke extensively throughout the country. The most dominant issue in this campaign was imperialism. Critical of U.S. acquisitions following the Spanish-American War (1898), Democratic candidate Bryan cried, "Imperialism finds no warrant in the Bible." There was "no gatling gun attachment," Bryan declared, to Christ's command to go into the world and preach the gospel to every creature (Harbaugh, p. 37).

Roosevelt's response to criticism of U.S. foreign policy under McKinley was "The simple truth is that there is nothing even remotely resembling 'imperialism' or 'militarism' involved in the present development of that policy of expansion which has been part of the his-

tory of America from the day she became a nation." To those advocating Philippine independence he retorted that conditions would only worsen for the masses. In Roosevelt's view it was the duty of the United States to educate the Filipinos so that at some future day they could enjoy self-government.

In November the Republicans won the election handily. McKinley and Roosevelt captured 52 percent of the popular vote with a total of 7,218,491. Bryan and Stevenson wound up with 6,356,734 votes, or 46 percent. The Republicans' electoral vote was 292 to 155 for the Democrats. Roosevelt took the oath of office for vice president on March 4, 1901. In September Roosevelt became president when anarchist Leon F. Czolgosz fatally shot McKinley in Buffalo, New York.

The Campaign of 1904

In 1904 the Republicans unanimously nominated Theodore Roosevelt to be their standard-bearer in the November general election. Any opposition Roosevelt might have encountered in gaining the nomination ended when popular Ohio senator Mark Hanna died on February 15, 1904. The Republicans chose Senator Charles W. Fairbanks to be Roosevelt's running mate. Until Fairbanks assumed office, the United States had no vice president, for unlike today there was no provision made to name a vice president if a U.S. president failed to complete his term. (It was not until 1965, when the Twenty-fifth Amendment was passed, that provisions were made to name a new vice president in situations such as this.)

The Democrats in 1904 seemed willing to concede the election when they nominated the conservative and colorless Alton B. Parker for president, and then teamed him with West Virginia's Henry G. Davis who was almost 81 years old by election day.

The 1904 presidential campaign turned out to be rather dull. In those days the president did not take the stump campaigning for election as he does today, nor was Parker energized to go looking for votes. Parker railed against Roosevelt's usurpation of authority and "aggrandizement of personal power," while the Democratic platform called for gradual reduction of tariffs and a more powerful Interstate Commerce Commission. Late in the campaign the Democrats charged that Republican national chairman George B. Cortelyou, while secretary of commerce and labor, had used his office to extort significant sums of money from large industrial trusts. Allegedly he was using these funds to insure Roosevelt's election. When Parker used the word "blackmail," Roosevelt thundered, "Mr. Parker's accusations against Mr. Cortelyou and me are monstrous. If true, they would brand both of us forever with infamy; and inasmuch as they are false, heavy must be the condemnation of the man making them" (Pringle, p. 256).

On November 8, 1904, election day, Roosevelt demolished Parker with a popular majority of over 2.5 million votes. No candidate in U.S. history had ever enjoyed that kind of majority. Roosevelt garnered 336 electoral votes to 140 for Parker.

On the night of his momentous victory Roosevelt with the two-term tradition in mind disavowed another term saying, "Under no circumstances will I be a candidate for or accept another nomination" (Mowry, 180). While some historians described this statement as the worst political blunder of Roosevelt's career, others praised his victory as one of his greatest contributions to his country.

Supposedly, on the day before the inauguration Roosevelt declared, "Tomorrow I shall come into my office in my own right. Then watch out for me" (Pringle, p. 253). If Roosevelt did not make that statement, in the days following the 1905 inauguration he acted like it. In his message to Congress in December 1904, Roosevelt laid before Congress an extensive agenda that seemed to embrace much of the reform movement that was now afoot.

Fast Fact

At his 1905 inauguration Roosevelt wore a ring that had been worn by President Lincoln. His secretary of state John Hay, who had been Lincoln's private secretary, gave it to him.

(Source: Joseph Nathan Kane. *Facts About the Presidents*, 1993.)

The Campaign of 1912

Immediately following his campaign victory in 1904 Roosevelt declared that he would not seek reelection to a third term. He firmly believed that the tradition of not seeking a third term begun by George Washington was one that he should not violate. He heartily approved the nomination of William H. Taft, who won the election of 1908 and became president when Roosevelt stepped down in 1909.

Almost immediately Taft proved to be disappointing to Roosevelt and other Progressives. In 1911 the Taft administration decided to file an antimonopoly suit against the United States Steel Corporation. United States Steel had merged with Tennessee Coal and Iron Company with Roosevelt's blessing while he had been in office. The suit thoroughly enraged Roosevelt and contributed significantly to an open rift between Roosevelt and Taft. Urged by other Progressives to seek the Republican presidential nomination in 1912, Roosevelt actively sought his party's endorsement. When at its 1912 convention the Republicans renominated Taft, Roosevelt formed the Progressive, or Bull Moose, Party. As a third-party presidential nominee, Roosevelt finished second behind Woodrow Wilson, the Democratic nominee, in the 1912 general election. William H. Taft was a distant third.

Roosevelt's Advisers

Because of Roosevelt's commanding personality and ego, presidential advisers had less influence than they have had on weaker presidents or presidents with less political experience. This is not to say that Roosevelt's cabinet was singularly undistinguished, but as an experienced public servant Roosevelt knew how things operated and what he wanted to do. Thus he recruited advisers with an eye towards those who could carry out his Square Deal reform program.

Fast Fact

During the 1912 presidential campaign, a man named John Schrank shot Roosevelt in the chest as he was leaving Milwaukee's Hotel Gilpatrick. Roosevelt, on his way to deliver a speech, persisted in delivering his oration. As he began his speech he said, "Friends, I shall ask you to be very quiet and please excuse me from making you a long speech. I'll do the best I can, but, you see, there is a bullet in my body. But, it's nothing. I'm not hurt badly." Only after finishing his hour-and-a-half-long speech did he go to the hospital.

(Source: Paul F. Boller, Jr. *Presidential Campaigns*, 1996.)

Both John Hay, an Abraham Lincoln biographer, and Elihu Root served as secretary of state. Hay formulated much of the Open Door policy in China, insisting that China be open to commercial and railroad development by all nations, without carving up its territory. Most major nations reluctantly accepted this position. He negotiated the Hay-Pauncefote Treaty, an agreement by which the British gave the United States the exclusive right to construct what came to be the Panama Canal. With Colombia he concluded the Hay-Herran Treaty giving the United States title to land in Panama for a canal that would connect North and South America (*See also,* Foreign Issues).

Root, a 1912 Nobel Peace Prize winner, served as secretary of war until February 1, 1904. He was then appointed secretary of state on July 1, 1905. As secretary of war he reorganized the army. As secretary of state he toured Latin America in 1906 in an effort to cultivate better relations with those nations. Later he negotiated the "Gentlemen's Agreement" with Japan by which Japan agreed to limit immigration to the United States, thus forestalling passage of exclusionary immigration legislation.

Attorney General Philander C. Knox, despite some conservative tendencies, skillfully and successfully prosecuted the Northern Securities Company under the 1890 Sherman Antitrust Act, the United States's first antimonopoly legislation (*See also,* Domestic Issues). He also helped draft legislation that led to the creation of the Department of Commerce and Labor in 1903.

Two advisers that worked with Roosevelt in advancing the conservation cause were Secretary of Interior James R. Garfield, the son of former president James A. Garfield, and Gifford Pinchot, head of the U.S. For-

est Service. Lauding Garfield the president said, "His administration of the Interior Department was beyond comparison the best we have ever had. It was based primarily on the conception that it is as much the duty of public land officials to help the honest settler get title to his claim as it is to prevent the looting of the public lands." To Gifford Pinchot, Roosevelt wrote, "I am a better man for having known you . . . and I cannot think of a man in the country whose loss would be a more real misfortune to the nation than yours would be" (Harbaugh, p. 349).

A group of companions with whom Roosevelt sometimes played tennis and more often went riding or walking came to be called the Tennis Cabinet. These included Leonard Wood, Thomas H. Barry, Robert Bacon, James Garfield, and Gifford Pinchot. Official matters were often informally discussed, and the president at times sought the advice of these trusted friends.

Roosevelt and Congress

The Fifty-seventh session of Congress was sitting when Roosevelt assumed the presidency. He went on to preside over the Fifty-eight, Fifty-ninth, and Sixty sessions before he retired in March 1909. In the early twentieth century the Republicans held control of both houses of Congress. In the Fifty-seventh Congress there were 56 Republicans, 32 Democrats, and 2 Populists in the Senate. In the House of Representatives there were 200 Republicans, 151 Democrats, 5 Populists, and one Silver Republican who backed bimetallism. This changed little throughout Roosevelt's tenure.

During the Roosevelt years Congress, particularly the Senate, tended to be more conservative than the chief executive. Historian George Mowry wrote that by 1901 "the power of Nelson W. Aldrich of Rhode Island, John C. Spooner of Wisconsin, Orville H. Platt of Connecticut, and William B. Allison of Iowa was practically unchallenged." Other influential senators included Pennsylvania's Matthew Quay, New York's Thomas C. Platt, Ohio's Mark Hanna, and Roosevelt's good friend Henry Cabot Lodge of Massachusetts. In the House of Representatives Joseph G. Cannon of Illinois ruled that body with authority from the time he was elected Speaker in 1902. The badly outnumbered Democrats were also divided so that they provided little effective opposition during the Roosevelt administration.

Because he had no popular mandate during his first term, having succeeded to the office upon McKinley's death, and realizing that in Congress there were several persons of power and influence, Roosevelt was careful to develop a good relationship with congressional leaders. Roosevelt also worked hard and effectively at gaining public support. Historian Lewis Gould wrote that Roosevelt used the presidency as a "bully pulpit," whereby the president uses his office and prestige to rally public support by making "his ideas clear, his language direct, and his message striking" (Gould, p. 10).

After Roosevelt scored an impressive victory in the 1904 election, he had more leverage with Congress. Many members of Congress were used to the presidents of the late nineteenth century, administrators who for the most part had not sought to initiate change. With his impressive public support, Roosevelt could make Congress consider the issues he wanted. As a result, some significant pieces of progressive legislation were adopted by Congress. At the same time, Roosevelt was a seasoned politician, and he knew that the art of politics is compromise. Even with his public support, Roosevelt was careful to work with congressional leaders, compromising at times, to avoid alienating them. For example, the Hepburn Act to reform the Interstate Commerce Commission (ICC) and broaden its powers would not have passed had Roosevelt proved to be inflexible. Other significant pieces of legislation initiated by the Roosevelt administration were the Meat Inspection Act, the Pure Food and Drug Act, and several initiatives on conservation (*See also,* Domestic Issues).

During his presidency Roosevelt exercised the veto 82 times. Forty-two were regular vetoes and 40 were pocket vetoes, indirect vetoes accomplished by retaining a bill without signing it until Congress is adjourned. None of his vetoes concerned major legislation. Only once did Congress override a veto.

Roosevelt and the Judiciary

Roosevelt named three Supreme Court justices. In 1902 he picked Oliver Wendell Holmes to sit on the supreme tribunal. At the time of his appointment Holmes was chief justice of Massachusetts. A highly literate, progressive justice, he would serve on the Court for 30 years. In 1903 Roosevelt chose William Rufus Day, of Ohio, and in 1906 he named William Henry Moody of Massachusetts. Both Day and Moody, like Roosevelt, believed in strict enforcement of antitrust legislation.

Although President Roosevelt enforced the Sherman Antitrust Act more vigorously than any of his predecessors, he did not believe that bigness, per se, violated antitrust legislation. Only corporations that seemed to have no regard for the public's welfare deserved to be prosecuted in the nation's courts. The Northern Securities Company, the Standard Oil Company, and the American Tobacco Company, Roosevelt believed, were three such companies, and thus legal action was taken against each of them (*See also,* Domestic Issues).

The Supreme Court ruled in a number of important cases on labor and labor law during Roosevelt's term in office. In 1905 in *Lochner v. New York* the Court declared unconstitutional a New York law limiting the number of hours that bakery employees could be compelled to work.

The Court felt that limiting the ability of bakery employees to enter into contracts for long working hours was a violation of the Fourteenth Amendment. However, in 1908 the Supreme Court declared in *Muller v. Oregon* that an Oregon law limiting a woman's working day to 10 hours was constitutional. In this case the Court's reasoning was based on the idea that women enjoyed a special place in society, and needed the protection of the law. Another important 1908 Court ruling was set forth in *Adair v. United States,* which struck down a law making it illegal for railroad companies to require their employees to sign contracts promising not to join a labor union. In general, then, the judiciary did not support the progressive movement.

Changes in the U.S. Government

As the United States became more industrialized, the need for new federal agencies became apparent. On February 14, 1903, Roosevelt signed legislation establishing the Department of Commerce and Labor. The first secretary of commerce and labor was George B. Cortelyou, who then became the ninth person in Roosevelt's cabinet. Within this department existed the Bureau of Corporations, with the purpose of investigating the operations and conduct of interstate corporations. On March 6, 1902, Congress created the U.S. Bureau of the Census. Before then a temporary organization was formed each time decennial census needed to be conducted as prescribed by the Constitution.

Roosevelt also believed that the federal government should play a greater role in preserving the nation's environment, and he developed a number of agencies to do so. The U.S. Forest Service was established in 1905 under the umbrella of the Agriculture Department, with Gifford Pinchot as its first chief. In 1906 both the Bureau of Chemistry and the Bureau of Immigration and Naturalization came into being. On March 14, 1907, Roosevelt appointed the Inland Waterways Commission declaring that "the time has come for merging local projects and uses of the inland waters in a comprehensive plan designed for the benefit of the whole country" (Harbaugh, p. 316). And on June 8, 1908, Roosevelt appointed the National Commission for the Conservation of Natural Resources, which was charged with charting all of the United States's natural resources. Pinchot later headed this commission.

On November 16, 1907, Oklahoma was admitted as the 46th state.

Domestic Issues

As the twentieth century dawned the United States was undergoing significant changes. A rural, pastoral nation was giving way to one that was more urban and industrial. New immigrants from southern and eastern Europe were flocking into U.S. cities. During the previous century the country felt quite self-sufficient, safely separated from the troubles of the rest of the world by the Atlantic and the Pacific Oceans. As a new century began the United States sought to build an empire beyond the seas. Ravenous U.S. machines needed sources of raw materials and overseas markets to sell manufactured products.

Economically, a few Americans were accumulating great wealth, but there were many others who lived in dire poverty. Life in the ghettos of the major cities could be incredibly harsh. Politically, there were questions about government that truly represented the people. In his Gettysburg Address President Abraham Lincoln said that the American Civil War had tested whether any "government of the people, by the people, for the people" and "dedicated to the proposition that all men are created equal" can long endure. As the century ended, U.S. democracy was being tested not by civil war, but by a concentration of wealth and power in a few hands. Special interests rather than the public's interest sometimes seemed to hold sway.

In the late nineteenth century a reform movement, called the Progressive movement, began on the state and local level. On the state level, governors like Wisconsin's "Battlin' Bob" La Follette, New York's Charles E. Hughes, and California's Hiram Johnson provided leadership. In city government, mayors like Toledo's "Golden Rule" Jones, Detroit's Hazen Pingree, and Cleveland's Tom Johnson provided the spark leading to urban reforms. Progressives, determined to revitalize democracy by giving more power to the people, called for such reforms as popular election of U.S. senators and greater regulation of powerful interests that seemed little concerned with the public good. Roosevelt, who firmly believed that he embodied the people's interest, stepped forward to give the Progressive movement publicity, popularity, and propulsion on the national level.

Roosevelt, who had become president by "accident" following the assassination of President William McKinley, ruffled a few feathers among party faithfuls. Some Republicans had hoped that by nominating him for vice president they had placed him in a position where he could do little harm. Ohio senator Mark Hanna said, "I told William McKinley it was a mistake to nominate that wild man at Philadelphia. I asked him if he realized what would happen if he should die. Now look, that damned cowboy is president of the United States" (Goldman, 161).

Upon taking office Roosevelt promised "to continue, absolutely unbroken the policy of President McKinley for the peace, the prosperity, and the honor of our beloved country." At the same time he knew that if U.S. democracy was to prosper, the national government and particularly the president had to act decisively to effect some changes. Roosevelt declared, "I have always maintained that our worst revolutionaries today are those reac-

tionaries who do not see and will not admit that there is any need for change" (Harbaugh, p. 144). By the beginning of his second term in office, an increasingly popular Roosevelt would launch the nation into a series of reforms to address the concerns of Progressives, that would become known as the Square Deal.

Roosevelt Challenges the Northern Securities Company

One of the "vital questions" with which Roosevelt had to deal when he became president was the attitude of the nation toward big corporations. Roosevelt said, "When I became President, the question as to the method by which the United States Government was to control the corporations was not yet important. The absolutely vital question was whether the Government had power to control them at all" (Roosevelt, p. 465). Between 1896 and 1900 there had been almost 2,000 mergers in the United States, resulting in gigantic companies controlling entire industries. With no competition, prices for manufactured goods were high and wages were low, and it was easy to intimidate the unions. With almost no governmental restraint industry grew unfettered while the U.S. government, supposedly representing the interest of the people, did very little.

The new president waited for the right moment to demonstrate that the government and therefore the people were again in charge. In late 1901 an opportunity to act presented itself with the formation of the Northern Securities Company. A merger of three large northwestern railroads, the Northern Pacific; the Great Northern; and the Chicago, Burlington and Quincy, merged to become the Northern Securities Company. This new holding company seemed powerful enough to create a transportation monopoly in the Northwest. Involved were Rockefeller interests, J.P. Morgan and Company, James J. Hill, and E. H. Harriman, all of whom were among the richest and most powerful businessmen in the country. Thus, if Roosevelt were to take on Northern Securities successfully he would bring down an unpopular giant, not a mere pygmy.

Lightning struck the business community when on February 18, 1902, without advanced warning, President Roosevelt's attorney general, Philander C. Knox, announced that his boss had directed him to invoke the Sherman Antitrust Act against the Northern Securities Company. Roosevelt had acted without consulting anyone except Knox. The Sherman Antitrust Act, enacted on July 2, 1890 (during the Benjamin Harrison administration), was the first federal legislation directed against industrial combination and monopoly. It prohibited combinations that restrained commerce between states or with foreign nations. This action stunned J. P. Morgan, but he recovered sufficiently to suggest that Roosevelt send Knox to meet with one of Morgan's lawyers "and they can fix it up." "That can't be done," Roosevelt responded while Knox shot back that the suit was not concerned with fixing anything up but ending illegal monopolies. Apparently sensing the president meant business, Morgan asked whether the Roosevelt administration planned to "attack my other interests." Roosevelt replied that he had no intention of doing so "unless we find they have done something that we regard as wrong" (Pringle, p. 180).

On March 10, 1902, the U.S. government filed its suit against Northern Securities in St. Paul, Minnesota. The case worked its way through to the Supreme Court. On March 14, 1904, the Court in a five-to-four decision ruled in favor of Roosevelt and the government. The Northern Securities Company must be dissolved.

Trust Busting

Roosevelt came to be called the "trust buster." More than 40 antitrust suits were initiated during the years Roosevelt was president, including those against the American Tobacco Company and the Standard Oil Company. Nonetheless, throughout his entire administration Roosevelt made it clear that he did not oppose large corporations simply because of their size. He summed up his attitude toward large corporations when he wrote, "Where a company is found seeking its profits through serving the community by stimulating production, lowering prices or improving service, while scrupulously respecting the rights of others (including its rivals, its employees, its customers, and the general public), and strictly obeying the law, then no matter how large its capital, or how great the volume of its business it would be encouraged to still more abundant protection, or better service by the fullest protection that the Government could afford it" (Roosevelt, p. 472).

According to Roosevelt large corporations could become partners in making the United States a great nation. It was the duty of the president not necessarily to break them up, but to regulate them so that the interest of the public was enhanced and not harmed. To aid the government in fulfilling this obligation, Roosevelt pushed through Congress legislation that created a new department of Commerce and Labor. The first head of this department was George B. Cortelyou. Within the department existed a Bureau of Corporations charged with investigating the operations and the conduct of interstate corporations (*See also,* Changes in the U.S. Government).

The Anthracite Coal Strike of 1902

Roosevelt saw himself as a steward, or manager, of the American people. According to Roosevelt the nation's steward is not neutral but always seeks to advance the welfare of the people. The steward, Roosevelt believed, "has the legal right to do whatever the needs of the people demand, unless the Constitution or the laws explicitly forbid him to do it" (Roosevelt, 504).

Roosevelt applied this theory in 1902 when the anthracite coal fields were shut down by a strike in north-

eastern Pennsylvania. The United Mine Workers led by John Mitchell struck on May 12, 1902. They demanded a 10 to 20 percent pay increase, an eight-hour day, union representation, and other benefits. The owners, led by George F. Baer, were uncompromising.

As the strike dragged on, a fellow named W. F. Clark sent a letter to Baer reminding him that it was his religious duty to end the strike. On July 17 Baer arrogantly replied by begging Clark not to be discouraged. He said, "The rights and interest of the laboring man will be protected and cared for—not by the labor agitators, but by Christian men to whom God in his infinite wisdom has given the control of the property interests of the country" (Pringle, p. 188). To some observers Baer seemed to suggest that he and the other owners ruled the coal mines by Divine right.

Roosevelt Intervenes

As summer turned to autumn with cooler days and nights, the need for coal to heat homes became more acute. With the welfare of the American people paramount, Roosevelt acted. He arranged an October 3 meeting at the Blair House in Washington, D.C., to which he invited the leaders from both sides. The president began by requesting "an immediate resumption of operations" so that "the crying needs of the people" might be fulfilled (Harbaugh, p. 171).

John Mitchell, representing the miners, responded by agreeing to accept the findings of a tribunal named by Roosevelt, even if it went against the strikers' claims. The owners would have none of this. Instead, Baer chided the president for asking the operators to "deal with a set of outlaws." There was to be no compromise (Harbaugh, p. 172).

After the meeting Roosevelt praised Mitchell as the "only one man in the conference who behaved like a gentleman." Alluding to Baer he said, "If it wasn't for the high office I hold, I would have taken him by the seat of the breeches and the nape of the neck and chucked him out of the window." Baer said in retrospect, "We object to being called here to meet a criminal, even by the President of the United States" (Pringle, p. 190–91).

Independent Arbitration

Although the conference failed, the people's steward persisted. Roosevelt now turned to J. Pierpont Morgan, one of the United States's richest men, and suggested that an independent arbitration commission be established. Morgan endorsed this suggestion and used his influence to gain the acceptance of the operators.

A prime reason for accepting this proposal was the president's decision to take over the mines and operate them if arbitration failed. In times past the U.S. government had moved in to break strikes. This time the government would take over the management of the mines from the owners. To the operators this smacked of socialism, and they wanted none of that.

On March 22, 1903, the commission advised a 10 percent wage increase. A nine-hour day became standard with limitations of eight hours for a few jobs. The commission also created an Anthracite Board of Conciliation to settle future differences, but the operators were not forced to recognize the United Mine Workers as a bargaining agent.

Roosevelt's handling of the strike set many important precedents. For the first time a president used his influence to bring about a negotiated settlement between labor and management. For the first time a president appointed an arbitration commission whose recommendations both sides agreed to accept. And for the first time a president threatened to send in troops not to act as strikebreakers but to take over and operate a private enterprise. As the people's steward Roosevelt felt that these actions were entirely justifiable. When Roosevelt was questioned as to whether his actions were constitutional, he retorted, "The Constitution was made for the people and not the people for the Constitution" (Harbaugh, p. 176).

The Hepburn Act, the Meat Inspection Act, and the Pure Food and Drug Act

With the nation so dependent on railroads for transportation, railroad rate regulation had become a major issue by 1905. The Congress in 1903 had passed the Elkins Act, which prohibited railroads from giving rebates to favored customers. In 1905 Roosevelt asked for more. Among the president's proposals was one that would give the Interstate Commerce Commission (ICC) more power. He told Congress that while he would not suggest to give the commission general authority to fix rates, the ICC should be allowed to monitor rates to make sure they are reasonable. Congress responded on March 18, 1906, with the passage of the Hepburn Act, called "a landmark in the evolution of federal control of private industry" (Mowry, p. 205).

The Hepburn Act gave the ICC power to nullify a railroad rate if the commission, after a shipper complained, determined that the rate charged was unreasonable. To determine the fairness of the rate, the law gave the ICC authority to examine the financial records of a company and to prescribe uniform bookkeeping. The findings of the ICC were subject to court review.

In pushing for this legislation, Roosevelt was no wild-eyed radical. In fact, while discussing the Hepburn Act Roosevelt said that when "a road is managed fairly and honestly, and when it renders a real and needed service, then the Government must see that it is not so burdened as to make it impossible to run it at a profit" (Roosevelt, p. 477). Nonetheless, he recognized that this was a new era and that the laissez-faire law of supply and demand that prevailed in the nineteenth century had to change when an industry vital to the welfare of so many Americans was involved. Oftentimes the people by themselves were

unable to battle big corporations effectively. As the people's steward the president and the U.S. government had to help. "The public, the shippers, the stock and bondholders, and the employees, all have rights, and none should be allowed unfair privileges at the expense of the others," Roosevelt said. Only a strong government could insure this (Roosevelt, p. 477).

Two other laws that were passed during Roosevelt's administration and are still on the books are the Meat Inspection Act and the Pure Food and Drug Act, both passed in June 1906. After reading Upton Sinclair's 1906 novel *The Jungle,* which described the atrocious conditions in the Chicago meat packing plants, Roosevelt went to work. He pushed through Congress the Meat Inspection Act, which called for enforcement of sanitary regulations in packing establishments and federal inspection of all companies selling meat in interstate commerce. The Pure Food and Drug Act, also backed by Roosevelt and passed the same day, prohibited the adulteration or misbranding of foods or drugs shipped in foreign or interstate commerce. The passage of these bills again signaled a significant change concerning the role of government in the lives of all Americans. Whereas the "let the consumer beware" philosophy seemed to prevail in the nineteenth century, now in an age that seemed more impersonal than the America of the nineteenth century a more apt adage was "let the producer beware."

Roosevelt and African Americans

The Progressive movement was concerned with revitalizing democracy in the United States. The Progressives believed that the rights and privileges of each and every American should be respected—the public's interest and not special interests should hold sway. Nonetheless, the record of the Progressive movement on civil rights for minorities is spotted. In the late nineteenth century Justice John Marshall Harlan had said that the Constitution is color-blind, which means there should be no discrimination because of skin color. However, the Progressives did not always promote this cause.

Roosevelt, who did much to propel the Progressive movement and called the White House a "bully pulpit," did not champion this cause. Soon after he assumed the presidency he invited Booker T. Washington, the well-known African American leader of Tuskegee Institute in Alabama, for dinner. For this Roosevelt was soundly scolded. "White men of the South, how do you like it?" cried the New Orleans *Times-Democrat.* The Memphis *Scimitar* charged Roosevelt with perpetrating "the most damnable outrage ever." Roosevelt retorted that he would have Washington "to dine just as often as I please." However, Booker T. Washington never received a second invitation (Pringle, p. 175).

Roosevelt's appointment of an African American, Dr. William Crum, as collector of customs at Charleston, South Carolina, and his determination to retain Crum in office by interim appointment when the Senate refused to approve the appointment, appeared to make Roosevelt a champion of equal opportunity. He named another African American, Cox, as postmaster of Indianola, Mississippi. When townspeople forced Minnie Cox to resign, he closed the post office for a time rather than appoint a successor. Concerning the appointment of African Americans, Roosevelt said, "It is in my mind equally an outrage against the principles of our party and of our government to appoint an improper man to a position because he is a Negro, or with a view of affecting the Negro vote; or on the other hand, to exclude a proper man from an office or as a delegate because he is a Negro. I shall never knowingly consent to either doctrine" (Blume, p. 46). Nevertheless, appointments of African Americans often seemed to be dictated more by politics than by high principle.

The Brownsville Affair

On August 14, 1906, a group of African American soldiers stationed at Fort Brown, Texas, allegedly entered nearby Brownsville, and before the night ended killed a white bartender and wounded a policeman. No one admitted committing the crime; no soldier ever was positively identified as a perpetrator. With some reluctance the soldiers' commanding officer concluded that his troops were involved. No African American soldier in three companies pointed to a culprit; thus, all were charged with a conspiracy of silence. President Roosevelt ordered all the African American soldiers in the three companies dishonorably discharged.

This action obviously provoked a great deal of reaction. While southern newspapers approved the action, northern newspapers and African American leaders soundly condemned it. Whereas, said the pastor of the Abyssinian Baptist Church in New York, Roosevelt was "once enshrined in our love as our Moses," he is today "enshrouded in our scorn as our Judas" (Harbaugh, p. 291). Not until 1972 did the U.S. Army clear the names of the African American soldiers by changing their dishonorable discharges to honorable discharges.

Roosevelt had sensed that a U.S. president was more than a political leader. This was clear when he referred to the White House as a "bully pulpit." A president unlike Congress speaks with a single voice and thus can encourage people to do right. All during the time of the Progressive movement, African Americans continued to be lynched. Although Roosevelt expressed misgivings about such outrages as well as other violations of civil rights, he never took up this cause as he did the cause of conservation. From the bully pulpit he did not thunder like an Old Testament prophet against the evils that were perpetrated against helpless victims.

Roosevelt and Conservation

Roosevelt demonstrated that he was a visionary when as president he became a staunch advocate of conservation. During the nineteenth century the United States's natural resources seemed inexhaustible. For example, Americans heading west slew huge numbers of buffalo until there were hardly any left. With a concern for future generations Roosevelt threw himself into the battle. One of his best soldiers in this campaign was Gifford Pinchot, chief forester of the United States during the Roosevelt era. Roosevelt recognized Pinchot's efforts when he wrote, "Gifford Pinchot is the man to whom the nation owes most for what has been accomplished as regards the preservation of the natural resources of our country" (Roosevelt, p. 429).

Roosevelt stated that the work of reclamation was what he first chose to address when he became President. A concrete result of this work came when Congress passed the Newlands Reclamation Act, which Roosevelt signed on June 17, 1902. This act channeled funds from the sale of western land into the construction of large dams and irrigation projects in the hot and dry regions of the West. When Roosevelt left office in 1909, 30 irrigation projects were already progressing including Arizona's Roosevelt Dam. This "helped powerfully to prove to the nation that it can handle its own resources and exercise direct and business-like control over them," Roosevelt declared (Roosevelt, p. 434).

The National Forests

In 1905 Congress authorized the creation of the U.S. Forest Service and transferred the care of the national forests from the Interior Department to the Department of Agriculture. Under Pinchot's supervision, the government encouraged supervised settlement by small-time settlers while discouraging unbridled exploitation by wealthy entrepreneurs for, as Roosevelt put it, "It is better for the Government to help a poor man to make a living for his family than to help a rich man make more profit for his company." In the summer of 1906, for the first time, those "rich men" had to pay a fee when they allowed their cattle to graze in the national forests. It was collected, said Roosevelt in the face of bitter opposition. In 1907 by presidential proclamation some 43 million acres were added to the national forests, bringing the total size of the national forests to more than 300 million acres.

After doing this Congress sought to rein in Roosevelt by attaching an amendment to the 1907 Agricultural Appropriation Bill. The amendment prohibited the president from setting aside any additional national forests in six northwestern states. This meant, Roosevelt said, that some 16 million acres of forest land could be exploited by special interests at the expense of the public interest. Yet Roosevelt had no desire to veto the entire bill, much of which dealt with other matters. With the aid of Pinchot the president outfoxed the opposition by quickly setting aside the 16 million acres and only then signing the Agricultural Appropriation Bill. When this became known, the proponents of the amendment "turned handsprings in their wrath," Roosevelt said. "Dire" threats were made against the president but "the threats could

Biography:

Gifford Pinchot

Governor; Conservationist (1865-1946) Gifford Pinchot was a Yale graduate when he traveled to Europe on his own to study forestry. He brought back with him everything he learned about scientific forestry and used it to institute the first systematic forest program in the United States. In 1896 Pinchot served on the National Forest Commission and, after only two years, was named head of the Department of Agriculture's Division of Forestry. A driving, zealous man, Pinchot enjoyed substantial influence within the administration of President Theodore Roosevelt. He was the driving force behind Roosevelt's landmark decision to transfer millions of acres of forest lands to protected reserves. Unlike other, more radical environmentalists of his time, Pinchot pushed for an understanding and a balance between environmental needs and the needs of people. Pinchot battled unbridled exploitation of U.S. resources, and taught and encouraged managed utilization. He educated some of the nation's largest lumber harvesters about the practice of

selective-cutting and its principle, "perpetuation of forests through use." He is credited, alongside Roosevelt, for some of the greatest advances in forestry and conservation between 1901 and 1909. After Roosevelt left office, Pinchot found himself working for President William Howard Taft, a man who regarded conservation as a lower priority than his predecessor. The heated debates between Pinchot and members of Taft's administration resulted in Pinchot being fired. Pinchot settled in Pennsylvania and served two terms, both marked by controversy, as the state's governor. Despite this controversy, Pinchot did succeed in passing through considerable progressive environmental legislation.

---

not be carried out, and were really only a tribute to the efficiency of our action" (Roosevelt, p. 440).

The conviction that the chief executive is the steward of the public welfare became the cornerstone of Roosevelt's conservation policy. Under this theory railroads and other corporations were subject to rules and regulations set forth by the Forest Service. "In short," Roosevelt, said "the public resources in charge of the Forest Service were handled frankly and openly for the public welfare under the clear-cut and clearly set forth principle that public rights come first and private interest second" (Roosevelt, p. 443).

Further Efforts

Keeping in mind those generations yet unborn, Roosevelt took steps to conserve the United States's forests and natural resources. During his administration five new national parks, four big game refuges, and 51 bird reservations were created. Under the National Monuments Act of June 8, 1908, places like Muir Woods in California and Mount Olympus National Monument in Washington were set aside for the public to enjoy. Congress passed laws regulating the export of heads and trophies from Alaska as well as legislation appropriating funds for the preservation of the buffalo nearly exterminated in an earlier era.

Roosevelt admitted that the conservation movement would have been unsuccessful without the support of public sentiment. To win the support of the public and

to give the conservation cause publicity and credibility Roosevelt late in his second term invited governors of several states and presidents of various important societies concerned with natural resources to the White House Conservation Conference, which ran from May 13 through May 15, 1908. This was followed by another conference, the Joint Conservation Conference, in December, which was attended by 20 state governors, representatives of 22 state conservation commissions, and representatives from 60 national organizations enlisted in the cause. This in turn gave rise to a North American Conservation Conference in February 1909, to which Canada and Mexico were invited. "It is evident," Roosevelt said, "that natural resources are not limited by the boundary lines which separate nations, and that need for conserving them upon this continent is as wide as the area upon which they exist" (Roosevelt, p. 447).

The Panic of 1907

In 1907 a year-long panic or recession hit the United States. In January the stock market experienced a jolt when John D. Rockefeller warned that because of President Roosevelt's hostility towards big business, hard times lay ahead. The stock market endured a more severe shock when in March it was rumored that the federal government planned to move against E. H. Harriman and his railroad empire. Through the summer stock prices continued to decline, and in September industrial production began to wane. Business leaders faulted the government for this turn of events, while Roosevelt in late summer blamed moneyed interests inducing panic as a means of undoing his policies.

In the twentieth century the federal government became much more involved in dealing with economic dislocations than it ever had in the past. Thus, when New York's Knickerbocker Trust Company failed in October, secretary of the Treasury George B. Cortelyou deposited $25 million in New York national banks to help them weather the storm. In November the government sold to the banks $100 million in Treasury certificates and $50 million in bonds at low interest rates on credit. The banks then could issue currency with the bonds as collateral. Finally Roosevelt allowed the merger of Tennessee Coal and Iron Company with the United States Steel Corporation. Roosevelt became convinced that a failure to agree to the merger might worsen the panic. A large New York brokerage firm held stock in Tennessee Coal and Iron and the demise of the brokerage house could generate shock waves throughout the entire financial community. In keeping with the theory that in the twentieth century the federal government has some responsibility for the public wealth and cannot simply stand idly by, Roosevelt acted.

The merger of Tennessee Coal and Iron with United States Steel had a significant, far-reaching political ramification. Historian George Mowry described the effect as "catastrophic" both for Roosevelt's hand-picked successor, William H. Taft, and the Republican Party, when the Taft administration later filed an antimonopoly suit against this merger angering Roosevelt.

The panic of 1907 made responsible leaders painfully aware of faults in the banking and currency system. As a result Congress passed the Aldrich-Vreeland Act in 1908. This established a National Monetary Commission authorized to examine the banking and currency systems of both the United States and European countries. Its 1912 report to Congress led to the Federal Reserve Act of 1913 and the establishment of the Federal Reserve system.

Foreign Issues

During the nineteenth century the United States grew and expanded by pushing westward, on the North American continent, but the country did not seem to be interested in a world empire such as Great Britain's. However, by the end of the century the nation was poised to go further. The United States began creating an empire far from her North American shores with the acquisition of Hawaii in the early 1890s. After the Spanish-American War that realm grew when Spain ceded the Philippine Islands, Guam, and Puerto Rico to the United States. In 1899 Germany and the United States each took a slice of the Samoan Islands.

There are various reasons why the United States became concerned about a far-ranging empire. Some were economic. With the growth of industry and trade the United States began to feel that if it hoped to remain strong and prosperous, it needed control over foreign markets. Other major nations sought possessions too. The United States did not want to be left out as these countries established colonies throughout the world. Nationalism also played a part. If United States wanted to claim greatness, many felt that it would have to build an overseas empire like the great powers of Europe.

When Roosevelt became president he had become convinced that his nation had to become a world player. He had been influenced by writers like Alfred T. Mahan who in 1890 published *Influence of Sea Power upon History, 1660–1783.* Mahan argued that if a nation expected greatness, a strong navy was vital. This meant naval bases throughout the world and a canal through Panama. Roosevelt set forth to build a powerful navy and the canal espoused by Mahan.

Roosevelt was also a staunch moralist. He believed that he and the country should "take up the white man's burden" as the British writer Rudyard Kipling had urged. "He shared the conviction of many Americans of his day that the superior white man must bear the burden of civilizing colonial peoples of the world, if necessary against the will of those peoples" (Beale, p. 34).

Finally, Roosevelt understood better than some of his constituents the world was shrinking and that events in Europe or Asia could affect their interests and security. Thus, the United States had to play a greater role in world affairs. Just as he became involved as a mediator in a coal strike at home because he felt the public's interests dictated it, so he became involved in Asian and European conflicts because he felt that the welfare of the United States demanded it.

The Roosevelt Corollary

The Roosevelt Corollary to the Monroe Doctrine had its beginnings soon after Roosevelt assumed the presidency. In South America an unscrupulous Venezuelan dictator named Cipriano Castro had borrowed significant sums of money from European lenders and then refused to repay. Great Britain, Germany, and later Italy instituted a blockade that finally forced Castro to arbitrate. The European allies seized several Venezuelan gunboats and the Germans sank two. During the arbitration process the Germans bombarded Fort San Carlos in Venezuela. The *New York Times,* in its January 23, 1903, edition, strongly condemned this destruction, stated, "Worse international manners than Germany had exhibited from the beginning of this wretched Venezuela business have rarely come under the observation of civilized men." The German action had annoyed Roosevelt who feared further intervention from an increasingly powerful Germany. When in 1904 the Venezuelans also seemed to invite

Biography:

John Pierpont Morgan

Banker; Financier (1837–1913) John Pierpont Morgan, commonly referred to as J. P. Morgan, was easily the most powerful U.S. banker of his time, and arguably the most accomplished industrialist. Today, Morgan is more closely associated with his founding of U.S. Steel (the largest industrial concern of its time) and his capitalization of turn-of-the-century railroad expansion, but his contributions to the nation's banking system twice proved to be the financial salvation of the federal government. During President Grover Cleveland's administration, an economic downturn combined with questionable monetary policies to strain the U.S. Treasury's gold reserves. In 1895, as the strain worsened, Morgan stepped in to sell government bonds for gold, both at home and overseas, virtually guaranteeing the solvency of the gold reserve. During President Theodore Roosevelt's administration, it was Morgan to the rescue again, this time to solve a much bigger crisis: the panic of 1907. As no central bank

existed at that time, the New York financial community responded to the panic by rallying around Morgan and his successful commercial and investment bank, J. P. Morgan and Co. Morgan averted disaster by quickly identifying and saving still-solvent institutions and transferring all federal government deposits into his bank. In the

wake of these near disasters, the need for a central bank became apparent. In 1913 the Federal Reserve was established. Never again would a private power be entrusted with so much public responsibility. Of course, Morgan's acts were not wholly altruistic and the sharp banker profited handsomely on both occasions.

European intervention by a failure to meet its financial obligations, Roosevelt advanced what came to be called the Roosevelt Corollary to the Monroe Doctrine.

The Monroe Doctrine was an idea first put forward by President James Monroe in the early 1820s that became a major component of subsequent U.S. foreign policy. The Monroe Doctrine declared that the United States would not tolerate the involvement of European nations in the Western Hemisphere. However, the Monroe Doctrine said nothing about the right of the United States to intervene in the affairs of a New World nation. In his 1904 annual message to Congress Roosevelt assumed that right, when he said:

> Chronic wrongdoing, or an impotence which results in a general loosening of the ties of civilized society, may in America, as elsewhere, ultimately require intervention by some civilized nation, and in the Western hemisphere the adherence of the United States to the Monroe Doctrine may force the United States, however reluctantly, in flagrant cases of such wrongdoing or impotence, to the exercise of an international police power.

In essence, Roosevelt was stating that the United States would take responsibility for the Western Hemisphere. The United States would ensure that disputes between Europe and the nations of South and Latin America were resolved, without the need for direct intervention by those European nations. Roosevelt hoped that the Roosevelt Corollary would nullify any legitimate reason for European intervention.

The Roosevelt Corollary was soon implemented vis-á-vis the Dominican Republic. "After a show of force by the United States," said U.S. historian Thomas A. Bailey, "the island government rather resignedly invited the Yankee big brother to step in" (p. 505). An American became the director of national finance and the United States took over the collection of tariffs, allocating 45 percent for Dominican expenses and placing 55 percent in a trust fund out of which international obligations could be met. A reluctant U.S. Senate did not approve the agreement until February 1907.

The Alaskan Boundary Dispute

In 1896 gold was discovered in Canada's Klondike region. Prospective miners found that the best water route to this area meant traversing the Alaskan panhandle. A problem arose when neither the Canadians nor the Americans seemed to know exactly what the boundaries of the panhandle were. The Anglo-Russian Treaty of 1825 and the treaty by which the United States purchased Alaska in 1867 apparently failed to mark the boundary clearly.

Secretary of State John Hay negotiated the Convention of 1903 whereby six impartial jurists of repute would meet in London England. A majority vote would decide where the line should be drawn. Each side named three representatives. Roosevelt named Secretary of State Elihu Root, former senator George Turner of Washington, and Senator Henry C. Lodge of Massachusetts, hardly "impartial jurists of repute."

The other side was represented by two Canadians and Lord Alverstone of Great Britain. When Roosevelt indicated that he would run the line where he thought it should be if the six-man tribunal did not recommend a solution the United States could accept, Lord Alverstone voted with the United States. The tribunal's findings so favored the United States that the Canadian representatives voted against the decision handed down. They charged that Lord Alverstone had caved in to pressure applied by Roosevelt and the United States.

The United States Acquires the Canal Zone

When, during the Spanish-American War, the U.S. battleship *Oregon* had been forced to sail all the way from Washington's Puget Sound around the southern tip of South America to Cuba, the United States became more aware of what might happen if there was no isthmian, or interoceanic, canal through Central America. According to the Clayton-Bulwer Treaty of 1850, Great Britain and the United States agreed to cooperate in the construction and control of any isthmian canal with the understanding that the canal could never be fortified. A half century later the United States wanted exclusive control of any canal. In 1900 Secretary of State John Hay and Britain's ambassador to the United States, Lord Pauncefote, concluded a treaty giving the United States the exclusive right to build, own, and operate an isthmian canal with the understanding that it was not to be fortified. Some Americans objected to the no-fortification clause, "Another of the Administration's 'great diplomatic victories,'" sneered the *Detroit News,* as cited in Bailey (p. 487), "has been won—by the British government" (Bailey, p. 487). Hay and Pauncefote went back to the drawing board and soon after Roosevelt assumed the presidency produced a treaty giving the United States authority to fortify as well as construct and operate a canal.

The United States now had to decide whether to build the canal through Nicaragua or Panama, then a part of Colombia. Both routes had advantages. The one through Nicaragua would be longer but would not require the construction of locks. The one through Panama would be shorter and would only require completion of work that the French had begun but had been forced to abandon.

Colombia Rejects an Offer

Another French company, the New Panama Canal Company, had acquired the rights to build a canal from the defunct company. One of its large stockholders was Philippe Bunau-Varilla who was prepared to sell those rights to the United States for $40 million. The deal was made. Only Colombia stood in the way of work beginning.

Again Hay went to work and this time concluded an agreement with the Colombian representative in Washington. Under the terms of this pact, the United States

President Roosevelt (right) *followed his own "walk softly and carry a big stick" policy in Panama. Negotiations for the construction of the canal were a major accomplishment of the Roosevelt administration.*

(The Library of Congress.)

obtained rights to a canal zone six miles wide for $10 million and an annual payment of $250,000, beginning in nine years. As the U.S. Senate considered the agreement, however, Colombia's senate unanimously rejected the treaty.

Roosevelt was outraged. He stormed that the "cut throats" and "blackmailers" of Bogotá (the Colombian capital) should not be allowed "permanently to bar one of the future highways of civilization." Roosevelt railed that, "you could no more make an agreement with the Colombian rulers than you could nail currant jelly to a wall" (Bailey, p. 491).

Roosevelt Aids Revolution in Panama

As chagrined as Roosevelt was Bunau-Varilla, who stood to lose $40 million. This persistent fellow now plotted a revolution in Panama. He conferred with Roosevelt who tacitly agreed to cooperate. Said Roosevelt about the scheming Frenchman, "He is a very able fellow, and it was his business to find out what he thought our Government would do. I have no doubt that he was able to make a very accurate guess, and to advise his people accordingly. In fact, he would have been a very dull man had he been unable to make such a guess" (Bailey, p. 493).

On November 3, 1903, a revolution in Panama began. In 1846 the United States had concluded a treaty with Colombia by which both nations had agreed to maintain the neutrality of the isthmus so that "free transit" would be unhindered. This treaty now was used against Colombia. The U.S.S. *Nashville* moved into place helping to prevent the landing of Colombian troops to quell the revolution. On November 6 Roosevelt recognized Panama as an independent nation. On November 18 the Hay-Bunau-Varilla Treaty granted the United States a zone ten miles wide for $10 million and an annual payment of $250,000 to begin in 1913. Construction of the Panama Canal began on May 4, 1904. The United States opened the canal to commerce on August 15, 1914.

Roosevelt and Relations with Japan

Nobel Peace Prize Awarded to Roosevelt

In February 1904 war broke out between Russia and Japan when Japan unleashed a surprise attack against the Russian fleet anchored at Port Arthur, Manchuria. The Japanese went on to win a series of victories. However, by the spring of 1905, the Japanese were running dangerously short of troops and money and secretly invited Roosevelt to act as peacemaker.

Roosevelt agreed to mediate the conflict. He convinced both sides to send representatives to Portsmouth, New Hampshire. Japan demanded a large war indemnity from Russia of at least $600 million and the cession of the island of Sakhalin. However, they were forced to compromise and wound up with no indemnity and settled on the southern half Sakhalin. Predictably, the Japanese public was not elated with the settlement and blamed Roosevelt and the United States. Nonetheless, throughout the world Roosevelt's efforts were hailed so that in 1906 the Nobel Peace Prize was awarded to the old Rough Rider who long had advocated speaking softly and carrying a big stick.

One significant effect of this war was the conclusion of an accord called the Taft-Katsura Memorandum. Fearful that a confident Japan might have designs on the Philippine Islands, Secretary of War William H. Taft with Roosevelt's blessing agreed to allow Japanese control over Korea in return for a promise by the Japanese to refrain from threatening the Philippines.

The Gentleman's Agreement

In 1906 the San Francisco Board of Education, in California, strained relations between the United States and Japan by ordering all Asian American students to attend a segregated public school. After just scoring a military victory in the Russian-Japanese war, many Japanese were in no mood to accept this humiliation. "Stand up, Japanese nation!" the Japanese newspaper *Mainchi Shimbun* urged on October 22, 1906. Roosevelt, who had little control over any local school board, admit-

ted that he was "horribly bothered about the Japanese business" and fretted that "the infernal fools in California" by insulting the Japanese endangered the welfare of the entire nation (Bailey, p. 522).

Roosevelt charmed the board by inviting all of them to Washington, D.C. From the board he exacted a promise to end the segregation of Asian students from the board, and in return the president agreed to take steps to curb Japanese immigration. Out of this came the so-called Gentlemen's Agreement. Japan agreed to sharply limit the number of laborers immigrating from Japan to the United States through a series of diplomatic conferences that took place in 1907 and 1908. The agreement became effective in 1908.

The Great White Fleet

Roosevelt never wanted any person or any nation to think he was afraid. Thus, he wrote to a friend:

> I am exceedingly anxious to impress upon the Japanese that I have nothing but the friendliest possible intentions toward them, but I am none the less anxious that they should realize that I am not afraid of them and that the United States will no more submit to bullying than it will bully (Bailey, p. 524).

With this in mind, Roosevelt in 1907 decided to send a U.S. fleet of 16 battleships around the world. "To observe such an armada plowing the Pacific," wrote Roosevelt biographer H. W. Brands, "would give pause to even the most reckless fire-eaters in the Japanese admiralty" (Bailey, p. 611).

Preparations went forward throughout all of 1907. When the chairman of the Senate Committee on Naval Affairs, angered that Roosevelt had not first sought congressional approval, threatened to stop the entire venture by withholding necessary funds, Roosevelt retorted by declaring that he had enough appropriated to send the fleet to the Pacific, and there it would remain if Congress refused to make available the money needed for the journey around the world. After that, Roosevelt, said "There was no further difficulty about money" (Roosevelt, p. 598).

The Great White Fleet sailed from Hampton Roads, Virginia, on December 16, 1907. The fleet steamed around South America to lower California and then to Australia and Japan. In Japan the battleships were warmly welcomed. Large numbers of Japanese children lined the way singing the U.S. national anthem in English.

The armada sailed home by way of the Mediterranean Sea. It reached U.S. shores in February 1908, the month before Roosevelt retired. Roosevelt was jubilant. Notwithstanding the Nobel Peace Prize he had won in 1906, he believed that the Great White Fleet's circumnavigation of the world was one of his most important services rendered to peace.

One evidence that this venture may have contributed to better relations between Japan and the United States was the conclusion of the November 30, 1908, Root-Takahira agreement. In this accord, reached after full discussions between the Japanese ambassador to the United States and Secretary of State Elihu Root, the two nations promised to respect each other's territorial possessions in Asia, to maintain the status quo in that area, to uphold the Open Door policy of allowing free access to China, and to support by peaceful means the "independence and integrity of China."

Roosevelt and the Algeciras Conference

In 1905 Germany and France seemed on the verge of war over Morocco. In 1880, 14 nations including the United States signed the Madrid Convention guaranteeing that all 14 nations have equal commercial opportunity in Morocco. However, France sought to gain the upper hand, and when in 1904 she announced that she would intervene in the politics of Morocco, Germany reacted angrily.

At first Roosevelt remained aloof. To William H. Taft he wrote, "We have other fish to fry and we have no real interest in Morocco" (Mowry, p. 193). However, as tensions increased, Roosevelt realized more than ever that he had to act. He persuaded both sides to meet at Algeciras, Spain, on January 16, 1906. The United States, too, sent representatives.

The conference provided no permanent solution to the conflict between Germany and her European neighbors, but did temporarily end conflict over Morocco. U.S. participation demonstrated that Roosevelt fully realized that in the twentieth century events in Europe and elsewhere significantly affected the United States. As a rising world power, his nation had to play a significant role, this time in keeping the peace.

The Roosevelt Administration Legacy

Henry Steele Commager and Richard B. Morris, two well-known and highly respected U.S. historians, state in the "Editor's Introduction" to George Mowry's *The Era of Theodore Roosevelt* that Roosevelt "ushered in a revolution—a revolution as significant in its way as the industrial revolution of almost a century earlier." They go on to say that the revolution inaugurated by Roosevelt "has gone on, not without challenge but without serious interruption, to our time, and in a very real sense we can say that the modern age began when Roosevelt took over the Presidency on September 14, 1901." Roosevelt was able to successfully inaugurate this revolution partially by the force of his personality, which won the hearts and the allegiance of many of his fellow citizens. Roosevelt himself recognized that without pub-

Fast Fact

The teddy bear got its name from Roosevelt. While Roosevelt was on a 1902 hunting expedition in Mississippi, he saved the life of a young bear that was threatened with great harm. Political cartoonist Clifford K. Berryman drew a delightful cartoon depicting the bear quizzically peeking up at the president who stood with arms outstretched signaling that no one was to hurt the bear. He was "drawing the line." After Morris and Rose Mitchom of Brooklyn, New York, saw the cartoon, they asked the president's permission to manufacture a brown toy bear and name the bear after Roosevelt. Teddy bears have existed ever since.

(Source: Vincent Tompkins, ed. *American Decades, 1900–1909*, 1996.)

lic support no significant changes could be effected. He also was a skilled politician knowing how and when to wield presidential power.

Laissez-faire, or nonintervention, had been the watchword so far as the federal government was concerned since the American Civil War. Few U.S. presidents from Abraham Lincoln to Roosevelt had been dynamic leaders. Most of them had been content to be administrators, advancing no programs to alter the status quo. Roosevelt changed all of this, and in doing so he set a new example of aggressive leadership for all presidents to follow. Roosevelt also believed a strong and active government was necessary to protect the land and people of the United States from exploitation, and he used his substantial political skill to bring such a government into being. Most significantly, he broadened the government's power to regulate industry, ensuring fair prices and competition. He was also a pioneer in conservation. His efforts protected vast tracts of land and many threatened species from destruction, so that future generations of Americans could enjoy them.

In his foreign policy Roosevelt believed that the president more than Congress could act decisively in protecting and furthering the interests of the people. Mindful of this he sought to safeguard U.S. security by laying the groundwork for an interoceanic canal and through pronouncements like the Roosevelt Corollary. Roosevelt made his constituents aware that as a world power the interests of the United States were affected by developments in faraway places like Asia and Europe. He acted to insure that the United States's interests would be protected at home and abroad, breaking the tendency of U.S. leadership to isolate the United States from the rest of the world. At times he worked hard to establish peace, but he could also be very aggressive. His treatment of Latin American nations damaged the U.S. relationship with those countries in a way that has never been fully repaired.

In sum, Roosevelt did much to restore the power and prestige of the presidency that it had lost in the late nineteenth century. In acting as he did, Roosevelt also enhanced the strength and the breath of the federal government. In various ways the federal government has become a much more vital force in the lives of all Americans during the twentieth century than it ever was in the nineteenth century. In some sense the reform movement of Theodore Roosevelt continued through the twentieth century in programs like Franklin Roosevelt's New Deal, Truman's Fair Deal, and Lyndon Johnson's Great Society.

Sources

Bailey, Thomas A. *A Diplomatic History of the American People.* New York: Appleton-Century-Crofts, 1969.

Beale, Howard K. *Theodore Roosevelt and the Rise of America to World Power.* Baltimore: The John Hopkins Press, 1956.

Blum, John Morton. *The Republican Roosevelt.* New York: Atheneum, 1962.

Boller, Paul F., Jr. *Presidential Campaigns.* New York: Oxford University Press, 1996.

Brands, H. W. *T. R.: The Last Romantic.* New York: Basic Books, 1997.

Gould, Lewis L. *The Presidency of Theodore Roosevelt.* Lawrence, Kans: University Press of Kansas, 1991.

Harbaugh, William Henry. *The Life and Times of Theodore Roosevelt.* New York: Oxford University Press, 1975.

Historic World Leaders. Vol. 5. Detroit: Gale Research, Inc., 1994.

Kane, Joseph Nathan. *Facts About the Presidents.* New York: H. W. Wilson Co., 1993.

La Follette, Robert M. *La Follette's Autobiography.* Madison, Wis.: University of Wisconsin Press, 1960.

Miller, Nathan. *Theodore Roosevelt.* New York: Morrow, 1992.

Mowry, George E. *The Era of Theodore Roosevelt.* New York: Harper and Row, 1958.

Pringle, Henry F. *Theodore Roosevelt.* New York: Harcourt, Brace and World, 1956.

Roosevelt, Theodore. *An Autobiography.* New York: Macmillan Co., 1913.

Teichman, Howard. *Alice, the Life and Times of Alice Roosevelt Longworth.* Englewood Clifts, N.J.: Prentice Hall, 1979.

Tompkins, Vincent, ed. *American Decades, 1900–1909.* Detroit: Gale Research, 1996.

Further Readings

Chessman, G. Wallace. *Theodore Roosevelt and the Politics of Power.* Boston: Little, Brown and Co., 1969.

Cooper, John Milton, Jr. *The Warrior and the Priest: Woodrow Wilson and Theodore Roosevelt.* Cambridge, Mass.: Belknap Press of Harvard University, 1983.

Hofstadter, Richard. *The Age of Reform.* New York: Random House, 1955.

———. *The American Political Tradition.* New York: Random House, 1948.

Keller, Morton, ed. *Theodore Roosevelt: A Profile.* New York: Hill and Wang, 1967.

McCullough, David. *Mornings on Horseback.* New York: Simon and Schuster, 1981.

Morison, Elting E., ed. *The Letters of Theodore Roosevelt.* 8 vols. Cambridge, Mass.: Harvard University Press, 1951–54.

Morris, Edmund. *The Rise of Theodore Roosevelt.* New York: Coward, McCann and Geoghegan, 1979.

Sinclair, Upton. *The Jungle.* New York: Doubleday, Page and Co., 1906.

Taft Administration

Biography

A congenial man with a passion for the law, William Howard Taft devoted his life to public service. His intelligence and hard work impressed Theodore Roosevelt, who gave Taft a place in his cabinet and went on to endorse him as his successor to the presidency. Taft fared poorly as president, however. He was seen as inept and conservative in comparison to Roosevelt, and disputes between his supporters and Roosevelt's cost him any chance at a second term. After the presidency Taft went on to achieve his lifelong dream by becoming the chief justice of the U.S. Supreme Court.

Early Life

From an early age, William Howard Taft was very large. As he matured, Taft might have been the butt of many a joke because of his size, but his good-naturedness instead made him well liked rather than taunted and teased. That characteristic was apparent all through his life.

Taft's father, Alphonso Taft, was, like his more famous son, a Yale graduate, lawyer, judge, and cabinet officer, serving Ulysses S. Grant as both secretary of war and attorney general in the 1870s. Taft was very much like his father and shared his father's aspirations to be a lawyer and a judge, rather than a politician. Taft's mother, Louise Taft, in some sense may have known her son better than he did himself for she discouraged him from entering politics, believing that a political career would make her son miserable.

Full name: William Howard Taft

Personal Information:
Born: September 15, 1857
Birthplace: Cincinnati, Ohio
Died: March 8, 1930
Death place: Washington, D.C.
Burial place: Arlington National Cemetery, Arlington, Virginia
Religion: Unitarian
Spouse: Helen Herron (m. 1886)
Children: Robert Alphonso; Helen Herron; Charles Phelps II
Education: Yale College, B.A., 1878; Cincinnati Law School, LL.B., 1880
Occupation: Lawyer; judge; politician
Political Party: Republican Party
Age at Inauguration: 51 years

William Howard Taft. (The Library of Congress.)

Education

William H. Taft began his formal education at Cincinnati's Sixteenth District public school. In 1870 he enrolled in Woodward High School, graduated in 1874, second in his class. In 1874 he entered Yale, graduated in 1878, again second in his class. One of his instructors was William Graham Sumner, a well-known sociologist who had popularized social Darwinism (an extension of Darwinism to social phenomena). About Sumner Taft later wrote, "I have felt that he had more to do with stimulating my mental activities than anyone under whom I studied during my entire course" (Pringle). In his junior year he was elected class orator. Taft completed his formal education by spending two years at Cincinnati Law School. In 1880 he both graduated from law school and passed the state bar examination.

Family Life

William Howard Taft married Helen Herron of Cincinnati, Ohio, on June 19, 1886. Well-bred and gracious, Helen Herron Taft was also strong-willed and ambitious when it came to her husband's career. Even though her spouse would have preferred a Supreme Court seat, she convinced Taft to turn down several such offers and instead seek the presidency in 1908. Unfortunately

Nellie, as her husband affectionately called her, suffered a stroke two months after her husband became president. She would partially recover and entertained at the White House with the aid of her sister. One of her most lasting accomplishments as first lady was arranging for the planting of the three thousand Japanese cherry trees that have graced the Washington Tidal Basin ever since.

The Tafts had three children. The oldest was Robert A. Taft who became a well-known U.S. senator from Ohio. Daughter Helen Herron Taft earned a doctorate in history from Yale and then went on to become a dean and later a history professor at Bryn Mawr College in Pennsylvania. The Taft's third child, Charles Phelps Taft, was, among other things, a county prosecutor, president of the Federal Council of Churches, and mayor of Cincinnati.

Career

Law

After Taft received his law degree and was admitted to the bar, he became assistant prosecutor of Hamilton County, Ohio. He was appointed collector of internal revenue for Ohio's First District in 1882. He practiced law in Cincinnati, Ohio, with Harlan Page Lloyd from 1883 to 1884. He became Hamilton County's assistant solicitor in 1885. In 1887 he was appointed judge of Ohio's Superior Court. Following his term as judge he served as U.S. solicitor general from 1890 to 1892, and then judge of the Sixth U.S. Circuit Court until 1900.

Politics

After the Spanish-American War (1898), the United States acquired the Philippine Islands in the Pacific Ocean as a colony. President William McKinley wanted Taft to become president of the Philippine Commission, so Taft left the bench and for the first time in his life became an executive. As commissioner and then governor-general of the Philippines, Taft was known for his able and enlightened leadership. Twice while he served in the Philippines, President Theodore Roosevelt offered Taft a seat on the Supreme Court. Although he forever aspired to be a Supreme Court justice, Taft put aside his own ambitions and remained in the Philippines, where he felt he still had work to do.

On February 1, 1904, Taft became Roosevelt's secretary of war. He accepted this position with the stipulation that as secretary of war he would continue to have supervision in the Philippines. In his new office he oversaw the early construction of the Panama Canal, connecting the Atlantic and the Pacific Oceans, and again impressed Roosevelt with his skill and intelligence.

Although Taft continued to covet a Supreme Court appointment, he gave in to the wishes of Roosevelt and his own wife and in 1908 accepted the Republican pres-

President Taft traveled to Panama to inspect the progress being made on the Panama Canal. As secretary of war under his predecessor, Theodore Roosevelt, Taft supervised the construction of the canal and established the U.S. Canal Zone. The Panama Canal was opened to traffic in 1914. (Corbis. Reproduced by permission.)

idential nomination. He won the November election, in large part because of his association with the popular Roosevelt, becoming the 27th president of the United States.

President

Taft became president at the age of 51. He was the second of the three presidents of the Progressive Era, and to his misfortune he suffers in comparison to his predecessor, Theodore Roosevelt, and to his successor, Woodrow Wilson. While Taft could claim some successes in his term, particularly for his conservation efforts and antitrust prosecutions, his lack of political skill and relative conservatism made him a poor leader for the reform-minded Republican Party. The Progressive reform movement continued under Taft, but its slower pace frustrated many Republicans. The resulting split in the party helped Democrat Wilson defeat Taft in 1912.

Post-presidential Years

After he lost the 1912 election, Taft retired from politics when he returned to Yale University to become Kent Professor of Constitutional Law. Although he continued

to teach as a law professor until 1921, he also found time to serve as joint chairman of the National Labor Board during World War I (1914–18).

On June 30, 1921, President Warren Harding named Taft chief justice of the United States. He presided over the Supreme Court until his health forced him to retire in February 1930, just one month before his death on March 8, 1930.

The William Howard Taft Administration

William H. Taft, the second U.S. president of the Progressive Era, suffered during and since his presidency from comparisons with his predecessor, Theodore Roosevelt, and his successor, Woodrow Wilson. During his presidency Taft was a supporter of the Progressive agenda, which included conservation of the nation's resources and wildlife, the break up of business trusts and monopolies that stifled the free market, and an increased responsiveness of the federal government to the will of the people. While his accomplishments were not insignificant, Taft is best remembered for his failures. Unable

Administration

Administration Dates
March 4, 1909–March 4, 1913

Vice President
James Schoolcraft Sherman (1909–12)

Cabinet
Secretary of State
Robert Bacon (1909)
Philander C. Knox (1909–13)

Secretary of the Treasury
George B. Cortelyou (1907–09)
Franklin MacVeagh (1909–13)

Secretary of War
Luke E. Wright (1908–09)
Jacob M. Dickinson (1909–11)
Henry L. Stimson (1911–13)

Attorney General
Charles J. Bonaparte (1906–09)
George W. Wickersham (1909–13)

Secretary of the Navy
Truman H. Newberry (1908–09)
George V. Meyer (1909–13)

Postmaster General
George V. Meyer (1907–09)
Frank H. Hitchcock (1909–13)

Secretary of the Interior
James R. Garfield (1907–09)
Richard A. Ballinger (1909–11)
Walter L. Fisher (1911–13)

Secretary of Agriculture
James Wilson (1897–13)

Secretary of Commerce and Labor
Oscar S. Straus (1906–09)
Charles Nagel (1909–13)

and to some extent unwilling to follow the example set by Roosevelt, Taft upset many within his own Republican Party with his actions. This split not only ensured his defeat in the 1912 election, but helped Democrat Wilson to capture the presidency.

Taft Becomes President

The Campaign of 1908

With Theodore Roosevelt's blessing, Taft had little difficulty winning the 1908 Republican presidential nomination. The Republicans chose Senator James "Sunny Jim" Sherman of New York as Taft's running mate. The Democrats for the third time called upon William Jennings Bryan to be their candidate. Bryan ran with vice presidential candidate John W. Kern of Indiana.

Because of Roosevelt's popularity, Bryan did not strongly attack the Roosevelt administration but argued that he more than Taft could carry on the reform movement. However, to many Americans Bryan seemed too radical, especially when he came out for nationalization of the railroads.

In spite of some criticism of his Unitarian religion, and a campaign that was somewhat lackluster, Taft had little difficulty winning the November election. In 1908 Taft garnered 7.6 million, or 52 percent, of the popular vote. Bryan received 6.4 million, or 43 percent, of the popular vote. Third party candidate Socialist Eugene V. Debs got three percent, or approximately 420,800 votes. In the electoral college Taft had 321 votes and Bryan had 162. On March 4, 1909, a winter storm hit Washington, D.C., so that for the first time since Andrew Jackson's 1833 inauguration the ceremony was held indoors in the Senate chamber. In his inaugural address the new president promised to advance the Progressive programs and policies established by Roosevelt.

The Campaign of 1912

By 1912 Theodore Roosevelt was so unhappy with Taft, the man he had picked as his successor in 1908, that he challenged him for the Republican presidential nomination. The reasons for Roosevelt's action were several. Roosevelt was annoyed with Taft's ineptness as a politician, his cautious conservatism, and failure to retain certain Roosevelt appointees in his own administration.

When Taft decided to run for a second term in 1912, he faced a difficult task. The Republicans had not done well in the 1910 congressional elections, and many Republicans began to wish for Roosevelt's return to the presidency. Although Taft had not enjoyed the presidency, he decided to run for the office again in 1912 in order to protect his policies. Taft felt that Roosevelt had become too radical and that the nation would not be well served by such a president.

Although Roosevelt proved to be popular in presidential primaries, Taft had the support of many of the more conservative Republicans. At the Republican National Convention, in Chicago, Illinois, this support secured the Republican nomination for Taft. The next day Roosevelt and his supporters declared the formation of a new party, the National Progressive, or Bull Moose,

Party, with Roosevelt as the party's presidential nominee. Between them, Roosevelt and Taft captured more than 50 percent of the popular vote. But neither of them won as much individually as the Democratic candidate, Woodrow Wilson. Wilson won the election with 41.9 percent of the vote, compared to 27.4 percent for Roosevelt, and 23.2 percent for Taft. With only 8 electoral college votes in his name, Taft suffered the worst defeat ever for an incumbent president.

Taft's Advisers

Unlike his predecessor, Taft relied primarily on his cabinet for advice on policy. Taft had a number of excellent advisers, particularly in the realm of foreign affairs and defense. However, his decision to replace some of Roosevelt's most favored appointees in charge of conservation, including Roosevelt's secretary of the interior, James Garfield, proved a serious political mistake. Taft's secretary of the interior, Richard Ballinger, was unpopular with many of the Progressive's strongest supporters of conservation. In particular, Gifford Pinchot, the Roosevelt appointee who headed the Department of Agriculture's Forestry Department, challenged Ballinger and Taft at every opportunity. This dispute, which lasted for the first two years of Taft's presidency and eventually forced him to fire Pinchot, played no small part in turning Roosevelt and other Progressives against Taft (*See also,* Domestic Issues).

Secretary of State Philander C. Knox was an important adviser to Taft in both domestic and foreign affairs. With Taft's blessing Knox thoroughly reorganized the State Department. He also did much to formulate and implement the dollar diplomacy policy that Taft's administration followed. Dollar diplomacy is a foreign relations strategy that emphasizes the use of economic pressure and economic aid instead of military force to achieve one's goals.

Although Taft did not strongly support recommendations for reforms in army reorganization made by his first secretary of war, Jacob M. Dickinson, Taft more willingly went along with the "Stimson Plan" devised by his second secretary of war, Henry L. Stimson. Stimson, later secretary of state under Herbert Hoover and secretary of war under Franklin Roosevelt, began the implementation of a comprehensive defense policy, while Secretary of the Navy George Meyer went about reorganizing the U.S. Navy to make it more efficient.

Attorney General George W. Wickersham played a significant role in formulating what came to be called the Mann-Elkins Act, which strengthened and extended the powers of the Interstate Commerce Commission (*See also,* Changes in the U.S. Government). The bill originally written by Wickersham was submitted to Congress where it was amended.

Fast Fact

On April 14, 1910, Taft began a presidential tradition when he threw out a baseball at the opening game of the major league baseball season. In this first game of the season the famed Washington pitcher, Walter Johnson, pitched a one-hitter as his team defeated the Philadelphia Athletics.

(Source: Joseph Nathan Kane. *Famous First Facts,* 1997.)

Taft and Congress

Taft presided over the Sixty-first and the Sixty-second sessions of Congress. In the Sixty-first session the Republicans controlled both houses of Congress. In the Sixty-second session, however, the Democrats took control of the House, 230 to 162, while the Republicans retained control of the Senate, 52 to 44. Republicans in Congress included both the reform-seeking Progressives and the older, conservative wing of the party, which considered many of the changes proposed by the Progressives to be too radical.

While Taft tended to be more conservative than his predecessor, he was still a Progressive. At the beginning of his presidency he sought to limit the power of Speaker of the House of Representatives, Joseph G. Cannon, a conservative Republican who used his authority as Speaker to control House proceedings as he saw fit (*See also,* Domestic Issues). Taft also immediately called Congress into a special session to consider tariff reform. Both efforts met with mixed results, as conservative Republicans such as Cannon resented his attacks, while Progressive Republicans saw these same efforts as too weak. Over the course of his term, Progressives came to resent Taft and his unwillingness to take the bold steps that they desired.

Although often at odds with Progressive Republicans and the Democratic opposition, Taft kept the Progressive reform movement alive, both by his support of some reform legislation and by not standing in the way of other measures favored by Progressives in Congress. Taft's support of the Mann-Elkins Act, the Postal Savings Bank system, the income tax amendment, the establishment of the Children's Bureau and the Bureau of Mines demonstrates that he was a moderate conservative (*See also,* Changes in the U.S. Government). Taft exercised the veto 39 times, nine of which were pocket vetoes. (If Congress adjourns before the president can return the vetoed bill, it is considered "pocketed.") Only once was his veto overridden.

Taft and the Judiciary

William Howard Taft appointed six Supreme Court justices. The six included Horace H. Lurton, Charles Evans Hughes, Edward D. White, Willis Van Devanter, Joseph R. Lamar, and Mahlon Pitney. Taft especially admired Lurton saying that the Lurton appointment was one of the great pleasures of his administration.

The most significant action taken by the Supreme Court during the Taft administration was the establishment of the so-called "Rule of Reason." In the 1911 *Standard Oil Company v. United States* and *United States v. American Tobacco Company* cases the Court ruled that the prohibition of all combinations in restraint of trade set forth in the Sherman Antitrust Act of 1890 really meant only unreasonable combinations in restraint of trade. This implied that there were good trusts and there were bad trusts.

In a case significantly affecting the cause of conservation, the Court in *United States v. Grimaud* (1911) ruled that the federal government and not individual states control the United States's great forest preserves.

Changes in the U.S. Government

The United States saw a number of changes in government operations during Taft's presidency. The Mann-Elkins Act (1911) recommended by Taft and passed by Congress gave the Interstate Commerce Commission unprecedented regulatory power over telephone, telegraph, cable, and wireless companies as well as railroad terminals, bridges, and fences.

At the very end of Taft's term the Department of Commerce and Labor was divided into two separate departments. In 1912 Congress passed a bill establishing a federal Children's Bureau, which publicized some of the evils wrought by child labor. When Taft chose Julia C. Lathrop to head the newly established agency, she became the first woman to lead a federal bureau. This bureau, as well as the Bureau of Mines established in 1910, represented some of the federal government's first efforts to protect the safety of workers in the United States.

In Taft's day the federal government had no central unified budget. Taft sought to change that by insisting that all budgetary estimates first go through his office. He pruned $92 million from the estimates and then sent the first modern budget to Congress.

Although one cannot argue that Taft strongly supported the Sixteenth and Seventeenth Amendments, both were proposed during his presidency. The Sixteenth Amendment, allowing a federal income tax, was adopted on February 25, 1913, just days before Taft left office. Later in 1913 the Seventeenth Amendment was adopted, allowing the people to directly elect U.S. senators. Previously senators were elected by the state legislatures. Furthermore, both Arizona and New Mexico gained statehood while Taft held office. Taft held up the admission of Arizona until that state revoked clauses in its state constitution allowing the recall of judges.

Domestic Issues

By the time William H. Taft assumed the presidency, the United States was rapidly becoming a more urban and industrialized nation. The rise of this modern society presented new challenges, which by the beginning of the twentieth century many people felt the federal government should address. In particular certain powerful collections of companies, called trusts, had developed into giant monopolies, with the ability to unfairly control prices in the marketplace and exploit resources and people on a vast scale. Furthermore, many journalists, called muckrakers because they "dug up" unpleasant facts and presented them to the public, were publicizing social ills ranging from unsafe foods and products to corruption and bribery in government. These too led to public calls for reform. The most powerful of the reform movements to arise in response to these conditions was called the Progressive movement.

The Progressive movement called for a better distribution of wealth, reforms of the political system to eliminate corruption and allow more truly democratic participation, conservation of natural resources, and limitations on the power of big business. The federal government was expected to play a major role in achieving these ends. Theodore Roosevelt, the first Progressive to become president, had begun to address many of the movement's concerns during his presidency. In the eyes of Progressives, however, many problems remained.

Taft and the Payne-Aldrich Tariff Act

For some time Progressive Republicans and Democrats had talked of tariff reform, or lowering taxes on imports. Tariff reforms were a popular idea with Progressives and among the general population because it was believed that lowering tariffs would encourage competition and cause prices to drop. However, tariff reform was opposed by businesses and by many conservatives, including conservative Republicans. As a result Roosevelt had decided not to divide the party by pushing for it. Nonetheless, the Republicans had promised to reform the tariff as part of their campaign platform, and Taft made it one of his first priorities. Soon after taking office he called Congress into a special session to face the issue.

On March 16, 1909, the day after the special session convened, Taft sent a brief 324-word message to Congress making no specific recommendations for downward revision but urging Congress to make haste in dealing with tariffs. In Taft's message, droned by a clerk, there was little electricity or a stirring call to arms. Initially, the House Ways and Means Committee, chaired by Sereno Payne of New York, proposed a bill that would have modestly reduced tariffs on four hundred items, while increasing tariffs on 75. This was not as substantial a change as many had hoped for, but despite the requests of Wisconsin senator Robert La Follette and Vice President Sherman, Taft refused to pressure the House into larger cuts. The Payne Bill passed the House on April 9, 1909. In the Senate conservative Republicans, led by Rhode Island senator Nelson W. Aldrich of the Finance Committee, took charge of the tariff issue. The bill they eventually produced contained 847 changes, six hundred of which were increases. Ten Republican senators voted against the bill, but it still passed the Senate.

Clearly, there was significant difference between the House and the Senate versions of the tariff bill. These had to be resolved by a conference committee made up of representatives from both houses. Although Taft was able to gain some reductions on some significant items along with the inclusion of a federal tax on corporations, the bill was far from the kind of sweeping reforms some had hoped for.

After signing the Payne-Aldrich Tariff Act on August 5, 1909, Taft in September embarked upon a transcontinental speaking tour. His goal was to try and win support for the unpopular act, but his speeches went over so poorly as to make matters worse. A notorious procrastinator, Taft made little preparation for his speeches, and in Winona, Minnesota, this lack of preparation showed. Speaking to a crowd of people who had hoped for much larger reductions than those made by the Payne-Aldrich Act, Taft blundered when he said that the Payne bill was the best tariff bill that the Republican Party ever passed. This claim made Taft sound ignorant and uncaring to the interests of the public, and he alienated many.

Reforming the House of Representatives

In 1903 Republican Joseph G. Cannon, often called Uncle Joe, became Speaker of the House of Representatives. At this time the Speaker could control how much time was given to debating proposals in the House, through chairmanship of the Rules Committee. The Speaker also determined who chaired the standing committees of the House, where most legislation is originally written. From the start Cannon, much like one of his pre-

decessors Thomas "Czar" Reed, presided over the House dictatorially, aggressively using his powers to prevent voting on bills he did not like. A conservative Republican, Cannon often used this power to stall or kill measures supported by Progressives.

When William Howard Taft became president, he made known his desire to remove Cannon, or if that was not possible, to at least limit his power. Progressive Republicans thought they had found an ally in the White House who would use the influence of his office to support their efforts to limit the power of the Speaker. Heartened by Taft's stance, 30 Progressive Republican congressmen in March 1909 broke with the party caucus, which had pledged to support the current system.

In spite of Taft's tough talk about dethroning Cannon, however, he ultimately followed the counsel of Theodore Roosevelt and former secretary of state Elihu Root who advised that he not seek to bring "Uncle Joe" down. Cannon could not be beaten, they said, and ultimately more harm than good would come from any attempt to unseat the Speaker. On March 9, 1909, Speaker Cannon, Senate leader Nelson W. Aldrich, and other powerful conservative Republicans met with Taft. They warned Taft that if he were to persist in the movement to restrict Cannon's power, they would block the tariff reforms that Taft was trying to achieve. After this Taft surrendered and decided to back the man that at one point he was determined to unseat. Many Progressive Republicans saw this action as strong evidence that Taft really was not on their side. They felt betrayed and this, combined with Taft's failure to support them fully in the debate on tariff reforms, made them increasingly unhappy with his leadership of the party.

In 1910 a coalition of Progressive Republicans and Democrats were successful in changing the rules of the House. The Speaker lost the power to appoint committee chairs and was no longer allowed to serve on the Rules Committee. Taft's original goal was accomplished, but in spite, rather than because, of his efforts.

The Ballinger-Pinchot Affair

The Ballinger-Pinchot controversy began the day Taft named Richard A. Ballinger secretary of the interior as a replacement for James Garfield who had served under Theodore Roosevelt. During the Roosevelt years Garfield had done much to advance the conservation cause. Both Roosevelt and Garfield hoped Taft would keep Garfield at his post. While replacing Garfield with Ballinger, Taft did retain Gifford Pinchot as chief forester even though he did not approve of Pinchot's activities under Roosevelt.

Ballinger soon angered ardent conservationists by convincing Taft that Roosevelt had erred by withdrawing from the public domain millions of acres of land and hundreds of water-power sites. Roosevelt had hoped to prevent exploitation of these resources by private entre-

Biography:

Joseph Gurney Cannon

Politician (1836–1926) Joseph Gurney Cannon was a colorful, outspoken politician who enjoyed playing the familiar, colloquial role of a common constituent. "I am," he said, "one of the great army of mediocrity which constitutes the majority." Elected to Congress in 1872, the "hayseed member from Illinois" was regarded as arrogant, reckless, and at the same time familiar and accessible. The unabashed representative was known also as "foul-mouthed Joe" and, later in his career, as "Uncle Joe." The brash Cannon fought bitterly with President Theodore Roosevelt. Roosevelt's swing to a more progressive political position conflicted sharply with Cannon's own agenda. Cannon fought Roosevelt's conservation program maintaining that the government should spend "not one cent for scenery." In 1912 Cannon was one of four Republicans to champion a proposal of an anti-third-term resolution aimed at Roosevelt. As Speaker of the House during President William Taft's administration, the controversial Cannon wasted no time

making friends with the incoming president. President Taft called Cannon's criticism of the tariff reciprocity with Canada, "the lowest politics I have ever seen in Congress." Taft tried to confront and limit Cannon's power, but to no avail. Despite his bitter disposition and clashes with other politicians, Cannon was an effective politician himself and an ardent nationalist. "This country," he

would say, is one "hell of a success." His power as a congressman was derived primarily from the strength of his personality. During his tenure, Cannon enjoyed long terms in powerful positions such as chairman of the Committee on Appropriations, chairman of the House Committee on Rules, and Speaker of the House.

---

preneurs. Taft now ordered that the land and water-power sites be returned to the public domain. Pinchot publicly attacked Ballinger's decision in August 1909, and he intimated that Ballinger was opposed to the conservation policies favored by Progressives. In November Pinchot stepped up his attacks by claiming that Ballinger was corrupt. In articles in *Collier's Weekly* he claimed that Ballinger had abused his powers as commissioner of the General Land Office in 1907 to help friends gain claims to valuable, publicly owned coal fields in Alaska. This was after Taft and his attorney general, George Wickersham, had reviewed investigations into the incident and concluded that Ballinger had done nothing wrong.

After Pinchot openly attacked Taft in January 1910, Taft decided to fire him. Taft did this even though he knew such action would hurt his relationship with Roosevelt, and at the same time cause the Taft administration to appear anticonservation. As for Ballinger, a joint congressional committee exonerated him from all charges of fraud and corruption. Nonetheless, Ballinger resigned as secretary of the interior in March 1911.

Taft Prosecutes the U.S. Steel Corporation

During the panic of 1907 President Theodore Roosevelt had allowed the merger of the U.S. Steel Corporation with the Tennessee Coal, Iron, and Railroad Com-

pany. At the time Roosevelt was convinced that the marriage of the two companies was necessary to combat the 1907 economic recession.

When Taft became president he believed that the U.S. Steel Corporation had violated the Sherman Antitrust Act, established in 1890 to deter monopolies, and therefore should be prosecuted. Taft felt that competition had been stifled and that the government should take action to restore it. Thus on October 26, 1911, the Taft administration filed suit calling for dissolution of the U.S. Steel Corporation.

Roosevelt believed this action slapped him in the face. The man that he had chosen to succeed him now had turned on him. He felt the suit was directed as much against him as it was against the U.S. Steel Corporation. Although relations between Taft and his mentor in 1911 had already become strained, the suit against U.S. Steel is what finally caused a true break. The rift now became open and public, and Roosevelt began to think of wresting the 1912 Republican presidential nomination from Taft.

Foreign Issues

Around the turn of the twentieth century, the United States began building an empire that stretched around the globe. In the late nineteenth century the United States had acquired Hawaii, the Philippines, Guam, Puerto Rico, and part of Samoa. Theodore Roosevelt had acted as arbitrator in conflicts between Russia and Japan and then later in one involving Britain, France, and Germany. This desire to acquire territories far from U.S. shores and to become involved in settling disputes in Europe and Asia reflected a change in policy from the isolationism of the United States during the nineteenth century. At the beginning of the twentieth century, Americans increasingly believed that the United States had to become more concerned about events across the seas.

William Howard Taft, Roosevelt's secretary of war and then his successor, continued the policy of involvement. Taft's policy came to be called dollar diplomacy which, among other things, meant the utilization of financial strength rather than military force to accomplish U.S. goals. To Taft, a man who abhorred war, this was a more enlightened means of advancing U.S. interests than a resort to violence.

Taft and the Open Door in China

In the Far East the United States had advocated an "Open Door" policy in China since the McKinley administration. This policy called for Chinese trade to be open to all nations. It also stipulated that China should not be carved up into spheres controlled by foreign governments, as many European nations were interested in doing.

In China's Manchuria region, Russia and Japan were each establishing spheres of influence that threatened the Open Door policy and Chinese control of the area. Secretary of State Philander Knox attempted, as he put it, to "smoke Japan out" (Bailey) by convincing U.S. and European bankers to loan China enough so that China could gain control of two railroads that were essential to Japanese and Russian dominance. However, these efforts to keep Japan out served primarily to stiffen Japanese and Russian resistance to the United States. The two nations signed a treaty of friendship on July 4, 1910.

Dollar Diplomacy and Nicaragua

Nicaragua was one nation that the United States did not wish to see fall under the dominance of some major world power, because through Nicaragua a canal to rival the Panama Canal might be constructed. Thus, the U.S. government feared that Nicaraguan dictator Jose Zelaya, who had often expressed his contempt for the United States, might enter into an agreement with a European power. After Zelaya was driven from power in 1909, with some assistance from private U.S. sources, the Taft administration insisted on reorganizing Nicaragua's finances. This was accomplished by persuading Nicaragua to arrange a large loan from U.S. bankers to pay off debts owed the British. Nicaragua was then coerced into naming an American as collector general of customs, which

would help ensure that the debts to U.S. banks would be paid on time. After extensive disorder in 1912, some 2,500 U.S. Marines landed in Nicaragua to protect U.S. lives and property.

Taft and Canada

In 1911 the Taft administration pushed through Congress a reciprocal trade agreement reducing tariffs between the United States and Canada. Unfortunately for Taft and his agreement, certain Americans, including Speaker of the House Champ Clark, convinced some Canadians that this treaty was the first step towards annexation of Canada by the United States. In the Canadian general elections of 1911, this fear of annexation by the United States helped to bring the Conservative Party, which was opposed to the trade agreement, into power. The newly elected Canadian Parliament rejected the pact.

The Taft Administration Legacy

William Howard Taft, the second president during the Progressive movement in the United States, came to office in 1909 fully intending to advance the reform movement. He had been handpicked by his predecessor, Theodore Roosevelt, who certainly expected Taft to forward his policies. Taft so disappointed Roosevelt that in 1912 Roosevelt sought to retake the White House.

Although Taft tended to be more conservative than Roosevelt, Taft's major weakness was that he lacked the sort of political skill that Roosevelt had used to advance his policies. Because he was a good politician, Roosevelt was able to hold his party together even though not all Republicans were always enthralled with him. Taft, on the other hand, alienated Progressives in his own party. The dynamic Roosevelt also gained widespread popular support that aided him in his relations with Congress. Taft never won the admiration and affection of either the American people or Congress as Roosevelt had. The U.S. public saw President Taft as overweight and overwhelmed. These considerations overshadowed Taft's legitimate Progressive accomplishments as president.

Lasting Impact

Despite his disputes with the Progressives, Taft was not a conservative and his administration boasts many reforms. He, like Roosevelt, believed that corporations should be regulated and that the cause of conservation was one that should be promoted by the federal government. Taft initiated almost twice as much antitrust legislation in four years as Roosevelt did in eight. Taft put almost as much land under federal protection as Roosevelt had, despite the fact that he also removed from protection some of the land that Roosevelt had set aside earlier. Although constantly and consistently concerned about constitutional limitations on the federal government's power, he believed the national government should concern itself with checking exploitation of those who are weak. The creation of the Children's Bureau and the Bureau of Mines provides evidence of this. Taft's attempt at tariff reform, while ultimately a failure, was also a sincere effort to improve the life of the average American. Taft favored the constitutional amendment calling for the popular election of U.S. senators (Seventeenth Amendment), and supported the income tax amendment (Sixteenth Amendment).

In sum, the Progressive movement may have lost some momentum under Taft, but it did not stop nor was it undone by his presidency. Taft's reputation no doubt suffers by comparison to the other Progressive presidents, Theodore Roosevelt and Woodrow Wilson. Together with these men, however, Taft helped to establish new political principles, directly involving the federal government in the protection and improvement of American lives.

Taft's foreign policy legacy is less impressive. Taft believed that the United States had to be more involved in world affairs than it had been throughout most of the nineteenth century. However, his attempts to exert U.S. power internationally met with mixed success at best. His efforts to support the Open Door policy in China heightened tensions with Russia and especially with Japan. Under Taft the United States also continued its trend of treating Latin American nations condescendingly rather than as equals. U.S. intervention in Nicaragua convinced many Latin Americans that Taft's dollar diplomacy was no more friendly than earlier, more militaristic, strategies.

Sources

Anderson, Judith I. *William Howard Taft: An Intimate History.* New York: W. W. Norton, 1981.

Bailey, Thomas A. *A Diplomatic History of the American People.* Englewood Cliffs, N.J.: Prentice Hall, 1980.

Coletta, Paolo E. *The Presidency of William Howard Taft.* Lawrence, Kans.: The University Press of Kansas, 1973.

Encyclopedia of World Biography. Vol. 15. Detroit: Gale Research Inc., 1998.

Kane, Joseph Nathan. *Famous First Facts.* New York: H.W. Wilson, 1997.

Mowry, George E. *The Era of Theodore Roosevelt, 1900–1912.* New York: Harper and Row, 1958.

Pringle, Henry F. *The Life and Times of William Howard Taft.* 2 vols. New York: Farrar and Rinehart, Inc., 1939.

Tompkins, Vincent, ed. *American Decades, 1910–1919.* Detroit: Gale Research Inc., 1996.

Further Readings

Anderson, Donald F. *William Howard Taft: A Conservative's Conception of the Presidency.* Ithaca, N.Y.: Cornell University Press, 1973.

Barker, Charles E. *With President Taft in the White House.* Chicago: A. Kroch and Son, 1947.

Burton, David H. *The Learned Presidency: Theodore Roosevelt, William Howard Taft, Woodrow Wilson.* London: Associated University Presses, 1988.

Butt, Archibald Willingham. *Taft and Roosevelt, the Intimate Letters of Archie Butt, Military Aide.* 2 vols. Garden City, N.Y.: Doubleday, Doran, 1930.

Penick, James, Jr. *Progressive Politics and Conservation: The Ballinger-Pinchot Affair.* Chicago: University of Chicago Press, 1968.

Sullivan, Mark. *Our Times: The United States, 1900–1925.* 6 vols. New York: Charles Scribner's Sons, 1926–35.

Taft, William H. *Our Chief Magistrate and His Powers.* New York: Columbia University Press, 1916.

Wilson Administrations

Biography

A strong and persuasive speaker, Woodrow Wilson used these talents throughout his life to encourage reform and improvement of U.S. government, education, and society. A political scientist who made important contributions to the study of U.S. government, Wilson spent many years at Princeton University as a professor and president, helping to lead the reform of U.S. higher education. After Princeton, Wilson took his passion for reform to the governorship of New Jersey and then to the presidency of the United States. Wilson's ideals were translated into many important innovations, including the institution of an income tax, suffrage for women, and reforms to the U.S. fiscal system. Wilson also guided the nation through World War I (1914–18), but in the peace that followed, Wilson's devotion to his ideals and unwillingness to compromise contributed to the Senate's failure to ratify the Treaty of Versailles and the rapid deterioration of Wilson's health.

Full name: Woodrow Wilson
Given name: Thomas Woodrow Wilson

Personal Information:

Born: December 29, 1856
Birthplace: Staunton, Virginia
Died: February 3, 1924
Death place: Washington, D.C.
Burial place: National Cathedral, Washington, D.C.
Religion: Presbyterian
Spouse: Ellen Louise Axson (m. 1885); Edith Bolling Galt (m. 1915)
Children: Margaret; Jessie; Eleanor
Education: Princeton University, BA; attended University of Virginia Law School; Johns Hopkins University, PhD, 1886
Occupation: University president; professor; lawyer; governor
Political Party: Democratic Party
Age at Inauguration: 56 years

Early Life

Wilson was born five years before the outbreak of the American Civil War (1861–65) in the Shenandoah Valley town of Staunton, Virginia. His family was deeply religious. Wilson's father, Joseph Ruggles Wilson, was a Presbyterian minister and later a seminary professor. His mother, Jessie Janet Woodrow Wilson, was of Scottish descent. Because of Pastor Wilson's duties, the family moved frequently. When young "Tommy," as he was known as a child, was just two, they moved to Augusta, Georgia. Later, they went to Columbia, South Carolina.

Woodrow Wilson. *(The Library of Congress.)*

College of New Jersey, later renamed Princeton. Wilson's oratorical abilities soon became evident. He won several public speaking contests, founded the Liberal Debating Club, and became managing editor of the campus newspaper, the *Princetonian.* Enrolling at the University of Virginia Law School upon graduation in 1879, he withdrew due to ill health in his second year. He passed the bar anyway in 1882. Following his long-standing interest in U.S. government, Wilson pursued graduate work at Johns Hopkins University in Baltimore, Maryland, where he earned one of the first PhDs in political science in 1886. His thesis, which he expanded into a book, *Congressional Government,* won him praise and remains in print over 120 years later.

Family Life

In 1885 Woodrow Wilson married Ellen Axson, a Georgian lady who was devoted to him totally in spite of his seemingly poor prospects as a graduate student. Their marriage was a grand love affair, and the couple had three daughters. Ellen Wilson made her own clothes and dresses for her daughters during the years of financial stringency, and continued doing so long after Wilson had achieved success and financial security. A woman ahead of her time, Ellen Wilson did not confine herself to domestic matters. She was involved in most of her husband's business transactions and reviewed his lectures and articles prior to their publication. Ellen Wilson died of kidney failure on August 6, 1914. The couple's eldest daughter, Margaret Wilson, assumed duties as White House hostess.

Barely six months after Ellen Wilson's death, the president began courting Edith Galt, a 42-year-old widow. She owned Washington's most fashionable jewelry store and was famous as the first woman in the city to drive her own car. The couple married on December 18, 1915. Edith Wilson became known as a gracious hostess in the White House. As first lady during World War I (1914–18), she set a good example for the country by observing meatless, gasless, and wheatless days at the White House, and volunteering with the Red Cross.

In 1919, after Wilson suffered his incapacitating stroke while touring the nation to promote his peace policies, Edith Wilson took on a highly controversial role as her husband's spokeswoman and go-between with government officials. For eight months she jealously controlled all access to Wilson and issued orders and directives in his name. While Edith Wilson claimed to be simply following her husband's wishes, she was his only source of information and thus exercised a powerful influence on those decisions. While insisting that the president was mentally sound and his physical recovery was just around the corner, the country had only her word on it.

The family was fortunate in that no family member actually had to fight during the war, although the Wilson home and church did sometimes serve as a camping ground for Confederate, or southern, soldiers. Nevertheless, the war made a deep impression on young Wilson. Later, he viewed the war as a dividing line, one after which the original constitutional structure of the nation's founders had become unworkable. Something new and different was needed to rise in its place.

Joseph Wilson had a domineering personality, demanded total loyalty from family and friends, and often seemed to want others to think him infallible. These qualities, many argue, were transferred to his son. Pastor Wilson placed no great priority on his son's education and, incredibly, the future president did not learn to read until he was nearly 12. He may have been dyslexic, and reading was always a chore for him. But he made up in doggedness and determination what he lacked in natural ability. A lighthearted youth, he joked easily and lived a rich fantasy life, imagining himself a great ship captain sent to sea to battle pirates.

Education

Wilson enrolled in Davidson College in Davidson, North Carolina, in 1873, but he withdrew the next year complaining of digestive disorders that would bother him on and off throughout his life. He soon enrolled in the

The vice president, Thomas R. Marshall, refused to force the issue of removing the president. The cabinet was suitably intimidated when Secretary of State Robert Lansing was fired (by Edith Wilson, who detested him) for suggesting that the president ought to temporarily step aside.

Wilson's health began to improve in the spring of 1920, and he once again assumed his duties as president. Edith Wilson continued to watch over him closely, however, and he remained an invalid for the rest of his term and his life.

Opinion is divided on Edith Wilson's actions during her husband's illness. One reporter called her "the finest argument for (women's) suffrage," and many felt she was simply acting as a good spouse by safeguarding her husband's health while allowing him to continue his work. But others said her appointment and dismissal of cabinet members, and her forging of the president's signature on bills were unconstitutional and a disservice to the country. Edith Wilson lived on in Washington until her own death in 1961.

Career

Wilson's father wanted his son to either follow him into the ministry or become a successful lawyer, and young Woodrow (as he began calling himself in his early adulthood) sought to satisfy that ambition by enrolling in the University of Virginia Law School. He dropped out after the first year for health reasons, but after passing the bar in 1882 he set up a practice in Atlanta, Georgia. Wilson was more interested in politics and statesmanship than the law, however, and he abandoned his practice after less than three years. He resolved to further his ambitions by returning to graduate school at Johns Hopkins University in Maryland to study and teach his first love: U.S. government. After stints of teaching at Bryn Mawr in Pennsylvania and Wesleyan in Connecticut, Wilson was named professor of jurisprudence and political economy at his own alma mater, Princeton University, in 1890.

Wilson at Princeton

At this time Princeton was still primarily a training ground for Presbyterian clergymen, a fact that Wilson hoped to change. His close study of U.S. government led him to believe that it could be further improved, and that a good place to start was by modernizing U.S. higher education. Instead of concentrating on theological subjects, he thought the mission of the modern university should be to create a corps of idealistic young men who wanted to perform public service. Wilson quickly established himself as the most popular lecturer on campus and a leader among the more liberal faculty members. In 1902 he became the university's president.

As president Wilson pushed for dramatic changes in almost every aspect of Princeton's affairs. He succeeded in raising academic standards and shifting the focus of the school away from theology and religious studies. Later efforts to reform the social atmosphere of the school brought him into conflict with students and alumni. These and other disagreements led to his resignation in 1910.

Governor of New Jersey

Wilson had attracted attention from the Democratic Party in New Jersey during his tenure as Princeton University president, and even before his resignation some of them had been encouraging him to run for governor. New Jersey politics at this time were notably corrupt, dominated by politicians who used their control over money and jobs to convince people to vote for them. These political bosses thought that the upright, straight-laced Wilson could attract the support of reformers, but be easy for them to control once in office.

Wilson won easily and, just as quickly, turned on his surprised backers. He pushed through progressive political reforms such as a direct primary law, a law regulating public utilities, a corrupt-practices act, and a workman's compensation act, which instantly made him popular with Democratic liberals across the country, and brought him the party's 1912 presidential nomination. With the Republican Party split between support for incumbent president William Taft, and former president Theodore Roosevelt, Wilson won the presidential election easily.

President

Wilson's first term represented the high point of the Progressive movement, which had begun gaining strength under President Theodore Roosevelt. Wilson significantly expanded the size and scope of government, creating the Federal Reserve Board to stabilize the currency and prevent "panics," such as the one in 1907 that had crashed Wall Street. The first peacetime federal income tax was instituted, and the Underwood Tariff Act lowered tariff schedules. Prohibition—the ban on imports, production, and sales of alcohol—was also enacted under Wilson, and women were granted the right to vote.

While Wilson sent U.S. troops into Mexico, Haiti, and the Dominican Republic to support U.S. interests, neutrality and nonintervention marked Wilson's policy in the European war, soon called World War I (1914–18). This stance was popular and helped him win a second term in 1916 on the slogan, "He Kept Us Out of War." Less than a month after being sworn in for a second term, however, Wilson asked Congress for a declaration of war on Germany, because of the latter's continued policy of sinking merchant vessels without warning. U.S. troops helped turn the tide of battle in favor of the Allies, and Germany agreed to an armistice in November 1918 on

Biography:

Edith Wilson

First Lady (1872–1961) First lady Edith Wilson commands center stage in what is certainly one of the most bizarre episodes in U.S. presidential history. In late 1919 President Woodrow Wilson became ill while on a speaking tour. Days later a stroke paralyzed the left side of his body and adversely affected his vision. More important than the changes to his physical condition were the changes to his personality and a deterioration of his decision-making ability. Certain that he would recover, Edith Wilson immediately insisted that he be secluded from everyone except herself and their doctor, a family friend. Arguing for protection of his health, Edith Wilson stood personal guard outside of her husband's door, turning away all visitors including the vice president, Thomas Marshall. For months she alone would accept documents that required the president's perusal or signature. Upon finally learning that the secretary of state had not spoken to the president in months, Republican leaders demanded a meet-

ing. To Edith Wilson's great relief, her husband pulled himself together for the short time required to say a few angry words to his skeptics. Edith Wilson was criticized by many and accused by some of filtering information before it reached her husband, even directing policy. Some say her "takeover" caused the United States to lose Sen-

ate approval for membership in Wilson's own League of Nations. Historians disagree and to her death Edith Wilson denied all such claims. Arguing for her stewardship, Edith Wilson once said, "Woodrow Wilson was first my beloved husband whose life I was trying to save, after that he was the president of the United States."

the basis of Wilson's liberal "fourteen points" (an outline of what Wilson believed necessary for world peace).

The president's efforts to negotiate a moderate peace and institute a League of Nations would be frustrated, however, by the other Allied powers (Great Britain, France, Russia, and Italy) and the U.S. Senate, neither of whom he consulted on major decisions. The U.S. Senate refused to ratify the Treaty of Versailles, which put an end to World War I and which Wilson had been instrumental in developing. Further, Wilson's attempt to generate support for the treaty with a public speaking tour in 1919 led to a stroke. His wife's decision to restrict access to Wilson during his recovery, and essentially act as president in his name, nearly provoked a constitutional crisis. Wilson would spend the rest of his term as an invalid.

Post-presidential Years

Wilson had, despite his illness, entertained thoughts of seeking a third term as president in 1920. The Democratic Party refused to consider it, however, and Wilson left office in March 1921, embittered by the Senate's unwillingness to ratify the Treaty of Versailles. He had won the Nobel Peace Prize in 1920, however, and used the money to purchase a comfortable townhouse in the Georgetown neighborhood of Washington, D.C. He thus became the only retired president to remain in Washing-

ton after the expiration of his term. He served as a law partner with Bainbridge Colby, who had served in his cabinet, but his physical debilitation prevented active work. He emerged publicly on several occasions, notably Armistice Day 1921, when he was cheered by thousands as he rode in his carriage to the funeral of the Unknown Soldier of World War I (1914–18). For the most part, however, he lived a quiet life and died on February 3, 1924. Wilson is the only president buried in the national capital, resting in the National Cathedral in northwest Washington, D.C.

The Woodrow Wilson Administrations

Wilson's presidency was dominated by World War I (1914–18), a fact that he himself found ironic given his preference for domestic affairs. Early on he stressed U.S. nonintervention and sought to mediate the conflict, but his efforts were rebuffed by both sides. After taking the United States into the war in 1917, he raised an army of more than four million people and a powerful navy. He sought a just peace at the conference table after the war, but was frustrated when his high ideals came up against the hard reality of international diplomacy and politics and his plans, as well as his health, collapsed. Domesti-

Administration

Administration Dates
March 4, 1913–March 4, 1917
March 4, 1917–March 4, 1921

Vice President
Thomas Riley Marshall (1913–21)

Cabinet
Secretary of State
Philander C. Knox (1909–13)
William J. Bryan (1913–15)
Robert Lansing (1915–20)
Bainbridge Colby (1920–21)

Secretary of the Treasury
Franklin MacVeagh (1909–13)
William G. McAdoo (1913–18)
Carter Glass (1918–20)
David F. Houston (1920–21)

Secretary of War
Henry L. Stimson (1911–13)
Lindley M. Garrison (1913–16)
Newton D. Baker (1916–21)

Attorney General
George W. Wickersham (1909–13)
James C. McReynolds (1913–14)

Thomas W. Gregory (1914–19)
Alexander M. Palmer (1919–21)

Secretary of the Navy
George V. Meyer (1909–13)
Josephus Daniels (1913–21)

Postmaster General
Frank H. Hitchcock (1909–13)
Albert S. Burleson (1913–21)

Secretary of the Interior
Walter L. Fisher (1911–13)
Franklin K. Lane (1913–20)
John B. Payne (1920–21)

Secretary of Agriculture
James Wilson (1897–1913)
David F. Houston (1913–20)
Edwin Thomas Meredith (1920–21)

Secretary of Labor
William B. Wilson (1913–21)

Secretary of Commerce
Charles Nagel (1909–13)
William C. Redfield (1913–19)
Joshua W. Alexander (1919–21)

---

cally, Wilson expanded the scope and reach of the federal government more than any president since Abraham Lincoln, instituting the Federal Reserve Board, the first peacetime income tax, and other progressive legislative initiatives.

Wilson Becomes President

The Campaign of 1912
Wilson was one of the strongest candidates for the presidential nomination of the Democratic Party as the 1912 campaign season opened. For one of the few times since the American Civil War (1861–65), the party's prospects in the November election appeared bright. The Republicans were bitterly divided between their Progressive leader, former president Theodore Roosevelt, and the conservative leader, President William Howard Taft.

Wilson's major opponents for the Democratic nomination were House Speaker James Beauchamp "Champ" Clark of Missouri, who had the backing of newspaper publisher William Randolph Hearst; House Ways and Means Committee Chairman Oscar Underwood of Alabama, a proponent of lowering tariffs who had a sizable following; and Governor Judson Harmon of Ohio, who was a favorite of the conservative faction. William Jennings Bryan, who had been the unsuccessful candidate of the Democrats in the 1896, 1900, and 1908 elections, also had many loyal supporters.

The June 1912 convention in Baltimore, Maryland, was dominated by Clark, who initially had Bryan's support. Clark held a majority of delegates in the early going, but two-thirds were needed for nomination. Wilson, back home in New Jersey, wanted to withdraw from the contest. But William G. McAdoo and Alexander McCombs, Wilson's managers, thought the contest winnable and refused to follow orders. Bryan eventually shifted his support to Wilson, and others began to fol-

Fast Fact

Wilson was the first president to hold a doctorate. His thesis, *Congressional Government: A Study in American Politics,* earned him one of the first political science doctorates granted in the United States.

(Source: Joseph Nathan Kane. *Facts About the Presidents,* 1993.)

low suit. On the 46th ballot Wilson won the necessary two-thirds and received the nomination. Governor Thomas R. Marshall of Indiana was chosen as the vice presidential nominee.

The Election

In the fall campaign Wilson realized his actual opponent was Roosevelt and his "Bull Moose" Progressive Party, as opposed to the colorless and fading Republican candidate Taft. The two men disagreed most obviously on the tariff, which was then the government's primary source of revenue, with Wilson favoring sharp reduction and Roosevelt favoring only minor changes. Both men favored banking and currency reform, with relatively little disagreement on how that should be achieved. Another major point of contention was over what to do about the "trusts," or large industrial combines that dominated entire industries, such as oil, steel, and tobacco.

Theodore Roosevelt proposed fighting bad behavior by the trusts, rather than their mere size. He favored strict enforcement of safety rules, child labor laws, and workmen's compensation for on-the-job injuries. Above all, he urged the creation of a "national industrial commission" with the power to regulate and control the activities of the trusts. The commission would be similar to the regulation the Interstate Commerce Commission (ICC) was supposed to accomplish with the railroads. Wilson took a somewhat different approach. Believing that the trusts would eventually get control of any regulatory body, the only realistic approach was to ban the practices that enabled trusts to come together in the first place, and break up existing monopolies. Early in October Wilson almost offhandedly coined a campaign slogan for this policy, "The New Freedom," which came to stand for his entire domestic program.

The campaign was thrown temporarily into confusion when an insane saloon keeper attempted to assassinate Roosevelt in Milwaukee, Wisconsin, on October 14. The bullet was stopped by the former president's eye-

glass case and the copy of the speech he was about to give. He talked for an hour before seeking medical attention. The wound proved superficial, however, and after a brief flurry of excitement, the race returned to the pre-attack pattern.

In the elections Wilson scored an impressive victory in the electoral college. Wilson had 435 electoral votes from 40 states, compared to 88 from six states for Roosevelt, and eight votes from two states for Taft. Democrats also managed to win a majority in both houses of Congress. These victories were due in no small part to the divisions within the Republican Party. Wilson's 42 percent of the popular vote was the lowest percentage for any successful presidential nominee since Abraham Lincoln's 39 percent in 1860, and was less than the 50 percent of the votes that went to Roosevelt (27 percent) and Taft (23 percent). Eugene V. Debs and the Socialist Party also had a significant showing, with 6 percent of the votes.

The Campaign of 1916

The campaign of 1916 centered dramatically on the Great War, or World War I (1914–18), then raging in Europe, and the issue of whether or not the United States should get involved. There was no question that Wilson would be the Democratic nominee. The Republican nomination went to Charles Evans Hughes, a Progressive former governor of New York who resigned his seat on the Supreme Court to run for president.

As U.S. war fever mounted, Wilson insisted on continuing his policy of neutrality, though he beefed up the armed forces in response to demands for "preparedness" from, among others, Theodore Roosevelt. Wilson's initial plan was to campaign on this theme of "preparedness," but delegates at the convention reacted so wildly to pacifist statements from the platform by the likes of William Jennings Bryan that Wilson's fall theme was switched to "He Kept Us Out of War." Wilson also sought to win over Republican Progressives with domestic legislation such as a bill mandating an eight-hour day for railroad workers, federal loans for farmers, a federal child-labor bill, heavy new income taxes on the rich, and the first estate tax in U.S. history. The Democratic platform also endorsed women's suffrage, or the right to vote.

Although the Republicans were united again and Roosevelt campaigned actively for Hughes, they could not find a way to dent Wilson's popular "He Kept Us Out of War" slogan. The Republican platform was evasive on the issue of intervention, and Roosevelt's angry attacks on the administration's neutrality policy played into Wilson's hands. Hughes's dull and legalistic oratory failed to excite the public.

Even so, the election was extremely close. Every eastern state north of the Potomac River, except Maryland and New Hampshire, went for Hughes, as did the whole Midwest except for Ohio. Wilson dominated the South and the West, however, and won 277 electoral college votes to Hughes's 254. Without the electoral votes of California, which went to Wilson by only four thousand votes, he would have lost the election.

Wilson's Advisers

Wilson was surrounded by a group of exceptionally strong and able advisers, both in his cabinet and among his informal "kitchen" cabinet. His closest adviser for most of his administration was "Colonel" Edward M. House, who accepted no official post but carved out a role for himself as Wilson's alter ego and all-around sounding board. (A wealthy Texan, House was not a military man; the title was a political moniker given to him by a friend.) House idealized Wilson, whom he first met in 1911 in New York, but House was extremely insecure with his unofficial, but highly influential position. He frequently worked to undermine and obstruct the president's other advisers, including Treasury secretary William G. McAdoo. His desire for importance in foreign affairs often caused him to disregard and exceed his instructions. Eventually these habits caught up with him, and in 1919 Wilson fired House from the delegation to the Paris Peace Conference, which negotiated an end to World War I (1914–18).

Also in the White House at Wilson's side was his secretary (the modern-day equivalent would be chief of staff) Joseph Tumulty, a New Jersey political operative who had served Wilson when Wilson was governor. Although totally loyal to Wilson, the newly elected president was uncertain Tumulty was ready for Washington. The young man had also drawn public fire for his Catholicism, and Wilson did not initially offer him a post in the new administration. House prevailed upon Wilson to rethink his position and appoint Tumulty his secretary. Tumulty's political skills proved invaluable to his patron.

The 28th president was essentially a loner. He preferred making decisions by himself rather than in consultation with others. Few cabinet members became intimate with the president, and newspaper stories sometimes leaked, especially early in the administration, that the president did not consult the cabinet enough.

In general, then, Wilson allowed his cabinet officers to run their own departments. Fortunately for him, the cabinet he chose, with a few exceptions, was more than up to the task at hand. Stellar among them was Treasury secretary William G. McAdoo, the key man inside the administration, who had run Wilson's 1912 campaign and would soon marry one of his daughters. In the cabinet, he shepherded to passage the bills creating the Federal Reserve Board and the first peacetime federal income tax (*See also,* Domestic Issues). During World War I he created the War Finance Corporation, which organized the effort to pay the immense costs of the war.

Also superb was Josephus Daniels, the North Carolina newspaperman who ran Wilson's 1912 publicity machine and was named secretary of the navy. With the help of the young assistant secretary Franklin D. Roosevelt, he built the United States Navy from a small, coastal defense force in 1913 to a war-winning, world-class operation by the end of World War I.

Inevitably, there were some mistakes. Wilson appointed William Jennings Bryan to be secretary of state, in large part because he owed Bryan for his support during the 1912 campaign. Bryan's deeply felt Christian and pacifistic beliefs were poorly suited to wartime diplomacy, however. Bryan did negotiate several successful treaties with Latin American nations, but he resigned in 1915 as a protest against the increasingly pro-Allied (including Great Britain, France, Russia, and Italy) direction of Wilson's policies. Robert Lansing replaced Bryan as secretary. Lansing proved another poor choice. His proposal to the British to disarm their merchant ships in return for an end to German surprise attacks met with outrage. He also publicly differed with Wilson on the League of Nations, Wilson's brainchild for an international peacekeeping organization of member nations, and was fired in February of 1920.

While he never served in Wilson's cabinet, Louis D. Brandeis was also an important source of advice. An attorney and a Progressive, Brandeis was famous for his support of those suffering from economic and political inequality. Wilson consulted with Brandeis on issues such as antitrust and labor policy during his 1912 campaign and first term, and he eventually appointed Brandeis to the Supreme Court.

No catalogue of Wilson's advisers would be complete without mentioning Edith Bolling Galt Wilson, the president's second wife, whom he married in 1915 after his first wife, Ellen Wilson, died in August 1914. During the winter of 1919 to 1920, with Wilson incapacitated by a stroke, Edith Wilson controlled all access to the president. Edith Wilson later claimed that she made no decisions in Wilson's name during his sickness that he was not consulted upon, but her influence was clearly enormous in terms of what the president saw and did not see. She deliberately shielded him from anything that might be unpleasant and encouraged unrealistically positive ideas, such as the possibility that Wilson could be elected to a third term. Of her "stewardship," as she later described it, it can be said that many issues and decisions were simply ignored, or put off for months. To describe her as "the first woman president," as some overenthusiastic admirers have done, is an exaggeration.

Wilson and Congress

Wilson held office during the Sixty-third, Sixty-fourth, Sixty-fifth, and Sixty-sixth Congresses. Probably no other president saw his relations with Congress deteriorate so much during his time in office, from near dominance at the start to icy and virtually total estrangement at the end. Democrats had won control of the House of Representatives in 1910, and in 1912 the Democrats added control of the Senate as well as the White House. The stage was thus set for the passage of one of the most ambitious domestic agendas of any president since Abraham Lincoln.

Wilson quickly established himself as the leader of his party and the nation, by actively working to direct the activities of Congress in a way few presidents before him had managed. Hendrick A. Clements, in his important study *The Presidency of Woodrow Wilson,* noted that there is no great secret to Wilson's early success with the Congress. "He set definite priorities," Clements writes, "made absolutely clear the principles he wanted the legislation to embody, consulted regularly and extensively with legislative leaders on the details and timing of proposals, compromised on non-essentials when necessary, and conducted effective campaigns to publicize issues and to mobilize public opinion behind what he wanted to accomplish."

The president also showed a capacity to seize politically promising opportunities. When lobbyists descended on Washington in an effort to frustrate tariff reform, his top legislative priority, he publicly attacked them in an almost unprecedented display of presidential pique. This led to a Senate investigation of lobbying that revealed several senators as having personal financial interests in halting the tariff bill. Thoroughly embarrassed, Congress gave Wilson most of what he wanted in the tariff act. By keeping Congress in special session throughout the long, hot Washington summer, he persuaded it to pass landmark bills creating the Federal Reserve Board, the first peacetime income tax in the nation's history, and the pro-labor Clayton Antitrust and the Federal Trade Commission (FTC) Acts.

The onset of the European war and the consequent uncertainty, combined with an economic recession that set in around the end of 1913, caused unemployment to soar. Wilson, newly widowed, refrained from campaigning in the 1914 midterm elections, and the Democrats were punished at the polls in November. Although they gained Senate seats and retained control of the House, their loss of 59 seats in the latter chamber stung. In 1915 Wilson was preoccupied with his remarriage and the spreading European war. In 1916, however, he put himself behind a renewed legislative push for progressive legislation. He eventually enacted a farm credit program, an eight-hour day for railroad workers, and the child-labor law that had eluded many previous reformers. On foreign policy and the war, the Congress generally fell into line behind Wilson's priorities.

Wilson's Relationship With Congress Sours

In the 1916 elections the Democrats once again lost House seats while keeping control of the chamber. The declaration of war on April 6, 1917, seems to have hardened Wilson's attitudes toward Congress, and he began to interpret all opposition to him as personal. Because of their prewar criticism of his neutrality policy, Wilson refused to work with Republicans such as former president Theodore Roosevelt or Massachusetts senator Henry Cabot Lodge. Even moderate Republicans such as former president William Howard Taft could make little impression. Democrats who opposed the war resolution and who questioned his policies were targeted by Wilson for defeat. He mostly excluded Congress from war planning, and in the process Wilson violated the principle of consultation that was so effective in his first term. To be sure, the pressures of war meant that Wilson had great freedom of action, but this very personal style of leadership meant trouble down the road.

Wilson's relations with Congress began its final plunge with the fall 1918 campaign. Republicans successfully baited Wilson into making an explicit appeal for the public to elect Democrats to office. This descent from the seemingly above politics position of a national leader during wartime to party chieftain not only failed to convince voters to choose Democrats, but actively turned them towards Republicans. The Republicans won both houses of Congress—the Senate by two seats and the House by 50.

The new political lineup guaranteed that Wilson would be in a difficult situation with Congress for the last two years of his administration. He could have lessened the damage by taking Lodge and other leading Republicans into his confidence, especially with regard to the Paris peace negotiations at the end of World War I (1914–18). This would have made it difficult for the Republicans to reject any treaty. But Wilson's insistence on conducting the negotiations by himself, and further insisting that no changes be made in the Senate, doomed the Treaty of Versailles' chances in Congress (*See also,* Foreign Issues: The Paris Peace Conference). Wilson's stroke in September 1919 meant there was little he could do to effectively oppose the Republican Congress.

Wilson and the Judiciary

Around the time of his inauguration, Wilson told Navy secretary Josephus Daniels that the federal courts needed "a very different sort of men," who were free from ties and biases "in favor of the Big Interests rather than the superior rights of all the public." Historians differ as to how well he succeeded at this goal, but Wilson certainly did appoint a higher percentage of federal judges who were members of his own political party than any president since Grover Cleveland (Abraham, p. 60). Still, at least in his High Court appointments, Wilson seems to have cared little for a candidate's nominal politics and placed more weight on his actual inclinations. That Louis D. Brandeis was a registered Republican from

Biography:

Louis Dembitz Brandeis

Jurist (1856–1941) First as an attorney, and later as a U.S. Supreme Court justice, Louis Dembitz Brandeis was one of the most effective people in protecting individuals' liberties and their right to opportunity against the inequities that were part of the industrialization of the United States. Brandeis successfully defended state laws which imposed wage controls and hour limits for workers. He led opposition to transportation monopolies and spawned the creation of alternative insurance programs with his investigation of the inequities of existing programs. In 1916 President Woodrow Wilson appointed Brandeis as a justice of the Supreme Court. As the first Jewish person to sit on the bench of the High Court, many felt that the opposition he faced during Senate confirmation hearings was the product of anti-Semitism. President Wilson's appointment was upheld and Brandeis served on the bench with distinction for more than 23 years. During his tenure he often led the way in defend-

ing civil liberties. In *Whitney v. California* (1927), Brandeis shot down a California law suppressing free speech. In the wiretapping case of *Olmstead v. United States* (1928), Brandeis argued for the right to privacy, saying that those who wrote the Constitution, as evidence of their effort, "to protect Americans in their beliefs, their

thoughts, their emotions and their sensations . . . conferred, as against the Government, the right to be let alone the most comprehensive of rights and the right most valued by civilized men." In his personal life, Brandeis was a leading Zionist, strong in his support of the development of a Jewish nation in Palestine.

Massachusetts, for example, made little impression on Wilson. Broadly, Wilson required a liberal-progressive outlook on issues generally, with a particular dedication to trust-busting in particular.

Wilson named three justices to the nation's highest court. His first appointee was his attorney general, James Clark McReynolds of Tennessee, who, like Wilson, had attended the University of Virginia Law School. Although easily confirmed in 1914, McReynolds quickly became one of the Court's most conservative, even reactionary, members. His manner and activities over the next 27 years became the stuff of Court legend. An unapologetic anti-Semite (someone who discriminates against Jews), he refused to associate with Justice Louis D. Brandeis, would not sit next to him (as seniority demanded), and left the room whenever the first Jewish justice entered. On the occasion of the 1932 swearing in of the second Jewish justice, Benjamin Cardozo, McReynolds conspicuously read a newspaper and was heard to mutter under his breath, "another one."

In contrast with McReynolds's easy confirmation, Louis D. Brandeis's nomination a year-and-a-half later was greeted with a storm of controversy. Wilson's decision to nominate the first Jewish justice provoked bitter criticism and insults against Brandeis. Factory owners, New Haven Railroad stockholders, the owners of the Boston transit system, insurance and gas industries—all of whom had lost cases to Brandeis—banded together to fight his nomination. While the opposition claimed to

be based on social and political concerns, it is clear that much of it was anti-Semitic in character. In the end, Brandeis's opponents could find no valid reason to deny him his seat, and he was confirmed by a Senate vote of 47 to 22.

Brandeis spent over 22 years on the bench, carving out for himself what most agree was one of the most important Supreme Court careers of all time, particularly in the area of civil liberties. Brandeis kept the Wilsonian faith alive long after his patron had left office and died. For that reason, he certainly can be ranked as one of Wilson's most successful appointments of any kind, and his best Supreme Court appointment.

Wilson's third and final Supreme Court nominee, John Hessin Clarke, raised none of the passions that his first two did. Just nine days after Brandeis was confirmed, Justice Charles Evans Hughes resigned from the Court to seek the Republican presidential nomination. Wilson appointed Clarke to replace him. An old friend and associate of Secretary of War Newton Baker, Clarke was then just into his second year as a U.S. district court judge in Ohio, a post to which he had been appointed by Wilson. Clarke, too, remained faithful to the ideals of the man who appointed him during his relatively brief (six years) court career. Indeed, he was to the left of Wilson and Brandeis on many issues, being the sole dissenter on a child-labor case where even Brandeis joined the majority. He resigned in 1922 to devote himself to the cause of convincing the United States to enter the League of Nations.

Significant Supreme Court decisions that affected Wilson administration policies included *Bushaber v. Union Pacific Railroad Inc.* (1916), which upheld the constitutionality of the federal income tax enacted in 1913. A series of cases in 1918 upheld the institution of a military draft and stated that such a draft did not violate the Thirteenth Amendment's ban on "involuntary servitude." *Schenck v. United States* (1919) was an important case that clarified the scope of the First Amendment in wartime. In his majority opinion, Justice Oliver Wendell Holmes offered his famous "clear and present danger" test for the limits of free speech guarantees by the government.

Changes in the U.S. Government

Prior to the first years of the twentieth century, most Americans continued to share the view of the nation's founders that large, powerful governments, such as Great Britain's during the American Revolution (1775–83), were an invitation to tyranny. But starting in the 1890s views began changing, as rural-based Populists, and later the more urban and well-educated Progressives, began boosting government as the only force that could stand up to the large industrial combines known as trusts.

Wilson fell within the Progressive camp. This is not to say that all his actions were in favor of larger government, but the overall trend of the Wilson administration was to increase the federal government's power. Wilson established the Federal Reserve Bank to bring order to the nation's money and banking system and to soften, or, better still, prevent altogether, "panics" such as that of 1907. The Federal Trade Commission (FTC) was established with the power to demand annual reports from corporations and to investigate allegedly unfair business practices. The Clayton Antitrust Act filled gaps left by the Sherman Antitrust Act of 1890 (*See also,* Benjamin Harrison Administration) and granted labor unions certain exemptions from the antitrust laws, causing labor leader Samuel Gompers to call it labor's charter of freedom. The cabinet-level Department of Commerce and Labor was split into the separate Departments of Commerce and of Labor. The Adamson Act mandated an eight-hour workday for railroad workers, an idea that quickly spread throughout the economy. Wilson also saw to the institution of the personal income tax. For the first time, individual Americans were directly responsible for the financial maintenance of the federal government.

World War I (1914–18) also was crucial in changing the relationship of Americans to their government. Its staggering cost—ten times more than the American Civil War (1861–65), not counting loans to the Allied powers (the United States's World War I allies)—was unprecedented in U.S. history. The federal budget, which was just $1 billion in 1916, doubled to $2 billion in 1917, soared to $14 billion in 1918 and a staggering $19 bil-

lion in 1919. Despite proclamations by Treasury secretary William McAdoo that the war would be financed 50 percent via taxation, the national debt leapt from $1 billion in 1915 to $24 billion in 1920.

Two constitutional amendments were passed under the Wilson administration. The Eighteenth Amendment, often called the Prohibition Amendment, banned the import, manufacture, or sale of alcoholic beverages. The Nineteenth Amendment granted women in the United States the right to vote. Both of these amendments were the result of long public campaigns and popular support, rather than action by Wilson. In fact, Wilson opposed Prohibition and doubted its feasibility. After the Eighteenth Amendment passed over his protest, he vetoed the Volstead Act that Congress passed to enforce it, but Congress overrode his veto. Wilson did not place a high priority on women's suffrage, or the right to vote, but his modest support may have helped the Nineteenth Amendment pass Congress by a narrow margin. In addition to these amendments, the Seventeenth Amendment, which had been passed by Congress in 1912, was ratified and went into effect early in Wilson's first term. The Seventeenth Amendment provided that U.S. senators be voted for directly by the electorate, rather than chosen by the state legislature as originally called for by the Constitution.

Domestic Issues

The United States was changing more rapidly in the early decades of the twentieth century than ever before. National wealth doubled between 1890 and 1900, as the United States rapidly shifted from an agricultural to an industrial economy. Between 1900 and 1913 exports leaped from $1.2 billion to $2.4 billion, with manufactured goods rising from 35 percent of this total to nearly 50 percent. A nation that had not long before been almost entirely agricultural was now the world's largest producer of coal, iron, and steel.

The tremendous changes in the U.S. economy had equally enormous social consequences. Americans flooded from their farms in the country to seek employment at urban factories, and were joined by huge numbers of immigrants from Europe. This led to overcrowding in the cities, and desolation and unrest in rural areas. In business itself, the rise of industrial capitalism and finance had led to the formation of huge trusts, combinations of businesses that controlled entire industries. These trusts and the men who ran them, such as John D. Rockefeller's oil trust, and Andrew Carnegie's steel trust, held great power not only over the U.S. economy, but over politics as well. Many politicians were unable to resist the rich monetary rewards offered by the trusts if they would use their political power to support big business.

Faced with this situation, a powerful reform movement was built across the United States in the late nineteenth and early twentieth century. Farmers and industrial workers sought protection and assistance from the government, and many in the urban middle class, calling themselves Progressives, demanded that the power of the federal government be used to reform the economy and defend the people and the so-called national interest from exploitation by big business.

By the time Wilson became president in 1912, many important reforms had been initiated. Presidents Theodore Roosevelt and William H. Taft both supported Progressive ideals to varying degrees, and they took action to break up monopolistic trusts, increase the accountability of elected officials to the public, and protect the natural resources of the United States from exploitation. The demand for change was still strong, however, and Wilson, a lifelong supporter of governmental reform, entered office with the intention of leading the movement for further change.

The Underwood Tariff

In 1913 the U.S. government derived the bulk of its revenues from taxes, called tariffs, on imported foreign goods. The tariff rates varied, but they generally ranged from 37 to 40 percent of a product's value. The effect of such tariffs was to prevent foreign producers of items ranging from shoes to sugar to steel from selling goods at lower prices than U.S. producers. High tariffs were generally supported by Republicans, who predominated in the Northeast and the Midwest and who represented industrial interests. They were opposed by Democrats from the South and the West, where there were few industries and the cost of consumer goods was high. The agricultural and mineral products of the South and the West also tended to be the target of tariffs in foreign countries in retaliation for U.S. tariffs on their goods. These latter regions had harbored long-standing resentment against the tariffs, and when Democrats got control of the federal government they aimed to do something about it.

The result was the Underwood Tariff Act of 1913. While by no means a free trade bill that eliminated tariffs, the act did propose to reduce tariffs to an average of 26 percent of value, and the list of "free" goods, not subject to tariffs, was greatly expanded.

The reduction of tariffs by the Underwood Bill meant that new sources of revenue for the government needed to be found. This was accomplished by the enactment of the first peacetime income tax system in U.S. history, made possible by the ratification of the Sixteenth Amendment to the Constitution shortly before Wilson's presidency. An earlier attempt to enact an income tax in the 1890s had been declared unconstitutional by the U.S. Supreme Court, which is what necessitated the passage of the Sixteenth Amendment.

The main threat to the passage of the income tax sections of the Underwood Tariff Act came from Pro-

gressives such as Wisconsin Republican senator Robert La Follette, who wanted a top rate of 10 percent on incomes over $100,000 annually. Wilson and his allies feared that such a rate (though hardly high by today's standards) would arouse the anger of conservatives and doom the entire bill. Wilson managed to get the Progressives to accept a top rate of 7 percent. As a result, the Underwood Tariff Act passed Congress and was signed into law by Wilson.

Banking and Currency Reform

Wilson's next priority was the modernization of the U.S. banking and currency system, which was designed for an early nineteenth-century economy rather than the world power that was now emerging. U.S. economic history in the late nineteenth and early twentieth centuries was punctuated by periodic "panics," or depressions, that threw many people out of work. By 1913 there was virtually unanimous agreement that a central reserve bank was necessary to raise and lower interest rates and make currency available to banks that were under pressure. The reserve bank was to regulate credit and banking and therefore help avoid panic situations in the future.

Wilson steered a clever middle course between southern and western Democrats who wanted a powerful government central bank and the New York bankers themselves, who favored a largely private system. On June 22, 1913, Wilson announced his decision in his second personal appearance before Congress, saying the new bank "must be public, not private, must be vested in the Government itself, so that the banks may be the instruments, not the masters of business, and of individual enterprise and initiative." In the end, what was passed was a decentralized system of regional Federal Reserve Banks under the overall supervision of a governmental body, the Federal Reserve Board in Washington, D.C. This successfully combined public control with private participation, and centralized responsibility with regional input.

Clayton Antitrust Act and Federal Trade Commission

As the Federal Reserve Act was nearing passage, Wilson turned his attention to the two competing antitrust proposals before him. One was the approach favored by Wilson's close friend and adviser Louis D. Brandeis and would ban particular business practices that were said to lead to monopolies. The other would establish a federal regulatory body to oversee business practices and would have the power to ban those it deemed "anticompetitive."

Wilson appeared for the third time before Congress in early 1914 and seemed to be in favor of a regulatory body. He advocated the creation of an "interstate trade commission" to act as a "clearinghouse" for information for businesses and the public and to impose "corrective" policies that would break large trusts into competing units.

The bill that ultimately passed bore the name of Representative Henry Clayton of Alabama, the chairman of the House Judiciary Committee, and was less than almost every advocate of strong antitrust action had wanted. No longer containing a list of prohibited practices, the bill did little more than restate the general provisions of the 1890 Sherman Antitrust Act. Wilson himself admitted when he signed it that it was "so weak you cannot tell it from water." Labor unions did win a partial exemption from the Sherman Act's prohibition of organizations that acted in restraint of trade, a significant victory although not the total exemption they had hoped for.

The criticism leveled at the Clayton Act increased Wilson's support for an industrial commission. A new bill was introduced in June 1914 to create a nonpartisan Federal Trade Commission (FTC) of five members empowered to investigate and halt anticompetitive practices and to enforce its authority through the courts. Wilson was heavily criticized by conservatives who denounced the idea as "socialist" and from a few Progressives who feared that business would soon capture control of the commission. But Wilson defended the bill on the grounds that no law could ever define prohibited business practices. The FTC Bill was passed by both houses largely as Wilson wanted it, and he signed it into law on September 26, 1914.

At the same time that the administration sought new laws, the Wilson Justice Department pursued a vigorous antitrust policy in the federal courts. While the Taft administration had largely restricted itself to attacking so-called "bad trusts," notably John D. Rockefeller's Standard Oil Company, Wilson moved against "good trusts" as well. (The latter were defined as trusts that dominated their industries, but were thought to refrain from anticompetitive practices.) These included suits to break up United States Steel, National Cash Register, and International Harvester. The Wilson Justice Department won most of the suits, either in court or by settlement. The FTC brought 224 restraint of trade cases between 1915 and 1920.

Labor Legislation

Relations between organized labor and business in the early twentieth century were poor. Unions had little in the way of legal protections, and the use of strikebreakers by businesses was common. While Wilson himself was not a supporter of labor unions, nor they supporters of Wilson, his administration fundamentally altered the relationship between labor and capital in the United States.

Wilson's first term saw the infamous 1914 Ludlow Massacre, in which striking Colorado miners and their families were machine-gunned by antiunion strikebreakers employed by Rockefeller mining interests, killing five miners, two women, and 12 children. At the request of Colorado's governor, Wilson sent federal troops into the area to disarm all parties and prevent the company from using strikebreakers. The Wilson administration thus gained credibility with organized labor that it had lacked to that point.

The first important labor legislation of Wilson's administration was the Seamen's Act of 1915. Sponsored by Progressive senator Robert La Follette, it improved pay and conditions for the nation's seafarers. In 1916 Wilson actively pushed for new labor legislation, in an effort to win support for his reelection campaign. Wilson urged the passage of the Keatings-Owen Child Labor Act, which forbade the export across state lines of goods made by children under the age of 14 (the act was later declared unconstitutional by the Supreme Court). He also signed the Kern-McGillicuddy Workmen's Compensation Act, which provided assistance for workers injured on the job. Faced with a threatened railroad strike, Wilson also signed the Adamson Act, which mandated an eight-hour day for railroad workers.

Despite his support of pro-labor legislation, the Wilson administration saw a great deal of labor strife as the United States entered World War I (1914–18). With immigration suddenly cut off, millions of men being drafted into the armed forces, and demand for labor high, unions took advantage of the situation and staged a wave of strikes. From 979 strikes in 1914, that number soared to 4,233 in 1917. After much trial and error, Wilson established the National War Labor Board, which helped guarantee labor peace in exchange for a promise of no resistance to unions by business. That, and other measures, helped calm the home front during the war and laid the groundwork for similar efforts in the Great Depression and World War II (1939–45).

Agricultural Policy

Farmers in the South and the West were an important Wilson administration constituency. Farmers had been leaving the land for industrial jobs in large cities for several decades before the Wilson administration, a process that led to much upheaval both in urban areas with unions and for those remaining on the farm. The Populist Party was fed by rural discontent with tight credit policies. Farmers generally have to borrow money in the spring to put in their crop and—hopefully—repay the loan after the fall harvest. But crop failures or low crop prices often meant the loans could not be repaid, and farmers had to take out new loans and a never-ending cycle was repeated.

In 1915 Congress reorganized the Department of Agriculture, centralizing authority in the department secretary and changing the mission of the department from primarily that of conducting agricultural research to educating farmers and improving farm living conditions. "Demonstration farms," which brought scientists and farmers into regular contact for the first time, were a feature of the Wilson agriculture policy.

The most significant piece of farm legislation of the Wilson term was the Federal Land Bank Act of 1916.

Wilson had originally opposed getting the government into the banking business, and had specifically opposed a bank aimed at a particular constituency. "I have a very deep conviction that it is unwise and unjustifiable to extend the credit of the Government to a single class of the community," he wrote in a letter to Republican Carter Glass of Virginia in 1913 (Clements, p. 64). The reality of reelection in 1916, however, swept away Wilson's doubts. He signed a bill providing federal loans at low interest rates to farmers on July 17, 1916, justifying it on the grounds that farmers were victims of credit discrimination.

Civil Rights

By any measure the Wilson administration was a backward step in the history of African Americans. Although a southerner by birth, Wilson's views on race were relatively mild. However, he was not willing to buck what he saw as popular opinion on the issue when he needed southern support in Congress. Wilson looked the other way when secretary of the Treasury William G. McAdoo of Georgia and Postmaster General Albert S. Burleson of Texas instituted segregated working conditions in their departments. They sought to dismiss African American employees where possible and, in those instances where African Americans enjoyed civil service protection, to separate them from whites. When a delegation of African American leaders came to visit him in the White House in 1914 to protest his administration's racial policies, Wilson made an absurd declaration that African Americans were full citizens treated like any other Americans and lost his temper when they disagreed (Cooper, pp. 273–4).

The "Red Scare" and the Palmer Raids

The Bolshevik Revolution of 1917, when Communists took control of Russia, inspired fear among the Allied powers (including Great Britain, France, and Italy) that their governments might also fall to Communist revolutions. This fear was strengthened by anger towards Communists, as the Bolsheviks made peace with Germany, allowing that nation to concentrate its armies on the western front of World War I, where U.S. soldiers were stationed. These concerns continued to build, and in 1919 they erupted into what became known as the Red Scare, as many Americans in their fear of Communism turned against radicals, pacifists, and foreigners of all kinds. Wilson's Espionage Act of 1917 and his Sedition and Alien Acts of 1918 allowed for the prosecution of U.S. leftists, Socialists, and pacifists who were in the forefront of antiwar activity. Mail was opened and telephones were bugged. Eventually, three thousand people were prosecuted under these laws, and many more were harassed by the American Protective League (APL), a semiofficial organization formed to boost feelings of patriotism and support for the war. Socialist Party leader and former presidential candidate Eugene V. Debs was probably the most prominent defendant, sentenced to 10 years in prison for claiming the United States was not a democracy. Other suspected Communists and revolutionaries were killed by lynch mobs.

By 1919 a wave of labor unrest and the discovery of several bombs in packages addressed to prominent Americans fed the atmosphere of paranoia. One of the bombs, carried by the bomber, exploded prematurely outside of the home of new attorney general A. Mitchell Palmer just before he went to bed. This inspired Palmer to go to work combating what he saw as a terrorist menace to U.S. society. Concentrating his attention on foreign-born radicals, who could be quickly deported under the Alien Act following a simple administrative hearing (native-born radicals required costly and time-consuming trials), more than four thousand people were arrested in a series of sweeps that came to be known as "the Palmer Raids." Many of these individuals, however, were guilty of nothing more than labor activism and had been targeted by employers eager to be rid of them. The Department of Labor, under Secretary William Wilson and Assistant Secretary Louis Post, courageously voided most of the arrest warrants. This led to hearings on whether Post should be impeached. His calm and rational testimony before a congressional committee proved a successful defense of his actions and contributed to an end to the Red Scare in the summer of 1920.

Prohibition

Prohibiting the sale of alcoholic beverages was an idea that had been growing in the United States in the late nineteenth and early twentieth century. It was promoted primarily by religious fundamentalists in the rural areas of the South and the Midwest as a pro-family measure and was led by such activists as the hatchet-wielding saloon-smasher Carrie A. Nation. The movement also exhibited an antiurban flavor (cities being the presumed site of most drinking) as well as anti-immigrant, and particularly anti-Roman Catholic Irish, impulse (again because immigrants were thought to be heavier drinkers). A Prohibition Party was established and ran unsuccessful presidential candidates but did elect some candidates to lower offices.

The onset of U.S. intervention in World War I provided Prohibitionists with an opportunity to make headway. Alcohol was prohibited in the vicinity of army bases and forbidden on board U.S. Navy vessels. Prohibitionists successfully argued that a nationwide ban on brewing would save grain needed to feed the war effort, and a temporary ban on alcohol production was passed in the summer of 1917.

The Prohibitionists built on these successes, and continued pressure on Congress led that body to pass a constitutional amendment prohibiting the sale, manufacture, or transportation of alcoholic beverages. This

A consignment of beer being destroyed during Prohibition. Wilson did not feel that Prohibition was pragmatic. (The Library of Congress.)

Eighteenth Amendment was sent to the states for ratification, which was achieved on January 16, 1919. Prohibition was scheduled to go into effect exactly one year later.

Wilson believed that Prohibition would be difficult if not impossible to enforce. He opposed the amendment, but without much vigor. Wilson vetoed the Volstead Act, which would have established a system for enforcing the Prohibition. Congress went on to pass the act over Wilson's veto, however, and Prohibition was implemented as scheduled. It is reasonable to believe that the millions of young Americans serving in Europe during the passage of the Eighteenth Amendment would have taken action to prevent Prohibition if they had been in the United States when it was debated. Certainly they, and many others, resented Prohibition, and defied it from the outset.

Women's Suffrage

The movement to grant women the right to vote grew out of the abolitionist movement against slavery in the mid-nineteenth century, in which women played a prominent role. Late in the nineteenth century many western states granted suffrage, or the right to vote, to women, in an attempt to attract women settlers. Jeannette Rankin, a Democrat from Montana, was elected to the U.S. House of Representatives in 1916, becoming the first woman to serve in Congress.

World War I helped give impetus to the suffrage movement. The drafting of millions of young men, combined with wartime restrictions on immigration, led to labor shortages. Women took advantage of the situation to enter the labor force in much larger numbers, and in more occupations, than ever before.

The Democratic platform of 1916 pledged the vote for women, a goal that Wilson officially supported but did not personally attach much importance to. Although both his first and second wife and all three of his daughters supported suffrage and may have influenced his thinking, Wilson's views on the opposite sex were somewhat patronizing and typical of Wilson's upbringing as a genteel southerner. With the war in Europe taking up much of his attention, Wilson took little action on the suffrage issue early in his presidency. Women's suffrage supporters responded with increased pressure on Wilson. Beginning in 1917 the White House was picketed 24-hours a day, and some of the more militant suffragettes engaged in hunger strikes. These actions forced Wilson to confront the issue, and in January 1918 Wilson spoke out, urging Congress to reward the heroism and loyalty of women in the United States during the war effort by passing a suffrage amendment.

The House of Representatives passed a suffrage amendment that month with only one more vote than the required two-thirds majority. The Senate for a time refused to act, but in June 1919 it too passed a suffrage amendment. Sent to the states for ratification, the Nineteenth Amendment was ratified and went into effect in time for the 1920 elections.

Foreign Issues

The end of the nineteenth century saw fundamental changes in the role of the United States in world politics. The crushing defeat of the (already much weakened) European power of Spain in the Spanish-American War (1898) impressively demonstrated U.S. military strength. The war also resulted in the establishment of an overseas empire for the United States, as it gained control of Puerto Rico and the Philippine Islands. The United States, which had long held to a policy of avoiding involvement in international affairs, was now establishing itself as a major power.

This new aggressive approach continued throughout the first decade of the twentieth century. President Theodore Roosevelt sent the U.S. navy around the world in a show of strength and began construction of a canal across the isthmus of Panama (which opened during the Wilson administration). The willingness of Roosevelt and President William H. Taft to use military force to protect U.S. interests in Central and South America understandably angered the nations of the region. Many in the United States also were uncomfortable with the new role being adopted by the United States, as the nation struggled to reconcile its history of rebellion against a repressive empire with foreign policy that some considered imperialistic.

Shortly before his inauguration, Wilson is supposed to have said to a friend, "It would be the irony of fate if my administration had to deal chiefly with foreign affairs" (Clements, p. 93). If so, fate was indeed ironic, for, almost from the first, Wilson was enmeshed in foreign policy affairs. Wilson felt that the strength of the United States could be used to support the interests of all humankind, by which he meant liberty, justice, and democracy. These beliefs would be tested, at first by unrest in Latin America, but soon afterwards by the outbreak of World War I (1914–18) in Europe. From August 1914 on, Wilson became increasingly occupied with the U.S. response to and eventually involvement in the war in Europe.

Latin America

Latin America, and Mexico in particular, formed the most important aspect of U.S. foreign policy for the first 16 months of the Wilson administration. Wilson had hoped to open a new era of good relations south of the border, but this was not to be. In the end, Wilson frequently resorted to the use of U.S. armed forces to intervene in, and in some cases occupy, Latin American and Caribbean nations.

Intervention in Mexico

Wilson's first challenge was Mexico, which had been plunged into revolution in 1911 and was in a state of near chaos. The Mexican dictator, Victoriano Huerta, had seized power following the assassination of his predecessor. Wilson refused to recognize the legitimacy of his regime. Wilson sought support among anti-Huerta rebels, and lifted his arms embargo on Mexico in hopes that weapons would reach them. But in April 1914, he seized on a minor incident in the Mexican port of Tampico, when Mexican authorities arrested some U.S. sailors, as an excuse for direct action. He ordered one thousand U.S. Marines and sailors to occupy the port of Vera Cruz and prevent the landing of German munitions destined for Huerta's forces. The landing instantly united the entire Mexican political spectrum behind Huerta. A worse result from Wilson's standpoint would be hard to imagine.

This outcome, along with the casualties of the Vera Cruz operation (19 Americans killed and 71 wounded) persuaded the new president that he had boxed himself in, and he now began looking for a diplomatic way out. Argentina, Brazil, and Chile almost immediately offered mediation, and Wilson gratefully accepted. Huerta was forced out of office in the summer of 1914, and U.S. forces withdrew from Vera Cruz four months later. But Mexico continued to bedevil Wilson.

Two years later, Washington recognized the Mexican government established by Venustiano Carranza as legitimate. Pancho Villa, a guerrilla/bandit in northern Mexico who had shown pro-U.S. inclinations previously, flew into a rage and attacked the border town of Columbus, New Mexico, in March 1916. Eighteen Americans were killed and eight wounded before Villa's band was driven off by U.S. cavalry. A U.S. force under Gen. John J. "Black Jack" Pershing was quickly dispatched to pursue Villa, an operation that soon grew to 10,000 and might have resulted in full-scale war. But it was quickly obvious that Villa had slipped away, and a sharp clash with Mexican troops at Carrizal, Mexico, convinced Wilson to close down the operation.

Pan-American Non-Aggression Treaty

Another example of Wilsonian idealism in foreign affairs that did not work out was Secretary of State William Jennings Bryan's idea for a Pan-American Non-Aggression Treaty as a symbol of the new U.S. attitude toward the region. The treaty would be a mutual agreement between the nations of North and South America that they would not attack each other. Wilson thought little of it until December 1914, when he thought he could use it as a model for a postwar treaty in Europe. He personally drafted the main clauses, calling for respect of national borders and the reduction of armaments. Chile, however, quickly rejected the idea, since it had territorial claims on Peru. Argentina, which had initially been receptive, turned it down because of Wilson's intervention in Mexico.

Mexican revolutionaries who raided Columbus, New Mexico, under the command of Pancho Villa, are apprehended by U.S. soldiers in the Mexican mountains in 1916. Clashes with Villa and his followers nearly launched the United States into war with Mexico during the Wilson administration. (Corbis. Reproduced by permission.)

Intervention in Haiti and the Dominican Republic

Wilson also invaded and occupied Haiti and the Dominican Republic during his administration, the former in July 1915 and the latter in May 1916. The motives behind each intervention were almost purely Wilsonian: a desire to bring democracy and good government to nations racked by seemingly interminable revolutions and instability. Economic and security interests were distant secondary considerations. Although the United States built roads, sewers, schools, hospitals, and other

public works in each country, and gave each relatively honest governments, the fact is these good intentions were neither wanted nor appreciated by the Haitians or the Dominicans.

Promise of Independence for the Philippines

Secretary of State Bryan had opposed the U.S. annexation of the Philippines following the Spanish-American War in 1898 and had based much of his unsuccessful 1900 presidential campaign on the issue. Bryan, like many Americans, felt that the United States, founded in opposition to the injustices of the British Empire, should not possess colonies of its own. As secretary of state, he hoped to free the islands from U.S. control. Wilson, however, was not in agreement on immediate independence, although he did instruct his new U.S. governor of the islands to publicly read a letter from him promising eventual self-government. In 1917 Wilson signed the Jones Act, formally committing the United States to this promise. While actual independence would have to wait another three decades, with a bloody war and occupation intervening, no one doubted the basic direction of U.S. policy after 1913.

World War I

The greatest test of Wilson's presidency began as his first wife Ellen lay on her deathbed in early August 1914. The war began as a conflict between Austria-Hungary and Serbia, but it quickly spread to include most of Europe. Germany, Austria-Hungary, and the Ottoman Empire (which included Turkey, Syria, Mesopotamia, Egypt, Palestine, and other states) allied together and became known as the Central Powers. They were opposed by the Allied Powers (also simply called the Allies): Britain, France, Russia, and (in 1915) Italy. Many smaller nations also participated, on both sides. As the nations of Europe went to war, Wilson read the mood of the U.S. public perfectly: whatever the causes of the war, most Americans wanted no part of it. The European war was physically distant and involved no obvious U.S. interest. Wilson proclaimed U.S. neutrality, and on August 18 urged Americans to be "neutral in thought as well as deed."

From the start, this neutrality policy was threatened by the popularity of the Allied cause with the bulk of the U.S. public and opinion makers. Though the United States had no historical or immediate quarrel with Germany, the latter's militarism and semidictatorial form of government alienated most Americans. While there were significant exceptions, such as the large German American and Irish American populations, most Americans were far more sympathetic towards Britain and its allies than towards Germany. The sense was widespread that the Allies (with the exception of Czarist Russia) were supporting values more like those of the United States: freedom and representative democracy. Thus, while they did not want to risk American lives in a European war, they hoped for an Allied victory.

Americans also found that their extensive overseas trade made neutrality easier to talk about than to accomplish. Britain applied its overwhelming sea power to blockade Germany, and the Germans retaliated by using their submarine fleet to attack and sink British shipping. Both of these actions interfered greatly with U.S. shipping and exports, particularly the blockade of Germany. By 1916 U.S. trade with Germany had fallen to scarcely 1 percent of its 1914 level, while trade with the Allied powers more than tripled. However, the British blockade only seized ships and goods, while German submarine warfare required the sinking of ships and the death of passengers and crew. These attacks created much more anger in the United States than British activities.

The United States Struggles with Neutrality

The *Lusitania*: On May 7, 1915, the British passenger liner *Lusitania* was sunk by a German U-boat (submarine) off the coast of Ireland. More than 1,200 passengers died, including 128 Americans. This loss of American lives angered much of the U.S. public, as well as Wilson himself. The president insisted on making a strong protest to the German government over the sinking that demanded reparations and an end to submarine attacks on shipping. Secretary of State Bryan, the strongest supporter of neutrality in Wilson's cabinet, was unable to convince him to modify his position and resigned on June 8.

In the short term, Wilson's response to the *Lusitania* sinking was successful. While submarine attacks continued for the next year, Wilson's approach eventually convinced the Germans that the risk of war with the United States was too great, and in May of 1916 Germany restricted the operations of its U-boats. Remarkably, this relative quiet held throughout Wilson's 1916 reelection campaign and allowed the president to run on the "He Kept Us Out Of War" slogan. Wilson's strong defense of U.S. shipping rights, however, pushed the United States further towards the Allied side and away from true neutrality.

Attempts at Mediation: Throughout the early part of World War I, Wilson tried to help the warring nations reach a settlement. On August 4, 1914, as the nations of Europe were preparing for war, Wilson dispatched a note to the European powers offering to mediate the imminent conflict. His beloved wife Ellen, however, lay on her deathbed and died just two days later, plunging Wilson into deep mourning, and he did not pursue his offer vigorously. Wilson's trusted adviser, Col. Edward House, traveled to Europe several times in 1915, as part of the continued effort to help the warring nations make peace. House was a strong supporter of Britain and the Allies, however, and it is likely that his attitude convinced the Allies that the United States would support them.

Wilson made a major attempt at mediation following his 1916 reelection. Just before Christmas he dispatched a note to the combatants once more asking them to publish the terms on which they would agree to make peace. He also offered mediation as well as U.S. participation in some sort of international league to ensure future peace, an idea he had first put forth seven months earlier. But the wording was insensitive (it suggested the war aims of the two sides were "practically the same") and failed to win any converts in Europe's capitals.

On January 22, 1917, Wilson went public with his vision of a lasting peace in what came to be known as his "peace without victory" speech to the Senate. In it, he pleaded with the combatants to forgo their hopes of victory and abandon their traditional concepts of maintaining peace through a "balance of power." He called for an equality of rights among nations and pledged that the United States would involve itself in maintaining the peace. This last point was a major change in U.S. policy, and while the speech did not succeed in its immediate object, it laid the groundwork for U.S. participation in the war on its own terms. That the United States was seeking no selfish gains in the war, unlike the other participants, was the implicit message.

The Decision to Intervene

Unbeknownst to Wilson, two weeks before his "peace without victory" address to the Senate, Germany's Kaiser Wilhelm II approved a resumption of unrestricted submarine warfare to begin on February 1, 1917. Any vessel approaching the British Isles, regardless of its flag, was liable to be attacked and sunk without warning by German U-boats. The German government was well aware that this was in violation of the pledges that had been made to Wilson the year before, and that it would likely lead to, at the very least, a rupture in relations with Washington and, at worst, a U.S. declaration of war. But the situation in Germany, suffering and starving behind the British blockade, was sufficiently dire for its government to take the risk that Germany could win the war before the United States could become militarily involved.

When the German's decision to resume unrestricted submarine warfare was announced, many Americans were angry or dismayed. Wilson broke off diplomatic relations with Germany on February 3, a step that is almost always a prelude to declaring war. But in 1917, despite the German provocations, public opinion was still against war, reflecting the isolationist mood of the public. Relatively few U.S. ships were sunk in February, and Congress refused Wilson's request to arm U.S. merchant vessels.

The Zimmerman Telegram: Meanwhile, Britain intercepted and provided to the U.S. government a telegram from the German foreign minister Arthur Zimmerman to the German ambassador in Mexico. Reflecting his country's growing desperation, the telegram instructed the ambassador to ask Mexico to ally with Germany if the United States went to war. The telegram said that after the United States was defeated, Mexico would be rewarded for its efforts with the territory it had lost to the United States during the Mexican War (1846–48): Texas, New Mexico, and Arizona.

The Zimmerman Telegram, as it came to be known, was released to the press by Wilson late in February. The telegram further worsened relations between the United States and Germany, but no action was taken at the time. What finally pushed Wilson over the edge to declare war remains somewhat mysterious to this day. He met with his cabinet on March 20 and polled its opinion, which

was in favor of war. Wilson then called Congress into special session.

In his address to Congress on April 2, Wilson declared that it was "recent actions of the Imperial German Government" that had forced the United States into the war. At the same time, Wilson made it clear that he had not abandoned the ideals in his "peace without victory" speech. For this reason, Wilson insisted that the United States was not actually joining the Allies, but was acting as merely an "Associated Power." He pledged that the United States would fight to "make the world safe for democracy." The House of Representatives and the Senate both voted in favor of war by large margins, and on April 6 Wilson signed an official declaration of war with Germany. For the first time in U.S. history, a large conscript, or drafted, army would be raised and sent overseas to fight. Initial plans called for the new income tax to pay for 50 percent of the war's cost, so as to avoid saddling future generations with the bill. Some observers, such as Theodore Roosevelt, immediately spotted the contradiction between the all-out war raging in Europe and the peace without victory that Wilson sought, but few paid attention at the time. This unresolved contradiction would prove Wilson's undoing after the armistice.

At War in Europe

The fighting on the western front, where the German army faced primarily French and British forces, had been a bloody stalemate since 1915. Millions of soldiers from both sides had died fighting in the trenches in France. Relatively few U.S. troops saw action before the fall of 1918, as the U.S. commander, Gen. John "Black Jack" Pershing, refused to place his forces on the front line mixed with other Allied troops. He wanted to wait until there were enough trained and equipped U.S. soldiers to form a separate U.S. army holding its own designated sector of the front. There were two reasons for this. First, Wilson thought that integrating the U.S., British, and French armies would weaken his claim to unselfish aims at the eventual peace conference. Second, the incredible loss of life in the first three years of the war led Pershing and Wilson to suspect that U.S. lives would simply be wasted where British and French lives had been wasted before them. Meanwhile, Germany and the new Communist government in Russia made a separate peace in late 1917, and the Germans reinforced their western armies with troops from the east.

With their increased strength, the German armies attacked the Allies repeatedly in early 1918, and U.S. troops were sometimes called in to help hold off these powerful attacks. By the mid-1918, however, U.S. soldiers were arriving in Europe in large numbers, and U.S. armies moved into the front lines. The United States finally staged its offensive in September to October 1918 in the Meuse-Argonne sector in France, helping push back the exhausted Germans while incurring heavy casualties themselves. The U.S. troops helped turn the tide against Germany, and the Allies gradually drove German army back. By early October the Germans began to seek peace. On November 9 Kaiser Wilhelm II of Germany abdicated and fled to the Netherlands. Germany signed an armistice and the fighting ceased on November 11, 1918. A total of 53,000 U.S. soldiers and sailors had died in battle. As in previous wars, more U.S. servicemen died of disease than enemy action, in this case, the influenza epidemic that gripped the world in the fall and winter of 1918–19. More than 61,000 U.S. soldiers and sailors were fatally stricken, bringing the total number of U.S. casualties in the war to 115,000 dead, and just over 200,000 wounded.

The Home Front

The United States that entered World War I had truly graduated to great power status. It possessed more than half of the world's manufacturing capacity and was financially supporting the Allied cause. Already more than $2 billion had been loaned to the British and French governments to buy U.S. munitions and supplies. Before the conflict was over, it would lend more than $7 billion more.

The Draft: One of the most controversial aspects of the Wilson administration's war effort was Wilson's plan to draft hundreds of thousands of Americans to serve in Europe. The draft had proved massively unpopular in the American Civil War (1861–65), leading to the New York draft riots. House Speaker Champ Clark was leery, saying that many Americans viewed the draft as little better than being sent to a penitentiary, and that it seemed like the very type of militarism and regimentation that the United States claimed to be fighting.

But conscription, or the draft, proved to be, if not popular, at least accepted by most Americans as the most democratic and fair way of filling the ranks. For the many immigrants in the country, it proved an "Americanizing" experience, especially for the Germans and the Irish, many of whom were not, respectively, eager to fight against Germany or at the side of Great Britain. To lessen opposition, more than four thousand local draft boards were set up to decide who would actually serve. More than 24 million men registered, and 2.7 million men were actually drafted.

The Wartime Economy: Arming and supplying such an enormous force and transporting it across three thousand miles of ocean patrolled by hostile submarines was a daunting undertaking. It required such never-before-used expedients as nationalizing the nation's railroads and establishing a Food Administration to allocate foodstuffs among the needs of the U.S. Armed Forces, the Allies, and the general population of the United States. Also new was a Shipping Board to allocate merchant shipping as required. The Council of National Defense, established in 1916, oversaw the government's economic planning and wartime supply efforts. Under this organization were the War Industries Board and the War Labor Board. While these bodies did not have the legal author-

ity to dictate to industry and labor, they successfully used public sentiment to convince the nation's manufacturers and unions to cooperate with each other and the government to help the war effort.

One possible explanation for most Americans' acceptance of the decision to go to war was the Wilson administration's decision not to impose rationing or end the production of consumer goods. The economy boomed. The draft and the wartime cutoff of immigration caused a labor shortage with a resulting rise in wages. Farmers, seeing crop prices soar, had some of their best years ever. Treasury Secretary William McAdoo's plan to finance 50 percent of the war by direct taxation proved impractical, but more than 60 million Americans ultimately bought war bonds.

Morale: Maintaining support for the war on the home front was a high priority, so the Wilson administration established the Committee of Public Information (CPI) under journalist George Creel. Its dual purpose was to censor the news and to whip up public enthusiasm and patriotism. It employed writers, photographers, and cartoonists to create thousands of pamphlets extolling the absolute righteousness of the U.S. cause. Mostly, however, it is recalled for the many speakers it trained, the so-called "four-minute men," who would give short, crisp addresses exhorting the public to ever-greater efforts.

Such efforts were not all wholesome, however. A distinct anti-German feeling was encouraged, much to the discomfort of the substantial German community in the United States. Sauerkraut became "Liberty Cabbage" and hamburgers became "Liberty Steaks." Cartoonists could not resist depicting the Kaiser and his soldiers as barbarians. The American Protective League (APL), a voluntary organization of superpatriots, deputized themselves to help suppress "subversive" activities by Socialists, pacifists, and German sympathizers. While Wilson claimed to be disturbed by the APL's vigilante-like actions, he was not sufficiently discomfited to stop Attorney General Thomas W. Gregory from using it to enforce the Sedition Act (*See also*, Domestic Issues). Postmaster General Albert Burleson vigorously enforced authority that allowed him to deny the use of the mails to any publication he deemed "subversive" or "disloyal."

The Fourteen Points and the Armistice

Nine months after the United States entered World War I, Wilson went before Congress and outlined his version of a peace settlement. The speech, which came to be known as "The Fourteen Points," was motivated by several factors. It was meant to further underline that the U.S. aims in the war differed from those of Great Britain, France, and Italy. Further, the Bolshevik government in Russia was in the midst of negotiating with Germany for a separate peace. Wilson hoped that by reemphasizing "peace without victory" and including the evacuation of all Russian territory in the Fourteen Points, he could convince Russia to stay in the war. The Fourteen Points would have a profound effect on the war's outcome and the subsequent peace conference. The points were:

1. An end to secret treaties; open agreements among nations, openly arrived at.

2. Freedom of the seas.

3. Free international trade.

4. Reduction of national armaments.

5. Impartial adjustment of colonial claims.

6. Evacuation of Russian territory.

7. Evacuation of Belgium.

8. Evacuation of French territory and the return of Alsace-Lorraine to France.

9. Readjustment of Italian frontiers.

10. Autonomy for Austria and Hungary.

11. Evacuation of Romania, Serbia, and Montenegro, and security for the Balkan states.

12. Self-determination of the peoples of the Turkish empire.

13. Independence for Poland.

14. Formation of a general association of nations.

Wilson did not consult his allies or Europe's neutrals before he issued the points, for they would not be in favor of all of them. Britain, in particular, was wary of point number two, "freedom of the seas." An island nation, Britain had long relied on the strength of its navy and control of the seas for its security. The second of the Fourteen Points seemed to imply, for example, that Britain could not stage a repeat of the blockade of Germany that had greatly weakened that nation.

The Germans did not take public note of the Fourteen Points until late September 1918, when it became clear that the Allied counterattacks in the summer and fall were pushing the German armies back, and victory for Germany was no longer attainable. A new civilian government took office in Germany and appealed directly to Wilson for an armistice based on the Fourteen Points. A complex and delicate series of negotiations now commenced between Wilson and the new German administration under Prince Max of Baden. With the other Allies watching warily from the sidelines, Wilson ultimately negotiated a settlement that amounted to virtual German surrender including the evacuation of all occupied territories, and Allied occupation of portions of western Germany as a guarantee against the resumption of the war. The war ended at the 11th hour of the 11th day of the 11th month: November 11, 1918.

The Paris Peace Conference

The victorious Allies now had to gather and determine the fate of their defeated enemies. On December 4, 1918, Wilson and his handpicked delegation of associates set sail for France, where the peace conference was to be held in Paris beginning on January 18, 1919. Wilson was the first serving U.S. president ever to visit Europe. While many of those he brought with him, notably Colonel House, were able and the delegation was probably the best prepared and briefed of any of those present, the president did not bring any Republicans with him. This would prove to be a serious mistake. The Democrats had lost control of Congress in the elections of the previous month, and a Republican Senate would have to ratify any treaty that Wilson brought home.

Wilson was one of the most popular men in the world in the late fall of 1918. When he arrived in Paris, enormous crowds greeted him chanting "Wil-son! Wil-son!" His professed idealism and liberalism and promises of a new era of world peace were music to the ears of a war-weary continent.

Wilson was determined to formalize the Fourteen Points, but his negotiating partners—Prime Minister David Lloyd George of Great Britain, Premier's Georges Clemenceau of France, and Vittorio Orlando of Italy—were lukewarm at best about the Fourteen Points and were interested in them only to the extent that their purposes were served.

Wilson's Fourteenth Point, his proposal for a League of Nations, proved to be what he was most interested in. He was made the chairman of the committee in charge of drafting a covenant for the league, which he accomplished within a month. A trip back to Washington, however, should have warned him that he was getting out of touch with public opinion back home. Republican leaders in charge of Congress were not flat-out opposed to a league, but they were concerned about U.S. sovereignty and "entangling alliances." Upon his return to France, Wilson discovered that House, whom he had deputized to negotiate for him in his absence, had made a number of concessions Wilson felt he could not accept. The pressures on Wilson reached the point where he became sick and took to his bed. This illness, and reports that Wilson was suffering a number of odd hallucinations (he thought someone was stealing the furniture from the house where he was staying, for example) undermined his standing in Paris.

The Treaty of Versailles

The negotiations concluded on June 28, 1919, with the signing of a treaty at Versailles, not far from Paris. The Treaty of Versailles followed Wilson's Fourteen Points in many areas but violated them in others. While Wilson was able to prevent France from dismembering western Germany or imposing a permanent occupation of its territory, these concessions hardly made up for what Germany lost: its overseas colonies, navy, air force, and most of its army. Germany was saddled with reparations no nation could afford to pay and was forced to accept sole guilt for starting the war. While the treaty

President Wilson (far right) *outside the Palace of Versailles during the Versailles Treaty negotiations with the other heads of state who, with Wilson, make up "The Big Four": David Lloyd George of Great Britain, Vittorio Orlando of Italy, and Georges Clemenceau of France* (left to right). *(The Library of Congress.)*

has always been presented as having been given to the Germans on a "take it or leave it" basis, this is not quite true. They received the text on May 7, and there followed nearly two months of back-and-forth negotiations that resulted in several key concessions to Germany. Still, the treaty was harsher than the German public had been led to expect, given that Germany had agreed to the November 1918 armistice on the basis of the Fourteen Points. A young corporal in a Bavarian regiment named Adolf Hitler would ride this sense of having been cheated to power 15 years later. The Treaty of Versailles did include the covenant for the Wilson's League of Nations, however.

The U.S. Senate Rejects the Treaty of Versailles

Wilson fought hard to include the league covenant in the treaty because he believed it would provide a permanent institution for resolving conflict between nations without resorting to war. Despite the fact that the Treaty of Versailles included provisions with which Wilson did not agree, such as very heavy reparations on Germany, he supported it in part because he believed the League of Nations would allow the problems with the rest of the document to be addressed. But Wilson now began paying the price for failing to bring the Republicans into his peace delegation. By keeping them out, Wilson ensured that he bore sole responsibility for a treaty that, even though he generally liked it, he admitted was "less than ideal."

Senate majority leader and Foreign Relations Committee chairman Henry Cabot Lodge believed the United States should remain engaged in world affairs, but he found Wilson's moralizing a poor foundation on which to base a system of international security. He objected to the Treaty of Versailles because he feared that it would threaten U.S. sovereignty, and draw the United States into dangerous and impractical obligations. Article 10 of the League of Nations covenant was particularly worrisome to Lodge; it appeared to commit the United States to go to war in support of the territorial integrity of any member state of the League of Nations.

The president tried to woo senators to his side but was unsuccessful largely because he refused to attach to the treaty any reservations or amendments. He demanded that the treaty be accepted as it stood. Wilson did this even though many changes were favored by almost as many Democrats as Republicans. Wilson then embarked on a nationwide speaking tour, which he firmly believed would reveal a nationwide consensus in favor of his own position.

Leaving Washington on September 3, 1919, Wilson headed for the western states, which had given him his narrow margin of victory in 1916. The president was greeted by large, and mostly enthusiastic, crowds. But

What They Said . . .

On April 2, 1917, President Wilson went before Congress to request a declaration of war against Germany. In this speech Wilson said:

"The world must be made safe for democracy. . . . It is a fearful thing to lead this great peaceful people into war, into the most terrible and disastrous of all wars, civilization itself seeming to be in the balance. But the right is more precious than the peace, and we shall fight for the things we have always carried nearest our hearts—for democracy, for the right of those who submit to authority to have a voice in their own governments, for the rights and liberties of small nations, for a universal dominion of right by such a concert of free peoples as shall bring peace and safety to all nations and make the world itself at last free. To such a task we can dedicate our lives and our fortunes, everything that we are and everything that we have, with the pride of those who know that the day has come when America is privileged to spend her blood and her might for the principles that gave her birth and happiness and the peace which she has treasured. God helping her, she can do no other."

(Source: John Bartlett. *Familiar Quotations: a collection of passages, phrases, and proverbs traced to their source in ancient and modern literature,* 1992.

the strain of the trip on his already weakened constitution was great (his doctor had recommended that he stay home), and on September 25, after a poorly delivered speech in Pueblo, Colorado, Wilson suffered a stroke. Edith Wilson canceled the remainder of the excursion, but after returning to Washington Wilson suffered a second, more massive stroke on October 2. Wilson was left paralyzed and unable to manage the government effectively for months. From his sickbed, Wilson continued to refuse to compromise, insisting that changes, especially to Article 10, would cut the heart out of the treaty.

On November 19, 1919, the Senate rejected the treaty. In the final vote, on the treaty without reservations, it lost with 38 votes in favor and 53 opposed. Attempts to revive the treaty later by the president's allies, including former secretary of state William Jennings Bryan, were unavailing because the president continued to refuse compromise of any sort. The League of Nations was established by the signatories of the Treaty of Versailles, but the United States was not among them.

The Wilson Administration Legacy

Wilson's presidency ended in drift and disarray. Although Wilson had recovered to some extent from his stroke by the spring of 1920, he was still far from capable of the strong leadership and policy making he had once exhibited. Given that Wilson had spent much of the year before his illness in Europe or battling for the Treaty of Versailles in the United States, he was out of touch with the concerns of many Americans.

There was no real plan for demobilizing the U.S. economy after the war. The armistice meant the cancellation of orders for war material from the Allies, and as a consequence farm prices collapsed. Millions of returning veterans could not find jobs and unemployment rose. Inflation soared (postwar prices were 77 percent above their prewar levels), and with it came strikes throughout the economy, as workers demanded higher wages to keep up with higher prices.

Not only was the economy a mess, but many Americans were unhappy with the results of Wilson's foreign policies. Despite his call for "open covenants openly arrived at," Wilson had permitted the Paris Peace Conference to be conducted under a press blackout. As a result, few Americans were prepared for the aspects of the Treaty of Versailles that ran against the principles of the Fourteen Points. Although Wilson carried hopes of a third term even after his stroke, his infirmity led the Democrats instead to run the ticket of James M. Cox and Franklin D. Roosevelt. They were soundly defeated by Republican Warren G. Harding, who based his campaign largely on criticism of Wilson, the poor economy, and his call for a return to "normalcy."

Lasting Impact

The Wilson administration had a tremendous impact on the future of the United States, both at home and abroad. In the decades immediately after World War I (1914–18), Wilson's methods of attaching moral principles and idealism to foreign policy, known as "Wilsonianism," was seen as a failure and a mistake. In particular, the collapse of the Treaty of Versailles in the U.S. Senate, and the inability of the League of Nations to halt aggression by Germany, Italy, and Japan in the 1930s, seemed to underline the death of "Wilsonianism." Wilson's own mistakes were largely responsible for this situation. In promising to make the world safe for democracy and a war to end all wars, he raised unrealistic expectations for the postwar peace process. A backlash set in against the wartime propaganda, which had glorified the Allies and demonized the Germans beyond all reality. The former were soon reviled by the U.S.

public for falling short of perfection, and the latter came to be seen as a scapegoat. The belief took hold that the United States had somehow been hoodwinked into the war by clever British and French diplomats, and that arms manufacturers, the "merchants of death," had sacrificed U.S. boys for profit. These half-truths acquired great force and fed an ardent "never again" attitude among large segments of the U.S. public. By 1935 a Gallup Poll revealed that 70 percent of those polled believed that intervention in the war had been a mistake (O'Neill, p. 10–11).

But the man who would be Wilson's political heir, his assistant navy secretary Franklin D. Roosevelt, was an ardent supporter of the League of Nations, and when he became president himself in 1933, he modified Wilson's precepts in many ways without abandoning them. Roosevelt never allowed his idealism to get too far ahead of public opinion. When Roosevelt was faced with a European war and a United States uneasily maintaining its neutrality, Roosevelt made no pretense of neutrality "in thought as well as deed." Roosevelt favored Britain and made no secret of it. The Atlantic Charter, agreed to by British prime minister Winston Churchill and Roosevelt in August 1941 before the United States entered World War II (1939–45), was Roosevelt's way of avoiding Wilson's mistake of issuing the Fourteen Points unilaterally. Roosevelt wanted Britain's agreement in advance about Allied aims in World War II, aims that were utterly Wilsonian: freedom of the seas, self-determination for peoples, disarmament, and some kind of world security organization.

Still, the skepticism that surrounded Wilson's policies made it very difficult for Roosevelt to intervene in the war until the Japanese attacked Pearl Harbor in Hawaii in December 1941. Once the war was won and the United Nations (an international peacekeeping organization similar to the League of Nations) established, Roosevelt made certain that its important functions were exercised by the Security Council, which was dominated by the great powers. Successful U.S. efforts to maintain the moral high ground in the struggle with Nazi Germany and later the Soviet Union showed that Roosevelt had learned from Wilson's mistakes and had found a way to institute a sort of practical Wilsonianism: idealism, leavened by a great deal of realism.

Domestically, Wilson changed the United States as much if not more than any president since Abraham Lincoln. His Federal Reserve System centralized control over the nation's money and credit system in the hands of government, and continues to operate as Wilson designed it more than 80 years later. The income tax instituted under Wilson also became a fundamental part of the U.S. political system. The establishment of the Federal Trade Commission (FTC), combined with antitrust lawsuits, firmly committed the government to policy established by former president Theodore Roosevelt of defending the public interest from big business. While Prohibition and women's suffrage were not Wil-

Fast Fact

Wilson was very concerned about the possibility that, if he were to lose his bid for reelection in 1916, during his remaining four months in office he would lack the credibility necessary to handle the United States's tense relations with Mexico and the warring nations of Europe. Leaving the United States without an effective foreign policy leader during such a critical period seemed to Wilson to be asking for disaster. To ensure that this would not occur, Wilson developed a plan that he outlined in a secret memorandum to Secretary of State Robert Lansing two days before the November election. In the memorandum, Wilson told Lansing that if Wilson lost the election to Republican Charles Evans Hughes, then he planned to appoint Hughes to be secretary of state. Wilson would then resign his office along with Vice President Thomas R. Marshall. As the secretary of state was at that time second in line to succeed to the presidency, these resignations would immediately make Hughes president. This drastic plan proved unnecessary, however, as Wilson won reelection by a small margin.

(Source: Joseph Nathan Kane. *Facts About the Presidents*, 1993.)

son's initiatives, they too had a tremendous impact on the life of the nation. On the minus side, Wilson's acceptance of segregation in government was a major step backwards, which would not be reversed for more than four decades.

Wilson's strong leadership style, of both the nation and his party, set important precedents, and helped to transform the Democratic Party into a liberal organization. The extreme activity of the reformist Wilson administration led, perhaps inevitably, to a conservative backlash after he left office. The Republican administrations that followed consciously sought to avoid social upheavals or domestic or foreign crusades. But the basic structure that Wilson put in place both at home and abroad could not be completely eradicated.

Sources

Bartlett, John. *Familiar Quotations: a collection of passages, phrases, and proverbs traced to their sources in ancient and modern literature.* 16th ed., Boston: Little, Brown, and Company, 1992.

Clements, Hendrick A. *The Presidency of Woodrow Wilson.* Lawrence, Kans.: University Press of Kansas, 1992.

Cooper, John Milton. *The Warrior and the Priest: Woodrow Wilson and Theodore Roosevelt.* Cambridge, Mass.: Belknap Press/Harvard University Press, 1983.

The Dictionary of American Biography. New York: Scribner, 1959.

Heckscher, August. *Woodrow Wilson: A Biography.* New York: Charles Scribner's Sons, 1991.

Kane, Joseph Nathan. *Facts About the Presidents.* New York: H.W. Wilson Co., 1993.

Further Readings

Fromkin, David. *In the Time of the Americans.* New York: Random House, 1995.

Johnson, Paul. *A History of the American People.* New York: HarperCollins, 1998.

Link, Arthur S. *Wilson.* 5 vols. Princeton, N.J.: Princeton University Press, 1947–65.

Olasky, Marvin. *The American Leadership Tradition.* New York: The Free Press, 1999.

Shenkman, Richard. *Presidential Ambition.* New York: HarperCollins, 1999.

Harding Administration

Biography

Warren G. Harding was born the year the American Civil War (1861–65) ended, and he grew to maturity in the years when the Republican Party dominated U.S. politics. The party's strength was based in the rural North, where Harding was born and raised. It also had the support of business, of which Harding was also a part as owner and operator of a small newspaper in Ohio that grew into a successful publishing venture. Harding was a prototype of many successful Republican politicians in the decades following the end of the Civil War.

Early Life

Warren G. Harding was born on November 2, 1865, on a farm near Corsica (later, Blooming Grove, Ohio). He was the first of six children of George and Phoebe Harding. The Hardings were proud of their ancestral heritage, and George Harding claimed that his family could be traced back to an early Puritan immigrant from England who had settled in Braintree, Massachusetts, in 1623. Over the next two centuries the family gradually migrated west, and one branch of the Hardings arrived in Ohio about 1820.

Warren Harding's parents were married shortly after his father returned from military service during the American Civil War (1861–65). In 1873 when Harding was seven years old his family moved to nearby Caledonia in Marion County, Ohio. Here Harding's father established a full-time medical practice. After the birth of her last child, Phoebe Harding entered medical practice with her husband. Warren Harding learned from his parents and

Full name: Warren Gamaliel Harding

Personal Information:

Born: November 2, 1865
Birthplace: Corsica, Ohio
Died: August 2, 1923
Death place: San Francisco, California
Burial place: Marion Cemetery, reinterred in Harding Memorial Tomb, Marion, Ohio
Religion: Baptist
Spouse: Florence Mabel Kling De Wolfe (m. 1860)
Education: Iberia College (later Ohio Central College), A.B., 1882
Occupation: Teacher; insurance salesman; journalist; politician
Political Party: Republican Party
Age at Inauguration: 55 years

Warren G. Harding. (The Library of Congress.)

from the successful businesspeople of Caledonia the virtues of hard work and upward striving.

Education

Warren Harding attended local schools in Caledonia, Ohio. He never brought the same energy to his studies as he did to physical labor. His grades were average.

In the fall of 1880 he entered Iberia College in Iberia, Ohio (also known as Ohio Central College)—a small two-year school only six miles from his hometown. Iberia had gone into decline by the time Harding attended the school and had little to offer in the way of advanced education.

The most important experience of Harding's college years was his coeditorship of the school newspaper. It became the basis for his interest in journalism and publishing, activities that were to dominate his life in the decades after his graduation from college.

Family Life

In 1891 Warren Harding married Florence "Flossie" Mable Kling De Wolfe, a divorced woman who was four years older than him. (A few years into the marriage,

Harding assigned the nickname "Duchess" to his wife—referring to her dominant personality.)

Soon after their marriage, Florence Harding began work at her husband's newspaper, the *Star.* She saw to matters of circulation and made sure that the newsboys who distributed the paper collected from their customers. Her contribution was important in making what had been a small struggling paper a financially successful one.

Their childless marriage was not a happy one. Florence Harding " . . . was shrewish and sharp . . . . Her personality soon began to jar upon the easy habits of her husband. Gradually there was a drifting apart, though it was not often apparent to outsiders" (Trani and Wilson, p. 33).

Despite their differences and the lack of intimacy, Florence Harding was, nonetheless, a positive force behind her husband's career. Besides contributing to the success of the *Star,* she also strongly supported Harding's political career when he might have withdrawn from politics.

Florence Harding also proved to be a very successful first lady following her husband's election as president in 1920. From 1917 until Harding was sworn in as president in March 1921, the White House had been a gloomy place due to World War I (1914–18) and later President Woodrow Wilson's serious illness. The Hardings changed this situation immediately. Less than two hours after his inauguration, Harding had the gates of the White House opened for the first time since 1917 so that the public could watch the comings and goings. Florence Harding ordered the blinds on the windows to be opened at night and revived the practice of allowing the public to tour parts of the White House. Occasionally she would come downstairs from her living quarters and greet visitors. She also had flowers placed throughout the White House and planted bulbs in its gardens. She gave teas and garden parties and resumed the practice of holding Christmas receptions. On most evenings during the first year of Harding's presidency the White House was the scene of either public or private parties. Florence Harding was a frequent visitor to veterans' hospitals that housed the wounded from the world war. This intense round of activities stopped in 1922, however, when Florence Harding became seriously ill.

Perhaps because of the problems with his marriage, Harding often sought the company of his male friends on golf courses and at the poker table (with a glass of liquor, even though the sale of liquor in the United States had been illegal since 1919). He also sought the company of other women.

Harding's Extramarital Affairs

One of Harding's alleged affairs was with Carrie Fulton Phillips, the wife of one of Harding's best friends. In 1963 love letters written between 1905 and 1920 from Harding to Carrie Phillips were discovered. There is also evidence that the National Republican Party made cash payments to the Phillips so that they would not disclose the affair. (Phillips's husband had learned of the romance while it was still going on.)

A second alleged romance was even more scandalous. The woman was Nan Britton who was 30 years younger than Harding. The affair allegedly began in 1917 and continued up until the time of his death in August 1923. In October 1919 Britton had a daughter, Elizabeth Ann Christian, which she claimed was Harding's. When Britton's attempts to have the Harding estate create a trust fund for the child failed, she published a best-selling book, *The President's Daughter,* in 1927.

Career

The Harding family had moved to Marion, Ohio, in 1882. Marion boasted three railroads passing through the town and several small manufacturers. George Harding's medical practice flourished.

During his first years in Marion, Warren Harding studied law in the office of a family friend. However, he did not care for the study of law and left the profession when he realized that he was not turning a profit and had to ask his father for financial aid to pay his bills.

Harding tried his hand at teaching school and sold insurance for a short time. Finally, he obtained employment as a reporter at the Marion *Mirror.* The newspaper, like the town of Marion, strongly supported the Democratic Party. Even as a young man, however, Harding was a Republican. In 1884 this led to his dismissal from his reporter's job at the *Mirror* when the editors of the paper learned that he was spending time working for the election of the Republican presidential candidate, James Blaine. Harding was again adrift and looking for work.

The Marion Star

Soon after his dismissal from the *Mirror,* Harding and two friends bought a small, failing, daily Marion newspaper, the *Star,* for a few hundred dollars. The paper had to compete with two more successful publications, the weekly *Mirror* and the biweekly *Independent.* The former supported the Democratic Party, the latter the Republican Party. The *Star* claimed to be independent in its political views. The prospects for success were not bright for the trio of owners, but Harding had finally found in publishing an activity that he enjoyed.

Harding soon became the sole owner of the *Star.* He improved the quality of the news stories run in the paper, and within a relatively short time he increased the circulation and advertising space. Within seven months Harding launched a new publishing venture—the *Weekly Star,* a paper that identified itself as Republican in its politics. Over time Harding's Star Publishing Company grew increasingly successful and became a fixture in Marion, Ohio, and the future president became one of the young successful business leaders of the community.

Years later, after Harding had been elected president of the United States, his newspaper background helped him in dealing with members of the press. As president Harding restored the practice of holding biweekly press conferences, a practice President Wilson had suspended while he held office. Harding genuinely enjoyed his dealing with reporters and they, in turn, liked and respected him. Few presidents in U.S. history have had as cordial a relationship with the press as Harding.

Harding Enters Politics

As a leading citizen in his hometown of Marion, Ohio, it was natural that Harding would run for political office. He had gained wide recognition in the area for his many activities promoting the development of Marion. His frequent editorials in the *Star* provided a forum for reaching the citizens of the area with his ideas about civic growth and improvement. He also gave public speeches and joined local organizations to advance his generally pro-business ideas.

Harding's chances of winning either city or county office were small, however, since these areas usually voted Democratic in elections. In 1892 Harding was defeated in his first attempt to win an elective office when he ran for the position of county auditor.

In 1899 a vacancy occurred in a state senate district. The district was much larger than Marion County and included areas that were heavily Republican. In this election Harding was elected to the state legislature. He was reelected for a second term and served as the senate Republican majority leader.

While a state legislator, Harding met Harry Daugherty, the person who would help guide him to election to the U.S. Senate and to the U.S. presidency. Daugherty was an Ohio Republican politician, lawyer, and lobbyist for several large corporations. Early in Harding's political career he became Harding's chief political strategist. Daugherty is alleged to have said of Harding when he first saw him: "What a great looking president he'd make."

In 1903 Harding was elected lieutenant governor of Ohio and held that position until 1905. But he was overwhelmingly defeated in 1910 when he sought election as governor. Four years later, however, Harding's fortunes changed when he was elected to the U.S. Senate from Ohio.

Harding as a U.S. Senator

Harding's one-term career in the Senate was characterized by absenteeism; he was present for less than one third of the votes taken during his six-year term. He supported the United States's entry into World War I

(1914–1918) in 1917 but avoided taking clear stands on two of the most controversial issues of his day, the prohibition of liquor and the right of women to vote. (He ultimately did support both the Eighteenth and Nineteenth Amendments to the Constitution that established these policies.) He was also an opponent of the Versailles Treaty, which ended World War I in 1919. It was eventually defeated in the Senate (*See also,* Foreign Issues).

Harding as President

Warren Harding was nominated by the Republican Party to run for president of the United States at its national convention in June 1920. The party turned to Harding as its candidate when several other leading contenders for the nomination were unable to obtain the vote of a majority of the delegates. Calvin Coolidge, then governor of Massachusetts, was chosen by the party as Harding's vice presidential running mate. The Harding-Coolidge ticket was overwhelmingly elected in the November 1920 general election, defeating the Democratic ticket of James M. Cox of Ohio and Franklin D. Roosevelt of New York.

Harding became president at the age of 55. The Harding presidency has been viewed unfavorably by most historians. While it had a few successes, especially in international affairs, it was plagued by scandals, most of which became fully known only after Harding's death in August 1923. Corruption was rampant and ultimately a number of persons he had appointed to his cabinet and to agency positions left in disgrace. Several were later convicted of crimes.

President Harding Dies in Office

Harding died on a transcontinental train. He was returning from Alaska when he became ill and died on August 2, 1923. A diagnosis was never determined.

The president's body was taken to Washington, D.C., where a public viewing and services were held. Following the services, the president's body was carried by train to his hometown of Marion, Ohio. Tens of thousands of mourning Americans lined the route. The body was interred in a large oval Grecian-style structure—the Harding Memorial—that was built in Marion with money contributed by many admiring constituents.

Post-presidential Years

Vice President Calvin Coolidge succeeded to the office of president upon the death of President Harding. Florence Harding lived for only 16 months after the death of her husband. She had suffered from a variety of illnesses and died on November 21, 1924.

It was not long after Harding's death that Congress and the courts uncovered widespread corruption in his administration. Although no evidence ever showed that the president was personally involved in any wrongdoing, several of his advisers were convicted and served time in jail.

The Warren G. Harding Administration

Warren G. Harding's good looks, resonant voice, and success as a small-town businessman in Ohio made him an attractive presidential candidate for the Republicans. Beyond his background and appearance, however, Harding had few other qualifications for the presidency. Personally affable and honest, Harding foolishly appointed to his administration a number of people who were corrupt and used their offices to enrich themselves financially. Unfortunately the distinguishing characteristic of the Harding presidency proved to be political corruption on a scale that this nation had almost never before—or since—witnessed.

Harding Becomes President

The Republicans grew increasingly confident of victory as the 1920 presidential election drew closer. They were convinced that the nation would turn away from the Democrats after the years of sacrifice and turmoil caused by World War I (1914–18), which had recently concluded in Europe. But the Republicans lacked a candidate who had the clear support of a majority of party members. The situation was ripe for a compromise candidate—one who would not alienate any wing of the party and could also gain the support of enough delegates to win the party's nomination at its 1920 national convention.

The Campaign of 1920

Warren Harding and his supporters believed that he would be the ideal compromise candidate for the convention, despite being a relatively obscure Ohio senator who had served only one term and had few legislative accomplishments to his credit. After a poor showing in states that held primary elections for delegates to the national convention, and not even gaining the support of the entire Ohio delegation, Harding thought about withdrawing from the contest and running for reelection to the Senate. But his wife and his political strategist Harry Daugherty convinced him that he could still win his party's presidential nomination.

No candidate was able to receive a majority of the convention vote on the first four ballots. It was then that Daugherty and a small group of other Republican leaders met in the early morning of June 12, 1920, in a smoke-filled Chicago hotel room and decided to try and have

Administration

Administration Dates
March 4, 1921–August 2, 1923

Vice President
Calvin Coolidge (1921–23)

Cabinet

Secretary of State
Bainbridge Colby (1920–21)
Charles E. Hughes (1921–25)

Secretary of the Treasury
Andrew W. Mellon (1921–32)

Secretary of War
Newton D. Baker (1916–21)
John W. Weeks (1921–25)

Attorney General
Alexander M. Palmer (1919–21)
Harry M. Daugherty (1921–24)

Secretary of the Navy
Josephus Daniels (1913–21)
Edwin Denby (1921–24)

Postmaster General
Albert S. Burleson (1913–21)
William H. Hays (1921–22)
Hubert Work (1922–23)
Harry S. New (1923–29)

Secretary of the Interior
John B. Payne (1920–21)
Albert B. Fall (1921–23)
Hubert Work (1923–28)

Secretary of Agriculture
Edwin T. Meredith (1920–21)
Henry C. Wallace (1921–24)

Secretary of Labor
William B. Wilson (1913–21)
James J. Davis (1921–30)

Secretary of Commerce
Joshua W. Alexander (1919–21)
Herbert C. Hoover (1921–28)

Harding nominated by the convention. After consulting with other state party leaders and gaining their approval, Harding received the necessary majority of delegate votes on the 10th ballot and was chosen to be the party's presidential nominee. Calvin Coolidge, the governor of Massachusetts, was selected as Harding's vice presidential running mate.

The Democrats Nominate Cox and Roosevelt

The Democratic Party nominated the governor of Ohio, former newspaperman and member of the House of Representatives, James M. Cox. Cox was a compromise choice, selected on the party convention's 44th ballot. His vice presidential running mate was the young and relatively unknown New Yorker, Franklin D. Roosevelt.

The Presidential Campaign

Cox traveled extensively and gave many speeches during the presidential campaign. He valiantly supported President Wilson's domestic record and the United States's entry into the League of Nations (an international organization of world communities with the purpose of promoting peace) and opposed the prohibition of liquor. Harding, to the contrary, largely remained at home in Ohio and conducted a campaign from his front porch. He spoke in generalizations and avoided taking clear stands on such controversial issues as the prohibition of liquor.

The presidential election produced a huge victory for Harding. He captured 61 percent of the popular vote and 404 electoral votes to Cox's 35 percent of the popular vote and only 127 votes in the electoral college. Harding won all of the states except for 11 in the then traditionally Democratic South.

Mark Sullivan wrote of the 1920 presidential election in *Our Times* that the huge victory for Harding was in reality a vote against President Wilson who by 1920 had already become " . . . the symbol both of the war we had begun to think about with disillusion, and of the peace we had come to think about with cynicism."

Fast Fact

On the morning of November 11, 1921—the day the war in Europe had ended three years earlier—President Harding presided at the internment of the United States's Unknown Soldier at the National Cemetery in Arlington, Virginia. The custom of selecting one unknown soldier to represent all those who had died in the world war had begun in England and had quickly been adopted by the other victorious Allied nations. Harding's speech was amplified so that all of the people at Arlington Cemetery would hear, but it was also carried by telephone wires to large crowds in Washington, D.C., New York, and San Francisco. "Never before in history had so many thousands simultaneously heard the sound of a human voice."

(Source: Francis Russell. *The Shadow of Blooming Grove: Warren G. Harding in His Times,* 1968.)

Harding's Advisers

President Harding delegated to Secretary of State Charles Evans Hughes broad authority over matters related to foreign affairs. Secretary of the Treasury Andrew Mellon and Secretary of Commerce Herbert Hoover played similarly important roles in regard to finance and business respectively. Hoover, already famous for his humanitarian work during and after World War I (1914–18), would further boost his image with his excellent work in the Commerce Department under Harding and Coolidge, so much so that he was elected president in 1928.

The men closest to the president, however, were his friends—the so-called "Ohio Gang"—especially his attorney general, Harry M. Daugherty. Daugherty, in turn, brought his friend and associate, Jesse Smith, into the Justice Department. (Smith never held any official government position but he nonetheless had an office near Daugherty in the Justice Department building.) Daugherty and Smith shared a house in Washington that became the base of their operation in Washington. Other friends from Ohio also came to the nation's capital to profit from their association with the president and with Daugherty and Smith. Historian Robert K. Murray wrote of the Ohio Gang:

> The Ohio Gang had very few of the characteristics of a gang because it had no concrete form, no cohesion, and no plan . . . [It] was simply a collection of rank oppor-

tunists who worked together as a matter of expediency . . . They looked for the quick buck, not sustained graft. Each new batch of boodle was from a completely different operation or deal. Division of the profits occurred on a haphazard basis.

Harding and Congress

The Republicans maintained majority control of both houses of the national legislature during Harding's years as president. His term encompassed the Sixty-seventh (1921–23) and the Sixty-eighth (1923–25) Congresses. The Republican Party had long been split between its old guard conservatives and its more progressive wing. Harding had always been associated with the old guard. Despite this division within the party, the new president was able to obtain congressional support for most of his legislative policies.

Harding adopted generally conservative, pro-business policies during his years as president. He was successful in having Congress lower taxes on the wealthy and repeal the excess profits tax that had been imposed during the war. Harding also signed the Fordney-McCumber Act of 1922 that raised tariffs on imported goods an average of almost 40 percent, a change favored by U.S. business. The Fordney-McCumber Act changed the direction of tariff policy that had been adopted during the Woodrow Wilson administration. Harding vetoed the bonus bill for veterans of World War I (1914–18) that had been passed by Congress, and he packed the regulatory agencies of government with persons having a conservative pro-business philosophy.

One of the first laws signed by Harding after becoming the nation's chief executive was the Emergency Quota Act of 1921. Reflecting his isolationist views, the law sharply limited immigration into the United States and imposed a quota system based on the 1910 U.S. census that favored immigration from the nations of western and northern Europe. The quota system became a part of U.S. immigration policy that was to last for more than four decades.

But there were some exceptions to his conservative domestic philosophy. He backed increased federal financial aid to the states to reduce infant mortality and proposed the creation of a department of public welfare to coordinate and increase federal spending on child welfare, public health, education, and recreation.

Harding also commuted the prison sentence of Eugene V. Debs, the leader of the Socialist Party, who had been imprisoned for a speech he gave opposing the United States's involvement in World War I, a step Wilson had refused to take while he was president.

Harding and the Judiciary

Warren Harding made four appointments to the U.S. Supreme Court during his two and one-half years as president—an usually large number for a president who held office so briefly. Each appointee was staunchly conservative in his legal outlook, and this fact influenced the character of the Court's work for the next two decades. William Howard Taft, who had served as president of the United States between 1909 and 1913, was appointed chief justice of the Supreme Court in 1921 and held that position until declining health compelled him to resign in 1930. Other appointees were George Sutherland of Utah (1922–38), Pierce Butler of Minnesota (1922–39), and Edward T. Sanford of Tennessee (1923–30).

Changes in the U.S. Government

The most important change in the structure of the U.S. government during Harding's administration was the passage of the Budget and Accounting Act of 1921. Originally conceived during the Taft administration, this law created the first federal budget office, the Bureau of the Budget, as part of the president's executive office. It reduced the power of Congress over the federal budget, and for the first time gave U.S. presidents a major role in the creation of this important annual document. The law passed because Congress had come to realize that the national government and its budget had grown too large for it to manage, and the process needed to be centralized.

The Veterans' Bureau Act of 1921 was another important change, which established a single agency to administer veterans' benefits.

Domestic Issues

Warren G. Harding was elected president at a time when most Americans wanted to forget the domestic reforms that had marked the first years of Woodrow Wilson's presidency—his campaign against large monopoly corporations that had grown up in this country, for example—and the hardships and suffering they had endured during World War I (1914–18). They were generally uninterested in political reform, and they were becoming increasingly disillusioned with the consequences of the war. Wilson had promised lasting peace and democracy in Europe, and these objectives were already beginning to fade by 1920.

Business and Labor

Harding proposed pro-business legislation: lower taxes, a balanced budget, and higher tariffs to protect the nation's industries from foreign competition.

The Strikes of 1922

U.S. business in the early twentieth century opposed labor unions, collective bargaining (negotiations between an employer and union representatives), and the right of workers to strike. (It was not until 1935 that the Wagner Act recognized the right of workers to form unions.) Harding's policies toward labor closely mirrored the prevailing views of business, which became most apparent in the response he took toward two major strikes that occurred during his presidency. One was in the coal fields of Pennsylvania and Ohio and the second was in the U.S. railroads.

In April 1922 over 600,000 coal miners went on strike over wages and their right to have the United Mine Workers as their union. At first Harding took no action in regard to the strike. However he changed his position after several months when the nation's coal supplies began to run low and widespread violence broke out in the coal fields between union and nonunion workers hired by the mine owners. When his attempt to resolve the dispute by arbitration failed, the president came to the support of the mine owners. He contacted the governors in the affected states and told them that they should use the state militia to protect the right to work for any person who wanted to work, and he promised that the federal government would provide whatever support was necessary to keep the coal mines opened. Members of the state militia were sent to the mine fields in Pennsylvania and Ohio, and the workers' strike came to an end.

Also in 1922 the railroad mechanics went on strike against the railroad owners over a proposed cut in their wages. Although none of the other railroad unions supported the strike, the mechanics were successful in interfering with the operation of U.S. railroads for several months. When all attempts to settle the strike failed, Harding ordered his attorney general, Harry Daugherty, to obtain a court injunction against the strikers. Federal judge James Wilkerson, a Harding appointee, issued a very broad order that made it illegal for officials of the union to picket or to use any means of communication—letters, telephone calls, person-to-person conversations—to encourage workers to strike against the railroads. Although the injunction was of doubtful constitutionality, it brought a quick end to the strike.

Teapot Dome and Other Scandals

The first clear evidence of corruption in the Harding administration came in January 1923 when the person Harding had appointed to run the newly formed Veterans' Bureau—Charles Forbes—resigned and fled the country. In March 1925 Forbes's general counsel committed suicide. Forbes was returned to the United States and in 1925 was convicted of stealing or wasting vast sums of money that had been appropriated to assist veterans. (It is impossible to know exactly how much money was misused; estimates have been made of between $200 and $250 million.)

The Teapot Dome Scandal involved the sale of U.S. government-owned oil reserves to private oil industries, without competitive bidding. A Senate investigation led to the indictment of three of Harding's cabinet members. Details of the scandal did not become known until after Harding's death. (Corbis. Reproduced by permission.)

In 1927 there was evidence of widespread graft in the branch of the Treasury Department charged with enforcing the prohibition laws. It was alleged that the Justice Department provided protection for violators of the prohibition laws, and that Attorney General Daugherty had profited from the sale of supplies of government-owned alcohol.

But the largest and most disgraceful corruption had to do with the sale of government-owned oil reserves, a scandal known to history as Teapot Dome. In 1921 Secretary of the Navy Edwin Denby convinced Harding to transfer certain navy oil reserves from the control of the navy to the Department of the Interior. The reserves were located in Wyoming at a place called Teapot Dome and in Elk Hills, California. In 1922 the secretary of the interior, Albert B. Fall, leased the land to friends in the oil industry without competitive bidding. A Senate investigation revealed that Fall had received more than $400,000 from the beneficiaries of the leases. Denby resigned from office and Fall was tried and convicted in a federal court. He was sentenced to one year in prison and a fine of $100,000.

No evidence ever showed that Harding knew the details of the corruption in his administration, and he was not directly involved in any wrongdoing. Most of the corruption was revealed after Harding's death in August 1923. But almost from the beginning of his administration rumors of scandal circulated in Washington, and Harding made the mistake of not taking action to deal with these problems. Of course the major cause of these scandals was the selection of unqualified people to staff some of the departments and agencies of the federal government, and Harding alone was responsible for these unwise appointments.

Foreign Issues

President Harding's opposition to U.S. membership in the League of Nations (the international organization that came into being at the end of World War I (1914–18) tarnished his reputation, and as a consequence he has often been viewed as an isolationist in his foreign policy. His secretary of state, Charles Evans Hughes, however, was very much an internationalist, and the president gave Hughes broad freedom to shape U.S. foreign policy. Although the Senate had refused to approve the Treaty of Versailles that ended World War I, in 1921 Harding signed a resolution ending the state of war between the United States and Germany. While not joining the League of Nations, the United States did cooperate with some of the nonpolitical activities of the league.

Harding also improved relations between the United States and Mexico that had been damaged during the Wilson administration, and he ended the U.S. military intervention in Haiti and the Dominican Republic. Colombia was paid for its loss of Panama that had occurred early in the twentieth century, and the Harding administration backed the territorial integrity of China and the "Open Door" policy of allowing all nations wishing to trade with China to do so.

The Washington Conference of 1921

Harding's most important contribution to foreign policy during his presidency was the Washington Conference of 1921. The meeting was designed to prevent future wars by reducing the naval power of the world's major powers. To achieve this objective Harding invited representatives of Great Britain, France, Japan, and Italy to attend a conference in Washington during the summer of 1921 to discuss disarmament.

The five major powers negotiated a treaty that reduced the number of capital ships each possessed and also provided that for the next 10 years no new capital ships would be constructed by the parties to the agreement. Another provision of the treaty restricted the number and size of aircraft carriers each nation could possess. The agreement did not, however, apply to cruisers, destroyers, submarines, and other smaller ships. (Other conferences of this type were held in Geneva, Switzerland; Washington, D. C.; and London, England, during the next 15 years.)

Other treaties were also negotiated at the Washington Conference with Belgium, Portugal, Holland, and China that were intended to guarantee peace in the Far East. The main concern was over the expansion of Japan in this part of the world. Japan had fought a largely successful war against Russia between 1904 and 1905 and had annexed Korea in 1910. China and Southeast Asia loomed as the next possible targets for Japanese expansion. Many believed that the ultimate goal of Japan was to gain naval supremacy over the United States in the Pacific Ocean and thus be the dominant military force in this area of the world.

The best that can be said about the Washington Conference of 1921 is that it may have temporarily slowed the race to build larger navies by the world's major powers and placed obstacles in the way of Japanese expansion in Asia. But in 1931 Japan conquered Manchuria and a few years later invaded China. When Japan bombed the U.S. naval base at Pearl Harbor in the Hawaiian Islands on December 7, 1941, a general war broke out in Asia and the Pacific Ocean.

The Harding Administration Legacy

The Death of Warren Harding

Amidst rumors of widespread corruption in his administration, Harding, determined to maintain his popularity with the U.S. public, undertook a transcontinental trip in June 1923 that was to end in Alaska. He made many personal appearances and scores of speeches along the way. On his trip back from Alaska to San Francisco, California, the president suffered stomach cramps and indigestion. At 7:30 P.M. on August 2, the president suddenly died while resting in his bed.

The Senate investigation of Teapot Dome did not begin until after Harding's death. But he understood the worsening situation of his administration, and he spoke with sadness to Commerce Secretary Herbert Hoover and other associates about his betrayal by his best friends. It is possible that Harding's early death was brought about in part by his growing anxiety over the developing scandals involving men whom he appointed to positions of responsibility in his administration.

Harding's legacy to his successor Calvin Coolidge was that of a tarnished presidency. It would fall to Coolidge to restore confidence in the executive office.

Lasting Impact

During his years as the nation's chief executive, President Harding was very popular with both the press and the U.S. public. When he died in San Francisco, California, in August 1923, the nation mourned his loss.

Historians, however, have evaluated Harding's presidency much differently. They have generally agreed that his administration was a failure and have ranked him as one of the nation's worst presidents. Their negative view concerns the corruption in the Harding administration, especially the Teapot Dome scandal.

But there is another view of the Harding presidency that also deserves recognition. He made several distinguished appointments to his cabinet—Charles Evans Hughes as secretary of state, Andrew Mellon as secretary of the treasury, and Herbert Hoover as secretary of commerce—and one to the Supreme Court—Chief Justice William Howard Taft. Hughes negotiated a major world treaty at the Washington Conference of 1921. This treaty delayed Japanese aggression in the Pacific Ocean for a decade though it failed to prevent Japan from beginning a war against China in the 1930s and against the United States in the early 1940s. Harding also improved U.S. relations with Mexico and with other nations in Central America and the Caribbean. Harding's pardon of the convicted Socialist leader Eugene V. Debs was an act of political courage by the president. Finally, Harding was an early supporter of increased federal aid to the states for child welfare, education, and public health.

Sources

Downes, Randolph C. *The Rise of Warren Gamaliel Harding, 1865–1920.* Columbus, Ohio: Ohio State University Press, 1970.

Murray, Robert K. *The Harding Era: Warren G. Harding and His Administration.* Minneapolis: University of Minnesota Press, 1969.

Russell, Francis. *The Shadow of Blooming Grove: Warren G. Harding in His Times.* New York: McGraw-Hill, 1968.

Trani, Eugene P., and David L. Wilson. *The Presidency of Warren G. Harding.* Lawrence, Kans.: Regents Press of Kansas, 1977.

Further Readings

Adams, Samuel Hopkins. *Incredible Era: The Life and Times of Warren Gamaliel Harding.* Boston: Houghton Mifflin Co., 1939.

Hicks, John D. *The Republican Ascendancy, 1921–1933.* New York: Harper and Row, 1960.

Murray, Robert K. *The Politics of Normalcy: Government Theory and Practice in the Harding-Coolidge Era.* New York: W. W. Norton and Co., 1973.

Sferrazza, Carl. *Florence Harding: The First Lady, the Jazz Age, and the Death of America's Most Scandalous President.* New York: William Morrow and Co., 1998.

Sinclair, Andrew. *The Available Man: The Life Behind the Masks of Warren G. Harding.* New York: Macmillan, 1965.

White, William Allen. *The Autobiography of William Allen White.* New York: Macmillan, 1946.

Coolidge Administrations

Full name: Calvin Coolidge
Given name: John Calvin Coolidge
Popular name: Silent Cal

Personal Information:

Born: July 4, 1872
Birthplace: Plymouth Notch, Vermont
Died: January 5, 1933
Death place: Northampton, Massachusetts
Burial place: Plymouth Notch Cemetery, Plymouth, Vermont
Religion: Congregational
Spouse: Grace Anna Goodhue (m. 1905)
Children: John C.; Calvin Jr.
Education: Amherst College, B.A., 1895
Occupation: Attorney; mayor; governor; vice president of the United States
Political Party: Republican Party
Age at Inauguration: 51 years

Biography

Calvin Coolidge grew up in a small, rural community in Vermont in the late nineteenth century. He embodied all of the traits that are associated with rural New England life: independence, frugality, integrity, and personal reserve. Combined with these characteristics was a wry sense of humor that not everyone appreciated. Coolidge acquired from his father an interest in public affairs and devoted most of his adult life to politics. It was an odd choice for a man who was as shy and private as Coolidge and who over the course of his life had few close friends. Despite these apparent handicaps, Coolidge was remarkably successful in politics at the local, state, and national levels.

Early Life

Calvin Coolidge was the oldest child of John Calvin Coolidge and Victoria Josephine Moor. He was born in the back room of his father's general store in the small village of Plymouth Notch, Vermont, on July 4, 1872. His only sibling, Abigail Coolidge, was born three years later but died in 1890 at the age of 15. Coolidge's father was a hardworking, thrifty man who prospered as a shopkeeper and farmer. He also held several local governmental positions, and served several terms in the Vermont House of Representatives and one term in the state Senate. Coolidge had a close relationship with his parents. His mother died in 1885 when Coolidge was only 12 years old. It was a blow that was to remain with him throughout his life.

As a boy, Coolidge was shy and sensitive. When his parents called him to the kitchen of their family home to greet friends, he would enter the room only with great difficulty. It was a problem he had to face throughout his life.

Education

Coolidge attended the local elementary school in Plymouth Notch, Vermont, and then the Black River Academy in Ludlow, Vermont, beginning in 1887. He briefly attended St. Johnsbury Academy in St. Johnsbury, Vermont, in order to qualify for admittance to Amherst College. In 1891 he began undergraduate study at Amherst College in Amherst, Massachusetts. Coolidge was very much a loner. He was shy, quiet, and spent much of his time studying during his first years at the college, though he did join the Amherst Republican club. His favorite areas of study were French and Italian, political science, philosophy, and modern history. Coolidge's grades were good, and he eventually graduated cum laude. Somewhat oddly given his quiet demeanor, Coolidge developed into an excellent public speaker. He became a skilled debater, won a prize for oration, and was asked to give one of the six student speeches at his college graduation—the humorous one—in 1895.

Legal Training

Coolidge was not entirely sure of the direction he would take after receiving his undergraduate degree. He could have returned to his Vermont home and worked in his father's business. His father, however, encouraged him to pursue a career in law, and this is the route that the young Coolidge took.

Rather than attend law school, an Amherst classmate helped Coolidge obtain an opening in the law offices of two Northampton, Massachusetts, attorneys. He read law for a year and a half and was admitted to legal practice in 1897. Coolidge then made a decision that would chart the course of his career: he would not return to Vermont to practice law but would stay in Massachusetts and open a law office in Northampton. He maintained that practice for the next two decades—until the time he was elected governor of the Commonwealth of Massachusetts.

Family Life

In 1905, at the age of 33, Coolidge married Grace Anna Goodhue, a graduate of the University of Vermont and a teacher at a school for deaf children. The couple had two children, John and Calvin Jr. Calvin died in 1924 at the age of 16 after developing a blister on his foot while playing tennis at the White House, which progressed into blood poisoning. Many observers felt that

Calvin Coolidge. (The Library of Congress.)

President Coolidge never overcame this loss. Indeed, in his autobiography Coolidge wrote: "When he [Calvin, Jr.] went, the power and the glory of the presidency went with him. I do not know why such a price was exacted for occupying the White House."

Grace Coolidge's personality was the direct opposite of her husband's. He was quiet, private, and dour; she was lively, outgoing and, a gracious hostess. Grace Coolidge broke with the tradition that required presidential spouses to remain in the background and not to engage in public affairs. She held a few press conferences and occasionally spoke out on issues that concerned her. In his autobiography Coolidge said of her, "For almost a quarter of a century she has borne with my infirmities, and I have rejoiced in her graces."

Career

Calvin Coolidge followed in his father's footsteps by becoming active in local Republican Party politics. His republicanism was never in doubt. Coolidge had grown up in a Republican household in a state—Vermont—that was then strongly Republican. He had later moved to Massachusetts, a state that was also controlled by the Republican Party at the turn of the twentieth century. As a result, his political philosophy closely mirrored the generally conservative ideas of the Republican Party in his area of the country.

Fast Fact

Coolidge's reputation for silence followed him throughout his lifetime. He earned the particular nickname "Silent Cal" as a result of his behavior during the cabinet meetings of President Warren Harding. Harding invited Coolidge to attend these meetings but Coolidge rarely, if ever, spoke except when questions were put to him. But even in these circumstances Coolidge's comments tended to be brief and to the point. Seated at the far end of the conference table, the vice president often seemed to be only a spectator at the meetings. It can be safely concluded that Coolidge had little influence on the policies of the Harding administration.

(Source: Donald R. McCoy. *Calvin Coolidge: The Quiet President,* 1988.)

Coolidge was a member of the Northampton City Council in 1899 and 1900, after which the council appointed him city solicitor. He held that position for two years and then briefly served as clerk of the courts in Hampshire County, Massachusetts. In 1904 Coolidge was chosen to head the local Republican Party organization. The only election he ever lost came in 1905 when he was defeated in a race to become a member of the Northampton School Board.

Coolidge in Massachusetts Politics

In 1907 Coolidge's political career began its rapid rise that was to culminate in his election as vice president and then president of the United States. He served two terms as a member of the Massachusetts General Court (1907–08) and compiled a record as a progressive in this legislative body. Coolidge supported laws to protect children and women in the workplace. He also backed amendments to the U.S. Constitution that would provide for the direct election of U.S. senators and grant women the right to vote. At the same time that he served in the General Court Coolidge also held the position of mayor of Northampton.

Coolidge was elected to four terms in the Massachusetts State Senate (1912–15) and served as president of that chamber in 1914 and 1915. He backed minimum wage legislation for women, the creation of a workman's compensation for persons injured on the job, a state income tax, and the legalization of labor picketing. He also continued his support for the direct election of sen-

ators and women's suffrage. (Both became part of the U.S. Constitution, the former as the Seventeenth Amendment in 1913 and the latter as the Nineteenth Amendment in 1920.)

In 1916 Coolidge was elected lieutenant governor of Massachusetts. He held this position until 1918. When he was elected governor of the Commonwealth in 1918 and 1919, he signed legislation limiting the time women and children could work to 48 hours a week and created the first state budget system. But some of the most difficult problems Coolidge faced were those derived from the aftermath of World War I (1914–18). Housing was scarce and public workers demanded an increase in their salaries. The governor acted to reduce the shortage of housing, and he granted government employees an increase in their pay.

It was the Boston police strike that occurred in September 1919 that projected Coolidge into national prominence. When the city's police commissioner, Edwin Curtis, refused to recognize the union as the legal representative of the policemen, a large majority of the officers went on strike. The crime rate in Boston quickly grew. Boston mayor Andrew Peters asked Coolidge to assist the city. Coolidge responded by sending in state police to restore order. Further, he backed Curtis in his decision not to recognize the police union. The president of the American Federation of Labor (AFL), Samuel Gompers, asked Governor Coolidge to reconsider his actions. Coolidge quickly sent Gompers a telegram that declared, "There is no right to strike against the public safety by anybody, anywhere, anytime" (as quoted in: McCoy, p. 94).

Coolidge's Assent to the Presidency

The telegram made Coolidge a hero to many Americans, and it led directly to his nomination as vice president at the Republican National Convention in 1920. The Massachusetts delegation to the convention made Coolidge its favorite son for the vice-presidential nomination, but he had little support. A favorite son candidate at a national convention is one who has the support of his state delegation, but he's often not a serious contender for the presidential or vice-presidential nomination. The nomination is used for strategic reasons, especially in situations in which there are several strong candidates. The state is then in a position to bargain with those candidates for its vote.

When U.S. senator Warren Harding of Ohio was nominated as the party's presidential candidate, Coolidge's name did not receive active consideration by the nominee and his advisers. When the first nominations for the vice-presidential candidate began, however, shouts of "Coolidge" began to be heard from the convention floor. The cries grew louder and a rush to support Coolidge swept through the various state delegations. The delegates voted overwhelmingly to make the Massachusetts governor the party's vice-presidential candidate. The Republican ticket of Warren Harding and Calvin Coolidge easily won the national election in November 1920. (Interestingly, the losing Democratic ticket consisted of another Ohio politician, then-governor James Cox, and his running mate, future four-term president Franklin D. Roosevelt.) The new vice president and his wife moved to Washington, and Coolidge began his career in national politics.

Coolidge as Vice President

Few vice presidents have left lasting marks on U.S. government while holding this office, and Coolidge is no exception. Except for the exercise of a few constitutional duties—presiding over sessions of the Senate and casting a vote in case of a tie in that chamber—vice presidents have little opportunity to influence policymaking without the president's expressed consent. President Harding invited Coolidge to attend cabinet meetings, but the vice president rarely spoke. Further, Coolidge never had the chance to cast a tie-breaking vote in the Senate, and he took a very narrow view of the vice president's power as president of the Senate. A quiet, unassuming man, Coolidge seemed utterly out of place in a chamber noted for the strong personalities of its members and their tendency to speak at great length.

Vice presidents are often called upon by the president to make public appearances on ceremonial occasions. This type of activity was more suited to Coolidge's personality, though it was not one he especially enjoyed. Nonetheless, his somber and reserved demeanor was perfectly suited to these state occasions. Coolidge was also frequently called upon to give speeches at various political and public events. Sometimes he chose patriotic or moral themes, and other times he defended the policies of the Harding administration.

Coolidge as President

Coolidge became president at the age of 51 after President Harding's sudden death from heart failure on August 2, 1923. Scandals surrounding crimes and improprieties committed by several of Harding's advisers, including his attorney general and secretary of the interior, dominated the early months of Coolidge's first term. With his natural honesty, integrity, and reserve, Coolidge quickly dealt with the scandals and restored the faith of the American people in the presidency and the Republican Party. He easily won reelection in 1924. For the most part, Coolidge kept to the policies and programs that Harding had begun and which Coolidge had always supported. He pursued a policy of limited government throughout his time in office, a policy that resulted primarily in tax reductions and tariff protections for industry. His impact on daily life in the United States was, by design, minimal, and in a time of general prosperity this strategy proved very popular. In foreign affairs Coolidge also followed the lead of his predecessor, working to

ensure that the war debts of European nations would be paid and forming peace pacts and arms limitations treaties in an attempt to prevent future war.

Post-presidential Years

In 1929 after announcing that he would not seek a third term and passing the reins to his successor Herbert Hoover, Calvin and Grace Coolidge returned to their home in Northampton, Massachusetts. During his retirement Coolidge wrote his autobiography, *The Autobiography of Calvin Coolidge,* and published articles in some of the popular magazines of the day in which he reiterated his philosophy of limited government. He served as a member of the Board of Trustees of Amherst College and the New York Life Insurance Society. Grace Coolidge resumed her activities in the local Congregational Church and her work for the Red Cross and other community organizations. The Great Depression that began in late 1929, as well as President Hoover's defeat in the 1932 presidential election by Franklin D. Roosevelt, caused Coolidge much distress. He did not live long enough to see the great expansion in government instituted by President Roosevelt as part of his New Deal reform program, but if he had, Coolidge would undoubtedly have opposed this development since it ran counter to his entire philosophy of government.

Coolidge died in his Northampton, Massachusetts home on January 5, 1933, of a coronary thrombosis. A service was held in Northampton that was attended by the president and Mrs. Hoover and many other political dignitaries. Coolidge's body was then taken to Plymouth, Vermont, for burial in the family cemetery. A simple stone bearing the president's name marks the place. Grace Coolidge died in 1957 at the age of 78 and was buried next to her husband.

The Calvin Coolidge Administrations

Calvin Coolidge was a popular president who held office during a carefree time of growing national prosperity. He brought to the presidential office the characteristics of his small town New England background—thrift, honesty, and integrity. The people of the United States appreciated these qualities in the wake of the unfolding scandals of the Harding years. Coolidge saw only a limited role for government in the U.S. economy. His policies of cutting taxes and maintaining tight control over government spending were especially popular with U.S. business. In 1927 Coolidge suddenly announced that he would not run for reelection as president in 1928. At the time he provided no explanation for

Administration

Administration Dates

August 3, 1923–March 4, 1925
March 4, 1925–March 4, 1929

Vice President

Charles G. Dawes (1925–29)

Cabinet

Secretary of State
Charles Evans Hughes (1921–25)
Frank B. Kellogg (1925–29)

Secretary of the Treasury
Andrew W. Mellon (1921–32)

Secretary of War
John W. Weeks (1921–25)
Dwight F. Davis (1925–29)

Attorney General
Harry M. Daugherty (1921–24)
Harlan F. Stone (1924–25)
John G. Sargent (1925–29)

Secretary of the Navy
Edwin Denby (1921–24)
Curtis D. Wilbur (1924–29)

Postmaster General
Harry S. New (1923–29)

Secretary of the Interior
Hubert Work (1923–28)
Roy O. West (1928–29)

Secretary of Agriculture
Henry C. Wallace (1921–24)
Howard M. Gore (1924–25)
William M. Jardine (1925–29)

Secretary of Labor
James J. Davis (1921–1930)

Secretary of Commerce
Herbert C. Hoover (1923–28)
William F. Whiting (1928–29)

---

his decision. Less than a year after he left office, the United States descended into a decade-long economic depression, and Coolidge and his governmental philosophy were discredited in the minds of most Americans.

Coolidge Becomes President

Vice President Calvin Coolidge was on vacation in Vermont when the announcement of President Harding's death reached him. At 2:47 A.M. on the morning of August 3, 1923, the oath of office was administered to him by his father—a notary public and justice of the peace—in the sitting room of his father's home in Plymouth Notch, Vermont. A second oath of office was given in Washington, D.C., on August 21, 1923.

Between August 3, 1923, and March 3, 1925,—while Coolidge completed Harding's term—the United States had no vice president. The original Constitution made no provision for filling the office when a vice president succeeded to the presidency following the removal, death, or resignation of the president. It was not until 1965, when the Twenty-fifth Amendment, giving the

president power to nominate a successor who becomes vice president after approval by both houses of Congress, was added to the Constitution, that this oversight was addressed. (In October 1973, U.S. representative Gerald R. Ford of Michigan was the first person to become vice president under the Twenty-fifth Amendment, following Vice President Spiro Agnew's resignation.)

Coolidge's succession to the presidential office did not produce major changes in personnel, policies, or practices. He initially kept all of Harding's cabinet members and only made gradual changes. The new president repeatedly stated during his first weeks in office that he would continue the policies of Harding.

The Election of 1924

The 1924 Republican Party Convention

With thoughts of a second term for Harding looming, some Republican Party leaders had thought of replacing Coolidge as the president's running mate on the national ticket in 1924. But the death of Harding and the emerging scandals of that administration eliminated all thought of dropping Coolidge from the national

Republican ticket. His unquestioned honesty enabled the party to defuse claims that it was the party of corruption.

Thus when the Republicans held their national convention in Cleveland, Ohio, in June 1924, Coolidge was the overwhelming choice of the delegates to be their presidential candidate. Coolidge was nominated on the convention's first ballot with only a handful of dissenting votes. The party platform adopted by the convention called for economy in government, tax reduction, a high tariff, aid to farmers, limitations on armaments, and support for the World Court (the Permanent Court of International Justice at the Hague, the Netherlands, established to resolve disputes between nations by judicial means rather than by resorting to force).

The 1924 Democratic Party Convention

The Democratic Party, to the contrary, took 103 ballots at its New York City convention to select John W. Davis of West Virginia as its presidential candidate. Davis had been a conservative congressman from that state and had been active in Democratic Party affairs. At the time of his nomination, Davis was a very successful New York City attorney. The Democrats nominated Nebraska governor Charles W. Bryan as its vice-presidential candidate. (He was the brother of William Jennings Bryan, who had run unsuccessfully as the Democratic Party's candidate for president on three separate occasions.)

Not only did the Democratic Party have difficulty agreeing on a candidate at its 1924 convention, it was also deeply divided over its program. A resolution condemning the Ku Klux Klan group was narrowly defeated after a bitter floor debate at the convention. (The white supremacist Klan had originally been formed in the South after the American Civil War (1861–65). It had grown in strength and spread its influence to some northern states after the end of World War I [1914–18] and had added Jews and Catholics to its list of hated groups.) A declaration of support for the League of Nations (an international peacekeeping organization made up of independent states conceived by Woodrow Wilson) was defeated by a wide margin, although the convention did support the idea of a national referendum on U.S. membership in the world organization. The Democrats did agree on some general themes: the party attacked Republican corruption in Washington, favored aid for the U.S. farmer, supported the rights of labor, and criticized large monopolistic U.S. corporations.

The 1924 Progressive Party Convention

The 1924 presidential election also produced a significant third party movement. U.S. senator Robert M. La Follette, a Republican from Wisconsin, and Senator Burton K. Wheeler, a Democrat from Montana, were nominated at the Cleveland convention of the Progressive Party. The party was composed of Republicans, Democrats, and independents who opposed what they

Fast Fact

Soon after Ronald Reagan became the nation's chief executive in January 1981, he entered the Cabinet Room in the White House and saw the portraits of Jefferson, Lincoln, and Truman on the wall. The new president ordered that Truman's portrait be taken down and one of Coolidge be taken from storage and hung in its place. This symbolic act showed Reagan's admiration of Coolidge and his conservative philosophy of government.

Robert Sobel. *Calvin Coolidge: An American Enigma,* 1988.

believed to be the conservatism of the two major political parties. The party platform strongly condemned the emergence of large corporations that dominated many areas of the U.S. economy and exercised undue control of government. It also called for public ownership of the nation's railroads and the right of Congress to override decisions of the U.S. Supreme Court.

The Campaign of 1924

Coolidge took an unusual approach to the 1924 presidential campaign; he campaigned very little and did not address any specific political issues. His speeches dealt with broad, general topics such as peace, education, citizenship, and religious freedom. The Republican Party used the slogans "Keep Cool with Coolidge" and "Coolidge or Chaos" to promote the president's election. It was enough to give Coolidge an easy victory. The Democratic Party's candidate, John W. Davis, proved to be a very dull campaigner. Furthermore, given the general prosperity of much of the nation, voters were in no mood for the progressive policies of Senator La Follette and his Progressive Party.

Coolidge received 382 electoral votes and 54 percent of the popular vote, while Davis garnered 136 electoral votes and 29 percent of the popular vote. Davis's Electoral College victories came in 12 solidly Democratic states in the South. La Follette polled an impressive 17 percent of the popular vote and ran ahead of Davis in 11 western states, but he won only the 13 electoral votes of his home state of Wisconsin. La Follette's campaign was hurt by the growing prosperity of much of the nation in 1924; his voting strength came largely from those states in the West whose depressed economies were based on farming.

Biography:

Robert Marion La Follette

Politician; Attorney (1855–1925) Like many politicians, Robert M. La Follette began his career as an attorney. It was as an attorney that La Follette was offered a bribe by a Republican Party supporter to "fix" a court case. Then and there, the principled La Follette declared war on the political party machine. La Follette traveled the state speaking at country fairs and any place else there was likely to be a crowd. His message was a progressive one that denounced existing politics and its unprincipled corruption. His impassioned efforts convinced the public and, in 1900, he was elected to the first of his three terms as governor of Wisconsin. In 1906 La Follette was elected to the U.S. Senate where he soon made a name for himself with his outspoken, contrary positions. He defied Senate tradition at every turn and angered "Old Guard" senators by refusing to concede on legislation he opposed. La Follette was an isolationist who first fought President Howard Taft on tariff issues and later Presi-

dent Woodrow Wilson on his decision to enter World War I (1914–18). After the war La Follette played a prominent role in exposing scandals in President Warren Harding's administration and then went head-to-head against his successor, Calvin Coolidge, in the 1924 run for the presidency. La Follette was the Progressive Party's candidate and carried the support of groups like the American Federation of Labor, the Socialist Party, and the railroad unions. Though he lost the election to Coolidge, La Follette won five million votes, carried his home state, and forever seated the Progressive Party's influence in the country.

Coolidge's Advisers

Coolidge kept all of the members of Harding's cabinet in office upon his succession to the presidency in August 1923. The major criticism that can be made of Coolidge's cabinet is that he failed to act quickly to remove several most corrupt members of the Harding cabinet. His unexpected accession to the presidency partly explains his inaction; he was simply dependent upon those more knowledgeable about the inner workings of the executive office. Further, the worst of the Harding scandals were yet to be revealed in August 1923 when Coolidge took office. However, the president most likely had heard rumors of impending problems, and he had a firsthand opportunity as Harding's vice president to know of the personal shortcomings of both Harry Daugherty (attorney general) and Edwin Denby (secretary of war). Under pressure from Coolidge, both men submitted their resignations early in 1924.

Coolidge nominated Harlan Fiske Stone to be Daugherty's successor as attorney general. Stone brought unquestioned honesty and integrity to an office that had been enmeshed in scandal. Stone acted quickly to eliminate all traces of corruption from the Justice Department. Herbert Hoover remained as secretary of commerce until 1928 when he resigned the post to seek the Republican presidential nomination. Two Harding appointees—Secretary of the Treasury Andrew Mellon and Secretary

of Labor James J. Davis—remained in office throughout Coolidge's presidency.

Coolidge appointed Frank Kellogg from Minnesota as secretary of state following the resignation of Charles Evans Hughes in 1925. He relied heavily on Kellogg for foreign policy decisions—an area in which Coolidge had no experience. Secretary of the Treasury Mellon played a dominant role in shaping economic policy. Both Mellon and Coolidge held conservative pro-business philosophies, and the two men worked closely together during the Coolidge presidency. Indeed, Mellon was the only member of the cabinet with whom Coolidge was personally friendly. Secretary of Commerce Hoover shared the conservative economic ideas of Coolidge and Mellon, but his influence on Coolidge's domestic policy was much less significant. Coolidge and Hoover disliked each other and each shared a low estimate of the other's abilities.

The four men who were closest to President Coolidge and whose advice he respected were not to be found in his cabinet. They were Frank Stearns, Dwight Morrow, William Butler, and Frederick Gillette. Stearns was the owner of a large Boston department store who had worked with Coolidge since his race for lieutenant governor of Massachusetts in 1915. Morrow had been a friend and classmate at Amherst College and they had remained close since that time. Both Butler and Gillette were Massachusetts politicians whom Coolidge had known since the time he had held public office in the Commonwealth. These four men were the "Massachusetts gang" and were among the few friends Coolidge had in Washington.

Coolidge's cabinet from 1924 to 1929 contained many successful Republican businesspeople whose government philosophy was quite conservative. They tended to mirror Coolidge's own political and economic ideas. Coolidge's personal honesty and dedication to public service was reflected in the character of the men who served in his administration. It was possible to criticize their ideas and policies, but there was never any question about their honesty.

Coolidge and Congress

The Republican Party had majority control of both houses of Congress throughout President Coolidge's time as the nation's chief executive. This included the Sixty-eighth Congress that had been elected while Harding was president and the Sixty-ninth and Seventieth Congresses that were chosen in 1924 and 1926 respectively.

The fact that the Republicans controlled both houses of Congress throughout the Coolidge years is somewhat misleading, however. It suggests more unity among Republicans than was actually present. This was especially true during the period when Coolidge served out the unexpired term of Warren Harding. The divisions in the party between old guard conservatives and progressives were very strong. Led by Wisconsin senator Robert La Follette, the Progressives often sided with Democrats in Congress and clashed with the new president. This coalition twice passed a veteran's bonus bill that the president had vetoed; it revised Coolidge's tax program and delayed several cabinet nominations. In 1924 when Coolidge was overwhelmingly elected president, Americans elected a Republican-controlled Congress that was far more sympathetic to the president than the prior Congress had been. La Follette, the Progressive leader, had died in June 1925, and the Democrats were dispirited following their crushing defeat in the 1924 elections.

The improved relations between Coolidge and the Republican Congress had several explanations. The president presented few important proposals to Congress for its consideration, and Congress proposed little in the way of significant new legislation. Weak leadership in Congress and the general prosperity of the Coolidge years also contributed to the absence of rancor between Congress and the president. Politics was reduced to "secondary importance" during this time, and the "normalcy" Harding had spoken of but had not produced finally became a reality during the Coolidge era.

This is not to say that Coolidge and Congress were in complete agreement. Agricultural policy often caused friction between the president and Congress, and in 1925

Coolidge's nominee for attorney general—Charles B. Warren—was rejected. Congress and Coolidge also disagreed over the fate of electrical power generating facilities at Muscle Shoals, Alabama. Coolidge wanted to firmly place the facilities into private hands, but Congress failed to approve such a step. As a result Coolidge was forced to use a pocket veto (failing to act before Congress adjourned) to stop a bill that would have solidified government control over the facilities. For the most part, however, Coolidge and Congress worked well together. Coolidge himself wrote: "My personal and official relations have all been peculiarly pleasant. The Congress has not always done all that I wished, but it has done very little that I did not approve."

Coolidge and the Judiciary

President Coolidge made one appointment to the Supreme Court during his tenure in office, Harlan Fiske Stone. Stone had been dean of the Columbia University Law School and was serving as U.S. attorney general at the time of his appointment. He served as an associate justice of the nation's highest court between 1925 and 1941. President Franklin D. Roosevelt elevated him to the position of chief justice in 1941, a position he held until his death in 1946. Integrity, moderation, and great legal skill characterized Justice Stone's years of distinguished service on the Supreme Court.

Changes in the U.S. Government

No significant changes in the structure of the U.S. governmental system occurred during Coolidge's presidency. This was understandable given his basic philosophy of keeping government as limited as possible. Further, the policies adopted during his administration were not unique to the Coolidge presidency; his predecessor, Warren Harding, had initiated many. Cutting taxes and balancing the federal budget were policies adopted during Harding's years as president. Restricting immigration to the United States also began under Harding; and in 1924 Coolidge signed legislation that imposed further limitations (*See also,* Domestic Issues). In the area of foreign relations the pattern was the same. Harding began the process of seeking world peace by means of naval disarmament, and Coolidge tried to extend this approach to ships not covered by the original treaty of 1921 (*See also,* Foreign Issues).

Changes that did occur during the Coolidge administration included the first law regulating commercial aviation which was passed by Congress in 1926 and signed by Coolidge. Known as the Air Commerce Act, it placed aviation under the control of the Commerce Department and established the first commercial air routes. In February 1927 the federal Radio Commission was established to regulate use of airwaves by radio stations. Finally, the Foreign Service, which represents U.S. interests abroad, was also created during the Coolidge administration.

Domestic Issues

From the beginning of his presidency in August 1923, Coolidge vowed that he would continue the policies of his predecessor, Warren Harding. To a great extent Coolidge achieved this objective. Like Harding, Coolidge favored lowered taxes, a balanced budget, higher tariffs, restricting immigration into the United States, and reducing the level of government intrusion into the nation's economic system. With Republicans holding majorities in both houses of Congress during his years in office, Coolidge was remarkably successful in achieving his domestic policy objectives.

Coolidge Backs Business

President Coolidge never presented to Congress a large program of domestic legislative proposals, and the number of his programs actually declined during his years in office. Largely as a result of keeping government spending under tight control and better management of the budget by both the Congress and the president, the Coolidge years saw a significant reduction in the size of the national debt. Coolidge was successful in 1924 and again in 1926 in obtaining congressional approval for a package of tax changes designed by Secretary of the Treasury Mellon. Income taxes were cut, estate taxes were halved, the gift tax was abolished, and some excise taxes left over from World War I (1914–18) were ended. The purpose of these changes was to make more money available for investment in U.S. business, thus raising standards for the general population. This was called the "trickle down effect." Eventually these changes may have contributed to the economic crash of 1929 in that it encouraged speculative investment in the U.S. stock markets.

The president's pro-business policies were also shown in his appointments to the federal regulatory agencies of government such as the Federal Trade Commission (FTC) that had been created in 1914 to regulate business. Coolidge's appointees actually had little interest in any such regulation, and thus the agencies did little or nothing to restrain business practices. Further, Coolidge opposed any proposals to reduce the high tariff rates that were favored by U.S. businesses.

Immigration Policy

In the shaky peacetime economy that followed World War I, Americans, especially organized labor, feared economic competition from immigrants, who willingly worked for low wages. White Protestants resented the flood of Catholics and Jews from southern and eastern Europe into the United States. Although the United States already restricted Asian immigration, it had always had an open-door policy in regard to the European immigrants. In 1921, during the Harding presidency, legislation was adopted that limited immigration and established a quota system for establishing the annual number of immigrants from each nation. In 1924 Coolidge signed legislation that further restricted immigration into the United States. The quota system that had been created under Harding was changed to favor immigrants from northern Europe and to restrict the number of immigrants arriving from southern and eastern Europe. This was accomplished in two ways: (1) the overall quota was cut from 3 to 2 percent of each nationality group living in the United States; and (2), even more significantly, the 1890 census replaced the census of 1910 as the basis for determining quotas. This meant that 20 years of heavy immigration from eastern and southern Europe was ignored when it came to determining the quotas.

Policy Defeats: Coolidge Vetoes the McNary-Haugen Bills

The most intense conflict between Coolidge and Congress came over agricultural legislation. The farmers in the West had failed to share in the postwar domestic prosperity of the nation. The abundance of U.S. agriculture led to overproduction and to falling prices paid to farmers. The major farm organizations and members of Congress from agricultural states—Republicans and Democrats—passed the McNary-Haugen Bill in 1927 and again in 1928, and both times Coolidge vetoed the laws. The proposed laws would have created a government corporation empowered to purchase certain major agricultural products for sale overseas. The purchase price would have been high enough to guarantee farmers a profit. The corporation could then either sell the products abroad at a loss or hold them until world prices increased. In his first veto message Coolidge denounced the proposed legislation as an unconstitutional form of price fixing that would produce more, not less, production of agricultural produce and would disrupt world agricultural markets. His second veto was even more scathing in its attack on the farm bill. Coolidge referred to the proposed legislation as "cumbersome," "bureaucracy gone mad," "intolerable tyranny," "futile," and "nonsense" (McCoy, p. 327).

The economic problems of the U.S. farmer would continue and then worsen when the world slipped into the Great Depression of the 1930s. In 1933 President Franklin D. Roosevelt signed the Agricultural Adjustment Act that drew on the ideas first proposed in the McNary-Haugen Bill and created a system of increasing commodity prices by limiting their production.

Farming did not enjoy the postwar prosperity that other U.S. industries did. Farmers were negatively affected during Coolidge's term when he vetoed the McNary-Haugen Bill twice, in both 1927 and 1928. (Corbis. Reproduced by permission.)

Foreign Issues

Coolidge generally followed the foreign policies set by his predecessor, Warren Harding. Coolidge opposed U.S. entry into the League of Nations and, like Harding, gave lip service to the United States becoming a member of the Permanent Court of International Justice (the World Court), though he made no attempt to gain Senate approval for this step. Coolidge also pressed for the payment of Allied war debts and reparations by Germany for the damages it inflicted on the Allies during World War I. He strongly opposed the cancellation of the war debts owed to the United States by its European allies. "They hired the money, didn't they? Let them pay it!" he is supposed to have said (White, p. 384).

The Geneva Conference of 1927

The public's desire for peace remained very strong during the years following the end of World War I. President Warren Harding had responded to this strong public sentiment in 1921 by bringing together representatives of the five great world powers of the time—the United States, Great Britain, France, Japan, and Italy—to negotiate a reduction in the number of naval ships each possessed. The Washington Conference of 1921 did reach agreement about capital ships— battleships and aircraft carriers—but not with respect to other smaller warships. Coolidge decided to respond to the public's demand for

the prevention of another world war—and also to establish the Republican Party as the party of peace—by calling for a new conference on naval disarmament. The meeting would be held in Geneva, Switzerland, and be a follow-up to the Washington Conference of 1921. The world's five major naval powers would try to negotiate a reduction in the number of their smaller ships— submarines, destroyers, and cruisers. Unfortunately the Geneva Conference was unable to produce any positive results. France and Italy refused to attend, and the representatives of the United States, Great Britain, and Japan failed to reach an agreement.

The Dawes Plan

The administration's efforts to collect war debts and German reparations were not successful. While the United States continued to press for payments of these obligations, it increasingly became clear that they were never going to be paid in full. The Dawes Plan was conceived during the Wilson administration by Charles G. Dawes, a former Chicago banker and later Coolidge's vice president. The Dawes Committee met throughout the Harding administration, and its plan for addressing the escalating international debt crisis was completed in April 1924. It scaled down German reparations payments and called on U.S. bankers to make substantial loans to Germany in order to stabilize its currency and help it meet its reparations obligations to the Allied nations. These nations, in turn, would use the money to repay their war debts to the United States. This met with Coolidge's approval because private money was to be used to finance the loans, and the goal remained for debtor nations to repay their debts to the United States. Between 1925 and 1927 the plan worked well, and Dawes was awarded the Nobel Peace Prize in 1925 for his contributions. However, it became apparent by 1927 that the plan was only a stopgap measure, and that Germany would need to continue borrowing from outside to meet its obligations. Without those payments, payments to the United States by Allied nations could not be made. By the early 1930s each of the debtor nations (except Finland) had stopped making payments to the United States.

The Kellogg-Briand Pact

The foreign policy event most associated with the Coolidge administration is the Kellogg-Briand Pact, also known as the Pact of Paris. In 1927, the 10th anniversary of the United States's entry into World War I, French Foreign Minister Aristide Briand proposed a treaty between the United States and France outlawing war as a means of resolving future disputes between the two nations. The Coolidge administration had important reservations about the Briand proposal. First, a two-nation agreement might be interpreted as an alliance between France and the United States, and second, it would probably require the negotiation of similar agreements with many other countries. On December 28, 1927, Secretary of State Kellogg wrote the French foreign minister and suggested that the treaty be expanded to include other nations. After some delay Briand agreed to the change. A draft of the treaty was circulated to the other major world powers—Great Britain, Germany, Japan, and Italy—and each quickly gave its consent. The treaty was signed in Paris by 15 nations on August 27, 1928. By a vote of 85 to one the U.S. Senate gave its advice and consent to the treaty, although not all the senators who voted in favor of the agreement believed that it would be an effective means of preventing wars (Hicks, pp. 150–52). Ultimately almost all the nations of the world became party to the agreement. Both Kellogg and Briand received the Nobel Peace Prize in 1929 because of their efforts in connection with the pact.

The provisions of the Kellogg-Briand Pact required its members to renounce force as an instrument of international policy, condemned the use of force as a means of settling all international disputes, and demanded that all conflicts be resolved by peaceful means. The pact cannot be understood without appreciating the strength of antiwar sentiment in the United States and in Europe following World War I. The enormous loss and injury to human life and the devastation of property that took place during the war came as a great shock to many. The naval disarmament conferences of the 1920s and 1930s were one manifestation of the antiwar movement. The Kellogg-Briand Pact was another.

The agreement was, however, fatally defective. While Kellogg-Briand expressed noble sentiments, there was no way of enforcing its provisions. The League of Nations, for example, had no effective means of halting military actions begun by member nations. Both President Coolidge and Secretary of State Kellogg realized the treaty's shortcoming and were not optimistic about its future effectiveness. But they backed the treaty because public opinion strongly supported it as a means to prevent the reoccurrence of world war.

Within a few years two nations that had signed the agreement began wars. Japan invaded Manchuria in 1931, and Italy invaded Ethiopia in 1935. With only the force of world opinion to enforce it, the futility of the Kellogg-Briand Pact became apparent. A little more than a decade after the treaty was signed in Paris, World War II (1939–45) broke out in Europe, and the agreement became only a memory of a more innocent time.

Latin America and the Caribbean

Despite the failures of Coolidge's peace efforts, his administration had a number of small but significant accomplishments in foreign affairs. This was especially true with regard to the relations between the United States and the nations of Latin America and the Caribbean. Coolidge faced widespread distrust and hatred by many governments and people in this part of the world. These attitudes were the result of U.S. imperialism at the end of the nineteenth century and in the first decades of the twentieth century. The United States had acquired possessions (Puerto Rico and the Philippine Islands, for example), supported military dictators, and on a number of occasions sent U.S. military personnel into countries in Latin America and in the Caribbean when their own governments were not able to maintain order.

Coolidge was perhaps the first U.S. president who appreciated the problems and costs of being a colonial power (i.e., one that controls a smaller power) and he began to change U.S. policy toward the nations south of its border. In 1924 he withdrew the U.S. marines that had been sent to Santo Domingo, on the Dominican Republic, in 1916. For a brief period in 1925, Coolidge also withdrew U.S. marines from Nicaragua who had been present in that nation since 1912. He had to return them almost immediately as violence broke out.

U.S. policy toward Mexico provided the most important evidence of the changing nature of U.S. policy toward its southern neighbors during the Coolidge years. Anti-U.S. sentiment was particularly strong in Mexico. A crisis developed in 1927 when the Mexican president, Plutarco Elias Calles, demanded that all mineral deposits and oil owned by U.S. companies in his nation become the property of the Mexican government. To defuse this situation, President Coolidge sent Dwight Morrow to Mexico with instructions to main-

The Kellogg-Briand Act, drafted by U.S. secretary of state Frank Kellogg and French foreign minister Aristide Briand, went into effect on August 27, 1928. The pact expressed the strong antiwar sentiment of the general public after World War I. (Corbis. Reproduced by permission.)

tain peace. Morrow was a New York banker and friend of Coolidge from their days as students at Amherst. His mission was successful. Morrow was able to avoid war and maintain U.S. property rights in Mexico— at least for the time being. His flexibility and more pragmatic approach to resolving problems served to moderate U.S.-Mexican differences and provided a basis for future improvements in the relations between the two countries.

The Coolidge Administration Legacy

Republican Party leaders were confident that the Coolidge-Dawes ticket would be reelected in the 1928 presidential election. The nation was at peace, its economy strong, and wealth was increasing at an unheard-of pace. Then on August 2, 1927—the fourth anniversary of his succession to the presidency—Coolidge made a short statement to the press reporters who were called to a meeting at the president's summer office in the Black Hills of South Dakota: "I do not choose to run for president in nineteen twenty-eight." Not even his wife knew of his intention, and Coolidge never gave a clear explanation for his decision. Certainly one important reason for his choice was the death of his sixteen year-old son, Calvin Jr. Though later, in his autobiography, he expressed concern over the public's view of a president seeking a third term, even though his first term was less than two years. "A president should not only not be selfish, but he ought to avoid the appearance of selfishness. The people would not have confidence in a man that appeared to be grasping for the office."

With Coolidge out of the race for president in the 1928 election, the Republicans turned to Herbert Hoover as the party's candidate. At its 1928 national convention the Republicans nominated Hoover for president and Senator Charles G. Curtis of Kansas for vice president. This ticket easily won election in November 1928.

Popularity and Public Opinion

Calvin Coolidge's presidency coincided with a time of growing prosperity and technological innovation in the United States. The wealthy were becoming richer and the middle class was increasing in number as many poor people were able to achieve greater economic security. The price of mass-produced automobiles and kitchen refrigerators came within the financial reach of more Americans, and motion pictures and radio provided new forms of entertainment for millions of U.S. citizens.

The mid-1920s was a period of general optimism about the future of the United States. Certainly Coolidge's quiet, almost melancholic personality did little to convey this mood of hope. But there were other features of the president that made him very popular in his time. His belief in small government and in not using its power to introduce significant changes in society contributed to his reputation. His philosophy of government was especially popular with business, but many in the United States also accepted this view of government. Most importantly he restored honesty and integrity to the presidency at a time when the scandals of the previous Harding administration had lowered the public's regard for the executive branch of government.

Press and Media

Following the lead of his predecessor, President Harding, Coolidge held biweekly press conferences throughout his term in office. It has been estimated that he held 520 such meetings during his six years as president. (The questions had to be submitted to the president in writing before the conference and he selected which ones to answer and which to ignore.) Like Harding, Coolidge, according to presidential historian Robert

Sobel, enjoyed great popularity among the members of the Washington press corps.

Lasting Impact

History, however, has not been kind to Calvin Coolidge. While his personal honesty has been admired, the American people through much of the remaining decades of the twentieth century rejected his philosophy of government. The onset of the economic depression in 1929 convinced many Americans that a larger, more positive government in Washington was necessary to protect the needs of the public. Thus, the 1930s produced President Franklin D. Roosevelt's New Deal with its many new agencies and its network of rules to regulate the U.S. economy. Its many laws were designed to protect the nation's citizens in times of financial need. This philosophy of positive government was extended even further during the Great Society programs of President Lyndon Johnson between 1964 and 1968.

World War II (1939–45), the Korean War (1950–53), and the Vietnam War (1959–75), along with the long Cold War against the former Soviet Union, also contributed to the growth of government in Washington. War draws power to the nation's capital and further concentrates that power in the hands of the president and the executive branch of government.

While the great peace treaties and conferences undertaken by Coolidge's administration ultimately failed, many of the seemingly less significant policy changes began under Coolidge produced important long-term benefits. Coolidge, for example, made a very serious attempt to improve U.S. relations with Mexico. His choice of Dwight Morrow to be ambassador to Mexico in 1927 was an especially inspired one. Morrow was remarkably successful in reducing the high level of tensions, bordering on war, that then existed between the two countries. In the 1930s President Roosevelt set forth his famous "Good Neighbor" policy toward Latin America, which drew upon Coolidge's ideas for developing a new type of relationship between the United States and its southern neighbors—one based more on cooperation than on dominance.

As a result of many domestic and international developments that took place over the course of the second half of the twentieth century, the U.S. governmental system today is very different from that of Coolidge's era. The huge size of the federal budget and the wide scope of government activities would have been outside the comprehension of Coolidge and of most Americans of his day. Coolidge's philosophy of government looked back to his roots in late nineteenth century, small town New England. He believed that the functions of government should be limited and that government should be frugal with the public's tax money. Not even the most conservative presidents since Coolidge have espoused such a limited view of government, and it is not likely to be put into practice again in this country's near future.

Coolidge was fortunate to have been president at a time when the United States was prosperous and at peace. These conditions enabled him to govern on the basis of his political philosophy.

Sources

Coolidge, Calvin. *The Autobiography of Calvin Coolidge.* New York: Cosmopolitan Book Corp., 1929.

Hicks, John D. *Republican Ascendancy: 1921–1933.* New York: Harper and Row, 1960.

McCoy, Donald R. *Coolidge: The Quiet President.* Lawrence, Kans.: University Press of Kansas, 1988.

Sobel, Robert. *Calvin Coolidge.* Washington, D.C.: Regnery Publishing Co., 1998.

White, William A. *A Puritan in Babylon: The Story of Calvin Coolidge.* New York: Macmillan, 1938.

Further Readings

Ables, Jules. *In The Times of Silent Cal.* New York: G. P. Putnam's Sons, 1969.

The Calvin Coolidge Memorial Foundation. 1999. <http://www.calvin-coolidge.org> (7 July, 1999).

Ferrell, Robert H. *The Presidency of Calvin Coolidge.* Lawrence, Kans.: University Press of Kansas, 1998.

Fuess, Claude M. *Calvin Coolidge: The Man From Vermont.* Boston: Little-Brown, 1940.

Ross, Isabel. *Grace Coolidge and Her Era.* New York: Dodd, Mead, 1962.

Hoover Administration

Full name: Herbert Clark Hoover
Given name: Herbert Hoover
Popular name: The Great Engineer

Personal Information:

Born: August 10, 1874
Birthplace: West Branch, Iowa
Died: October 20, 1964
Death place: West Branch, Iowa
Burial place: West Branch, Iowa
Religion: Society of Friends (Quaker)
Spouse: Lou Henry (m. 1899)
Children: Herbert Clark, Jr.; Allan Henry
Education: Stanford University, Stanford, California, B.A., 1895
Occupation: Mining engineer; public administrator; cabinet member
Political Party: Republican Party
Age at Inauguration: 54 years

Biography

Before earning an international reputation as a humanitarian and administrator, Herbert Hoover achieved renown as a mining engineer, amassing a large fortune in the process. Self-disciplined and ambitious, he first entered politics by heading the Belgian Relief Commission at the start of World War I (1914-18) and went on to serve as secretary of commerce for Presidents Harding and Coolidge. Hoover was a man of extraordinary intelligence, dedication, and integrity, and was far from the "do-nothing" president of legend. Throughout his presidency he promoted financial stability overseas while acting swiftly to combat economic ruin at home. However, because of his belief in a balanced budget and refusal to foster direct aid to the unemployed, he left office without the gratitude of a nation.

Early Life

On August 10, 1874, Herbert Clark Hoover was born in West Branch, Iowa, a small Quaker settlement about 25 miles from Iowa City. Herbert was the third and last child of Jesse Hoover and Hulda Randall Minthorn Hoover. Jesse was a village blacksmith, then a merchant. Hulda was a lay minister in the Society of Friends (Quakers). In his memoirs, Hoover called her "serious minded, even for a Quaker." Speaking of village life, Hoover recalled: "We ground our own meat and corn at the mill. We slaughtered our own hogs for meat; we wove at least part of our own clothing. . . . We erected our own buildings; we made our own soap."

When young Hoover reached the age of six, his thirty-four year-old father died of heart trouble. At age nine, he saw his mother, who was not quite 36, die of typhoid. Because of these losses, the suddenly orphaned Hoover developed a certain protective shell around him, a detachment that masked a loneliness that remained the rest of his life. Hoover was always a reserved man, abrupt, taciturn, and little given to small talk.

Within a year after Hulda Hoover's death, the Hoover children were scattered among relatives. Young Herbert was sent to live with his uncle, Henry John Minthorn, in the Quaker village of Newberg, Oregon, 20 miles southwest of Portland. Minthorn was a man of many talents—Quaker minister, doctor, Indian agent, missionary—who ran the Friends Pacific Academy, which Hoover attended. At age 14, young Hoover worked as an office boy for the Oregon Land Company, a real estate firm Minthorn launched in nearby Salem. Finding Minthorn a repressive figure, Hoover turned inward, nursing his grievances in private and becoming even more introverted and self-disciplined. At the same time, he developed a driving ambition. He once stated while in the White House, "My boyhood ambition was to be able to earn my own living, without the help of anybody, anywhere." Much of his career would be occupied, as biographer David Burner notes, "with getting power and control for himself, and with creating order and stability around him." Part of this drive involved achieving financial independence at any cost.

Education

In 1891 Hoover was part of the 559 member charter class of Leland Stanford Junior University, an institution endowed by the prominent California senator and railroad magnate. The university was located 30 miles south of San Francisco, where the village of Palo Alto was soon founded. Graduating in 1895, Hoover made his mark in college politics, being particularly active behind the scenes by holding such offices as student body treasurer. He was a capable student, not a brilliant one, shining far more in his major, geology, than in German or English.

Only after graduation did Hoover's bookish side appear. In a sense reacting to a college training that concentrated on the sciences, he would read widely for the rest of his life. While not exactly a man of letters, Hoover wrote extensively on the mining industry, his chosen career after graduation from college. His *Principles of Mining* (1909) shows Hoover quite advanced for his time, endorsing collective bargaining and an eight-hour work day and denouncing "reactionary capitalists." The translation of the late medieval mining tome, *De Re Metallica,* made him and his wife Lou Henry Hoover, (who worked with him on the project) highly respected figures in the history of science.

Herbert Clark Hoover. (The Library of Congress.)

Family Life

At Stanford, Hoover met Lou Henry, daughter of a Monterey, California, banker and the university's first female engineering graduate. Though he was a Quaker and she was an Episcopalian, they were married by a Roman Catholic priest who was their personal friend in 1899. Tall, lithe, and athletic, Lou was as outgoing as Herbert was introverted. Always more articulate and charming than her husband, Lou Hoover made it her specialty to, in a sense, explain her shy and complicated husband to the outside world. She would forever be protecting his privacy while arranging elaborate formal social affairs that could both display and shield him. The couple had two children, Herbert Clark, Jr. in 1903 and Allan Henry in 1907.

Career

Upon graduation from college in 1885, Hoover worked in a gold mine near Nevada City, California, pushing an ore cart below the ground on the night shift. The future president labored 10 hours a stretch, seven days a week, for the princely wage of two dollars a day. In 1896 he began work as an office boy for the prominent San Francisco mining firm of Louis Janin, but within a year he became the assistant manager of Janin's Steeple Rock Development Company, another mining company, in New Mexico. He was soon surveying mines and examining territories in Arizona, Nevada, and Wyoming.

In 1897, at age 23, Hoover was hired by the prominent British mining firm of Bewick, Moreing, to work at Coolgardie, a mining camp in the outback of Western Australia. There he lived a strenuous life, experiencing heat, dust storms, flies—even blood poisoning. He traveled close to five thousand miles, mostly by camel and horse. "Every man here talks of when to go home," Hoover wrote a friend of back country mining life. "None come to stay except those who die, and a few go away as well off as they came." Starting out as a mere clerk, he soon proved his worth as a mining engineer, in the process coming across a fabulously rich vein of gold called the Sons of Gwalia mine. In no time, Hoover was earning the then staggering salary of $10,000 a year.

Bewick, Moreing sent Hoover to China in 1898, just in time for the nationalist uprising known as the Boxer Rebellion to break out. During the siege of Tientsin, he took part in the city's defenses. In China, Hoover excelled in inspecting and evaluating mines, and at age 26 he ran the giant Kaiping coal mines, the largest industrial enterprise in all China.

At age 27 Hoover became a partner in Bewick, Moreing, representing the firm in such far-flung areas as Ceylon (Sri-Lanka), Russia, Egypt, Rhodesia (Zimbabwe), and the Malay States (Malaysia). Indeed it was in Burma that he made his first of several million dollars. He later remarked, "If a man has not made a fortune by 40, he is not worth much" (Nash, vol. 1, p. 569).

A resident in London, England, from 1901 to 1915, he lived in a spacious country villa, with a paneled library, large garden, and half a dozen servants. By 1914, however, Hoover was claiming that he was leading "a dog's life." "Just making money isn't enough," he told a friend. He found himself as rich "as any man has a right to be," but he realized something was missing.

Hoover Enters Politics

Hoover found his new mission in 1914, when World War I (1914–18) broke out. He headed the Commission for Relief in Belgium (CRB), which provided two and a half million tons of food to nine million Belgians and two million more to people in northern France. Flying its own flag over a fleet of 35 ships, the CRB became the equivalent of an independent state. Eventually it involved four thousand committees worldwide, recruited 130,000 volunteers, and raised $200 million in gifts and subsidies. As Belgium was under German occupation all during Hoover's effort, he had to combine extraordinary diplomatic skill with equally extraordinary perseverance, risking his life during his frequent visits to the war zones.

In May 1917, just a month after the United States entered the conflict, President Woodrow Wilson appointed Hoover food administrator for the United States. Here he stimulated agricultural production, con-trolled surging farm prices, and in the process was able to ship two hundred million bushels of wheat to a famished Europe. He developed the slogan, "Food will win the war," while telling fellow citizens to observe "the gospel of the clean plate."

During the Paris Peace Conference of 1919, Hoover held a variety of positions: chairman of the Inter-Allied Food Council, director general of the American Relief Administration, economic director of the Supreme Economic Council, chairman of the European Coal Council, and personal adviser to President Woodrow Wilson. In 1921 Hoover directed a massive program for famine relief inside the Soviet Union. Russian novelist Maxim Gorky credited him with having saved three and a half million children and five and a half million adults.

In 1922, taking full advantage of his newly found status as international hero, Hoover published *American Individualism,* in which he attacked laissez-faire (or hands off) economics, opposed the twelve hour work day and child labor, and he called upon the nation's economic organizations to combine "self-interest" with a "sense of service" and to submit to government regulation designed to preserve the one condition he treasured above all— equality of opportunity.

Hoover as Secretary of Commerce

In the meantime, Hoover maintained his role as bureaucratic entrepreneur par excellence. There were rumblings among both Republicans and Democrats in 1920 of a possible presidential candidacy for Hoover, but nothing ever materialized. Instead, Hoover endorsed the Republican standard-bearer, Warren Gamaliel Harding, who, upon election, appointed Hoover secretary of commerce. He retained the position under President Calvin Coolidge. In this office Hoover encouraged the formulation of trade associations, pushed cooperative markets for farmers, and was particularly aggressive in seeking markets overseas. In 1927 the Mississippi River flooded, an event Hoover called "the greatest peace-time calamity in the history of the country" (Burner, p. 193). Twenty-five thousand square miles lay under water, leaving 350,000 people destitute. Dominating the headlines, Hoover directed the feeding, clothing, and housing of the stricken families. Such publicity, which he did little to discourage, helped make him undoubtedly the most famous secretary of commerce in U.S. history.

The Presidency

In March 1929 Hoover was inaugurated president, having defeated Democratic candidate Al Smith of New York. Entering office in a time of unparalleled prosperity, he and his fellow citizens were brought short when, beginning on October 24, 1929, the stock market plunged. Soon the United States was in the grips of the greatest depression in its history, Hoover advanced a series of relief measures, including mortgage aid to farmers and homeowners, and public works and flood control projects. Increasingly administration expectations were centered upon the Reconstruction Finance Corporation (RFC), a federal agency that administered massive loans to banks, railroads, insurance companies, and individual states. He also signed the Smoot-Hawley Tariff of 1930, which radically raised duties on numerous imports. Despite his arduous efforts, the economy steadily worsened. Hoover refused to sanction direct relief to the unemployed, claiming it would lower wages to a bare minimum and reward laziness. He was also averse to any policies that might unbalance the budget; deficits, he believed, were the road to ruin. Blamed increasingly by his countrymen for the increasing poverty, he reached the depth of his career in the summer of 1932, when federal troops routed a "bonus army" of unemployed veterans from shacks outside Washington, D.C. (*See also,* Domestic Issues).

His foreign policy included the Stimson Doctrine, by which Secretary of State Henry L. Stimson announced that the United States would not recognize any unilateral change in Asia imposed by force (a slap to the recent Japanese penetration of Manchuria); a one-year moratorium on the payment of war debts and reparations; and support for the agreements made at the London Disarmament of 1930. In November 1932 Hoover was defeated in his bid for reelection by New York governor Franklin D. Roosevelt.

Post-presidential Years

Although Hoover was never again close to the reins of power, his post-presidential career was far from anticlimactic. In 1934 he wrote *The Challenge to Liberty,* in which he attacked Franklin Roosevelt's New Deal as "the most stupendous invasion of the whole spirit of Liberty that the nation has witnessed since the days of colonial America." In 1936 and 1940 he hoped that a deadlocked Republican convention would again nominate him for president, but tensions between him and his party remained.

As World War II (1939–45) approached, Hoover was frequently labeled an "isolationist," though such a designation does not do justice to his position. His preference for peaceful settlement of all disputes derived from his conviction that military action created far more problems than it solved. In 1919 the future president had established the Hoover War Collection, renamed the Hoover War Library in 1922, originally housed in the Stanford University Library in California. By 1926 it contained the largest collection dealing with World War I (1914–18). In 1941 the documents were housed in a new building, a ten-story tower that still dominates the Stanford campus. In 1957 it was renamed the Hoover Institution on War, Revolution and Peace.

During World War II (1939–45) Hoover launched relief efforts for occupied Poland and Finland, then engaged in an abortive effort to feed the invaded democracies of Western Europe. His book *The Problems of Lasting Peace* (1942), written with diplomat Hugh Gibson, contained many suggestions for international organization, and he pursued these eagerly in Republican quarters.

In 1946, less than a year after Harry S. Truman acceded to the presidency, the new chief executive appointed Hoover honorary chairman of the Famine Emergency Committee. In this capacity he journeyed around the world to survey food needs. A year later the former president undertook another relief mission, this one limited to Germany and Austria. From 1947 to 1949, at Truman's request, Hoover headed the Committee on Organization of the Executive Branch of the Government, a special task force to streamline the federal government commonly called the Hoover Commission. From 1953 to 1955 he performed a similar service for President Dwight D. Eisenhower.

Until the end of his life, Hoover was a prolific author, his books often serving as justifications of his policies. Major works included three volumes of memoirs and four volumes on his various relief activities. On October 20, 1964, at the age of ninety, Herbert Hoover died in New York City.

The Herbert Hoover Administration

Shortly after Herbert Hoover took office, the United States faced a crisis that would cast a shadow over his entire administration. When the stock market crashed on October 24, 1929, a downward economic slide was sparked that led to the Great Depression. Although Hoover attempted to infuse hope in the American public by touting the phrase, "Prosperity is just around the corner," economic conditions worsened. Federal recovery measures were undertaken to alleviate America's problems including the Reconstruction Finance Corporation and the Federal Farm Board, but by the end of Hoover's term, the American public felt that the administration had done "too little, too late" and were more than eager to embrace Franklin Roosevelt's "New Deal."

Hoover Becomes President

The Campaign of 1928

In 1928 Hoover was strongly favored for the Republican presidential nomination after President Calvin Coolidge announced that he would not seek another term. Aside from President Coolidge, Hoover was the most well-known Republican in the nation and lost only three

Administration

Administration Dates
March 4, 1929–March 4, 1933

Vice President
Charles Curtis (1929–33)

Cabinet

Secretary of State
Frank B. Kellogg (1925–29)
Henry L. Stimson (1929–33)

Secretary of the Treasury
Andrew W. Mellon (1921–32)
Ogden L. Mills (1932–33)

Secretary of War
Dwight F. Davis (1925–29)
James W. Good (1929)
Patrick J. Hurley (1929–33)

Attorney General
John G. Sargent (1925–29)
William D. Mitchell (1929–33)

Secretary of the Navy
Curtis D. Wilbur (1924–29)
Charles F. Adams (1929–33)

Postmaster General
Harry S. New (1923–29)
Walter F. Brown (1929–33)

Secretary of the Interior
Roy O. West (1928–29)
Ray L. Wilbur (1929–33)

Secretary of Agriculture
William M. Jardine (1925–29)
Arthur M. Hyde (1929–33)

Secretary of Labor
James J. Davis (1921–30)
William N. Doak (1930–33)

Secretary of Commerce
William F. Whiting (1928–29)
Robert P. Lamont (1929–32)
Roy D. Chapin (1932–33)

---

state primaries. On the very first ballot of the convention, which met in mid-June in Kansas City, Missouri, Hoover won a majority of votes, making him the party's candidate. His running mate, Senator Charles Curtis of Kansas, was a bland party regular, whose advice Hoover seldom followed. The Democrats nominated Governor Alfred Emanuel Smith of New York, a moderate reformer and superb administrator who, like Hoover, rose from modest circumstances, in Smith's case from the Lower East Side of Manhattan. Always having cigar in hand, sporting a brown derby, and speaking in a distinctive New York City accent, Smith was designated "the Abe Lincoln of the tenement people." The candidates had a surprising amount in common. Both were self-made men, highly efficient administrators, and surrounded themselves with experts. In the campaign both drew upon labor support, obtained millionaire backing, worked to obtain the women's vote, and strongly defended U.S. capitalism.

In his acceptance speech of the presidential nomination, delivered on August 11, 1928, at Palo Alto, California, Hoover took credit for the existing prosperity carrying over from his days as secretary of commerce and warned against "state socialism." "We shall soon . . . be

in sight of the day," he claimed, "when poverty will be banished from this nation." He publicly endorsed the 1919 Eighteenth Amendment banning the manufacture, sale, and transportation of alcoholic beverages, known as Prohibition. Though personally opposed to the amendment he referred to it as "a great social and economic experiment, noble in motive and far-reaching in purpose." Smith had no use for the measure and made no secret of his vehement opposition. Though the candidates sparred over tariffs, price-fixing for farmers, and public ownership of hydroelectric power sites, the campaign lacked substantive issues.

Hoover easily won the election, with 21.4 million popular votes to Smith's 15 million. In the electoral college he did even better, with 444 votes to Smith's 87. For the first time since the American Civil War (1861–65), some southern states voted Republican: Virginia, North Carolina, Tennessee, Florida, and Texas. Though much attention has been given to Smith's Roman Catholicism as a factor in his defeat, almost any Republican could have beaten Smith under almost any circumstances that year. In his memoirs Hoover wrote that general prosperity was on his side, and he was right. The Republicans might have been wise to note one fact: the

Democrats captured practically every city housing over 400,000 people. It was not a good omen.

The Campaign of 1932

Four years later it was not just the urban masses that felt little sympathy for the president. The outcome of Hoover's second campaign was almost predetermined by the Great Depression. Hoover was skillful in advancing his nomination in 1928 and renomination in 1932, and he could bestow patronage most effectively, but he really possessed few political skills. When, on June 14, 1932, the Republican Party renominated Hoover for president, the cause was already lost. The Democratic nominee was virtually assured victory. The fact that Hoover's opponent, Governor Franklin D. Roosevelt of New York, possessed a magnetic personality and exuded tremendous confidence only made Hoover's defeat the more bitter.

In a series of nine speeches, Hoover boasted that he had waged "battles on a thousand fronts" and had fought "the good fight to protect our people in a thousand cities from hunger and cold." To the unemployed he promised jobs, to farmers he promised enlarged tariff protection and additional credit, and to investors he promised the continuation of the gold standard. Claiming that recovery was well underway, he pointed to a decline in unemployment of 700,000 as well as increases in certain economic indexes, such as farm products, textile output, iron and steel production, and the value of common stock. But Hoover was ignoring crucial evidence that the economy was still spiraling downward towards collapse, including a sharp drop in credit, a steep decline in bank deposits, and ten million still unemployed. As far as Prohibition was concerned, Hoover ran on a party platform that would allow individual states to "deal with the problem as their citizens may determine."

During the campaign Franklin Roosevelt attacked the president for failing to balance the budget and, upon taking office, signed the Economy Act of 1933, which was designed to balance the budget by cutting veterans' pensions and the salaries of civil servants. Far from innovative, the Democrats had a most conservative platform, calling for the reduction of federal spending, a balanced budget, states's rights, a lower tariff, a sound currency, and an end to Prohibition.

On November 8, nevertheless, Roosevelt swept the country, carrying seven million more popular votes, 413 more electoral votes and 36 more states than Hoover. The Democrats also gained control of both houses of Congress.

Hoover's Advisers

Hoover exercised some care in picking his cabinet. Although it was not a spectacular body, it usually served him well. To an exceptional degree, Hoover kept his own counsel. Major advisers within the cabinet included Treasury Secretary Odgen Mills and Secretary of State Henry L. Stimson. Also close to the president were Assistant Secretary of the Treasury Walter E. Hope; Los Angeles banker Henry M. Robinson; Edward Eyre Hunt, economist with the Commerce Department; journalist Mark Sullivan; Undersecretary of State William R. Castle Jr.; and Henry J. Allen, Republican senator from Kansas. Hoover's personal staff was very supportive. Walter H. Newton directed executive appointments, government reorganization, and contacts with Congress. Lawrence Richey supervised personal affairs and office management. George E. Akerson was in charge of press relations.

Secretary of State Henry L. Stimson had a long record of distinguished service, serving as secretary of war under President William Taft and governor-general of the Philippines under President Calvin Coolidge. Hoover and Stimson differed in temperament, for the president found his secretary—who would often only put in two or three hours at the State Department—lethargic. More significantly, they differed in policy, for Hoover found his secretary irresponsibly adopting a threatening diplomatic posture as seen by his stridency in the Manchurian crisis (*See also,* Domestic Issues).

Until February 1932 Hoover retained Andrew W. Mellon, who had been Coolidge's secretary of the Treasury, at which point he appointed him ambassador to Great Britain. A Pittsburgh, Pennsylvania, banker who made a fortune in aluminum, Mellon held views on fighting the Depression that over time proved too conservative for Hoover. Hoover replaced Mellon with assistant Treasury secretary Ogden L. Mills, whose intelligence Hoover greatly respected.

Ray Lyman Wilbur, physician, president of Stanford, and a man personally close to Hoover, became secretary of the interior. The president held the Interior Department in particularly high regard, seeing it as possessing great influence in such matters as natural resources, children, housing, and the condition of American Indians. Wilbur, fortunately, met Hoover's expectations.

U.S. agriculture was in a desperate condition throughout the 1920s. Hoover first hoped that Republican senator Charles L. McNary of Oregon would become secretary of agriculture, a surprising choice given McNary's co-authorship of a controversial farm bill that Hoover detested. However, Hoover eventually awarded the post to Arthur Hyde, former Ford dealer and governor of Missouri, who knew little about farming.

For attorney general Hoover chose William D. Mitchell, formerly solicitor general and a Democrat, who served him well. Hoover kept on James J. Davis (Puddler Jim), originally a Harding appointee, as secretary of labor. Supreme Dictator and Reorganizer of the Loyal Order of Moose, Davis was an arch conservative. Resigning in 1930 to run for the Senate from Pennsylvania, he was replaced by William N. Doak, a leader in the railroad trainmen's union. Neither man was equal to the task, particularly in times of depression.

Charles Francis Adams, a cultivated financier, philanthropist, and yachtsman, became secretary of the navy. Hoover found Adams so competent he wished he had made the Massachusetts native secretary of state. Adams's counterpart in the War Department, James W. Good of Iowa, died within a year of taking office. He had been a prominent Republican congressman. His replacement, Patrick J. Hurley, was a Tulsa, Oklahoma, businessman who had helped carry his home state for Hoover in the recent election. His conduct during the Bonus March (*See also,* Domestic Issues) would seriously embarrass the president.

Robert P. Lamont, an engineer-turned-businessman like the president, disappointed Hoover as secretary of commerce, a post in which he held a proprietary interest. In July of 1932, Roy D. Chapin, president of the Hudson Motor Company, assumed the post. The Post Office Department, traditionally a font of political patronage, went to Walter F. Brown, who had been assistant secretary of commerce when Hoover was secretary. As expected, he was a great source of political advice.

Hoover and Congress

The Seventy-first Congress lasted from March 4, 1929, to March 3, 1931. The Senate was composed of 59 Republicans and 39 Democrats, plus one member of the Farmer-Labor Party of Minnesota. In the House the Republicans possessed a majority of 103 seats.

Contrary to myth, Hoover did not always have trouble with Congress. True, in 1929 he and his Senate majority leader, James E. Watson of Indiana, shared a mutual contempt. Watson's extreme isolationism and high tariff views, as well as his courting of the Ku Klux Klan, a white supremacy group, drew little respect from the president. In the House, however, the president's relationships with key party members were not colored by such personal animosity.

Although known for his early-day progressivism (he had fought for an income tax and the Federal Reserve system), Hoover had no plan for preventing the Great Depression. Moreover, he was surprisingly inept at imposing discipline upon an unruly body.

Coming after the beginning of the Great Depression (*See also,* Domestic Issues), the November 1930 congressional elections greatly weakened Hoover's control of Congress; nevertheless, the election was not a mass repudiation of his leadership. In the Seventy-second Congress, which met from March 4, 1931, to March 3, 1933, the Republicans at first retained the House by only one vote; but over the course of the following year enough Republican incumbents had died to give control

to the Democrats. Although the Senate that was elected comprised 48 Republicans, 47 Democrats, and one Farmer-Laborite, so many Republican progressives opposed the president's measures to deal with the Depression that an insurgent Democratic coalition became dominant. Until then, however, Hoover remained in charge. Congress even backed the presidential veto of a bill creating a vast federal hydroelectric development in the Tennessee Valley, a project close to the heart of the highly respected Republican senator George Norris of Nebraska. In only one major instance did Congress override Hoover, this involving a bill to permit World War I veterans to borrow up to 50 percent on their allocated bonus, a life insurance policy payable in 1945 (*See also,* Domestic Issues).

Labor received a boost when, in March 1932, Hoover signed the Norris-LaGuardia Bill, outlawing yellow-dog contracts and injunctions, which were court orders banning a particular strike. By greatly enhancing labor's right to bargain collectively, the bill was deservedly seen as a landmark in labor relations. It passed Congress easily.

Until March 1932, when Congress balked over Hoover's proposal of a sales tax, even the Democratic leadership was generally supportive of the president. The administration was able, in fact, to ride roughshod over its disparate foes, obtaining its entire program in the process. Only after March, when Hoover felt forced to veto various bills embodying massive relief efforts, did friction really begin.

Hoover and the Judiciary

During his term, Hoover was able to appoint three justices to the Supreme Court. In 1930 he appointed Charles Evans Hughes, who had been appointed associate justice in 1910, to be chief justice. Despite a strong judicial record, Hughes met with some opposition. His corporate associations as a Wall Street lawyer, and his resignation from the Court in 1916 to run for the presidency, resulted in the 68-year-old jurist receiving confirmation by only 52 to 26.

Hoover's next choice, John J. Parker, met with defeat by a Senate vote of 41 to 39. A Republican circuit judge from North Carolina, Parker was opposed by organized labor for decisions upholding the "yellow dog" labor contract, which required a no-strike pledge from a prospective employee, and the right of mining companies to evict strikers from the company towns in which they lived. African Americans opposed Parker for a remark made in 1920, that blacks were not yet ready to participate actively in state politics. At this point Hoover nominated Owen Roberts, formerly a law professor at the University of Pennsylvania and a special government attorney in the Teapot Dome Scandal (*See also,* Warren Harding Administration). Roberts was unanimously confirmed.

In 1932 Hoover chose Benjamin Cardozo to serve on the bench. Cardozo was a legal scholar who served on the New York Court of Appeals. A Democrat and a liberal, he became a bulwark of much New Deal legislation.

During the Hoover presidency all the landmark decisions lay in the area of civil liberties. The Supreme Court decided on a number of cases that expanded application of the "due process" clause of the Fourteenth Amendment of the Constitution, which reads "nor shall any State deprive any person of life, liberty, or property, without due process of law." Originally the Bill of Rights had applied only to federal activities. Now the courts were using the Fourteenth Amendment to apply the Bill of Rights to the states as well and thereby widely extending the scope of civil liberties.

In *Stromberg v. California* (1931), the Court declared invalid a state statute prohibiting the display of the red flag as an emblem of anarchism or of opposition to organized government. "The concept of liberty under the due process clause of the Fourteenth Amendment," said Chief Justice Hughes, "embraces the right of free speech," as embodied in the First Amendment. In *Near v. Minnesota* (1931), the Court struck down a state law providing for the suppression of any malicious, scandalous, or defamatory newspaper. Hughes, again speaking for the Court, found the Minnesota law transcending existing standards of responsibility under libel law and thereby violating the due process clause. The same clause was again expanded in *Powell v. Alabama* (1932). Here the Court ruled that the state of Alabama had denied nine young African Americans, who were convicted of raping two white girls, the right of access to counsel, as specified in the Sixth Amendment.

Changes in the U.S. Government

Hoover saw government primarily in terms of administration, not legislation, a view that obviously won few backers in Congress. To Hoover, major economic and social problems should be solved by conferences composed of disinterested experts, who would gather immense amounts of data and make appropriate recommendations. For example, the White House Conference on Health and the Protection of Children of 1929 called together some 2,500 delegates and issued 35 volumes of findings. During his presidency, Hoover also held conferences on waste, housing, public-land policy, and oil conservation. Possibly even more significant were certain commissions the president sponsored, such as the one investigating *(See also, Domestic Issues)* Prohibition enforcement. One commission, the Research Committee on Social Trends, issued a two-volume report that became a Bible for social scientists and set a standard that has seldom, if ever, been equaled.

As with similar bodies, however, little follow-up machinery was produced.

During Hoover's tenure the Twentieth Amendment, popularly known as the "lame duck amendment," was passed. Before it was adopted, a president elected in November did not take office until the following March. Congressman in office before the election also continued to legislate in the short and ineffective December-to-March session. This amendment stipulated that congressmen elected in November assume their duties on January 3, and the elected president assumes office on January 20.

Domestic Issues

Overall, the impact of World War I (1914–18) on the economy was beneficial. Demand for manufactured goods rose in a spectacular fashion as U.S. steel and all sorts of raw materials and other goods flowed toward Europe. Another impact of the war was the development of technology under the force of demand and through generous federal military spending. By 1920 automobiles, airplanes, and radios were being produced in large quantities, and the workforce in these industries had accumulated vast experience in assembling these products. Plants were in place, and a sophisticated infrastructure of support existed: thousands of rural workers had moved to the industrial centers. When the war ended and demand for goods associated with the war lessened, production was aimed at consumers who had seen goods manufactured in previous years directed at the war effort. Backed fully by the hands-off policy of government led by Presidents Warren Harding and Calvin Coolidge, by the late 1920s U.S. business was experiencing growth unequaled in its history.

However, prosperity was far from evenly distributed around the country. The Northeast, the Upper Midwest industrial belt, and the West Coast were booming, but the South and the agricultural Midwest were doing poorly. With the war over, African Americans, coal miners, and other traditionally ill-paid workers had drifted back into their prewar status.

When inventories began to build up, in order to sustain continued consumption, manufacturers and retailers encouraged purchases on the "installment plan," a system of credit by which one could purchase the most expensive of items—such as automobiles or refrigerators—by making periodic payments that included interest. In effect, such consumers were mortgaging their future, for if one stopped payments at any point, the creditor would confiscate the item. During this time corporate profits reached 63 percent, and those of financial institutions rose 150 percent.

The stock and bond market became more active, and by the middle of the decade thousands of Americans who

Biography:

Charles Evans Hughes

Supreme Court Justice; Secretary of State (1862–1948) Charles Evans Hughes was a lawyer for twenty years and approaching his mid-forties before he entered politics as a Republican nominee for the governorship of the state of New York. After a bitter race against publisher William Randolph Hearst, Hughes won the job and then worked hard through two terms, successfully bringing about beneficial reforms, such as cleaning out corruption in New York City boroughs. Hughes then served briefly on the Supreme Court before resigning in 1916 to accept the Republican presidential nomination. He lost the race to Woodrow Wilson. In 1920 he campaigned for Warren Harding and later accepted President Harding's appointment as secretary of state. Hughes served a single but brilliant term, orchestrating the Washington Conference on the Limitation of Armaments. He was not called to public duty again until 1930 when President Herbert Hoover nominated him as chief justice of the U.S. Supreme Court. Shortly after Hughes's appointment, President Franklin D. Roosevelt arrived on the

scene with an extensive list of radical reforms for a hungry, ailing nation. The New Deal, and all of the legislation it brought forth, found both friend and foe amongst Hughes's panel of justices, the men charged with ruling on the constitutionality of each piece. In spite of the Court's often hostile division, rulings were made against key pieces of New Deal legislation like the National Recovery Act of 1934 and the Agricultural Recovery Act of 1935, prompting disagreement between President Roosevelt and Judge Hughes. For the duration of his multi-faceted career, Hughes was consistent in his support of both civil rights for African Americans and freedom of the press. He retired from the bench in 1941.

---

had never invested before were following the market avidly leading to speculation of the most irresponsible sort. The price of stocks absolutely skyrocketed. Radio Corporation of America (RCA), for example, sold for $85 dollars a share in 1928 and $549 a year later. Many Americans were buying these stocks by a process called "margin," by which the purchaser pays the broker only a fraction of the purchase price, borrowing the rest from the brokerage house. If the stock increases in price, the buyer can sell the stock, pay off the borrowed money, and pocket a large profit on a small investment. If, however, the price of the stock decreased, the broker would demand immediate payment from the investor, who—if unable to meet the "margin"—would lose the entire investment. The proliferation of slipshod banking loans made a precarious situation even more risky.

The Great Depression

The bubble suddenly burst when on October 24, 1929, a day known as "Black Thursday," stock prices plummeted. About thirteen million shares changed hands. As investors scrambled to sell off their stocks, prices were forced even lower. On the 28th and 29th 16.5 million shares were sold. Within two more weeks, the industrial index of the New York Stock Exchange (NYSE) had fallen by over half. Just before the crash Hoover had privately complained about the scope of market operations.

It soon became obvious that the Wall Street crash was no mere panic but the catalyst of what later would be called the Great Depression. Seldom had a single disaster led to so much misfortune. It was, in the words of historian Robert H. Ferrell, "like a global tornado that sucked up everything in its track." Within weeks, the market disaster blew thirty billion dollars into thin air, a sum almost equaling the entire cost of U.S. participation in World War I (1914–18).

Early Hoover Remedies

Beginning on November 19, 1929, and for several days thereafter, Hoover convened the five-day Conference for Continued Industrial Progress. Railroad, labor, and construction leaders, mayors and governors each met with the president. In December he met with larger groups of business, labor, and farm leaders. To all the message was the same. Warning of a serious recession and placing the responsibility for avoiding major catastrophe in their hands, he asked them to foster industrial expansion, avoid strikes, share work when possible, stabilize prices, and provide relief where needed. Most important of all, he stressed that there must be no drastic wage cuts. He soon was pushing national and state public works, whereby government bodies set up projects that would employ people who are out of work. He asked both Congress and state governors to appropriate the needed funds.

By the spring of 1930 it appeared as if Hoover's policies were working. Early in March, he predicted an end to the economic crisis within 60 days. Two months later he said, "We have passed the worst and with continued unity of effort we shall rapidly recover." In June he told a visiting delegation, "The depression is over." For Hoover, such optimism made perfect sense. If business regained its confidence, there would be investments in new plants; these factories would start rehiring workers. Once the new labor force drew pay checks, it would start buying consumer goods, thereby reviving the economy.

By mid-1930 Congress had allocated $800 million for public works—river and harbor improvements, public buildings, and highways. In the fall, construction began on the massive Boulder (later renamed Hoover) Dam, on the Colorado River between Arizona and Nevada.

Disaster Worsens

Despite Hoover's efforts, the economic situation continually worsened. Employers—faced with huge surpluses—felt they had to cut production. In September 1930 the United States Steel Corporation announced a 10 percent wage cut, and other major firms soon followed suit. Similarly General Motors cut salaries by 10 to 20 percent. In October approximately four million Americans were unemployed; by January 1931 approximately six million. In response, Hoover established the President's Emergency Committee for Unemployment, composed of 30 prominent business leaders and economists. The committee was headed by former New York City police commissioner Arthur Woods, who had been active in relief during the depression of 1921. Establishing three thousand local committees, the Emergency for Unemployment Committee pushed local and private relief efforts. By June some $2 billion was being spent and a million men were being employed on federal projects.

Despite occasional rallies in the various economic indicators—those centering on employment, payrolls, and production—by 1932 some twelve million people, over 20 percent of the labor force, was unemployed, and of this number only about one-quarter were actually receiving relief. Limited mainly to fuel, all such aid was on a disaster basis. The relief fund of New York City could only care for about half of the unemployed heads of families; the average allocation per family was $2.39 per week. In Chicago, half the labor force was jobless. For months, municipal workers there received no wage. If there was little outright starvation, there was much hunger. Coal miners in Pennsylvania lived on weed roots and dandelions, those in Kentucky ate wild onions and weeds. In the South poor whites and African Americans existed on salt pork and hominy.

Agriculture

From the time he took office, Hoover had sought to curb a long-standing depression in agriculture, an enter-

prise involving nearly half the population. In his 1928 presidential nomination acceptance speech, he called the predicament of the farmer "the most urgent economic problem in our nation today." Tremendous overproduction glutted the agricultural markets, causing much misery in the West and the South.

At Hoover's prompting, Congress passed the Agricultural Marketing Act of 1929, which established an eight-man Federal Farm Board. Its purpose was to establish a $500-million fund that would makes loans to farm cooperatives. The cooperatives in turn would control crop production in order to avoid massive surpluses and low prices. It also sought ways to produce and market crops more efficiently.

Although agriculture had long been failing, the stock market crash made a bad situation worse, as demand for farm products decreased even further. From 1929 to 1931 the Federal Farm Board took on a greater task: to combat rural depression by purchasing surplus crops outright and selling them at the best prices. Because it lacked the power to directly limit production, its efforts were bound to fail. The depression in Europe added to the problem by creating a sudden shrinking of foreign markets. The Soviet Union, Argentina, and Australia engaged in "dumping" (selling huge quantities at a low price). Board purchases could not make up for the continuing decline in demand. When board chairman Alex Legge, president of International Harvester, called for farmers to voluntarily take acreage out of production, they balked, fearing that their competitive neighbors would not cooperate. Hence the price of all of the United States's major crops—wheat, corn, cotton, tobacco—plummeted. By the summer of 1932, having lost some $354 million in market operations, the board conceded failure. In December 1932 it called upon Congress to regulate production directly. Hoover's farm program, with its stress on voluntary cooperation, had failed.

Finance and Banking

The crash of 1929 reflected widespread mismanagement of the economy. Hoover had cautioned the Federal Reserve Board to restrict credit and deter speculation, but banking and finance remained virtually unregulated. Unsound bank practices included encouraging speculation by lending money to buy stocks, making risky loans, and being open to fraudulent investment schemes.

Between June 1931 and June 1932, bank deposits shrank almost nine billion dollars. Many Americans, fearful for their savings (bank deposits were not insured at that time), were withdrawing their deposits on a massive scale. The banking situation was exacerbated when the banks in Europe began to fail (*See also*, Foreign Issues).

On October 4, 1931, Hoover met secretly with leading New York bankers and insurance executives, includ-

What They Said . . .

"We in America today are nearer to the final triumph over poverty than ever before in the history of any land. The poorhouse is vanishing among us. We have not yet reached the goal, but, given a chance to go forward with the policies of the last eight years, we shall soon with the help of God be in sight of the day when poverty will be banished from this nation."

(Source: Herbert Hoover, Speech Accepting the Republican Nomination for President, August 11, 1928.)

---

ing representatives of J. P. Morgan and Company, Chase National Bank, and the National City Bank. During the year 2,300 banks had closed their doors. On October 31, 1931, the governor of Nevada declared a 12-day banking "holiday," in effect closing his banks for that time. In February Louisiana and Michigan did the same, with nine other states following suit. Panicking depositors continued to withdraw their deposits simply compounding the problem. Hoover called upon the banks to form an emergency credit pool of $500 million and urged the insurance firms to offer mortgage relief. The bankers, fearful of Hoover's threat of congressional action, pledged support, establishing the National Credit Corporation. Within a month, this body failed, with the bankers lending sums too paltry to save banks and ease credit. They feared that they would jeopardize their own position by taking over the assets of the weaker banks.

Seeking a Balanced Budget

Faced with a continuing economic crisis, early in December of 1931 Hoover offered a battery of proposals to bring relief, including a balanced budget, expansion of federal public works, and increased lending powers for Federal Land Banks. When the Depression first emerged, Hoover believed that budget-balancing could wait until prosperity returned. It was his secretary of the Treasury, Ogden Mills, who convinced Hoover to balance the budget and to do so by raising taxes. As early as February 1930, Hoover called for government economy. In July 1931 he deplored a national deficit of $500 million out of a total federal budget of $4 billion. In December he recommended a tax increase to balance the federal books. When, in March 1932, Congress delayed, he told a press conference that a balanced budget was "the very keystone of recovery. It must be done." He con-

tinued, "The Government no more than individual families can continue to expend more than it receives without inviting serious consequences." Congress in turn balked at his proposal for a national sales tax, a levy that would disproportionately hit people of lower income, turning it down that very month.

The Reconstruction Finance Corporation

The linchpin of Hoover's recovery program was the Reconstruction Finance Corporation (RFC), established in January 1932. It was patterned after the War Finance Corporation, which financed the United States during World War I. It also capitalized $500 million and was given authority to borrow up to $2 billion more, The RFC established offices in 30 cities. Charles G. Dawes, Coolidge's vice president and Chicago banker, was the RFC's first president. In late July Dawes was replaced by former Democratic senator Atlee Pomerene of Ohio. During 1932 it provided loans to over five thousand banks, railroads, life insurance companies, farm mortgage associations, and building and loan associations, in the process saving many businesses from failure, restoring much public confidence, and halting further undermining of the U.S. financial structure. In January 1932 the U.S. experienced 346 bank failures, in April only 46.

Emergency Powers

To confront the increasing unemployment, now numbering eight million, Hoover established the President's Unemployment Relief Organization headed by Walter Gifford, president of the American Telephone and Telegraph Company. It basically continued the Emergency Committee for Unemployment's activity, launching an advertising campaign designed to stimulate private charity but never recommending the direct federal relief programs increasingly demanded by Congress.

At Hoover's prompting, Congress passed other relief measures. In January 1932 it provided $125 million for Federal Land Banks. A month later it adopted the Glass-Steagall Act, making about $750 million of government gold available to business. In July it passed the Emergency Relief and Reconstruction Act, which empowered the RFC to provide $1.5 billion in loans for state and local construction of public works, to furnish $300 million in temporary loans to states otherwise unable to finance relief measures, and to give $200 million to assist in liquidating closed banks. By the end of 1932, however, the RFC was so cautious that only $30 million of the $300 million allotted to the states for relief had been spent, and none of that sum was allocated for public works.

The Depression Deepens

As far as direct aid to the unemployed went, Hoover drew the line. Refusing to budge any further, in July 1932 he vetoed the Wagner-Garner Bill, extending the work of federal employment agencies to states that lacked such units, and even resisted a congressional appropriation to

One of the many results of the Great Depression was the appearance of soup kitchens to provide a small measure of relief to the unemployed. This one was opened in Chicago by mobster Al Capone in 1931. (National Archives and Records Administration.)

the Red Cross. His proposals to Congress in July 1932, a month after he had been renominated for president, conspicuously omitted any mention of direct relief. By the summer of 1932 Hoover saw his recovery program as complete. He would go no further. True, the president did urge citizens to back private charities, refused to take any salary himself, and fostered private help for the unemployed. Using the most idealistic language, he continually called on his fellow citizens to aid the less fortunate.

It was this opposition to direct relief that, more than anything else, gave him a negative image that lasted for decades. The makeshift shack villages of the unemployed were called Hoovervilles. When a jobless man wrapped a newspaper around him for warmth, he called the paper a Hoover blanket. When a broken-down automobile was being hauled by mules, the vehicle was a Hoover wagon. A man would turn a pocket inside out and call it a Hoover flag. Jackrabbits were called Hoover hogs.

The Smoot-Hawley Tariff

The economy was not helped by the Smoot-Hawley Tariff, signed by Hoover on June 17, 1930. A tariff is a tax or duty placed on goods imported from another country, protecting U.S. workers by assuring that U.S.-made goods will not be undersold by foreign competition. At the same time, by taking foreign-produced goods off the markets, U.S. consumers are forced to pay higher prices for the protected products. The bill's sponsors, Republican senator Reed Smoot of Utah and Republican congressperson Willis C. Hawley of Oregon, were fervent protectionists, men who believed that the U.S. economy had to be protected from foreign competition by the government. The tariff involved 75 increases for farm products, and 925 for manufactured goods. Hoover strongly opposed its high schedules, and retaliation eventually occurred. In 1932 the British responded by establishing its own protective tariff within the British Empire, and other U.S. trading partners followed suit. As far as its domestic consequences went, it did little to raise agricultural prices, something that Hoover sought above all.

The Bonus March

By the spring of 1932, while most of the country remained calm, signs of social disruption were breaking out. In Dearborn, Michigan, hunger marches took place and the unemployed rioted. Farmers around the country organized to prevent foreclosure. By far, however, the most dangerous outbreak took place in Washington, D.C., where the Bonus Expeditionary Force (BEF) had gathered. Some eleven thousand World War I veterans, homeless and unemployed, refused to budge until Congress voted some $2.4 billion dollars as immediate payment on the remaining 50 percent of a promised bonus. Technically the "bonus" was not a "bonus" at all. Depending on length of service and time overseas, a veteran could borrow up to a thousand dollars on free government life insurance policies maturing in 1945. They wanted their money now, not 20 years in the future, for their homes, businesses, and in some cases elementary nourishment.

As the nation was experiencing a daily deficit of several million dollars, payment could have been ruinous. Most marchers cooperated with Washington police chief Pelham D. Glassford and were quite well behaved. On June 15 the House passed the BEF proposal in the form of a bill advanced by Democratic representative Wright Patman of Texas. Hoover, deeply alarmed over a budget already unbalanced and with a fear of inflation, strongly opposed the proposal, and the Senate backed him 62 to 18. At the same time, Hoover did defend the BEF's civil liberties and signed a $100,000 authorization to pay their way home. About half the marchers took advantage of the president's offer.

Some marchers, however, occupied buildings scheduled to be razed so that long-awaited public works projects would be carried out. On July 28 police attempted to clear a throng of marchers out of a construction area. Two veterans were killed and several police injured. Hoover refused to declare martial law but ordered Sec-

retary of War Patrick J. Hurley to remove the occupants from the buildings to their camps nearby. Acting on his own authority, Hurley instructed General Douglas MacArthur to move marchers not to their camps but rather across the Potomac River to Camp Marks on Anacostia Flats. MacArthur in turn directed his forces to drive the BEF remnants beyond Camp Marks, using tanks, guns, and tear gas in the process. Hoover attempted, via high ranking officers, to stop the army from driving the BEF across the Anacostia bridge, but MacArthur disobeyed the president. Though Hoover was appalled by both the treatment of the veterans and the insubordination of MacArthur and Hurley, he kept silent amid nationwide criticism. Indeed, speaking in St. Paul, Minnesota, as the presidential campaign was coming to an end, he remarked, "Thank God, you have got a government in Washington that knows how to deal with a mob."

Prohibition

For many Americans, particularly those who did not perceive their jobs at risk, the nation's number one problem was not jobs but alcohol. In October 1919 Congress had passed the National Prohibition Enforcement Act, also known as the Volstead Act, which provided the enforcement apparatus for the Eighteenth Amendment to the Constitution. The amendment had outlawed "the manufacture, sale, or transportation of intoxicating liquors." Americans violated the Volstead Act on a massive scale, as a huge illegal traffic fell under the control of organized crime. By 1927, for example, Chicago gang leader Al Capone grossed $60 million a year.

The Prohibition Bureau, which numbered under three thousand agents, could not possibly arrest all violators, and in areas where public opinion was hostile, enforcement remained sporadic. Realizing that Prohibition enforcement had broken down completely, Hoover increased the number of federal officers, transferred supervision from the Treasury to the Justice Department, and implored the states to share the policing. In private he deplored the legislation and toyed with the idea of revising the Eighteenth Amendment. Although personally he had been a moderate drinker in Europe, he believed firmly that he was obligated to enforce the law and that he must set a national example of total abstinence.

Most important of all, Hoover appointed a blue-ribbon investigating panel, headed by George W. Wickersham, who had been attorney general under William Howard Taft. Within the next two years the commission issued 14 separate reports totaling almost three and a half million words and covering all aspects of the subject. In January 1931, in offering its conclusions, it reported that enforcement was a farce and that in reality local option (enforcement in some areas and tacit permitting of alcohol in other areas) existed everywhere. Beyond that point the panel was divided. Two commissioners favored repeal. Five sought adoption of a national and state

This political cartoon reflects public sentiment over the two-year investigation on Prohibition enforcement led by George W. Wickersham. The report concluded in January 1931 that law enforcement was almost nonexistent and that local option existed everywhere.

monopoly of liquor sales. Two favored revision and further trial. Only two wanted to keep the amendment intact. The report satisfied neither "wets" (who sought repeal) nor "dries" (who desired continuation of the Eighteenth Amendment). One paper called it "Wickershambles." In transmitting Wickersham's report to Congress, Hoover inaccurately claimed that the commission supported the amendment and that punishing violators had been improved under his presidency.

Foreign Issues

When Hoover first assumed the presidency, he was highly optimistic concerning international affairs. U.S. capital not only underwrote much of Europe's prosperity but that of Latin America as well. Asia was experiencing greater turmoil, particularly as China's efforts to gain both unity and genuine autonomy left much instability in its wake. Japan appeared more focused on economic expansion than on territorial conquest.

Even the existence of a nation-state dedicated to Communism did not appear that alarming. Ever since the Bolshevik Revolution took place in October 1917, the U.S. had refused to recognize Russia's Communist government. Possessing an ideological abhorrence to the

regime, Hoover strongly supported U.S. policy of his predecessors. He did, however, tacitly support indirect financing of U.S. exports to the Soviet state.

Of course, few realized that the world was on the verge of a depression so massive that it would leave no region untouched. By the time Hoover left office, Germany was facing a Nazi takeover, Japan had seized Manchuria, and Britain was ruled by a coalition "national" government that had abandoned the gold standard. With much of the globe sinking into impoverishment, the future course of democracy itself as a viable form of government was subject to questioning everywhere.

European Affairs

During World War I (1914–18) and particularly in its aftermath, the United States had extended massive loans to the Allies that were popularly called "war debts." In particular, U.S. loans to Germany enabled the new Weimar Republic to pay its war reparations to the Allies. So long as the credit flowed, Europe seemed stable. When the economic crisis became worldwide, various nations started to default on these loans. U.S. taxpayers, however, saw their own government operating at a deficit and were insistent concerning repayment of the loans. Of the nation's high officials, only Secretary of State Henry L. Stimson appeared willing to write off the debts alto-

Fast Fact

Hoover did not take a salary when he was president and used his own money for entertaining.

(Source: Barbara Seuling. *The Last Cow on the White House Lawn.* New York: Ivy Books, 1978.)

gether. Incurred in a common struggle, the debts—he believed—could not possibly be repaid, particularly given the high U.S. tariffs. Efforts to force the issue would simply compound international bitterness. Hoover, like his rival in the 1932 presidential election Franklin Roosevelt, realized that no politician could publicly endorse cancellation.

Hoover Declares Moratorium on the Payment of War Debts

On May 11, 1931, just when Hoover thought he finally had the Depression licked, the largest bank in Austria (the Kreditanstalt) failed, tottering the national banks of Austria, Hungary, and Yugoslavia and unleashing a financial crisis in Germany. It also resulted in large-scale withdrawals of foreign gold deposits from the United States, thereby threatening the stability of U.S. banks. If Germany, which owed the victor powers billions of gold marks in reparations, went under, the entire European economy faced ruin. Hoover responded on June 21 by recommending a moratorium on all intergovernmental debts for one year, including the payment of German reparations. If, thought Hoover, the Europeans had more money in their pockets, they could buy more U.S. goods. Despite the objections of some congressional leaders, who feared that the obligations would never be repaid, in December Congress backed the president. Hoover's move blocked the downward spiral of trade and prices, but it came too late to prevent Germany's slide into depression.

The London Naval Conference

In January 1930 Secretary of State Henry L. Stimson led a seven-member delegation to the London Naval Conference, a meeting called by British prime minister Ramsay MacDonald and consisting of Britain, the United States, France, Japan, and Italy. On April 22, after several months of negotiation, the London Naval Treaty was signed. The treaty extended the informal ban on battleship construction, agreed at the Washington Conference in 1922 (*See also,* Warren Harding Administration);

specified a 5:5:3 ratio for the United States, Britain, and Japan in large cruisers; denoted a 10:10:7 ratio for the three powers in small cruisers and destroyers; and granted equality among the three in submarines. All ratios were binding until 1936. The treaty included an "escalator clause," by which each power could exceed established levels if it felt threatened.

The Conference for the Limitation and Reduction of Armaments

In February 1932 the Conference for the Limitation and Reduction of Armaments convened in Geneva, Switzerland. It was the largest international assemblage held up to that time. Hoover strongly supported the conference, believing that a peaceful world would be one receptive to U.S. goods. Besides, if the western European nations could be alleviated of their arms burden, they could resume payment of reparations and war debts. Stimson chaired the U.S. delegation, though entrusting most duties to Hugh Gibson, U.S. ambassador to Belgium. Almost immediately the meeting reached a familiar impasse: the French insisted on "disarmament through security," meaning international guarantees of protection against Germany; the United States sought "security through disarmament." In June, Hoover, frustrated by the conference's "dawdling," proposed that all nations reduce their arms by one-third. Bombs, tanks, large guns, and chemical warfare would be abolished. As far as navies went, submarines and battleships would be reduced by a third and cruisers, destroyers, and aircraft carriers by one-fourth. Italy, Germany, and the Soviet Union were highly receptive. France delayed its counterproposal until November, at which point it offered a complicated scheme for an international police force. Although they were essentially deadlocked, sessions continued until 1934 to no avail.

Latin America

The Good Neighbor Policy

If there was a marked success to Hoover's diplomacy, it lay in his Latin American policy. It was really Hoover, not his successor, Franklin Roosevelt, who launched the "good neighbor policy," though Roosevelt has been given the credit. Good neighbor policy is a catchall phrase implying that the United States would not meddle in Latin American affairs and acknowledging that its past interventions had been less than neighborly.

More significantly, in September 1930 Secretary of State Stimson reversed President Woodrow Wilson's policy that the United States would only recognize governments that were based on fair elections and the rule of law, and not those based on the use of force and suppression. As there had been so many revolutions in recent months, with the likelihood of more in sight, such requirements appeared most impractical. Henceforth, asserted the secretary, the United States would grant recognition to any regime that had de facto, or actual, control of a country; that intended to fulfill international obligations; and that intended to hold elections "in due course."

To show his sincerity in January 1933 Hoover withdrew U.S. marines from Nicaragua, where they had been since 1927. In 1927 President Coolidge had dispatched some five thousand U.S. troops to Nicaragua at the appeal of its president, who was threatened by a general revolt. The troops remained to help the local government suppress the bandit leader August Sandino. Hoover was also prepared to order U.S. marines out of Haiti where President Wilson had sent them 16 years earlier to establish normalcy after a mob had assassinated its president. In 1932 the Haitian government itself refused protectorate status and U.S. terms for withdrawal, and the United States occupied the country.

The Clark Memorandum

In 1930 Hoover published the Clark Memorandum, a document prepared two years earlier by President Calvin Coolidge's undersecretary of state, J. Reuben Clark Jr. Clark challenged a policy known as the Roosevelt Corollary to the Monroe Doctrine. The Monroe Doctrine was issued in 1823 by President James Monroe, closing the Western Hemisphere to further European colonization. In 1904 President Theodore Roosevelt had warned Latin American nations that "chronic wrongdoing" might force U.S. intervention. At the time Roosevelt was specifically referring to the activity of the Dominican Republic, which had defaulted on $32 million of foreign debts and thereby risked European military intervention. According to Clark, the Roosevelt Corollary was not justified by the Monroe Doctrine itself, "however much it may be justified by the application of the doctrine of self-preservation." Stimson elaborated, declaring that "the Monroe Doctrine was a declaration of the United States versus Europe—not that of the United States versus Latin America." If the memorandum really did not rule out the option of U.S. intervention, it still helped to alleviate much resentment.

The Manchurian Crisis

Japan Invades Manchuria

Undoubtedly the major foreign policy crisis of Hoover's presidency took place when, in September 1931, Japanese troops occupied Mukden, the leading city of Manchuria. A region of northern China at the time, Manchuria was under only nominal control of the Republic of China. Within a few months troops for the Kwantung army (as the Japanese army in China was called) had occupied most of the rest of Manchuria.

At first Stimson was cautious, merely asking both belligerents to negotiate without outside aid. Hoover strongly supported the secretary's desire not to become directly involved. Neither believed that Japan would be

able to hold on to its new territory, as they felt the huge population of native Chinese would be impossible for the Japanese to control. But as the Japanese continued to expand, Hoover and Stimson changed their views. The Japanese had long controlled much of Manchuria economically, but outright domination would supply Japan with vital raw materials, serve as a strategic base against the Soviet Union, and increase the power and influence of the Kwantung army's leaders in the Japanese government and military.

On January 3, 1932, the Japanese entered the city of Chinchow, the last outpost of organized Chinese resistance in Manchuria. Four days later, Stimson, acting with Hoover's full approval, released a statement declaring that the United States would not recognize any new agreements "which relate to the sovereignty, the independence, or the territorial and administrative integrity of China, or to the international policy relative to China, commonly known as the open-door policy." The open-door policy had been announced by Secretary of State John Hay during the Theodore Roosevelt administration (1901–1909) and assured all nations equal trading rights in China.

The move was a largely symbolic gesture. The United States did not suggest it would send troops to aid the Chinese in defeating Japan. Futhermore, Britain and France, the two European nations with the greatest stake in China, were unresponsive to the January 7 note. They were sufficiently fearful of their lucrative trade and investments, not to mention colonial holdings including Hong Kong and Indochina (Cambodia, Laos, Myanmar, Vietnam), that they did not want to antagonize Japan.

For both the Hoover administration and opinion-leaders, neither the welfare of the Chinese people per se nor the territorial integrity of China as a nation-state was deemed crucial. At stake was what is now called "the Washington system," a carefully crafted series of agreements made during the Washington Conference of 1922 (*See also,* Warren Harding Administration). In some ways an Asian counterpart to the new European order established by the Versailles Treaty of 1919, the Washington system committed all the major Pacific powers to a new diplomacy based on multilateral cooperation by which all signers to the Washington agreements agreed to resolve all disputes by peaceful means. Certainly change on the Asian mainland was not ruled out, but it had to be made peacefully. Japan, by acting both unilaterally and violently, had placed the Washington system in grave jeopardy.

Shanghai

Japan further antagonized the United States on January 27, 1932, when its navy bombarded the city of Shanghai, a major port on the east coast of China, south of Manchuria. Varied incidents in Shanghai had convinced the Japanese naval commander stationed in the city's harbor that the Chinese there were planning to drive

27,000 Japanese residents away. Angered by the Japanese invasion of Manchuria, Chinese citizens in Shanghai had boycotted Japanese goods, refused to sell to Japanese customers, burned Japanese merchandise, and assaulted Japanese citizens.

But many Western powers had interests in Shanghai as well. A center of foreign trade with China, Shanghai was a city with many separate foreign sectors, including British, French, Italian, and Japanese sections, as well as a U.S. marines sector and a sector jointly occupied by British and U.S. troops. Over 3,500 Americans lived in the city, often engaged in large-scale commercial and missionary enterprises. On January 31 Hoover dispatched six destroyers and a cruiser to Shanghai, along with a thousand infantrymen and four hundred more marines. Early in February the annual maneuvers of the U.S. Fleet were held off Shanghai, an event involving over two hundred war vessels. The maneuvers had been scheduled well in advance but obviously bore strong political implications. Stimson hoped that such action would serve several functions: protect American lives and property, maintain the open door, and strengthen the government of China's nominal ruler, Generalissimo Chiang Kaishek.

On February 24, Stimson wrote, and Hoover approved, a public letter to Republican senator William E. Borah of Idaho, the powerful chairman of the Senate Foreign Relations Committee. In what became known as the Borah letter, Stimson reaffirmed the January 7 note but added something quite ominous as well. Further Japanese aggression, he said, might well cause the United States to enlarge its fortifications in Guam and the Philippines and increase naval tonnage beyond the limits specified at the Washington Conference. Early in May the Japanese reached a truce with China and ceased their aggression in Shanghai. The Borah letter, though, had little impact on the situation. Acting on their own, Japan's military and civilian leaders had sought to terminate the affair.

International Response

All this time, particularly after the Shanghai incident, U.S. opinion-leaders debated economic sanctions. The problem was compounded in March 1932, when the Japanese established a puppet state called Manchukuo (the name given the old Manchuria by the Japanese). Stimson and Hoover remained opposed to sanctions, however, feeling that they would only further provoke Japan, perhaps to the point of war with the United States. The United States refused to recognize the new Manchukuo state, and in March of 1932 the League of Nations, an international peacekeeping organization set up after World War I, endorsed this policy.

When the League of Nations went on to propose new administrative arrangements for Manchuria, which would protect Japan's long-standing special rights there and at the same time uphold the general principle of China's

formal sovereignty, Japan left the organization in protest. On May 31, 1933, Japanese and Chinese officials met in the town of Tankgu near the Great Wall of China. The negotiators accepted a truce, thereby alleviating the need for further U.S. action. Japanese troops would remain in Manchuria until the end of World War II (1939–45).

Philippine Independence Veto

When Hoover became president the Philippines were a U.S. possession, having been annexed after the Spanish-American War (1898) during the William McKinley administration. The Jones Act of 1916 (also known as the Organic Act of the Philippine Islands) provided for male suffrage, an elected senate, and a bill of rights. The supreme executive power was vested in a governor-general appointed by the U.S. president. From 1927 to 1929 Hoover's secretary of state, Henry L. Stimson, held the position.

During Hoover's administration a bill was introduced to grant independence to the Philippines. Certain U.S. business firms, especially those producing sugar, encouraged Philippine freedom. By giving the Philippines independence their sugar production could be protected from Philippine competition by a tariff. U.S. military leaders advocated Philippine independence because the distant location made them a burden to defend. In January 1933 Hoover vetoed the bill providing for Philippine independence. The president stated the need to protect the islands from foreign encroachment, particularly given what he called "the present political instability in the Orient." Stimson feared that U.S. withdrawal would lead to eventual Japanese or Chinese domination. Congress, reflecting a public that found the islands too heavy a financial burden, overrode the president. The Filipino leadership realized that their economy could little afford sovereignty and secretly backed the president. Congress was adamant on the matter, and hence in 1934 the Filipinos had to accept the Tydings-McDuffie Act, an almost exact replication of the independence act of 1933. This act offered the Filipinos independence after a transition period and empowered them to write a constitution and establish a democratic government.

The Hoover Administration Legacy

The election of 1932 turned Hoover out of office. As soon as the election was over, Hoover sought immediate face-to-face meetings with his successor. At issue were such matters as war debts, banking, and ultimately Franklin Roosevelt's reform agenda, a diverse series of measures that would go down in history as the New Deal.

Although Franklin Roosevelt established a state relief agency in 1931 and advocated unemployment insurance, the New York governor certainly had no reputation for radicalism. He had roundly criticized Hoover the previous year for departing from laissez-faire and pouring money into public works.

On December 15, 1932, a semiannual installment of $150 million owed the United States in war debts came due, for the Hoover moratorium had expired (*See also,* Foreign Issues). The British agreed to pay their full installment of $95 million in gold, although they warned that the sum was not a resumption of the annual payments. The Italians followed suit. Both Poland and France, however, defaulted. Hoover was particularly distressed with France. As French citizens held over half a billion dollars in New York banks, he thought they could easily make their $20 million payment. When he met with Roosevelt on November 22, Hoover claimed the United States must insist on the December remuneration. He suggested that both he and the president-elect jointly urge the revival of a World War I (1914–18) debt commission of presidential appointees, all of whom must be acceptable to Roosevelt. The commission would reduce the debt tally, but not cancel it. By making concessions on debt payments, Hoover hoped that a forthcoming World Economic Conference, to be held that spring in London, England, would produce an integrated settlement that would lower tariffs, stabilize currencies, and foster disarmament. Above all, he believed, Britain had to be persuaded to return to the gold standard.

Roosevelt balked at Hoover's proposal, refusing to bind himself to any foreign economic arrangements in advance of entering the White House. He later told reporters that the debt question was "not his baby." The new administration did not intend to buttress Hoover's claim that the U.S. Depression was part of a larger worldwide one and hence could not be blamed on the outgoing president.

Even before Roosevelt's election, the nation's banking system was on the verge of collapse. Low trade levels, general business failures—all had made bank investments unproductive and bank loans uncollectible. As Hoover told Congress on December 6, 1932, "Clearly we must secure sound organization of our financial system as a prerequisite of the functioning of the whole economic system. The first steps in that system are sound currency, economy in government, balanced budgets, whether national or local." Once the election was over, Hoover sought immediately to enlist president-elect Roosevelt behind these policies, realizing full well that his program would cause Roosevelt to continue basic Hoover policies. Hoover wrote Senator David A. Reed (Rep.-Pa.), "If these declarations be made by the president elect, he will have ratified the whole major program of the Republican Administration; that is, it means the abandonment of 90% of the so-called new deal."

In particular, Hoover wrote Roosevelt, there must be "prompt assurance that there will be no tampering or inflation of the currency," by which he meant maintaining the gold standard. Roosevelt, who had already decided to inflate the currency, correctly sensed that

Fast Fact

Hoover was tireless at the beginning of his presidency. Often putting in 18-hour days, he would rise at six every morning, join a group of friends for a brisk half-hour session with a five-pound medicine ball, have breakfast, and be at his desk by 8:30. He would then work all day and usually well into the night smoking incessantly. Often he only got three hours sleep. Sometimes he would wake up in the middle of the night, pore over papers, and write for an hour or two. By the end of his presidency, his hand shook, his shoulders sagged, and his hair had turned white. He appeared to have aged 20 years while in the White House.

(Source: Carl N. Degler. "The Ordeal of Herbert Hoover." *Yale Review*, June 1963.)

Hoover was trying to tie his hands in advance. Again, Roosevelt proved uncooperative, and a final meeting of the two men the day before the inauguration proved futile. By then fifteen million people were unemployed. On March 4, 1933, as he left office, Hoover commented privately, "We are at the end of our string. There is nothing more we can do."

Lasting Impact

More than any chief executive from George Washington to Calvin Coolidge, Hoover met economic crisis with governmental action. Certainly, he was one of the United States's truly activist presidents. His was the first administration to use federal power to intervene directly in the nation's economy. In fact, it was Hoover himself who told the American Bankers Association in October 1930 that depressions were not to be borne uncomplaining. The nation, he continued, should treat an "economic pestilence" in the same manner it coped with typhoid, cholera, and smallpox, that is to engage in positive efforts to eliminate such scourges.

At the same time, Hoover stressed the primacy of voluntary and local activity. Through summit meetings of business and labor leaders and through fact-finding committees and commissions, he worked ceaselessly to return prosperity through voluntary initiative. Because of such efforts, U.S. business and voluntary agencies could not deny that they had been given a chance to act independently of federal intervention. Only after all else failed would he even advance a measure as radical as the Reconstruction Finance Corporation (RFC).

As president, Hoover accomplished far more than he was ever given credit for. He energetically fought the Depression with such measures as mortgage aid to farmers and homeowners, increased public works and flood control, and oversaw the Agricultural Marketing Act and the RFC, causing several pundits later to talk of a "Republican New Deal."

In regards to foreign policy, Hoover advanced disarmament, withdrew U.S. forces from Nicaragua, promoted the "good neighbor" policy in Latin America, and issued a moratorium on foreign debts. If he was unable to prevent Japanese penetration of Manchuria, it is doubtful whether any world leader or world power could have been able to do so. Though in retrospect his diplomacy was ill-suited to confronting the rise of totalitarian aggression, his successor did not start off much better.

Even the most avowed Hoover partisan, however, would be hard put to find his presidency a success. Part of the problem lay in Hoover's bad luck to be president during a time of widespread misery. Part lay in Hoover's own leadership. He took bold and imaginative steps to save the nation's financial structure. He would not, indeed refused, to take equally bold steps to save the unemployed and the farmers. To many Americans, Hoover's programs could be summed up in the words, "Too little, too late."

Sources

Best, Gary Dean. *Herbert Hoover: The Postpresidential Years, 1933–1964.* 2 vols. Stanford, Calif.: Hoover Institution Press, 1983.

Burner, David. *Herbert Hoover: A Public Life.* New York: Alfred A. Knopf, 1979.

Degler, Carl N. "The Ordeal of Herbert Hoover." *Yale Review* 52 (June 1963): 563–83.

Fausold, Martin L. *The Presidency of Herbert C. Hoover.* Lawrence, Kans.: University Press of Kansas, 1985.

Fausold, Martin L., and George T. Mazuzan *The Hoover Presidency: A Reappraisal.* Albany, N.Y.: State University of New York Press, 1974.

Ferrell, Robert H. *American Diplomacy in the Great Depression: Hoover- Stimson Foreign Policy, 1929–1933.* New Haven, Conn.: Yale University Press, 1957.

Hoover, Herbert. *Memoirs.* 3 vols. New York: Macmillan, 1952.

Myers, William Starr, ed. *The State Papers and Other Writings of Herbert Hoover.* 2 vols. Garden City, N.Y.: Doubleday, Doran, 1934.

Nash, George H. *The Life of Herbert Hoover.* 3 vols. New York: W.W. Norton, 1996.

Romasco, Albert U. *The Poverty of Abundance: Hoover, the Nation, the Depression.* New York: Oxford University Press, 1995.

Schwarz, Jordan A. *The Interregnum of Despair: Hoover, Congress, and the Depression.* Urbana, Ill.: University of Illinois Press, 1970.

Smith, Richard Norton. *An Uncommon Man: The Triumph of Herbert Hoover.* New York: Simon and Schuster, 1984.

Warren, Harris Gaylord. *Herbert Hoover and the Great Depression.* New York: Oxford University Press, 1959.

Wilson, Joan Hoff. *Herbert Hoover: Forgotten Progressive.* Boston: Little Brown, 1975.

Further Readings

Daniels, Roger. *The Bonus March: An Episode of the Great Depression.* Westport, Conn.: Greenwood, 1971.

DeConde, Alexander. *Herbert Hoover's Latin-American Policy.* Stanford, Calif.: Stanford University Press, 1951.

Doenecke, Justus D. *When the Wicked Rise: American Opinion-Makers and the Manchurian Crisis of 1931–1933.* Lewisburg, Pa.: Bucknell University Press, 1984.

Link, Arthur S. *American Epoch: A History of the United States Since the 1890s.* New York: Knopf, 1955.

Lisio, Donald J. *The President and Protest: Hoover, Conspiracy and the Bonus Riot.* Columbia, Mo.: University of Missouri Press, 1974.

O'Brien, Patrick. *Herbert Hoover: A Bibliography.* Westport, Conn: Greenwood, 1993.

Patterson, James T. *America in the Twentieth Century: A History.* 3rd ed. New York: Harcourt Brace Jovanovich, 1989.

Rappaport, Armin. *Henry L. Stimson and Japan, 1931–33.* Chicago: University of Chicago Press, 1963.

Rosin, Elliot A. *Hoover, Roosevelt, and the Brains Trust: From Depression to New Deal.* New York: Columbia University Press, 1977.

Schlesinger, Arthur M. Jr. *The Crisis of the Old Order, 1919–1933.* Boston: Houghton Mifflin, 1957.

Throne, Christopher. *The Limits of Foreign Policy: The West, the League, and the Far Eastern Crisis of 1931–1933.* New York: Putnam, 1972.

Franklin D. Roosevelt Administrations

Biography

Raised according to the tenets of the gospel of wealth, Roosevelt assumed social responsibility upon entering the world of politics. As an activist politician—even when only a freshman state senator—he honed his political skills. In 1921 he was forced to retire from public life due to a debilitating case of poliomyelitis. However, when he returned to politics he was warmly welcomed and his charisma and political skill enabled him to deal with the fallout of the Great Depression and, eventually, as president, to meet the challenges of World War II.

Early Life

There was absolutely nothing in Franklin Delano Roosevelt's background that would have supported a prediction of his future greatness. He was born on January 30, 1882, in Hyde Park, Duchess County, in upstate New York. He was the only child of James and Sara Roosevelt, people of considerable wealth and privilege. James was of Dutch descent—the family having come to America in the seventeenth century—and had prospered through investments in mining, shipping, and railroads. Sara Delano Roosevelt was descended from Flemish immigrants. She had wealth of her own derived from her father's investments in the tea and opium trade in China. She was a strong-willed woman who exerted a dominant influence on Roosevelt, not only during his childhood, but throughout his life. James, who was 26 years older than Sara, died in 1900; Sara lived on until 1941.

The home where Roosevelt spent his early years is called Springwood. It is in the village of Hyde Park on

Full name: Franklin Delano Roosevelt
Popular name: FDR

Personal Information:
Born: January 30, 1882
Birthplace: Hyde Park, New York
Died: April 12, 1945
Death place: Warm Springs, Georgia
Burial place: Family plot, Hyde Park, New York
Religion: Episcopalian
Spouse: Anna Eleanor (m. 1905)
Children: Anna Eleanor; James; Franklin; Elliott; Franklin Delano, Jr.; John
Education: Harvard College, BA, 1903; attended Columbia Law School
Occupation: Lawyer; politician
Political Party: Democratic Party
Age at Inauguration: 51 years

Franklin D. Roosevelt. *(The Library of Congress.)*

the eastern bank of the Hudson River about five miles north of the city of Poughkeepsie. Members of the Roosevelt family had owned property in the area for many years, but the house where Roosevelt was born in 1882 was purchased by his father just 15 years earlier in 1867. It continued to be the family home until Roosevelt's death in 1945, at which time it became the property of the National Park Service. Roosevelt's wife, Eleanor, lived nearby at Val-Kill until her death in 1962. Since then the Roosevelt family has had no connection with the Hyde Park property.

During the first seven years of his life his father spent considerable time with young Roosevelt, especially in outdoor pursuits. Even after his health began to fail in 1891, from a series of debilitating heart attacks, James Roosevelt continued to encourage his son and to follow his activities closely. It was Sara Roosevelt, however, who was most devoted to the boy. She threw herself into his upbringing with a single-minded devotion. She read to him by the hour, carefully screened his playmates, and supervised his play. She also saw to it that her son developed all the personal qualities so admired by the upper classes of that day. These included good manners, noblesse oblige—the obligation of the rich to help and share with those less fortunate—and most of all the determination that he should succeed at anything he tried.

Education

Roosevelt's early days reflected the privileged life of the rich during the so-called Gilded Age. This is a term used by historians to describe the period from the end of the Civil War (1861–65) to the turn of the century when the economic system of the nation became industrialized. There was considerable expansion and economic growth during this time, and the people who made large sums of money often flaunted their wealth while at the same time imposing upon themselves an obligation to give something back to society.

Another aspect of Roosevelt's privileged station was his education by private tutors. The first, in 1890, was Jeanne Sandoz, a French-speaking Swiss woman who developed a curriculum that emphasized both science and the arts and, in fact, provided more scientific information than Roosevelt received at any other time during his education. Sandoz also preached about the Social Gospel to her young pupil. This is another term used to describe the acceptance of social responsibility by the privileged. She succeeded admirably. Roosevelt loved her and learned much from her. He later said that in the three years they were together she did more than any other teacher to lay the foundation of his education. Sandoz was succeeded by another talented teacher, Arthur Dumper, who taught Roosevelt between 1893 and 1896.

In the fall of 1896 14-year-old Roosevelt enrolled at the prestigious Groton School in Groton, Massachusetts. Many teachers influenced Roosevelt at Groton, but Endicott Peabody, the headmaster, made the biggest impression. Peabody was a man of enormous self-confidence and integrity who became somewhat of a father figure to Roosevelt as James's strength diminished. Peabody was also an elitist who undoubtedly molded Roosevelt's paternalistic view of society more than any other person.

The young Roosevelt enrolled at Harvard in 1900. Here he found excellent scholars, but unlike those at Groton they offered no guidance. As a result his performance declined and he made mostly Cs with an occasional B. He was not excited by the intellectual life as he had been at Groton. His curriculum included political science, history, English, and literature. He took practically nothing in science, mathematics, philosophy, or economics.

Extracurricular activities commanded Roosevelt's attention while he was at Harvard. Although he failed to make either the football or rowing teams, he did become a cheerleader. He also joined several clubs, but his main interest was the student newspaper, *The Crimson,*, where he became managing editor in his junior year. He graduated with a B.A. in only three years.

In 1905 Roosevelt enrolled in the Columbia University Law School in New York City. He studied there until 1907, at which time he passed the bar examination without completing his degree.

Family Life

Franklin Delano Roosevelt married Anna Eleanor Roosevelt, his distant cousin, in 1905. Together they had six children, five of whom lived to maturity. The children were: Anna Eleanor Roosevelt (1906–75); James (1907–91); Franklin, who lived from March 18 to November 1, 1909; Elliott (1910–90); Franklin Delano, Jr. (1914–88); and John (1916–81). The Roosevelt children were involved in numerous divorces, scandals, financial difficulties, and controversies, especially during the White House years, but Franklin and Eleanor always forgave them, appearing to some critics to be unconcerned.

Anna was always closest to Roosevelt, and was with him on his last great diplomatic venture to Yalta in 1945, which laid the groundwork for an end to World War II (1939–45). James served his father as a White House aide and later served in Congress representing a district from California. Elliott became a rancher. Franklin Delano Roosevelt Jr. was a lawyer who served in Congress and once ran unsuccessfully for governor of New York. John eventually became a Wall Street lawyer.

Eleanor Roosevelt faced severe problems in the marriage. She never got along with Roosevelt's domineering mother Sara Roosevelt (who lived until 1941), and her heart was broken by Roosevelt's faithlessness. In 1917 Eleanor discovered that her husband was involved in an affair with her social secretary, Lucy Mercer. Eleanor was devastated and demanded that Roosevelt never see Mercer again. She remained in the marriage, but her relationship with Franklin was henceforth characterized by respect and cooperation but not intimacy. After Roosevelt was stricken by polio in 1921, Eleanor assisted with his recovery and subsequently worked hard to promote the rebirth of his political career as well as her own interest in social reform.

Throughout the 1920s, groomed by Louis Howe, Roosevelt's personal secretary, Eleanor Roosevelt worked diligently to develop her political skills and to keep Roosevelt's contacts with Democratic Party leaders alive during his convalescence. The culmination of her efforts during this period came in 1928 when she served as chairperson of the Democratic Party Women's Committee in Alfred E. Smith's bid for the presidency.

Roosevelt was elected governor of New York in 1928. During the next four years, as first lady of the Empire State, Eleanor Roosevelt continued her pattern of intense activity on behalf of both her husband and the many reform movements that interested her. She also continued to learn the intricacies of politics and to cultivate innumerable personal contacts. Thus she was well-suited to become first lady of the United States in 1933. In fact, during the 12 years of Roosevelt's administration, Eleanor Roosevelt redefined the role of the first lady. She served as Roosevelt's eyes and ears, she made numerous suggestions for program development, and she continued to pursue her own interests in the field of social reform, especially civil rights and women's rights.

Career

After passing the bar in 1907 Roosevelt became a clerk in the Wall Street law firm of Carter, Ledyard and Milburn. He was a competent attorney and could have made a fine career in the law, but his ambition lay in politics. He made this clear on many occasions, often remarking that he wanted to be president. He clearly intended to model his political career on that of his distant cousin, former president Theodore Roosevelt. He would seek election to the state legislature, then become governor, and finally move on to the White House. His plan was destined to work remarkably well.

Roosevelt's chance came in 1910 when he was elected to the New York State Senate. Even though his district was traditionally a Republican stronghold, Roosevelt won because the GOP (Grand Old Party, as the Republican Party is often referred) was split. From this point onward, as long as his political career was centered in New York, Roosevelt had to deal with Tammany Hall.

Tammany Hall, headquartered in New York City, was the New York state Democratic party machine. In the campaign of 1910, Tammany neither supported nor opposed Roosevelt, although its leaders did not like him. Immediately after the election, however, Roosevelt crossed swords with the "bosses" when he joined with a group of upstate legislators who opposed the Tammany candidate for the U.S. Senate. These rebels were successful in forcing the selection of another candidate and the episode brought Roosevelt considerable publicity as a crusader for progressive politics.

Roosevelt's political career began during a period of U.S. history known as the Progressive Era. This was a time when many leaders advocated greater use of the powers of government to promote the general welfare, the regulation of business, and greater honesty in politics. Roosevelt generally subscribed to these views and this put him at odds with the Tammany leaders who he perceived to be conservative and corrupt.

As time went on, however, Roosevelt's perceptions changed. He came to realize that he could not hope for higher state office without Tammany support, and he came to be impressed with the more progressive views of certain party leaders like Alfred E. Smith and Robert F. Wagner who were closely associated with the machine. Thus Roosevelt forged a truce with Tammany in 1917, which generally continued throughout the rest of his career. He was always a reformer, but for political reasons he also was willing to work with rather than against the party bosses. This relationship with the powerful machine never adversely affected his image with the public.

Biography:

Eleanor Roosevelt

First Lady; Humanitarian (1884–1962) Eleanor Roosevelt is widely regarded as the most effective woman in the history of U.S. politics. As first lady of the United States, Roosevelt broke the "social hostess" mold her predecessors had cast. She held weekly press conferences for women reporters, she wrote newspaper and magazine columns that addressed personal and political issues, she had a highly successful radio program, and she commanded exorbitant fees for biannual lecture tours. Even people within her husband's administration never knew where she would turn up next. The most famous political cartoon about her depicts a miner laboring in the bowels of the earth. He's looking up with astonishment saying, "For gosh sakes, here comes Mrs. Roosevelt." For depression-era work-relief programs, Roosevelt fought for equal access by African American citizens to available jobs. Roosevelt said, "It is a question of the right to work and the right to work should know no color lines." She found government posts for many qualified women and used her unique access to the president to lobby for

legislation and programs that would benefit the oppressed. In a politically intuitive move, Roosevelt, fearing that the continued depression may drive some young people to extremist movements, lobbied for the creation of the National Youth Administration of 1935, which employed thousands of high school and university students and allowed them to continue their studies. Following her husband's death, Eleanor Roosevelt main-

tained an active and high-profile role in both national and world political arenas. At her funeral in 1962, former presidential candidate Adlai Stevenson said of Roosevelt, "She would rather light candles than curse the darkness."

From almost the beginning of his career in politics, until 1936, Roosevelt was associated with Louis McHenry Howe. Howe served as a close adviser and political mentor to both Roosevelt and his wife. Howe was a rather unsuccessful journalist who in 1906 decided to become a political strategist. He learned his trade by simply watching the behavior of politicians on a daily basis. Attracted to Roosevelt by the latter's leadership of the anti-Tammany revolt in 1911, he helped Roosevelt win reelection in 1912, thus beginning an association that lasted for the rest of Howe's life.

Roosevelt Enters National Politics

The Tammany fight made Roosevelt famous in New York but also earned him many enemies. Nevertheless, he was reelected in 1912, the same year that Woodrow Wilson won the U.S. presidency. Roosevelt campaigned for Wilson and was noticed by Josephus Daniels, a prominent Democrat from North Carolina. Wilson appointed Daniels to his cabinet as secretary of the navy and Daniels in turn made Roosevelt assistant secretary.

As assistant secretary, Roosevelt angered his superiors with his support for U.S. involvement in World War I (1914–18) because the administration's policy was that

of neutrality. He also made an unsuccessful bid for the U.S. Senate in New York. When the United States finally entered the war in 1917, Roosevelt threw himself into the task of administering the navy. Louis Howe came to Washington to assist him and together they did an excellent job. Roosevelt tried on several occasions to leave his civilian job and join the armed forces, but each time his superiors persuaded him to remain.

Disillusionment with Wilson's wartime policies and the results of the Versailles Peace Conference, which helped to settle the end of World War I, filled the Republicans with hope for the presidential election of 1920. They nominated Warren G. Harding, a conservative senator from Ohio, as their candidate. Wilson was gravely ill and out of favor so the Democrats nominated Governor James Cox of Ohio. Roosevelt received the vice presidential nomination largely because of his name.

Although the Democrats had little hope of victory and Cox campaigned ineffectively, Roosevelt made the most of this opportunity. He toured the nation by train, making numerous speeches and becoming acquainted with party leaders everywhere. The defeat of the Democratic ticket was decisive, but Roosevelt emerged from the experience as one of the leading members of the party.

After the election Roosevelt returned to New York City to practice law. In the summer of 1921, while vacationing in Canada, he became gravely ill. He had polio, but it was not immediately diagnosed. The result was devastating. He was paralyzed from the waist down. His political career appeared to be over, and his mother insisted that he return to Hyde Park and the life of a country gentleman, but Eleanor Roosevelt and Howe encouraged him to go on and his ambitions were renewed.

Roosevelt's convalescence was long and hard but he persevered, showing great strength of character. In 1923 he discovered the warm mineral waters of Warm Springs, Georgia, and purchased the site now called the Warm Springs Foundation, a facility where polio victims could come for recreation and therapy. After Roosevelt became president, it was called the "Little White House," because he spent so much time there.

From Governor to the White House

By 1924 Roosevelt had recuperated sufficiently to return to politics. He made the nominating speech on behalf of Al Smith, who was then the governor of New York, at the Democratic convention. Smith did not win, but he and Roosevelt maintained a close relationship. In 1928 when Smith left his post as governor to run for president, he persuaded Roosevelt to run for governor himself. Smith was defeated by Herbert Hoover, but Roosevelt won New York's governorship. He was now a likely presidential candidate.

As governor Roosevelt fostered programs to improve both rural and urban life. He did not maintain his alliance with ex-governor Smith, splitting over patronage and Roosevelt's unwillingness to allow him a major voice in party affairs. Smith and others condemned Roosevelt for his allegedly dictatorial ways. Nevertheless, the people adored Roosevelt and he was easily reelected in 1930.

During his second term as governor, Roosevelt dealt with the effects of the Great Depression on his state and set his sights on the presidency. He surrounded himself with an able group of advisers: people like Frances Perkins, Henry Morgenthau Jr., and James A. Farley, and they devised a program that in many ways anticipated the New Deal of his presidential years. Roosevelt declared that one duty of the state was to care for those who could not care for themselves. He called for unemployment relief, farm relief, old age pensions, improved conditions for workers, tax increases, and other reforms. Under his leadership New York became the first state to provide major assistance to those affected by the economic collapse.

Roosevelt was elected president in 1932 and was subsequently reelected three times, thus becoming the only person ever to be elected to the highest office in the

Fast Fact

The Franklin Delano Roosevelt Memorial occupies 7.5 acres in West Potomac Park, Washington, D.C. The monument, as originally conceived, had four outdoor gallery rooms containing statuary, inscriptions, waterfalls and thousands of plants, shrubs, and trees. None of the sculptures of Roosevelt depicted him as disabled. It was argued that during his lifetime Roosevelt always tried to hide his disability.

After organizations representing disabled Americans protested vehemently, President Bill Clinton proposed legislation that required a statue of Roosevelt showing his disability be commissioned for the memorial. On July 2, 1998, Vice President Al Gore announced that the main entrance to the memorial would be reconfigured to accommodate an additional outdoor room that would contain a life-size statue of Roosevelt seated in the small wheelchair he had invented.

(Source: "FDR Memorial Homepage," <*http://www.hps.gov*>, 1999.)

United States more than twice. During these turbulent years—from 1933 to 1945—Roosevelt successfully led the nation through two of its greatest crises—the Great Depression and World War II.

Post-presidential Years

Franklin Delano Roosevelt was still president when he died of a cerebral hemorrhage on April 12, 1945, at his summer cottage at Warm Springs, Georgia. He had been rumored to be in ill health for many months, at least since the presidential campaign of the previous year, but no one knew the true extent of his problems. He suffered from extremely high blood pressure and advanced arteriosclerosis.

By the evening of April 12, the shocking news had spread around the world to be received by most people in silent disbelief. The train carrying the president's body left Warm Springs on April 13 for Washington where a funeral service took place in the White House on April 14. The following day the president was buried at Hyde Park in his beloved rose garden. Eleanor Roosevelt was buried beside him after her death in 1962.

The Franklin D. Roosevelt Administrations

Franklin Delano Roosevelt is regarded by historians as one of the greatest U.S. presidents. He was in office longer than any other person and he successfully led the nation through two of the most serious crises in U.S. history—the Great Depression and World War II. Only George Washington and Abraham Lincoln faced greater challenges and were successful in overcoming them.

Roosevelt Becomes President

The Campaign of 1932

Roosevelt's quest for the presidency in 1932 came at a time when the Great Depression was at its worst. An estimated 13 million people were out of work, many great industries—like steel—were operating at a fraction of capacity, banks were failing, and the Hoover administration had proved unable to cope effectively with the catastrophic conditions. Roosevelt had many assets working in his favor. He had been reelected governor of New York in 1930, had an excellent record, and had extremely shrewd advisers including his secretary Louis Howe and James A. Farley, a career politician with innumerable contacts in the West and the South. Although Roosevelt could not walk as a result of polio, which he had contracted in 1921, he hid his infirmity exceptionally well and projected an image of vigor.

The only serious opponent to Roosevelt's ambitions was the Speaker of the House, John Nance Garner of Texas, who had the support of William G. McAdoo and William Randolph Hearst of California. McAdoo had been secretary of the Treasury in the Wilson administration and a presidential contender in 1920 and 1924. In 1932 he was the chairman of the California delegation to the national convention. Hearst was an influential newspaper publisher with control of papers in major cities across the country.

Another opponent of Roosevelt was his onetime New York ally, Alfred E. Smith. Smith knew he could not win the nomination, but hoped to keep it from Roosevelt. At the convention Roosevelt won a majority on the first ballot, but not the necessary two-thirds. However, McAdoo then announced the shift of the Garner delegates to Roosevelt thus assuring him victory. The following day Garner was nominated for vice president. Roosevelt startled the convention by flying from Albany to Chicago to give the acceptance speech in person. This had never been done, but it was a master stroke of politics. Roosevelt's apparent vigor, his fine voice, his warm personality, and his liberal creed endeared him to most of the party faithful.

Roosevelt endorsed the party platform that called for repeal of the Eighteenth Amendment (Prohibition, which outlawed the manufacture and sale of alcoholic beverages), reduction of government spending, a balanced budget, sound currency, competitive tariffs, and reciprocal trade agreements. As for the Depression, the platform prescribed federal credits to the states for unemployment relief; an expanded public works program; a reduction of the length of the work week; and unemployment and old age insurance. For the farmer there were promises of mortgage refinancing; promotion of cooperatives; and efforts to bring prices above the cost of production. Finally, the Democrats declared their intention to enforce the antitrust laws; conserve natural resources; and regulate public utilities, holding companies, and the stock market.

Republican president Herbert Hoover was in many ways the antithesis of Roosevelt. Although highly intelligent, he was not a skilled politician. Moreover, he lacked a sense of humor and his personality, while not introverted, was quite reserved. Even before the Depression he was not popular with the press. Also, Progressive Republicans, like Senator George Norris of Nebraska, disliked Hoover's policies. The president had vetoed Norris's cherished plan for federal development of a hydroelectric power project at Muscle Shoals, Alabama. Hoover had also failed, in Progressive eyes, to support agriculture sufficiently, and he vehemently opposed direct federal relief to the unemployed. His persistent declaration that "prosperity is just around the corner," intended to boost consumer confidence, had become the object of ridicule.

The Republican platform equivocated on Prohibition by calling for a referendum on an amendment allowing the states to decide the issue individually. The document went on to blame the Depression on the European bankers and in general to offer no new solutions, with one exception. The plank on agriculture called for plans to balance production against demand and specified that it would be necessary for farmers to decrease the amount of land under production in order to achieve the desired result. This seemed to foreshadow the policy adopted later by Roosevelt and the New Dealers.

In spite of his major problems and deficiencies, Hoover was renominated with little opposition. The incumbent president at first did not intend to campaign vigorously but the situation soon looked so gloomy that he took to the road. In a brave but colorless whistle-stop campaign he attempted to save his presidency by arguing that things would only be worse if the Democrats won. The only chance he had was for the Depression to show some sign of lifting, but that did not happen.

Roosevelt's campaign was very energetic and his ebullient personality seemed to lift people's spirits wherever he went. He promised the people a "New Deal" without offering many specifics, but at the same time his "brain trust" advisers were working diligently on the

Administration

Administration Dates

March 4, 1933–January 20, 1937
January 20, 1937–January 20, 1941
January 20, 1941–January 20, 1945
January 20, 1945–April 12, 1945

Vice President

John Nance Garner (1933–41)
Henry A. Wallace (1941–45)
Harry S. Truman (1945)

Cabinet

Secretary of State

Cordell Hull (1933–44)
Edward R. Stettinius Jr. (1944–45)

Secretary of the Treasury

William H. Woodin (1933)
Henry Morgenthau Jr. (1934–45)

Secretary of War

George H. Dern (1933–36)
Harry H. Woodring (1936–40)
Henry L. Stimson (1940–45)

Attorney General

Homer S. Cummings (1933–39)

Francis W. Murphy (1939–40)
Robert H. Jackson (1940–41)
Francis B. Biddle (1941–45)

Secretary of the Navy

Claude A. Swanson (1933–39)
Charles Edison (1940)
William F. Knox (1940–44)
James V. Forrestal (1944–47)

Postmaster General

James A. Farley (1933–40)
Frank C. Walker (1940–45)

Secretary of the Interior

Harold L. Ickes (1933–46)

Secretary of Agriculture

Henry A. Wallace (1933–40)
Claude R. Wickard (1940–45)

Secretary of Commerce

Daniel C. Roper (1933–38)
Harry Lloyd Hopkins (1938–40)
Jesse H. Jones (1940–45)
Henry A. Wallace (1945–46)

Secretary of Labor

Frances Perkins (1933–45)

---

development of policy (*See also,* Roosevelt's Advisers). Raymond Moley sketched out the broad outlines of what the New Deal should be while Rexford Tugwell worked mostly on agriculture and Adolph Berle on business and finance. Meanwhile, Samuel I. Rosenman, Roosevelt's counsel who had earlier served on the New York State Supreme Court, wrote many of Roosevelt's speeches.

The outcome of the election was a monumental victory for the Democrats. Roosevelt polled close to 23 million popular votes to under 16 million for Hoover. Moreover, the Democrats gained firm control of both the House and the Senate. Also adding to the field for this election were six minor party candidates including the Socialists, the Communists, Prohibition, Liberty, Socialist-Labor, and Farmer-Labor. They performed very poorly. Even the Socialists, revitalized by the Depression and led by Norman Thomas, one of the founders of the American Civil Liberties Union (ACLU) and a prominent social reformer, polled fewer than one million votes.

In March 1933, when Franklin Delano Roosevelt began his first term, the nation lay in the depths of the Depression. Millions of Americans looked to the president for leadership. The mood was one of desperation tinged with hope. Roosevelt could attempt practically anything. It mattered only that he do something, and he did. "Debate might rage over the correctness of Roosevelt's actions, but his decisiveness had captured the imagination and the loyalty of the American people. . . . Bonds had been joined between them and the President that were to endure throughout the remainder of his life" (Miller, p. 325).

The Campaign of 1936

When the Democrats assembled in Philadelphia the renomination of President Roosevelt was a foregone conclusion. The platform defended all the existing New Deal programs (*See also,* Domestic Issues), but also promised a balanced budget as soon as possible. In foreign policy the platform promised to continue the Good Neighbor policy in Latin America (*See also,* Foreign Issues) and to avoid involvement in any war anywhere. There were no surprises at the convention and most of it was taken up with endless speech-making.

The Opposition

When the Republicans gathered in Cleveland in June 1936, they were experiencing mild optimism. The economy had yet to recover, and there was substantial sentiment that Roosevelt's New Deal was intrusive. However, the Republicans had no strong candidates. The party regulars finally agreed on Governor Alfred M. Landon of Kansas. He was a successful businessman with a mildly progressive reputation and he had carried the state of Kansas impressively in his two campaigns for governor. The Republican platform of 1936 called for the preservation of liberty and individual opportunity, and indicted the New Deal for its misdeeds, especially deficit spending and the alleged failure of the relief programs that included the proposed locally controlled unemployment relief programs and a reduction in federal regulations. The foreign policy section reflected extreme isolationism.

There was another politically dangerous group that represented a source of opposition to the New Deal from the Left. It had grown out of a loose coalition of the forces led by Father Charles E. Coughlin of Michigan, Dr. Francis E. Townsend of California, and Huey P. Long of Louisiana. Each of these men had substantial popular support for their own radical ideas, and for a time it appeared that they would be able to band together to challenge Roosevelt and his policies.

Long was the only true politician of the group. A senator from Louisiana, he was also the former governor, and his political machine in that state gave him near dictatorial political power. Long's so-called Share-Our-Wealth movement, which promised $5,000 a year to every family, was quite popular. Coughlin had developed a large following through his radio broadcasts from Royal Oak, Michigan, in which he demanded complete government control of currency and credit. Even more popular was the Townsend Plan. Townsend proposed a federal pension that would pay every person over 65 $200 per month provided they spent the money within 30 days.

In September of 1935, Huey Long was assassinated. Without Long, his so-called Union Party had no true presidential candidate. Congressman William Lemke, a Nonpartisan League Republican from North Dakota, would eventually run on the Union Party ticket, with the nominal support of the Longites, Coughlinites, and Townsendites. In reality the different groups could not settle on a general policy, and the Union Party failed to present a serious challenge to Roosevelt.

The Presidential Campaign

The Democrats were better organized than the Republicans and ran a more effective campaign even though they had less money. They successfully countered most Republican criticism by urging citizens to compare 1932 with 1936. Although the Depression was not over, most people believed they were better off. Roosevelt was a charismatic speaker and projected his magnetic personality in stark contrast to the unexciting Landon. While some conservative Democrats broke with Roosevelt, they had little effect on public opinion.

On November 8, 1936, Roosevelt swamped his opponent with over 27 million popular votes to 16.5 million for the Kansas governor. Lemke polled a mere 800,000. The president carried every state except Maine and Vermont. In Congress the Democratic majorities increased while at the state and local level thousands of Democratic candidates were swept into office on Roosevelt's coattails. Roosevelt had hoped for a mandate, but the result of the election was beyond his wildest dreams.

The Campaign of 1940

In 1940 Roosevelt ran for an unprecedented third presidential term. There were no other serious Democratic candidates and Roosevelt was easily renominated. The real battle swirled around the selection of a new vice president. Political differences with Roosevelt precluded Garner from running again. Roosevelt wanted Secretary of Agriculture Henry A. Wallace as his new running mate, but old line regular Democrats resisted. Wallace was after all a former Republican and was thought by many to be a spiritualist. Moreover, there was great resentment on the part of those who claimed that the "New Deal Crowd" had taken over the party. The opposition, however, was weak and Wallace was nominated on the first ballot.

Wendell L. Willkie was an Indiana-born attorney who lived in New York City. While a successful businessperson who opposed Roosevelt, he had been a Democrat until 1938 and had never held public office. He was thus an unlikely candidate for the Republican nomination. As in 1936, however, the Republicans lacked any strong candidates with a more conventional political background and certainly not anyone that was considered a real possibility to defeat Roosevelt. Willkie reinforced this impression of his Republican opponents with a very extensive and active campaign, and at the Republican convention he was rewarded with the nomination on the sixth ballot.

The Presidential Campaign

Willkie conducted an energetic campaign during which he traveled over 30,000 miles and delivered 540 speeches. His major theme was the third-term issue. In the United States, he argued, power should not be concentrated in the hands of one man. This was Willkie's only major issue; he agreed with Roosevelt's foreign policies and would not criticize his popular New Deal domestic programs. Most of the Democratic campaigning for the national ticket was conducted by Wallace, but late in the game Roosevelt did give five very effective speeches in the East and Middle West.

The election proved to be another landslide for Roosevelt. He defeated Willkie by 5 million votes in the popular election and 449 to 82 in the electoral college. Most of Willkie's support came from the agricultural Middle West where many farmers were growing tired of new government regulations. Roosevelt, however, retained the bulk of his urban support showing that New Deal labor policies were still popular.

The Campaign of 1944

Thomas E. Dewey, a Republican who had contended for the nomination in 1940, had become governor of New York and was in a strong position to challenge for the Republican nomination. Initially, he appeared to have several serious challengers, including Wendell Willkie, General Douglas MacArthur, and Governors John W. Bricker of Ohio and Harold E. Stassen of Minnesota. In the end, only Bricker could generate any lasting support. He campaigned vigorously but could not overcome Dewey's supporters and was forced to accept second place on the ballot.

Roosevelt was easily nominated for the presidency by the Democrats, but there were serious divisions within the party. Conservative southern Democrats were now opposed to Roosevelt and his policies. They were particularly unhappy with Vice President Wallace, who had openly advocated equal opportunity for all regardless of race. Desiring the support of the southerners, Roosevelt stood by and allowed the convention to select a new running mate for him, Senator Harry S. Truman of Missouri.

The campaign was brief. Concentrating for the most part on radio addresses, Dewey called for a more efficient administration, the relaxation of regulations, and the stimulation of private enterprise. Roosevelt also spoke mostly over the radio but, in fact, made very few speeches. Again, the result was a Roosevelt sweep. The president garnered over 25 million popular votes to 22 million for Dewey. Roosevelt lost some of the farm vote but retained the urban labor vote. Dewey realized most of his support in New England and the Middle West. Unbeknownst to the public, Roosevelt was seriously ill at the time of his January 20, 1945, inauguration. He would die of a cerebral hemorrhage only three months later.

Roosevelt's Advisers

There were several people not in Roosevelt's cabinet who influenced the president in significant ways. Among these were his personal secretary Louis Howe, Eleanor Roosevelt, Justice Felix Frankfurter, counsel Samuel I. Rosenman, Hugh Johnson, Thomas G. Corco-

ran, and Benjamin V. Cohen. The latter two were especially important because they drafted important legislation that included the Truth in Securities Act, the Securities and Exchange Act, the Public Utilities Holding Company Act, the Rural Electrification Act, and the Fair Labor Standards Act.

In the spring of 1932 at the suggestion of Rosenman, Roosevelt surrounded himself with a group of advisers known as the brain trust. This group included Rexford Tugwell, Raymond Moley, and Adolph A. Berle, Jr., and played a vitally important role between the election and Roosevelt's first inauguration. The advice provided by these three men became the basis of Roosevelt's overall domestic policy that came to be known as the "New Deal," a term coined by Moley.

Moley argued that both major political parties had grown too conservative and that the Democrats should move to the left with a liberalization based on progressive principles. Specifically, Moley proposed a large-scale relief program, old age pensions and unemployment insurance, the regulation of banking and securities exchange, heavy taxation of corporate wealth, federal ownership and operation of public utilities, and higher wage rates.

Tugwell offered the outline of what would become the New Deal farm program. It was based on the idea that farm commodity prices could be raised by inducing farmers to cultivate less land. This idea is known as acreage allotment. Adopted in 1933 this policy—with various modifications—has continued to be the basis of U.S. federal farm policy until the present day.

Berle made many technical proposals dealing with securities exchange, mortgages, lending policies, and banking. A number of his ideas made their way into important legislation. After the brain trust was dissolved following the election of 1932, Berle continued on as unofficial adviser to the president and finally joined the State Department in 1938. He was serving as ambassador to Brazil at the time of Roosevelt's death.

Moley was appointed assistant secretary of state in 1933 and served until September of that year when he left government service to become editor of *Today* magazine. In the mid-1930s he broke with Roosevelt over the court-packing scheme (*See also,* Roosevelt and the Judiciary) and his belief that the New Deal had become far too anti-business. He spent the balance of his career in the publishing industry.

Tugwell joined the administration in 1933 as assistant secretary of agriculture. Until 1935 he helped administer the first Agricultural Adjustment Act (AAA), which helped to increase farm income by reducing surpluses. In that year he was appointed head of the Resettlement Administration (RA), an agency designed to assist poor farmers to acquire better land. He was very liberal in his views and became a prime target of the conservative press. He left the Roosevelt administration in 1936.

What They Said . . .

Following Japan's attack on Pearl Harbor, President Roosevelt appeared before Congress to ask for a declaration of war against Japan.

"Yesterday December 7, 1941—a date which will live in infamy—the United States of America was suddenly and deliberately attacked by naval and air forces of the Empire of Japan.

"The United States was at peace with that nation and, at the solicitation of Japan, was still in conversation with its Government and its Emperor looking toward the maintenance of peace in the Pacific. Indeed, one hour after Japanese air squadrons had commenced bombing in Oahu, the Japanese Ambassador to the United States and his colleague delivered to the Secretary of State a formal reply to a recent American message. While this reply stated that it seemed useless to continue the existing diplomatic negotiations, it contained no threat or hint of war or armed attack. . . .

"Japan has, therefore, undertaken a surprise offensive extending throughout the Pacific area. The facts of yesterday speak for themselves. The people of the United States have already formed their opinions and well understand the implications to the very life and safety of our nation. . . .

"Hostilities exist. There is no blinking at the fact that our people, our territory and our interests are in grave danger.

"With confidence in our armed forces—with the unbonded determination of our people—we will gain the inevitable triumph—so help us God.

"I ask that the Congress declare that since the unprovoked and dastardly attack by Japan on Sunday, December seventh, a state of war has existed between the United States and the Japanese Empire."

(Source: Franklin D. Roosevelt, as quoted in *DISCovering U.S. History,* 1996.)

Many of Roosevelt's cabinet members also had the president's ear at one time or another, but Vice President Garner was unusual among Roosevelt's close associates. Garner was a conservative Democrat from Uvalde in southern Texas who had been elected to the House in 1902. He became minority leader in 1928 and Speaker in 1931 after the Democrats gained the majority. As a southern Democrat he was very conservative and disapproved of much of the New Deal from the start. His distaste for Roosevelt's policies grew as time passed, but because of party loyalty he did not openly oppose the president until 1937. After that, the court-packing scheme, and Garner's perception that Roosevelt favored civil rights for African Americans, put the vice president in the opposition camp. By mutual consent he was replaced in 1940.

Roosevelt and Congress

Roosevelt presided over an administration that included the Seventy-third through the Seventy-ninth Congresses. During that entire period Congress was dominated by the Democratic Party; however, the party was not a monolithic organization. Southerners tended to be conservative and there was a limit to their willingness to support liberal legislation.

Until 1937 the majority party in Congress supported practically everything Roosevelt proposed. As time went on, however, conservatives in both parties became increasingly uneasy as New Deal programs became more and more intrusive, as even greater regulations were imposed upon business, and as ever higher taxes seemed to be in the offing. By 1938 a loose coalition had formed that was powerful enough to obstruct virtually all of the president's efforts, and it is generally agreed that at that time the creative phase of the New Deal came to an end. As a result of this change election issues were diverted from the Depression back to local matters and also more to foreign policy. This accounts for the gains made by the Republicans in Congress during the latter years of the Roosevelt administration. However, the Democrats never lost their numerical majority.

Congress remained isolationist (avoiding involvement in foreign affairs) from 1933 to 1939, but after World War II began in September 1939, the legislators tended to support Roosevelt's international approach. Increased defense spending was approved and the Neutrality Acts, which were aimed at keeping the United States out of war, in order to encourage trade with friendly nations, were revised. During World War II Congress supported Roosevelt's defense programs by authorizing the creation of numerous war agencies and allowing certain controls such as rationing when the U.S. government issued coupons to limit the number of items a person could buy thus reducing the demand of scarce goods.

After the election of 1942, the conservative coalition rallied against Roosevelt's efforts to increase taxes and terminated many New Deal agencies. The conservatives were thwarted somewhat by the election of 1944, which increased the Democratic majority in the House. In 1946, after Roosevelt's death and the end of World War II, the conservatives seized control of Congress.

Historians agree that Roosevelt altered the relationship between the executive and legislative branches of government more than any other president. The essence of the change was to shift the initiative for legislation to the executive branch. Clearly, Roosevelt thought the presidency was the most important of the three branches, and his experience convinced him that both the Congress and the Supreme Court were largely obstructionist. However, Roosevelt never gained enough power to completely override the other branches and thus a long period of intergovernmental warfare was instituted. This trend continues to the present day.

During his long tenure Roosevelt vetoed 635 bills most of which dealt with individual pensions and other insignificant matters. Very few of Roosevelt's vetoes were aimed at substantive legislation during the pre-war period because there were no serious efforts to pass conservative bills. During the war the struggle between Roosevelt and the conservative coalition was mirrored in two episodes involving the veto. In 1943 Roosevelt vetoed an antilabor bill, the Smith-Connally Act. This veto was overridden. In 1944 Congress sliced $10 billion from an administrative tax bill. When Roosevelt vetoed the altered measure, he was overridden again by the legislative branch.

Roosevelt and the Judiciary

When Roosevelt was elected president the Supreme Court consisted of nine justices: Willis Van Devanter, James McReynolds, George Sutherland, Pierce Butler, Owen J. Roberts, Louis D. Brandeis, Benjamin N. Cardozo, and Harlan F. Stone, and Chief Justice Charles Evans Hughes. There was a clear philosophical divergence on the Court. Van Devanter, McReynolds, Sutherland, and Butler were conservatives, while Brandeis, Cardozo, and Stone were liberals. Roberts and Hughes were regarded as "swing men," meaning they alternated their votes from one position to the other. During Roosevelt's first term the justices generally regarded much of the New Deal legislation as an unwarranted assault on private property, contract rights, and the time-honored fundamentals of the American economic system.

The Court and the New Deal

Many of the early New Deal measures were hastily thrown together and were of dubious constitutionality. Many of them were inevitably challenged in court cases that gradually made their way to the Supreme Court. The Supreme Court struck down numerous New Deal measures in 1935 and 1936, often citing constitutional contradictions as their reason for invalidation (*See also,* Domestic Issues). In January 1935 in the case of *Panama Refining Co. v. Ryan,* the court struck down a portion of the National Industrial Recovery Act on grounds that it was an improper delegation of legisla-

tive power to the executive. In May, in *Schecter v. U.S.,* the National Recovery Act (NRA) was invalidated in its entirety on grounds that it was an improper regulation of intrastate business. Then in early 1936 the justices destroyed the Agricultural Adjustment Administration in *U.S. v. Butler.* Here the grounds cited were that the processing tax for regulating agricultural production was not supported by the general welfare clause of the Constitution.

Court-packing

President Roosevelt was furious over the judicial attack on his programs, and he resolved to neutralize the power of the Court. He believed the justices were far behind the needs of the time and the country, and he accused them of making "horse and buggy" decisions.

After his overwhelming victory in the election of 1936, Roosevelt instructed Attorney General Homer S. Cummings to find a legal precedent he could use to thwart the Supreme Court. Cummings delved into the archives of the Justice Department and came up with a precedent for action based on a long forgotten proposal made by the attorney general in 1913. This proposal would empower the president to appoint a new judge for every federal magistrate who reached the age of 70 and had not retired. The plan had not been intended to apply to the Supreme Court, Roosevelt nevertheless believed it met his needs. Because there was no law or constitutional precedent governing the number of justices, he saw no reason not to apply this idea to the highest court. In 1937 six justices were over 70—including the four conservatives—and this meant that if the proposal became law Roosevelt could appoint enough new justices to gain control of the Court.

Presented to Congress in the form of the Judicial Reform Act of 1937, the bill caused an instant furor. Conservatives condemned it and even many pro-Roosevelt Democrats were incredulous. The opposition claimed that Roosevelt was trying to subvert the Constitution and there was little the president's friends could offer in response. Roosevelt attempted to rally support for his plan in Congress and took his case to the American people with a speaking tour. Nevertheless, he could not rally sufficient votes to secure passage.

Quite suddenly, in the midst of the controversy, the Court reversed itself and began to uphold New Deal legislation. In quick succession in March and April 1937, the Court sustained the National Labor Relations Act and the Social Security Act. The former was decided in the case of *National Labor Relations Board v. Jones-Laughlin Steel Corp.,* whereby the Court used the interstate commerce clause of the Constitution to uphold the right of workers to organize unions. The Social Security system was sustained in *Stewart Machine Co. v. Davis.* Here the Court held that federal tax for old-age pensions is a valid use of the power to tax for the general welfare.

THE INGENIOUS QUARTERBACK!

In his drive to ensure approval of his New Deal programs, FDR attempted to alter the political makeup of the Supreme Court. This cartoon depicts President Roosevelt as the quarterback choosing justices like football players.

(Pen and ink drawing, by C. K. Berryman. The Library of Congress.)

The new direction taken by the Court was caused by the fact that Chief Justice Hughes began voting with the liberals. Historians have wondered what prompted this change and have generally concluded that Hughes voted against the New Deal legislation before the election of 1936 hoping to undermine Roosevelt's policies. When Hughes saw that Roosevelt had the overwhelming support of the people, he capitulated to the popular will.

In addition to Hughes's change of direction, the personnel of the Court also changed due to retirements and deaths, and Roosevelt was given the opportunity to appoint his own Court. In May Justice Van Devanter retired and was replaced by Hugo Black. Then in January 1938 Sutherland resigned and was replaced by Stanley F. Reed. In December of the same year Cardozo died and was replaced by Felix Frankfurter. In 1939 Brandeis resigned and Butler died. They were replaced by William O. Douglas and Frank Murphy, respectively. In 1941 McReynolds retired and Hughes resigned. Robert H. Jackson and Harlan F. Stone were their replacements. All the new justices were liberals and loyal New Dealers. Roosevelt eventually won the court battle, but at heavy cost to his prestige. Moreover, since New Deal legislation was effectively blocked by the conservative coalition after 1938, there were no liberal measures for the Court to approve.

Changes in the U.S. Government

No new cabinet positions were created under Roosevelt's leadership, but numerous government agencies came into being and many became permanent. Among these was the Federal Deposit Insurance Corporation (FDIC) created in 1935, which is regarded by many authorities as the most important banking reform of all time. It was designed to restore public confidence in banks by providing federally guaranteed insurance on deposits. At first the maximum deposit that could be insured was $2,500 per deposit; it has risen to $100,000.

Another important agency that endured was the Securities and Exchange Commission (SEC). The United States had no strict standards governing the sale of stocks and bonds, but that changed in 1933 with this very significant reform. It made securities fraud illegal under federal law, provided for the strict regulation of securities dealers, made corporate officers responsible for their claims, and provided for the strict monitoring of all exchanges.

The Federal Communications Commission (FCC) was established in 1934 to oversee the communications industry, which had grown rapidly since the early 1920s with little supervision. Radio and television remain subject to federal licensure and supervision. The FCC's role continues to broaden as it takes up the issue of Internet regulation.

Also created were the Federal Housing Administration (FHA) and the National Labor Relations Board (NLRB). The FHA, established in 1934, continues to provide long-term low interest loans to home buyers. The NLRB, established in 1935, supervises the relationship between employers and organized labor. The original bill gave unions legal standing and required collective bargaining. During the first years of its existence (1935–41) this agency was extremely powerful, but its importance diminished during World War II and was permanently reduced by the Taft-Hartley Act of 1947. Nevertheless, it still exists and represents the commitment of the U.S. government to the rights of workers to organize and bargain with their employers.

In order to administer these new agencies and programs the powers of the government were expanded dramatically under Roosevelt. As a result the size of the federal government expanded as a large bureaucracy was created to carry out federal mandates, leading to an effort by Roosevelt to reorganize the executive branch. A committee was appointed in 1936 to study and to make recommendations for a reorganization. The plan they presented in 1937 sparked a firestorm of opposition from conservatives. The original plan called for the president to have more assistants to lighten his work load, for the civil service system to be reorganized, for the Bureau of the Budget to be under the president's direct control, for two new cabinet posts to be created, and for the creation of a permanent National Planning Board. Conservatives feared that Roosevelt was planning to form a dictatorship similar to those in Italy and Germany.

The plan failed when it was met with strong opposition in Congress during 1937 and 1938, but Roosevelt succeeded in obtaining passage of a milder version of the bill in 1939. Under the second bill the president could appoint six new assistants and could propose organizational changes to Congress. The powers defined in this bill remain substantially the same today, and most historians agree that their use since Roosevelt's time has made the executive branch of government somewhat more efficient.

Domestic Issues

When Roosevelt entered the White House the nation was in the grip of the worst Depression of all time. The government under President Herbert Hoover had tried to stimulate the economy by appropriating large sums of money for public works—like big dams—and making large loans to businesses, but this strategy failed. The economy spiraled ever downward between 1930 and 1932, and the American people were overcome with frustration, rage, and fear. They blamed the government for their troubles and looked for new answers.

Roosevelt attempted to provide these answers. During the five-year period between 1933 and 1938, a whirlwind of legislative activity took place that is collectively known as the New Deal. This did not end the Depression—prosperity did not return until the United States entered World War II—but it did change the nature and direction of American society. The government accepted a much greater responsibility for the general welfare of its citizens and the regulation of the economy. The overall effect of all these changes can still be seen in government operations.

Roosevelt knew on his first day in office that he must do something dramatic to establish the credibility of the government and he chose to declare a bank holiday and close the banks. The public had lost confidence in the nation's banking system and many banks had ceased operations—some because they were insolvent (had insufficient funds) and some because they were shut down by state authorities. By closing all the banks and allowing them to reopen only after being certified by the Treasury to be solvent, Roosevelt restored a measure of confidence. Never before had the government taken such drastic nonmilitary actions to meet a domestic crisis. It worked but there was still much more to do.

Biography:

Sir Winston Leonard Spencer Churchill

Prime Minister; Author (1874–1965) Sir Winston Churchill was a British statesman whose service during the years of World War II prompted people to refer to him as the "savior of his country." Churchill was a man born to fit the needs of an exact circumstance, place, and time. In a retrospective look at World War II, Churchill wrote, "I felt as if I was walking with destiny, and that all my past life had been but a preparation for this hour." Elected prime minister in the war's infancy, Churchill's leadership role was less pragmatic and militaristic as it was inspirational and symbolic. Wrote author Anthony Storr, "In 1940 Churchill became the hero he had always dreamed of being. . . . In that dark time, what England needed was not a shrewd, equable, balanced leader. She needed a prophet, a heroic visionary, a man who could dream dreams of victory when all seemed lost." In the especially anxious years prior to the United States entering the war, Churchill was the man for the job. It is

impossible to overstate the importance of Prime Minister Churchill's relationship with U.S. President Franklin D. Roosevelt. Before the United States entered the war, that relationship was a factor in Roosevelt's decision to push, despite strong, domestic isolationist sentiment, to secure critical weapon and supply aid for the outmatched British. While Churchill's political performance prior to, and after the war was undistinguished, and while some of his tactical leadership decisions during the war have been criticized, his critical importance as a symbol of resistance and as an inspiration to victory, will never be disputed.

Phase One—The Hundred Days or the First New Deal

The first one hundred days of Roosevelt's administration is sometimes called the First New Deal. Between March and June 1933 there came a flood of legislation falling into three categories: relief, recovery, and reform. Relief measures were designed to assist unemployed workers and also farmers who faced impossible financial conditions. Recovery measures were designed to bring the economy back toward normal activity. Reform measures were aimed at protecting consumers by regulating businesses—like banking and the public utilities—whose activities directly affected individuals on a daily basis, and protecting the elderly and unemployed by providing for social instruments such as old-age pensions and health insurance.

Relief

During the first phase of the New Deal the major relief legislation included the creation of the Civilian Conservation Corps (CCC), the Federal Emergency Relief Act (FERA), and the Civil Works Administration (CWA).

The CCC was established in 1933. Its purpose was to put young men (mostly between the ages of 18 and 24) to work in forests and parks. This program was the most popular of all the New Deal relief programs. It lasted until 1943 and eventually employed 2,750,000 men for temporary periods—usually about a year.

Also in 1933 the FERA was passed. Its purpose was to make loans and grants to the states so they could create programs to reduce unemployment. It was administered by Harry L. Hopkins, a native of Iowa who had spent many years as a social worker in New York and had assisted Roosevelt when he was governor of that state. Hopkins was highly competent and energetic and was determined to bring immediate assistance to the unemployed. He believed that a federally administered work program was also required, so he persuaded Roosevelt to create a new work relief agency. Thus the CWA was born on November 15, 1933.

Designed to be temporary, the idea of the CWA was to put as many people as possible to work during the winter of 1934. Before long over four million people had government jobs. Many of the jobs created were not necessary and were called "make work jobs," attracting severe criticism. Nevertheless, much was accomplished. The CWA workers built and repaired numerous schools, streets, and airports. Overall, the CWA showed that federally sponsored work relief programs could succeed. By late 1934 Roosevelt became worried about spending and attacks from conservatives, and thus he terminated the program.

Recovery

The very first legislation introduced in Congress by Roosevelt's advisers was intended to assist farmers. It was called the Agricultural Adjustment Act (AAA) and was proposed on March 16, 1933. After two months of debate, it was passed on May 12. Its purpose was to increase farm income by reducing surpluses, thus offering both relief and recovery to the nation's farmers. It paid farmers to cultivate fewer acres, and it was financed by a tax on food processors such as the millers who ground wheat into flour.

The AAA was administered by Secretary of Agriculture Henry A. Wallace. Wallace came from an Iowa family very well known in agricultural circles. The young Wallace was an effective administrator and the AAA experienced some success. Farmers all over the country complied with the new acreage reduction regulations during the first growing season and farm prices showed a slight increase by the end of 1933. However, benefits were very uneven. Small farmers gained far less than large operators and tenants were not helped much at all. In fact, many were forced off the farm because land owners retired the acreage the tenants had been working. Nevertheless, the benefits outweighed the difficulties, and by 1935 farm income had increased by nearly 50 percent.

The food processors, who were taxed to finance the AAA, were unhappy and challenged the law in the courts. In 1935 the Supreme Court ruled that the tax was invalid and the AAA was struck down. However, it was soon replaced by another, similar program called the Soil Conservation and Domestic Allotment Act (*See also,* Domestic Issues: The Second New Deal).

The second major recovery law was the National Industrial Recovery Act (NIRA) which created the National Recovery Administration (NRA). The NRA supervised industry in creating rules—"codes of fair competition"—to govern production and marketing. Areas covered included minimum wages, maximum hours, price-fixing production controls, and collective bargaining. Title II of the NIRA created a separate agency—the Public Works Administration (WPA)—to support large construction projects, especially buildings and dams.

The NRA was headed by Hugh Johnson, one of Roosevelt's early advisers. He was a former army officer and lawyer who also had considerable experience in business, having served as chairman of the board of the Moline Implement Company during the late 1920s. Unfortunately, Johnson was very erratic and was not a good administrator, thus he contributed to the failure of the NRA.

At the outset Johnson had to conduct an extensive public relations campaign in order to convince all businesses to join the program. Many were reluctant and some flatly refused. Still, the plan went into operation. For success it had to reconcile the desires and the needs of all the workers and all the operators in every industry. This proved to be practically impossible. Businesspeople never trusted each other or the government, and workers often complained that management sought to avoid the labor provisions of the law. Cumbersome and eventually unworkable, the NRA collapsed even before it was struck down by the Supreme Court on May 27, 1935. The high court held in *Schecter v. United States* that the code system was an unconstitutional delegation of legislative power to the executive branch and an unconstitutional effort to regulate intrastate commerce. This meant that none of the codes any longer had the force of the law and so could not be enforced. With no more power and nothing to do, the NRA was abolished on January 1, 1936.

Reform

Another significant and ambitious program of the early New Deal was the Tennessee Valley Authority (TVA). It was conceived as a multipurpose agency that would develop the entire watershed of the Tennessee River and its tributaries. The area was a region of eroded soil and cutover forests that experienced flooding. Its rural areas had almost no electricity. Under the TVA a series of dams and locks were built to make the river navigable. Later the TVA would generate electricity using coal and nuclear power. The TVA produced nitrates for cheap fertilizer. Overall the TVA greatly improved the standard of living for the people living in the region.

Because it was a government agency, the TVA inevitably came into conflict with private business, especially those large utility companies that also produced electric power. This created a great debate over the question of whether or not there was any justification for the government to compete with private enterprise. The courts decided in favor of the government. In *Ashwander v. TVA* (1936), the Supreme Court held that the agency could sell electric power because it was property that had been legally acquired.

There were other reform measures passed during the early New Deal. These included the Truth in Securities Act, which required people selling stocks and bonds to provide buyers with complete and accurate information, and the Securities Exchange Act, which created the Securities Exchange Commission (SEC) to regulate the stock market. Congress also passed the Home Owners Loan Act, which created the Home Owners Loan Corporation (HOLC) with a revolving fund of $2 million to make low interest loans to homeowners so they could keep up their mortgage payments.

Finally, Roosevelt tinkered with the money and banking system of the nation during the early stages of the New Deal. In March 1933 he was authorized by Congress to stimulate inflation by reducing the gold content of the dollar and printing more money. Controlled inflation was a time-honored mechanism for dealing with recession or depression because reducing the value of the dollar automatically tended to increase prices. In April 1933 Roosevelt took the nation off the gold standard by prohibiting the export of gold. Thus he allowed the dollar to reach its own level with other world currencies. In May Congress repealed the gold clause in all public and private contracts. Thus debts could be paid with currency lacking any specific gold content. These actions also were designed to produce inflation. In May the Glass-Steagall Act was enacted, which required bankers to get out of the investment business. It also established the Federal Deposit Insurance Corporation (FDIC), which provided federally guaranteed insurance on deposits.

The Second New Deal

Another flurry of legislation beginning in the mid-1930s is often called the Second New Deal. Similar to the First New Deal, most of the laws and new agencies can be classified under the headings of relief and recovery, or reform.

Relief and Recovery

Creating Jobs: Realizing that the existing relief programs were inadequate, Roosevelt supported the creation of a more elaborate and broad-based effort in 1935. This new effort grew out of the Emergency Relief Appropriations Act—which provided initial funding of $4.8 billion—and created the Works Program Administration (WPA) headed by Harry Hopkins (who had administered the FERA and CWA).

Although subject to withering criticism by conservatives, the WPA was the largest and most successful relief program in U.S. history. By the time it was terminated in 1944, it had employed nearly eight million people. These people were not only rescued from disaster, they made significant contributions to American life. They built highways, schools, hospitals, and airports; staffed schools and clinics; and even promoted the arts.

One of the most unusual features of the WPA was the Federal Arts Project—a program designed to provide work for unemployed musicians, actors, artists, and writers. This program marked the first time that the U.S. government had given direct support to the arts. The workers in the program took classical music and the theater to small towns all over the country where they had opened art centers, and they produced elaborate guide books for all the states, some of which are still in print.

Another unusual and very popular feature of the WPA was the National Youth Administration (NYA), which provided opportunities for young people. Nearly one-third of the unemployed were under the age of 24, yet the Civilian Conservation Corps (CCC), established during the First New Deal, could not possibly assist them all and offered nothing for young women. The NYA, led by Harry Hopkins's associate Aubrey Williams, helped to close this gap. It offered jobs to unemployed youth who were out of school and created part-time positions for those who were still in school so they could stay there. Between 1935 and 1942 about 1.5 million youths were employed by the NYA.

The WPA and its associated programs operated on the basis of the so-called doctrine of "pump-priming"

designed to stimulate recovery as well as provide immediate relief. These programs did not do enough in this regard to end the Great Depression, but they did make important and lasting contributions.

Agriculture: Relief and recovery programs for farmers continued during this period. In 1936 Congress passed the Soil Conservation and Domestic Allotment Act. It did much the same thing as the Agricultural Adjustment Act (AAA), but it was financed by direct appropriations, a technique that could not be challenged in the courts. Two years later, in 1938, Congress passed a second Agricultural Adjustment Act. This legislation limited the volume of farm products that could be marketed and added a new twist called the Ever Normal Granary. Under this plan farm products could be stored rather than sold at once. Theoretically, this would ensure adequate food supplies in times of low production and guarantee farmers reasonable prices at the same time.

Two additional programs designed to help farmers were the Resettlement Administration (RA) and the Farm Security Administration (FSA). The RA operated during 1935 and 1936 and was designed to help farmers improve land use techniques, or help them move to better, more productive land. The FSA was designed to help people living on small farms (under 100 acres) improve their techniques or acquire more land. It also made loans to tenants to enable them to buy their own land. Both programs received severe criticism by conservatives who opposed social planning and thus they accomplished little.

Finally, there was the Rural Electrification Administration (REA), which many historians regard as one of the most important of all the New Deal programs. It provided funding for the establishment of cooperatives to build electric transmission lines to the rural areas of the country. The program commenced in 1936 and took several decades to complete, but it literally changed the nature of society by electrifying the American farm.

Reform

Labor: Most of the important reform legislation of the Roosevelt era was conceived between 1935 and 1938. One of the first and most significant of these measures was the National Labor Relations Act, a proposal that had been submitted somewhat earlier by Senator Robert P. Wagner of New York and is often called the Wagner Act. The bill incorporated the provisions of the defunct National Recovery Administration (NRA), especially those that guaranteed labor the right to organize and bargain collectively. It called for the creation of the National Labor Relations Board (NLRB) to ensure that workers were allowed to choose unions to represent them and were not discriminated against because they joined unions. This is considered one of the most important laws ever passed by Congress, and—with some modifications—still defines labor-management relations in the United States.

The last major labor law passed during this period was the Fair Labor Standards Act of 1938. This law, frequently amended but still in effect, established the minimum wage, the maximum work week, and abolished child labor.

Social Security: Social Security was another major New Deal reform. Every industrialized nation except for the United States had some form of old-age pension and unemployment insurance system and Roosevelt set out to remedy this problem. At first the president envisioned an all-encompassing program that would provide various forms of insurance for all Americans from infancy to old age. In the end, however, he had to settle for a compromise. As finally adopted, the Social Security Act of 1935 provided a small pension for retired workers, limited unemployment insurance, and some support for survivors. The universal health insurance that Roosevelt had wanted was dropped. Moreover, not everyone was covered by Social Security. Largely to assuage the South, farm workers and domestics were not included in the original package. Later, Social Security was expanded dramatically by President Lyndon Johnson's Great Society program of the 1960s.

Big Business: Major regulatory laws were also passed during this period that infuriated the business community. Chief among these measures were the tax and banking bills. In the tax bill of 1935, Roosevelt proposed an inheritance tax, a gift tax, and higher individual and corporate taxes. Again he had to settle for a compromise. The final version of the act scaled back general increases and dropped the inheritance tax altogether. Even so, conservatives were outraged at its passage.

The Banking Act of 1935 was more important. It increased the power of the Federal Reserve Board (created in 1913) to adjust the money supply by controlling rediscount rates and reserve requirements. This was a very significant development and the exercise of this power has affected the national economy dramatically on many occasions since.

Even more startling was the Public Utilities Holding Company Act. It reflected the beliefs of people like Justice Louis D. Brandeis that "big business" was evil. The law gave the Securities Exchange Commission (SEC) considerable power to regulate such gigantic businesses as the electric utilities. In its original form it included the famous "death sentence" clause that would have enabled the SEC to dissolve a utility company if it could not justify its own existence. This power was substantially modified before the bill was passed. Even so, conservatives and the business community in general accused Roosevelt of trying to wreck the capitalist system.

Housing: The last area in which major reforms took place was that of public and private housing. The problems faced by homeowners resulting from the Depression were recognized very early by the Roosevelt administration and dealt with temporarily by means of such

Roosevelt delivers an address to the nation over the radio. His fireside chats were an important way for the president to communicate directly with the entire country. (The Library of Congress.)

legislation as the Home Owners Loan Corporation Act (1933). During the Second New Deal, the Federal Housing Administration (FHA) was created in 1934. The FHA provided home loans at low interest on long mortgages (30 years), and required very low down payments. This permitted people with moderate incomes to buy houses and thus changed the parameters of home ownership in the United States. The FHA still finances mortgages today.

For the very poor the New Deal began a program of subsidized housing aimed mostly at the cities. The U.S. Housing Act of 1937 provided for federal housing complexes to be built in connection with slum clearance projects. There has been subsequent legislation and modifications since Roosevelt's day, but essentially his federal housing program still exists.

The most unusual aspect of the New Deal's housing policy was the Greenbelt Towns Program administered by the Resettlement Administration (RA). It provided for the construction of three planned communities: one in Maryland (Greenbelt); one in Ohio (Greenbelt); and one in Wisconsin (Greenbelt). The idea behind this project was to build complete, attractive suburban communities with affordable homes. They were highly successful even though conservatives attacked the use of government funds to back the program as a form of socialism.

Fighting the Reactionaries

By 1938 a coalition of Republicans and conservative Democrats in Congress had become strong enough to prevent the passage of any more liberal legislation. Roosevelt was furious with the Democrats in this group whom he considered disloyal, and he attempted to rid himself of at least some of them by intervening in the primary elections of 1938. To the dismay of Democratic Party "regulars," Roosevelt toured the country in opposition to some of the more conservative Democratic members of Congress.

Roosevelt's attempts to oust conservative Democrats from office failed, as only one of the targeted politicians wasn't renominated. The events of 1937 and 1938 foreshadowed the end of the creative period of the New Deal. Republicans made substantial gains in the November general election of 1938. They gained 81 seats in the House and eight in the Senate. They also enjoyed some important victories in state and local elections. Still, the Democrats retained control of Congress and Roosevelt's popularity, although tarnished, was still immense.

Foreign Issues

When Roosevelt assumed power in 1933 changes were already underway that would lead to World War II. In 1931 the Japanese, desperate for the raw materials needed to support their rapidly industrializing economy, invaded and occupied Manchuria. Later, in 1937, they commenced their effort to gain control of the entire Chinese mainland. In 1935, Italy, under the leadership of the fascist dictator Benito Mussolini, invaded Ethiopia. Mussolini, who had come to power in 1923, harbored delusions of grandeur and hoped to restore the might of the ancient Roman Empire. In Germany Adolf Hitler and the National Socialists (Nazis) came to power in 1933. Hitler promised the German people that he would restore their country to its rightful position of leadership in Europe, which was lost when Germany was defeated in World War I (1914–18). He soon embarked on a policy of expansion. He reoccupied the Rhineland in 1935, occupied Austria in 1938, and took a portion and then all of Czechoslovakia in 1939.

Throughout these events the predominant mood in the United States was isolationist. Neither the people nor the political leaders wanted to become involved in overseas affairs that might lead to war. Moreover, since Britain and France, the leading European democracies, took no action against the aggressors, Roosevelt was in no position to act independently. Even the outbreak of World War II, triggered by the German invasion of Poland in September 1939, did not jar the American people sufficiently enough for them to support any dramatic change in U.S. policy. It was not until December 7, 1941, when the Japanese launched their attack on Pearl Harbor, Hawaii, that everything changed. Within a few weeks after that cataclysmic event, Roosevelt found himself cast as the leader of the free world in a life-or-death struggle against aggression.

Early Developments in Foreign Policy

In his first inaugural address Roosevelt dedicated the United States to a "good neighbor" policy especially with reference to Latin America. He wanted to diminish the perception that the United States would intervene in the affairs of other nations whenever it suited its purposes. "In the field of world policy," said Roosevelt, "I would dedicate this nation to the policy of the good neighbor—a nation who resolutely respects himself and, because he does so, respects the rights of others." At the Montevideo (Uruguay) Conference later that year Secretary of State Cordell Hull supported an international agreement renouncing intervention. The Good Neighbor Policy was initially well received and successful, but since World War II it has been violated on many occasions.

Not so neighborly was U.S. behavior at the London Economic Conference during the summer of 1933. Earlier, President Herbert Hoover had promised U.S. participation in the conference which was aimed at international currency stabilization. But Roosevelt had taken the United States off the gold standard and did not support such a policy. He instructed Secretary Hull to discuss only tariff matters. Thus the conference failed and some economic historians believe the failure contributed to the continuation of the international financial crisis.

On the other hand, Roosevelt made a significant break with traditional U.S. policy by granting diplomatic recognition to the Soviet Union. Since the Bolshevik Revolution in 1917, which ushered in Communism to Russia, the United States had declined to recognize the Russian government, but Roosevelt believed this to be an erroneous policy. In November 1933, the two nations exchanged notes promising mutual noninterference in internal affairs and increased trade. Thus recognition was achieved although neither country kept its promises and the relationship remained chilly.

World War II

By the mid-1930s the attention of the United States began to shift toward the building crisis in Europe. Opinion in the United States was divided between those known as isolationists and those known as internationalists. The former remembered the disasters of World War I and wanted a policy of total noninvolvement in European affairs. The latter favored world peace but argued that ignoring Europe's problems could lead to even more serious difficulties.

Efforts to Remain Neutral

Between 1934 and 1939 the isolationist viewpoint dominated public opinion and was reflected in Congress.

The result was the passage of several laws designed to avoid U.S. involvement in any war. The first of these was the Johnson Debt Default Act (1934), which prohibited loans to any country that had not fully repaid its debt to the United States from the last war. Because only Finland had paid up fully, U.S. credit was essentially unavailable to any European nation that needed it for the war effort.

The Neutrality Act was passed by Congress when Italy invaded Ethiopia in 1935. This law prohibited arms shipments to belligerents (warring nations) and travel by U.S. citizens on belligerent vessels. Despite his opposition, Roosevelt signed the bill because of the overwhelming public support for the isolationist viewpoint.

In 1936 Congress extended the law and added a provision forbidding loans or credit to nations at war. After the Spanish Civil War broke out in 1936, Congress passed a law aimed directly at this conflict. It forbade shipments of arms to either side. Since Italy and Germany were supplying the rebels led by General Francisco Franco, this law most directly hurt the Loyalists—those fighting to defend the existing government. Moreover, since the Catholic Church supported the rebels, Roosevelt could not oppose them openly for fear of political repercussions at home.

To test public opinion, Roosevelt made a speech in Chicago—the heart of isolationism—in October 1937, in which he declared that aggressor nations should be "quarantined" in order to ensure peace. By this he meant that such nations should be denied normal trade relationships. The speech was not well received, so Roosevelt backed off.

Meanwhile, world conditions deteriorated rapidly. The Japanese, who had attacked China in 1932, renewed its aggression in 1937. In Europe Hitler's Germany occupied the Rhineland (lost after World War I), annexed Austria (1938), and then seized a portion—followed by all—of Czechoslovakia. At a conference at Munich in September, 1938, Hitler promised British prime minister Neville Chamberlain that if the German portion of Czechoslovakia (the Sudetenland) were ceded to Germany, this would satisfy him. Chamberlain believed Hitler, but when the Nazi dictator seized all of Czechoslovakia in March 1939, it was clear that he could not be trusted.

In August 1939, mortal enemies Germany and the Soviet Union (USSR) surprised the world by signing a nonaggression agreement. Shortly thereafter, on September 1, 1939, Germany invaded Poland. This event marked the official beginning of World War II.

Phase One: Aiding the Allies

When the hostilities began Roosevelt proclaimed American neutrality but he also asked Congress to repeal the arms embargo. They did so in the Neutrality Act of 1939, which authorized the sale of arms to those nations who could pay cash and transport the goods on their own ships. Soon, Roosevelt also asked Congress for increased

defense appropriations and called for increased production of military equipment. After the conquest of France by Germany in June 1940, Congress increased taxes and the national debt limit in order to finance greater defense spending.

Late in the summer of 1940 the Battle of Britain occurred. The German air force (the Luftwaffe) launched a massive bombing attack designed to soften up the British Isles for an invasion. The effort failed as the Royal Air Force (RAF) exacted a horrible toll upon the invaders, but Britain was desperate nevertheless. Practically all of Europe had by this time come under German control. Roosevelt knew that assisting Britain was vital to U.S. interests, but he still faced the obstructionist attitudes of the isolationists. In September 1940, he transferred ownership of 50 obsolete destroyers to the British in exchange for U.S. bases in British territory in the Western Hemisphere. This did not violate any law, but it excited harsh criticism from Roosevelt's opponents. Meanwhile, Prime Minister Winston Churchill of Great Britain pleaded with Roosevelt for even more aid. His country was approaching bankruptcy.

The Lend-Lease Program: Roosevelt responded to Churchill's pleas with the famous "Lend-Lease" proposal. If the United States could not legally sell arms to her friends on credit, the country could "lend" or "rent" them with the understanding they would be "returned" later. Roosevelt proposed this scheme to Congress in January 1941, and after considerable debate it passed in March. In the end support for the proposal was overwhelming. It was originally intended to provide aid to Great Britain but was soon expanded to include 38 nations. Even the Russians received substantial aid after they were invaded by Germany in June 1941. The total value of the Lend-Lease aid proffered by the United States during World War II has been estimated at $48 billion. Only a small fraction has ever been repaid, mostly by the British and the French. Nevertheless, most historians agree that it was a policy vital to the successful conclusion to the war.

The Atlantic Charter: In August 1941, Roosevelt and Churchill met secretly in Argentia Bay near Newfoundland, Canada, aboard the warships *Augusta* and *Prince of Wales*. This meeting produced a statement of aims acceptable to both nations. It was called the Atlantic Charter and it denounced aggression, supported the right of all people to choose their own government, called for cooperative efforts to improve the lives of all people, endorsed freedom from want and fear, and called for freedom of the seas and for efforts to disarm the aggressors.

During the fall of 1941, U.S. naval forces became involved in an undeclared war against the Germans in the Atlantic, and U.S. diplomats, led by Secretary of State Cordell Hull, attempted to negotiate a settlement with Japan. This effort did not go well because neither side was willing to compromise. The Japanese wanted the United States to recognize their dominant position in East

Asia, while the United States wanted the Japanese to withdraw from their occupied territories in Southeast Asia and China and promise there would be no further aggression. The negotiations failed completely, and on December 7, 1941, Japan launched an attack on the U.S. fleet at Pearl Harbor, Hawaii.

The United States Enters World War II

The strategy for World War II was conducted essentially by Roosevelt, Winston Churchill, and Joseph Stalin, leader of the Soviet Union. Roosevelt and Churchill remained in close contact and consulted with Stalin periodically. In late December 1941, Churchill traveled to Washington to develop plans for the war. He and Roosevelt agreed to concentrate their efforts first in Europe and then aim stronger blows against the Japanese after Hitler was defeated. During these meetings the two leaders also drafted the Declaration of the United Nations, calling for the creation of an international peace-keeping organization after the war.

1943 Conferences: There were several important international conferences in 1943 at which the Allied leaders discussed plans to end World War II. Roosevelt and Churchill decided early on that there would be no negotiated peace with the Axis coalition. The Axis powers, which included Germany, Italy, and Japan, would be required to submit an "unconditional surrender." Roosevelt and Churchill also discussed the "second front" issue, and agreed to a preliminary invasion of Sicily and Italy with a major assault in Western Europe to come later. The main invasion would be scheduled for the spring of 1944. The post-war status of Poland was another issue that commanded attention during these conferences (there was considerable disagreement concerning Poland's borders and government), as well as the leaders' commitment to the creation of the United Nations.

By the fall of 1943 Roosevelt decided to place overall command of the invasion of Western Europe in the hands of U.S. General Dwight D. Eisenhower. Roosevelt and Churchill assured Stalin their plans for the invasion were underway, and Stalin promised to declare war on Japan after the defeat of the Germans.

IMF and World Bank Established: There were four major conferences in 1944. In July at Bretton Woods, New Hampshire, representatives of 44 nations met to discuss post-war world trade and finance. They established the International Monetary Fund (IMF) and set up the International Bank for Reconstruction and Development (IBRD). The purpose of the IMF was to permit member nations to make short-term loans in order to prevent long-term balance of payment trade deficits. This, it was hoped, would help to prevent currency devaluation and thus support international trade. But this system, known as the fixed-exchange rate, never worked and was suspended in 1971. Since then the IMF has served mainly to moderate currency and exchange decisions made by individual nations.

The IBRD, also known as the World Bank, was initially created to fund the reconstruction of the war-torn world. More recently it has functioned primarily to make loans for development in lesser-developed nations and has played a vital role in the growth of many of these countries. Although many nations contribute to the World Bank, the United States is the largest single supporter.

Later in the summer of 1944 the second conference took place at Dumbarton Oaks in Washington, D.C. Representatives of the United States, Britain, China, and the USSR discussed the creation of the United Nations. The draft resolution issued by the conference served as the basis for the Charter of the United Nations, which was formally organized in San Francisco in April 1945, shortly after Roosevelt's death.

Roosevelt and Churchill met in Quebec in September 1944, to discuss zones of occupation in post-war Europe. A month later Churchill was in Moscow to discuss similar matters with Stalin. The United States was not represented at this meeting and Roosevelt made it known that his country would not be bound by any agreements reached there.

The Yalta Conference of 1945: The last and most famous of all the war-time conferences took place in the city of Yalta in the region of the Soviet Union known as Crimea, in February 1945. Roosevelt, Churchill, and Stalin were there accompanied by many of their top aides. The specific agreements reached at Yalta caused much controversy later, when it was charged by Roosevelt's critics that he had given too much to the Russians. Roosevelt apologists countered that the agreement was the best that could be expected given that the Russians had made a massive contribution to the war effort; they had already occupied most of Eastern Europe; and the Western Allies desperately wanted the Russians to declare war on Japan.

The major agreements at Yalta gave the USSR control of certain islands occupied by Japan and a zone of occupation in Korea. The British and the Americans also recognized Russian influence in Outer Mongolia, formerly a part of China. In Europe, Russian control of eastern Poland was recognized and Poland was given territories in the west at the expense of Germany. A plan for elections in Poland was also adopted. Finally, the Big Three reaffirmed their policy of unconditional surrender and worked out an agreement concerning voting rights for Russian satellite nations in the United Nations.

When Roosevelt returned to Washington from this journey he was exhausted and fatally ill. He lived only two more months and did not witness the end of a war whose course he had charted.

The Homefront During World War II

The war changed American life in many ways. It ended the Great Depression and brought prosperity, it

During World War II, President Roosevelt sought peace through communication; here he is flanked by Prime Minister Winston Churchill of Great Britain (left, seated) and Premier Joseph Stalin of the USSR. The February 1945 Yalta Conference was a major step in wartime relations. (National Archives and Records Administration.)

stimulated a further expansion of executive authority in the federal government, it caused very large numbers of people to relocate, it encouraged quick marriages and easier divorces, and it dramatically affected both race and gender relations.

Government spending for the war effort, of course, was the key factor in the return of prosperity. Unemployment dropped from 17 percent to one percent between 1939 and 1944, while personal income doubled during the same period. Hence, people had more to spend, even though the government halted the production of nonessential goods such as refrigerators and cars and rationed many other products. This contributed to massive savings.

Expansion of Executive Authority: The rapid increase in executive power was dramatic and was evident in several ways, such as the draft. In September 1940, Congress passed the Burke-Wadsworth Act creating the first peacetime military service program in U.S. history. Roosevelt and most politicians were at first reluctant to support such an act because it went against the American tradition of a volunteer army. However, as the world crisis worsened, the president came to believe that he had no choice.

In its original form the law provided that a maximum of 900,000 men could be called up to serve for one year. The program was to be administered by a new agency called the Selective Service System, but the actual work of drafting people would be handled by local boards. Individuals were to be chosen by means of a lottery. The program was extended for another year in 1941, and Roosevelt worried about the political repercussions of extending it indefinitely. When the Japanese attack on Pearl Harbor catapulted the nation into war, the peacetime draft was no longer an issue.

Managing Resources

Roosevelt created many other new agencies to conduct the war. In January 1942, he appointed Donald M. Nelson head of the War Production Board (WPB), with power to mobilize the nation's resources for all-out war. This agency functioned until October 1945. In June 1942, the WPB established a system of priorities for the allocation and use of all strategically important materials. A little later control of essential materials was transferred to the Board of Economic Warfare (BEW) headed by Vice President Wallace. In July 1943, the BEW was replaced by the Office of Economic Warfare (OEW). Other agencies created to administer critical materials included the Rubber Administration, the Petroleum Administration, the Solid Fuels Administration, and the Smaller War Plants Corporation.

The Office of Price Administration (OPA) was created in January 1942, to establish price ceilings and control rents. The first director was Leon Henderson, followed by Prentiss Brown and Chester Bowles. Rationing began in late 1941 starting with automobile tires followed by shoes, sugar, coffee, gasoline, meat, butter, and other foods. The main reason for rationing was to support price controls and thus check inflation. It also helped the public to develop a shared feeling of sacrifice in support of the war effort. It functioned through thousands of local rationing boards that issued the stamps needed to obtain limited quantities of the rationed products. The system worked very well until it was terminated in 1946.

Relocation: More than 25 million people relocated during the war, some because they were in the military and some in search of higher paying jobs. The farm population dwindled, although production increased, and many cities, especially those on the coast where shipbuilding boomed, exploded in size. This led to major housing and public service problems that were not always effectively handled. Associated with this significant migration, many families were dislocated or actually separated. This led to increasing instances of divorce and juvenile delinquency. Furthermore, many more women than ever before entered the workforce and some believed this was a permanent trend—although large numbers of women returned to the home at war's end.

Labor: It was imperative that the labor force be adequately managed for the duration of the war and that called for the quick and amicable settlement of disputes. Early in the war such disputes were handled by the National Defense Mediation Board (NDMB), headed by William H. Davies, but this agency failed to adequately resolve a dispute between the United Mine Workers (UMW) and the steel companies. The NDMB was replaced by the National War Labor Board (NWLB). This agency successfully handled several major disputes during the rest of the war. Overall, it can be said that while labor-management relations were by no means smooth during the war, production was seldom affected. Before 1945 it reached almost unbelievable levels.

Race Relations: Race relations during World War II often turned ugly, especially in rapidly growing industrialized cities. Blacks wanted the benefits of wartime employment as much as whites but often experienced discrimination. When the blacks threatened a march on Washington in 1941, Roosevelt responded by creating the Fair Employment Practices Commission that banned discrimination in any industry with a government contract. This helped a little, but there were still major confrontations such as the horrendous race riot in Detroit in June 1943. This tragic conflict, in which scores were killed or injured, was only quelled after the president ordered in 6,000 troops.

The worst racial indignity generated by the war was the relocation of practically all the Japanese Americans residing on the West Coast. Under this program, which began in early 1942, over 100,000 people were forced to leave their homes and businesses to be sent to camps in the interior of the country. This unspeakable act reflected the long-standing hatred of Asians by whites in the western United States. It was fueled by the media and public officials who declared that it was incumbent upon the Japanese Americans to "prove their loyalty" by submitting. The excuse was that many of these people might support Japan; however, the program was almost entirely racially motivated as demonstrated by the fact that nothing even remotely resembling these relocations was carried out against Italian Americans or German Americans. Most of the people who were affected by this utterly cruel and unnecessary program lost everything. They were not reimbursed by the government until nearly 40 years later.

Impact of U.S. Participation in World War II

The United States's participation notwithstanding, World War II was almost lost by the Allies. Only a serendipitous combination of luck, poor planning by the enemy, and extraordinary fortitude brought the war to a successful conclusion for the Western powers. In this complex and frightening process, Roosevelt played a major role. Early in the conflict his support of Britain was crucial to the survival of the island nation. Later, the sheer force of his personality and his determination helped to forge the direction of grand strategy and buoyed up morale at home.

Although Roosevelt has been criticized for his insistence on unconditional surrender and for assuming he had more influence over Stalin than was actually the case, he has been credited by most historians with exerting a predominately positive influence upon the outcome of the great conflict.

The Roosevelt Administration Legacy

On April 12, 1945, Franklin Delano Roosevelt died of a cerebral hemorrhage at his summer cottage in Warm Springs, Georgia. Harry S. Truman was inaugurated as president that evening. The entire allied world mourned his passing. In the years after his death, the rumors of Roosevelt's ill-health that had started during his last presidential campaign were discovered to have been true; Roosevelt was already suffering from serious heart and artery problems when he was inaugurated to his last term in January of 1945. This has led many to question if Roosevelt truly served the best interests of the nation by continuing as president in his weakened state. Of particular controversy is whether his weakness may have led to inappropriate U.S. concessions to the Soviet Union at the Yalta Conference, only two months before his death.

Popularity and Public Opinion

When Roosevelt assumed office in 1933 the nation awaited his actions with great anticipation. Within two years he had launched a sufficient enough attack upon the Depression to establish himself as one of the most popular presidents of all time. This resulted specifically from his New Deal relief programs such as the Civilian Conservation Corps (CCC), the Works Progress Administration (WPA), and the various loan programs for home owners and farmers that restored both hope and confidence for millions.

During the middle years of the 1930s, especially in 1937 and 1938, Roosevelt's stature declined somewhat due to controversy over his reform programs, especially those aimed at the regulation of banking and business, but his presidency was never seriously threatened. As the international crisis deepened, people rallied to his leadership and, after the Japanese attack on Pearl Harbor on December 7, 1941, his position as commander in chief was practically unquestioned. He remained popular and retained the confidence of the vast majority of people throughout the war, and when he died on April 12, 1945, mourning was practically universal.

Press and the Media

Generally Roosevelt was very popular with the press and he used the media effectively. His popularity was generated by the press conferences that began early in his administration and went on regularly until the end.

He averaged about two press conferences per week for a total of nearly 1,000 by 1945. Unlike his immediate predecessors, presidents Herbert Hoover and Calvin Coolidge, Roosevelt was friendly and forthcoming with reporters and addressed most of their important questions directly and honestly, thereby gaining the confidence of the press corps.

Roosevelt also used newsreels and radio effectively to communicate. On numerous occasions he talked directly to the American public by means of radio broadcasts that came to be known as his fireside chats. His radio talents were so good that many people had the impression that he was talking to them personally. The fireside chat technique was used when the president wanted to explain critical legislation or an important decision, such as his banking and financial policies early in the New Deal, or his Lend-Lease policy early in the war. The enormous success of the fireside chats derived from the fact that Roosevelt's voice was soothing and attractive. Moreover, he had the uncanny ability to explain complicated matters in terms that practically anyone could understand. Later presidents, notably Jimmy Carter and Bill Clinton, attempted to replicate the fireside chat technique, but with little success.

Although Roosevelt generally received support and praise from the media, there were those in the press who became his implacable foes. Among these were newspaper publishers like Robert McCormick of the Chicago *Tribune*. McCormick hated strong federal governments, government spending, and anything he termed "socialistic." Therefore, he opposed practically everything the Roosevelt administration did. He was also an avowed isolationist and accused Roosevelt of dragging the United States into war. He did, however, support the government once the war began. Publishers with similar views included William Randolph Hearst of San Francisco and Henry Luce who published *Time* and *Life* magazines.

Historians' Viewpoints

Among historians there are generally two interpretative views regarding Roosevelt's domestic policies. One school holds that the New Deal marked a new departure in American life. These historians argue that the power and activities of the government inaugurated during the 1930s marked a significant break with the past. This view is represented by Richard Hofstadter in his book, *Age of Reform* (New York: Knopf, 1995). The other school holds that Roosevelt's policies reflected continuity; that far from signaling a new departure, they simply followed a course that had been clearly marked out by earlier reformers such as the Populists and the Progressives.

With respect to Roosevelt's foreign policy the greatest controversy has always swirled around U.S. entry into World War II. One quite vocal group of historians (a minority to be sure) known as the Revisionists, have always argued that Roosevelt goaded the

Japanese into their attack on Pearl Harbor in a desperate effort to enter the conflict against the fascist dictatorships. According to their view Roosevelt believed that fighting the Nazis was absolutely imperative to save Western civilization, an opinion that many Revisionists do not share.

In opposition to the Revisionists is the majority of historians who believe that the worst that can be said is that Roosevelt and his aides bungled their negotiations with the Japanese. They argue that there is no evidence of a conspiracy.

Lasting Impact

In both foreign and domestic affairs, Roosevelt stands as one of the most influential presidents in U.S. history. In combating the Depression and the Axis powers, Roosevelt's actions continued to influence the United States long after his death.

In foreign affairs Roosevelt's legacy is supremely important. He recognized the threat of Nazi Germany to world civilization before most leaders and realized that Hitler had to be stopped. He was thwarted by the isolationist political climate of the United States, but when the war finally came he led the nation in support of the democracies and ultimately altered the course of world history. The United States emerged from the war with a powerful army and a new, more active outlook on its place in world affairs.

In terms of his domestic policy the legacy of Franklin Delano Roosevelt is considered one of the greatest contributions of any U.S. president. Roosevelt came into office in the middle of the worst economic crisis in history. While it is true that his New Deal policies failed to end the Depression, they had a lasting effect nationwide. The New Deal restored the confidence of the people in government, and many New Deal policies and agencies remain in operation today and continue to benefit millions.

Roosevelt was highly significant in a long-term economic sense, for even though his enemies called him a Socialist and a dictator, he was in fact a moderate, and his administration worked to save the capitalist system. When he came into office conditions were so bad that he could have done practically anything. He could have nationalized banking and industry, for example, but he did not. Instead he sought to establish policies that would restore the industrial and financial system to normal operations. While Roosevelt was president there also began a long and gradual process of strengthening the power of the executive branch of the government, which continued throughout the twentieth century.

While it is true that many people continue to benefit from programs initiated during the New Deal, these programs remain controversial. Many Americans still believe that the government has intruded too far into private enterprise and personal affairs. Roosevelt's policies

remain a subject of fierce debate five decades after his death, further demonstrating his tremendous impact on the nation he governed for 12 years.

Sources

Beard, Charles A. *President Roosevelt and the Coming of the War.* New Haven, Conn.: Yale, 1948.

Burns, James M. *The Lion and the Fox.* New York: Harcourt, Brace and World, 1956.

Conklin, Paul. *The New Deal.* New York: Crowell, 1967.

Dallek, Robert. *Franklin D. Roosevelt and American Foreign Policy, 1932–1945.* New York: Oxford, 1979.

DISCovering U.S. History. [CD-ROM]. Detroit.: Gale Research, 1996.

Divine, Robert. *Roosevelt and World War II.* Baltimore: Johns Hopkins, 1969.

Freidel, Frank. *Franklin D. Roosevelt.* 4 vols. Boston: Little, 1952–73.

Goldman, Eric. *Rendezvous With Destiny.* New York: Vintage, 1955.

Historic World Leaders. Gale: Detroit, 1994.

Lash, Joseph P. *Eleanor and Franklin.* New York: Norton, 1971.

Miller, Nathan. *FDR: An Intimate History.* New York: Meridian, 1983.

Morgan, Ted. *FDR: A Biography.* New York: Grafton, 1985.

Schlesinger, Arthur M., Jr. *The Age of Roosevelt.* 3 vols. Boston: Houghton, 1957–60.

Worlstetter, Roberta. *Pearl Harbour: Warning and Decision.* Stanford: 1962.

Further Reading

Cox, James M. *Journey Through My Years.* New York: Simon and Schuster, 1946.

Daniels, Josephus. *The Wilson Era.* 2 vols. Chapel Hill: University of North Carolina Press, 1944–46.

Feis, Herbert. *Churchill—Roosevelt—Stalin.* Princeton, N.J.: Princeton University Press, 1957.

Hickock, Lorena. *Reluctant First Lady.* New York: Dodd, 1962.

Hofstadter, Richard. *Age of Reform.* New York: Knopf, 1995.

Hull, Cordell. *Memoirs.* 2 vols. New York: Macmillan, 1948.

Ickes, Harold L. *The Secret Diary of Harold L. Ickes.* 3 vols. New York: Simon and Schuster, 1953–54.

Johnson, Hugh. *The Blue Eagle From Egg to Earth.* Garden City, N.Y.: Doubleday, 1935.

Lash, Joseph P. *Love, Eleanor: Eleanor Roosevelt and her Friends.* Garden City, N.Y.: Doubleday, 1982.

Moley, Raymond. *After Seven Years.* New York: Harcourt, 1966.

———.*The First New Deal.* New York: Harcourt, 1966.

Perkins, Frances. *The Roosevelt I Knew.* New York: Viking, 1946.

Roosevelt, Eleanor. *This I Remember.* New York: Harper, 1949.

Roosevelt, Franklin D. *His Personal Letters.* Edited by Elliott Roosevelt. 4 vols. New York: Duell, 1947–50.

———. *The Public Papers and Addresses of Franklin D. Roosevelt.* Edited by Samuel I. Rosenman. 3 vols. New York: Macmillan, 1938–50.

Schlesinger, Arthur M., Jr. *Crisis of the Old Order.* Boston: Houghton-Mifflin, 1957.

Tugwell, Rexford. *Roosevelt's Revolution.* New York: Macmillan, 1977.

Truman Administrations

Full name: Harry S. Truman

Personal Information:

Born: May 8, 1884

Birthplace: Lamar, Missouri

Died: December 26, 1972

Death place: Kansas City, Missouri

Burial place: Courtyard of the Truman Presidential Library, Independence, Missouri

Religion: Baptist

Spouse: Elizabeth "Bess" Virginia Wallace (m. 1919)

Children: (Mary) Margaret

Education: High school graduate, Independence, Missouri, 1901

Occupation: Bank clerk; farmer; soldier; politician; legislator

Political Party: Democratic Party

Age at Inauguration: 60 years

Biography

Harry Truman grew up among farmers in small Missouri towns. A struggling businessman during his 20s and 30s, he entered local politics in his mid-thirties and quickly became a success. Elected to the U.S. Senate in 1934, Truman supported President Franklin Roosevelt's New Deal, and developed a national reputation as a representative of the common people. Elected to serve as vice president for Roosevelt's fourth term in office, he succeeded to the presidency after Roosevelt's death in April 1945. As president, Truman became known for his tireless work, insistence on a strong U.S. foreign policy, and attempt to extend the domestic policies of the New Deal.

Early Life

Truman's father was a small farmer and livestock trader in Lamar, Missouri, in the Ozarks south of Kansas City, Missouri. The family, descended from Kentucky farmers, moved frequently in the years following Truman's birth. In 1890 they settled in the western Missouri town of Independence when he was six years old. That year he was diagnosed as nearsighted and had to wear glasses, which at the time was unusual among children. The glasses, and a severe attack of diphtheria when he was 10 (which meant that for a year he was confined to a modified baby carriage in lieu of a wheelchair), made him feel like an outsider among his peers.

Truman practiced the piano for two hours every morning as a teenager and remained an accomplished amateur pianist throughout his life. He also worked in a drugstore, but devoted as much time as possible to reading. He claimed later to have read every book in the Independence town library. There was little in his early life to predict his later political eminence.

Education

Truman attended Independence High School and graduated in 1901. Among his classmates was Bess Wallace, his future wife. He hoped to attend the U.S. Military Academy at West Point in New York for army officer training or the U.S. Naval Academy at Annapolis, Maryland, but he was barred because of his poor eyesight. Although his family could not afford to send him to college Truman continued his extensive independent reading and concentrated on history, including Edward Gibbon's *Decline and Fall of the Roman Empire* and the novels of Mark Twain.

Family Life

Truman married Elizabeth (Bess) Virginia Wallace on June 28, 1919, at the Episcopal Church in Independence, after a nine-year engagement. He had known her since their school days in Independence but Truman came from a distinctly lower social class than Bess, and had not been part of her social circle. Bess's mother, Madge Wallace, disapproved of Truman. Truman and Bess Wallace began courting in 1910, but at a distance because he was working on his family's farm outside town. She had several other suitors whereas he was devoted to Bess. In his hundreds of letters to Bess Truman throughout his life he treated her with great respect and restraint, seeing her willingness even to consider him as an act of generosity. Her rejection of his first proposal of marriage in 1911 was gentle and did not discourage him. But even after becoming an honored war veteran and rising businessman, and finally winning Bess's hand, Bess's mother remained a disapproving and intrusive presence. She lived either with them or nearby for most of the next 20 years.

Truman called his wife "The Boss" and remained very close to her throughout his life, first in Kansas City, Missouri, and later in Washington. She worked in his senatorial office after his 1934 election, and they wrote each other almost daily letters when political business forced them to spend time apart. They nicknamed the White House "the Great White Jail" and he claimed, in letters to her when she was back in Missouri, that it was haunted—that his lonely work was plagued by unexplained knocks on the door and footsteps in deserted rooms. She disliked politics, was shy, and spent long periods away from Washington, trying to stay out of the limelight.

Harry S. Truman. (The Library of Congress.)

In 1948 Truman angered architectural critics by having a balcony built off the second floor of the White House, adjacent to his study. Later that year a series of cracks in the fabric and floorboards showed that the whole executive mansion was in danger of collapsing and needed to be renovated. A government panel, the Commission on the Renovation of the Executive Mansion, studied the problem and concluded that the whole interior should be gutted and rebuilt from the ground up, which would make it uninhabitable for three or four years. Therefore, just after his reelection in 1948, Truman was obliged to move to Blair-Lee House, across Lafayette Square, until the White House renovations were finished in 1952. Often working himself to the brink of exhaustion, Truman liked to get away from Washington a few times every year and relax at the "Little White House," a navy station at Key West, Florida, or on the navy yacht *Williamsburg.*

The Trumans' only child, Margaret, was born in 1924 and grew up first in Missouri and then, after age 10, in Washington D.C. A talented musician whose first piano teacher was her father, she began a career as a singer. Her mother's shyness in Washington's public life meant that although she was only 21, Margaret often took on the role of White House hostess when her father took office. In the 1950s she abandoned music as a profession in favor of writing and became an established mystery novel writer. She married a New York journalist, Clifton Daniel, in 1956 and had four sons.

Career

The Truman family was ruined in 1902 when Harry's father lost out in grain futures speculation. The family moved to Kansas City, Missouri, and 18-year-old Harry, recently out of high school, got work as a clerk in the National Bank of Commerce. He proved effective but unambitious. Moving to another bank, Union National, he lived at a nearby boardinghouse. By an odd coincidence his roommate there, Arthur Eisenhower, was the older brother of the man who would later succeed him in the White House.

Between 1906 and 1917 Truman worked on the family's farm near Grandview, Missouri, due to another reversal in his hapless father's business fortunes. The farm, owned by his grandparents, required long hours of work every day. Truman took an interest in scientific agriculture and modern farm management methods, kept careful records of his work, and gradually increased crop yields. Ambitious and energetic, he also took on the job of local postmaster. Following his father's death in 1914 he accepted sole care of the farm. He was able to afford a car in 1911 (still a luxury in those early days) and by 1917 was prosperous enough that Bess Wallace accepted his second proposal of marriage.

Always gregarious and a "joiner," Truman became a Freemason in 1908. The Freemasons, originally a semi-secret fraternal society of Protestant men, had become more of a businessmen's social club by the early twentieth century, although they retained a series of elaborate rituals for initiation. Truman organized a new Masonic lodge in Grandview, Missouri, became its first master, and kept up his membership throughout his later life.

Military

Truman also joined an artillery battery of the National Guard in Kansas City, Missouri, in 1905, and continued, after his move to the farm, to spend a few weeks each summer on maneuvers at Camp Girardeau, Missouri. Truman's military ambitions intensified when the United States entered World War I (1914–18) in 1917, and he volunteered for service. By then he was 33 but his experience in the National Guard made him valuable to the army. He was elected lieutenant (later promoted to captain) and trained at Camp Doniphan, Oklahoma, before being sent to Europe, where he served as an artillery officer on the western front. The experience gave him an aversion to regular army officers whom he regarded as fanatics for meaningless details of discipline, spit and polish, and slavish adherence to the rule book for its own sake. Like most reservists he approached military life democratically rather than autocratically.

Truman distinguished himself in the war, entering combat for the first time in September 1918 and staying in action with his battery until the armistice of November 11 that year. His unit, the 129th Field Artillery, spent five months in France after the armistice before going home on the *Zeppelin,* a former German ship acquired by the United States. He was demobilized in May 1919.

Business and Politics

Like his father, Truman was unlucky in business. He lost out in a speculative zinc mining venture in 1915 and, the next year, in an attempt to drill for oil. After World War I he and an army friend, Eddie Jacobson, set up a men's clothing and haberdashery store in Kansas City, Missouri, but, after a promising start in 1919, it collapsed during a business recession in 1922. After the failure of his shop he was entitled to declare bankruptcy but, feeling responsible to his creditors, he refused to do so and worked throughout the next 15 years to repay his debts in full. Jacobson became a traveling shirt salesman, but the two men remained friends. Jacobson, who was Jewish, would later encourage President Truman to recognize the new state of Israel, which Truman did within minutes of its formal independence in 1948.

Among Truman's acquaintances was Kansas City's Democratic political boss Thomas J. Pendergast. "Boss" Pendergast had a well-deserved reputation for political corruption. His political "machine" worked sometimes by bribing voters directly, sometimes by exchanging practical favors for votes, and sometimes by stuffing the ballot box, creating fictitious votes for his candidates. Despite this political chicanery Pendergast proved a good friend to Truman, who returned the favor. His machine in Kansas City was supported mainly by Catholics, and he understood that Truman, a rock-ribbed rural Protestant, a Freemason, and a war veteran, could extend the reach of the machine into the surrounding countryside. With Pendergast's help Truman was elected administrator of Jackson County, which includes Kansas City, in 1922, taking this first step into politics at age 38. Despite his official title, "judge," he was not a lawyer. He played a leading role over the next decade in planning, financing, and building western Missouri's road network. He lost his reelection bid in 1924 but won again in 1926 (this time as presiding judge), and never again lost an election. He continued this work for the county through the late 1920s and early 1930s, renovating the courthouse, building a new hospital and prison, and becoming federal reemployment director for Missouri when President Franklin Roosevelt's New Deal began in the spring of 1933.

Senator

In 1934 Pendergast helped secure Truman's victory in the state Democratic primary over two rivals and then his election to the U.S. Senate over the Republican incumbent, Roscoe Patterson. Now 50, Truman was leaving Missouri for the first time, other than his year in France, and moving into the sphere of national politics. He never forgot the importance of local political support, however, and he never tried to distance himself from his roots.

In his first six-year term in Washington he was a member of the Interstate Commerce Committee, which oversaw federal regulation of railroads, shipping, and road transport, and of the Senate Appropriations Committee, which had suddenly gained in importance because it was responsible for allocating tax money to the big New Deal projects. A supporter of the New Deal, with its suspicion of greedy big businesspeople whom Roosevelt nicknamed the "economic royalists," he undertook an investigation of U.S. railroads' financial structure in 1937. Railroads, central to U.S. transport and commerce in the days before civil aviation and interstate highways, were widely suspected of illegal monopoly practices. Truman's report urged tighter political control of railroads, and he joined Senator Burton Wheeler of Montana in introducing legislation to assure it, which Roosevelt signed into law in 1940. His campaign for reelection in 1940 proved difficult, but he was again able to overcome Democratic rivals in the primary and narrowly beat out his Republican opponent, Manvel Davis, at the polls. In that election Roosevelt ran a successful, precedent-breaking bid to be elected president for the third time.

Truman gained a wider reputation as the United States was drawn into World War II (1939–45) the following year as a result of the Japanese attack on Pearl Harbor. He headed a Senate special committee to investigate the National Defense Program, designed to prevent wasteful spending practices in defense industries and war profiteering. His sensible reports and regulation proposals made him steadily more popular among the public; his face appeared on the cover of *Time* magazine in March 1943, and his 19-year-old daughter Margaret was invited to christen the battleship *Missouri* when it was launched in January 1944.

Vice President

His reputation as a defender of ordinary citizens' rights and as a protector of taxpayers' dollars made Truman an attractive running mate to Franklin Roosevelt in the presidential election of 1944. The vice president of the last four years, Henry Wallace, proved unacceptable to Roosevelt because he lacked political skill and was disliked by most senior Democrats in Washington. Truman's newfound popularity made him a useful compromise figure to Democratic leaders who realized that Roosevelt might not survive a fourth term and that the vice president was likely to become president. Despite Truman's reluctance (he was now 60 and enjoyed life as a senator), he was nominated at the Chicago convention that summer. He campaigned hard by train because Roosevelt was too sick to travel, and the two were elected in November.

In January 1945 his old friend and patron Thomas Pendergast, recently released from jail after serving a term for tax evasion, died. Truman flew in a government aircraft to Kansas City, Missouri, for the funeral despite the fears of some Democratic strategists that it

was unwise for the new vice president to align himself so closely with a figure synonymous with the old style of corrupt urban politics. He found his work as vice president largely that of a figurehead and far less taxing and tiring than his years of investigative work in the Senate.

President

Only 82 days after Roosevelt's fourth inauguration, during which Truman and his chief rarely met, the president died on April 12, 1945. Thus the man from Missouri, who had no prior experience in foreign affairs, was left to bring a world war to an end. Truman presided over the Allies' victory in the European theater of war and announced the Germans' surrender on May 8, 1945. He also supervised the San Francisco, California, conference at which the United Nations (UN) was founded that spring and early summer. The war against Japan was not yet finished, and his most momentous decision of 1945 was to use the new atomic bomb, just developed in secret, against the cities of Hiroshima and Nagasaki. They had the effect of forcing a Japanese surrender.

Despite victory on both fronts, Truman's diplomatic situation remained fraught with difficulty. In the immediate postwar years he realized that the Soviet Union, until recently the United States's powerful ally, was determined to control the nations of Eastern Europe rather than return them to their pre-Hitler governments. Tension over Europe, over whether nuclear information should be shared, over Communist militancy in Western Europe, and over the Soviets' exclusion from the reconstruction of Eastern Asia and Japan, led to the rapid deterioration of Soviet-U.S. relations and the start of the Cold War.

Second Administration

Truman was elected president in 1948, winning an upset victory over Republican New York governor Thomas Dewey. In pursuit of his new policy of "containment" (preventing Communism from spreading any further than its 1945 boundaries), Truman committed U.S. forces in the Korean War (1950–53), which broke out in the summer of 1950, and fought there against North Korean and Chinese Communist troops until after the end of his administration. At home he imposed loyalty programs on all government officials but still had to deal with Republican allegations that he was "soft on Communism" and knowingly harbored traitors at high levels of his government.

In domestic affairs Truman supervised the reconversion of the U.S. economy to peacetime conditions (albeit at a high level of military readiness), and was relieved to find that the United States did not revert to the depression conditions that had dogged the nation throughout the 1930s. He was successful in maintaining many of the social programs and policies Roosevelt had begun but yielded to a powerful Republican attack

Fast Fact

In 1971 the U.S. House of Representatives considered bestowing the Congressional Medal of Honor (the nation's highest military award) on former president Truman. Truman declined the offer, as he did not feel he had done anything to deserve it.

(Source: Barbara Seuling. *The Last Cow on the White House Lawn & Other Little-Known Facts About the Presidency*, 1978.)

on trade unions called the Taft-Hartley Act of 1946 (*See also*, Truman and Congress). He was unsuccessful in advancing an ambitious new social agenda, the Fair Deal, because of Republican opposition in Congress and because of poorly-substantiated allegations that his advisers were accepting bribes in return for federal contracts.

Post-presidential Years

After deciding not to run for the presidency again, Truman retired from office in January 1953. He then set to work on his memoirs, which were published as *Year of Decisions* (1955) and *Years of Trial and Hope* (1956). He also supervised the building of the Truman Library in Independence, Missouri, making it one of the first presidential libraries (whose role in preserving political records was endorsed by Congress in 1955). He remained active in Democratic politics, supporting Adlai Stevenson's unsuccessful bid for office in 1956 against Dwight D. Eisenhower and John F. Kennedy's successful bid in 1960. The Kennedys invited him to a White House reception in 1961, where he was treated as the grand old man of the Democratic Party and entertained the guests on the White House's Steinway grand piano (which was later given to him by President Nixon). An enthusiastic supporter of President Lyndon Johnson's "Great Society" programs in the 1960s, he was the first American to be enrolled in the Medicare program when Johnson signed it into law at the Truman Library in 1965. Truman died in 1972 at the age of 88, in a Kansas City, Missouri, hospital. He was survived by his wife Bess, who died at the age of 97 in 1982.

The Harry S. Truman Administrations

Harry Truman inherited the presidency from Franklin D. Roosevelt just before the end of World War II (1939–45), and made the fateful decision, three months later, to use atomic bombs to end the war against Japan. He helped create the United States's superpower role in the Cold War and led the nation into the Korean War (1950–53), while maintaining the tradition of Roosevelt's New Deal in his domestic "Fair Deal" program.

Truman Becomes President

After presiding in the Senate on Thursday, April 12, 1945, as it debated a water rights treaty with Mexico, Vice President Truman was summoned to the White House by Steve Early, President Franklin Roosevelt's press secretary. On his arrival Roosevelt's wife, Eleanor Roosevelt, told him the president, who had been in office since 1933, had died. Truman at once telephoned his wife and daughter, chief justice of the Supreme Court Harlan Stone, and the members of the Roosevelt cabinet who were in Washington at the time. Then, in the White House cabinet room, he was sworn in as president at 7:09 in the evening, under a portrait of Woodrow Wilson.

The Campaign of 1948

The Democratic Party was subject to severe stresses in 1948. Its left wing, led by Henry Wallace, who had been Franklin Roosevelt's vice president until 1944, believed that Truman was being unnecessarily confrontational toward the Soviet Union, and that a more peaceful resolution of the postwar situation was possible. Wallace decided to run as an independent candidate for president and won an eager following from U.S. radicals and the Democratic Left. At the same time the Democratic Party's southern white conservatives were dissatisfied by Truman's concessions to African Americans, particularly his executive orders for the desegregation of the armed forces and the federal government (*See also*, Domestic Issues). Under the leadership of South Carolina governor Strom Thurmond many of them broke away from the party and ran Thurmond for president as a states's rights or "Dixiecrat" candidate. Another group of Democrats, the Americans for Democratic Action (ADA), feeling sure that Truman would lose, tried unsuccessfully to replace him with World War II general Dwight Eisenhower.

Truman campaigned hard, concentrating his fire against the obstructive Congress and even called it back into an extraordinary session in July 1948, challenging it to make good on its promises to solve the domestic inflation and housing crises. Nicknamed "The Turnip Congress" because it met on the day Missourian farmers tra-

Administration

Administration Dates

April 12, 1945–January 20, 1949
January 20, 1949–January 20, 1953

Vice President

Alben William Barkley (1949–53)

Cabinet

Secretary of State

Edward R. Stettinius Jr. (1944–45)
James F. Byrnes (1945–47)
George C. Marshall (1947–49)
Dean G. Acheson (1949–53)

Secretary of the Treasury

Henry Morgenthau Jr. (1934–45)
Frederick M. Vinson (1945–46)
John W. Snyder (1946–53)

Secretary of War

Henry L. Stimson (1940–45)
Robert P. Patterson (1945–47)
Kenneth C. Royall (1947)

Attorney General

Francis B. Biddle (1941–45)
Thomas C. Clark (1945–49)
James H. McGrath (1949–52)
James P. McGranery (1952–53)

Secretary of the Navy

James V. Forrestal (1944–47)

Secretary of the Interior

Harold L. Ickes (1933–46)
Julius A. Krug (1946–49)
Oscar L. Chapman (1949–53)

Secretary of Agriculture

Claude R. Wickard (1940–45)
Clinton P. Anderson (1945–48)
Charles F. Brannan (1948–53)

Secretary of Commerce

Henry A. Wallace (1945–46)
William A. Harriman (1946–48)
Charles Sawyer (1948–53)

Secretary of Labor

Frances Perkins (1945)
Lewis B. Schwellenbach (1945–48)
Maurice J. Tobin (1948–53)

Secretary of Defense

James V. Forrestal (1947–49)
Louis A. Johnson (1949–50)
George C. Marshall (1950–51)
Robert A. Lovett (1951–53)

---

ditionally planted their turnips, and given insufficient time to carry out its members' plans, it passed no legislation. The session seemed, to Truman's opponents, no more than a cheap political ploy. Undaunted by criticism, Truman hit back by claiming that Republicans were the party of the privileged few, and were responsible for housing shortages, inflation, and other woes.

The Republican Party, delighted at the disarray of its foes, anticipated an easy victory for its candidate Thomas Dewey, the governor of New York, who had lost to Roosevelt in 1944. Polls and pundits were virtually unanimous that Truman would lose, and the *Chicago Daily Tribune* even ran as its November 4, 1948, headline "Dewey Defeats Truman" before the votes had all been counted. The headline was wrong. Truman held on to the presidency in the biggest election surprise of the century. A famous news photograph shows Truman gleefully waving a copy of the November 4 *Tribune,* with its

false headline and beaming at the knowledge that he was assured another four years in office. His running mate, Kentucky senator Alben Barkley, kept most of the "Solid South" in the Truman camp (the segregationist Dixiecrats gained only one million votes against Truman's 24 million), and his own vigorous campaigning held together Roosevelt's New Deal coalition. To complete Truman's triumph, the Democrats regained control of both houses of Congress.

Truman's Advisers

Truman chose some of the most talented people in Washington as his political advisers, and they lent their prestige to his administration. By contrast he stayed with people he had known throughout his life to work on his

President Truman enjoys a laugh over an early election night edition of the Chicago Tribune, *which erroneously proclaimed that he had lost the 1948 presidential election to New York governor Thomas E. Dewey. Truman rallied to win the election after initial polls indicated that he was headed for defeat.* (AP/Wide World Photos. Reproduced by permission.)

domestic staff, of whom some were unsuitable while others found the temptations of high office more than they could resist.

Among his political advisers Secretary of State George Marshall was outstanding. He joined the administration after two legacies from Roosevelt, Edward Stettinius and James Byrnes, left the office in quick succession. Marshall, who had been chief of staff of the army throughout World War II (1939–45), despised electoral politics, and had a reputation for absolute integrity. This quality helped him assemble the congressional votes to assure support for the Truman Doctrine, which structured U.S. policy in the early Cold War years, and the Marshall Plan, to aid the postwar recovery of Europe's industrial economy. Retiring in early 1949, at the beginning of Truman's second administration, Marshall was called back into service as secretary of defense during the Korean War crisis of 1950, and continued to enjoy Truman's absolute confidence.

Clark Clifford, special counsel to the president, and Dean Acheson, Marshall's successor as secretary of state, also became close and trusted confidantes of the president, and were present at nearly all the crucial policy meetings of his second administration. Acheson had had a long career in the State Department during the New Deal years of Franklin Roosevelt. He was a career diplomat, extraordinarily well educated, experienced, and

familiar with every detail of U.S. foreign policy. He was a worthy successor to Marshall.

Truman's domestic staff were mostly Missourians. Press secretary Charles Ross was an old school friend from Independence who had gone on to a distinguished career in journalism at the *St. Louis Post-Dispatch* and had won a Pulitzer Prize in 1931. He wielded a significant influence over Truman, moderating his outbursts against opponents and often restraining the president from sending angry letters he had drafted in the heat of controversies. The day after Ross's sudden death from a heart attack in 1950 Truman wrote a bitterly angry and threatening letter to music critic Paul Hume, who had criticized his daughter's singing. He then sent it, to the embarrassment of other advisers. Their mutual friend George Elsey remarked, "Charlie Ross would never have let the Paul Hume letter get out . . . he was a calming fine influence on Truman, a tempering influence" (McCullough, p. 828).

Military aide Harry H. Vaughan was an old army friend who had stayed in touch with Truman through the interwar years and had been his executive secretary while Truman was in the Senate. Vaughan's frequent indiscretions, salty humor, shabby appearance, and frequent wisecracks caused adverse publicity, and many Democrats urged Truman to fire him. Truman believed in standing by his friends, however, and refused. Republicans took advantage of allegations in 1949 that Vaughan was corrupt, and had sold his White House influence to lobbyists and accepted a deep freezer for himself and one for Bess Truman in return for political favors. A Senate investigation was unable to prove any wrongdoing by Vaughan, but the Republicans wove insinuations of corruption around Vaughan in the election campaign of 1952.

Appointments secretary Matthew J. Connelly, another trusted adviser, who controlled access to the president in person and by telephone, also drew allegations of corruption and was indicted by a federal grand jury in 1951 on charges of corruption, bribery, and perjury. He was convicted for his involvement in a tax evasion scheme and for accepting gifts of clothing and oil company shares in exchange for influence. He served six months of a two-year prison sentence after the end of the Truman administration. Truman, by then out of office, spoke at fund-raising dinners to help pay his legal bills.

Truman and Congress

The Congress Truman inherited with his presidency had Democratic majorities in both houses. Congress, after 12 years of the New Deal and World War II (1939–45), often had been subservient to the centralizing, power-building government of Franklin Roosevelt. It was eager to regain the initiative many of its members felt they had lost. It began by passing the Legislative Reorganization Act of 1946, giving itself new investigative powers. These powers were used in the following years to investigate Communism, organized crime, and the controversy over the dismissal of General MacArthur in the Korean War (1950–53) (*See also,* Foreign Issues).

Truman, despite his 10 years as a well-liked senator, endured strained relations with Congress during his entire term. His administration encompassed the Seventy-ninth, Eightieth, Eighty-first, and Eighty-second Congresses, and even though the first, third, and fourth Congresses had Democratic majorities, this did not make it any easier for the president. He eventually used the presidential veto 83 times, the third most frequent of any president in history, and had 11 of those vetoes overruled by Congress.

The midterm elections of 1946, the first since Truman's inauguration, returned big Republican majorities to both houses. The Republicans hoped to dismantle the apparatus of the New Deal and put a stop to inflation and labor militancy. Among the new Democratic members was John F. Kennedy, a Massachusetts freshman, later to be the United States's 35th president. Among the new Republicans were California freshman Richard Nixon, later the United States's 37th president, and Wisconsin junior senator Joseph R. McCarthy, soon to be scourge of the Truman administration's anticommunist policy.

This Congress's most dramatic legislation was the Taft-Hartley Act of 1947, which aimed to curb the power of trade unions. Trade unions had grown rapidly in the New Deal and war years and called a wave of strikes for better pay and conditions once the wartime emergency had ended. The act included provisions for the president to order "cooling off" periods when a strike was threatened in a vital national industry, and for legal injunctions to prevent strikes. Truman vetoed the first version of the act but a second passed quickly through both houses of Congress over his veto, with conservative southern Democrats swelling the Republican majority.

The Eightieth Congress also passed two tax-reduction acts, both of which Truman vetoed, fearing that they would worsen an already serious inflation problem. It did everything it could to prevent his further extension of the New Deal's social welfare legislation and to begin rolling it back. Sixty of Truman's 83 vetoes came against Eightieth Congress legislation in 1947 and 1948.

In his election campaign of 1948 Truman artfully made "The do-nothing Eightieth Congress" shoulder the blame for such domestic and foreign crises as the worsening Cold War and the continued problem of inflation, by calling it into an emergency summer session that he knew would be too short for any real accomplishments (*See also,* Truman Becomes President). Throughout his second term in office he enjoyed Democratic majorities in both houses. They were, however, dependent on the votes of conservative southerners who looked askance at Truman's New Deal liberalism and support for civil rights. He found them almost as intractable as the Republicans of the Eightieth Congress. In fact Truman rarely enjoyed support on Capitol Hill except on his foreign policy measures, which won a large measure of bipartisan support once he had convinced Republican senators Arthur Vandenberg of Michigan and Robert Taft of Ohio that a permanent U.S. role in Europe was essential. Even on foreign policy he angered Congress by neglecting to ask it for a declaration of war before committing U.S. troops to Korea in the summer of 1950.

Among the preeminent figures in his Congresses were Democrats Sam Rayburn of Texas, Speaker of the House, and Alben Barkley of Kentucky, the Senate Majority leader who became Truman's vice president during his second term. On the Republican side there was Arthur Vandenberg and Robert Taft, senators whose cooperation with Truman's foreign policy enabled key Cold War policies: containment, the Marshall Plan, NATO, and the Rio Pact to be approved in the upper house (*See also,* Foreign Issues).

Truman and the Judiciary

The Supreme Court had suffered a scare in the mid 1930s when President Roosevelt threatened to increase the number of justices from nine to 15 if that was what it took to get judicial support for his New Deal programs. The Constitution did not specify any particular number of Supreme Court justices, but nine had been the standard for over one hundred years by then. The public outcry at this violation of tradition led Roosevelt to abandon the plan. Meanwhile one judge, Justice Owen Roberts, had begun voting to uphold the New Deal innovations, prompting the jest: "A switch in time saves nine." Truman, inheriting the Roosevelt Court, was able to make four appointments: Harold Burton, Frederick Vinson, Thomas Clark, and Sherman Minton. Burton was a Republican and the other three were Democrats, but all were conservative in outlook and deplored judicial activism. Hugo Black and William O. Douglas were the most liberal members of the Court but could rarely find majorities while Vinson was chief justice (between 1946 and 1953).

Ironically, however, conservative decisions do not always have conservative consequences, as became clear in the Court's civil rights decisions during Truman's administration. The Court found in *Morgan v. Virginia* (1946) that state-enforced segregation in interstate commerce was unconstitutional. In *Shelley v. Kraemer* (1948) it added that restrictive housing covenants (designed to prevent African Americans from buying houses in white neighborhoods) were also unconstitutional. Three cases relating to higher education also rejected southern states's attempts to segregate graduate and professional schools, and paved the way for the famous *Brown v. Board of Education of Topeka, Kansas* decision of 1954, which outlawed racial segregation at all levels of education. These decisions, along with Truman's desegregation of the United States's armed forces in 1948, laid the foundation for the more dramatic civil rights era of the 1950s and 1960s.

In the tense political atmosphere of early Cold War Washington, civil liberties and First Amendment rights often came into conflict with McCarthyism, the reckless allegation of Communist influence in the government, and loyalty programs that required oaths swearing allegiance to the U.S. government. The Court also ruled that the Taft-Hartley Act of 1947 did not violate the Constitution when it required noncommunist pledges from trade union members in *American Communication Association v. Douds* (1950). It added that loyalty oaths for public employees were also constitutional in *Adler v. Board of Education* (1952). In two church-state cases, *Everson v. Board of Education* (1947) and *McCollum v. Board of Education* (1948) it expanded the principle of a "wall of separation" between religion and public education by forbidding state subsidies for children attending religious schools and by denying religious groups the right to hold classes in public school buildings.

In 1952 the Korean War (1950–53) prompted a judicial crisis. Steelworkers were demanding higher wages while owners, who wanted to raise the price of steel in violation of price-control legislation, denied that Congress was entitled to set prices. Truman sympathized with

the workers and believed that the owners were using the dispute as an excuse for profiteering. With the war in progress, however, the president could not afford to have a major strike in this basic industry. After 80 days of anxious negotiations Truman, claiming that he was justified by his right to use emergency powers to protect national security, authorized government seizure of the steel factories. Supreme Court justices Vinson and Clark (Truman's former attorney general) both advised Truman that the seizure was constitutional.

The steelmill owners reacted by seeking a legal injunction against the government, which they received. The Supreme Court went on to uphold the injunction in its six-to-three decision in *Youngstown Sheet and Tube Company v. Sawyer.* The Court ruled that the president was not constitutionally entitled to seize the industry as he did because his action, legislative as much as executive, violated the principle of the "Separation of Powers." They also rejected the idea that the Constitution's granting of emergency powers to the president during wartime extended to the ability to seize private property to settle a domestic dispute. Truman noted indignantly that Clark, despite his earlier advice, now voted with the majority and against Vinson. With the government excluded, a strike began and dragged on for seven costly weeks. When the workers finally agreed to return, it was with a pay raise of 21 cents per hour rather than the 26 cents Truman had favored.

Changes in the U.S. Government

The rapid escalation of the Cold War led to the expansion of the Department of Defense and the creation of a National Security Council in 1947 to coordinate all defense-related activities and agencies. By the same legislation the World War II Office of Strategic Services (OSS) was reorganized and became the Central Intelligence Agency (CIA), charged with maintaining U.S. interests throughout the world, covertly if necessary. In its first years the CIA tried to boost anticommunist political factions in Italian elections, where Truman feared the possibility of a Communist victory, and it funded U.S. anticommunist organizations such as the Congress for Cultural Freedom.

The National Defense Act of 1949 tried to bring order to intense rivalries among the military services by creating a chairman of the Joint Chiefs of Staff. In the preceding years, for example, the U.S. Air Force had argued that it deserved the maximum of research and development funds to perfect nuclear weapon delivery systems, while the navy argued that new generations of ships were imperative to U.S. safety. Each lobbied hard against the others, and the lack of a supreme arbiter had made the arguments drag on inconclusively. Truman's first appointee to that post was a fellow Missourian, World War II army veteran General Omar Bradley, who took office in time to preside over administration of the Korean War crisis (1950–53) and supported Truman's controversial decision to dismiss General MacArthur (*See also,* Foreign Issues).

Truman appointed former Republican president Herbert Hoover to lead a commission on restructuring the federal government. Its report of 1949 recommended simplification of the complex federal government structure and creation of unified departments of Labor, Housing, Transportation, and Urban Development. Most of its proposals were carried out in the following years. Truman also approved the Twenty-second Amendment, which passed through Congress in 1947 and was ratified by two-thirds of the states by 1951. It specified that no one after Truman could serve as president for more than two terms. Franklin Roosevelt's decision to run for a third and then a fourth term in 1940 and 1944 had been controversial, and this amendment guaranteed that no successor would preside for more than eight years. The related Presidential Succession Act specified that if a president died or left office prematurely, he would be succeeded first by the vice president and then by the Speaker of the House of Representatives.

The federal government was swept by fears of espionage during the Truman years. He initiated loyalty policies in early 1947, ordering all federal employees to swear oaths that they were not Communists or conspirators against the government. Federal employees with radical pasts, particularly those who had been Communists, lost their jobs and did not always know who had testified against them. This situation raised serious questions of due process—the right of all accused men and women to a fair trial in open court—and civil liberty—the First Amendment right to hold any opinions and express them openly. In a few instances, these purges cost the government some of its most experienced people, such as the Far East experts at the State Department, and may have affected policy decisions over the Korean War and, later, the United States's involvement in Vietnam (1959–75).

One useful and lasting reform was the creation of the Council of Economic Advisers in 1946. This is a body of experts ready to provide the president with impartial advice on economic issues and to suggest ways to promote economic growth and avoid a recurrence of the Great Depression. Its creation signaled the federal government's acceptance of the principle that one of its tasks is to guide the economy rather than leaving it to the mercies of the free market.

Domestic Issues

Soon after Truman became president, the U.S. economy went through an immense transition from emergency wartime production of munitions to peacetime production of consumer goods. This process of "conversion"

brought benefits to millions of people, who were able to spend money they had earned and saved in the high-employment, high-wage years of the war, when consumer goods were unavailable. Much of the population wanted to preserve the gains it had made in basic social welfare during the New Deal years but feared the return of depression conditions now that the war was over. These years saw the start of the "baby boom" and the anxious pursuit of suspected Communists, who replaced Nazis as the United States's new presumptive enemy.

Truman presided over the period of rapid economic growth as the United States became the world's first consumer-oriented affluent society. The Depression did not return but growth was uneven and was accompanied by social stresses, frequent strikes by labor unions, high rates of inflation, rapid population growth, and a severe housing shortage. These economic challenges were coupled with continued agitation over civil rights for African Americans and widespread fears of Communist subversion.

Labor

Truman's worst economic problem grew out of wartime conditions, when U.S. industrial might had been dedicated to war production and consumer goods were rationed. The end of the war meant the end of rationing, but industry could not convert to consumer production overnight. Scarcities drove up consumer goods prices, which pleased manufacturers but hurt ordinary citizens. Inflation in turn led to wage demands from unionized workers. Strikes broke out, first by steel workers in the fall of 1945, then by railroad workers in May 1946, and finally by mine workers throughout that summer. Truman settled the steel strike by offering the workers an 18 1/2 cent per hour raise, which then became the demand of all other dissatisfied workers and tended to stoke the inflationary furnace.

Railroad Strike of 1946

Although Truman, as a New Dealer, had enjoyed good relations with organized labor—which had benefited from Roosevelt's policies—he soon showed that he was willing to act decisively against strikers. When the railroad unions called a strike in May 1946, paralyzing the entire economy, he responded by declaring in a nationwide broadcast that he would order the army to take over the railroads if the strikers did not return to work. He understood that lack of rail transportation would create a nationwide emergency since nearly all commodities traveling long distances still went by rail. Speaking to Congress the next day he added that he would ask for emergency legislation to draft the railroad workers themselves into the army and put them under military discipline. As his speech came to an end an aide hurried in with news that the union leaders, learning of these threats, had finally agreed to Truman's proposed pay settlement. Congress cheered Truman and learned from the episode that he was as willing as any union leader to play political hardball. The House passed the emergency legislation, even though it was no longer needed. The Senate, however, held back, aware of the grave constitutional implications of such a step, which would have, in effect, given the president legislative as well as executive authority.

Lewis Leads Mine Workers' Strike

John L. Lewis, the charismatic leader of the Union of Mine Workers (UMW) frequently came into conflict with Truman. Nearly every year of the Truman administration the president and the union chief were in conflict. In 1946, for example, Truman ordered the secretary of the interior, Julius Krug, to take over U.S. coal mines to avert a strike and to run them under federal government authority. Truman's reasoning was that since coal was essential to the whole economy and could be regarded as a strategic resource it was within his authority. Miners faced some of the worst working conditions and greatest health threats of any workers in the United States and Krug, recognizing the truth of Lewis's complaints against the mine owners, accepted the principle that long-term health and pension benefits should be negotiated as part of mine workers' contracts. Details of the contract still had to be hammered out in hard bargaining sessions, with the government as an arbitrator. When Lewis resumed the strike that November, Krug took him to court for violating an injunction. Lewis was convicted of contempt and was forced to pay a personal fine of $10,000 and a union fine of $3.5 million. Most Americans not involved in coal mining detested Lewis. Truman, aware of the fact, often profited from his confrontations with the union leader, since they enabled him to deny Republican claims that he was unwilling to stand up to the power of organized labor. Later in the early 1950s Truman sought to support steel workers but ran into opposition (*See also,* Truman and the Judiciary).

GIs Return to Civilian Life

The rapid demobilization of soldiers at the end of World War II (1939–45) was another source of anxiety. Many of the soldiers remembered the Great Depression conditions of the 1930s in which they had grown-up and feared that the end of the war would mean a return to depression and unemployment. In fact the dramatic redistribution of incomes during the high-wage war years had strengthened the economy's foundation. Pent-up consumer demand and the industrial demands made by the early Cold War combined to prevent a new depression. Demobilized GIs benefited from a wide array of advantages legislated on their behalf during the war: the right to subsidized college education, the right to low-interest loans for housing, and advantages in gaining civil service employment. The fact that 16.5 million Americans had been in uniform at some time during the war made them a potentially powerful lobby. Truman, himself a veteran and a member of the American Legion (a veter-

ans' organization), was sympathetic to their needs and did all he could to smooth their return to civilian life, though the buoyancy of the postwar economy was decisive in aiding him.

Civil Rights

Truman's ancestors had fought for the Confederacy and his mother supported segregation. Nevertheless Truman believed that U.S. race relations, especially in the South, where African American war veterans returning home were lynched in a series of notorious incidents in 1945 and 1946, should be reformed. Racism as official policy in the South mocked the United States's human rights rhetoric at the newly formed United Nations (UN), and gave leverage to Soviets' anti-U.S. propaganda. He appointed a commission in December 1946 to investigate civil rights and supported its report, *To Secure These Rights,* when it was published in October 1947. It recommended an end to the poll tax (a fee that is required in order to vote), desegregation of the military, anti-lynching laws, and a permanent Fair Employment Practices Commission. Endorsing the report was a daring step because Truman needed not only the votes of African Americans to be reelected in 1948 but also the votes of the "Solid South," the traditionally Democratic white power structure of the southern segregated states.

By executive order Truman created a Committee on Equality of Treatment and Opportunity in the Armed Forces, which upheld the principle of racial integration for reasons of efficiency and humaneness, and overcame strong opposition within the services (especially the army and the navy) to abolish segregation and African American enlistment quotas. As a result the U.S. military fought with desegregated units for the first time when it entered combat in Korea.

Truman's support for civil rights reforms, strongly encouraged by his adviser Clark Clifford, led to a protest movement by Democratic white segregationist southerners who refused to vote for a pro-integration Democratic president. Known by the media as the "Dixiecrats," they ran Strom Thurmond of South Carolina for president in 1948 instead of Truman. The Dixiecrat votes Truman lost were offset by the praise he won from civil rights groups and by his assurance of nearly all African American votes cast in that election. After the election congressional conservatives blocked passage of most civil rights legislation, but Truman's actions had laid the groundwork for the more radical civil rights movement of the 1950s and 1960s.

The Fair Deal

After his reelection in 1948 and before his reinauguration, Truman declared his policy of a Fair Deal in his State of the Union address to Congress. In language reminiscent of Roosevelt's New Deal, Truman proposed an ambitious series of social reforms. Most of the Fair

Biography:

Douglas MacArthur

General (1880–1964) General Douglas MacArthur was 65 years old when he accepted a Japanese surrender on the deck of the USS *Missouri* in Tokyo Bay on September 2, 1945. This dramatic moment capped, but did not end, a long distinguished U.S. military service career. With World War II ended, President Harry Truman appointed MacArthur supreme commander of the Allied Power in Japan. To the astonishment of many observers, the hardened military general's occupation was surprisingly benevolent and encouraged religious freedom, civil liberties, land reform, emancipation of women, and formation of trade unions. When fighting flared in Korea in 1950, President Truman appointed MacArthur as commander of the United Nations' forces. When he was defeated in battle by intervening Chinese armies, an angered MacArthur made public statements advocating a policy change that would extend the war into China. President Truman, furious over MacArthur's open statements that contradicted public policy, relieved the general of his command in 1951. Nonetheless, MacArthur

returned to the United States a hero and public sentiment for President Truman plummeted. MacArthur presented his case before a joint session of Congress and testified at great length before the Senate Armed Services and Foreign Relations committees. MacArthur then toured the country blasting President Truman and his administration for selling out to communism. When President-elect Dwight Eisenhower consulted MacArthur for his sug-

gestions on ending the Korean War, MacArthur recommended a peace conference which, if unsuccessful, would be followed by widespread nuclear bombing of North Korea and China with the, "sowing of fields of suitable radioactive materials." MacArthur was not consulted again.

Deal proposals were defeated in Congress, which contained many conservative Democrats unsympathetic to Truman's domestic liberalism. One proposal was a national health insurance scheme comparable to Britain's new National Health Service. The American Medical Association (AMA) lobbied against it as a socialist measure and intimidated many congresspeople into blocking it. A second proposal was a program of federal aid to education, which ran into religious controversy on the question of supporting Catholic parochial schools as well as those run by the states. A third proposal, also defeated, was for a powerful Federal Employment Practices Commission (FEPC) to assure equal access to work for African American citizens. One provision which did succeed was the extension of Social Security benefits. The average benefit was almost doubled, and another 10 million people were added to the list of beneficiaries. Truman was also able to get congressional assent to an ambitious public housing scheme, at a time when housing was in very short supply, and an increase in the national minimum wage to 75 cents per hour.

Assassination Attempt

While the White House was being renovated Truman was living at nearby Blair House. On November 1, 1950, two Puerto Rican nationalists, resentful that their home territory belonged to the United States, broke into the

house and attempted to shoot him while he was taking an early afternoon nap. Due to the quick response of Truman's bodyguards, both Griselio Torresola and Oscar Collazo were shot and the president unharmed, although one of his bodyguards, Leslie Coffelt, was killed in the rapid exchange of fire, and two others were wounded. Torresola died from a bullet wound to his head. Collazo recovered from his wounds, was tried, and sentenced to death. His sentence was later commuted to life imprisonment by his intended victim. Ironically Truman had been more sympathetic to Puerto Ricans than any predecessor: appointing a Puerto Rican native as governor and extending New Deal programs like Social Security to the island. But as Collazo said, the attack was on the symbol, not the man. From then on security around the president was tightened. He was obliged to drive back and forth across Lafayette Square in a specially reinforced car rather than walk as before, and he felt more than ever that he was perpetually hemmed in by the presidency.

Anticommunist Fervor

The Hiss-Chambers Case

The House Committee on Un-American Activities (HUAC) had been established in the late 1930s to investigate possible subversion from the extreme right (pro-Nazi German-Americans) and the extreme left (the Communist Party). It took on a new lease of life in the late 1940s when one of its junior members, California representative Richard Nixon, used it to investigate allegations that Alger Hiss, a senior New Deal bureaucrat and head of the Carnegie Endowment for International Peace, was a secret member of the Communist Party who had passed classified information to Soviet espionage couriers throughout the 1930s and 1940s. Hiss was accused by Whittaker Chambers, one of these couriers, who had renounced Communism and become an outspoken anticommunist in articles for *Time* magazine.

These investigations of Hiss led to his trial for perjury (the statute of limitations prevented him from being tried for treason or espionage, charges he denied under oath). Hiss had been one of President Roosevelt's senior advisers at the Yalta summit with Stalin, which had decided on the disposition of post-World War II Europe. Truman understood that the case affected the credibility of his foreign policy, especially since Secretary of State Dean Acheson was a personal friend of Hiss. If one of his and Roosevelt's foreign policy advisers was pro-communist, how effective could the United States's anticommunist policies be? The first jury could not reach a decision, but on retrial a second jury found Hiss guilty and he was imprisoned for five years in January 1950. The case, full of symbolic significance for the legacy of the New Deal and U.S. Communism, remains controversial up to the present and has been the subject of dozens of books.

Other spies were identified by Igor Gouzenka, a clerk in the Russian embassy in Ottawa, Canada, who defected to the West in 1945, and by U.S. ex-Communists Elizabeth Bentley and Louis Budenz. Among the more scandalous revelations were that Klaus Fuchs, a scientist at the Los Alamos nuclear bomb project throughout World War II, had passed top secret information to the Russians, helped by a ring of U.S. Communists including Harry Gold, David Greenglass, Morton Sobell, and Julius and Ethel Rosenberg. This latter couple, tried and convicted of treason in 1951, were later executed in the electric chair.

"The Hollywood Ten"

HUAC began other investigations, including an excursion to Hollywood, California, to investigate the influence of Communists in the movie industry. The studios, frightened by this external interference, cooperated with HUAC and, in addition, expelled several current or former Communist Party members and sympathizers. The best known of these "blacklisted" actors, screenwriters, musicians, and directors included Alvah Bessie, Ring Lardner Jr., Dalton Trumbo, and John Howard Lawson, known by their supporters as The Hollywood Ten. They were excluded from film projects for the next 10 years while Cold War tensions and anticommunist suspicions were at their height. Most Hollywood stars and businesspeople cooperated with the purging of Communists and ex-Communists. Among the most enthusiastic

was Ronald Reagan, then president of the Screen Actors' Guild (the movie actors' trade union), and later 40th president of the United States.

Truman, aware that the Republicans would allege that he was "soft on Communism" as a political tactic, was determined not to be outdone. He authorized loyalty checks on all federal employees in 1947 and approved a Justice Department prosecution of the American Communist Party's leadership. In 1948 they were convicted of conspiracy to overthrow the government under the Smith Act of 1940, which outlawed the organizing of a group to, or incitement of, overthrowing the government by force and violence. Their conviction was upheld by the Supreme Court. Truman also approved the dismissal of nearly four hundred federal civil servants, not because loyalty checks showed them to be Communists, but because their previous membership or their association with Communists now made them "security risks."

While sometimes succumbing to the anticommunist phobia of those years, Truman was also willing at times to resist it, especially when he believed that the Republicans were using allegations of Communism as a way to discredit the social legislation and achievements of the New Deal. For example, he appointed David Lilienthal head of the new Atomic Energy Commission (AEC) in late 1946. Lilienthal had previously headed the Tennessee Valley Authority (TVA), one of the most controversial New Deal programs because it had brought the federal government into the electricity generation business in competition with private utilities. The TVA was regarded by conservatives as a form of "creeping socialism." Republicans in the Senate, led by Robert Taft of Ohio, insinuated that Lilienthal was "soft on Communism" and that he had harbored known Communists in the TVA. Lilienthal, a technocratic liberal who believed in the ability of technology and expertise to solve all political and technical problems, stoutly denied the charge at his confirmation hearings. He made a ringing speech in defense of democracy and against Communism. Truman was delighted and the senators confirmed Lilienthal's AEC nomination.

McCarthyism

Anticommunist fears, already high, intensified when the United States went to war against North Korea in 1950. Joseph R. McCarthy, the Republican junior senator from Wisconsin, profited from the war by intensifying these fears. Just before the war began he asserted that he possessed a list of 205 names of known Communists at work in sensitive federal jobs, including the State Department. He changed that number several times and later admitted that he was talking about "security risks" rather than actual Communist Party members. Even then he refused to publish the list. Other Republicans, including Taft, were skeptical but recognized the electoral benefits of discrediting the Democrats and did nothing to discourage McCarthy. His sweeping charges, and his assertion that anyone who opposed him was involved in

Sen. Joseph McCarthy of Wisconsin alleged Communist infiltration of the federal government and that the Truman administration harbored Communists. Numerous congressional hearings, held at his behest, probed the lives of many prominent U.S. citizens. (UPI/Corbis-Bettmann. Reproduced by permission.)

a worldwide Communist conspiracy, created the phenomenon of "McCarthyism."

Aiming high he accused Secretary of State Dean Acheson of being part of Alger Hiss's spy ring, denounced Truman's policy of "containment" as cowardly and communist-inspired, and described the president himself as a drunkard. He called Professor Owen Lattimore of Johns Hopkins University, an Asian Studies expert, the "top Russian spy" in the United States. Truman detested McCarthy and retorted that he was one of those men "who mistake notoriety for fame, and would rather be remarked for their vices and follies than not

be noticed at all" (Kirkendall, p. 227). In the end McCarthy's exaggerations undermined his credibility, but not before Truman's second term of office ended with mutual recriminations about disloyalty and Communist sympathizing.

Foreign Issues

Truman came to power as World War II (1939–45) neared its end. He supervised the Western Allies' victory in Europe over Hitler, and later in 1945 made the decision to use atomic bombs against Japan, which ended the Pacific War. Recognizing the Soviet Union's reluctance to relinquish its gains in Eastern Europe and its resistance to self-determination for nations it had liberated from the Nazis, Truman then presided over the reorientation of U.S. foreign policy in the opening days of the anti-Soviet Cold War. He matched his rhetoric with action, first in the Berlin crisis of 1948 and then, more dramatically, by going to war to prevent South Korea from falling to a Communist North Korean invasion in 1950.

Truman was the first U.S. president to consider every part of the world relevant to U.S. foreign policy and the first to maintain a large military force and arms industry during peacetime. The late 1940s and the early 1950s witnessed the transformation of the geopolitical world, and Truman made certain that the United States was its preeminent power.

End of World War II in Europe

When Truman became president in 1945, Germany's armies were in retreat on all fronts. The last effective German counteroffensive, the Battle of the Ardennes (or "Battle of the Bulge") had failed to stop Allied advances in Belgium. U.S. and British tanks were rolling across Germany toward Berlin. The Russian armies, after a rapid advance across Eastern Europe, beat them to it, and when hostilities ended with the suicide of Nazi leader Adolf Hitler and the surrender of his successor Admiral Karl Doenitz a week later, Berlin and the rest of Germany was occupied by the Soviet armies. Despite pleas from British Prime Minister Winston Churchill, Truman honored President Roosevelt's earlier pledge to withdraw U.S. soldiers from this Soviet-dominated zone.

Post-war Negotiations

Although the United States and the Soviet Union had been allies against Hitler, there were tensions in the alliance over the future of Europe. Truman favored free elections for countries newly liberated from the Germans, and he promoted them in Western Europe. The Soviets had agreed to this principle at the Yalta Conference held in 1945 but proved, in practice, reluctant. Relations between the victors deteriorated sharply when Soviet leader Joseph Stalin prevented participation in Polish elections by the provisional democratic government of Poland, which had spent the war years exiled in London. Meanwhile, Stalin interpreted Truman's abrupt ending of wartime "lend-lease" aid in the summer of 1945 as a hostile act (though it was as damaging to Britain, the United States's closest Western ally, as it was to the Soviet Union). Lend-lease had been the U.S. policy of sending war-related goods and materials to Britain and Russia even when they were unable to pay, with the promise of a later settlement (*See also,* Franklin D. Roosevelt Administrations). Stalin was also aware, thanks to his

spies, of the maturing atomic bomb project and was indignant at Truman's refusal to share nuclear weapons information at a time when both superpowers were turning their attention to defeating Japan.

The United States and the Soviet Union both joined the new United Nations (UN), created at a San Francisco conference during the final weeks of the war in Europe, but neither of the new superpowers was willing to surrender any sovereignty to this new organization. As relations between the two superpowers deteriorated Europe, recently freed from the Nazis, was divided all over again by what former British prime minister Winston Churchill described as an "Iron Curtain" stretching "from Trieste in the Adriatic to Stettin in the Baltic" (McCullough, p. 489). Churchill, speaking in Fulton, Missouri, on March 5, 1946, and standing beside Truman, had always regarded Soviet Communism as evil on the same magnitude as German Nazism. Truman, after an early feeling of gratitude and friendship for the wartime Soviet ally, gradually came to agree with Churchill's view.

The Atomic Bomb

One of the most momentous decisions of Truman's administration was his decision to use atomic weapons against Japan during the first months of his first term. Scientists and technologists had been working throughout the war years at 37 sites around the nation, including Hanford, Washington; Oak Ridge, Tennessee; and Los Alamos, New Mexico; to translate theoretical nuclear physics into a portable and functional explosive. By June 1945 this secret operation, code-named The Manhattan Project, had succeeded. A test at Alamogordo, New Mexico, on July 16, 1945, proved that the bomb would work and that it would be immensely destructive, having the power of 20,000 tons of conventional high explosive. Truman, who had known little of the project before Roosevelt's death, now had to decide whether to use it against Japan. Some advisers feared that it would inaugurate a series of earthquakes; others feared that it would set off an unmanageable chain reaction in the atmosphere; and others again felt that it was too lethal for use by a humane and idealistic nation. On the other hand Truman himself and those advisers who favored using the bomb believed that a massive nuclear explosion, by its sheer power, would prompt a Japanese surrender and spare thousands of American and Japanese lives that would otherwise be lost in continued conventional warfare.

Truman decided to use the bomb after his ultimatum to Japan to surrender or be totally destroyed met no response. The first bomb, carried by the B-29 Superfortress *Enola Gay,* exploded over the Japanese city of Hiroshima on August 6, 1945, with immense destructive effect, flattening the city and killing nearly 80,000 people. A second bomb detonated over Nagasaki three days later was even more destructive and finally prompted a Japanese surrender, which was signed on the deck of the USS *Missouri* in Tokyo harbor on September 2, 1945.

Biography:

John Llewellyn Lewis

Union Organizer; Labor Leader (1880–1969) In 1920 at the age of 40, John Llewellyn Lewis was president of the half-a-million-member strong United Mine Workers of America (UMWA). His dictatorial lust for power and his Republican willingness to sacrifice jobs for higher wages, alienated many members throughout the 1920s. Following the crash of 1929, the Great Depression brought the birth of President Franklin Roosevelt's union-friendly New Deal program. Lewis capitalized on this new, benign attitude and quickly moved to rebuild the UMWA. In 1935 he created the Committee for Industrial Organizations (CIO) to organize industrial workers of the automobile, steel, and rubber industries who had been turned away by the American Federation of Labor (AFL). Through militant, well-financed organizing efforts, the power of the CIO grew and Lewis became a national figure. Though he donated heavily to the Democratic Party, Lewis turned sharply against President Roosevelt when Roosevelt failed to heed his every demand. On a national radio program that aired during the 1940 presidential campaign, Lewis called on all workers to vote Republican, promising to resign as president of the CIO if Roosevelt won the election. Lewis's punitive actions failed and in 1941 he resigned from the CIO. He continued to lead the UMWA until 1960, a thorn in the side of other labor leaders, employers, and public officials. During President Harry Truman's administration, Lewis abused his power by calling frequent strikes during times of national emergency. Though his conduct in the final years diminished public support for labor unions and resulted in anti-labor legislation, his overall contribution to the power of this country's labor movement is significant.

Historians since then have debated the merits of the decision in moral and strategic terms, with some emphasizing that the atomic bomb struck not only the last blow of World War II but also the first blow of the Cold War. It was, they argue, designed as a warning to the United States's ally, the Soviet Union, which had also declared war on Japan, to stay out of the United States's new Pacific sphere of influence.

The Cold War

The chilling of relations between the two superpowers began soon after the end of World War II. A highly influential telegram from Moscow sent by diplomat George Kennan in early 1947, arguing the need for perpetual vigilance against a vicious Soviet regime, confirmed Truman's recognition that the United States could no longer risk detaching itself from European affairs. The policy developed in the following years, drawing on Kennan's insights, was named "containment." It was based on the hope that the Soviet Union would eventually either mellow, recognizing the need for permanent coexistence, or even collapse from its own internal weaknesses. Containment required perpetual U.S. vigilance against Communist expansion wherever it might occur, coupled with the rebuilding of an economically and militarily strong Western Europe.

The Truman Doctrine

Britain had been weakened by the war and was no longer able to play its traditional strong role in the Eastern Mediterranean. When Winston Churchill's successor, the Labour Party prime minister Clement Attlee, told Truman that Britain could not assure the survival of democratic, anticommunist institutions in Greece and Turkey, Truman agreed to take over the responsibility. This decision of March 1947, soon titled "The Truman Doctrine," was a key part of the United States's resolve to become a permanent participant in European affairs, even during peacetime, and to do everything it could to assure that the spread of Communism would go no further. It showed that the long U.S. tradition of peacetime isolation was ending. Truman watched with dismay as the last Eastern European democracy, Czechoslovakia, succumbed to Soviet pressure in 1948 and became a one-party Communist state. The Czech crisis had the effect of increasing U.S. politicians' willingness to become permanently involved in safeguarding the Western European democracies.

NATO

In 1949 a new Western military alliance was formed. This new alliance—which included German soldiers, many of whom had fought with Hitler against the United States just a few years before—brought together 11 nations in the North Atlantic Treaty Organization (NATO) and was backed by the force of U.S. nuclear weapons. It was designed to fight Soviet advances in Europe if necessary. The National Security Council's memorandum NSC 68, published the following year, explained that the United States had to face down a worldwide Communist plan of aggression, and remained the operational principle of U.S. foreign policy throughout the following decade.

The Marshall Plan

The economic side of U.S. aid to Western European recovery took shape in the Marshall Plan of 1947. First announced at a commencement speech at Harvard College in Cambridge, Massachusetts, that year by Secretary of State George Marshall, it was a series of subsidies designed to revive European economic vitality by rebuilding the industrial infrastructure, such as factories and railroads, that years of bombing and fighting had shattered. Remembering the economic weakness of Germany after World War I (1914–18), which had contributed to the Great Depression and the rise of Hitler, U.S. policymakers and economists understood the need to avoid a punitive policy towards its defeated enemy. They also needed Britain, their leading war ally and still the strongest European nation, to be economically powerful. Truman offered Marshall aid to Russia and its satellites fully expecting Stalin's rejection of it as a form of Western meddling in his sphere of influence. The 16 Western nations that did participate in the Marshall Plan enjoyed $17 billion of U.S. aid. By the 1950s and 1960s Western Europe was markedly wealthier and more productive than the East. The "Iron Curtain" marked not only a political barrier but a wealth barrier too, which many people to its east longed to cross.

The Berlin Crisis

Berlin, as the capital of Nazi Germany, had a symbolic significance to all the World War II victors and was divided into zones at the end of the war. The East went to the Soviets and the West was shared by Britain, France, and the United States. The city itself, however, was well inside the Soviet zone, which became East Germany. As relations between the United States and the Soviet Union deteriorated in the course of the next two years, Berlin became the front line of the new Cold War standoff, an advanced Western listening post for the Western allies inside the Soviet sphere of influence.

In June 1948 Stalin, eager to dislodge the Americans and take over all of Berlin, decided to blockade its western access routes. Truman's advisers were reluctant to oppose the blockade by force, which might begin a new land war in Europe. Instead they suggested flying over it, carrying supply cargoes into Berlin by air rather than by road. This "Berlin Airlift," at first a mere gesture, soon proved realistic. Truman persisted for 10 months until Stalin admitted defeat by lifting his blockade in April 1949. Without firing a shot, Truman had secured a moral victory in the Cold War at one of its most sensitive flashpoints.

The Arms Race

Nuclear weapons development continued after World War II and gave the United States an immense advantage in the early years of the Cold War. Rapid demobilization of conventional armies meant that the U.S. military shrank from 12 million in 1945 to just 1.3 million by early 1947. At one point the United States had only one division ready for combat in Europe versus 240 Soviet divisions. The threat of the bomb, however, compensated for this manpower imbalance and showed, as it was often to do later, that it had a powerful deterrent effect.

Early hopes that nuclear weapons might be regulated by the UN or an international control group were soon dashed by the deterioration of U.S.-Soviet relations. Truman did, however, sign legislation ensuring civilian control of nuclear research, reserving to the president, not the armed forces, the right to decide on their military use. An arms race developed in the late 1940s, with the Soviet Union exploding its own nuclear weapon in 1949. News of this Soviet advance, coming in the same year as the Chinese Communist Revolution, prompted Truman to approve development of another generation of even more powerful nuclear weapons, the hydrogen bombs, which were perfected and tested in 1954.

Truman, always a foreign policy realist, hoped to avoid open nuclear conflict but never doubted the need to continue developing the weapons and to stay ahead of the Soviets. The bombs as well as the aircraft to "deliver" them if necessary were perpetually updated. The U.S. Air Force, independent of the army from 1947, campaigned hard for intense and expensive aircraft development. The world's first supersonic flight, made by test pilot Charles Yeager in 1947, opened up the possibility of supersonic bombing planes, while U.S. and ex-Nazi rocket scientists were hard at work on missile-based delivery systems. From the late 1940s into the late 1980s the two superpowers confronted each other with immense nuclear arsenals, each capable of annihilating life in the other country and each depending on mutual deterrence to prevent the Cold War from turning hot.

Postwar Japan

After the Japanese surrender at the end of World War II, Truman gave war hero General Douglas MacArthur almost dictatorial powers in reconstructing Japan and turning it from an arch enemy into a strongpoint of U.S. policy in the Pacific. MacArthur supervised redistribution of land to poor farmers, broke up the biggest industrial combines, the Zaibatsu, which had encouraged Japanese aggression, and wrote out a democratic constitution on the U.S. model, with such differences as the continuation of the Emperor Hirohito on his throne. Women were given the vote and the army was abolished in an effort to ensure no resumption of Japanese aggression. The Korean War (1950–53), which broke out in 1950, made Japan strategically vital to the U.S. war effort and provided an immense economic stimulus to Japanese industrial growth. In 1951 the United States and Japan signed a peace treaty (there had been no general treaty at the end of World War II), whose provisions gave the United States bases in Japan itself while bringing the U.S. occupation to an end in April 1952.

The "Loss" of China

China had been in upheaval since the early twentieth century. Japanese invasion in the 1930s and heavy fighting in many parts of the country had worsened conditions of recurrent famine and poverty. U.S. policy during and after World War II aimed at creating a strong, stable China under the leadership of the Chinese nationalist Chiang Kai-shek. Chiang's leadership was, however, ineffective, compromised by internal corruption, weak leadership, and reluctance to fight. General George Marshall spent a year in China trying unsuccessfully to conciliate Chiang and his chief rival, the revolutionary Communist leader Mao Tse-tung. Despite $2 billion worth of U.S. military and civilian aid, Chiang's army, the Kuomintang, was defeated by Mao in 1949 and driven off the mainland to the island of Formosa (Taiwan). This event, described in the United States as the "loss of China," dismayed Truman and his foreign policy advisers, though it hardly surprised those who understood the real weakness of the Chinese nationalists. In the prevailing atmosphere of fervent anticommunism, however, it fueled Republican charges that Communist spies in the U.S. government had contributed to the defeat. An alliance between Mao's China and Stalin's Soviet Union, signed the next year, intensified these suspicions.

The Korean War and the Truman-MacArthur Controversy

The next year Communism appeared to make another forward stride when North Korean soldiers attacked South Korea across the 38th parallel, on June 25, 1950. Korea had been conquered by Japan during World War II and temporarily partitioned at the war's end between a pro-U.S. south and a Communist north. Ambiguous remarks by Secretary of State Acheson appear to have misled the North Korean leadership into thinking that the United States, despite its policy of containment, would not go to the aid of South Korea, just as it had not committed troops to China. In fact, however, Acheson and Truman agreed that the United States must react. They forced a resolution through the UN Security Council (unanimous due to the absence of the Soviet Union) and, using the resolution as their mandate, committed UN troops and ships, led by the United States, to Korea.

The handful of U.S. troops already there, and their South Korean allies, were in desperate straits after six

Fast Fact

weeks of fighting, besieged on the Pusan Peninsula. General Douglas MacArthur, the U.S. commander in the Pacific, managed to stabilize the Pusan situation with air attacks on the North Koreans, and then, in September, mounted a daring amphibious counterattack at Inchon, close to the enemy-held capital of South Korea, Seoul, and far behind enemy lines. His armies landed in strength and forced the North Koreans to retreat with heavy losses. Rather than ceasing his pursuit at the 38th parallel, however, MacArthur, sensing the possibility of defeating North Korean Communism once and for all, continued to harry his enemy into North Korea. Truman approved, and at a meeting with MacArthur on Wake Island in the Pacific, learned from his general that the war was virtually over and the whole of Korea reunited.

But MacArthur had miscalculated. China reacted to the United States's success by joining the war on the North Koreans' side. Their counterattack drove the U.S. troops back down the Korean peninsula once more, in the bitter winter of 1950–51. By March 1951 the U.S. armies had recovered and retaken Seoul for the second time. Truman now proposed negotiating a truce lest the war spread throughout Asia and involve the Soviet Union. MacArthur, on the other hand, sensed a new opportunity for victory, especially if he could coordinate a new U.S. advance with an attack on China by Chiang Kai-shek from Taiwan. His supporters in Congress publicized his declaration that "there is no substitute for victory" (McCullough, p. 850).

Truman, furious at MacArthur for challenging his authority and fearful that the war might escalate into a third world war, dismissed him and sent General Matthew Ridgway, a World War II parachute commander, to replace him. Ridgway scared his headquarters staff by wearing live grenades on his uniform even when he was far from combat lines, but he proved more obedient to the president's orders. MacArthur, meanwhile, returned to the United States, addressed a packed and enthusiastic joint session of Congress in a speech justifying his recent conduct in Korea, and became the darling of Republican anticommunists who opposed the idea of negotiated truces with Communists. To them, a policy of permanent coexistence seemed cowardly, and they were delighted by MacArthur's daring.

Despite an angry reaction by the public at MacArthur's dismissal, Truman was vindicated in his action by a subsequent congressional investigation. The inquiry showed that MacArthur had indeed violated his commander in chief's orders. Omar Bradley, chairman of the Joint Chiefs of Staff, added that MacArthur could easily have involved the United States in a large-scale Asian land war against China and possibly Russia as well. It would, he said, have been "the wrong war, at the wrong place, at the wrong time, and with the wrong enemy" (Grantham, p. 65). Influential and popular Secretary of Defense George Marshall also supported Truman's decision.

Eventually 16 nations, all members of the UN, participated in the Korean War (1950–53), but the U.S. contributions, especially of air and naval power, were the greatest. The war, no longer so mobile as in its early phases, dragged on through the closing years of the Truman administration and was only stabilized by a truce early in the Dwight Eisenhower presidency.

France and Vietnam

Southeast Asia was part of the French colonial empire before World War II (1939–45). Overrun by the Japanese, it was occupied in 1945 by U.S. and British troops. A Vietnamese nationalist leader, Ho Chi Minh, had fought a sustained anti-Japanese guerrilla war and hoped that the United States, which had once fought an anticolonial war of its own against a great European power, would now guarantee Vietnamese independence. In fact, however, Ho's Communism made him an object of suspicion in early Cold War Washington. Moreover the French, humiliated by Hitler in the war, were determined to resume their position as a major world power with a colonial empire. The French government notified Washington that U.S. support for the French empire in Asia and Africa was the price of French cooperation in NATO. Truman and his secretaries of state, George Marshall and Dean Acheson, believed the price was worth paying, and between 1947 and 1952 they heavily subsidized the French military effort to regain control of Vietnam from Ho's force, the Viet Minh. When Truman left office the war was still going on but the French were on the brink of a defeat at Dien Bien Phu, which finally forced them to abandon the colony. Vietnam was to play a major role in subsequent U.S. foreign policy.

The Truman Administration Legacy

The last years of Truman's administration were soured by McCarthyism and by the bloody, inconclusive fighting in Korea. Truman was determined not to run for president again and reflected on the difficulties of the job in a 1952 memorandum. "The president," he wrote, "should embody the virtues of all the great leaders of the past; he should be a Cincinnatus, Marcus Aurelius Antoninus, a Cato, Washington, Jefferson and Jackson all in one. I fear there is no such man" (Ferrell, p. 221). Under no illusions about being such a man himself he tried to persuade the nearest approximation he could find, Illinois governor Adlai Stevenson, to run for president in his place. Stevenson at first refused, then, at the Democratic Convention in Chicago, he changed his mind and entered the race late. A highly intelligent man, he was nominated on the third ballot over Truman's own vice president Alben Barkely, but then ran a lackluster campaign against a powerful Republican rival, war hero and General of the Army Dwight D. Eisenhower. Far from refuting Republican allegations about corruption and Communism in the Democratic Party, Stevenson acted as though they were accurate and tried to detach himself from Truman's record, much to the president's annoyance. Truman made a few campaign speeches, concentrating less on praise for Stevenson than on criticism of the Republicans, especially McCarthy. Even so, Eisenhower swept to victory in the election of November 1952.

Popularity and Public Opinion

While he was president Harry Truman was rarely popular with either Congress or the electorate. Consumers blamed him for high inflation after World War II (1939–45), while trade unionists blamed him for his high-handed attempt to seize first the railroads and later the steel industry to prevent strikes. They were unenthusiastic about his plan for universal military training and, after the euphoric Inchon campaign, disliked the costly and inconclusive fighting of the Korean War (1950–53). His doggedness, forthright speech, and adherence to the New Deal legacy of Franklin Roosevelt, however, assured him sufficient popular support to win reelection to the White House in 1948.

Press and Media

Truman held a press conference most weeks and prepared for a frantic half-hour before each one, fielding trial questions from his press secretary Charles Ross and trying to memorize appropriate facts on leading topics of the moment. Even so, his impromptu answers to some journalists' questions got him in trouble, especially when, in 1950, he implied off the cuff that he might use nuclear weapons in Korea. As a result Ross had to issue frequent "clarifications" of Truman's statements. Unlike his successors Truman did not court the press assiduously and was outspokenly critical of journalists he might profitably have courted, like the influential columnist Walter Lippmann and Drew Pearson. He was delighted at the embarrassment felt by nearly all the media and polling organizations for their incorrect prediction that he would be defeated in the election of 1948.

According to Contemporaries

Most contemporaries expected Truman's historical reputation to be weak. Few could see much to praise in his conduct, and most regarded him as a muddling second-rater. The exception, in his own time, were his close friends, advisers, and cabinet members, such as Dean Acheson, George Marshall, and Clark Clifford, who recognized that Truman actually possessed many excellent qualities: dedication, a willingness to work hard and learn the contours of every issue, decisiveness in decision making, ability to isolate key issues, and a flinty personal integrity. Truman, unlike many later presidents, never suffered from hostile, indiscreet "inside the White House" biographies from disappointed advisers.

Lasting Impact

Truman brought World War II to a decisive close, permanently eliminating Nazism and Japanese military dictatorship. His decision to bomb Hiroshima, Japan, illustrated his belief that the use of nuclear weapons could be justified in extremity. His later caution with nuclear weapons, placing their ultimate control in civilian hands and using them as deterrents rather than battlefield weapons, set the pattern for their history up to the present.

It was Truman above all who transformed U.S. foreign policy. He recognized very soon after 1945 that the United States could no longer be isolationist but must play an active role in the geopolitics of the entire world. His policy of "containment" against the Soviet Union prevented its further expansion and set the stage for the next four decades, until the collapse of Soviet Communism in 1989 retrospectively justified this approach.

His administration upheld the legacy of the New Deal at home, the principle that the federal government ought to be stronger than the governments of the states, and the principle that a limited welfare state and regulated economy ought to displace the old "hands-off" principles of social and economic laissez-faire. For both his domestic and his foreign policies his reputation has steadily improved among historians, most of whom now recognize him as an excellent twentieth-century president. "Revisionist" historians in the Vietnam era, those who were inclined to be harsher on the United States and more lenient toward the Russians, blamed him for the intransigence of his anticommunism and argued that he missed opportunities for Cold War reconciliation. A broad historian's consensus since the 1970s, however, has credited Truman with an appropriate blend of force-fulness and restraint at a time of great political upheaval and potential catastrophe. The general public opinion of Truman seems equally upbeat—Truman is often mentioned favorably as the ideal Cold War president.

Sources

Commire, Anne, ed. *World Leaders.* Detroit: Gale Research, Inc., 1996.

Donovan, Robert J. *Conflict and Crisis: The Presidency of Harry S. Truman.* New York: Norton, 1977.

Ferrell, Robert. *Truman: A Centenary Remembrance.* London: Thames and Hudson, 1984.

Gosnell, Harold F. *Truman's Crises: A Political Biography of Harry S. Truman.* Westport, Conn.: Greenwood Press, 1980.

Grantham, Dewey. *Recent America.* 2d ed. Wheeling, Ill.: Harlan Davidson, 1998.

McCullough, David. *Truman.* New York: Simon and Schuster, 1992.

Seuling, Barbara. *The Last Cow on the White House Lawn & Other Little-Known Facts About the Presidency.* New York: Ivy Books, 1978.

Truman, Harry S. *Harry S. Truman Encyclopedia.* Edited by Richard S. Kirkendall. Boston: G. K. Hall and Co., 1989.

Further Readings

Acheson, Dean. *Present at the Creation.* New York: Norton, 1969.

Fried, Richard. *Nightmare in Red: The McCarthy Era in Perspective.* New York: Oxford University Press, 1990.

Harry S. Truman Library & Museum. 1999. <http://www.trumanlibrary.org> (7 July 1999).

Lacey, Michael, ed. *The Truman Presidency.* Cambridge: Cambridge University Press, 1989.

Miller, Merle. *Plain Speaking: An Oral Biography of Harry S. Truman.* New York: Putnam, 1973.

Truman, Harry S. *Memoirs.* 2 vols. New York: Doubleday, 1955/1956.

———. *The Truman Administration: Its Principles and Practice.* Edited by Louis Koenig. New York: New York University Press, 1956.

Whelan, Richard. *Drawing the Line: The Korean War, 1950–53.* Boston: Little Brown, 1990.

Eisenhower Administrations

Full name: Dwight David Eisenhower
Popular name: Ike

Personal Information:

Born: October 14, 1890
Birthplace: Denison, Texas
Died: March 28, 1969
Death place: Washington, D.C.
Burial place: Chapel beside his boyhood home and
    presidential library, Abilene, Kansas
Religion: Presbyterian
Spouse: Marie (Mamie) Geneva Doud (m. 1916)
Children: Dwight Doud; John Sheldon Doud
Education: U.S. Military Academy at West Point; Army
    Command and General Staff School, Fort Leavenworth,
    Kansas; Army War College, Washington, D.C.
Occupation: Soldier; general; university president
Political Party: Republican Party
Age at Inauguration: 62 years

Biography

Dwight D. Eisenhower, a small town Kansas boy, became a football star at West Point then rose through the ranks of the army, becoming the United States's supreme commander in World War II (1939–45) Europe. Shrewd, genial, hardworking, and a brilliant organizer, he based his successful political career on the appearance of being unconcerned about politics.

Early Life

It is ironic that Eisenhower, the career soldier and war hero, should be the son of Mennonites, a German Protestant immigrant group famous for their radical pacifism. In his childhood the family continued to read every night from the Bible but seemed to have lost the sharp condemnation of war their ancestors had brought from Europe. Eisenhower's grandparents had emigrated from Pennsylvania to Kansas in the 1870s and their son, Eisenhower's father, became a shopkeeper in Hope, Kansas. He was bankrupted in the business depression of 1888. Mortified by this failure, he was a grim and humorless figure to his six sons, of whom Dwight was the third.

The future president was born in Denison, Texas. His family lived there for a short time but he was raised in Abilene, Kansas. As a child Eisenhower had a hot temper and recalled later that he sometimes hurt himself in a fury when he did not get his own way. Learning from his mother Ida the importance of self-control, he was to become a superbly self-restrained and tactful adult, a master of both military and civilian politics. His father worked on the railroads for a time, then at a creamery in

Abilene. Eisenhower also worked there for two years after finishing high school and before starting college, helping to pay his brother Edgar's fees at the University of Michigan.

Education

At the age of 21 Eisenhower, who was a gifted student when he concentrated on his work, won a merit scholarship to West Point in New York in a competitive exam. He did not, at that point, have strong military ambitions, but West Point was attractive because it offered a free, high-quality technical education to young men unable to afford private college fees. He was a talented and enthusiastic football player and soon became a West Point star. He was devastated when a knee injury ended his playing career. Eisenhower studied the traditional curriculum, a blend of military history, English composition, mathematics, and army technology. He graduated from West Point in 1915, popular among his fellow cadets but without a strong academic record.

Disappointed at not being chosen to serve at the Western Front in World War I (1914–18), Eisenhower was posted to Panama where he became the protege of Fox Connor, one of the U.S. Army's most highly educated and gifted officers. Connor encouraged Eisenhower to study the history of war, Carl von Clausewitz, and other great military writers, and to make himself an expert on military organization. Thanks to Connor's intervention, Eisenhower was able to move from Panama to the Army Command and General Staff School at Fort Leavenworth, Kansas, in 1925, where he studied and played elaborate war games. After a period of concentrated hard work and fierce competition he graduated first in his class, which marked him for promotion. He completed his education in 1927 by studying strategy at the Army War College in Washington, D.C., after delighting his superiors by completing a well-written history of the U.S. Army in France during World War I.

Family Life

In January 1916, when he was 25 years old and stationed in San Antonio, Texas, Eisenhower met Mamie Geneva Doud, the 18-year-old daughter of a prosperous Denver meat packer. After an eight-month courtship they married. It was a social step down for Mamie, and a big step up for Eisenhower. She had grown up with servants and found it difficult to adjust to the constant moves and shabby billets assigned to junior officers' families, especially on the tropical stations such as Panama and the Philippines. Nevertheless she played the role of a devoted army wife, entertained fellow officers and their families, and was a steady help in his success.

Dwight David Eisenhower. (The Dwight D. Eisenhower Library.)

Their son David was born in 1917 and his death from scarlet fever just three years later left a permanent mark of sorrow on them both. They were consoled by the birth of their second child, John, in 1922. John grew up to follow his father to West Point and to active service in the World War II (1939–45) and in the Korean War (1950–53). Another strain on the Eisenhowers' marriage was the rumor that Eisenhower, during his long absence from home in World War II, had a love affair with Kay Summersby, his Irish chauffeur. She was certainly in love with him, as she showed in an emotional book of memoirs, *Eisenhower Was My Boss.* It is unlikely that they had an affair. Mamie Eisenhower countered the rumors by publishing Eisenhower's letters to her from the same years, espousing the constant theme that he was eager to be reunited with her.

As first lady Mamie Eisenhower was more interested in smoothing her husband's domestic life than in playing an independent political role. She slept late, vacationed often, appeared only rarely in public on her own account, and tried to shield Eisenhower from the press and from overwork, especially after his heart attack in 1955. Even so she agreed with his doctors that he should run for reelection in 1956 and that the anticlimax of being out of office would be even more harmful than the stress of the presidency.

The Eisenhowers had not owned a home of their own until 1953. Then they bought a farm in Gettysburg, Pennsylvania, in the area from which the Mennonite Eisenhowers had first emigrated to Kansas. Mamie Eisenhower devoted a lot of time to modifying and decorating their home, and they retired there when Eisenhower left the White House in 1960. Their son John and his wife Barbara, with their children, often stayed for long visits with the president and Eisenhower in the White House and at Gettysburg. Ironically, in view of his frequently strained relations with his vice president, Richard Nixon, Eisenhower ultimately became related to Nixon when his grandson David Eisenhower married Nixon's daughter Julie Nixon in 1969.

Career

Eisenhower graduated from West Point in 1915 when World War I (1914–18) was raging in Europe. The United States entered the conflict in 1917 when Germany declared unrestricted submarine warfare against U.S. ships. Eisenhower, an ambitious junior officer, was eager to get to the western front as soon as possible but never managed it. Instead he was assigned to training other soldiers in the use of tanks, then a brand-new weapon. Late in 1918 he was ordered to Europe, but the armistice of November 11 brought the war to an end before he could set sail.

The army, much reduced in size after the war, offered few prospects of advancement to ambitious junior officers in the 1920s, but Eisenhower impressed every senior officer for whom he worked. He served a term in Panama, where he was coached by General Fox Connor in military history, army politics, and ways of advancing his career.

In the mid 1920s he worked for the Battle Monuments Commission, which gave him a chance to visit the European battlefields of World War I. Stationed in Paris he wrote a history of the U.S. Army's role in that war. His advanced studies at the Army Command and General Staff School and at the War College followed, between 1924 and 1927. In 1929, after frequent moves (the Eisenhowers lived in 35 different places in as many years), he was appointed to the staff of the charismatic General Douglas MacArthur in Washington, D.C. MacArthur was a fearless soldier with an impressive leadership record from World War I, and he was a man known to be politically ambitious. He became notorious among unemployed men in the worst days of the Great Depression when he led troops in forcibly dispersing a demonstration of World War I veterans, the "Bonus Marchers," who had come to Washington to appeal for early payment of promised benefits. Photographs of the incident show Eisenhower standing uncomfortably at MacArthur's side amid clouds of smoke and dust.

In 1935 Eisenhower went to the Philippines, where MacArthur had been seconded to President Manuel Quezony Molina as a military adviser. Eisenhower was a skillful staff officer, efficient, tactful, and always informative. MacArthur appreciated his work and blocked Eisenhower's frequent requests for a transfer back to the United States and a job leading troops. Relations became strained between them because Eisenhower disliked MacArthur's flamboyant manner and his tendency to cross the line between military and political affairs.

The outbreak of World War II (1939–45) in Europe in September 1939 convinced Eisenhower that the United States would soon become involved in the conflict. Over MacArthur's pleas to remain, he returned home. His skillful work in large-scale Louisiana war game exercises the next year, where he was chief of staff of the Third Army (responsible for its organization, movement, and engagement with the enemy), finally opened the way to his rapid promotion. Moving up the ladder had been impossible in the small army of the previous 20 years.

World War II

Summoned to Washington after the Japanese attack on Pearl Harbor, Eisenhower won the trust of the army's chief of staff, George Marshall, who gave him a series of rapid promotions. Visiting Britain in 1942 to discuss preliminary schemes for an invasion of Europe, he also won the confidence of British commanders and Prime Minister Winston Churchill. Marshall promoted him to the acting rank of major general and decided to put him in command of all U.S. troops in the African and European theaters of the war.

Eisenhower's first battle experience came in November 1942, when he led "Operation Torch," the U.S. invasion of Oran, Casablanca, and Algiers in North Africa, to neutralize pro-Nazi French forces. A sharp defeat by the Germans at Kasserine Pass in Tunisia in February 1943 raised the possibility that he would be made a scapegoat for the U.S. failure. He retained Marshall's confidence, however, was promoted to four-star general, and went on to join the British in a successful battle for Tunisia. British and U.S. troops under his command next turned to attack Sicily and Italy. In the invasion campaigns that followed, Eisenhower specialized in meticulous planning, strong naval and aerial support of invading forces, and a conciliatory style of leadership, getting the best out of egotistical subordinates (George Patton, Bernard Montgomery, and such politicians as the exiled French general Charles de Gaulle) and trying to prevent their personality clashes from harming the war effort.

Overlord

His greatest military challenge was D-day, the invasion of western Europe, code-named "Overlord." U.S., British, and Canadian troops under his command attacked a line of beaches in Normandy, France, on June 6, 1944. It was the biggest amphibious (land, sea, and air) assault in the history of the world, and succeeded despite heavy casualties at some of the invasion beaches. In the fol-

Gen. Dwight D. Eisenhower gives the command, "Full victory—nothing else," to paratroopers on D-day, June 6, 1944. This was the largest military land, air, and sea assault in the history of the world. (National Archives and Records Administration.)

lowing month a huge buildup of supplies, troops, trucks, and tanks made certain that the Germans would not be able to drive the invaders back into the sea. Through late 1944 Eisenhower's armies retook France from the Germans, and advanced across Holland and Belgium. Temporarily halted by the Germans in the Ardennes Forest in western Europe at the "Battle of the Bulge" that winter, they finally joined Soviet troops advancing from the east at the Elbe River on April 18, 1945. The war ended triumphantly for Eisenhower in May with the suicide of Adolph Hitler.

Post-war Service

Eisenhower returned in triumph to the United States and enjoyed a ticker tape parade in his honor from the city of New York. He addressed a joint session of Congress to tumultuous applause and visited his home town of Abilene, Kansas. Back in Europe the next month he served as commander of the U.S. occupation zone in Germany, trying to carry out the U.S. side of the Yalta agreement with Soviet leader Joseph Stalin. The Yalta accord specified self-government for all countries liberated from the Germans and democratic elections. Stalin's refusal to honor the accord began the deterioration of U.S.-Soviet relations. Among Eisenhower's many tasks was the de-Nazification of Germany, repatriation of prisoners of war and refugees, and relieving famine conditions in war-ravaged Germany.

Eisenhower returned to Washington in November 1945 when President Truman appointed him army chief of staff, the single highest post in the army, in charge of all army affairs throughout the world. He held the post until February 1948 and witnessed the continuing deterioration of U.S.-Soviet relations and the creation of the United States's Cold War apparatus, which he would inherit as president. He was dismayed at the speed with which the victorious U.S. armies of 1945 were dismantled as the nation converted back to civilian life. Despite his urging and the support of President Truman, he was unable to convince Congress of the need for universal military training—and two years of army service—for all 18-year-old men. Most drafted men had been willing to fight for their country in the emergency of World War II, (1939–45), but few young men wanted to be forced into two years of service in a peacetime army. Eisenhower could never find the congressional support for such a reform.

In 1948, retiring from the army at the age of 58, Eisenhower wrote his wartime memoirs, *Crusade in Europe.* An excellent account of the war from his vantage point, it remains highly valuable to historians. Later that year he accepted the presidency of Columbia University in New York. As a university president he began to meet the wealthy business people who would play a key role in promoting and supporting his presidency. At the same time he continued to advise the president and the Joint Chiefs of Staff over recurrent Cold War crises, such as the Berlin Air Lift of 1948–49 in which over two hundred thousand flights carrying relief to West Berliners in Germany were flown in an effort to avoid a Soviet blockade.

He declined offers from both major parties to run for political office in the election of 1948 but accepted President Truman's call for him to return to active service in 1950 as the first supreme commander of the North Atlantic Treaty Organization (NATO). His task was to create a real fighting force from the armies of the 12 western nations that had joined the anti-Soviet alliance in 1949. He found, and gradually overcame, the same problems that had confronted him in World War II: conciliating commanders, developing effective communication lines with numerous rival governments, and creating a unified force with interchangable equipment.

Presidency

In 1948 both the Republicans and Democrats urged him to run for the presidency on their ticket. He declined both. After months of equivocation he entered the 1952 race, believing that Truman's foreign policy was largely right and that it should be protected from the alternative offered by his chief Republican rival, Robert Taft. Taft was an isolationist who favored United States disengagement from all European affairs. Eisenhower won the nomination then the November election against Democrat Adlai Stevenson. He secured a truce in the Korean War (1950–53) in mid 1953 and throughout the 1950s managed to avoid U.S. participation in any major conflict, despite sustained Cold War tensions. Recurrent crises with China, the Soviet Union, and Indochina (comprising Laos, Cambodia, Thailand, and Vietnam) were all resolved by a mix of negotiations and mutual threats.

At home, Eisenhower presided over a period of sustained economic growth and the rapid spread of affluence through the growing U.S. middle class. The civil rights movement began with the Supreme Court's decision in *Brown v. Board of Education of Topeka, Kansas* (1954), which ruled that the prevailing law "separate but equal" was not equal, and the Montgomery, Alabama, bus boycott of 1955–56. Eisenhower was unenthusiastic about changing the South's racial mores, but he did believe in upholding the law. After the Supreme Court called for the integration of public schools he sent the 101st Airborne Division to enforce the desegregation of public schools in Little Rock, Arkansas, in 1957. Reelected over Stevenson in 1956, his second administration suffered two embarrassments: first when the Soviet Union beat the United States in launching an artificial satellite, *Sputnik,* in 1957, and again when the pilot of a U.S. spy plane, Francis Gary Powers, was shot down over the Soviet Union in 1960 and captured. His two-term vice president Richard Nixon lost a close race in November 1960 to Democratic challenger John F. Kennedy.

Post-presidential Years

Eisenhower retired to his farm at Gettysburg, Pennsylvania. Bombarded with requests for interviews and advice, he remained a figure in the public eye. He also devoted more time than ever to his favorite pastimes of painting, golf, and bridge, and he dabbled in raising cattle and feed crops. Forty-three-year-old president John F. Kennedy, whom Eisenhower regarded as too young, vulgar, and inexperienced to run the country, asked for Eisenhower's advice after the disastrous failure of the Bay of Pigs invasion in Cuba (*See also,* Kennedy Administration), but otherwise Kennedy did not draw on Eisenhower's experience. Eisenhower continued to fear the dangers of war in Asia, but once the United States was committed to the Vietnam War (1959–75) under Lyndon Johnson (who had been Senate majority leader through many of Eisenhower's years in office), he argued for decisive strokes to achieve victory.

Eisenhower published his White House memoirs in two volumes, *Mandate for Change* and *Waging Peace,* but they lacked the literary flair and distinctiveness of his earlier book *Crusade in Europe.* By an odd coincidence the publication of each volume was overshadowed by Kennedy. The first appeared in November 1963, the month of Kennedy's assassination. The second appeared at the same time as biographies of Kennedy by his friends and advisers Theodore Sorensen and Arthur Schlesinger Jr. were published. His later and more personal book *At Ease* (1967) showed renewed evidence of his literary skill.

Eisenhower, who had suffered his first heart attack in 1955, faced a complicated series of challenges to his health in the mid- and late-1960s. By the time of the Republican Convention of 1968 in Miami Beach he was too weak to attend. He did make a televised speech to the delegates from his hospital bed, and he was pleased to see his former vice president, Richard Nixon, win the nomination. He died on March 28, 1969, soon after Nixon's inauguration and the marriage of his grandson David Eisenhower to Nixon's daughter Julie Eisenhower.

The Dwight D. Eisenhower Administrations

Eisenhower, the first Republican president for 20 years, was a skilled army politician and showed, by winning two elections, that he could transfer his political talent to the civilian world. He avoided U.S. involvement in foreign wars but demonstrated a firm resolve in the continuing Cold War face-off with the Soviet Union and China. At home he accepted much of the legacy of the New Deal, which annoyed the Republican Right Wing but conciliated the majority of newly affluent voters.

Eisenhower Becomes President

The Campaign of 1952

In the tradition of other war-heroes-turned-president, such as Andrew Jackson and William Henry Harrison, Eisenhower won the personal support of voters not normally pro-Republican. Portraying himself as above the fray of ordinary politics, he delayed his official entry into the race until write-in voters in New Hampshire and other primaries had shown that he stood a good chance of winning. At the Republican Convention of 1952, in Chicago, Illinois, his supporters outmaneuvered the Republican right wing's favorite, Senator Robert Taft of Ohio, and won him the nomination. To mollify the Republican right wing's "Old Guard," he selected Senator Richard Nixon of California as his running mate.

Nixon was already renowned as a tough political fighter who had made his name in the McCarthyite atmosphere of early Cold War Washington during the Harry S Truman administration (*See also,* Domestic Issues). Another concession to the Republican Right was a party platform criticizing the Democrats' foreign policy of anticommunist "containment," which it described as negative, futile, and immoral. In fact Eisenhower had helped design and carry out that policy and believed in it, though he was less enthusiastic about the embryonic welfare state created by his predecessors Franklin Delano Roosevelt and Harry S Truman.

Eisenhower and Nixon campaigned against the Democrats, portraying them as the party of "Korea, Communism, and Corruption," taking advantage of the unpopular Korean War (1950–53), of allegations that Truman's administration was sheltering Communists, and of rumors that Truman's advisers accepted bribes. Halfway through the campaign the Democratic candidate, Adlai Stevenson, discovered that Nixon had received gifts and financial favors from supporters. Eisenhower was on the brink of dropping him from the ticket but Nixon, speaking on national radio to clear his name, made a brilliant speech in his own defense. Denying any improprieties and declaring his willingness to have all his financial affairs investigated, he challenged all other candidates for office that year to do the same. He ended by admitting that a supporter had given his two young daughters a dog, Checkers, and that whatever anyone said, he was going to keep it. The "Checkers" speech, a masterpiece of political survivalism, brought a torrent of favorable telegrams and phone calls to the Republican Party. Eisenhower relented and Nixon stayed on the ticket, which won the November election and brought with it Republican majorities in both houses of Congress.

The Campaign of 1956

Eisenhower frequently wrote in his diary that he had doubts about his position as president, but most reporters who knew him, and his close friends, agreed that he enjoyed the power, status, and authority of the presidency. He was uncertain of whether to run for reelection in 1956 after suffering a heart attack in September 1955. His health then became a major political issue. His advisers disguised its seriousness in press releases, however, and in February 1956 he declared that he was going to run. He doubted whether any other Republican could win, and he was eager to prevent the Democrats' return to power. He had never liked Nixon, his vice president, and hoped to drop him from the ticket. Nixon, with his eye on becoming president in the 1960 election, was determined to stay, and he politely declined the offer of another cabinet post. The Republican Right, disheartened by the discovery that Eisenhower was carrying on much of the Roosevelt-Truman domestic and foreign policies, was also eager to keep Nixon on the ticket. If Eisenhower's heart gave way (as Roosevelt's had a decade before, opening the door to Truman), Nixon would be

Administration

Administration Dates
January 20, 1953–January 20, 1957
January 20, 1957–January 20, 1961

Vice President
Richard Milhous Nixon (1953–61)

Cabinet

Secretary of State
John F. Dulles (1953–59)
Christian A. Herter (1959–61)

Secretary of the Treasury
George M. Humphrey (1953–57)
Robert B. Anderson (1957–61)

Attorney General
Herbert Brownell Jr. (1953–57)
William P. Rogers (1957–61)

Postmaster General
Arthur E. Summerfield (1953–61)

Secretary of the Interior
Douglas McKay (1953–56)
Frederick A. Seaton (1956–61)

Secretary of Agriculture
Ezra T. Benson (1953–61)

Secretary of Labor
Martin P. Durkin (1953)
James P. Mitchell (1953–61)

Secretary of Commerce
C. Sinclair Weeks (1953–58)
Frederick H. Mueller (1959–61)

Secretary of Defense
Charles E. Wilson (1953–57)
Neil H. McElroy (1957–59)
Thomas S. Gates Jr. (1959–61)

Secretary of Health, Education and Welfare
Oveta C. Hobby (1953–55)
Marion B. Folsom (1955–58)
Arthur S. Flemming (1958–61)

---

president. The health issue was revived in June 1956 when Eisenhower underwent another operation for an intestinal ailment.

The Democratic candidate was again Adlai Stevenson, who beat off challenges from Averell Harriman and Estes Kefauver in the primaries. He found campaigning against a popular war hero and well-loved president in prosperous times very difficult. He tried in vain to capitalize on the issue of Eisenhower's health and some early fears of atmospheric radiation from nuclear tests but was defeated by more than nine million votes at the polls. The autumn run-up to the election also witnessed two foreign policy crises: in Hungary and over the Suez Canal in Egypt. Eisenhower's handling of them enabled him to profit from the appearance of expertise and experience in emergency conditions. His campaign claimed that the Republican Party "is again the rallying point for all Americans of all callings, ages, races and incomes" (Grantham, p. 92.) In fact the Republican Party had lost control of Congress in the midterm elections of 1954 and was unable to recover it in 1956. It fared even worse in 1958, showing that Eisenhower's personal popularity did not translate into popularity for the Republican Party as a whole.

Eisenhower's Advisers

Eisenhower's White House chief of staff was Sherman Adams, former governor of New Hampshire, to whom the president entrusted the running of everyday business. Adams once told Vice President Nixon that "Ike always had to have someone else who could do the firing, or the reprimanding, or give any order which he knew people would find unpleasant to carry out. Ike always had to be the nice guy" (Brendon, p. 233). He controlled access to Eisenhower and often had the job of saying "no" in response to requests for interviews—journalists nicknamed him "the Abominable No-Man."

Press Secretary James Hagerty was more friendly towards journalists, a master of the new medium of television. He knew how to "spin" political stories to shine a favorable light on all Eisenhower's dealings, giving even defeats the appearance of victory. For example, Adolphe Wenzell, an adviser to the Bureau of the Budget, was found in 1954 to have a conflict of interest; he was also an adviser to Dixon-Yates, a corporation that won a big government contract on his recommendation. At first Eisenhower wrongly denied that Wenzell had any connection to the government, but when evidence of the link was produced Hagerty was able to cover this embarrassing slip with a "clarification." In it he asserted the administration's high-minded determination to expose all such conflicts, and then arranged for Eisenhower to pointedly cancel the contract.

With his return to civilian life in 1948, Eisenhower had befriended many wealthy business executives, with whom he socialized, played golf and bridge, and from whom he learned about economic affairs. As a result his outlook was notably pro-business and he was sometimes insensitive to the needs of the poor and the working class. Many of his choices for the cabinet came from the private business sector. Secretary of Defense Charles "Engine" Wilson, formerly head of General Motors, for example, made headlines when he declared that "what was good for our country was good for General Motors, and vice versa" (Parmet, p. 170). Eisenhower also had great faith in his Treasury secretary George Humphrey, an Ohio industrialist, who thought along lines familiar and congenial to Eisenhower, favoring a balanced budget, restraint in spending, and a relaxed regulatory system.

A conspicuous exception was his first secretary of labor, Martin Durkin, the president of the American plumbers' trade union, who was always out of place in the White House and refused to take a broader view of labor affairs than that afforded by his union standpoint. An editorial in *The New Republic* joked that the administration consisted of "eight millionaires and a plumber" (Ambrose, p. 291). Durkin was soon maneuvered into resigning when Eisenhower refused to endorse his plans for a revision of the anti-union provisions of the Taft-Hartley Act, which had passed in 1947.

His secretary of agriculture, Ezra Taft Benson, was one of the 12 apostles of the Mormon Church as part of its administrative Council. He was a severe, humorless man dedicated to reviving the free market and ending 20 years of federal support for the prices of farm goods. He wanted to start every cabinet meeting with a prayer. According to historian Piers Brendon the prayer "was occasionally omitted and Ike was liable to exclaim, . . . we forgot the prayer'" (Brandon, p. 232). Benson caused great anxiety to midwestern farmers, who voiced a rock-ribbed Republicanism in theory but remembered that farm price supports (a New Deal innovation) had saved many of them from disaster in the Great Depression years of the 1930s.

Eisenhower and Congress

Eisenhower's first Congress, the Eighty-third, had Republican majorities in both houses. He treated it deferentially to conciliate the Senate majority leader, Robert Taft, nicknamed "Mr. Republican," who had expected to win the presidential election of 1952. Eisenhower was eager to win congressional Republicans over to a more internationalist foreign policy of the sort created by the Democratic presidents Roosevelt and Truman over the past 12 years (and stubbornly opposed by Taft). That job became easier when Taft, the last great Republican isolationist, died in 1953.

Eisenhower worked to prevent passage of the "Bricker Amendment," a proposed constitutional amendment introduced by Republican senator John Bricker of Ohio that would have severely restricted the president's right to negotiate treaties and make executive decisions on foreign policy. Bricker and his supporters were afraid that too many powers, reserved to the individual states by the Tenth Amendment, were being centralized in the presidency. Although they were Eisenhower's fellow Republicans, they believed that his predecessors in the White House, Roosevelt and Truman, had exceeded their authority. They aimed to make sure that no subsequent president, of whatever party, would do the same. By calling in favors and lobbying hard against it, Eisenhower was able to prevent congressional majorities from endorsing the amendment. He feared that if it passed he would be unable to coordinate international organizations like the North Atlantic Treaty Organization (NATO) against the Soviet threat.

His campaigning in 1954, which he hoped would lead to the election of another Republican Congress, yielded disappointing results. The Democrats regained control of both houses, with majorities of just one in the Senate and 29 in the House of Representatives. The Democrats then fought vigorously to uphold elements of Roosevelt's New Deal that were threatened by Republicans. In 1956 these Democratic majorities increased by another seat in the Senate and another four seats in the House. The worst setback for the Republicans, however, came in 1958, when the administration was fighting allegations that senior officials were involved in influence-peddling, selling lobbyists access to the president. In that election the Senate went to the Democrats 64 to 34 and in the House 282 to 154, the biggest Democratic majorities since Roosevelt's landslide reelection in 1936.

With Eisenhower's active encouragement Congress passed an act extending the reach of Social Security in 1954, enabling the self-employed and many more working people than ever before to obtain coverage and benefits. Ten million more Americans entered the scheme, making it close to universal, and greatly easing aging Americans' anxieties about their later years. He also approved a rise in the minimum wage in 1956, from $.75 to $1 per hour. In general, however, he did not push hard for radical changes in domestic legislation, and he did not find Democratic Congresses as intractable as he had expected. His last Congress, for example, overwhelmingly Democratic, was led by Lyndon Johnson in the Senate and Sam Rayburn in the House, both Texans who saw eye-to-eye with the president on the need for financial restraint.

Eisenhower and the Judiciary

Eisenhower appointed Earl Warren chief justice of the Supreme Court in October 1953. Warren had been attorney general of California during World War II (1939–45) and had authorized the mass deportation of Japanese-American citizens to internment camps after Pearl Harbor. He seemed an unlikely figure to become a civil rights hero, but within months of his confirmation he led an activist Supreme Court in overturning the legal basis of southern racial segregation. Eisenhower's other appointments to the Supreme Court were John M. Harlan (1955), William Brennan (1956), Charles Whittaker (1957), and Potter Stewart (1958), most of whom had reputations as moderate conservatives but who, under pressure of circumstances, made some of the most radical judicial judgments of the twentieth century in the following years.

The unanimous school desegregation decision in *Brown v. Board of Education of Topeka, Kansas* (1954), was that the old policy of "separate but equal" facilities for African Americans and whites was inherently discriminatory against African Americans. The Warren Court admitted sociological as well as legal evidence in reviewing the case and gave notice of its willingness to approach divisive social issues in a broad and creative way. A subsequent decision on education ruled that schools must be desegregated "with all deliberate speed." This ambiguous phrasing was used by southern white segregationists as an opportunity for delay, and actual desegregation took another 10 or 15 years to enforce (*See also,* Domestic Issues). Federal judges in lower courts were among the few committed agents of racial change in many southern states during the Eisenhower years.

The Supreme Court also made several decisions limiting the reach of McCarthyism, or anticommunist investigations (*See also,* Domestic Issues). It found, for example, that the government could not arbitrarily withhold the granting of passports (then a standard method of regulating suspected radicals), and that it could only convict citizens of antigovernment conspiracy if it had specific evidence of their intent to use violence against the United States.

In an obscenity case, *Roth v. United States* (1957), the Court reduced the power of censorship laws by arguing that printed material could only be regarded as obscene if it offended "contemporary community standards," as held by "the average person." As standards changed, in other words, so would the legal definition of pornography. In a related case two years later, *Kingsley International Pictures Corporation v. Regents* (1959), the Court also relaxed film censorship by overturning a New York censorship law. In that case a film version of D. H. Lawrence's novel *Lady Chatterley's Lover* had been banned because it made an argument in favor of adultery. In the Court's view the ban violated the First Amendment free speech right. These cases were consonant with the Warren Court's activism on behalf of equal rights and free expression for all, an activism that led to bitter criticism from conservatives and, by 1960, frequent calls for the impeachment of Chief Justice Warren.

Changes in the U.S. Government

Alaska and Hawaii, both federal territories since the nineteenth century, were admitted to the Union as states in 1959, raising the number of states (and hence, the number of stars on the flag) to 50.

Another change during the Eisenhower years was passage of the Twenty-third Amendment, to permit residents of the District of Columbia to vote in national elections. When the District had been created, just after the American Revolution (1775–83), it was as a special political enclave. By the twentieth century, however, it had a large permanent population as well, and their inability to vote in presidential elections (because they were not residents of any state) seemed arbitrary and unjust. The draft amendment passed through Congress in June 1960 with Eisenhower's approval and rapidly won the assent of two-thirds of the states, being officially included in the Constitution on March 29, 1961.

Eisenhower was also the first president to be elected since national endorsement of the Twenty-second Amendment (1951). It barred any president from holding the office more than twice and meant that, following his reelection in 1956, he was the first "lame duck" president in U.S. history. Only Franklin Roosevelt had ever broken the unofficial two-term limit first imposed by George Washington (Roosevelt was elected four times); from now on even the most ambitious presidents could only serve to two terms.

In the Cold War environment, and in the confrontation with what was often referred to as "Godless Communism," Eisenhower tried to emphasize the religious character of the United States, but without making the case for any particular faith or denomination. He rarely made reference to the Mennonite tradition from which he came. He befriended religious celebrities of the day, Billy Graham and Norman Vincent Peale, and he encouraged Congress's decision to add the words "under God" in the Pledge of Allegiance, and the motto "In God We Trust" on coinage and banknotes, in 1954 and 1955 respectively.

Domestic Issues

The civil rights revolution began with the Supreme Court's decision in the *Brown* case (1954) and the Montgomery Bus Boycott (1955), and intensified with the standoff over desegregating schools in Little Rock, Arkansas (1957). Eisenhower, despite his conservative rhetoric, had no intention of permitting the blatant racial

Biography:

Earl Warren

Lawyer; Politician; Supreme Court Justice (1891–1974) Earl Warren was a successful county and state prosecutor before he was elected governor of California for an unprecedented three terms. When the call to national politics came, Warren ran as Thomas Dewey's running mate in the 1948 presidential election. Four years later, he was edged out of the running by the popular Gen. Dwight Eisenhower. It was President Eisenhower who, in 1953, appointed Warren justice on the U.S. Supreme Court. By that time, Warren's reputation had been secured by political observers who had called him, "the most intelligent and politically independent district attorney in the United States." Upon taking the bench, Warren's place in history was secured when he wrote a landmark decision for the court stating that public facilities described as "separate but equal" (regarding race) were inherently unequal and therefore in violation of the Constitution. Warren's stay on the Court spanned a tumultuous time in U.S. history during which decisions

were handed down limiting the powers of government to investigate citizens based upon their political affiliations, disallowing state electoral apportionment that unduly favored lightly populated rural districts, and instating new rights for criminal suspects including notification of their rights at the time of arrest and the right to legal counsel at the time of questioning. Because his and the

Court's opinions and decisions so directly affected the lives of so many Americans, critics were quick to attack. But it is perhaps Justice Warren's legacy that he effectively demonstrated the means and range by which the Supreme Court might intervene in major questions of American public life.

---

injustice of segregation to continue, and he did much to affirm the central place of the federal government in U.S. domestic life that had begun under Franklin Delano Roosevelt. His government maintained and extended most New Deal programs, including the controversial Social Security program, and showed itself willing to manipulate the currency and interest rates to assure favorable economic trends.

The 1950s was an era of sustained economic growth and entrepreneurial daring, now backed by government initiatives. Eisenhower authorized the building of the St. Lawrence Seaway linking the Great Lakes to the Atlantic Ocean, a nationwide interstate highway system, and a network of airports, all of which contributed to the decline of railroads and the rise of ship, road, and air transportation. These massive internal improvements stimulated trade and were, in effect, government subsidies to business and industry. Apart from a sharp recession in 1958 his government enjoyed sustained prosperity; it was in the 1950s that economist John Kenneth Galbraith described the United States as "the Affluent Society" and pointed out that for the first time in history, the nation was suffering as much from the problems brought by wealth as from the problems brought by poverty.

McCarthyism

Senator Joseph McCarthy had scourged Truman Democrats in the early 1950s, alleging that they know-

ingly sheltered Communists in high government positions, and that even such high officials as former and current secretaries of state George Marshall and Dean Acheson might well be Communists. McCarthy's threats and bluster made other politicians reluctant to denounce him for fear that he would turn on them and accuse them of Communist conspiracy. Even Eisenhower, who was above suspicion and could have put a stop to McCarthy's excesses, shied away from doing so. After approving a vivid paragraph in favor of George Marshall in one of his 1952 campaign speeches, he omitted it when he spoke in Wisconsin, McCarthy's home state. Journalists criticized Eisenhower for the omission. In the early days of his administration he again refused to intervene to save officials smeared by McCarthy's allegations, observing merely that he did not want to "get into a contest with that skunk" (Pach and Richardson, p. 67).

The Eisenhower administration, indeed, was as zealous as its predecessor in hunting for "security risks" and dismissed 3,000 people from their government jobs even though none was shown to be a spy. The most famous was Robert J. Oppenheimer, who had been one of the masterminds of the atomic bomb during World War II (1939–45). In 1954, however, McCarthy finally provoked a counterattack from Eisenhower when he alleged that even the U.S. Army was infiltrated by Communist spies and told one general, Ralph Zwicker, that he was not fit to wear his army uniform. The Senate Permanent Subcommittee on Investigations, of which McCarthy

What They Said . . .

Although many people associate U.S. involvement in Vietnam with the presidents of the 1960s, U.S. commitments in the region actually began under Eisenhower. These commitments reflected the views of Eisenhower on the potential spread of Communism and its threat to U.S. security, views which he was called on to explain in a 1954 press conference. In the following quote, Indochina refers to the region now known as Vietnam.

Q. Robert Richards, Copley Press: "Mr. President, would you mind commenting on the strategic importance of Indochina to the free world? I think there has been, across the country, some lack of understanding on just what it means to us."

President Eisenhower: "You have, of course, both the specific and the general when you talk about such things. Then you have the possibility that many human beings pass under a dictatorship that is inimical to the free world. Finally, you have broader considerations that might follow what you would call the "falling domino" principle. You have a row of dominoes set up, you knock over the first one, and what will happen to the last one is the certainty that it will go over very quickly. So you

could have a beginning of a disintegration that would have the most profound influences. But when we come to the possible sequence of events, the loss of Indochina, of Burma, of Thailand, of the Peninsula, and Indonesia following, now you begin to talk about areas that not only multiply the disadvantages that you would suffer through loss of materials, sources of materials, but now you are talking about millions and millions and millions of people.

"Finally, the geographical position achieved thereby does many things. It turns the so-called island defensive chain of Japan, Formosa, of the Philippines and to the southward; it moves in to threaten Australia and New Zealand. It takes away, in its economic aspects, that region that Japan must have as a trading area or Japan, in turn, will have only one place in the world to go that is, toward the Communist areas in order to live. So, the possible consequences of the loss are just incalculable to the free world."

(Source: Dwight D. Eisenhower, Press Conference, 1954.)

---

himself was chair, held an inquiry into these allegations, which were televised in April 1954. For many Americans the sight of McCarthy bullying witnesses, shouting, and intervening rudely to prevent testimony, was a shock. The army, with Eisenhower's support, came out of the hearings largely unscathed but McCarthy was censured, or officially reprimanded, by the Senate, on the motion of another Republican, Ralph Flanders of Vermont. After that his assertions lost their impact and he went into a rapid alcoholic decline, dying at the age of 49 in 1957.

Civil Rights

A series of Supreme Court decisions in the late 1940s and early 1950s had begun to erode the structure of racial segregation in the southern states. President Truman had desegregated the U.S. military in 1948. He recognized that racism tarnished the United States's reputation as the homeland of freedom in the propaganda exchanges of the Cold War. A decisive event in the history of U.S. race relations took place with the Supreme Court's decision in *Brown v. Board of Education of Topeka, Kansas* (1954), which found that segregation was inherently discriminatory. Even separate schools that

were equal, said the Court, discriminated against African Americans who, as a minority, felt themselves singled out as an inferior caste. A subsequent decision ordered schools throughout the south to desegregate "with all deliberate speed," a phrase that many southern authorities construed as license to delay.

Late in 1955 Martin Luther King, Jr., a Baptist minister in Montgomery Alabama, drew nationwide headlines by leading a boycott of the city's buses until they abandoned their policy of segregation. The boycott had started after an African American woman named Rosa Parks refused to surrender her seat in the front of a bus to a white man. King went on to found a new organization, the Southern Christian Leadership Conference, which began to campaign for racial integration in other southern communities. The National Association for the Advancement of Colored People (NAACP) had been leading the legal struggle against segregation for half a century by then. Now, under the inspiration of the charismatic King, such newer organizations as the Congress of Racial Equality (CORE) and the Student Nonviolent Coordinating Committee (SNCC) took up energetic campaigns. The southern white press criticized them and defended segregation but the African American press,

Federal troops escort African American students into Central High School in Little Rock, Arkansas, in 1957. This action underscored Eisenhower's strong stance against segregated schools and upheld the Supreme Court's ruling in the Brown vs. Board of Education *case (1954). (AP/Wide World Photos. Reproduced by permission.)*

north and south, and such national media as the *New York Times* and the growing television networks, sympathized with the African American protestors.

Eisenhower was no enthusiast for racial integration. His southern friends were mainly rich whites. He passed on their racist jokes to other friends and was untroubled, on frequent golfing visits to Augusta, Georgia, by the prevailing system of segregation. He never publicly expressed his support for the *Brown* decision, and he gave only lukewarm support to the mild Civil Rights Acts passed through Congress in 1957 and 1960. The first of these acts extended federal protection to African American voters in segregated southern counties and established a civil rights commission to investigate racial abuses. The second act added federally appointed referees in civil rights cases and increased the criminal penalties for preventing free elections. Neither act, however, had the enforcement powers that Martin Luther King, Jr., and other civil rights leaders wanted. Attorney General Herbert Brownell was more supportive of civil rights reforms than Eisenhower and encouraged federal prosecution of illegal election tactics throughout the south in the late 1950s.

Eisenhower, despite his lukewarm opinions on civil rights, did believe in upholding the law of the land and the Court's decisions. In 1957 Little Rock, Arkansas, ordered its schools to be desegregated. The first day of

school witnessed a riot as diehard segregationists promised to resist the new policy at all costs. In response to the rioting Eisenhower sent members of the 101st Airborne Division to Arkansas and was enraged when he learned that Arkansas Governor Orval Faubus was himself trying to thwart the desegregation of public schools. He underlined his policy by placing local National Guard units under federal command and compelling the desegregation plan to go forward, whatever the views of local whites.

White citizens' councils were formed in many southern states, aiming to resist desegregation by all possible means, and the Ku Klux Klan, a secret society of white supremacists begun in the South, gained new members. Technically legal obstructions included school closings, enforcement of century-old black codes, and segregation statutes. Illegal obstruction included intimidation, harassment, and direct violence against demonstrators and protestors. One hundred and one southern representatives and senators announced a policy of "massive resistance" to desegregation in March 1956, declaring that if necessary they would close public schools down rather than see them integrated. Prince Edward County, Virginia, did exactly that in 1959, and its public schools remained closed for the next four years. Most southern communities however, backed down when the federal government retaliated against their intransigence by withdrawing funds from other state projects.

Education

Eisenhower shared the general sense of shock and dismay when a Soviet satellite, *Sputnik,* went into space before any U.S. spacecraft. He signed into law the National Defense Education Act later in 1958, by which he hoped to stimulate rigorous education in mathematics and science, and funded it with a total of $887 million. The act provided $295 million for college student loans (repayable at low interest rates), and gave incentives to young adults willing to become teachers of science, mathematics, and foreign languages. His administration witnessed an immense expansion of higher education, as ever larger percentages of 18-year-olds elected to go to college. Federal subsidies and the GI Bill made it possible for working-class youths, previously excluded for financial reasons, to study beyond the high school level.

Foreign Issues

Americans felt a strange mixture of confidence and fear in the Eisenhower years of the 1950s. Their war victories in World War II (1939–45) and the Korea War (1950–53), their ability to avoid a new Great Depression, and their sense of greater wealth and power than ever before made them proud and self-assured in their dealings with other countries. But the knowledge that the Soviet Union regarded them as destined for extinction, and had the nuclear weapons to back up its threats, created an undercurrent of alarm and dread. It seemed reasonable to U.S. civil authorities to hold regular air raid drills for schoolchildren, and even for entire cities. Concerned communities began building antinuclear air raid shelters and stocking them with food—even do-it-yourself shelters came on the market, and magazine articles discussed the grim necessity of shooting neighbors who had neglected to build their own shelters, rather than admitting them to one's own.

Ideological differences, nuclear bombs, and the unresolved European situation left over from World War II kept relations between the United States and the Soviet Union tense throughout the Eisenhower years. The Chinese Communist revolution of 1949, and the U.S. assumption (not always accurate) that China and Russia were natural allies, intensified Cold War feelings of mutual mistrust. Eisenhower had been military head of the North Atlantic Treaty Organization (NATO): now he was Commander in Chief of NATO's strongest member. He aimed to cement the alliance but came into conflict with two other members, Britain and France, when he forcibly restrained them from military action against Egyptian seizure of the Suez Canal in 1956. He also made use of covert operations by authorizing CIA-backed coups in Guatemala and Iran. On the other hand, he was powerless to intervene against the Soviet Union behind the Iron Curtain when Hungarian rebels appealed for U.S. help in 1956.

Cold War

Since the end of World War II (1939–45) the United States, leader of the NATO alliance, had confronted the Soviet Union, leader of the Warsaw Pact, across what Winston Churchill had nicknamed the "Iron Curtain" in Central Europe. Mutual mistrust and ideological conflict between the two superpowers made each one fearful of the other's intentions, and the arms race escalated after the Soviets exploded their own nuclear weapon in 1949. The next stage in weapons escalation came with the successful test of a U.S. hydrogen bomb in November 1952 and its Soviet counterpart the following year. Within the Western alliance Eisenhower had to overcome French suspicions that they should remain more afraid of Germany, which had invaded France three times in the last century, than of NATO's ostensible foe, the Soviet Union.

Development of aircraft and missile delivery systems moved ahead rapidly in the 1950s. Intercontinental Ballistic Missiles (ICBMs) were perfected in the late 1950s and the first nuclear-powered Polaris submarine armed with nuclear missiles was put to sea in 1960. Eisenhower realized that a defense policy based on the threat of nuclear retaliation, though expensive, cost less than one based on conventional field armies. He also realized that this would be popular among taxpayers, who enjoyed a tax cut in 1954. He favored balanced budgets and believed that the nation could not be strong if it constantly ran up deficits. And he was among the first Cold War leaders to see that arms races are self-defeating; the more weapons the United States acquired the more the Soviets would acquire to stay equal—a pointless and costly treadmill. He was not able to act on this perception, however, because of national fears of falling behind in the arms race. He was certainly politician enough to see the need for actions which, from a strictly logical approach, were pointless.

His policy of cutting conventional forces and relying chiefly on the Strategic Air Command (SAC) was nicknamed the "New Look" by Pentagon propagandists, who borrowed the term from a recent trend in women's fashions. They also referred to the effect of this reliance on nuclear bombs as "more bang for the buck." But, said Democratic critics, it denied the United States the flexibility it needed in responding to less-than-catastrophic challenges around the world. By the late 1950s Democrats were also becoming afraid that Eisenhower had taken the principle of economizing much too far. Democratic aspirants like John F. Kennedy and Lyndon Johnson alleged that there was now a missile gap between the Americans and the Russians, and that while Eisenhower fussed over balancing the books, the Soviets had surged ahead with their costly rocket programs. Eisenhower knew, from spy-plane intelligence, that there was no "missile gap," but he could not say so without exposing the existence of the flights themselves.

In the same years Secretary of State John Foster Dulles, a senior Presbyterian layman with a high moral sense of the United States's role in the world, aimed to improve on President Truman's policy of containment. This required U.S. vigilance on all the frontiers of the Soviet empire to prevent its expansion. Containment, said Dulles, was too negative. Instead, the United States should aim at liberating the nations of Eastern Europe. He understood the importance of nuclear threats and practiced what he termed "brinksmanship," a willingness to step to the brink of the nuclear precipice without flinching, as a way of gaining diplomatic and strategic advantage over the adversary. Despite the rhetoric, however, and a good deal of bluster in the early days of the administration, he and Eisenhower were constrained by the realties of power and found themselves maintaining most of Truman's policies.

Trouble within the Warsaw Pact

In response to the creation of NATO the Soviet Union, in 1955, had organized its Eastern European satellite nations, East Germany, Hungary, Poland, Czechoslovakia, Rumania, and Bulgaria, into a military alliance, the Warsaw Pact. In October 1956 two Warsaw Pact members, Poland and Hungary, tried to throw out their Soviet masters and regain genuine independence. Worker riots broke out in Poznañ, Poland. In response to the unrest a new Polish Politboro introduced liberalizations that restored a measure of peace. In Hungary patriotic rebels actually expelled the pro-Soviet government and set up an indigenous government led by Imre Nagy. Broadcasts by a CIA-supported radio station, Radio Free Europe, had encouraged uprisings of this kind and led Hungarian nationalists to expect U.S. help. However, the Russians promptly answered with a military expedition against Hungary and warned Eisenhower that any U.S. intervention in their sphere of influence would provoke a general war. Eisenhower and Dulles were forced to admit that they were powerless to help in a place so far from U.S. resources and so central to the Soviet establishment. As a result the Hungarian rebellion was crushed with 30,000 victims, its leaders killed and imprisoned, and a puppet Soviet regime was reestablished.

Summit Meetings

Between the death of Soviet leader Joseph Stalin in 1953 and the Hungarian revolution of 1956 a thaw in the Cold War seemed possible. Stalin's successor Nikita Khrushchev criticized Stalin's legacy in a speech at the Twentieth Soviet Party Congress and began a program of de- Stalinization, while Eisenhower began to express the hope that the superpowers could manage peaceful coexistence. Many friction points remained, however, even in the years before the Hungarian crisis led to renewed animosity. In a speech at the United Nations (UN) on December 8, 1953, for example, Eisenhower won enthusiastic applause for his proposal to turn atomic power from warlike to constructive, peaceful uses. This "Atoms for Peace" speech included the idea of all the nuclear nations placing stocks of uranium at the disposal of the United Nations. But the speech, watered down from its original boldness by anxious foreign policy staffers, made clear Eisenhower's intention of maintaining U.S. nuclear superiority. As a result the Soviet Union declined to participate, and the plan came to nothing.

The 1955 Geneva Summit

Similarly, at a summit meeting in Geneva, Switzerland, in July 1955 Eisenhower expressed his goodwill towards the Soviet Union's post-Stalin leadership group, Khrushchev, Nikolay Bulganin, and his old military friend Marshal Georgy Zhukov. It was the first U.S.-Soviet summit since the Yalta and Potsdam meetings at the end of World War II, 10 years before. It was at these meetings, many Republicans believed, that the United States had unnecessarily surrendered Eastern Europe into the hands of the Soviet Union. Eisenhower had to be careful to show that in his concern for world peace he would not let himself be overawed by the Soviets. He proposed an "Open Skies" policy, by which the Soviet Union and the United States would each establish air bases in the other's country, with the right to overfly and photograph military installations. In this way, he argued, neither would have any incentive to build up massive and futile stockpiles of secret nuclear weapons, and the level of mutual trust between the Cold War rivals would increase. As he and his advisers had expected the Soviet leaders refused this proposed infringement of their sovereignty. They also refused Eisenhower's second major proposal at Geneva, the reunification of Germany, which had been divided into eastern and western zones at the end of World War II.

The Hungarian crisis prevented further progress between the superpowers for the next two years, but in 1959 Vice President Nixon visited the Soviet Union and Khrushchev visited the United States. On the first of these exchanges Nixon and Khrushchev paused beside a model American kitchen at an exhibition of U.S. consumer goods in Moscow. Nixon pointed to it as an example of the superior technology generated by the United States's free market economy, but in a series of good-natured, finger-wagging disagreements Khrushchev emphasized that Russia had plenty of its own special strengths to answer the challenge of the West. In 1958 each side suspended atmospheric testing of nuclear weapons and each recognized the desirability of a treaty to prevent further nuclear contamination of the air.

The U-2 Incident

In 1960, his last year as president, Eisenhower hoped to build a lasting peace agreement with the Soviet Union, and he arranged a summit meeting in Paris, France, with Premier Khrushchev for the middle of May. He hoped the two sides could agree to limit arms production and to formalize the ban on atmospheric tests. He planned it as the crowning achievement of his popular presidency, and an event to assure his dignified place in the history books. Yet he contributed to undermining it needlessly. Since 1955 the CIA had been flying spy-plane missions

Fast Fact

The Interstate Highway Act of 1956 authorized a network of federally funded, multi-lane highways 42,000 miles long. Complications with urban clearance, land acquisition, suburban sprawl, pollution, and local political resistance, meant that only 7,500 miles had been built by the time Eisenhower left office.

(Source: Robert F. Burk. *Dwight D. Eisenhower*, 1986.)

over the Soviet Union with special aircraft, the U-2s, which flew at the very high altitude of 15 miles and could not be brought down by Soviet air defenses (though their radar could spot them). Photographs taken by the U-2s proved that an alleged "missile gap" between the United States and the Soviet Union (a theme exploited by Democratic candidates in the 1958 and 1960 elections) was nonexistent.

Just two weeks before the summit Eisenhower authorized another flight, with the pilot taking off from Turkey on May 1, 1960, and heading for a landing in Norway after making his photographic runs over defense areas. It was an act of foolish provocation, whose yield of photographic information was unlikely to equal the embarrassment if something went wrong. Something did go wrong. The Russians managed to shoot down the plane with an improved surface-to-air missile. At first the Pentagon would admit only that it was a weather forecasting plane that had flown off course. Just before the Paris summit meeting, however, Khrushchev announced that the pilot, CIA agent Francis Gary Powers, had survived the destruction of his plane and was now a prisoner. He and cameras recovered from the plane's wreckage revealed the true nature of his mission.

Eisenhower went to Paris hoping to bluff his way around this diplomatic embarrassment but he was unable to do so. Khrushchev, who had got on well with the president in previous meetings, was personally affronted and mortified, and he condemned the Americans in a harsh, implacable speech that destroyed the possibility of treaties relating to arms limitation or an atmospheric test ban.

Asian Affairs

Korea

At the beginning of his administration Eisenhower tried to make good on his election rhetoric of "rolling back Communism" by escalating the level of the Korean War (1950–3). He visited U.S. troops there after his election but before his inauguration. After early mobile phases in 1950–1 it had become a horribly costly and static war of attrition. He authorized nationalist leader Chiang Kai-shek to intervene against the Communist Chinese (North Korea's chief ally) and Dulles, putting his promise of "brinksmanship" into action, threatened that the United States would resort to tactical nuclear weapons, some of which were actually sent to U.S. Air Force bases in Okinawa off the coast of Japan. The Chinese and North Koreans responded by negotiating a truce with the UN forces in July 1953. The hoped-for next stage, a peace treaty, remained elusive. The truce restored the 38th parallel as the line between the Communist north and the anticommunist south. Heavily fortified on both sides, it remained a potential Cold War flashpoint.

China

The Chinese mainland, under Communist control since the success of Mao Tso-tung's revolution in 1949, was eager to destroy the remains of Chiang Kai-shek's Chinese Nationalists, who had been overthrown and retreated to the island of Formosa (Taiwan). Eisenhower, like Truman, was pledged to preserve Chiang as the great Chinese anticommunist. In September 1954 he also had to decide whether to defend Nationalist outposts on the islands of Quemoy, Matsu, and the Tachen islands, just off the mainland, when Mao's forces began to bombard them. Although the islands were strategically worthless, and although their fall would have no direct affect on the security of Formosa, Eisenhower feared a propaganda defeat. After requesting and receiving from the Eighty-fourth Congress a resolution (the Formosa Resolution) giving him power to use military force; Eisenhower ordered the Seventh Fleet to patrol the strait off mainland China, forestalling any Communist invasion attempt. The Chinese had no fleet to match the U.S. fleet and so were unable to move. To underline his determination, Eisenhower permitted Secretary of State Dulles to threaten the use of tactical atomic weapons against the Chinese if they invaded. The bombardment ceased.

Although U.S. and Chinese negotiations over the islands began in August 1955, the area remained a potential flashpoint. Congress had authorized Eisenhower to use all necessary force to prevent Communist advances, and a flare-up of Communist bombardment of the islands caused another war scare in 1958. The Communist Chinese hoped to force the United States away, but Eisenhower, eager to mollify Chiang and prevent him from launching a rash reinvasion of the Chinese mainland, again sent his fleet and up-to-date missiles for Nationalist Chinese aircraft. The Communists backed off and contented themselves with no more than an occasional shelling of the islands, which remained in Nationalist hands.

Vietnam

The French were colonial masters of Vietnam from the late nineteenth century to the mid- twentieth century.

Japan invaded Vietnam during World War II but France regained its colony in 1945 when Japan was defeated. Ho Chi Minh, a French-educated Communist and Vietnamese nationalist, had fought against the Japanese and then led his country's war of independence against the French in the late 1940s and early 1950s. The United States aided the French in return for French support of NATO in Europe. In 1954 the French stronghold of Dien Bien Phu, under strong attack by Ho's forces, was in imminent danger of collapse. Eisenhower's defense advisers suggested U.S. Air Force strikes to save it, possibly including nuclear weapons. Eisenhower refused and Dien Bien Phu fell to the Communists, effectively ending the French empire in Vietnam.

In July 1954 a treaty formulated at Geneva, Switzerland, involving the French, Vietnamese, and other Asian colonial powers arranged for a temporary division of the country into a Communist North Vietnam, governed by nationalist leader Ho Chi Minh, and a southern zone under Ngo Dinh Diem, a French-speaking Catholic and anticommunist. After the settlement of refugees and a general pacification, elections for the newly unified and independent Vietnam were scheduled for 1956.

Eisenhower and Dulles, foreseeing that Ho Chi Minh would win these elections, refused to endorse the treaty and notified Diem that they would support his effort to keep South Vietnam independent. As a result guerrilla fighting resumed in the late 1950s, with the procommunist Viet Minh, Ho Chi Minh's army, attacking Diem's southern soldiers, who were armed with U.S. weapons. Eisenhower was willing to send aid to Diem but, mindful of the Korean quagmire, was determined not to become directly involved.

To fortify Asia he and Dulles arranged a South East Asian Treaty Organization (SEATO), a regional equivalent of the European NATO pact, which was signed in 1954 at Manila in the Philippines. Its members; the United States, Britain, France, Australia, New Zealand, Pakistan, Thailand, and the Philippines, were pledged to mutual defense in the area against Communist aggression, but unlike NATO they lacked the coordinated armed forces to carry out this pledge in the event of a crisis.

The Middle East

Another site of international tensions in the Eisenhower era was the Middle East, in which anticolonial feeling and Arab nationalism were blended with intense hatred for the new, postwar nation of Israel. Egypt had been under British control until World War II but was now ruled by an Arab nationalist, Gamel Abdel Nasser, who played the superpowers against each other and was able, for a time, to win promises of support from both to build the Aswan Dam across the River Nile. In July 1956, however, he fell out with the Western powers, gave diplomatic recognition to Communist China, and made an arms deal with Communist Czechoslovakia. The Eisen-

hower government reacted by withdrawing its offer of help with the dam. Nasser in turn retaliated by seizing the strategically vital Suez Canal (the gateway from the Mediterranean Sea to the Arabian Gulf and Indian Ocean, and a major oil supply route) from its British and French owners.

Britain and France negotiated secretly with Israel for a joint military mission to regain control of the canal and launched their attack that October. British Prime Minister Anthony Eden had not assured himself of Eisenhower's support, however, and the president, preoccupied with the Hungarian crisis and afraid that the Soviet Union would use the incident as an excuse for direct intervention, was furious at this display of independent action by his chief NATO ally. Angry though he was at Nasser, he had to acknowledge that the canal ran through Egyptian territory, and he regarded the Anglo-French mission as the kind of imperialist aggression that was no longer internationally acceptable. He sent an ultimatum to Eden, declaring that if the attacks did not stop at once, the United States would withdraw its support from the British economy, including its vital oil supply. Faced with the prospect of an economic catastrophe, Eden complied, and the half-completed mission ground to a halt. British and French forces gave way to a United Nations peacekeeping force in the area.

The Suez fiasco marked the last time that Britain would attempt an independent imperial adventure. Its world influence and its empire had shrunk dramatically since World War II, and there was no further room for doubt that it had become a second-rate power, dependent on U.S. goodwill. Prime Minister Eden resigned in disgrace. Eisenhower tried to restore good diplomatic relations with Britain by meeting Eden's successor as prime minister, Harold Macmillan, who had been one of his military aides during World War II. Macmillan, more attuned to the realities of world power than Eden, cooperated with Eisenhower in 1958 in sending peacekeeping forces to Lebanon and Jordan against the threat of Communist subversion.

Covert Operations

The Central Intelligence Agency (CIA), established in 1947, flourished in the conspiratorial atmosphere of the Cold War and soon moved from mere intelligence-gathering to active but secret operations. Its chief, Allen Dulles, was brother of Secretary of State John Foster Dulles. Eisenhower allowed the CIA to flourish because it permitted him to achieve numerous Cold War objectives while posing as a high-minded man of peace.

Iranian Coup Aided by CIA

In August 1953 the CIA contributed money and expertise to an Iranian coup, in which Prime Minister Mohammad Mosaddeq (suspected of negotiating for Soviet aid) was overthrown by supporters of Shah Mohammad Reza Pahlavi. Mosaddeq had nationalized oil fields held by British oil companies, seizing them from their owners and declaring them the property of the Iranian nation. He then diverted the profits to his own treasury. Eisenhower aided the coup against Mosaddeq because he recognized that oil was now one of the world's premier strategic resources, to which the Western powers must have the best access. The Shah became, in effect, the tool of U.S. and British oil companies, because the price of U.S. aid had been to give them a 40 percent share in Iran's oil development consortium. With the oil flowing, Iran and the Shah were rich—without it they were destitute—but it would only flow when conditions suited the Western oil companies.

Guatemala

A similar situation took place in Guatemala the next year. When Jacobo Arbenz Guzman was elected premier of the Central American republic in 1951, Eisenhower's intelligence agencies treated him as a Communist, though most observers saw him as a moderate Social Democrat. Guatemala had been dominated through much of the twentieth century by the U.S.-based United Fruit Company (UFCO). It was, literally, a banana republic, whose only profitable business was the export of fruit in the hands of this foreign corporation. In 1953 and early 1954 the Guatemalan leader nationalized much of the UFCO land and gave it to peasant farmers. He compensated UFCO but the company's officials became convinced that their entire operation was in jeopardy, and, after spending millions of dollars to lobby sympathetic Republicans, they prevailed on Eisenhower to intervene. He authorized a campaign of press smears against Arbenz and a naval blockade, and then gave financial and weapons support to a right-wing alternative to Arbenz named Castillo Armas, who seized power and restored UFCO's privileges.

Cuba

Cuba, under U.S. influence since the Spanish-American War at the turn of the century, was another focus of U.S. covert operations in the last years of the Eisenhower administration. The island was divided between a rich minority, closely tied to U.S. businesses, including organized crime, and a huge, wretchedly poor minority. In 1959, after years of jungle campaigning, revolutionary armies led by the romantic figure of Fidel Castro, a former lawyer and a passionate Cuban nationalist, descended on the capital city, Havana, and expelled the corrupt regime of dictator Fulgencio Batista. As with Arbenz in Guatemala it was not clear that Castro was a Communist, but his grisly public executions of old Batista supporters, his anti-U.S. rhetoric, and his negotiations with the Soviet Union soon soured U.S.-Cuban relations.

Castro and his lieutenant, Che Guevara, an idealistic doctor and guerrilla fighter, became existentialist heroes to a generation of young leftists and anti-imperialists throughout the world. Meanwhile, thousands of Cubans associated with the Batista regime fled the island and sailed to the nearest U.S. landfall, Miami, Florida, which became the headquarters of a thriving exile community. U.S. military and CIA advisers urged Eisenhower to launch an invasion of Cuba and retake it, rather than permit a pro-Soviet Communist regime to take root so close to the U.S. mainland. Eisenhower's anti-communist zeal and his caution about military adventures clashed, but before long he was giving approval to plans for covert operations against Castro. He was out of office before the disastrous Bay of Pigs operation could be launched, for which President Kennedy got the blame instead (*See also,* Kennedy Administration). But most historians believe that Eisenhower would have undertaken a similar venture rather than let a potential enemy thrive so near to the continental United States.

The Space Race

Closely related to nuclear weapons was the rapid development in the 1950s of rocket and missile technology. The United States and the Soviet Union alike linked rocket research to space exploration and travel, while knowing perfectly well that each was equally interested in missiles as bomb delivery systems. To Eisenhower's dismay the Soviets were first to launch an artificial satellite, *Sputnik,* which went into orbit in October 1957. A series of humiliating setbacks, launch pad explosions, and failures to take off, hamstrung the U.S. space program in the mid and late , 1950s, until the first successful launch of a U.S. satellite, *Explorer I,* on January 31, 1958. That year Congress created the civilian-controlled National Aeronautics and Space Administration (NASA) to run the space program, but it was not able, in the short run, to overcome the Soviets' advantage. Just before Khrushchev's visit to the United States in 1959, the Russian *Lunik I* was intentionally crash-landed in the Sea of Tranquillity, becoming the first terrestrial object to reach the moon. Khrushchev gave a model of it to Eisenhower in the Oval Office at the White House, partly as a gesture of goodwill, partly as a reminder that there were areas in which Russia still had the edge.

The Eisenhower Administration Legacy

Eisenhower, aged 70, was the oldest president in U.S. history when he left office in the winter of 1961, handing over to John F. Kennedy, who, at the age of 43, was the youngest. Kennedy's inaccurate allegation that Eisenhower had permitted a missile gap to develop annoyed the retiring president. The new president's inaugural address included a section about passing the torch to a new generation of Americans born in the twentieth century. Kennedy supporters loved it, but Eisenhower (born in 1890), found it hurtful and rather pointed, as though he were a relic of bygone ages. And although he had never been close to his own vice president, Richard Nixon, the Republicans' 1960 candidate and loser in one of the century's closest election races, Eisenhower regretted that his party had not retained the White House.

Observers at the time and historians since 1960 have disagreed about the strengths and weaknesses of the Eisenhower administration. On the one hand he successfully extricated the United States from the costly and destructive Korean War (1950–3) and prevented U.S. soldiers from fighting in remote parts of the world; he was always convinced that the United States could not win a land war in Asia. His successors, Kennedy and Lyndon Johnson, were not so cautious. On the other hand he missed several opportunities to thaw the Cold War; once after the death of Joseph Stalin, and again with the provocative U-2 spy planes just before the Paris summit conference of 1960. Rhetoric of liberation notwithstanding, he did nothing to help the Hungarian rebels, and his rebuke to Britain and France in the Suez crisis threatened the stability of the Western alliance.

Covert operations continued to flourish through the 1950s and 1960s. Ironically their effectiveness came into question when several senior British intelligence agents were shown to be Soviet spies, feeding information about U.S. and British military plans to the Soviet Union. Defection, double cross, and amoral dealings made espionage a fertile subject for fiction in the Eisenhower era.

Eisenhower, in his farewell address, made reference to the "military-industrial complex" as a potentially threatening set of interlocking agencies and corporations that might come to dominate U.S. life. The escalation of the United States's role in Vietnam during the 1960s made his remark seem prophetic, and the military-industrial complex became a leading target of New Left critics during the 1960s. His domestic policy as a whole was successful, if unremarkable. His role in the Civil Rights movement was the opposite of heroic, but he did enable to the nation to consolidate the social and economic gains it had begun with the New Deal. He had the good fortune to preside over a period of sustained economic growth, when the United States became the world's most affluent society.

Lasting Impact

When Eisenhower's term of office ended, few historians gave him high marks, and he was ranked 21st among historic presidents in a poll. Later, however, in light of the Vietnam and Watergate disasters of the 1960s and 1970s, he began to look better, and he became ninth among presidents in another historians' poll held in the early 1980s. His restraint was remarkable. Throughout his first term of office he was pressured by his military advisers and the Joint Chiefs of Staff to use nuclear weapons against China, Korea, and Vietnam. In every instance he refused, just as he refused to become involved in a land war in Asia. This forbearance seemed very com-

mendable by the 1980s, and it wins high praise for him from historians and biographers today.

On the other hand his use of the CIA and covert operations, highly praised by those who knew about them at the time, came to seem a sinister precedent in light of later events in Vietnam, Iran, and Central America. For example, British historian and Eisenhower biographer Piers Brendon writes: "His intervention [in Guatemala] had disastrous long-term effects. It inspired future U.S. presidents to pursue hidden and sometimes iniquitous policies abroad, from which Congress was excluded and press and people were kept in ignorance or deceived . . . and it did not quell, as much as foster, Communism elsewhere in Latin America" (Brendon, p. 286).

Another dangerous trend was his invocation of "executive privilege" to prevent his advisers from being subpoenaed by Senator Joseph McCarthy. Executive privilege, which is not mentioned in the Constitution and has always been ambiguous, is the claim that a president needs to be exempt from the usual forms of legal process so that he can concentrate on work of national importance. Unlike President Nixon in the Watergate scandal, however, he did not abuse the privilege as a way of covering up law-breaking and abuse of power. But he certainly did try to increase the powers of the presidency, as when he persuaded Congress to grant him war-making discretion in the Quemoy-Matsu crisis of 1954 (*See also*, Foreign Issues).

Eisenhower's failure to achieve clear victories in foreign or domestic affairs made him seem lackluster at the time, but his restraint has won high praise from such later historians as Herbert Parmet and Stephen Ambrose. Ambrose finishes his biography of Eisenhower with the declaration that "Eisenhower gave the nation eight years of peace and prosperity. No other president in the twentieth century could make that claim," adding that "whether or not one agrees with his decisions . . . there is no doubt that he was an inspiring and effective leader, indeed a model of leadership."

Sources

Ambrose, Stephen. *Eisenhower: Soldier and President.* New York: Simon and Schuster, 1991.

Beschloss, Michael R. *Eisenhower: A Centennial Life.* New York: Edward Burlingame/HarperCollins, 1990.

Brendon, Piers. *Ike: His Life and Times.* New York: Harper and Row, 1986.

Burk, Robert F. *Dwight D. Eisenhower: Hero and Politician.* Boston: Twayne, 1986.

Goldman, Eric. *The Crucial Decade and After: America 1945–1960* New York: Vintage, 1960.

Grantham, Dewey W. *Recent America: The United States Since 1945.* 2d ed. Wheeling, Illinois: Harlan Davidson, 1998.

Halberstam, David. *The Fifties.* New York: Villard, 1993.

Historic World Leaders. Detroit: Gale Research, 1994.

Pach, Chester, and Elmo Richardson. *The Presidency of Dwight D. Eisenhower.* Lawrence, Kans.: University Press of Kansas, 1991.

Parmet, Herbert. *Eisenhower and the American Crusades.* New York: Macmillan, 1972.

Roark, James, et al. *The American Promise.* Vol 2. Boston: Bedford, 1998.

Further Readings

Dwight D. Eisenhower Library. <http://www.eisenhower.utexas.edu> (7 July 1999).

Eisenhower, Dwight. *Crusade in Europe.* Garden City, NY: Doubleday, 1948.

————. *Mandate for Change.* Garden City, NY: Doubleday, 1963.

Fried, Richard M. *Nightmare in Red: The McCarthy Era in Perspective.* New York: Oxford University Press, 1990.

Greenstein, Fred I. *The Hidden Hand Presidency: Eisenhower as Leader.* New York: Basic, 1982.

Larson, Arthur. *Eisenhower, the President Nobody Knew.* New York: Charles Scribner's, 1968.

Kennedy Administration

Biography

John F. Kennedy was raised in a privileged background and shaped by his ambitious father who wanted to establish the Kennedys in positions of influence and power in the United States. Though somewhat detached and ironic in personality, Kennedy served with distinction in World War II, was elected to both the U.S. House and Senate and was a Pulitzer Prize winning author. As president, Kennedy proved a dynamic leader in a time of crisis, a figure who captured the imagination of the public, and one of the nation's most discussed presidents.

Early Life

Descended from Irish-Catholic immigrants, John Kennedy's achievements capped a four-generation long struggle for ascendancy in their adopted homeland. His great-grandfather, Patrick Kennedy, a barrel maker fleeing the famine in Ireland, emigrated to Boston, Massachusetts in 1849 from Dunganstown in County Wexford. His grandfather, Patrick J. Kennedy Jr., owned three saloons and branched out into banking and Boston politics. Intent on breaking the social barriers erected by Boston's Yankee Protestant elite, Kennedy's son, Joseph Patrick Kennedy (1888–1969), gained admission to Harvard College, announced his goal of being a millionaire by age 30, and, in 1914, married Rose Elizabeth Fitzgerald, the spirited and attractive daughter of Boston mayor John "Honey Fitz" Fitzgerald.

Full name: John F. Kennedy
Given name: John Fitzgerald Kennedy
Popular name: JFK; Jack

Personal Information:
Born: May 29, 1917
Died: November 22, 1963
Burial place: Arlington National Cemetery, Arlington, Virginia
Religion: Roman Catholic
Spouse: Jacqueline Lee Bouvier (m. 1953)
Children: Caroline Bouvier Kennedy Schlossberg; John F. Jr.; Patrick
Education: Harvard College, B.S., 1940
Occupation: Author; journalist; politician
Political Party: Democratic Party
Age at Inauguration: 43 years

John F. Kennedy. (The Library of Congress.)

Joseph P. Kennedy Founds a Dynasty

Joseph P. Kennedy compiled an immense fortune in banking, real estate, stock market speculation, motion pictures, and liquor imports. He earned a reputation for a brusque, profane manner and ruthless business practices. For helping finance Franklin D. Roosevelt's 1932 presidential campaign, Kennedy was appointed chairman of the Securities Exchange Commission (1934–36), chairman of the Maritime Commission (1937), then ambassador to Great Britain (1937–40). Kennedy's public career ended abruptly in 1940 when he alienated President Roosevelt by advocating coexistence with Nazi Germany and by bluntly asserting that England's weaknesses gave them little chance of defeating Nazi leader Adolf Hitler. Thereafter, he focused on business and his sons' political careers.

JFK Growing Up

John Fitzgerald Kennedy, born May 29, 1917, in his parents' home at 83 Beals Street in the middle-class suburb of Brookline, Massachusetts, was the second of nine children. In 1927 the Kennedys moved to a large estate in the Bronxville section outside New York City where, except for two years in London, England, they resided until 1941. Thereafter, they summered in Hyannis Port, Massachusetts, wintered in Florida or on the French Riviera, and kept apartments in New York City.

Remarkably similar in appearance, each with shocks of auburn or brown hair, bright toothy smiles, strong chins, and high cheekbones, the Kennedy children created their own intensely competitive, prank-filled inner world. Joe Jr., the eldest and his father's favorite, took charge of the younger children, teaching them sports and discipline. Robert Kennedy would later say that he was their role model. John regaled his younger brothers and sisters with stories of heroes, the epic tales of great men in history gleaned from the many books he read during his numerous childhood illnesses.

Health

John Kennedy's poor health was a closely held family secret. Surviving several life-threatening illnesses, Kennedy was given the last rites of the Catholic Church on at least four occasions. He suffered throughout life from chronic stomach disorders, recurrent venereal disease, debilitating back problems, frequent and severe allergic reactions, and the undiagnosed, until 1947, effects of Addison's disease, a failure of the adrenal glands, which sapped his energy, weakened his immune system, and left him vulnerable to infections and dangerously high fevers. His father, fearing an adverse public reaction, covered up John's illnesses (and also daughter Rosemary's mental retardation), persistently portraying John as fit and vigorous and attributing his many afflictions to athletic or war injuries.

From 1951 to the end of his life, Kennedy treated his Addison's disease with regular cortisone and steroid injections. The medications created a puffiness in his face, heightened his sexual desires, and discolored his skin, giving him the appearance of a perpetual tan. Chronic back pain forced him onto crutches several times during his presidency. To endure long public appearances he wore a metal-reinforced back brace and, as on the day of his assassination, heavy bandages wrapped around his torso and thighs.

Education

John attended Choate, an Episcopal preparatory school in Connecticut, where he earned a reputation as a charming womanizer and fun-loving prankster. In 1935 Kennedy enrolled at the London School of Economics and Princeton University in New Jersey but attended neither because of illness. He entered Harvard College in the fall 1936, taking leave in 1938 to travel through Europe, serving as personal secretary to his father, the U.S. ambassador to Great Britain.

Kennedy graduated from Harvard in June 1940, winning honors in history for his thesis analyzing England's slow reaction to German rearmament. With help from his father's powerful friends in publishing, the thesis was published in 1941 under the title, *Why England Slept*. At

22 and the author of a best-selling book, Kennedy looked toward a career in history, journalism, or public service.

Informal Education

Joseph Kennedy deliberately prepared all of his sons for public service and politics, constantly impressing on them the exceptional status they enjoyed as his sons and their obligations to bring prestige to the family. For John he arranged trips abroad as a newspaper correspondent so he could tour foreign capitals, meet political leaders, and gain an appreciation for the complexities of international affairs. He discouraged John from adhering to absolute political beliefs that might lessen or restrict his appeal and effectiveness. Believing that appearances were very important, Joseph Kennedy skillfully enhanced the Kennedy image, cultivating reporters, publishers, and media leaders and garnering a great deal of publicity for himself and his sons.

Family Life

As a young man Kennedy enjoyed bachelor life and earned a reputation as a ladies' man. In January 1953, when he was 35 and a newly elected U.S. senator, Kennedy began seriously courting 23-year-old Jacqueline (Jackie) Bouvier, then a reporter for a Washington newspaper. Born in Southampton, New York, accustomed to wealth and privilege, she was educated at fashionable finishing schools, Vassar College, the Sorbonne in Paris, France, and George Washington University. Attractive and demure, she possessed a biting wit and independent spirit that both complemented and challenged Kennedy. Their spectacular Newport, Rhode Island, wedding that September was hailed as the social event of the year.

Although a legal, voting resident of Boston, Massachusetts, where he maintained a small apartment on Bowdoin Street, Kennedy never lived there and visited rarely. When Congress was in session John and Jacqueline Kennedy lived in Georgetown, an upscale section of Washington, D.C. To satisfy Jacqueline Kennedy's love of horses, they rented a large country house called Glen Ora located near Middleburg, Virginia, about 40 miles from the capital, where they spent many weekends during Kennedy's presidency.

Far from perfect, the Kennedys' marriage faltered badly at times. Jacqueline Kennedy disliked politics and most politicians. She also struggled to win acceptance in the close-knit Kennedy family. Jacqueline Kennedy was deeply hurt by her husband's continued involvements with other women. He ignored her feelings and, according to evidence uncovered after his death, persisted in a series of reckless sexual liaisons. On several occasions the marriage appeared in dire straits, particularly in 1956 when Jacqueline Kennedy faced alone the trauma of the stillbirth of their first child while John was partying with friends in Europe. Happily two healthy children followed, Caroline Bouvier Kennedy in 1957 and, John Fitzgerald Kennedy Jr. in 1960. A fourth child, Patrick Bouvier Kennedy, born August 7, 1963, died two days later. Patrick's death, close friends of the Kennedys agreed, profoundly affected the couple's relationship, as, ironically, after years of marital tension, they drew closer together in the months just prior to Kennedy's assassination.

Career

In 1941, with U.S. entry into World War II (1939–45) approaching, John Kennedy put his career on hold and in September followed his brother Joe Jr. into the U.S. Navy. Assigned initially to Naval Intelligence in Washington, he became sexually involved with a woman the Federal Bureau of Investigation (FBI) suspected (later cleared) of being a Nazi spy and was transferred to a patrol torpedo (PT boat) squadron and sent to the Pacific theater of war. In the Solomon Islands on August 2, 1943, a boat under his command, *PT-109,* was rammed and sunk by the Japanese destroyer *Amagiri.* Some authorities questioned Kennedy's seamanship and command abilities prior to the sinking of his craft. No one, however, doubted his genuine heroism in rescuing injured crew members or his courage in sustaining his crew behind enemy lines pending their rescue. Awarded the Navy and Marine Corps Medal and the Purple Heart, and proclaimed a hero by the *New York Times,* he soon returned home for treatment of recurring back problems that should have disqualified him for military service in the first place.

Discharged from the navy for medical reasons in April 1945, Kennedy was immediately thrust into politics by his father who, a year earlier, was devastated by the death of his oldest son, Joe Jr., during a volunteer bombing mission in Europe. It now fell to John Kennedy to fulfill his father's avowed goal of making one of his sons the first Irish-Catholic president of the United States.

Congressman

In 1946 John Kennedy won election to the U.S. Congress from Massachusetts' 11th District, representing parts of Boston and Cambridge, the same seat his grandfather John Fitzgerald once held. Kennedy ran on his family's name, his youth, and his war record. His father spent exorbitant sums on the campaign and involved the entire Kennedy family (except sister Rosemary, who was mentally retarded).

In 1952, at his father's urging, Kennedy challenged Henry Cabot Lodge Jr. for the U.S. Senate from Massachusetts. Most observers gave Kennedy little chance.

Fast Fact

Although fewer than 50 percent voted for him in 1960, JFK's effect on the U.S. public was so great and his death such a shock that 65 percent of those polled in 1964 claimed to have voted for him.

(Source: William Manchester. *The Death of a President,* 1967.)

Lodge, scion of a venerable Boston family and a national figure, seemed unbeatable. With the popular Gen. Dwight D. Eisenhower, hero of the Allied victory in Europe during World War II, at the top of their ticket, Republicans expected to sweep most offices in 1952.

The 1952 campaign featured sophisticated, often unique methods of reaching the voters. Among the first to make extensive use of television for advertising and fund-raising, Kennedy enrolled in a special CBS-TV seminar on how to use TV effectively. His naturally poised and unrestrained manner fitted the new medium perfectly. Highlighting the campaign were the appearances of the candidate's mother and sisters at hundreds of invitation-only social events where the Kennedy women served tea and charmed an estimated 70,000 women voters. A record turnout gave Kennedy a slim 76,000 vote margin over Lodge. Kennedy attracted large support from Boston, Irish Catholics, Jews, labor union members, and some disaffected Republicans who thought Kennedy more conservative than Lodge.

Poised for the Presidency

By the late 1950s John Kennedy had garnered a great deal of publicity, much of it based on the allure of his good looks and his family name. His reputation was enhanced by his participation in the televised hearings of investigations into criminal influences in the labor movement by the Senate Rackets Committee, for which his brother Robert served as chief counsel. In 1955 he published a best-selling book, *Profiles in Courage,* which contained biographical sketches of eight political leaders who had risked everything for the sake of their convictions. The book stamped Kennedy as something exceptional, an intellectual in politics. His father lobbied his influential friends and the book won the Pulitzer Prize for biography. Kennedy had help in writing the book, but he accepted the prize as though the work were wholly his own, thus arousing suspicions about how much sub-

stance existed behind the image. Those suspicions lingered throughout his life and into the historical assessments beyond.

Kennedy campaigned for the vice presidential nomination at the 1956 Democratic National Convention. He tried to persuade Adlai Stevenson, the Democratic presidential nominee, that a Catholic running mate from the Northeast would greatly strengthen the ticket. However, Eleanor Roosevelt, wife of President Franklin D. Roosevelt, spoke for many liberals when she refused to support Kennedy, suggesting that he show less profile and more courage. Kennedy narrowly lost the vice presidential nomination to Senator Estes Kefauver of Tennessee. He won reelection to the Senate in 1958 by a record 874,000 vote margin. After that Kennedy spent virtually full time running for the presidency.

Presidency

In the tough Democratic presidential primary campaigns of 1960 Kennedy persuaded doubtful politicians that a Catholic could indeed win Democratic votes, even in heavily Protestant states like West Virginia. He won the nomination on the first ballot at the convention and promised to lead the United States toward a New Frontier. He was pitted against President Dwight D. Eisenhower's vice president, Richard Nixon. Kennedy's telegenic looks, oratorical skills, and remarkable poise won a number of converts during the first televised presidential debates. Otherwise, voters found little of substance to separate Kennedy and Nixon.

Kennedy won the election by the narrowest of margins without building a strong base within his own party. Neither liberals nor conservatives felt great allegiance to Kennedy, thus limiting Kennedy's domestic policy achievements. His most important domestic accomplishment was his belated but earnest endorsement of civil rights for African Americans, including a comprehensive bill that, in a modified form, became the Civil Rights Act of 1964.

For Kennedy the real test of presidential greatness lay in international affairs. An admiring nation approved of his bravado and coolness in leading the country through a series of frightening confrontations with the Soviet Union over Berlin and Cuba. Determined to contain Communism everywhere, Kennedy presided over the largest peacetime expansion of the U.S. military, which included a significant commitment to aid the government of South Vietnam.

Post-presidential Years

At 12:30 P.M., Friday, November 22, 1963, while riding in a motorcade through downtown Dallas, Texas, John F. Kennedy was assassinated by high-powered rifle fire. The largest mass experience in the nation's history, the news of the president's death simultaneously spread by radio and television to a profoundly shocked and disbelieving country. On November 24, the president's suspected assassin, Lee Harvey Oswald, a disgruntled leftist who had defected to the Soviet Union and then returned, was himself shot to death by Jack Ruby, a Dallas nightclub operator, as a startled national television audience and scores of Dallas police officers looked on. An enormous emotional reaction reverberated for decades after Kennedy's assassination, sometimes manifesting itself in bizarre conspiracy theories about his death.

Vice President Lyndon B. Johnson, who was driving two cars behind President Kennedy when he was assassinated, took the oath of office as president of the United States at 2:30 P.M. that same day. The oath was administered by District Judge Sarah T. Hughes aboard the presidential airplane Air Force One, which had flown the president and his wife to Dallas from Fort Worth, Texas, earlier in the day.

Jacqueline Bouvier Kennedy witnessed the horrible violence of her husband's death seated next to him in the limousine. Images of her disembarking from Air Force One later that evening with her husband's blood caked to her dress are burnished in American memories. Her majestic grace and dignity throughout the long ordeal endeared her to the American people. In 1968, following the assassination of her brother-in-law Robert F. Kennedy, she left the United States to marry the Greek millionaire Aristotle Onassis. After Onassis's death in 1975 she returned to New York City, took on many charitable and civic tasks, and worked as an editor. She died of cancer in May 1994 and is buried next to her husband and two dead infant children in Arlington National Cemetery in Arlington, Virginia.

Both Kennedy children, Caroline Kennedy Schlossberg and John F. Kennedy Jr., went on to successful careers and families of their own. They continued to live in the limelight that followed their father and mother and the rest of the Kennedy clan, prompting many in the media to dub the Kennedys the United States's royal family. The death of John F. Kennedy Jr. in a 1999 plane crash led to nationwide mourning.

The John F. Kennedy Administration

John F. Kennedy, the first Catholic and the youngest elected president, left indelible marks on the presidency and on a nation's psyche. A product of his father's ambition and a reflection of mid-twentieth century U.S. culture and values, Kennedy transformed U.S. politics. He led the country through the most perilous crises of the Cold War, hesitated but then committed himself and the presidency to the Civil Rights movement, and at the peak of his powers was assassinated, to remain, for all his

Following the funeral of President Kennedy in Washington, D.C., his casket was taken by caisson to Arlington National Cemetery for burial. John Kennedy Jr., stood with his mother, Jacqueline Kennedy, and his sister, Caroline Kennedy, saluting the passing processional. (AP/Wide World Photos. Reproduced by permission.)

strengths and weaknesses, a fascinating icon in U.S. political culture.

Kennedy Becomes President

The Campaign of 1960

Kennedy benefited from a well-financed and well-organized campaign. His father's wealth allowed him to outspend his opponents in the primaries and to remain competitive in the general election. Kennedy's campaign organization was the first to include professional pollsters and experts in television advertising. Winning primary elections in New Hampshire, Wisconsin, and West Virginia, amid losers' charges that his father's money bought the elections, Kennedy persuaded skeptical Democratic leaders that he was a viable candidate. He secured the nomination on the first ballot at the Los Angeles Democratic National Convention, with only 806 delegate votes (just 45 more than the required minimum). On July 15, 1960, Kennedy delivered his acceptance speech, promising to

Administration

Administration Dates
January 20, 1961–November 22, 1963

Vice President
Lyndon Baines Johnson (1961–63)

Cabinet
Secretary of State
David D. Rusk (1961–69)

Secretary of the Treasury
Clarence D. Dillon (1961–65)

Attorney General
Robert F. Kennedy (1961–64)

Postmaster General
J. Edward Day (1961–63)
John A. Gronouski, Jr. (1963–65)

Secretary of the Interior
Stewart L. Udall (1961–69)

Secretary of Agriculture
Orville L. Freeman (1961–69)

Secretary of Labor
Arthur J. Golberg (1961–62)
William W. Wirtz (1962–69)

Secretary of Commerce
Luther H. Hodges (1961–65)

Secretary of Defense
Robert S. McNamara (1961–68)

Secretary of Health, Education, and Welfare
Abraham A. Ribicoff (1961–62)
Anthony J. Celebrezze (1961–65)

"get America moving again" and to lead the United States towards a "New Frontier."

Surprisingly, Kennedy selected longtime Texas senator Lyndon Baines Johnson as his running mate. As Senate majority leader, Johnson's skills in securing compromises on controversial legislation earned him the title of Washington's second most powerful man during the second Dwight D. Eisenhower administration, so few expected him to be interested in the mostly ceremonial post of vice president. Johnson, moreover, had personally attacked Kennedy at the convention, citing his lack of experience, his poor health, and his father's isolationist record before World War II (1939–45). Many liberals distrusted Johnson, regarding him as a slippery wheeler-dealer. Therefore, most Democrats were shocked when Kennedy offered and Johnson accepted the vice presidency. However, Johnson's selection proved extremely wise. No other Democrat could have balanced the ticket so effectively, because Johnson enjoyed strong support among white southerners where Kennedy as a New Englander had little strength.

The Republicans nominated Richard M. Nixon at their Chicago convention. A navy veteran and California native, Nixon, only 47, had entered Congress the same year as Kennedy, won election to the Senate in 1950, and served for eight years as Dwight D. Eisenhower's vice president. A champion of anticommunist causes, Nixon was a solemn representative of the middle class to which the Republican Party directed its appeals. He was also a tenacious defender of the Eisenhower record and the status quo. For his running mate Nixon selected Henry Cabot Lodge Jr., the man Kennedy defeated for the Senate in 1952.

Essentially the candidates differed little on the issues. Both were staunch anticommunists who would grant no quarter to the Soviet Union or permit Communist expansion anywhere. Both also hugged the political center; that is, neither candidate endorsed significant expansion or contraction of federal authority beyond the limits set during the previous decade. The real issues of the 1960 campaign were religion, race, and the candidates' contrasting styles.

Religion
Before Kennedy only one Catholic, Governor Al Smith of New York, had won the nomination of either major party for the presidency, and Smith was beaten in a landslide by Herbert Hoover in 1928. Leading Protestant clergy, dismayed at Kennedy's nomination, argued that no Catholic could be president because, according to their understanding of Catholicism, no Catholic could place the United States above the Roman Catholic Church. Kennedy was not a devout Catholic, nevertheless he realized that if he did not confront the issue squarely a Catholic might never be elected president. Kennedy told a gathering of Protestant clergy in Houston, Texas, that he was not the Catholic candidate for president—he did not speak for the Catholic Church, and the Church did not speak for him. Affirming his absolute belief in the separation of church and state, he promised to resign the presidency before allowing religious pressures to violate the national interest. Kennedy, in effect, challenged Protestant voters to prove they were not bigots by voting for him. Estimates are that Kennedy carried only 38 to 46 percent of the

The televised debates between Vice President Richard M. Nixon (left) *and Senator John F. Kennedy in the 1960 presidential election changed forever the form and content of national elections in the United States. Candidates would henceforth be judged on their stage presence as well as their character. (UPI/Corbis-Bettmann. Reproduced by permission.)*

Protestant vote but 78 to 80 percent of the Catholic vote and large numbers of other sympathetic ethnic groups, which helped him carry several of the urban-industrial states in the electoral college.

Race

African American voters, initially inclined toward Nixon, changed their minds late in the campaign because of two telephone calls. In late October Martin Luther King Jr., the United States's most influential civil rights leader, was arrested in Georgia during a civil rights protest. John Kennedy telephoned King's wife, Coretta Scott King, to express his personal concern. The next day his campaign manager and brother, Robert Kennedy, telephoned the presiding judge in the case and demanded that he release King, which he did. King's father publicly expressed his thanks to Kennedy. Just before the election special campaign pamphlets describing Kennedy as the candidate with a heart were distributed throughout African American communities. Kennedy carried an estimated 70 percent of the African American vote, which proved pivotal in several northern cities.

Style

Another turning point occurred during the first of four nationally televised debates. Seemingly fitter and more relaxed, Kennedy's telegenic good looks projected an informed confidence, contrasted to Nixon's pale coun-

tenance and wooden demeanor. Radio listeners thought Nixon, a trained debater, had won; but television audiences gave the edge to Kennedy on the basis of his poise and eloquence. The debates revitalized Kennedy's campaign and boosted him in the polls.

On election day the largest number of eligible voters (64.5 percent) to turn out since 1916 delivered 34,226,731 (49.7 percent of the total vote cast) for Kennedy to 34,108,157 (49.6 percent) for Nixon, making it the closest margin ever in a presidential election. Kennedy carried 22 states (narrowly winning the middle Atlantic states, six states in the Deep South, Illinois, and Texas) and 303 electoral college votes (Johnson had delivered Texas and the six other southern states.) Nixon won 26 Midwest, border, and western states and 219 electoral votes. Largely in protest against Kennedy's religion, 15 electors (eight in Mississippi, six in Alabama, and one in Oklahoma) voted for the conservative Democratic senator Harry F. Byrd of Virginia.

Kennedy took office January 20, 1961, a cold, bright day, following an overnight snowstorm. His inaugural address, notable for its brevity, soaring oratory, and bellicose content, made no mention of civil rights or domestic issues. Instead, Kennedy promised to preserve and expand U.S. influence in world affairs in the face of a "long twilight struggle" against the Soviet Union. Kennedy committed the United States to "pay any price, bear any burden, meet any hardship" in the preservation of freedom. And he demanded sacrifice with the immortal words: "And so, my fellow Americans: ask not what your country can do for you—ask what you can do for your country." Few inaugural addresses have so clearly set the tone for their administrations.

Kennedy's Advisers

Kennedy perceived the lines of governmental authority like the spokes of a wheel all coming to him and going from him. Abandoning formal staffing policies and bureaucratic lines of authority, he sought out ideas from an imposing array of devoted crises managers and problem solvers who shared his values and outlook. Taken from the upper strata of academia and industry, these highly educated men prided themselves, like the president, on their cool temperaments, toughness of mind, and competitive successes.

Theodore Sorensen, a reserved Nebraskan who worked for Kennedy in the Senate, became White House counsel, chief speech writer, and adviser on many foreign and domestic policy matters. McGeorge Bundy, a former Harvard dean, was named special assistant for national security affairs, with the brilliant economic historian Walt W. Rostow as his deputy. R. Sargent Shriver, the president's brother-in-law, directed the civil rights section during the 1960 campaign and headed the Peace Corps. Harris Wofford left the law faculty at the University of Notre Dame to be special counsel on civil rights and later to serve in the Peace Corps. Arthur Schlesinger Jr., prize-winning historian, became special assistant to the president on Latin American affairs and the administration's unofficial historian, as well as its intellectual link to the liberal community.

All major national security decisions involved Gen. Maxwell Taylor, the president's personal adviser on military affairs, and Secretary of Defense Robert McNamara, the brilliant, Harvard-trained 44-year-old president of the Ford Motor Company. No one, however, was closer to the president or involved in a wider range of decisions than Robert Kennedy. Appointed attorney general, some say at his father's insistence, he was the one person on whom John Kennedy could invariably rely. Robert Kennedy's responsibilities overlapped every department. Insiders knew him as chief overseer of his brother's administration.

Kennedy expanded his cabinet by inviting to its meetings Vice President Lyndon Johnson and U.S. ambassador to the United Nations, Adlai E. Stevenson, the Democratic nominee for the presidency in 1952 and 1956. But Kennedy seldom asked the cabinet to resolve major issues. For example, in times of foreign crises, rather than turn to the State Department, which he considered slow and clumsy, he relied upon select advisers, some from the Executive Committee of the National Security Council (called ExComm), and some from outside the government, including Dean Acheson, secretary of state under President Truman, and John J. McCloy, former U.S. high commissioner to Germany.

Kennedy and Congress

When the Eighty-seventh Congress convened in January 1961 President Kennedy's party held majorities of 64 to 36 in the Senate and 262 to 175 in the House. In the 1960 elections Democratic congressional candidates averaged 54.7 percent of the vote (compared to John Kennedy's 49.7 percent), yet the Democrats lost two Senate and 22 House seats. Kennedy's place at the top of the ticket, therefore, actually hurt Democrats in Congress, and they knew it.

Kennedy did not have much influence with individual members of Congress. Although popular during his 14 years in Congress, he paid scant attention to the legislative process, purposely avoided leadership responsibilities, and remained apart from partisan disputes. Kennedy had asked very little of other members of Congress. He owed them little, and they owed him less.

Kennedy's record with Congress was mixed. He gained passage of an impressive list of important new initiatives in foreign policy and national security, but his record on domestic legislation was marginal, leaving much to be completed after his death.

Kennedy's 1961 legislative agenda included five high-priority bills: federal assistance to public schools, hospital insurance for the aged, legislation for housing, aid to depressed areas, and increased minimum wages. He managed to get three of the five passed, failing on federal aid to education and hospital insurance for the aged. Additional domestic issues he came to consider high priorities included a civil rights bill, a tax reduction package, and a proposal to create a Department of Urban Affairs. None passed while he was president.

Surprisingly Kennedy seemed to lack the energy and will to fully engage in the legislative process. He disliked the intense bargaining and time-consuming follow-up required of lawmakers. Rather than deal directly with Congress on normal legislative matters, Kennedy established a congressional liaison office headed by Lawrence F. O'Brien. An advertising executive and expert in political campaigning, O'Brien had no prior experience on Capitol Hill, where Congress holds its sessions, and was seen by legislators as an unnecessary buffer between Congress and the president. Members of Congress wanted and expected personal contact with the president and felt frozen out by the president's surrogates.

Entrenched Opposition

There was a stalemate in the Kennedy Congress caused by a conservative coalition of about 70 Republicans and southern Democrats (many with long years of seniority) who had succeeded since 1938 in blocking liberal-activist programs of the type Kennedy proposed. Southern Democrats who were opposed to the further expansion of federal power at the expense of the states (especially over civil rights for African Americans), frequently aligned with conservative and moderate Republicans who were against regulation of business, increased taxes, deficit spending, and any expansion of presidential authority.

Early in 1961 House Speaker Sam Rayburn developed a plan to unblock a conservative bottleneck, the House Rules Committee, which decided which bills went to the House floor and imposed limits on debate for each bill. Its chairman, Virginia Democrat Howard Smith, supported by Republican conservatives, had frequently blocked liberal initiatives from reaching the floor during the 1950s. Under Rayburn's prodding and with the full exertion of the president's influence, the House, by a narrow 217 to 212 vote, enlarged the Rules Committee, adding three liberals to outnumber the conservatives.

The 1962 elections produced a net gain for the Democrats in the Eighty-eighth Congress of three Senate seats, giving them 67, including Edward (Teddy) Kennedy, who was elected to fill his brothers unexpired Senate term. House Democrats lost four seats, far fewer than the usual drop-off for the presidential party in midterm elections, leaving them with a 259 to 175 margin over the Republicans. Still, the president was unable to demonstrate a clear mastery of the legislative process, particularly when compared to the avalanche of legislation passed after Lyndon Johnson became president. In fairness to Kennedy, however, two things must be considered: first, much of Johnson's success was owing in large measure to the sentimental momentum created by Kennedy's death and; second, Kennedy's overall record with Congress, when considering both domestic and foreign policy issues, was not as bad as some critics suggest.

Kennedy and the Judiciary

Despite the brevity of his tenure in office, Kennedy substantially influenced the makeup of the federal judiciary, appointing 126 federal judges in less than three years, compared to 175 by Eisenhower in eight years. The large number of Kennedy appointments was largely because of the May 1961 enactment of an omnibus judiciary act, which administratively reformed the judiciary and created more than 70 new federal judgeships.

Each Kennedy nomination for a federal judgeship involved political bargaining, because each nomination had to be approved by the Senate and its Judiciary Committee, chaired by Senator James Eastland of Mississippi. Eastland was a states rights advocate and staunch opponent of racial integration. For example, Eastland held up

the confirmation of Thurgood Marshall, the most distinguished African American member of the American Bar Association (later appointed to the Supreme Court by President Johnson), until Attorney General Robert Kennedy agreed to nominate Eastland's college roommate, Harold Cox, an avowed segregationist. Once appointed Cox openly expressed racist views, refused to accept higher court rulings on desegregation, and placed obstacles in the path of the Civil Rights movement. Many liberals and civil rights advocates considered the Cox appointment one of Kennedy's biggest mistakes.

Kennedy made two Supreme Court appointments. To replace Associate Justice Charles E. Whittaker in April 1962 Kennedy named a member of his presidential campaign team, Deputy Attorney General Byron Raymond ("Whizzer") White of Colorado. A former All-American football player with moderate to conservative views, White was easily confirmed by the Senate. To replace Associate Justice Felix Frankfurter, who retired in October 1962, Kennedy nominated and the Senate confirmed Secretary of Labor Arthur J. Goldberg of Illinois, the former general counsel of the AFL-CIO (American Federation of Labor and Congress of Industrial Organizations). Goldberg, like Frankfurter, was Jewish; thus Kennedy followed an unwritten tradition began earlier in the century with the appointment of Louis D. Brandeis of having at least one Jew on the Supreme Court.

During the Kennedy presidency the Supreme Court under Chief Justice Earl Warren handed down a series of important decisions, including *Baker v. Carr* (1962), which forced states to reapportion legislative districts to give urban and suburban voters a representation appropriate to their growth in numbers, thereby reducing the power of rural conservatives in legislatures. In *Engel v. Vitale* (1962), the Court held that it was unconstitutional, a violation of the separation of church and state doctrine, for public schools to require children to recite a nondenominational prayer. A year later in *Abingdon School District v. Schempp* (1963), it ruled against the practice of daily Bible readings in public schools. All three decisions appalled conservatives.

Changes in the U.S. Government

Kennedy's greatest impact on government came from the special aura he brought to the presidency. He increased the presidency's power and authority and expanded the public's respect for the office during his brief service. Kennedy fixed the focus of attention within the U.S. government firmly on the presidency and, so, when someone mentioned the U.S. government, most Americans thought first of the poised and eloquent man sitting in the White House Oval Office.

Rarely has the presidency been as highly celebrated as during the Kennedy years. The pomp and circumstance of the presidency, the elegant state dinners, the high style of the first lady, all gave the president and his family an air of royalty.

Kennedy's changes in the executive office of the president were mostly subtle managerial preferences, not substantive changes. For example, he abandoned President Dwight D. Eisenhower's staff system for managing the presidency, and during the early part of his presidency he made little formal use of the National Security Council, preferring instead to rely on a more collegial approach to foreign policy decision making.

Kennedy did propose a new cabinet-level department—the Department of Housing and Urban Development—in response to the growing problems of U.S. cities. Congress did not pass the necessary legislation during Kennedy's presidency, but a similar proposal was enacted in 1965.

Two constitutional amendments passed during the Kennedy presidency. The Twenty-third Amendment on March 29, 1961, gave District of Columbia residents the right to vote for president and vice president.

In August 1962 Congress passed a provision outlawing poll taxes, which were instituted by white southerners to prevent African Americans and other poor minorities from voting. When approved by the states in January 1964, it became the Twenty-fourth Amendment to the U.S. Constitution.

Executive Orders and Commissions

Partly because he was unable to break the congressional stalemate (*See also,* Kennedy and Congress), President Kennedy created policy through enactment of 214 executive orders. These were presidential proclamations that had been used by modern presidents, such as Franklin D. Roosevelt, to accomplish their agendas. The premise was that Article II of the U.S. Constitution grants power to the president to take action in the nation's best interest as long as the action is not prohibited by the law or by the Constitution. Kennedy built on that tradition by using executive orders to launch new programs, such as the Peace Corps; the Alliance for Progress (a program of economic and technical assistance for Latin American countries); and emergency awareness, and civil defense, and civil rights programs (*See also,* Domestic Issues).

He also assembled presidential commissions to examine a wide range of issues, including the arts, the status of women, narcotic and drug abuse, youth physical fitness, aging, employing the handicapped, juvenile delinquency, and equal employment opportunity.

Domestic Issues

When Kennedy took his oath of office in 1961, the United States still enjoyed the unprecedented prosperity begun after World War II (1939–45). Production of U.S.

goods and services increased by 37 percent during the 1950s, boosting the Gross National Product (GNP—the value of goods and services produced and sold each year) to $488 billion by 1960, or almost five times what it had been in 1940. More families than ever before (80 percent) owned automobiles and their own homes (61.9 percent), many of which were now located in the rapidly expanding suburbs. Unemployment remained low compared to prior decades. Family incomes (up 30 percent since 1950) provided real purchasing power, because prices remained stable and inflation was negligible.

There was a slight recession in the country when Kennedy became president. Conservative Republican policies had kept inflation below 2 percent, but the annual growth rate measured in terms of the GNP was only between 2 and 3 percent which, Kennedy observed, was well below the Soviet Union's growth rate of between 6 and 10 percent.

Kennedy knew that beneath the affluence of the recent past lay a host of new challenges and unsolved economic and social problems for which the government had to assume increased responsibility.

Social Legislation

Between 1950 and 1960 the U.S. population increased from 151.7 to 180.7 million Americans, a growth rate of 19.7 percent. This "baby boom", which began after World War II, increased demand for almost everything, but especially for more housing and schools. Several medical breakthroughs in the 1940s and 1950s offered Americans the prospect of longer, healthier lives, but this was accompanied by rising health care costs that most of the United States's aged population could not afford.

To meet many of the social problems, Kennedy in 1961 presented a domestic legislative agenda that was an amalgam of proposals drawn from congressional liberals and from previous Democratic administrations. Although not always aligned with the liberal activists when he was in Congress, Kennedy increasingly came to appreciate the significance of their proposals. Lacking many specific proposals of his own (at least initially), he appropriated theirs.

Labor

When Kennedy came to office the United States was gradually changing from a country engaged principally in the production of industrial goods by blue-collar workers to one relying on new technologies for delivering goods, services, and information provided by white-collar workers. For U.S. cities this deindustrialization process meant the abandonment of manufacturing centers, loss of employment, and physical decay. This in turn bred unrest among urban inhabitants, particularly unemployed minorities who felt unfairly deprived of the comforts enjoyed by most other Americans.

Biography:

Martin Luther King, Jr.

Minister; Civil Rights Activist (1929–68) Almost overnight, 27–year-old Dr. Martin Luther King Jr., a small town minister and active member of the National Association for the Advancement of Colored People (NAACP), was catapulted into the national spotlight as the recognized leader of the Civil Rights movement. When the 1955–56 Montgomery, Alabama, bus boycott that began his career ended, King continued in earnest his life's mission to protest racial inequality. He traveled the country speaking out for justice and refining his legendary speaking skills. All the while, King's life was in constant danger. His home was bombed and he was constantly threatened, harassed, arrested, and jailed. In 1960, while he attended a nonviolent sit-in at an Atlanta, Georgia, lunch counter, King was arrested and then imprisoned for violating his probation related to a traffic offense conviction. John F. Kennedy, then a presidential hopeful, made an urgent telephone call to King's wife before following up with other calls that resulted in King's release. The scope of King's nonviolent protest expanded. He delivered one of the most passionate addresses of his career at the historic march on Washington in 1963. Angry whites became violent towards the passive protestors on several occasions and televised films of these encounters appeared in living rooms across the country until President Lyndon Johnson signed the 1964 Civil Rights Bill. Across the country, and over the years thousands of people participated in peaceful marches related to the struggle. Unfortunately, the struggle was still far from over when King was assassinated at age 39. In the months preceding his death, King's time and energies were divided between the civil rights cause and the equally compelling cause for peace in Vietnam.

Kennedy succeeded almost immediately in enacting three of his five highest priority economic programs. In February 1961 Congress accepted Kennedy's proposal to amend the Fair Labor Standards Act of 1938 and increase the minimum wage to $1.25 an hour. Southern Democrats and Republican conservatives blocked efforts to extend coverage to workers in intrastate commercial facilities, which Kennedy regarded as a personal rebuff because during the 1960 campaign he had specifically pledged to secure coverage for exploited laundry workers. Still Kennedy managed to add nearly four million workers to the lists of those guaranteed a minimum wage.

Kennedy also won quick approval of a program, originally proposed by Senator Paul Douglas of Illinois, to aid depressed areas plagued by chronic unemployment. The $394 million Area Redevelopment Act of 1961 established technical assistance and job training programs to bring new industry and created jobs in depressed areas such as Appalachia, in the southeastern United States. These programs created 26,000 jobs by late 1962. Similarly, the Manpower Development and Training Act of 1962 established programs in 40 states to retrain workers with inadequate or obsolete skills.

Poverty

Poverty was another emerging problem. Socialist Michael Harrington's influential book, *The Other Amer-*

ica (1962) warned of the systemic effects of deprivation in the midst of affluence, documenting the persistence of poverty in the decaying industrial cities and rural areas such as those Kennedy visited during his West Virginia campaign. Stunned by Harrington's observations, Kennedy directed his staff to begin work in October 1963 on a comprehensive, coordinated attack on poverty. Nothing substantial was formulated by the time of Kennedy's death. However, his successor, Lyndon Johnson, took many of Kennedy's ideas and turned it into his own domestic program known as the War on Poverty (*See also,* Lyndon Johnson's Administration).

Low-cost housing was another triumph for the president. In June 1961 the administration gained passage of a $4.88 billion omnibus housing act to broaden and extend programs in urban renewal, public housing, and housing for the elderly and for college students.

Health Care

Kennedy responded to rising health costs by proposing a medical insurance program similar to one proposed by President Harry Truman in 1949. Kennedy's bill provided hospital and nursing care for Americans over 65, to be financed by a 0.25 percent increase in social security payroll taxes. His plan enjoyed wide public support but met adamant opposition from the American Medical Association, the main lobbying group for U.S. physi-

---

cians, whose spokespersons labeled it "socialized medicine." In 1961 the Senate tabled the bill by a 52 to 48 vote, with 27 Democrats, mostly from the South, turning against the administration. Kennedy never reintroduced it, but a similar bill establishing the Medicare system passed early in the Johnson presidency.

Mental Health: Kennedy, whose sister Rosemary Kennedy was mentally retarded, took exceptional interest in a proposal to advance the cause of mental health through the Mental Retardation Facilities and Community Mental Health Centers Act of 1963. The act provided $329 million in grants for research and treatment and for construction of local mental health centers so mentally ill people could be removed from large state hospitals, considered no more than human warehouses, and placed into treatment programs. An unintentional consequence was to fling many severely and chronically ill mental patients onto the mercies of local communities without the resources to help them, thus exacerbating other social problems, such as drug addiction and homelessness.

The Economy

Anxious to stimulate economic growth, Kennedy was a proponent of English economist John Maynard Keynes's theories for controlling the business cycle by coordinating government spending, taxing, and monetary policies. Walter Heller, chairman of Kennedy's Council of Economic Advisers, convinced the president that the economy would escape recession if the government temporarily spent more than it collected in taxes. To free funds for investment and thereby promote economic growth, Kennedy recommended a cut in personal income and corporate taxes.

A tax cut proved unnecessary in 1962 because the recession ended in February, due largely to Kennedy's large increases in federal expenditures (over $7.2 billion alone in military spending). A tax cut passed in 1964 and had a noticeable impact on the economy. Economists since have debated whether such cuts are truly beneficial. What is important, however, is that the proposal itself marked a significant departure—the first time a U.S. president publicly professed the principles of Keynesian economics.

Business

Kennedy was also successful in negotiating the passage of the first major trade bill since 1934. The Trade Expansion Act of 1962, an earlier version of which he had drafted while a senator, granted the president authority to reduce tariffs (the federal tax on imported goods) by 50 percent and, if necessary, to retaliate with higher tariffs against countries that tried to restrict U.S. imports.

The Steel Crisis

Kennedy also feared that rampant inflation could wipe out solid economic gains by cheapening the buy-

ing power of the dollar. Controlling inflation meant keeping prices and wages at a level not to exceed the productivity rate (output per worker) for any given industry. In early 1962 Kennedy asked labor unions, including the United Auto Workers and the Steelworkers of America, two of the country's largest, to limit their demands for wage increases and asked large corporations to agree not to raise their prices beyond the amounts granted to workers in pay increases. This way, Kennedy reasoned, the economy could grow at a steady rate and workers could gain a reasonable share of the prosperity; they could, for example, afford to buy the cars they were building.

But shortly thereafter the United States Steel Corporation announced a 3.5 percent price increase; other steel companies soon followed suit.

It seemed to Kennedy that greedy steel companies were grabbing for profits at the expense of their workers while at the same time threatening U.S. economic stability by raising prices. More importantly to Kennedy, the steel companies personally insulted him by flaunting their disrespect for his guidelines. Feeling double-crossed, Kennedy brought the full weight of the presidency down on the steel companies and was able to force them temporarily to roll back the price hike, but not without stepping on toes in the process.

But, except for the steel crisis, business had little reason to be angry with Kennedy. When examined in a broader perspective, economists regard Kennedy's business policies, which included generous investment tax credits, accelerated depreciation allowances, and lenient enforcement of antitrust laws, as very favorable to business.

Agricultural Policy

Troubled by perpetual farm surpluses and attendant increases in government expenditures to pay for them, a program initiated during the New Deal of the 1930s, Kennedy proposed to grant price supports only to those farmers who agreed to divert a portion of their acreage from production (thus reducing the supply of agricultural products and increasing demand for them).

Kennedy's plan for mandatory acreage controls was defeated by congressional Republicans and conservative Democrats who, with pressure from farmers, called it an unwarranted extension of federal authority and an invasion of individual freedom. Kennedy dropped his plan, surpluses continued, and so did large federal expenditures for farm subsidies.

To make use of the food surpluses, Kennedy issued an executive order increasing the distribution of surplus food to the needy, established a pilot food stamp program (the first since World War II), and increased the federal school lunch and milk programs started by Eisenhower. Acting on a proposal put forth by Minnesota senator Hubert Humphrey in 1960, Kennedy established the

Food for Peace Program and appointed George McGovern (the Democratic Party's 1972 presidential nominee) as its first director. The Food for Peace Program distributed $2 billion a year in surplus food to impoverished countries in the Third World, feeding 92 million people a day. Trumpeting the superiority of U.S. agricultural production, Kennedy won a major propaganda victory (and at the same time further reduced the surplus) by authorizing a private sale of excess wheat to the Soviet Union.

Youth

John Kennedy had a profound effect on American youth, serving as a catalyst for what historians regard as the most politically active generation of high school and college students in U.S. history. By the early- to mid-1960s the first wave of baby boomers (born after 1945) was making its way through high school into college. The explosive leap during the 1960s in the numbers of 18 to 24 year olds (from 16.5 million to 24.7 million, a 50 percent increase) inspired talk of a "youth rebellion" and "youth culture." Kennedy's speeches evoking idealism and sacrifice and appealing to the nation's noblest traditions, resonated with American youths. From Kennedy's Peace Corps program (*See also,* below) to his programs to combat juvenile delinquency and aid to education, Kennedy began to address this burgeoning population with innovation and foresight. However, it would take the Johnson administration to see many of his ideas to fruition.

The Peace Corps

Established by executive order in March 1961 and headed by the president's brother-in-law, R. Sargent Shriver, the Peace Corps remains Kennedy's most innovative program and one of the most positive and enduring aspects of his presidency. Kennedy first publicly spoke of the idea of a Peace Corps (previously proposed by Minnesota senator Hubert Humphrey) during a 2:00 A.M. appearance at a 1960 campaign rally at the University of Michigan. Sensing the emerging idealism among college youth, Kennedy asked the students if they were prepared to give years of their lives to service in Asia, Africa, or Latin America. Their enthusiastic response convinced Kennedy to make the Peace Corps one of his first priorities.

After intense training, Peace Corps volunteers served two-year terms in one of 44 countries requesting service. The objectives of Peace Corps service were to provide a needed skill to an interested country, to increase the understanding of Americans by other people, and to increase Americans' understanding of other people. The Peace Corps showed the United States's idealistic side to the world, making the volunteers goodwill ambassadors and winning many friends.

Women

Kennedy, the only president since Herbert Hoover not to appoint a woman to his cabinet, was heedless of women's rights in his private life. His political instincts, however, sensed the beginnings of feminist activism, and he took a few steps that later advanced the interests of women. In 1961 he appointed former first lady Eleanor Roosevelt to chair a presidential commission on the status of women. Esther Peterson, assistant secretary of labor and director of the Women's Bureau, the highest-ranking woman in the Kennedy administration and the driving force behind the commission, was instrumental in the passage of the Equal Pay Act of 1963. The act made significant concessions to working women on the issue of comparable pay, guaranteeing equal pay to women doing work equal to what men did. That meant little, however, to women engaged in sexually segregated occupations and to women working in small businesses (fewer than 25 employees). Still, historians recognize it as a milestone in antidiscrimination legislation, marking the federal government's concerns for safeguarding the right of women to hold employment on the same basis as men. By the summer of 1963, when Betty Friedan's *The Feminine Mystique* appeared advocating meaningful work outside the home as women's solution for "the problem that has no name," the Kennedy administration had given the women's movement a political starting point.

Civil Rights

Civil rights was the issue that was the most difficult for Kennedy to confront. At the beginning of his presidency millions of African Americans living in the South were legally prohibited by state or local laws (so-called Jim Crow laws) from using the same public facilities as whites and, despite federal court rulings, were denied the right to vote and the right to send their children to public schools with whites. Kennedy neither appreciated the extent to which African Americans were losing patience with drawn-out legal strategies and with white people like the president, who counseled them to accept gradually change, nor did he comprehend that the civil rights leadership, with unwavering determination, intended to force the end of legal segregation of the races through direct action protests (sit-ins, protest rallies, marches, boycotts).

Kennedy was caught in a political dilemma: he wanted to advance the interests of African Americans without surrendering his slim electoral hold on the South, where legal segregation of the races (Jim Crow laws) defined the culture. He also feared that a major domestic disruption would divert attention from foreign affairs.

Whatever changes were to occur, Kennedy knew he could not get them through Congress, where for decades southern Democrats had used various devices to thwart legislation. Relying, instead, on executive actions, the

What They Said . . .

"The world is very different now. For man holds in his mortal hands the power to abolish all forms of human poverty and all forms of human life. And yet the same revolutionary beliefs for which our forebears fought are still at issue around the globe—the belief that the rights of man come not from the generosity of the state, but from the hand of God.

"We dare not forget today that we are the heirs of that first revolution. Let the word go forth from this time and place, to friend and foe alike, that the torch has been passed to a new generation of Americans—born in this century, tempered by war, disciplined by a hard and bitter peace, proud of our ancient heritage—and unwilling to witness or permit the slow undoing of those human rights to which this Nation has always been committed, and to which we are committed today at home and around the world.

"Let every nation know, whether it wishes us well or ill, that we shall pay any price, bear any burden, meet any hardship, support any friend, oppose any foe, in order to assure the survival and the success of liberty.

"This much we pledge—and more."

(Source: John F. Kennedy, Inaugural Address, January 20, 1961.)

Kennedy administration took a number of positive steps, hiring more African Americans in government and, in effect, introducing the concept of affirmative action employment; creating the Committee on Equal Employment Opportunities, chaired by Vice President Johnson, to probe discriminatory practices in government contracts; bringing lawsuits to integrate school districts in southern states; and originating the Voter Education Project to register African Americans in southern states and following up with lawsuits in 145 counties.

Kennedy disappointed civil rights leaders when he refused to introduce a civil rights bill in 1961 and, despite an explicit campaign pledge, delayed until November 1962 issuing an executive order banning racial discrimination in federally funded housing. Reverend Martin Luther King Jr., cochair of the Southern Christian Leadership Conference (SCLC), decided not to wait for Kennedy.

Racial Confrontations in the South

In the spring of 1961 a group of "freedom riders" boarded two buses in Washington, D.C., bound for cities in the Deep South with the intention of testing a Supreme Court ruling declaring segregated interstate bus terminals unconstitutional. White mobs savagely attacked the riders throughout the South, while Kennedy attempted to isolate himself and his reputation from these events.

The freedom riders' episode had some success in September 1961 when, with prodding from Attorney General Robert Kennedy, the Interstate Commerce Commission (ICC) prohibited interstate bus and train companies from using segregated facilities.

White southerners, fearing even greater interference in local affairs, severely criticized the Kennedy administration's handling of the freedom rides. Civil rights activists, on the other hand, were also far from pleased with the Kennedy approach. Young, militant civil rights activists volunteering for the Student Nonviolent Coordinating Committee (SNCC) pressed for the end of racial discrimination throughout the South, demanding that Kennedy protect them from white terrorists. But the Kennedy administration rarely intervened, citing lack of federal jurisdiction over local matters and preferring instead to strike deals with southern politicians. Only reluctantly and in extreme cases did Kennedy order the use of force.

Mississippi and Alabama: In September 1962 James Meredith, an African American, was denied the right to enroll at the University of Mississippi. Governor Ross Barnett defied a federal court order to integrate the university and refused to guarantee Meredith's safety, leaving the U.S. attorney general no choice except to send U.S. marshals to protect Meredith and to enforce the integration order. Violent riots resulted in two deaths and 160 injuries, becoming the most extreme confrontation between federal and state authority since the Reconstruction era. Ultimately the federal government prevailed; Meredith enrolled at the University of Mississippi and other African Americans followed thereafter.

Meanwhile, in the spring of 1963, civil rights demonstrations in Birmingham, Alabama, led by Martin Luther King Jr., brought a savage response by Police Commissioner Eugene "Bull" Connor, who arrested thousands of protestors, including two thousand children, and used fire hoses and police dogs to brutally suppress marches and demonstrations. The ghastly scenes, carried throughout the country by television, sickened the president and awoke the nation. Public opinion for the first time shifted in the direction of the civil rights advocates. Shocked by these scenes and urged on by his brother Robert, Kennedy put aside political considerations and declared the time had arrived for the federal government to assume authority over civil rights.

On the evening of June 11, 1963, after a confrontation that morning with Alabama governor George C. Wallace ended in the peaceful integration of the University of Alabama, Kennedy placed the power of the presidency firmly on the side of civil rights. Announcing his intention to send Congress a comprehensive civil rights bill, Kennedy for the first time since the American Civil War (1861–65) put the presidency on the side of expanding African American civil rights.

Civil Rights Bill

Kennedy's 1963 Civil Rights Bill guaranteed all citizens equal access to public accommodations, challenged (but did not outlaw) the denial of black voting rights, and gave the federal government authority in school desegregation matters. Liberals and civil rights leaders said the proposal lacked teeth because Kennedy failed to include provisions for the federal government to institute lawsuits for civil rights violations and to end discrimination by employers and labor unions. The president believed a stronger bill would fail to pass Congress, given the strength of southern opposition.

Congress finally passed Kennedy's bill in the summer of 1964, following Kennedy's death and after hundreds of thousands of Americans, black and white, converged on the U.S. capital for the March on Washington. The march took place in August 1963 to awaken the country to the civil rights cause.

Foreign Issues

Kennedy's presidency framed the most frightening years of the Cold War. He took the United States closer to the abyss of World War III than any other president. Viewed decades later, many of his foreign policies seem dangerously provocative, but, at the time, most Americans looked with pride upon those policies, which were executed with courage and conviction.

Kennedy accepted the interventionist foreign policy approaches of former presidents Woodrow Wilson, Franklin Roosevelt, and Harry Truman. Kennedy's goal was a stable world order, held in place by strategic security agreements. Influenced by pre-World War II failures to check the aggression of totalitarian regimes, Kennedy granted Communist aggressors no leeway. After World War II (1939–45), under the threatening cloud of Communist expansion, U.S. foreign policy focused on containing Communism.

Kennedy's foreign policies were based on two basic assumptions. First, he believed that all Communists were united and all took directions from Moscow, the capital of the Soviet Union, even though he knew of growing tensions between Communist China and the Soviet Union. Second, he accepted the "domino theory," first enunciated by President Dwight Eisenhower in 1954, that when one country became Communist, its neighbor was likely to fall next.

To block the fall of nations to Communism or to buttress those in Communism's path, Kennedy sought imaginative new approaches. One of them was the Alliance for Progress, a bold program that provided billions of dollars in aid to Latin American countries on the edge of revolution. The Alliance for Progress was only marginally successful, with few countries participating, because it provided loans, not grants, and the loans had to be used to purchase U.S. goods.

However, Kennedy still tended to rely primarily on the use of the military as a political instrument. To meet Soviet challenges, wherever they might occur, Kennedy broke away from total reliance on nuclear weapons, which had limited Eisenhower's foreign policy responses, and created a military that offered a "flexible response," a "wider choice than humiliation or all-out war." Kennedy increased spending on both nuclear and conventional weapons. During his presidency military expenditures rose 13 percent, from $47.4 billion to $53.6 billion annually; military personnel increased from 2.5 million in 1960 to 2.7 million in 1964.

Cuba

The Bay of Pigs

Throughout his presidency Kennedy was obsessed with the continual presence 90 miles from U.S. shores of the Communist regime in Cuba and its leader, Fidel Castro. During the 1960 campaign Kennedy criticized the Eisenhower administration for failing to end the Communist threat. Eisenhower's Central Intelligence Agency (CIA), however, had not been idle. They hired the Mafia, a secret criminal society, to plan the assassination of Castro to be timed with the invasion of the island by Cuban exiles, called the Cuban Brigade, recruited and trained by the CIA. What Kennedy knew about the assassination plans remains unclear, but no documentary evidence exists to connect him with their planning. However, he did approve its execution later in 1961.

After Castro took over U.S. holdings without compensation and then aligned Cuba with the Soviet Union, Kennedy embargoed Cuban goods and told the CIA to proceed with a "quiet landing," one that could be plausibly denied and that would under no circumstances commit U.S. military personnel. Richard Bissell, CIA deputy director of plans, told the president that the 1,400-man Cuban landing force, even if initially defeated on the beaches, could stay in Cuba, melt into the countryside, and make a guerrilla war against Castro drawing on the support of presumably thousands of Cubans who wanted to see Castro overthrown. Kennedy's military advisers were skeptical of the plan, but, reassured by the CIA, the president and practically all of the president's advisers (including Attorney General Robert Kennedy) thought the operation involved minimal risk.

April 17, 1961, was the low point of the Kennedy presidency. Within minutes of the landings at the ill-chosen Cochinos Bay (Bay of Pigs), the CIA's abundant failures and miscalculations, especially their lack of secrecy and flawed intelligence reports, were evident. When Kennedy refused to authorize U.S. air strikes and thus broaden the engagement, as the CIA planners had cynically presumed would occur, the Cuban Brigade was forced to surrender. Critics immediately attacked Kennedy, blaming him for the fiasco, calling him timid and indecisive. Few, however, questioned the assumptions behind the U.S.-sponsored invasion of a sovereign country.

Despite the Bay of Pigs fiasco, Kennedy remained enamored of covert and clandestine operations against Communist regimes. An investigation into the failures of the Bay of Pigs operation, chaired by Gen. Maxwell Taylor, recommended not that such efforts be discontinued but, rather, that their coordination be centered in the White House. Kennedy would go on to oversee U.S. efforts in assisting selected foreign governments (Laos, South Vietnam, and Thailand) threatened by guerrilla insurrection. Its purpose was to prevent any more Castros from emerging and to figure out a way to prevent the spread of Communism (*See also,* Southeast Asia).

Kennedy so gracefully acknowledged his responsibility for the Bay of Pigs disaster that his approval rating in the Gallup Poll jumped to 83 percent. Feeling personally responsible for the fate of the Cuban Brigade, he had his brother Robert Kennedy negotiate an exchange of drugs and food for the release of the captured. On their release in December 1962, Kennedy addressed them in Miami's Orange Bowl.

Kennedy's outwardly amiable, thoughtful, carefully controlled demeanor masked an inner hardness and a sometimes volatile anger toward those he blamed for his humiliating defeat at the Bay of Pigs. Shaken and disillusioned and feeling poorly served by his intelligence officers, Kennedy relieved Allen Dulles and Richard Bissell of their duties and appointed John A. McCone CIA director. Refusing to be dependent on the so-called experts, Kennedy centralized decision making in the White House, creating a personal national security apparatus built around the people he could trust, starting with his brother and including Theodore Sorensen, Robert McNamara, Maxwell Taylor, and McGeorge Bundy, whom he put in charge of a revived National Security Council (NSC) (*See also,* Kennedy's Advisers).

Cuban Missile Crisis

Still obsessed with Castro, Kennedy in November 1961 established Operation Mongoose, a CIA operation under the leadership of Robert Kennedy. Its purpose, said the attorney general, was to "stir things up on the island with espionage, sabotage, general disorder" (and possibly assassination). Tipped off by Mongoose, Castro and Soviet leader Nikita Khrushchev became convinced that the United States was planning another invasion, this time involving the U.S. military. Thus, in the summer of 1962 the Soviet Union (USSR) increased its military forces in Cuba and began installation of medium nuclear range missiles with a range of 1,100 miles.

Suspicious of Soviet activities, Kennedy publicly warned Khrushchev not to put nuclear missiles on Cuban soil. Foreign Minister Andrei Gromyko assured Kennedy of the USSR's peaceful mission on the island of Cuba. But aerial photographs over Cuba on October 15 confirmed that 24 nuclear missile sites were under construction. For 13 days the nation and the world faced its most extreme nuclear crisis, as Kennedy's top advisers, known as ExComm, short for Executive Committee, debated U.S. options.

Sensitive to Republican charges that Kennedy had been lax in dealing with Cuba, yet refusing to engage in an attack without warning, Kennedy knew that allowing the missiles to remain would damage U.S. credibility and prestige around the world. The missiles had to go.

On October 22, Kennedy announced a naval blockade of the island and demanded the withdrawal of the Soviet missiles. Any nuclear missile launched from Cuba at places in the Western Hemisphere, he warned, would be regarded as an attack on the United States and provoke a full retaliatory response on the Soviet Union.

Unparalleled fear and tension gripped the country as the president awaited Khrushchev's response. The U.S. military went into final preparations for nuclear war.

U-2 spy flights observed that construction of the missile sites continued as did the uncrating of Soviet bombers. Kennedy demanded the missiles be removed and the sites inspected. In a long rambling letter to Kennedy on October 26, Khrushchev appeared to agree to the missiles' withdrawal, but he wanted the United States to end the blockade and promise not to invade Cuba. While ExComm was considering the proposal, another letter arrived, this one adding a demand that the United States remove its Jupiter missiles in Turkey. At this crucial juncture word arrived that a U-2 plane had been shot down over Cuba killing the pilot. The Joint Chiefs demanded immediate retaliation, but Kennedy wisely decided not to react. Struggling to hold his military advisers in check, Kennedy decided, on Robert Kennedy's advice, to accept the first Khrushchev letter and ignore the second.

All the while Kennedy had authorized secret talks between his brother and Anatoly Dobrynin, the Soviet ambassador in Washington. That evening Robert Kennedy told Dobrynin of the pressures placed on the Kennedys by the Joint Chiefs, of how ExComm was exhausted and losing patience. He set a deadline of 24 hours for the removal of the missiles in Cuba, in return for which the United States, Kennedy promised, would remove its Jupiter missiles in Turkey and Italy. President Kennedy had planned to remove the Jupiters anyway, because the new Polaris submarines now made them obsolete. The next morning, Sunday, October 28, 1962, Khrushchev wired his acceptance of the terms.

Having made no visible concessions to the Soviets (the removal of the Jupiter missiles remained secret), Kennedy emerged looking like a winner, to be congratulated for his skills at crisis management. Only many years later, however, when U.S., Cuban, and Soviet leaders conferred on the crisis, was it learned how close to nuclear war Kennedy had taken the United States. Unknown at the time, the Soviets already had nuclear warheads for the medium range missiles and nuclear bombs for their IL-29 bombers in Cuba; they had amassed 42,000 troops, or four times as many troops as U.S. intelligence estimated; they had installed nine tactical missiles with nuclear warheads and a 30-mile range to repel invasion forces; and they were a week away from completing installation of the medium range missiles on Cuba. Moreover, the Soviet commander on Cuba, not the Cubans and not the military commanders in Moscow, had authority to launch missiles, such as the surface-to-air missile that brought down the U.S. U-2 plane. Secretary of Defense Robert McNamara acknowledged in 1995 that a U.S. attack would have been disastrous.

It was neither a managed nor a manageable crisis. Kennedy's brilliance extricated the country from the crisis, but it was, after all, his policies on Cuba that provoked it.

Berlin

Believing Kennedy vulnerable after the failure of the Bay of Pigs, Khrushchev increased the pressure over Berlin in what was then Soviet-controlled East Germany. West Berlin, occupied by the western powers, was an irritation that Khrushchev wanted removed. Unable to stop the flow of refugees leaving East Germany, an estimated 20,000 to 30,000 refugees a month by 1961, Khrushchev threatened to conclude a separate peace treaty with East Germany and to drive the western powers out of Berlin.

Both sides said they would fight over Berlin. Neither believed the other. Kennedy asked Congress for another increase in military spending and mobilized 200,000 reservists. Khrushchev responded with a military buildup of his own and in August ordered construction of a wall separating the two Berlins and the two Germanies.

In the summer of 1961 the Kennedy administration reverted to the brinkmanship and massive retaliation approaches of the Eisenhower administration. Hardliners among Kennedy's advisers called for a showdown, and that meant nuclear war. Shaken by the prospect, Kennedy lost his temper with one adviser, "What we are talking about is seventy million dead Americans" (Reeves, pp. 175–76). Tension peaked in Berlin on October 27, when Soviet and U.S. tanks faced off against each other at Checkpoint Charlie, the U.S. name for a military station on Friedrichstrasse (a street) connecting East and West Berlin. Kennedy convinced Khrushchev that the United States would stand its ground. Khrushchev

Fast Fact

Robert F. Kennedy's appointment as attorney general marked the first and last time in U.S. history that a president appointed his brother to such high office. The Postal Revenue and Federal Salary Act of 1967, enacted into law by President Lyndon Johnson, prohibits the president from appointing family members to high office.

(Source: "Bill to Bar Nepotism Approved." *New York Times*, December 13, 1967.)

decided that it was not worth war and pulled back his tanks and dropped his demands for a separate treaty.

Kennedy traveled to West Berlin in June 1963 and expressed solidarity with the West Berliners, "All free men, wherever they may live, are citizens of Berlin, and, therefore, as a free man, I take pride in the words, *Ich bin ein Berliner.*" The Berlin Wall remained until the reunification of Germany in 1989.

Space

One of Kennedy's most dramatic and memorable actions was his pledge to land a man on the moon before 1970. He wanted to get there before the Soviets. Dating from the launch of the first satellite (*Sputnik*) in October 1957, the Soviets had achieved one startling success after another, while the U.S. program languished. During the 1960 campaign Kennedy repeatedly warned Americans of the potential costs, militarily and otherwise, by the U.S. failure to be number one in space. To invigorate the program he appointed James Webb, an energetic and aggressive administrator, to head the National Aeronautics and Space Administration (NASA) and boosted its 1962 budget by 30 percent, doubling it the year after.

Russian Yuri Gagarin's orbit of the earth on April 12, 1961, alarmed Kennedy. He demanded to know what the United States could do to catch and leapfrog over the Soviets. Fortunately NASA's Project Mercury manned space program produced two timely triumphs, launching Alan Shepard on a suborbital flight in May 1961, and orbiting John Glenn around the earth the next February. Convinced by his scientific advisers that a manned lunar exploration could be achieved by 1970, and persuaded that it was politically necessary (even though opinion polls indicated that 58 percent opposed the $40 billion projected costs), Kennedy threw his full political weight behind NASA's Apollo program. Space exploration perfectly symbolized Kennedy's commitment to excellence and his admiration of courage embodied in his idea of the United States's New Frontier (*See also,* Kennedy Becomes President).

Southeast Asia

Laos

Southeast Asia was becoming a proving ground for Kennedy's policy regarding the containment of Communism. In 1962 the Joint Chiefs advised Kennedy to send U.S. troops into Laos, where Communists were thought to be on the verge of taking over. Kennedy vetoed their proposal. If it had not been for the Bay of Pigs, Kennedy told adviser Arthur Schlesinger Jr., "I might have taken this advice (the Joint Chiefs') seriously." Kennedy turned instead to negotiations, and in June 1962 a 14-nation Geneva conference reached an agreement for a neutral Laos. Events in neighboring Vietnam, however, were not as easily settled.

Vietnam

U.S. involvement in the Vietnam War (1959–75) is for Americans one of the most painful experiences of recent times, leaving 59,000 Americans dead and the country bitterly divided over the causes and the consequences of the war.

Under French colonial rule until Ho Chi Minh's Communist forces defeated the French in 1954, Vietnam was then divided in two at the 17th parallel by a Geneva agreement, with North Vietnam continuing under Communist leadership and South Vietnam aligning itself with the United States. Soon Viet Cong (Vietnamese Communist) forces launched insurgent attacks against the South with the purpose of unifying the two Vietnams. President Eisenhower propped up the South Vietnamese government with substantial economic and military aid.

Kennedy expanded that commitment, broadening the U.S. military role because he believed that Ho Chi Minh was part of a general Communist expansion. Like most Americans, he believed that North Vietnam was controlled by the Soviets and the Communist Chinese. Knowing the political burden President Truman faced over charges that he had lost China when the Communist revolution succeeded during his presidency, Kennedy did not want to be seen as losing Vietnam to the Communists.

When Kennedy entered office approximately one thousand U.S. military advisers were serving in South Vietnam. During his second week in office he approved $42 million in new aid to South Vietnam for a basic counterinsurgency plan to combat an increase in Viet Cong terrorist activities. After the Bay of Pigs, Kennedy decided that the place to demonstrate U.S. firmness was Vietnam. Yet he seldom gave his full attention to Vietnam until the final months of his administration. In no hurry to send troops to Vietnam, Kennedy rejected a

November 1961 Pentagon proposal for 40,000 regular troops, but he did increase economic and military aid to Vietnam from $215 to $337 million annually. Intended or not, the Americanization of the war had begun. No one around Kennedy challenged the morality of the presumptive right of the United States to interfere in an internal war or an insurgency.

A few South Vietnamese victories in 1962 raised expectations, as the number of U.S. advisers reached nine thousand. Nonetheless, the U.S. counterinsurgency schemes failed in Vietnam, thwarted by a repressive South Vietnamese government and by a corrupt South Vietnamese army.

In the summer of 1963 South Vietnamese prime minister Ngo Dinh Diem regime's repression sunk to new depths, as reports of widespread violations of personal freedoms and political rights filtered out of the country. Then Washington learned that Diem's brother, Ngo Dinh Nhu, had secretly contacted North Vietnam, apparently with ideas of arranging a settlement of his own. Realizing that victory under Diem's leadership was unlikely, Kennedy directed his new ambassador, Henry Cabot Lodge Jr., to tell Diem to rid himself of Nhu. If Diem refused, Lodge was instructed to tell dissident South Vietnamese generals that they had U.S. support for a coup. The Kennedy administration then went through an "agonizing reappraisal" of U.S. policy towards Vietnam, during which Kennedy tried to pull together his divided advisers. "Confronted with a choice among evils," Robert McNamara wrote in 1995, John Kennedy "remained indecisive far too long" (McNamara with VanDeMark, p. 70).

In November 1963 the coup in South Vietnam unfolded. When word came that Diem and his brother Nhu had been captured and summarily executed by a military junta, Kennedy literally blanched, then rushed from the room in shock. When Kennedy himself was killed a few weeks later, his administration still lacked a firm policy on Vietnam.

No one can be certain what Kennedy would have done had he lived. However, this much is clear: Kennedy proclaimed South Vietnam a sovereign state, enveloping it in the prestige and protection of the United States. He fostered the notion that insurgency in South Vietnam had to be countered by U.S. efforts.

Peaceful Overtures

The cumulative effects of the many crises Kennedy faced during his presidency brought him to reconsider the risks of seemingly perpetual confrontation with the Soviet Union. Following the Cuban missile crisis, Kennedy and Khrushchev realized the enormous role played by chance during those 13 days. To avert future miscalculations, they agreed to install a telephone "hot line" connecting Moscow and Washington. The following spring John Kennedy took the first U.S. steps toward arms reduction by initiating the Limited Test Ban Treaty. Ratified by the Senate in September 1963, it prohibited aboveground nuclear testing. Kennedy said, it was "a step toward reason—a step away from war."

The Kennedy Administration Legacy

For the first few years after John F. Kennedy's death, his administration and its accomplishments were widely celebrated. The Kennedy White House was even referred to as "Camelot" (the mythical court of King Arthur). No politician thereafter captured the public's imagination to the same degree as Kennedy. Forgotten, at least momentarily, were the mistakes and shortcomings. When economic prosperity blossomed forth in 1965, many credited Kennedy's prudent policies and foresight. When Americans landed on the moon in 1969, many saw it as a Kennedy victory. When the United States later turned seriously in the 1970s to the business of arms reduction and peaceful coexistence with the Soviet Union, many remembered Kennedy's first tentative steps in that direction. Americans proudly recalled his toughness during the Cuban missile crisis, his leadership (however belatedly) on civil rights, and his call to national service in the Peace Corps.

As the realities of the Vietnam War set in, as the youth culture turned to a youth rebellion, as the Civil Rights movement radicalized and the nation's cities burned each summer, as the covert power of the presidency expanded to threatening proportions, as new gender roles and standards of sexual conduct changed, Americans reassessed not only Kennedy but all presidents, setting new expectations and behavioral standards and often imposing them retroactively.

Kennedy and the Press

A respectful tone characterized reporting on President Kennedy. The elite of U.S. print and television journalism considered themselves Kennedy's friends and believed they shared in shaping the country's sense of itself and its future. Using flattery to keep them in his debt, Kennedy charmed his favorite reporters, reminded them of his gratitude for their support, and thanked them for the things they did not publish about him. He also cagily played reporters off one another, shrewdly exerting influence to get his versions of stories printed and unfavorable ones suppressed. Few reporters complained: one said the president "either overwhelmed you with decimal points or disarmed you with a smile and a wisecrack."

Lasting Impact

Intensely private and unknowably complicated, Kennedy left a perplexing legacy built mostly on what might have been. Given more time Kennedy may have secured many of the same programs passed during Lyndon Johnson's presidency, such as the Civil Rights Act of 1964 and an antitpoverty program, dubbed by Johnson the War on Poverty.

Vietnam

Long after the end of the Vietnam War (1959–75) historians pondered what effect Kennedy might have had on the war's outcome had he lived. Shortly after Kennedy's death the Johnson administration instituted a plan written by Kennedy advisers to expand covert action against North Vietnam (*See also,* Lyndon Johnson Administration). Whether Kennedy would have gotten in as deep as Johnson did cannot be stated with certainty. Johnson was responsible for the massive commitment of U.S. troops to Vietnam, but he did so on the advice of a team of national security and foreign policy advisers carried over from the Kennedy administration.

Assassination Controversies

John Kennedy's assassination is a source of continuing perplexity. Almost immediately after Kennedy's death President Lyndon B. Johnson appointed a commission headed by Chief Justice Earl Warren to conduct an investigation. The Warren Commission, as it was known thereafter, submitted its report in September 1964, concluding that the shots killing President Kennedy and wounding Texas governor John B. Connally were fired by one man, Lee Harvey Oswald, and that he was not part of a conspiracy to assassinate the president. Those findings have been bitterly challenged by legions of independent investigators who have published alternative explanations of the crime. For example, the House Select Committee's 1979 report affirmed the Warren Commission's substantive findings, but also deduced from some audio evidence (later discredited) that a second gunman fired at Kennedy from Dealey Plaza's "grassy knoll" in Dallas, Texas. Uncovering FBI records of electronic surveillance of various Mafia figures overheard plotting revenge against the Kennedys, the committee investigators concluded that President Kennedy was assassinated probably as the result of a conspiracy involving organized crime (*See also,* Career).

The Kennedy Family

Despite the shocks registered by disclosures of John Kennedy's personal failings, the U.S. public's fascination with the Kennedy family lingers, as Kennedy offspring, siblings, heirs, and mementoes of the Camelot years attract exceptional interest decades after Kennedy's assassination.

After President Kennedy's death his brother Robert F. Kennedy carried the family torch (a metaphor uniquely associated with John Kennedy and his family because of an eternal flame burning at his grave site). In 1968 Robert Kennedy challenged Johnson for the presidency, and the evening of his victory in the California Democratic presidential primary, he was assassinated at a hotel in Los Angeles. Following a funeral mass at St. Patrick's cathedral in New York City, Kennedy's body was taken by train to Washington and buried in Arlington National Cemetery only a few yards from his brother.

Edward (Teddy) Kennedy's dreams of another Kennedy presidency disintegrated in the summer of 1969 when a young woman, Mary Jo Kopechne, a passenger in Kennedy's automobile, drowned when he drove the car off a bridge at Chappaquiddick, Massachusetts. Unable to shake the effects of the scandal caused by his inept attempt to cover up his involvement in the accident, Kennedy nevertheless challenged incumbent president Jimmy Carter during the 1980 presidential primaries and suffered almost total rejection by Democratic voters. Kennedy went on to compile a respectable record for length of service, legislative leadership, and perseverance as a lawmaker in the U.S. Senate.

Carrying on the Kennedy tradition of public service, a fifth generation of Kennedys born in the U.S. won elected office in the 1980s. Robert Kennedy's oldest son, Joseph P. Kennedy II, won election to Congress representing the same Boston district that his uncle John and grandfather John Fitzgerald had earlier, and his oldest daughter, Kathleen Kennedy Townsend, won election as lieutenant governor of Maryland. Edward Kennedy's son, Patrick, was elected to the House of Representatives from Rhode Island.

Historians versus General Public

Early assessments of the Kennedy presidency, written mostly by Kennedy advisers and confidants, romanticized his contributions and exaggerated Kennedy's place in history and his influence on later events. While late twentieth-century historians generally regard Kennedy as overrated, focusing on his major character flaw (his marital infidelities) and his father's dynastic aspirations, the general public continued to rate him the most popular president of the twentieth century.

Sources

Bernstein, Irving. *Promises Kept: John F. Kennedy's New Frontier.* New York: Oxford University Press, 1991.

Beschloss, Michael R. *The Crisis Years: Kennedy and Khrushchev, 1960–1963.* New York: Harper Collins, 1991.

"Bill to Bar Nepotism Approved." *New York Times,* 13 December 1967.

Encyclopedia of World Biography. Detroit: Gale Research, Inc., 1997, pp. 502–6.

Fairlie, Henry. *The Kennedy Promise: The Politics of Expectation.* New York: Dell Book, 1973.

Giglio, James. *The Presidency of John F. Kennedy.* Lawrence, Kans.: University Press of Kansas, 1991.

Goodwin, Doris. *The Fitzgeralds and the Kennedys: An American Saga.* New York: St. Martin's, 1987.

Hilty, James W. *Robert Kennedy, Brother Protector.* Philadelphia: Temple University Press, 1997.

Historic World Leaders. Detroit: Gale Research, 1994.

Kane, Joseph Nathan. *Facts About the Presidents: A Compilation of Biographical and Historical Information.* 6th ed. New York: H. W. Wilson, 1993.

Kennedy, John F. *Profiles in Courage.* Memorial edition with special foreword by Robert F. Kennedy. New York: Harper and Row, 1964.

Kennedy, Robert F. *Robert Kennedy in His Own Words: The Unpublished Recollections of the Kennedy Years.* Edited by Edwin O. Guthman and Jeffrey Shulman, introduction by Arthur M. Schlesinger Jr. New York: Bantam, 1988.

Kennedy, Rose. *Times to Remember: Rose Fitzgerald Kennedy.* London: William Collins Sons, 1974.

Manchester, William. *The Death of a President.* New York: Harper & Row, 1967.

May, Ernest R., Philip D. Zelikow, eds. *The Kennedy Tapes: Inside the White House During the Cuban Missile Crisis.* Cambridge, Mass.: Harvard University Press, 1997.

Morris, Dan, and Inez Morris, eds. *Who Was Who in American Politics.* New York: Hawthorn Books, 1974.

Patterson, Thomas G., ed. *Kennedy's Quest for Victory: American Foreign Policy 1961–1963.* New York: Oxford University Press, 1989.

Reeves, Richard. *President Kennedy: Profile of Power.* New York: Simon and Schuster, 1993.

Schlesinger, Arthur Meier, Jr. *A Thousand Days: John F. Kennedy in the White House.* Boston: Houghton Mifflin, 1965.

Sorensen, Theodore C. *Kennedy.* New York: Harper and Row, 1965.

Whalen, Richard J. *The Founding Father: The Story of Joseph P. Kennedy and the Family He Raised to Power.* New York: Signet, 1964.

Further Readings

Collier, Peter, and David Horowitz. *The Kennedys: An American Drama.* New York: Warner Books, 1984.

Davis, John H. *The Kennedys: Dynasty and Disaster 1848–1984.* New York: McGraw Hill, 1984.

Hamilton, Nigel. *JFK: Reckless Youth.* New York: Random House, 1992.

John F. Kennedy Library and Museum. 1999. <http://www.cs.umb.edu/jfklibrary> (7 July 1999).

Klein, Edward. *Just Jackie: Her Private Years.* New York: Ballantine, 1998.

Leuchtenburg, William. *In the Shadow of FDR: From Harry Truman to Ronald Reagan.* Ithaca, N.Y.: Cornell University Press, 1983.

Mailer, Norman. *Oswald's Tale: An American Mystery*. New York: Random House, 1995.

Matusow, Allen J. *The Unraveling of America: A History of Liberalism in the 1960s*. New York: Harper and Row, 1984.

O'Donnell, Kenneth P., David F. Powers, and Joe McCarthy. *"Johnny, We Hardly Knew Ye": Memories of John Fitzgerald Kennedy*. Boston: Little, Brown, 1972.

Parmet, Herbert. *Jack: The Struggles of John F. Kennedy*. New York: Dial, 1981.

———. *JFK: The Presidency of John F. Kennedy*. New York: Dial, 1983.

Posner, Gerald. *Case Closed: Lee Harvey Oswald and the Assassination of JFK*. New York: Random House, 1993.

Schlesinger, Arthur M., Jr. *Robert Kennedy and His Times*. Boston: Houghton Mifflin, 1978.

Shannon, William V. *The American Irish: A Political and Social Portrait*. Amherst, Mass.: University of Massachusetts Press, 1989.

Sundquist, James L. *Politics and Policy: The Eisenhower, Kennedy, and Johnson Years*. Washington, D.C.: Brookings Institution, 1968.

Wyden, Peter. *Bay of Pigs*. New York: Simon and Schuster, 1979.

Lyndon Johnson Administrations

Full name: Lyndon Baines Johnson
Popular name: LBJ

Personal Information:
Born: August 27, 1908
Died: January 22, 1973
Burial place: LBJ Ranch, near Johnson City, Texas
Religion: Disciples of Christ
Spouse: Claudia Alta "Lady Bird" Taylor (m. 1934)
Children: Lynda Bird; Luci Baines
Education: Southwest Texas State Teachers College, San Marcos, Texas, BS, 1930
Occupation: Teacher; politician
Political Party: Democratic Party
Age at Inauguration: 55 years

Biography

Throughout his career Lyndon Johnson was known as a man who got things done. Some observers saw him as a pompous, overbearing bully, while others saw him as a skilled negotiator. Perhaps he was all these things. In any case, his personality was very strong and played a significant role in all the momentous decisions that he made. Molded by his own experiences of the Great Depression and the New Deal programs that attempted to alleviate American suffering, Johnson viewed the government as a tool of reform. This made Johnson an unabashed liberal. His decisions as president would greatly influence the future of liberalism in the United States.

Early Life

Lyndon Baines Johnson was born in Gillespie County, Texas, on August 27, 1908, the first of five children of Sam and Rebekah Johnson. His younger siblings were sisters, Rebekah, Josefa, and Luci, and brother Sam Houston. Later in his life Johnson was fond of recalling that his family was unhappy and poverty-stricken. This was one of his numerous exaggerations. In fact, his family was middle class, and his parents doted on their oldest boy. If anything, Johnson was spoiled. His mother was particularly attentive and tried diligently to fulfill his every whim. She introduced him to the "finer things" of life. His father was somewhat more distant but did instill Johnson with a passion for politics. Sam was active in Texas politics most of his life and served six terms in the state legislature. Sam Johnson was from the

southern populist wing of the Democratic Party. He was an honest politician who never made much money but who did his best to serve his constituency. He would occasionally take Lyndon along with him during campaign trips.

Education

Johnson began his education at age four in a one-room school near his rural home. In 1913 the family moved to Johnson City where he enrolled in the first grade. Johnson graduated from Johnson City High School in 1921, finishing second in a class of six. Always yearning for leadership and recognition he was senior class president, leader of the school debate team, and he gave the student oration at the graduation ceremony.

Because he graduated from an unaccredited high school, Johnson had to pass an entrance examination to be accepted at a state college. During the summer and fall of 1924 he attended several remedial classes at Southwest Texas State Teachers' College in San Marcos, Texas, but he did not do well and did not enroll in regular college classes.

From November 1924 to September 1927, Johnson traveled and worked. For a while he lived in California, and later did manual labor in Johnson City and Blanco County, Texas. Finally, in February 1928, he enrolled in regular classes at Southwest Texas State, but he soon experienced financial difficulties and had to withdraw.

Though he was still without a college degree, during 1928 and 1929 Johnson taught at an all-Hispanic high school in Cotulla, Texas. He threw himself wholeheartedly into his work and was very popular with his students. His experience as a teacher of Mexican American students gave him insight into the problems of education and poverty.

When Johnson returned to Southwest Texas State in 1930 he worked part-time and became heavily involved in campus politics. He was obviously ambitious, and some people found him boorish. One student said, "He'd just interrupt you,—my God, his voice would just ride over you until you stopped" (Dallek, p. 68). Others admired his pluck and predicted great things for his future. One friend said, "He was the only fellow I ever knew who could see around corners" (Dallek, p. 67). Graduating with a bachelor's degree in 1930, Johnson accepted a position at Sam Houston High School in Houston, Texas. He taught public speaking, geography, and arithmetic and became involved in local politics. His career as a high school teacher lasted just one year.

Lyndon Baines Johnson. *(Photograph by Arnold Newman. AP/Wide World Photos. Reproduced by permission.)*

Family Life

Johnson was always ambitious and hardworking, but he found some time for socializing. As a result of a blind date he met and courted Claudia Alta Taylor. Johnson gave her the nickname "Lady Bird" Johnson, so that his wife and later his daughters (Lynda Bird and Luci Baines), would all have the LBJ monogram. Johnson proposed to Lady Bird only 24 hours after they met. She held him off for two months, but they were married on November 17, 1934, in San Antonio, Texas. Lady Bird was a loving wife and mother and also became a valuable political adviser to the sometimes overbearing Johnson. She also provided the family with financial stability. In the early 1940s she inherited $36,000, which became the basis of the Johnson family fortune. In 1943, while a member of Congress, Johnson used his influence, and that of powerful friends on the Federal Communications Commission (FCC), to permit Lady Bird Johnson to buy a small radio station in Austin, Texas. KTBC grew into a vast radio and television empire. Later, the Johnsons bought a ranch near Johnson City, Texas, where they retired after Johnson left the White House. Their two daughters, Lynda Bird, born in 1944, and Luci Baines, born in 1947, filled out what to all appearances was a close family, although the personalities of the girls differed. Lynda was quiet, studious, and conventional, while Luci was outspoken, witty, and sometimes rebellious.

Career

Having worked as a teacher for two years before returning to school to earn his bachelor's degree in 1930, Johnson went back to the classroom for his first postgraduate job. Within a year he resigned to become secretary to the newly elected congressman from Texas's 14th District, Richard M. Kleberg. Thus, Johnson's political career began in 1931. He moved to Washington, D.C., where he served Congressman Kleberg for three years. Kleberg was mainly interested in the trappings of office and Johnson did most of the work. Johnson dominated the small staff and also tried to dominate the so-called "Little Congress," an organization of young congressional staffers. He met and ingratiated himself with many people who were important or destined for importance. He also learned how to use his personal contacts to get things done.

National Youth Administration Director

Johnson's early career flourished under the New Deal programs of President Franklin Roosevelt. In 1936 Johnson promoted himself for the New Deal position of Texas state director of the National Youth Administration (NYA). He got the job, thus becoming the youngest state director in the country. Soon he made the Texas NYA the best in the nation. He cultivated all the right people, such as the influential utilities lawyer Alvin J. Wirtz; mastered the crazy quilt of federal rules and regulations governing the NYA; and developed an excellent program of work-study for those youths who were still in school and work relief for those who were not. He provided as much assistance as he could for needy African Americans while at the same time maintaining segregation. In this way, he was able to satisfy the administration in Washington which more or less demanded equality, and the white people of Texas who were still not ready for racial mixing.

Congressman

In 1937 Johnson ran for Congress. Campaigning hard as a New Deal Democrat, he was elected. As the representative from Texas's 10th Congressional District, Johnson exhibited the same habits of hard work and served his constituents well. He voted for practically all New Deal legislation, and he attended to special requests. Making skillful use of the franking privilege (free mail for congressmen), Johnson kept his constituents informed in glowing terms of his labors on their behalf.

His first and perhaps most notable success on behalf of a Texas constituent concerned the building of the Marshall Ford Dam by the Lower Colorado River Authority (LCRA). The LCRA was but one of what would eventually be 14 river authorities in Texas. These were smaller projects on the model of the Tennessee Valley Authority (TVA), the mammoth New Deal electrification and mining project on the Tennessee River (*See also,* Franklin Roosevelt Administration). Johnson also worked hard to bring electricity to the farmers of Texas through a Rural Electrification Administration (REA) co-op.

These projects involved large-scale earth moving and dam construction. Using all the influence that a freshman congressman could muster, and drawing upon his acquaintanceship with President Roosevelt, Johnson helped the Austin, Texas-based Brown and Root Construction Company obtain the needed authorizations for the construction contracts awarded in these projects. Over the years Brown and Root made millions of dollars through their association with Johnson. In return, Johnson gained a loyal campaign contributor. Thus was established a mutually beneficial relationship that would last for the rest of Johnson's life.

Johnson did not regard the House of Representatives as the culmination of his political career. In 1941 he ran for the Senate in a special election. He lost the race to Texas governor W. Lee O'Daniel, who won by means of fraud. Johnson did not demand an inquiry, however, fearing that an investigation would uncover improprieties in the financing of his own campaign. He also expected to have another chance to enter the Senate in the near future.

Military Service

When the Japanese attacked Pearl Harbor on December 7, 1941, Johnson applied for a leave of absence from Congress and went on active duty as a lieutenant commander in the navy. He took a job inspecting and reporting on operations in the Pacific theater. While there he flew as an observer on one bombing mission against the Japanese, and, since his plane came under attack during the raid, he was awarded the Silver Star for heroism. A little later President Roosevelt ordered all members of Congress serving in the military to either resign their seats in Congress or else return to Washington. Johnson returned as a decorated veteran.

Senator

In 1948 Johnson ran against former Texas governor Coke Stevenson in the Democratic primary election for the United States Senate, a campaign in which it would later be demonstrated that Johnson engaged in ballot-stuffing. His supporters in several south Texas counties altered enough of the returns to give Johnson an 87 vote margin of victory. In the halls of Congress this earned Johnson the humorous nickname of "Landslide Lyndon." Nevertheless, Johnson demonstrated that he was an effective campaigner. He used the radio extensively, and he rented a helicopter to campaign in outlying parts of his district. The helicopter made an enormous impression on the people of these little towns. Lyndon Johnson had now reached what for him, at the time, was his highest political goal. He was a member of the United States Senate.

Johnson entered the Senate in January 1949. Using techniques that had worked well for him in the past—cultivation of powerful colleagues like Senator Richard Russell of Georgia, deference to the strong, intimidation of the weak, vast knowledge of the system, and inhumanely hard work—Johnson in swift succession became minority whip (1951), minority leader (1953), and by 1955 majority leader. By then he was also the most powerful senator.

Johnson's goal in the Senate was to serve Texas while at the same time making a name for himself in the national political arena so that he could take advantage of any opportunities that might later arise. To do this, he supported issues important to powerful constituencies in Texas, such as the deregulation of natural gas and the high oil depletion allowance, while straddling the fence on certain inflammable issues like labor and race. This allowed him to avoid being labeled a "true believer," either liberal or conservative.

As the Senate majority leader, Johnson measured success in terms of getting bills passed, not trumpeting causes, and, depending upon the popularity of the legislation in question, he sought compromise and consensus in order to achieve results. In some cases, such as the Civil Rights Act of 1957, this meant passing a weak bill, devoid of enforcement language. In others, like the National Aeronautics and Space Act of 1958, the popularity of the cause allowed for a stronger bill. Because of his standing in the Senate, Johnson sometimes had to take up matters related to the decorum and integrity of the Senate itself. In the case of the red-baiting Republican Senator Joseph McCarthy of Wisconsin, who in the early 1950s was terrorizing public figures with unsubstantiated accusations of radical associations in the past, Johnson instructed Senate Democrats not to attempt to turn McCarthy's growing unpopularity into a partisan issue. Then, when they voted on the resolution censuring, or formally reprimanding, McCarthy, every senator was able to argue that he had voted his conscience, rather than the party line.

Vice President

Senator Johnson allowed his followers to work on his behalf for the presidential nomination of 1960, but he did not formally announce as a candidate until early July. Meanwhile, Senator John F. Kennedy of Massachusetts campaigned vigorously and won most of the primaries. At the Democratic National Convention in Los Angeles, California, Johnson joined in a momentary flurry of "stop Kennedy" activity, but this collapsed early and the Massachusetts senator won easily on the first ballot. What happened after that has always been the subject of intense speculation. After his victory, Kennedy offered Johnson second place on the ticket. Kennedy probably saw Johnson as a useful complement

to his candidacy. As a Protestant southerner Johnson might buffer the obstacles to success posed by Kennedy's urban, eastern, Catholicism. The Kennedy-Johnson ticket was a formidable one, and some observers have always argued that Johnson's presence in the campaign was the key to success. When the votes were counted the election was very close. Kennedy and Johnson defeated Vice President Richard Nixon and United Nations Ambassador Henry Cabot Lodge of Massachusetts by little more than one hundred thousand votes.

Even though he was galled by his removal from the limelight and jealous of the adulation enjoyed by Kennedy for the expenditure of so little effort, Johnson served loyally as vice president. His power and influence were practically gone. Kennedy gave him little of importance to do. Still, he had a few responsibilities that allowed him to make meaningful contributions. As chairman of the Space Council he supported the growing commitment of the government to the National Aeronautics and Space Administration (NASA). His work in this arena led Kennedy to endorse the idea of landing a man on the moon before the end of the 1960s. As roving ambassador Johnson represented the nation and the president when and wherever Kennedy could not. He traveled to the Far East, Europe, Africa, and South America, and, although little of significance came out of these excursions, he performed his largely ceremonial duties with dignity.

Johnson's most important contribution as vice president stemmed from his chairmanship of the President's Committee on Equal Employment. The purpose of this committee was to monitor the employment practices of government agencies and contractors to ensure that minorities (not yet including women at this date) received fair employment opportunities. Johnson worked hard at this job and established for himself more believable credentials as a civil rights advocate than he had previously enjoyed. He came to be identified as the primary administration spokesperson for African Americans.

By the fall of 1963 the Kennedy administration was in trouble in the South and also faced potential problems occasioned by the constant infighting between the conservative and liberal wings of the Democratic Party in Texas. Determined to ease these tensions, President Kennedy planned a fence-mending trip to Texas in November. There, hosted by Vice President Johnson and Governor John Connally, he would attempt to charm the warring factions back together. Kennedy might have succeeded, but in one hideous instant his life was snuffed out and everything was changed by the actions of an assassin (*See also,* John Kennedy Administration). Kennedy was declared dead at Parkland Hospital in Dallas, Texas, at 1:30 P.M., on November 22, 1963. Johnson was sworn in as president at 2:40 P.M. on Air Force One by his friend U.S. District Court Judge Sarah T. Hughes.

Lyndon B. Johnson was sworn in as president on Air Force One as he returned to Washington, D.C., following President Kennedy's assassination on November 22, 1963. His wife, Lady Bird Johnson left *and Kennedy's widow, Jacqueline Kennedy* right *look on.* (AP/Wide World Photos. Reproduced by permission.)

President

From November 22, 1963, to January 20, 1969, Johnson served as president of the United States. During this time his two great obsessions were social reform and the Vietnam War. Both were passionate crusades among their supporters as well as their detractors. The former would mark him for greatness while the latter would simultaneously destroy him. In both of these struggles, Johnson exhibited remarkable singlemindedness. But the contradictory nature of these two crusades created severe strains on his presidency.

Post-presidential Years

After leaving the White House Johnson retired with his wife, Lady Bird Johnson, to his ranch near Johnson City, Texas, where he devoted himself to three interests: raising cattle, writing his memoirs, and overseeing the construction of the Johnson Library on the campus of the University of Texas at Austin. Johnson had suffered two previous heart attacks in 1955 and 1972. On January 22, 1973, he suffered a third heart attack and died en route to the hospital. After the funeral service in Washington,

D.C., Johnson was buried at the Johnson family plot on the LBJ Ranch near Johnson City, Texas.

The Lyndon B. Johnson Administrations

Lyndon Johnson inaugurated new initiatives in health, education, human rights, and conservation with his Great Society program that served the needs of the U.S. middle class. With the War on Poverty he also attacked the problems of urban blight, unemployment, and job training among the poor. His effectiveness in passing social reform legislation is matched by few other U.S. presidents. But, his foreign policy—and especially the Vietnam War (1959–1975)—undermined the constructive aspects of his domestic agenda.

Johnson Becomes President

At 12:30 P.M., Friday, November 22, 1963, President John F. Kennedy was assassinated while riding in his motorcade through Dallas, Texas. News of his death shocked the nation and sent many Americans into mourning. Johnson, too, was in Dallas at the time trying to repair party relations. As he began his return trip to Washington, D.C., accompanied by President Kennedy's widow Jacqueline Kennedy (later Onassis), he was sworn into office by a personal friend, Judge Sarah T. Hughes. The ceremony took place on the presidential plane, Air Force One, at Love Field, the main Dallas airport. He returned to Washington that night and began his presidency.

The Campaign of 1964

The Republicans

Although the outcome of the 1964 election was never in doubt, it was nevertheless very interesting. The Republicans sealed their own fate early on when they allowed the ultraconservative faction to gain temporary control of the party and engineer the nomination of Senator Barry Goldwater of Arizona.

Goldwater had emerged as the darling of the extreme right wing in 1960. But he was a not a good campaigner, and he frequently made off-the-cuff comments that hurt his already slim chances. For their vice presidential candidate the Republican delegates at the San Francisco, California, convention named William E. Miller, an obscure congressman from western New York. During the campaign Goldwater spoke out against big government, civil rights, Social Security, and arms control. He stood for the old American virtues of self-reliance, frugality, and rugged individualism. But Goldwater was his own worst enemy, as when he declared in his Republi-

can Party nomination acceptance speech that "extremism in the defense of liberty is no vice . . ." This, after the Republicans had engaged in a more or less open discussion during the campaign about the possibility of using tactical nuclear weapons against the Russians. The American people were not about to vote for an extremist who might start a nuclear war.

The Democrats

As Johnson assessed his chances of winning his own presidential term in 1964, he was more worried about John Kennedy's brother Robert Kennedy than about Goldwater. Kennedy, whom Johnson had kept on as attorney general after John Kennedy's assassination, wanted the vice presidency in 1964, obviously regarding it as a stepping-stone to the White House. But Johnson would not oblige. He did not want his presidency to be remembered as the interregnum between two Kennedys. The problem was how to rid himself of Kennedy without causing a public outcry. He did this by announcing that no member of his cabinet would be considered. In the end Johnson tapped Senator Hubert Humphrey of Minnesota as his running mate.

While campaigning against Goldwater during the summer and fall, Johnson played down the war in Vietnam and promised the people that he would not send U.S. ground troops to the area. Johnson, who had wrestled with feelings of inadequacy as vice president under John Kennedy, now wanted to win the greatest landslide in history. He campaigned vigorously. He traveled extensively and behaved as if he thought the race would be close. Johnson attacked Goldwater on all the issues but focused particularly on civil rights, Social Security, and arms control. He tried—successfully—to make Goldwater look like an insensitive, racist warmonger.

In part through his skillful exploitation of these major issues and also because President Johnson was still riding the great wave of sympathy over the Kennedy assassination, the result of the election was a Democratic landslide. Johnson polled over 43 million popular votes to 27 million for Senator Goldwater. In the best traditions of Franklin Roosevelt's several landslide victories, Johnson was supported by white and black workers in both the North and the South. The electoral college result was 486 to 52. Johnson believed that he now had a mandate to move the country forward.

The Campaign of 1968

The situation in 1968 was very different. When President John Kennedy's assassination brought Johnson to power, he had deployed an ambitious set of domestic social reforms rivaled only by Franklin Roosevelt's New Deal. These programs—collectively called the Great Society—did not solve all of the problems that they addressed, but they served as a kind of down payment on the goodwill and patience of the American people. But as the ghettos went up in flames beginning with the

Administration

Administration Dates
November 22, 1963–January 20, 1965
January 20, 1965–January 20, 1969

Vice President
Hubert Horatio Humphrey (1965–69)

Cabinet
Secretary of State
David D. Rusk (1961–69)

Secretary of the Treasury
C. Douglas Dillon (1961–65)
Henry H. Fowler (1965–68)
Joseph W. Barr (1968–69)

Attorney General
Robert F. Kennedy (1961–64)
Nicholas D. Katzenbach (1965–66)
William R. Clark (1967–69)

Postmaster General
John A. Gronouski Jr. (1963–65)
Lawrence F. O'Brien (1965–68)
William M. Watson (1968–69)

Secretary of the Interior
Stewart L. Udall (1961–69)

Secretary of Agriculture
Orville L. Freeman (1961–69)

Secretary of Labor
William W. Wirtz (1962–69)

Secretary of Commerce
Luther H. Hodges (1961–65)
John T. Connor (1965–67)
Alexander B. Trowbridge (1967–68)
Cyrus R. Smith (1968–69)

Secretary of Defense
Robert S. McNamara (1961–68)
Clark M. Clifford (1968–69)

Secretary of Health, Education and Welfare
Anthony J. Celebrezze (1962–65)
John W. Gardner (1965–68)
Wilbur J. Cohen (1968–69)

Secretary of Housing and Urban Development
Robert C. Weaver (1966–68)

Secretary of Transportation
Alan S. Boyd (1967–69)

Watts riot in Los Angeles, California, in 1965, and as civil rights leader Martin Luther King, Jr.'s nonviolent civil rights movement faced challenges from black separatist northern leaders like the Nation of Islam's charismatic spokesperson Malcolm X, and from young "Black Power" militants on the front lines of the civil rights struggles in the South, the public support for Johnson's programs began to erode.

By the 1968 presidential campaign Johnson's foreign policy in Southeast Asia also was under siege by a growing antiwar movement. What the antiwar militants shared with the civil rights militants was a common disdain for traditional "liberals." The most visible liberal of the age was Lyndon Johnson, and all the contradictions of liberalism loomed large in Johnson's public image and in his domestic and foreign policies.

Johnson, facing the fact that his policy of limited war in Vietnam was both failing and highly unpopular with the American people, reached a momentous decision in the spring of 1968. On March 31, 1968, Johnson gave a televised address to the nation. He began by announcing a partial halt to the bombings in Vietnam, and invited the North Vietnamese government to join in negotiations to end the war. Johnson followed this shocking news with another surprise, when he declared that he would not seek the Democratic nomination for the presidency.

The Democratic Convention of 1968

The Democrats had their 1968 national convention in Chicago, and experienced what can only be described as a nightmare. The party was badly split between those who supported Johnson's conduct of the war, and the smaller group of Democrats, led by Senator Eugene McCarthy of Minnesota, who favored peace. Outside the convention hall, thousands of student radicals and others gathered to protest against the unpopular Vietnam War, Johnson, and the status quo. The situation rapidly broke down into violence, as Chicago police and protestors clashed repeatedly. Thousands were injured during the rioting that week, many of them the very evening that Hubert Humphrey, Johnson's vice president, won the nomination.

The Election

Although President Johnson had pulled out of the race, he had a major influence on the Democratic campaign. Behind the scenes, the still powerful Johnson warned Humphrey that financial support for his campaign might be cut off if the vice president opposed Johnson's wishes. Unwilling to allow the Democrats to break with his earlier policies, which would be essentially admitting that Johnson had been wrong, Johnson insisted that the official party platform include a commitment to a continued U.S. presence in Vietnam until a settlement could be negotiated. In a bitter, brooding mood, Johnson weakened Humphrey by refusing to allow him to announce a lull in the bombing of North Vietnam until very late in the campaign. When Humphrey was finally allowed to announce a cessation of bombing in October, his support increased noticeably, but it was too late. Republican Richard M. Nixon won the election with 43.4 percent of the vote against the 42.7 percent for Humphrey, and 13.5 percent for Independent candidate George Wallace. By tying Humphrey's hands until so late in the campaign, Johnson allowed his bruised ego to cripple Humphrey's chances and damage the viability of the moderate wing of the Democratic Party.

Johnson's Advisers

Johnson's style was to solicit advice from a variety of people both inside and outside his cabinet. While in Congress he also had built up a set of rich and powerful supporters who financed his political career and advised him along the way—and for whom he did favors whenever he could. Among his benefactors were the Brown Brothers of Brown and Root Construction; Alvin Wirtz, an influential Texas utilities lawyer; Ed Clark, a successful Austin attorney who would later receive the post of United States ambassador to Australia; and Charles Marsh, the multimillionaire owner of two Austin newspapers. John Connally, later governor of Texas, also played a major role in Johnson's career, as did Robert "Bobby" Baker, Johnson's former Senate aide and trusted adviser.

Other advisers included Walter Jenkins, Johnson's longtime legal aide; Horace Busby, a speech writer; Jack Valenti, Johnson's trusted companion, valet, and sounding board; Abe Fortas, a highly successful Washington lawyer whom Johnson would later appoint to the Supreme Court; Joseph Califano; and Clark Clifford. Califano and Clifford advised Johnson on both domestic and foreign affairs, and Johnson eventually appointed Clifford to the cabinet as secretary of defense. Most influential in Johnson's cabinet were Secretary of State Dean Rusk and Secretary of Defense Robert McNamara. Both were "hawks" who urged Johnson onward as he became

more and more obsessed with events in Southeast Asia. (The term "hawk" means a person who favors a very aggressive military policy.) Rusk did not alter his views until many years later, but by 1968 McNamara realized that promoting the escalation of the war had been a catastrophic error, and he resigned. Clark Clifford, McNamara's successor, was previously a hawk, but he had concluded by early 1968 that the war was unwinnable.

Among Johnson's inner circle of advisers were three who openly opposed expanding the war. These were press secretary Bill Moyers, Undersecretary of State George Ball, and State Department official James Thompson. Vice President Hubert Humphrey was also concerned about the unfavorable results that might accompany military escalation, but Johnson was not interested in a critique of his obsessions. Hence, his advisers found it necessary to speak carefully or risk exclusion from the inner circle.

Other advisers who did not hold cabinet posts but who consistently told Johnson what he wanted to hear (what the president wanted to hear was that everything was going well) were McGeorge Bundy, William Bundy, and Walt Whitman Rostow. General William Westmoreland, commander of all forces in Vietnam, also had Johnson's ear. He consistently tried to persuade the president that the war could be won if only several thousand more troops would be committed. Until early 1968 Johnson was open to Westmoreland's entreaties. When, however, after the Tet Offensive the general asked for 206,000 additional troops, Johnson finally refused (*See also,* Foreign Issues).

Johnson and Congress

One of Johnson's great strengths as an activist president was his intimate familiarity both with the way that Congress worked and also with the representatives and senators who worked there. He knew who to intimidate and who to placate. He knew who owed him favors, and he knew how to reward those who cooperated. He presided over the astonishingly productive Eighty-eighth, Eighty-ninth, and Ninetieth Congresses, which all had diminishing Democratic majorities. But Johnson could have his way even with Republicans. The "Johnson treatment" consisted of having the president (who stood over 6 feet, 4 inches) harangue someone at close quarters, appealing to his or her vanity, patriotism, or any other motive in order to get his way.

Under Johnson's leadership these Congresses, especially the Eighty-ninth, were among the most active in history. They passed an amazing amount of domestic legislation, which was designed to change American life. Collectively, this legislation is known as the Great Society. Johnson's success in leading Congress was attributable to the enormous influence he had built up during his tenure in the Senate coupled with his powerful person-

Protests and demonstrations in favor of civil rights and against the Vietnam War were commonplace during the Johnson administration. Thousands were injured when protestors and the Chicago police clashed outside the Democratic National Convention in August 1968. (UPI/Corbis-Bettmann. Reproduced by permission.)

ality and the fact that many people were demanding change. During his administration Johnson vetoed a total of 30 bills, of which 16 were regular vetoes and 14 were pocket vetoes (an indirect veto of a bill by leaving it unsigned until after the legislature adjourns). None were overridden and none of these vetoes dealt with legislation of any great significance.

Johnson and the Judiciary

When Johnson assumed the presidency on November 22, 1963, the nine members of the Supreme Court under the leadership of Chief Justice Earl Warrren, a Republican, were generally thought of as liberals.

Johnson made two appointments to the High Court. These were Abe Fortas in 1965, and Thurgood Marshall in 1967. Fortas possessed a fine mind and would certainly have made a good justice. Unfortunately, he came under fire because of allegations that he had engaged in inappropriate financial dealings. Eventually in 1969 the pressure became so great that he resigned from the Court.

Marshall had long been one of the leading attorneys for the National Association for the Advancement of Colored People (NAACP). It was Marshall who had argued *Brown v. Topeka Board of Education* back in 1954. (The case that ruled school segregation unconstitutional.) Marshall was the first African American to be appointed to the High Court. He was to have a distinguished career and retired in 1991.

There were several important decisions rendered by the Supreme Court during Johnson's presidency. *New York Times Co. v. Sullivan* (1964) was a libel case growing out of disturbances in connection with desegregation efforts in Alabama. Here the Court ruled that unless public officials could prove that a defamatory statement regarding the conduct of their duties was made with actual malice, such a statement was protected by the First Amendment provision regarding freedom of speech and the press. This decision was significant to the civil rights revolution because it permitted journalists to criticize the behavior of southern officials who were attempting to use their positions to prevent the free exercise of civil rights by U.S. citizens.

Reynolds v. Sims (1964) was the famous "one man-one vote" decision concerning the apportionment of state legislatures. The Court held that the system of electing members to a state legislature had to be on as equitable a basis as possible in terms of the distribution of population in order to meet the provisions of the Fourteenth Amendment guaranteeing equal protection of the law.

Biography:

Thurgood Marshall

Lawyer; Supreme Court Justice (1908–1993) Despite strenuous opposition from southern senators on the Judiciary Committee, President Lyndon Johnson nominated NAACP counsel Thurgood Marshall for an appointment on the Supreme Court in 1967. Marshall took a seat on the bench later that year and became the first African American justice to sit on the court. Marshall's thirty-four year professional history preceding his appointment was courageous and stellar, earning him both death threats and the title of, "America's outstanding civil rights lawyer." Marshall was named the national counsel of the NAACP in 1938 and helped found the NAACP's Legal Defense and Educational Fund. His most important cases were hailed as landmarks in the destruction of segregation. *Brown v. Board of Education,* Marshall's most famous victory, outlawed segregation in public schools. During his quarter century on the High Court, Marshall played a key part of the Court's pro-

gressive majority that upheld a woman's right to abortion and made significant inroads toward protecting the civil liberties of all Americans. In a real, measurable sense, the progress of African Americans toward equal opportunity turned upon Marshall's legal victories. By the time he retired from the bench in 1991, Judge Mar-

shall had risen to the stature of mythic hero. Although he vowed to serve until he was 110 years old and then die "shot by a jealous husband," Marshall succumbed to illness at the age of eighty-four. Said journalist Juan Williams, "Marshall is the most important Black man of this century."

In *Escobedo v. Illinois* (1964) the Court dealt with the rights of suspected criminals in the hands of the authorities. Here the High Court overturned the decision of a state court when it ruled that confessions obtained by police from a suspect who is not advised of his right to have an attorney present is a violation of the Sixth Amendment, which guarantees legal representation to any person under arrest.

Griswold v. Connecticut (1965) dealt with the sensitive issue of birth control. In this case the Court overturned a state law that forbade the advising of an individual in any way in the use of birth control devices. The Court based its decision on the grounds that the law violated the implied protection in the Bill of Rights of the "right of personal privacy."

Miranda v. Arizona (1966) was the famous and precedent-setting case in which the Court ruled that a suspect in a criminal case must be advised of his right to remain silent and his right to an attorney before interrogation.

Finally, there was the Warren Commission. Johnson appointed this commission, headed by Chief Justice Earl Warren, on November 27, 1963, to conduct a thorough investigation of the assassination of President Kennedy. On September 27, 1964, the commission issued an 888 page report concluding that Lee Harvey Oswald was the lone assassin. This report generated significant controversy, which continues to the present day.

Changes in the U.S. Government

There was substantial growth and organizational change in the federal government between 1963 and 1969. The number of civilian jobholders (excluding the Post Office) increased from 1.9 million to 2.3 million—20 percent—and there was a huge increase in the use of outside consultants, agencies, and think tanks. Also, there were two new departments created—Housing and Urban Development, and Transportation. An attempt to merge the Department of Commerce and the Department of Labor failed.

In the long run these trends led to considerable inefficiency and a top-heavy bureaucracy that did not do well in administering the many new programs initiated by Johnson's domestic agenda known as the Great Society. In fact, according to some observers, the problems of structure and coordination that grew out of these developments were more severe than at almost any other time in U.S. history.

Two amendments were added to the Constitution during Johnson's presidency. The Twenty-fourth Amendment (1964) struck down the poll tax (a tax some southern states imposed before someone was allowed to vote), and the Twenty-fifth (1967) provided that the vice president may assume the office of acting president in case the president should be incapacitated. It also provided that the president may appoint a new vice president should the office become vacant.

Domestic Issues

The Johnson administration's domestic program benefited from the fact that the majority of the voters in the 1960s had grown up during the Depression and the New Deal. Not only did they remember the social dislocation of the 1930s, many of them had benefited from the social reform federal programs of the New Deal. This, plus the fact that the 1960s were years of economic expansion, made the U.S. voters during this decade more willing to go along with big government programs of social reform. Johnson promoted legislation known as the Great Society and the War on Poverty. These reform programs addressed some of the major problems in U.S. society: racial discrimination, the need for education reform and for more schools, the need for better medical care, and the recognition that poverty was a prominent feature of U.S. society.

Practically all of the problems that the War on Poverty attempted to address still haunt the United States. Still, measured in terms of sheer speed and magnitude of the legislation, the War on Poverty and the Great Society were impressive, even breathtaking efforts. Moreover, some of the programs did improve the lives of the recipients, even though the United States never approached an egalitarian society.

The Great Society

Johnson's domestic agenda was labeled the Great Society, a term he uttered frequently after assuming office, but which did not come into general usage until after his State of the Union message of 1964. In this message Johnson also announced his "declaration of war on poverty." When the president spoke of a Great Society for the United States he meant programs that targeted the poor, but also programs that improved the lives of everybody. Thus the Great Society encompassed civil rights for minorities, an end to poverty, improved educational opportunities for all, improved health care for the poor and the aged, an improved quality of life in the cities, protection for the consumer, conservation, and environmental regulation. The president launched his crusade in early 1964, and even before his momentous victory in the presidential election that year he experienced three remarkable legislative successes. These were the Tax Reform Act, the creation of the Office of Economic Opportunity, and the Civil Rights Act.

Tax Reform

Kennedy had been working with little success to achieve tax cut legislation. His economic adviser, Walter Heller, had convinced him that lower taxes, combined with controlled deficit spending, would promote long-

term growth. This was the program that Kennedy had called "fine tuning" the economy. Now, Johnson gave his unqualified support to the plan and secured passage of the Tax Reform Act, a tax-cut bill in early 1964, thereby triggering an era of prosperity that would last until late in the decade.

Economic Opportunity Act

The Economic Opportunity Act (EOA) really marked the beginning of the Great Society. It had no distinct focus but instead authorized a variety of programs that were intended to eliminate and prevent poverty. The key program was the Community Action Program (CAP). CAP required that local antipoverty projects be developed, conducted, and administered to the greatest extent possible by the people to be served. CAP would then provide grant funding to local Community Action Agencies (CAA's) set up by these people, who would then implement the program. Johnson argued that this was best because local people were most familiar with their own problems and knew how to deal with them. The idea was sound, but in practice many CAA's did relatively little to alleviate poverty and a great deal to heighten tensions with city administrations, police departments, and school boards, because the local CAAs administrators were often people already at odds with established institutions.

The Equal Opportunity Act also authorized Project Head Start, a preschool program for underprivileged children; Upward Bound, designed to assist poor but talented youth to prepare for college; a Legal Services program; and Neighborhood Health Centers. Far more significant in terms of its intentions and far more controversial in terms of its results than any of these was the Job Corps.

President Johnson was very fond of the Job Corps idea because it reminded him of his two favorite New Deal programs, the Civilian Conservation Corps (CCC) and the National Youth Administration (NYA). The Job Corps provided funds for the creation of camps for youths between the ages of 16 and 21 in which they would receive education, vocational training, and work experience. There were a few rural camps in the West set up by the Park Service, the Forest Service, and the Bureau of Land Management, which were reminiscent of the CCC camps of the 1930s. However, most of the sites were in urban areas, usually occupying old military bases. Participants had to be out of school and unemployed. Hence they tended to come from the most impoverished levels of society and were mostly African American and Hispanic American. The idea was to provide them with marketable skills. They received a $30-per-month allowance and a $50-per-month credit to be paid upon completion of the course. Unfortunately, many of the targeted youth were already caught up in the cycle of unemployment and crime. The Job Corps was characterized by a high dropout rate, generally low morale, and internal problems and conflict. Few who completed the Job Corps program found their lives substantially improved.

Civil Rights Act of 1964

The most important of all the Great Society legislation was that which dealt with civil rights. The first was the Civil Rights Act of 1964. Johnson had nothing to do with the contents of the bill—it had been essentially written earlier during the Kennedy administration. Johnson's role was to maneuver the bill through Congress, and this he did with consummate skill. He subjected Republican minority leader Everett Dirksen of Illinois to the "Johnson treatment," putting him in a position from which he could either claim credit for the passage of the bill or accept responsibility for its defeat. Dirksen chose the former course because he recognized that public opinion at long last was demanding action on this vital issue. As a result of Dirksen's efforts, the Senate voted cloture (a two-thirds Senate vote to close debate) on a southern filibuster, or legislative delay, for the first time ever, and the bill passed with no weakening amendments.

This law prohibited racial, religious, and gender discrimination in private business and public facilities, and established a sixth grade education as the basic requirement for literacy. This was designed to prevent the use of unfair literacy tests against African Americans who attempted to register to vote. However, this law did not give federal agents specific authority to intervene in obvious cases of discrimination. Therefore it was followed by the Voting Rights Act of 1965, which allowed the government to send federal examiners to register voters in any county where there was *prima facie,* or obvious, evidence of discrimination. Prima facie means something that is immediately obvious or clear. This law was effective, and soon the number of African American registered voters in the South began to increase dramatically.

These civil rights acts were vitally important and produced results that were profoundly significant to the U.S. electoral system and to U.S. society, but they had little immediate effect upon the economic and social conditions experienced by poor minorities. Johnson hoped to address these issues through other facets of the Great Society program.

Education Acts

The desire to improve the U.S. educational system was very close to Johnson's heart because he had never forgotten his experiences as a teacher. His efforts to improve education were embodied in several important pieces of legislation, including the Elementary and Secondary Education Act and the Higher Education Act of 1965. The former began as an attempt to provide funds for improvement in schools situated in low-income districts, but it was written in such a way that nearly 90 percent of all school districts qualified. It also provided for the purchase of library and instructional supplies, special education programs, and research and development. The law was carefully worded so as to avoid any semblance of interference with local control.

What They Said . . .

A week after deadly racial violence broke out in Selma, Alabama, President Lyndon Johnson went before a joint session of Congress to request the passage of new voting rights legislation. Speaking to a national television audience, Johnson said:

"But even if we pass this bill the battle will not be over. What happened in Selma is part of a far larger movement which reaches into every section and state of America. It is the effort of American Negroes to secure for themselves the full blessings of American life. Their cause must be our cause too. Because it's not just Negroes, but really it's all of us, who must overcome the crippling legacy of bigotry and injustice.

"And we shall overcome."

(Source: Lyndon B. Johnson, Address to Congress, March 15, 1965.)

The Higher Education Act funded community service programs, library improvements, professional exchanges, fellowships, and struggling institutions. However, its main purpose was to broaden educational opportunities for low-income families. Hence, it provided for scholarships, loans, and recruiting funds. It also expanded the work-study program, which had begun in 1963.

Medicare and Medicaid

Improved medical care, especially for the aged and the poor, was important to Johnson. His commitment resulted in Medicare and Medicaid. The former came in the form of an amendment to the Social Security Act of 1935. It included a hospitalization plan and a plan to cover physicians' fees, both tied to the Social Security income deduction. Medicare was followed by Medicaid, also an addition to the original Social Security Act, which provided grants to the states to partially subsidize the major medical costs of the poor, who were also frequently aged.

Urban Development and Housing

Johnson's concern with the quality of urban life in the United States was reflected in a stack of legislation aimed at improving practically every urban service. Included here were the Mass Transportation Act of 1964, and the Solid Waste Disposal Act of 1966, and the Safe Streets and Law Enforcement Assistance Acts of 1967, all of which offered financial assistance to cities in the form of grants. Most important to the urban improvement phase of the Great Society, however, were the Housing and Urban Development Acts of 1965 and 1968, and the Demonstration (or Model) Cities Act of 1966. Intended to be administered by the newly created Department of Housing and Urban Development, the Model Cities Act was designed to improve the quality of urban life by providing what were to become known as "block grants" to cover 80 percent of the cost of approved projects. These could be in just about any area of urban life such as housing construction, rental subsidies, employment, education, health care, crime prevention, and recreation. Like CAP, the Model Cities program emphasized local initiation and administration.

The Housing Act of 1968 was the most ambitious public housing scheme in U.S. history. After housing was first recognized as a public responsibility in the early 1930s, Congress created a temporary program to guarantee mortgages. This approach was expanded by the New Deal in 1937, and again by the Urban Renewal Act of 1949. The Housing Act of 1968 expanded on its forerunners dramatically. It called for the annual construction of hundreds of thousands of units of subsidized housing, and it provided an expanded mortgage insurance plan. The hope was to overcome the problems associated with earlier efforts that had bypassed the most needy, but unfortunately this program did the same thing. The Federal Housing Administration (FHA), which cleared all applicants for assistance, tended to approve those closest to the upper limits of eligibility, while participating contractors tended to build cheap and shabby housing. Hence the dream of making livable housing available to all Americans was not realized. Public housing projects all over the country continue to fester with poverty, crime, and disease.

Conservation

The Great Society produced a vast array of legislation dealing with conservation, the environment, and consumer protection. Included were the Federal Pollution Control Act, the Water Quality Act, the Water Resources Planning Act of 1965, the Clean Water Restoration Act of 1966, the Air Quality Act of 1967, and the Water Pollution Act of 1968. Johnson also created a large number of new national parks, scenic areas, recreational sites, wildlife refuges, and wilderness areas. These initiatives, which benefited the broad mass of society, not just the poor, struck at the heart of the country's conscience regarding the frontier and the relationship between man and nature, and were among the most popular programs of the Johnson years.

Consumer Affairs and Labor

Among the Great Society laws designed to protect the consumer were: the Automobile Safety Act of 1966; the Fair Packaging and Labeling Act of 1967; the Meat Inspection Act of 1967; and the Coal Mine Safety Act of 1968. Perhaps the most ambitious piece of regulatory legislation—this in the area of labor and workplace safety—was the Occupation Health and Safety Act of 1968. This law created the Occupational Health and Safety Administration (OSHA). Altogether these laws nearly doubled the regulatory responsibilities of the federal government. In the eyes of supporters, it represented the culmination of the progressive response to industrialism of the late nineteenth century. For critics these efforts were an unwarranted and unwise intrusion into the private sector, which could only result in the growth of a massive bureaucracy, increased costs, and confusion. There were plenty of jokes about the reams of OSHA regulations regarding the operation of a stepladder. But few of the complaining spokespeople from management were willing to contemplate the alternative of broadening labor's right to strike over unsafe working conditions.

Culture

Of interest to middle-class consumers were the cultural aspects of the Great Society. These included the National Museum Act, the Public Broadcasting Act of 1967, and the creation of the National Endowments for the Arts and Humanities. These represented only the second effort in national history by the federal government to support the arts; the other was the temporary Federal Arts Project of the New Deal and early World War II periods.

Unrest and Violence

As the Great Society grew it sparked demands for even more fundamental social change, especially in the area of race relations. As masses of people woke up to the possibility that institutions and social customs might change, they called for more rapid and dramatic changes than were occurring. These demands were often strident and sometimes violent. They arose from the fact that minorities—especially African Americans—still felt cut off from the image of affluence portrayed on nightly television. Many worked at menial, low paying jobs and lived in substandard housing. Victory over social segregation meant little to people experiencing double the average unemployment rate and paid a fraction of the average wages. They demanded more and responded to activists who told them that they deserved better. This led to violent urban insurrections, beginning with the Watts rebellion of August 1965. (Watts was an African American section of Los Angeles, California, where the police clubbing of African American bystanders at a traffic arrest sparked several days of rioting involving perhaps 10,000 people and inflicting $45 million in property damage and 34 deaths.) In addition, the women's liberation movement was posing demands that seemed to shake the pillars of society, and student radicals were challenging every aspect of the U.S. system. The increasingly unpopular Vietnam War was also a major source of discontent. Rallies, protests, and even riots became a common occurrence, especially on college campuses and in major cities. As cries rang out for revolution, it seemed to some as though the shared values necessary to maintain a viable society were collapsing.

Foreign Issues

When Johnson became president in 1963, most American's were indifferent to the conflict in Vietnam. During the 1964 campaign Johnson promised that no more U.S. troops would be sent to Southeast Asia. This was not true. In fact, Johnson had already come to believe that a Communist victory in Vietnam would eventually lead to Communist domination of other nations in the region, a process known as the "domino effect." In 1947 the U.S. foreign policy establishment had called for the "containment" of Communism. This view of the world had been confirmed in the "fall of China" to the Communists in 1949, and it had been tested in the Berlin Airlift in 1948 and 1949 and in the bloody stalemate in Korea of the early 1950s (*See also,* Harry Truman Administration). Johnson did not intend to see the process repeated in Vietnam. His attempt to contain the spread of Communism in Southeast Asia became an obsession that utterly overwhelmed his efforts in other arenas. In his defense it must be noted that Johnson shared this obsession with the majority of American's. Communism was the U.S. nightmare of the mid-century. The United States was aware—and vaguely concerned about—its own prosperity relative to the rest of the world, longing for a return to an isolationist past and yet conscious of the fact that in the post-Hiroshima world this was no longer possible. (Hiroshima refers to one of the atomic bombs used by the United States to end World War II [1939–45].)

At first more Americans generally supported Johnson when, in 1965, he went back on his pledge not to commit more troops. However, as the war dragged on over the next three years and victory seemed nowhere in sight, attitudes began to change. More and more troops were committed, casualties mounted, and Johnson's constant assertion that the war could be won caused people to doubt his honesty. Protests increased, and by 1968 Johnson had lost his credibility.

Dominican Republic

Johnson's first foray into foreign policy exhibited these well-worn anticommunist reflexes. In the wake of the 1959 Cuban revolution led by Fidel Castro, U.S. foreign policy in Latin America was on a permanent emergency basis. In April 1965 a group of liberal army officers in the Dominican Republic began a revolt hoping to restore their exiled leader—Juan Bosch—to power. Bosch had been elected in 1963, but his regime was toppled by a conservative coup after less than a year in power. At first bloodless and successful, the liberal coup of 1965 soon ran into opposition from the upper classes who allied themselves with older, more conservative

senior officers. It appeared that a full-scale civil war was imminent.

U.S. officials in the country sided with the conservatives and informed Johnson that U.S. interests would be threatened by the return of Bosch. At the same time fighting broke out and nearly one thousand Americans found themselves trapped in the capital, Santo Domingo. U.S. Ambassador to the Dominican Republic W. Tapley Bennett cabled Washington that a Castro-like takeover was possible and that American lives were in danger. Johnson responded immediately by sending a detachment of marines to Santo Domingo. After the cease-fire they continued to occupy the country until the following spring when they were replaced by a multinational force sponsored by the Organization of American States (OAS).

Johnson justified this action to the nation by stating that he had acted to prevent a Communist takeover. Informed persons found this assertion hard to believe, and it damaged the president's credibility among liberals who hoped to prevent the spread of Communism through a policy of encouraging domestic reform in developing nations rather than the traditional U.S. posture of siding with the plantation owners and the military. As a result, many began to suspect that Johnson's ability to conduct foreign policy was not on a par with his seeming mastery of domestic issues.

The Cold War

The Cold War—the competition between the United States and the Soviet Union (USSR) for world domination—still raged during Johnson's presidency. On both sides success was measured in terms of nuclear weapons superiority. When Johnson became president the military policy of the United States was—and had been for some time—known as the strategy of the flexible response. This meant that in case of a threat from the USSR the United States could send a part of its missile force against the Russians while keeping a secondary force of missiles and bombers in reserve. If the Russians failed to back down a second strike could be sent that would specifically target cities.

This strategy was regarded as sound as long as the U.S. nuclear force was superior to that of the Soviets. In the mid-1960s, however, the Soviets began a nuclear arms buildup hoping to achieve parity. This, in turn, triggered a response from the United States. In early 1965 Defense Secretary Robert S. McNamara announced a new strategy known as assured destruction. This meant that in case of a threat to the United States or Europe, the United States would not limit its response in any way but would launch an all-out nuclear attack on the USSR, which would suffer complete destruction. Soon the Soviets adopted a similar strategy, and the combined policies of the two superpowers came to be known as mutually assured destruction, or MAD.

In spite of these hair-trigger policies, the relationship between the USSR and the United States during the Johnson years was relatively tranquil, even though the Russians supported the North Vietnamese in the war. This seemingly inconsistent situation resulted from the fact that neither side wanted a nuclear confrontation. Moreover, the Russians were concerned about a possible threat from China, and this increased their desire to reduce friction with the United States.

North Atlantic Treaty Organization (NATO)

The North Atlantic Treaty Organization (NATO), an alliance founded in 1949 to provide a defense against the potential Soviet threat to Europe, presented the Johnson administration with some difficulties. Britain, facing severe economic problems, constantly threatened to reduce its manpower on the mainland, while West Germany and other nations complained of U.S. domination in the organization. The worst problems, however, were with France. Led by French President Charles de Gaulle, the French resented U.S. leadership of the free world and wanted to establish what de Gaulle called a "third force." To this end he withdrew French forces from NATO and demanded that NATO personnel be withdrawn from France by April 1967. In response the Johnson administration cooperated with other NATO allies in relocating NATO political and military headquarters to Belgium. These developments put a chill in U.S.-French relations.

Vietnam

In November 1963 the United States had already been involved in Vietnam for nearly 20 years. U.S. intelligence officers had worked closely with nationalist leader Ho Chi Minh to drive out the Japanese during World War II (1939–45), and Ho dreamed of an independent Vietnam developed with U.S. support.

The advent of the Cold War in 1945 quashed Ho's ambitions (Ho was a Communist national), and when France reoccupied the country in 1946 full-scale war erupted. The United States did not intervene directly, but gave France considerable military and economic aid in order to bolster the French government at home and further U.S. aims in postwar Europe.

Between 1950 and 1954 U.S. policy was to support French efforts in Vietnam while at the same time urging France to recognize Vietnamese independence. But France refused and at the same time threatened to withdraw from the burgeoning European Alliance unless U.S. aid continued. The result was that U.S. involvement deepened.

The crucial battle for Vietnam occurred in 1954 at a lonely French outpost near Hanoi in northern Vietnam known as Dien Bien Phu. There, 12,000 of France's best troops were besieged and beaten by the forces of Ho Chi Minh. Desperately, France begged for direct U.S. intervention, but public opinion and Congress would not sup-

port it. Ironically, however, on the same day that Dien Bien Phu fell an international conference opened in Geneva, Switzerland, to consider the fate of all Indochina.

Because the Russians were in a mood to relax international tensions, they persuaded the Vietminh (the Communist nationalists) to accept a temporary division of the country at the 17th parallel, with reunification to occur in two years after national elections. The United States government, however, balked at the idea.

Eisenhower refused to sign the Geneva Accords and instead sought to maintain the southern portion of Vietnam in permanent division. The United States had no intention of allowing reunification to take place under the leadership of Ho Chi Minh and the Communists. Hence, the United States supported Ngo Dinh Diem, a puppet of the French, to form a government in Saigon, South Vietnam. Diem declared the 17th parallel to be a permanent boundary and, with massive U.S. aid, set out to build his army, restore the economy, and create a viable nation-state. He held a referendum on his policies that produced a favorable vote of 98.2 percent. This vote, of course, was rigged.

In fact, Diem was rigid, corrupt, and incompetent. Hence, his chances for success were slim. He had no intention of implementing needed reforms, especially land redistribution. And as a Catholic, he discriminated against the Buddhist majority. Invoking the need for "security," he persecuted all dissidents.

Kennedy's Policies

By the time John F. Kennedy and Lyndon Johnson took office in January 1961, the Diem regime in South Vietnam was already crumbling, yet Kennedy regarded it as one of the keys to containment of worldwide Communism. As a result, United States involvement deepened. Kennedy sent helicopters, pilots, advisers, and massive amounts of aid and equipment to South Vietnam in order to bolster the government efforts against the Communist guerrillas from the North, the Viet Cong.

At first Kennedy's strategy seemed to be working, but by 1963 optimism gave way to concern, as it finally became clear that the Diem regime could not be persuaded to change its ways. By then there were 15,000 U.S. troops in Vietnam, billions had already been spent, and lives had been lost, yet the war was obviously at a stalemate. Kennedy began to have doubts. He appointed Henry Cabot Lodge as his new ambassador to Vietnam, and Lodge soon concluded that Diem had to be replaced. Soon thereafter a group of South Vietnamese military leaders staged a coup that resulted in Diem's murder. This took place on November 1, 1963. Just three weeks later John F. Kennedy also was assassinated, and Lyndon Johnson found himself in the White House.

Johnson and the Gulf of Tonkin Resolution

When Johnson assumed the presidency the situation in Vietnam was highly unstable and it appeared that the Viet Cong and the North Vietnamese might overrun the

President Johnson visited U.S. troops in Vietnam in 1966. At this early stage of the war, Johnson was optimistic about a U.S. victory in the small Asian nation. (Corbis. Reproduced by permission.)

country very soon. In 1964 Johnson made up his mind to act. He began looking for an excuse to increase the U.S. military involvement in Vietnam while at the same time assuring the American people during his campaign speeches that there would be no expansion of U.S. troop commitment in Vietnam. Finally, on August 4, 1964, an incident occurred in the Gulf of Tonkin off North Vietnam that provided the excuse Johnson was looking for. In a televised address Johnson announced to all Americans that the U.S. destroyer *Maddox* had come under attack by North Vietnamese torpedo boats in the Gulf of Tonkin. Johnson said that the U.S. ship was in international waters and the attack unprovoked. (Others have since claimed that the *Maddox* was engaged in helping South Vietnam commando forces conduct a raid on North Vietnam.) In any case, Johnson asked Congress for carte blanche authority to defend American lives in Vietnam. Congress granted the "blank check" Tonkin Gulf Resolution with only two dissenting votes. While not a declaration of war the Tonkin Gulf Resolution became the legal basis for U.S. in the Vietnam War (1959–75). Whether the gulf incident represented a real or serious threat has always been subject to question. Hence, Johnson's credibility was an issue in Vietnam from the very beginning.

The United States Fully Committed

At first the president continued to move cautiously, merely authorizing occasional air strikes to retaliate for Viet Cong raids against U.S. installations. However, in

March 1965, believing an attack from the North was imminent, Johnson authorized sustained bombing raids above the 17th parallel. This proved to be the critical decision—the beginning of a full-scale U.S. commitment. Johnson had no offensive designs on North Vietnam. He only wished to prevent the reunification of Vietnam under the leadership of Ho Chi Minh. He apparently believed these objectives could be reached in a short time, so he did nothing to prepare the American people for a long and costly war. Nor did he put the U.S. economy on a wartime footing, in the apparent belief that this would complicate and weaken his Great Society plans.

But Johnson's strategy of massive bombing in the North, coupled with limited ground action in the South, was flawed. The bombing campaign was supposed to avoid civilian targets yet cut off the flow of men and supplies into the South. In reality, while the bombing may have hampered the enemy supply lines, it never cut them off. Moreover, it was responsible for the death of thousands of civilians. As for the North Vietnamese morale, the bombing seemed to strengthen rather than weaken their resolve to carry on the struggle. Some analysts argue that the bombing ultimately forced the enemy to the bargaining table, but the process took much longer than Johnson or most of his advisers had envisioned.

The ground-fighting phase of the war was a calamity. The U.S. committed more than twice the number of U.S. servicemen that Gen. William Westmoreland had originally projected, and even then the enemy could only be slowed down. In December 1968 the U.S. troop level peaked at 536,100. By the time that Johnson's successor, Richard Nixon, finally made peace with the victorious North Vietnamese, 58,000 Americans were killed and thousands more were physically or emotionally wounded. As for the Vietnamese killed and wounded, it can only be estimated, but, considering both military and civilian personnel on both sides, it is certainly in the millions.

The Home Front

The Vietnam War was fought mostly by draftees from the lower echelons of U.S. society who served one-year tours of duty. Their morale was low and support at home diminished as the years passed. The American people watched an edited, tape-delayed version of the war on television, but this was nonetheless a horrible image that contributed to the erosion of U.S. support for the war effort. Since the troops served their tours on a rotating basis, those who returned home while the war continued received little or no attention except from their own families. By the time the war finally ended, public opinion had become so alienated that the returning men were received not as heroes but with scorn and indifference. The folks at home were exhausted by the length and horror of the conflict, and besides, there had been no victory.

The Vietnam War era in the United States was dominated in one sense by economic growth and prosperity. Encouraged by the twin supports of tax cuts and increased spending, the economy expanded substantially between 1963 and 1968. Unfortunately, this expansion resulted in a runaway inflation that extended into the 1970s. But before it spiraled out of control the "boom" of the 1960s benefited many people.

In another sense the period was dominated by protest and dissent at home (*See also,* Domestic Issues). Led on by radical thinkers like the maverick socialist from Columbia University, C. Wright Mills, many young people, especially the well educated, began to harshly criticize U.S. society. Their main targets were "materialism" (they argued that U.S. society had become devoted to things rather than ideals), racial discrimination, and the war. The protest was nationwide although it was concentrated in certain large cities like San Francisco, California, and New York, and on large university campuses, and it was divided into two groups: the New Left political radicals, and the "counterculture." The New Left believed in attacking the undemocratic aspects of U.S. society by means of radical political action like demonstrations and violence, while the counterculture—sometimes known as "hippies"—demonstrated their disdain for society by ignoring it, "dropping out" as they called it. Both groups opposed the war.

Attempts at Peace

By the end of 1965 Johnson believed that the United States had gone too far into Vietnam to withdraw. With-

drawal would tarnish U.S. honor and cast doubt on its willingness and ability to keep U.S. treaty commitments and protect the world from Communism. Thus Johnson's only options were complete victory or negotiated peace. The first of these was really no more feasible than withdrawal since the military strategy employed was not calculated to produce a complete victory. Anyway, Johnson feared that an all-out war might lead to Chinese or Russian intervention with disastrous results. So negotiation was the only out, yet Johnson had a weak hand to play in trying to initiate a dialogue. The United States had nothing to offer the North Vietnamese except an end to hostilities, but since the war had been going in their favor to this point, there was no reason to believe the North Vietnamese wanted to end it. Furthermore, the government in South Vietnam was utterly unreliable and thus a poor partner for the U.S. to be negotiating with. Still, the president made some halfhearted and predictably unsuccessful efforts to get talks started. In December 1965 he ordered a bombing halt that lasted until the end of January 1966. During that time several foreign governments began efforts to bring the two sides together but nothing happened and, in fact, the North Vietnamese government responded only with a demand for unconditional U.S. withdrawal.

Another failed effort to open peace talks occurred in late 1966, when the Poles attempted to broker secret negotiations in Warsaw, Poland. Januscz Lewendowski, a Polish diplomat, devised a ten point proposal that he hoped would bring the two sides together. Johnson appointed former commerce secretary and U.S. ambassador to Great Britain Averell Harriman to represent the United States in the projected talks, but nothing happened. Inexplicably, the United States intensified the bombing in the Hanoi area at the very time the talks were supposed to begin. The North Vietnamese used this as an excuse to withdraw; perhaps they had never intended to participate. In any case, this effort failed.

Yet another chance to open peace talks was bungled in 1967. During a brief bombing halt early in the year Prime Minister Harold Wilson of Great Britain and Chairman Alexi Kosygin of the USSR attempted to facilitate negotiations on the basis of a sustained bombing halt in exchange for reduced infiltration by the North. This effort failed when the Americans, apparently fearful that the North Vietnamese would actually step up their activities during a prolonged halt in the bombing, demanded a promise to de-escalate within 24 hours.

Throughout 1967, in the face of mounting criticism, Johnson doggedly insisted that the situation in Vietnam was improving. This was an illusion based on inaccurate reports from the field, and the president fell into the trap of proclaiming that the end might be in view. Then came the Tet Offensive of January 31, 1968, a massive and unexpected attack launched by the North Vietnamese and the Viet Cong that penetrated well into South Vietnam. While the attack stopped short of all-out victory for the North Vietnamese, the widespread destruction it wreaked marked the beginning of the end for the United States and the South Vietnamese.

On March 1, 1968, Johnson's old friend Clark Clifford took over as Secretary of Defense. He had always supported the Vietnam policy of the government, but now, as he studied conditions more thoroughly, he concluded that it could not succeed. He advised Johnson to begin serious efforts to secure a negotiated peace. Almost simultaneously the military asked Johnson for permission to commit another 206,000 U.S. troops to Southeast Asia, another major escalation.

Johnson Opts for Peace

The president was now faced with a critical policy decision as to whether he should continue to back, or even expand, the war despite mounting opposition at home. By the summer of 1968 Johnson's approval rating was plummeting. His supporters in Congress were defecting to the peace movement, and Senator Eugene McCarthy of Minnesota and Senator Robert Kennedy of New York were both campaigning for the Democratic presidential nomination on peace platforms. Campus antiwar activities continued to expand in size and scope, and the major news media demanded change. In the face of these pressures, Johnson finally gave in. He rejected the request for more troops, and he announced in his momentous speech of March 31, 1968, that he had ordered a partial halt to the bombing of North Vietnam. Johnson went on to stun the nation by announcing that he would not seek re-election. Many rejoiced in the belief that an end to the war was near. In truth, it would take another five years before the war's conclusion.

The Johnson Administration Legacy

Johnson came into office with the sympathy and the support of the entire nation behind him. This was a considerable advantage and he used it—combined with his great political skills—to push a monumental reform program through Congress. At first this made him one of the most popular presidents of all time, but this status was temporary. Following his triumph in the election of 1964, and the passage of the Great Society legislation in 1965 and 1966, Johnson's popularity declined precipitously. This was the result of the unfulfilled short-run expectation of minorities for changes in their status, increasing discontent over the president's Vietnam policy, and the "backlash" of many mainstream citizens to the new militancy of minorities.

Popularity and Public Opinion

Johnson was very sensitive to public opinion. In fact, he was the first president to hire a private polling firm to keep him apprised of the public's views. However, he did not always interpret polling results correctly or use the information wisely. Desperate to be loved but at the same time stubborn and arrogant, he often responded to unfavorable poll results with efforts to persuade people that his policies were correct rather than adjusting those policies. This practice only led to escalating difficulties and Johnson's momentous decision to step aside in March 1968.

Johnson's relationship with the people was, of course, mediated by his relationship with the press. The president craved attention, as well as approval, and he found both with the journalists. In some ways he related well to them and attempted, for the most part, to treat them kindly and fairly. But he expected them to reciprocate, which to him meant positive discussions of himself and his policies, and no criticism. This made for an impossible situation because even when the journalists tried to be objective he regarded it as a betrayal. From 1967 on, as criticism of his Vietnam policy mounted, the relationship deteriorated rapidly.

Lasting Impact

Johnson's long-term impact on the nation has been mixed. Johnson's domestic program was hailed by liberals who saw in it the fulfillment of the promises of the New Deal. Conservatives who were for the moment discredited and in the minority, bemoaned practically all aspects of Johnson's agenda as damaging to the American character. For most people, however, it appeared to be a new beginning, the opening for the first time for millions of the pathway to the fulfillment of the American dream. This positive appraisal of Johnson's programs did not last long. The rising antiwar movement coupled with the agitation of those for whom the War on Poverty and the Great Society did not move fast enough soon cast a pall over Johnson's domestic program. Liberalism's harshest critics were, paradoxically, the very people whom Johnson's program was supposed to help. In the end, Johnson was left to question why the people he served no longer loved him. Johnson never understood that many people were bitter because they continued to suffer from discrimination, low pay, poor housing, and inadequate education despite the changes wrought by the Great Society programs.

Nevertheless, with respect to his domestic policy, Johnson was the most important president of the twentieth century save Franklin Roosevelt. Under Johnson's leadership Congress passed more important social legislation than at any other time except the New Deal period (1933–38). Moreover, despite the difficulties and problems, many Great Society measures bore significant long-term importance. These included Medicare and Medicaid, which have provided health care for millions who would otherwise not have it; federal aid to education, which upgraded the educational facilities and allowed many to go to school who might otherwise not have had the opportunity; and, perhaps most important of all, the civil rights laws, which ended segregation once and for all and allowed African American citizens to exercise their constitutional right to vote.

As for Johnson's foreign policy, all his efforts in this arena were overwhelmed by his disastrous Vietnam policy. His strategy in Vietnam was hopelessly flawed from the outset. By fighting a limited war he practically guaranteed a long conflict and failure because the Communists were aware of U.S. plans and were prepared to resist indefinitely at any cost. Had Johnson sought a quick victory, had he defeated the Communists by 1967, he may well have been regarded as a great hero. Of course it is by no means clear that this victory could have been won. Two means to win in Vietnam—a massive and sudden commitment of troops or the use of tactical nuclear weapons—may not have been politically feasible. In any case, this was not to be. Instead, the Vietnam War (1959–75) must be regarded as one of the greatest disasters in U.S. history. It divided the people more drastically than any crisis since the American Civil War (1861–65), it diminished the reputation of the United States in the eyes of the international community, and it caused the United States to lose its confidence and sense of purpose.

Perhaps the worst tragedy of the war was the effect upon those who fought it, the Americans and the Vietnamese people. Millions of Vietnamese from both sides were killed. Some 58,000 young Americans were killed in a losing cause. The U.S. soldiers who fought the war were hardly noticed when they returned and certainly not received as heroes like the veterans of all other wars fought by the United States. Many, in fact, were treated as pariahs—as if they had done something wrong.

Historians who have considered Lyndon Johnson are often struck by the importance of Johnson's conflicted personality in his rise and fall from power. Robert Dallek argues in *Flawed Giant* that Johnson's personality determined his performance as president in very significant ways. Johnson tended to see public problems as the enlargement of personal concerns, either real or imagined. Thus with respect to domestic policy the Great Society reflected Johnson's vision of himself as an underdog who overcame many difficulties to achieve success. He had done it on his own, but now he would use the great power that had fallen into his hands to provide avenues of advancement for others. Essentially, this was all to the good, but on the foreign policy side, Johnson's personality quirks spelled disaster.

Dallek holds that Johnson could not have walked away from the Vietnam War early in his administration because he was obsessed with proving himself. Later, deluded by his own wishful thinking that the war could be won, and his obsessive fear of failure, he would not back down, even in the face of overwhelming opposition. Indeed, it was opposition from people like senators J. William Fulbright of Arkansas, Robert Kennedy of New York, and Eugene McCarthy of Minnesota, that

drove him to dig in his heels. Suspicion and anger distorted his judgment and led him to decisions that could not possibly result in success.

The feeling of the people towards the presidency is a part of Johnson's impact on the United States. The outcome of the Vietnam War left both the public and the politicians with a fear and mistrust of presidential leadership. Even as late as 1990, when the United States found it vitally important to go to war in the Middle East to protect their petroleum interests, Congress demanded to have at least a token voice in making the decision.

Because of the scrutiny to which Johnson's personality has been subjected by scholars and journalists alike, to say nothing of public perception, and because of the additional mistrust of politicians fostered by Johnson's successor, Richard M. Nixon, the character of would-be leaders has become more of an issue than ever before in U.S. history.

Sources

Caro, Robert. *The Years of Lyndon Johnson: The Path to Power.* New York: Knopf, 1982.

———. *The Years of Lyndon Johnson: Means of Ascent.* New York: Knopf, 1984.

Conkin, Paul. *Big Daddy from the Pedernales: Lyndon Baines Johnson.* Boston: Twayne, 1986.

Dallek, Robert. *Flawed Giant.* New York: Oxford, 1998.

———. *Lone Star Rising.* New York: Oxford, 1990.

Divine, Robert A. *Exploring the Johnson Years.* Austin, Tex.: UT Press, 1981.

Dugger, Ronnie. *The Politician: The Life and Times of Lyndon Baines Johnson: The Drive for Power from the Frontier to Master of the Senate.* New York: Norton, 1982.

Goodwin, Richard N. *Remembering America.* Boston: Little Brown, 1988.

Further Readings

Goldman, Eric. *The Tragedy of Lyndon Johnson.* New York: Knopf, 1968.

Kearns, Doris. *Lyndon Baines Johnson and the American Dream.* New York: Harper, 1976.

Lyndon B. Johnson Library and Museum. 1999. <http://www.lbjlib.utexas.edu/> (6 July, 1999).

Miller, Berle. *Lyndon: An Oral Biography.* New York: Putnam, 1980.

Rulon, Phillip. *The Compassionate Samaritan.* Chicago: Nelson-Hall, 1982.

Steinberg, Alfred. *Sam Johnson's Boy: A Close up of the President from Texas.* New York: Macmillan, 1968.

Nixon Administrations

Biography

Few figures in U.S. history have been as controversial as Richard Nixon. A passionate and aggressive politician, Nixon came to national attention first as a representative and senator, and then as vice president to Dwight D. Eisenhower from 1953 to 1961. In that time, Nixon established a reputation for ruthless campaigning, anticommunism, and foreign policy expertise. Seemingly finished after electoral defeats in 1960 and 1962, Nixon made a remarkable political comeback to capture the presidency in 1968. As president Nixon enjoyed many successes, particularly in foreign affairs, but the scandalous actions of Nixon and his supporters in the election of 1972 led to his resignation in disgrace.

Early Life

Richard Milhous Nixon was born on January 9, 1913, in Yorba Linda, California, the son of Frank and Hannah Nixon. Frank Nixon, who had grown up in poverty and ran away from home when he was 13, worked as a farmer and then tried the grocery business, but he was never very successful. Frank and Hannah Nixon married over her parents' objections. The Milhouses were Quakers and Frank Nixon was not. Richard and his five brothers enjoyed a reasonably happy childhood. There was a lot of hard work, however, because of Frank Nixon's business failures, and most of the time the family was barely able to make ends meet.

In spite of his misgivings, Hannah's father loaned the young couple money with which Frank built a house and started a lemon orchard at Yorba Linda. The orchard

Full name: Richard Milhous Nixon
Popular name: Dick Nixon

Personal Information:

Born: January 9, 1913
Birthplace: Yorba Linda, California
Died: April 22, 1994
Death place: New York, New York
Burial place: Nixon Library Grounds, Yorba Linda, California
Religion: Quaker
Spouse: Thelma Catherine (Patricia) Ryan (m. 1940)
Children: Patricia (Tricia); Julie
Education: Whittier College, B.A., 1934; Duke University Law School, 1937
Occupation: Lawyer, naval officer, politician
Political Party: Republican Party
Age at Inauguration: 56 years

Richard Milhous Nixon. *(The Library of Congress.)*

devoted himself mostly to debate. He astounded most observers with his debating skills and won numerous contests. He was an honor student and upon his graduation he was given a tuition scholarship to Harvard. He was forced to decline the scholarship, however, because his family could not afford travel and living expenses. Instead, Nixon enrolled at Whittier College.

At Whittier College Nixon was encouraged to read widely and deeply and to think independently, and this had a profound affect on his life. He had been born and reared as a Quaker; taught to accept the literal correctness and infallibility of the Bible. But, as he wrote in his senior essay, his education made this impossible. From that point on, religion was less important to him.

In June 1934 Nixon graduated from Whittier College, second in his class. He applied for a scholarship to Duke University Law School in Durham, North Carolina, and was accepted.

Throughout his time at Duke Nixon continued to be a top student even though he had to work in order to meet expenses. He served on the law review and was president of the student bar association. He graduated third in his class in 1937.

After considering jobs in New York and thinking about a career in the Federal Bureau of Investigation, Nixon at length returned to California. He passed the bar in December 1937 and joined the law firm of Wingert and Bewley in Whittier.

never did well, largely because of cold weather, and the Nixons never prospered from it. Later Frank Nixon tried a number of other jobs but was not particularly successful in any of them.

Hannah Nixon, a Quaker, seems to have had the greatest influence over the children, and her influence on her son Richard continued to be strong throughout her life. She died in 1967 just before he ran for president. Some observers believe that her absence permitted the darker side of Nixon's personality to emerge and that, had she lived, his presidency might have been different.

There was tragedy in the Nixon family. Two of Frank and Hannah Nixon's sons, Arthur and Harold, died within a ten year period. Their deaths dealt the family a devastating blow. Neither parent fully recovered. What is more, the loss of Nixon's brothers seems to have affected him for the rest of his life. Although he rarely spoke of these tragedies, he was overcome with emotion whenever he did so.

Education

Nixon began his formal education in 1918 at age five. He proved to be a precocious student with a photographic mind. He read voraciously. At Whittier High School in Whittier, California, Nixon participated in some sports but

Family Life

After returning to Whittier to practice law in 1938, Nixon met Patricia Ryan when both were auditioning for parts in a play with the Whittier Community Players. They were married in 1940. Born Thelma Catherine Ryan in 1912, Pat (who legally changed her name in 1930) grew up in a poor, unhappy home. Her mother died in 1926 and her father in 1930, so at the age of 18 she was on her own. She gradually worked her way through college and graduated from the University of Southern California in 1937 with a teaching certificate. She began her first job at Whittier High School in September 1937, and met Nixon the following January. They were married more than 50 years and had two children: Patricia (1946) and Julie (1948).

Julie married David Eisenhower, grandson of President Dwight D. Eisenhower, in 1967, and Tricia married Edward Cox, a student who later became a successful lawyer, in 1971.

First Lady Pat Nixon

As first lady Pat Nixon championed volunteerism and was especially concerned with programs designed to improve literacy. She also pushed for the establishment of new recreational areas near cities for those people who could not afford to visit faraway national parks. Pat Nixon reached out to the U.S. public by inviting them to the White House and, in partnership with White House Curator Clement Conger, she worked hard to beautify it. Conger inaugurated a significant program of collecting and displaying American art and furniture, most of which remains in the White House. Pat Nixon also arranged the first White House tours for the disabled, the famous candlelight tours for those who worked during the day, and for the White House to be lit at night like the other great monuments in Washington.

Pat Nixon often accompanied the president on his foreign junkets and also made several trips abroad on her own. She was with her husband on the historic trips to China and the Soviet Union (*See also,* Foreign Issues) and made solo trips to Africa and South America. When traveling she always tried to keep formal gatherings to a minimum so she could visit schools, hospitals, orphanages, and nursing homes. In 1969 while accompanying Nixon to Vietnam, she became the only first lady thus far to visit a combat zone.

Career

From 1937 to 1941 Nixon practiced law in Whittier. In 1939 he was made a partner in the firm of Wingert and Bewley and was regarded as a highly competent attorney. He did not make much money though, never exceeding $4,000 in the years before World War II (1939–45). He became active in community affairs, including involvement in Whittier College and Duke alumni organizations. His greatest triumph was his appointment to the Whittier Board of Trustees. Undoubtedly, his political ambitions also developed during this period. In fact, he had a mentor, Herman Perry, a prominent banker, who began grooming him for elective office.

Military Service

When the United States entered World War II (1939–45) in December 1941, Nixon took a job with the Office of Price Administration (OPA) where he worked in the tire rationing division. In April 1942 he applied for Naval Officer Candidate School (NOCS). This was a decision he was not required to make. As a civil servant he could have had a deferment, and as a birthright Quaker he could have avoided the military altogether, but he felt strongly that it was his duty to serve.

Nixon served in the U.S. Navy for three and one-half years. He was an assistant operations officer at an airstrip on the island of New Caledonia, in command of a small group of men whose job was to load and unload cargo planes. Nixon was regarded by his men as a good leader and showed courage under fire.

U.S. Representative

In the summer of 1944 Nixon returned to California where he worked for four months as a maintenance officer at a naval air base near Alameda. Then he was transferred to the Pentagon in Washington, D.C., where he served as a contracts officer. While he was there he received a letter from his old friend Herman Perry asking him to run on the Republican ticket for Congress in 1946. Amongst the Committee of 100—the local group of power brokers who would choose the candidate—Nixon was the unanimous choice.

The seat in California's 12th Congressional District was held by Jerry Voorhis, a liberal Democrat who had been in office for five terms. Voorhis was regarded by most observers as unbeatable, so Nixon faced a formidable challenge. But Voorhis was vulnerable. He was not a good campaigner—he had never faced a serious challenge—and he thoroughly underestimated the skill and determination of Richard Nixon. In fact he had never heard of Nixon, nor had anyone else in the 12th District with the exception of people in the immediate Whittier area.

In the campaign Nixon's speaking skills and the obvious research that went into his preparations far outdistanced Voorhis's efforts. Nixon ridiculed Voorhis's poor record and labeled him a radical. Communism, Nixon asserted again and again, was the great challenge to democracy, and Voorhis was essentially a Communist. Of course Voorhis was not a Communist at all but merely a liberal Democrat. Nixon's charges were excessive and showed that he was capable of being meanspirited and even unethical. Yet on election day Nixon won a decisive victory, polling 57 percent of the vote. Nixon, Pat, and their friends were overjoyed. Nixon later remarked that November 6, 1946, was the happiest day of his political career.

Nixon came into Congress well connected and was given excellent committee assignments, including the Education and Labor Committee; the House un-American Activities Committee (HUAC); and the Herter Committee. It was his work on the House un-American Activities Committee that brought Nixon to the attention of the nation, particularly his involvement in the case of Alger Hiss.

One of the people testifying to HUAC about Communist spies in government was Whittaker Chambers, a former Communist then working as a senior editor for *Time* magazine. In his testimony Chambers named several people who had been involved in a spy ring, including Alger Hiss.

Hiss had worked for the Department of Agriculture during the 1930s and later went to the State Department. There he became a foreign policy adviser to President Franklin D. Roosevelt and accompanied him to Yalta at the end of World War II. Later he was involved in the formation of the United Nations (UN) and finally left government service to become president of the Carnegie Endowment for International Peace. With Hiss's background the charges caused a sensation throughout the nation. Hiss responded to the charges with a demand that he be allowed to testify. When he did he categorically denied that he was a Communist or that he ever knew Whittaker Chambers. Hiss received so much support from influential people around the country that the committee looked foolish and considered dropping the matter. But Nixon, a junior member of the committee, persuaded them to push on.

As the committee hearings continued Hiss and Chambers confronted each other, and Hiss was forced to admit that he did know Chambers, but under the name of Crosley. This and other revelations diminished Hiss's credibility, but there was no hard evidence to prove his guilt. Hiss was later convicted for perjury and eventually sent to jail. He could not be tried for espionage because the statute of limitations had run out (*See also,* Truman administration).

The legacy of the Hiss case was very significant to Nixon's career. Nixon's handling of the Hiss affair catapulted him into the Senate and eventually the vice presidency of the United States.

U.S. Senator and Vice Presidential Candidate

In 1950 Nixon ran for the Senate against Helen Gahagan Douglas. He won, but in the process his reputation for political ruthlessness was enhanced.

In the campaign Nixon and his backers smeared Douglas by saying the liberal Democrat was soft on Communism. They called her "the pink lady," and they tried to make her voting record appear to be that of a "left winger" who was out of step with her own party. Douglas did not defend herself very effectively and Nixon won a resounding victory.

Almost immediately after entering the Senate in 1951, Nixon was touted by many Republicans as a potential vice presidential candidate. He was attractive, smart, articulate, had a good war record and, of course, was well-known for his anticommunist views.

When General Dwight D. Eisenhower won the presidential nomination in 1952, he immediately chose Nixon as his running mate.

In the campaign that followed, Nixon almost lost his chance for national office. A group of his friends in California had established a fund to support his political activities. His enemies discovered the existence of this fund and set out to make it appear that there was something corrupt about it. Soon there were demands that Nixon be removed from the Republican ticket. In fact, there was nothing illegal about the fund, and many politicians had similar support. Such funds were used to pay necessary expenses that were not covered by the salary or expense account of an officeholder.

Nixon was under great pressure to withdraw, but he did not. Instead, he went on television to explain himself to the American people.

On the night of September 23, 1952, Nixon made his most famous speech. It has gone down in history as "The Checkers Speech." Before a nationwide television audience estimated at nearly 60 million people, Nixon laid bare his personal finances. He listed everything that he had ever earned, and everything that he owed. Then came the coup de grace. He went on to explain that a supporter in Texas had given his children a dog—a little cocker spaniel named Checkers. "The children love that dog," Nixon said, "and regardless of what 'they' (his enemies) might say, we're going to keep it."

After the Checkers' speech, there was such an overwhelming outpouring of public support for Nixon that Eisenhower had no choice but to leave Nixon on the ticket. In November Eisenhower and Nixon were elected.

Vice President

Nixon was an active vice president who is thought by many scholars to have transformed the office from one that was merely ceremonial to one of importance. Eisenhower was partly responsible for this because he kept Nixon well informed and often gave him important things to do in both the domestic and foreign policy arenas.

Nixon often represented the United States abroad. During his eight years in office he made 12 overseas journeys for various purposes and always performed with skill and dignity.

The most famous of all Nixon's trips took him to Moscow in 1959, where he was the highest-ranking U.S. representative at the Soviet international trade fair. At the fair he encountered Nikita Khrushchev, and the two leaders engaged in a spirited debate over the relative merits of their two economic systems: Communism and capitalism. Eisenhower's popularity at home and Nixon's skill at foreign policy made them a popular combination, and Nixon's position as Eisenhower's successor was now pretty well established.

On the domestic front Nixon served as liaison between the White House and Capitol Hill, and he served as a sort of deputy leader of the Republican Party. Eisenhower delegated to Nixon the task of dealing with Wisconsin senator Joseph McCarthy, who accused many both inside and outside of government of Communist affiliations between 1950 and 1954 (*See also,* Eisenhower administration).

Eisenhower's policy created a problem for Nixon. Nixon generally agreed with the idea of unmasking Communism, but he disagreed with McCarthy's tactics. Hence he tried to follow a middle course of only fending off McCarthy's most outrageous charges. This more or less worked although it further weakened Nixon's standing with liberals. McCarthy finally went too far when he attacked the army, declaring that Communists had been promoted. This was too much for Eisenhower and he ordered Nixon to go on television to inform the public that the senator did not have the support of the administration. Nixon did this, but in his speech many thought he was harsher on the Democrats than on McCarthy. The Democrats were furious and in the congressional election campaign of 1954 they used Nixon as a specific target in their efforts to gain a victory over the Republicans. The Democrats succeeded in regaining control of Congress, and Nixon was so upset by this that he considered resigning but did not. He was bitter, however, because he felt that Eisenhower had essentially sacrificed him to the onslaught of the opposition.

While trying to maintain a tough anticommunist policy and at the same time distance the administration from McCarthy, many in both parties felt Nixon bumbled the job. Under pressure Eisenhower suggested to Nixon that he might want to consider accepting a cabinet post rather than running for vice president in the 1956 election. Since this would have been perceived by the nation as a demotion and hence would have ruined his career, Nixon did not want to do it. He wanted the president's endorsement, which Eisenhower hesitated to give saying instead that Nixon should make his own decision. Even though Nixon interpreted this as an invitation to resign, he courageously stuck to his guns and eventually told Eisenhower that he intended to run. Eisenhower agreed, and they were overwhelmingly reelected to a second term in 1956.

Campaigning for the Presidency

During 1960—the last year of his vice presidency—Nixon spent most of his time preparing for the presidential election scheduled for November. Nixon and his running mate, Senator Henry Cabot Lodge of Massachusetts, lost to John F. Kennedy and Lyndon Johnson, in one of the closest presidential elections of all time. With 68.8 million votes cast Kennedy claimed 34.2 million (49.7 percent), and Nixon claimed 34.1 million (49.6 percent). The difference was a mere 112,881 votes, or less than one-tenth of one percent. However, Kennedy's victories were concentrated in states with large electoral college votes so he came out with 303 electoral votes to 219 for Nixon. Allegedly there was election fraud committed in some of the big states, especially Illinois and Texas. Some of Nixon's advisers urged him to demand a recount, but because it would have taken a long time and might have caused a constitutional crisis, he declined. Many observers regard this decision as his highest act of statesmanship in his entire career.

Running for Governor

When Nixon left Washington in 1961, he took a position in a law firm in California. He also wrote a book entitled *Six Crises,* which chronicled his career up to 1960. This book soon became a best-seller, and by 1962 Nixon could contemplate a comfortable future and possibly a return to politics. Against his better judgment, he

was persuaded to run for governor of California in 1962. Nixon was out of touch with the needs of California residents and lost to Pat Brown by nearly 300,000 votes.

The campaign turned out to be bitter and much more difficult than Nixon had anticipated. Tired and angry by the end of the campaign, Nixon made a statement to the press late on election night that was to haunt him for years. It was a rambling address that contained numerous references to journalistic bias and concluded with Nixon declaring that the reporters would not "have Nixon to kick around anymore . . . because . . . gentlemen, this is my last press conference" (Patterson, p. 450).

Following the debacle of 1962 practically all political observers were certain that Nixon would never return to national politics, but Nixon never gave up. He returned to law and joined a New York City law firm in 1963. But he still kept in touch with the party power brokers. Whenever the opportunity presented itself he spoke and traveled on behalf of Republican candidates. By 1967 he had emerged as the front-runner for the Republican nomination, and in 1968 he won it easily.

Presidency

Nixon defeated Vice President Hubert Humphrey in the election of 1968. He was 56 years old. He promised to end the Vietnam War (1959–75) and end the factionalism and polarization at home that had been caused by the war and the race issue. He did indeed end the war, but it took five years—much longer than he had anticipated. His efforts on the domestic scene, however, were not successful, and his presidency was eventually destroyed by the Watergate scandal (*See also,* Domestic Issues).

Post-presidential Years

Nixon resigned the presidency on August 9, 1974, and returned to San Clemente, California, where he and his wife lived for the next six years. In 1980 they moved to New York City and a little later to New Jersey where they resided until their deaths. After his resignation, Nixon feared prosecution but was pardoned by President Gerald Ford. This was a unique and unprecedented action because there was considerable evidence that Nixon might have been guilty of several crimes.

Although he was utterly disgraced, Nixon began to write and to travel throughout the United States and the world again, working hard to rebuild his reputation as a foreign policy expert and make himself a recognized and influential elder statesman. Many of his books became best-sellers.

As he worked on his books Nixon traveled extensively. He received and accepted hundreds of invitations to speak at college campuses and before a variety of

What They Said . . .

"The American people love a fighter, and in Dick Nixon they found a gallant one. In her wonderful biography of her mother, Julie recalls a discussion where Pat Nixon expressed astonishment at her husband's ability to persevere in the face of criticism. To which the president replied, 'I just get up every day to confound my enemies.'"

(Source: Robert Dole, eulogy for Richard M. Nixon, April 27, 1994.)

groups. He also traveled in Europe, the Middle East, and Asia. His books were his calling cards, and they opened many doors and opportunities, all of which he exploited shrewdly.

By 1985 Nixon had achieved his comeback and continued extensive travel in the name of international peace. In the course of this work he wrote articles, gave speeches, consulted with the Reagan. Bush, and Clinton administrations, and made annual visits to Russia.

In 1994 he announced the establishment of the Nixon Center for Peace and Freedom, a policy center of the Nixon Foundation dedicated to promoting his principles of enlightened national interest in foreign policy and pragmatic idealism at home.

Richard M. Nixon died on April 22, 1994, in New York City. He was buried on the grounds of the Nixon Library in Yorba Linda, California, beside his wife. Eulogists at his funeral included President Bill Clinton, Senator Robert Dole of Missouri, California governor Pete Wilson, and Nixon's second secretary of state Henry Kissinger.

The Richard M. Nixon Administrations

Richard M. Nixon came into office determined to end the Vietnam War (1959–75) and bring the people together at home. He succeeded in an ironic way. He ended the war, although the process took much longer than he imagined, and he united the country not by persuading people to accept his policies but by turning them against him as a result of his scandalous behavior in what

came to be known as Watergate. Subsequently, he became the only president in U.S. history to resign.

Nixon Becomes President

The Campaign of 1968

Nixon began his drive for the presidency in January 1968. He chose his issues shrewdly. It was time for new leadership, he said, to deal with the salient problems of the day: inflation, crime, and the Vietnam War (1959–75). He would hammer at these points time and time again throughout the year, and his efforts proved successful.

At the Republican Convention in Miami, Florida, Nixon was easily nominated. His selection of Governor Spiro T. Agnew of Maryland as his running mate caused some consternation because Agnew was little known nationally and there was some questions about his honesty. These fears were quickly overcome, however, as Nixon doggedly insisted that the convention approve his choice.

During the campaign against Democratic nominee Vice President Hubert Humphrey, Nixon made "law and order" his primary theme. This was appropriate because during the summer of 1968 it appeared that the United States was about to come unraveled. Protesters and hecklers were everywhere, and Nixon handled it by remaining calm and cool on the surface. As far as the war issue was concerned, he was silent and would say only that he wanted the peace talks to succeed. (President Lyndon Johnson was attempting to facilitate negotiations during the fall of 1968 without much luck.)

Nixon's opponents in the campaign were at opposite ends of the political spectrum. Hubert Humphrey, the Democratic candidate, was a liberal who represented all that was best in the appeal of the old-fashioned New Deal Democratic Party. Unfortunately that appeal had been tarnished by the anti war movement and the backlash against Johnson's Great Society (*See also,* Lyndon Johnson administration). On the domestic side he could only call for more government programs—an approach that was losing its appeal—and on the war issue Humphrey was hamstrung by President Johnson who told him that if he criticized the bombing of North Vietnam, he would lose party funding. Hence, Humphrey had nothing new to offer.

George Wallace of Alabama, the third-party candidate, called his organization the American Independent Party. He was a firm believer in racial segregation and appealed strongly to the racial bias of many Americans, especially in the South. He also called for harsh measures against dissidents and increasing rather than decreasing the war effort. Although Wallace's campaign was a nuisance and an embarrassment, Nixon welcomed his participation believing that Wallace would draw more votes from Humphrey than from himself.

Administration

Administration Dates
January 20, 1969–January 20, 1973
January 20, 1973–August 9, 1974

Vice President
Spiro Theodore Agnew (1969–73)
Gerald Rudolph Ford (1973–74)

Cabinet

Secretary of State
William P. Rogers (1969–73)
Henry A. Kissinger (1973–77)

Secretary of the Treasury
David M. Kennedy (1969–71)
John B. Connally (1971–72)
George P. Shultz (1972–74)
William E. Simon (1974–77)

Attorney General
John N. Mitchell (1969–72)
Richard G. Kleindienst (1972–73)
Elliot L. Richardson (1973)
William B. Saxbe (1974–75)

Postmaster General
Winton M. Blount (1969–71)

Secretary of Interior
Walter J. Hickel (1969–70)
Rogers C. B. Morton (1971–75)

Secretary of Agriculture
Clifford M. Hardin (1969–71)
Earl L. Butz (1971–76)

Secretary of Labor
George P. Schultz (1969–70)
James D. Hodgson (1970–73)
Peter J. Brennan (1973–75)

Secretary of Commerce
Maurice H. Stans (1969–72)
Peter G. Peterson (1972–73)
Frederick B. Dent (1973–75)

Secretary of Defense
Melvin R. Laird (1969–73)
Elliot L. Richardson (1973)
James R. Schlesinger (1973–75)

Secretary of Health, Education and Welfare
Robert H. Finch (1969–70)
Elliot L. Richardson (1970–73)
Caspar W. Weinberger (1973–75)

Secretary of Housing and Urban Development
George W. Romney (1969–73)
James T. Lynn (1973–75)

Secretary of Transportation
John A. Volpe (1969–73)
Claude S. Brinegar (1973–75)

In the final analysis Nixon polled over 31.5 million votes (43.42 percent) to 31 million (42.7 percent) for Humphrey. Wallace garnered 9.9 million (13.5 percent). In the electoral college, however, it was not so close. Nixon had 301 votes to 191 for Humphrey and 46 for Wallace. Nixon had finally achieved his dream. He was the president of the United States.

The Campaign of 1972

Nixon's popularity had sagged dramatically in 1971 due to frustration over the peace process and the nation's economic problems. By 1972, however, all that had changed, and it was generally agreed by observers that the president was assured of reelection. This was because of his foreign policy triumphs in Moscow, Russia, and Peking, China, and his handling of the economy. By the spring of 1972 inflation was down, the Gross National Product (GNP) was rising, incomes were rising, taxes were down, and the stock market was soaring.

Wallace could have been a serious problem. His popularity was growing in the North, and potentially he could have cost Nixon needed electoral votes in that region. However, before the president could develop a strategy to deal with Wallace, fate intervened. While he was campaigning in Maryland, Wallace was shot by a would-be assassin. The governor was paralyzed from the waist down by this attack and forced to withdraw. Nixon was now unbeatable.

Meanwhile, the Democrats seemed bent upon committing political suicide. After 1968 they had made new rules for the selection of convention delegates, which required quotas based on age, sex, and ethnicity. Thus the party was no longer dominated by power blocs like the unions and the state and local machines, but by interest groups. These groups were more concerned with their own agendas than in party harmony.

Senator George McGovern, a liberal from South Dakota, was the Democratic nominee. He favored immediate withdrawal from Vietnam, women's liberation, homosexual equality, amnesty for draft dodgers, special rights for migrant farm workers, an improved welfare program for single mothers, and compensation for dispossessed Indian tribes, among other things. The trouble was that these issues did not appeal to the mainstream of the U.S. population in 1972. Thus McGovern was hobbled by his own agenda.

McGovern campaigned vigorously, often lashing out at Nixon with vicious personal attacks, but it gained him little. The president for his part allowed his party workers to smear McGovern and other Democrats with a campaign of "dirty tricks" (unfair and untrue charges) while he himself stood majestically above and apart from it all. Nixon campaigned little because there was not much need. Most polls showed him leading by overwhelming percentages. He was not hurt at all by the Watergate break-in. It was kept in the news by the *Washington Post* (See also, Domestic Issues), but as yet had no affect on the president or his administration.

Nixon's victory in 1972 was breathtaking. He polled 47 million votes (60.7 percent) to 29 million (37.5 percent) for McGovern. It was the second greatest landslide of all time. Only Lyndon Johnson had done better when he defeated Barry Goldwater in 1964. Ironically, though, the Democrats maintained their control of Congress with a majority of 59 to 43 in the Senate and 243 to 192 in the House. This was because local rather than national issues were the deciding factors in congressional elections.

With this great victory Nixon should have felt secure, but he did not. He worried about Congress; he was beginning to worry about Watergate; and worst of all his paranoia caused him to have nightmares about his real and imagined enemies in the population at large, the government and the media. Some of these nightmares, largely because of his own behavior, were about to come true.

Nixon's Advisers

Nixon was a loner and had few friends. As president he did not rely much on his cabinet or other advisory groups such as the National Security Council in foreign affairs or the Council of Economic Advisers on domestic matters. Instead, he sought out individuals who seemed to have ideas similar to his own and drew upon their expertise for specific projects.

One such person was Daniel Patrick Moynihan. Moynihan was a Harvard professor and an Irish Catholic

Democrat, but he was moderately conservative. This appealed to Nixon, and the president began to listen to the professor's ideas. Moynihan persuaded Nixon that he could secure his place in history just as Benjamin Disraeli had done as prime minister of England a century earlier. Disraeli had succeeded in the 1870s in promoting social reform even though he was a conservative. Thus Nixon embraced Moynihan's proposal for welfare reform (See also, Domestic Issues), though he became embittered when the plan failed in Congress.

Kevin Phillips was another of Nixon's advisers. He was an aide to Nixon's closest political adviser, John Mitchell. Phillips wrote a book entitled *The Emerging of a Republican Majority* in which he argued that Americans were sick of New Deal liberalism supported by the intellectual elite of the Northeast who dominated the Democratic Party. Phillips predicted that a new conservative majority was emerging in U.S. politics. It was made up of the Catholic working class, white southerners, and average middle-class Americans, all of whom were revolted by militant minority groups, radical students, and arrogant intellectuals.

Nixon decided that he would appeal to these people, many of whom lived in the South—the so-called Sun Belt—through an approach that came to be known as the Southern Strategy. This involved appeals to those he called the "forgotten" or "silent majority" of Americans who longed for "law and order."

During his successful campaign for the presidency, Nixon gathered around him a small cadre of people who later served as presidential advisers and most of whom were eventually caught up in the Watergate scandal. Few could be said to have been friends of the president—he had very few real friends—but they all served him loyally. Most important in this group were H. R. "Bob" Haldeman and John Ehrlichman.

Haldeman was Nixon's chief of staff. A former advertising executive, he gained a reputation as a very difficult person. Haldeman was deeply involved in the Watergate cover-up, and many of the "White House tapes" that ended Nixon's presidency record damning conversations between Haldeman and Nixon. Haldeman resigned his White House post in April 1973, and he was later convicted of conspiracy and obstruction of justice. Like Ehrlichman, he served 18 months in prison.

John Ehrlichman was Nixon's chief assistant for domestic affairs. As director of the so-called "plumbers' unit" he approved the break-in at the office of Daniel Ellsberg's psychiatrist. Ellsberg was the defense analyst who leaked the Pentagon Papers to the press (See also, Nixon and the Judiciary). Ehrlichman also was deeply involved in the Watergate cover-up. He resigned his White House position in 1973, and he subsequently was convicted of perjury and obstruction of justice.

Another man who was fairly close to Nixon was Charles W. Colson who served as special counsel to the president. Colson was so mean that he was known in the administration as the "evil genius." He was deeply involved in the Watergate cover-up and the Ellsberg case, as well as numerous other shenanigans generally known as "dirty tricks." This term refers to the publication of false and often damaging information about other people. He left the White House in 1974 and was indicted, whereupon he pleaded guilty to obstruction of justice and was sent to prison.

John Mitchell was Nixon's former law partner and served as attorney general until 1972, when he resigned to become chairman of the Committee to Reelect the President (CREEP). During 1972 it was discovered that Mitchell controlled a secret campaign fund that paid for the Watergate break-in and other illegal activities. He denied these allegations, but they were later substantiated in court and Mitchell went to jail for 19 months.

Maurice Stans was Nixon's secretary of commerce and later finance chairman for CREEP. In this capacity he raised nearly $60 million for the campaign of 1972, and some of the money was used to finance Watergate and other irregularities. As a result Stans was indicted on charges of conspiracy, perjury, and obstruction of justice. He maintained that he had no knowledge of how the money he raised was used, and he was acquitted. Later Stans wrote several books about his experiences. He always remained loyal to Nixon and later raised nearly $30 million to finance the Nixon Library at Yorba Linda, California.

John W. Dean III, in his capacity as special counsel, was another of Nixon's advisers who was deeply involved in Watergate. Nixon told him to lie about it, which he did at first, but then he changed his mind and told the truth in his testimony before the Ervin Committee (the Senate committee investigating Watergate). His statement ultimately led to Nixon's fall, but Dean received no immunity. He was charged with obstruction of justice for his role in the Watergate cover-up and spent four months in jail.

One of Nixon's advisers who was generally untouched by the Watergate affair was Pat Buchanan, who served as a speech writer and researcher from 1966 to 1974. Later he worked for both Presidents Ford and Reagan. Buchanan is extremely conservative and has made a living as a right-wing author and commentator on television. He also continues to be very interested in politics and has sought the Republican presidential nomination on two occasions (1992 and 1996).

One of Nixon's most important advisers was Henry A. Kissinger. His expertise was in foreign policy, and he had nothing to do with Watergate or any other problems that plagued Nixon on the domestic scene. Kissinger was German-born and was brought to the United States by his parents in 1938. Brilliant and well-educated, he began his career as a professor at Harvard in 1954. His first book on nuclear weapons and foreign policy, published in 1957, gained attention, and he was occasionally called upon to advise Presidents Eisenhower, Kennedy, and Johnson. In 1969 he was named Nixon's national security affairs adviser, and in 1973 he became secretary of state. While serving Nixon, Kissinger was very influential in establishing and implementing foreign policy, and his highest achievement came in negotiating an end to the Vietnam War (1959–75) in 1973. For this he received the Nobel Peace Prize. Kissinger also served as secretary of state in the Ford administration before leaving public service in 1977.

Leonard Garment first met Nixon when the latter joined the New York City law firm in 1963. Garment at once became convinced that Nixon had a political future and began to advise him and introduce him to influential people. During the 1968 campaign Garment was one of Nixon's closet advisers and later became his personal counsel during Watergate.

Nixon and Congress

The very close election of 1968 that brought Nixon to the White House also resulted in Democratic majorities in both houses of Congress. Nixon was to preside over the Ninety-first, Ninety-second, and part of the Ninety-third Congresses between 1969 and 1974, where there were Democratic majorities. Nixon never worked well with them and so did not accomplish as much, especially in domestic policy, as he might have otherwise.

Nixon always complained that it was because he was stuck with a Democratic Congress that limited his achievements. Many analysts have countered that his efforts to move Congress in the direction he wanted it to go were ineffective. In fact, it has been said that Nixon was the least effective president in dealing with Congress since Herbert Hoover. The best example of this is the Family Assistance Program, a welfare reform of historic significance (*See also,* Domestic Issues). Nixon supported the plan and got it through the House, but he failed to lay the groundwork effectively for maneuvering it through the Senate. Then, when he ran into obstacles, he simply gave up and a great opportunity for social reform was lost. Once the Watergate scandal broke in 1973, Nixon's relationship with Congress soured even further, and the last 18 months of his administration were consumed by this issue.

During his presidency Nixon vetoed 43 bills, most of which were either appropriations measures of one sort or another, or personal relief bills. Seven of Nixon's vetoes were overridden, but of those, the only one of major significance was the War Powers Act of 1973, which requires the president to seek congressional approval to wage war even if war is not formally declared.

Biography:

Henry Kissinger

Statesman (b. 1923) Henry Kissinger's influence on American foreign policy began when he served as a special consultant to the National Security Council and the Department of State in 1961 and 1962. Kissinger emerged during the 1968 presidential election as the leading Republican foreign policy expert. After his victory in the 1968 presidential election, Nixon named Kissinger his special assistant for national security affairs. His first objective was ending U.S. involvement in the Vietnam War. Kissinger was instrumental in negotiating the peace settlement between the North and South Vietnamese in 1973. During 1972 and 1973, not only was a cease fire negotiated in Vietnam, but the United States initiated diplomatic relations with China and the United States and the Soviet Union signed the Strategic Arms Limitation Treaty (SALT), which estab-

lished, for the first time, limits on offensive and defensive weapons. For these accomplishments, and also for his role in attempting to bring settlement to the conflicts between Israelis and Palestinians, Kissinger won the Nobel Peace Prize in 1973. With President Gerald Ford's defeat in the 1976 election, Kissinger too left the government. Since then he has written his memoirs, started a private consulting firm, and has continued to serve as a leading commentator on international affairs.

Nixon and the Judiciary

When Nixon became president in 1969, the nine members of the Supreme Court were dominated by broad constructionist liberals (jurists who believe the Constitution should be interpreted as being very flexible). Nixon generally did not agree with this view. He wanted to change the nature of the Court by appointing constructionist judges, or judges who believed in a very strict and conservative interpretation of the Constitution.

Nixon's opportunity soon presented itself when Earl Warren retired as chief justice. Nixon replaced him with Warren Burger, a distinguished jurist with a conservative reputation, especially in criminal cases. At about the same time in the spring of 1969, Justice Abe Fortas (Lyndon Johnson's choice for the chief justiceship) resigned in the wake of allegations against him of inappropriate behavior. Thus Nixon was given a second chance to appoint a justice to the Court very early in his administration. His next choice was Judge Clement F. Haynsworth. Haynsworth fit Nixon's job description almost perfectly. He was a southerner and a strict constructionist who was also regarded by his peers as a distinguished jurist.

No sooner had the appointment been announced than there was a storm of criticism. Liberals charged that Haynsworth was a racist, and the Jewish lobby argued that this seat on the Court belonged to them since it had been held in succession by Louis Brandies, Felix Frankfurter, Arthur Goldberg, and Abe Fortas, all Jews.

Haynsworth also ran into trouble in the confirmation process. Democrats dug up every crumb of dirt they could find, and even though the sum total amounted to very little, it soon became clear that Haynsworth's nomination was doomed. Nixon did not have the votes. So, even though Judge Haynsworth was perfectly qualified to join the Court, his nomination had to be withdrawn and everyone knew the real reason; he was a southerner and a conservative.

Nixon was furious, and he instructed his aides to find another southern nominee who was even more conservative than Haynsworth. The name that surfaced was that of Judge G. Harrold Carswell of Florida. Carswell was an unfortunate choice. He really was a racist who was also a second-rate jurist at best. Again, there was a storm of criticism that was this time quite justified. The Justice Department, especially Attorney General John Mitchell, had moved too fast in an effort to satisfy Nixon and had created an embarrassing problem. In no way could Carswell's nomination be justified. Still, Nixon dug in his heels and defended his man to the end. The Senate rejected the nomination in April 1970.

Despite his disappointment Nixon turned this defeat to his own advantage. Soon after the Senate vote he addressed the nation saying that he had concluded that it would be impossible for him to appoint a southern, strict constructionist to the Court. This saddened and angered him because strict constructionism was his philosophy of constitutional law, and his nominees had been subjected to excessive criticism simply because of their viewpoints—legitimate viewpoints. This statement instantly gave Nixon very high credibility in the South and would eventually enable him to achieve notable political and policy successes that would otherwise have been impossible without support from the South.

Eventually Nixon had his way with the Supreme Court. He appointed Harry Blackmun in 1970, and then Lewis F. Powell Jr. and William H. Rehnquist in 1971. Blackmun was a distinguished jurist who was regarded as a moderate in matters of civil liberties and civil rights and a conservative in criminal matters. Lewis Powell Jr. was regarded as "moderately conservative" and so fulfilled Nixon's search for a conservative southerner. William Rehnquist was an outspoken, conservative Republican, and for many years after his appointment in 1971 he was generally regarded as the most conservative member of the Court.

There were several notable decisions handed down by the Supreme Court during Nixon's administration. One of the first of these was *Swann v. Charlotte-Mecklenburg Board of Education* (1971). In this decision, one of several concerning desegregation of public schools to be handed down over the years, the Court once again declared that de jure (state imposed) segregation was unacceptable, and it established a broad set of guidelines for the elimination of de jure segregation by such means as busing.

Another important case was *New York Times v. United States* (1971). This decision involved the Pentagon Papers, classified documents relating to the Vietnam War (1959–75) that were stolen and given to the press by former Defense Department staff member Daniel Ellsberg. When these documents began to appear in the *New York Times* and other newspapers, the attorney general secured a restraining order to stop publication. This order, and others, were subsequently overturned by the Court as violations of the First Amendment right of freedom of the press.

The most sensational decision handed down by the Court during Nixon's presidency, and the one with by far the most far-reaching consequences, was *Roe v. Wade* (1973). This was a Texas case arising from a state law prohibiting abortion. The Court held that such a law was a violation of the right of personal privacy guaranteed by the due process clause of the Fourteenth Amendment, as well as a violation of rights set forth in the First, Third, Fourth, Fifth, and Ninth Amendments. Their ruling, in effect, made abortion a legal procedure. Ironically, this decision represented an extreme use of judicial flexibility and broad constructionist philosophy such as Nixon opposed, and he was not pleased.

Another of the important court decisions of this period involved Nixon himself. It was *United States v. Nixon* (1974) and was the famous decision involving the White House tapes of Nixon's conversations, which led directly to the president's decision to resign. In this case the Court weighed the due process requirements of crim-

inal trials in which anyone may be required to testify, against the claim of absolute privilege on the part of the president to withhold evidence obtained in confidential exchanges among officials of the executive branch. This doctrine of "executive privilege" had never been challenged in the courts before, and in this landmark decision the Court held that while the privilege exists, it is qualified and limited, not absolute.

Changes in the U.S. Government

Nixon contemplated a major structural reorganization of the government, but it did not materialize. However, he did create two important agencies. The first was the Urban Affairs Council, created in 1969 and chaired by Daniel Patrick Moynihan. Its purpose was to advise the president concerning domestic policy with special reference to the needs of people living in cities. Moynihan's only major effort was the Family Assistance Program, which failed. The second agency was the Environmental Protection Agency (EPA), which still exists and which plays a major role in the lives of many Americans (*See also,* Domestic Issues). It is very controversial because of the widespread belief that it has too much power to interfere in private business matters.

The Twenty-sixth Amendment was proposed and ratified during Nixon's administration. In the social and political turmoil of the 1960s and early 1970s, young people had shown themselves to be remarkably astute and articulate—even to those who disagreed with their views. Moreover, young people were being called upon in large numbers to fight for their country. Hence, it occurred to many people that they should be allowed to vote. This amendment, which lowered the voting age from 21 to 18, was proposed on March 23, 1971, and ratified on June 30, 1971. This was a record for the ratification of a constitutional amendment.

Domestic Issues

When Nixon was elected president in November 1968, the nation was still reeling from the shocking events of that tumultuous year. Leaders like Robert Kennedy and Martin Luther King Jr. had been assassinated, the presidency of Lyndon Baines Johnson had collapsed under the strain of the antiwar movement, and the Democratic National Convention in Chicago, Illinois, had been the scene of rioting and bloodletting. The nation had become polarized in several ways. There were those who still supported the Vietnam War (1959–75) and those who demanded its end. There were those who demanded more rapid changes on the domestic scene, and those who were adamantly opposed to these developments—especially in such arenas as race relations. This polarization cut across class, race, and gender lines.

Nixon's plan was to present himself to the people as a consensus figure who would promote the kind of reform at home and policy abroad that would bring the people together. In his campaign he said this would be his first great objective. His would be an "open administration." It would be open to people of both parties, open to new ideas, open to critics as well as friends. This was high-sounding rhetoric that proved to be quite misleading. Nixon's administration was not an open one—except perhaps during the first few months, and while it did bring the American people together, it did so in ways that Nixon did not intend. Nevertheless he experienced some notable successes as well as some disappointing failures in domestic policy.

Ending the Draft

Even before his election Nixon had considered the idea of an all-volunteer army, and by the time of his election the appeal of the idea had grown considerably. Early in his administration he turned the issue over to a blue-ribbon committee and in the spring of 1970 the committee recommended an end to the military draft. Although there was considerable opposition in Congress, Nixon was able to maneuver a bill through, and it became law in September 1971.

The Environment

Nixon had never been a great advocate of conservation, indeed he had never given the matter much attention. However, he realized that the issue had a large constituency when Earth Day 1970 produced rallies, seminars, "clean-ups," teach-ins, and vigils all over the nation. Within 60 days he announced the creation of the Environmental Protection Agency (EPA), which centralized the essential functions of several government agencies and was given significant power to regulate industry in order to control pollution. He told the people and the Congress that all Americans were entitled to clean air and water, and he proposed an array of environmental legislation. Included were such laws as the Clean Air Act, which imposed emission restrictions on cars, the Oil Spill Act, the Noise Control Act, the Clean Water Act, the Ocean Dumping Act, and other antipollution laws. Passed in 1971 and 1972, these laws represented the most thorough effort of its kind by any president before or since.

Nixon's policy on national parks was also a positive contribution. He felt strongly that parks should be available to as many Americans as possible. Since people of modest means could not afford to embark on long journeys to visit places like Yellowstone in the northwestern United States, Nixon, inspired by his wife Pat Nixon's commitment to expand recreational opportunities, believed that parks should be brought to them. Thus he decreed that any federal land released for use by the Property Review Board should be made into a park. This order resulted in the creation of 642 new parks during Nixon's presidency.

Nixon's record with respect to environmental issues has been the subject of considerable debate. His critics claim it was self-serving and insincere—merely an effort to gain political advantage. His supporters claim that he developed a real interest. The truth may never be known, but the results were significant.

The Economy

With respect to the country's financial structure and economy, Nixon made several important moves. Among Nixon's economic policies were his directives that government contracts should be concentrated as much as possible in depressed areas, that prices of major commodities should be kept as low as possible, and most importantly that the free-market economy should be regulated if necessary. On this latter issue Nixon took action in the summer of 1971. Worried about rising inflation and unemployment, he imposed wage and price controls and suspended the convertibility of the dollar into gold. These policies were in effect for three months, were very unpopular, and may or may not have worked. This has been a matter of debate ever since. In any case, the economy was under control by 1972 (temporarily it turned out), and this helped Nixon immensely in his reelection campaign.

Civil Rights

The civil rights revolution made significant gains by 1969. The Supreme Court had quashed the "separate but equal" doctrine in 1954 (*See also,* Eisenhower administration) and the weak Civil Rights Acts of 1957 and 1960 had been replaced by the more effective Civil Rights Act of 1964 and Voting Rights Act of 1965. Nevertheless, there was still far to go, especially in the arena of school desegregation. Presidents Kennedy and Johnson had devoted themselves to solving this problem but had achieved little. Ironically, it would be Nixon who would succeed.

In 1969 only about five percent of the nation's African American children were in desegregated schools; by 1972 the figure was near 90 percent. Nixon was undoubtedly a complex figure, and often his motives are difficult to discern. He certainly harbored a sympathy for both the South and for the needs of the people, and he also had political ambition. He saw desegregation as both the right and the politically expedient thing to do. He accomplished it by stealth and indirection, not frontal assault. He confronted it as a national problem—there was in fact both de jure (without support of law) and de facto (legislated) segregation all over the country. He encouraged the redrawing of school district lines with generous offers of federal aid, and he made the matter an issue of education—and the need to improve it—not race. He was particularly adept at working with southern whites, not confronting them or denouncing them, and his policy succeeded. Of course his critics pictured him as a cunning, shallow, and unethical politician throughout the process, and perhaps there is some truth to these allegations. Even so, his policies worked.

Welfare Reform

Nixon's greatest failure and greatest disappointment in the domestic arena was welfare reform. He was influenced by Daniel Patrick Moynihan, a Harvard professor who had written extensively on the subject and whom Nixon appointed the first director of the new Urban Affairs Council. The idea of this council was that it would be the domestic equivalent of the National Security Council in foreign affairs. In August 1969 Moynihan persuaded Nixon to support a proposal for the creation of a new system called the Family Assistance Program (FAP). Under this proposal all families in need would be guaranteed an income of $1,600 by the federal government. The idea quickly came under fire from both conservatives and liberals in Congress. The former opposed it as an unwarranted expense, and the latter claimed it did too little. Soon the idea simply died and Nixon was bitter. He concluded that the plan had been scuttled by his enemies—mostly the Democrats—because they could not stand to see a Republican president achieve any results in the field of social reform. This was no doubt an exaggerated view, but Nixon really believed it, and it contributed to the growth of his general hatred for his "enemies."

Watergate

In the early morning of June 17, 1972, police arrested five men attempting a break-in at Democratic National Headquarters in the Watergate, a fashionable residential and office complex in Washington, D.C. The culprits were attempting to install electronic listening equipment in several offices. When Nixon was informed of the incident he announced that he deplored such actions, and he assured the public that the White House had no involvement. Later in the summer, however, the *Washington Post* published the names of several White House aides who allegedly were involved. To this the president responded by announcing later in August that his counsel, John W. Dean, had conducted a thorough investigation and concluded that no one in the administration was in any way connected with the break-in.

During the summer of 1972 the *Washington Post* continued to publish stories by reporters Carl Bernstein and Robert Woodward arguing that in spite of official denials many members of the Committee to Reelect the President (CREEP), several of Nixon's close associates, and maybe even Nixon himself, had been party to the Watergate break-in. Much of their information was provided by an informant who came to be known only as "Deep Throat." The identity of this person has never been revealed, and it has been suggested that Woodward and Bernstein simply invented him and that he never existed.

White House counsel John Dean, shown here taking the oath before the Ervin Committee (the Senate committee investigating Watergate). Dean was the most important witness in the Watergate cover-up investigation.

(UPI/Corbis-Bettmann. Reproduced by permission.)

In January 1973 the Watergate culprits were tried and found guilty, but the judge in the case, John J. Sirica, was not satisfied. He believed there was much more to the incident. Accordingly he urged a congressional investigation. Responding to Sirica's plea, the Senate formed the Select Committee on Presidential Campaign Activities (the Ervin Committee) with Sam J. Ervin of North Carolina as chairman. Meanwhile in March 1973, Judge Sirica sentenced the Watergate players to prison.

The Senate Hearings

Soon the Senate Select Committee and a federal grand jury began to hear testimony. In April 1973 Nixon announced that he had ordered new inquiries and that soon there would be major new developments. Meanwhile, Jeb Stuart McGruder, who had been chairman of CREEP, testified that Attorney General John N. Mitchell and Nixon's counsel John Dean had both been involved in the break-in. In fact they had helped plan it and then had attempted to buy the silence of the burglars. Then the *Washington Post* revealed that Haldeman and Ehrlichman had ordered Dean to ensure that the break-in could never be connected to the White House. In the aftermath of these events, Nixon fired Dean and forced both Haldeman and Ehrlichman to resign.

On April 30, 1973, President Nixon addressed the nation. He categorically denied having any foreknowledge of Watergate or any involvement in a cover-up. He told the American people that the presidency was a sacred trust and that he was worthy of that trust. However, serious doubts were mounting, and three weeks later Attorney General Elliott L. Richardson, responding to a Senate resolution, appointed a special prosecutor, Harvard law professor Archibald Cox, to take over all aspects of the Watergate case. At the same time Nixon issued a statement now admitting there had been a cover-up but insisting that he had known nothing about it.

Meanwhile, the matter of Daniel Ellsberg came to light. Ellsberg, a former Pentagon employee, had in 1971 stolen classified documents on U.S. policy in Southeast Asia and given them to the *New York Times*. These documents, which were in many ways not flattering to the U.S. government, came to be known as the Pentagon Papers. Ellsberg said he gave this material to the newspaper because he was upset by what the United States was doing in Vietnam.

Although the material in the Pentagon Papers ended with 1968 and thus had nothing to do with Nixon, the president was furious with this leak and others, and he instituted an "anti-leak" project whose members came to be known as the "plumbers." In September 1971 the plumbers broke into the office of Ellsberg's psychiatrist trying to find information that would discredit him. At least two of the plumbers were men who would later be involved in the Watergate break-in. All of this became public in April 1973 during Ellsberg's trial for conspiracy, espionage, and theft in connection with the publication of the Pentagon Papers, and the connection between this incident and Watergate was all too clear. The presiding judge in the trial, W. M. Byrne, was so disgusted by these revelations that he dismissed the charges and Ellsberg went free.

Meanwhile, the Ervin Committee held hearings. James W. McCord, security coordinator for CREEP, testified that he had been asked to lie. Magruder testified that Attorney General John Mitchell had approved the break-in. Mitchell denied it, and both Haldeman and Ehrlichman proclaimed that there had been no illegal activity at all.

The most important witness to testify in the spring of 1973 was John Dean. He said that contrary to Nixon's assertions there had been no thorough investigation of the Watergate incident in the summer of 1972. Instead there had been a cover-up, and Nixon was guilty of obstruction of justice. Moreover, Dean said that Nixon had approved the payment of hush money to the Watergate conspirators and had ordered government agencies such as the Internal Revenue Service (IRS) to harass those people he regarded as enemies.

Dean's testimony, damning as it was, could not be verified. Nixon might have survived if it had not been for the testimony of the next witness, former presidential appointments secretary, Alexander Butterfield. Butterfield revealed that all activities in the Oval Office had, at Nixon's direction, been taped since 1970. This was the most startling revelation of the entire Watergate episode for if true it meant that the president himself was in possession of a detailed record that could establish his guilt or innocence once and for all.

When Nixon heard of Butterfield's testimony he was tempted, of course, to destroy the tapes, but he was persuaded not to do so by White House Chief of Staff Alexander M. Haig. Haig argued that to destroy the tapes would create an impression of guilt that could never be overcome. Later Nixon would suggest that he believed there was more material on the tapes that would vindicate him than would damn him. He was wrong.

At about the same time that Butterfield revealed the existence of the tapes, the news media disclosed that Vice President Spiro Agnew faced charges of bribery, conspiracy, and income tax evasion stemming from his career as a public official in Maryland. Agnew vigorously denied the charges but resigned anyway. Later, in the face of overwhelming evidence of his guilt, he entered a no contest plea and was fined and put on probation. He never went to jail. Nixon appointed Congressman Gerald Ford of Michigan as his new vice president.

On July 23, 1973, Nixon refused to turn the tapes over to Senator Ervin. As his reasons he cited the constitutional doctrine of separation of powers and the principle of executive privilege. He also defied a subpoena issued by Special Prosecutor Cox. But the pressure continued, and in October Nixon agreed to deliver a summary of the tapes to the committee. At the same time he ordered Cox to limit his efforts to obtain the tapes and other material related to the Watergate incident. When Cox refused Nixon ordered Attorney General Richardson to fire him. Richardson refused and resigned, as did Deputy Attorney General William D. Ruckelshaus. Solicitor General Robert H. Bork, the next official in the line of authority at the Justice Department, finally agreed to dismiss Cox.

This event came to be known as the "Saturday Night Massacre." It had a devastating effect on Nixon's approval ratings which now fell below 30 percent. In response the president appointed a new special prosecutor, Leon Jaworski of Houston, Texas. Apparently Nixon thought Jaworski would be less aggressive than Cox, but he was wrong.

As the summer and autumn of 1973 passed, events began to overwhelm Nixon. First it was announced that two of the nine tapes were missing. Then it was revealed that one of the remaining tapes had an eighteen minute gap—apparently the result of an erasure. Worse, it was revealed that in 1970 and 1971 Nixon had paid less than $1,000 in income taxes although his income was over $400,000. He claimed this was perfectly legal because he had donated his vice presidential papers to the National Archives, but most people were not convinced.

In any case it appeared that Nixon's donation had been executed after the repeal of the law permitting such deductions and then the instrument of transmittal was backdated. In connection with this episode Nixon held a press conference on November 17, 1973, in which he made the famous assertion, "Well, I'm not a crook."

By early 1974 it had become clear that Leon Jaworski was very aggressive indeed. In March a federal grand jury indicted Ehrlichman, Haldeman, Mitchell, and others on charges of obstruction of justice. Later it was revealed that the grand jury named Nixon as an unindicted coconspirator. He was not indicted because the Constitution protects the president from any legal action save impeachment.

However, the House Judiciary Committee was gathering evidence to support a possible impeachment proceeding, whereby a government official is charged with "treason, high crimes, or misdemeanors." As a part of this process the committee subpoenaed the tapes. Advised by his legal and political counsel that defiance of this subpoena would create an intolerable situation, Nixon agreed to release transcripts of portions of the tapes to the committee and the public. In a televised address on April 29, 1974, he told the public that he was convinced this material would establish his innocence.

Again Nixon was wrong. The transcripts of the 46 tapes not only clearly established the president's involvement, they showed him to be capable of vindictive, shabby, and immoral behavior. In the immediate wake of these events many leading newspapers, which had previously supported Nixon, urged him to resign. To make matters worse, when Nixon refused to turn over other tapes and potentially incriminating materials to Jaworski, the latter appealed to the Supreme Court and was upheld.

Near the end of July 1974 Nixon reluctantly turned the tapes over to Jaworski, and the House Judiciary Committee voted on articles of impeachment. Specifically, Nixon was charged with obstruction of justice, abuse of power, and impeding the impeachment process by defying the committee's subpoenas. Nixon still hoped that somehow he could triumph, but when the recently released tapes revealed that he had discussed the cover-up with his aides before telling the American people that he knew nothing about Watergate, the end had come.

On August 5, 1974, Nixon was advised that he could not survive an impeachment proceeding in the Senate and that he should resign. Reluctantly he agreed. Three days later he advised Vice President Ford of his decision, and that evening he announced to the nation that he would surrender his office the following day at noon. The next morning Nixon signed his letter of resignation and then made a speech to the White House staff. Shortly after 10:00 A. M. Nixon boarded an army helicopter for the short trip to Andrews Air Force Base in Maryland. There he and his family boarded the presidential airplane, Air Force One, for the flight into exile in California. At the stroke of 12:00 on August 9, 1974, while the plane soared somewhere over the U.S. heartland, Richard M. Nixon ceased to be president.

Foreign Issues

The world was a dangerous place when Nixon became president in 1969. The war still raged in Vietnam; China, the largest nation on earth, was still ruled by Communist revolutionaries led by Mao Tse-tung and was not favored by U.S. diplomatic recognition; and the Cold War with the Soviet Union showed no signs of abating.

Nixon was committed to peace. In fact he wanted to be the architect of a new and peaceful world. Hence, he devoted himself to three major foreign policy issues: ending the Vietnam War (1959–75), opening relations with China, and improving relations with the Soviet Union by inaugurating a dialogue on disarmament.

Although they were eventually overshadowed by the disgrace stemming from the Watergate scandal, Nixon's foreign policy achievements were remarkable. He ended the Vietnam War, opened relations with China, and at the same time provided a bit of a thaw in the Cold War with the Soviet Union.

China

Before World War II (1939–45) China was ravaged by a civil war pitting the so-called "Nationalists" led by Chiang Kai-shek against the Communists led by Mao Tse-tung. Chiang had the upper hand in the beginning, and Mao's followers had retreated into virtual exile deep in the interior of the country. Then came the Japanese invasions—first in 1932 and again in 1937—which precipitated the outbreak of World War II. During the conflict the United States aided and supported Chiang in the hope that China could be stabilized in the aftermath of a Japanese defeat.

The United States's hopes were dashed soon after the war when the conflict between the Nationalists and the Communists resumed. By 1949 the Communists had driven Chiang off the continent to the island of Taiwan, where he reestablished his government. Meanwhile, Mao and his henchmen proclaimed the People's Republic of China with its capital in Peking. The United States declined to grant diplomatic recognition, and for the next two decades pretended that Taiwan was China. Ironically Nixon was one of the foremost advocates of nonrecognition, so it came as a great surprise to many people when he articulated a new China policy and actually visited the country in 1972.

It has been said that Nixon's trip to China and its results mark the most significant achievement in U.S. foreign policy since the end of World War II, because it shifted the global balance of power in favor of the United States.

President Nixon embarked on a major shift in U.S. foreign policy with his 1972 visit to China. The trip, which included a walk on the Great Wall, opened Chinese-U.S. relations for the first time since the Asian nation fell to Communism in 1949. (National Archives and Records Administration.)

The idea of reconciliation between the United States and China occurred to Nixon at least as early as 1967, when he published an article in the prestigious journal, *Foreign Affairs,* in 1967, in which he argued persuasively that relations with China should be normalized. Moreover, soon after assuming the presidency he ordered that a report be prepared discussing ways and means to proceed. There were many people in the U.S. government who disliked the idea, but Nixon persisted.

The problems were immense. For one, there was no official way to communicate with China. All diplomatic channels had been closed since 1949. If a world emergency should arise, the U.S. government could not consult with the leaders of the most populous nation on earth. In order to change this—Nixon believed it was imperative—the president had to move indirectly and very discreetly lest his actions offend or startle the leaders of other nations, both friend and foe, to say nothing of the right-wing extremists at home.

To achieve his goal Nixon resorted to a technique known as "triangular diplomacy." This involved offering something of value to the Chinese, through intermediaries, and the Soviets at the same time, without frightening one or the other into some precipitous and potentially dangerous response. At the time China and the Soviet Union, the two Communist giants in the world, were not friends. The antagonism between them—which involved boundary disputes as well as ideological differences—was a matter of great concern.

In the early stages of his efforts Nixon moved cautiously. He sent Secretary of State Henry Kissinger on a secret mission to Peking, China, to ascertain whether the Chinese leaders would welcome a presidential visit. They agreed. Then on July 15, 1971, Nixon stunned the entire world by announcing that he had been invited to visit China and had accepted. Practically everyone except the Nationalist Chinese on Taiwan and the Japanese viewed the announcement favorably. The Russians had been told in advance that no matter what the United States might do with China, they need not be concerned.

In China Nixon met with the old Chinese revolutionary leaders, Mao Tse-tung and Chou En-lai. These talks, along with considerable pageantry and travel to historic sites, were all covered by the press. The major agreements that emerged from the talks dealt with Vietnam, Taiwan, and the Soviet Union. With respect to the former, the final communique suggested that the United States would reduce its military presence in Taiwan if China would decrease her support for the North Vietnamese. As for the Soviets, it was agreed that the United States would not permit the military domination of Asia by the Russians. Thus a new alliance aimed at deterring Russian expansion or aggression was created.

Russia

The Soviet leaders feared Nixon when he came to power because of his reputation as a ferocious anticommunist. As time passed, however, they found him to be very businesslike in his diplomacy and their fears subsided somewhat. Eventually the United States and the Soviet Union made several major agreements during Nixon's presidency, which produced a slight thaw in the Cold War and contributed significantly to the peace process. These included arms control treaties, various cooperative agreements, and in general an improved atmosphere that is usually called "detente."

On May 20, 1972, Nixon traveled to Moscow, the capital of the former Soviet Union. The most important item on the agenda was arms reduction. Negotiating directly with Leonid Brezhnev, the Soviet leader, Nixon succeeded in finalizing an agreement that had been worked out earlier by the technical experts. Known as the Antiballistic Missile Defense System Treaty (ABM), it was the first arms control agreement of the nuclear age. It provided that both sides would reduce missile size and fleets. It was only a beginning and was to be followed by numerous future agreements.

Vietnam

While dealing with the Chinese and the Russians, Nixon also sought to end the Vietnam War (1959–75). This proved to be a long, tedious, and very controversial process, but it would ultimately be successful. Nixon came into office fully intending to end the war, but he miscalculated the length of time it would take. He also underestimated the power and intensity of the antiwar movement at home, which would limit his options and restrict his diplomacy. Peace talks actually began in early 1969, but they were to drag on until 1973.

By 1969 the antiwar movement in the United States had become so intense that the North Vietnamese had come to the conclusion that time alone would force their enemy to undertake a unilateral withdrawal. Therefore, they did not respond at first to Nixon's proposals for negotiations. The president reacted to their unresponsiveness in two ways: he ordered the bombing of the North Vietnamese Army strongholds in Cambodia—this to be done secretly because Cambodia was supposedly neutral—and he ordered the withdrawal of 25,000 U.S. troops as an act of good faith. He also put forth his first formal peace proposals. He called for phased withdrawals of U.S. and North Vietnamese army forces from South Vietnam, internationally supervised elections, and an end to hostilities. The North Vietnamese ignored these proposals, and the intensity of the antiwar movement at home escalated.

Nixon had long since determined that "peace with honor" was the only possible option. This meant that both the United States and North Vietnam would withdraw, and that South Vietnam would be kept strong enough to defend itself. Nixon did not intend to be dissuaded from this policy. He believed it was important to have the support of the people, so he prepared a speech that he delivered on November 3, 1969. It was one of his most important and controversial statements. In it he declared that the United States wanted peace, but that it would not withdraw until the South Vietnamese were able to defend themselves or until the North Vietnamese agreed to a reasonable settlement. He called upon the American people to support his policy, referring to them as the "silent majority." If we withdraw unilaterally, he warned, the word of the United States that it would defend her allies would become meaningless and would spark outbreaks of violence everywhere: in the Middle East, in Germany, and even in the Western Hemisphere. On the other hand, if the people would support his policies, then he could negotiate a just peace in Vietnam and end the war quickly.

Although the speech was severely criticized by the press, it generated the result Nixon had sought—at least in the short run. Public opinion polls showed a very high approval rating, and Congress voted its support. Nixon believed that the speech had enabled him to temporarily derail the antiwar movement and buy some time to move the peace process forward.

By the spring of 1970 Nixon's peace initiative was in serious trouble. In Paris, France, the North Vietnamese negotiators were stalling, in Southeast Asia the North Vietnamese Army was massing troops and supplies in Cambodia, and in the United States the time the president had bought with the "silent majority" speech was running out as the antiwar movement gained a second wind. The early months of 1970 featured a rising tide of violent antiwar outbursts all over the country, especially on college campuses.

To throw the critics of his policies off stride, Nixon announced the withdrawal of 150,000 U.S. troops from Vietnam in April 1970 . This had the desired affect, but it frightened the U.S. military, which believed that a massive North Vietnamese Army offensive was imminent. Faced with a very difficult problem Nixon decided to authorize an invasion of Cambodia by U.S. and Army of the Republic of Vietnam (ARVN) forces. On the night of April 30, 1970, the president went on national television to explain his decision. It generated a fire storm of protest.

The violence on college campuses reached its tragic climax on May 4, 1970, at Kent State University near Cleveland, Ohio. There the governor called out the National Guard to maintain order, and the young soldiers lost their composure and opened fire on a crowd of students. Four were killed and 11 were wounded. This drove antiwar activists into a frenzy. Scores of students rioted all over the country. In some cities workers clashed with students. Property destruction mounted into the millions, and there were many injuries. Nixon was appalled, but he was also determined to pursue the policy he believed to be correct.

The Cambodian invasion and the reaction to it at home were public relations disasters for Nixon. In view of that it is ironic that militarily it was not a total failure. U.S. and ARVN forces captured tons of equipment, reduced the ability of the Russians and the Chinese to import more, and probably saved the pro-Western government of Cambodia from falling into Communist hands. Moreover, on this occasion the ARVN fought reasonably well, thus encouraging Nixon to think that Vietnamization might really work.

From the summer of 1970 through 1971, Nixon's efforts to secure a just peace continued to produce few results. Then, about the middle of 1972, changes began to occur. Neither the Russians nor the Chinese were giving the North Vietnamese as much aid as before, the ARVN was fighting surprisingly well, and it looked like Nixon was going to win reelection. Henry Kissinger, Nixon's representative at the Paris peace talks, reported that the enemy seemed to be changing its attitude and signaling a willingness to settle.

In October 1972 the North Vietnamese for the first time offered terms that were considered a reasonable basis for meaningful negotiations. The plan called for the withdrawal of U.S. forces, an exchange of prisoners, and no further infiltration of the South by the North. Nixon wanted to accept these terms, but he could not do so without the consent of the South Vietnamese government. When the plan was laid before South Vietnamese president Nguyen Van Thieu, he objected. He was frightened because the plan did not call for the withdrawal of all North Vietnamese forces already in South Vietnam. Nixon pointed out that this was a practical impossibility, but he attempted to reassure Thieu, president of South Vietnam (1967–75) with a guarantee that the United States would not permit a Communist takeover of South Vietnam.

Meanwhile, as the negotiators attempted to work out the final details, it became clear that the North Vietnamese were going to stall in authorizing a cease-fire based upon their own proposal. Nixon and Kissinger were furious, and Nixon decided that his only option was to use force to persuade the enemy to bargain in a more reasonable fashion. Hence he ordered an intensive bombing campaign of North Vietnam during the Christmas holiday period. The president was harshly criticized for this but it worked. In January 1973 the North Vietnamese signaled their willingness to get on with the negotiations. Thereafter, terms were quickly agreed upon and the cease-fire was declared in effect on January 27, 1973.

The Nixon Administration Legacy

Nixon's domestic achievements were not as impressive as they could have been for two reasons: he could not handle a Congress controlled by the Democrats; and his personality, which drove him to excessive behavior, significantly mitigated his administrative abilities. He had many good ideas, but few of them materialized. Nevertheless, his successes were significant and should not be discounted. The most important of these was desegregation.

The antiwar movement reached a crescendo of violence in 1970 and 1971, due in part to Nixon's inability or unwillingness to explain himself adequately to the American people. However, it is debatable whether by smooth presentation of his policies through the media he could have calmed the public temper which had gotten out of hand.

The Watergate scandal caused a constitutional crisis, tarnishing the presidency, and in fact the entire executive branch because of the numerous indictments and convictions that emanated from it.

Unlike his domestic policy efforts, Nixon's foreign policy had a significant immediate impact. The opening of China was a remarkable achievement, and it tipped the world balance of power away from the Soviet Union almost at once.

Nixon's Soviet policy was also very important. By reassuring the Russians and concluding the first nuclear arms reduction treaty with them, Nixon began the era of detente (relaxation of strained relations).

Many believe that ending the Vietnam War (1959–75) was Nixon's greatest achievement, even though the process did not occur as quickly or as cleanly as he had hoped. Nevertheless, when the announcement finally came in early 1973, and the last U.S. troops and the prisoners of war finally came home, the feeling was one of overwhelming relief. Unfortunately for Nixon, he was unable to enjoy the fruits of his triumph for very long because by the spring of 1973 the Watergate affair was rapidly heating up.

Nixon's Relations with the Press

Nixon's relationship with the press can only be described as a disaster, though it was the media that initially catapulted him to fame in 1946 during his involvement in the Alger Hiss affair (*See also*, Career).

Long before he was rocked by scandal, Nixon believed that he was to be locked in an adversarial relationship with the press. Nixon's strategy in dealing with the press was to tell them as little as possible. This reflected his general belief that he was not required to reveal what he was doing to anyone—even members of his own administration. It soon became apparent to reporters that Nixon was obsessed with secrecy. This in turn led to increased tensions between the press and the administration.

Nixon's Public Image

Even though he was elected to the highest office in the land twice, Nixon was never a popular president. This unhappy state of affairs derived largely—although not entirely—from his own behavior. His obvious malice toward the press made it practically inevitable that he would find antagonism there and this, of course, had some effect on public opinion. But there was more to it than that. Nixon simply did not possess the grace and manners in public that had been exhibited by some of his predecessors like John Kennedy. He always appeared to be uncomfortable when he made public appearances or when he addressed the nation on television, and his discomfort was so obvious that it affected people's attitudes towards him. Many people were so put off by his performances that they assumed he was lying even when he was not.

The regrettable result of all this was that Nixon's reputation suffered even before it was ruined by scandal. It also made Nixon's comeback even more remarkable because it must be remembered that even though he was totally discredited in 1974, by 1985 his reputation had been substantially, if not fully, restored. In the end Nixon was tough, well-educated, willing to work hard, and absolutely obsessed with a desire to regain public influence. Most men, crushed as he was, would have been incapable of summoning the strength necessary to fight back. Nixon not only possessed this strength, he applied

What They Said . . .

"I know many fair-minded people believe that my motivations and action in the Watergate affair were intentionally self-serving and illegal. I now understand how my own mistakes and misjudgments have contributed to that belief and seemed to support it. . . .That the way I tried to deal with Watergate was the wrong way is a burden I shall bear for every day of the life that is left to me."

Richard Nixon's response to being pardoned of all crimes by President Ford, September 8, 1974.

it vigorously to all his activities and never gave up. Hence, ironic as it may be, he captured the attention of the very press with whom he had fought such remorseless battles before and they, admiring his tenacity, covered his activities and assisted in his recovery.

Lasting Impact

As historian Stephen E. Ambrose noted in his book *Nixon: Ruin and Recovery, 1973–1990,* Richard Nixon craved power and he achieved it, but he was unable to use this power to achieve greatness. Because of his character flaws, it was virtually inevitable that he would destroy himself, thus leaving the quest for greatness unfulfilled. He had a goal—world peace—that would certainly have qualified him for greatness if he had achieved it, but he never did. The reason is that even though Nixon had power, he could not use it effectively because his paranoia and his mistrust of practically everyone prevented him from exercising the long-term moral leadership that might have made him more successful. To attain world peace under his leadership required that he first be recognized as the undisputed leader of his own nation. This he could not do.

Instead of greatness, the legacy of Nixon is to be found in the long-term implications of Watergate and the heartbreaking speculation about what might have been.

The legacy of Watergate is profoundly significant. First and foremost it weakened the office of the presidency. By remaining in office as long as he did, Nixon achieved only this, and the executive branch has never fully recovered.

Watergate also produced many legislative changes. These include, among others, the Privacy Act of 1974, which permits people to use information in the federal agency files; the Ethics in Government Act of 1978, which provides the legal basis for the office of special prosecutor; and the War Powers Act of 1973, which requires the president to seek congressional approval to wage war, even if war is not formally declared.

As a result of Watergate investigative reporting became an integral part of political life. The public also became more cynical about politics and politicians.

In spite of his flaws and weaknesses it is possible to argue that much was lost by Nixon's resignation. It has been suggested that Nixon's resignation resulted in the loss of South Vietnam. He had promised that any violation of the cease-fire would be met with an immediate and massive response by the United States, however, by the time the violations came Nixon was so involved with Watergate that he could not persuade Congress to act.

With respect to China and the Soviet Union much was lost with respect to the further pursuit of peace. This is especially true concerning the Russians. If Nixon had remained in office, he might have successfully pursued a policy of cooperation. Instead, the two great powers spent the next decade and a half at each other's throats, and it was not until the late 1980s that things changed. Nixon might have achieved the same results in the 1970s.

With respect to domestic policy there is much that Nixon might have achieved. He might have, for example, expanded the Basic Opportunity Education Act, thus providing a chance for a college education to many young Americans who, in fact, never enjoyed such an opportunity. He might have resurrected and pushed through his welfare reform program or his universal health insurance plan. Finally, he might have prevented the Republican Party from sliding even farther to the right as it did under Ronald Reagan a few years later.

Nixon's legacy is in many ways unique. He was the only president ever to resign, he is the only president ever to be so thoroughly disgraced, and he is one of the few to leave so much potential unfulfilled.

Sources

Aitken, Johnathan. *Nixon: A Life.* Washington, D.C.: Regency Press, 1993.

Ambrose, Stephen E. *Nixon.* 3 vols. New York: Simon and Schuster, 1987–91.

Larsa, Rebecca. *Richard Nixon: Rise and Fall of a President.* New York: Franklin Watts, 1991.

Parmet, Herbert S. *Richard Nixon and His America.* Boston: Little, Brown, 1990.

Patterson, James T. *America in the Twentieth Century: A History.* Fort Worth, Tex.: Harcourt Brace College Publishers, 1994.

Wicker, Tom. *One of Us: Richard Milhous Nixon and the American Dream.* New York: Random House, 1991.

Further Readings

Friedman, Leon, and William F. Levanstrosser, eds. *Cold War Patriot and Statesman: Richard M. Nixon.* Westport, Conn.: Greenwood, 1993.

Greene, John R. *The Limits of Power: The Nixon and Ford Administrations.* Bloomington, Ind.: Indiana University Press, 1992.

Hoaf, Joan. *Nixon Reconsidered.* New York: Basic Books, 1994.

Richard Nixon Library & Birthplace Foundation. 1999. <http://www.nixonfoundation.org/> (25 June 1999).

Thompson, Kenneth W., ed. *The Nixon Presidency.* New York: University Press of America, 1987.

Volkan, Vamik D., Norman Itzkowitz, and Andrew W. Dod, *Richard Nixon: A Psychobiography.* New York: Columbia, 1997.

White, Theodore H. *The Making of a President, 1972.* New York: Atheneum, 1973.

Ford Administration

Biography

Gerald R. Ford earned a reputation for loyalty, integrity, and teamwork in his long career of public service. From his early involvement in sports, through his 25 years as a member of the U. S. House of Representatives, Ford sought to bring people together and formulate solutions to problems through cooperation and compromise. His moderate to conservative views and values helped him avoid the political and personal pitfalls of extremism.

Early Life

Gerald Ford was born to the former Dorothy Gardner and Leslie Lynch King on July 14, 1913, in Omaha, Nebraska. Two weeks after he was born his parents separated, and he and his mother returned to Grand Rapids, Michigan, to live with her parents. After her divorce from King, Dorothy married Gerald R. Ford in 1916, and they began calling her son Gerald R. Ford Jr., although his name was not changed legally until 1935. The future president grew up in a close-knit family that grew to include his three younger half brothers, Thomas, Richard, and James. The Fords lived a comfortable life and Ford learned the values of hard work, honesty, and teamwork at home, as an active boy scout, and as an excellent student and athlete. Ford only saw his biological father a few times and considered Ford Sr. his father.

Full name: Gerald Rudolph Ford
Given name: Leslie Lynch King, Jr.

Personal Information:
Born: July 14, 1913
Birthplace: Omaha, Nebraska
Religion: Episcopalian
Spouse: Elizabeth "Betty" Bloomer Warren (m. 1948)
Children: Michael; John; Steven; Susan
Education: University of Michigan, B.A., 1935; Yale University Law School, 1941
Occupation: Coach; attorney; legislator; vice president
Political Party: Republican Party
Age at Inauguration: 61 years

Gerald R. Ford. (The Library of Congress.)

States, and the elegant themes and decor that highlighted everything from Native American traditions to Art Deco.

As first lady Betty Ford was a strong advocate of equal economic and civil rights for women and spoke out in favor of the passage of the Equal Rights Amendment. (While the amendment was approved by Congress in 1972, it failed to gain ratification by the states.) While Betty Ford's outspokenness at first brought criticism, by l975 her public approval rating had risen to 75 percent—much higher than her husband's. Shortly after becoming first lady, Betty Ford was diagnosed with breast cancer and underwent a radical mastectomy to remove cancerous tissue. By speaking publicly about a disease that had often been treated as a private and somewhat shameful condition, Betty Ford heightened public awareness and encouraged testing for early diagnosis and proper treatment of cancer. In the late 1970s Betty Ford publicly discussed her battles with alcoholism and prescription drug dependency. Again, her example helped many Americans admit their own problems and seek treatment. To aid the treatment process, she established the Betty Ford Center in Rancho Mirage, California, which still serves as a model for successful programs and facilities that help people control their substance abuse problems.

Career

When Gerald Ford graduated from law school at Yale in 1941, he returned to Grand Rapids, Michigan, passed the bar exam, and became an attorney in a partnership with his college friend, Philip Buchen. In 1942, after the United States entered World War II (1939–45), Ford enlisted in the U.S. Naval Reserve and received a commission as an ensign. He was assigned to the USS *Monterey* in the South Pacific and served as an athletic director, a gunnery division officer, and an assistant navigator. Ford was discharged in 1946 as a lieutenant commander and returned to Grand Rapids to join the law firm of Butterfield, Keeney, and Amberg.

With support and encouragement from Republican U.S. senator Arthur Vandenburg (R-Mich.), who had sponsored Ford's application to work as a ranger at Yellowstone National Park in l936 and continued to take an interest in Ford's plans after that initial interaction, Ford decided to challenge the incumbent U.S. representative Bartel J. Jonkman for the Republican nomination in 1948. Jonkman was a Republican who was growing increasingly unpopular with young Republicans like Ford. Ford won the nomination and was elected to the U. S. House of Representatives on November 2 after receiving 61 percent of the vote.

Ford's Years in Congress

Ford continued to serve in Congress for the next 25 years, being reelected 12 times with more than 60

Education

Ford was gifted in athletics and scholastics and his skills earned him a scholarship to the University of Michigan, which he attended from 1931 to 1935. He majored in economics and political science. Ford was named a college all-star football player and graduated with a B.A. in 1935. Ford turned down offers to play professional football to take a coaching job at Yale University in New Haven, Connecticut, and attend law school there. He graduated with a law degree in 1941.

Family Life

Gerald Ford was discharged from the army in 1946 after serving four years. He returned to Grand Rapids, Michigan, where he met, courted, and married Elizabeth "Betty" Bloomer Warren in 1948, just before Ford took his seat in Congress for the first time. It was Warren's second marriage. By 1957 the couple had four children—Michael, John, Steven, and Susan—and had moved to a home in Alexandria, Virginia.

Betty Ford—an intelligent, vivacious woman who was very interested in dance and culture—was a smash as a hostess in Washington. The Ford White House was greatly admired for the varied entertainments provided, the interesting guests from all walks of life in the United percent of the vote. He gained a reputation for moderation, integrity, and openness and rose through the ranks to become a member of the powerful House Appropriations Committee, which oversees budget issues, the Defense Appropriations Subcommittee, and was an appointee to the Warren Commission that investigated the assassination of President John F. Kennedy. In 1963, with the support of other young Republicans, Ford became the chairman of the House Republican Conference. Two years later he was elected minority leader of the House. During his tenure as a member of Congress, he gave over two hundred speeches supporting the Republican Party and Republican candidates.

Nixon Appoints Ford Vice President

When Vice President Spiro Agnew resigned in 1973 amidst accusations that he had taken bribes as governor of Maryland, Gerald Ford's record of loyalty to his party and personal integrity made him the perfect man to replace Agnew. Ford was nominated for the position by President Nixon and approved by Congress on December 6, 1973, thus becoming the nation's first unelected vice president. In his short term as vice president Ford traveled the country speaking in support of Nixon. Nixon's presidency was unraveling due to charges that he had covered up his role in the Watergate scandal, which involved a burglary at the Democratic Party headquarters during the presidential election of 1972.

When Nixon resigned under mounting pressure, Gerald Ford, at age 61, became the country's first unelected president on August 9, 1974. As president, Ford struggled to move the country forward and put the Watergate scandal to rest. He sought to heal the country by avoiding a long trial of former president Nixon, providing an amnesty program for draft dodgers and deserters, and attempting to address the nation's economic problems. As a man of honesty and integrity, Ford also returned some measure of respect to the office that Nixon had tarnished.

But the outcry from his pardoning of Nixon and a failing economy resulted in few successes for Ford as president. When Ford lost the presidential election of 1976 to Jimmy Carter, his supporters as well as many of his critics claimed the loss was due to the Nixon legacy rather than Ford's lack of skills or abilities.

Post-presidential Years

In 1977 Ford and his wife moved to Rancho Mirage, California. He supported his wife as she struggled successfully to cope with her alcoholism and addiction to painkillers. Betty Ford went on to establish the Betty Ford Center in Rancho Mirage, a treatment facility for those addicted to alcohol and other chemicals.

What They Said . . .

"To the peoples and the governments of all friendly nations, and I hope that could encompass the whole world, I pledge an uninterrupted and sincere search for peace. America will remain strong and united, but its strength will remain dedicated to the safety and sanity of the entire family of man, as well as to our own precious freedom.

"I believe that truth is the glue that holds government together, not only our Government but civilization itself. That bond, though strained, is unbroken at home and abroad. In all my public and private acts as your President, I expect to follow my instincts of openness and candor with full confidence that honesty is always the best policy in the end. My fellow Americans, our long national nightmare is over."

(Source: Gerald Ford, Inaugural Address, August 9, 1974.)

None of Ford's children entered politics. Mike Ford became a minister; John (Jack) Ford a park ranger; Steve Ford a rancher; and Susan Ford a photographer. All married and had children. In 1979 Ford published his memoirs, titled *A Time To Heal: The Autobiography of Gerald R. Ford.* He also has built a lucrative post political career as a speaker and a member of several corporate boards, remaining active in Republican Party politics and supporting the Gerald R. Ford Presidential Library in Ann Arbor, Michigan, and the Gerald R. Ford Museum in Grand Rapids, Michigan.

The Gerald R. Ford Administration

President Ford inherited an administration that was faced with the ongoing Vietnam War (1959–75), domestic energy shortages and economic problems, and the mistrust of the people in their government after the Watergate scandals. During his short term as president, Ford worked diligently to maintain the United States's strong presence in foreign affairs and to resolve the problems at home.

Administration

Administration Dates
August 9, 1974–January 20, 1977

Vice President
Nelson Aldrich Rockefeller (1974–77)

Cabinet

Secretary of State
Henry A. Kissinger (1973–77)

Secretary of the Treasury
William E. Simon (1974–77)

Attorney General
William B. Saxbe (1974–75)
Edward H. Levi (1975–77)

Secretary of the Interior
Rogers C. B. Morton (1971–75)
Stanley K. Hathaway (1975)
Thomas S. Kleppe (1975–77)

Secretary of Agriculture
Earl L. Butz (1971–76)
John A. Knebel (1976–77)

Secretary of Labor
Peter J. Brennan (1973–75)
John T. Dunlop (1975–76)
William J. Usery Jr. (1976–77)

Secretary of Commerce
Frederick B. Dent (1973–75)
Rogers C. B. Morton (1975–76)
Elliot L. Richardson (1976–77)

Secretary of Defense
James R. Schlesinger (1973–75)
Donald H. Rumsfeld (1975–77)

Secretary of Health, Education and Welfare
Caspar W. Weinberger (1973–75)
F. David Mathews (1975–77)

Secretary of Housing and Urban Development
James T. Lynn (1973–75)
Carla A. Hills (1975–77)

Secretary of Transportation
Claude S. Brinegar (1973–75)
William T. Coleman Jr. (1975–77)

Ford Becomes President

Initially Ford did not believe that Richard Nixon had been involved in the Watergate cover-up, but he was concerned about the negative impact the scandal was having on the reputation of Republican politicians. As Nixon's involvement became more apparent Ford supported Nixon from a distance, not wanting to become too allied with Nixon in the public's mind, but also not wanting it to appear he was angling to be president. (Ford makes no mention of ever discussing resignation with Nixon.)

On August 9, 1974, Richard M. Nixon resigned as the president of the United States and his vice president, Gerald R. Ford, was sworn in as president. Thus, Ford became the first U.S. president to be designated as president, rather than elected by the people. In accordance with the Twenty-fifth Amendment to the Constitution, which allows the president to nominate and the Congress to confirm a vice president in case that office becomes vacant, Ford had been approved by Congress to become vice president in 1973, when Spiro Agnew resigned in the middle of his term. As vice president, Ford was next in line to become president when Nixon resigned.

The Campaign of 1976

While still a member of Congress in 1974, Ford had decided to retire at the age of 63 when his congressional term was up, for personal and financial reasons. His wife and family wanted more of his time, and he needed to think about long-term finances because congressional salaries at that time did not provide a secure retirement. In 1976 Ford initially felt committed to retiring for these same reasons and also because the Republican Party seemed divided by supporters of former California governor Ronald Reagan and of Ford. Only after lengthy meetings with Republican leaders was Ford convinced he should run in 1976.

Ford faced some tough competition within his own party when Reagan challenged him for the Republican Party's nomination. Reagan chose a liberal running mate, Senator Richard S. Schweiker, a Pennsylvania Republican, for the vice presidency and directed his views toward liberal Republicans to counteract Ford's appeal to conservatives. At the Kansas City, Missouri, convention, the conservatives rallied behind Ford and he became the Republican Party's candidate for president by only 57 more votes than was needed. Robert Dole of Kansas was selected as his running mate.

The U.S. public was concerned about Reagan's challenge because if Ford's own party did not fully support him from the beginning, it made the public unsure of Ford's ability to lead the country. Polls also showed that the public did not feel that as president Ford had done anything impressive or meaningful enough that would warrant his presidency continuing. Ford also faced the problem of his growing reputation as a klutz after he slipped and fell on a rain-slicked ramp, and it was captured on film and broadcast. After that incident, the media publicized several other mishaps when Ford fell on the ski slopes, bumped his head on helicopter doors, and got tangled in his dogs' leashes. Even though they were exaggerated, Ford became famous for his accidents and was often made fun of in the media. The public perceived Ford as physically inept and, whether fairly or unfairly, as politically inept as well.

When Ford faced off against the Democratic candidate, former Georgia governor Jimmy Carter, in the November election, he lost a fairly close election by 1.7 million votes. Inflation, the Watergate scandal, and Ford's pardon of Nixon weighed heavily on the minds of voters. Ford did not campaign vigorously. He chose to stay close to the White House taking care of business to remind the voters that he was the president and that he should remain in office due to the fact that he was experienced in the job. This style of campaign is often referred to as a Rose Garden strategy.

Jimmy Carter's election and the election of an overwhelmingly Democratic Congress were as much, if not more, a judgment on Republicans than support for individual candidates. When Ford lost the presidential election to Carter in 1976, only 54 percent of those eligible to vote did so. Americans did not so much support Carter or Ford as they did express their lack of support for politicians in general. Despite small improvements in the economy, many Americans felt that the Ford administration had spent more time quarreling with Congress over fiscal matters than providing a real plan for economic recovery.

Ford's Advisers

When Ford became president he stressed the importance of keeping the United States on the steady course set by Nixon, of coping responsibly with domestic economic problems, and working with foreign nations to promote world peace and improved international relations. One way he sought to achieve continuity was by maintaining Nixon's cabinet and conferring with them to learn the state of domestic and foreign affairs. With little more

than a 24-hour notification that he would become president, Ford felt that he must trust the officials in place to advise him in his new role. Ford relied especially on Secretary of State Henry Kissinger to guide him through negotiations to end the Vietnam War (1959–75) and continue peace talks with the Soviet Union.

As the months passed and officials appointed by Nixon moved to other positions or left their offices for personal reasons, Ford did appoint several of his own choices to cabinet positions. However, with little time to work together and many position changes in such a short time, Ford had little opportunity to develop a strong group of advisers or his own unique style of governing.

Ford and Congress

As one of their own, Ford had many close personal ties and had established close-working relationships with members of Congress. He also understood the intricate way that Congress worked to get legislation passed and the need for a balance of power to be observed in the congressional relationship with the executive branch. Yet, despite his experience with the legislative processes, Ford was unable to develop a smooth-working relationship with Congress.

Ford's term as president began about halfway through the Ninety-third Congress where the political balance in the Senate was 56 Democrats and 46 Republicans and 242 Democrats and 192 Republicans in the House of Representatives. When the Ninety-fourth Congress opened on January 14, 1975, the Democratic majority had increased to 61 seats in the Senate and 291 seats in the House. With such a huge majority, Democratic members of Congress grew increasingly aware of their power to pursue their agenda and had little need to work cooperatively with their Republican opponents. Congress as a whole felt that their power exceeded that of the president because they had been elected, not merely appointed. The days of working out bipartisan compromises were largely gone. Intent on resolving the country's economic problems through government intervention, Democrats in Congress passed measure after measure to increase spending on existing programs and to create new ones. As president, Ford was as fiscally conservative as he had been as a member of the House, and he pushed legislation that would reduce government spending and taxes. With little hope of finding common ground, Ford resorted to the presidential veto to block congressional spending plans. During his first 14 months as president alone, Ford vetoed 39 measures, most of which were sustained (while Congress controlled the majority of the votes, they could not always muster the two-thirds needed to override a presidential veto). This pattern of legislation being passed in Congress, then vetoed by the president, continued throughout Ford's term.

Ford and the Judiciary

President Ford's relationship with the judiciary was uneventful during his short term. When William O. Douglas left the Supreme Court in 1975, Ford had the opportunity to fill the liberal Douglas's seat with a more conservative jurist. His choice was the U.S. Court of Appeals judge John Paul Stevens. Stevens was confirmed with little debate and was seated on the Supreme Court in 1975, where he maintained a centrist, or moderate, position.

Changes in the U.S. Government

In 1974 President Ford signed the Federal Elections Campaign Act into law, which took effect in 1975. As a response to the campaign finance abuses of Watergate, it limited the amount of individual contributions to presidential campaigns and put strict limits on campaign expenditures. The law also created a system whereby the public would fund presidential campaigns by checking off a one dollar donation box on their federal tax returns, if they chose to donate.

That same year Ford signed the Privacy Act of 1974, which was intended to limit the federal government's ability to invade the privacy of U.S. citizens through such activities as wiretapping and obtaining confidential records. This act was also in response to Watergate revelations that Nixon had used such tactics on people he perceived to be his enemies.

Domestic Issues

When Gerald Ford succeeded Richard Nixon as president in 1974 after Nixon's resignation, he faced overwhelming challenges. Public demonstrations against government policies and societal traditions were occurring almost daily. Political protesters such as antiwar, women's rights, gay rights, and civil rights activists were becoming increasingly militant and demanding that the government respond to their issues. Most Americans were feeling the effects of rising inflation, unemployment, and spiraling energy costs and expected the federal government to find relief for their growing economic problems. And as the Watergate scandal unfolded, Americans learned how devious their highest elected officials could be and began to lose their faith in the government's ability to act in the best interests of the people and solve the country's problems.

As president, Ford would try to heal the country by reestablishing faith in the government, moving beyond the troubles caused by the Vietnam War (1959–75), and reviving a stalled economy. He responded to women's rights activists by signing an executive order establishing a National Commission on the Observance of International Women's Year 1975 and a proclamation supporting the Equal Rights Amendment, which called for equal rights for women. Ford also met with the Congressional Black Caucus to listen to their opinions on issues concerning African Americans. In his usual style, Ford showed courtesy and respect to minority activists without committing himself to any significant activities on their behalf.

Nixon Pardon

Little more than a month after taking office, Ford took what may have been his most significant action as president and granted a full pardon to Richard Nixon on September 8, 1974. Nixon resigned as president after it was made public that he had lied about his role in covering up the burglary at the Democratic headquarters in the Watergate Hotel in Washington, D.C. Ford felt that being forced to resign was punishment enough for Nixon, and that the country would only be damaged further by Watergate if the ex-president went through a lengthy and public criminal trial. Many Americans disagreed with Ford's reasoning and felt that Nixon should face the same investigation, prosecution, and possible sentencing as his coconspirators. It was virtually impossible to convince the public that the pardon was not part of some corrupt, secret deal between Ford and Nixon whereby Ford had agreed to pardon Nixon in exchange for Nixon resigning and clearing the way for Ford to become president. Ford went before the House Judiciary Subcommittee on Criminal Justice to explain his reasons for the pardon and assure the committee and the public that there had been no secret deal. Ford repeated that his intention in pardoning Nixon was to shift attention from the past to the present and future needs of the nation. Despite Ford's apparent sincerity, his credibility suffered so much after the Nixon pardon that he was never able to fully regain the public trust.

Amnesty Program

A week after the Nixon pardon, on September 16, 1974, Ford made a presidential proclamation announcing an amnesty program for those who had fled the country rather than serve in the Vietnam War (1959–75) or had deserted while in the service. Ford offered freedom from prosecution to draft evaders if they would swear an oath of allegiance to the United States and perform two years of public service. Deserters were also required to swear an allegiance oath and to give two years of service to the military branch from which they had fled. Once again a measure Ford took in an attempt to heal wounds created by the Vietnam War and restore trust in government. Ford's amnesty program created fresh wounds as segments of the public reacted quickly and angrily. Conservatives and veterans felt the program was too lenient for men who had refused to serve as their country directed. Antiwar activists and many evaders and deserters felt the program would make men who had followed their conscience and done the right thing out to be criminals and wrong. Ford believed it was a fair compromise, although liberals felt it did not go far enough and conservatives felt it went too far.

Whip Inflation Now (WIN)

After the Nixon pardon and the announcement of his amnesty program, Ford introduced his economic plan as another way to move the country forward. The campaign was titled Whip Inflation Now, or WIN, and it was presented to Congress with great fanfare that included WIN buttons and banners. While the program called for some federal actions including limiting the federal budget and raising taxes, it centered on the efforts of average people to curb inflation, which occurs when prices keep going up and the average consumer's wages stay the same so they have less buying power. Americans were asked to become WIN volunteers by sending enlistment papers to the White House. These papers said volunteers were committed to WIN's anti-inflation activities such as taking inventory of office and household trash to reduce waste and purchasing and eating only as much food as would be eaten with no waste. While several hundred thousand citizens joined up, and Ford's intentions were good, the recession deepened and the program was criticized as a public relations maneuver and not a serious economic plan. Even Ford admitted that WIN was probably too "gimmicky." Furthermore, Congress did not support Ford's economic policies and passed measures that increased government spending.

Energy

Contributing to inflation in the 1970s were skyrocketing energy costs and increasing energy shortages. The Middle East dominated oil production and so controlled the flow and prices of oil and gas. As oil consumption rose, so did prices. Ford attempted to reduce consumption by imposing taxes on foreign oil in February 1975. Ford's energy plan also included developing more domestic sources of energy, and he signed a bill to deregulate control over domestic oil prices over several years. By relaxing control of domestic oil prices, oil companies could price their products more competitively, increase their profits, and use the profits to increase their oil production. Congress did not agree with Ford's proposals and they argued back and forth until December 1975 when they agreed on a compromise bill called the Energy Policy and Conservation Act. The bill did not provide any solutions, and it was soon replaced by other energy policies during the Carter administration.

Ford also signed legislation creating the Energy Research and Development Administration and converting the Atomic Energy Commission to the Nuclear Regulatory Commission. These two government offices were charged with streamlining and expanding efforts to provide Americans with domestic sources of energy and reduce reliance on foreign products.

Foreign Issues

When Ford became president after Nixon resigned, there was great uncertainty in the world over the United States's commitment to providing leadership in foreign affairs. Nixon had established a strong role for the United States in foreign affairs on issues such as cooperative economic and energy plans, arms reduction, and East-West diplomacy. Ford lost no time in assuring Americans and the world that he intended to continue on Nixon's course. Ford became the first incumbent U.S. president to travel to Japan, he made goodwill trips to other countries, pursued favorable trade agreements, and continued arms control talks. Ford relied heavily on Secretary of State Henry Kissinger to continue meeting with Soviet and Middle Eastern leaders to lay the groundwork for formal summit meetings. Ford's and Kissinger's frequent travels came to be known as "shuttle diplomacy" as they went back and forth between other countries and the United States.

The Mayaguez *Incident*

On May 12, 1975, Cambodian gunboats seized the U.S. merchant ship *Mayaguez,* declaring that the vessel was within their territorial waters (water areas off the coastline of a country that country has control over). Given the additional fact that the *Mayaguez* was a U.S. ship and that the United States and Cambodia had a very poor relationship at the time, Cambodia may have been concerned that the *Mayaguez* was involved in military or spying operations. The U.S. government claimed the *Mayaguez* was actually 60 miles off the Cambodian coast, and Ford decided to use military force to prevent the ship and its 39-member crew from being taken to the mainland of Cambodia. Two U.S. destroyers and an aircraft carrier sped to the scene and sank three Cambodian gunboats. U.S. planes dropped bombs on the mainland to prevent Cambodian interference with the rescue operation. On May 14, 1975, Ford ordered a marine attack on an island where the crew was believed to be held. Later that day marines boarded and recovered the empty *Mayaguez* and a small Cambodian boat delivered the crew to another U.S. boat in the area. Despite the fact that 41 American lives were lost in the recovery of the 39-member crew, the U.S. public was supportive of Ford's show of United States's military strength.

The Helsinki Agreement

In July of 1975 President Ford met with Soviet leaders and leaders of 35 other countries in Helsinki, Finland. At the conference the Soviet Union agreed to observe international human rights principles. In exchange the United States and other Western countries agreed to recognize the Eastern European boundaries created by Soviet influence after World War II (1939–45) as legitimate. This recognition was significant because it marked the West's acceptance of Communist countries in Europe

A crowd of South Vietnamese attempt to climb the wall of the U.S. embassy in Saigon trying to reach U.S. helicopters. After South Vietnam surrendered to North Vietnam on April 30, 1975, many South Vietnamese tried to escape to the United States. (Photograph by Neil Ulevich. Corbis. Reproduced by permission.)

and their decision not to interfere in the internal affairs of the Communist countries. Prior to the Helsinki Agreement the West had, at least informally, resisted Soviet domination of Eastern Europe because it felt that U.S. president Franklin Roosevelt had allowed the Soviets to simply take by force these countries of Eastern Europe and then gave them away in the Yalta agreement at the end of World War II. In essence the United States was

accepting Soviet influence in the Eastern bloc countries. By formally recognizing the Communist countries' legitimacy, Ford hoped to move past border disputes and expand the flow of ideas and diplomatic agreements. Once again, much of the U.S. public did not see things Ford's way. They felt that recognizing the postwar boundaries as legitimate was a sellout to the Communists and a retreat from democratic ideals.

The Ford Administration Legacy

In 1976 Ford's own pollster found that 61 percent of people polled felt that Ford had done nothing particularly impressive as president, while 41 percent felt that he had not done anything they particularly did not like. The media viewed Ford as a bumbling puppet of Nixon and Kissinger at worst and a nice guy without much influence or vision at best. Members of his own party, including former California governor Ronald Reagan, who would become president in 1981, capitalized on his limited successes in either domestic or foreign affairs to advance their own political careers. And Democrats painted Ford's policies as continuations of Nixon's whenever possible to convince the country that its problems were the fault of Republicans.

When Ford left office in 1977 his presidency was widely considered a temporary appointment between a disgraced, but elected, Nixon and the people's next elected choice, Jimmy Carter. Ford left Carter the same issues he had struggled with, a troubled economy, energy problems, and a lack of meaningful advances in foreign relations. Inflation had dropped, but not much. Employment had dropped, but not much. No new military conflicts with Communist governments had arisen, but no new progress had been made in arms reductions. And oil and gas prices kept rising. Ford had provided the nation with a leader they could respect, but he had not proved to be a president of action, creating bold and innovative solutions to the nation's continuing problems. Ford conducted himself as Congressperson Ford had, by being honest and straightforward, always taking the middle or moderate road in an effort to offend no one.

Lasting Impact

Had Gerald Ford retired from the House of Representatives at 63 as he had intended, he would be remembered as a dedicated public servant who advocated moderation and compromise as a skilled legislator. By becoming the first appointed vice president in the United States and then the first president to hold office due to his successor's resignation, his legacy became that of a caretaker. Historians view his short time in office as a period of stewardship, or management, rather than one in which he made his mark. Ford's pardoning of Nixon and his continuation of Nixon's policies branded him a president with few ideas of his own who could not read public opinion accurately. At the same time even Ford's critics concede that he had very little preparation to be president and very little time to develop his own system of governing. He was forced into a situation where perhaps no one could have succeeded. In the end, although it is unfair, it is impossible to separate the Ford administration from the Nixon administration, which created a distrust of politics and politicians from which the United States has never recovered.

Sources

Barber, James David. *The Presidential Character: Predicting Performance in the White House.* Englewood, N.J.: Prentice Hall, 1992.

Boyer, Paul S., et al. *The Enduring Vision: A History of the American People.* Lexington, Mass.: D.C. Heath and Co., 1990.

Cannon, James. *Time and Chance: Gerald Ford's Appointment With History.* New York: HarperCollins Books, 1994.

Ford, Gerald R. *A Time to Heal.* New York: Harper and Row, 1979.

Nash, Gary, et al. *The American People: Creating a Nation and a Society.* New York: Harper and Row, 1990.

TerHorst, Jerald F. *Gerald Ford and the Future of the Presidency.* New York: Third Press, 1974.

Further Readings

Ford, Betty. *The Times of My Life.* New York: Harper and Row, 1978.

Sidey, Hugh. *Portrait of a President.* New York: Harper and Row, 1975.

Carter Administration

Full name: Jimmy Carter
Given name: James Earl Carter, Jr.

Personal Information:

Born: October 1, 1924
Birthplace: Plains, Georgia
Religion: Southern Baptist
Spouse: Rosalynn Smith (m. 1946)
Children: John William (Jack); James Earl (Chip); Donnel
  Jeffrey (Jeff); Amy Lynn
Education: United States Naval Academy, B.S., 1946
Occupation: Farmer; warehouseman; governor
Political Party: Democratic Party
Age at Inauguration: 52 years

Biography

Jimmy Carter was a deeply religious man who entered politics believing that he could make decisions to serve the public good. His morality and compassion appealed to a nation seeking healing from the social turmoil of the 1960s, the Vietnam War (1959–75), and Watergate.

Early Life

James Earl Carter, Jr., was born in the agricultural town of Plains, Georgia, on October 1, 1924. His father, James Earl Carter, Sr., was a farmer and businessman, his mother, Lillian Gordy Carter, a nurse. When Carter—who had three younger siblings—was four years old, his family moved to Archery, a rural community west of Plains, to run a peanut farm. Although the family was relatively well-off by rural Georgia standards, the family home was not equipped with electricity or running water. When he was not in school Carter helped out on the farm and sold boiled peanuts in Plains.

Education

Carter attended elementary and high school in Plains, Georgia, graduating in 1941. He enrolled at Georgia Southwestern College, in Americus, Georgia, but left in 1942 after receiving a much desired appointment to the U.S. Naval Academy in Annapolis, Maryland. At Annapolis Carter excelled in electronics and naval tactics, graduating towards the top of his accelerated wartime class of 1946. He served in the navy from 1946 to 1953, working on the world's first nuclear-powered submarines.

Family Life

Carter married Rosalynn Smith on July 7, 1946. Rosalynn Carter also grew up in Plains, Georgia, and began dating Carter while he was home on leave from Annapolis in 1945. The two married soon after Carter's graduation from Annapolis. The couple had four children.

They moved to Norfolk, Virginia, for Carter's first tour of duty. For the next six years, they lived up and down the eastern seaboard. When Carter's father died in 1953, he decided to resign his commission and return to run the family peanut business. Rosalynn Carter, who enjoyed living away from Plains, first opposed Carter's decision. After their return, however, she kept the books and provided invaluable help in expanding the family operations into a million dollar business.

Rosalynn Carter also brought the same involvement to her husband's career in politics. She was a strong voice in Carter's political decision making from early in his career. When she became first lady, Rosalynn Carter continued to offer policy advice to her husband. She also became an outspoken advocate for her own public issues. Like Eleanor Roosevelt, she testified before Congress promoting policies and initiatives that she favored, particularly advocating for increased mental health program funding. After Carter left office she continued to serve with her husband, spending summers building houses and raising funds for Habitat for Humanity. In 1984 she published her memoir, *First Lady from Plains*, which became a national best-seller.

Career

Carter served in the navy from 1946 to 1953, working first as an electronics instructor and then attending submarine school in 1948 in New London, Connecticut. In 1951 he joined the nuclear-powered submarine program, studying nuclear physics at Union College in Schenectady, New York. He was then chosen by Adm. Hyman Rickover to serve as engineering officer aboard the *Sea Wolf,* one of the nation's early nuclear submarines. Rickover's drive and diligence greatly inspired the young Carter, who vowed to work as hard in his pursuits as did his mentor. Working as an engineer for Rickover, Carter came to believe that he could solve even the most intractable problems through hard work and intelligent thinking. This conviction would have a distinct effect on his approach to politics in later years.

After returning to Plains, Georgia, to manage the family's farm and peanut brokerage business, ever the

Jimmy Carter. (Jimmy Carter Library. Reproduced by permission.)

engineer, Carter studied modern farming techniques at the Agricultural Experimental Station in Tifton, Georgia, and applied them to his own farm. He increased production, expanding the family peanut warehouse into a million dollar business. Carter also became active in the community, sitting on the Sumter County (Georgia) Board of Education, serving as a church deacon, and participating in various other civic organizations. Carter's involvement in the community and his sense of public duty led naturally to a growing involvement in politics. Amid the racial unrest of the South in the late 1950s, Carter distinguished himself by his liberal views on race, calling for tolerance and spurning an invitation to join the segregationist White Citizens' Council. Carter's increasing involvement in politics seemed to stem from a combination of his growing religious convictions and his engineering background. He came to believe he could successfully apply his intelligence and problem-solving skills to issues of government and morality in the same way he had mastered nuclear submarines and the peanut business.

Georgia Politics

In 1962 Carter ran for the Georgia senate but lost to his Democratic opponent, Homer Moore, in the Democratic primary. Carter proved Moore had committed voter fraud and emerged victorious, going on to win easily in the general election. Carter was a dedicated and diligent state senator, promising to read every single bill on which he voted and taking a speed reading course when his workload threatened to overwhelm him. In the state senate he earned a reputation as an effective, outspoken, moderate liberal legislator and was reelected for another two-year term in 1964.

In 1966 Carter ran for the office of Georgia governor. He finished third in the Democratic primary, losing to Governor Lester Maddox. Disappointed and demoralized after losing the primary, Carter, a devout Southern Baptist, after meditation and reflection, became a "born again" Christian. With an even greater zeal towards using politics as a tool to achieve good works, Carter traveled Georgia between 1966 and 1970 studying the state's problems and making close to 1,800 speeches. Carter won the 1970 gubernatorial election handily.

Carter had positioned himself as a racial conservative in the race for governor—he spoke against busing to achieve racial integration in schools and campaigned with segregationist Alabama governor George Wallace. But in his inaugural address as governor, he immediately dispelled the fears of the civil rights community, announcing that he intended to aid all poor and needy Georgians, regardless of race. He called for an end to racial discrimination and "simple justice" for the poor. The speech won him national attention as a rising Democratic star in the New South—the modern, post-segregation South—and positioned him as a moderate reformer. As governor Carter increased the number of African American appointees on major state boards and agencies from three to 53 and increased the number of African American state employees by 40 percent. He pushed a law through the legislature stipulating that the poor and the wealthy areas of Georgia must have equal school funding. He also streamlined the state government, consolidating agencies and introducing strict budget controls to the state.

National Politics

Carter also became increasingly involved in national Democratic Party politics during his time as Georgia governor. In 1972 he headed the Democratic Governors Campaign committee, and in 1974 he chaired the Democratic National Committee. The same year that the Watergate scandal (in which members of Republican president Richard Nixon's campaign staff had broken into Democratic campaign headquarters) shook the foundations of U.S. politics (*See also,* Nixon Administration), the still obscure southern governor declared that he would run for the presidency. And in the campaign of 1976 he came out of nowhere to sweep the New Hampshire primary and win the nomination.

On November 2, 1976, Carter defeated incumbent Republican president Gerald Ford and became the first president from the Deep South since before the American Civil War (1861–65). He was 52 years old. Carter would be a one-term president, however, presiding over the nation in a time of profound disorder and change. After he seemed to stumble in the handling of a series of domestic and foreign crises, Carter lost the presidency to California governor Ronald Reagan in the 1980 election, stepping down from office as one of the most unpopular incumbents in U.S. history.

Post-presidential Years

Jimmy Carter retired from office amid a barrage of criticism and derision. By the late 1980s Carter came into the news again as he championed and worked for the causes he believed in. He committed himself to humanitarian issues around the world and wrote policy books, memoirs, and poetry. After the constant stream of presidential scandals in the two decades following Carter's retirement, Americans came to admire Carter's honesty and his unwavering morality.

After he left the White House in 1981, Carter established the nonprofit Carter Center in Atlanta, Georgia. He took an active role in the organization, raising private funds and public grants for its programs, which ranged from promoting human rights and health care in Third World countries to monitoring democratic elections abroad and maintaining databases of immunization records for Atlanta children. Carter and his wife Rosalynn also built houses with Habitat for Humanity, which constructed low-income housing around the world.

Carter came to enjoy a new prominence as a freelance statesman in his retirement. In 1990 he persuaded Nicaraguan Sandinista leader Daniel Ortega to cede power to newly elected President Violeta Chamorro. In 1993 Carter brought messages from Somali warlord Mohammed Farah Aidid to President Clinton in order to avert a military confrontation between the two countries. In June 1994 Carter convinced North Korean dictator Kim Il Sung to freeze his country's nuclear program and allow inspection of its nuclear facilities. Clinton was not always pleased when Carter waged his own diplomacy outside of the traditional machinery of the State Department. Nonetheless, Clinton sent Carter to Haiti in September 1994 on a mission to persuade that nation's military junta, who had ousted Haitian president Jean-Bertrand Aristide in a 1991 coup, to step down in order to avoid a U.S. invasion. Carter, along with former Joint Chiefs of Staff chairman Colin Powell and former Georgia senator Sam Nunn, negotiated an agreement with Haitian revolutionary leader Lt. Gen. Raoul Cédras to allow Aristide, Haiti's first democratically elected president, to return to power.

Carter's successes in the international arena were made possible by his continuing concern for issues of international peace and by his reputation for integrity and neutrality both in the United States and abroad. In many ways Carter's post-political career was more successful

than his presidency: his work for humanity redefined the role of ex-president, ensuring his place in history.

The Jimmy Carter Administration

Jimmy Carter campaigned as a Washington outsider and Americans, disillusioned by Watergate and the other scandals of previous years, heeded his message. As president, however, Carter's unwillingness to play politics made for poor relations with Congress, the press, and American voters. Carter spoke of limits and lowered expectations to voters seeking reassurance, not candor, and Americans came to see his idealism as arrogant naiveté, his honesty as weakness.

Carter Becomes President

The Campaign of 1976

The 1976 election was a unique opportunity for the Democratic Party to recapture the presidency. Many Americans were still voting against the permissiveness and turmoil of the Democratic 1960s, but by 1976 voters were even more shaken by the Watergate scandal and Richard Nixon's resignation. Jimmy Carter capitalized on the anti-Washington sentiment of the years after Watergate (when President Richard Nixon's supporters attempted to install listening devices in Democratic headquarters located in the Watergate Apartments in Washington, D.C.) by campaigning as an outsider who would act independently of the entrenched interest groups in Washington. He campaigned on the twin themes of "competence and compassion," insisting that he could run the nation effectively while still acting in the interest of morality and the public good.

Americans responded to Carter's call for principle in politics. Carter, a virtual unknown before 1976, swept 10 other Democratic candidates in the February New Hampshire primary, going on to win 17 of 30 primary contests. He won the Democratic nomination on the first ballot at his party's national convention in New York City. Minnesota senator Walter Mondale was chosen as his running mate. Mondale, a popular liberal two-term U.S. senator, was considered an experienced Washington hand who would please liberal interest groups and could offset Carter's inexperience in Washington.

Carter spoke of reconciliation and honesty in his speech accepting the Democratic nomination. In a period of economic slowdown, he made unemployment a central issue in his campaign, urging increased federal spending to create jobs. Carter also promised to pardon

Fast Fact

Jimmy Carter was the first president to send his mother on a diplomatic mission. His mother, Lillian Gordy Carter, headed the U.S. delegation attending the funeral of India's president Fakhruddin Ali Ahmed in 1977. "Miss Lillian," as Americans knew her, had served as a Peace Corps nurse in India in the late 1960s.

(Joseph Nathan Kane. *Facts About the Presidents,* 1993.)

Vietnam draft evaders, to reorganize and cut the federal bureaucracy, to reform taxes, to introduce national health insurance, and to return the Panama Canal (a sore spot in U.S.-Latin American relations) to Panamanian control while protecting U.S. interests.

In the general election Carter ran against incumbent President Gerald Ford, who had been elevated to president when Richard Nixon resigned in 1974. Ford had not proven his electability: appointed to succeed Vice President Spiro Agnew, who resigned in 1973 under a cloud of corruption, Ford had never won a national election. In addition, the nation was in the throes of a severe economic slowdown and soaring inflation rates. Ford was also tainted by having served as Richard Nixon's vice president, and for having given Nixon an absolute pardon for any crimes he may have committed during the Watergate scandal. After fighting off a strong challenge from former California governor Ronald Reagan, however, Ford managed to secure the Republican nomination, choosing Kansas senator Robert Dole as his running mate.

Ford entered the general election battle more than 30 percentage points behind Carter in the polls. With little to lose Ford made a decision to become the first incumbent president to participate in a televised debate with his opponent, challenging Carter to three televised debates. Ford, not known as a particularly talented public speaker, seemed to prevail in the first debate on domestic issues, but he stumbled in the later meetings with Carter. In the second debate he made the mistaken assertion that, "There is no Soviet domination of eastern Europe, and there never will be under this administration" (presidential debate, October 6, 1976.) Carter, meanwhile, uttered his own gaffes, the most famous of which was an interview with *Playboy* in which he confessed, "I've looked on a host of women with lust. I've committed adultery in my heart many times" (*Playboy,* November 1976.) The interview confirmed the press'

Administration

Administration Dates
January 20, 1977–January 20, 1981

Vice President
Walter Frederick Mondale (1977–81)

Cabinet
Secretary of State
Cyrus R. Vance (1977–80)
Edmund S. Muskie (1980–81)

Secretary of the Treasury
W. Michael Blumenthal (1977–79)
G. William Miller (1979–81)

Attorney General
Griffin B. Bell (1977–79)
Benjamin R. Civiletti (1979–81)

Secretary of the Interior
Cecil D. Andrus (1977–81)

Secretary of Agriculture
Robert S. Bergland (1977–81)

Secretary of Labor
F. Ray Marshall (1977–81)

Secretary of Commerce
Juanita M. Kreps (1977–79)
Philip M. Klutznick (1980–81)

Secretary of Defense
Harold Brown (1977–81)

Secretary of Health, Education and Welfare
Joseph A. Califano Jr. (1977–79)
Patricia R. Harris (1979–80)

Secretary of Housing and Urban Development
Patricia R. Harris (1977–79)
Maurice E. "Moon" Landrieu (1979–81)

Secretary of Transportation
Brockman "Brock" Adams (1977–79)
Neil E. Goldschmidt (1979–81)

Secretary of Energy
James R. Schlesinger (1977–79)
Charles W. Duncan Jr. (1979–81)

Secretary of Health and Human Services
Patricia R. Harris (1980–81)

Secretary of Education
Shirley M. Hufstedler (1979–81)

---

impression of Carter's bumbling naiveté, but Americans still seemed to prefer Carter's earnestness to four more years with a Republican Party that had betrayed the nation's trust.

While Carter's campaign attracted strong backing from Georgia's African American leaders, he had little initial support from national civil rights leaders. Many national black leaders saw Carter's antigovernment orientation as an attack on liberal principles, including civil rights. Carter also earned the mistrust of civil rights groups because his church in Plains did not admit blacks and because of a comment during the 1976 primary campaign that he was opposed to forced integration of neighborhoods. Despite his initial stumbles, however, Carter received enormous support from black voters—African Americans provided general election victory margins in Ohio, Pennsylvania, Louisiana, Mississippi, and North and South Carolina (Dumbrell, p. 88).

On November 2, 1976, Carter defeated Ford by 1.6 million votes, winning the electoral college by 297 votes to Ford's 240. He became the first president from the Deep South since Zachary Taylor in 1849. Ford won the West and prevailed among upper-income white voters. Carter collected the highest number of southern votes for a Democratic candidate since President Franklin Roosevelt and carried the industrial north, while losing ground with Catholics and Italians.

The Campaign of 1980

Carter entered the 1980 election in a tremendously weakened position. Inflation was higher than ever, the economy had stalled, and angry voters questioned Carter's competence to lead (*See also,* Domestic Issues). Carter also faced a strong primary challenge within his own party from Senator Edward Kennedy, who won a number of primaries and withdrew from the race only when it became clear during the Democratic National Convention that he would not marshal the votes to defeat Carter.

Carter faced a devastating array of crises at the end of his presidency that contributed to his unpopularity. In addition to the debilitating inflation and economic stagnation that Carter had failed to halt, the president had been frustrated in his efforts to free 52 U.S. citizens who had been held hostage in Iran for over a year. Carter had staked much of his personal and political capital on freeing the hostages, with no success. In addition, the Soviets invaded Afghanistan in 1980, making a mockery of Carter's efforts at cooperation and conciliation with the Soviets. By July 1980 Carter's public opinion ratings measured at 31 percent, the lowest recorded for any president.

Carter's opponent in the general election was former California governor Ronald Reagan, a popular, charismatic former movie actor who won the Republican nomination as the most conservative of the Republican candidates for president. Reagan called for tax cuts and increased defense spending, opposed abortion, and enjoyed lucrative support from the increasingly powerful bloc of New Right evangelical Christian voters who called for "pro-family" policies and a revival of religion in public life.

Carter attempted to stave off Reagan's challenge by adopting a Rose Garden strategy, working for reelection by attending to his duties as president and avoiding traditional campaigning. Reagan, meanwhile, exercised great skill in his use of the media, looking relaxed and confident in his public appearances and in the campaign's one televised debate. In the debate and in campaign speeches and advertisements Reagan repeatedly asked Americans if they were better off than they were four years ago. Carter, beset by the nation's economic and foreign policy difficulties, was hard pressed to respond to Reagan's attacks on the nation's faltering position in the world.

Reagan won the election by a landslide, with 51 percent of the popular vote, or 44 million votes, to Carter's 41 percent, or 35 million votes. John Anderson, a liberal Republican who had lost to Reagan in the primaries and reentered the campaign as an independent, won more than five and a half million votes, most of them from Carter's former supporters. Carter left Washington on January 20, 1981, turning the government over to Reagan and returning to Georgia. On the same day Iran finally freed the U.S. hostages.

Reagan's election not only reflected the public's loss of faith in Carter's leadership, it represented a realignment of the political parties that finally broke the Democratic coalition of southern and industrial states that Franklin Roosevelt had built in the 1930s. Ronald Reagan and the "new right" who brought him to power were more conservative on social issues than the moderate Republicans who had controlled the party for years. Campaigning for tax cuts for the middle class and the wealthy, funding cuts for programs for the poor, decreased regulation of business, and anticommunist and anti-abortion policies, Reagan won the traditionally Democratic South and swept the western United States. He also made significant inroads into the working-class, white voters who had once been loyal Democrats. It was these so-called Reagan Democrats who now decided elections.

Fast Fact

Jimmy Carter participated in the first presidential call-in television program on the "Ask President Carter" show broadcast from the Oval Office in 1977.

(Joseph Nathan Kane. *Facts About the Presidents,* 1993.)

Carter's Advisers

Carter was notorious for micromanagement—paying personal, detailed attention to the issues he considered most important. One consequence of his deep involvement in policy issues was that Carter initially believed that he did not need a chief of staff to prioritize and simplify the issues the president decided. Carter preferred a "spokes in the wheel" configuration of government, with Carter at the hub, receiving information from cabinet officers and other advisers who made decisions and spoke to Carter directly.

Although he consulted with his cabinet secretaries, none were particularly influential in domestic policy, where Carter considered himself an expert. Energy Secretary James R. Schlesinger helped Carter formulate his energy package, and Attorney General Griffin Bell was influential in his selection of appointments to the federal judiciary, but Carter trusted his own opinion above all, and his most trusted advisers were generally longtime associates, not Washington insiders. Between 1977 and 1979 the White House's top personnel was composed mostly of holdovers from Carter's 1976 campaign staff, many of them from Georgia. Carter's unwillingness to surround himself with a hierarchy of Washington insiders who understood the intricacies of policy left critics with the sense that White House business was being conducted by a group of arrogant, inexperienced Georgians who knew nothing about the workings of Washington. The president, overworked and duplicating effort, was seen as unable to delegate tasks and as being mired in details without understanding the larger picture. In July 1979 Carter finally appointed a chief of staff, Hamilton Jordan. But the chaotic image remained.

In foreign policy Carter also assumed the role of central policymaker. While Secretary of State Cyrus Vance and National Security Adviser Zbigniew Brzezinski offered their opinions and advice, they left the ultimate decisions up to Carter. This configuration worked well at times, but Carter faltered in regions where he lacked the personal knowledge to make informed decisions, such as Iran. Vance and Brzezinski initially agreed that the nation must stress international human rights over what Brzezinski termed the United States's "hysterical preoccupations" with the containment of Soviet Communism. As time went on, however, they began to disagree on the issue of the Soviet Union, with Vance pushing for conciliation and Brzezinski pushing for a harder line in arms treaty negotiations. Carter generally sided with Vance, but when the Soviet Union invaded Afghanistan, he began leaning towards the revived militarism that Brzezinski believed was necessary to battle the Soviet threat. The result, as in domestic affairs, was vacillation and confusion. Ironically, Carter's knowledge of the issues and his personal involvement in addressing them eroded public confidence in his actions (Brzezinski, pp. 441–2).

Carter and Congress

Carter presided during the Ninety-fifth and Ninety-sixth Congresses. Both Congresses had strong but fractured Democratic majorities. Carter did manage to shepherd a number of important legislative proposals through Congress, but he also saw many bills die there. This was in part because of Carter's ambitious agenda. Carter proposed a number of complicated bills, often simultaneously, that he did not have the resources to support. Other bills that did become law, such as his first energy package, emerged from Congress in a very different form than what the White House had requested. This was because of the disorganized way Carter's office prioritized legislation, and, more importantly, because of his difficult relationship with the Democratic leaders in Congress.

When Carter entered office in 1977 he faced an extremely independent-minded Congress that was determined not to allow another "imperial" president such as Lyndon Johnson or Richard Nixon to shape U.S. policy. In addition, high turnover rates in Congress after the Watergate scandal had resulted in a fractured Democratic majority with little party discipline. The Democrats in Congress were also considerably more liberal than Carter, who had campaigned as a moderate. The result was a Democratic leadership that was rarely willing to cooperate with their Democratic president. Carter's domestic policy adviser, Stuart Eizenstat, joked in 1979 that Moses would have had difficulty getting the Ten Commandments through Congress unscathed. In 1980 Carter suffered two veto overrides, the first since 1952 in a Congress controlled by a president's own political party.

Carter also considered himself a foe of the "interest group liberalism" so rampant in government, whereby members of Congress voted for the good of the specific interest groups who funded their campaigns rather than for the good of the whole. Carter believed he could persuade Congress to vote with him by lecturing them about the ultimate good of the legislation. In reality, however, winning votes in Congress required "horsetrading" favors and promises in exchange for votes. To members of Congress who were accustomed to being catered to by presidents who wanted their votes, Carter appeared insensitive, high-handed, and arrogant. In addition, his unwillingness to bring experienced Washington players into his legislative staff was seen as a sign of how out of touch he was with the culture of Capitol Hill.

Carter's first altercation with Congress came early, when, in 1977, he attempted to eliminate $5 billion worth of water projects from the 1978 budget. Carter used the confrontation over what he considered wasteful pork barrel projects—budget appropriations that deliver money and patronage to a politician's home district—as an opportunity to chide Congress into exercising budgetary discipline. Members of Congress, however, considered federal spending in their districts their ticket to reelection, and they considered Carter's artless political efforts an affront. Carter first agreed to compromise, then vetoed a bill containing the appropriations for the projects. He was ultimately forced to accept the dams. In the process, he alienated key Democratic figures whose help he would need in later battles.

Carter, according to historian Erwin Hargrove, operated with an "instinct for the future," but little for his political present. Thus many of his biggest battles were political liabilities for him. As time went on, however, Carter would learn the importance of compromise and trading favors. By the end of his presidency he lobbied more effectively and entered into a partnership with the Democratic leadership, consulting them on his proposals and becoming more flexible in accepting their changes.

Carter and the Judiciary

In 1978, faced with a huge backlog of cases in the federal courts, Congress passed a law creating 152 new federal judgeships—117 on the district court and 35 on the circuit courts of appeal. It was the greatest expansion of the federal judiciary in the nation's history. Carter filled these new posts and other federal judicial vacancies with more women, African Americans, and Hispanic Americans than any previous president. Carter made no Supreme Court appointments.

Perhaps the most important Supreme Court decision made during the Carter presidency was the 1978 *Bakke v. Board of Regents of California* case. Allan Bakke, a white man, was rejected twice for admission to the University of California at Davis medical school, despite the fact that he was more qualified than some minority students who were admitted. He sued the university, claiming that the racial quota reserving 16 of 100 places for minority-group applicants was a form of "reverse discrimination" that violated the Civil Rights Act of 1964. In 1978 the Supreme Court ordered Bakke's admission to the medical school, ruling that quotas could no longer be imposed, but that schools could still consider race in their admissions policies. The case received widespread attention and seemed to signal a departure from the Court's activism in the civil rights arena, but it still upheld the principle of affirmative action.

Changes in the U.S. Government

During the 1976 campaign Carter promised to cut the number of federal agencies from 1,900 to two hundred, and he entered the White House committed to cuts in the federal government. Carter was not opposed to big government, he simply hoped to eliminate waste. He believed that a thoughtful reorganization of government could save taxpayer dollars and, at the same time, dilute the influence of special interests. Carter authorized the consolidation of several agencies and jurisdictions, though nowhere near the 1,700 he had promised to eliminate.

Despite his campaign against bureaucracy, Carter also created two new cabinet departments: Energy and Education. In 1977 Carter selected former Defense Secretary James R. Schlesinger as the nation's first secretary of energy. The department absorbed the energy-related functions of more than 50 government agencies, including the defunct Federal Power Commission and the Federal Energy Administration (*See also,* Domestic Issues). In 1979 Carter, believing education was neglected, divided the Department of Health, Education and Welfare (HEW) into two separate cabinet-level bodies: Health and Human Services (HHS), and Department of Education (DOE). Shirley M. Hufstedler, a California judge, became the first secretary of education in 1979. The DOE absorbed 150 programs from HEW and from the education wing of the Defense Department.

Carter's most lasting contribution to the shape of the federal government, however, was the 1978 Civil Service Reform Act, which governed nonappointed employees of the federal government. The act created a performance evaluation system for civil service managers, linked performance and pay, committed the civil service to equal employment opportunity and affirmative action, and extended protection to "whistle blowers," federal employees who reported on waste and corruption. The act was lauded at the time as one of Carter's most impressive domestic achievements.

However, the Civil Service Reform Act also brought about some unintended consequences, such as providing less flexibility and making it very difficult to replace employees who were not doing their jobs. In addition, the ethics provisions of the act designed to keep appointees from lobbying their departments for one year after leaving the government, the so-called "revolving door" provision, proved nearly impossible to enforce.

In 1978 Congress also passed the Independent Counsel Act. The statute, a response to the firings of Justice Department officials investigating Richard Nixon during

What They Said . . .

"He's come back, he's really made us see that being a private citizen can be a great thing and a high office in its own self.

The way he's handled himself, refusing to sit on the boards of corporate directors, refusing to take any money for speeches, not just talking about the poor but working to build houses with Habitat for Humanity, not just talking about health care problems but working to eradicate guinea worm disease in Africa, not just talking about how great democracy is but monitoring elections in places like Nicaragua and Panama . . . makes him a hero because he's raised the bar on how one handles himself out of office."

(Source: Carter historian Douglas Brinkley. *Scripps Howard News Service,* 1999.)

the Watergate scandal, was passed with the intentions of promoting good government, policing the executive branch, and restoring public faith in elected officials. The law created a position for an "independent" prosecutor to be appointed to investigate public officials. Like the Civil Service Reform Act, however, the Independent Counsel Statute spawned some very destructive, unintended consequences. Aiming to free investigations from politics, it became a political tool in itself. In its 20 years of existence, the Justice Department authorized 20 separate investigations, many of them protracted, few with any significant convictions. The investigations cost U.S. taxpayers total of $150 million over the 20 years. In 1998 after a $50 million, three-year investigation into President Bill Clinton ended in a divisive and fruitless impeachment trial in Congress, Congress decided not to renew the law, and on June 30, 1999, it expired.

Carter also signed the 1980 Alaska Land Act, which set aside 104 million acres in national parks, wildlife refuges, and wilderness areas in the nation's largest state.

Domestic Issues

Carter believed that he had come to power in an age of limits, and that his role was to steer the country through what he called the United States's "crisis of confidence."

The nation was, indeed, in dire straits. The economy, battered by simultaneous economic stagnation and inflation, was in the worst shape of recent years, and Americans distrusted the government immensely. Carter's interest in long-term policy making and his insistence on sacrifice, however, did little to bolster Americans' confidence.

Carter was a moderate centrist, and much of the legislation he proposed, such as welfare reform and tax reform, were issues the Democrats generally avoided. Between 1977 and 1980 Carter signed legislation deregulating natural gas, cargo airlines, commercial airlines, and the trucking industry, which had been favored by Republicans. Carter's centrist orientation often meant that he appeared too conservative for his own party and too liberal to work with the Republicans.

The Economy

For the three decades after World War II (1939–45), the U.S. standard of living rose steadily. The U.S. economy, in those years, produced as much as a third of the world's industrial goods, and the U.S. dollar was the strongest currency in the world. When Carter came to office, however, two conditions of that prosperity had changed. First, large increases in the federal deficit due to the Vietnam War (1959–75) and the increased social spending of Lyndon Johnson's War on Poverty had created unprecedented rates of inflation. And second, the nation could no longer be certain of access to the cheap raw materials that had helped fuel the growth of the post–World War II economy. By the late 1960s with domestic petroleum resources no longer sufficient to meet the huge U.S. demand, the nation grew increasingly dependent on imports from the Middle East and Africa.

In addition, in the early 1970s, while Richard Nixon was president, the Organization of Petroleum Exporting Countries (OPEC), which had been a weak coalition of Third World oil-producing nations, began to assert itself as a formal bargaining unit for the sale of oil. In 1973 Arab members of OPEC announced that they would no longer ship petroleum to nations supporting Israel in the Yom Kippur War (October 1973). At the same time OPEC nations agreed to raise their prices by 500 percent, from $3 to $15 a barrel. The United States suffered its first fuel shortage since World War II, and the price of energy skyrocketed.

At the same time the U.S. economy found its manufacturing base threatened by increased productivity in other nations. Europe and Japan had, by the late 1960s, begun to recover from the damage to their manufacturing sectors during World War II, and they began competing with U.S. firms in the sales of automobiles and other products.

Stagflation

The oil shock and the structural changes in the manufacturing sector meant that during Richard Nixon's first two and a half years in office, the cost of living rose 15 percent while economic growth declined. Economists came to describe the nation's new economic difficulties as "stagflation," a combination of inflation—rising consumer prices and a decline in the dollar's purchasing power—and economic stagnation. Both Nixon and Ford seemed unsure of how to respond—they lurched from a tight money policy at one moment to increased government spending at the next, unable to decide whether it was more important to curb inflation or to battle the economic slowdowns of recession. These erratic patterns helped create the largest budget deficit since World War II but did little to produce any substantial change in either the inflation rate or the stagnant economic growth rate. By 1976 the inflation rate stood at 11 percent, and the economy was at a standstill.

Although Jimmy Carter was a fiscal conservative at heart who spoke of balancing the federal budget and fighting inflation, he was initially convinced by his advisers that recession, and not inflation, was the United States's greatest problem. He first moved to reduce unemployment by raising public spending and cutting federal taxes. Unemployment did decline for a time, but the inflation rates, already high, began to soar. In response, Carter, like Nixon and Ford before him, shifted his policies, calling for a tighter money supply and appointing two conservative economists, G. William Miller and Paul Volcker, to the Federal Reserve Board to ensure a policy of high interest rates and reduced currency supplies. Inflation continued to climb at an annual rate of well over 10 percent, however, while productivity continued to decline. By 1980, as the nation's economy stagnated, interest rates soared to the highest levels in U.S. history. At times they exceeded 20 percent.

Energy

The Arab oil embargo of 1973 and 1974 and the formation of the Organization of Petroleum Exporting Countries (OPEC) made evident the United States's increasing dependence on costly foreign oil at the same time that domestic oil production was declining. The Nixon and Ford administrations, however, continued to keep the price of domestic oil artificially low through price controls and did little to penalize excessive consumption by taxing oil and gas. Nor did Carter's predecessors seriously consider enacting conservation programs and conversion to other energy sources that would help curtail the nation's dependence on foreign oil.

Shortly after Carter took office, he concluded that the nation needed a comprehensive energy policy. He appointed James L. Schlesinger, head of the Atomic Energy Commission under Nixon, to help him develop a package that Carter unveiled to the nation on April 20, 1977, 90 days after his inauguration. The energy bill called for a tax on gasoline pegged to rise to consumption, a tax on automobiles that burned excessive amounts of fuel, and several conservation measures including tax

Automobiles converge on a gas station during the energy crisis of the late 1970s. The crisis crippled President Carter's domestic agenda and his public approval rating slipped dramatically. (UPI/Corbis-Bettmann. Reproduced by permission.)

credits for installation of insulation and investments in more fuel-efficient buildings. It also called for taxation of domestic crude oil to raise domestic prices to world levels, federal control of intrastate natural gas sales, incentives to install solar heating, an end to gasoline price controls, and the deployment of nuclear reactors.

Carter had a difficult task of convincing Americans that there was truly an oil shortage when most Americans believed that the oil-producing countries and oil companies were simply gouging the public. In addition, the package included a number of long-term solutions that offered little short-term benefit for politicians, and

thus it was a difficult sell in Congress. The bill passed the House of Representatives without serious modification, but the Senate passed it only after a protracted 18-month struggle, with a much more gradual schedule of natural gas and crude oil deregulation and a greatly reduced tax on energy.

OPEC Triggers a Second Oil Crisis

In the summer of 1979 the fall of the Shah of Iran (*See also,* Foreign Issues) precipitated a second energy crisis for the United States, with another round of OPEC oil increases. Without Iran, one of the United States's largest suppliers of oil, oil prices soared while the nation faced severe short-term shortages, and Americans found themselves waiting in long lines at gasoline stations. Responding to this, Carter proposed another energy package. Prefacing the introduction of the bill, he made what was perhaps the most famous speech of his presidency. In his speech he said Americans had an inability to discipline themselves in their energy use and that they were no longer willing to sacrifice for the greater national good. Critics came to call the address the "malaise" speech (although Carter never actually used the word "malaise"), and Americans attacked Carter for blaming his problems on the nation.

Still, with the soaring oil prices and gasoline rationing that the Iranian Revolution brought about, Americans finally rallied behind the second package, passed by Congress in 1980. The second energy bill lifted controls on crude oil prices and imposed a tax on the profits from imported oil sales. The program also introduced incentives for conservation along with a plan for developing new sources of energy.

Three Mile Island

Carter, who had begun his professional life as an engineer on a nuclear submarine, was a strong proponent of nuclear energy. However, an accident at the Three Mile Island (Pennsylvania) nuclear power plant made Carter, and Americans, reconsider the safety of nuclear plants. On March 28, 1979, a year-old reactor overheated, raising fears that it might explode and release radioactive cesium. The reactor shut down automatically, but plant operators, misled by ambiguous indicators, believed that water pressure was building and shut down the remaining cooling pumps, causing the reactor to heat up further. The reactor core did not melt down, despite significant damage, and little radiation was released. Still, some 144,000 people, mostly pregnant women and small children, were evacuated from the area. It was the most serious domestic nuclear accident in the nation's history.

The combination of human error, mechanical breakdowns, and design flaws at Three Mile Island prompted Carter to appoint a commission to study the incident. It recommended that the government suspend nuclear plant construction until stricter safety standards were adopted. After Three Mile Island the nation changed its policy toward nuclear energy. With both the public and the politicians now less optimistic about the future and the safety of nuclear energy, nuclear construction slowed to a standstill. Many reactors that had begun construction in 1978 were simply abandoned.

Civil Rights

Despite some concern from African American leaders during the 1976 campaign that Carter, a southerner, would not respond to the needs of minority communities, Carter proved to be deeply committed to civil rights during his presidency.

As president, Carter appointed a number of African Americans to high-profile positions. Patricia Harris became head of the Department of Housing and Urban Development (HUD); Eleanor Holmes Norton, the former head of New York City's Human Rights Commission, became the chair of the Equal Employment Opportunity Commission (EEOC); and Georgia congressperson Andrew Young became ambassador to the United Nations (UN). Carter also appointed African Americans to a number of important spots in the Justice Department.

In policy the Carter administration was strongly committed to desegregation and affirmative action. The administration did initially oppose the use of quotas, but after much debate it ultimately supported the use of racial classifications for affirmative action.

Carter also consolidated and strengthened the EEOC, giving it new powers to enforce civil rights in the workplace. His administration filed "friend of the court" briefs to lend support to African Americans in a number of federal civil rights suits. Carter supported limited, restricted busing of schoolchildren across school district boundaries to achieve integration. In a symbolic gesture of solidarity, the president also sent his daughter Amy to a desegregated public school in Washington, D.C.

Carter, however, was also a fiscal conservative who was confronted with escalating inflation and budget deficits, and he requested few increases in federal spending for social programs that would benefit minorities. His lack of support for increased social programs for the poor, strained African American loyalty to the Democratic Party, and Carter received far fewer black votes in his 1980 race against Ronald Reagan.

Foreign Policy

One of Jimmy Carter's first actions upon taking office was to pardon the estimated 10,000 draft evaders who had fled or gone into hiding rather than fight the unpopular war in Vietnam (1959–75). Although organizations representing veterans who had fought the war condemned the move, Carter considered it a unifying gesture that would signal a shift in foreign policy: the Vietnam era was over. Further, the U.S. government would no longer pursue its Cold War rivalry with the Soviet Union at the expense of the nation's domestic stability. Carter's foreign policy team sought to modify what National Security Advisor Brzezinski called the United States's "hysterical preoccupations" with the containment of Communism (*See also,* Truman Administration).

Instead, Carter hoped to incorporate the notion of "human rights"—the universal respect for the civil liberties of individuals—into the nation's foreign policy. Carter attacked a number of difficult, complicated foreign policy issues such as Middle East peace and the Panama Canal, and he tackled these problems with the passionate belief, similar to Woodrow Wilson's, that morality was fundamental to foreign policy. Following the human rights policy he had endorsed, Carter suspended or reduced U.S. aid to nations that chronically violated human rights, including Argentina, Uruguay, Chile, Nicaragua, Brazil, Venezuela, Ethiopia, and South Africa (Nash, p. 999).

This moralism, however, may have ultimately complicated Carter's diplomatic efforts. He criticized the Soviet Union for its treatment of dissidents, for instance, at the same that the two superpowers were engaged in sensitive negotiations over arms control—and was surprised when the Soviets balked. And in the end, deteriorating Soviet relations and the Soviet invasion of Afghanistan forced Carter to commit the nation to new militarism reminiscent of the early Cold War. Carter's humanitarian vision for U.S. foreign policy became a casualty of the turbulent times.

Panama Canal

In 1977 Carter signed two treaties that transferred the control and sovereignty of the Panama Canal to the nation of Panama. The canal, the man-made waterway that cut across the isthmus of Panama and linked the Atlantic and the Pacific Oceans, had once served as one of the crucial trade routes in the Western Hemisphere. Built in the days of Theodore Roosevelt, the waterway had been U.S. territory for nearly 75 years, but it was the subject of increasing resentment on the part of Panamanians who felt U.S. control of the canal was an encroachment on their sovereignty. Negotiations to transfer the canal's ownership had been ongoing since the Lyndon Johnson administration (1963–69), and Carter believed strongly in returning the canal to Panama.

In September 1977 Carter signed the treaties, which gave complete control of the canal to Panama on December 31, 1999, and guaranteed the canal's neutrality while retaining the United States's right to defend the canal. The ratification of the treaty, however, met with strong opposition from conservatives, led by former California governor Ronald Reagan, who argued that the cession of the canal was a sign of U.S. weakness. The canal, they insisted, was vital to U.S. prestige and to its hemispheric defenses, and an American presence in Central America was a deterrent to the growth of Cuban-Soviet Marxism in the region. Carter's protreaty forces, meanwhile, maintained that the waterway no longer held strategic importance because of increased air freight and because of the fact that neither the largest aircraft carriers nor supertankers could travel through the canal's locks. After a prolonged, bitter debate, the Senate approved the treaties in 1978 by only one vote.

China

In 1978 the United States extended diplomatic recognition to the People's Republic of China. Carter's overtures to China were a continuation of Richard Nixon's strategy of improving relations with China in order to strengthen the U.S. hand against the Soviet Union. In addition, U.S. farm and business interests had eyed the Chinese market of nearly a billion people with enthusiasm. In reestablishing diplomatic relations with China for the first time since 1949, the United States recognized the Communists in the Chinese capital of Beijing as the legitimate government of China and agreed to withdraw U.S. forces from Taiwan. In 1979 China's vice premier Deng Xiaoping, attempting to modernize his nation and open it to the world, became the first Chinese Communist leader to visit the United States.

The Soviet Union

For nearly a decade, the United States had been working toward a gradual thawing of relations with the Soviet Union, called détente—the easing of Cold War hostilities between the two nations. From 1969 to 1972 the Americans and the Soviets participated in the Strategic Arms Limitations Talks (SALT) to negotiate an agreement to limit missile stockpiles, to work together in space, and to ease long-standing restrictions on trade. In 1972 Nixon met with Soviet premier Leonid Brezhnev in Moscow to sign the Anti-Ballistic Missile (ABM) treaty and the Interim Agreement on the Limitation of Strategic Offensive Arms.

Also in 1972 the Americans and the Soviets initiated a second round of negotiations, called SALT II. When Carter became president he continued the negotiations. In 1978 he traveled to Vienna, Austria, to meet with Brezhnev to finish drafting the SALT agreement. Carter did not have an easy time, in part because of his own unyielding philosophy on human rights. Carter antagonized the Soviets by offering outspoken support for Soviet dissidents Anatoly Shcharansky, Alexander Ginzburg, and Andrei Sakharov at the same time that he was engaging in the sensitive SALT negotiations. The Soviets charged Carter with meddling in their internal affairs and refused, for a time, to cooperate further in the talks. Misjudging the willingness of the Russians to disarm, Carter also offered new weapons reductions that went further than the Soviet Union was prepared to accept. When this threw matters into confusion, Carter backed off and through patient negotiation signed the SALT II agreement with Brezhnev in June 1979. The SALT II treaty set limits on the number of long-range missiles, bombers, and nuclear warheads for each side.

The ratification of SALT II proved even more difficult. Despite the decade of détente, the treaty met fierce opposition among U.S. conservatives distrustful of any relations with the Soviet Union and any reduction in U.S. military strength. Thus the treaty was already in deep trouble in Congress when the Soviets invaded Afghanistan in late December 1979. Carter, feeling betrayed by the invasion, withdrew SALT II from consideration in Congress. The demise of the treaty also signaled the end of a decade of U.S.-Soviet détente, and the beginnings of a renewed arms race that would define U.S.-Soviet relations in the next decade.

Afghanistan Invasion

The Soviet Union had been a power in Afghanistan (the mountainous nation that was surrounded by the Soviet Union, Iran, and Pakistan) for years, and it established formal ties to the country after a Soviet-backed Communist coup in 1978. In late 1979 Russian troops invaded Afghanistan in order to quell an Islamic insurgence that was threatening the Soviet-supported puppet regime of President Babrak Karmal. The rebels, who fought to establish a Muslim state, soon found themselves confronted with an overwhelming display of Russian firepower.

The Soviets said they intervened in Afghanistan because of their concern about the rise of Islamic fundamentalism inside and outside the territorial Soviet Union—which the Soviets believed was a threat both to the survival of Communism and to the Soviet Union's territorial integrity. Carter, however, saw the invasion as an expansionist move—a step toward possible Soviet control over much of the world's oil supplies. Calling the invasion the gravest threat to world peace since World War II, Carter imposed economic sanctions, suspending the sale of high-technology goods and grain to the Soviet Union. He also won passage of a United Nations General Assembly resolution calling for the withdrawal of all foreign troops from Afghanistan and joined 63 other nations in boycotting the Olympic Games in Moscow, the capital of the former Soviet Union.

The war in Afghanistan was, in many ways, Moscow's Vietnam: the unpopular and costly war in Afghanistan, like the United States's escalation in Vietnam, precipitated a disastrous rise in inflation and a shortage of funds for domestic initiatives. Thus when Carter, and then Ronald Reagan, increased U.S. defense spending in response to the Afghanistan invasion, the Soviet Union could not both keep up with U.S. spending and continue pouring resources into the central Asian war. The Soviets withdrew in 1988 and 1989 after an immense loss of lives—13,000 dead and 35,000 wounded—and an even greater decline in world prestige. The most significant casualty, however, was the Soviet economy, which collapsed soon after the war ended.

The struggle over Afghanistan also ultimately injured U.S. interests in the region. The United States poured money and weapons into neighboring Pakistan to support the Mujaheddin, the Islamic rebels fighting the Soviet army in Afghanistan. But the anticommunist sentiment that inspired the rebels was also markedly anti-western, and the money that fed the rebel forces would also help fuel Islamic fundamentalism in the Persian Gulf. In the next decades it would be Islamic revolutions—and not the world Communist revolution—that would concern U.S. foreign policymakers the most.

Mideast Peace

Camp David Accords

On September 17, 1978, Prime Minister Menachem Begin of Israel and President Anwar Sadat of Egypt signed the Camp David Accords. The peace treaty ended a 31-year state of war between Israel and Egypt, and set a framework for the return of lands that Israel had captured from Egypt in the "Six Days War" of 1967. Carter considered the accords essential to maintaining stability in the oil-rich region.

President Carter, who signed the accords as a witness, was instrumental in the negotiations. After talks between Sadat and Begin had stalled in September 1978, Carter invited the two leaders to the Camp David retreat in Maryland, where they spent 13 days hammering out the details of the treaties. The final treaty, signed in March 1979, implemented a timetable for Israeli withdrawal from the Sinai Desert. The United States, for its part, promised financial aid to both countries and pledged to defend Israel—which ceded significant strategic lands in exchange for peace—if Egypt broke the terms of the treaty.

The accords also provided for future negotiations that would prove to be less fruitful, such as the question of Palestinian self-rule, an issue brought to the forefront after the Palestinian Liberation Organization (PLO) began to agitate for an independent Palestine. The guerilla group demanded the return of the West Bank, the Gaza Strip, and East Jerusalem—lands that Israel had also captured in the 1967 war. It would take 15 years to produce any significant headway on that issue.

Iran

For years the United States had considered Iran one of its friendliest allies among the nations in the Persian Gulf. The Shah Reza Pahlavi had succeeded to Iran's throne in 1945, forging an immediate alliance with the United States and their European allies. The Shah's reign was threatened briefly in 1953, when the Shah dismissed Prime Minister Mohammad Mosaddeq, a popular leader of a coalition of nationalist groups. When Mosaddeq's followers rioted, the Shah fled briefly to Rome, Italy. After three days, however, the royalists regained control of Teheran, the Iranian capital, the Shah returned, and Mosaddeq was sentenced to prison.

As time went on the Shah became increasingly repressive. He dissolved the parliament in 1961, tolerating less and less internal dissent. Nonetheless, the Shah enjoyed unwavering military and financial support from the United States, in order to conciliate the Shah who would in turn make his nation a bulwark against Soviet expansion in the Middle East. Indeed, by the early 1970s, the Nixon administration had given the Shah open-ended control over arms purchases and restricted the operation of U.S. intelligence activities in Iran.

By 1979 Iranians had come to resent the Shah's repressive, authoritarian regime, and the Islamic clergy

President Carter signs the Mideast Peace Treaty at the White House in 1979, flanked by Egyptian president Anwar Sadat (left) and Israeli prime minister Menachem Begin. (UPI/Corbis-Bettmann. Reproduced by permission.)

had begun to oppose his efforts to modernize and westernize Iran. The zealous religious leader, the Ayatollah Ruhollah Khomeini, who envisioned the birth of a radical Islamic republic in Iran, led a revolt against the Shah. In January 1979 the Shah fled the country.

The Hostage Crisis: Carter, who had little intelligence information on developments in Iran because of limited U.S. intelligence there, attempted to establish cordial relations with the increasingly militant new regime. In November 1979, however, after the United States admitted the Shah into the country to be treated for cancer, an armed, enraged mob stormed the U.S. embassy in Teheran and seized the diplomats and military personnel inside, demanding the return of the Shah to Iran. The raid, which was ostensibly about the Shah's return to Iran to stand trial on criminal charges, was also an expression of anger at the United States, which Iranians saw as a force of evil in their history. The 52 U.S. hostages remained captive for 444 days. Americans, already battered by the economic turmoil of the 1970s, were outraged and frustrated at Carter's inability to free the hostages.

Carter invested much personal and political capital in solving the crisis. He suspended oil imports from Iran and froze Iranian assets in the United States. He also dispatched a military force to rescue the hostages in April 1980, but after the expedition landed in Iran, the mal-

function of three helicopters caused the commander to abort the raid. During evacuation, two aircraft collided and eight U.S. servicemen died. The raid was a public relations fiasco, and Secretary of State Cyrus Vance resigned a few days after the debacle, protesting Carter's decision to mount the rescue mission.

After the failed U.S. raid, the Iranians scattered the hostages among locations throughout Iran, and negotiations reached a stalemate. The death of the Shah did little to change the situation. Iran simply changed its demands, asking for the return of the late Shah's assets, the cancellation of all U.S. claims against Iran, the unfreezing of Iranian assets in the United States, and a U.S. pledge of noninterference in Iranian affairs. In November 1980, however, Khomeini finally agreed to release the hostages in exchange for releasing Iranian assets in the United States.

The hostages emerged relatively unscathed, but Carter did not. The president, already seen as having failed in his efforts to revive the economy, now appeared helpless before a smaller, poorer, and weaker Third World country, and the failure of the military's rescue mission only increased the perception of incompetence.

The hostage crisis was not only a symbol of the United States's decline in the world, it was a symptom of the nation's blind policies towards the Third World during the Cold War. Foreign policymakers did not realize how dependent the nation had become on oil-producing countries until the OPEC oil embargo opened their eyes. In addition, the United States had for years enlisted Third World dictators in the fight against communism without regard for their often authoritarian policies and the backlash that would occur. As a result, Carter, and the United States, did not anticipate a revolution in Iran. Nor did they have any understanding of a revolution inspired by Islam rather than by Marxism. The result was a 444-day paralysis that ended, fittingly, on the day Carter's presidency ended. The hostages left Iran on January 20, 1981—Ronald Reagan's inauguration day.

The Carter Administration Legacy

When Jimmy Carter lost the 1980 election, interest rates were soaring, Soviet troops were in Afghanistan, and 52 U.S. hostages were scattered throughout Iran. Carter's idealism and his long-term visions for the country, it seemed, were ultimately defeated by the widespread perception that his presidency, at least in the short term, had been a failure.

Popularity and Public Opinion

One of the great weaknesses of Carter's presidency was his inability to communicate with the press and with the public. Unlike his successor Ronald Reagan, Carter could not connect with the public, because of his unwillingness to simplify his message and because of a speaking style that was not particularly forceful or television-friendly. In addition, Carter developed an antipathy for the Washington press corps that he saw as hostile to him—a reflection, in part, of a new aggressiveness towards presidents as a result of the Watergate scandal. As Carter's relations with the press deteriorated, so did public perceptions of him.

Carter's average approval rating during his presidency was 47 percent, and there were times when his Gallup Poll ratings exceeded those of Lyndon Johnson and Ronald Reagan at the same point in their presidencies. By the election of 1980, however, Carter's approval ratings had dipped to 31 percent, even lower than Nixon's before his 1974 resignation.

The most obvious explanation for Carter's falling popularity was the rising inflation rate—as a general rule presidential popularity rises and falls with economic indicators. In addition, Carter too often appeared to the American people as a bearer of bad news regarding the economy and the United States's declining power in the world. Carter often said that he had little fear of becoming a one-term president if that meant doing what was right instead of what won votes. Carter's desire to solve the United States's politically unpopular issues, in combination with the faltering economy and the foreign policy crises, all but ensured that he would become a one-term president.

Lasting Impact

Jimmy Carter was remembered as a good man, if not always a good president. Carter was seen as an ineffectual leader during his presidency, who was overwhelmed by the crises of the late 1970s—skyrocketing inflation rates and gasoline prices, the hostage situation in Iran, and the invasion of Afghanistan. Carter told the nation in his inaugural address on January 20, 1977, that more is not necessarily better, that the United States could "neither answer all questions nor solve all problems." The majority of Americans, however, believed otherwise, and in 1980 they sought a more reassuring, if less candid, voice.

Still, Carter's reputation would improve with time. Carter had always believed in tackling the nation's long-term issues rather than focusing on short-term political salves. His energy package, for instance, was a serious attempt to introduce an ethic of conservation into U.S. energy policy and to wean the nation from its dependence on foreign oil, despite the political unpopularity of any move to limit Americans' gasoline consumption. In addition, Carter's humanitarian and diplomatic work after his presidency contributed immensely to his reputation for honesty and morality. His earnestness and principles came to seem all the more important after the presidential scandals of the 1980s and 1990s.

Sources

Brinkley, Alan. *The Unfinished Nation: A Concise History of the American People.* Vol.2, *From 1865.* New York: McGraw Hill, 1997.

Brzezinski, Zbigniew. *Power and Principle.* London: Wiedenfeld and Micolson, 1983.

Dumbrell, John. *The Carter Presidency: A Re-evaluation.* New York: Manchester University Press, 1985.

Encyclopedia of World Biography. 2d ed. Detroit: Gale Research, 1998.

Hargrove, Erwin C. *Jimmy Carter as President: Leadership and the Politics of the Public Good.* Baton Rouge, La.: Louisiana State University Press, 1988.

Kane, Joseph Nathan. *Facts About the Presidents.* New York: The H. W. Wilson Co., 1993.

Lang, John. "Public Views Reagan, Carter as Heroic Leaders," *Scripps Howard News Service.* 1999.

Nash, Gerald, et al. *The American People: Creating a Nation and a Society.* New York: Harper Collins, 1994.

U.S. Government Printing Office. *The Presidential Campaign 1976.* Vol. 1., Washington D.C.: U.S. Government Printing Office, 1978.

Further Readings

Carter, Jimmy. *Keeping Faith: Memoirs of a President.* New York: Bantam Books, 1982.

———. *The Blood of Abraham: Insights into the Middle East.* Fayetteville: University of Arkansas Press, 1993.

Glad, Betty. *Jimmy Carter: In Search of the Great White House.* New York: Norton, 1980.

Jimmy Carter Library. 1999. <carterlibrary.galileo.peachnet. edu> (6 July, 1999).

Kucharsky, David. *The Man From Plains: The Mind and Spirit of Jimmy Carter.* New York: Harper and Row, 1976.

Wooten, James. *Dasher: The Roots and the Rising of Jimmy Carter.* New York: Summit Books, 1978.

Reagan Administrations

Full name: Ronald Reagan

Given name: Ronald Wilson Reagan

Popular name: Dutch; The Gipper; Bonzo; The Great
Communicator

Personal Information:

Born: February 6, 1911

Birthplace: Tampico, Illinois

Religion: Disciples of Christ (mother's side); Catholic
(father's side)

Spouse: Jane Wyman (m. 1940); Nancy Davis (m. 1952)

Children: Maureen; Michael; Patricia; Ronald Jr.

Education: Eureka College, B.A.

Occupation: Radio sports commentator, film actor, television
actor, state governor

Political Party: Republican Party

Age at Inauguration: 69 years

Biography

Handsome and charismatic, Ronald Reagan had
already made a name for himself in movies and television by the time he entered politics in the 1960s. Reagan's sincere manner and straightforward speeches
appealed to voters, and helped him win election to the
governorship of California, and later the presidency of
the United States. Highly popular while in office, as a
conservative Republican, Reagan sought to shift the federal government away from the large and active style of
governing that had dominated U.S. politics since the
1940s, while also providing for a strong defense against
the Soviet Union.

Early Life

Ronald Reagan spent his childhood in a succession
of small towns in Illinois. His father, a salesman, was a
heavy drinker, but his mother provided guidance, stability, and a commitment to the Disciples of Christ Church.
The family settled in Dixon, Illinois in 1920 and Reagan
spent the rest of his childhood there. He was student body
president at Dixon High, a good all around athlete, and
an especially good swimmer. He spent the summers
working as a lifeguard, and a plaque commemorating the
77 people he saved between 1927 and 1933 is now on
display in the Loveland Museum.

A conventional, handsome, and popular young man,
Reagan learned and accepted the Protestant values and
work ethic of the small midwestern town and held to them
throughout his later life. Reagan's father began working
for the Federal Emergency Relief Administration

(FERA), a New Deal agency, in 1933, and throughout the Depression decade the Reagans were staunch Democrats. Ironically, in view of President Reagan's later opposition to federal bureaucracy, the large-scale government of the New Deal provided stability and a way out of poverty to his own family in those years. Reagan himself was a New Deal Democrat in the 1930s and supported the Democratic incumbent, Harry S. Truman, for the presidency in 1948 before joining the Republican Party in the 1950s.

Education

Reagan was a sociology and economics major at Eureka College in Eureka, Illinois, but did not study hard. He held a partial athletic scholarship and lettered in two sports, washed dishes in his fraternity house and, when only a freshman, played a leading role in a student strike to fire an unpopular college president. He acted in seven college plays and impressed his drama coaches with a confident stage manner. In his senior year Reagan was president of the students' booster club. He graduated with a B.A. in 1932 when the Depression was at its worst.

Ronald Reagan. (The Library of Congress.)

Family Life

Reagan married Jane Wyman, a Hollywood actress, in 1940, at a time when he was also a rising movie star. Their daughter Maureen was born the following year, and in 1945 they adopted a son, Michael. Jane Wyman continued to work in films through much of the 1940s and was more successful than he, winning an Oscar in 1948 for her role as a deaf-mute in *Johnny Belinda.* Her successful career and the infant death of a third child in 1947 contributed to the deterioration of their marriage, which ended with a divorce in 1948.

In 1952 Reagan married another actress, Nancy Davis, who abandoned her own career for the sake of her husband's. They had two children, a daughter Patricia born in 1952 and a son Ronald in 1958. Fiercely protective of Reagan, and as ambitious as he, she contributed to his political career and enjoyed the limelight, first as governor's wife in California in the late 1960s, later as first lady in the White House in the 1980s. With extravagant tastes in fashionable clothes and furnishings, she gained a reputation for insensitivity among the Washington press during the 1980s by her lavish spending on White House redecoration and parties at a time of economic depression and widespread unemployment.

Her special project as first lady was working to prevent children and teenagers from taking drugs, and she popularized the slogan "Just say no!" Newcomers to the Reagans' Washington scene, such as Interior Secretary James Watt, were surprised to discover how active Nancy

Reagan was in political business and how much weight her opinions carried with her husband.

The Reagans lived in Hollywood until 1967 and then moved to Sacramento, the state capital of California, when he was elected governor. Nancy Reagan was dissatisfied with the official governor's mansion, an old Victorian home, which she claimed was a fire trap, and the Reagans accepted the offer of a new modern-style governor's mansion, to be built at the expense of some wealthy friends. While it was being prepared, however, they lived in a third Sacramento house, also bought for them by Republican sponsors. Between the end of Reagan's governorship in 1974 and the start of his presidency in 1981 they lived in Santa Barbara near the central Californian coast, and returned there in 1989 following the end of Reagan's presidency.

Career

Reagan graduated from Eureka College in the worst year of the Great Depression, 1932, and was unable to carry out his plan of finding work in Chicago. He finally got a job as a radio announcer in Davenport, Iowa. Radio was then a fast-growing business and this first foot in the door soon led to a better radio job with station WHO in Des Moines, Iowa. Reagan described, or rather reenacted, professional baseball games for his radio audience, even though he was sitting in a studio. Telegraph messages would arrive from the Chicago Cubs' stadium indicating that a batter had struck out, singled, stolen a base, or scored, and Reagan would then imaginatively recreate the scene, making up the details as though he were present, and adding colorful touches about the weather, the crowd, and the players.

Movies

After four years in Des Moines, and with a growing reputation as a local celebrity, he traveled to California early in 1937, ostensibly to watch the Cubs in spring training but really to take a Hollywood screen test. Warner Brothers, one of the era's big studios, was impressed by this attractive midwesterner and awarded him a movie contract at a salary of $200 per week. His film debut was *Love is on the Air* (1937), in which he played the role of a small town radio reporter, just the job he had abandoned in favor of Hollywood. He had taken a risk by giving up a high paying job and a good reputation in the middle of the Depression, and moving west to start over without any assurance of stardom, but his confidence in his abilities seemed justified by a string of minor film successes in the next three years.

In most of his early films Reagan played the role of a good natured and rather innocent young man. Hollywood's own polls showed that he was more popular with women than with men (the opposite of his polls as president), and that he was most popular with teenage girls. His first breakthrough came in *Knute Rockne—All American* (1940), the story of the University of Notre Dame's great football coach. His own role was that of star player George Gipp. His greatest success came the following year in *King's Row*. In this film he played a man whose legs are amputated after a railroad accident. His cry of alarm on discovering what had happened, "Where's the rest of me?" was to become the title of his autobiography, written 25 years later in 1965. The film's success enabled him to renegotiate his contract and turned him into a millionaire.

King's Row came out shortly before the Japanese attack on Pearl Harbor. Reagan entered the army as a junior officer when war was declared, but poor eyesight prevented him from becoming an aviator or combat soldier. The military decided to leave him in Hollywood, where he made propaganda and instructional films. In fact Reagan was afraid of flying, and after a terrifying flight from Los Angeles to Catalina Island in 1937 he avoided flying altogether until late 1960s. Only when his developing political career made it essential did he take to the air once more.

Screen Actors' Guild

After the war, in 1947, Reagan was elected president of the Screen Actors' Guild (SAG), the Hollywood trade union. He served in that position until 1952 and on the Guild's board until 1959—the longest term in the

SAG's history. By 1947, the American wartime alliance with the Communist Soviet Union had broken down and the Cold War had begun. Many Americans, including President Harry S. Truman, suspected that Communist traitors in the United States were threatening national security and a congressional committee, the House Committee on un-American Activities, began searching for Communists or ex-Communists in the government and other prominent areas of American life. Hollywood was one place they investigated, and Reagan, of the same mind, worked to purge the Screen Actors' Guild of all current or former Communists. Several actors and screenwriters had been idealistic Communists in the 1930s, nevertheless it is doubtful that any of them had been Russian spies. If they refused to denounce their old Communist friends they were "blacklisted," denied the chance to work for any of the Hollywood studios. In Reagan's view the threat of Communism was so great that it was necessary to blacklist people. In the eyes of many liberals, however, Reagan showed himself as the enemy of free speech and free expression. From then on he was identified as an outspoken anticommunist, and it was the issue around which he built his political career.

Early Political Moves

Reagan's film career did not blossom as he had expected after *King's Row*. There were various reasons, including the war, a life-threatening attack of pneumonia in 1947, his work for the Guild, and an ugly divorce in 1948. Although he continued to make films into the 1950s (including *Bedtime for Bonzo* in 1951), he switched to what was then the new medium of television. In 1954 he became the host of *General Electric Theater*, a television drama show, and coupled his on-screen duties with tours of General Electric (GE) industrial plants, where he gave inspirational speeches to GE workers. He was a devout believer in honest hard work, private enterprise, minimal government intervention in the economy, and a strong anticommunist foreign policy. These principles formed the basis of "The Speech," an address he gave, with minor variations, all over the country in the late 1950s and early 1960s. GE fired him in 1962 over a conflict of interest controversy, but he was soon back on television as host of another drama show, *Death Valley Days*. By then, however, he was turning his attention from entertainment to politics.

Reagan delivered "The Speech" on television shortly before the presidential election of 1964, in which he supported Republican candidate Barry Goldwater. Goldwater lost that election to Lyndon B. Johnson, but Reagan's speech, which had created a favorable public reaction, was a turning point in his political career. Unlike Goldwater, whose personality seemed abrasive and threatening to many voters, Reagan projected a mood of confident relaxation to offset his tough anticommunist message. Republican strategists offered to turn him into a politician and tested the value of his image by nominating him for Governor of California in 1966 against the incumbent, Democrat Edmund Brown. The Free Speech movement at the University of California, Berkeley, in the fall of 1964 had set off a wave of campus unrest across the state, and the university became one of Reagan's favorite targets. His speeches portrayed the activist students as ungrateful louts and Governor Brown as a patsy unable to deal with them. These themes played well with voters whose taxes supported the state's university system. Brown underestimated the seriousness of Reagan's threat and found to his dismay, on election day, that the actor had outwitted him and won.

Governor of California

Buoyed by this success Governor Reagan risked ordering a dramatic state tax increase in 1967, then worked hard to cut the state's expenses and balance its budget. He also signed a permissive abortion law reform bill, though he would later be closely associated with the anti-abortion movement. He continued his rhetorical war against the university and ordered state troopers onto the Berkeley campus when anti–Vietnam War demonstrations threatened the peace. He supported a strong American role in Vietnam.

Reagan, gaining political confidence rapidly, made his first presidential bid in 1968. Still close to the Goldwater legacy, and not yet experienced as a national campaigner, he was outwitted and easily defeated for the presidential nomination by Richard Nixon at the Republicans' Miami convention. Nixon went on to win the presidency. In 1970 Reagan was reelected California governor, defeating veteran California assemblyman Jesse Unruh. He stood aside from the national campaign in 1972, not challenging the incumbent, Nixon, but he made a serious bid for the nomination in 1976 against Nixon's successor, Gerald Ford. Ford had become president when the Watergate scandal forced Nixon to resign the presidency in 1974, and although he had played no part in that scandal, Ford's connection with Nixon was a serious obstacle to his candidacy. After beating Reagan in the primaries, Ford lost the presidency to Democrat Jimmy Carter that November. Reagan became the Republicans' heir apparent. He campaigned successfully for the Republican nomination in 1980 and defeated President Carter in the November election of that year.

President

During his presidency Reagan set about drastically cutting domestic spending and taxation in the hope of stimulating an economic "supply-side" revolution to lift the nation out of a period of economic stagnation. At the same time he increased defense spending, believing that the Soviet Union, which he named the "Evil Empire" in a foreign policy speech, was as dangerous now as at any time in the long Cold War standoff. Economic recovery made him an attractive candidate for reelection in 1984, and he defeated Walter Mondale in the presidential campaign of that year. During his second term there was less

anticommunist rhetoric because major reforms were taking place in the Soviet Union under the leadership of Mikhail Gorbachev. At the same time, however, Reagan's second administration came under congressional scrutiny when his national security advisers were shown to have illegally traded arms for hostages with Iran, and illegally supported the Contra guerrillas in Nicaragua.

Post-presidential Years

Leaving Washington in January 1989 at the end of his second term, Ronald Reagan retired to his ranch in the hills above Santa Barbara, California. He had often vacationed there during his presidential years, and the estate became known as the "Western White House." Reagan, like all other recent presidents, was eager to establish a presidential library and supervised its construction in nearby Simi Valley. Already in his late seventies when he left Washington, however, he was diagnosed with Alzheimer's disease, which afflicts the memory. He and Nancy Reagan helped publicize the plight of Alzheimer's disease patients in the early and mid-1990s, contributing money to research into corrective medicines and lending their names and influence to organizations concerned with Alzheimer patients' special needs.

The Ronald Reagan Administrations

President Ronald Reagan is best remembered for being more aggressive than his predecessors in confronting the Soviet Union. He built up all departments of the U.S. military and took a hard line on negotiations. At home he cut taxes and government spending in the hope that these changes, the "supply-side revolution," would enhance economic growth. His popularity assured reelection in 1984, but his second administration was hamstrung by congressional investigations into Iran-Contra arms and hostages deals made by his national security advisers.

Reagan Becomes President

The Campaign of 1980

Reagan was one of eight candidates for the Republican nomination in 1980. His leading rivals were John Anderson, George Bush, Howard Baker, and Bob Dole. Reagan was the most conservative of them all and enjoyed the support of the Moral Majority, a political organization of evangelical Christians, led by the Rev-

Administration

Administration Dates

January 20, 1981–January 20, 1985
January 20, 1985–January 20, 1989

Vice President

George Herbert Walker Bush (1981–89)

Cabinet

Secretary of State

Alexander M. Haig Jr. (1981–82)
George P. Shultz (1982–89)

Secretary of the Treasury

Donald T. Regan (1981–85)
James A. Baker III (1985–88)
Nicholas F. Brady (1988–93)

Attorney General

William F. Smith (1981–85)
Edwin Meese III (1985–88)
Richard L. Thornburgh (1988–91)

Secretary of the Interior

James G. Watt (1981–83)
William P. Clark (1983–85)
Donald P. Hodel (1985–89)

Secretary of Agriculture

John R. Block (1981–86)
Richard E. Lyng (1986–89)

Secretary of Labor

Raymond J. Donovan (1981–85)
William E. Brock III (1985–87)
Ann D. McLaughlin (1987–89)

Secretary of Commerce

Malcolm Baldrige (1981–87)
C. William Verity (1987–89)

Secretary of Defense

Caspar W. Weinberger (1981–87)
Frank G. Carlucci (1987–89)

Secretary of Housing and Urban Development

Samuel R. Pierce Jr. (1981–89)

Secretary of Transportation

Andrew L. Lewis Jr. (1981–83)
Elizabeth H. Dole (1983–87)
James H. Burnley IV (1987–89)

Secretary of Energy

James B. Edwards (1981–82)
Donald P. Hodel (1982–85)
John S. Herrington (1985–89)

Secretary of Health and Human Services

Richard S. Schweiker (1981–83)
Margaret M. Heckler (1983–85)
Otis R. Bowen (1985–89)

Secretary of Education

Terrel H. Bell (1981–84)
William J. Bennett (1985–88)
Lauro F. Cavazos (1988–90)

---

erend Jerry Falwell of Lynchburg, Virginia. Moral Majority voters saw in Reagan their best hope for the restoration of prayer in public schools, an end to legalized abortion, and other "pro-family" policies.

Reagan, having secured the necessary delegates in the primaries, was nominated at the convention held in Detroit, Michigan, and chose one of his disappointed rivals, George Bush, as vice-presidential candidate. During the campaign Bush, a more liberal Republican, had called Reagan's policies for economic recovery "voodoo economics" (Berman, p. 77), but from the time of his nomination he became an untiring Reagan loyalist.

Reagan campaigned against President Jimmy Carter. The economy in the Carter years had struggled with a previously unknown combination of rising prices (inflation) and lack of economic growth (stagnation), a combination that economic journalists nicknamed "stagflation." As a result Carter, who was unable to correct the problem, had steadily lost popularity. Two foreign policy crises, the seizure of American embassy personnel in Tehran, Iran, by revolutionary students, and the Soviet invasion of Afghanistan in 1979, had created a temporary surge in his popularity as the nation rallied behind its chief. He tried to make the most of it by adopting a "Rose Garden" strategy, working for reelection by posing as a man too busy with affairs of state to run a traditional campaign. However, Carter's inability to solve either foreign policy crisis and a worsening recession was the end of his hopes. Reagan argued that U.S. citizens

---

were worse off than they had been four years earlier and that Carter's leadership had failed. Skilled in his use of the media, Reagan appeared relaxed and confident throughout the campaign's one televised debate and easily outshone Carter. In the polling he won 51 percent of the popular vote, against 41 percent for Carter. John Anderson, one of his rival Republicans in the primaries, ran an independent presidential campaign that eventually won more than five and a half million votes, but Anderson's liberal Republicanism probably took more votes from Carter's election total than from Reagan's.

Reagan took office on January 20, 1981, at the age of 69, the oldest man to be inaugurated as president. Carter had continued negotiating with the Iranian revolutionaries right up to the last moments of his administration, and an agreement to release the hostages was reached on inauguration day. In a generous gesture, President Reagan appointed the outgoing President Carter as his delegate to meet the freed hostages in Europe.

The Reagans at once drew attention to the style they would bring to Washington with a series of lavish inauguration parties. Forty-three thousand guests were invited to ten separate balls, all of which the Reagans visited during a four hour period. Nancy Reagan at once began extensive renovations of the White House and adjacent buildings, which she regarded as unpardonably shabby.

The Election Campaign of 1984

A strong economic recovery in 1983 and 1984 gave plausibility to claims that Reagan's daring economic policies were paying off. The Republican Party, recognizing its incumbent leader's strengths, made no serious efforts to dislodge him and renominated him and Vice President Bush at their Dallas convention. The Democrats, by contrast, indulged in months of strife during the primaries. The three principal candidates were former vice president Walter Mondale, who had served under President Carter, Colorado senator Gary Hart, and the Reverend Jesse Jackson, a colleague of Martin Luther King Jr. during the civil rights movement. Jackson claimed to speak for the "Rainbow Coalition," comprising people of all colors and varieties of minority status. His breathtaking oratory and charisma, credited to his years of experience as a preacher, earned him a loyal and eager following. However, he scared off voters who were more middle-of-the-road Democrats in the primaries. As a result Mondale won the nomination at the Democrats' San Francisco convention. As a gesture to the constituency Jackson had represented, Mondale took the unprecedented step of choosing a woman as his running mate, Geraldine Ferraro, a congressperson from New York. Ferraro, a new hero to American feminists, began to lose her luster in the later months of the campaign when journalists discovered that her husband, John Zaccaro, had been involved in a succession of unsavory land speculation deals. Ferraro claimed no knowledge of these

events, but that in turn laid her open to charges of naiveté and dented her image as a tough, no-nonsense politician.

In the candidates' first televised debate, Mondale attacked vigorously while Reagan seemed demoralized, and for a moment it seemed a genuine contest might result. But Reagan was in top form for the second and final debate and scored a succession of strong debaters' points. To Mondale's assertion in an October 7, 1984 debate that tax-increases were inevitable, whichever one of them won, Reagan answered that Democrats "see every day as April 15th (when tax returns are due)" but that Republicans "see an America where every day is the fourth of July." Democratic miscues and Reagan's personal and political popularity contributed to making the November 1984 election a lopsided affair, with Reagan winning 59 percent of the popular vote, which translated into an overwhelming 525 of the electoral college's 538 votes. Mondale won only his home state of Minnesota and the District of Columbia.

Reagan's Advisers

Reagan, unlike Carter, delegated authority very well and did not work excessively long hours. He quipped: "It's true that hard work never killed anybody, but I figure why take a chance at this late age" (Cannon, p. 125). Ably advised by a series of White House advisers, Michael Deaver, Edwin Meese III, and James Baker, (and later Donald Regan and Howard Baker), he trusted his cabinet secretaries to run their departments in accordance with his general philosophy. James Baker was a seasoned Washington professional while Meese and Deaver, who had been with Reagan since the early days of his California governorship, understood how he and Mrs. Reagan liked to work. They presented the president with detailed schedules of each day's activities and wrote out one-page summaries of all the issues on which he was required to make decisions or hold meetings. They then trusted him to use his disarming blend of charm and common sense to garner support for their positions.

Like all administrations, Reagan's was full of strong, ambitious personalities, often clashing and feuding. The president's easy going manner, sometimes bordering on passivity, made the feuds more intense because he didn't interfere and Reagan's vagueness introduced an element of uncertainty into them. In their study of Reagan, Gary Paul Gates and Bob Schieffer note that "Reagan's people came to see him more as an abstract idea than as a flesh and blood leader." Budget Director David Stockman wrote that "His conservative vision was only a vision. He had a sense of ultimate values and a feel for long term directions, but he had no blueprint for radical governance" (Schieffer and Gates, p. 89).

Personality clashes obliged Reagan to change several of his Cabinet secretaries. For example, Secretary of State Alexander Haig, who came highly recommended by former presidents Nixon and Ford, and had worked under former Secretary of State Henry Kissinger, proved to be awkward and uncompromising in his relations with the rest of the White House staff. Hard-working and dedicated, he was also considered egotistical, insensitive, and too eager to resort to arms in foreign policy crises. Early on he reacted to news of Cuban aid to Communist rebels in Latin America by declaring "Give me the word and I'll make that island a ... parking lot" (Cannon, p. 196). His reaction to the assassination attempt on Reagan, soon afterwards, was to seize the microphone from press spokesman Larry Speakes in the middle of a press briefing, and declare "I'm in control here!" In mid-1982, during a dispute over a crisis in Lebanon, Reagan accepted one of Haig's many threats to resign, and replaced him with the more even-tempered and equally experienced George Shultz.

Reagan employed fiery conservative speechwriters, notably Patrick Buchanan and Peggy Noonan, to craft speeches that would reassure his conservative supporters that his ideological resolve was strong. When it came to delivering speeches written by these and other professional speechwriters, Reagan rehearsed carefully and outshone all his recent predecessors. Press conferences were another story, however, and he gave fewer of them as his two administrations progressed, since thinking on his feet was not his strong suit.

There were several embarrassing incidents that might have fatally weakened a less popular leader. In 1985, for example, shortly after his second inauguration, Reagan, on a visit to Europe, visited Bitburg, a German war cemetery, and laid a wreath there, even though the cemetery contained the graves of 49 of Hitler's fanatical SS soldiers. The visit was a major diplomatic blunder but caused no lasting damage. On another occasion he told Israeli premier Menachem Begin that he had been present at the liberation of Nazi death camps in the last days of World War II (1939–1945). Begin, impressed by the story, repeated it to the Knesset (Israeli parliament), only to learn later that it was a pure fabrication.

Reagan and Congress

Reagan was in office during the 97th, 98th, 99th, and 100th congresses. Republicans riding Reagan's coattails made gains in the congressional elections of 1980 and won the Senate majority for the first time in 26 years, but the House of Representatives retained a Democratic majority. Reagan recognized that he would have to work with them, and find ways to win Democrats over to his policy initiatives. He was able to cultivate a group of southern Democrats, nicknamed the "Boll Weevils," after the pests whose larvae are born in cotton bolls and burrow from within to destroy the crop. Despite their party allegiance, their conservative constituents made them sympathetic to Reagan's policy agenda. For the first six

years of his administration his personal popularity made all Democrats wary of thwarting his pet projects, lest they lose the support of their own districts. The Republicans retained control of the Senate in the midterm election of 1982 and the presidential election of 1984. Reagan's relations with Congress were generally cordial, at least outwardly. He enjoyed enthusiastic ovations when he came to Capitol Hill to deliver his annual State of the Union addresses.

Both houses in the 100th Congress, unlike the preceding ones, were dominated by the Democrats, who were able to push through long-deferred legislation of the kind Reagan and his ideological followers disliked. They allocated more federal money to education, food stamps, health care, mass transit, and aid to the homeless. This Congress also passed major welfare reform bills in 1988. By then Reagan's administration was mired in scandals that had cut into his popularity. Hampered by the Iran-Contra investigation he also found it more difficult to impede the congressional Democrats' passage of their bills. Even then, however, loyal congressional Republicans fought for him during the Iran-Contra investigation and prevented it from damaging his reputation directly.

Reagan and the Judiciary

Reagan, like most of his fellow conservatives, was annoyed by the Supreme Court's activism in the 1960s and 1970s. Ever since the Court's decision in *Brown v. Board of Education of Topeka, Kansas* in 1954, which desegregated public schools, the Court had made precedent-breaking decisions that angered conservatives, such as the elimination of prayer and Bible reading in schools, the creation of a Constitutional right to privacy, and the decision (*Roe v. Wade*, 1973) that abortion, at least in the first three months of pregnancy, was constitutionally protected under this privacy doctrine. Conservative jurists and legal scholars were critical of judicial activism. They favored judicial restraint, by which the justices confined themselves to deciding cases strictly according to the Constitution, the written law, and precedent.

Reagan, hoping to end this era of judicial activism, had three opportunities to change the composition of the Court. His first, and most noteworthy nominee, was the first woman ever to serve, Sandra Day O'Connor, an Arizona judge and former state senator. She was appointed in September 1981. He had promised during the 1980 campaign to appoint a woman, and now he made good on that promise (even though the number of women he appointed to federal judgeships overall was under 10 percent, while over 20 percent of President Carter's appointments were women). When Chief Justice Warren Burger resigned in 1986 Reagan promoted William Rehnquist, already a Supreme Court justice, and reputedly the most conservative of the justices, to the position of chief justice. At the same time he nominated Antonin Scalia, another conservative, to the empty seat, and both these nominees won congressional approval.

Reagan's final opportunity to make an appointment came in the summer of 1987 when Justice Lewis Powell announced his resignation. Reagan's nominee, Robert Bork, was already a federal judge in the District of Columbia and an outspoken political conservative, who had a distinguished but controversial record of legal teaching and scholarship at Yale Law School. Bork believed that the Court should consider the "original intent" of the founding fathers when making their decisions in constitutional law cases. If they did so, he implied, they would never have "found" new constitutional rights, such as the right to privacy that had played a key role in *Roe v. Wade*.

It was Bork's misfortune to be nominated at a time when President Reagan's reputation was in decline, and congressional Democrats were strong enough to thwart him for the first time in seven years. First the Senate's Judiciary Committee and then the whole of the Senate rejected Bork. Reagan had no better luck with his second nominee, Douglas Ginsburg, when background checks showed that he had broken the law by smoking marijuana, first as a student and later as a Harvard Law School professor. After these two embarrassments, he was finally able to win confirmation for his third choice, the quiet and scholarly Anthony Kennedy, a Californian whose personal life appeared to be spotless, and who joined the Court with the Senate's approval in February 1988. Ironically, judicial restraint, because it meant upholding the laws and adhering to precedents, actually worked in favor of maintaining legal abortion and maintaining the ban on school prayer. The justices, unwilling to tamper further with precedents, upheld even those precedents for which they had no personal liking and would not have approved in the first place. Kennedy, and Reagan's other nominees, did not carry out the judicial counterrevolution his strongest supporters had anticipated.

Changes in the U.S. Government

During his campaign, Reagan proposed eliminating much of the federal bureaucracy and simplifying government. He found it very difficult to do so in practice because of bureaucratic inertia, the tendency for organizations to carry on working in the same way once a routine is established, and to resist efforts at reform from outside. Reducing bureaucracy proved difficult also because of the intensity with which groups of federal employees who felt threatened pulled strings and called in political favors to retain their positions. Although he had called for the abolition of both the Department of Education and the Department of Energy, strong opposition from Republicans and Democrats prevented Reagan from carrying out this plan. Reagan even added a

What They Said . . .

"If we look to the answer as to why for so many years we achieved so much, prospered as no other people on earth, it was because here in this land we unleashed the energy and individual genius of man to a greater extent than has ever been done before. Freedom and the dignity of the individual have been more available and assured here than in any other place on earth. . . . It is no coincidence that our present troubles parallel and are proportionate to the intervention and intrusion in our lives that result from unnecessary and excessive growth of government."

Ronald Reagan's first inaugural address, as quoted in *Reagan as President,* January 20, 1981.

new department, the Department of Veterans' Affairs, in response to fierce lobbying. Far from making his department disappear, the first secretary of education, Terrell Bell, produced an influential report, *A Nation at Risk* (1983), which many conservatives hailed as a straightforward account of current deficiencies in schooling, and of necessary reforms. When Bell retired early in Reagan's second administration a more influential conservative, William Bennett, took his place and the department's continuity was assured.

Reagan periodically appointed commissions to study particular issues. For example the Kissinger Commission of 1983–84 was a bipartisan group (six Democrats and six Republicans) set up to study U.S. policy towards Central America. It was chaired by former president Nixon's secretary of state, Henry Kissinger, who was by now one of the grand old men of the Republican Party. In early 1984 the commission recommended a mixture of incentives and threats to help Central American development and prevent Communist victories. In practice, however, Reagan failed to follow its recommendations, and his own wayward policy in the region (secretly funding Nicaraguan Contra guerrillas against an explicit congressional ban) marred his second administration.

Another special commission of 1983 declared that the United States government had committed a "grave injustice" in interning Japanese American citizens in concentration camps during World War II. That report led to a congressional grant of about $20,000 to each surviving internee, along with an official apology.

Domestic Issues

Reagan's principal interest in domestic policy was to decrease federal taxes and federal regulation of the economy, believing that a freer economic environment would stimulate investment, productivity, and economic growth. He made some headway with these economic reforms, especially when, in the first year of his presidency, he won a great deal of political goodwill by surviving an assassination attempt. A tight monetary policy brought inflation down from its high Carter-era levels, and then in 1985 the collapse of the Organization of Petroleum Exporting Countries (OPEC) price controls brought a sudden reduction in world oil prices. OPEC was formed in the 1960s to coordinate the petroleum policies of its members. It had succeeded for the previous 12 years in limiting the supply of oil coming into the world market, causing its price to rise. Political disputes among its members ended this era of regulation, and as more oil became available, prices fell. That in turn helped restrain inflation further, since transport costs are a major component of market prices for nearly everything. The Reagan years witnessed sustained economic growth, though the severe stock market fall of 1987 dampened market euphoria.

Despite its anti-big-government rhetoric, the Reagan administration was unable to shift policy in many areas of government, where bureaucratic inertia proved too strong. The number of federal employees actually grew, despite the president's efforts, and federal expenditures continued to rise because of a massive military buildup. Reagan was also committed to "pro-family" legislation, to prohibit abortion and pornography, to bring back school prayer, and to encourage public decency. But to the bitter disappointment of pro-life groups there was no change in the legal status of abortion. Reagan's advisers warned him that the issue would do more harm than good to his reputation because opinions about abortion did not follow party lines—there were plenty of Democrats against abortion and Republicans who supported the right to choose. He published a book on the subject, *Abortion and the Conscience of the Nation* (1984), but the law remained unchanged. Neither was the administration able to halt cross-district busing of schoolchildren as an effort to achieve racially balanced schools which had caused political friction through the 1970s, and against which he had campaigned.

Economy

Reagan believed that his economic policies, if enacted, would achieve a balanced budget and a reduction of the federal deficit. The "supply side" principles from which he and budget director David Stockman worked were based on the work of economist Arthur Laffer. They included the idea that a lighter tax burden would free up more money for investment. That in turn would increase productivity and stimulate economic growth,

with the result that the government would actually be able to gather more tax revenue, even though the rate had been lowered. U.S. senator Howard Baker (R-TN), who later became Reagan's chief of staff, described the plan as a "riverboat gamble" but helped make sure it passed the Senate. Like Reagan he understood that tax cuts for individuals and corporations were very popular among the voters.

Assassination Attempt

Reagan was shot and seriously injured on March 30, 1981, by John Hinckley Jr., a deranged young man who was trying to win the attention of movie actress Jodie Foster. Reagan was rushed to the hospital, and to most people's amusement and admiration, joked with the doctors and nurses: "I hope you're all Republicans," before they operated to remove a bullet that had punctured his lung and lodged just an inch from his heart. Emerging from the hospital on April 11, apparently well on the way to recovery, he made an emotional State of the Union address to Congress, which soon afterwards welcomed his return and, in effect, extended the traditional new president's "honeymoon" by passing his first tax reform bill.

Gramm-Rudman-Hollings Act

High expenditures and reduced tax revenues at first made it seem that the government was heading for catastrophe. By the time of the 1984 election, the annual federal budget deficit had ballooned to $200 billion and was causing concern throughout Washington. Reagan remained confident that economic recovery would take care of the deficit, however, and did not make his 1984 rival Walter Mondale's mistake of insisting to the voters that if elected he would raise taxes.

The deficit rose to $226 billion in 1985, prompting a bipartisan deficit reduction plan in Congress, the Gramm-Rudman-Hollings Act. According to Gramm-Rudman, if budget planners could not balance the figures, automatic spending reductions would kick in, and the deficit would dwindle down to a balance point in 1991. The attraction of this act to lawmakers was that no particular congressperson would be held responsible for making cuts, an action that always angered the section of the electorate most directly affected. The first version of the act was declared unconstitutional by the Supreme Court, however, because it violated the separation of legislative and executive powers. A revised, weaker version made it unlikely that an actual balanced budget could be achieved in the foreseeable future. When Reagan left office in early 1989 the national debt, which he had inherited at $834 billion, had risen to $2.3 trillion and the deficit was still running at $160 billion per year.

Tax Reform Act

Treasury Secretary Donald Regan, a multimillionaire and former head of the brokerage house Merrill-

Lynch, worked out a tax-reform bill intended to streamline the Internal Revenue Service (IRS), by reducing tax rates and the number of tax brackets. He and White House Chief of Staff James Baker exchanged jobs at the beginning of Reagan's second term of office, enabling Regan to advise the president as the legislation was guided through Congress. It was eventually embodied in law as one of the Reagan administration's lasting legislative achievements. Regan had told the president that tax reform was vital, if only to close the loopholes enjoyed by the rich. "The tax system we have now is designed to make the avoidance of taxes easy for the rich and has the effect of making it almost impossible for people who work for wages and salaries to do the same" (Cannon, p. 566). Congressional Democrats favored tax reform too, especially the section that exempted the poor from income tax and closed loopholes for the rich. Bipartisan support (after much bickering over the details) assured the law's passage through Congress in 1986. In its final form, the act reduced the maximum tax rate on personal incomes to 28 percent (down from 50 percent) and reduced the maximum rate on businesses from 48 to 34 percent.

Business and Labor

Businesses benefited during the Reagan years from a relaxation in federal regulation—the Occupational Health and Safety Administration (OSHA), for example, prosecuted safety violators far less often and levied smaller fines than it had in the 1970s. Reagan and his appointees insisted that they were not protecting the rich against the poor (as their opponents alleged) but helping to stimulate more economic activity, whose benefits would "trickle down" to the whole population. The Department of Commerce's antitrust division was particularly reluctant to prosecute violators of the antimonopoly laws with the result that the 1980s saw a long succession of mergers and takeovers in oil, steel, airlines, banking, and other primary areas of the economy.

The Savings and Loans Crash

Deregulation of banking and savings and loan institutions (S & Ls) also led to a rash of lucrative but risky investments that had been sheltered by federal government insurance plans. For a while the bankers and investors thrived, but a dip in housing values led to widespread bankruptcy among S & Ls after 1986. The damage to ordinary investors was so widespread that Congress voted to bail out the S & Ls, which meant, in reality, transferring the cost of the failures to ordinary taxpayers—a total cost estimated in the hundreds of billions of dollars. Anyone who had invested in a S & L that went bankrupt was assured of recovering his or her investment because the federal government had backed them and could cover the losses through general tax revenues. This policy meant that lower income members of the middle class were often subsidizing the failed investments of higher income members (those more likely to have

invested in the first place), with obvious inequitable consequences.

PATCO Strike

Meanwhile, the position of American trade unions weakened steadily, partly because a severe economic recession had raised the unemployment rate to 11 percent in 1980 and left nearly twelve million workers searching for jobs. In 1981 the Professional Air Traffic Controllers' Union (PATCO) called a strike for higher wages and better working conditions; they feared that overwork diminished air safety. The strike threatened to bring civil aviation to a standstill throughout the nation. Reagan retaliated by firing all 12 thousand members of the union, replacing them temporarily with military air traffic controllers, and then hiring and training new recruits. He and the Federal Aviation Administration (FAA) refused to rehire any of the strikers, and this hard-line action sent a shudder of alarm through U.S. trade unions.

Throughout the 1980s trade unions' positions became weaker as the National Labor Relations Board (NLRB) showed little zeal on their behalf and the courts often interpreted contract disputes against them and in favor of employers. Lane Kirkland, president of the AFL-CIO, remarked in 1983 that the administration appeared to be seeking economic recovery by "dismantling the federal government until it is left with no function but to raise armies and coddle big business" (Dallek, p. 101).

Black Monday

Years of favorable economic conditions set off a speculative boom. Deregulated businesses and banks, less troubled by federal supervision than they had been for half a century, began reckless overexpansion and the stock market rose in 1986 and 1987 to new highs. On August 17, 1987, the Dow Jones Industrial Average (DJIA) closed at above 2,700 for the first time ever. A few analysts warned that share prices were unrealistically high, and that investments were not secure, but the investment frenzy remained high. In October 1987 the bubble burst and share prices began to fall catastrophically, first on Japanese markets, then in Europe, and finally in America. For a time on October 19, 1987, everyone wanted to sell and it was impossible to find buyers—the Dow Jones fell 508 points that day. Thousands of investors were ruined, and banks were swamped by demands that could not be met, and consequently were forced into bankruptcy. Part of the problem was caused by computer systems which had been designed to trigger "sell" messages if particular share prices dropped below a certain limit. In the ordinary to and fro of a stable market such systems make sense, but when all prices were falling they had the effect of worsening the crisis by pitching millions more shares onto an already flooded market and driving prices even further down.

The Federal Reserve Board decided it must step in to prevent a catastrophe like the Wall Street crash of

Fast Fact

Family income for the richest one-fifth of the population increased by 11.1 percent between 1979 and 1987. The number of millionaires doubled during the decade (of the 1980s), and the number of billionaires grew from thirteen to fifty one.

(Source: James Roark, et al. *American Promise,* 1998.)

1929, and it began buying government securities and trying to reestablish business confidence. President Reagan was slow to realize the seriousness of the situation and seemed unsure of how to respond. Journalists and congressional Democrats compared him to Herbert Hoover, the president in 1929 who had seemed like a hero during boom times but became the scapegoat of the Great Depression. *Washington Post* journalist Haynes Johnson wrote later: "Reagan's reputation suffered grievously during the days of the crisis. Even many of his strongest supporters had come to accept the popular picture of him as a president not in charge created during the Iran-Contra affair. His actions during and immediately after the market's near disintegration reinforced those impressions" (Johnson, p. 385).

Environment

Reagan's first secretary of the interior, James Gaius Watt, was a controversial choice from the start. A Colorado attorney already notorious for his aversion to environmentalists, Watt faced continuous opposition from environmental organizations. These organizations had gained in popularity and power through the 1970s and become permanent parts of the Washington scene. They now threw their weight against Watt's pro-business policies, depicting him as an anti-environmental extremist and a lackey of big corporations.

Interior Department Controversies

Watt believed that the United States ought to be self-sufficient in energy so that it would not need to depend on oil supplies from the Middle East. He therefore approved exploratory drilling permits for oil and coal in national wilderness areas, described the moderate members of the National Wildlife Federation and the Audobon Society as a "chanting mob," and declared his intention

to "mine more, drill more, cut more timber" (Cannon, p. 531). His blunt approach aroused intense opposition, with the result that the environmental organizations' membership lists swelled during his tenure. Among the beneficiaries were the Sierra Club, the Environmental Defense Fund, the Wilderness Society, and the Friends of the Earth. Their lawyers were able to block several of Watt's proposed drilling permits in court, and they were successful in lobbying even Republican congresspeople to oppose Watt's threatened assault on the national parks, forests, and wilderness areas.

EPA and Superfund

Watt's choice for Environmental Protection Agency (EPA) administrator, Anne Gorsuch, was controversial. She could be effective when she perceived a genuine environmental risk. For instance, she moved quickly to evacuate the Missouri town of Times Beach when it was shown to be polluted with high levels of toxic dioxin in 1983. More often, however, she seemed reluctant to do her job. She and her adviser Rita Lavelle, who had previously worked in the private sector on behalf of industrialists, made "sweetheart" deals with companies accused of polluting the environment. Meeting the executives whose companies were under investigation, at lavish Washington restaurants rather than in their offices, they would give the companies lenient schedules for fulfillment of toxic waste cleanups to ease the corporations' ability to comply. Both women were forced to resign under threat of prosecution in 1983 when they refused to hand over to Congress documents dealing with these arrangements. The General Accounting Office had identified 378,000 toxic waste sites in need of clean up by 1980, but lack of political will and bargaining with owners meant that only six of them had been cleaned up by 1985.

Watt too was obliged to step down after telling an off-color joke that lampooned the principle of diversity in government commissions. Later secretaries of the interior, William Clark, and Donald Hodel, were much more conciliatory, and tried to repair the public relations damage Watt had caused. Even so, when George Bush ran for president in 1988, he carefully dissociated himself from Reagan's environmental record and said that, if elected, he would chart new territory as the first "environmental president."

Immigration Reform and Control Act

Throughout the 1960s and 1970s growing numbers of illegal immigrants had been coming to the United States, chiefly from Mexico and other parts of Latin America, but also from southeast Asia in the aftermath of the Vietnam War (1959–75). They were lured by high wages in the United States and freedom from poverty and persecution. They usually held the worst jobs and lacked Social Security benefits and job security. Some were blackmailed by unscrupulous employers who threatened to turn them in to the Immigration and Naturalization Service (INS). The important Immigration Reform and Control Act, passed in 1986 by Congress and signed by the president, made it illegal for employers to hire foreigners who could not prove that they were legal immigrants. This provision had the effect of ending the blackmail and preventing illegal immigrants from taking priority in jobs over legal citizens. At the same time, knowing that hundreds of thousands of illegal immigrants were struggling to build a decent life for themselves in the United States, the act offered an amnesty to all illegal immigrants who could prove that they had already been in the United States since before 1982. An astonishingly high two million illegal immigrants took advantage of the amnesty clause and registered— the first step on their road to legal immigration and citizenship.

Administration Upheaval

On several occasions Reagan's appointees had to resign under threat of prosecution. Reagan himself appears to have been above the financial temptations of power (he had been a rich man for more than 30 years by 1980). Many of those around him, by contrast, went to prison for insider dealing, cronyism, and related actions that crossed the border of legality—six senior appointees were jailed in his first administration alone. For example, Paul Thayer, a deputy secretary of defense, was sentenced to four years for insider trading. Rita Lavelle, head of the EPA's Superfund program, was jailed for contempt of Congress when she refused to turn over documents that, allegedly, would have shown her making "sweetheart" deals with corporations accused of pollution. Even Reagan's second term attorney general Edwin Meese got into legal trouble for his connection to the Wedtech Corporation, a defense contractor, which enjoyed favorable patronage arrangements with the federal government. The head of the Department of Justice, Meese, was forced into the humiliating situation of having to appoint an independent counsel to investigate himself. Based on the findings of the independent counsel, he resigned under a cloud of suspicion in the summer of 1988.

Numerous Reagan officials got into legal trouble soon after leaving the president's service, too. Michael Deaver, Reagan's deputy chief of staff and assistant, left the administration at the beginning of Reagan's second term. He at once set up a lobbying business in Washington, D.C., which won lucrative business from clients who knew that Deaver was a personal friend of the president and had good personal access to him. Federal law made lobbying by recent administration employees illegal. A special prosecutor investigated Deaver's business, he lied under oath, and he was tried and convicted of perjury. As Reagan's biographer Garry Wills recounts, "Twenty five high officials were fired, resigned, or had their nominations withdrawn for allegations of financial misconduct or lax standards. There were famous resig-

nations (Raymond Donovan, Rita Lavelle, Max Hugel, Richard Allen, J. Lynn Helms), and many quieter withdrawals, many cases where the interplay of interests brought no punitive action, or penitence" (Wills, pp. 304–5). Through it all Reagan retained his belief in the selflessness of businesspeople and their commitment to the national interest. Despite the fervent efforts of his political and media opponents, none of the mud they threw at Reagan during these scandals seemed to stick to him, and journalists began to repeat Colorado Representative Patricia Schroeder's witticism that Reagan was the "Teflon President."

Foreign Issues

President Reagan had the same anticommunist passion in the 1980s that had been common in the late 1940s and early 1950s, the pre-Vietnam War days of the Cold War. Determined to face down the Soviet Union, he undertook an ambitious defense program, expanding the navy, updating weapons systems, and developing ambitious new ones, in the hope of gaining the strategic advantage. Fear of Communist advance influenced his policy towards Latin American policy too, where he supported all anticommunist regimes, even if they were authoritarian, and opposed all regimes that accepted Soviet or Cuban aid. Like his predecessors he found it difficult to make the Middle East fit into this ideological framework, but like them he too was forced to engage in Middle East maneuvering because of the worldwide importance of the area's oil supplies.

Soviet Relations

The centerpiece of President Reagan's foreign policy was militant anticommunism. The détente policies (aimed at lessening tensions between the two countries) of the Nixon, Ford, and Carter administrations, and the growing antinuclear movement in the United States and Europe, had led some analysts to regard the sharp antagonism of the early Cold War era, the 1950s, as a thing of the past. President Nixon had signed the first Strategic Arms Limitation Treaty (SALT I) back in 1972 and President Jimmy Carter's negotiators had signed a SALT II agreement with the Soviets by 1978 (though anger at the Soviet invasion of Afghanistan in early 1979 had prevented it from being ratified by the Senate). Reagan and his foreign policy advisers, including Alexander Haig (secretary of state), Jeanne Kirkpatrick (ambassador to the United Nations), and Casper Weinberger (secretary of defense), regarded the Soviet Union under Leonid Brezhnev as no less dangerous than it had been under Joseph Stalin 30 years earlier, and they were less conciliatory than their predecessors. They pointed to Soviet persecution of Jews and dissenters at home, to Soviet warfare in Afghanistan, and to a dramatic Soviet military and naval buildup during the 1970s.

The Soviet Union remained Reagan's chief source of concern. After the Afghan invasion in 1979 President Carter had begun to increase military spending, and Reagan now accelerated it further, deploying a new generation of nuclear missiles—Pershing II—moving the B1 Bomber and the MX missile system from prototype to full production, and creating a Rapid Deployment Force for actions in the Arabian Gulf. He even took the remaining U.S. battleships out of mothballs. Battleships are not much use for combat missions in an era of long-range guided missiles and nuclear submarines, but Reagan and his defense advisers believed that their symbolic power as monarchs of the ocean outweighed their impracticality. The mere fact of them putting to sea would send a message of American military resolve to the Soviets.

Strategic Defense Initiative

The most dramatic of Reagan's anti-Soviet policies, however, was the Strategic Defense Initiative (SDI), a planned series of satellite-based defense systems, designed to intercept and destroy Soviet nuclear weapons fired against American targets. Democratic and press critics of the plan, who pointed to its technological shortcomings and its staggering cost in research, development, and deployment, gave it the derisive nickname of "Star Wars," after the popular science-fiction movie series. The explosion of the space shuttle *Challenger* on January 28, 1986, soon after take off, with the death of its seven-member crew, underlined critics' doubts about the possibility of a fail-safe, space-based program.

Soviet premier Leonid Brezhnev died in 1982, but Reagan's opinion of his successor, Yuri Andropov, was that he was a man in the same mold, uncompromising in his ambitions for Soviet expansion and dedicated to ultimate Communist conquest of the world. Reagan's fears seemed ominously justified in September 1983 when a Korean airliner that had accidentally strayed over Soviet airspace was shot down by Russian missiles, killing all 269 people on board including 60 Americans. Unapologetic, the Soviets claimed that the unarmed Boeing 747 had been on an American espionage mission.

Arms Control Negotiations

In 1984, however, Soviet Premier Yuri Andropov also died as did his successor Constantin Chernenko a year later. The next Soviet chief, Mikhail Gorbachev, really did appear to be a new kind of leader. His stated policies of glasnost (openness) and perestroika (economic reform) were accompanied by a relaxation of internal persecution and an effort to reduce the arms race of the early 1980s. Reagan and his fellow conservatives were suspicious at first and doubted that any genuine change was taking place in Russia. Central to their outlook throughout the Cold War era had been the idea that the Soviets, although they might temporize and conciliate at times, ultimately wanted to gain power over the United States. By contrast, Gorbachev gained a highly favorable reception from most Americans for breaking

out of the traditional Soviet mold of repression and persecution. Reagan began to soften in his view of the new leader, and the two men met at Geneva in late 1985. Secure in the knowledge of the United States's growing military might, Reagan expressed a willingness to negotiate arms reduction talks.

At a second, hastily arranged meeting in Reykjavik, Iceland, in October 1986, Reagan dismayed many of his closest advisers by appearing to agree to a complete phasing out of nuclear weapons over the next decade. Reagan's advisers were opposed to such a treaty, because U.S. defense policy depended on a nuclear strike capability to counteract the Soviet Union's advantages in conventional weapons. They felt that the Senate would reject any treaty that eliminated this capability, and would suggest that the president did not really understand the issues and their wider implications. In the end Reagan's refusal to eliminate SDI as part of the treaty proved to be unacceptable to the Soviet Union, and the conference ended with no new agreement.

Reagan and Gorbachev did achieve a more realistic agreement on the control of intermediate-range nuclear forces (the INF treaty) in November 1987, after careful planning and preparation, and began discussing a strategic arms reduction treaty (START) later in the same year. When Gorbachev visited the United States in December 1987 to sign the INF treaty he found he was a popular hero, cheered by appreciative crowds for taking real steps to thaw the Cold War. The following summer Reagan returned the favor by visiting Moscow and making a conciliatory speech at Moscow State University.

By the time he left office in January 1989, Reagan had shifted the emphasis of his foreign policy. He had come to believe that Gorbachev was sincere, that the Russian armies were withdrawing from Afghanistan, that arms reduction was a real possibility, and that what he had earlier called the "Evil Empire" really was capable of internal change. He also believed, nevertheless, that these changes had come about because the intensified threat from the United States had overpowered the rickety Soviet economy's ability to compete. His conclusion, one shared by his friends and supporters, was that his arms buildup of the early and mid 1980s had, in effect, won the Cold War.

Central and South America

The United States, as senior member of the Organization of American States (OAS), organized in 1948 to promote Latin American economic development, sought good relations with its neighbors in the Western Hemisphere, but generally on its own terms. President Reagan and his advisers looked at affairs throughout the Americas as a reflection of the Cold War conflict with Communism, and reacted sharply against perceived Communist influence in Grenada, El Salvador, and Nicaragua. Congress took a more nuanced view, recognizing that the issue in Latin America was more often a conflict between

Biography:

Mikhail Sergeevich Gorbachev

President (b. 1931) On Christmas Day 1991, Mikhail Sergeevich Gorbachev resigned his political office and signified the formal end of the Union of Soviet Socialist Republics (USSR). Gorbachev's thirty-two year ascent to the highest office in the Communist Party was steady from the time of Joseph Stalin's death in 1953 to the time he took power in March of 1985. He launched energetic campaigns to improve economic productivity among the working class and to "wake up" sleeping bureaucrats. He made personal and direct contact with people on the streets and in the factories. He charmed world leaders with his charismatic personality and met with U.S. President Ronald Reagan the same year he came to power. In 1988, while on a visit to New York City, Gorbachev made a demonstration of reduced tensions between the two superpowers when he broke rank to enter a crowd of spectators to shake hands. President Reagan contin-

ued relations with two consecutive visits to Moscow in May and June of the same year. Not surprisingly, it was Gorbachev's light-handed treatment of his own Soviet states and the hard economic times that were so slow in healing, that eventually resulted in widespread uprising

and various states eventually seceding from the USSR. Critics claim Gorbachev's failure to end strife among the more than 100 different ethnic groups is the underlying cause of the breakup of the Soviet Union. Regardless of opinion, history will irrevocably link Gorbachev with the end of communism and the Cold War.

---

wealthy oligarchies and poor peasants. It was reluctant to fund anticommunist wars in the region, but when it prohibited Reagan from sending military aid to the Nicaraguan Contras, fighting the pro-Soviet Sandinistas in that country, Reagan encouraged, or at least permitted, his advisers to do so secretly. One inter-American conflict with no apparent Cold War relevance was the war between Argentina and Britain over the south Atlantic's Falkland Islands. In that instance the United States backed the successful campaign of its North Atlantic Treaty Organization (NATO) ally Britain to retake the islands.

The countries of Central America were sources of continual concern to President Reagan's administration. The corrupt but pro-American regime of Anastasio Somoza in Nicaragua had been overthrown in 1979, and its place taken by the left wing Sandinista regime of Manuel Ortega, whom Reagan perceived as pro-Soviet and anti-American. Against the Sandinistas he was eager to aid the Contras, a group made up partly of former Somoza supporters and partly of other anticommunist groups. In neighboring El Salvador, meanwhile, a repressive but pro-American government was under attack by left wing guerrillas. Congress was willing to send helicopters, guns, and advisers to the government of El Salvador and humanitarian aid to the Contras, but not troops. Members of Congress feared that Nicaragua and El Salvador might easily prove to be Vietnam-style quagmires, easy to enter but difficult to leave, and more complicated than Reagan's polarized anticommunist views admitted. The congressional Boland Amendment expressly pro-

hibited U.S. military aid to the Contras. President Reagan, using the Central Intelligence Agency (CIA), covertly channeled supplies to them anyway.

The 1983 Invasion of Grenada

A principle of anticommunist politics that Reagan had learned in the 1950s was the need to stop Communism while it was weak and far away rather than letting it spread and move closer to the United States. (This is sometimes called the Domino Theory.) Despite the memory of Vietnam, which had given many policymakers second thoughts about this principle, Reagan acted on it by authorizing a U.S. invasion of the Caribbean island of Grenada in October 1983. There had been a left wing coup on the island (formerly a British colony) and there was evidence that Cuban workers were arriving to build an airfield that could accommodate modern military aircraft. The administration feared that it might become a base for Soviet or Cuban spy planes. Intervening ostensibly to safeguard American medical students on the island, Reagan's real purpose was to ensure that Grenada would be politically neutralized and that other pro-Soviet or pro-Cuban regimes in the area would be warned of American willingness to intervene against them.

The Falkland Islands War

When Communism was the enemy President Reagan's cabinet members were united, but over conflicts without a Communist aspect they were divided, as they showed during the Falkland Islands War of 1982. The

---

Fast Fact

The national debt rose from under $500 billion in 1974 to almost $3 trillion ($3,000,000,000,000) in 1989.

(Source: James Roark, et al. *American Promise,* 1998.)

Falklands, off the east coast of South America, was one of the world's few remaining British colonies, but was also claimed by Argentina. An unpopular Argentinian dictator seized the islands in April 1982, in the hope of gaining popularity at home and international recognition for what he called the Islas Malvinas. The British government, under its powerful prime minister Margaret Thatcher, sent an expeditionary force to regain the islands and presented the American government with a dilemma. On the one hand, Argentina was a key member of the Organization of American States (OAS). The tradition of the Monroe Doctrine dictated an anti-European, anti-colonial policy—one favored by UN Ambassador Jeanne Kirkpatrick. On the other hand, Britain was the United States's most loyal partner in NATO, an anchor of the western anti-Soviet alliance, and Reagan often expressed his admiration and friendship for Thatcher. British and U.S. armies, navies, and air forces trained regularly together and had been allies in the century's two world wars. These Anglo-Saxon ties—strongly supported by the secretaries of defense and state, Weinberger and Haig—proved more durable. Reagan himself was steadily pro-British and in June 1982 became the first U.S. president to address a combined session of the Houses of Commons and the Lords in London. As the war progressed, U.S. satellites kept the British ships well informed about enemy movements and the weather, and U.S. tankers refueled them, prior to their successful campaign to retake the islands.

The Middle East

The politically volatile Middle East, source of much of the world's oil supply, caused President Reagan's foreign policy staff perpetual anxiety. The Camp David treaty between Egypt and Israel, signed in 1978, had peacefully resolved one conflict in the area but left many others unresolved, including the revival of revolutionary Islamic fundamentalism in Iran; the aggressive dictatorships of Saddam Hussein in Iraq and Muammar Qaddafi in Libya; chronic civil war in Lebanon; displaced Palestinian refugees in Lebanon, Syria, and Jordan; and the immense wealth and power of the oil-producing Arabian Gulf states.

Iran and Iraq

Iran remained a thorn in the United States's side throughout the two Reagan administrations. The Ayatollah Khomeini, Iran's revolutionary Moslem ruler, was fanatically anti-American. After securing his revolution at home, Khomeini plunged Iran into a brutal war against its western neighbor Iraq in 1980, a war as catastrophic in the region as World War I (1914–18) had been in Western Europe. Like its predecessor, it saw immense armies mired in static trench warfare and dreadful casualty rates on both sides, with little possibility of strategic gain for either. Reagan's first impulse was to arm and support the Iraqis. Fortunately he didn't because in the 1990s the United States found itself embroiled in direct conflict with Iraq. The Iraq-Iran war imperiled shipping in the Arabian Gulf and in mid-1987 Reagan sent a navy task force to the Gulf to protect Kuwait's oil tankers from the forces of both sides.

Lebanon

President Reagan intervened in Lebanon when Israeli forces invaded it and attacked Palestinian camps in 1982. The Israelis were retaliating against attacks by Palestinian terrorists on northern Israel. Lebanon had been in a state of recurrent civil war since the mid-1970s and was riven by political and religious factions, internal strife, and overbearing neighbors like Israel and Syria. It did not contain any internal force or population strong enough to unify the country and exclude foreign invaders. In the late summer of 1982 Reagan, hoping to restore order and stability as a prelude to general pacification and elections, sent 800 U.S. Marines to Lebanon as part of a United Nations (UN) force. The Marines' original authorization for a thirty day stay stretched on when no short-term solution seemed possible. On October 23, 1983, 241 of them were killed by a suicide bomber who drove a truck loaded with explosives into the midst of their compound and detonated it. The apparent futility of the Marines' deaths in a region endlessly at war made the Lebanon disaster particularly difficult for the government to justify. Even so Reagan recognized that he must not immediately recall the remaining troops; that would be a sign of weakness. Only after a decent interval did he withdraw American troops in the spring of 1984, leaving the internal Lebanese situation almost as unsettled as before.

Reagan Combats Terrorism

Reagan promised never to negotiate with terrorists, or regimes that used terrorism. When a German discotheque was bombed in April 1986, killing two American off-duty soldiers and wounding several hundred others, American intelligence traced the attack to Libyan agents. Libya's leader, Muammar Qaddafi, was another militantly anti-American Moslem. American warplanes, some carrier-based and some flying from U.S. bases in Britain, retaliated by bombing the Libyan cities of Benghazi and Tripoli, and only narrowly missed killing Qaddafi himself. The ensuing years saw a marked decline in Libyan-backed terrorism and Reagan counted the raid as a foreign policy success, even though its violation of international law led to a spate of adverse criticism from congressional Democrats and from European allies. On the face of it Reagan was showing his stern determination against terrorism.

The Iran-Contra Scandal

Reagan's administration broke its "no deals with terrorists" promise by bargaining with Iran for the release of hostages. In 1984 and 1985, without the knowledge of Congress, CIA director William Casey arranged for the sale of arms to Iran through Israel, in return for the release of hostages held by pro-Iranian guerrillas in Lebanon. To make matters worse, Casey's operation then channeled part of the proceeds to the Nicaraguan Contras, in explicit violation of the Boland Amendment, which provided only for humanitarian aid. The man in charge of these activities was a marine colonel, Oliver North, who worked from National Security Council offices in the basement of the White House.

In 1986 Casey and North's secret operations began to unravel when an aircraft carrying aid to the Contras was shot down over Nicaragua and a surviving crew member, Eugene Hasenfus, explained to his Sandinista captors the source of his plane's cargo. Secretary of State George Shultz and other senior officials all denied knowledge of the affair. In fact Shultz did know about the operations and had warned Reagan and Casey against undertaking them lest an incident of this kind expose them. The scandal widened when a Lebanese newspaper, *Al Shiraa,* reported in November 1986 that senior U.S. national security officials had visited Teheran to negotiate arms sales. Knowing that they would soon come under public scrutiny, Oliver North and his superiors, Admiral John Poindexter and Robert McFarlane, the current and former national security advisers, set to work destroying as many incriminating documents as possible with a paper shredder.

Iran-Contra Investigations

Reagan fired Poindexter and North but made a point of telling North that he was a "national hero" for his work. He then appointed an investigative commission to study the whole affair, headed by former Texas senator John Tower. For the first time the "Teflon" president found that his popularity was slipping. A poor showing at a press conference hurt him further. Members of the administration were scrambling to save themselves even at the expense of each others' reputations, and numerous times their stories conflicted, damaging Reagan's reputation further. CIA director Casey developed a brain tumor and died in May 1987, taking vital information

Oliver North testified before Congress at the Iran-Contra hearings about his part in the arms-for-hostages deal. It was later revealed that the marine lieutenant colonel and National Security Council employee was the person in charge of the illegal dealings. (UPI/Corbis-Bettmann. Reproduced by permission.)

about the affair with him to the grave. Former national security adviser McFarlane, after initially trying to escape the blame, decided to tell all but found the process so humiliating that in February 1987 he attempted suicide by drug overdose and almost died.

The Tower Commission report, published at the end of February, blamed White House Chief of Staff Donald Regan for negligence and dereliction of duty, although placing the blame squarely on his shoulders was questionable. He was forced to resign, and former Senator Howard Baker (R-TN) took his place. The Tower Commission report also confirmed the president's claim that he had not known what was taking place in the Iran-Contra affair. Senator Barry Goldwater (R-AZ), the 1964 Republican presidential candidate and a powerful conservative figure, found this conclusion incredible and said that Reagan was "either a liar or incompetent," but journalists Bob Schieffer and Gary Paul Gates, in their book on the administration, believe Reagan might well have been telling the truth. He had never paid close attention to policy issues, being content to let his staff take care of them. "The incredible thing," they wrote, "is how lucky Reagan had been all those years before the Iran-Contra scandal. Until then his passive approach had always worked like a charm, so it's no wonder that he himself was bewildered when his longtime habit of letting others make crucial decisions for him finally led him and his presidency into deeply troubled waters" (Schieffer and Gates, pp. 304–5).

A joint congressional committee convened to review the available evidence, but it was hampered by clumsy procedures and by the fact that Republican members obstructed its investigation out of loyalty to the president and the fear that humiliating him would weaken all other aspects of the administration. Everyone involved was aware of the parallel with the Watergate hearings on the Nixon administration from 14 years before, and of the possibility that they might lead to a presidential resignation or impeachment; the hearings were nicknamed "Irangate" by much of the press. In any event, Admiral Poindexter resolutely held to his story that he had made the crucial decisions, that the president had not known, and that the activities had all been undertaken from the highest patriotic motives.

The Reagan Administration Legacy

Even without the Iran-Contra scandal Reagan's image was tarnished before he left office in 1989. Former senior members of his government began publishing their memoirs in the latter days of his second term. David Stockman's *The Triumph of Politics* and Alexander Haig's *Caveat* had already drawn unflattering portraits of the president as a man who could not understand the operations of a government he was supposed to lead. Then Michael Deaver, Larry Speakes (former press secretary), and former White House chief of staff Donald Regan, whom Reagan had fired in the midst of the Iran-Contra scandal, added to the growing number of Reagan era memoirs that depicted the president in a less-than-flattering light. Reagan's age, the residual effects of the assassination attempt and subsequent surgery (in 1985) for cancer polyps, his hearing impairment and his failing memory, all caused concern during the closing days of his second administration.

The media had played an increasing role in politics throughout the twentieth century and the Reagan years marked an acceleration of the process. Reagan's earlier career as an actor, his good looks, and his charismatic screen presence had made him an attractive candidate from the outset, and had shown that image could be very important. The many Republicans who had thought he was far too extreme in his right wing views ever to be elected were proven wrong—his manner and image offset his ideas. His staff included pollsters who tested policies not solely for their intrinsic worth but for their popularity among the voters. Issues, as they developed, were studied for their attractiveness in the media, and Reagan's cabinet members tried to speak in "sound bites" to be sure of favorable coverage on television news. Commentators

were baffled to discover that even voters who thought Reagan was wrong on the issues and compromised by the Iran-Contra scandal still expressed their faith and confidence in him as a decent and honorable president. Candidates throughout the United States learned that media plausibility often mattered as much as the intrinsic wisdom of policies, with the result that the Reagan legacy includes an intensified attention to image building.

Lasting Impact

Soon after Reagan's retirement, the Berlin Wall was demolished, the Iron Curtain itself rusted away, and the era of the Soviet empire ended, with its numerous republics declaring their independence. There is little doubt that President Reagan's intense pressure on the Soviet Union, coupled with its own internal economic and political weaknesses, and its doomed role in the Afghan War, had combined to bring it down. The end of the Cold War after 44 years, and the end of Communism as a world-threatening ideology, are the most lasting legacies of the Reagan administration.

In domestic affairs the legacy was more ambiguous. Reagan had posed as the champion of conservative family values, yet he was the first divorced president in the nation's history. Turmoil in his own family came to light when Reagan's daughter, Patty, denounced many of her father's policies. He was the champion of the Christian right, and yet Evangelical Christianity, which had played an important role in his election campaigns, lost much of its political credibility as its leaders became involved in a series of sex and corruption scandals during the late 1980s. During Reagan's eight years in office, the gap between the rich and the poor in the United States widened, and the number of people listed as officially below the poverty line rose from 11.7 percent to 13.5 percent of the whole population, which was greater than in any other industrialized nation. Female-headed households and minorities remained extremely prone to poverty.

The Iran-Contra scandal left a permanent blemish on Reagan's record, and suggested that, even after Watergate, Congress and the judiciary must keep a close watch on executive branch activities. His confidence in the goodness of businesspeople appeared naive after the savings and loan failures, the 1987 Wall Street crash, and the extensive revelations of corruption and crime among his own trusted officials. He passed on to President George Bush a society still burdened by a gigantic national debt, staggering annual budget deficits, and a growing gap between the rich and the poor.

Sources

Boyer, Paul, ed. *Reagan as President.* Chicago: Ivan Dee, 1990.

Cannon, Lou. *President Reagan: The Role of a Lifetime.* New York: Simon & Schuster, 1991.

Dallek, Robert. *Ronald Reagan: The Politics of Symbolism.* Cambridge, Mass.: Harvard University Press, 1984.

Ehrenreich, Barbara. *The Worst Years of Our Lives: Irreverent Notes from a Decade of Greed.* New York: Harper Perennial, 1991.

Grantham, Dewey. *Recent America: The United States Since 1945.* New York: Harlan Davidson, 1998.

Historic World Leaders. Detroit: Gale Research, 1994.

Johnson, Haynes. *Sleepwalking Through History: America in the Reagan Years.* New York: Norton, 1991.

Reagan, Nancy, with William Novak. *My Turn: The Memoirs of Nancy Reagan.* New York: Random House, 1989.

Roark, James, et al. *The American Promise.* Vol. 2. Boston: Bedford, 1998.

Schieffer, Bob, and Gary Paul Gates. *The Acting President.* New York: Dutton, 1989.

Wills, Garry. *Reagan's America: Innocents at Home.* Garden City, N.Y.: Doubleday, 1987.

Further Readings

Mayer, Jane, and Doyle McManus. *Landslide: The Unmaking of the President, 1984-1988.* Boston: Houghton Mifflin, 1988.

Reagan, Ronald. *Where's The Rest of Me?* New York: Dell, 1965.

Reeves, Richard. *The Reagan Detour.* New York: Simon & Schuster, 1985.

Ronald W. Reagan Presidential Library and Museum. <http://www.webportal.com/reaganlibrar> 1999.

Stockman, David. *The Triumph of Politics: How the Reagan Revolution Failed.* New York: Harper and Row, 1986.

Bush Administration

Full name: George Bush
Given name: George Herbert Walker Bush
Popular name: Poppy

Personal Information:
Born: June 12, 1924
Birthplace: Milton, Massachusetts
Religion: Episcopalian
Spouse: Barbara Pierce (m. 1945)
Children: George Walker; Robin; John Ellis (Jeb); Neil
    Mallon; Marvin Pierce; Dorothy Pierce
Education: Yale College, B.A., 1948
Occupation: Oil company executive, congressman,
    Republican Party chairman, ambassador, CIA director,
    vice president
Political Party: Republican Party
Age at Inauguration: 64 years

Biography

A U.S. senator's son, George Bush considered politics both a personal duty and an innate privilege. Bush left his native New England for a career as a Texas oilman with an eye, always, to public service and the political future. He won the presidency in 1988, after eight years as vice president and a lifetime of Republican politics.

Early Life

Born in Milton, Massachusetts, on June 12, 1924, George Bush hailed from a prominent New England family. His father, Prescott Bush, was a managing partner at the Wall Street investment firm, A. V. Harriman, and served as U.S. senator from Connecticut from 1952 to 1962. His mother, Dorothy Walker Bush, was the daughter of another prominent Wall Street banker, George Herbert Walker. Bush grew up in the affluent New York City suburb of Greenwich, Connecticut, and spent the summers vacationing in Kennebunkport, Maine. As a senator's son and a natural leader, a career in politics was never far from the young Bush's mind.

Education

Bush was educated at some of the most elite private schools in the nation, attending Greenwich Country Day School and Phillips Academy in Andover, Massachusetts. After graduating from preparatory school in 1942, he enrolled in the U.S. Navy Reserve. At the age of 18, Bush was commissioned as a navy flight pilot in 1943, and served in the Pacific for the duration of World War II (1939–45). He flew 58 combat missions during his 39 months of service and was shot down twice while flying missions over the Pacific.

In September 1945, after the war, Bush enrolled at Yale University in New Haven, Connecticut. An ambitious, highly competitive student, Bush was active in campus social and athletic activities. He was the captain of the baseball team and a member of Skull and Bones, Yale's most venerated "secret society." He graduated with honors in 1948, earning a Bachelor of Arts degree in economics in three years.

Family Life

Bush met Barbara Pierce, then a student at Smith College, at a Christmas dance in Greenwich, Connecticut, in 1942, while he was on leave from the U.S. Navy. She left Smith during her sophomore year, and the two married in Rye, New York, on January 6, 1945. Throughout Bush's career, Barbara Bush volunteered for a variety of causes including improving adult literacy, increasing breast cancer awareness, and improving education. Many Americans admired her direct style and her straightforward demeanor. Despite a reputation for independence and strong opinions, she disagreed publicly with her husband only on two occasions—in 1989, when she supported a ban on assault weapons that her husband opposed, and in 1992, when the Republican Party included a strict antiabortion plank in its convention platform.

The Bushes had six children, including a daughter, Robin, who died of leukemia at the age of three. All of Bush's children followed their father into business—Neil, the youngest, went into the oil business in Denver and was implicated in the failure of a Denver savings and loan in 1988. They were also active in their father's political campaigns, and his two oldest sons, George and Jeb, began rising to political prominence themselves in the 1990s.

Career

After graduating from Yale in 1948, Bush opted not to follow his father into investment banking. Instead, he moved his family to Odessa, Texas, and went to work for Dresser Industries, an oil company owned by a family friend. Bush started his own oil and gas drilling firm in 1953 and moved his corporate headquarters to Houston, Texas, in 1958.

Bush was active in local Republican politics from the time he moved to Texas. He served as Houston

George Bush. *(The Library of Congress.)*

County Republican Party chairman from 1963 to 1964. In 1964 he took a leave of absence from his firm, Zapata Petroleum, to challenge incumbent Democrat Ralph Yarborough for his seat in the U.S. Senate. Bush campaigned as a western conservative, following the lead of Arizona senator Barry Goldwater, the Republican presidential nominee. Goldwater was an avid anti-Communist who believed in a strong national defense and wanted to roll back the social programs that had proliferated in the years after the Great Depression. Goldwater, Bush, and others who embraced this "new right" conservatism opposed civil rights legislation, called for the United States to withdraw from the United Nations (UN) if the Communist People's Republic of China was admitted, demanded a cutback in foreign aid spending, and opposed any new domestic spending.

Bush's New England conservative tradition emphasized a hands-off policy on social matters, while the new right's conservatism championed a forceful return to traditional social values after the turmoil of the 1960s. Bush's natural sympathies seemed to lie with the more moderate conservatism of his privileged New England upbringing, but he recognized that Republican voters, especially in the West, were coming to embrace a new, more aggressive sort of politics, and that the growing western states would be increasingly influential in U.S. elections. Bush's first election campaign foreshadowed the future president's vacillating sympathies between the new right social conservatives and the more moderate wing of his party. In 1964 Bush cast his lot with the Gold-

Fast Fact

Bush was the youngest aviator in the Navy when he received his wings in 1943. During his service in the military, he was awarded the Distinguished Flying Cross and three air medals.

(Source: Joseph Nathan Kane. *Facts About the Presidents*, 1993.)

water Republicans, and he lost decisively in the nationwide Democratic landslide of that year.

In 1966 Bush won election to the U.S. House of Representatives in a suburban Houston district. A two-term congressman, Bush served from 1966 through 1970. He championed anti-labor union legislation and freedom of choice legislation to end forced school busing. Generally, Bush was conservative in economic matters but more moderate on social issues. He forcefully advocated housing desegregation and family planning and supported much of President Richard Nixon's moderate domestic legislative initiatives.

In 1970 Bush again sought election to the Senate, campaigning as an outspoken Nixon supporter on a law and order theme. His election chances, however, dimmed when the moderate Lloyd Bentsen defeated Ralph Yarborough, the more liberal incumbent, in the Democratic primary. After losing to Bentsen, Bush refrained from seeking elective office again until his first run for the presidency in 1980.

Statesman and Party Leader

In February 1971 President Nixon appointed Bush U.S. Ambassador to the United Nations (UN). Bush proved to be an able and popular diplomat. In December 1972 Bush resigned his UN appointment to accept, again at Nixon's request, the post of chairman of the Republican National Committee (RNC). Not long afterwards, scandal broke out when the Democratic campaign offices at the Watergate complex in Washington, D.C., were broken into. Despite mounting evidence that Nixon had been involved in the break in and the growing likelihood that Nixon would be impeached, Bush publicly championed President Nixon and sought to minimize the scandal's impact on the Republican Party image.

In September 1974, after Nixon was forced to resign, President Gerald Ford appointed Bush to serve as head of the U.S. diplomatic liaison office in Communist China.

Bush left that post in December 1975 to accept appointment as director of the Central Intelligence Agency (CIA), where he was credited with shoring up the agency's crumbling morale. Following Democrat Jimmy Carter's inauguration as president in 1977, Bush resigned the CIA directorship and returned to Texas to accept the chairmanship of the First National Bank of Houston.

The Election of 1980

Bush became an undeclared candidate for the Republican 1980 presidential nomination beginning in 1977. He raised a remarkable amount of campaign money and endorsements through his RNC connections, as well as through his family and corporate contacts in Texas and in the East. Bush formally announced his candidacy in May 1979 and quickly emerged as former California governor Ronald Reagan's principal opponent.

While as conservative as Reagan on economic and foreign policy matters, Bush was more moderate on social issues. Bush supported the Equal Rights Amendment (ERA), which sought constitutional equality for women and defended limited access to abortion, while Reagan adamantly opposed both abortion and the ERA. Bush derided Reagan's plan to increase defense spending sharply while reducing taxes and balancing the budget, calling it "voodoo economics." Reagan, however, proved a much smoother campaigner, and Bush's bid for the nomination faltered. Bush remained in the race until Reagan won the nomination at the Republican National Convention. Reagan then selected Bush as his vice presidential running mate.

Vice President

After Reagan's decisive victory over incumbent Jimmy Carter in 1980, Bush served as vice president for the entire eight years of the Reagan administration. Bush was a loyal, deferential vice president, never disagreeing in public with Reagan. He took over the duties of the president briefly in 1981, when Reagan was shot in an assassination attempt and again in 1985, when the president underwent surgery for intestinal cancer, but Bush deferred all policy decisions until the president returned. Bush also chaired several presidential task forces, including one on combating terrorism, which recommended that the U.S. government institute a policy of making no concessions to terrorists.

Only a few years later, revelations that the Reagan administration broke this no-arms-for-hostages policy led to the most damaging scandal of the Reagan years. In 1987 the *Washington Post* revealed that the Reagan administration arranged the sale of arms to Iran in return for the release of hostages held by pro-Iranian guerrillas in Lebanon and then illegally channeled the profits from these sales to the anticommunist Nicaraguan Contras.

Bush maintained throughout the investigation of the Iran-Contra scandal that he was out of the loop, but there was some evidence that he had attended meetings in which the issue was discussed. He admitted knowing of the arms sales and of the efforts to release the hostages but claimed that he was not aware that the two were linked. He also claimed to know nothing of the illegal diversion of funds to the Contras. According to Lawrence Walsh, the independent prosecutor who was appointed to look into the matter, Bush also was involved in efforts to encourage the Honduran government to aid the Contras, circumventing a congressional ban on military aid to the Nicaraguan rebels. The allegations against Bush were never proven. Shortly before he left office in 1992, President Bush pardoned former Defense Secretary Caspar Weinberger and five others facing criminal charges for their roles in the Iran-Contra scandal, a move which many critics saw as further evidence that Bush was involved in the affair.

President

When the election of 1988 rolled around, Bush was not assured the Republican presidential nomination. While the vice president had proven himself quite capable of handling difficult administrative assignments in his 25 years of public service, he had yet to develop a national constituency. Bush did have the advantage of his years in the Reagan administration, however, and he harnessed Reagan's lingering popularity to propel him to victory in the Republican primaries. Bush then won a hard-fought general election campaign against Democratic nominee Michael Dukakis and was inaugurated as the 41st president of the United States on January 20, 1989.

Bush came into office in a time of prosperity, and in 1989, as Communist governments across the world came tumbling down, Bush saw his public opinion ratings rise to extraordinary heights. In 1991, as Bush led an international coalition to victory in the war against Iraq, his polls soared even higher. At the same time, however, his domestic fortunes began to fade. By late 1991 the nation had plunged into an economic downturn. By the election of 1992, an electorate disillusioned with Bush's handling of domestic affairs chose Democrat Bill Clinton over Bush. Bush became the first Republican president to serve only one term in the post–World War II era.

Post-Presidential Years

In retirement Bush kept a relatively low profile, muting his criticism of the Clinton administration and making occasional public appearances. In November 1997 he attended the dedication of the George Bush Presidential Library and Museum on the campus of Texas A & M University in College Station, Texas.

Bush also quietly supported the political careers of his sons, George and Jeb, both Republicans. Both ran for governorships in 1994, with George winning in Texas and Jeb losing a close race in Florida. In 1998 Jeb ran in Florida again and this time was successful, while George was reelected to a second term in Texas. George's background and strong showings in the state of Texas brought him national attention. He declared his intentions to seek the Republican Party's 1999 presidential nomination.

The George Bush Administration

A cautious conservative, both by philosophy and by nature, Bush believed that the role of the president was to address issues and crises in a competent manner as they arose; to serve as a "guardian" over a country that he believed had nothing fundamentally wrong with it. Soon after his inauguration, however, the world that Bush had known changed profoundly, both at home and abroad.

Bush Becomes President

The Campaign of 1988

Although Bush, after eight years as vice president, was the obvious front-runner to succeed Ronald Reagan to the presidency, he was a less than inspired campaigner who had never developed a national constituency. His only electoral victory in his 25 years of public service, in fact, had come as a candidate in a safe Republican congressional district. After finishing third place in the Iowa caucuses behind Senator Bob Dole of Kansas and Rev. Pat Robertson, a conservative television evangelist, Bush's campaign launched a negative advertising campaign that attacked Dole's record in the Senate and his unwillingness to pledge not to raise taxes if he became president. Bush went on to win the New Hampshire primary, and, with his large fundraising advantage, outpaced his opponents—former Delaware Governor Pierre "Pete" duPont, New York representative Jack Kemp, former secretary of state Alexander Haig, Dole, and Robertson—to capture the Republican nomination.

In what was perhaps the most roundly criticized decision of his campaign, Bush chose a little-known junior senator from Indiana, James Danforth (Dan) Quayle III, as his vice-presidential running mate. Critics saw Quayle as an inexperienced lawmaker, unsuited to lead the country. He had a tendency to make ill-advised comments and gaffes that earned him ridicule from the media. Early in the campaign, for instance, Quayle clumsily called the murder of six million Jews in Europe during World War II an "obscene moment in

Administration

Administration Dates
January 20, 1989–January 20, 1993

Vice President
James Danforth Colfax Quayle III (1989–93)

Cabinet

Secretary of State
James A. Baker III (1989–92)
Lawrence S. Eagleburger (1992–93)

Secretary of the Treasury
Nicholas F. Brady (1988–93)

Attorney General
Richard Lewis Thornburgh (1988–91)
William P. Barr (1991–93)

Secretary of the Interior
Manuel Lujan Jr. (1989–93)

Secretary of Agriculture
Clayton Yeutter (1989–91)
Edward Madigan (1991–93)

Secretary of Labor
Elizabeth H. Dole (1989–90)
Lynn Morley Martin (1991–93)

Secretary of Commerce
Robert A. Mosbacher (1989–92)
Barbara H. Franklin (1992–93)

Secretary of Defense
Richard Cheney (1989–93)

Secretary of Housing and Urban Development
Jack Kemp (1989–93)

Secretary of Transportation
Samuel K. Skinner (1989–91)
Andrew Card Jr. (1992–93)

Secretary of Energy
James Watkins (1989–93)

Secretary of Health and Human Services
Louis Sullivan (1989–93)

Secretary of Education
Lauro F. Cavazos (1988–90)
Lamar Alexander (1991–93)

Secretary of Veterans Affairs
Edward J. Derwinski (1989–92)

---

our nation's history," and later in the same appearance asserted that he "didn't live in this century" (*New York Times*, October 5, 1988). Quayle did enjoy a small, loyal constituency among religious conservatives, but he commanded consistently low opinion ratings among the broader public. Bush, always loyal, stood by his selection even when it became clear that it pleased few of the voters whom he had hoped Quayle's youthful energy would attract.

The Republican Convention of 1988

At the Republican National Convention in New Orleans, Louisiana, Bush delivered an unusually moving, well-received acceptance speech, describing his long career in public service since World War II as a series of missions accomplished. "The most important work of my life is to complete the mission we started in 1980," he said. His mission as president, he told Americans, would be to create 30 million jobs in eight years. He

would be the "education president"; he would be "the environmental president." He would work towards a "drug-free America"; and push the nation to rely not on government for social services for the needy, but on voluntary organizations, "a brilliant diversity spread like stars, like a thousand points of light in a broad and peaceful sky." He implored Americans to eschew what some saw as the uncaring materialism of the Reagan years, to become a "kinder, gentler nation." In the same speech, Bush also made the pledge that ultimately may have cost him reelection in 1992. He had, on the advice of economic advisers concerned with the massive federal budget deficit, refused throughout the primaries to make a commitment not to raise taxes. In his acceptance speech, however, he followed the advice of his political advisers, who believed such a pledge was essential to winning the election. "The Congress will push me to raise taxes, and I'll say no," he said, "and they'll push me again, and I'll say to them, 'Read My Lips, No New Taxes'" (*New York Times*, August 19, 1988).

The Campaign for the Presidency

Bush's opponent in the general election was Massachusetts' governor Michael Dukakis, a son of Greek immigrants who had first won the governor's seat in 1974, losing his job in 1978 but regaining it in 1982. Dukakis was credited with bringing about the "Massachusetts miracle," the turnaround of the state's economy from years of industrial decay to a new era of high-tech prosperity. A classic liberal, Dukakis believed that government could serve as a useful tool in solving social problems, and as Massachusetts' governor he introduced a number of employment programs and policies to foster new industry. After learning that Massachusetts Senator Edward Kennedy would not run in 1988, Dukakis declared his candidacy, defeating a host of other Democratic candidates in the field. At the Democratic convention he invoked the liberal idealism of John Kennedy and Lyndon Johnson, and lambasted the inequities of wealth of the 1980s. Dukakis chose Texas Senator Lloyd Bentsen, a well-respected Senate veteran (who had defeated Bush in the 1970 Texas Senate race), as his running mate.

The campaign of 1988 was mostly negative and image-driven. Dukakis' early lead in the polls evaporated under a barrage of Republican advertisements that attacked Dukakis as a "tax-and-spend" Democrat who would raise taxes at any opportunity in order to pay for unnecessary government programs. According to the Bush campaign, Dukakis was an out-of-touch liberal who was soft on crime because he opposed the death penalty. Bush accused Dukakis of being unpatriotic because he vetoed a bill requiring that Massachusetts schoolchildren pledge allegiance to the U.S. flag; Bush also said Dukakis showed weakness on national defense because he opposed Reagan's "Star Wars" space-based defense program. Dukakis, in turn, questioned Bush's involvement in the Iran-Contra scandal and attacked Bush's decision-making capacities in choosing the inexperienced Dan Quayle as a vice-presidential running mate. Bush won the battle of perceptions, however, creating images of the Democratic candidate as a weak "technocrat," a politician more concerned with policies than with actual people.

Bush won the election by a substantial margin, winning 54 percent of the popular vote to Dukakis' 46 percent. Bush made inroads into the traditionally Democratic Jewish and African American vote, as well as winning the electoral votes of every state in the south. Dukakis split the states on the East Coast with Bush, and won Washington and Oregon, the first western states to vote Democratic since the 1964 presidential election.

The Campaign of 1992

In the aftermath of the Persian Gulf War (1991), President Bush seemed headed for easy reelection. His near-90 percent approval ratings dissuaded many nationally prominent Democrats, such as Senator Bill Bradley of New Jersey and Governor Mario Cuomo of New York, from entering the race. But by election season, the nation had plunged into a damaging and prolonged recession—an economic downturn resulting in job losses and higher prices—and voters were unhappy.

Arkansas Governor Bill Clinton emerged as a contender early in the Democratic race, pressing on to win the Democratic nomination despite allegations of womanizing, draft-dodging, and marijuana use. As Clinton approached the Democratic convention, he stood a distant third in national polls. President Bush, whose approval ratings had fallen dramatically as the nation became mired in recession, had also fallen in the polls.

In the lead was Ross Perot, a diminutive, sharp-tongued Texas billionaire who had entered the race as an independent on a whim during an appearance on a cable-television talk show, and who preached about the evils of the $4 trillion national debt and the corrupting influence of money in politics. The independent candidate offered plain-spoken solutions to the nation's dilemmas, saying a president should fix the country's problems like a good mechanic tinkering "under the hood" of a car, and promising to rid Washington of lobbyists "in thousand-dollar suits and alligator shoes" (*New York Times*, October 12, 1992). Perot, who financed his own "United We Stand" party to campaign for him and spearhead a petition drive to place him on the ballot in all 50 states, held no convention and made few public appearances. Instead, he paid for half-hour time slots on the major television networks to present his case. On the same day that Clinton prepared to give his acceptance speech for the Democratic nomination, Perot announced that he was dropping out of the race. Perot explained that he believed that the Democratic Party had sufficiently revived to challenge Bush, and that deficit reduction was now an issue in the campaign. Months later Perot would reenter the race, stating that the American people had demanded he rejoin the campaign. His support never approached its earlier levels, but in the debates he was a vocal critic of Bush's leadership and the country's economic footing.

The Issues

When Perot left the race, Clinton's polling numbers shot up and President Bush trailed his Democratic opponent for the first time. Throughout the general election campaign, Clinton focused on Bush's economic performance. In the "War Room" at the center of Clinton's campaign headquarters in Little Rock, Arkansas, one of Clinton's campaign managers had pasted a slogan on the wall reminding his staff about the issue that drove their campaign: "the economy, stupid" (Woodward, p. 54). The Clinton campaign criticized Bush's economic performance and promised activist measures to improve Americans' economic outlook.

Clinton believed that the government could play a constructive role in fixing the nation's social problems and stimulating economic growth. Bush, by contrast, argued that government should play a limited role. He insisted that the recession was ebbing and would end of its own accord. His one prescription for economic revitalization—a cut in the capital gains tax on the appreciation of investments, such as stocks—was seen as primarily benefiting the rich. The idea that a tax cut that helped the wealthy would stimulate the entire economy was a notion that recalled Ronald Reagan's policy that tax cuts on the rich would "trickle down" to the less fortunate. Clinton, campaigning as a champion of the middle class, supported an increase in the taxes on the wealthiest Americans. Clinton also supported such traditionally Republican measures as welfare reform and stronger law enforcement, making it difficult for Republicans to attack him as a "tax-and-spend" liberal, as they had successfully done to Dukakis in 1988. With Clinton matching Bush on many social issues, Bush's inactivity on the economy stood out even more starkly: to voters, Bush seemed more interested in preserving the status of the wealthy than addressing the concerns of the middle class.

When the Republican National Convention convened in Houston in August 1992, Bush faced a divided party, with economic conservatives on one side, and social and religious conservatives on the other. Bush was torn between his moderate background on social issues and his need for the support of the social conservatives who dominated the convention. Trying to hold to a middle ground, Bush satisfied neither branch of his party. His efforts to move to the right on social issues still were not enough for social conservatives and led him to support policies more conservative than those of other Republicans or the average American voter. Many women were offended by the Republican hard-line stand on abortion. Bush also suffered for having approved a 1990 tax increase, which reneged on his 1988 "Read My Lips, No New Taxes" campaign pledge and angered many Republicans. Heading into the elections, Bush could not claim the unqualified support of any major voting block.

The Election

On Election Day, November 5, 1992, George Bush became the first Republican president since World War II not to win a second term of office. Clinton defeated Bush and Perot, winning most of the electoral votes (370 to 168) but only 43 percent of the popular vote. Clinton had maintained the traditional Democratic coalition of the poor and middle class, African-Americans, labor, and liberals, and won the votes of a large proportion of women and voters under the age of 25. Bush's strongest support was in the South, reflecting the continuing realignment of that region from Democratic to Republican after 1964. Perot won 19 percent of the popular vote but won no electoral votes. Nonetheless, his showing was the best for an independent candidate since 1912, when Theodore Roosevelt ran as the "Bull Moose" candidate.

Bush's Advisers

During his tenure as president, on domestic issues in particular, Bush relied heavily on his advisers. His first chief of staff, John Sununu, and his budget director, Richard Darman, were widely credited with (and blamed for) convincing Bush to reverse his "no new taxes" pledge and agree to the 1990 budget deal. Darman, the budget director, considered the budget deficit—the increasing disparity between what the government spent and what it collected in taxes every year, which was driving the federal government further and further into debt—the nation's most pressing problem. Sununu, the chief of staff, had a strong personality and alienated many Bush staffers and members of Congress, and tightly controlled access to the president. Sununu resigned in late 1991 amid allegations that he had used White House planes for personal trips and golf outings. Sununu was an efficient manager, however, and when Transportation Secretary Samuel Skinner replaced Sununu in 1991—just as the president's polling numbers began a steep decline—Skinner found it difficult to impose order on what was by then a demoralized staff and a hostile Congress.

Bush's most influential adviser, however, was Secretary of State James Baker, a longtime friend from Texas, who had run Bush's 1980 presidential campaign, served as chief of staff and Treasury secretary under Reagan, and again joined Bush to run his campaign in 1988. Baker was an adviser to Bush on all matters, and was the president's point man on foreign policy for all but the last few months of Bush's presidency. Baker was lauded for his work in negotiating a settlement in Nicaragua and for helping Bush build the international coalition that joined in the Persian Gulf War. Bush's heavy reliance on his friend's competent leadership was especially apparent when Bush asked Baker to resign as secretary of state—a post he loved—in order to take over Bush's sputtering reelection campaign in August 1992.

Bush and Congress

Upon assuming the presidency, Bush sought to cultivate a friendlier relationship with Congress than had Ronald Reagan. Both the 101st and 102d Congresses were controlled by Democrats, where they maintained advantages of at least 10 seats in the Senate and 80 seats in the House throughout Bush's term. Facing this largest opposition majority in Congress of any newly elected president in history, Bush embarked on a strategy of conciliation towards his opposition in the Democrat-controlled Congress, inviting senators and representatives to his living quarters and bestowing attention upon opposition leaders. Personal relations and loyalty had always been important to Bush, and he hoped to overcome the difficulties of divided government by maintaining what he called a civilized relationship with the Democrats in Congress.

As the inaugural glow faded, however, Bush was surprised to find that the Democrats he had considered his friends now placed partisan politics above personal loyalty. The Republicans were also displeased with what they considered Bush's appeasement of the Democrats, decrying his well-mannered reluctance to use the presidential "bully pulpit" to deliver high profile speeches that would pressure Congress into cooperating. There was, in the words of House Minority Whip Newt Gingrich, a "cultural war" going on in America between the forces of liberalism and conservatism, and Bush needed to "pick a side" (*New York Times,* June 22, 1992). Bush was torn between his tendency towards prudence, personal loyalty, and moderation, and the right-wing social conservatism that he had endorsed in order to get elected.

The Tower Nomination

Bush's first defeat at the hands of Congress came early: the Senate rejected Bush's nominee for secretary of defense. John Tower, a former senator from Texas, had seemed a sound choice: he had served 24 years in the Senate, which generally confirmed its members to executive posts without problem, and he was a close, longtime political ally of Bush. But the Democratic members of the Senate Armed Services Committee believed that allegations of womanizing, conflict of interest problems, and excessive drinking made Tower a poor candidate to control the nation's armed forces. "I cannot in good conscience vote to put an individual at the top of a chain of command when his history of excessive drinking is such that he would not be selected to command a missile wing," said Georgia Democrat Sam Nunn, the chairman of the Senate committee (Mervin, p. 91).

For Bush, who had lobbied hard for Tower's confirmation, the rejection was a stunning defeat. Tower's rejection was the first of any cabinet nominee since 1959, only the ninth in the history of the nation. The Tower battle opened Bush's eyes to the trouble he would have in facing an opposition Congress, regardless of how congenial their personal relations. It also made the president more averse to taking political risks in the future.

Legislation

The result of Bush's continuous standoff with Congress was a historically unproductive legislative session. Bush supported and passed fewer bills than any other president since World War II. This was, in part, due to the difficulty of governing with a legislature that opposed him at every turn. And in part, it was due to the fact that he considered himself, in the words of presidential scholar David Mervin, a "guardian" whose role was to address crises as they arose rather than to offer grand visions and expensive programs for the nation. An activist legislative record was not, in Bush's estimation, necessarily a sign of success. In addition, Bush had inher-

Fast Fact

Bush was the first sitting vice president to win the presidency since Martin Van Buren was elected in 1836.

(Source: Joseph Nathan Kane. *Facts About the Presidents,* 1993.)

ited the bloated deficit of the Reagan years, which left little money to devote to new programs (Mervin, p. 8).

Bush was also a lackluster lobbyist. Although he did offer proposals on health, crime, energy, education, and banking, he did little to build public support for his ideas. The president did achieve some important legislative victories (see also Domestic Issues). He acted quickly and competently to bail out the faltering savings and loans that threatened the financial security of the nation. He broke with the conservative wing of his party and signed revisions of the Clean Air Act, the most comprehensive and expansive environmental statute enacted to that date. He also shaped and signed the Americans with Disability Act (ADA), important legislation granting new rights to disabled persons, and appropriated increased funding for education, farming, and housing programs. In foreign policy, Bush ended years of partisan dispute over the United States' policy in Central America and persuaded an unconvinced Congress to support the war in the Persian Gulf. His most forceful legislative statements may have come in the form of the 44 vetoes he exercised during his term. While presidents, on average, see about one quarter of their vetoes overridden, Congress overturned only one of Bush's vetoes. On a number of occasions, however, the president signed bills similar to those he had vetoed when it became clear that Congress had the votes to override them.

Ultimately, his legislative victories were overshadowed by his most staggering defeat—the 1990 budget showdown with Congress that forced Bush to renege on his "no new taxes" campaign promise. Conservatives in Congress were appalled when Bush agreed to a deal that included $137 billion in new taxes. And while this modest but important step in bringing the deficit under control was probably in the best interest of the nation, the budget deal also succeeded in propelling Congress out of Bush's control for good. It was perhaps the crucial turning point in Bush's presidency, shattering morale among Republicans who believed that Bush had abandoned the Republican economic creed and exposing Bush's weakness before the Democrats in Congress.

Bush and the Judiciary

The Bush administration built on Reagan's policy of carefully screening nominations to the federal bench in order to exercise a conservative influence on the interpretation of the law. Like Reagan's appointees, Bush's nominees tended to be young and white and could be expected to hold their lifetime appointments long after Bush stepped down from the presidency. Bush appointed a record number of women to the federal bench.

The Bush and Reagan appointees tended to construe laws very narrowly and to side with conservatives who sought to restrict abortion, affirmative action (special benefits intended to improve the lives of underprivileged minorities and women), and the rights of criminal defendants, and to increase the influence of religion in public life. While Bush's policies were not always conservative in other arenas, Bush and C. Boyden Gray, the White House counsel who screened judicial nominees, were faithful to the idea of shifting the federal courts to the right, ensuring that the conservative philosophy would survive electoral setbacks. When Bush left office in 1993, nearly a quarter of federal judges were his appointees.

Supreme Court Appointments.

Bush made two Supreme Court appointments: Justice David Souter and Justice Clarence Thomas. A reclusive intellectual, Souter's confirmation hearings were uneventful. To the dismay of many conservatives, who hoped Souter would provide a crucial conservative swing vote for the Court, Souter formed a moderate conservative bloc with Justices Sandra Day O'Connor and Anthony Kennedy, both Reagan nominees. This alliance held the balance in decisions preventing a reversal of the Court's positions on abortion, school prayer, and prisoners' rights.

Clarence Thomas, an African American judge whom Bush selected to replace retiring Justice Thurgood Marshall, was elevated to the court after a sensational round of confirmation hearings. When a former employee, law professor Anita Hill, publicly accused Thomas of sexual harassment after hearing of his nomination to the high court, the Senate held televised hearings in which they grilled both Hill and Thomas about the unseemly details of the allegations. Bush continued to support Thomas, who won confirmation by the slimmest of margins. Once joining the Court, Thomas proved to be one of its most consistently conservative judges.

Changes in the U.S. Government

Bush, in line with his conservative philosophy and with his eight years as vice president, made few changes to the federal government. The largest regulatory shift in Bush's tenure was the revamping of the nation's bank-

ing system in response to the savings-and-loan crisis. The savings-and-loan bailout legislation that Bush signed soon after coming to office dissolved the agencies in charge of regulating the thrifts and created a new agency, the Resolution Trust Corporation, to oversee the closing of banks that had become insolvent.

Domestic Issues

The Bush presidency began with widespread contentment with the status quo, which Bush was satisfied to maintain. While there was some controversy surrounding issues such as civil rights, the environment, and taxes, ill-feeling on these issues was largely overshadowed by dramatic world events and crises. As international affairs cooled off, however, Americans became increasingly dissatisfied with the state of the economy. What had seemed at one point to be a minor downturn was proving to be a serious recession.

The economy performed worse under Bush than under any president who had served since World War II. Economic growth stagnated, businesses failed, fewer jobs were created, and the national debt soared to a record high. Social programs expanded under Bush as the recession caused economic hardships for millions of Americans. Some programs grew because Bush proposed increases—as in the case of the Head Start preschool program and the $1.1 billion urban aid package passed in the wake of the 1992 Los Angeles riots; more of them grew automatically because the recession qualified more Americans for government aid. Between 1989 and 1992, for instance, the number of people receiving food stamps increased 37 percent, to an unprecedented 25.8 million, and the number of people receiving Aid For Families with Dependent Children rose 25 percent, to 13.6 million, the highest number of families on welfare in American history. Bush was conspicuously silent about the growth in social programs, however, knowing he could satisfy neither his conservative constituency nor the liberals for whom his commitment to social spending was never enough. Furthermore, the average salaries of college graduates and of managerial and professional workers had fallen steadily since Bush took office. By 1992 only 16 percent of Americans in a *New York Times* poll approved of Bush's handling of the economy, a lower rating than even President Carter had received in an administration that was widely considered a failure (*New York Times,* June 22, 1992).

Recession

A comparison of economic growth figures in the Reagan and the Bush years offers a startling contrast. The economy grew by 14 percent in the Reagan years, and 2.5 percent in Bush's four years. Americans saw 9.8 percent job growth and a 6.6 percent increase in personal income in the Reagan years, compared to an 0.7 percent job increase and 1.2 percent rise in personal income under Bush. Industrial production, which grew moderately under Reagan, decreased under Bush. And even as tax rolls shrank in the recession of the early 1990s, government spending grew because of the mounting interest on the trillion-dollar debt. Despite the Reagan administration's favorable economic performance, many of Bush's economic troubles grew directly from Reagan administration policies. In the 1980s companies, households, and most of the federal government went deeply into debt, in large part because of changes in the tax and banking codes in the 1980s. This borrowing tended to finance day-to-day consumption rather than long-term investments. By the time Bush came to office, many of these debts had come due. Americans came to learn that much of the prosperity of the 1980s was borrowed from the future, the so-called "hangover" from the Reagan years. Bush could not criticize Reagan's policies, however, without contradicting the opinions he had held as vice president.

The economic slump was not entirely the fault of either president; beginning as far back as the 1970s, the United States' new technology-based economy produced enormous disparities in income, wealth, and opportunity. From 1973 to 1989 median family income increased less than two percent after inflation, even though many families had two wage earners. And while the middle class was stagnating, the rich were growing richer at an astounding rate. Over 94 percent of the wealth created by the U.S. economy in the 1980s went to the richest 20 percent of the population, and over 50 percent accrued to the top one percent. By the time Bush left office in 1993, 47 percent of the total income in the United States went to the wealthiest 20 percent of the population.

While Bush could not be blamed for many of these long-term trends in the American economy, he never adequately explained them to the public. In fact, Bush seemed blindsided by the recession himself. The economy had been stagnating since shortly after Bush took office in 1989 and was in full recession by the time the Persian Gulf War started. Bush, preoccupied with the war and convinced the economic downturn was temporary, was consistently upbeat about the nation's economic growth even as the economy slipped further and further into recession.

Bush blamed the country's economic problems on Congress and on Federal Reserve Bank chairman Alan Greenspan, who kept long-term interest rates high. Greenspan had done this because of the bloated budget deficit and rising fears that the inflation rate would surpass the nation's economic growth. Bush refused to take any action himself, however, and ignored Democratic prescriptions to stimulate the economy by introducing government programs that might cushion the impact of the recession. The best role the government could play was to keep its hands off, Bush insisted. This determination not to intervene with the economy was consistent with Bush's political philosophy, but it did not sit well with voters deeply concerned with both their short-term

finances and with the prospects for future generations. To many Americans, Bush, who was by all accounts a warm and caring man, seemed disinterested in the needs of ordinary Americans. By the time Bush left office, he appeared to voters, who were struggling to deal with the recession, to be lacking in compassion, vision, and the resolve necessary to combat the nation's woes.

The Savings and Loan Crisis

In the wake of banking deregulation passed in the 1980s, hundreds of savings and loan associations began to risk depositors' money on hazardous investment schemes. Banks began to branch out into the stock market and land deals in the hopes of creating larger returns on their investments. Many bank directors, who were both inexperienced in financial markets and sometimes corrupt, extended sweetheart loans to cronies or financial contributors. And when land prices in the southwest collapsed in the late 1980s at the same time that a building boom produced a glut of excess commercial real estate, many of the get-rich-quick land developers financed by the local thrifts defaulted on their debts. The savings and loans soon found themselves insolvent, and the nation was confronted with the threat of massive bank failures similar to those that had helped bring about the Great Depression in the 1930s. Because of Depression-era reforms to the banking system the federal government now insured bank deposits, but there were not enough reserve funds to cover all of the losses.

The bank failures reached a crisis point just as Bush took office, and the savings and loan bailout would be one of the most successful bipartisan efforts of Bush's presidency. Bush acted quickly to enact a comprehensive plan to bail out the failing thrifts. In 1989 Bush and Congress approved a package providing more than $150 billion to refund deposits from failed thrifts. The total cost of the bailout, including the increased fees Congress imposed on banks that survived, was estimated to cost taxpayers as much as $500 billion over 40 years. The bailout plan dissolved both the Depression-era Federal Home Loan Bank Board, which had supervised the savings and loans, and the Federal Savings and Loan Insurance Corporation (FSLIC), which had guaranteed deposits. Congress transferred these agencies' responsibilities to a new Office of Thrift Supervision and to the Federal Deposit Insurance Corporation (FDIC). The bill also created the Resolution Trust Corporation (RTC) in order to close and sell off the assets of the failed institutions.

A number of high-profile Americans would find themselves caught in the savings and loan disaster. Five U.S. Senators were investigated for their involvement in the failure of an Arizona bank; George Bush's son, Neil, was implicated in the failure of a Denver bank; and Bush's successor, Bill Clinton, spent much of his presidency fighting off allegations stemming from his involvement in a land deal funded by a failed Arkansas thrift.

Biography:

Alan Greenspan

Chairman of the Federal Reserve Board (1926–) As chairman of the Federal Reserve, Alan Greenspan is arguably the most powerful man in the world. If Greenspan comments off-hand on the state of the economy or even whether he liked his breakfast analysts and investors around the world scramble to interpret those comments as indication of Greenspan's intentions. "Will he raise interest rates on the U.S. money supply? Will he lower them?" A very slight movement one direction or the other sends ripples across the global economic landscape. As a college student studying economics, Alan Greenspan became involved with a tightly knit group of less than a dozen young people who, like himself, were inspired by the philosophy and teachings of writer Ayn Rand. Rand's objectivist philosophy expounded the virtues of *laissez-faire* capitalism, a condition whereby market forces regulate the economy rather than government intervention. As chairman of the Federal Reserve since his appointment by President Ronald Reagan in 1987, Greenspan's strict adherence to the tenants of

laissez-faire capitalism has been credited with perpetuating the longest-running bull market in our nation's history. Surprisingly, given the power Greenspan wields, he is not elected by the public, but appointed by presidents. One of Greenspan's outstanding assets is his apolitical approach to his job. Though it has frustrated some presidents, Greenspan insulated himself from politics that might dictate his actions despite disagreements about

measures that should be taken to heal an ailing economy, such as when he refused to lower interest rates when the economy went into decline during the Bush administration. President George Bush reappointed Greenspan chairman in 1991. In 1996 Clinton did the same despite similar differences.

The 1990 Budget Crisis

Once Bush came to office, two of his most trusted advisers, Budget Director Richard Darman and Chief of Staff John Sununu, insisted that it was vital to bring the ballooning deficit under control. During Bush's campaign he had promised not to raise taxes, against their advice. Once in office, Bush was eventually persuaded by their arguments, and he entered budget negotiations with Democratic leaders in 1990 with a statement that he had "no precondition," a signal that he might be willing to budge on taxes. After a set of long, tense negotiations, Bush agreed to reduce the deficit by $492 billion. The deal included $137 billion in new taxes, $99 billion in budget cuts, and $184 in future appropriations cuts. Congress raised income taxes on the wealthiest Americans from 28 percent to 31 percent. Bush was also forced to abandon the centerpiece of his economic plan, a reduction in the capital gains tax—the levy on the appreciation of stocks, real estate, and other investments.

Bush received criticism from all sides after the deal. Conservative Republicans believed Bush's lack of resolve on his "no new taxes" pledge undermined his credibility as a Reagan Republican. Bush's political advisers were angered that much of the negotiations had been conducted behind closed doors, with "deficithawks" Darman and Sununu monopolizing the process. And moderates in both parties who had supported the

budget deal were also angered when, only two days later, Bush stated that his support of the budget had been a mistake. As his reelection campaign neared, he continued to broadcast his regret for a move that many considered essential to the long-term health of the country, but that he seemed to address in purely political terms. "If I had to do that over," he said in a 1992 radio address, "I wouldn't do it. Look at all the flak it's taking" (Mervin, p. 156). Bush's presidency never recovered from his apparent lack of resolve. Many took his willingness to compromise (and then immediately to apologize) as a sign of how he would respond to political pressures in a multitude of other circumstances.

Bush Backs the Voucher System

Bush proclaimed in the 1988 campaign that he would be the "education president," insisting that the answer to America's poor test scores and underachieving schools lay not with the federal government but with local initiative. As president, Bush supported conservative efforts to win federal support for vouchers that would allow parents to use public funds to pay private or parochial school tuition. He also pushed for "magnet" and "charter" schools—selective, focused public schools students could choose to attend in the place of their local institutions. The attempt to introduce "choice" into public schooling won Bush the enmity of education advocates everywhere, who feared vouchers and magnet schools would hurt ordinary public education, drawing resources—and the remaining middle-class students—away from local institutions. Both the National Education Association and the American Federation of Teachers—the nation's largest teachers' unions—vigorously opposed Bush's proposals. Although magnet and charter schools did begin to proliferate in larger districts, Bush's ideas never sold well with the American public, in part because Bush, believing that school policy was a local issue, refused to offer a detailed agenda or money to pay for the proposals.

Despite the fact that Bush believed education programs should pay for themselves, he did show more commitment to education than had Reagan, restoring money to existing programs that had been slashed in the Reagan years. Department of Education budgets increased 22 percent after inflation during Bush's term, and federal spending for college tuition grants and the successful Head Start preschool program for four-year-olds grew as well.

The Civil Rights Act of 1990

The Bush administration did more for minorities than the Reagan administration. The Bush Justice Department sided with minority groups in civil rights litigation much more often than had the Reagan attorney general's office. It acted more forcefully to enforce the Voting Rights Act, blocking many state and local redistricting plans on the ground that they discriminated against people who were African American or Hispanic American, and it pushed for more vigorous enforcement of housing laws. Bush also worked with Congress to secure approval of the Americans with Disabilities Act (ADA), a landmark law that prohibited discrimination against people with physical or mental disabilities. The legislation provided legal protection for disabled people in the workplace and required that all buildings open to the public be accessible to the handicapped.

But Bush's credibility with civil rights groups was effectively destroyed when he vetoed the Civil Rights Act of 1990, which was intended to protect workers from job discrimination. The legislation effectively overruled six U.S. Supreme Court decisions that had limited the legal options for employees who experienced discrimination in the workplace. The Civil Rights Act effectively shifted the burden of proving whether or not discrimination had occurred from the worker to the employer. Bush initially vetoed the bill, complaining that it would force employers to adopt "quotas" for hiring and promoting members of minority groups. After a bitter fight with civil rights groups and Democratic members of Congress, however, Bush signed a slightly revised version in November 1991 when it became clear that Congress had the votes to override his veto. Bush had effectively squandered his goodwill with civil rights groups, who had been angered by Bush's veto and his use of the racially charged

term "quota." After the bill became law, civil rights advocates became even more incensed when White House counsel C. Boyden Gray attempted to use the legislation to undermine longtime federal affirmative action programs. In the face of the furor, Bush eventually declared his support of affirmative action and ordered Gray to leave the programs intact.

The Environment

Bush had campaigned in 1988 as the future "environmental president," and in his first two years in office he made a number of moves that pleased environmental activists. He approved steep increases in the budget of the Environmental Protection Agency (EPA), refused to authorize an unpopular dam in Colorado that would have flooded a scenic canyon, and added more than $100 million to the federal budget for buying land for parks and refuges. In his last two years as president, however, as his popularity waned, Bush began to favor business interests over environmental concerns, placing a much higher priority on reducing the costs of complying with environmental regulation. In his last years in office, Bush backed proposals to limit the public's ability to block timber cutting, dam construction, and mining and oil exploration on public lands. He also approved a plan to develop 50 million acres of wetlands, half the nation's total, and was the last head of state to announce he would attend the international Earth Summit in Rio de Janeiro, Brazil. When he did attend, he drew widespread criticism for weakening a treaty to combat global warming and for refusing to sign a treaty to protect endangered species.

This same contradictory attitude on the environment was evident in Bush's approach to the ambitious revision of the Clean Air Act of 1990, the most comprehensive and expensive environmental statute ever enacted. Bush initially supported the rigorous new standards on air pollution that the law imposed, but when the recession hit and Bush's popularity plummeted, he allowed business interests to attack the law's enforcement at every turn. As the EPA prepared to write the new regulations called for by the act, the White House attempted to influence the process and soften the new clean air standards, refusing to meet numerous regulatory deadlines. The White House's foot-dragging in implementing the Clean Air Act won Bush the enmity of environmentalists despite his sincere interest in environmental protection.

Foreign Issues

United States foreign policy had, since the beginning of the Cold War, focused on containing Communism and countering the Soviet threat, and President Bush sold himself to the American public in 1988 as a seasoned statesman. In the first three years of his presidency, Bush won accolades for a number of foreign policy triumphs. He ended years of partisan dispute over U.S. policy in Central America, he presided over the fall of Communism in Eastern Europe, and he persuaded an unconvinced Congress to support the war in the Persian Gulf. Bush also reacted constructively and creatively to the end of the Cold War, and in 1990 he proclaimed that the old framework of American policy had given way to a new era of international cooperation, a "New World Order." (Graff, p. 600)

Because of the Soviet Union's declining power it was no longer the source of tension that it was during the Cold War years. But deadly conflicts in Haiti, Panama, and Bosnia defied the old Cold War formula, and a final resolution to the problems with Iraq came to seem more and more elusive. As international conflicts became more complex, Americans became less and less convinced that Bush was the right person to lead the nation into the post-Cold War era.

The Soviet Union Collapses

When Mikhail Gorbachev became the General Secretary of the Communist Party of the Soviet Union (its head of state) in 1985, few people anticipated the revolution in world politics he was set to bring about. In the face of the Soviet Union's increasingly severe economic difficulties, Gorbachev introduced two dramatic new initiatives into Soviet politics. Glasnost (openness) resulted in the dismantling of many of the repressive mechanisms of Soviet government, and perestroika (reform) attempted to restructure the ailing Soviet economy by introducing some elements of capitalism such as private ownership. Gorbachev also initiated a warming of relations with the United States by holding a series of summits with President Reagan.

Without money to sustain Soviet commitments abroad, the Soviet government also began loosening its grip on Communist governments across the world. The result, as Bush took power in 1989, was the collapse of nearly every Communist government in Eastern Europe. Marxist governments in Poland, Czechoslovakia, Hungary, Yugoslavia, Romania, Bulgaria, and Albania came tumbling down, replaced by incipient Western-style democracies. In October 1990 the Berlin Wall separating East and West Germany also came tumbling down, and Germany was reunited. The Soviet Union itself began to come apart in 1991 after Gorbachev called for free elections and granted independence to many of the former Soviet republics. Gorbachev dissolved the Soviet Union and on Christmas Day, 1991, leaving Russian president Boris Yeltsin to lead Russia in the post-Soviet era.

A Cautious Response

Bush responded to these staggering changes with his characteristic prudence. He cautiously supported Gorbachev in his reforms, applauded free elections in various Eastern bloc countries, worked very effectively behind the scenes to bring about the peaceful unification of Germany, and, after some prodding from former President Richard M. Nixon, pledged $1.5 billion in food aid to the Soviet Union (*New York Times*, June 26, 1992). He also held a series of summit meetings to formalize the changes that were happening in Eastern Europe. In the spring of 1990, Bush and Gorbachev agreed to reduce atomic and chemical stockpiles. In November 1990 the North Atlantic Treaty Organization (NATO) and the Warsaw Pact—the military alliances of the Western nations and the Eastern bloc, respectively—signed a mutual nonaggression pledge, proclaiming an end to the Cold War. The Warsaw Pact disbanded in March 1991.

Bosnia

If Bush's foreign policy expertise was formed in the atmosphere of the Cold War, the civil war in the former Yugoslavia illustrated the changing landscape of the post–Cold War world. After the fall of the Soviet bloc, foreign policy issues abroad were increasingly "intrastate" ethnic and national disputes, such as civil wars, rather than the "interstate" confrontations Bush had experience dealing with in the past. Since 1991 a war between the Christian Serbs and the ethnic Muslims of Bosnia over control of the multiethnic state had resulted in the murder of hundreds of thousands of Muslims and the displacement of two million refugees. The "ethnic cleansing" campaigns and concentration camps reminded Americans too much of the World War II Holocaust in Europe, and the public clamored to end the genocide. But U.S. politicians were haunted equally by the specter of the Vietnam War (1959–75) and were loathe to make the mistake again of risking American lives in a civil war in a place with little strategic importance to the United States. Bush refused to commit significant troops to participate in U.N. peacekeeping efforts, and many critics believed that Bush's lack of leadership in responding to the crisis in Bosnia was a sign of his inability to articulate the American mission after the Cold War.

Latin America

The end of the Cold War also precipitated challenges closer to home—political changes in the Central American countries that had long battled Communism—and military crises in Panama and Haiti. With the Soviet Union no longer providing aid for its client states, Marxism faltered not only in Eastern Europe, but also in Latin America, where Nicaragua and the rebels of El Salvador had long relied on Soviet assistance to support their revolutions. And without the threat of Communism in its backyard, the U.S. government no longer felt compelled to support corrupt dictatorships that had held the line against Communism.

Nicaragua

Americans had been particularly divided over the nation's foreign policy in Central America in the 1980s. The Reagan administration supported anticommunist forces in civil wars throughout Latin America, often in defiance of Congress. When Bush came to office, he concluded that Reagan's confrontational posture in Latin America had failed, particularly his policy of re-arming the anticommunist Contra rebels in Nicaragua after their defeat by socialist forces. Bush instead struck a compromise with Congress, extending humanitarian aid to the Contras and permitting the peaceful repatriation of the Contras in Nicaragua, but slashing funding for their political and military activities in exile. Bush's gamble on a more hands-off policy in Central America paid off when the Soviet bloc collapsed and Nicaragua's socialist Sandinista government also began to falter. In 1990 Nicaraguan opposition presidential candidate Violeta Chamorro surprised both the Americans and Sandinista president Daniel Ortega by leading the National Opposition Union, a 14-party anti-Sandinista coalition, to victory in Nicaragua's elections. In response, Bush lifted economic sanctions against Nicaragua.

Invasion of Panama

With Marxism ebbing in Latin America, the problem of drug trafficking became an increasingly high priority. On December 20, 1989, U.S. forces invaded Panama to capture General Manuel Antonio Noriega, Panama's unpopular military leader, who had been indicted for drug trafficking in Florida in 1987 and 1988. Bush had been criticized for failing to support an October 1989 coup attempt against Noriega, and after a U.S. military officer was killed by the Panamanian defense forces in 1989, Bush took the opportunity to unseat the Panamanian strongman. American troops invaded Panama shortly thereafter, and Noriega surrendered to U.S. forces on January 3, 1990. Noriega was tried in Florida and found guilty of eight counts of cocaine trafficking, racketeering, and money laundering. He was sentenced to 40 years in prison.

Bush's decision to invade Panama met with mixed reactions both at home and abroad, in part because the United States had, to various degrees, tolerated Noriega's obvious involvement in the drug trade for years, all the while keeping him on intelligence payrolls to provide information on Cuba and Nicaragua. Critics saw the invasion as a violation of international law and of the U.S. Constitution. The invasion was attacked by all of the Latin American states and all but the United States's most staunch allies in Europe.

Haitian Refugees Turned Back

After Haiti's first elected president, Jean-Bertrand Aristide, was deposed by a military junta, the island nation's military leaders imposed a reign of terror that unleashed a flood of refugees to U.S. shores. A U.S. embargo against Haiti failed to persuade the military dictators to step aside peacefully. Bush refused to intervene, and he also refused to allow the flood of refugees leaving Haiti on rickety boats to land in U.S. shores. Rather, he initiated a policy of intercepting the refugees on the open seas and escorting them to refugee camps at the U.S. military base in Guantanamo Bay, Cuba, where the Haitians' requests for asylum were processed in an excruciatingly slow manner. Critics, including Bill Clinton, asserted that the camps were more like prisons than immigration facilities. When Clinton won the presidential election in 1992, he did initially continue the policy of interning the refugees. In 1994, however, Clinton finally committed U.S. troops to Haiti. The junta, negotiating through former president Jimmy Carter, agreed to step down and allow Aristide to return and resume his presidency.

Conflict in the Middle East

In the 1980s the Persian Gulf nations of Iran and Iraq engaged in a long, costly war over their mutual border. The Reagan administration had sided with Iraq during the war, believing that the great menace to peace in the Gulf was Iran. The United States provided weapons, money, and technical support to Iraqi leader Saddam Hussein during the conflict. When Bush came to office, his administration continued to isolate Iran and extend Iraq political and economic favors, even as U.S. intelligence reports noted Hussein's increasingly threatening behavior. Hussein was spending $10 billion, 40 percent of Iraq's oil revenues, in 1988 and 1989 on military equipment and personnel, and mounting evidence suggested Iraq was developing nuclear and biological weapons. Even as Iraq grew steadily more belligerent, the Bush administration provided Baghdad with $500 million in agricultural credits that were widely diverted to kickbacks and arms buying, and sold high technology equipment to Hussein that could be useful in military programs. Even with U.S. support, however, the expensive eight-year-war left Iraq short on hard currency and in need of better access to shipping routes on the Persian Gulf. Iraq invaded the small, oil-rich emirate of Kuwait on August 2, 1990, in the mistaken belief that the United States would continue to support Iraqi aggression in the Persian Gulf.

Operation Desert Shield

Concerned with the destabilization of the Persian Gulf and with U.S. oil interests in Kuwait, President Bush responded forcefully to the Iraqi invasion, building an international coalition in support of Kuwait unlike any since World War II (1939–45). Bush and his allies launched "Operation Desert Shield," a defensive military operation headquartered in Saudi Arabia. The alliance, under the umbrella of the United Nations (UN), imposed a January 15, 1991, deadline for Iraqi withdrawal from Kuwait. The coalition also imposed an economic embargo on Iraq—halting oil purchases and other transactions with Iraq—and froze Iraqi and Kuwaiti assets in the hopes of forcing Hussein to withdraw peacefully from Kuwait. Bush's work in persuading an unprecedented number of international leaders to support the coalition against Iraq may have been his greatest diplomatic feat,

The U.S. flag being raised at the U.S. embassy in Kuwait at the conclusion of Operation Desert Storm in 1991. (The Library of Congress.)

pulling together a world community that had been polarized by ideological divisions since World War II.

Dissent

While many in the United States supported a military commitment against Iraq, there were also many vocal critics. "No Blood for Oil" banners appeared across the nation to voice the protest that the American commitment in the Gulf was based purely on the desire for cheap oil. Congressional Democrats criticized Bush's policies on Iraq before the war, pointing out that the Rea-

gan administration's unwavering support of Hussein in the Iran-Iraq war led the Iraqi president to believe Americans would tolerate an invasion of Kuwait. And when Iraq amassed 100,000 troops on Kuwait's northern border, Bush, believing Hussein was bluffing, still sent conciliatory messages to Iraq.

The Persian Gulf War

When Hussein remained in Kuwait past the January 15, 1991 deadline, the UN coalition prepared for a war that would include troops from the United States, Saudi Arabia, Great Britain, Egypt, France, Syria, Kuwait-in-exile, Pakistan, Morocco, Bangladesh, Canada, Italy, Senegal, Niger, and Argentina. Those industrialized nations that did not contribute troops, including the Soviet Union, provided naval vessels or money. The coalition was an unprecedented display of international cooperation, leading Bush to proclaim that a "New World Order" had risen from the ashes of the Cold War, defending against "naked aggression" in the world wherever it arose (Graff, p. 600).

Operation Desert Storm commenced on January 16, 1991, with a massive aerial bombing campaign against Iraq. A little more than a month later, the international force commenced a ground war. With such a massive commitment of forces, the UN troops led by U.S. general Norman Schwarzkopf liberated Kuwait in a matter of days. On February 27, only four days after the ground war began, the U.S. Marines liberated Kuwait City and began to press on into southern Iraq. A total of 148 Americans were killed in the war, with 467 wounded, and 15 percent of the U.S. casualties were injuries inflicted by their own troops. Only 141 servicemen from other allied nations were killed in the war. Meanwhile Iraq suffered immense losses: 100,000 dead and 300,000 wounded.

On April 3, 1991, Iraq accepted the UN Security Council's terms for a cease-fire. The agreement restored Iraq's pre-war boundary with Kuwait, required that Iraq pay reparations to a war-scarred Kuwait, and mandated the elimination of Iraq's weapons of mass destruction. In the United States the operation was hailed as a success and proof that the country had recovered from the divisiveness and shame that surrounded its defeat in the Vietnam War (1959–75).

The Aftermath

The pinnacle of George Bush's political career may have occurred on March 7, 1991 when his approval ratings soaring to nearly 90 percent in several polls. On that date he also received a three-minute standing ovation from a joint session of Congress in deference to his skillful handling of the war. The adulation, however, was short-lived, in part because of the recession; in part because of increasing criticism of Bush's blindness towards Hussein's aggressions before the war; and in part because of lingering difficulties in Iraq.

Iraq repeatedly violated cease-fire terms by threatening UN patrol planes and barring UN weapons inspectors from examining Iraqi arsenals. Hussein ruthlessly quashed internal rebellions among Kurds in the north and Shiite Moslems in the south, and continued to threaten Kuwait. Bush, however, fearing a protracted engagement in Iraq, remained reluctant to invade Iraq and unseat Hussein. Hussein's unwillingness to comply with the terms of the cease-fire would persist well into the Clinton administration. These ongoing struggles quickly dampened the initial public enthusiasm about the victory over Iraq.

World Trade

Bush was an outspoken advocate for more open and free trade in the international sphere, and the Bush administration was instrumental in negotiating two of the most far-reaching international trade agreements in history. Bush's trade representatives hammered out the details of both the North American Free Trade Agreement (NAFTA), which Congress approved in Bill Clinton's first year in office in 1993, and the General Agreement on Tariffs and Trade (GATT), ratified a year later. NAFTA did away with all trade barriers between the United States, Mexico, and Canada, creating one huge free trade zone. GATT negotiated a lowering of trade barriers throughout the world. Both agreements, but particularly NAFTA, met with vehement opposition among unions and working-class people worried that jobs would flow to poorer countries where workers would command significantly lower salaries. Labor advocates pointed to the low-wage, poorly-regulated Mexican *maquiladoras*—factories that manufactured American goods in a narrow free trade zone just south of the Mexican border—as an example of the abuses workers could expect from unfettered global trade. Environmentalists attacked the accords as well, out of concern that local environmental legislation would be nullified by international agreements that saw environmental protection as a "trade barrier."

The Bush Administration Legacy

George Bush stepped down from office in a very different world from that in which he had been elected. The Cold War was over and the prosperity of the Reagan years was gone. Americans had come to feel that Bush, a competent manager, had been too reactive in a time when the nation needed a creative, forward-looking leader.

Bush succeeded one of the most immensely popular presidents in American history, and for a time it seemed that Bush would surpass Ronald Reagan's public standing. Bush, however, also inherited the economic problems caused by Reagan's reign, and even as Bush's popularity soared to almost 90 percent during the 1991

Persian Gulf War, the nation had entered a prolonged and deepening recession. As the 1992 election loomed and the recession settled in, Bush's foreign policy achievements came to be overwhelmed by his failure to address the faltering economy. By the spring of 1992 Bush's popularity had dropped below 35 percent, and voters expressed a sense that the Bush administration was drifting without clear priorities. In a June 1992 *New York Times* poll, only one percent of voters questioned about Bush's most important accomplishment mentioned the economy or his leadership abilities. The largest number—29 percent—said the President's most memorable achievement had been the Persian Gulf War, 18 percent mentioned foreign policy in general, and 39 percent could think of nothing at all that Bush had done that they would consider an accomplishment (*New York Times*, June 25, 1992).

Lasting Impact

By his own design, George Bush left little impact on the nation's laws. Bush was a true conservative who believed a president's role should be that of a "guardian" seeking stability, not change. Unfortunately, the country, and the world, changed without him, and Americans faulted Bush for not responding decisively enough to those transformations, particularly with regards to the ailing economy. Having served as vice president for eight years, Bush was also hard-pressed either to radically reverse the policies of his predecessor or to blame the previous administration for his own difficulties.

Bush's greatest accomplishments were in the realm of foreign affairs, but even here time has shown his achievements to be less than originally imagined. The allied forces spent $61 billion in the Persian Gulf War, critics said, to drive Saddam Hussein out of Kuwait. Hussein, however, was still causing problems for the United States long after Bush left office. Some believe that the war simply inaugurated a new era of American impotence in the Persian Gulf. After a decade of standoffs with its onetime ally Iran, the United States would spend the 1990s in frustrating conflict with Iraq. Bush's most lasting contribution to the global picture was probably not the stalemate in the Persian Gulf, but his work leading to the ratification of the NAFTA and GATT free trade accords, which lowered international trade barriers and effectively legitimized the increasing globalization of the U.S. economy.

Sources

Duffy, Michael, and Dan Goodgame. *Marching in Place: The Status Quo Presidency of George Bush*. New York: Simon & Schuster, 1992.

Encyclopedia of World Biography. 2d ed. Detroit: Gale Research, 1998.

Graff, Henry F., ed. *The Presidents: A Reference History*. New York: McMillan, 1997.

Kane, Joseph Nathan. *Facts About the Presidents.* 6th ed. New York: H.W. Wilson, 1993.

Mervin, David. *George Bush and the Guardianship Presidency.* New York: St. Martin's Press, 1996.

Woodward, Bob. *The Agenda: Inside the Clinton White House.* New York: Simon & Schuster, 1992.

Further Readings

Bush, Barbara. *Barbara Bush: A Memoir.* New York: Scribner's Sons, 1994.

Bush, George H. W. *Looking Forward: An Autobiography.* Garden City, N.Y.: Doubleday, 1987.

George Bush Presidential Library and Museum. 1999. <http://www.csdl.tamu.edu/bushlib/> (25 June 1999).

Graubard, Stephen R. *Mr. Bush's War: Adventures in the Politics of Illusion.* New York: Hill & Wang, 1992.

Pamet, Herbert. *George Bush: The Life of a Lone Star Yankee.* New York: Scribner, 1997.

Stewart, James B. *Den of Thieves.* New York: Simon & Schuster, 1991.

Woodward, Bob. *The Commanders.* New York: Simon & Schuster, 1991.

Clinton Administrations

Biography

The first U.S. president born after World War II, Bill Clinton in many ways personified the polarization of the baby boom generation. Born in rural Arkansas, Clinton attended the nation's best universities, became involved in the social protests of the 1960s, and possessed both striking ambition and remarkable political skills. Often embroiled in controversy, Clinton's path to the presidency was a reflection of the personal and political turbulence of the postwar era.

Early Life

William Jefferson (Bill) Clinton was born in Hope, Arkansas, on August 19, 1946. Clinton's mother, Virginia Kelley, named him after his father, William Jefferson Blythe IV, who was killed in an automobile accident several months before young Clinton's birth. When the boy was four years old, he went to live with his maternal grandparents, Harkey and Mattie Hawkins, while his mother trained to become a nurse-anesthetist in New Orleans. His grandparents ran a small grocery store in a predominantly African American neighborhood outside Hope. Despite the racism that pervaded the U.S. South in the early 1950s, Clinton's grandparents treated their customers with respect and dignity, and impressed upon the future president the idea that segregation was wrong.

When Clinton was eight, his mother married Roger Clinton, a car salesman, and the family moved to Hot Springs, Arkansas, to a house that had no indoor plumbing. Although Clinton took his stepfather's last name when he was 16 in a gesture of family solidarity, the

Full name: William Jefferson Clinton
Given name: William Jefferson Blythe, IV
Popular name: Bill Clinton

Personal Information:

Born: August 19, 1946
Birthplace: Hope, Arkansas
Religion: Baptist
Spouse: Hillary Diane Rodham (m. 1975)
Children: Chelsea Victoria
Education: Georgetown University, B.S., 1968; attended Oxford University, 1968–70; Yale Law School, L.LD.,1973
Occupation: Law professor; Arkansas attorney general; Arkansas governor
Political Party: Democratic Party
Age at Inauguration: 46 years

Bill Clinton. *(The White House.)*

household was a troubled one. Roger Clinton was an alcoholic, who often flew into drunken rages, beating his wife and once firing a gun inside the house. At the age of 14, young Clinton stood up to his stepfather, making it clear that he would protect his mother and half-brother, Roger, Jr., from any further assaults.

Clinton traced the empathy that he communicated so well to voters (he was frequently lampooned for his oft-repeated campaign phrase, "I feel your pain") to his chaotic childhood. His peacemaking skills and his tendency to emphasize compromise over conflict (or, as some critics said, his habit of telling people what they wanted to hear), was a trait Clinton believed he inherited from the years of living with an abusive stepfather. Biographers also linked Clinton's tremendous political skills to his mother's optimism, tenacity, and resilience in response to the less than optimal circumstances of her life. Virginia Kelley (who married a third time after Roger Clinton's death) always accentuated the positive: "when bad things do happen," she wrote in *Leading with My Heart,* her posthumously-published memoirs, "I brainwash myself to put them out of my mind." Clinton, like his mother, demonstrated a remarkable ability to brush off his defeats (Kelly, 1994).

Intelligent and driven, Clinton considered several careers as a child. At one point he wanted to play the saxophone for a living, at another he hoped to become a doctor. Clinton was a natural leader from an early age, and in 1963, as part of a delegation of the American

Legion Boys' Nation, he met then-President John F. Kennedy. That meeting had a profound affect on Clinton who decided thereafter he wanted a career in politics.

Education

Clinton entered Georgetown University in 1964. As a college student coming of age in the heat of the social turmoil of the 1960s, he was committed to the movement against the Vietnam War (1959–75) and to the civil rights struggle. In 1966 he worked as a summer intern for Arkansas senator J. William Fulbright, who was at that time the leading antiwar spokesman in the U.S. Senate. Clinton was still a college student in Washington, D.C., when Martin Luther King Jr., was killed, and during the riots that followed King's assassination he and a friend used Clinton's car to deliver food and medical supplies to besieged neighborhoods.

Clinton graduated from Georgetown University in 1968 with a Bachelor of Science in International Affairs. It was already clear to those who knew him that he was a natural politician. Clinton had served as president of his freshman and sophomore class at Georgetown, although he lost the election for student body president when he was a senior. That same year, he was awarded a Rhodes scholarship and spent the next two years as a postgraduate student at Oxford University. In 1969, while at Oxford, Clinton was classified as eligible for the Vietnam draft. He signed a letter of intent to join the Army Reserve Officers Training Corps program at the University of Arkansas in order to avoid the draft. After Clinton drew a lottery number high enough to avoid being shipped to Vietnam, he wrote a letter to a colonel in the University of Arkansas ROTC program thanking him "for saving me from the draft" and expressing his opposition to the war in Vietnam. In his 1969 letter, he said that he had only submitted himself to a draft system that he considered "illegitimate" in order "to maintain my political viability within the system . . . to prepare myself for a political life characterized by both practical political ability and concern for rapid social progress." At the age of 23 Clinton was already concerned with his electability.

In 1970 Clinton entered law school at Yale University. In his first year at Yale Clinton served as a campaign coordinator for Joe Duffy, an antiwar candidate for the U.S. Senate from Connecticut. While still a law student, Clinton worked with writer Taylor Branch (best known for *Parting the Waters,* the 1989 Pulitzer-prize-winning first volume in a planned trilogy of the U.S. civil rights movement) as campaign coordinator in Texas for antiwar presidential candidate George McGovern. At Yale, Clinton also met Hillary Rodham, a fellow law student, who would soon become his wife.

Family Life

After graduation from Yale, Clinton returned to Arkansas while Rodham went to work on the staff of the House of Representatives committee that was considering the impeachment of President Richard Nixon. Clinton went into private practice in Fayetteville, the center of Arkansas politics, and also began teaching at the University of Arkansas Law School. Rodham followed Clinton to Fayetteville in 1974 and also began teaching at the University of Arkansas Law School. On October 11, 1975, Bill Clinton and Hillary Rodham were married. On February 27, 1980, they had a daughter, named Chelsea Victoria.

Early in the presidential campaign of 1992, Hillary Rodham Clinton became a target of criticism from conservatives opposing Clinton's candidacy, who liked to refer to the Democratic ticket as "Clinton and Clinton." Her detractors claimed that Rodham-Clinton's strong opinions, her professional credentials, and her "radical feminism," would mean that the White House would soon be occupied by a powerful, unelected "Lady Macbeth with a headband." Criticisms of Hillary's influential role in her husband's career only grew stronger when the Clintons moved to Washington and the new first lady broke precedent by occupying an office in the West Wing of the White House, the area where presidential policy is usually made.

Rodham-Clinton eventually scaled down her public role after criticism escalated surrounding her involvement in the policy decisions at the White House, which included an unsuccessful attempt to overhaul the nation's health care system. She moved her office away from the West Wing and assumed a lower, more traditional profile. Rodham-Clinton stood by her husband through all of the scandals and allegations of womanizing that dogged his presidency, and her steadfast defense helped him weather the storm any number of times. She was also the subject of numerous allegations, and was investigated for her involvement in firings at the White House travel office, in commodities trading in Arkansas in the late 1970s, and in the collapse of the Whitewater real estate venture.

Career

In 1974, soon after graduating from law school and moving back to Arkansas, Clinton ran for Congress against incumbent John Paul Hammerschmidt, a Nixon supporter. Although he was a skillful campaigner, Clinton lost the election in a surprisingly close vote. Running in a heavily Republican district, Hammerschmidt received only 51.5 percent of the vote. In 1976 Clinton again set his sights on public office, this time winning a race for attorney general for the state of Arkansas, an office he held from 1977 to 1979. Clinton maintained a high profile, developing a reputation as a reformer and consumer advocate who fought against utility rate raises and crusaded for environmental protection.

Clinton was elected governor of Arkansas in 1978. At the age of 32, Clinton was the state's youngest-ever governor, the second youngest governor of any state since 31-year-old Harold E. Stassen was elected to govern Minnesota in 1938. Clinton brought an ambitious agenda to the governor's office. He surrounded himself with inexperienced young aides, however, and attempted to institute a series of measures, such as raising the state gasoline tax and automobile registration fees, without gauging the support of Arkansas voters. Perhaps more importantly, he also offended the state's influential poultry and trucking industries—the major financiers of Arkansas political candidates and their campaigns—when he attempted to tax truck payloads in order to pay for road improvements.

In 1980, the same year Ronald Reagan swept President Jimmy Carter from office, Clinton lost his bid for reelection. Republican Frank White, who was backed by the business interests that Clinton had angered, wrested the governor's seat from Clinton. While Clinton's strong support for Carter in the presidential election may have accounted for his loss, the youngest ex-governor in U.S. history also recognized that many of his own policies had cost him reelection, especially those that alienated Arkansas big business. It was a lesson that profoundly influenced Clinton's career in politics. When a chastened Clinton campaigned to regain the governorship in 1982 against White, he reemerged as a pragmatic politician, explaining to voters that he had learned the price of his arrogance and the importance of adaptability and compromise. The affable, engaging Clinton, who always displayed a tremendous ability to communicate with voters, took 55 percent of the vote, and won every other election in which he ran.

Clinton served as governor of Arkansas until 1992. He was considered an activist, pushing for school reform and for health care and welfare reform in a state that included some of the poorest and least educated constituencies in the union. While his initiatives saw mixed results, Arkansas' national ranking in terms of education and salary levels improved under Clinton's watch. Advertising the state's low wage base, Clinton offered tax breaks to entice new businesses into the state, creating more than 200,000 new manufacturing jobs during his time as governor. He also became increasingly active in national Democratic politics. Clinton attracted more and more interest as a new, pragmatic voice in post-segregation Southern politics. In 1988 the governor took the national spotlight at the Democratic convention when he was selected to deliver the nominating speech for Massachusetts Governor Michael Dukakis as the party's presidential candidate. The now-notorious 32-minute address bored the convention's delegates so much that they began to chant "Get off, Get off," cheering only when Clinton finally said, "In conclusion . . ."

Biography:

Hillary Rodham-Clinton

Lawyer; First Lady (b. 1947) With the arguable exception of Eleanor Roosevelt, no previous first lady of the United States has both figured so prominently in a presidential administration and been widely regarded as a major U.S female political figure, as Hillary Rodham-Clinton. In the first year of her husband's presidency, Rodham-Clinton was appointed to head the Task Force on National Health Care with the responsibility of preparing legislation, lobbying proposals before Congress, and marshaling strategy for passage of a comprehensive reform package. In the twilight of her husband's second term in office, Rodham-Clinton launched an exploratory committee to look into the viability of her running for a soon-to-be vacant New York Senate seat. Wellesley and Yale-graduated, Rodham-Clinton came to the White House with prior professional experience as a corporate lawyer, a tenacious fighter for educational reform, a nationally recognized expert on children's legal rights, and a director of both corporate and non-

profit boards. She continued to champion children's issues from her office in the west wing of the White House. In 1995 Rodham-Clinton was invited to deliver the keynote address at the United Nations International Conference on Women near Beijing, China. The following year, she and her daughter Chelsea made a goodwill trip to Asia to address women's issues in Pakistan

and India. In 1996 Rodham-Clinton also wrote her bestseller, *It Takes a Village: And Other Lessons Children Teach Us.* With her unique background and her demonstrated strength and ambition, many expect Rodham-Clinton to have redefined the role of first lady for the twenty-first century.

Clinton, however, showed resilience in the face of his humiliating national debut, much as he would throughout his campaign and presidency. He shrugged off the embarrassment and continued his activities in national politics. In 1990 he was chosen as chair of the moderate Democratic Leadership Conference. Along with other southern Democrats such as Senator Albert Gore of Tennessee and Sam Nunn of Georgia, Clinton worked to shift control of the party away from the northeastern liberal wing toward more centrist policies and political constituencies. By 1991 Clinton had achieved national prominence, and was voted most effective governor in the nation in a *Newsweek* poll of state governors.

President

In October of 1991 Clinton announced that he was entering the race for president of the United States, and in 1992 he beat incumbent Republican President George Bush in a three-way race to become the 42nd president. As president, Clinton presided over an era of unprecedented prosperity, and easily won reelection for a second term in 1996. Despite Clinton's political genius, however, he also was a lightning rod for the criticism of the political right, who saw him as a symbol of the promiscuous values of the 1960s, and pursued him with a zeal previously unseen in presidential politics.

Clinton was embroiled in scandal from the moment he took office. Both Bill and Hillary Clinton were sub-

ject to a three-year, $50 million Independent Counsel investigation of a failed real estate deal Clinton was involved with in Arkansas in the 1970s. Although investigators turned up no evidence of criminal wrongdoing by the Clintons, they did uncover evidence that the president had an affair with a White House intern in late 1995 and 1996, and had provided evasive answers in a court deposition about the affair. Accusing him of perjury and obstruction of justice, in 1998 the House of Representatives voted along party lines to impeach Clinton. In 1999, however, he was acquitted by the Senate, which could not muster a majority to convict the president—much less the two-thirds vote needed to unseat Clinton. Only a handful of Democrats in the House, and none in the Senate, voted for conviction. The proceedings were seen by a large majority of Americans less as an attempt to punish "high crimes and misdemeanors" as a public war waged along partisan lines.

The Bill Clinton Administration

Bill Clinton came to power in a time of profound economic restructuring and anxiety, and promised to use the power of the presidency to help the struggling American middle class return to prosperity. The Clinton

Administration

Administration Dates

January 20, 1993–January 20, 1997
January 20, 1997–

Vice President

Albert Gore (1993–)

Cabinet

Secretary of State

Warren M. Christopher (1993–97)
Madeleine Albright (1997–)

Secretary of the Treasury

Lloyd M. Bentsen (1993–94)
Robert E. Rubin (1995–)

Secretary of Defense

Les Aspin (1993–94)
William J. Perry (1994–97)
William Cohen (1997–)

Attorney General

Janet Reno (1993–)

Secretary of the Interior

Bruce Babbitt (1993–)

Secretary of Agriculture

Mike Espy (1993–94)
Daniel Glickman (1994–)

Secretary of Commerce

Ronald H. Brown (1993–96)
Mickey Kantor (1996–97)
William M. Daley (1997–)

Secretary of Labor

Robert B. Reich (1993–97)
Alexis M. Herman (1997–)

Secretary of Health and Human Services

Donna E. Shalala (1993–)

Secretary of Housing and Urban Development

Henry G. Cisneros (1993–97)
Andrew M. Cuomo (1997–)

Secretary of Transportation

Federico Peña (1993–97)
Rodney Slater (1997–)

Secretary of Energy

Hazel R. O'Leary (1993–97)
Federico Peña (1997–98)
Bill Richardson (1998–)

Secretary of Education

Richard W. Riley (1993–)

Secretary of Veteran Affairs

Jesse Brown (1993–97)
Togo D. West Jr. (1997–)

---

administration was marked by tremendous economic growth, but also by unprecedented political warfare. The election of an ideological, hostile Republican Congress in 1994 spelled the end of Clinton's activist programs: he spent the rest of his presidency defending himself from both political and personal attacks.

Clinton Becomes President

The Campaign of 1992

In the aftermath of the Persian Gulf War (1991), President George Bush seemed headed for easy reelection. His near 90 percent approval rating dissuaded many nationally prominent Democrats, such as Senator Bill Bradley of New Jersey and Governor Mario Cuomo of New York, from entering the race. But by election sea-

son, the nation had plunged into a damaging and prolonged recession—an economic downturn—and voters were unhappy. Clinton, campaigning as an economic populist fighting for the interests of the middle class, emerged as a contender early in the Democratic race, winning second place in the New Hampshire primary behind the local favorite, former Massachusetts Senator Paul Tsongas.

In the weeks before the primary, the tabloid newspaper *The Star* published allegations that Clinton had a 12-year affair with an Arkansas woman named Gennifer Flowers. It was the first of many "bimbo eruptions," as one loyal Clinton aide came to call the allegations of infidelity and womanizing that would bedevil Clinton's campaign and presidency. In addition, stories broke about Clinton's use of marijuana and his attempts to avoid the Vietnam draft. Newspapers found and published a letter Clinton had written to the ROTC commander expressing his antiwar sentiments, but saying that he had submitted himself to the draft in order to maintain his "political viability." Despite these allegations Clinton pressed on. The fact that Clinton sidestepped the damaging allegations and took second place in the New Hampshire primaries demonstrated his tremendous resilience in the face of controversy and defeat that would serve him throughout his presidency. Clinton soon became the clear front-runner, outpolling and outfund-raising most of his competition, which included Senator Bob Kerrey of Nebraska, Senator Tom Harkin of Iowa, Virginia Governor L. Douglas Wilder, and Tsongas, the winner of the New Hampshire primary. He went on to win most of the Southern primaries. Only Jerry Brown, the former governor of California, remained in the race until the Democratic convention, long after Clinton had locked up the nomination.

Ross Perot

Despite his success in the Democratic primaries, Clinton stood a distant third in national polls as he approached the Democratic convention. President Bush, whose approval ratings had fallen dramatically as the nation became mired in recession, had also fallen in the polls. In the lead was H. Ross Perot, a diminutive, sharp-tongued Texas billionaire who had entered the race as an independent on a whim during an appearance on a cable-television talk show. Perot preached about the evils of the $4 trillion national debt and the corrupting influence of money in politics. The independent candidate offered plain-spoken solutions to the nation's dilemmas, saying a president should fix the country's problems like a good mechanic tinkering "under the hood" of a car, and promising to rid Washington of lobbyists "in thousand dollar suits and alligator shoes" (*New York Times*, 1992).

Perot, who financed his own "United We Stand" party that spearheaded a petition drive to place him on the ballot in all 50 states, held no convention and made few public appearances. Instead, he paid for half-hour time slots on the major television networks to present his case. On the same day that Clinton prepared to give his acceptance speech for the Democratic nomination, however, Perot announced that he was dropping out of the race. Perot explained that he believed the Democratic Party had revived to challenge Bush, and that deficit reduction had finally become a central issue in the campaign. With Perot out of the race, and Clinton in the spotlight at his party's national convention, Clinton's polling numbers shot up. For the first time, President Bush trailed his Democratic opponent.

The Democratic Ticket

The selection of Albert Gore Jr., a Democratic senator from Tennessee, as Clinton's running mate also improved the Democratic ticket's standing in the polls. Clinton defied the tradition of seeking regional balance on the presidential ticket by selecting Gore, who was,

like Clinton, a youthful, moderate Southern Democrat. Gore, the son of a longtime Tennessee congressman and senator, had won his father's congressional seat in 1976 and won election to the Senate in 1984. In many ways, Gore served as the perfect electoral counterpoint to Clinton. The vice presidential candidate's record was strong in areas where Clinton was considered weak. Unlike Clinton, Gore was an old Washington hand, an expert on foreign affairs and the environment, and had served in Vietnam despite his opposition to the war.

Gore had mounted his own unsuccessful bid for the presidential nomination in 1988, but failed to win enough delegates outside of the South to win the nomination. He opted out of the 1992 race in part because his young son was still recovering from a near fatal 1989 car accident. In 1991 Gore wrote *Earth in the Balance,* a national best-seller that called "rescuing the environment the central organizing principle for civilization." Gore's seriousness on issues like the environment, and his earnest public demeanor, lent Clinton, viewed as the consummate politician, a gravity that helped their campaign immensely. Together, the two men, both well over six feet tall, projected an image of youthful vigor and generational change that appealed to many voters. The Clinton-Gore candidacy was the youngest combined presidential ticket in U.S. history.

Both Clinton and Gore considered themselves to be "New Democrats," and both were key members of the Democratic Leadership Conference, the group of moderate, mostly Southern Democrats who hoped to move the Democratic Party back to the center. The New Democrats sought to convince middle class voters that the Democratic Party could be, in the words of journalist Robert Woodward, "strong on foreign and defense policy, moderate in social policy, and disciplined in spending tax dollars and taming runaway government." These "Reagan Democrats," the middle class and working class white Democrats who had defected to Republican presidential candidates in 1980s, were the people who held the balance in national elections. Clinton's campaign specifically targeted these swing voters in the hopes of wooing them back into the Democratic fold (Woodward, p. 25).

The Economy, Stupid

At the Democratic convention, Clinton framed the race as a referendum on President Bush's economic performance, contending that Bush refused to take active steps to fix the economy. Clinton argued that the president should use the power of his office in an active manner to restart the stalled economy. "I know how President Lincoln felt when General McClellan wouldn't attack in the Civil War," Clinton said in his nomination acceptance speech. "He asked him, 'If you're not going to use your army, may I borrow it?' And so I say: George Bush, if you won't use your power to help people, step aside, I will" (Woodward, p. 11).

Bush did not take Clinton's July surge in the polls seriously until after the Republican convention. When the party convened in Houston in August, the president received less of the traditional "bounce" after the convention than he had anticipated. This was in part because his convention proved to be a divisive one. The Republican Party's traditional "big tent" was pulled in two different directions, with economic conservatives on one side and social and religious conservatives like Pat Buchanan, who had challenged Bush in the Republican primaries, on the other. Bush was torn between his moderate background on social issues and the religious delegates who dominated the convention. Bush seemed unable to satisfy either wing of his party. Despite his efforts to move to the right on social issues, he remained more moderate than the religious activists who had come to hold considerable power in the party. Bush's attempts to placate the right wing of the Republican Party meant that he was captive to a party faithful that was far more conservative than the average American voter.

Throughout the last months of the general election campaign, Clinton continued to focus on Bush's economic performance. In the "War Room" at the center of Clinton's campaign headquarters in Little Rock, Arkansas, one of Clinton's campaign managers had pasted a slogan on the wall reminding his staff about the issue that drove their campaign: "It's the economy, stupid" (Woodward, p. 54). The Clinton campaign promised activist measures to improve the economic outlook of the United States and, ultimately, it was the candidates' positions on the economy that decided the election. The 1992 campaign, unlike that of 1988, was one of the more issue-driven elections in recent years. In a time of recession, Clinton believed that the federal government could play a constructive role in fixing the nation's social problems and stimulating economic growth.

Bush, by contrast, argued that the federal government should play a limited role. He insisted that the recession was ebbing and would end of its own accord, and called for a cut in the capital gains tax—the prohibitively high tax on the appreciation of investments—as his only answer for economic revitalization. The idea that a tax cut, which would primarily benefit the wealthy, would also stimulate the entire economy was a notion that recalled Ronald Reagan's prescription that tax cuts on the rich would "trickle down" to the less-fortunate. Clinton, campaigning as a champion of the middle class, supported an increase on taxes for the wealthiest Americans.

Clinton also called for health care reform and for investments in the national "infrastructure" of roads, communications systems, and common public assets. At the same time, Clinton attempted to defuse the Republican strategy of painting Democratic candidates as "tax-and-spend" liberals. Clinton made it difficult for Republicans to accuse him of coddling the poor by arguing for traditionally Republican measures such as welfare reform. He deflected calls that Democrats were "soft on crime" by calling for 100,000 new police officers on U.S.

streets. With Clinton matching Bush on many social issues, Bush's inactivity on the economy stood out even more starkly: to voters, Bush seemed more interested in preserving the status of the wealthy than in ensuring the survival of the middle class.

To compound Bush's difficulties, Ross Perot reentered the race in October, choosing a political neophyte, retired Rear Adm. James Stockdale, as his running mate. Perot's support never approached the levels it had before he withdrew from the race in June, but he nonetheless influenced the election, participating in the debates and running 30-minute television "infomercials" attacking Bush's leadership and questioning the country's economic footing. Bush responded by ignoring Perot and attacking Clinton's character, particularly his avoidance of the draft and his antiwar activism of the Vietnam years. He lambasted Clinton's tendency toward evasive responses, and derided what he said were Clinton's frequent changes of position. One Bush aide, Mary Matalin, went so far as to publicly attack Clinton as a "philandering, potsmoking, draft dodger." Clinton's campaign staff, however, responded promptly with a media blitz of faxes and telephone calls, deflecting most of Bush's barbs (Woodward, p. 97).

On Election Day, November 5, 1992, Clinton defeated Bush and Perot, winning most of the electoral votes (370 to 168) but only 43 percent of the popular vote. Clinton had maintained the traditional liberal coalition of the poor and middle class, African Americans, labor, and liberals, and won the votes of a large proportion of women and voters under the age of 25. He lost the South, however, reflecting the continued realignment of that region from Democratic to Republican after 1964. Perot won 19 percent of the popular vote, the largest percentage of the popular vote received by an independent candidate since 1912, when Theodore Roosevelt ran as the "Bull Moose" candidate.

The Campaign of 1996

In 1996 Clinton ran for reelection against former senate majority leader Robert Dole. Although Dole moderated the conservative rhetoric of the 1992 campaign and seemed more sympathetic to the concerns of ordinary Americans than Bush, Clinton won an easy victory against Dole, a perennial presidential candidate who appeared too dour and pessimistic to many voters. Independent candidate H. Ross Perot also entered the race, this time winning only eight percent of the vote. Brushing off allegations of fund-raising improprieties and a sex scandal involving Clinton's campaign adviser Dick Morris, Clinton won handily by once again offering voters a referendum on the economy. This time, the nation had undergone a remarkable economic recovery, and the economy was in better shape than it had been in 30 years. Clinton won the election with 49 percent of the popular vote and 379 electoral votes.

Clinton's Advisers

While Clinton appointed a number of influential cabinet secretaries and surrounded himself with loyal aides, his administration was in a constant state of flux. Aides and appointees came and went as Clinton's policy's shifted from liberal to moderate and as the investigations that culminated in impeachment continued to mount. Indeed, by the time Clinton's second term began, many of his most loyal followers from Arkansas and the 1992 campaign had left, many of them pulled into the vortex of White House scandal (*See also,* The Clinton Administration Legacy).

In part, this shifting personnel pool reflects the divisiveness of Washington politics during this period, particularly after the Republicans won both houses of Congress in 1994. Clinton's political ambitions and his magnetic personality had always stirred up a remarkable amount of enmity throughout his career in politics, but the highly partisan politics of a divided government contributed to the hostility that Clinton and his advisers faced.

The transience of his advisers also reflects Clinton's tendency to tack in the shifting political winds. After a storm of controversy surrounding the "liberal" policies Clinton initiated when he first arrived at the White House, the president began a gradual shift away from the left wing of his party. In part, the chaos in the Clinton administration reflected a battle within the White House walls. Liberals such as Labor Secretary Robert Reich and adviser George Stephanopoulos stood on one side, while more moderate voices like Treasury Secretary Robert Rubin and Budget Director and then-Chief of Staff Leon Panetta stood on the other. It was the moderates, preaching deficit reduction, who emerged victorious, and many of the liberals departed during and after Clinton's first term.

Clinton did rely on a few people throughout his presidency, including Vice President Al Gore, longtime friend and adviser Vernon Jordan, and first lady Hillary Clinton. The first lady broke precedent by occupying an office in the West Wing of the White House, the area where presidential policy is usually made. In the face of withering criticism, Mrs. Clinton scaled down her public role, which included involving herself in policy decisions such as an unsuccessful attempt to overhaul the nation's health care system. Despite the high-profile difficulties with their marriage, however, she remained Clinton's closest adviser.

Clinton appointed more women and members of minority groups to his cabinet and other high-level positions than any other president. Included among his appointees was the first female secretary of state in U.S. history, Madeleine Albright. He was often criticized, however, for his willingness to abandon nominees who generated unexpected controversy, as he did with Lani Guinier, a law professor who Clinton chose to head the Justice Department's civil rights division. When her past writings drew fire from conservatives, he withdrew his support, and left many civil rights advocates angered at his lack of resolve.

Clinton and Congress

Clinton came to the White House with a Democratic Congress and high expectations that he could advance his agenda with the help of his willing congressional partners. Clinton and the Democratic leadership, however, overestimated the depth of Clinton's public support and the discipline of the Democratic Congress to pass controversial legislation. Almost immediately, conservative Democrats defected from the Clinton camp over issues such as the new president's attempt to allow gays to serve in the military, and over the White House's 1993 budget proposal.

Still, the 103rd Congress was more active than any since the 1960s. It eventually passed a hard-fought deficit-cutting budget deal with only Democratic votes, approved two major trade deals, enacted a Family and Medical Leave Act that allowed family members to take unpaid time to care for their loved ones, and created a National Service program that repaid college loans for young people who took low-paying community service jobs after graduation. The Congress's successes, however, were overshadowed in the public mind by the defeat of Clinton's ambitious plan to reform the nation's health care system.

Although Clinton's relationship with Congress was rocky even before the Republicans won control of the House and Senate in 1994, relations reached a new low when the highly partisan and ideological 104th Congress convened in early 1995. The Republicans had won control of the House of Representatives for the first time in a generation, and they believed it was their mandate to enact a revolution in government. The new Speaker of the House, conservative Georgia Congressman Newt Gingrich, came to power brandishing a "Contract with America," a campaign document that many of the freshman congressmen had signed which sought to restructure or even do away with huge segments of the federal government.

Ironically, Clinton was in many ways more successful with a Republican Congress, in part because he scaled back his ambitions and supported more moderate, gradual legislation. After he vetoed a 1995 Republican budget with spending cuts that Clinton said were too extreme, the Republicans refused to pass the customary stopgap measures to keep the federal government open. The two resulting government shutdowns in late 1995 and early 1996 left the Republicans looking reckless. Clinton, meanwhile, prevailed by championing the popular middle class entitlement programs like Medicare that Republicans sought to reform. The Republicans eventually backed down and gave Clinton a bill he was more amenable to signing. In the course of the budget battle,

Clinton learned that the veto and the use of the "bully pulpit" to deliver high profile speeches to pressure Congress into cooperating gave him power to alter the shape of the Republican bills he signed. The 104th Congress's bills on welfare, agriculture, telecommunications, health insurance, and another deficit reduction budget deal all bore Clinton's imprint, despite their origins in the Republican Congress.

After winning the 1996 election, Clinton pledged to work from the "vital center" of U.S. politics in his second term. Having failed to carry a Democratic Congress back into office with him, he extolled the benefits of bipartisan legislation. Clinton would continue to shape legislation through vetoes and act as a defensive buffer, rebuffing attacks on popular New Deal and Great Society programs. His final term in office, however, was considerably less productive, in large part because of the personal and political scandals that began to increasingly impact Clinton's presidency. After the revelations about Clinton's affair with intern Monica Lewinsky and the allegations of perjury and obstruction of justice, Clinton's relationship with the Republicans in Congress reached a new low.

Although congressional Democrats initially joined Republicans in condemning Clinton's actions, they ultimately rallied to support him, especially after voters made it clear that they were not happy with the Independent Counsel investigation and that they did not believe Clinton should be forced to leave office. Republicans and Democrats alike were taken by surprise in the 1998 elections when Americans expressed their anger at the scandals by voting against the Republicans and narrowing the Republican majority in the House. In the wake of the elections, controversial House Speaker Newt Gingrich resigned his speakership and his seat in Congress, citing the unexpected losses and dissent among Republican ranks. After Speaker-elect Robert Livingston was accused of his own adulterous affairs and also resigned his seat, Illinois Congressman Dennis Hastert, a conservative with a much more unblemished reputation, won the position.

When the House of Representatives voted to impeach Clinton in December 1998, only a handful of Democrats voted with the Republicans, and when the Senate voted not to unseat Clinton, no Democrat voted against him. Still, Clinton would serve the remainder of his term as a lame duck president contending with hostile Republicans who expressed their mistrust of Clinton at every opportunity, and reluctant Democrats still resentful of Clinton's reckless behavior.

Clinton and the Judiciary

Bill Clinton appointed the highest percentage of minorities and women to the federal bench than any U.S. president. Clinton did face the same controversial battles over Supreme Court nominees as Presidents Reagan and Bush, in part because Clinton's nominees for the high court were moderate in their judicial philosophies. In 1993 Clinton nominated the second woman to the Supreme Court, federal appeals court judge Ruth Bader Ginsburg, to succeed the retiring Justice Byron White. In 1994, Clinton appointed former federal appeals court judge Stephen Breyer to succeed the retiring justice, Harry Blackmun. Both were known as moderate liberals, who fell in the middle of the ideological spectrum between the conservative appointees of Reagan and Bush and liberal judges that Jimmy Carter chose for the court. In the lower courts, too, Clinton avoided choosing judicial nominees who might attract opposition.

When Clinton took office, 15 percent of the nation's judicial slots were not filled. When the Republicans won the Senate two years later, they brought the confirmation process of judicial nominees for the lower courts almost to a standstill in order to preserve any vacancies in the hopes that Republicans would recapture the White House. In 1996, for the first time in a century, the Senate did not confirm any judges for the appeals courts, the level just below the Supreme Court, and confirmed only 17 district court judges. After Clinton won reelection, some Republican members of the Senate Judiciary committee still refused to allow Clinton to shape the courts, expressing their desires to keep certain seats permanently vacant because there were "too many judges." This prompted Supreme Court Chief Justice William H. Rehnquist, a Republican appointee, to note that the growing number of vacancies was slowing the administration of justice and creating a huge backlog of federal cases. Rehnquist urged Congress to speed up the process of confirming federal judges. Still, the Republicans on the Judiciary Committee dragged their feet.

Of the cases that the Supreme Court considered during Clinton's term of office, perhaps the most important lay in the realm of civil rights law. The courts were still in the process of interpreting many of the laws that had been created in the 1960s and 1970s to ensure the fair treatment of women and minorities. The court agreed to hear two important cases on affirmative action. The first, the 1995 case of *Adarand v. Pena,* restricted the use of race as a consideration in awarding federal contracts, requiring the government to reform the "set-aside" programs that guaranteed minority businesses a first crack at federal construction projects.

The court also agreed to hear a second case, *Taxman v. Piscataway Board of Education,* in which a New Jersey school board, faced with the need to lay off one teacher, chose to fire a white teacher while retaining an African American teacher with the same seniority and qualifications. The Bush administration had initially supported the fired schoolteacher's claim, but the Clinton administration switched positions on the case. The court never issued an opinion, however: fearful that an unfavorable decision would overturn affirmative action, a coalition of civil rights groups paid to settle the case.

What They Said . . .

"Indeed, I did have a relationship with Ms. Lewinsky that was not appropriate. In fact, it was wrong. It constituted a critical lapse in judgment and a personal failure on my part for which I am solely and completely responsible. But I told the grand jury today and I say to you now that at no time did I ask anyone to lie, to hide or destroy evidence, or to take any other unlawful action. I know that my public comments and my silence about this matter gave a false impression. I misled people, including my wife. I deeply regret that."

(Source: Bill Clinton. Remarks following his grand jury testimony, August 17, 1998.)

The court was faced with a number of cases that attempted to interpret the increasingly murky issues surrounding sexual harassment, particularly the issue of what constitutes a "hostile work environment." Sexual harassment directly affected Clinton's presidency when an Arkansas woman, Paula Jones, claimed that Clinton had propositioned her when she was an Arkansas state employee and he was governor. The Supreme Court ruled, for the first time, that a sitting president could stand trial in civil cases, and as Jones's lawyers began to take depositions in the harassment case, Clinton found his presidency wracked by allegations of marital infidelity and perjury (*See also,* Domestic Issues).

Changes in the U.S. Government

Clinton came to office in an atmosphere of public outcry against the growth of federal government, and most of the changes at the federal level came in the form of downsizing. Upon taking office, Clinton did form the National Economic Council, which would serve in the same advisory capacity as the National Security Council for defense issues, briefing the president every day on the nation's economic situation. This would be Clinton's only major administrative change, however. Clinton had hoped to elevate the Environmental Protection Agency to cabinet status, but backed off from his promise after congressional opponents objected. When the Republicans took over Congress, they proposed doing away with the Departments of Energy and Commerce. Confronted with the monumental task of reapportioning the duties of those

departments, however, the Republicans abandoned their efforts.

In 1999, after the Senate failed to convict Clinton of the articles of impeachment passed by the House of Representatives, Congress also considered abolishing the Office of the Independent Counsel. The office was formed in 1978 by the passage of the Independent Counsel Act. The statute, a response to the firings of Justice Department officials investigating President Richard Nixon during the Watergate scandal, was intended to promote good government, police the executive branch, and restore public faith in elected officials. The law created a position for an independent prosecutor to investigate public officials. The Independent Counsel Act, however, spawned some very destructive, unintended consequences.

Aiming to free investigations from politics, the Independent Counsel law became a political tool in itself. In the law's almost 21 years of existence, the Justice Department authorized 20 separate investigations, many of them long-term, few with significant convictions. The investigations cost U.S. taxpayers an aggregate of $150 million over the 20-year period. The investigation that led to Clinton's impeachment prompted almost universal criticism of the act—after a $50 million, three-year investigation ended in a publicly volatile and divisive impeachment trial. In June of 1999, the law expired and was not renewed by Congress. The top officials in the office reverted to the Justice Department.

Domestic Issues

Clinton took office in 1993 arguing that the nation needed dramatic change to undo the policies of 30 years of deficit spending. He argued that the nation needed to reverse an economic process that allowed a small percentage of the U.S. population to grow very rich while the middle and working classes saw their wages diminish and their prospects dim. The 1994 Republican takeover of Congress, however, ensured that Clinton's activist program, already crumbling under the pressures of the existing Congress, would come to a standstill. For the rest of Clinton's presidency, the Republicans sought to undo the legacy of Democratic Congresses dating from the New Deal and the 1960s. Clinton's vision of new Democratic activism was instead redirected into the project of defending and reforming the social programs of his predecessors (*See also,* Clinton and Congress).

Clinton's administration began in the midst of a deep recession that had, by the 1996 election season, been replaced by one of the most sustained periods of economic health in years. Unemployment, inflation, and interest rates dropped to 30-year lows, and the stock market, in the middle of its biggest boom in history, rose to record levels. Clinton's early decision to reduce the deficit at the expense of his proposed social programs both hurt and helped his presidency. The 1993 deficit reduction plan, which raised taxes, was the key campaign issue that helped Republicans recapture Congress in 1994. But by the time Clinton ran for reelection in 1996, the reduction of the deficit had prompted low interest rates and a Wall Street boom that was enormously popular with voters. The economy's health in many ways insulated Clinton from the stream of accusations and scandals that battered his administration.

The Economy

Beginning in the 1970s and becoming more marked in the 1990s, the United States developed a new technology-based economy that produced enormous disparities in income, wealth, and opportunity. In the first 20 years after World War II (1939–45), most Americans could survive on a single income. By 1992, however, more and more families depended on two incomes to maintain their standard of living. From 1973 to 1989, median family income increased less than two percent after inflation, even though many families now had two parents who were wage earners. And while the middle class was stagnating, the rich were growing richer at an astounding rate. Over 94 percent of the wealth created by the U.S. economy in the 1980s went to the richest 20 percent of the population, and over 50 percent was earned by the top one percent. In 1993, 47 percent of the total income in the United States accrued to the wealthiest 20 percent of the population. The recession of the early 1990s and the anxieties of working and middle class voters were reflections of these changes.

Bill Clinton won the 1992 election in part because Americans of modest means, insecure about their position in this increasingly disparate, two-tiered economy, had become convinced that President Bush was insensitive to their needs. Clinton campaigned as the champion of the "forgotten middle class," offering detailed programs that included cutting the deficit, enacting a middle class tax cut, and spending heavily on measures like job training, education, and research that would help American workers adjust to the changes of the new, information-based economy.

Deficit Reduction and Alan Greenspan

In office, however, Clinton soon discovered that he could not reduce the deficit and offer the middle class new tax cuts and entitlement programs. He had to choose one or the other. Even before he took office, Clinton met with Alan Greenspan, the chairman of the Federal Reserve Board, who impressed upon Clinton the importance of deficit reduction to the economy's health. If the budget gap increased, Greenspan said, so would interest rates, which would frighten the inflation-wary Wall Street bond traders, which would in turn stall economic growth. Greenspan, the man who controlled the interest rates, insisted that if the deficit was low, interest rates would remain low, which would stimulate investment in

new businesses and capital expansion, put money in the pockets of ordinary Americans who could refinance their mortgages, and give the stock market a boost.

Faced with a difficult choice, Clinton opted for the deficit reduction route favored by Greenspan and the bond traders on Wall Street, rather than the tax cuts he had conceived to help ordinary voters. He presented Congress with a deficit reduction package that included $250 billion in tax increases. The bill raised taxes on the wealthiest Americans from 31 percent to 40 percent of their income and instituted a 4.3 cent gasoline tax, while abandoning the middle class tax cuts and spending on "human capital" that Clinton had promised during the campaign. Alan Greenspan, with the control he exercised over interest rates, was the force behind this decision: the Federal Reserve Chairman was, according to political writer Bob Woodward "in some ways the ghostwriter of the Clinton plan" (Woodward, p. 135).

Balancing the Budget

While Clinton was often criticized for his tendency to sway in the political winds, the budget he submitted in 1993 represented a difficult decision to emphasize the nation's long-term economic health over short-term political gain. Knowing his budget would be highly unpopular with middle class voters and would give the Republicans an easy campaign issue for the mid-term elections, Clinton chose to pursue it anyway. Indeed, when the budget passed the House of Representatives with no votes to spare, the last representative to vote, Marjorie Margolies Mezvinsky, heard chants of "Bye bye, Marjorie" as she cast her vote with the president. She lost her seat in the 1994 elections (*New York Times,* 1992).

Government Shutdowns

After the Republicans won the majority of congressional seats in 1994, Clinton found himself fending off conservative bills. He vetoed Republican measures to cut taxes, limit social programs, and emphasize business profits over environmental protection. When the Republicans forced a government shutdown rather than pass stopgap spending bills to keep the government running during budget negotiations, Clinton refused to back down, and for several weeks government offices, parks, and other services across the United States were closed, at an enormous expense to taxpayers. Clinton won the public relations battle by insisting on preserving the New Deal and Great Society programs like Social Security and Medicare that the Republicans aimed to cut or reform. Voters, angered by the shutdowns, agreed with Clinton and the Republicans found themselves forced to accept a more bipartisan solution. Ultimately, Congress passed the first balanced budget bill in 17 years.

The struggle for deficit reduction produced a political payoff for Clinton, who won reelection in 1996 with unemployment and inflation at a 30-year low, with interest rates down, and the stock market surging. By 1998 the economy was so strong that, for the first time in decades, the taxes collected exceeded spending, and the federal government found itself with a budget surplus. While some Republicans wanted to refund the surplus by passing out tax cuts, Clinton argued that the money should go to restructuring the Social Security trust fund, which would go bankrupt by 2010 when the baby boomers began to retire. While Congress was slow to decide how to reform Social Security, the difficult political decision to save the surplus for the nation's long-term health rather than for immediate tax relief proved a popular one with voters.

Health Care

In his 1992 campaign "War Room," Clinton's campaign staff had pasted their campaign mantra, "It's the economy, stupid," along with a less famous slogan: "Don't forget health care." Along with his economic agenda, health care reform was the campaign promise closest to Clinton's heart. Democratic leaders from Truman on had failed to produce guaranteed, affordable health care, and by 1993 the problem had reached a critical point. In 1992, 37 million Americans were without health insurance, and insurers, concerned with profitability, had developed a system that could help only the healthy. Those who had "preexisting" medical conditions were often not able to find coverage.

The Task Force on Health Care Reform

After his election, Clinton assigned the first lady, Hillary Rodham Clinton, to create legislation guaranteeing universal health care to all Americans, and to shepherd it through Congress. The selection of his wife for such a monumental task, despite her obvious competence and ability, proved to be one of the biggest tactical errors of Clinton's presidency. Mrs. Clinton and consultant Ira Magaziner envisioned a system of "managed competition" in which networks of doctors, hospitals, and other health care providers competed for patients, overseen by a National Health Board. The team working on the bill, however, worked in secrecy, allowing neither Republicans nor the businesses affected to have any input into the reforms. When Mrs. Clinton's health care task force unveiled its complicated 240,000-word bill in September of 1993, insurance companies and medical associations immediately went on the attack.

The Republicans in Congress also seized the opportunity to assail the administration, calling the bill a system of "socialized medicine." The public, bombarded with criticism portraying Clinton as a tax-and-spend liberal trying to impose more big government on Americans, came to see the Clintons' plan for health care reform as a bid to replace their family doctor with a huge, impersonal bureaucracy. Clinton also made his task more difficult by promising to veto any bill that did not include universal coverage. Unable to compromise, Clinton watched his most ambitious legislation die in Congress as the 1994 mid-term elections neared. After the Republicans took control of Congress, Clinton found himself, ironically, the defender of the health care status quo, protecting Medicare and Medicaid from the cuts and overhauls that Republicans proposed.

The Clintons' spectacular defeat on health care overshadowed many of the administration's other goals, destroyed Hillary Clinton's attempt to remake the role of first lady into one of policymaker and partner, and left the president nearly mute on the pressing subject of health care reform. In 1996 Congress finally passed the Kennedy-Kassebaum health care reform act, a much less ambitious attempt at reform that allowed workers to take their insurance with them when they changed jobs and required insurance companies to cover both healthy applicants and those with preexisting conditions. By then, the number of uninsured Americans had grown to 40 million.

Criminal Justice

Perhaps Clinton's most sterling credential as a moderate "New Democrat" was his public stance on crime. Clinton abandoned the Democratic Party's traditional approach to criminal justice, which often emphasized the rights of criminal defendants over those of victims, and instead embraced a series of punitive measures that gave him conservative credentials and threatened the Republican Party's ownership of the "law and order" mantle. In his first campaign, Clinton endorsed expanding the federal death penalty, limiting death row appeals, and spending billions of dollars for prison construction. The Crime Bill he pushed through Congress in 1994 allocated $8.8 billion to meet his campaign promise of 100,000 more police officers on the streets; imposed a "Three-Strikes-and-You're-Out" provision to put violent criminals behind bars for life after three felonies; and expanded the death penalty for almost 60 federal crimes.

Clinton's tough stand on crime frustrated some civil libertarians who believed he had overstepped the constitutional bounds ensuring prisoners' rights. Clinton also cemented his support on liberal criminal issues such as gun control. Clinton supported the Brady Bill, which in an attempt to deter felons from buying handguns, required a five-day waiting period with background checks for prospective handgun buyers. He also supported a ban prohibiting the manufacture and importation of 19 assault weapons. Both laws passed Congress by very close votes in 1994.

By the 1996 election, crime rates had dropped substantially, in part because of the waning crack cocaine epidemic and the booming economy, and in part because of increased numbers of law enforcement officers and new approaches to policing. Clinton used these figures to point out that his 1994 Crime Bill was a substantive achievement of his first term.

Welfare

As the 1996 election approached, President Clinton reluctantly signed a bill that cut $55 billion from welfare programs for needy Americans. While the bill did fulfill Clinton's campaign promise to "end welfare as we know it," it did not end welfare in the way he had envisioned. In the wake of his disastrous defeat on national health care, Clinton had submitted a bill that would increase welfare spending by $10 billion in order to provide education, training, and child care to reintegrate women on welfare into the work force. When the Republicans won Congress, however, they proposed their own welfare bill that many considered to be the most sweeping reversal of domestic social policy since the New Deal.

While both Clinton and the Republicans believed welfare should be the means to a job, not an open-ended entitlement or a way of life, the Republicans sought to impose a strict two-year deadline on welfare benefits and to turn responsibility for the needy over to the states. Clinton vetoed two welfare bills that imposed time limits and limited federal involvement, but as the election approached, he finally signed another slightly less punitive bill that still contained the two-year deadline. In a speech that accompanied the signing, he noted that he had "deep reservations" about measures in the bill that cut the food stamp program significantly and blocked legal immigrants from receiving social services. Clinton said that he hoped Congress would reconsider those aspects in the next term.

The Environment

With the debate on the environment often framed as a choice between economic forces and ecological imperatives, the Clinton White House sought to tread the thin line between environmental and business concerns. Clinton did not initiate or sign any landmark environmental laws, but after the Republicans took Congress in 1994, he vetoed a series of anti-regulatory bills that would have dismantled an entire generation of rules preserving public lands and wilderness areas. While in office, Clinton also signed into law measures imposing strict new health protections on the use of pesticides and supporting the expansion of the National Park system into California's desert. He also signed executive orders enforcing new environmental policies on ocean dumping, recycling paper, and managing fisheries. In addition, he negotiated a number of compromises between the timber industry and environmentalists to restrict, but not prohibit, forest logging, and he attempted, with little success, to restructure the system of subsidized logging, mining, and grazing on public lands.

While Vice President Al Gore was known as a committed environmentalist, having written a best-selling treatise on the importance of environmental protection, Clinton was not initially seen an advocate for the environment. However, by the time the Republican Congress began threatening to dismantle the Clean Air Act, the Clean Water Act, and the Endangered Species Act, and to allow increased mining and logging on public lands, Clinton had learned the political power of mainstream environmentalism. Protecting the environment, Clinton's pollsters learned, appealed even to voters who considered themselves conservative on other issues. Realizing that the Republicans had miscalculated the public support for weakening environmental regulation, Clinton began to trumpet his protection of the environment. Clinton proposed few laws that would in any way rival Theodore Roosevelt's establishment of the national forest system or the environmental legislation of the 1960s and 1970s. Instead he focused on producing compromises to defuse hostilities on issues like logging and land rights, and on enforcing and defending existing regulation.

Civil Rights

Clinton displayed a passionate concern for civil rights throughout his presidency. He appointed more women and minorities to high-ranking posts in the executive branch than any prior president, and backed measures to end discrimination against homosexuals. Despite Clinton's strong record on civil rights, however, he did make efforts in his campaign and early in his administration to distance himself somewhat from the civil rights establishment. He trumpeted his disagreements with civil rights leader and perennial presidential candidate Jesse Jackson, and accused the women's groups who criticized him for not appointing more women of being "bean counters." Clinton also lost an important symbolic battle early in his first term when he attempted to issue orders to allow gays in the military. When the top military brass and congressional Republicans—and many Democrats—balked, Clinton quickly backed down, allowing the military to institute a "don't ask, don't tell" policy that essentially kept things as they had been.

Nonetheless, the Clinton administration made a monumental effort to ensure diversity in their appointments, to the point where the nomination process often dragged on for months, leaving important positions vacant. Due to conflicts with Congress and pressure from civil rights activists, the administration often took a particularly long time to fill important civil rights posts.

Affirmative Action: Proposition 209

By the 1996 election season, Clinton's stout defense of affirmative action in the face of a number of court challenges won him the praise of civil rights groups. A case in point occurred in 1996 with California's Proposition 209, a ballot proposal that stated race or color "could not be a criteria for either discriminating against or granting preferential treatment to anyone." Clinton came out strongly against it, while his opponent Bob Dole quietly supported the referendum. The measure passed, and after the Supreme Court ruled further that steps needed to be taken to ensure that affirmative action programs were justified and respected the rights of whites,

President Clinton's "don't ask, don't tell" policy on gays in the military ignited a controversy immediately following his inauguration in 1993. (Political cartoon by Neil R. King. Reproduced by permission of Neil R. King.)

Clinton again defended the importance of affirmative action, insisting that Americans should "mend it, not end it." Clinton also advocated for affirmative action in two cases that came before the Supreme Court. His support of affirmative action and diversity in important government posts ultimately won him the most unqualified praise he would receive from liberals who felt he had abandoned them on many other fronts (*See also,* Clinton and the Judiciary).

Sexual Harassment: The Paula Jones Case

The Supreme Court considered important cases on sexual harassment during Clinton's second term. As more and more women joined the workforce, they began to call attention to sexism and sexual politics in the workplace. In 1998 the Supreme Court agreed to consider two cases that many hoped would clarify the murky, frequently invoked law that attempted to define a "hostile work environment."

Clinton himself became caught in the debate on sexual harassment when a former Arkansas state employee, Paula Jones, sued the president, claiming he had propositioned her in a hotel room while he was the governor of Arkansas. Jones further asserted that because she rebuffed Clinton's overtures, she had not advanced professionally. Jones said Clinton had created a "hostile work environment" that constituted sexual harassment. The case threatened to undermine Clinton's presidency as it brought his alleged sexual escapades into the public forum. Clinton, the first sitting president to be deposed in federal court, found his personal life under immense and unprecedented public scrutiny. Clinton's lawyers, meanwhile, sought to prove that Jones had not suffered as a consequence of the alleged sexual advance, and thus had not encountered a hostile work environment.

A federal judge threw out the case in 1998, but not before it had permanently altered the course of Clinton's presidency. It was eventually revealed that Clinton had an affair with a White House intern and that he had provided evasive answers about it under oath during his deposition in the Jones case. The Republican Congress impeached Clinton for perjury and obstruction of justice. Although Paula Jones's initial lawyers quit, she continued to appeal the case, insisting all she wanted was an apology, which Clinton refused to offer, although he had offered a $750,000 settlement. As the impeachment proceedings continued, Clinton finally settled the case for $850,000—without an apology. While it was unlikely that the case would prevail, it would continue to wreak immense damage on Clinton's reputation and his presidency. Far from resolving anything, the Jones case only made the debate over sexual harassment more confused.

Impeachment

Midway through Clinton's second term, the various allegations of misconduct had grown to a fever pitch. When Clinton was deposed in the Paula Jones sexual harassment case, Jones's lawyers asked him questions about his relationship with a White House intern, Monica Lewinsky. Clinton denied having any "sexual relations" with Lewinsky. The following week Independent Prosecutor Kenneth Starr uncovered secret tapes of Lewinsky confiding in a friend about an affair with Clinton. The tapes raised questions of whether Clinton had perjured himself in his deposition and encouraged Lewinsky to lie when she appeared in the Jones case. Starr began investigating the Lewinsky matter before a federal grand jury.

In August 1998, after physical DNA evidence linked Clinton to Lewinsky, Clinton agreed to testify before the grand jury, admitting that he had an "inappropriate" relationship with Lewinsky and that he had provided "misleading" answers to the grand jury and to the American public. He denied, however, having committed actual perjury, and lashed out angrily at Kenneth Starr for what he saw as the political tenor of the investigation.

Starr then referred the matter to the House of Representatives for impeachment proceedings on charges of perjury and obstruction of justice. He also, at the same time, acknowledged that he had found no concrete evidence to charge Clinton on the original Whitewater matter. Clinton instead faced new charges that were uncovered—indeed created—through the sheer breadth and persistence of the three-year, $50 million investigation. And although U.S. voters disapproved of Clinton's behavior, they seemed to disapprove even more of the level of scrutiny to which he was subjected. In the November 1998 elections, they surprised Republicans and Democrats alike by unseating a number of Republicans and narrowing the Republican majority in the House of Representatives. At the same time, Clinton's approval ratings climbed as high as 70 percent. Americans in some ways seemed more sophisticated than the politicians that represented them—they made it clear that they were able

Newspaper headlines following the impeachment of President Clinton on December 19, 1998. President Clinton was the first elected president ever to be impeached. He was acquitted of the charges by the U.S. Senate. (AP/Wide World Photos. Reproduced by permission.)

to separate Clinton's obvious personal failings from his presidential performance.

In December 1998 the House of Representatives voted to impeach Clinton on a vote that fell almost entirely along party lines, further confirming the partisan nature of the impeachment proceedings. In January 1999 the Senate voted to acquit Clinton of the charges. Not one Democrat voted for conviction. While the Republicans argued that they had stood up for the Constitution and the principle of equal justice for all, most Americans saw the impeachment proceedings as an attempt to overturn a lawful election, and they clamored for an end to the scandal mongering.

Foreign Issues

Clinton had campaigned in 1992 accusing George Bush of paying too much attention to foreign affairs and not enough to the state of the U.S. economy and other domestic concerns. But Clinton found himself early in his presidency faced with the reality that foreign and domestic affairs, in an age of multinational corporations and a global economy, were inextricably linked. After several highly public and profoundly disturbing incidents—including the murder of 18 American soldiers on a United Nations Peacekeeping mission in Somalia, including one soldier whose corpse was dragged through the streets of Mogadishu while television cameras rolled—Clinton learned the importance of projecting a forceful voice in global politics.

Clinton also understood the importance of coordinating foreign and domestic economic policy, and created the National Economic Council as a counterweight to the National Security Council. Faced with the reality that the United States could no longer sustain prosperity just on sales within its borders, the Clinton administration aggressively targeted the enforcement of trade agreements as an essential element of foreign policy.

Trade Pacts: NAFTA and GATT

In 1993 Clinton lobbied Congress for the passage of the North American Free Trade Act (NAFTA), and the General Agreement on Tariffs and Trade (GATT), two trade pacts that lowered international trade barriers. Free trade was traditionally a Republican issue, and both agreements were negotiated by the previous Republican administrations and were very unpopular with organized labor. Labor advocates feared that the creation of a free trade zone would speed up relocation of factories and industry to developing countries with low wages and few labor laws. Clinton won passage of the legislation with the support of Republicans and moderate Democrats.

Mexico

Perhaps one of Clinton's most important foreign policy moves was his decision to overrule Congress and provide aid to Mexico after its currency fell precipitously in 1994. Mexico was the fastest growing consumer of U.S. goods, particularly after the NAFTA agreement had lowered trade barriers between the United States and Mexico. Clinton believed the peso crisis threatened to destabilize the entire region, and that Texas and California could expect a flood of illegal immigrants if the Mexican economy was allowed to collapse. Clinton approved

$12.5 billion in aid to Mexico despite congressional objections to the corruption and drug trafficking endemic in Mexico. Clinton's gamble paid off. Mexico stuck to a stringent fiscal and monetary policy, triggering joblessness at home but persuading private investors to return. Mexico paid off three-quarters of its debt years ahead of schedule.

Haiti

After a military junta deposed Haiti's first elected president, Jean Bertrand Aristide, in 1991 the island nation's military leaders imposed a reign of terror that unleashed a flood of refugees to U.S. shores. An embargo against Haiti was initiated by the Organization of American States (OAS) and led by the United States under President Bush, but failed to persuade the military dictators to step aside peacefully. After an embarrassing misstep in which an American troop transport heading for Haiti turned around when confronted with an unruly mob in Haiti's capital, Port-au-Prince, Clinton committed a larger force to Haiti. American troops arrived in 1994, and the junta, negotiating through former President Jimmy Carter, agreed to step down and let Aristide return. Haiti eventually held new elections, which represented the first legitimate transfer of power from one democratically elected president to another in the island's history.

Bosnia

Perhaps the most troubling issue in U.S. foreign policy was the protracted civil war in Bosnia, in the former Yugoslavia. Since 1991, a war between the Christian Serbs and the ethnic Muslims of Bosnia for control of the multiethnic state had resulted in a brutal campaign of genocide that saw the relentless murder of hundreds of thousands of Muslims and the displacement of two million. Haunted by the specter of the World War II Holocaust in Europe, Americans clamored to end the slaughter, but, haunted equally by the memory of Vietnam, they were loathe to commit significant troops to participate in United Nations peacekeeping efforts. Bush and Clinton offered little significant help in the conflict, in part because Colin Powell, the chairman of the Joint Chiefs of Staff for the armed forces, opposed sending troops unless the United States committed a massive display of force.

When Powell retired, however, the new chairman of the Joint Chiefs, General John Shalikashvili, embraced the carefully limited use of U.S. military might, and Clinton was able to push for limited air strikes against the Bosnian Serbs, which ultimately led the warring parties in Bosnia to the negotiating table. In November 1995, the Serbs, Muslim, and Croats of Bosnia signed a U.N.-brokered peace accord that resulted in the partition of the country under a multiethnic leadership, with NATO peacekeeping troops to enforce the cease-fire, including 20,000 U.S. soldiers.

Secretary of State Madeleine Albright termed the American policy in Bosnia an example of "assertive multilateralism"—building international coalitions that would act aggressively to resolve violent conflicts around the world. Under this strategy, the United Nations remained the only repository of legitimacy for the use of force in situations like Bosnia, but required forceful U.S. leadership to shape the U.N.'s decisions. The decision to commit troops to Bosnia during an election year was a risky one, but if it was not wildly popular with voters, it also did not draw significant criticism. (*New York Times,* 1996)

Kosovo

Conflict in the former Yugoslavia continued to affect U.S. foreign policy throughout the Clinton administration. In the summer of 1998 the Kosovo Liberation Army began an armed campaign to gain independence for the Kosovo region from Serbia, the largest most powerful republic in the Yugoslav federation. Serbian president, Slobodan Milosevic responded to the campaign for Kosovo's independence by launching a brutal attack against the Albanian descendants who populated the region. Many civilians were killed and many more were forced from their homes as Serb forces destroyed whole towns and villages.

President Clinton, believing that the United States had an ethical obligation to prevent crimes against humanity and concerned that the conflict would spread to other areas of Europe where ethnic tensions existed, called on the international community to take action. The United Nations demanded a cease-fire and discussions to resolve the conflict. The North Atlantic Treaty Organization (NATO), a mutual defense group made up of the United States, Canada, and several European nations, took further steps and threatened Serbia with military action if it did not stop the attacks in Kosovo. Under the threat of NATO intervention, Milosevic signed a cease fire agreement with U.S. envoy Richard Holbrook in October 1998.

During the winter of 1998–99, U.S. diplomats tried to bring about a long-lasting political settlement between Kosovo and Serbia as violent incidents continued to erupt on both sides. In March 1999, the Kosovo Albanians agreed to sign a peace agreement calling for their autonomy, to be implemented by NATO troops, but the Serbs refused to sign.

Despite last ditch efforts by Holbrook, Serbia refused to agree to any plan for autonomy for Kosovo and NATO launched bombing raids against Serbia. After two months of air strikes, the Serbian parliament approved the peace plan and the NATO bombings were suspended in June 1999 when Serbian forces withdrew from Kosovo. Once again, a very fragile peace existed in Eastern Europe, under the watchful eyes of international peacekeeping forces.

Many Americans supported Clinton's insistence on strong NATO actions in Kosovo and agreed with the president that widespread conflict in Europe would adversely affect U.S. interests. Many citizens were also deeply affected by the visual images of thousands of Kosovan refugees and evidence of Serbian war crimes. However, there were also many critics of Clinton's position, who pointed out that the United States had not responded to similar ethnic conflicts in Africa. Some critics suggested that economics and public relations, not ethics, were the real basis for Clinton's policy in Kosovo.

Russia

Clinton considered the U.S. relationship with post-Soviet Russia an important priority. Clinton supported Russian President Boris Yeltsin against a resurgent Communist Party in elections and offered aid to the Russians. When Yeltsin's severe health problems became evident, it was unclear who would take the reigns as the Russian president's health continued to deteriorate. While Clinton supported strong relations with the Russians, who still held a formidable, if decaying, nuclear arsenal, he also supported NATO expansion into the former eastern bloc countries despite Moscow's opposition. The relationship between the two former Cold War antagonists had warmed significantly since the fall of Communism, but it continued to be a wary one.

The Middle East

Israeli/Palestinian Peace Accords

When Israeli Prime Minister Yitzhak Rabin and Palestinian leader Yassar Arafat signed a peace accord in the White House Rose Garden in September 1993, relations between Israel and its Arab antagonists seemed to have entered a new era of reconciliation. The peace soon fell apart, however, when Rabin was assassinated by a Jewish extremist in November 1995. Clinton supported Rabin's successor Shimon Peres in the subsequent elections, but right-wing *Likud* Party leader Benjamin Netanyahu won a close race that in effect unraveled the hard-won peace between Israel and the Palestinians. After the election, Netanyahu ceased the transfer of lands to the Palestinians, claiming that they had not done enough to apprehend anti-Israeli terrorists within the Palestinian borders.

Clinton would continue to press for Israel to uphold its side of the accords, and in 1998 he persuaded Netanyahu and Arafat to sign a second treaty in Wye River, Maryland. The Wye River Accord also promised an Israeli withdrawal from Palestinian lands in exchange for a Palestinian promise to arrest terrorists and revoke the section of the Palestinian charter calling for the destruction of Israel. Netanyahu, however, pressured by religious conservatives in his party and in Parliament, was again slow to live up to his end of the bargain.

Iraqi Air Strikes

In Iraq, relations with Saddam Hussein continued on their rocky course after President Bush defeated him in war but failed to unseat him as Iraq's leader. Clinton threatened Iraq with air strikes numerous times because of the Arab nation's failure to comply with United Nations inspectors seeking to dismantle its chemical and biological weapons program, and in response to the Iraqi army's occasional forays toward the Kuwait border and against Kurdish rebels on Iraqi soil. In late 1998, as Clinton's impeachment trial got underway, the United Nations withdrew all of its inspectors from Iraq and the United States and Great Britain, acting without the agreement of the United Nations, commenced a sustained four-day air strike against Iraqi military targets. The raid met with condemnation from every nation. After the raid, the Iraqis began a calculated campaign to disregard the U.N.-enforced "no fly" zone in southern Iraq, prompting a series of skirmishes and air strikes from U.S. forces. While the air strikes were the inevitable result of the U.S. policy toward Iraq since the 1991 war, they were increasingly unpopular in the global community, particularly among the Arab nations. In addition, some Americans came to believe that Clinton's campaigns against Iraq were coordinated to distract the world from Clinton's political troubles at home.

The Clinton Administration Legacy

The Clinton administration will be remembered both for its poisonous political atmosphere, including the constant stream of scandals and allegations leveled at Clinton and his advisers, and for the political situation that created such a hostile environment. Clinton was president during a period that had, thanks to the Watergate scandal of the 1970s, seen a marked decline of public confidence in government and government officials, and a passionate national debate about the federal role in solving America's social and economic problems.

Clinton's Scandals

Since the New Hampshire primary, Clinton had been dogged by allegations of womanizing, draft-dodging, bank fraud, perjury, even murder. Beginning with the 1992 campaign attacks about Clinton's alleged philandering through his 1998 impeachment, Clinton saw a nonstop drumbeat of allegations about improprieties in either his personal life or his professional activities. Almost immediately after Clinton took office, Congress initiated investigations into the firing of the White House travel office employees, the suicide of long-time friend and White House aide Vincent Foster, and the Clintons' investments in Arkansas in the years when Clinton was governor.

Many of these scandals came to fall under the investigative umbrella of the "Whitewater" investigation, which involved a 1978 land deal in Arkansas and the bankruptcy of a savings and loan that had extended a questionable loan to the Clintons' business partner, James MacDougal. The proposed development, Whitewater Estates, collapsed, and MacDougal defaulted on the loan that he and others claimed was made at the behest of then-Governor Clinton. The scandal grew from the initial allegations to more significant charges that Clinton and his aides had broken the law in attempting to cover up the scandal. To Clinton's opponents in Congress, the U.S. public, and the media all of these doings seemed reminiscent of Richard Nixon's illegal "dirty tricks" in the Watergate scandal.

In the Media

Since the Watergate scandal, and since 1988, when Democratic candidate Gary Hart withdrew from the presidential race after newspaper reporters uncovered photos of the married Hart frolicking with model Donna Rice, the Washington media had begun to air personal details about politicians that the press had previously refused to publish. Investigative journalists since Watergate had come to consider it their duty to subject the presidency to intense scrutiny. In the past, the press had overlooked the personal affairs of presidents, but by the time Clinton took office this had changed. Such a shift in journalistic ethics may have started in part after Gary Hart challenged reporters to uncover his sins, but they exploded during the Clinton administration.

Clinton, according to biographer Stanley Renshon, was "a man of enormous appetites—for information, for attention, for food, for activity." His large personality, his talk-show appearances, and, perhaps most importantly, his striking ambition, made him an easy target for journalists and for the well-organized right-wing opposition that coalesced almost as soon as Clinton announced he would run for office. This, combined with Clinton's tendency toward evasive replies to questions—what critics termed his propensity to "play fast and loose with the truth"—made his personal life fodder for public debate.

Like Richard Nixon, whom critics called "Tricky Dick," Clinton seemed a magnet for criticism of a personal sort. He even earned his own Nixonian nickname, "Slick Willie," dubbed by an Arkansas reporter during Clinton's gubernatorial days. While Clinton's tendency toward evasive answers and his obvious ambition were among the reasons for the constant attacks, the fact that he was the first baby boomer president may also have accounted for some of the criticism. Clinton's life situations including his avoidance of the military draft, his admitted marijuana use (including his assertion that "I didn't inhale"), his sexual escapades, the Clintons' financial speculation in the 1980s seemed a direct reflection of his generation. The constant challenges to the legitimacy of Clinton's presidency, too, were in many ways a reflection of what was for many the most important political event of his generation, the shattering of political innocence of the Watergate scandal. This new lack of respect for the presidency was both a personal indictment of a young president whose ambitions always seemed slightly incompatible with his ideals, and a sign of a larger decline of public confidence in government's ability to solve the nation's problems.

Atmosphere of Scandal

Clinton was not the only person to fall prey to the nation's fixation with personal scandal. Many of his aides were implicated, or at the very least questioned before the grand jury in the Whitewater case, contracting immense legal bills and even greater damage to their reputations. In addition, many members of Clinton's cabinet were the subject of their own inquiries. Agriculture Secretary Mike Espy, Interior Secretary Bruce Babbitt, and Energy Secretary Hazel O'Leary were all subjects of investigations that turned up little criminal wrongdoing but exacted a great personal cost.

An investigation into the Democratic Party's fundraising practices during the 1996 also resulted in legal bills for Clinton aides and jail terms for some Democratic Party donors, although Clinton and his staff were exonerated. In addition, as the accusations of sexual misconduct began to fly, the media also began to scrutinize the behavior of some of Clinton's accusers. A number of Republican congressman—among them House Judiciary Committee chairman Henry Hyde, Judiciary Committee member and zealous Clinton detractor Robert Barr, and Robert Livingston, who had been slated to become Speaker of the House—also found their own extramarital activities aired in the press. As the situation degenerated and the call of "scandal" became more and more petty and outlandish, the media, the politicians, and citizens of all persuasions began to clamor for an end to what had been dubbed the "politics of personal destruction." There appeared, however, to be no end in sight.

Popularity

One Clinton biographer, Stanley Renshon, termed Clinton's presidency a "presidency of persistence" (Renshon, p. 268). Clinton's popularity in the face of the constant scandals was a testament to his ability to brush off damaging attacks and allegations and persevere. Like Ronald Reagan, whom one observer termed the "Teflon president," Clinton had a remarkable ability to survive both crushing political defeats and extraordinarily damaging personal allegations. Clinton, who was elected with only 43 percent of the vote and reelected again with only 49 percent, saw his popularity ratings swing wildly. They plunged from a low of 36 percent in 1993 to numbers as high as 70 percent in 1998 and 1999.

Nothing seemed to phase U.S. voters as Clinton consistently polled well. His high poll numbers, even after he was impeached, confirmed his campaign advisers' insistence in 1992 that it was "the economy, stupid," that voters cared about. The remarkable economic recovery seemed to make Clinton's constant political recoveries and resurrections possible, as he lurched from one policy change or political defeat to another, picked himself up, and moved on.

Lasting Impact

It is too early to know whether the Clinton administration's reputation will survive the impact of its scandals and earn a place in the history books. Clinton campaigned on the economy and it was the nation's economic performance that kept Clinton in Americans' good graces. His decision in his first budget to choose deficit reduction over tax cuts made possible the historic economic surge of the mid-1990s.

Clinton was also the first president of the baby boom generation, bringing many of the issues and controversies of the postwar years with him to the White House. It may, in the end, be the controversy he inspired that will leave the most lasting impression—Clinton, only the second U.S. president to be impeached, was both a victim of the vicious partisanship of his era, and of his own personal failings.

Sources

Brice, Ch'i Pai–Shih. *Encyclopedia of World Biography,* Second Edition. Detroit: Gale, 1998.

Brinkley, Alan. *The Unfinished Nation: A Concise History of the American People.* New York: McGraw Hill, 1997.

The Columbia Dictionary of Quotations. New York: Columbia University Press, 1993.

Kane, Joseph Nathan. *Facts About the Presidents: A Compilation of Biographical and Historical Information.* New York: The H.W. Wilson Company, 1993.

Kelly, Michael. "The President's Past." *New York Times Magazine,* July 31, 1994.

Nash, Gerald, et al. *The American People: Creating a Nation and a Society.* New York: Harper Collins, 1994.

Renshon, Stanley A. *High Hopes: The Clinton Presidency and the Politics of Ambition.* New York: New York University Press, 1996.

Woodward, Robert. *The Agenda: Inside the Clinton White House.* New York: Simon & Schuster, 1994.

Further Readings

Kelley, Virginia. *Leading With My Heart.* New York: Simon & Schuster, 1994.

Maraniss, David. *First In His Class: A Biography of Bill Clinton.* New York: Simon & Schuster, 1995.

Stewart, James B. *Blood Sport: The President and his Adversaries.* New York: Simon & Schuster, 1996.

Appendixes, Glossary, & Subject Index

The Oath of Office

I do solemnly swear or affirm that I will faithfully execute the Office of President of the United States, and will to the best of my ability, preserve, protect and defend the Constitution of the United States.

The oath of office is prescribed by Article II section 1 of the Constitution of the United States. The oath of office is taken by the president-elect with his hand upon a Bible opened to a scripture that he has selected.

Constitution of the United States of America

We the People of the United States, in Order to form a more perfect Union, establish Justice, insure domestic Tranquility, provide for the common defense, promote the general Welfare, and secure the Blessings of Liberty to ourselves and our Posterity, do ordain and establish this Constitution for the United States of America.

Article I

Items in italic have since been amended or superseded. A portion of Article I, Section 2, was modified by Section 2 of the Fourteenth Amendment; Article I, Section 3, was modified by the Seventeenth Amendment; Article I, Section 4, was modified by Section 2 of the Twentieth Amendment; and Article I, Section 9, was modified by the Sixteenth Amendment.

Section 1. All legislative Powers herein granted shall be vested in a Congress of the United States, which shall consist of a Senate and House of Representatives.

Section 2. The House of Representatives shall be composed of Members chosen every second Year by the Peo-

The seal of the president of the United States. (Archive Photos. Reproduced by permission.)

ple of the several States, and the Electors in each State shall have the Qualifications requisite for Electors of the most numerous Branch of the State Legislature.

No Person shall be a Representative who shall not have attained to the Age of twenty five Years, and been seven Years a Citizen of the United States, and who shall not, when elected, be an Inhabitant of that State in which he shall be chosen.

Representatives and direct Taxes shall be apportioned among the several States which may be included within this Union, according to their respective Numbers, which shall be determined by adding to the whole Number of free Persons, including those bound to Service for a Term of Years, and excluding Indians not taxed, three fifths of all other Persons. The actual Enumeration shall be made within three Years after the first Meeting of the Congress of the United States, and within every subsequent Term of ten Years, in such Manner as they shall by Law direct. The Number of Representatives shall not exceed one for every thirty Thousand, but each State shall have at Least one Representative; and until such enumeration shall be made, the State of New Hampshire shall be entitled to chuse three, Massachusetts eight, Rhode-Island and Providence Plantations one, Connecticut five, New-York six, New Jersey four, Pennsylvania eight, Delaware one, Maryland six, Virginia ten, North Carolina five, South Carolina five, and Georgia three.

When vacancies happen in the Representation from any State, the Executive Authority thereof shall issue Writs of Election to fill such Vacancies.

The House of Representatives shall chuse their Speaker and other Officers; and shall have the sole Power of Impeachment.

Section 3. The Senate of the United States shall be composed of two Senators from each State, *chosen by the Legislature thereof* for six Years; and each Senator shall have one Vote.

Immediately after they shall be assembled in Consequence of the first Election, they shall be divided as equally as may be into three Classes. The Seats of the Senators of the first Class shall be vacated at the Expiration of the second Year, of the second Class at the Expiration of the fourth Year, and of the third Class at the Expiration of the sixth Year, so that one third may be chosen every second Year; *and if Vacancies happen by Resignation, or otherwise, during the Recess of the Legislature of any State, the Executive thereof may make temporary Appointments until the next Meeting of the Legislature, which shall then fill such Vacancies.*

No Person shall be a Senator who shall not have attained to the Age of thirty Years, and been nine Years a Citizen of the United States, and who shall not, when elected, be an Inhabitant of that State for which he shall be chosen.

The Vice President of the United States shall be President of the Senate, but shall have no Vote, unless they be equally divided.

The Senate shall chuse their other Officers, and also a President pro tempore, in the Absence of the Vice President, or when he shall exercise the Office of President of the United States.

The Senate shall have the sole Power to try all Impeachments. When sitting for that Purpose, they shall be on Oath or Affirmation. When the President of the United States is tried, the Chief Justice shall preside: And no Person shall be convicted without the Concurrence of two thirds of the Members present.

Judgment in Cases of Impeachment shall not extend further than to removal from Office, and disqualification to hold and enjoy any Office of honor, Trust or Profit under the United States: but the Party convicted shall nevertheless be liable and subject to Indictment, Trial, Judgment and Punishment, according to Law.

Section 4. The Times, Places and Manner of holding Elections for Senators and Representatives, shall be prescribed in each State by the Legislature thereof; but the Congress may at any time by Law make or alter such Regulations, except as to the Places of chusing Senators.

The Congress shall assemble at least once in every Year, and such Meeting shall *be on the first Monday in December,* unless they shall by Law appoint a different Day.

Section 5. Each House shall be the Judge of the Elections, Returns and Qualifications of its own Members, and a Majority of each shall constitute a Quorum to do Business; but a smaller Number may adjourn from day to day, and may be authorized to compel the Attendance of absent Members, in such Manner, and under such Penalties as each House may provide.

Each House may determine the Rules of its Proceedings, punish its Members for disorderly Behaviour, and, with the Concurrence of two thirds, expel a Member.

Each House shall keep a Journal of its Proceedings, and from time to time publish the same, excepting such Parts as may in their Judgment require Secrecy; and the Yeas and Nays of the Members of either House on any question shall, at the Desire of one fifth of those Present, be entered on the Journal.

Neither House, during the Session of Congress, shall, without the Consent of the other, adjourn for more than three days, nor to any other Place than that in which the two Houses shall be sitting.

Section 6. The Senators and Representatives shall receive a Compensation for their Services, to be ascertained by Law, and paid out of the Treasury of the United States. They shall in all Cases, except Treason, Felony and Breach of the Peace, be privileged from Arrest during their Attendance at the Session of their respective Houses, and in going to and returning from the same; and for any Speech or Debate in either House, they shall not be questioned in any other Place.

No Senator or Representative shall, during the Time for which he was elected, be appointed to any civil Office under the Authority of the United States, which shall have been created, or the Emoluments whereof shall have been increased during such time; and no Person holding any

Office under the United States, shall be a Member of either House during his Continuance in Office.

Section 7. All Bills for raising Revenue shall originate in the House of Representatives; but the Senate may propose or concur with Amendments as on other Bills.

Every Bill which shall have passed the House of Representatives and the Senate, shall, before it become a Law, be presented to the President of the United States: If he approve he shall sign it, but if not he shall return it, with his Objections to that House in which it shall have originated, who shall enter the Objections at large on their Journal, and proceed to reconsider it. If after such Reconsideration two thirds of that House shall agree to pass the Bill, it shall be sent, together with the Objections, to the other House, by which it shall likewise be reconsidered, and if approved by two thirds of that House, it shall become a Law. But in all such Cases the Votes of both Houses shall be determined by yeas and Nays, and the Names of the Persons voting for and against the Bill shall be entered on the Journal of each House respectively. If any Bill shall not be returned by the President within ten Days (Sundays excepted) after it shall have been presented to him, the Same shall be a Law, in like Manner as if he had signed it, unless the Congress by their Adjournment prevent its Return, in which Case it shall not be a Law.

Every Order, Resolution, or Vote to which the Concurrence of the Senate and House of Representatives may be necessary (except on a question of Adjournment) shall be presented to the President of the United States; and before the Same shall take Effect, shall be approved by him, or being disapproved by him, shall be repassed by two thirds of the Senate and House of Representatives, according to the Rules and Limitations prescribed in the Case of a Bill.

Section 8. The Congress shall have Power To lay and collect Taxes, Duties, Imposts and Excises, to pay the Debts and provide for the common Defence and general Welfare of the United States; but all Duties, Imposts and Excises shall be uniform throughout the United States;

To borrow Money on the credit of the United States;

To regulate Commerce with foreign Nations, and among the several States, and with the Indian Tribes;

To establish an uniform Rule of Naturalization, and uniform Laws on the subject of Bankruptcies throughout the United States;

To coin Money, regulate the Value thereof, and of foreign Coin, and fix the Standard of Weights and Measures;

To provide for the Punishment of counterfeiting the Securities and current Coin of the United States;

To establish Post Offices and post Roads;

To promote the Progress of Science and useful Arts, by securing for limited Times to Authors and Inventors the exclusive Right to their respective Writings and Discoveries;

To constitute Tribunals inferior to the supreme Court;

To define and punish Piracies and Felonies committed on the high Seas, and Offences against the Law of Nations;

To declare War, grant Letters of Marque and Reprisal, and make Rules concerning Captures on Land and Water;

To raise and support Armies, but no Appropriation of Money to that Use shall be for a longer Term than two Years;

To provide and maintain a Navy;

To make Rules for the Government and Regulation of the land and naval Forces;

To provide for calling forth the Militia to execute the Laws of the Union, suppress Insurrections and repel Invasions;

To provide for organizing, arming, and disciplining, the Militia, and for governing such Part of them as may be employed in the Service of the United States, reserving to the States respectively, the Appointment of the Officers, and the Authority of training the Militia according to the discipline prescribed by Congress;

To exercise exclusive Legislation in all Cases whatsoever, over such District (not exceeding ten Miles square) as may, by Cession of particular States, and the Acceptance of Congress, become the Seat of the Government of the United States, and to exercise like Authority over all Places purchased by the Consent of the Legislature of the State in which the Same shall be, for the Erection of Forts, Magazines, Arsenals, dock-Yards, and other needful Buildings;—And

To make all Laws which shall be necessary and proper for carrying into Execution the foregoing Powers, and all other Powers vested by this Constitution in the Government of the United States, or in any Department or Officer thereof.

Section 9. The Migration or Importation of such Persons as any of the States now existing shall think proper to admit, shall not be prohibited by the Congress prior to the Year one thousand eight hundred and eight, but a Tax or duty may be imposed on such Importation, not exceeding ten dollars for each Person.

The Privilege of the Writ of Habeas Corpus shall not be suspended, unless when in Cases of Rebellion or Invasion the public Safety may require it.

No Bill of Attainder or ex post facto Law shall be passed.

No Capitation, or other direct, Tax shall be laid, *unless in Proportion to the Census or enumeration herein before directed to be taken.*

No Tax or Duty shall be laid on Articles exported from any State.

No Preference shall be given by any Regulation of Commerce or Revenue to the Ports of one State over those of another; nor shall Vessels bound to, or from, one State, be obliged to enter, clear, or pay Duties in another.

No Money shall be drawn from the Treasury, but in Consequence of Appropriations made by Law; and a regular Statement and Account of the Receipts and Expenditures of all public Money shall be published from time to time.

No Title of Nobility shall be granted by the United States: And no Person holding any Office of Profit or Trust under them, shall, without the Consent of the Congress, accept of any present, Emolument, Office, or Title, of any kind whatever, from any King, Prince, or foreign State.

Section 10. No State shall enter into any Treaty, Alliance, or Confederation; grant Letters of Marque and Reprisal; coin Money; emit Bills of Credit; make any Thing but gold and silver Coin a Tender in Payment of Debts; pass any Bill of Attainder, ex post facto Law, or Law impairing the Obligation of Contracts, or grant any Title of Nobility.

No State shall, without the Consent of the Congress, lay any Imposts or Duties on Imports or Exports, except what may be absolutely necessary for executing it's inspection Laws: and the net Produce of all Duties and Imposts, laid by any State on Imports or Exports, shall be for the Use of the Treasury of the United States; and all such Laws shall be subject to the Revision and Controul of the Congress.

No State shall, without the Consent of Congress, lay any Duty of Tonnage, keep Troops, or Ships of War in time of Peace, enter into any Agreement or Compact with another State, or with a foreign Power, or engage in War, unless actually invaded, or in such imminent Danger as will not admit of delay.

Article II

Article II, Section 1, was superseded by the Twelfth Amendment; Article II, Section 1, was modified by the Twenty-fifth Amendment.

Section 1. The executive Power shall be vested in a President of the United States of America. He shall hold his Office during the Term of four Years, and, together with the Vice President, chosen for the same Term, be elected, as follows:

Each State shall appoint, in such Manner as the Legislature thereof may direct, a Number of Electors, equal to the whole Number of Senators and Representatives to which the State may be entitled in the Congress: but no Senator or Representative, or Person holding an Office of Trust or Profit under the United States, shall be appointed an Elector.

The Electors shall meet in their respective States, and vote by Ballot for two Persons, of whom one at least shall not be an Inhabitant of the same State with themselves. And they shall make a List of all the Persons voted for, and of the Number of Votes for each; which List they shall sign and certify, and transmit sealed to the Seat of the Government of the United States, directed to the President of the Senate. The President of the Senate shall, in the Presence of the Senate and House of Representatives, open all the Certificates, and the Votes shall then be counted. The Person having the greatest Number of Votes shall be the President, if such Number be a Majority of the whole Number of Electors appointed; and if there be more than one who have such Majority, and have an equal Number of Votes, then the House of Representatives shall immediately chuse by Ballot one of them for President; and if no Person have a Majority, then from the five highest on the List the said House shall in like Manner chuse the President. But in chusing the President, the Votes shall be taken by States, the Representation from each State having one Vote; A quorum for this purpose shall consist of a Member or Members from two thirds of the States, and a Majority of all the States shall be necessary to a Choice. In every Case, after the Choice of the President, the Person having the greatest Number of Votes of the Electors shall be the Vice President. But if there should remain two or more who have equal Votes, the Senate shall chuse from them by Ballot the Vice President.

The Congress may determine the Time of chusing the Electors, and the Day on which they shall give their Votes; which Day shall be the same throughout the United States.

No Person except a natural born Citizen, or a Citizen of the United States, at the time of the Adoption of this Constitution, shall be eligible to the Office of President; neither shall any Person be eligible to that Office who shall not have attained to the Age of thirty five Years, and been fourteen Years a Resident within the United States.

In Case of the Removal of the President from Office, or of his Death, Resignation, or Inability to discharge the Powers and Duties of the said Office, the Same shall devolve on the Vice President, and the Congress may by Law provide for the Case of Removal, Death, Resignation or Inability, both of the President and Vice President, declaring what Officer shall then act as President, and such Officer shall act accordingly, until the Disability be removed, or a President shall be elected.

The President shall, at stated Times, receive for his Services, a Compensation, which shall neither be increased nor diminished during the Period for which he shall have been elected, and he shall not receive within that Period any other Emolument from the United States, or any of them.

Before he enter on the Execution of his Office, he shall take the following Oath or Affirmation:—"I do solemnly swear (or affirm) that I will faithfully execute the Office of President of the United States, and will to the best of my Ability, preserve, protect and defend the Constitution of the United States."

Section 2. The President shall be Commander in Chief of the Army and Navy of the United States, and of the Militia of the several States, when called into the actual Service of the United States; he may require the Opinion, in writing, of the principal Officer in each of the executive Departments, upon any Subject relating to the Duties of their respective Offices, and he shall have Power to grant Reprieves and Pardons for Offences against the United States, except in Cases of Impeachment. He shall have Power, by and with the Advice and Consent of the Senate, to make Treaties, provided two thirds of the Senators present concur; and he shall nominate, and by and with the Advice and Consent of the Senate, shall appoint Ambassadors, other public Ministers and Consuls, Judges of the supreme Court, and all other Officers of the United States, whose Appointments are not herein otherwise provided for, and which shall be established by Law: but the Congress may by Law vest the Appointment of such inferior Officers, as they think proper, in the President alone, in the Courts of Law, or in the Heads of Departments.

The President shall have Power to fill up all Vacancies that may happen during the Recess of the Senate, by granting Commissions which shall expire at the End of their next Session.

Section 3. He shall from time to time give to the Congress Information of the State of the Union, and recommend to their Consideration such Measures as he shall judge necessary and expedient; he may, on extraordinary Occasions, convene both Houses, or either of them, and in Case of Disagreement between them, with Respect to the Time of Adjournment, he may adjourn them to such Time as he shall think proper; he shall receive Ambassadors and other public Ministers; he shall take Care that the Laws be faithfully executed, and shall Commission all the Officers of the United States.

Section 4. The President, Vice President and all civil Officers of the United States, shall be removed from Office on Impeachment for, and Conviction of, Treason, Bribery, or other high Crimes and Misdemeanors.

Article III

A portion of Section 2 was modified by the Eleventh Amendment

Section 1. The judicial Power of the United States shall be vested in one supreme Court, and in such inferior Courts as the Congress may from time to time ordain and establish. The Judges, both of the supreme and inferior Courts, shall hold their Offices during good Behaviour, and shall, at stated Times, receive for their Services a Compensation, which shall not be diminished during their Continuance in Office.

Section 2. The judicial Power shall extend to all Cases, in Law and Equity, arising under this Constitution, the Laws of the United States, and Treaties made, or which shall be made, under their Authority;—to all Cases affecting Ambassadors, other public Ministers and Consuls;—to all Cases of admiralty and maritime Jurisdiction;—to Controversies to which the United States shall be a Party; to Controversies between two or more States;—*between a State and Citizens of another State;*—between Citizens of different States; between Citizens of the same State claiming Lands under Grants of different States, and between a State, or the Citizens thereof, and foreign States, Citizens or Subjects.

In all Cases affecting Ambassadors, other public Ministers and Consuls, and those in which a State shall be Party, the supreme Court shall have original Jurisdiction. In all the other Cases before mentioned, the supreme Court shall have appellate Jurisdiction, both as to Law and Fact, with such Exceptions, and under such Regulations as the Congress shall make.

The Trial of all Crimes, except in Cases of Impeachment, shall be by Jury; and such Trial shall be held in the State where the said Crimes shall have been committed; but when not committed within any State, the Trial shall be at such Place or Places as the Congress may by Law have directed.

Section 3. Treason against the United States, shall consist only in levying War against them, or in adhering to their Enemies, giving them Aid and Comfort. No Person shall be convicted of Treason unless on the Testimony of two Witnesses to the same overt Act, or on Confession in open Court.

The Congress shall have Power to declare the Punishment of Treason, but no Attainder of Treason shall work Corruption of Blood, or Forfeiture except during the Life of the Person attainted.

Article IV

A portion of Section 2 was superseded by the Thirteenth Amendment.

Section 1. Full Faith and Credit shall be given in each State to the public Acts, Records, and judicial Proceedings of every other State. And the Congress may by general Laws prescribe the Manner in which such Acts, Records and Proceedings shall be proved, and the Effect thereof.

Section 2. The Citizens of each State shall be entitled to all Privileges and Immunities of Citizens in the several States.

A Person charged in any State with Treason, Felony, or other Crime, who shall flee from Justice, and be found in another State, shall on Demand of the executive Authority of the State from which he fled, be delivered up, to be removed to the State having Jurisdiction of the Crime.

No Person held to Service or Labour in one State, under the Laws thereof, escaping into another, shall, in

Consequence of any Law or Regulation therein, be discharged from such Service or Labour, but shall be delivered up on Claim of the Party to whom such Service or Labour may be due.

Section 3. New States may be admitted by the Congress into this Union; but no new State shall be formed or erected within the Jurisdiction of any other State; nor any State be formed by the Junction of two or more States, or Parts of States, without the Consent of the Legislatures of the States concerned as well as of the Congress.

The Congress shall have Power to dispose of and make all needful Rules and Regulations respecting the Territory or other Property belonging to the United States; and nothing in this Constitution shall be so construed as to Prejudice any Claims of the United States, or of any particular State.

Section 4. The United States shall guarantee to every State in this Union a Republican Form of Government, and shall protect each of them against Invasion; and on Application of the Legislature, or of the Executive (when the Legislature cannot be convened), against domestic Violence.

Article V

The Congress, whenever two thirds of both Houses shall deem it necessary, shall propose Amendments to this Constitution, or, on the Application of the Legislatures of two thirds of the several States, shall call a Convention for proposing Amendments, which, in either Case, shall be valid to all Intents and Purposes, as Part of this Constitution, when ratified by the Legislatures of three fourths of the several States, or by Conventions in three fourths thereof, as the one or the other Mode of Ratification may be proposed by the Congress; Provided that no Amendment which may be made prior to the Year One thousand eight hundred and eight shall in any Manner affect the first and fourth Clauses in the Ninth Section of the first Article; and that no State, without its Consent, shall be deprived of its equal Suffrage in the Senate.

Article VI

All Debts contracted and Engagements entered into, before the Adoption of this Constitution, shall be as valid against the United States under this Constitution, as under the Confederation.

This Constitution, and the Laws of the United States which shall be made in Pursuance thereof; and all Treaties made, or which shall be made, under the Authority of the United States, shall be the supreme Law of the Land; and the Judges in every State shall be bound thereby, any Thing in the Constitution or Laws of any State to the Contrary notwithstanding.

The Senators and Representatives before mentioned, and the Members of the several State Legislatures, and all executive and judicial Officers, both of the United States and of the several States, shall be bound by Oath or Affirmation, to support this Constitution; but no religious Test shall ever be required as a Qualification to any Office or public Trust under the United States.

Article VII

The Ratification of the Conventions of nine States, shall be sufficient for the Establishment of this Constitution between the States so ratifying the Same.

Attest William Jackson Secretary

Done in Convention by the Unanimous Consent of the States present the Seventeenth Day of September in the Year of our Lord one thousand seven hundred and Eighty seven and of the Independence of the United States of America the Twelfth In witness whereof We have hereunto subscribed our Names,

G°. Washington Presidt and deputy from Virginia

Delaware: Geo: Read, Gunning Bedford jun, John Dickinson, Richard Bassett, Jaco: Broom

Maryland: James McHenry, Dan of St Thos. Jenifer, Danl. Carroll

Virginia: John Blair—, James Madison Jr.

North Carolina: Wm. Blount, Richd. Dobbs Spaight, Hu Williamson

South Carolina: J. Rutledge, Charles Cotesworth Pinckney, Charles Pinckney, Pierce Butler

Georgia: William Few, Abr Baldwin

New Hampshire: John Langdon, Nicholas Gilman

Massachusetts: Nathaniel Gorham, Rufus King

Connecticut: Wm. Saml. Johnson Roger Sherman

New York: Alexander Hamilton

New Jersey: Wil: Livingston, David Brearley, Wm. Paterson, Jona: Dayton

Pennsylvania: B Franklin, Thomas Mifflin, Robt. Morris, Geo. Clymer, Thos. FitzSimons, Jared Ingersoll, James Wilson, Gouv Morris

Amendments to the Constitution

The first 10 amendments to the Constitution were ratified December 15, 1791, and form what is known as the "Bill of Rights."

Amendment I

Congress shall make no law respecting an establishment of religion, or prohibiting the free exercise thereof; or abridging the freedom of speech, or of the press; or the right of the people peaceably to assemble, and to petition the Government for a redress of grievances.

Amendment II

A well regulated Militia, being necessary to the security of a free State, the right of the people to keep and bear Arms, shall not be infringed.

Amendment III

No Soldier shall, in time of peace be quartered in any house, without the consent of the Owner, nor in time of war, but in a manner to be prescribed by law.

Amendment IV

The right of the people to be secure in their persons, houses, papers, and effects, against unreasonable searches and seizures, shall not be violated, and no Warrants shall issue, but upon probable cause, supported by Oath or affirmation, and particularly describing the place to be searched, and the persons or things to be seized.

Amendment V

No person shall be held to answer for a capital, or otherwise infamous crime, unless on a presentment or indictment of a Grand Jury, except in cases arising in the land or naval forces, or in the Militia, when in actual service in time of War or public danger; nor shall any person be subject for the same offence to be twice put in jeopardy of life or limb; nor shall be compelled in any criminal case to be a witness against himself, nor be deprived of life, liberty, or property, without due process of law; nor shall private property be taken for public use, without just compensation.

Amendment VI

In all criminal prosecutions, the accused shall enjoy the right to a speedy and public trial, by an impartial jury of the State and district wherein the crime shall have been committed, which district shall have been previously ascertained by law, and to be informed of the nature and cause of the accusation; to be confronted with the witnesses against him; to have compulsory process for obtaining witnesses in his favor, and to have the Assistance of Counsel for his defence.

Amendment VII

In suits at common law, where the value in controversy shall exceed twenty dollars, the right of trial by jury shall be preserved, and no fact tried by a jury, shall be otherwise reexamined in any Court of the United States, than according to the rules of the common law.

Amendment VIII

Excessive bail shall not be required, nor excessive fines imposed, nor cruel and unusual punishments inflicted.

Amendment IX

The enumeration in the Constitution, of certain rights, shall not be construed to deny or disparage others retained by the people.

Amendment X

The powers not delegated to the United States by the Constitution, nor prohibited by it to the States, are reserved to the States respectively, or to the people.

Amendment XI

Passed by Congress March 4, 1794. Ratified February 7, 1795. A portion of Article III, Section 2, was modified by the Eleventh Amendment.

The Judicial power of the United States shall not be construed to extend to any suit in law or equity, commenced or prosecuted against one of the United States by Citizens of another State, or by Citizens or Subjects of any Foreign State.

Amendment XII

Passed by Congress December 9, 1803. Ratified June 15, 1804. A portion of Article II, Section 1, was superseded by the Twelfth Amendment. A portion of the Twelfth Amendment was superseded by Section 3 of the Twentieth Amendment.

The Electors shall meet in their respective states and vote by ballot for President and Vice-President, one of whom, at least, shall not be an inhabitant of the same state with themselves; they shall name in their ballots the person voted for as President, and in distinct ballots the person voted for as Vice-President, and they shall make distinct lists of all persons voted for as President, and of all persons voted for as Vice-President, and of the number of votes for each, which lists they shall sign and certify, and transmit sealed to the seat of the government of the United States, directed to the President of the Senate;—the President of the Senate shall, in the presence of the Senate and House of Representatives, open all the certificates and the votes shall then be counted;—The person having the greatest number of votes for President, shall be the President, if such number be a majority of the whole number of Electors appointed; and if no person have such majority, then from the persons having the highest numbers not exceeding three on the list of those voted for as President, the House of Representatives shall choose immediately, by ballot, the President. But in choosing the President, the votes shall be taken by states, the representation from each state having one vote; a quorum for this purpose shall consist of a member or members from two-thirds of the states, and a majority of all the states shall be necessary to a choice. *And if the House of Representatives shall not choose a President whenever the right of choice shall devolve upon them, before the fourth day of March next following, then the Vice-President shall act as President, as in case of the death or other constitutional disability of the President.*—The person having the greatest number of votes as Vice-President, shall be the Vice-President, if such number be a majority of the whole number of Electors appointed, and if no person have a majority, then from the two highest numbers on the list, the Senate shall choose the Vice-President; a quorum for the purpose shall consist of two-thirds of the whole number of Senators, and a majority of the whole number shall be necessary to a choice. But no person constitutionally ineligible to the office of

President shall be eligible to that of Vice-President of the United States.

Amendent XIII

Passed by Congress January 31, 1865. Ratified December 6, 1865. A portion of Article IV, Section 2, was superseded by the Thirteenth Amendment.

Section 1. Neither slavery nor involuntary servitude, except as a punishment for crime whereof the party shall have been duly convicted, shall exist within the United States, or any place subject to their jurisdiction.

Section 2. Congress shall have power to enforce this article by appropriate legislation.

Amendment XIV

Passed by Congress June 13, 1866. Ratified July 9, 1868. A portion of Article I, Section 2, was modified by Section 2 of the Fourteenth Amendment. A portion of the Fourteenth Amendment was modified by Section 1 of the Twenty-sixth Amendment.

Section 1. All persons born or naturalized in the United States, and subject to the jurisdiction thereof, are citizens of the United States and of the State wherein they reside. No State shall make or enforce any law which shall abridge the privileges or immunities of citizens of the United States; nor shall any State deprive any person of life, liberty, or property, without due process of law; nor deny to any person within its jurisdiction the equal protection of the laws.

Section 2. Representatives shall be apportioned among the several States according to their respective numbers, counting the whole number of persons in each State, excluding Indians not taxed. But when the right to vote at any election for the choice of electors for President and Vice-President of the United States, Representatives in Congress, the Executive and Judicial officers of a State, or the members of the Legislature thereof, is denied to any of the male inhabitants of such State, *being twenty-one years of age,* and citizens of the United States, or in any way abridged, except for participation in rebellion, or other crime, the basis of representation therein shall be reduced in the proportion which the number of such male citizens shall bear to the whole number of male citizens twenty-one years of age in such State.

Section 3. No person shall be a Senator or Representative in Congress, or elector of President and Vice-President, or hold any office, civil or military, under the United States, or under any State, who, having previously taken an oath, as a member of Congress, or as an officer of the United States, or as a member of any State legislature, or as an executive or judicial officer of any State, to support the Constitution of the United States, shall have engaged in insurrection or rebellion against the same, or given aid or comfort to the enemies thereof. But Congress may by a vote of two-thirds of each House, remove such disability.

Section 4. The validity of the public debt of the United States, authorized by law, including debts incurred for payment of pensions and bounties for services in suppressing insurrection or rebellion, shall not be questioned. But neither the United States nor any State shall assume or pay any debt or obligation incurred in aid of insurrection or rebellion against the United States, or any claim for the loss or emancipation of any slave; but all such debts, obligations and claims shall be held illegal and void.

Section 5. The Congress shall have the power to enforce, by appropriate legislation, the provisions of this article.

Amendment XV

Passed by Congress February 26, 1869. Ratified February 3, 1870.

Section 1. The right of citizens of the United States to vote shall not be denied or abridged by the United States or by any State on account of race, color, or previous condition of servitude—

Section 2. The Congress shall have the power to enforce this article by appropriate legislation.

Amendment XVI

Passed by Congress July 12, 1909. Ratified February 3, 1913. A portion of Article I, Section 9, was modified by the Sixteenth Amendment.

The Congress shall have power to lay and collect taxes on incomes, from whatever source derived, without apportionment among the several States, and without regard to any census or enumeration.

Amendment XVII

Passed by Congress May 13, 1912. Ratified April 8, 1913. Portions of Article I, Section 3, were modified by the Seventeenth Amendment.

The Senate of the United States shall be composed of two Senators from each State, elected by the people thereof, for six years; and each Senator shall have one vote. The electors in each State shall have the qualifications requisite for electors of the most numerous branch of the State legislatures.

When vacancies happen in the representation of any State in the Senate, the executive authority of such State shall issue writs of election to fill such vacancies: Provided, That the legislature of any State may empower the executive thereof to make temporary appointments until the people fill the vacancies by election as the legislature may direct.

This amendment shall not be so construed as to affect the election or term of any Senator chosen before it becomes valid as part of the Constitution.

Amendment XVIII

Passed by Congress December 18, 1917. Ratified January 16, 1919. Repealed by the Twenty-first Amendment.

Section 1. After one year from the ratification of this article the manufacture, sale, or transportation of intoxicating liquors within, the importation thereof into, or the exportation thereof from the United States and all territory subject to the jurisdiction thereof for beverage purposes is hereby prohibited.

Section 2. The Congress and the several States shall have concurrent power to enforce this article by appropriate legislation.

Section 3. This article shall be inoperative unless it shall have been ratified as an amendment to the Constitution by the legislatures of the several States, as provided in the Constitution, within seven years from the date of the submission hereof to the States by the Congress.

Amendment XIX

Passed by Congress June 4, 1919. Ratified August 18, 1920.

The right of citizens of the United States to vote shall not be denied or abridged by the United States or by any State on account of sex.

Congress shall have power to enforce this article by appropriate legislation.

Amendment XX

Passed by Congress March 2, 1932. Ratified January 23, 1933. A portion of Article I, Section 4, was modified by Section 2 of the Twentieth Amendment. In addition, a portion of the Twelfth Amendment was superseded by Section 3 of the Twentieth Amendment.

Section 1. The terms of the President and the Vice President shall end at noon on the 20th day of January, and the terms of Senators and Representatives at noon on the 3d day of January, of the years in which such terms would have ended if this article had not been ratified; and the terms of their successors shall then begin.

Section 2. The Congress shall assemble at least once in every year, and such meeting shall begin at noon on the 3d day of January, unless they shall by law appoint a different day.

Section 3. If, at the time fixed for the beginning of the term of the President, the President elect shall have died, the Vice President elect shall become President. If a President shall not have been chosen before the time fixed for the beginning of his term, or if the President elect shall have failed to qualify, then the Vice President elect shall act as President until a President shall have qualified; and the Congress may by law provide for the case wherein neither a President elect nor a Vice President shall have qualified, declaring who shall then act as President, or the manner in which one who is to act shall be selected, and such person shall act accordingly until a President or Vice President shall have qualified.

Section 4. The Congress may by law provide for the case of the death of any of the persons from whom the House of Representatives may choose a President whenever the right of choice shall have devolved upon them, and for the case of the death of any of the persons from whom the Senate may choose a Vice President whenever the right of choice shall have devolved upon them.

Section 5. Sections 1 and 2 shall take effect on the 15th day of October following the ratification of this article.

Section 6. This article shall be inoperative unless it shall have been ratified as an amendment to the Constitution by the legislatures of three-fourths of the several States within seven years from the date of its submission.

Amendment XXI

Passed by Congress February 20, 1933. Ratified December 5, 1933. Repealed the Eighteenth Amendment.

Section 1. The eighteenth article of amendment to the Constitution of the United States is hereby repealed.

Section 2. The transportation or importation into any State, Territory, or Possession of the United States for delivery or use therein of intoxicating liquors, in violation of the laws thereof, is hereby prohibited.

Section 3. This article shall be inoperative unless it shall have been ratified as an amendment to the Constitution by conventions in the several States, as provided in the Constitution, within seven years from the date of the submission hereof to the States by the Congress.

Amendment XXII

Passed by Congress March 21, 1947. Ratified February 27, 1951.

Section 1. No person shall be elected to the office of the President more than twice, and no person who has held the office of President, or acted as President, for more than two years of a term to which some other person was elected President shall be elected to the office of President more than once. But this Article shall not apply to any person holding the office of President when this Article was proposed by Congress, and shall not prevent any person who may be holding the office of President, or acting as President, during the term within which this Article becomes operative from holding the office of President or acting as President during the remainder of such term.

Section 2. This article shall be inoperative unless it shall have been ratified as an amendment to the Constitution by the legislatures of three-fourths of the several States within seven years from the date of its submission to the States by the Congress.

Amendment XXIII

Passed by Congress June 16, 1960. Ratified March 29, 1961.

Section 1. The District constituting the seat of Government of the United States shall appoint in such manner as Congress may direct:

A number of electors of President and Vice President equal to the whole number of Senators and Representatives in Congress to which the District would be entitled if it were a State, but in no event more than the least populous State; they shall be in addition to those appointed by the States, but they shall be considered, for the purposes of the election of President and Vice President, to be electors appointed by a State; and they shall meet in the District and perform such duties as provided by the twelfth article of amendment.

Section 2. The Congress shall have power to enforce this article by appropriate legislation.

Amendment XXIV

Passed by Congress August 27, 1962. Ratified January 23, 1964.

Section 1. The right of citizens of the United States to vote in any primary or other election for President or Vice President, for electors for President or Vice President, or for Senator or Representative in Congress, shall not be denied or abridged by the United States or any State by reason of failure to pay poll tax or other tax.

Section 2. The Congress shall have power to enforce this article by appropriate legislation.

Amendment XXV

Passed by Congress July 6, 1965. Ratified February 10, 1967. A portion of Article II, Section 1, was modified by the Twenty-fifth Amendment.

Section 1. In case of the removal of the President from office or of his death or resignation, the Vice President shall become President.

Section 2. Whenever there is a vacancy in the office of the Vice President, the President shall nominate a Vice President who shall take office upon confirmation by a majority vote of both Houses of Congress.

Section 3. Whenever the President transmits to the President pro tempore of the Senate and the Speaker of the House of Representatives his written declaration that he is unable to discharge the powers and duties of his office, and until he transmits to them a written declaration to the contrary, such powers and duties shall be discharged by the Vice President as Acting President.

Section 4. Whenever the Vice President and a majority of either the principal officers of the executive depart-

ments or of such other body as Congress may by law provide, transmit to the President pro tempore of the Senate and the Speaker of the House of Representatives their written declaration that the President is unable to discharge the powers and duties of his office, the Vice President shall immediately assume the powers and duties of the office as Acting President.

Thereafter, when the President transmits to the President pro tempore of the Senate and the Speaker of the House of Representatives his written declaration that no inability exists, he shall resume the powers and duties of his office unless the Vice President and a majority of either the principal officers of the executive department or of such other body as Congress may by law provide, transmit within four days to the President pro tempore of the Senate and the Speaker of the House of Representatives their written declaration that the President is unable to discharge the powers and duties of his office. Thereupon Congress shall decide the issue, assembling within forty-eight hours for that purpose if not in session. If the Congress, within twenty-one days after receipt of the latter written declaration, or, if Congress is not in session, within twenty-one days after Congress is required to assemble, determines by two-thirds vote of both Houses that the President is unable to discharge the powers and duties of his office, the Vice President shall continue to discharge the same as Acting President; otherwise, the President shall resume the powers and duties of his office.

Amendment XXVI

Passed by Congress March 23, 1971. Ratified July 1, 1971. A portion of the Fourteenth Amendment, Section 2, was modified by Section 1 of the Twenty-sixth Amendment.

Section 1. The right of citizens of the United States, who are eighteen years of age or older, to vote shall not be denied or abridged by the United States or by any State on account of age.

Section 2. The Congress shall have power to enforce this article by appropriate legislation.

Amendment XXVII

Originally proposed Sept. 25, 1789. Ratified May 7, 1992.

No law, varying the compensation for the services of the Senators and Representatives, shall take effect, until an election of representatives shall have intervened.

The United States Government

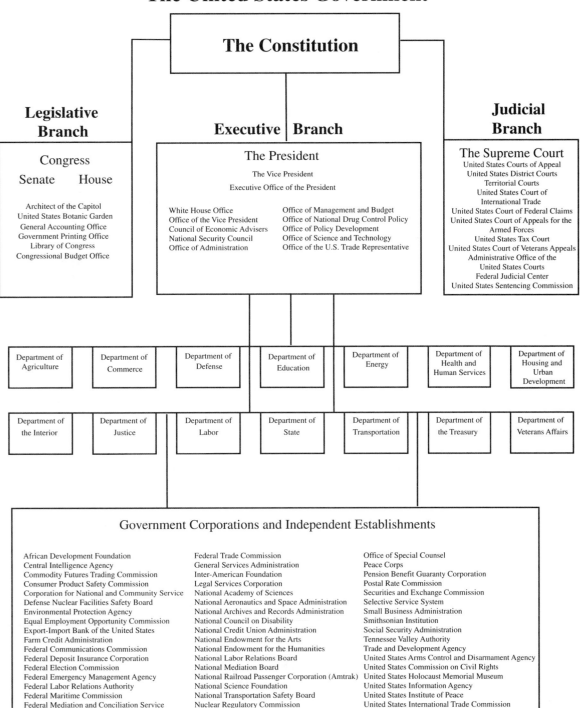

The Constitution

Legislative Branch

Congress

Senate   House

Architect of the Capitol
United States Botanic Garden
General Accounting Office
Government Printing Office
Library of Congress
Congressional Budget Office

Executive | Branch

The President

The Vice President

Executive Office of the President

White House Office
Office of the Vice President
Council of Economic Advisers
National Security Council
Office of Administration

Office of Management and Budget
Office of National Drug Control Policy
Office of Policy Development
Office of Science and Technology
Office of the U.S. Trade Representative

Judicial Branch

The Supreme Court
United States Courts of Appeal
United States District Courts
Territorial Courts
United States Court of
International Trade
United States Court of Federal Claims
United States Court of Appeals for the
Armed Forces
United States Tax Court
United States Court of Veterans Appeals
Administrative Office of the
United States Courts
Federal Judicial Center
United States Sentencing Commission

Department of Agriculture	Department of Commerce	Department of Defense	Department of Education	Department of Energy	Department of Health and Human Services	Department of Housing and Urban Development

Department of the Interior	Department of Justice	Department of Labor	Department of State	Department of Transportation	Department of the Treasury	Department of Veterans Affairs

Government Corporations and Independent Establishments

African Development Foundation
Central Intelligence Agency
Commodity Futures Trading Commission
Consumer Product Safety Commission
Corporation for National and Community Service
Defense Nuclear Facilities Safety Board
Environmental Protection Agency
Equal Employment Opportunity Commission
Export-Import Bank of the United States
Farm Credit Administration
Federal Communications Commission
Federal Deposit Insurance Corporation
Federal Election Commission
Federal Emergency Management Agency
Federal Labor Relations Authority
Federal Maritime Commission
Federal Mediation and Conciliation Service
Federal Reserve System

Federal Trade Commission
General Services Administration
Inter-American Foundation
Legal Services Corporation
National Academy of Sciences
National Aeronautics and Space Administration
National Archives and Records Administration
National Council on Disability
National Credit Union Administration
National Endowment for the Arts
National Endowment for the Humanities
National Labor Relations Board
National Mediation Board
National Railroad Passenger Corporation (Amtrak)
National Science Foundation
National Transportation Safety Board
Nuclear Regulatory Commission
Office of Government Ethics

Office of Special Counsel
Peace Corps
Pension Benefit Guaranty Corporation
Postal Rate Commission
Securities and Exchange Commission
Selective Service System
Small Business Administration
Smithsonian Institution
Social Security Administration
Tennessee Valley Authority
Trade and Development Agency
United States Arms Control and Disarmament Agency
United States Commission on Civil Rights
United States Holocaust Memorial Museum
United States Information Agency
United States Institute of Peace
United States International Trade Commission
United States Postal Service

Federal Government System of Checks and Balances

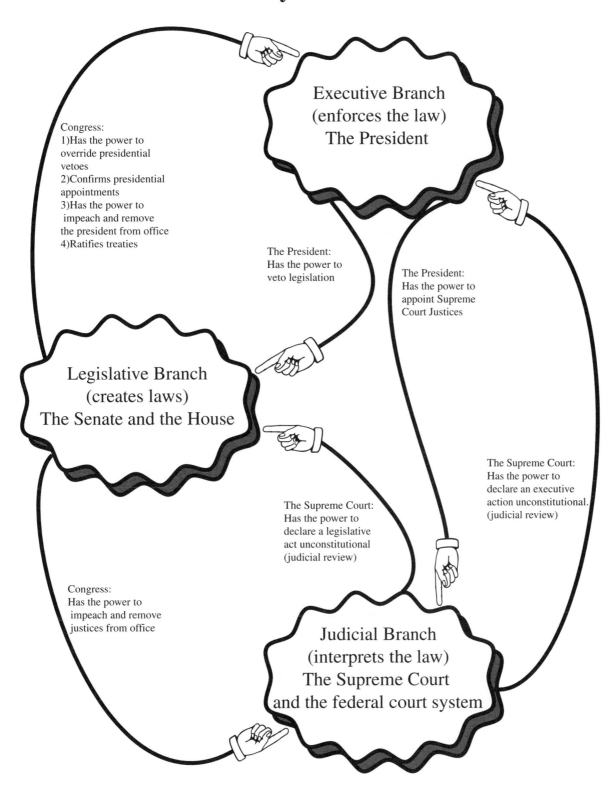

Congress:
1)Has the power to
override presidential
vetoes
2)Confirms presidential
appointments
3)Has the power to
 impeach and remove
the president from office
4)Ratifies treaties

Executive Branch
(enforces the law)
The President

The President:
Has the power to
veto legislation

The President:
Has the power to
appoint Supreme
Court Justices

Legislative Branch
(creates laws)
The Senate and the House

The Supreme Court:
Has the power to
declare an executive
action unconstitutional.
(judicial review)

The Supreme Court:
Has the power to
declare a legislative
act unconstitutional
(judicial review)

Congress:
Has the power to
 impeach and remove
justices from office

Judicial Branch
(interprets the law)
The Supreme Court
and the federal court system

Electoral College Votes by State for U.S. President

Appendix D: Electoral College Representation

The president and the vice president of the United States are elected by the Electoral College. These are the only federal elective offices that are not voted on directly by the people. The number of electors for each state is equal to the number of each states' congressional representatives. (Membership in the House of Representatives is determined by the census conducted every 10 years. The above map is based on the 1990 census.)

Maine 4
N.H. 4
Mass. 12
R.I. 4
Conn. 8
N.J. 15
Del. 3
Md. 10
D.C. 3

Vt. 3
New York 33
Pennsylvania 23
W.Va. 5
Virginia 13
North Carolina 14
S.C. 8
Georgia 13
Fla. 25

Michigan 18
Ohio 21
Ind. 12
Kentucky 8
Tennessee 11
Ala. 9
Miss. 7
La. 9

Minnesota 10
Wisconsin 11
Illinois 22
Iowa 7
Missouri 11
Arkansas 6

N. Dakota 3
S. Dakota 3
Nebraska 5
Kansas 6
Oklahoma 8
Texas 32

Montana 3
Wyoming 3
Colorado 8
New Mexico 5

Idaho 4
Utah 5
Arizona 8

Washington 11
Oregon 7
Nevada 4
California 54

Alaska 3

Hawaii 4

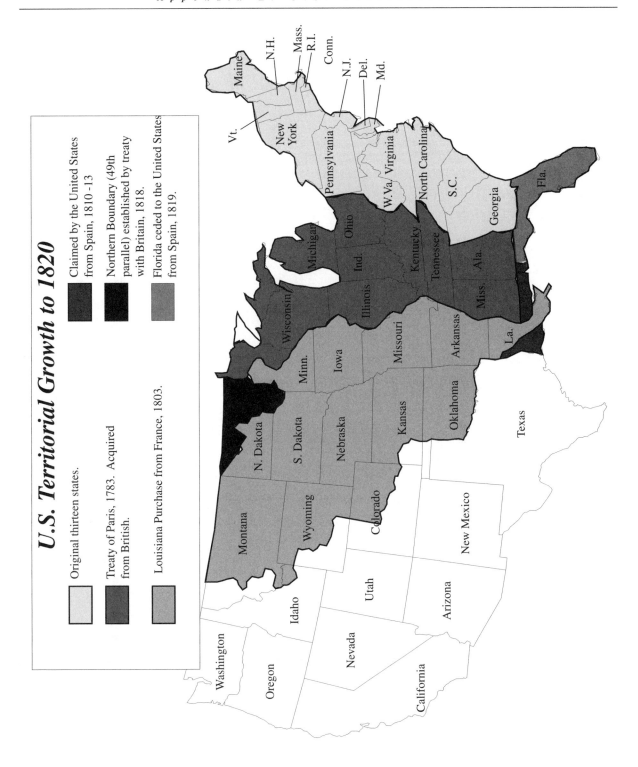

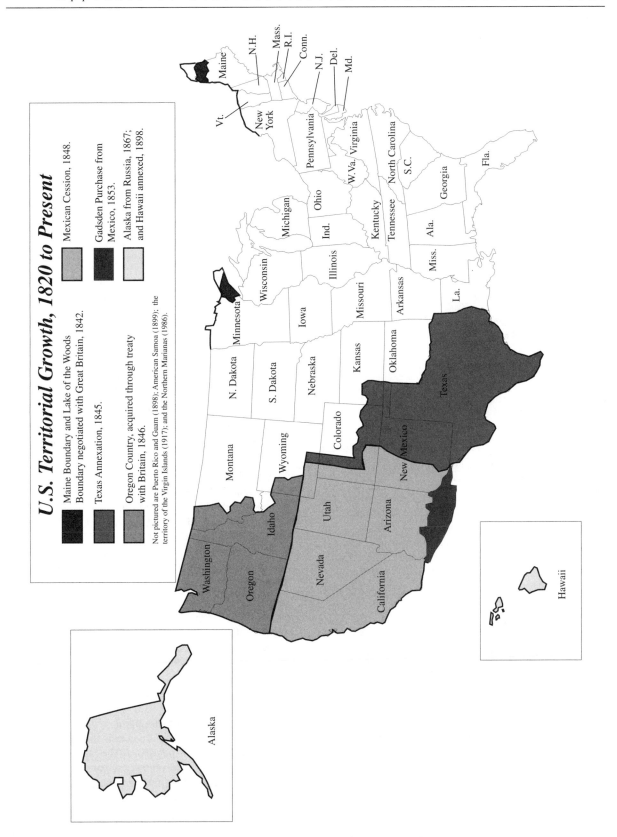

U.S. Territorial Growth, 1820 to Present

Maine Boundary and Lake of the Woods Boundary negotiated with Great Britain, 1842.

Texas Annexation, 1845.

Oregon Country, acquired through treaty with Britain, 1846.

Mexican Cession, 1848.

Gadsden Purchase from Mexico, 1853.

Alaska from Russia, 1867; and Hawaii annexed, 1898.

Not pictured are Puerto Rico and Guam (1898); American Samoa (1899); the territory of the Virgin Islands (1917); and the Northern Marianas (1986).

Appendix F: U.S. Territorial Growth 1820 to Present

Glossary

A

abolitionist: A person who supports the elimination of slavery.

accession: The process by which a country becomes a member of an international agreement, such as the General Agreement on Tariffs and Trade (GATT) or the European Community.

administration: In the U.S. federal government, the executive branch is responsible for the administration (or carrying out and enforcing) of the laws. For this reason, the word administration is frequently used to refer to the executive branch. "The administration" refers to the sitting president and the executive officers and agencies that operate under his authority.

admiral: The commander in chief of a navy or coast guard.

affirmative action: The policy of affording special opportunities or advantages to members of groups that have been the historic victims of discrimination; taking positive steps to remedy past acts of discrimination.

agency: Term used to define any governmental body.

alien: An individual who is not a citizen of the country in which he or she is living. In the United States, aliens may not hold public office or vote, but are provided with civil rights under the Constitution and do pay taxes.

Allies: Nations or states that form an association to further their common interests. The United States's partners against Germany during World War II (1939–45) are often known collectively as "The Allies" and included Great Britain and the Soviet Union. (*See also* Axis powers)

ambassador: An official of a country or organization who formally represents that country or organization. In U.S. government, an ambassador is the top ranking diplomat and personal representative of the president to another country.

amendment: Changes or additions to an official document. In U.S. government, the word Amendment is often used to refer to an amendment to the Constitution. They may only be proposed only by a two-thirds vote of both houses of Congress or by a convention called by Congress at the request of two-thirds of the state legislators. A constitutional amendment must be accepted both by the states and by Congress to be effective.

American Party: A secretive fraternal organization, the American Party was commonly called the Know-Nothing Party because its earliest members answered questions about the group with "I know nothing." The American Party developed as a national party in the early 1850s, and based its appeal on an anti-immigrant and anti-catholic stance. It had significant power in the early and mid-1850s. Internal disputes over the slavery issue and the rise of other new parties such as the Republicans led to a rapid decline for the American Party, it was effectively dead by 1860.

American System: The domestic economic program advanced by Henry Clay and the Whig party which called for active governmental supervision and intervention in the economy. Its prime components were a high protective tariff to develop manufacturing industries; a national bank; and federally funded internal improvements.

Americans with Disabilities Act (ADA): A landmark law that prohibited discrimination against people with physical or mental disabilities. The legislation provided legal protection for disabled people in the workplace and required that all buildings open to the public be accessible to the handicapped.

amnesty: An act of government by which pardons are granted to individuals or groups who have violated a law. Generally, amnesty is a power exercised by the president when a federal law is violated, but Congress may also grant amnesties.

annexation: The addition of new territory to a particular unit of government.

antitrust (laws): Laws designed to prevent a company from completely dominating portions of the economy by the elimination of competitors through unethical business practices. Antitrust laws are designed to maintain competition in a market economy.

anti-federalist: The term most commonly used to describe those who opposed the formation of a strong national government in the late eighteenth century. After the adoption of the U.S. Constitution, many anti-federalists continued to oppose the concentration and development of power in the federal government. (*See also* Democratic-Republican Party)

apportionment: The process by which a state's number of seats in the House of Representatives is determined. Each state is allotted one representative, then a formula based on population is used to determine how many additional seats a state is entitled to.

appropriations: Funds for specific government and public purposes as determined by legislation.

armistice: An agreement or truce that ends military conflict in anticipation of a peace treaty.

arms control: Reducing, eliminating, or otherwise restricting the production, use, or sale of weapons of war. During the Cold War the United States and the former Soviet Union developed numerous treaties to control such weapons as nuclear, biological, chemical, and space-based arms.

Articles of Confederation: The compact made among the thirteen original colonies to form the basis of their government. Prepared in 1776, the Articles were adopted by all states in 1781. The Articles of Confederation provided for a relatively weak national government, leaving most power at the state level. They were replaced by the U.S. Constitution in 1789.

atomic (weapons): Weapons of mass destruction with violent explosive power that results from the splitting of the nuclei of atoms (usually uranium or plutonium) by neutrons in a rapid chain reaction.

attaché: A representative of a government, typically stationed at an embassy, who serves the diplomatic staff in a support position.

attorney general: The chief legal officer of a state or nation. In the government of the United States, the attorney general is the legal adviser to the president and to all agencies of the executive branch and is the highest law enforcement officer in the country. The attorney general is also head of the Department of Justice and a member of the president's cabinet. (*See also* cabinet)

Axis Powers: The countries aligned against the Allied nations in World War II (1939–45). The term originally applied to Nazi Germany and Fascist Italy (Rome-Berlin Axis), and later extended to include Japan. (*See also* Allies)

B

ballot: Instrument used for casting a secret vote. It may be a paper or electronic system.

bicameral: A legislative body consisting of two chambers; an example is the U.S. Congress, which consists of the House of Representatives and the Senate.

bilateral negotiations: Discussions between, and problem solving efforts of, two parties or nations.

bill: A proposed law. In the United States bills may be drawn up by anyone, including the president or citizen groups, but they must be introduced in Congress by a senator or representative.

Bill of Rights: The first ten amendments to the Constitution of the United States. Proposed shortly after the adoption of the Constitution, they list the rights a U.S. citizen is entitled to that cannot be interfered with by the government, including freedom of speech and religion.

bipartisan: Cooperation between the two major political parties; for example, Republican and Democratic. (*See also* partisan)

blockade: Isolating an area belonging to an enemy, such as a harbor, by a nation or warring force to prevent supplies and people from entering or leaving the area.

bond: A type of loan, such as savings bonds, issued by the government to finance public needs that cost more than existing funds can pay for. The government agrees to pay lenders back the initial cost of the bond, plus interest.

brain trust: A group of official or unofficial advisers who assist a politician with planning and strategy.

brinkmanship: Pushing a dangerous or tense situation towards confrontation to force an opponent to concede. In U.S. government brinkmanship usually refers to threatening another country with military action if they do not comply with the United States' wishes.

Brown vs. Board of Education: A landmark decision by the Supreme Court in 1954 that ruled that segregation of the races in public schools violates the equal protection clause of the Fourteenth Amendment and that separate educational facilities are inherently unequal.

budget deficit: Occurs when the money spent by the government or other organization is more than the money coming in.

"Bull Moose" Party: A popular nickname for the Progressive Party during the presidential campaign of Theodore Roosevelt. (*See also* Progressive Party)

bully pulpit: When a president makes use of the high visibility of his office to publically and aggressively call for change and generate public support for his policies, he is said to be using his office as a bully pulpit.

bureau: A working unit of a department or agency with specific functions.

bureaucracy: An administrative system, especially of government agencies, that handles day-to-day business and carries out policies. Workers within a bureaucracy create and process forms, implement procedures, exist in chains of command, and establish routines that must be followed in order to get work accomplished.

business cycle: A widely accepted theory in economics which holds that the economy naturally and endlessly shifts from a period of growth to decline to recession or depression to recovery and then back to growth.

C

cabinet: A group of senior advisers. In the federal government the cabinet is made up of advisers who offer assistance to the president. Each president determines the make up and role of their cabinets, although most include the heads of major departments such as State, Treasury, and Justice, and the vice president.

campaign: The organized activities of candidates seeking office to convince voters to vote for them, rather than their opponents.

capital gains tax: A tax levied on the profit from the sale of assets, such as stocks or real estate, that have increased in value from the time they were bought to the time they were sold.

capitalism: An economic system based on private ownership of industry and property. Suppliers seek to sell products for profit and buyers determine which products they will purchase and at what cost.

carpetbagger: A disparaging term used to describe an outsider or non-resident who gets involved in the politics of a specific region. First used to describe northerners who became involved in southern politics after the Civil War. Supposedly they came south with no more possessions than would fit in a small bag made of carpet, hoping to exploit the defeated southern states.

cartel: An organization of independent producers formed to regulate or fix the production, pricing, or marketing practices of its members in order to limit competition and maximize their market power.

caucus: The meeting of a political or other organized group in order to decide upon issues and policies or to choose a political candidate; also refers to the group itself.

censure: A measure by which legislative bodies can discipline their own members with punishments ranging from withdrawal of privileges to expulsion.

census: An official counting of the inhabitants of a state or country; compiled data usually includes such details as gender, age, family size, and occupation.

centrist: An individual or political group that advocates a moderate approach to politics and political decision making that is neither liberal or conservative.

Certiorari, writ of: The primary method by which cases reach the Supreme Court of the United States. The writ is discretionary and allows the Court to pick and choose which lower court cases it deems appropriate for a full hearing and possible decision.

checks and balances: A system, particularly in government, where equal branches must cooperate with each other, oversee each other, and enforce and support each others' decisions according to established rules. (*See also* separation of powers)

chief executive: The head of a nation or state. The chief executive is the acknowledged leader of government and is responsible for policy decisions and implementation. In the United States the president is the chief executive.

chief of state: A ceremonial head of government whose duties center on "affairs of state" such as greeting foreign dignitaries and hosting state dinners, the chief of state may also be the chief executive. In the United States the president is the chief of state.

citizen: An individual who is a legal member of a political unit by birth or naturalization and is entitled to all the protections and privileges of its laws.

civil disobedience: Refusal to obey the law on the grounds that the law is morally wrong. Civil disobedience may also encompass actions to change such laws.

civil law: The code that governs interactions between private persons as opposed to the code known as criminal law that governs individual conduct. Civil law provides a forum to settle disputes involving contracts, business dealings, and accidents. (*See also* criminal justice system)

civil liberties: Those recognized principles of American law that limit the powers of government and also guarantee the privileges of citizenship, such as voting and equality of treatment. (*See also* citizen)

civil rights: The privileges of all individuals to be treated as equals under the laws of their country; specifically, the rights given to U.S. citizens by certain amendments to the U.S. Constitution.

civil servant: A member of the civil service, the administrative service of a government.

civil service: A term describing an organized official system for employing people in non-military government jobs. The modern U.S. system is based on merit classifications.

civilian: An individual who is not on active duty in the military.

classified: Information or documents withheld from the public because their circulation could threaten national security. (*See also* declassify; secured document)

cloture: A parliamentary procedure used by a decision making body, such as Congress, to end discussion on a matter and move to a vote.

coalition: An alliance between several groups forged to pursue shared interests and agendas.

cold war: Conflict over ideological differences that is carried on by words and diplomatic actions, not by military action. The term is usually used to refer to the tension that existed between the United States and the USSR from the 1950s until the breakup of the USSR in 1991.

collective bargaining: The negotiations between workers who are members of a union and their employer for the purpose of deciding upon such as issues as fair wages and work-day hours.

colony: A territory ruled over by a foreign country without becoming a part of that country, especially in the case where natives of that country move to the territory in large numbers to become permanent residents.

commander in chief: The officer who is in command of a major armed force; in the United States the role of the president as the supreme commander of the nation's military forces and the national guard when it is called into federal service.

committee: A group of individuals charged by a higher authority with a specific purpose such as investigation, review, reporting, or determining action. In the U.S. Congress, standing and special committees are where most legislation is developed.

commonwealth: A free association of sovereign independent states that has no binding charter, treaty, or constitution. The association promotes cooperation, consultation, and mutual assistance among members.

communism; communist: A political, economic, and social theory that promotes common ownership of property for the use of all citizens. All profits are to be equally distributed and prices on goods and services are usually set by the state. Communism also refers directly to the official doctrine of the former Soviet Union.

Communist bloc: Refers to a group of countries in Eastern Europe with Communist governments that supported and were influenced by the former Soviet Union. In the 1990s, many of these countries, such as Poland and Czechoslovakia overthrew Communist regimes and established democratic systems of government.

Compromise of 1820: Commonly called the Missouri Compsomise, this agreement prohibited slavery north of Missouri's southern border with the exception of Missouri itself, which was allowed to enter the union as a slave state. This preserved the balance between slave and free states in the Union, and at the same time addressed the future of slavery in the United States.

Compromise of 1850: A series of bills passed by Congress in 1850 that determined the status of slavery in the large amounts of new land captured from Mexico in the Mexican War (1846–48). The compromise temporarily subdued, but did not truly eliminate, conflict between the northern and southern United States over slavery.

comptroller: An official who oversees spending to determine whether funds have or have not been spent on purchases they were intended for. The federal title is Comptroller General and the responsibility is to oversee funds to be spent according to legislative approval.

Confederacy: The government formed by the southern states that seceded from the United States prior to the Civil War.

confederation: A unified group of independent states or nations where a central body makes decisions about matters of common concern but units make decisions affecting individuals.

confirmation: The process by which the Senate approves of presidential appointees to offices.

conflict of interest: When an individual's actions in a business or political situation are affected or motivated by their personal interest. Examples include politicians who vote on particular issues to gain financial support from like minded groups, or a federal official in charge of regulating an industry owning businesses in that industry.

Congress: The term used to describe the combined Senate and House of Representatives of the United States.

congressional appropriation: Money that Congress approves for a specific purpose. (*See also* appropriations)

congressional district: The geographic area that a member of the House of Representatives is elected from and represents in Congress. Congressional districts are drawn up to include a nearly equal number of voters.

conscription: The mandatory enlistment of citizens to serve in the military. (*See also* draft)

consensus: Agreement that is supported by all parties involved.

conservative: In general, one who opposes change or wishes to see old ways reestablished. In the modern United States, a political philosophy that generally favors state over federal action, and opposes regulation of the economy, extensive civil rights legislation, and federally funded social programs.

consortium: A group of business organizations that join together to achieve things they did not have the resources to accomplish individually.

constituent; constituency: The registered voters in a governmental district; a group of people who support a position or a candidate.

constitution: Fundamental laws that establish government organization, determine the roles and duties of segments of government, and clarify the relationship between the people and their government. The U.S. Constitution was created in 1787 and ratified in 1788.

constructionist: A method of interpreting the U.S. Constitution which seeks to confine the powers of the government strictly to those specifically mentioned. Belief that a governmental power does not exist if the Constitution does not explicitly name it.

consul: Government officials sent to other countries to assist and provide support to citizens of the country the official represents who are staying in the foreign country. (*See also* consulate)

consulate: The official residence and place of business of a consul in a foreign country. (*See also* consul)

Consumer Price Index (CPI): The change in the cost of certain current goods and services used by the average consumer compared to the cost for the same goods and services in a chosen base year. Legislators use the CPI when considering wage and subsidy increases as well as other legislation affected by economic factors.

containment: Generally, the process of limiting or restraining something. Specifically, a policy adopted during President Harry Truman's administration (1945–53) to build up areas of U.S. military strength around the world to isolate and intimidate communist nations. The belief behind the policy was that communism would eventually collapse on its own if it was not allowed to spread and expand its power.

Continental Congress: The body formed by American colonists in 1774 to protest British treatment of the colonies. The group eventually became the first government of the United States after adopting the Declaration of Independence.

corporate welfare: A negative phrase used to describe tax breaks and favorable laws the government creates for industry. The implication is that such supports are "charity" for big business. (*See also* welfare)

counterinsurgency: Military force directed at a revolutionary group that tries to overthrow an established government.

criminal justice system: The United States court system that deals with criminal violations and punishment. Criminal law differs from civil law in that it regulates individual actions and not conduct between parties. (*See also* civil law)

customs: The fees imposed by a country on items imported and exported. In the United States, the word customs can also apply to the agency that collects these fees. (*See also* tariff)

D

dark horse candidate: A politician not known to be a candidate who, at a deadlocked convention, unexpectedly receives the nomination. Phrase derives from racing slang for a little-known horse that unexpectedly goes to the front.

declassify; declassification: The process of making previously secret information available to the public by removing or reducing its security classification. (*See also* classified)

decommission: When something is removed from active military service. Usually refers to military vessels such as ships and submarines.

deficit: The amount by which spending exceeds income over a given period.

demobilize: To disband or discharge military troops.

democracy: A form of government in which the power lies in the hands of the people, who may govern directly, or govern indirectly by electing representatives.

Democratic Party: One of the oldest political parties in the United States. Developed out of the Democratic-Republican Party established early in the nineteenth century, the party became known as the Democrats during the presidency of party member and leader Andrew Jackson. In the years before the Civil War, the Democrats became increasingly associated with the South and slavery. After the Civil War, the Democratic Party gradually transformed and became associated with urban voters and liberal politics. In the twentieth century, the Democratic Party has generally stood for freer trade, more international commitments, greater government regulations, and social programs. (*See Also* Democratic-Republican Party, Republican Party, Whig Party)

Democratic-Republican Party: One of the first political parties in the United States, developed around opposition to the Federalist policies of George Washington and John Adams. In general, the Democratic-Republicans sought to restrict the power and influence of the national government in favor of state and local control, and support for individual freedoms. Democratic-Republicans were particularly opposed to government support for business. The party was at times referred to as the Democrats or the Republicans, but while the modern Democratic Party is an off-shoot of the Democratic-Republicans, the Republican Party is not. (*See also* Democratic Party, Federalist Party, Jeffersonian Republicanism)

demographic(s): Statistics about human populations including such categories as age, density, income, and distribution.

department: An administrative unit with responsibility for a broad area of an organization's operations. Federal departments include Labor, Interior, Health and Human Services, and State.

deposit insurance: Government-regulated protection for interest-bearing deposits, such as savings accounts, to protect the depositor from failure of the banking institution.

depression: An economic term used to describe an extended period of poor performance by the economy. A depression is usually marked by high unemployment, decreased purchasing power for consumers, and a slowdown of production.

deregulation: The process of removing government restrictions and regulations.

détente: An easing of strain and confrontations between two or more nations. Often used to describe the improved relationships between the United States and the Soviet Union and the Peoples Republic of China in the 1970s.

diplomacy: The process by which nations carry out political relations with each other. In the United States, diplomacy is the primary responsibility of the president and the Department of State.

diplomatic envoy: A person sent to represent their nation in dealings with another nation.

dissident: Someone who disagrees with an established political system or organization. A member of an organization who opposes its leadership.

domestic: Of, relating to, or originating within a particular country. When referring to the United States, the term implies something which is made within

(for example, domestic goods) or is restricted in scope to (for example, domestic politics) the United States itself.

domestic policy: Policies that focus on issues internal to the United States. (*See also* foreign policy).

Domino Theory: A political and military theory advanced in the 1950s that assumes that if a key nation in a region falls under Communist control, surrounding weaker nations will also succumb to communism.

dove: Someone who opposes war and seeks a peaceful resolution to conflict.

draft: A draft is the process of selecting, out of a pool of qualified individuals, people who will be compelled to serve in the military. (*See also* conscription)

***Dred Scott* case:** An 1857 case in which the Supreme Court ruled that African Americans could not become citizens of the United States and were not entitled to any of the rights and privileges of citizens. The ruling also declared that the Missouri Compromise, which had banned slavery in most of the northwest United States, was unconstitutional because citizens had the right to own slaves as property.

due process: The judicial standard that laws and the application of the law be fair, that no individual should be dealt with arbitrarily or unreasonably by the law or its officers. For example, the principle of due process prevents the government from seizing people or their property without a warrant or other legal justification.

E

economic forecast: Predictions about a country's economic future including projected revenues, employment statistics, and interest rates.

electoral college: The group of qualified voters chosen to represent their individual states, who ultimately elect the president and vice president of the United States. Each state has a number of votes in the electoral college equal to their representation in Congress; their votes are based on the popular vote within their state.

electorate: The individuals who are qualified to vote in an election.

embargo: A legal restriction on commercial ships from entering a country's ports; any legal restriction of trade. One example of an embargo would be for a government to prevent any shipments of a commodity, such as oil, to other countries. Another example would be for a government to restrict all trade with a particular country.

embassy: The office or residence of the ambassador of a foreign country; also collectively refers to an ambassador and his staff.

emergency powers: Powers given to the president for a limited time by Congress or the Constitution for use only during a crisis.

ethics: The principles and morals that govern an individual or group and clarify right behavior and wrong behavior.

excise tax: A tax or duty on the sale of specific commodities or groups of commodities; for instance, tobacco or liquor.

executive agreement: An agreement made between the United States and another country by officials in the executive branch of government.

executive branch: In the United States, the branch of government charged with administering the laws and policies of the nation or state. In contrast, the legislative and judicial branches of government have the respective powers of creating and interpreting the laws.

executive order: A rule or regulation issued by the president or a governor that has the effect of law. Presidential executive orders are limited in scope to those that implement provisions of the Constitution, treaties, and regulations governing administrative agencies.

executive privilege: The right of executive officials to keep information from or refuse to appear in front of a court or legislative body. In the United States only the president and officials designated by the president enjoy executive privilege.

expansionist: Someone who supports the growth of a nation by adding new territory.

export: Goods sold to foreign buyers; the act of selling goods to foreign buyers. (*See also* import)

F

faction: A group of people who have ideas or goals in common, especially a group which is part of a larger whole. Political parties are sometimes referred to as factions within government.

fair housing laws: Group of laws that make discrimination in renting, purchasing, or selling housing, illegal.

fair labor practices: Group of laws that guarantee fair treatment of employees by employers including the right to unionize and the right to pursue grievances according to established personnel policies.

favorite son: A favorite son is a candidate at a national convention who has the support of his home state's delegation but little national support. Often the candidate is not a serious contender for the presidential or vice-presidential nomination and the nomination is used for strategic reasons, especially in situations in which there are several strong candidates and the state is then in a position to bargain with those candidates for its vote.

federal aid: Funds collected by the federal government (generally through taxes) and distributed to states or individuals for a variety of reasons including education and disaster relief.

federal budget: The annual financial plan of the United States government including all sources and amounts of income and items and amounts of expenditure. The federal budget must be approved by Congress and the president.

federal government: The national government of the United States of America under the Constitution, including the executive, legislative, and judicial branches, as opposed to state or local governments.

federalism: The system of government in the United States, in which the power of government is distributed between a central authority and its constituent units.

Federalist Papers, The: A famous and influential series of articles believed to be written by Alexander Hamilton, John Jay, and James Madison. The Federalist Papers were published during the period that ratification of the U.S. Constitution was being debated, in an attempt to justify and explain the Constitution.

Federalist Party: One of the first parties in the United States. The party developed during the later part of George Washington's (1789–96) administration to support the national financial and economic programs being developed by Washington and Alexander Hamilton. The party desired the United States to have a powerful national government. (*See Also* Democratic-Republican Party)

federal poverty guidelines: Federal guidelines that define the maximum amount of income that families can earn to be considered living in poverty.

felony: A serious criminal offense, usually punishable by a year in prison or more.

filibuster: A tactic used in the U.S. Senate, where there is no limit on the time a bill can be debated. Opponents of a bill insist on continuing to speak, thereby preventing the bill from coming to a vote. The purpose of a filibuster is to defeat proposed legislation by forcing the Senate to move on to other business, leaving the disputed measure unresolved.

fiscal: Relating to financial matters.

floor leader: Representatives and Senators who are selected by their party to carry out party decisions during legislative battles by influencing and working with undecided members.

foreign aid: Funds provided by the U.S. government to assist other countries.

foreign policy: The plans and course of actions that the United States develops regarding other nations. (*See also* domestic policy)

free enterprise system: The system of economics in which private business may be conducted with minimum interference by the government.

free market economy: An economic system that relies on the market, as opposed to government planners, to set the prices for wages and products.

free silver: In the later half of the nineteenth century, the term free silver was used to describe the political movement for the use of silver as currency. The "free and unlimited coinage of silver," which was expected to greatly increase the amount of money in circulation, was one of the most significant political issues of the 1880s and 90s.

Free-Soil Party: A party of the late 1840s and early 1850s. The Free-Soil Party was the first serious anti-slavery party, it also supported a number of measures intended to improve life for laborers and farmers in general, and western settlers in particular. While the party had only modest electoral success, many of its members and ideas were later incorporated into the Republican Party.

free trade(rs): Trade between two entities, particularly the United States and another country, that is not limited by regulations and other restrictions.

friendly fire: When a military unit mistakenly shoots at its own forces.

front porch campaign: A political campaign in which the nominee stays close to home and does not actively participate in efforts to secure his or her election beyond giving speeches to visitors.

G

GDP: *See* Gross Domestic Product

gender bias: Discrimination against or favoritism toward someone because of his or her sex.

general: A high ranking official in the army, marine corps, or air force.

gerrymandering: Apportionment of voters in such a way as to give unfair advantage to a political party or racial group.

Gilded Age: This is a term used by historians to describe the period from the end of the Civil War to the turn of the century when the economic system of the United States became industrialized and there was considerable expansion and economic growth. This growth came at the same time that many laborers and city dwellers endured low wages and poor working conditions. Hence the use of the word gilded, which means something which is attractive only on the surface.

glasnost: Policy of openness and freedom of expression. Embraced by Mikhail Gorbachev in the late 1980s as part of his attempt to reform the Soviet Communist system.

globalization: Expanding a policy or activity to apply worldwide.

global market(place): The buying and selling of products throughout the world, rather than limiting sales within a country or region.

global warming: Also called the greenhouse effect. The supposed gradual warming of the earth's climate as a result of various environmental factors including the burning of fossil fuels, the use of man-made chemicals, and deforestation.

GNP: *See* Gross National Product

gold standard: A fiscal system in which all currency is backed by gold reserves, and can be exchanged for a set amount of gold.

government: The political and administrative system of a nation or state including legislative, executive, and judicial functions.

government securities: Certificates issued by the government as guarantees to repay loans.

grand jury: In the United States, a group of 12 to 23 people who hear evidence presented by a prosecuting attorney against someone accused of a serious crime. Based on this evidence, they decide whether the person should be indicted, or charged with the crime.

grant: Money provided by a government or organization to an individual or group for a specific purpose. For example, the federal government makes education grants to students for college expenses and to states to improve schools.

grassroots organizing: Organizing the general public to collectively act on political issues. As opposed to organizing politicians or other prominent and influential individuals.

Great Depression: Period in U.S. history from 1929 until the early 1940s when the economy was so poor that many banks and businesses failed and millions of people lost their jobs and their homes. The terrible business problems were combined with a severe drought that ruined many farms and contributed to the economic disaster.

Great Society: Term used by Lyndon Johnson during his presidential administration (1963–69) to describe his vision of the United States as a land without prejudice or poverty, that would be made possible by implementing his series of social programs.

greenbacks: Paper money issued by the United States government during the American Civil War (1861–65). Unlike most paper money of the time, greenbacks were not backed by gold or other precious metal. They are the direct forerunners to modern U.S. currency. (*See also* soft money, hard money)

Gross Domestic Product (GDP): A measure of the market value of all goods and services produced within the boundaries of a nation, regardless of asset ownership. Unlike gross national product, GDP excludes receipts from that nation's business operations in foreign countries, as well as the share of reinvested earnings in foreign affiliates of domestic corporations.

Gross National Product (GNP): A measure of the market value of goods and services produced by the labor and property of a nation. Includes receipts from that nation's business operation in foreign countries, as well as the share of reinvested earnings in foreign affiliates of domestic corporations.

H

hard money: Currency which is made of precious metals, or specie. Also, a fiscal system in which all currency is either made of precious metals, or can be directly exchanged for it at a set value. (*See also* specie)

hawk: Someone who supports war as a means to resolving conflicts between nations.

House of Representatives: One of the two bodies with specific functions that make up the legislative branch of the United States government. Each state is allocated representatives based on population. (*See also* Congress; Senate)

humanitarian: A person who works for social reform and is concerned about the welfare of people. Anything which is done to aid or benefit a person or people, without expectation of payment or reward.

I

ICBM: *See* intercontinental ballistic missile

illegal immigrant: A person who comes from another country to live in the United States without applying for entrance or completing the appropriate documents.

immigration: The process of leaving one's native country to live in another country.

impeach(ment): To charge someone with an offense that may lead to removal from the office they hold. In the United States, the House of Representatives has the power to bring charges against federal officials, and the Senate tries impeachment cases to determine the outcome.

imperialism: The policy and practice of extending a nation's power over new territories and their economies.

implied powers: Authority granted to the federal government that is not specifically granted by the Constitution, but can be deduced from what is written in the Constitution.

import: Goods purchased from foreign suppliers; the act of purchasing goods from foreign suppliers. (*See also* export)

impressment: In the nineteenth century and earlier, it was not uncommon for "press gangs" from British naval vessels to take captives from costal cities or other ships, and force them serve on their vessels. This practice is known as impressment.

income tax: A tax levied on personal or corporate income, whether that income is in the form of wages or income from investments or property.

independent: A voter who does not belong to any political party and votes for individual candidates regardless of their party affiliation.

industrialization: The process of converting from an economy that is based primarily on agriculture and/or manual labor to one devoted to the manufacture of goods, with extensive use of heavy machinery.

inflation; inflation rate: An economic term which describes the tendency for prices to rise over time as more money circulates in an economy. Inflation generally causes the purchasing power of a currency to decline. The inflation rate is a measure of how much the value of a piece of currency (for example, a dollar) has changed over time due to inflation.

infrastructure: A basic system of public works such as roads, sewers, and power sources, and the people and resources needed to conduct activity.

insurgent: Someone in revolt against the leadership and policy of their group.

intelligence: Gathering information on another country's military capabilities and political plans. In the United States, these operations are conducted by the Central Intelligence Agency, the National Security Agency, and military intelligence units.

intercontinental ballistic missile (ICBM): Missiles that are capable of traveling from one continent to another.

interest rate: A percentage of money borrowed that must be paid back in addition to the sum of the original loan for the privilege of being able to borrow.

interstate (commerce): Interstate commerce is business that is conducted between two or more states.

interstate highway system: The system of major highways built by the federal government that crisscross the country.

internal improvements: Improvements to the infrastructure of a state, such as dams, roads, and canals, that are intended to boost commerce and improve the quality of life for residents, and do not cross over state borders.

isolationism; isolationist: A policy of avoiding political and/or economic interaction with other countries. One who supports such a policy

J

Jeffersonian Republicanism: The policies and ideas associated with the Democratic-Republican party which dominated U.S. politics from the time of Thomas Jefferson's election as president in 1801 until 1824. This was a movement to restore limited democratic government to the American polity after years of the extension of executive power and the reach of the national government under the Federalist party. (*See also* Democratic-Republican Party)

Jim Crow: A social and legal system instituted in the South after the Civil War to maintain segregation between races by physically separating blacks from whites in inferior housing, schools, jobs, and public facilities.

joint committee: A committee composed of members from both the House of Representatives and the Senate to address an issue of mutual concern.

joint resolution: A measure that must be approved by the House of Representatives and the Senate and signed by the president to become law. However, if a joint resolution proposes an amendment to the Constitution, the president does not have to sign for the measure to become law.

judicial branch: The segment of government that protects citizens against excessive use of power by the executive or legislature and provides an impartial setting for the settlement of civil and criminal cases. In the United States, the judiciary system is divided into state and federal courts with further divisions at those levels. State and federal courts are independent except that the Supreme Court of the United States may review state court decisions when a federal issue is involved. (*See also* executive branch; legislative branch)

jurisdiction: The right and authority of a court to hear and decide a case.

K

Kansas-Nebraska Act: The Kansas-Nebraska Act was a bill proposed by Senator Stephen Douglas in the U.S. Senate, and signed into law in 1854. It effectively repealed the Compromise of 1820 by allowing slavery to extend into the federal territories of Kansas and Nebraska. These territories would be allowed to enter the Union as either free or slave states, depending on what their inhabitants wanted. The Act led to armed struggles in Kansas over the slavery issue, and was met with disapproval throughout the North. The Republican Party organized itself around opposition to this Act. (*See also* Compromise of 1820, Republican Party, popular sovereignty)

"Know Nothing" Party: A popular and widely used nickname for the American Party. (*See also* American Party)

L

labor market: The people available for employment.

labor union: A group of organized workers who negotiate with management to secure or improve their rights, benefits, and working conditions as employees.

laissez faire: An economic theory that proposes that governments should not interfere in their economies and that natural economic laws should guide the production and consumption of goods.

lame duck: An elected official who is serving out the end of his term after failing to be re-elected.

League of Nations: The forerunner of the United Nations, envisioned by its originator, Woodrow Wilson, as a forum where countries could resolve their differences without resorting to war. Formed in 1919, the League also promoted economic and social cooperation. Congress did not support President Wilson's plan and the United States never joined the League, which contributed to its collapse in the late 1930s.

legislation: Measures that are intended to become law after approval by legislative bodies.

legislative branch: The branch of government that makes or enacts laws. In the U.S. government, Congress is the legislative branch. (*See also* executive branch; judicial branch)

liberal: A political philosophy that generally favors change and development of new ideas. Traditionally, U.S. liberals have pushed for political, economic, and social change to benefit individuals. In the twentieth century this has often included the expansion of the government's role in the every day life of Americans.

line-item veto: The power of the president to disapprove a particular expense (or line-item) in the federal budget while approving the budget as a whole.

lobby, lobbies: A group of people who conduct activities designed to influence legislators to vote the way the lobby wants them to, or to convince legislators to introduce bills that are favorable to lobby interests.

lobbyist: Someone who is paid to promote the interests of a particular group or industry in an attempt to influence the actions of legislators.

logrolling: An arrangement by which two or more members of a legislative body agree in advance to support each other's bills, particularly those that benefit each legislator's home district.

M

macroeconomics: The study of the economy as a whole terms of income, employment, output, price levels, and rates of growth. (*See also* microeconomics)

major party: A political party that has many supporters and a great deal of power and influence.

mandate: Popular support for a political program or politician. Candidates espousing particular political plans are considered to be given a mandate by the people if they are elected, meaning that people agree with the candidates plans and want them to be implemented.

Mandus, writ of: A court order demanding an action. The court has the right to order an individual to perform an act that someone else has a legal right to expect, such as the fulfillment of a business contract.

Manifest Destiny: Phrase coined by John L. O'Sullivan, Democratic editor, in 1845 to capture the growing public mood in the 1840s that America was destined—by God and history—to expand westward to the Pacific and beyond, spreading democracy and liberty in its wake.

Marshall Plan: Formally known as the European Recovery Program, a joint project between the United States and most Western European nations under which $12.5 billion in U.S. loans and grants was expended to aid European recovery after World War II (1939–45). Expenditures under the program, named for U.S. Secretary of State George C. Marshall, were made from fiscal years 1949 through 1952.

Maysville Road Veto: In 1830 President Andrew Jackson vetoed internal improvements legislation which sought federal funds for the construction of a road between Maysville and Lexington, Kentucky. Although Jackson's personal and political feelings influenced his decision to veto this particular bill, he justified his opposition to internal improvements in general on the grounds that it was unconstitutional for the U.S. government to pay for construction occurring within the confines of only one state.

McCarthy Era: Period in American history from the late 1940s to the 1950s when Senator Joseph McCarthy of Wisconsin headed a committee investigating communist influence in the United States. Begun as a legitimate investigation, the committee began questioning individuals about their activities with little or no evidence that they had been involved in communist activities. The excesses of the committee and McCarthy created widespread suspicion and hysteria concerning national security. McCarthy was censured by the Senate in 1954 and the committee's activities were severely restricted.

mediation: The intervention of an unbiased party to settle differences between two other disputing parties; any attempt to act as a go-between in order to reconcile a problem.

merchant marine: The ships of a nation, whether privately or publicly owned, that are involved in commercial business. The term may also refer to someone who works on such ships.

metropolitan area: A large important city and the outlying suburbs that are connected to it geographically and economically.

microeconomics: The study of the economy of a particular unit such as a business, or of a specific activity such as pricing. (*See also* macroeconomics)

military junta: The small military group in control of a country, especially after a coup.

military regime: A government which maintains control of its own people through the use of military force.

minimum wage: The wage established by law as the lowest amount to be paid to workers in particular jobs.

minor party: A small political party with little influence that is very often created around a single issue.

Missouri Compromise: *See* Compromise of 1820.

monopoly, monopolies: The exclusive control of goods and services in a particular market by a business or group of businesses, often leading to complete control over prices of those commodities.

Monroe Doctrine: U.S. foreign policy statement issued by President James Monroe in 1823 declaring that the United States would not tolerate European interference in the Western Hemisphere. It established the idea of American hegemony in the region that later U.S. governments used to justify American intervention in Latin America.

moratorium: An official delay or stoppage of some activity.

most-favored-nation: A trading system in which all participants receive the same tax benefits. Although the term implies special treatment for one nation, it actually guarantees fair treatment of all trade participants.

multilateral negotiation: Discussions and meetings to resolve conflicts in which many countries participate.

multiparty system: Political system in which many political parties representing different viewpoints are participants. (*See also* two-party system)

N

NAFTA: *See* North American Free Trade Agreement

nation: A large group of people united by bonds of geography, language, customs, and shared collective experiences. Some nations that have developed governmental systems are also referred to as states. (*See also* state)

national security: Ensuring that a country is protected from internal and external attacks.

NATO: *See* North Atlantic Treaty Organization

naturalization: The legal process by which an alien becomes a citizen. An individual who is at least 18 may become a U.S. citizen after meeting certain qualifications including: residing in the United States for five years; reading, writing, and speaking English; and taking an oath of allegiance to the United States. (*See also* alien; citizen)

nepotism: Showing favoritism toward someone because they are related to you. For example, granting a family member a job only because he or she is a family member.

New Deal: The name given to Franklin Roosevelt's plan to save the nation from the devastating effects of the Great Depression. His programs included direct aid to citizens and a variety of employment and public works opportunities sponsored by the federal government. It began shortly after his inauguration in 1933.

nonpartisan: An action free from political party influence or undertaken by members of all political parties involved.

nonproliferation: Stopping the increase in the number and spread of something, especially nuclear weapons.

North American Free Trade Agreement (NAFTA): A 1994 agreement between the United States, Canada, and Mexico that removes all trade barriers between the three countries. For purposes of trade, all boundaries disappear and the nations conduct business as if one country, rather than as foreign nations.

North Atlantic Treaty Organization (NATO): An organization formed in 1949 by countries bordering and near the north Atlantic Ocean, most notably the United States and the nations of Western Europe. Member nations agreed to come to each others defense if any member is attacked. For much of its history, NATO was primarily concerned with defending Western Europe against invasion by the Soviet Union and its Eastern European allies. (*See also* Warsaw Pact)

Northwest Ordinance of 1787: Law passed in 1787 creating a single Northwest Territory out of U.S. lands north of the Ohio River. It guaranteed freedom of religion and the right to trial by jury to residents and prohibited slavery throughout the territory.

nuclear: Relating to radioactive materials that may be used for weapons, energy, or medicine.

nullification: A political doctrine which holds that state governments are sovereign in their own territory, and therefore have the ability to ignore and even block the enforcement of federal laws which they do not approve of. This controversial theory had many supporters in the early nineteenth century United States, but was largely discredited by the American Civil War (1861–65).

Nullification crisis: A conflict over states' rights that nearly led to civil war in the 1830s. During President Andrew Jackson's first term in office (1829–1833) a tariff bill was passed that the inhabitants of South Carolina disliked. In response the South Carolina legislature invoked the concept of nullification, and declared that the new law was not in effect in the state. South Carolina threatened to secede if the federal government attempted to collect the taxes. President Jackson indicated his willingness to lead a federal army into South Carolina to enforce the law, but a new tariff was enacted in 1833 and South Carolina backed down before violence broke out.

O

oligarchy: Any system of government in which a small elite group holds the ruling power.

ombudsmen: An appointed official who investigates private complaints against an organized group, such as a government.

omnibus: A term describing something that includes or involves many items. Used in government to describe bills that contain a variety of proposals.

P

paramilitary: An organization created along military lines that is not part of any official military unit.

parliamentary: Related to a supreme legislative body made up of many representatives and similar to the British system of government.

partisan: An action or person that adheres to a political party's platform or opinion. (*See also* bipartisan)

patent: An official document granted by the federal government to an inventor of a product that gives the inventor the exclusive right to make, use, or sell the product. A patent also enables an inventor to pursue legal action against anyone who interferes with their exclusive rights.

patronage: The power to make appointments to office, confer contracts, and give other special favors to individuals chosen by a politician. (*See also* spoils system)

peacekeeping: Describes military troops sent into conflict situations to keep the peace and restore order until a permanent resolution can be reached.

pension(s): Money given to an employee when they retire from a company. Pensions can be funded by the government, an employer, or through employee contributions.

per capita: Literally, per person; for each person counted.

perestroika: Mikhail Gorbachev's policy of economic and governmental reform instituted in the 1980s when he was the leader of the Soviet Union.

pocket veto: A special type of veto. If Congress passes a bill and the president neither signs nor vetoes it, the bill is normally enacted. But if Congress adjourns within 10 days of the passage of the bill, and the bill has not yet been signed or vetoed, the president is said to have "pocketed" the bill, and it is considered vetoed. Unlike an ordinary presidential veto, a pocket veto cannot be overridden.

political action committee: A group that raises money to support the election of politicians that the group feels will support their interests.

political party: A group of individuals who organize for the purpose of nominating candidates for office, winning elections, operating government, and determining public policies.

political science: The academic study of political systems and theories.

politician: A person experienced in government as an appointed official or officeholder or someone involved in party politics.

politics: Relating to government or the conduct of government especially the making of government policies and organization.

popular sovereignty: The political position that settlers in the federal territories should be allowed to determine for themselves if they wanted to allow slavery in their region. Its most famous proponent was Democratic senator Stephen A. Douglas, who saw it enacted in his Kansas-Nebraska Act of 1854.

popular vote: The actual vote of the population. (*See also* electoral college)

Populist Party: A political party which arose in the 1890s to be a significant force in U.S. politics, particularly in the western states. The Populist (or People's) Party drew its support primarily from farmers and urban laborers who wanted government to be more responsive to the will of the public, and hoped to use the power of government to benefit and protect citizens rather than business and industry. Many of the issues which the Populist party championed were later adopted by progressives in other parties.

Populist philosophy: (In reference to Andrew Jackson) Jackson's Democratic party was an outgrowth of Jefferson's Democratic-Republican party which built on its beliefs about presidential authority being derived from the will of the American people. Jacksonian Democracy was referred to as a populist political program because it embraced the notions that equality of opportunity and the elimination of special privileges were the necessary prerequisites for a truly democratic society to exist.

pork barrel: Local projects funded by Congress that are not of critical or national importance. Usually seen as a method through which congressmen can win further support in their home districts.

press secretary: Assistant to the president who interacts regularly with the media on the president's behalf through press conferences and briefings. The press secretary provides information on the president's activities and plans.

price support: A program in which the federal government helps stabilize prices by buying up surplus products and granting loans. Most often used to support agriculture.

primary: An election within a political party to determine the candidate that party will support in the general election. During a presidential campaign parties generally have primaries in many states, and their results help to determine which of that party's candidates will be nominated at their national convention.

privateer: A privately owned ship which has been given official permission by a government to arm itself and attack ships belonging to specified enemy nations. As opposed to military vessel owned by a government, or a pirate that is acting without any legal authority from any nation. In the nineteenth century and earlier privateers were common and operated under specific international laws and treaties.

private sector: The division of an economy in which production of goods and services is privately owned.

privatization: To change from public to private control or ownership.

progressive: A political term used especially in the early twentieth century. It described politicians or policies that support increased government control over the economy, increased government responsiveness to the general population, and the general principle that the power of government could and should be used to improve the lives of citizens. The Populist Party was based around ideas that would later become known by this term, such as the direct election of senators, labor legislation, lower tariffs, and consumer protection.

Progressive Party: Two separate political parties went by this name in the first half of the twentieth century. The first such party was the one which developed around Theodore Roosevelt's unsuccessful third presidential campaign in 1912, it was defunct by the time the second party was organized in the 1920s. Both parties called for labor legislation, consumer protection, and other progressive reforms. The first party was also known for supporting conservation, the second for nationalization of railroads and an isolationist foreign policy position.

progressive tax: Any tax in which the tax rate increases as the amount to be taxed increases. For example, a progressive income tax might have a tax rate of 10% on the first $10,000 of income, a tax rate of 15% on the second $10,000, and a 20% tax rate on all income above $20,000.

Prohibition: The sale, manufacture, or transportation of alcoholic beverages was made illegal by the Eighteenth Amendment to the Constitution in 1920. Both this Amendment and the time period in which it was in effect are known as Prohibition. The rapid repeal of this provision, by the Twenty-First Amendment in 1933, shows the unpopularity of the ban.

proliferation: The growth or expanse of something. Often refers to the increase in the number or spread of nuclear weapons. (*See also* nonproliferation)

proportional tax: Any tax wherein the tax rate remains the same no matter how much the amount to be taxed increases.

protectionist: Someone who supports the use of restrictive government regulations and trade barriers to help domestic products and companies compete against foreign imports.

protective tariff: Taxes on imported goods that are instituted primarily to protect domestic trade rather than raise money.

protectorate: A nation governed under the influence of a more powerful protector nation.

pro tempore: Literally means "for the time being." The vice president is technically the head of the Senate, but a president pro tempore presides on a daily basis.

public corporation: Industries or businesses that are owned by the public through stock purchases or investments.

public debt: The entire debt of a government or nation.

public domain: Land owned by the federal government including national parks, forests, and grazing lands.

public interest: On behalf of the people, or for the good of the people.

public opinion: The combined opinions, attitudes, or beliefs of a large portion of a community that influences public policy and legislation.

public sector: The people of a country or community. Differs from the private sector which is made up of industries and organizations controlled by a few individuals, not the public as a whole.

public works: Facilities that are built or improved using government funds to benefit the general public. Parks, roads, hospitals, and dams paid for by the government are all examples of public works.

Q

quorum: The minimum number of members that must be present for a decision making body to conduct business. The U.S. Constitution states that "a majority of each [house of Congress] shall constitute a quorum to do business."

R

ratification, ratified: To formally agree with. In the United States amendments to the Constitution that are proposed by Congress must be ratified by three-fourths of the states to become official. Also, treaties with foreign nations which have been signed by the president must be ratified by the Senate to be official.

rearmament: To rebuild or substantially expand a nation's military, especially when the rebuilding involves new and better weapons.

recession: An economic slowdown of relatively short duration (as compared to a depression). During a recession, unemployment rises and purchasing power drops temporarily.

reconnaissance: A maneuver to gain information or explore territory. Often describes a military operation, when troops investigate enemy positions and plans.

Reconstruction: The period following the American Civil War (1861–65), when the states which had been members of the Confederacy were under occupied by the U.S. military, and the white population of these states saw their voting rights restricted as punishment for their rebellion. Reconstruction also saw federal protection for the former slaves, including several constitutional amendments. Reconstruction was effectively over by 1878, as the Jim Crow system rapidly deprived African Americans of their rights through the use of segregation.

referendum: A process by which voters in a state can disapprove a bill passed by state legislators. In states providing for referendums, a bill passed by the legislature does not take effect for a certain time period. During this period a bill may be suspended if the required number of voters sign a petition to do so. A suspended bill is then voted on by the public to determine whether or not it will go into effect.

regressive tax: Any tax in which the burden to pay falls relatively more heavily upon lower income groups than upon more wealthy taxpayers. A sales tax is an example of a regressive tax. Although both the wealthy and the poor pay the same amount of tax on the same goods, this is more burdensome for those with less money, because the tax represents a larger portion of their funds.

regulatory agency: A government office that makes rules for or concerning a particular product or service. For example, the Food and Drug Administration (FDA) determines which new foods and drugs will be made available to the public, and what quality standards products must meet to be sold in the United States.

regulatory reform: Attempts to streamline the processes of regulatory agencies because they are creating too many rules, rules that are too restrictive, or taking too long to make decisions.

remediation: The process of pursuing legal action to prevent or reverse a wrong done to an individual.

representative: An elected member of the United States House of Representatives. Can also be used to refer to an elected member of a state House of Representatives.

Republican Party: The Republican Party emerged in the 1850s as a northern anti-slavery party. It quickly rose to become one of the most important parties in the United States, and the major opposition to the Democratic Party. The Republican Party has been associated with conservative fiscal and social policies since the 1920s, but historically it has represented a wide range of views. The Republican Party is not related to the older Democratic-Republican Party, although that party was often called the Republicans before the 1830s. (*See also* Democratic Party)

revenue: The total income collected by state or federal governments.

revenue tariff: Taxes on imported goods that are instituted to primarily to raise money for the national government, rather than protect domestic trade. In the eighteenth and nineteenth centuries, tariffs were one of the primary sources of government funding. (*See also* protective tariff)

rider: A provision, unlikely to pass on its own merits, that is added to a bill so it will "ride" into passage. Although there is no absolute difference between them, a rider is generally distinguished from an amendment by not being closely related to the primary subject of the bill it is attached to.

Rough Riders: The popular nickname of a famous regiment of volunteer cavalry that Theodore Roosevelt helped recruit just as the Spanish-American War began in April 1898. As a formal part of the U.S. military, their official name was the First United States Volunteer Cavalry. Leonard Wood commanded the Rough Riders, Roosevelt was second in command and held the rank of lieutenant colonel.

S

scalawags: White southerners who supported the Union in the American Civil War (1861–65) or participated in the northern controlled process of Reconstruction after the war was over.

secession: To withdraw from an organization. Most often used to refer to states leaving the United States, such as when the Southern states withdrew from the union to form their own government shortly before the American Civil War (1861–65).

sectionalism, sections: A term used in U.S. history to refer to the differences in politics and economy that developed between the northern and the southern United States in the decades before the American Civil War (1861–65). Certain issues, most notably slavery, divided politicians and the public along sectional lines, regardless of their political parties.

secretary: In the federal government, secretary is the title of the head of an executive department.

secured document: An official document that is protected from general viewing due to high level security classification. (*See also* classified)

securities: Documents that prove debts owed to the holder, or ownership of something, such as a stock certificate or bond.

selective service: The program in the United States that determines which men will be selected for mandatory military service, also known as the draft.

Senate: One of the two bodies with specific functions that make up the legislative branch of the United States government. Each state is allocated two Senators. (*See also* Congress; House of Representatives)

senator: An elected member of the United States Senate.

senatorial courtesy: An informal understanding in U.S. government that senators will be allowed to control the filling of federal positions within their state. The president is expected to consult with his party's senators and follow their advice on this matter. If there are no senators from the president's party in a state with openings, the president may consult state party leaders.

separation of powers: The cornerstone of U.S. government wherein power is divided among three branches of government—the executive, legislative, and judicial. Officials of each branch are selected differently, have different responsibilities, and serve different terms. The separation of power is not absolute, however, due to the system of checks and balances. (*See also* checks and balances)

social insurance: Benefits or subsidies provided to citizens fully or partially to prevent economic or health problems. Unemployment insurance and worker's compensation are examples.

socialized medicine: Medical and hospital services that are provided by state or federal agencies and paid for by taxes or donations.

Social Security: A public program that provides economic aid and social welfare for individuals and their families through social insurance or assistance. In the United States, Social Security was passed into law in 1935, as a life and disability insurance and old-age pension for workers. It is paid for by employers, employees, and the government.

sovereignty: In international politics, the independent authority of a governmental unit, in that it is not subject to the control of another nation. Any independent nation is referred to as a sovereign nation, as opposed to colonies or protectorates, which are controlled by other nations.

special interest group: A group that organizes to influence legislation and government policies to further their specific interests. Some examples of special interest groups include the National Rifle Association, which advocates the right to own guns responsibly, and the Sierra Club, which promotes protecting the environment.

specie: Money that is made of precious metal, such as gold or silver, and therefore has an inherent value. As opposed to paper money, which has no significant value by itself, and relies on the willingness of the general population to accept it as payment for goods and services. (*See also* hard money, soft money)

spoils system: A system wherein elected officials award their supporters with appointments to federal jobs, often without any consideration given to the qualifications of the people thus appointed. Developed from the phrase "to the victor go the spoils." The spoils system was a major part of U.S. politics in the mid-eighteenth century, but was replaced by a merit-based civil service system as it gradually came to be seen as encouraging corruption and incompetence in government. (*See also* civil service)

stagflation: A combination of inflation (rising prices and decline in the value of the dollar) and economic stagnation.

staggered term: System wherein only a portion of the Senate or House of Representatives is up for re-election at a time. This ensures that there are always experienced members at each session to guide new members through the legislative process.

state: A body of people, occupying a specific geographic location, that organize into a political unit. State can also refer to the smaller geographic and political units that make up a larger state. In U.S. politics state is generally used to refer to one of the 50 states that make up the union, but in international politics nations and governments are often called states.

statute: A law, whether enacted by Congress or a state or local legislature.

statutory: Something established or otherwise defined by law.

steering committee: Committees formed to direct the flow of work and the operations of a body. In legislative bodies, the steering committee determines in what order work will be addressed.

stewardship: The act of carefully managing and safeguarding something. In the United States government, the president not only has the right to administer the country, but the duty to protect the nation and its people.

stock market: A market where shares of stock, or certificates of ownership in a company, are bought and sold.

strict constructionist: *See* constructionist

subsidy, subsidies, subsidized: Money granted by one state to another or from a government to an individual or company for an activity that benefits the public. Something which is supported by subsidies.

suffrage: The right to vote.

T

tariff(s): Tax imposed on products brought into a country from abroad. Tariffs can be used to raise funds for the government or, if high enough, to protect domestic businesses from foreign competition by increasing the overall prices of foreign goods.

tax: A charge, in the form of money, imposed on people or property by an authority and used for public purposes.

terrorism: Systematic acts of violence designed to frighten or intimidate.

third-world: A term often used to describe less developed countries; as of the mid-1990s, it was being replaced by the United Nations designation less developed countries, or LDCs.

trade: The business of buying and selling goods and services.

trade sanction: A trade restriction imposed on another country by a government, to convince that country to reverse or amend a course of action that is unacceptable.

trade surplus: The extent by which a country's exports exceed its imports.

treaty: An agreement entered into by two or more nations that creates or limits mutual rights and responsibilities. In the United States treaties are negotiated by the president and approved by the Senate.

two-party system: A political system dominated by two major political parties; for instance, the Democratic and Republican parties in the twentieth century United States. (*See also* multiparty system)

U

unconstitutional: Something that violates the written or implied principles of a constitution.

unemployment insurance: Money paid into a fund by employers and paid out to employees for a limited time when the worker is laid off work.

Union, The: The United States, especially the group of states that remained the United States during the Civil War and did not secede to join the Confederacy.

United Nations: Assembly organized in 1945 to find peaceful resolutions to international disputes and encourage cooperation in dealing with worldwide social and economic issues. Nations from all over the world are represented at the United Nations.

V

veteran: A person with long term experience in a skill or occupation. Veteran often refers to a former member of the armed services.

veto: The ability to forbid or prohibit something. In U.S. politics, the president has the authority to veto bills passed by Congress, preventing their enactment.

W

Warsaw Pact: A military alliance made up of the Soviet Union, East Germany, and most of the other nations of eastern Europe. The Warsaw Pact lasted from the 1950s until the 1990s. The Warsaw Pact's declared purpose was to defend eastern Europe from NATO, but many in the United States saw it as a threat to western Europe. (*See also* North Atlantic Treaty Organization)

watchdog (agency): A government agency that is responsible for ensuring that laws and regulations are followed. Such agencies often focus on specific activities such as trade and commerce.

welfare: Aid, in the form of money or services, to people who are economically disadvantaged.

white-collar crime: Non-violent crime involving violations of law that often take place in a business setting.

workers' compensation: An insurance program that provides money to workers injured in the workplace from a fund created by employer payments.

World Court, The: Officially known as the Permanent Court of International Justice, it was associated with the League of Nations and later with the United Nations. It is located in The Hague, the Netherlands; its purpose is to settle disputes among nations by peaceful judicial means.

writ(s): A written order of a court commanding an individual or group to perform or cease a particular activity.

Z

zoning: The process of designating sections of a geographic area for specific purposes such as business or residential.

Subject Index

Subject Index